Less managing. More teaching. Greater learning.

 INSTRUCTORS...

Would you like your **students** to show up for class **more prepared**?
(Let's face it, class is much more fun if everyone is engaged and prepared...)

Want an **easy way to assign** homework online and track student **progress**?
(Less time grading means more time teaching...)

Want an **instant view** of student or class performance relative to learning objectives? *(No more wondering if students understand...)*

Need to **collect data and generate reports** required for administration or accreditation? *(Say goodbye to manually tracking student learning outcomes...)*

Want to **record and post your lectures** for students to view online?

 With McGraw-Hill's *Connect*™ *Plus Accounting*,

INSTRUCTORS GET:

- Simple **assignment management**, allowing you to spend more time teaching.

- **Auto-graded** assignments, quizzes, and tests.

- **Detailed Visual Reporting** where student and section results can be viewed and analyzed.

- Sophisticated **online testing** capability.

- A **filtering and reporting** function that allows you to easily assign and report on materials that are correlated to accreditation standards, learning outcomes, and Bloom's taxonomy.

- An easy-to-use **lecture capture** tool.

- The option to **upload course documents** for student access.

Want an online, **searchable version** of your textbook?

Wish your textbook could be **available online** while you're doing your assignments?

Connect™ Plus Accounting eBook

If you choose to use *Connect™ Plus Accounting*, you have an affordable and searchable online version of your book integrated with your other online tools.

Connect™ Plus Accounting eBook offers features like:

- Topic search
- Direct links from assignments
- Adjustable text size
- Jump to page number
- Print by section

Want to get more **value** from your textbook purchase?

Think learning accounting should be a bit more **interesting**?

Check out the STUDENT RESOURCES section under the *Connect™* Library tab.

Here you'll find a wealth of resources designed to help you achieve your goals in the course. You'll find things like **quizzes, PowerPoints, and Internet activities** to help you study. Every student has different needs, so explore the STUDENT RESOURCES to find the materials best suited to you.

Essentials of
Advanced
Financial
Accounting

Essentials of Advanced Financial Accounting

Richard E. Baker

Northern Illinois University

Theodore E. Christensen

Brigham Young University

David M. Cottrell

Brigham Young University

With contributions from:

Valdean C. Lembke

Professor Emeritus
University of Iowa

Thomas E. King

Professor Emeritus
Southern Illinois University, Edwardsville

Cynthia G. Jeffrey

Iowa State University

McGraw-Hill Irwin

ESSENTIALS OF ADVANCED FINANCIAL ACCOUNTING

Published by McGraw-Hill/Irwin, a business unit of The McGraw-Hill Companies, Inc., 1221 Avenue of the Americas, New York, NY, 10020. Copyright © 2012 by The McGraw-Hill Companies, Inc. All rights reserved. No part of this publication may be reproduced or distributed in any form or by any means, or stored in a database or retrieval system, without the prior written consent of The McGraw-Hill Companies, Inc., including, but not limited to, in any network or other electronic storage or transmission, or broadcast for distance learning.

Some ancillaries, including electronic and print components, may not be available to customers outside the United States.

This book is printed on acid-free paper.

1 2 3 4 5 6 7 8 9 0 QDB/QDB 1 0 9 8 7 6 5 4 3 2 1

ISBN 978-0-07-802564-8
MHID 0-07-802564-8

Vice president and editor-in-chief: *Brent Gordon*
Editorial director: *Stewart Mattson*
Publisher: *Tim Vertovec*
Senior sponsoring editor: *Dana L. Woo*
Executive director of development: *Ann Torbert*
Development editor II: *Katie Jones*
Vice president and director of marketing: *Robin J. Zwettler*
Marketing director: *Brad Parkins*
Senior marketing manager: *Kathleen Klehr*
Vice president of editing, design, and production: *Sesha Bolisetty*
Lead project manager: *Pat Frederickson*
Senior buyer: *Carol A. Bielski*
Lead designer: *Matthew Baldwin*
Senior media project manager: *Greg Bates*
Media project manager: *Suresh Babu, Hurix Systems Pvt. Ltd.*
Cover design: *Matthew Baldwin*
Cover image: © *Getty Images*
Interior design: *Matthew Baldwin*
Typeface: *10.5/12 Times New Roman*
Compositor: *Laserwords Private Limited*
Printer: *Quad/Graphics*

Library of Congress Cataloging-in-Publication Data

Baker, Richard E.
    Essentials of advanced financial accounting / Richard E. Baker, Theodore E. Christensen, David M. Cottrell; with contributions from Valdean C. Lembke, Thomas E. King, Cynthia G. Jeffrey.—1st ed.
        p. cm.
    Includes index.
    ISBN-13: 978-0-07-802564-8 (alk. paper)
    ISBN-10: 0-07-802564-8 (alk. paper)
    1. Accounting.   I. Christensen, Theodore E.   II. Cottrell, David M.   III. Title.
HF5636.B35 2012
657'.046—dc22   2010053791

About the Authors

Richard E. Baker

Richard E. Baker was a member of the faculty of Northern Illinois University for 26 years. His academic recognitions include having been named the Ernst & Young Distinguished Professor of Accountancy at Northern Illinois University. In addition, he has been recognized as an inaugural University Presidential Teaching Professor, the highest teaching recognition of his university. He received his B.S. degree from the University of Wisconsin at River Falls and his MBA and Ph.D. from the University of Wisconsin at Madison. His activities in the American Accounting Association have been continuous over many years and include service on the AAA's Executive Committee as the Director of Education of the AAA; as a member of the AAA's Council; as the Chair of the Teaching and Curriculum Section; and as the President of the Midwest Region. His lengthy service to the Federation of Schools of Accountancy (FSA) includes the offices of the President, the Vice President, and the Secretary. Many of his extensive professional and academic organization committee service efforts have involved research in assessing teaching and learning outcomes, designing innovative curriculum models, developing meaningful measurement criteria for evaluating accounting programs, and continually integrating new electronic technology into the accounting classroom. Professor Baker has received numerous teaching awards at both the undergraduate and graduate levels and has been selected as the Illinois CPA Society's Outstanding Accounting Educator. His most recent published research studies have concentrated on ways to make the learning/teaching experience as effective as possible.

Theodore E. Christensen

Ted Christensen has been a faculty member at Brigham Young University since 2000. Prior to coming to BYU, he was on the faculty at Case Western Reserve University for five years. He received a B.S. degree in accounting at San Jose State University, a M.Acc. degree in tax at Brigham Young University, and a Ph.D. in accounting from the University of Georgia. Professor Christensen has authored and coauthored articles published in many journals including *The Accounting Review,* the *Journal of Accounting and Economics, Accounting Organizations and Society, Review of Accounting Studies,* the *Journal of Business Finance & Accounting, Accounting Horizons,* and *Issues in Accounting Education.* Professor Christensen has taught financial accounting at all levels, financial statement analysis, both introductory and intermediate managerial accounting, and corporate taxation. He is the recipient of numerous awards for both teaching and research. He has been active in serving on various committees of the American Accounting Association and is a CPA.

David M. Cottrell

Professor Cottrell joined the faculty at Brigham Young University in 1991. He currently serves as the Associate Director of the School of Accountancy. Prior to coming to BYU he spent five years at The Ohio State University, where he earned his Ph.D. Before pursuing a career in academics he worked as an auditor and consultant for the firm of Ernst & Young in their San Francisco office. At BYU, Professor Cottrell has developed and taught a case-based accounting and auditing research course in the graduate program, and also has taught financial accounting and corporate financial reporting courses in the School of Accountancy, the MBA program, and the Finance program. He has won numerous awards from the alumni and faculty for his teaching and curriculum development. He has received the Outstanding Professor Award in the college of business as selected by the students in the Finance Society; he has received the Outstanding Teaching Award as selected by the Marriott School of Management; and he is a four-time winner of the collegewide Teaching Excellence Award for Management Skills, which is selected by the Alumni Board of the Marriott School of Management at BYU. In 2005 he was named as a University Faculty Fellow for Teaching and Learning with Technology. Professor Cottrell also has authored many articles about accounting and auditing issues. His articles have been published in *Issues in Accounting Education, The Journal of Accounting Case Research, The Quarterly Review of Distance Education, Journal of Accountancy, The CPA Journal, Internal Auditor, The Tax Executive,* and *The Journal of International Taxation,* among others.

NOTE FROM THE AUTHORS

Our objective in creating the "Essentials of Advanced Accounting" text was to give an additional option to instructors and students who have only one term or one semester to devote to advanced accounting topics. We have received several requests from Instructors and students for a resource which will help them cover in a single term or semester the core elements of the advanced accounting material that is most frequently represented on the CPA exam. Hence this text contains the essential information on consolidations, multinational entities, partnerships, and governmental and not-for-profit entities.

The subject matter of advanced accounting is expanding at an unprecedented rate. New topics are being added, and traditional topics require more extensive coverage. Most one-term courses are unable to cover all the topics included in a traditional comprehensive advanced accounting text. In recognition of time constraints, this text is structured to provide the most efficient use of the time available, while maintaining all the learning support and ancillary materials that cover these essential topics. For students and instructors who would like to cover a wider set of topics, we invite you to examine our comprehensive text, Advanced Accounting, which is now in its ninth edition.

The new authors, Ted Christensen and David Cottrell, are excited to be involved with this book and express their gratitude to Val Lembke, Tom King, and Cindy Jeffrey for their many years of hard work to the previous editions of the comprehensive text.

Preface

Essentials of Advanced Financial Accounting is an up-to-date, comprehensive, and highly illustrated presentation of the accounting and reporting principles and procedures used in a variety of business entities. Every day, the business press carries stories about the merger and acquisition mania, the complexities of modern business entities, new organizational structures for conducting business, accounting scandals related to complex business transactions, the foreign activities of multinational firms, the operations of governmental and not-for-profit entities, bankruptcies of major firms, and other topics typically included in advanced accounting. Accountants must understand and know how to deal with the accounting and reporting ramifications of these issues.

OVERVIEW

Essentials of Advanced Financial Accounting provides strong coverage of advanced accounting topics, with clarity of presentation and integrated coverage based on continuous case examples. The text is highly illustrated with complete presentations of worksheets, schedules, and financial statements so that students can see the development of each topic. Inclusion of all recent FASB and GASB pronouncements and the continuing deliberations of the authoritative bodies provide a current and contemporary text for students preparing for the CPA examination and current practice. This has become especially important given the recent rapid pace of the authoritative bodies in dealing with major issues having far-reaching implications. An overview of the contents and organization is illustrated below.

Multi-Corporate Entities

Business Combinations
1   Intercorporate Acquisitions and Investments in Other Entities

Consolidation Concepts and Procedures
2   Reporting Intercorporate Investments and Consolidation of Wholly Owned with No Differential
3   The Reporting Entity and Consolidation of Less-than-Wholly-Owned with No Differential
4   Consolidation of Wholly Owned Subsidiaries Acquired at More than Book Value
5   Consolidation of Less-than-Wholly-Owned Subsidiaries Acquired at More than Book Value

Intercompany Transfers
6   Intercompany Inventory Transactions
7   Intercompany Transfers of Services and Noncurrent Assets

Multinational Entities

Foreign Currency Transactions
8   Multinational Accounting: Foreign Currency Transactions and Financial Instruments

Translation of Foreign Statements
9   Multinational Accounting: Issues in Financial Reporting and Translation of Foreign Entity Statements

Partnerships

Formation, Operation, Changes
10   Partnerships: Formation, Operation, and Changes in Membership

Liquidation
11   Partnerships: Liquidation

Governmental and Not-for-Profit Entities

Governmental Entities
12   Governmental Entities: Introduction and General Fund Accounting

Special Funds
13   Governmental Entities: Special Funds and Government-wide Financial Statements

---

KEY FEATURES OF *ESSENTIALS OF ADVANCED FINANCIAL ACCOUNTING*

- **Introductory vignettes.** Each chapter begins with a brief story of a well-known company to illustrate why topics covered in that chapter are relevant in current practice. Short descriptions of the vignettes and the featured companies are featured in the Chapter-by-Chapter Changes section on page xvi.
- **A building-block approach to consolidation.** Virtually all advanced financial accounting classes cover consolidation topics. While this topic is perhaps the most important to instructors, students frequently struggle to gain a firm grasp of consolidation principles. Baker/Christensen/Cottrell 1e provides students with a learning-friendly framework to consolidations by introducing consolidation concepts and procedures more gradually. This is accomplished by a building-block approach that introduces consolidations earlier than in previous editions by beginning the consolidation discussion earlier in Chapters 2 and 3. The building-block approach can be summarized as follows:

  - *Chapter 2* begins with the most basic consolidation situation: the consolidation of a wholly owned subsidiary that is either created or purchased at an amount equal to the book value of net assets. Thus, students practice basic consolidation procedures without having to worry about the complications associated with a differential or noncontrolling shareholders.
  - *Chapter 3* introduces the notion of partial ownership of a subsidiary that is created or acquired at an amount equal to the book value of net assets. In this way students are exposed to the nuances associated with the existence of noncontrolling shareholders, but without the details associated with a differential.
  - *Chapter 4* exposes students to the intricacies of consolidation when the subsidiary is acquired for an amount that exceeds the book value of net assets. In order to isolate the new concepts and procedures that accompany the consolidation of a subsidiary with a differential, this chapter focuses on wholly owned subsidiaries.
  - *Chapter 5* finally brings students full circle to the point where they are ready to tackle more realistic situations where the parent company purchases a controlling interest in a subsidiary (but not 100% ownership) *and* the acquisition price exceeds the book value of net assets. Thus, students learn how to simultaneously handle all of the details associated with a differential and noncontrolling shareholders.

The overall coverage of the consolidation process by chapter is illustrated below:

- **Reorganization of consolidation elimination entries.** Consistent with the building-block approach to consolidation, the text includes a slight reorganization of the elimination entries used in consolidation to facilitate the elimination of the investment in a subsidiary in two steps: (1) first the book value portion of the investment and income from the subsidiary are eliminated and (2) then the differential portion of the investment and income from the subsidiary are eliminated with separate entries. This approach facilitates the building-block approach in Chapters 2–5. The text also uses frequent illustrations to help students visualize the steps in the elimination process.

- **Presentation of intercompany transactions.** Intercompany inventory transfers are presented before fixed-asset transfers. Inventory transfers are (1) far more common than fixed-asset transfers and (2) easier for students to understand. The fully adjusted equity method is presented in Chapters 6 and 7. This method links back to the building-block approach in Chapters 2–5.
- **New FASB codification.** All authoritative citations to U.S. GAAP include secondary citations to the new FASB codification. We also maintain the authoritative citations for clarity during this period of transition.
- **IFRS comparisons.** As the FASB and IASB work toward convergence to a single set of global accounting standards, the SEC is debating the wholesale introduction of international financial reporting standards (IFRS). The text summarizes key differences between current U.S. GAAP and IFRS to make students aware of changes that will likely occur if the SEC adopts IFRS in the near future.
- **AdvancedStudyGuide.com.** See page xv for details.
- **The use of a continuous case for each major subject-matter area.** This textbook presents the complete story of a company, Peerless Products Corporation, from its beginning, through its growth to a multinational consolidated entity, and finally to its end. At each stage of the entity's development, including the acquisition of a subsidiary, Special Foods Inc., the text presents comprehensive examples and discussions of the accounting and financial reporting issues that accountants face. The discussions tied to the Peerless Products continuous case are easily identified by the company logos in the margin:

The comprehensive case of Peerless Products Corporation and its subsidiary, Special Foods Inc., is used throughout the for-profit chapters. For the governmental chapters, the Sol City case has been used to facilitate the development of governmental accounting and reporting concepts and procedures. Using a continuous case provides several benefits. First, students need only become familiar with one set of data and can then move more quickly through the subsequent discussion and illustrations without having to absorb a new set of data. Second, the case adds realism to the study of advanced accounting and permits students to see the effects of each successive step on the financial reports of an entity. Finally, comparing and contrasting alternative methods using a continuous case allows students to evaluate different methods and outcomes more readily.

- **Extensive illustrations of key concepts.** The book is heavily illustrated with complete, not partial, workpapers, financial statements, and other computations and comparisons useful for demonstrating each topic. The illustrations are cross-referenced to the relevant text discussion. In the consolidations portion of the text, the focus is on the fully adjusted equity method of accounting for an investment in a subsidiary, but two other methods—the cost method and the modified equity method—are also discussed and illustrated in chapter appendices.
- **Comprehensive coverage with significant flexibility.** The self-contained units of subject matter allow for substantial flexibility in sequencing the course materials. In addition, individual chapters are organized to allow for going into greater depth on some topics through the use of the "Additional Considerations" sections. Several chapters include appendices containing discussions of alternative accounting procedures or illustrations of procedures or concepts that are of a supplemental nature.

- **Contemporary topical coverage.** The dynamic business environment requires accountants to continually learn about new types of transactions, new technologies available to the profession, and new requirements and standards for accounting and financial reporting. This textbook integrates the most recent professional standards and includes cases and examples from current practice. For example, the importance in recent years of topics such as the Sarbanes-Oxley Act, special-purpose entities (SPEs), variable interest entities (VIEs), derivatives, fair value reporting, and international financial reporting standards (IFRS) has led to significant coverage of these topics in the current and recent editions of the text. The GASB's recent focus on enhanced financial statement disclosures for governmental entities is discussed and illustrated. Students are presented with an abundance of current information and learning opportunities to see that the topics in their advanced financial accounting courses are a significant part of today's profession of accountancy.

- **Extensive end-of-chapter materials.** A large number of questions, cases, exercises, and problems at the end of each chapter provide the opportunity to solidify understanding of the chapter material and assess mastery of the subject matter. The end-of-chapter materials progress from simple focused exercises to more complex integrated problems. Cases provide opportunities for extending thought, gaining exposure to different sources of accounting-related information, and applying the course material to real-world situations. These cases include research cases where students are referred to authoritative pronouncements, and Kaplan CPA Review simulations. The American Institute of CPAs has identified five skills to be examined as part of the CPA exam: (*a*) analysis, (*b*) judgment, (*c*) communication, (*d*) research, and (*e*) understanding. The end-of-chapter materials provide abundant opportunities for students to enhance those skills with realistic and real-world applications of advanced financial accounting topics. Cases and exercises identified with a world globe icon provide special opportunities for students to access real-world data by using electronic databases, Internet search engines, or other inquiry processes to answer the questions presented on the topics in the chapters.

MCGRAW-HILL'S *CONNECT*™ *ACCOUNTING*
Less Managing. More Teaching. Greater Learning.

McGraw-Hill's *Connect*™ *Accounting* is an online assignment and assessment solution that connects students with the tools and resources they'll need to achieve success.

McGraw-Hill's *Connect*™ *Accounting* helps prepare students for their future by enabling faster learning, more efficient studying, and higher retention of knowledge.

McGraw-Hill's *Connect*™ *Accounting* Features

McGraw-Hill's *Connect*™ *Accounting* offers a number of powerful tools and features to make managing assignments easier, so faculty can spend more time teaching. With McGraw-Hill's *Connect*™ *Accounting*, students can engage with their coursework anytime and anywhere, making the learning process more accessible and efficient. McGraw-Hill's *Connect*™ *Accounting* offers you the features described below.

Simple Assignment Management

With McGraw-Hill's *Connect*™ *Accounting,* creating assignments is easier than ever, so you can spend more time teaching and less time managing. The assignment management function enables you to

- Create and deliver assignments easily with selectable end-of-chapter questions and test bank items.
- Streamline lesson planning, student progress reporting, and assignment grading to make classroom management more efficient than ever.
- Go paperless with the eBook and online submission and grading of student assignments.

Smart Grading

When it comes to studying, time is precious. McGraw-Hill's *Connect™ Accounting* helps students learn more efficiently by providing feedback and practice material when they need it, where they need it. When it comes to teaching, your time also is precious. The grading function enables you to

- Have assignments scored automatically, giving students immediate feedback on their work and side-by-side comparisons with correct answers.
- Access and review each response; manually change grades or leave comments for students to review.
- Reinforce classroom concepts with practice tests and instant quizzes.

Instructor Library

The McGraw-Hill's *Connect™ Accounting* Instructor Library is your repository for additional resources to improve student engagement in and out of class. You can select and use any asset that enhances your lecture. The McGraw-Hill's *Connect™ Accounting* Instructor Library includes

- eBook
- Solutions Manual
- Instructor's Resource Manual
- Instructor PowerPoint® Presentations
- Test Bank
- Excel Spreadsheet Solutions
- Supplemental Chapters
- Supplemental Problems

Student Study Center

The McGraw-Hill's *Connect™ Accounting* Student Study Library is the place for students to access additional resources. The Student Library

- Offers students quick access to lectures, practice materials, eBooks, and more.
- Provides instant practice material and study questions, easily accessible on the go.

Student Progress Tracking

McGraw-Hill's *Connect™ Accounting* keeps instructors informed about how each student, section, and class is performing, allowing for more productive use of lecture and office hours. The progress-tracking function enables you to

- View scored work immediately and track individual or group performance with assignment and grade reports.
- Access an instant view of student or class performance relative to learning objectives.
- Collect data and generate reports required by many accreditation organizations, such as AACSB and AICPA.

Lecture Capture

Increase the attention paid to lecture discussion by decreasing the attention paid to note taking. For an additional charge, lecture capture offers new ways for students to focus on the in-class discussion, knowing they can revisit important topics later. For more information on lecture capture capabilities in McGraw-Hill's *Connect™ Accounting,* see the discussion of Tegrity, below.

McGraw-Hill's Connect™ Plus Accounting

McGraw-Hill reinvents the textbook learning experience for the modern student with McGraw-Hill's *Connect™ Plus Accounting.* A seamless integration of an eBook and McGraw-Hill's *Connect*™ *Accounting,* McGraw-Hill's *Connect*™ *Plus Accounting* provides all of the McGraw-Hill's *Connect*™ *Accounting* features plus the following:

- An integrated eBook, allowing for anytime, anywhere access to the textbook.
- Dynamic links between the problems or questions you assign to your students and the location in the eBook where that problem or question is covered.
- A powerful search function to pinpoint and connect key concepts in a snap.

In short, McGraw-Hill's *Connect*™ *Accounting* offers you and your students powerful tools and features that optimize your time and energies, enabling you to focus on course content, teaching, and student learning. McGraw-Hill's *Connect*™ *Accounting* also offers a wealth of content resources for both instructors and students. This state-of-the-art, thoroughly tested system supports you in preparing students for the world that awaits.

For more information about McGraw-Hill's *Connect*™ *Accounting,* go to **www .mcgrawhillconnect.com,** or contact your local McGraw-Hill sales representative.

TEGRITY CAMPUS: LECTURES 24/7

Tegrity Campus is a service that makes class time available 24/7 by automatically capturing every lecture. With a simple one-click start-and-stop process, you capture all computer screens and corresponding audio in a format that is easily searchable, frame by frame. Students can replay any part of any class with easy-to-use browser-based viewing on a PC or Mac, an iPod, or other mobile device.

Educators know that the more students can see, hear, and experience class resources, the better they learn. In fact, studies prove it. Tegrity Campus's unique search feature helps students efficiently find what they need, when they need it, across an entire semester of class recordings. Help turn your students' study time into learning moments immediately supported by your lecture. With Tegrity Campus, you also increase intent listening and class participation by easing students' concerns about note taking. Lecture Capture will make it more likely you will see students' faces, not the tops of their heads.

To learn more about Tegrity, watch a two-minute Flash demo at **http://tegritycampus .mhhe.com**.

COURSESMART.COM

CourseSmart is a new way to find and buy eTextbooks. At CourseSmart you can save up to 45 percent off the cost of a print textbook, reduce your impact on the environment, and gain access to powerful Web tools for learning. CourseSmart has the largest selection of eTextbooks available anywhere, offering thousands of the most commonly adopted textbooks from a wide variety of higher-education publishers. CourseSmart eTextbooks are available in one standard online reader with full-text search, notes and highlighting, and e-mail tools for sharing notes between classmates.

MCGRAW-HILL/IRWIN CUSTOMER CARE
CONTACT INFORMATION

At McGraw-Hill, we understand that getting the most from new technology can be challenging. That's why our services don't stop after you purchase our products. You can contact our Technical Support Analysts 24 hours a day to get product training online. Or you can search our knowledge bank of Frequently Asked Questions on our support Website. For Customer Support, call **800-331-5094** or visit **www.mhhe.com/ support**. One of our Technical Support Analysts will be able to assist you in a timely fashion.

MCGRAW-HILL HIGHER EDUCATION AND BLACKBOARD HAVE TEAMED UP. WHAT DOES THIS MEAN FOR YOU?

1. **Your life, simplified.** Now you and your students can access McGraw-Hill's *Connect*™ and Create™ right from within your Blackboard course—all with one single sign-on. Say goodbye to the days of logging in to multiple applications.

2. **Deep integration of content and tools.** Not only do you get single sign-on with *Connect*™ and Create™, you also get deep integration of McGraw-Hill content and content engines right in Blackboard. Whether you're choosing a book for your course or building *Connect*™ assignments, all the tools you need are right where you want them—inside of Blackboard.

3. **Seamless gradebooks.** Are you tired of keeping multiple gradebooks and manually synchronizing grades into Blackboard? We thought so. When a student completes an integrated *Connect*™ assignment, the grade for that assignment automatically (and instantly) feeds your Blackboard grade center.

4. **A solution for everyone.** Whether your institution is already using Blackboard or you just want to try Blackboard on your own, we have a solution for you. McGraw-Hill and Blackboard can now offer you easy access to industry-leading technology and content, whether your campus hosts it, or we do. Be sure to ask your local McGraw-Hill representative for details.

SUPPLEMENTS FOR INSTRUCTORS

- *Online Learning Center (OLC).* We offer an Online Learning Center (OLC) that follows *Essentials of Advanced Financial Accounting* chapter by chapter. It doesn't require any building or maintenance on your part. It's ready to go the moment you and your students type in the URL: **www.mhhe.com/baker1e**.

  The OLC includes

  - Interactive chapter quizzes
  - PowerPoint® presentations
  - Excel worksheets
  - Check figures
  - Supplemental chapters
  - Supplemental problems

- *Instructor PowerPoints.* The authors have developed a comprehensive set of PowerPoint slides designed to accompany the text. These slides do much more than simply summarize the topics in each chapter. They illustrate key concepts but also include group exercises and practice quiz questions to give students hands-on practice in class to better prepare them for future homework and assessment experiences. Instructors benefit from proven interactive class discussions and exercises fully annotated by the authors.

- *Solutions Manual.* Created by the authors, solutions are provided for all questions, cases, exercises, and problems in the text. Solutions are carefully explained and logically presented. Answers for many of the multiple-choice questions include computations and explanations.

- *Test Bank.* Prepared by the authors, this comprehensive collection of both conceptual and procedural test items is organized by chapter and includes a large variety of multiple-choice questions, exercises, and problems that can be used to measure student achievement in the topics in each chapter. The test items are closely coordinated with the text to ensure consistency.

- *Instructors' Resource Manual.* The Instructor's Resource Manual includes chapter outlines, additional examples, teaching suggestions, and other materials to assist instructors in making the most effective use of the text.

- *Supplemental Problems.* Downloadable additional exercises and problems are provided for a number of chapters. Instructors can assign these additional exercises and problems to broaden their students' understanding of the topics in the chapters. The instructor side of the OLC includes downloadable solutions to those supplemental exercises and problems.
- *Supplemental Chapters.* Two chapters are available online: (*a*) accounting for home office and branch operations and (*b*) accounting and reporting for estates and trusts. Cases, exercises, and problems are also available for these two chapters and the Instructor Edition includes solutions to those end-of-chapter items.
- *Instructor Updates.* Contains timely discussions and illustrations of major accounting or financial reporting issues under deliberation by standard-setting bodies. Instructors can choose to share them with their students.

ASSURANCE OF LEARNING READY

Many educational institutions today are focused on the notion of *assurance of learning,* an important element of some accreditation standards. *Essentials of Advanced Financial Accounting* is designed specifically to support your assurance of learning initiatives with a simple, yet powerful solution.

Each test bank question for *Essentials of Advanced Financial Accounting* maps to a specific chapter learning outcome/objective listed in the text. You can use our test bank software, EZ Test and EZ Test Online, or in McGraw-Hill's *Connect™ Accounting* to easily query for learning outcomes/objectives that directly relate to the learning objectives for your course. You can then use the reporting features of EZ Test to aggregate student results in a similar fashion, making the collection and presentation of assurance of learning data simple and easy.

AACSB STATEMENT

The McGraw-Hill Companies is a proud corporate member of AACSB International. Understanding the importance and value of AACSB accreditation, *Essentials of Advanced Financial Accounting* recognizes the curricula guidelines detailed in the AACSB standards for business accreditation by connecting selected questions in the text and the test bank to the six general knowledge and skill guidelines in the AACSB standards.

The statements contained in *Essentials of Advanced Financial Accounting* are provided only as a guide for the users of this textbook. The AACSB leaves content coverage and assessment within the purview of individual schools, the mission of the school, and the faculty. While *Essentials of Advanced Financial Accounting* and the teaching package make no claim of any specific AACSB qualification or evaluation, we have within *Essentials of Advanced Financial Accounting* labeled selected questions according to the six general knowledge and skills areas.

SUPPLEMENTS FOR STUDENTS

- McGraw-Hill's *Connect™ Plus Accounting*
  This integrates all of the text's multimedia resources. Students can obtain state-of-the-art study aids, including an online version of the text.

- McGraw-Hill's *Connect™ Accounting*
  This Web-based software duplicates problem structures directly from the end-of-chapter material in the textbook. It shows students where they made errors. All applicable exercises and problems are available with McGraw-Hill's *Connect™ Accounting.*

Available on the Online Learning Center at www.mhhe.com/baker9e

- *Online Quizzes.* Interactive quizzes give students a variety of multiple-choice and true/false questions related to the text for self-evaluation.
- *Excel Worksheets.* These worksheets for use with Excel are provided to facilitate completion of problems requiring numerous mechanical computations.

- *Check Figures.* Prepared by the text authors, a list of answers is provided separately for many of the end-of-chapter materials in the text.
- *Microsoft PowerPoint Slides®.* Available by chapter to facilitate note taking and review.
- *Supplemental Problems.* Additional problem materials for a number of the chapters are available online to enhance students' learning of the topics in the chapters. These supplemental problems tend to be longer problems that present a more comprehensive fact situation and can extend understanding of the topics in the chapters to a broader scope.
- *Supplemental Chapters.* Two chapters are available online for those persons wishing extended learning: (*a*) accounting for home office and branch operations and (*b*) accounting and reporting for estates and trusts. Cases, exercises, and problems are also available for these two chapters.

HIGH TECH: *ESSENTIALS OF ADVANCED FINANCIAL ACCOUNTING* HAS KEY TECHNOLOGY RESOURCES TO BENEFIT BOTH STUDENTS AND INSTRUCTORS

Advanced
StudyGuide
.com

Essentials of Advanced Financial Accounting introduces the most cutting-edge technology supplement ever delivered in the advanced accounting market. **AdvancedStudyGuide.com** is a product created exclusively by the authors of the text that represents a new generation in study resources available to students as well as a new direction and options in the resources instructors can use to help their students and elevate their classroom experiences.

Traditional study guides offer students a resource similar to the text itself. That is more discussion like the text accompanied by more problems and exercises like the ones in the text, all of this at a fairly costly price to just give students the same type of materials that they already received with the text.

At its core **AdvancedStudyGuide.com** (ASG) offers materials that go beyond what a printed text can possibly deliver. The ASG contains dozens of narrated, animated discussions and explanations of materials aligned to key points in the chapter. Not only that, the ASG also contains animated problems just like key problems in the exercises and problems at the end of each chapter. For the student who would like a little help with *Essentials of Advanced Financial Accounting,* the ASG is like having private tutoring sessions from the authors who wrote the book (not a class TA) any time, day or night. This also can provide tremendous benefits for instructors, as outlined below.

For Students:

The Questions

- Have you ever had to miss a class and were then confused about what the book was trying to say about a topic?
- Even when you were in class, do things sometimes not make as much sense when you are reviewing on your own?
- Do you ever feel stuck when it comes to doing homework problems, even though you read the chapter?
- When the exam is a few weeks after you covered the material in class, do you ever wish someone could walk you through a few examples as you review for the exam?
- Have you ever purchased a study guide for a text and found it was very expensive and did not give the additional study help you needed?

The ASG Answer

- The Answer, at least in part, is the ASG: a new type of study guide designed for the way you like to study and the way that you learn best.
- It is our attempt as authors to really discuss the material in a way that a text-only approach cannot do.
- AND we can discuss your questions with you 24/7, anytime—day or night, at times when your regular instructor is not around.

- Through the ASG, we will bring you streaming media discussions where the authors of the book (not a class TA) explain key points of each chapter.
- The ASG will also show, explain, and illustrate for you the approach to solving key homework problems in the text. These explanations are *Like Problems*; that is, they are problems "just like" some in the text that you were assigned for homework.

The ASG Benefit

AdvancedStudyGuide.com brings you discussion and examples worked out in streaming video. While traditional study guides can *Tell* you what to do, the ASG will *Show You What to Do AND HOW to Do It.*

See the student page at AdvancedStudyGuide.com.

For Instructors:

The Questions

- Have you ever had a student miss class and then come to your office and ask you to go over the topics that were discussed in class the day the student was absent?
- Even when a student is in class, does he or she sometimes come to your office and ask you to repeat the discussion?
- Even when you have discussed the chapter concepts, do you have students who still get stuck when it comes to doing homework problems?
- When exams are approaching, do students sometimes ask you to go back over material you taught days or weeks before?
- Would it be helpful to you if, on occasion, the authors of the text offered to hold "office hours" with your students for you?

The ASG Answer

- The Answer, at least in part, is the ASG: the authors' attempt to partner with you in helping to better serve students' needs in some of the common situations where questions arise, without using more of your scarce time.
- The ASG will allow you to refer to streaming media discussions where the authors explain key points of each chapter.
- The ASG will show, explain, and illustrate for students the approach to solving key homework problems in the text. These explanations are *Like Problems*; that is they are problems "just like" some in the text that you can assign for homework.

The ASG Benefit

AdvancedStudyGuide.com (ASG) is a great tool to let the authors of the text partner with you, the instructor, in helping students learn *Essentials of Advanced Financial Accounting*. The ASG will (1) help your students learn more effectively, (2) improve your class discussions, and (3) make your student contact hours more efficient.

See the instructor page at AdvancedStudyGuide.com.

CHAPTER-BY-CHAPTER COVERAGE

- **Chapter 1** emphasizes the importance of business acquisitions and combinations based on the January 2010 acquisition of **Cadbury PLC** by **Kraft Foods, Inc.** The business world is complex, and frequent business combinations will continue to increase the complex nature of the business environment in the future. An understanding of the accounting treatment of mergers, acquisitions, and other intercorporate investments is an invaluable asset in our ever-changing markets.

BERKSHIRE HATHAWAY INC.

- **Chapter 2** summarizes the different types of intercorporate investments based on the 2009 investment portfolio of **Berkshire Hathaway.** This vignette also discusses issues such as ownership and control that are related to the accounting for investments.

- **Chapter 3** introduces the notion of special-purpose entities and accounting standards related to variable interest entities by discussing the well-known collapse of **Enron Corporation.** New accounting rules for determining when a business entity must be consolidated resulted from this and other scandals. We also explore how the basic consolidation process differs when a subsidiary is only partially owned.

- **Chapter 4** gives a "behind the scenes" look at the work that goes into the consolidation process based on **Disney Corporation.** We learn about value-added activities during the consolidation process. In addition, we introduce issues such as when a differential occurs when the acquiring company pays more than the book value of the acquired company's net assets.

- **Chapter 5** discusses majority ownership of subsidiaries based on the 80 percent acquisition of **Nuova Systems** by **Cisco Systems, Inc.** in 2006. We further the discussion of acquisitions with a differential with the added complexity of noncontrolling interest shareholders when they purchase less than 100 percent of the outstanding common stock.

- **Chapter 6** introduces intercompany inventory transfers based on **Toys Я Us** and its 100 percent owned subsidiary **Toysrus.com.** Transactions between the two are related-party transactions; therefore, the profit from intercompany inventory transfers is eliminated in preparing consolidated finanial statements. This elimination process can become complicated. Therefore, this chapter examines intercompany inventory transactions and the consolidated procedures associated with them.

- **Chapter 7** presents a real fixed-asset transfer that took place in 2009 between two of **Mircon** subsidiaries. This chapter explores the accounting for both depreciable and nondepreciable asset transfers among affiliated companies.

- **Chapter 8** discusses the accounting issues affecting companies like **Microsoft** that have international operations. Specifically, we discuss foreign currency transactions, financial instruments, and the effects that changes in exchange rates can have on reported results.

- **Chapter 9** resumes the discussion of international accounting by looking at **McDonald's** global empire and how differences in accounting standards across countries and jurisdictions can cause significant difficulties for multinational firms. This chapter summarizes current efforts to develop a global set of high-quality accounting standards and explores the translation of financial statements of a foreign business entity into U.S. dollars.

- **Chapter 10** summarizes the evolution of the **large accounting firms** with an emphasis on partnerships. This chapter focuses on the formation and operation of partnerships, including accounting for the addition of new partners and the retirement of a present partner.

LAVENTHOL & HORWATH

- **Chapter 11** illustrates the dissolution of partnerships with the example of **Laventhol & Horwath,** the seventh largest accounting firm in 1990. We present the concepts that accountants must know if they offer professional services to partnerships undergoing liquidation.

City of

San Diego

- **Chapter 12** introduces the topic of accounting for government entities by examining the complexity of the operations of <u>**San Diego, California.**</u> The chapter has two parts: the accounting and reporting requirements for state and local governmental units and a comprehensive illustration of accounting for the general fund of a city.

- **Chapter 13** resumes the discussion of accounting for governmental entities by specifically examining special funds and government-wide financial statements using the example of the state of <u>**Maryland.**</u> We present the accounting and financial reporting requirements for four remaining governmental fund types, two proprietary fund types, and the four fiduciary fund types.

Acknowledgments

This text includes the thoughts and contributions of many individuals, and we wish to express our sincere appreciation to them. First and foremost, we thank all the students in our advanced accounting classes, from whom we have learned so much. In many respects, this text is an outcome of the learning experiences we have shared with our students. Second, we wish to thank the many outstanding teachers we have had in our own educational programs, from whom we learned the joy of learning. We are indebted to our colleagues in advanced accounting for helping us reach our goal of writing the best possible essentials of advanced financial accounting text. We appreciate the many valuable comments and suggestions from the faculty who used recent editions of the text. Their comments and suggestions have contributed to making this text a more effective learning tool. We especially wish to thank Jane Ou from Santa Clara University, Mallory McWilliams from San Jose State University, Mary Callegari from San Jose State University, Pam Smith from Northern Illinois University, Larry Walther from Utah State University, and Han Stice, Cameron Flanders, and Melissa Larson, all from Brigham Young University.

We express our sincere thanks to the following individuals who provided reviews on the full version of the text:

Alexander K. Buchholz
Brooklyn College of the City University of New York

Mary Burnell
Fairmont State University

Steve Fabian
New Jersey City University

Earl Godfrey
Gardner-Webb University

Joshua Herbold
University of Montana

Mallory McWilliams
San Jose State University/University of California, Santa Cruz

Abe Qastin
Lakeland College

Chantal Rowat
Bentley University

Margaret Shelton
University of Houston, Downtown

Frank Shuman
Utah State University

Nathan Slavin
Hofstra University

James Yang
Montclair State University

Jian Zhou
Binghamton University

We are grateful for the assistance and direction of the McGraw-Hill/Irwin team: Stewart Mattson, Tim Vertovec, Dana Woo, Katie Jones, Alice Harra, Pat Frederickson, Michelle Gardner, Dean Karampelas, Matt Baldwin, Greg Bates, Carol Bielski, and Suresh Babu, who all worked hard to champion our book through the production process.

Permission has been received from the Institute of Certified Management Accountants of the Institute of Management Accountants to use questions and/or unofficial answers from past CMA examinations. We appreciate the cooperation of the American Institute of Certified Public Accountants for providing permission to adapt and use materials from past Uniform CPA Examinations. And we thank Kaplan CPA Review for providing their online framework for *Essentials of Advanced Financial Accounting* students to gain important experience with the types of simulations that are included on the Uniform CPA Examination.

Above all, we extend our deepest appreciation to our families who continue to provide the encouragement and support necessary for this project.

Richard E. Baker
Theodore E. Christensen
David M. Cottrell

Brief Table of Contents

Table of Contents

Chapter One

Intercorporate Acquisitions and Investments in Other Entities

KRAFT'S ACQUISITION OF CADBURY

In recent years as well as during the past several decades, the business world has witnessed many corporate acquisitions and combinations, often involving some of the world's largest and best-known companies. Some of these combinations have captured public attention because of the personalities involved, the daring strategies employed, and the huge sums of money at stake. In January 2010 Kraft Foods Inc. finalized a deal to acquire Cadbury PLC for $19.4 billion to form the second-largest confectionery, food, and beverage company in the world. At the time of the acquisition, Cadbury's net assets were only worth around $5 billion. During the three months preceding Kraft's final bid, rumors circulated of a potential counterbid by Hershey. While a bidding war seemed likely, Hershey decided not to counterbid when Kraft produced a "winning" offer. This highly visible transaction was really the next step in more than a century of regular acquisitions.

In 1896, inspired in part by his time in the Kellogg brothers' Battle Creek Sanitarium, C.W. Post founded Postum Cereal Company, Ltd. The following year he introduced Grape-Nuts brand cereal. Within five years, Postum employed 2,500 people and its Battle Creek facility was the largest of its kind in the world.

In 1903, James L. Kraft started selling cheese door to door from the back of a horse-drawn wagon. Although not immediately successful, he continued operations and was eventually joined by four of his brothers in 1909. By 1914 Kraft & Bros. Company (later Kraft Foods Inc.) had opened its first cheese manufacturing plant and in 1916 patented a new process for pasteurizing cheese, making the cheese resistant to spoilage and allowing it to be transported over long distances.

These two start-up companies (Kraft and Postum) continued to grow independently. Postum went public in 1922, followed by Kraft in 1924. In 1925 Postum acquired Jell-O Company and in 1928 Maxwell House Coffee. That same year (1928) Kraft merged with Phenix Cheese, maker of Philadelphia Brand cream cheese.

In 1929, Postum changed its name to General Foods Corporation and in 1930 Kraft was acquired by National Dairy Products. In 1937 Kraft launched its well-known macaroni and cheese dinners. By 1953 business was booming for General Foods and they acquired Perkins Products, maker of Kool-Aid. In 1981 General Foods made another acquisition, this time acquiring Oscar Mayer & Co.

Philip Morris acquired General Foods in 1985 and Kraft in 1988. A year later General Foods and Kraft were combined to form Kraft General Foods Inc., which was renamed

Kraft Foods Inc. in 1995. In 2000, Philip Morris acquired Nabisco Holdings and began integrating Nabisco and Kraft. The story does not end here. In August 2008 the Post Cereal portion of Kraft was spun off and merged with Ralcorp Holdings. The remaining portion of Kraft Foods Inc. is the company that took part in the 2010 acquisition of Cadbury PLC.

Of course, this is only half of the story. Cadbury took its own journey. It took 104 years and dozens of mergers and acquisitions to finally end up with the companies that took part in the 2010 acquisition. The business world is complex and frequent business combinations will continue to increase the complex nature of the business environment in the future. An understanding of the accounting treatment of mergers, acquisitions, and other intercorporate investments is an invaluable asset in our ever-changing markets. This chapter introduces the key concepts associated with business combinations.

LEARNING OBJECTIVES

When you finish studying this chapter, you should be able to:

LO1 Understand and explain different methods of business expansion, types of organizational structures, and types of acquisitions.

LO2 Make calculations and prepare journal entries for the creation and purchase of a business entity.

LO3 Understand and explain the differences between different forms of business combinations.

LO4 Make calculations and prepare journal entries for different types of business combinations through the acquisition of stock or assets.

LO5 Make calculations and business combination journal entries in the presence of a differential, goodwill, or a bargain purchase element.

LO6 Understand additional considerations associated with business combinations.

A BRIEF INTRODUCTION

Before launching into our discussion of business combinations, we pause to provide a brief overview of the text. First, we note that the book's title does not necessarily describe the level of *difficulty* of topics covered in the text. The concepts covered here are not necessarily harder to grasp than those covered in your intermediate-level financial accounting courses. This course introduces financial accounting topics associated with many different topics that are typically not covered in intermediate-level texts. It may be more accurate to simply say that the term "advanced" means that the text covers topics that are more appropriately introduced *after* you've established a solid foundation in your intermediate courses. While the topics covered here will probably not be more *difficult* than those covered in previous courses, they have been saved to help you to build on what you've learned in prior courses. They will certainly help you transition from simple, contrived accounting examples to more realistic settings found in real-world situations.

Figure 1–1 summarizes the six major sections of this text. Chapters 1–7 comprise the first major section of the text on multi-corporate entities. In this chapter, we introduce major topics related to business combinations, as illustrated with the Kraft-Cadbury example. Chapters 2–5 explain the basic concepts and procedures for preparing consolidated financial statements, the required financial reporting method of affiliated corporate groups. Chapters 6–7 describe the intricacies of preparing consolidated financial statements in the presence of intercompany asset or debt transfers within a controlled group of companies. This major portion of the book on multi-corporate entities comprises the first half of the text.

FIGURE 1–1 Topical Overview

Advanced Financial Accounting Overview

Section	Major Topic	Chapter #	Chapter Title
Multi-Corporate Entities	Business Combinations	1	Intercorporate Acquisitions and Investments in Other Entities
	Consolidation Concepts and Procedures	2	Reporting Intercorporate Investments and Consolidation of Wholly Owned Subsidiaries with No Differential
		3	The Reporting Entity and Consolidation of Less-than-Wholly-Owned Subsidiaries with No Differential
		4	Consolidation of Wholly Owned Subsidiaries Acquired at More than Book Value
		5	Consolidation of Less-than-Wholly-Owned Subsidiaries Acquired at More than Book Value
	Intercompany Transfers	6	Intercompany Inventory Transactions
		7	Intercompany Transfers of Services and Noncurrent Assets
Multinational Entities	Foreign Currency Transactions	8	Multinational Accounting: Foreign Currency Transactions and Financial Instruments
	Translation of Foreign Statements	9	Multinational Accounting: Issues in Financial Reporting and Translation of Foreign Entity Statements
Partnerships	Formation, Operation, Changes	10	Partnerships: Formation, Operation, and Changes in Membership
	Liquidation	11	Partnerships: Liquidation
Governmental Entities	Governmental Entities	12	Governmental Entities: Introduction and General Fund Accounting
	Special Funds	13	Governmental Entities: Special Funds and Government-Wide Financial Statements

The next major section of the text on multinational entities introduces two main topics. Chapter 8 explains the accounting for foreign currency transactions, which are increasingly becoming more common in today's global economy. Then, Chapter 9 explains the translation of financial statements of foreign entities into U.S. dollars.

The subsequent major section of this text introduces the accounting for partnerships. In particular, Chapter 10 covers the accounting for the formation and normal operation of a partnership as well as the nuances of accounting for changes in ownership. Chapter 11 explores the winding-up process of partnership liquidation.

The next major section of the text provides a brief overview of accounting for governmental entities. In particular, Chapter 12 introduces basic concepts related to governmental accounting and the notion of fund accounting. Chapter 12 uses the general fund to illustrate these basic accounting principles. Chapter 13 concludes the discussion of governmental accounting by explaining the accounting for special funds.

The locator bar at the beginning of each chapter will remind you of where you are relative to the topical overview illustrated in Figure 1–1.

THE DEVELOPMENT OF COMPLEX BUSINESS STRUCTURES

LO1

Understand and explain different methods of business expansion, types of organizational structures, and types of acquisitions.

The business environment in the United States is perhaps the most dynamic and vibrant in the world. Each day, new companies and new products enter the marketplace, and others are forced to leave or to change substantially in order to survive. In this setting, existing companies often find it necessary to combine their operations with those of other companies or to establish new operating units in emerging areas of business activity. Recent business practice has also experienced the creation of numerous less traditional types of enterprise structures and new, sometimes novel, entities for carrying out the enterprise's operating and financing activities. The creation of new structures and special entities is often a response to today's current operating environment, with its abundant operating risks, global considerations, and tax complexities. In some cases, however, as evidenced by numerous lawsuits, criminal investigations, congressional actions, and corporate bankruptcies, the legitimacy of the use of some of these structures and special entities has been questioned. The adequacy of some of the accounting methods has also been questioned.

Overall, today's business environment is one of the most exciting and challenging in history, characterized by rapid change and exceptional complexity. In this environment, regulators such as the Securities and Exchange Commission (SEC), the Financial Accounting Standards Board (FASB), and the Public Company Accounting Oversight Board (PCAOB) are scrambling to respond to the rapid-paced changes in a manner that ensures the continued usefulness of accounting reports to reflect economic reality.

A number of accounting and reporting issues arise when two or more companies join under common ownership or a company creates a complex organizational structure involving any of a variety of forms of new financing or operating entities. The first seven chapters of this text focus on a number of these issues. Chapter 1 lays the foundation by describing some of the factors that have led to corporate expansion and some of the types of complex organizational structures and relationships that have evolved. Then, it describes the accounting and reporting issues related to formal business combinations. Chapter 2 focuses on investments in the common stock of other companies and on selected other types of investments in and relationships with other entities. Moreover, it introduces basic concepts associated with the preparation of **consolidated financial statements** that portray the related companies as if they were actually a single company. The next six chapters systematically explain additional details related to the preparation and use of consolidated financial statements.

Today's business environment is complex. This complexity arises when companies do business across state and national boundaries. Each state and country has its own set of laws, tax provisions, and risks. Moreover, each jurisdiction has a myriad of different types of common business transactions and financial instruments, and various other factors that require unique managerial expertise. The simple business setting in which one company has two or three manufacturing plants and produces products for a local or regional market is much less common now than it was several decades ago. As companies grow in size and respond to their unique business environment, they often develop complex organizational and ownership structures.

Enterprise Expansion

Most business enterprises seek to expand over time in order to survive and become profitable. Both the owners and managers of a business enterprise have an interest in seeing a company grow in size. Increased size often allows economies of scale in both production and distribution. By expanding into new markets or acquiring other companies already in those markets, companies can develop new earning potential and those in cyclical industries can add greater stability to earnings through diversification. For example, in 1997, Boeing, a company very strong in commercial aviation, acquired McDonnell Douglas, a company weak in commercial aviation but very strong in military aviation and other defense and space applications. When orders for commercial airliners plummeted following a precipitous decline in air travel, increased defense spending, partially related to the war in Iraq, helped level out Boeing's earnings.

Corporate managers are often rewarded with higher salaries as their companies increase in size. In addition, prestige frequently increases with the size of a company and with a reputation for the successful acquisition of other companies. As a result, corporate managers often find it personally advantageous to increase company size. For instance, Bernard Ebbers started his telecommunications career as the head of a small discount long-distance telephone service company and built it into one of the world's largest corporations, WorldCom. In the process, Ebbers became well known for his acquisition prowess and grew tremendously wealthy—until WorldCom was racked by accounting scandals and declared bankruptcy and Ebbers was sentenced to prison in 2003.

Organizational Structure and Business Objectives

Complex organizational structures often evolve to help achieve a business's objectives, such as increasing profitability or reducing risk. For example, many companies establish subsidiaries to conduct certain business activities. A ***subsidiary*** is a corporation that is controlled by another corporation, referred to as a ***parent company,*** usually through majority ownership of its common stock. Because a subsidiary is a separate legal entity, the parent's risk associated with the subsidiary's activities is limited. There are many reasons for creating or acquiring a subsidiary. For example, companies often transfer their receivables to subsidiaries or special-purpose entities that use the receivables as collateral for bonds issued to other entities (securitization). External parties may hold partial or complete ownership of those entities, allowing the transferring company to share its risk associated with the receivables. In some situations, companies can realize tax benefits by conducting certain activities through a separate entity. Bank of America, for example, established a subsidiary to which it transferred bank-originated loans and was able to save $418 million in quarterly taxes.[1]

---

[1] "PNC Shakes Up Banking Sector; Investors Exit," *The Wall Street Journal*, January 30, 2002, p. C2.

Organizational Structure, Acquisitions, and Ethical Considerations

Acquisitions and complex organizational structures have sometimes been used to manipulate financial reporting with the aim of enhancing or enriching managers. Many major corporations, taking advantage of loopholes or laxness in financial reporting requirements, have used subsidiaries or other entities to borrow large amounts of money without reporting the debt on their balance sheets. Some companies have created special entities that have then been used to manipulate profits.

The term *special-purpose entity* has become well known in recent years because of the egregious abuse of these entities by companies such as Enron. A **special-purpose entity** (SPE) is, in general, a financing vehicle that is not a substantive operating entity, usually one created for a single specified purpose. An SPE may be in the form of a corporation, trust, or partnership. Enron Corp., one of the world's largest companies prior to its collapse in 2001, established many SPEs, at least some of which were intended to manipulate financial reporting. Some of Enron's SPEs apparently were created primarily to hide debt while others were used to create fictional transactions or to convert borrowings into reported revenues.

Accounting for mergers and acquisitions also is an area that can lend itself to manipulation. Arthur Levitt, former chairman of the SEC, referred to some of the accounting practices that have been used in accounting for mergers and acquisitions as "creative acquisition accounting" or "merger magic." For example, a previously widely used method of accounting for business combinations, **pooling-of-interests,** sometimes created earnings and, in the view of many, provided misleading financial reporting subsequent to a combination. WorldCom was a company built through acquisitions, many of which were accounted for using the pooling-of-interests method. Another approach used by many companies in accounting for their acquisitions was to assign a large portion of the purchase price of an acquired company to its in-process research and development, immediately expensing the full amount and freeing financial reporting in future periods from the burden of those costs. These practices have since been eliminated by the FASB. However, the frequency and size of business combinations, the complexity of acquisition accounting, and the potential impact on financial statements of the accounting methods employed mean that the issues surrounding the accounting for business combinations are of critical importance.

The scandals and massive accounting failures at companies such as Enron, WorldCom, and Tyco, leading to heavy losses suffered by creditors, investors, employees, and others, focused considerable attention on weaknesses in accounting and the accounting profession. In the past several years, Congress, the SEC, and the FASB have taken actions to strengthen the financial reporting process and to clarify the accounting rules relating to special entities and to acquisitions.

BUSINESS EXPANSION AND FORMS OF ORGANIZATIONAL STRUCTURE

Historically, businesses have expanded by internal growth through new product development and expansion of existing product lines into new markets. In recent decades, however, many companies have chosen to expand by combining with or acquiring other companies. Either approach may lead to a change in organizational structure.

Internal Expansion

As companies expand from within, they often find it advantageous to conduct their expanded operations through new subsidiaries or other entities such as partnerships, joint ventures, or special entities. In most of these situations, an identifiable segment of the company's existing assets is transferred to the new entity, and, in exchange, the transferring company receives equity ownership (as illustrated in the diagram on the next page).

Companies may be motivated to establish new subsidiaries or other entities for a variety of reasons. Broadly diversified companies may place unrelated operations in separate subsidiaries to establish clear lines of control and facilitate the evaluation of operating results. In some cases, an entity that specializes in a particular type of activity or has its operations in a particular country may qualify for special tax incentives. Of particular importance in some industries is the fact that a separate legal entity may be permitted to operate in a regulatory environment without subjecting the entire entity to regulatory control. Also, by creating a separate legal entity, a parent company may be able to protect itself from exposing the entire company's assets to legal liability that may stem from a new product line or entry into a higher-risk form of business activity.

Companies also might establish new subsidiaries or other entities, not as a means of expansion, but as a means of disposing of a portion of their existing operations through outright sale or a transfer of ownership to existing shareholders or others. In some cases, companies have used this approach in disposing of a segment of operations that no longer fits well with the overall mission of the company. In other cases, this approach has been used as a means of disposing of unprofitable operations or to gain regulatory or shareholder approval of a proposed merger with another company. A ***spin-off*** occurs when the ownership of a newly created or existing subsidiary is distributed to the parent's stockholders without the stockholders surrendering any of their stock in the parent company. Thus, the company divests itself of the subsidiary since it is owned by the company's shareholders after the spin-off. A ***split-off*** occurs when the subsidiary's shares are exchanged for shares of the parent, thereby leading to a reduction in the outstanding shares of the parent company. While the two divestiture types are similar, the split-off could result in one set of the former parent shareholders exchanging their shares for those of the divested subsidiary. Although a transfer of ownership to one or more unrelated parties normally results in a taxable transaction, properly designed transfers of ownership to existing shareholders generally qualify as nontaxable exchanges.

External Expansion through Business Combinations

Many times companies find that entry into new product areas or geographic regions is more easily accomplished by acquiring or combining with other companies than through internal expansion. For example, SBC Communications, a major telecommunications company and one of the "Baby Bells," significantly increased its service area by combining with Pacific Telesis and Ameritech, later acquiring AT&T (and adopting its name), and subsequently combining with BellSouth. Similarly, since the state of Florida has traditionally been very reluctant to issue new bank charters, bank corporations wishing to establish operations in Florida have had to acquire an existing bank to obtain a charter in the state.

A ***business combination*** occurs when ". . . an acquirer obtains control of one or more businesses."[2] The diagram on the next page illustrates a typical acquisition. The concept of ***control*** relates to the ability to direct policies and management. Traditionally, control over a company has been gained by acquiring a majority of the company's common stock. However, the diversity of financial and operating arrangements employed in recent years also raises the possibility of gaining control with less than majority ownership or, in some cases, with no ownership at all through other contractual arrangements.

The types of business combinations found in today's business environment and the terms of the combination agreements are as diverse as the firms involved. Companies

[2] *Financial Accounting Standards Board Statement No. 141 (revised 2007),* "Business Combinations," December 2007, para. 3e. (ASC 805-10-65-1)

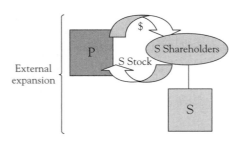

enter into various types of formal and informal arrangements that may have at least some of the characteristics of a business combination. Most companies tend to avoid recording informal agreements on their books because of the potential difficulty of enforcing them. In fact, some types of informal arrangements, such as those aimed at fixing prices or apportioning potential customers, are illegal. Formal agreements generally are enforceable and are more likely to be recognized on the books of the participants.

Informal Arrangements

Informal arrangements take many different forms. A simple gentlemen's agreement may be all that is needed to establish an amiable long-term relationship in a joint business venture. In other cases, companies with complementary products or services develop implicit working relationships. For example, a building contractor might always use a particular electrical or plumbing subcontractor. Some companies form *strategic alliances* for working together on a somewhat more formal basis. For example, Washington Mutual, the country's largest thrift organization, formed a strategic alliance with SAFECO Corporation to distribute SAFECO annuities through Washington Mutual's multistate branch network. Many airlines, such as American with Qantas and Delta with Air France-KLM, routinely enter into route-sharing or code-sharing agreements with one another, and many other well-known companies have entered into strategic agreements, such as Microsoft with Sun Microsystems, Microsoft with Nortel, eBay with VeriSign, Boeing with IBM, and AOL with Google. Companies that partially depend on each other may use interlocking directorates, in which one or more members serve on the boards of directors of both companies, as a means of providing a degree of mutual direction without taking formal steps to join together.

The informality and freedom that make informal arrangements workable also are strong factors against combining financial statements and treating the companies as if they were a single entity. Another key factor in most informal arrangements is the continuing separation of ownership and the ease with which the informal arrangements can be terminated. Without some type of combined ownership, the essentials of a business combination generally are absent.

Formal Agreements

Formal business combinations usually are accompanied by written agreements. These agreements specify the terms of the combination, including the form of the combined company, the consideration to be exchanged, the disposition of outstanding securities, and the rights and responsibilities of the participants. Consummation of such an agreement requires recognition on the books of one or more of the companies that are a party to the combination.

In some cases, a formal agreement may be equivalent in substance to a business combination, yet different in form. For example, a company entering into an agreement to lease all of another company's assets for a period of several decades is, in effect, acquiring the other company. Similarly, an operating agreement giving to one company full management authority over the operations of another company for an extended period of time may be viewed as a means of effecting a business combination.

Frequency of Business Combinations

Very few major companies function as single legal entities in our modern business environment. Virtually all major companies have at least one subsidiary, with more than a few broadly diversified companies having several hundred subsidiaries. In some cases, subsidiaries are created to incorporate separately part of the ongoing operations previously conducted within the parent company. Other subsidiaries are acquired through business combinations.

Business combinations are a continuing and frequent part of the business environment. A merger boom occurred in the 1960s. This period was characterized by frantic and, in some cases, disorganized merger binges, resulting in creation of a large number of conglomerates, or companies operating in many different industries. Because many of the resulting companies lacked coherence in their operations, they often were less successful than anticipated, and many of the acquisitions of the 1960s have since been sold or abandoned. In the 1980s, the number of business combinations again increased. That period saw many leveraged buyouts, but the resulting debt has plagued many of those companies over the years.

The number of business combinations through the 1990s dwarfed previous merger booms, with all records for merger activity shattered. This pace continued into the new century, with a record-setting $3.3 trillion in deals closed in 2000.[3] However, with the downturn in the economy in the early 2000s, the number of mergers declined significantly. Many companies put their expansion plans on hold, and a number of the mergers that did occur were aimed at survival. Toward the middle of 2003, merger activity again increased and accelerated significantly through the middle of the decade. During one period of less than 100 hours in 2006, "around $110 billion in acquisition deals were sealed worldwide in sectors ranging from natural gas, to copper, to mouthwash to steel, linking investors and industrialists from India, to Canada, to Luxembourg to the U.S."[4]

Through much of the middle of the last decade, merger activity was fueled by a new phenomenon, the use of *private equity* money. Rather than the traditional merger activity that typically involves one publicly held company acquiring another, groups of investors, such as wealthy individuals, pension and endowment funds, and mutual funds, pooled their money to make acquisitions. Most of these acquisitions did not result in lasting ownership relationships, with the private equity companies usually attempting to realize a return by selling their investments in a relatively short time. This activity was slowed dramatically by the credit crunch of 2007–2008. Nevertheless, business combinations will continue to be an important business activity into the foreseeable future.

Aside from private-equity acquisitions, business combinations have been common in telecommunications, defense, banking and financial services, information technology, energy and natural resources, entertainment, pharmaceuticals, and manufacturing. Some of the world's largest companies and best-known names have been involved in recent major acquisitions, such as Procter & Gamble, Gillette, Citicorp, Bank of America, AT&T, Whirlpool, Sprint, Verizon, Adobe Systems, Chrysler, Daimler-Benz, ConocoPhillips, British Petroleum, and Exxon.

Complex Organizational Structures

While a parent-subsidiary structure has been standard for major corporations for a number of decades, more complex structures have started to become common in recent years. Many companies now conduct at least part of their operations through entities other than subsidiaries. As is discussed in Chapter 3, special-purpose and variable interest entities, including trusts, have gained widespread use as financing vehicles. Corporate joint ventures and partnerships are commonly found in energy development and distribution, construction, motion picture production, and various other industries. For example, Cingular Wireless, the largest provider of mobile wireless communications in the United States and now part of AT&T, was operated as a joint venture of AT&T and BellSouth prior to AT&T's acquisition of BellSouth. The adoption of less traditional, innovative organizational structures provides many challenges for financial reporting.

---

[3] Dennis K. Berman and Jason Singer, "Big Mergers Are Making a Comeback as Companies, Investors Seek Growth," *The Wall Street Journal,* November 5, 2005, p. A1.

[4] Dennis K. Berman and Jason Singer, "Blizzard of Deals Heralds an Era of Megamergers," *The Wall Street Journal,* June 27, 2006, p. A1.

Organizational Structure and Financial Reporting

When companies expand or change organizational structure by acquiring other companies or through internal division, the new structure must be examined to determine the appropriate financial reporting procedures. Several approaches are possible, depending on the circumstances:

1. **Merger** A merger is a business combination in which the acquired company's assets and liabilities are combined with those of the acquiring company. Thus, two companies are merged into a single entity. In essence, the acquiring company "swallows" the acquired company.

2. **Controlling ownership** A business combination in which the acquired company remains as a separate legal entity with a majority of its common stock owned by the purchasing company leads to a parent–subsidiary relationship. Accounting standards normally require that the financial statements of the parent and subsidiary be consolidated for general-purpose reporting so the companies appear as a single company. The treatment is the same if the subsidiary is created rather than purchased. The treatment is also the same when the other entity is unincorporated and the investor company has control and majority ownership.[5]

3. **Noncontrolling ownership** The purchase of a less-than-majority interest in another corporation does not usually result in a business combination or controlling situation. A similar situation arises when a company creates another entity and holds less than a controlling position in it or purchases a less-than-controlling interest in an existing partnership. In its financial statements, the investor company reports its interest in the investee as an investment with the specific method of accounting for the investment dictated by the circumstances.

4. **Other beneficial interest** One company may have a beneficial interest in another entity even without a direct ownership interest. The beneficial interest may be defined by the agreement establishing the entity or by an operating or financing agreement. When the beneficial interest is based on contractual arrangements instead of majority stock ownership, the reporting rules may be complex and depend on the circumstances. In general, a company that has the ability to make decisions significantly affecting the results of another entity's activities or is expected to receive a majority of the other entity's profits and losses is considered to be that entity's *primary beneficiary.* Normally, that entity's financial statements would be consolidated with those of the primary beneficiary.

These different situations, and the related accounting and reporting procedures, will be discussed throughout the first seven chapters of the text. The primary focus will be on the first three situations, especially the purchase of all or part of another company's stock. The discussion of the fourth situation in Chapter 3 will be limited because of its complexity and the diversity of these contractual arrangements.

CREATING BUSINESS ENTITIES[6]

LO2

Make calculations and prepare journal entries for the creation and purchase of a business entity.

Advanced
StudyGuide
.com

Companies that choose to conduct a portion of their operations through separate business entities usually do so through corporate subsidiaries, corporate joint ventures, or partnerships. The ongoing accounting and reporting for investments in corporate joint ventures and subsidiaries are discussed in Chapters 2 through 7. This section discusses the origination of these entities when the parent or investor creates them rather than purchases an interest in an existing corporation or partnership.

---

[5] Majority ownership is generally a sufficient but not a necessary condition for the indicated treatment. Unlike the corporate case, percentage ownership does not fully describe the nature of a beneficial interest in a partnership. Investments in partnerships are discussed in later chapters.

[6] To view a video explanation of this topic, visit advancedstudyguide.com.

When a company transfers assets or operations to another entity that it has created, a vast number of variations in the types of entities and the types of agreements between the creating company and the created entity are possible. Accordingly, it is impossible to establish a single set of rules and procedures that will suffice in all situations. The discussion here focuses on the most straightforward and common cases in which the transferring company creates a subsidiary or partnership that it owns and controls, including cases in which the company intends to transfer ownership to its stockholders through a spin-off or split-off. In simple cases, the company transfers assets, and perhaps liabilities, to an entity that the company has created and controls and in which it holds majority ownership. The company transfers assets and liabilities to the created entity at book value, and the transferring company recognizes an ownership interest in the newly created entity equal to the book value of the net assets transferred. Recognition of fair values of the assets transferred in excess of their carrying values on the books of the transferring company normally is not appropriate in the absence of an arm's-length transaction. Thus, no gains or losses are recognized on the transfer by the transferring company. However, if the value of an asset transferred to a newly created entity has been impaired prior to the transfer and its fair value is less than the carrying value on the transferring company's books, the transferring company should recognize an impairment loss and transfer the asset to the new entity at the lower fair value.

The created entity begins accounting for the transferred assets and liabilities in the normal manner based on their book values at the time of transfer. Subsequent financial reporting involves consolidating the created entity's financial statements with those of the parent company. Overall, the consolidated financial statements appear the same as if the transfer had not taken place.

As an illustration of a created entity, assume that Allen Company creates a subsidiary, Blaine Company, and transfers the following assets to Blaine in exchange for all 100,000 shares of Blaine's $2 par common stock:

Item	Cost	Book Value
Cash		$ 70,000
Inventory	$ 50,000	50,000
Land	75,000	75,000
Building	100,000	80,000
Equipment	250,000	160,000
		$435,000

Allen records the transfer with the following entry:[7]

(1)			
	Investment in Blaine Company Common Stock	435,000	
	Accumulated Depreciation*	110,000	
	Cash		70,000
	Inventory		50,000
	Land		75,000
	Building		100,000
	Equipment		250,000

Record the creation of Blaine Company.
*$110,000 = ($100,000 − $80,000) + ($250,000 − $160,000)

[7] Journal entries used in the text to illustrate the various accounting procedures are numbered sequentially within individual chapters for easy reference. Each journal entry number appears only once in a chapter.

Blaine Company records the transfer of assets and the issuance of stock (at the book value of the assets), as follows:

(2)	Cash	70,000	
	Inventory	50,000	
	Land	75,000	
	Building	100,000	
	Equipment	250,000	
	Accumulated Depreciation		110,000
	Common Stock, $2 par		200,000
	Additional Paid-In Capital		235,000

Record the receipt of assets and the issuance of $2 par common stock.

BUSINESS COMBINATIONS

LO3

Understand and explain the differences between different forms of business combinations.

Advanced
StudyGuide
.com

A business combination occurs when one party acquires control over one or more businesses. This usually involves two or more separate businesses being joined together under common control. The acquirer may obtain control by paying cash, transferring other assets, issuing debt, or issuing stock. In rare cases, the acquirer might obtain control by agreement or through other means without an exchange taking place. Business combinations can take one of several different forms and can be effected in different ways.

Forms of Business Combinations

Figure 1–2 illustrates the three primary legal forms of business combinations. A *statutory merger* is a type of business combination in which only one of the combining companies survives and the other loses its separate identity. The acquired company's assets and liabilities are transferred to the acquiring company, and the acquired company is dissolved, or *liquidated.* The operations of the previously separate companies are carried on in a single legal entity following the merger.

A *statutory consolidation* is a business combination in which both combining companies are dissolved and the assets and liabilities of both companies are transferred to a newly created corporation. The operations of the previously separate companies are carried on in a single legal entity, and neither of the combining companies remains in existence after a statutory consolidation. In many situations, however, the resulting corporation is new in form only, and in substance it actually is one of the combining companies reincorporated with a new name. A *stock acquisition* occurs when one company acquires the voting shares of another company and the two companies continue to operate as separate, but related, legal entities. Because neither of the combining companies is liquidated, the acquiring company accounts for its ownership interest in the other company as an investment. In a stock acquisition, the acquiring company need not acquire all the other company's stock to gain control.

The relationship that is created in a stock acquisition is referred to as a *parent–subsidiary relationship.* A *parent company* is one that controls another company, referred to as a *subsidiary,* usually through majority ownership of common stock. For general-purpose financial reporting, a parent company and its subsidiaries present consolidated financial statements that appear largely as if the companies had actually merged into one.

The legal form of a business combination, the substance of the combination agreement, and the circumstances surrounding the combination all affect how the combination is recorded initially and the accounting and reporting procedures used subsequent to the combination.

Methods of Effecting Business Combinations

Business combinations can be characterized as either friendly or unfriendly. In a friendly combination, the managements of the companies involved come to agreement on the terms of the combination and recommend approval by the stockholders. Such combinations usually are effected in a single transaction involving an exchange of assets or

FIGURE 1–2
Types of Business Combinations

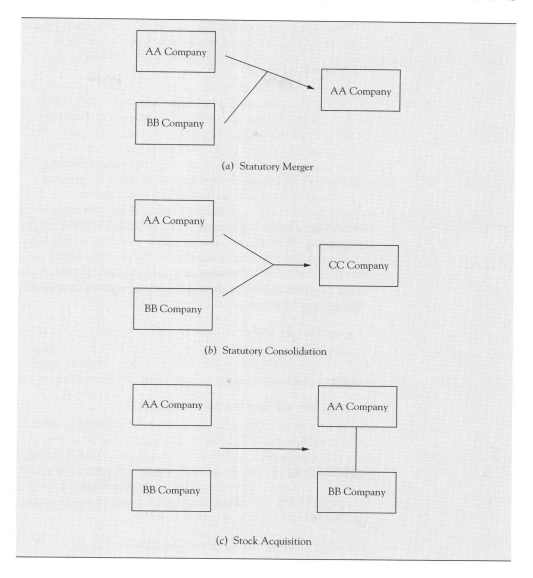

(*a*) Statutory Merger

(*b*) Statutory Consolidation

(*c*) Stock Acquisition

voting shares. In an unfriendly combination, or "hostile takeover," the managements of the companies involved are unable to agree on the terms of a combination, and the management of one of the companies makes a ***tender offer*** directly to the shareholders of the other company. A tender offer invites the shareholders of the other company to "tender," or exchange, their shares for securities or assets of the acquiring company. If sufficient shares are tendered, the acquiring company gains voting control of the other company and can install its own management by exercising its voting rights.

The specific procedures to be used in accounting for a business combination depend on whether the combination is effected through an acquisition of assets or an acquisition of stock.

Acquisition of Assets

Sometimes one company acquires another company's assets through direct negotiations with its management. The agreement also may involve the acquiring company's assuming the other company's liabilities. Combinations of this sort normally take form (*a*) or form (*b*) in Figure 1–2. The selling company generally distributes to its stockholders the assets or securities received in the combination from the acquiring company and liquidates, leaving only the acquiring company as the surviving legal entity.

The acquiring company accounts for the combination by recording each asset acquired, each liability assumed, and the consideration given in exchange.

Acquisition of Stock

A business combination effected through a stock acquisition does not necessarily have to involve the acquisition of all of a company's outstanding voting shares. For one company to gain control over another through stock ownership, a majority (i.e., more than 50 percent) of the outstanding voting shares usually is required unless other factors lead to the acquirer gaining control. The total of the shares of an acquired company not held by the controlling shareholder is called the ***noncontrolling interest.*** In the past, the noncontrolling interest was referred to as the ***minority interest.***

In those cases when control of another company is acquired and both companies remain in existence as separate legal entities following the business combination, the stock of the acquired company is recorded on the books of the acquiring company as an investment. Alternatively, the acquired company may be liquidated and its assets and liabilities transferred to the acquiring company or a newly created company. To do so, all or substantially all of the acquired company's voting stock must be obtained. An acquisition of stock and subsequent liquidation of the acquired company is equivalent to an acquisition of assets.

Acquisition by Other Means

Occasionally, a business combination may be effected without an exchange of assets or equities and without a change in ownership. In some cases, control might be acquired through agreement alone, or in rare cases, by other contractual arrangements.

Valuation of Business Entities

All parties involved in a business combination must believe they have an opportunity to benefit before they will agree to participate. Determining whether a particular combination proposal is advantageous can be difficult. Both the value of a company's assets and its future earning potential are important in assessing the value of the company. Tax laws also influence investment decisions. For example, the existence of accumulated net operating losses that can be used under U.S. tax law to shelter future income from taxes increases the value of a potential acquiree.

Value of Individual Assets and Liabilities

The value of a company's individual assets and liabilities is usually determined by appraisal. For some items, the value may be determined with relative ease, such as investments that are traded actively in the securities markets, or short-term payables. For other items, the appraisal may be much more subjective, such as the value of land located in an area where few recent sales have occurred. In addition, certain intangibles typically are not reported on the balance sheet. For example, the costs of developing new ideas, new products, and new production methods normally are expensed as research and development costs in the period incurred.

Current liabilities are often viewed as having fair values equal to their book values because they will be paid at face amount within a short time. Long-term liabilities, however, must be valued based on current interest rates if different from the effective rates at the issue dates of the liabilities. For example, if $100,000 of 10-year, 6 percent bonds, paying interest annually, had been issued at par three years ago, and the current market rate of interest for the same type of security is 10 percent, the value of the liability currently is computed as follows:

Present value for 7 years at 10% of principal payment of $100,000	$51,316
Present value at 10% of 7 interest payments of $6,000	29,211
Present value of bond	$80,527

Although accurate assessments of the value of assets and liabilities may be difficult, they form an important part of the overall determination of the value of an enterprise.

Value of Potential Earnings

In many cases, assets operated together as a group have a value that exceeds the sum of their individual values. This "going-concern value" makes it desirable to operate the assets as an ongoing entity rather than sell them individually. A company's earning power as an ongoing enterprise is of obvious importance in valuing that company.

There are different approaches to measuring the value of a company's future earnings. Sometimes companies are valued based on a multiple of their current earnings. For example, if Bargain Company reports earnings of $35,000 for the current year, the company's value based on a multiple of 10 times current earnings is $350,000. The appropriate multiple to use is a matter of judgment and is based on factors such as the riskiness and variability of the earnings and the anticipated degree of growth.

Another method of valuing a company is to compute the present value of the anticipated future net cash flows generated by the company. This requires assessing the amount and timing of future cash flows and discounting them back to the present value at the discount rate determined to be appropriate for the type of enterprise. For example, if Bargain Company is expected to generate cash flows of $35,000 for each of the next 25 years, the present value of the firm at a discount rate of 10 percent is $317,696. Estimating the potential for future earnings requires numerous assumptions and estimates. Not surprisingly, the buyer and seller often have difficulty agreeing on the value of a company's expected earnings.

Valuation of Consideration Exchanged

When one company acquires another, the acquiring company must place a value on the consideration given in the exchange. Little difficulty is encountered when the acquiring company gives cash in an acquisition, but valuation may be more difficult when the acquiring company gives securities, particularly new untraded securities or securities with unusual features. For example, General Motors completed an acquisition a number of years ago using a new Series B common stock that paid dividends based on subsequent earnings of the acquired company rather than on the earnings of General Motors as a whole. Some companies have used non-interest-bearing bonds (zero coupon bonds), which have a fair value sufficiently below par value to compensate the holder for interest. Other companies have used various types of convertible securities. Unless these securities, or others that are considered equivalent, are being traded in the market, estimates of their value must be made. The approach generally followed is to use the value of some similar security with a determinable market value and adjust for the estimated value of the differences in the features of the two securities.

ACCOUNTING FOR BUSINESS COMBINATIONS

LO4

Make calculations and prepare journal entries for different types of business combinations through the acquisition of stock or assets.

For over half a century, accounting for business combinations remained largely unchanged. Two methods of accounting for business combinations, *the purchase method* and *the pooling-of-interests method,* were acceptable during that time. However, major changes in accounting for business combinations have occurred over the past decade. First, the FASB eliminated the pooling-of-interests method in 2001, leaving only a single method, purchase accounting. Then, in 2007, the FASB issued the revised version of **FASB Statement No. 141,** "Business Combinations (revised 2007)" (FASB 141R, ASC 805), that replaced the purchase method with the *acquisition method,* now the only acceptable method of accounting for business combinations. The acquisition method must be used to account for all business combinations for which the acquisition date is in fiscal years beginning on or after December 15, 2008. **FASB 141R (ASC 805)** may not be applied retroactively.

Although all business combinations must now be accounted for using the acquisition method, many companies' financial statements will continue to include the effects of previous business combinations recorded using the purchase and pooling-of-interests methods. Thus, a general understanding of those methods can be helpful. Appendix 1A presents a numerical comparison of the three methods.

The idea behind a pooling-of-interests was that no change in ownership had actually occurred in the business combination, often a questionable premise. Based on this idea, the book values of the combining companies were carried forward to the combined company and no revaluations to fair value were made. Managers often preferred pooling accounting because it did not result in asset write-ups or goodwill that might burden future earnings with additional depreciation or write-offs. Also, reporting practices often made acquisitions appear better than they would have appeared if purchase accounting had been used.

Purchase accounting treated the purchase of a business much like the purchase of any asset. The acquired company was recorded based on the purchase price paid by the acquirer. Individual assets and liabilities of the acquired company were valued at their fair values, and the difference between the total purchase price and the fair value of the net identifiable assets acquired was recorded as goodwill. All direct costs of bringing about and consummating the combination were included in the total purchase price.

Acquisition accounting is consistent with the FASB's intention to move accounting in general more toward recognizing fair values. Under acquisition accounting, the acquirer in a business combination, in effect, values the acquired company based on the fair value of the consideration given in the combination and the fair value of any noncontrolling interest not acquired by the acquirer.

ACQUISITION ACCOUNTING

LO5

Make calculations and business combination journal entries in the presence of a differential, goodwill, or a bargain purchase element.

Advanced
StudyGuide
.com

As of the end of 2007, the FASB significantly changed the method of accounting for business combinations, requiring the use of the *acquisition method.* Under the acquisition method, the acquirer recognizes all assets acquired and liabilities assumed in a business combination and measures them at their acquisition-date fair values. If less than 100 percent of the acquiree is acquired, the noncontrolling interest also is measured at its acquisition-date fair value. Note that a business combination does not affect the amounts at which the assets and liabilities of the acquirer are valued.

Fair Value Measurements

Because accounting for business combinations is now based on fair values, the measurement of fair values takes on added importance. The acquirer must value at fair value (1) the consideration it exchanges in a business combination, (2) each of the individual assets and liabilities acquired, and (3) any noncontrolling interest in the acquiree. Normally, a business combination involves an arm's-length exchange between two unrelated parties. The value of the consideration given in the exchange is usually the best measure of the value received and, therefore, reflects the value of the acquirer's interest in the acquiree. However, the FASB decided in **FASB 141R (ASC 805)** to focus directly on the value of the consideration given rather than just using it to impute a fair value for the acquiree as a whole. In some cases, the value of the consideration given may be difficult to determine, or there may be no exchange, and valuation is better based on the value of the acquirer's interest in the acquiree or other valuation techniques. **FASB Statement No. 157,** "Fair Value Measurements" (FASB 157, ASC 820), provides a framework for applying fair value measurements in accounting.

Applying the Acquisition Method

For all business combinations, an acquirer must be identified, and that party is the one gaining control over the other. In the past, some business combinations occurred under the dubious assertion that neither party acquired the other. In addition, an acquisition date must be determined. That date is usually the closing date when the exchange transaction actually occurs. However, in rare cases control may be acquired on a different date or without an exchange, so the circumstances must be examined to determine precisely when the acquirer gains control.

Under the acquisition method, the full acquisition-date fair values of the individual assets acquired, both tangible and intangible, and liabilities assumed in a business combination are recognized. This is true regardless of the percentage ownership acquired by the controlling entity. If the acquirer acquires all of the assets and liabilities of the acquiree in a merger, these assets and liabilities are recorded on the books of the acquiring company at their acquisition-date fair values. If the acquiring company acquires partial ownership of the acquiree in a stock acquisition, the assets acquired and liabilities assumed appear at their full acquisition-date fair values in a consolidated balance sheet prepared immediately after the combination.

Several other points to remember related to assets and liabilities acquired in a business combination are as follows:

1. No separate asset valuation accounts related to assets acquired are recognized.
2. Long-lived assets classified at the acquisition date as held for sale are valued at fair value less cost to sell.
3. Deferred income taxes related to the business combination and assets and liabilities related to an acquiree's employee benefit plans are valued in accordance with the specific FASB standards relating to those topics.

Any excess of (1) the sum of the fair value of the consideration given by the acquirer in a business combination[8] and the acquisition-date fair value of any noncontrolling interest over (2) the acquisition-date fair value of the net identifiable assets acquired in a business combination is considered goodwill. The amount of goodwill arising in a business combination is unaffected by the percentage of the acquiree acquired.

All costs of bringing about and consummating a business combination are charged to an acquisition expense as incurred. The costs of issuing equity securities used to acquire the acquiree are treated in the same manner as stock issues costs are normally treated, as a reduction in the paid-in capital associated with the securities.

Goodwill

Conceptually, *goodwill* as it relates to business combinations consists of all those intangible factors that allow a business to earn above-average profits. From an accounting perspective, the FASB has stated that **goodwill** "is an asset representing the future economic benefits arising from other assets acquired in a business combination that are not individually identified and separately recognized."[9] An asset is considered to be *identifiable,* and therefore must be separately recognized, if it is separable (can be separated from the business) or arises from a contractual or other right.

Under the acquisition method, an acquirer measures and recognizes goodwill from a business combination based on the difference between the total fair value of the acquired company and the fair value of its net identifiable assets. However, the FASB decided, for several reasons, not to focus directly on the total fair value of the acquiree, but rather on the components that provide an indication of that fair value. The FASB identified three components that should be measured and summed for the total amount to be used in determining the amount of goodwill recognized in a business combination:

1. The fair value of the consideration given by the acquirer.
2. The fair value of any interest in the acquiree already held by the acquirer.
3. The fair value of the noncontrolling interest in the acquiree, if any.

[8] The fair value of any interest in the acquiree already held by the acquirer would also be included in this calculation.
[9] **FASB 141R,** para. 3j. (ASC 805-10-65-1)

The total of these three amounts, all measured at the acquisition date, is then compared with the acquisition-date fair value of the acquiree's net identifiable assets, and the difference is *goodwill.*

As an example of the computation of goodwill, assume that Albert Company acquires all of the assets of Zanfor Company for $400,000 when the fair value of Zanfor's net identifiable assets is $380,000. Goodwill is recognized for the $20,000 difference between the total consideration given and the fair value of the net identifiable assets acquired. If, instead of an acquisition of assets, Albert acquires 75 percent of the common stock of Zanfor for $300,000, and the fair value of the noncontrolling interest is $100,000, goodwill is computed as follows:

Fair value of consideration given by Albert	$300,000
+ Fair value of noncontrolling interest	100,000
Total fair value of Zanfor Company	$400,000
− Fair value of net identifiable assets acquired	(380,000)
Goodwill	$ 20,000

Note that the total amount of goodwill is not affected by whether 100 percent of the acquiree is acquired or less than that. However, the fair value of the noncontrolling interest does have an effect on the amount of goodwill recognized. In the example given, the fair values of the controlling and noncontrolling interests are proportional (each is valued at an amount equal to its proportionate ownership share of the total) and imply a total fair value of the acquired company of $400,000. This is frequently the case and will always be assumed throughout the text unless indicated otherwise. However, that may not always be the case in practice. Situations might arise in a stock acquisition, for example, where the per-share value of the controlling interest is greater than that of the noncontrolling interest because of a premium associated with gaining control.

Combination Effected through the Acquisition of Net Assets

When one company acquires all the net assets of another in a business combination, the acquirer records on its books the individual assets acquired and liabilities assumed in the combination and the consideration given in exchange. Each identifiable asset and liability acquired (with minor exceptions) is recorded by the acquirer at its acquisition-date fair value. Any excess of the fair value of the consideration exchanged over the fair value of the acquiree's net identifiable assets is recorded as goodwill by the acquiring company.

To illustrate the application of the acquisition method of accounting to a business combination effected through the acquisition of the acquiree's net assets, assume that Point Corporation acquires all of the assets and assumes all of the liabilities of Sharp Company in a statutory merger by issuing 10,000 shares of $10 par common stock to Sharp. The shares issued have a total market value of $610,000. Point incurs legal and appraisal fees of $40,000 in connection with the combination and stock issue costs of $25,000. Figure 1–3 shows the book values and fair values of Sharp's individual assets and liabilities on the date of combination.

The relationships among the fair value of the consideration exchanged, the fair value of Sharp's net assets, and the book value of Sharp's net assets are illustrated in the following diagram:

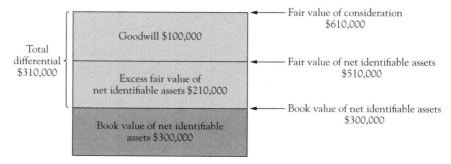

FIGURE 1–3
Sharp Company Balance Sheet Information, December 31, 20X0

Assets, Liabilities and Equities	Book Value	Fair Value
Cash and Receivables	$ 45,000	$ 45,000
Inventory	65,000	75,000
Land	40,000	70,000
Buildings and Equipment	400,000	350,000
Accumulated Depreciation	(150,000)	
Patent		80,000
Total Assets	$400,000	$620,000
Current Liabilities	$100,000	110,000
Common Stock ($5 par)	100,000	
Additional Paid-In Captial	50,000	
Retained Earnings	150,000	
Total Liabilities and Equities	$400,000	
Fair Value of Net Assets		$510,000

The total difference at the acquisition date between the fair value of the consideration exchanged and the book value of the net identifiable assets acquired is referred to as the ***differential.*** In more complex situations, the differential is equal to the difference between (1) the acquisition-date fair value of the consideration transferred by the acquirer, plus the acquisition-date fair value of any equity interest in the acquiree previously held by the acquirer, plus the fair value of any noncontrolling interest in the acquiree and (2) the acquisition-date book values of the identifiable assets acquired and liabilities assumed.

In the Point/Sharp merger, the total differential of $310,000 reflects the difference between the total fair value of the shares issued by Point and the carrying amount of Sharp's net assets reflected on its books at the date of combination. A portion of that difference ($210,000) is attributable to the increased value of Sharp's net assets over book value. The remainder of the difference ($100,000) is considered to be goodwill.

The $40,000 of acquisition costs incurred by Point in carrying out the acquisition are expensed as incurred:

(3)	Acquisition Expense	40,000	
	Cash		40,000
	Record costs related to acquisition of Sharp Company.		

Portions of the $25,000 of stock issue costs related to the shares issued to acquire Sharp may be incurred at various times. To facilitate accumulating these amounts before recording the combination, Point may record them in a separate temporary "suspense" account as incurred:

(4)	Deferred Stock Issue Costs	25,000	
	Cash		25,000
	Record costs related to issuance of common stock.		

On the date of combination, Point records the acquisition of Sharp with the following entry:

(5)	Cash and Receivables	45,000	
	Inventory	75,000	
	Land	70,000	
	Buildings and Equipment	350,000	
	Patent	80,000	
	Goodwill	100,000	
	Current Liabilities		110,000
	Common Stock		100,000
	Additional Paid-In Capital		485,000
	Deferred Stock Issue Costs		25,000
	Record acquisition of Sharp Company.		

Entry (5) records all of Sharp's individual assets and liabilities, both tangible and intangible, on Point's books at their fair values on the date of combination. The fair value of Sharp's net assets recorded is $510,000 ($620,000 − $110,000). The $100,000 difference between the fair value of the shares given by Point ($610,000) and the fair value of Sharp's net assets is recorded as goodwill.

In recording the business combination, Sharp's book values are not relevant to Point; only the fair values are recorded. Because a change in ownership has occurred, the basis of accounting used by the acquired company is not relevant to the acquirer. Consistent with this view, accumulated depreciation recorded by Sharp on its buildings and equipment is not relevant to Point and is not recorded.

The stock issue costs incurred by Point in connection with Sharp's acquisition are initially recorded in a temporary account as incurred. They are then treated in the normal manner as a reduction in the proceeds received from the issuance of the stock. Thus, these costs are transferred from the temporary account to Additional Paid-In Capital as a reduction. Point records the $610,000 of stock issued at its value minus the stock issue costs, or $585,000. Of this amount, the $100,000 par value is recorded in the Common Stock account and the remainder in Additional Paid-In Capital.

Entries Recorded by Acquired Company

On the date of the combination, Sharp records the following entry to recognize receipt of the Point shares and the transfer of all individual assets and liabilities to Point:

(6)			
	Investment in Point Stock	610,000	
	Current Liabilities	100,000	
	Accumulated Depreciation	150,000	
	Cash and Receivables		45,000
	Inventory		65,000
	Land		40,000
	Buildings and Equipment		400,000
	Gain on Sale of Net Assets		310,000

Record transfer of assets to Point Corporation.

Sharp recognizes the fair value of Point Corporation shares at the time of the exchange and records a gain of $310,000. The distribution of Point shares and the liquidation of Sharp are recorded on Sharp's books with the following entry:

(7)			
	Common Stock	100,000	
	Additional Paid-In Capital	50,000	
	Retained Earnings	150,000	
	Gain on Sale of Net Assets	310,000	
	Investment in Point Stock		610,000

Record distribution of Point Corporation stock.

Subsequent Accounting for Goodwill by Acquirer

Goodwill arising in a merger is recorded by the acquirer for the difference between the fair value of the consideration exchanged and the fair value of the identifiable net assets acquired, as illustrated in entry (5). Once goodwill has been recorded by the acquirer, it must be accounted for in accordance with **FASB Statement No. 142,** "Goodwill and Other Intangible Assets" (FASB 142, ASC 350). Goodwill is carried forward at the originally recorded amount unless it becomes impaired. Goodwill must be reported as a separate line item in the balance sheet. A goodwill impairment loss that occurs subsequent to recording goodwill must be reported as a separate line item within income from continuing operations in the income statement unless the loss relates to discontinued operations, in which case the loss is reported within the discontinued operations section.

Goodwill must be tested for impairment at least annually, at the same time each year, and more frequently if events that are likely to impair the value of the goodwill occur.

The process of testing goodwill for impairment is complex. It involves examining potential goodwill impairment by each of the company's reporting units, where a reporting unit is an operating segment[10] or a component of an operating segment that is a business for which management regularly reviews financial information from that component. When goodwill arises in a business combination, it must be assigned to individual reporting units. The goodwill is assigned to units that are expected to benefit from the combination, even if no other assets or liabilities of the acquired company are assigned to those units. To test for the impairment of goodwill, the fair value of the reporting unit is compared with its carrying amount. If the fair value of the reporting unit exceeds its carrying amount, the goodwill of that reporting unit is considered unimpaired. On the other hand, if the carrying amount of the reporting unit exceeds its fair value, an impairment of the reporting unit's goodwill is implied.[11]

The amount of the reporting unit's goodwill impairment is measured as the excess of the carrying amount of the unit's goodwill over the implied value of its goodwill. The implied value of its goodwill is determined as the excess of the fair value of the reporting unit over the fair value of its net assets excluding goodwill. Goodwill impairment losses are recognized in income from continuing operations or income before extraordinary gains and losses.

As an example of goodwill impairment, assume that Reporting Unit A is assigned $100,000 of goodwill arising from a recent business combination. The following assets and liabilities are assigned to Reporting Unit A:

Item	Carrying Amount	Fair Value
Cash and receivables	$ 50,000	$ 50,000
Inventory	80,000	90,000
Equipment	120,000	150,000
Goodwill	100,000	
Total assets	$350,000	$290,000
Current payables	(10,000)	(10,000)
Net assets	$340,000	$280,000

By summing the carrying amounts of the assets and subtracting the carrying amount of the payables, the carrying amount of the reporting unit, including the goodwill, is determined to be $340,000. If the fair value of the reporting unit is estimated to be $360,000, no impairment of goodwill is indicated. On the other hand, if the fair value of the reporting unit is estimated to be $320,000, a second comparison must be made to determine the amount of any impairment loss. The implied value of Reporting Unit A's goodwill is determined by deducting the $280,000 fair value of the net assets, excluding goodwill, from the unit's $320,000 fair value. The $40,000 difference ($320,000 − $280,000) represents Reporting Unit A's implied goodwill. The impairment loss is measured as the excess of the carrying amount of the unit's goodwill ($100,000) over the implied value of the goodwill ($40,000), or $60,000. This goodwill impairment loss is combined with any impairment losses from other reporting units to determine the total impairment loss to be reported by the company as a whole. Goodwill is written down by the amount of the impairment loss. Once written down, goodwill may not be written up for recoveries.

[10] An operating segment is defined in *Financial Accounting Standards Board Statement No. 131*, "Disclosures about Segments of an Enterprise and Related Information," June 1997 (ASC 280-10-50). Whereas U.S. GAAP assigns goodwill to reporting units, IFRS assigns goodwill to cash-generating units (GCU).

[11] The one-step impairment test for goodwill under IFRS is slightly different. The recoverable amount of the cash-generating-unit (GCU) is compared with its carrying amount. Any impairment loss is recognized in operating results as the excess of the carrying amount over the recoverable amount. Impairment losses are recognized in operating results. If the impairment loss exceeds the book value of goodwill, the loss is allocated first to goodwill and then on a pro rata basis to the other assets of the CGU.

Bargain Purchase

Occasionally, the fair value of the consideration given in a business combination, along with the fair value of any equity interest in the acquiree already held and the fair value of any noncontrolling interest in the acquiree, may be less than the fair value of the acquiree's net identifiable assets, resulting in a **bargain purchase.** This might occur, for example, with a forced sale.

When a bargain purchase occurs (rarely), the acquirer must take steps to ensure that all acquisition-date valuations are appropriate. If they are, the acquirer recognizes a gain at the date of acquisition for the excess of the amount of the net identifiable assets acquired and liabilities assumed as valued under **FASB 141R (ASC 805),** usually at fair value, over the sum of the fair value of the consideration given in the exchange, the fair value of any equity interest in the acquiree held by the acquirer at the date of acquisition, and the fair value of any noncontrolling interest. Along with the amount of the gain, companies must disclose the operating segment where the gain is reported and the factors that led to the gain.

To illustrate accounting for a bargain purchase, assume that in the previous example of Point and Sharp, Point is able to acquire Sharp for $500,000 cash even though the fair value of Sharp's net identifiable assets is estimated to be $510,000. In this simple bargain-purchase case without an equity interest already held or a noncontrolling interest, the fair value of Sharp's net identifiable assets exceeds the consideration exchanged by Point, and, accordingly, a $10,000 gain attributable to Point is recognized.

In accounting for the bargain purchase (for cash) on Point's books, the following entry replaces previous entry (5):

(8)			
	Cash and Receivables	45,000	
	Inventory	75,000	
	Land	70,000	
	Buildings and Equipment	350,000	
	Patent	80,000	
	Cash		500,000
	Current Liabilities		110,000
	Gain on Bargain Purchase of Sharp Company		10,000

This treatment is rather unusual because it recognizes a gain on an acquisition and, thus, represents an exception to the realization concept.

FASB 141R (ASC 805) does not state a treatment for the situation opposite to that of a bargain purchase, that is, an overpayment. Acquirers do not knowingly overpay for an acquisition. Any overpayment presumably would be the result of misinformation, and the overpayment would not be discovered until a later time. The FASB avoided this issue by basing the computation of goodwill on the consideration given by the acquirer rather than the acquiree's total fair value. Thus, any overpayment would be included in goodwill and presumably eliminated in future periods by testing for goodwill impairment.

Combination Effected through Acquisition of Stock

Advanced
StudyGuide
.com

Many business combinations are effected by acquiring the voting stock of another company rather than by acquiring its net assets. In such a situation, the acquired company continues to exist, and the acquirer records an investment in the common stock of the acquiree rather than its individual assets and liabilities. The acquirer records its investment in the acquiree's common stock at the total fair value of the consideration given in exchange. For example, if Point Corporation (*a*) exchanges 10,000 shares of its stock with a total market value of $610,000 for all of Sharp Company's shares and (*b*) incurs merger costs of $40,000 and stock issue costs of $25,000, Point records the following entries upon receipt of the Sharp stock:

(9)	Acquisition Expense	40,000	
	Deferred Stock Issue Costs	25,000	
	Cash		65,000

Record merger and stock issue costs related to acquisition of Sharp Company.

(10)	Investment in Sharp Stock	610,000	
	Common Stock		100,000
	Additional Paid-In Capital		485,000
	Deferred Stock Issue Costs		25,000

Record acquisition of Sharp Company stock.

When a business combination is effected through a stock acquisition, the acquiree may continue to operate as a separate company, or it may lose its separate identity and be merged into the acquiring company. The accounting and reporting procedures for intercorporate investments in common stock when the acquiree continues in existence are discussed in the next six chapters. If the acquired company is liquidated and its assets and liabilities are transferred to the acquirer, the dollar amounts recorded are identical to those in entry (5).

Financial Reporting Subsequent to a Business Combination

Financial statements prepared subsequent to a business combination reflect the combined entity only from the date of combination. When a combination occurs during a fiscal period, income earned by the acquiree prior to the combination is not reported in the income of the combined enterprise. If the combined company presents comparative financial statements that include statements for periods before the combination, those statements include only the activities and financial position of the acquiring company, not those of the acquiree.

To illustrate financial reporting subsequent to a business combination, assume the following information for Point Corporation and Sharp Company:

	20X0	20X1
Point Corporation:		
Separate income (excluding any income from Sharp)	$300,000	$300,000
Shares outstanding, December 31	30,000	40,000
Sharp Company:		
Net income	$ 60,000	$ 60,000

Point Corporation acquires all of Sharp Company's stock at book value on January 1, 20X1, by issuing 10,000 shares of common stock. Subsequently, Point Corporation presents comparative financial statements for the years 20X0 and 20X1. The net income and earnings per share that Point presents in its comparative financial statements for the two years are as follows:

20X0:	
Net Income	$300,000
Earnings per Share ($300,000/30,000 shares)	$10.00
20X1:	
Net Income ($300,000 + $60,000)	$360,000
Earnings per Share ($360,000/40,000 shares)	$9.00

If Point Corporation had acquired Sharp Company in the middle of 20X1 instead of at the beginning, Point would include only Sharp's earnings subsequent to acquisition in its

20X1 income statement. If Sharp earned $25,000 in 20X1 before acquisition by Point and $35,000 after the combination, Point would report total net income for 20X1 of $335,000 ($300,000 + $35,000).

Disclosure Requirements

FASB 141R (ASC 810)[12] requires extensive disclosures relating to a company's business combinations so that financial statement users may assess the impact of the combinations. These disclosures include, among others items:

1. Identification and description of the acquired company, the acquisition date, and the percentage ownership acquired.
2. The main reasons for the acquisition and a description of the factors that led to the recognition of goodwill.
3. The acquisition-date fair value of the consideration transferred, the fair value of each component of the consideration, and a description of any contingent consideration.
4. The acquisition-date amounts recognized for each major class of assets acquired and liabilities assumed.
5. The business combination–related costs incurred, the amount expensed, and where they were reported, along with any issue costs not expensed and how they were recognized.
6. The acquiree's revenue and net income included in the consolidated income statement for the period since acquisition, and the results of operations for the combined company as if the business combination had occurred at the beginning of the reporting period.
7. The total amount of goodwill, the amount expected to be deductible for tax purposes, changes in goodwill during each subsequent period, and, if the company is required to report segment information, the amount of goodwill assigned to each segment.
8. For less-than-100-percent acquisitions, the acquisition-date fair value of the noncontrolling interest and the valuation method used.

ADDITIONAL CONSIDERATIONS IN ACCOUNTING FOR BUSINESS COMBINATIONS

LO6

Understand additional considerations associated with business combinations.

FASB 141R (ASC 805) includes a number of requirements relating to specific items or aspects encountered in business combinations. A discussion of several of the more important situations follows.

Uncertainty in Business Combinations

Uncertainty affects much of accounting measurement but is especially prevalent in business combinations. Although uncertainty relates to many aspects of business combination, three aspects of accounting for business combinations deserve particular attention: the measurement period, contingent consideration, and acquiree contingencies.

Measurement Period

One type of uncertainty in business combinations arises from the requirement to value at acquisition-date fair value the assets and liabilities acquired in a business combination, the acquirer's interest in the acquiree, any noncontrolling interest, and the consideration given. Because the acquirer may not have sufficient information available immediately to properly ascertain fair values, **FASB 141R (ASC 805)** allows for a period of time, called the *measurement period,* to acquire the necessary information. The measurement period ends once the acquirer obtains the necessary information about the facts as of the acquisition date, but may not exceed one year.

[12] **FASB 141R,** para. 68. (ASC 810-10-50-1 through ASC 810-10-50-2)

Assets that have been provisionally recorded as of the acquisition date are retrospectively adjusted in value during the measurement period for new information that clarifies the acquisition-date value. Usually, the offsetting entry is to goodwill. Retrospective adjustments may not be made for changes in value that occur subsequent to the acquisition date.

As an illustration, assume that Baine Company acquires land in a business combination and provisionally records the land at its estimated fair value of $100,000. During the measurement period, Baine receives a reliable appraisal that the land was worth $110,000 at the acquisition date. Subsequently, during the same accounting period, a change in the zoning of a neighboring parcel of land reduces the value of the land acquired by Baine to $75,000. Baine records the clarification of the acquisition-date fair value of the land and the subsequent impairment of value with the following entries:

(11)	Land	10,000	
	Goodwill		10,000
	Adjust acquisition-date value of land acquired in business combination.		

(12)	Impairment Loss	35,000	
	Land		35,000
	Recognize decline in value of land held.		

Contingent Consideration

Sometimes the consideration exchanged by the acquirer in a business combination is not fixed in amount, but rather is contingent on future events. For example, the acquiree and acquirer may enter into a *contingent-share agreement* whereby, in addition to an initial issuance of shares, the acquirer may agree to issue a certain number of additional shares for each percentage point by which the earnings number exceeds a set amount over the next five years. Thus, total consideration exchanged in the business combination is not known within the measurement period because the number of shares to be issued is dependent on future events.

FASB 141R (ASC 805) requires contingent consideration in a business combination to be valued at fair value as of the acquisition date and classified as either a liability or equity. The right to require the return of consideration given that it is dependent on future events is classified as an asset. Contingent consideration classified as an asset or liability is remeasured each period to fair value and the change is recognized in income.[13] Contingent consideration classified as equity is not remeasured.

Acquiree Contingencies

Certain contingencies may relate to an acquiree in a business combination, such as pending lawsuits or loan guarantees made by the acquiree. Certainly, the acquirer considers such contingencies when entering into an acquisition agreement, and the accounting must also consider such contingencies. Under **FASB 141R (ASC 805),** the acquirer must recognize all contingencies that arise from contractual rights or obligations and other contingencies if it is more likely than not that they meet the definition of an asset or liability at the acquisition date. These contingencies are recorded by the acquirer at acquisition-date fair value.

For all acquired contingencies, the acquirer should provide a description of each, disclose the amount recognized at the acquisition date, and describe the estimated range of possible undiscounted outcomes. Subsequently, the acquirer should disclose changes in the amounts recognized and in the range of possible outcomes.

---

[13] Treatment of contingent consideration under IFRS is slightly different. While contingent consideration classified as an asset or liability will likely be a financial instrument measured at fair value with gains or losses recognized in profit or loss (or OCI, as appropriate), if the asset or liability is not a financial instrument, it is accounted for in accordance with the standard provisions for that class of asset or liability (i.e., not necessarily at fair value).

In-Process Research and Development

In normal operations, research and development costs are required to be expensed as incurred, except under certain limited conditions. When a company acquires valuable ongoing research and development projects from an acquiree in a business combination, a question arises as to whether these should be recorded as assets. The FASB concluded in **FASB 141R (ASC 805)** that these projects are assets and should be recorded at their acquisition-date fair values, even if they have no alternative use. These projects should be classified as having indefinite lives and, therefore, should not be amortized until completed or abandoned. They should be tested for impairment in accordance with current standards. Subsequent expenditures for the previously acquired research and development projects would normally be expensed as incurred.

Noncontrolling Equity Held Prior to Combination

In some cases an acquirer may hold an equity interest in an acquiree prior to obtaining control through a business combination. The total amount of the acquirer's investment in the acquiree subsequent to the combination is equal to the acquisition-date fair value of the equity interest previously held and the fair value of the consideration given in the business combination. For example, if Lemon Company held 10 percent of Aide Company's stock with a fair value of $500,000 and Lemon acquired the remaining shares of Aide for $4,500,000 cash, Lemon's total investment is considered to be $5,000,000.

An acquirer that held an equity position in an acquiree immediately prior to the acquisition date must revalue that equity position to its fair value at the acquisition date and recognize a gain or loss on the revaluation. Suppose that Lemon's 10 percent investment in Aide has a book value of $300,000 and fair value of $500,000 at the date Lemon acquires the remaining 90 percent of Aide's stock. Lemon revalues its original investment in Aide to its $500,000 fair value and recognizes a $200,000 gain on the revaluation at the date it acquires the remaining shares of Aide. Lemon records the following entries on its books in connection with the acquisition of Aide:

(13)	Investment in Aide Company Stock	200,000	
	Gain on revaluation of Aide Company Stock		200,000
	Revalue Aide Company stock to fair value at date of business combination.		

(14)	Investment in Aide Company Stock	4,500,000	
	Cash		4,500,000
	Acquire controlling interest in Aide Company.		

Acquisitions by Contract Alone

In rare instances, an acquirer may obtain control of an acquiree without transferring consideration or receiving an equity interest in the acquiree. Control is achieved by contract alone. In such cases, the amount of the acquiree's net assets at the date of acquisition is attributed to the noncontrolling interest and included in the noncontrolling interest reported in subsequent consolidated financial statements.

Summary of Key Concepts	Business combinations and complex organizational structures are an important part of the global business scene. Many companies add organizational components by creating new corporations or partnerships through which to carry out a portion of their operations. In other cases, companies may enter into business combinations to acquire other companies through which to further their objectives.
	When a company creates another corporation or a partnership through a transfer of assets, the book values of those assets are transferred to the new entity and no gain or loss is recognized. The creating company and the new entity will combine their financial statements for general-purpose

financial reporting to appear as if they were a single company as long as the creating company continues to control the new entity.

Over the decades, business combinations have been occurring with increasing frequency. A business combination occurs when an acquirer obtains control of one or more other businesses. The three types of business combination that are commonly found are: (*a*) statutory mergers, where the acquiree loses its separate identity and the acquirer continues with the assets and liabilities of both companies; (*b*) statutory consolidations, where both combining companies join to form a new company; and (*c*) stock acquisitions, where both combining companies maintain their separate identities, with the acquirer owning the stock of the acquiree.

The FASB recently issued **FASB 141R (ASC 805),** which requires the acquisition method be used to account for business combinations. Under the acquisition method, all of the assets acquired and liabilities assumed by the acquirer in a business combination are valued at their fair values. The excess of the sum of the fair value of the acquirer's consideration transferred, the fair value of any equity interest in the acquiree already held, and the fair value of any noncontrolling interest in the acquiree over the fair value of the net identifiable assets acquired is goodwill. In subsequent financial statements, goodwill must be reported separately. Goodwill is not amortized, but it must be tested for impairment at least annually. If goodwill is impaired, it is written down to its new fair value and a loss recognized for the amount of the impairment. If the fair value of the consideration transferred by the acquirer in a business combination, along with the fair value of an equity interest already held, and the noncontrolling interest is less than the fair value of the acquiree's net identifiable assets, a situation referred to as a bargain purchase, the difference is recognized as a gain attributable to the acquirer.

All costs associated with a business combination are expensed as incurred. Any stock issue costs incurred in connection with a business combination are treated as a reduction in paid-in capital. A business combination is given effect as of the acquisition date for subsequent financial reporting.

Key Terms

acquisition method, *16*
bargain purchase, *22*
business combination, *7*
consolidated financial statements, *4*
control, *7*
differential, *19*
goodwill, *17*
liquidated, *12*

measurement period, *24*
minority interest, *14*
noncontrolling interest, *14*
parent company, *5*
parent–subsidiary relationship, *12*
pooling-of-interests, *6*
primary beneficiary, *10*

special-purpose entity, *6*
spin-off, *7*
split-off, *7*
statutory consolidation, *12*
statutory merger, *12*
stock acquisition, *12*
subsidiary, *5*
tender offer, *13*

Appendix 1A Methods of Accounting for Business Combinations

As discussed in the chapter, several different methods of accounting for business combinations have been acceptable over the years. While acquisition accounting is the only method acceptable for business combinations occurring after 2008, many companies' financial statements include the results of past business combinations recorded using either the purchase or pooling-of-interests method. Thus, accountants should understand the effects of these earlier methods even though they are no longer acceptable.

We use the example presented earlier in the chapter to illustrate the differences between the methods of accounting for business combinations. Point Corporation acquires all of the assets and assumes all of the liabilities of Sharp Company in a merger by issuing to Sharp 10,000 shares of $10 par common stock. The shares issued have a total market value of $610,000. Point incurs legal and appraisal fees of $40,000 in connection with the combination and stock issue costs of $25,000. As discussed previously, Figure 1–3 gives the book values and fair values of Sharp's individual assets and liabilities on the date of combination.

Figure 1–4 shows the journal entries on Point's books to record the business combination under the acquisition, purchase, and pooling-of-interests methods. Under the acquisition method, Point records the identifiable assets and liabilities acquired in the business combination at their fair values and records goodwill for the $100,000 difference between the $610,000 fair value of the

[Handwritten margin note:]
– All costs expensed day 1
– Can be done on 12/31/12
* & still count whole year*
– All assets combined

FIGURE 1–4   Different Methods of Accounting for Business Combinations

Acquisition Accounting			Purchase Accounting			Pooling Accounting		
Merger Expenses	40,000		Deferred Merger Costs	40,000		Merger Expenses	65,000	
Deferred Stock Issue			Deferred Stock Issue			Cash		65,000
Costs	25,000		Costs	25,000				
Cash		65,000	Cash		65,000			

Acquisition Accounting			Purchase Accounting			Pooling Accounting		
Cash and Receivables	45,000		Cash and Receivables	45,000		Cash and Receivables	45,000	
Inventory	75,000		Inventory	75,000		Inventory	65,000	
Land	70,000		Land	70,000		Land	40,000	
Buildings and			Buildings and			Buildings and		
Equipment	350,000		Equipment	350,000		Equipment	400,000	
Patent	80,000		Patent	80,000		Accumulated Depreciation		150,000
Goodwill	100,000		Goodwill	140,000		Current Liabilities		100,000
Current Liabilities		110,000	Current Liabilities		110,000	Common Stock		100,000
Common Stock		100,000	Common Stock		100,000	Additional Capital		50,000
Additional Capital		485,000	Additional Capital		485,000	Retained Earnings		150,000
Deferred Stock Issue			Deferred Merger Costs		40,000			
Costs		25,000	Deferred Stock Issue Costs		25,000			

consideration transferred by Point and the $510,000 fair value of Sharp's net identifiable assets. Expenses related to the business combination are expensed, and the stock issue costs are treated as a reduction in the issue price of Point's stock.

The purchase method called for recording the acquired company at the amount of the total purchase price paid by the acquirer, including associated costs. Point records the identifiable assets and liabilities acquired at their fair values, as under the acquisition method. Point then records goodwill for the difference between the total purchase price paid for Sharp and the fair value of its net identifiable assets. The purchase method based the calculation of goodwill on the total purchase price while the acquisition method is based on the fair value of the consideration given. Also, the purchase method viewed the costs associated with bringing about the business combination as being part of the total purchase price, while the acquisition method expenses all such costs. The $140,000 of goodwill is calculated under the purchase method as the sum of the fair value of the consideration given by Point ($610,000) and the merger costs ($40,000), less the fair value of Sharp's net identifiable assets ($510,000).

The pooling-of-interests method assumed the view that the two companies were joining together and pooling their resources without either company acquiring the other and with a continuity of ownership. Thus, the book values of assets, liabilities, and equity were carried forward without adjustment to fair value. Consistent with the idea of the owners of both companies continuing as owners of the combined company, poolings could occur only when one company issued its common stock for the other combining company so that substantially all stockholders of both companies continued as owners. The issuing company recorded equity equal to that of the other combining company. The stock issued in the combination was recorded at the total amount of the other combining company's stock that it replaced, and the retained earnings of the other combining company was recorded on the books of the issuing company. All merger and stock issue costs were expensed. No goodwill was ever recorded in poolings, but unlike under purchase accounting, the retained earnings balances of both companies were carried forward. In this example, Point records on its books all of Sharp's recorded assets and liabilities at their book values from Sharp's books. Point records the stock it issues in the combination at the same total amount as Sharp's stock ($150,000, including both the par value and additional paid-in capital), and records Sharp's retained earnings ($150,000).

Questions

LO1   **Q1-1**   What types of circumstances would encourage management to establish a complex organizational structure?

LO1   **Q1-2**   How would the decision to dispose of a segment of operations using a split-off rather than a spin-off impact the financial statements of the company making the distribution?

LO1   **Q1-3**   Why did companies such as Enron find the use of special-purpose entities to be advantageous?

LO3   **Q1-4**   Describe each of the three legal forms that a business combination might take.

LO2   **Q1-5**   What basis of accounting normally is used in recording the assets and liabilities transferred to a new wholly owned subsidiary?

LO1   **Q1-6**   How might the concept of a beneficial interest impact the reporting of an interest in another company?

LO1   **Q1-7**   When does a noncontrolling interest arise in a business combination?

LO1   **Q1-8**   Why did corporate management often prefer pooling-of-interests accounting in recording business combinations?

LO5   **Q1-9**   How is the amount reported as goodwill determined under the acquisition method?

LO5   **Q1-10**   What impact does the level of ownership have on the amount of goodwill reported under the acquisition method?

LO5   **Q1-11**   How is the amount of goodwill assigned to the noncontrolling interest determined when less than full ownership is acquired?

LO5   **Q1-12**   What is a differential?

LO4, LO5   **Q1-13**   When a business combination occurs after the beginning of the year, the income earned by the acquired company between the beginning of the year and the date of combination is excluded from the net income reported by the combined entity for the year. Why?

LO4   **Q1-14**   What is the maximum balance in retained earnings that can be reported by the combined entity following a business combination?

LO4   **Q1-15**   How is the amount of additional paid-in capital determined when recording a business combination?

LO4, LO5   **Q1-16**   Which of the costs incurred in completing a business combination are capitalized under the acquisition method?

LO4   **Q1-17**   Which of the costs incurred in completing a business combination should be treated as a reduction of additional paid-in capital?

LO5   **Q1-18**   When is goodwill considered impaired following a business combination?

LO5   **Q1-19**   When does a bargain purchase occur?

LO5   **Q1-20***   Within the measurement period following a business combination, the acquisition-date fair value of buildings acquired is determined to be less than initially recorded. How is the reduction in value recognized?

LO4   **Q1-21***   P Company reports its 10,000 shares of S Company at $40 per share. P Company then purchases an additional 60,000 shares of S Company for $65 each and gains control of S Company. What must be done with respect to the valuation of the shares previously owned?

LO5   **Q1-22A**   P Company purchased 80 percent of the shares of S Company in 20X6 under the purchase method. How would the amount of goodwill reported under the purchase method differ from the amount to be reported under the acquisition method?

LO4   **Q1-23A**   What major differences occur between using pooling-of-interests accounting for a business combination and using the acquisition method?

Cases

LO5   **C1-1**   **Reporting Alternatives and International Harmonization**

Accounting procedures for business combinations historically have differed across countries. Pooling-of-interests, for many years a preferred method in the United States, was not acceptable in most countries. In some countries, accounting standards permit goodwill to be written off directly against stockholders' equity at the time of a business combination.

Understanding

Required

a. Over the years, many U.S. companies complained they were at a disadvantage when competing against foreign companies in purchasing other business enterprises because, unlike U.S. companies, many foreign companies either did not have to capitalize goodwill or could write it off immediately against stockholders' equity. Historically, why were U.S. companies opposed to

*Indicates that the item relates to "Additional Consideration."
"A" indicates that the item relates to "Appendix A."

capitalizing goodwill? What happened during the past decade to improve the situation from the perspective of U.S. companies?

b. Should U.S. companies care about accounting standards other than those that are generally accepted in the United States? Explain.

LO4, LO5   **C1-2**   **Assignment of Acquisition Costs**

Troy Company notified Kline Company's shareholders that it was interested in purchasing controlling ownership of Kline and offered to exchange one share of Troy's common stock for each share of Kline Company submitted by July 31, 20X7. At the time of the offer, Troy's shares were trading for $35 per share and Kline's shares were trading at $28. Troy acquired all of the shares of Kline prior to December 31, 20X7, and transferred the assets and liabilities of Kline to its books. In addition to issuing its shares, Troy paid a finder's fee of $200,000, stock registration and audit fees of $60,000, legal fees of $90,000 for transferring Kline's assets and liabilities to Troy, and $370,000 in legal fees to settle litigation brought by Kline's shareholders who alleged that the offering price was below the per share fair value of Kline's net assets.

Research

Troy is currently negotiating to purchase Lad Company through an exchange of common stock and expects to incur additional costs comparable to those involved in the acquisition of Kline. The acquisition of Lad is expected to close sometime late in 20X9.

Required

Troy Company's vice president of finance has asked you to review the current accounting literature, including authoritative pronouncements, and prepare a memo reporting the required treatment of the additional costs at the time Kline Company was acquired and the current requirements for reporting the additional costs of acquiring Lad Company. Support your recommendations with citations and quotations from the authoritative financial reporting standards or other literature.

LO1, LO2   **C1-3**   **Evaluation of Merger**

One company may acquire another for a number of different reasons. The acquisition often has a significant impact on the financial statements. In 2005, 3M Corporation acquired CUNO Incorporated. Obtain a copy of the 3M 10-K filing for 2005. The 10-K reports the annual results for a company and is often available on the Investor Relations section of a company's Web site. It is also available on the SEC's Web site at www.SEC.gov.

Research

Required

Use the 10-K for 2005 to find the answers to the following questions about 3M's acquisition of CUNO Inc. (*Hint:* You can search on the term CUNO once you have accessed the 10-K online.)

a. Provide at least one reason why 3M acquired CUNO.

b. How was the acquisition funded?

c. What was the impact of the CUNO acquisition on net accounts receivable?

d. What was the impact of the CUNO acquisition on inventories?

LO3   **C1-4**   **Business Combinations**

A merger boom comparable to those of the 1960s and mid-1980s occurred in the 1990s and into the new century. The merger activity of the 1960s was associated with increasing stock prices and heavy use of pooling-of-interests accounting. The mid-1980s activity was associated with a number of leveraged buyouts and acquisitions involving junk bonds. Merger activity in the early 1990s, on the other hand, appeared to involve primarily purchases with cash and standard debt instruments. By the mid-1990s, however, many business combinations were being effected through exchanges of stock. In the first decade of the new century, the nature of many business acquisitions changed, and by late 2008, the merger boom had slowed dramatically.

Analysis

a. Which factors do you believe were the most prominent in encouraging business combinations in the 1990s? Which of these was the most important? Explain why.

b. Why were so many of the business combinations in the middle and late 1990s effected through exchanges of stock?

c. What factors had a heavy influence on mergers during the mid-2000s? How did many of the business combinations of this period differ from earlier combinations? Why did the merger boom slow so dramatically late in 2008 and in 2009?

d. If a major review of the tax laws were undertaken, would it be wise or unwise public policy to establish greater tax incentives for corporate mergers? Propose three incentives that might be used.

e. If the FASB were interested in encouraging more mergers, what action should it take with regard to revising or eliminating existing accounting standards? Explain.

LO5

C1-5 **Determination of Goodwill Impairment**

Research

Plush Corporation purchased 100 percent of Common Corporation's common stock on January 1, 20X3, and paid $450,000. The fair value of Common's identifiable net assets at that date was $430,000. By the end of 20X5, the fair value of Common, which Plush considers to be a reporting unit, had increased to $485,000; however, Plush's external auditor made a passing comment to the company's chief accountant that Plush may need to recognize impairment of goodwill on one or more of its investments.

Required

Prepare a memo to Plush's chief accountant indicating the tests used in determining whether goodwill has been impaired. Include in your discussion one or more possible conditions under which Plush may be required to recognize impairment of goodwill on its investment in Common Corporation. In preparing your memo, review the current accounting literature, including authoritative pronouncements of the FASB and other appropriate bodies. Support your discussion with citations and quotations from the applicable literature.

LO1

C1-6 **Risks Associated with Acquisitions**

Analysis

Not all business combinations are successful, and many entail substantial risk. Acquiring another company may involve a number of different types of risk. Obtain a copy of the 10-K report for Google, Inc., for the year ended December 31, 2006, available at the SEC's Web site (**www.sec.gov**). The report also can be accessed through Yahoo Finance or the company's Investor Relations page.

Required

On page 21 of the 10-K report, Google provides information to investors about its motivation for acquiring companies and the possible risks associated with such acquisitions. Briefly discuss the risks that Google sees inherent in potential acquisitions.

LO1

C1-7 **Numbers Game**

Communication

Arthur Levitt's speech, "The Numbers Game," is available on the SEC's Web site at www.sec.gov/news/speech/speecharchive/1998/spch220.txt. Read the speech, and then answer the following questions.

Required

a. Briefly explain what motivations Levitt discusses for earnings management.

b. What specific techniques for earnings management does Levitt discuss?

c. According to Levitt, why is the issue of earnings management important?

LO1, LO3

C1-8 **MCI: A Succession of Mergers**

Research

MCI WorldCom, Inc. (later MCI), was known as a high-flying company, having had its roots in a small local company and rising to one of the world's largest communications giants. The company's spectacular growth was accomplished through a string of business combinations. However, not all went as planned, and MCI is no longer an independent company.

Required

Provide a brief history of, and indicate subsequent events related to, MCI WorldCom. Include in your discussion the following:

a. Trace the major acquisitions leading to MCI WorldCom and indicate the type of consideration used in the acquisitions.

b. Who is Bernard Ebbers, and where is he now?

c. What happened to MCI WorldCom, and where is it now?

LO3

C1-9 **Leveraged Buyouts**

Analysis

A type of acquisition that was not discussed in the chapter is the *leveraged buyout.* Many experts argue that a leveraged buyout (LBO) is not a type of business combination but rather just a restructuring of ownership. Yet some would see an LBO as having many of the characteristics of a business combination. The number of LBOs in recent years has grown dramatically and, therefore, accounting for these transactions is of increased importance.

Required

a. What is a leveraged buyout? How does an LBO compare with a management buyout (MBO)?

b. What authoritative pronouncements, if any, deal with leveraged buyouts?

c. Is a leveraged buyout a type of business combination? Explain.

d. What is the major issue in determining the proper basis for an interest in a company purchased through a leveraged buyout?

LO5

C1-10   Curtiss-Wright and Goodwill

Research

Accounting standards continually evolve. One area where significant change has occurred over the past decade is in recording and accounting for goodwill. Prior to 2002, companies were required to amortize goodwill over its useful life, not to exceed 17 years. Beginning in 2002, goodwill was no longer required to be amortized. One company that has been affected by the changes in accounting for goodwill is Curtiss-Wright.

Required

a. By what amounts did Curtiss-Wright's goodwill increase in 2001 and 2002, and what amounts did the company report at December 31, 2001 and 2002? What percentage of Curtis-Wright's total assets does goodwill represent at December 31, 2002? How does this compare to other companies?

b. What is the fair-value amount of assets Curtiss-Wright acquired in 2006 through business combinations? By what dollar amount did goodwill increase during 2006? What percentage increase does this represent? What percentage of Curtiss-Wright's total assets does goodwill represent at December 31, 2006?

c. What amount of goodwill impairment losses did Curtiss-Wright recognize for 2006 and 2005? What change did Curtiss-Wright make during 2006 in its goodwill impairment testing? Why was this change made? What effect did this change have on the financial statements for 2006 and prior years?

d. Do you think the management of Curtiss-Wright prefers the treatment that was required for goodwill before 2002 or the current treatment? Explain.

LO1

C1-11   Sears and Kmart: The Joining Together of Two of America's Oldest Retailers

Analysis

Kmart started in 1899 as the S. S. Kresge Company, better known as the five-and-dime store. Sears has its roots in the 1880s and incorporated as Sears, Roebuck and Company in 1893. In 2005, the two companies joined together in a business combination.

Required

a. What major event for Kmart occurred in 2002? How was that issued resolved?

b. What form of business combination brought Sears and Kmart together, and what was the resulting corporate structure?

c. In the business combination involving Sears and Kmart, which company acquired the other? On what basis was this determination made? What accounting implications did the choice of acquirer have?

Exercises

LO1, LO3

E1-1   Multiple-Choice Questions on Complex Organizations

Select the correct answer for each of the following questions.

1. Growth in the complexity of the U.S. business environment

   a. Has led to increased use of partnerships to avoid legal liability.

   b. Has led to increasingly complex organizational structures as management has attempted to achieve its business objectives.

   c. Has encouraged companies to reduce the number of operating divisions and product lines so they may better control those they retain.

   d. Has had no particular impact on the organizational structures or the way in which companies are managed.

2. Which of the following is *not* an appropriate reason for establishing a subsidiary?

   a. The parent wishes to protect existing operations by shifting new activities with greater risk to a newly created subsidiary.

   b. The parent wishes to avoid subjecting all of its operations to regulatory control by establishing a subsidiary that focuses its operations in regulated industries.

   c. The parent wishes to reduce its taxes by establishing a subsidiary that focuses its operations in areas where special tax benefits are available.

   d. The parent wishes to be able to increase its reported sales by transferring products to the subsidiary at the end of the fiscal year.

3. Which of the following actions is likely to result in recording goodwill on Randolph Company's books?

   a. Randolph acquires Penn Corporation in a business combination recorded as a merger.

   b. Randolph acquires a majority of Penn's common stock in a business combination and continues to operate it as a subsidiary.

   c. Randolph distributes ownership of a newly created subsidiary in a distribution considered to be a spin-off.

   d. Randolph distributes ownership of a newly created subsidiary in a distribution considered to be a split-off.

4. When an existing company creates a new subsidiary and transfers a portion of its assets and liabilities to the new entity

   a. The new entity records both the assets and liabilities it received at fair values.

   b. The new entity records both the assets and liabilities it received at the carrying values of the original company.

   c. The original company records a gain or loss on the difference between its carrying values and the fair values of the assets transferred to the new entity.

   d. The original company records the difference between the carrying values and the fair values of the assets transferred to the new entity as goodwill.

5. When a company assigns goodwill to a reporting unit acquired in a business combination, it must record an impairment loss if

   a. The fair value of the net identifiable assets held by a reporting unit decreases.

   b. The fair value of the reporting unit decreases.

   c. The carrying value of the reporting unit is less than the fair value of the reporting unit.

   d. The fair value of the reporting unit is less than its carrying value and the carrying value of goodwill is more than the implied value of its goodwill.

LO4, LO5

E1-2 Multiple-Choice Questions on Recording Business Combinations [AICPA Adapted]
Select the correct answer for each of the following questions.

1. Goodwill represents the excess of the sum of the consideration given over the

   a. Sum of the fair values assigned to identifiable assets acquired less liabilities assumed.

   b. Sum of the fair values assigned to tangible assets acquired less liabilities assumed.

   c. Sum of the fair values assigned to intangible assets acquired less liabilities assumed.

   d. Book value of an acquired company.

2. In a business combination, costs of registering equity securities to be issued by the acquiring company are a(n)

   a. Expense of the combined company for the period in which the costs were incurred.

   b. Direct addition to stockholders' equity of the combined company.

   c. Reduction of the otherwise determinable fair value of the securities.

   d. Addition to goodwill.

3. Which of the following is the appropriate basis for valuing fixed assets acquired in a business combination carried out by exchanging cash for common stock?

   a. Historical cost.

   b. Book value.

    c. Cost plus any excess of purchase price over book value of assets acquired.

    d. Fair value.

4. In a business combination, the fair value of the net identifiable assets acquired exceeds the fair value of the consideration given. The excess should be reported as a

    a. Deferred credit.

    b. Reduction of the values assigned to current assets and a deferred credit for any unallocated portion.

    c. Pro rata reduction of the values assigned to current and noncurrent assets and a deferred credit for any unallocated portion.

    d. No answer listed is correct.

5. A and B Companies have been operating separately for five years. Each company has a minimal amount of liabilities and a simple capital structure consisting solely of voting common stock. A Company, in exchange for 40 percent of its voting stock, acquires 80 percent of the common stock of B Company. This is a "tax-free" stock-for-stock (type B) exchange for tax purposes. B Company assets have a total net fair market value of $800,000 and a total net book value of $580,000. The fair market value of the A stock used in the exchange is $700,000 and the fair value of the noncontrolling interest is $175,000. The goodwill reported following the acquisition would be

    a. Zero.

    b. $60,000.

    c. $75,000.

    d. $295,000.

LO4, LO5   **E1-3** **Multiple-Choice Questions on Reported Balances [AICPA Adapted]**

Select the correct answer for each of the following questions.

1. On December 31, 20X3, Saxe Corporation was merged into Poe Corporation. In the business combination, Poe issued 200,000 shares of its $10 par common stock, with a market price of $18 a share, for all of Saxe's common stock. The stockholders' equity section of each company's balance sheet immediately before the combination was:

	Poe	Saxe
Common Stock	$3,000,000	$1,500,000
Additional Paid-In Capital	1,300,000	150,000
Retained Earnings	2,500,000	850,000
	$6,800,000	$2,500,000

In the December 31, 20X3, consolidated balance sheet, additional paid-in capital should be reported at

    a. $950,000.

    b. $1,300,000.

    c. $1,450,000.

    d. $2,900,000.

2. On January 1, 20X1, Rolan Corporation issued 10,000 shares of common stock in exchange for all of Sandin Corporation's outstanding stock. Condensed balance sheets of Rolan and Sandin immediately before the combination follow:

	Rolan	Sandin
Total Assets	$1,000,000	$500,000
Liabilities	$ 300,000	$150,000
Common Stock ($10 par)	200,000	100,000
Retained Earnings	500,000	250,000
Total Liabilities and Equities	$1,000,000	$500,000

Rolan's common stock had a market price of $60 per share on January 1, 20X1. The market price of Sandin's stock was not readily determinable. The fair value of Sandin's net identifiable assets was determined to be $570,000. Rolan's investment in Sandin's stock will be stated in Rolan's balance sheet immediately after the combination in the amount of

   a. $350,000.
   b. $500,000.
   c. $570,000.
   d. $600,000.

3. On April 1, 20X2, Jack Company paid $800,000 for all of Ann Corporation's issued and outstanding common stock. Ann's recorded assets and liabilities on April 1, 20X2, were as follows:

Cash	$ 80,000
Inventory	240,000
Property and equipment (net of accumulated depreciation of $320,000)	480,000
Liabilities	(180,000)

On April 1, 20X2, Ann's inventory was determined to have a fair value of $190,000 and the property and equipment had a fair value of $560,000. What is the amount of goodwill resulting from the business combination?

   a. $0.
   b. $50,000.
   c. $150,000.
   d. $180,000.

4. Action Corporation issued nonvoting preferred stock with a fair market value of $4,000,000 in exchange for all the outstanding common stock of Master Corporation. On the date of the exchange, Master had tangible net assets with a book value of $2,000,000 and a fair value of $2,500,000. In addition, Action issued preferred stock valued at $400,000 to an individual as a finder's fee in arranging the transaction. As a result of this transaction, Action should record an increase in net assets of

   a. $2,000,000.
   b. $2,500,000.
   c. $4,000,000.
   d. $4,400,000.

LO4, LO5   **E1-4**   **Multiple-Choice Questions Involving Account Balances**

Select the correct answer for each of the following questions.

1. Topper Company established a subsidiary and transferred equipment with a fair value of $72,000 to the subsidiary. Topper had purchased the equipment with an expected life of 10 years four years earlier for $100,000 and has used straight-line depreciation with no expected residual value. At the time of the transfer, the subsidiary should record

   a. Equipment at $72,000 and no accumulated depreciation.
   b. Equipment at $60,000 and no accumulated depreciation.
   c. Equipment at $100,000 and accumulated depreciation of $40,000.
   d. Equipment at $120,000 and accumulated depreciation of $48,000.

2. Lead Corporation established a new subsidiary and transferred to it assets with a cost of $90,000 and a book value of $75,000. The assets had a fair value of $100,000 at the time of transfer. The transfer will result in

   a. A reduction of net assets reported by Lead Corporation of $90,000.
   b. A reduction of net assets reported by Lead Corporation of $75,000.
   c. No change in the reported net assets of Lead Corporation.
   d. An increase in the net assets reported by Lead Corporation of $25,000.

3. Tear Company, a newly established subsidiary of Stern Corporation, received assets with an original cost of $260,000, a fair value of $200,000, and a book value of $140,000 from the parent in exchange for 7,000 shares of Tear's $8 par value common stock. Tear should record

   a. Additional paid-in capital of $0.
   b. Additional paid-in capital of $84,000.
   c. Additional paid-in capital of $144,000.
   d. Additional paid-in capital of $204,000.

4. Grout Company reports assets with a carrying value of $420,000 (including goodwill with a carrying value of $35,000) assigned to an identifiable reporting unit purchased at the end of the prior year. The fair value of the net assets held by the reporting unit is currently $350,000, and the fair value of the reporting unit is $395,000. At the end of the current period, Grout should report goodwill of

   a. $45,000.
   b. $35,000.
   c. $25,000.
   d. $10,000.

5. Twill Company has a reporting unit with the fair value of its net identifiable assets of $500,000. The carrying value of the reporting unit's net assets on Twill's books is $575,000, which includes $90,000 of goodwill. The fair value of the reporting unit is $560,000. Twill should report impairment of goodwill of

   a. $60,000.
   b. $30,000.
   c. $15,000.
   d. $0.

LO2

E1-5 Asset Transfer to Subsidiary

Pale Company was established on January 1, 20X1. Along with other assets, it immediately purchased land for $80,000, a building for $240,000, and equipment for $90,000. On January 1, 20X5, Pale transferred these assets, cash of $21,000, and inventory costing $37,000 to a newly created subsidiary, Bright Company, in exchange for 10,000 shares of Bright's $6 par value stock. Pale uses straight-line depreciation and useful lives of 40 years and 10 years for the building and equipment, respectively, with no estimated residual values.

Required

a. Give the journal entry that Pale recorded when it transferred the assets to Bright.
b. Give the journal entry that Bright recorded for the receipt of assets and issuance of common stock to Pale.

LO2

E1-6 Creation of New Subsidiary

Lester Company transferred the following assets to a newly created subsidiary, Mumby Corporation, in exchange for 40,000 shares of its $3 par value stock:

	Cost	Book Value
Cash	$ 40,000	$ 40,000
Accounts Receivable	75,000	68,000
Inventory	50,000	50,000
Land	35,000	35,000
Buildings	160,000	125,000
Equipment	240,000	180,000

Required

a. Give the journal entry in which Lester recorded the transfer of assets to Mumby Corporation.
b. Give the journal entry in which Mumby recorded the receipt of assets and issuance of common stock to Lester.

LO2, LO4

E1-7 Balance Sheet Totals of Parent Company

Foster Corporation established Kline Company as a wholly owned subsidiary. Foster reported the following balance sheet amounts immediately before and after it transferred assets and accounts payable to Kline Company in exchange for 4,000 shares of $12 par value common stock:

	Amount Reported			
	Before Transfer		**After Transfer**	
Cash		$ 40,000		$ 25,000
Accounts Receivable		65,000		41,000
Inventory		30,000		21,000
Investment in Kline Company				66,000
Land		15,000		12,000
Depreciable Assets	$180,000		$115,000	
Accumulated Depreciation	75,000	105,000	47,000	68,000
Total Assets		$255,000		$233,000
Accounts Payable		$ 40,000		$ 18,000
Bonds Payable		80,000		80,000
Common Stock		60,000		60,000
Retained Earnings		75,000		75,000
Total Liabilities and Equities		$255,000		$233,000

Required

a. Give the journal entry that Foster recorded when it transferred its assets and accounts payable to Kline.

b. Give the journal entry that Kline recorded upon receipt of the assets and accounts payable from Foster.

LO2

E1-8 Creation of Partnership

Glover Corporation entered into an agreement with Renfro Company to establish G&R Partnership. Glover agreed to transfer the following assets to G&R for 90 percent ownership, and Renfro agreed to transfer $50,000 cash to the partnership for 10 percent ownership.

	Cost	Book Value
Cash	$ 10,000	$ 10,000
Accounts Receivable	19,000	19,000
Inventory	35,000	35,000
Land	16,000	16,000
Buildings	260,000	200,000
Equipment	210,000	170,000

Required

a. Give the journal entry that Glover recorded at the time of its transfer of assets to G&R.

b. Give the journal entry that Renfro recorded at the time of its transfer of cash to G&R.

c. Give the journal entry that G&R recorded upon the receipt of assets from Glover and Renfro.

LO4, LO5

E1-9 Acquisition of Net Assets

Sun Corporation concluded the fair value of Tender Company was $60,000 and paid that amount to acquire its net assets. Tender reported assets with a book value of $55,000 and fair value of $71,000 and liabilities with a book value and fair value of $20,000 on the date of combination. Sun also paid $4,000 to a search firm for finder's fees related to the acquisition.

Required

Give the journal entries to be made by Sun to record its investment in Tender and its payment of the finder's fees.

LO5

E1-10   Reporting Goodwill

Samper Company reported the book value of its net assets at $160,000 when Public Corporation acquired 100 percent ownership for $310,000. The fair value of Samper's net assets was determined to be $190,000 on that date.

Required

Determine the amount of goodwill to be reported in consolidated financial statements presented immediately following the combination and the amount at which Public will record its investment in Samper if the amount paid by Public is

a. $310,000.
b. $196,000.
c. $150,000.

LO4

E1-11   Stock Acquisition

McDermott Corporation has been in the midst of a major expansion program. Much of its growth had been internal, but in 20X1 McDermott decided to continue its expansion through the acquisition of other companies. The first company acquired was Tippy Inc., a small manufacturer of inertial guidance systems for aircraft and missiles. On June 10, 20X1, McDermott issued 17,000 shares of its $25 par common stock for all 40,000 of Tippy's $10 par common shares. At the date of combination, Tippy reported additional paid-in capital of $100,000 and retained earnings of $350,000. McDermott's stock was selling for $58 per share immediately prior to the combination. Subsequent to the combination, Tippy operated as a subsidiary of McDermott.

Required

Present the journal entry or entries that McDermott would make to record the business combination with Tippy.

LO4, LO5

E1-12   Balances Reported Following Combination

Elm Corporation and Maple Company have announced terms of an exchange agreement under which Elm will issue 8,000 shares of its $10 par value common stock to acquire all of Maple Company's assets. Elm shares currently are trading at $50, and Maple $5 par value shares are trading at $18 each. Historical cost and fair value balance sheet data on January 1, 20X2, are as follows:

Balance Sheet Item	Elm Corporation		Maple Company	
	Book Value	Fair Value	Book Value	Fair Value
Cash and Receivables	$150,000	$150,000	$ 40,000	$ 40,000
Land	100,000	170,000	50,000	85,000
Buildings and Equipment (net)	300,000	400,000	160,000	230,000
Total Assets	$550,000	$720,000	$250,000	$355,000
Common Stock	$200,000		$100,000	
Additional Paid-In Capital	20,000		10,000	
Retained Earnings	330,000		140,000	
Total Equities	$550,000		$250,000	

Required

What amount will be reported immediately following the business combination for each of the following items in the combined company's balance sheet?

a. Common Stock.
b. Cash and Receivables.

c. Land.

d. Buildings and Equipment (net).

e. Goodwill.

f. Additional Paid-In Capital.

g. Retained Earnings.

LO5

E1-13   Goodwill Recognition

Spur Corporation reported the following balance sheet amounts on December 31, 20X1:

Balance Sheet Item	Historical Cost	Fair Value
Cash and Receivables	$ 50,000	$ 40,000
Inventory	100,000	150,000
Land	40,000	30,000
Plant and Equipment	400,000	350,000
Less: Accumulated Depreciation	(150,000)	
Patent		130,000
Total Assets	$440,000	$700,000
Accounts Payable	$ 80,000	$ 85,000
Common Stock	200,000	
Additional Paid-In Capital	20,000	
Retained Earnings	140,000	
Total Liabilities and Equities	$440,000	

Required

Blanket acquired Spur Corporation's assets and liabilities for $670,000 cash on December 31, 20X1. Give the entry that Blanket made to record the purchase.

LO4

E1-14   Acquisition Using Debentures

Fortune Corporation used debentures with a par value of $625,000 to acquire 100 percent of Sorden Company's net assets on January 1, 20X2. On that date, the fair value of the bonds issued by Fortune was $608,000. The following balance sheet data were reported by Sorden:

Balance Sheet Item	Historical Cost	Fair Value
Cash and Receivables	$ 55,000	$ 50,000
Inventory	105,000	200,000
Land	60,000	100,000
Plant and Equipment	400,000	300,000
Less: Accumulated Depreciation	(150,000)	
Goodwill	10,000	
Total Assets	$480,000	$650,000
Accounts Payable	$ 50,000	$ 50,000
Common Stock	100,000	
Additional Paid-In Capital	60,000	
Retained Earnings	270,000	
Total Liabilities and Equities	$480,000	

Required

Give the journal entry that Fortune recorded at the time of exchange.

LO5

E1-15 Bargain Purchase

Using the data presented in E1-14 determine the amount Fortune Corporation would record as a gain on bargain purchase and prepare the journal entry Fortune would record at the time of the exchange if Fortune issued bonds with a par value of $580,000 and a fair value of $564,000 in completing the acquisition of Sorden.

LO5

E1-16 Impairment of Goodwill

Mesa Corporation purchased Kwick Company's net assets and assigned goodwill of $80,000 to Reporting Division K. The following assets and liabilities are assigned to Reporting Division K:

	Carrying Amount	Fair Value
Cash	$ 14,000	$ 14,000
Inventory	56,000	71,000
Equipment	170,000	190,000
Goodwill	80,000	
Accounts Payable	30,000	30,000

Required

Determine the amount of goodwill to be reported for Division K and the amount of goodwill impairment to be recognized, if any, if Division K's fair value is determined to be

a. $340,000.

b. $280,000.

c. $260,000.

LO5

E1-17 Assignment of Goodwill

Double Corporation acquired all of the common stock of Simple Company for $450,000 on January 1, 20X4. On that date, Simple's identifiable net assets had a fair value of $390,000. The assets acquired in the purchase of Simple are considered to be a separate reporting unit of Double. The carrying value of Double's investment at December 31, 20X4, is $500,000.

Required

Determine the amount of goodwill impairment, if any, that should be recognized at December 31, 20X4, if the fair value of the net assets (excluding goodwill) at that date is $440,000 and the fair value of the reporting unit is determined to be

a. $530,000.

b. $485,000.

c. $450,000.

LO5

E1-18 Goodwill Assigned to Reporting Units

Advanced
StudyGuide
.com

Groft Company purchased Strobe Company's net assets and assigned them to four separate reporting units. Total goodwill of $186,000 is assigned to the reporting units as indicated:

	Reporting Unit			
	A	B	C	D
Carrying value of investment	$700,000	$330,000	$380,000	$520,000
Goodwill included in carrying value	60,000	48,000	28,000	50,000
Fair value of net identifiable assets at year-end	600,000	300,000	400,000	500,000
Fair value of reporting unit at year-end	690,000	335,000	370,000	585,000

Required

Determine the amount of goodwill that Groft should report at year-end. Show how you computed it.

LO5

E1-19 Goodwill Measurement

Washer Company has a reporting unit resulting from an earlier business combination. The reporting unit's current assets and liabilities are

	Carrying Amount	Fair Value
Cash	$ 30,000	$ 30,000
Inventory	70,000	100,000
Land	30,000	60,000
Buildings	210,000	230,000
Equipment	160,000	170,000
Goodwill	150,000	
Notes Payable	100,000	100,000

Required

Determine the amount of goodwill to be reported and the amount of goodwill impairment, if any, if the fair value of the reporting unit is determined to be

a. $580,000.

b. $540,000.

c. $500,000.

d. $460,000.

LO4, LO5

E1-20 Computation of Fair Value

Grant Company acquired all of Bedford Corporation's assets and liabilities on January 1, 20X2, in a business combination. At that date, Bedford reported assets with a book value of $624,000 and liabilities of $356,000. Grant noted that Bedford had $40,000 of research and development costs on its books at the acquisition date that did not appear to be of value. Grant also determined that patents developed by Bedford had a fair value of $120,000 but had not been recorded by Bedford. Except for buildings and equipment, Grant determined the fair value of all other assets and liabilities reported by Bedford approximated the recorded amounts. In recording the transfer of assets and liabilities to its books, Grant recorded goodwill of $93,000. Grant paid $517,000 to acquire Bedford's assets and liabilities. If the book value of Bedford's buildings and equipment was $341,000 at the date of acquisition, what was their fair value?

LO4, LO5

E1-21 Computation of Shares Issued and Goodwill

Dunyain Company acquired Allsap Corporation on January 1, 20X1, through an exchange of common shares. All of Allsap's assets and liabilities were immediately transferred to Dunyain, which reported total par value of shares outstanding of $218,400 and $327,600 and additional paid-in capital of $370,000 and $650,800 immediately before and after the business combination, respectively.

Advanced
StudyGuide
.com

Required

a. Assuming that Dunyain's common stock had a market value of $25 per share at the time of exchange, what number of shares was issued?

b. What is the par value per share of Dunyain's common stock?

c. Assuming that Allsap's identifiable assets had a fair value of $476,000 and its liabilities had a fair value of $120,000, what amount of goodwill did Dunyain record at the time of the business combination?

LO4

E1-22   Combined Balance Sheet

The following balance sheets were prepared for Adam Corporation and Best Company on January 1, 20X2, just before they entered into a business combination:

Item	Adam Corporation Book Value	Adam Corporation Fair Value	Best Company Book Value	Best Company Fair Value
Cash and Receivables	$150,000	$150,000	$ 90,000	$ 90,000
Inventory	300,000	380,000	70,000	160,000
Buildings and Equipment	600,000	430,000	250,000	240,000
Less: Accumulated Depreciation	(250,000)		(80,000)	
Total Assets	$800,000	$960,000	$330,000	$490,000
Accounts Payable	$ 75,000	$ 75,000	$ 50,000	$ 50,000
Notes Payable	200,000	215,000	30,000	35,000
Common Stock:				
$8 par value	180,000			
$6 par value			90,000	
Additional Paid-In Capital	140,000		55,000	
Retained Earnings	205,000		105,000	
Total Liabilities and Equities	$800,000		$330,000	

Adam acquired all of Best Company's assets and liabilities on January 1, 20X2, in exchange for its common shares. Adam issued 8,000 shares of stock to complete the business combination.

Required
Prepare a balance sheet of the combined company immediately following the acquisition, assuming Adam's shares were trading at $60 each.

LO4

E1-23   Recording a Business Combination

The following financial statement information was prepared for Blue Corporation and Sparse Company at December 31, 20X2:

Balance Sheets
December 31, 20X2

	Blue Corporation		Sparse Company	
Cash		$ 140,000		$ 70,000
Accounts Receivable		170,000		110,000
Inventory		250,000		180,000
Land		80,000		100,000
Buildings and Equipment	$ 680,000		$ 450,000	
Less: Accumulated Depreciation	(320,000)	360,000	(230,000)	220,000
Goodwill		70,000		20,000
Total Assets		$1,070,000		$700,000
Accounts Payable		$ 70,000		$195,000
Bonds Payable		320,000		100,000
Bond Premium				10,000
Common Stock		120,000		150,000
Additional Paid-In Capital		170,000		60,000
Retained Earnings		390,000		185,000
Total Liabilities and Equities		$1,070,000		$700,000

Blue and Sparse agreed to combine as of January 1, 20X3. To effect the merger, Blue paid finder's fees of $30,000 and legal fees of $24,000. Blue also paid $15,000 of audit fees related to the issuance of stock, stock registration fees of $8,000, and stock listing application fees of $6,000.

At January 1, 20X3, book values of Sparse Company's assets and liabilities approximated market value except for inventory with a market value of $200,000, buildings and equipment with a market value of $350,000, and bonds payable with a market value of $105,000. All assets and liabilities were immediately recorded on Blue's books.

Required

Give all journal entries that Blue recorded assuming Blue issued 40,000 shares of $8 par value common stock to acquire all of Sparse's assets and liabilities in a business combination. Blue common stock was trading at $14 per share on January 1, 20X3.

LO4

E1-24   Reporting Income

On July 1, 20X2, Alan Enterprises merged with Cherry Corporation through an exchange of stock and the subsequent liquidation of Cherry. Alan issued 200,000 shares of its stock to effect the combination. The book values of Cherry's assets and liabilities were equal to their fair values at the date of combination, and the value of the shares exchanged was equal to Cherry's book value. Information relating to income for the companies is as follows:

	20X1	Jan. 1–June 30, 20X2	July 1–Dec. 31, 20X2
Net Income:			
Alan Enterprises	$4,460,000	$2,500,000	$3,528,000
Cherry Corporation	1,300,000	692,000	—

Alan Enterprises had 1,000,000 shares of stock outstanding prior to the combination.

Required

Compute the net income and earnings-per-share amounts that would be reported in Alan's 20X2 comparative income statements for both 20X2 and 20X1.

Problems

LO2

P1-25   Assets and Accounts Payable Transferred to Subsidiary

Tab Corporation decided to establish Collon Company as a wholly owned subsidiary by transferring some of its existing assets and liabilities to the new entity. In exchange, Collon issued Tab 30,000 shares of $6 par value common stock. The following information is provided on the assets and accounts payable transferred:

	Cost	Book Value	Fair Value
Cash	$ 25,000	$ 25,000	$ 25,000
Inventory	70,000	70,000	70,000
Land	60,000	60,000	90,000
Buildings	170,000	130,000	240,000
Equipment	90,000	80,000	105,000
Accounts Payable	45,000	45,000	45,000

Required

a. Give the journal entry that Tab recorded for the transfer of assets and accounts payable to Collon.

b. Give the journal entry that Collon recorded for the receipt of assets and accounts payable from Tab.

LO2

P1-26   Creation of New Subsidiary

Eagle Corporation established a subsidiary to enter into a new line of business considered to be substantially more risky than Eagle's current business. Eagle transferred the following assets and accounts payable to Sand Corporation in exchange for 5,000 shares of $10 par value stock of Sand:

	Cost	Book Value
Cash	$ 30,000	$ 30,000
Accounts Receivable	45,000	40,000
Inventory	60,000	60,000
Land	20,000	20,000
Buildings and Equipment	300,000	260,000
Accounts Payable	10,000	10,000

Required

a. Give the journal entry that Eagle recorded for the transfer of assets and accounts payable to Sand.

b. Give the journal entry that Sand recorded for receipt of the assets and accounts payable from Eagle.

LO2

P1-27 Incomplete Data on Creation of Subsidiary

Thumb Company created New Company as a wholly owned subsidiary by transferring assets and accounts payable to New in exchange for its common stock. New recorded the following entry when it received the assets and accounts payable:

Cash	3,000	
Accounts Receivable	16,000	
Inventory	27,000	
Land	9,000	
Buildings	70,000	
Equipment	60,000	
Accounts Payable		14,000
Accumulated Depreciation—Buildings		21,000
Accumulated Depreciation—Equipment		12,000
Common Stock		40,000
Additional Paid-In Capital		98,000

Required

a. What was Thumb's book value of the total assets transferred to New Company?

b. What amount did Thumb report as its investment in New after the transfer?

c. What number of shares of $5 par value stock did New issue to Thumb?

d. What impact did the transfer of assets and accounts payable have on the amount reported by Thumb as total assets?

e. What impact did the transfer of assets and accounts payable have on the amount that Thumb and the consolidated entity reported as shares outstanding?

LO2

P1-28 Establishing a Partnership

Krantz Company and Dull Corporation decided to form a partnership. Krantz agreed to transfer the following assets and accounts payable to K&D Partnership in exchange for 60 percent ownership:

	Cost	Book Value
Cash	$ 10,000	$ 10,000
Inventory	30,000	30,000
Land	70,000	70,000
Buildings	200,000	150,000
Equipment	120,000	90,000
Accounts Payable	50,000	50,000

Dull agreed to contribute cash of $200,000 to K&D Partnership.

Required

a. Give the journal entries that K&D recorded for its receipt of assets and accounts payable from Krantz and Dull.

b. Give the journal entries that Krantz and Dull recorded for their transfer of assets and accounts payable to K&D Partnership.

LO2

P1-29 Balance Sheet Data for Companies Establishing a Partnership

Good Corporation and Nevall Company formed G&W Partnership in which Good received 75 percent ownership and Nevall received 25 percent ownership. The following assets were transferred by Good and Nevall:

	Good Corporation		Nevall Company	
	Cost	Book Value	Cost	Book Value
Cash	$ 21,000	$21,000	$ 3,000	$ 3,000
Inventory	4,000	4,000	25,000	25,000
Land	15,000	15,000		
Buildings	100,000	70,000		
Equipment	60,000	40,000	36,000	22,000

Required

a. Give the journal entry that Good recorded for its transfer of assets to G&W Partnership.

b. Give the journal entry that Nevall recorded for its transfer of assets to G&W Partnership.

c. Give the journal entry that G&W recorded for its receipt of assets from Good and Nevall.

LO4

P1-30 Acquisition in Multiple Steps

Deal Corporation issued 4,000 shares of its $10 par value stock with a market value of $85,000 to acquire 85 percent ownership of Mead Company on August 31, 20X3. The fair value of Mead was determined to be $100,000 on that date. Deal had earlier purchased 15 percent of Mead's shares for $9,000 and used the cost method in accounting for its investment in Mead. Deal later paid appraisal fees of $3,500 and stock issue costs of $2,000 incurred in completing the acquisition of the additional shares.

Required

Give the journal entries to be recorded by Deal in completing the acquisition of the additional shares of Mead.

LO4

Advanced
StudyGuide
.com

P1-31 Journal Entries to Record a Business Combination

On January 1, 20X2, Frost Company acquired all of TKK Corporation's assets and liabilities by issuing 24,000 shares of its $4 par value common stock. At that date, Frost shares were selling at $22 per share. Historical cost and fair value balance sheet data for TKK at the time of acquisition were as follows:

Balance Sheet Item	Historical Cost	Fair Value
Cash and Receivables	$ 28,000	$ 28,000
Inventory	94,000	122,000
Buildings and Equipment	600,000	470,000
Less: Accumulated Depreciation	(240,000)	
Total Assets	$ 482,000	$620,000
Accounts Payable	$ 41,000	$ 41,000
Notes Payable	65,000	63,000
Common Stock ($10 par value)	160,000	
Retained Earnings	216,000	
Total Liabilities and Equities	$ 482,000	

Frost paid legal fees for the transfer of assets and liabilities of $14,000. Frost also paid audit fees of $21,000 and listing application fees of $7,000, both related to the issuance of new shares.

Required

Prepare the journal entries made by Frost to record the business combination.

LO4

P1-32 Recording Business Combinations

Flint Corporation exchanged shares of its $2 par common stock for all of Mark Company's assets and liabilities in a planned merger. Immediately prior to the combination, Mark's assets and liabilities were as follows:

Assets

Cash and Equivalents	$ 41,000
Accounts Receivable	73,000
Inventory	144,000
Land	200,000
Buildings	1,520,000
Equipment	638,000
Accumulated Depreciation	(431,000)
Total Assets	$2,185,000

Liabilities and Equities

Accounts Payable	$ 35,000
Short-Term Notes Payable	50,000
Bonds Payable	500,000
Common Stock ($10 par)	1,000,000
Additional Paid-In Capital	325,000
Retained Earnings	275,000
Total Liabilities and Equities	$2,185,000

Immediately prior to the combination, Flint reported $250,000 additional paid-in capital and $1,350,000 retained earnings. The fair values of Mark's assets and liabilities were equal to their book values on the date of combination except that Mark's buildings were worth $1,500,000 and its equipment was worth $300,000. Costs associated with planning and completing the business combination totaled $38,000, and stock issue costs totaled $22,000. The market value of Flint's stock at the date of combination was $4 per share.

Required

Prepare the journal entries that would appear on Flint's books to record the combination if Flint issued 450,000 shares.

LO4, LO5   **P1-33**   **Business Combination with Goodwill**

Advanced
StudyGuide
.com

Anchor Corporation paid cash of $178,000 to acquire Zink Company's net assets on February 1, 20X3. The balance sheet data for the two companies and fair value information for Zink immediately before the business combination were:

	Anchor Corporation	Zink Company	
Balance Sheet Item	Book Value	Book Value	Fair Value
Cash	$ 240,000	$ 20,000	$ 20,000
Accounts Receivable	140,000	35,000	35,000
Inventory	170,000	30,000	50,000
Patents	80,000	40,000	60,000
Buildings and Equipment	380,000	310,000	150,000
Less: Accumulated Depreciation	(190,000)	(200,000)	
Total Assets	$ 820,000	$ 235,000	$315,000
Accounts Payable	$ 85,000	$ 55,000	$ 55,000
Notes Payable	150,000	120,000	120,000
Common Stock:			
$10 par value	200,000		
$6 par value		18,000	
Additional Paid-In Capital	160,000	10,000	
Retained Earnings	225,000	32,000	
Total Liabilities and Equities	$ 820,000	$ 235,000	

Required

a. Give the journal entry recorded by Anchor Corporation when it acquired Zink's net assets.

b. Prepare a balance sheet for Anchor immediately following the acquisition.

c. Give the journal entry to be recorded by Anchor if it acquires all of Zink's common stock for $178,000.

LO4, LO5 **P1-34** **Bargain Purchase**

Advanced
StudyGuide
.com

Bower Company purchased Lark Corporation's net assets on January 3, 20X2, for $625,000 cash. In addition, $5,000 of direct costs were incurred in consummating the combination. At the time of acquisition, Lark reported the following historical cost and current market data:

Balance Sheet Item	Book Value	Fair Value
Cash and Receivables	$ 50,000	$ 50,000
Inventory	100,000	150,000
Buildings and Equipment (net)	200,000	300,000
Patent	—	200,000
Total Assets	$350,000	$700,000
Accounts Payable	$ 30,000	$ 30,000
Common Stock	100,000	
Additional Paid-In Capital	80,000	
Retained Earnings	140,000	
Total Liabilities and Equities	$350,000	

Required

Give the journal entry or entries with which Bower recorded its acquisition of Lark's net assets.

LO4, LO5 **P1-35** **Computation of Account Balances**

Aspro Division is considered to be an individual reporting unit of Tabor Company. Tabor acquired the division by issuing 100,000 shares of its common stock with a market price of $7.60 each. Tabor management was able to identify assets with fair values of $810,000 and liabilities of $190,000 at the date of acquisition. At the end of the first year, the reporting unit had assets with a fair value of $950,000, and the fair value of the reporting entity was $930,000. Tabor's accountants concluded it must recognize impairment of goodwill in the amount of $30,000 at the end of the first year.

Required

a. Determine the fair value of the reporting unit's liabilities at the end of the first year. Show your computation.

b. If the reporting unit's liabilities at the end of the period had been $70,000, what would the fair value of the reporting unit have to have been to avoid recognizing an impairment of goodwill? Show your computation.

LO5 **P1-36** **Goodwill Assigned to Multiple Reporting Units**

The fair values of assets and liabilities held by three reporting units and other information related to the reporting units owned by Rover Company are as follows:

	Reporting Unit		
	A	B	C
Cash and Receivables	$ 30,000	$ 80,000	$ 20,000
Inventory	60,000	100,000	40,000
Land	20,000	30,000	10,000
Buildings	100,000	150,000	80,000
Equipment	140,000	90,000	50,000
Accounts Payable	40,000	60,000	10,000
Fair Value of Reporting Unit	400,000	440,000	265,000
Carrying Value of Investment	420,000	500,000	290,000
Goodwill Included in Carrying Value	70,000	80,000	40,000

Required

a. Determine the amount of goodwill that Rover should report in its current financial statements.

b. Determine the amount, if any, that Rover should report as impairment of goodwill for the current period.

LO4   **P1-37   Journal Entries**

On January 1, 20X3, PURE Products Corporation issued 12,000 shares of its $10 par value stock to acquire the net assets of Light Steel Company. Underlying book value and fair value information for the balance sheet items of Light Steel at the time of acquisition follow:

Balance Sheet Item	Book Value	Fair Value
Cash	$ 60,000	$ 60,000
Accounts Receivable	100,000	100,000
Inventory (LIFO basis)	60,000	115,000
Land	50,000	70,000
Buildings and Equipment	400,000	350,000
Less: Accumulated Depreciation	(150,000)	—
Total Assets	$ 520,000	$695,000
Accounts Payable	$ 10,000	$ 10,000
Bonds Payable	200,000	180,000
Common Stock ($5 par value)	150,000	
Additional Paid-In Capital	70,000	
Retained Earnings	90,000	
Total Liabilities and Equities	$ 520,000	

Light Steel shares were selling at $18 and PURE Products shares were selling at $50 just before the merger announcement. Additional cash payments made by PURE Products in completing the acquisition were

Finder's fee paid to firm that located Light Steel	$10,000
Audit fee for stock issued by PURE Products	3,000
Stock registration fee for new shares of PURE Products	5,000
Legal fees paid to assist in transfer of net assets	9,000
Cost of SEC registration of PURE Products shares	1,000

Required

Prepare all journal entries to record the business combination on PURE Products' books.

LO4, LO5   **P1-38   Purchase at More than Book Value**

Ramrod Manufacturing acquired all the assets and liabilities of Stafford Industries on January 1, 20X2, in exchange for 4,000 shares of Ramrod's $20 par value common stock. Balance sheet data for both companies just before the merger are given as follows:

	Ramrod Manufacturing		Stafford Industries	
Balance Sheet Items	Book Value	Fair Value	Book Value	Fair Value
Cash	$ 70,000	$ 70,000	$ 30,000	$ 30,000
Accounts Receivable	100,000	100,000	60,000	60,000
Inventory	200,000	375,000	100,000	160,000
Land	50,000	80,000	40,000	30,000
Buildings and Equipment	600,000 }	540,000	400,000 }	350,000
Less: Accumulated Depreciation	(250,000)		(150,000)	
Total Assets	$ 770,000	$1,165,000	$ 480,000	$630,000
Accounts Payable	$ 50,000	$ 50,000	$ 10,000	$ 10,000
Bonds Payable	300,000	310,000	150,000	145,000

(continued)

Common Stock:			
$20 par value	200,000		
$5 par value			100,000
Additional Paid-In Capital	40,000		20,000
Retained Earnings	180,000		200,000
Total Liabilities and Equities	$ 770,000		$ 480,000

Ramrod shares were selling for $150 on the date of acquisition.

Required
Prepare the following:

a. Journal entries to record the acquisition on Ramrod's books.

b. A balance sheet for the combined enterprise immediately following the business combination.

LO4

P1-39   **Business Combination**

Following are the balance sheets of Boogie Musical Corporation and Toot-Toot Tuba Company as of December 31, 20X5.

BOOGIE MUSICAL CORPORATION
Balance Sheet
December 31, 20X5

Assets		Liabilities and Equities	
Cash	$ 23,000	Accounts Payable	$ 48,000
Accounts Receivable	85,000	Notes Payable	65,000
Allowance for Uncollectible Accounts	(1,200)	Mortgage Payable	200,000
Inventory	192,000	Bonds Payable	200,000
Plant and Equipment	980,000	Capital Stock ($10 par)	500,000
Accumulated Depreciation	(160,000)	Premium on Capital Stock	1,000
Other Assets	14,000	Retained Earnings	118,800
Total Assets	$1,132,800	Total Liabilities and Equities	$1,132,800

TOOT-TOOT TUBA COMPANY
Balance Sheet
December 31, 20X5

Assets		Liabilities and Equities	
Cash	$ 300	Accounts Payable	$ 8,200
Accounts Receivable	17,000	Notes Payable	10,000
Allowance for Uncollectible Accounts	(600)	Mortgage Payable	50,000
Inventory	78,500	Bonds Payable	100,000
Plant and Equipment	451,000	Capital Stock ($50 par)	100,000
Accumulated Depreciation	(225,000)	Premium on Capital Stock	150,000
Other Assets	25,800	Retained Earnings	(71,200)
Total Assets	$347,000	Total Liabilities and Equities	$347,000

In preparation for a possible business combination, a team of experts from Boogie Musical made a thorough examination and audit of Toot-Toot Tuba. They found that Toot-Toot's assets and liabilities were correctly stated except that they estimated uncollectible accounts at $1,400. The experts also estimated the market value of the inventory at $35,000 and the market value of the plant and equipment at $500,000. The business combination took place on January 1, 20X6, and on that date Boogie Musical acquired all the assets and liabilities of Toot-Toot Tuba. On that date, Boogie's common stock was selling for $55 per share.

Required
Record the combination on Boogie's books assuming that Boogie issued 9,000 of its $10 par common shares in exchange for Toot-Toot's assets and liabilities.

LO4   **P1-40**   **Combined Balance Sheet**

Bilge Pumpworks and Seaworthy Rope Company agreed to merge on January 1, 20X3. On the date of the merger agreement, the companies reported the following data:

Balance Sheet Items	Bilge Pumpworks		Seaworthy Rope Company	
	Book Value	Fair Value	Book Value	Fair Value
Cash and Receivables	$ 90,000	$ 90,000	$ 20,000	$ 20,000
Inventory	100,000	150,000	30,000	42,000
Land	100,000	140,000	10,000	15,000
Plant and Equipment	400,000 }	300,000	200,000 }	140,000
Less: Accumulated Depreciation	(150,000)		(80,000)	
Total Assets	$540,000	$680,000	$180,000	$217,000
Current Liabilities	$ 80,000	$ 80,000	$ 20,000	$ 20,000
Capital Stock	200,000		20,000	
Capital in Excess of Par Value	20,000		5,000	
Retained Earnings	240,000		135,000	
Total Liabilities and Equities	$540,000		$180,000	

Bilge Pumpworks has 10,000 shares of its $20 par value shares outstanding on January 1, 20X3, and Seaworthy has 4,000 shares of $5 par value stock outstanding. The market values of the shares are $300 and $50, respectively.

Required

a. Bilge issues 700 shares of stock in exchange for all of Seaworthy's net assets. Prepare a balance sheet for the combined entity immediately following the merger.

b. Prepare the stockholders' equity section of the combined company's balance sheet, assuming Bilge acquires all of Seaworthy's net assets by issuing:

   1. 1,100 shares of common.
   2. 1,800 shares of common.
   3. 3,000 shares of common.

LO4, LO5   **P1-41**   **Incomplete Data Problem**

On January 1, 20X2, End Corporation acquired all of Cork Corporation's assets and liabilities by issuing shares of its common stock. Partial balance sheet data for the companies prior to the business combination and immediately following the combination are as follows:

	End Corp.	Cork Corp.	
	Book Value	Book Value	Combined Entity
Cash	$ 40,000	$ 10,000	$ 50,000
Accounts Receivable	60,000	30,000	88,000
Inventory	50,000	35,000	96,000
Buildings and Equipment (net)	300,000	110,000	430,000
Goodwill			?
Total Assets	$450,000	$185,000	$?
Accounts Payable	$ 32,000	$ 14,000	$ 46,000
Bonds Payable	150,000	70,000	220,000
Bond Premium	6,000		6,000
Common Stock, $5 par	100,000	40,000	126,000
Additional Paid-In Capital	65,000	28,000	247,000
Retained Earnings	97,000	33,000	?
Total Liabilities and Equities	$450,000	$185,000	$?

B) 126
247   100
       65   = 208 K
373 - 145

c) 96K
  -50K = 46K

D) 50K   46K
   48   - 220K
   96   6K   = 392K
  +430

E) 208K - 78K
   -130K

Required

126K-100K/$5=

a. What number of shares did End issue to acquire Cork's assets and liabilities? ~~20,200~~ 5,200

b. What was the market value of the shares issued by End? 208K

c. What was the fair value of the inventory held by Cork at the date of combination? 46K

d. What was the fair value of the net assets held by Cork at the date of combination? 130K

e. What amount of goodwill, if any, will be reported by the combined entity immediately following the combination? 78K

f. What balance in retained earnings will the combined entity report immediately following the combination? 49K

g. If the depreciable assets held by Cork had an average remaining life of 10 years at the date of acquisition, what amount of depreciation expense will be reported on those assets in 20X2?

LO4, LO5   **P1-42**   **Incomplete Data Following Purchase**

Advanced
StudyGuide
.com

On January 1, 20X1, Alpha Corporation acquired all of Bravo Company's assets and liabilities by issuing shares of its $3 par value stock to the owners of Bravo Company in a business combination. Alpha also made a cash payment to Banker Corporation for stock issue costs. Partial balance sheet data for Alpha and Bravo, before the cash payment and issuance of shares, and a combined balance sheet following the business combination are as follows:

	Alpha Corporation Book Value	Bravo Company Book Value	Fair Value	Combined Entity
Cash	$ 65,000	$ 15,000	$ 15,000	$ 56,000
Accounts Receivable	105,000	30,000	30,000	135,000
Inventory	210,000	90,000	?	320,000
Buildings and Equipment (net)	400,000	210,000	293,000	693,000
Goodwill				?
Total Assets	$780,000	$345,000	$448,000	$?
Accounts Payable	$ 56,000	$ 22,000	$ 22,000	$ 78,000
Bonds Payable	200,000	120,000	120,000	320,000
Common Stock	96,000	70,000		117,000
Additional Paid-In Capital	234,000	42,000		553,000
Retained Earnings	194,000	91,000		?
Total Liabilities and Equities	$780,000	$345,000	$142,000	$?

Required

a. What number of its $5 par value shares did Bravo have outstanding at January 1, 20X1?

b. Assuming that all of Bravo's shares were issued when the company was started, what was the price per share received at the time of issue?

c. How many shares of Alpha were issued at the date of combination?

d. What amount of cash did Alpha pay as stock issue costs?

e. What was the market value of Alpha's shares issued at the date of combination?

f. What was the fair value of Bravo's inventory at the date of combination?

g. What was the fair value of Bravo's net assets at the date of combination?

h. What amount of goodwill, if any, will be reported in the combined balance sheet following the combination?

LO4, LO5   **P1-43**   **Comprehensive Business Combination Problem**

Bigtime Industries Inc. entered into a business combination agreement with Hydrolized Chemical Corporation (HCC) to ensure an uninterrupted supply of key raw materials and to realize certain economies from combining the operating processes and the marketing efforts of the two companies. Under the terms of the agreement, Bigtime issued 180,000 shares of its $1 par common stock in exchange for all of HCC's assets and liabilities. The Bigtime shares then were distributed to HCC's shareholders, and HCC was liquidated.

Immediately prior to the combination, HCC's balance sheet appeared as follows, with fair values also indicated:

	Book Values	Fair Values
Assets		
Cash	$ 28,000	$ 28,000
Accounts Receivable	258,000	251,500
Less: Allowance for Bad Debts	(6,500)	
Inventory	381,000	395,000
Long-Term Investments	150,000	175,000
Land	55,000	100,000
Rolling Stock	130,000	63,000
Plant and Equipment	2,425,000	2,500,000
Less: Accumulated Depreciation	(614,000)	
Patents	125,000	500,000
Special Licenses	95,800	100,000
Total Assets	$3,027,300	$4,112,500
Liabilities		
Current Payables	$ 137,200	$ 137,200
Mortgages Payable	500,000	520,000
Equipment Trust Notes	100,000	95,000
Debentures Payable	1,000,000	950,000
Less: Discount on Debentures	(40,000)	
Total Liabilities	$1,697,200	$1,702,200
Stockholders' Equity		
Common Stock ($5 par)	600,000	
Additional Paid-In Capital from Common Stock	500,000	
Additional Paid-In Capital from Retirement of Preferred Stock	22,000	
Retained Earnings	220,100	
Less: Treasury Stock (1,500 shares)	(12,000)	
Total Liabilities and Equity	$3,027,300	

Immediately prior to the combination, Bigtime's common stock was selling for $14 per share. Bigtime incurred direct costs of $135,000 in arranging the business combination and $42,000 of costs associated with registering and issuing the common stock used in the combination.

Required

a. Prepare all journal entries that Bigtime should have entered on its books to record the business combination.

b. Present all journal entries that should have been entered on HCC's books to record the combination and the distribution of the stock received.

Chapter Two

Reporting Intercorporate Investments and Consolidation of Wholly Owned Subsidiaries with No Differential

BERKSHIRE HATHAWAY'S MANY INVESTMENTS

As of this writing (March 2010), Warren Buffett is the third richest man in the world, worth a staggering $47 billion. He is also the chairman, CEO, and primary shareholder of Berkshire Hathaway Inc. Over the past 44 years, Berkshire has grown at an average rate of 20.3 percent annually. Warren Buffett has achieved this success through his unparalleled business sense regarding investments and acquisitions of other companies.

Berkshire Hathaway was originally a textile manufacturing company. In 1962, Warren Buffett and his partners began buying large blocks of Berkshire stock. Within five years, Buffett began expanding into the insurance industry, and in 1985 the last of Berkshire's textile operations was shut down. In the late 1970s Berkshire began acquiring stock in GEICO insurance and in January 1996 bought GEICO outright. While Berkshire has extensive insurance holdings, it has not focused its investment activities solely on insurance. Since Buffett took the helm in the 1960s, Berkshire has made many acquisitions. Look at the list of selected Berkshire holdings as of the end of 2009 (on the next page). Do you recognize any of these companies?

Each item in Berkshire's portfolio has to be accounted for individually. For example, Wesco Financial and Comdisco Holdings are accounted for as equity method investments, while Wal-Mart, American Express, and Nike are classified as available-for-sale investments. Berkshire consolidates the fully owned companies as well as Wesco Financial. In addition, companies like GEICO have many subsidiaries of their own. As you can imagine, accounting for investments at Berkshire can be very complex. This chapter focuses on issues related to the accounting for investments.

BERKSHIRE HATHAWAY INC.

BERKSHIRE HATHAWAY SELECTED HOLDINGS
(as of 12/31/2009)

Fully owned subsidiaries:

Geico
Dairy Queen
See's Candies
Fruit of the Loom
The Pampered Chef

Partially owned companies:	Ticker	Holding Value	Stake
Wesco Financial Corporation	WSC	$ 2,235,610,104	80.1%
Comdisco Holdings Company	CDCO	$ 13,076,204	38.2%
The Washington Post Company	WPO	$ 774,038,720	18.4%
Moody's	MCO	$ 943,437,410	13.4%
American Express	AXP	$ 6,114,459,531	12.7%
Kraft Foods	KFT	$ 4,097,014,175	9.4%
The Coca-Cola Company	KO	$10,950,000,000	8.7%
Wells Fargo	WFC	$ 9,724,285,136	6.2%
Procter & Gamble	PG	$ 5,586,217,758	3.0%
Nike Inc.	NKE	$ 561,766,320	1.6%
Costco	COST	$ 319,022,880	1.2%
Walmart	WMT	$ 2,160,315,438	1.0%
Lowes Companies Inc.	LOW	$ 161,070,000	0.4%
United Parcel Service Inc.	UPS	$ 91,940,436	0.1%
General Electric	GE	$ 140,546,653	0.1%
Bank of America Corp.	BAC	$ 84,100,000	0.1%

LEARNING OBJECTIVES

When you finish studying this chapter, you should be able to:

LO1   Understand and explain how ownership and control can influence the accounting for investments in common stock.

LO2   Prepare journal entries using the cost method for accounting for investments.

LO3   Prepare journal entries using the equity method for accounting for investments.

LO4   Understand and explain differences between the cost and equity methods.

LO5   Prepare journal entries using the fair value option.

LO6   Make calculations and prepare basic elimination entries for a simple consolidation.

LO7   Prepare a consolidation worksheet.

ACCOUNTING FOR INVESTMENTS IN COMMON STOCK

LO1

Understand and explain
how ownership and control
can influence the accounting for investments in common stock.

The method used to account for investments in common stock depends, in part, on the level of influence or control that the investor is able to exercise over the investee. The investment must be reported on the investor's balance sheet using the cost method (adjusted to market value, if appropriate), the equity method, or the fair value option. Note that, while use of the cost or equity method is dictated by the level of influence, the investor can elect the fair value option in place of either method. Figure 2–1 summarizes the relationship between methods used to report intercorporate investments in common stock and levels of ownership and influence.

The ***cost method*** is used for reporting investments in equity securities when both consolidation and equity-method reporting are inappropriate. If cost-method equity securities have readily determinable fair values, they must be adjusted to market value at year-end under

FIGURE 2–1
Financial Reporting Basis by Level of Common Stock Ownership

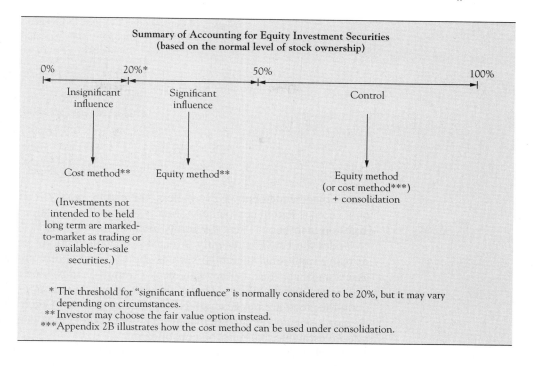

Summary of Accounting for Equity Investment Securities
(based on the normal level of stock ownership)

* The threshold for "significant influence" is normally considered to be 20%, but it may vary depending on circumstances.
** Investor may choose the fair value option instead.
***Appendix 2B illustrates how the cost method can be used under consolidation.

FASB Statement 115[1] **(ASC 320).** Under the cost method, the investor recognizes income from the investment when the income is distributed by the investee as dividends.

The *equity method* is used for external reporting when the investor exercises *significant influence* over the operating and financial policies of the investee and consolidation is not appropriate. This method is used most often when one company holds 20 percent or more of another company's common stock. Under the equity method, the investor recognizes income from the investment as the investee earns the income. Instead of combining the individual assets, liabilities, revenues, and expenses of the investee with those of the investor, as in consolidation, the investment is reported as one line in the investor's balance sheet, and income recognized from the investee is reported as one line in the investor's income statement. The investment represents the investor's share of the investee's net assets, and the income recognized is the investor's share of the investee's net income.

For financial reporting, consolidated financial statements that include both the investor and the investee must be presented if the investor can exercise control over the investee. *Consolidation* involves combining for financial reporting the individual assets, liabilities, revenues, and expenses of two or more related companies as if they were part of a single company. This process includes the elimination of all intercompany ownership and activities. Consolidation normally is appropriate when one company, referred to as the *parent,* controls another company, referred to as a *subsidiary.* We discuss the specific requirements for consolidation later in this chapter. A subsidiary that is not consolidated with the parent is referred to as an *unconsolidated subsidiary* and is shown as an investment on the parent's balance sheet. Under current accounting standards, most subsidiaries are consolidated. When intercorporate investments are consolidated for financial reporting, the investment and related income accounts are eliminated in preparing the

---

[1] *Financial Accounting Standards Board Statement No. 115,* "Accounting for Certain Investments in Debt and Equity Securities," May 1993. Because the provisions of **FASB 115 (ASC 320)** are normally discussed in Intermediate Accounting, detailed coverage is not provided here. Note, however, that equity investments accounted for using the cost method are accounted for as discussed in this chapter, with the provisions of **FASB 115 (ASC 320)** applied as end-of-period adjustments. **FASB 115 (ASC 320)** is not applicable to equity-method investments.

Summary of Consolidation Coverage in Chapters 2–5

	Wholly Owned Subsidiary	Partially Owned Subsidiary
Investment = Book value	Chapter 2	Chapter 3
Investment > Book value	Chapter 4	Chapter 5

consolidated statements. Nevertheless, the parent must still account for the investments on its books. Parent companies normally account for investments in consolidated subsidiaries on their books using the equity method.[2]

Under the FASB's recently effective fair value option,[3] companies have the choice of using traditional methods, such as the cost and equity methods, to report financial assets and liabilities, or they can elect to report at fair value some or all of their financial assets and liabilities. Under the fair value option, intercorporate investments in common stock are remeasured to fair value at the end of each period and the unrealized gain or loss is recognized in income. The fair value option does not apply to intercorporate investments that must be consolidated.

This chapter follows Figure 2–1 in summarizing the accounting for investments in other companies. It first discusses the cost and equity methods for accounting for investments. It then summarizes the fair value option. Finally, it introduces the preparation of consolidated financial statements using the most simple consolidation scenario (when a subsidiary is wholly owned and it is either created or purchased for an amount exactly equal to the book value of the subsidiary's net assets). Since consolidation is a major topic of this textbook, we use a building block approach to our coverage of consolidation in Chapters 2 through 5. Chapter 3 explains how the basic consolidation process changes when the parent company owns less than 100 percent of the subsidiary. Chapter 4 shows how the consolidation process differs when the parent company acquires the subsidiary for an amount greater (or less) than the book value of the subsidiary's net assets. Finally, Chapter 5 presents the most complex consolidation scenario (where the parent owns less than 100 percent of the subsidiary's outstanding voting stock and the acquisition price is not equal to the book value of the subsidiary's net assets). Chapters 6 and 7 delve into asset transfers among members of the same consolidated group of companies.

REASONS FOR INVESTING IN COMMON STOCK

Companies acquire ownership interests in other companies for a variety of reasons. For example, some companies invest in other companies simply to earn a favorable return by taking advantage of the future earnings potential of their investees. Other reasons for acquiring interests in other entities include (1) gaining voting control, (2) entering new product markets by purchasing companies already established in those areas, (3) ensuring a supply of raw materials or other production inputs, (4) ensuring a customer for production output, (5) gaining economies associated with greater size, (6) diversifying operations, (7) obtaining new technology, (8) lessening competition, and (9) limiting risk. Examples of intercorporate investments include IBM's acquisition of a sizable portion of Intel's stock to ensure a supply of computer components, AT&T's purchase of the stock of McCaw Cellular Communications to gain a foothold in the cellular phone market, and Texaco's acquisition of Getty Oil's stock to acquire oil and gas reserves.

[2] The cost method is also allowed for consolidated investments since (as explained later in this chapter) the investment account is eliminated in the consolidated financial statements.

[3] *Financial Accounting Standards Board Statement No. 159,* "The Fair Value Option for Financial Assets and Liabilities," February 2007.

THE COST METHOD

LO2

Prepare journal entries
using the cost method for
accounting for investments.

Intercorporate investments reported on the balance sheet using the cost method are carried by the investor at historical cost. Income is recorded by the investor as dividends are declared by the investee. The cost method is used when the investor lacks the ability either to control or to exercise significant influence over the investee. The inability of an investor to exercise either control or significant influence over an investee may result from the size of the investment, usually at common stock ownership levels of less than 20 percent. In some situations, other factors, such as the bankruptcy of the investee, prevent the investor from exercising control or significant influence regardless of the size of the investment.

Accounting Procedures under the Cost Method

The cost method is consistent with the treatment normally accorded noncurrent assets. At the time of purchase, the investor records its investment in common stock at the total cost incurred in making the purchase. Subsequently, the carrying amount of the investment remains unchanged under the cost method; the investment continues to be carried at its original cost until the time of sale. Income from the investment is recognized by the investor as dividends are declared by the investee. Once the investee declares a dividend, the investor has a legal claim against the investee for a proportionate share of the dividend, and realization of the income is considered certain enough to be recognized. Recognition of investment income before a dividend declaration is considered inappropriate because the investee's income is not available to the owners until a dividend is declared.

To illustrate the cost method, assume that ABC Company purchases 20 percent of XYZ Company's common stock for $100,000 at the beginning of the year but does not gain significant influence over XYZ. During the year, XYZ has net income of $60,000 and pays dividends of $20,000. ABC Company records the following entries relating to its investment in XYZ:

(1)	Investment in XYZ Company Stock	100,000	
	Cash		100,000
	Record purchase of XYZ Company stock.		

(2)	Dividends Receivable	4,000	
	Dividend Income		4,000
	Record dividend from XYZ Company ($20,000 × 0.20)		

Note that ABC records only its share of the distributed earnings of XYZ and makes no entry regarding the undistributed portion. The carrying amount of the investment remains at its original cost of $100,000.

Declaration of Dividends in Excess of Earnings since Acquisition

A special treatment is required under the cost method in situations in which an investor holds common stock in a company that declares dividends in excess of the income it has earned since the investor acquired its stock. The dividends received are viewed first as representing earnings of the investee from the purchase date of the investment to the declaration date of the dividend. All dividends declared by the investee in excess of its earnings since acquisition by the investor are viewed by the investor as ***liquidating dividends.*** The investor's share of these liquidating dividends is treated as a return of capital, and the investment account balance is reduced by that amount. Blocks of an investee's stock acquired at different times should be treated separately for purposes of computing liquidating dividends.

Liquidating Dividends Example

To illustrate the computation of liquidating dividends received by the investor, assume that Investor Company purchases 10 percent of the common stock of Investee Company on January 2, 20X1. The annual income and dividends of Investee, the amount of dividend income recognized by Investor each year under the cost method, and the reduction of the carrying amount of Investor's investment in Investee when appropriate are as follows:

	Investee Company			Investor Company		
Year	Net Income	Dividends	Cumulative Undistributed Income	Cash Received	Dividend Income	Reduction of Investment
20X1	$100,000	$ 70,000	$30,000	$ 7,000	$ 7,000	
20X2	100,000	120,000	10,000	12,000	12,000	
20X3	100,000	120,000	–0–	12,000	11,000	$1,000
20X4	100,000	120,000	–0–	12,000	10,000	2,000
20X5	100,000	70,000	30,000	7,000	7,000	

Investor Company records its 10 percent share of Investee's dividend as income in 20X1 because the income of Investee exceeds its dividend. In 20X2, Investee's dividend exceeds earnings for the year, but the cumulative dividends declared since January 2, 20X1, the date Investor acquired Investee's stock, do not exceed Investee's earnings since that date. Hence, Investor again records its 10 percent share of the dividend as income. By the end of 20X3, dividends declared by Investee since January 2, 20X1, total $310,000, while Investee's income since that date totals only $300,000. Thus, from Investor's point of view, $10,000 of the 20X3 dividend represents a return of capital while the remaining $110,000 represents a distribution of earnings. Investor's share of each amount is 10 percent. The entry to record the 20X3 dividend on Investor's books is:

(3)	Cash	12,000	
	Investment in Investee		1,000
	Dividend Income		11,000

Record receipt of 20X3 dividend from Investee
$12,000 = $120,000 × 0.10
$1,000 = ($310,000 – $300,000) × 0.10
$11,000 = ($120,000 – $10,000) × 0.10

Once the investor has recorded a liquidating dividend, the comparison in future periods between cumulative earnings and dividends of the investee should be based on the date of the last liquidating dividend rather than the date the investor acquired the investee's stock. In this example, Investor Company records liquidating dividends in 20X3 and 20X4. In years after 20X4, Investor compares earnings and dividends of Investee from the date of the most recent liquidating dividend in 20X4 rather than comparing from January 2, 20X1. The entire dividend paid in 20X5 is considered by Investor to be a distribution of earnings.

Liquidating Dividends following Switch from Equity Method

If the investor previously carried the investment using the equity method and, because of the sale of a portion of the investment, switches to the cost method, the date of the switch in methods replaces the date of acquisition as the reference date for distinguishing liquidating dividends. From that point forward, the investor should compare earnings and dividends of the investee starting at the date of the switch to the cost method.

Investee's View of Liquidating Dividends

Dividends received by an investor in excess of earnings since acquisition, while viewed as liquidating dividends by the investor, usually are not liquidating dividends from the investee's point of view. This type of dividend might occur, for example, when an investee's stock is acquired shortly before a dividend is declared. The investee does not consider a dividend to be a liquidating dividend unless the investee's retained earnings are insufficient or the investee specifically declares a liquidating dividend for all common shareholders.

Acquisition at Interim Date

The acquisition of an investment at other than the beginning or end of a fiscal period generally does not create any major problems when the cost method is used to account for the investment. The only potential difficulty involves determining whether some part of the payment received by the investor is a liquidating dividend when the investee declares a dividend soon after the investor purchases stock in the investee. In this situation, the investor must estimate the amount of the investee's earnings for the portion of the period during which the investor held the investee's stock and may record dividend income only on that portion.

Changes in the Number of Shares Held

Changes in the number of investment shares resulting from stock dividends, stock splits, or reverse splits receive no formal recognition in the accounts of the investor. The carrying value of the investment before the stock dividend or split becomes the carrying amount of the new, greater or lesser number of shares. Purchases and sales of shares, of course, do require journal entries but do not result in any unusual difficulties under the cost method.

Purchases of Additional Shares

The purchase of additional shares of a company already held is recorded at cost in the same way as an initial purchase of shares. The investor's new percentage ownership of the investee then is calculated, and other evidence, if available, is evaluated to determine whether the total investment still should be carried at cost or if the investor should switch to the equity method. When the additional shares give the investor the ability to exercise significant influence over the investee, the equity method should be applied retroactively from the date of the original investment, as illustrated later in this chapter.

Sales of Shares

If all or part of an intercorporate investment in stock is sold, the transaction is accounted for in the same manner as the sale of any other noncurrent asset. A gain or loss on the sale is recognized for the difference between the proceeds received and the carrying amount of the investment sold.

If shares of the stock have been purchased at more than one price, a determination must be made at the time of sale as to which of the shares have been sold. The specific shares sold may be identified through segregation, numbered stock certificates, or other means. When specific identification is impractical, either a FIFO or weighted-average cost flow assumption may be used. However, the weighted-average method seldom is used in practice because it is not acceptable for tax purposes.

THE EQUITY METHOD

LO3

Prepare journal entries using the equity method for accounting for investments.

The equity method of accounting for intercorporate investments in common stock is intended to reflect the investor's changing equity or interest in the investee. This method is a rather curious one in that the balance in the investment account generally does not reflect either cost or market value, and it does not necessarily represent a pro rata share of the investee's book value. Instead, the investment is recorded at the initial purchase price and adjusted each period for the investor's share of the investee's profits or losses and the dividends declared by the investee.

Use of the Equity Method

APB Opinion No. 18 (as amended, ASC 323 and 325), "The Equity Method of Accounting for Investments in Common Stock" (APB 18), requires that the equity method be used for reporting investments in common stock of the following:[4]

1. Corporate joint ventures. A *corporate joint venture* is a corporation owned and operated by a small group of businesses, none of which owns a majority of the joint venture's common stock.
2. Companies in which the investor's voting stock interest gives the investor the "ability to exercise significant influence over operating and financial policies" of that company.

The second condition is the broader of the two and establishes the "significant influence" criterion. Because assessing the degree of influence may be difficult in some cases, **APB 18 (ASC 323 and 325)** establishes a 20 percent rule.[5] In the absence of evidence to the contrary, an investor holding 20 percent or more of an investee's voting stock is presumed to have the ability to exercise significant influence over the investee. On the other hand, an investor holding less than 20 percent of an investee's voting stock is presumed not to have the ability to exercise significant influence in the absence of evidence to the contrary.

In most cases, an investment of 20 percent or more in another company's voting stock is reported under the equity method. Notice, however, that the 20 percent rule does not apply if other evidence is available that provides a better indication of the ability or inability of the investor to significantly influence the investee.

Regardless of the level of ownership, the equity method is not appropriate if the investor's influence is limited by circumstances other than stock ownership, such as bankruptcy of the investee or severe restrictions placed on the availability of a foreign investee's earnings or assets by a foreign government.

Investor's Equity in the Investee

Under the equity method, the investor records its investment at the original cost. This amount is adjusted periodically for changes in the investee's stockholders' equity occasioned by the investee's profits, losses, and dividend declarations. The effect of the investee's income, losses, and dividends on the investor's investment account and other accounts can be summarized as follows:

Reported by Investee	Effect on Investor's Accounts
Net income	Record income from investment Increase investment account
Net loss	Record loss from investment Decrease investment account
Dividend declaration	Record asset (cash or receivable) Decrease investment account

Recognition of Income

Under the equity method, the investor's income statement includes the investor's proportionate share of the investee's income or loss each period. The carrying amount of the investment is adjusted by the same amount to reflect the change in the net assets of the investee resulting from the investee's income.

[4] *Accounting Principles Board Opinion No. 18,* "The Equity Method of Accounting for Investments in Common Stock," March 1971, para. 16.
[5] Ibid., para. 17.

To illustrate, assume ABC Company acquires significant influence over XYZ Company by purchasing 20 percent of the common stock of the XYZ Company for $100,000 at the beginning of the year.

(4)	Investment in XYZ Company Stock	100,000	
	Cash		100,000
	Record purchase of XYZ Company stock.		

XYZ reports income of $60,000 for the year. ABC records its 20 percent share of XYZ's income ($12,000) in an account called "Income from XYZ Company" or "Equity in Net Income of XYZ Company" as follows:

(5)	Investment in XYZ Company Stock	12,000	
	Income from XYZ Co.		12,000
	Record income from XYZ Company ($60,000 × 0.20)		

This entry may be referred to as the ***equity accrual*** and normally is made as an adjusting entry at the end of the period. If the investee reports a loss for the period, the investor recognizes its share of the loss and reduces the carrying amount of the investment by that amount.

Because of the ability to exercise significant influence over the policies of the investee, realization of income from the investment is considered to be sufficiently ensured to warrant recognition by the investor as the income is earned by the investee. This differs from the case in which the investor does not have the ability to significantly influence the investee and the investment must be reported using the cost method; in that case, income from the investment is recognized only upon declaration of a dividend by the investee.

Recognition of Dividends

Dividends from an investment are not recognized as income under the equity method because the investor's share of the investee's income is recognized as it is earned by the investee. Instead, dividends of the investee are viewed as distributions of previously recognized income that already has been capitalized in the carrying amount of the investment. The investor must consider investee dividends declared as a reduction in its equity in the investee and, accordingly, reduce the carrying amount of its investment. In effect, all dividends from the investee are treated as liquidating dividends under the equity method. Thus, if ABC Company owns 20 percent of XYZ Company's common stock and XYZ declares and pays a $20,000 dividend, the following entry is recorded on the books of ABC to record its share of the dividend:

(6)	Dividends Receivable	4,000	
	Investment in XYZ Company Stock		4,000
	Record dividend from XYZ Company ($20,000 × 0.20)		

The following T-accounts summarize all of the normal equity method entries (journal entries 4–6) on the investor company's books:

	Investment in XYZ Co.				Income from XYZ	
Purchase	100,000					
20% of NI	12,000				12,000	20% of NI
		4,000	20% of Dividend			
Ending Balance	108,000				12,000	Ending Balance

While the "Investment in XYZ Company" account summarizes ABC's ownership of the net assets of XYZ Company, the "Income from XYZ" account summarizes ABC's share of XYZ Company's income.

Comparison of the Carrying Amount of the Investment under the Cost and Equity Methods

Because the investment account on the investor's books under the equity method is adjusted for the investor's share of the investee's income or losses and dividends, the carrying amount of the investment usually is not the same as the original cost to the investor. Only if the investee pays dividends in the exact amount of its earnings will the carrying amount of the investment subsequent to acquisition be equal to its original cost. If the earnings of the investee subsequent to investment by the investor exceed the investee's dividends during that time, the carrying amount of the investment will be greater than its original cost. On the other hand, if the investee's dividends exceed its income, the carrying amount of the investment will be less than its original cost.

To compare the change in the carrying amount of the investment under the equity method relative to the cost method, assume the same facts listed previously for ABC's 20 percent acquisition of XYZ's common stock. Recall that during the year XYZ earns income of $60,000 and pays dividends of $20,000. Under the equity method, the carrying amount of the investment starts with the original cost of $100,000 and is increased by ABC's share of XYZ's income ($12,000). The carrying amount is reduced by ABC's share of XYZ's dividends ($4,000). Thus, the carrying amount of the investment using the equity method at the end of the period is $108,000 ($100,000 + $12,000 − $4,000), compared to the original acquisition price of $100,000 under the cost method.

		Equity Method:				Cost Method:	
		Investment in XYZ Co.				Investment in XYZ Co.	
Acquisition:	Purchase	100,000				Purchase 100,000	
Share of Income:	20% NI	12,000					
Share of Dividends:			4,000	20% of Dividend			
	EB	108,000					

Investment income under the equity method (the balance in the "Equity in Net Income from XYZ" account) is $12,000 while investment income under the cost method is equal to dividend income, $4,000.

Acquisition at Interim Date

When an investment is purchased, the investor begins accruing income from the investee under the equity method at the date of acquisition. No income earned by the investee before the date of acquisition of the investment may be accrued by the investor. When the purchase occurs between balance sheet dates, the amount of income earned by the investee from the date of acquisition to the end of the fiscal period may need to be estimated by the investor in recording the equity accrual.

To illustrate, assume that ABC acquires 20 percent of XYZ's common stock on October 1 for $100,000. XYZ earns income of $60,000 uniformly throughout the year and declares dividends of $20,000 on December 20 (paid on December 31). The carrying amount of the investment is increased by $3,000, which represents ABC's share of XYZ's net income earned between October 1 and December 31 (1/4 of the year), and is decreased by $4,000 as a result of dividends declared at year end (resulting in a net *decrease* of $1,000 since the time of the stock purchase).[6]

---

[6] Note that we assume the entire dividend ($20,000) was declared and paid at the end of the year. If dividends had been declared and paid quarterly, we would only record dividends declared after ABC's acquisition of the XYZ shares.

	Investment in XYZ Co.		
Stock Purchase	100,000		
20% × NI × 1/4	3,000		
		4,000	20% Dividends
Ending Balance	99,000		

Changes in the Number of Shares Held

Some changes in the number of common shares held by an investor are handled easily under the equity method, but others require a bit more attention. A change resulting from a stock dividend, split, or reverse split is treated in the same way as under the cost method. No formal accounting recognition is required on the books of the investor. On the other hand, purchases and sales of shares do require formal recognition.

Purchases of Additional Shares

A purchase of additional shares of a common stock already held by an investor and accounted for using the equity method simply involves adding the cost of the new shares to the investment account and applying the equity method in the normal manner from the date of acquisition forward. The new and old investments in the same stock are combined for financial reporting purposes. Income accruing to the new shares can be recognized by the investor only from the date of acquisition forward.

To illustrate, assume that ABC Company purchases 20 percent of XYZ Company's common stock on January 2, 20X1, for $100,000, and another 10 percent on July 1, 20X1, for $50,000, and that the stock purchases represent 20 percent and 30 percent respectively of the book value of XYZ's net assets. If XYZ earns income of $25,000 from January 2 to June 30 and earns $35,000 from July 1 to December 31, the total income recognized in 20X1 by ABC from its investment in XYZ is $15,500, computed as follows:

Income, January 2 to June 30: $25,000 × 0.20	$ 5,000
Income, July 1 to December 31: $35,000 × 0.30	10,500
Investment Income, 20X1	$15,500

If XYZ declares and pays a $10,000 dividend on January 15 and again on July 15, ABC reduces its investment account by $2,000 ($10,000 × 0.20) on January 15 and by $3,000 ($10,000 × 0.30) on July 15. Thus, the ending balance in the investment account at the end of the year is $160,500, computed as follows:

	Investment in XYZ Co.				Income from XYZ Co.	
1/2/X1 Purchase	100,000					
20% NI to 6/30	5,000	2,000			5,000	20% NI to 6/30
7/1/X1 Purchase	50,000		20% Div. to 6/30			
30% NI from 7/1	10,500	3,000	30% Div. from 7/1		10,500	30% NI from 7/1
Ending Balance	160,500				15,500	Ending Balance

When an investment in common stock is carried using the cost method and purchases of additional shares give the investor the ability to significantly influence the investee, a retroactive switch from the cost method to the equity method is required. This change to the equity method must be applied retroactively to the date of the first acquisition of the investee's stock.

To illustrate a change to the equity method, assume that Aron Corporation purchases 15 percent of Zenon Company's common stock on January 2, 20X1, and another 10 percent on January 2, 20X4. Furthermore, assume that Aron switches to the equity method on January 2, 20X4, because it gains the ability to significantly influence Zenon. Given the following income and dividend data for Zenon, and assuming the purchases of stock are at book value, the investment income figures reported by Aron originally and as restated are as follows:

	Zenon		Aron's Reported Investment Income	
Year	Net Income	Dividends	Originally under Cost [a]	Restated under Equity [b]
20X1	$15,000	$10,000	$1,500	$2,250
20X2	18,000	10,000	1,500	2,700
20X3	22,000	10,000	1,500	3,300
	$55,000	$30,000	$4,500	$8,250

[a] 15 percent of Zenon's dividends for the year.

[b] 15 percent of Zenon's net income for the year.

Thus, in Aron's 20X4 financial report, the comparative statements for 20X1, 20X2, and 20X3 are restated to include Aron's 15 percent share of Zenon's profit and to exclude from income Aron's share of dividends recognized under the cost method. In addition, the investment account and retained earnings of Aron are restated as if the equity method had been applied from the date of the original acquisition. This restatement is accomplished on Aron's books with the following journal entry on January 2, 20X4:

(7)	Investment in Zenon Company Stock	3,750	
	Retained Earnings		3,750
	Restate investment account from cost to equity method: $8,250 − $4,500		

In 20X4, if Zenon reports net income of $30,000, Aron's investment income is $7,500 (25 percent of Zenon's net income).

Sales of Shares

The sale of all or part of an investment in common stock carried using the equity method is treated the same as the sale of any noncurrent asset. First, the investment account is adjusted to the date of sale for the investor's share of the investee's current earnings. Then, a gain or loss is recognized for the difference between the proceeds received and the carrying amount of the shares sold.

If only part of the investment is sold, the investor must decide whether to continue using the equity method to account for the remaining shares or to change to the cost method. The choice is based on evidence available after the sale as to whether the investor still is able to exercise significant influence over the investee. If the equity method no longer is appropriate after the date of sale, the carrying value of the remaining investment is treated as the cost of that investment, and the cost method is applied in the normal manner from the date of sale forward. No retroactive restatement of the investment to actual cost is made.

FIGURE 2–2
Summary Comparison of the Cost and Equity Methods

Item	Cost Method	Equity Method
Recorded amount of investment at date of acquisition	Original cost	Original cost
Usual carrying amount of investment subsequent to acquisition	Original cost	Original cost increased (decreased) by investor's share of investee's income (loss) and decreased by investor's share of investee's dividends
Income recognition by investor	Investor's share of investee's dividends declared from earnings since acquisition	Investor's share of investee's earnings since acquisition, whether distributed or not
Investee dividends from earnings since acquisition by investor	Income	Reduction of investment
Investee dividends in excess of earnings since acquisition by investor	Reduction of investment	Reduction of investment

COMPARISON OF THE COST AND EQUITY METHODS[7]

LO4

Understand and explain differences between the cost and equity methods.

Advanced
StudyGuide
.com

Figure 2–2 summarizes some of the key features of the cost and equity methods of accounting for intercorporate investments. The cost method is consistent with the historical cost basis for most other assets. This method is subject to the usual criticisms leveled against historical cost. In particular, questions arise as to the relevance of reporting the purchase price of an investment acquired some years earlier. The cost method conforms more closely to the traditional accounting and legal views of the realization of income in that the investee's earnings are not available to the investor until transferred as dividends. However, income based on dividend distributions can sometimes be manipulated. The significant influence criterion required for the equity method considers that the declaration of dividends by the investee can be influenced by the investor. Recognizing equity-method income from the investee without regard to investee dividends provides protection against manipulating the investor's net income by influencing investee dividend declarations. On the other hand, the equity method is sometimes criticized because the asset valuation departs from historical cost but stops short of a market value approach. Instead, the carrying amount of the investment is composed of a number of components and is not similar to the valuation of any other assets.

Over the years there has been considerable criticism of the use of the equity method as a substitute for the consolidation of certain types of subsidiaries. Although the equity method has been viewed as a *one-line consolidation,* the amount of detail reported is considerably different under the equity method than with consolidation. For example, an investor would report the same equity-method income from the following two investees even though their income statements are quite different in composition:

	Investee 1	Investee 2
Sales	$ 50,000	$ 500,000
Operating Expenses	(30,000)	(620,000)
Operating Income (Loss)	$ 20,000	$(120,000)
Gain on Sale of Land		140,000
Net Income	$ 20,000	$ 20,000

[7] To view a video explanation of this topic, visit advancedstudyguide.com.

Similarly, an investment in the stock of another company is reported under the equity method as a single amount in the balance sheet of the investor regardless of the asset and capital structure of the investee. In the past, some companies borrowed heavily through unconsolidated subsidiaries and reported their investments in the subsidiaries using the equity method. Because the debt was not reported in these situations, concerns were raised over the use of the equity method to facilitate "off-balance sheet" financing.

As a result of these concerns, the Financial Accounting Standards Board eliminated the use of the equity method for reporting investments in subsidiaries by requiring the consolidation of virtually all majority-owned subsidiaries.

THE FAIR VALUE OPTION

LO5

Prepare journal entries using the fair value option.

FASB 159 (ASC 825) permits, but does not require, companies to measure many financial assets and liabilities at fair value. Companies holding investments in the common stock of other companies have this option for investments that are not required to be consolidated. Thus, rather than using the cost or equity method to report nonsubsidiary investments in common stock, investors may report those investments at fair value.

Under the fair value option, the investor remeasures the investment to its fair value at the end of each period. The change in value is then recognized in income for the period. Although the FASB does not specify how to account for dividends received from the investment, normally the investor recognizes dividend income in the same manner as under the cost method.

To illustrate the use of the fair value method, assume that Ajax Corporation purchases 40 percent of Barclay Company's common stock on January 1, 20X1, for $200,000. Ajax prepares financial statements at the end of each calendar quarter. On March 1, 20X1, Ajax receives a cash dividend of $1,500 from Barclay. On March 31, 20X1, Ajax determines the fair value of its investment in Barclay to be $207,000. During the first quarter of 20X1, Ajax records the following entries on its books in relation to its investment in Barclay:

(8)	Investment in Barclay Stock		200,000	
	Cash			200,000
	Record purchase of Barclay Company stock.			

(9)	Cash		1,500	
	Dividend Income			1,500
	Record dividend income from Barclay Company.			

(10)	Investment in Barclay Stock		7,000	
	Unrealized Gain on Barclay Stock			7,000
	Record increase in fair value of Barclay stock.			

OVERVIEW OF THE CONSOLIDATION PROCESS

LO6

Make calculations and prepare basic elimination entries for a simple consolidation.

Advanced
StudyGuide
.com

The consolidation process adds together the financial statements of two or more legally separate companies, creating a single set of financial statements. Chapters 2 through 5 discuss the specific procedures used to produce consolidated financial statements in considerable detail. An understanding of the procedures is important because they facilitate the accurate and efficient preparation of consolidated statements. However, the focus should continue to be on the end product—the financial statements. The procedures are intended to produce financial statements that appear as if the consolidated companies are actually a single company.

The separate financial statements of the companies involved serve as the starting point each time consolidated statements are prepared. These separate statements are added together, after some adjustments and eliminations, to generate consolidated financial statements. The adjustments and eliminations relate to intercompany transactions and holdings. While the individual companies within a consolidated entity may legitimately report sales and receivables or payables to one another, the consolidated entity as a whole must report only transactions with parties outside the consolidated entity and receivables from or payables to external parties. Thus, the adjustments and eliminations required as part of the consolidation process aim at ensuring that the consolidated financial statements are presented as if they were the statements of a single enterprise.

CONSOLIDATION PROCEDURES FOR WHOLLY OWNED SUBSIDIARIES THAT ARE CREATED OR PURCHASED AT BOOK VALUE

We begin preparing consolidated financial statements with the books of the individual companies that are to be consolidated. Because the consolidated entity has no books, all amounts in the consolidated financial statements originate on the books of the parent or a subsidiary or in the consolidation worksheet.

The term *subsidiary* has been defined as "an entity . . . in which another entity, known as its *parent,* holds a controlling financial interest."[8] A parent company may hold all or less than all of a corporate subsidiary's common stock, but at least majority ownership is normally required for the presentation of consolidated financial statements. Most, but not all, corporate subsidiaries are wholly owned by their parents.

Because most subsidiaries are wholly owned, this chapter begins the in-depth examination of consolidation procedures for wholly owned subsidiaries. Moreover, we begin with the most basic consolidation scenario when the subsidiary is either created by the parent or purchased for an amount exactly equal to the book value of the subsidiary's net assets. This assumption simplifies the consolidation because there is no differential. We start with basic consolidation procedures applied to the preparation of a consolidated balance sheet immediately following the establishment of a parent–subsidiary relationship, either through creation or acquisition of the subsidiary. Then, we introduce the use of a simple consolidation worksheet for the balance sheet only. The chapter then moves to the preparation of a full set of consolidated financial statements in subsequent periods and the use of a three-part worksheet designed to facilitate the preparation of a consolidated income statement, retained earnings statement, and balance sheet. Chapter 3 extends the discussion by dealing with the preparation of consolidated financial statements for less-than-wholly-owned subsidiaries that are created or purchased at book value.

CONSOLIDATION WORKSHEETS

LO7

Prepare a consolidation worksheet.

The *consolidation worksheet* provides a mechanism for efficiently combining the accounts of the separate companies involved in the consolidation and for adjusting the combined balances to the amounts that would be reported if all consolidating companies were actually a single company. Keep in mind that no set of books exists for the consolidated entity. The parent and its subsidiaries, as separate legal and accounting entities, maintain their own books. When consolidated financial statements are prepared, the account balances are taken from the separate books of the parent and each subsidiary and placed in the consolidation worksheet. The consolidated statements are prepared, after adjustments and eliminations, from the amounts in the consolidation worksheet.

Worksheet Format

Several different worksheet formats for preparing consolidated financial statements are used in practice. One of the most widely used formats is the three-part worksheet, consisting of one part for each of three financial statements: (1) the income statement, (2) the statement of retained earnings, and (3) the balance sheet. In recent years, the

---

[8] *Financial Accounting Standards Board Statement No. 160,* "Noncontrolling Interests in Consolidated Financial Statements, an amendment of **ARB No. 51**," December 2007, para. B1. (ASC 810)

FIGURE 2–3
Format for
Consolidation
Worksheet

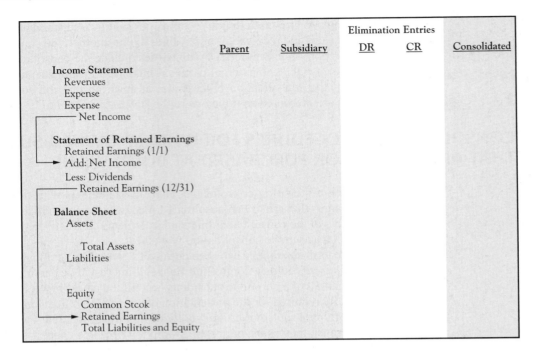

retained earnings statement has been dropped by many companies in favor of the statement of changes in stockholders' equity. Nevertheless, the information normally found in a retained earnings statement is included in the statement of stockholders' equity, along with additional information, and so the three-part worksheet described continues to provide a useful format. Figure 2–3 presents the format for the comprehensive three-part consolidation worksheet. Specifically, Figure 2–3 illustrates the basic form of a consolidation worksheet. The titles of the accounts of the consolidating companies are listed in the first column of the worksheet. The account balances from the books or trial balances of the individual companies are listed in the next set of columns, with a separate column for each company included in the consolidation. Entries are made in the columns labeled *Elimination Entries* to adjust or eliminate balances so that the resulting amounts are those that would appear in the financial statements if all the consolidating companies actually formed a single company. The balances in the last column are obtained by summing all amounts algebraically across the worksheet by account. These are the balances that appear in the consolidated financial statements.

The top portion of the worksheet is used in preparing the consolidated income statement. All income statement accounts are listed in the order they normally appear in an income statement.[9] When the income statement portion of the worksheet is completed, a total for each column is entered at the bottom of the income statement portion of the worksheet. The bottom line in this part of the worksheet shows the parent's net income, the subsidiary's net income, the totals of the debit and credit eliminations for this section of the worksheet, and consolidated net income. The entire bottom line is carried down to the "net income" line in the retained earnings statement portion of the worksheet immediately below.

The retained earnings statement section of the worksheet is in the same format as a retained earnings statement, or the retained earnings section of a statement of stockholders' equity. Net income and the other totals from the bottom line of the income statement

---

[9] An optional format lists accounts with credit balance accounts first and those having debit balances listed next.

portion of the worksheet are brought down from above. Similarly, the final line in the retained earnings statement section of the worksheet is carried down in its entirety to the retained earnings line in the balance sheet section.

The bottom portion of the worksheet reflects the balance sheet amounts at the end of the period.[10] The retained earnings amounts appearing in the balance sheet section of the worksheet are the totals carried forward from the bottom line of the retained earnings statement section. The examples in the following sections of this chapter demonstrate the use of the comprehensive three-part consolidation worksheet.

Nature of Eliminating Entries

Eliminating entries are used in the consolidation worksheet to adjust the totals of the individual account balances of the separate consolidating companies to reflect the amounts that would appear if all the legally separate companies were actually a single company. Eliminating entries appear only in the consolidating worksheets and do not affect the books of the separate companies.

For the most part, companies that are to be consolidated record their transactions during the period without regard to the consolidated entity. Transactions with related companies tend to be recorded in the same manner as those with unrelated parties, although intercompany transactions may be recorded in separate accounts or other records may be kept to facilitate the later elimination of intercompany transactions. Each of the consolidating companies also prepares its adjusting and closing entries at the end of the period in the normal manner. The resulting balances are entered in the consolidation worksheet and combined to arrive at the consolidated totals. Eliminating entries are used in the worksheet to increase or decrease the combined totals for individual accounts so that only transactions with external parties are reflected in the consolidated amounts.

Some eliminating entries are required at the end of one period but not at the end of subsequent periods. For example, a loan from a parent to a subsidiary in December 20X1, repaid in February 20X2, requires an entry to eliminate the intercompany receivable and payable on December 31, 20X1, but not at the end of 20X2. Some other eliminating entries need to be placed in the consolidation worksheets each time consolidated statements are prepared for a period of years. For example, if a parent company sells land to a subsidiary for $5,000 above the cost to the parent, a worksheet entry is needed to reduce the land amount by $5,000 each time consolidated statements are prepared for as long as an affiliate holds the land. It is important to remember that because eliminating entries are not made on the books of any company, they do not carry over from period to period.

CONSOLIDATED BALANCE SHEET WITH WHOLLY OWNED SUBSIDIARY

The simplest consolidation setting occurs when the financial statements of related companies are consolidated immediately after a parent–subsidiary relationship is established through a business combination or creation of a new subsidiary. We present a series of examples to illustrate the preparation of a consolidated balance sheet. Consolidation procedures are the same whether a subsidiary is created or acquired. We use the case of an acquired subsidiary to illustrate the consolidation procedures in the examples that follow. In each example, Peerless Products Corporation purchases all or part of the common stock of Special Foods Inc. on January 1, 20X1, and immediately prepares a consolidated balance sheet. Figure 2–4 presents the separate balance sheets of the two companies immediately before the combination.

In the discussion that follows, we discuss all journal entries and worksheet eliminating entries in the text of the chapter. To avoid confusing the eliminating entries with journal entries that appear on the separate books of the parent or subsidiary, all worksheet eliminating entries appearing in the text are shaded while journal entries recorded in the books of the parent company are not shaded.

[10] Optionally, accounts can be separated and listed with debits first and then credits.

FIGURE 2–4
Balance Sheets of Peerless Products and Special Foods, January 1, 20X1, Immediately before Combination

	Peerless Products	Special Foods
Assets		
Cash	$ 350,000	$ 50,000
Accounts Receivable	75,000	50,000
Inventory	100,000	60,000
Land	175,000	40,000
Buildings and Equipment	800,000	600,000
Accumulated Depreciation	(400,000)	(300,000)
Total Assets	$1,100,000	$500,000
Liabilities and Stockholders' Equity		
Accounts Payable	$ 100,000	$100,000
Bonds Payable	200,000	100,000
Common Stock	500,000	200,000
Retained Earnings	300,000	100,000
Total Liabilities and Equity	$1,100,000	$500,000

100 Percent Ownership Acquired at Book Value

In the first example, Peerless acquires all of Special Foods' outstanding common stock for $300,000, an amount equal to the fair value of Special Foods as a whole. On the date of combination, the fair values of Special Foods' individual assets and liabilities are equal to their book values shown in Figure 2–4. Because Peerless acquires all of Special Foods' common stock and because Special Foods has only the one class of stock outstanding, the total book value of the shares acquired equals the total stockholders' equity of Special Foods ($200,000 + $100,000). The $300,000 of consideration exchanged is equal to the book value of the shares acquired. This ownership situation can be characterized as follows:

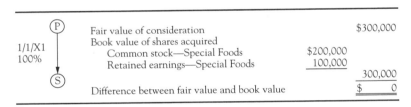

Peerless records the stock acquisition on its books with the following entry on the date of combination:

Figure 2–5 presents the separate financial statements of Peerless and Special Foods immediately after the combination. Special Foods' balance sheet in Figure 2–5 is the same as in Figure 2–4, but Peerless' balance sheet has changed to reflect the $300,000 reduction in cash and the recording of the investment in Special Foods stock for the same amount. Note that the $300,000 of cash was paid to the former stockholders of Special Foods and not to the company itself. Accordingly, that cash is no longer in the consolidated entity. Instead, Peerless' balance sheet now reflects a $300,000 Investment in Special Foods Stock account.

Investment Elimination Entry

Figure 2–6 presents a basic example of a consolidation worksheet. The only eliminating entry in the worksheet in Figure 2–6 removes the Investment in Special Foods Stock

FIGURE 2–5
Balance Sheets of Peerless Products and Special Foods, January 1, 20X1, Immediately after Combination

	Peerless Products	Special Foods
Assets		
Cash	$ 50,000	$ 50,000
Accounts Receivable	75,000	50,000
Inventory	100,000	60,000
Land	175,000	40,000
Buildings and Equipment	800,000	600,000
Accumulated Depreciation	(400,000)	(300,000)
Investment in Special Foods Stock	300,000	
Total Assets	$1,100,000	$500,000
Liabilities and Stockholders' Equity		
Accounts Payable	$ 100,000	$100,000
Bonds Payable	200,000	100,000
Common Stock	500,000	200,000
Retained Earnings	300,000	100,000
Total Liabilities and Equity	$1,100,000	$500,000

account and the subsidiary's stockholders' equity accounts. While this elimination entry is very simple, to be consistent with the discussion of more complicated examples later in the chapter, we illustrate the thought process in developing the worksheet entry. In this example, Peerless' investment is exactly equal to the book value of equity of Special Foods. Therefore, no goodwill is recorded and all assets and liabilities are simply combined from Special Foods' financial statements at their current book values. In Chapters 4 and 5, we will explore situations where the acquiring company pays more than the book value of the acquired company's net assets (i.e., when there is a positive differential). However, in Chapters 2 and 3, the excess value of identifiable net assets and goodwill will always be equal to zero. To maintain a consistent approach through all four chapters, we always illustrate the components of the acquiring company's investment, even though the acquiring company's investment will always be exactly equal to its share of the book value of net assets in Chapters 2 and 3. Therefore, the relationship between the fair value of the consideration given to acquire Special Foods, the fair value of Special Foods' net assets, and the book value of Special Foods' net assets can be illustrated as follows:

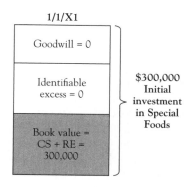

1/1/X1

Goodwill = 0

Identifiable excess = 0

Book value = CS + RE = 300,000

$300,000 Initial investment in Special Foods

The book value of Special Foods' equity as of the acquisition date is equal to the sum of common stock and retained earnings:

Book Value Calculations:

	Total Investment	=	Common Stock	+	Retained Earnings
Original book value	300,000		200,000		100,000

Therefore, the elimination entry simply credits the Investment in Special Foods Stock account (for the original acquisition price, $300,000) from Peerless' balance sheet. In this and all future examples, we use blue lettering to highlight the numbers from the book value analysis that appear in the basic elimination entry:

The corresponding debits eliminate the beginning balances in the equity accounts of Special Foods:

Basic elimination entry:

Common stock	200,000	← Original amount invested (100%)
Retained earnings	100,000	← Beginning balance in ret. earnings
Investment in Special Foods	300,000	← Book value in investment account

Remember that this entry is made in the consolidation worksheet, not on the books of either the parent or the subsidiary, and is presented here in general journal form only for instructional purposes.

The investment account must be eliminated because, from a single entity viewpoint, a company cannot hold an investment in itself. The subsidiary's stock and the related stockholders' equity accounts must be eliminated because the subsidiary's stock is held entirely within the consolidated entity and none represents claims by outsiders.

From a somewhat different viewpoint, the investment account on the parent's books can be thought of as a single account representing the parent's investment in the net assets of the subsidiary, a so-called *one-line consolidation.* In a full consolidation, the subsidiary's individual assets and liabilities are combined with those of the parent. Including both the net assets of the subsidiary, as represented by the balance in the investment account, and the subsidiary's individual assets and liabilities would double-count the same set of assets. Therefore, the investment account is eliminated and not carried to the consolidated balance sheet.

In this example, the acquisition price of the stock acquired by Peerless is equal to the fair value of Special Foods as a whole. This reflects the normal situation where the acquisition price paid by the parent is equal to the fair value of its proportionate share of the subsidiary. In addition, this example assumes that the subsidiary's fair value is equal to its book value, a generally unrealistic assumption. Given this assumption, however, the balance of Peerless' investment account is equal to Special Foods' stockholders' equity accounts, so this worksheet entry fully eliminates Peerless' investment account against Special Foods' stockholders' equity accounts.

Consolidation Worksheet

We present the worksheet for the preparation of a consolidated balance sheet immediately following the acquisition in Figure 2–6. The first two columns of the worksheet in Figure 2–6 are the account balances taken from the books of Peerless and Special Foods, as shown in Figure 2–5. The balances of like accounts are placed side by side so that they may be added together. If more than two companies were to be consolidated, a separate column would be included in the worksheet for each additional subsidiary.

FIGURE 2–6 Worksheet for Consolidated Balance Sheet, January 1, 20X1, Date of Combination; 100 Percent Acquisition at Book Value

	Peerless Products	Special Foods	Elimination Entries		Consolidated
			DR	CR	
Balance Sheet					
Cash	$ 50,000	$ 50,000			$ 100,000
Accounts Receivable	75,000	50,000			125,000
Inventory	100,000	60,000			160,000
Investment in Special Foods	300,000			$300,000	0
Land	175,000	40,000			215,000
Buildings & Equipment	800,000	600,000			1,400,000
Less: Accumulated Depreciation	(400,000)	(300,000)			(700,000)
Total Assets	**$1,100,000**	**$500,000**	**$ 0**	**$300,000**	**$1,300,000**
Accounts Payable	100,000	100,000			200,000
Bonds Payable	200,000	100,000			300,000
Common Stock	500,000	200,000	200,000		500,000
Retained Earnings	300,000	100,000	100,000		300,000
Total Liabilities & Equity	**$1,100,000**	**$500,000**	**$300,000**	**$ 0**	**$1,300,000**

The accounts are placed in the worksheet in the order they would normally appear in the companies' financial statements. The two columns labeled *Elimination Entries* in Figure 2–6 are used to adjust the amounts reported by the individual companies to the amounts appropriate for the consolidated statement. All eliminations made in the worksheets are made in double-entry form. Thus, when the worksheet is completed, total debits entered in the Debit Eliminations column must equal total credits entered in the Credit Eliminations column. We highlight all parts of each eliminating entry with the same color so that the reader can identify the individual elimination entries in the worksheet. After the appropriate eliminating entries have been entered in the Elimination Entries columns, summing algebraically across the individual accounts provides the consolidated totals.

The Consolidated Balance Sheet

The consolidated balance sheet presented in Figure 2–7 comes directly from the last column of the consolidation worksheet in Figure 2–6. Because no operations occurred between the date of combination and the preparation of the consolidated balance sheet, the stockholders' equity section of the consolidated balance sheet is identical to that of Peerless in Figure 2–5.

CONSOLIDATION SUBSEQUENT TO ACQUISITION

The preceding section introduced the procedures used to prepare a consolidated balance sheet as of the acquisition date. More than a consolidated balance sheet, however, is needed to provide a comprehensive picture of the consolidated entity's activities following acquisition. As with a single company, the set of basic financial statements for a consolidated entity consists of a balance sheet, an income statement, a statement of changes in retained earnings, and a statement of cash flows.

This section of the chapter presents the procedures used to prepare an income statement, statement of retained earnings, and consolidated balance sheet subsequent to the acquisition date.

The discussion that follows first deals with the important concepts of consolidated net income and consolidated retained earnings, followed by a description of the worksheet

FIGURE 2–7 Consolidated Balance Sheet, January 1, 20X1, Date of Combination; 100 Percent Acquisition at Book Value

PEERLESS PRODUCTS CORPORATION AND SUBSIDIARY				
Consolidated Balance Sheet				
January 1, 20X1				
Assets			**Liabilities**	
Cash		$ 100,000	Accounts Payable	$ 200,000
Accounts Receivable		125,000	Bonds Payable	300,000
Inventory		160,000		
Land		215,000	Stockholders' Equity	
Buildings and Equipment	$1,400,000		Common Stock	500,000
Accumulated Depreciation	(700,000)	700,000	Retained Earnings	300,000
Total Assets		$1,300,000	Total Liabilities and Equity	$1,300,000

format used to facilitate the preparation of a full set of consolidated financial statements. We then discuss the specific procedures used to prepare consolidated financial statements subsequent to the date of combination.

This and subsequent chapters focus on procedures for consolidation when the parent company accounts for its investment in subsidiary stock using the equity method. If the parent accounts for its investment using the cost method, the general approach to the preparation of consolidated financial statements is the same, but the specific elimination entries differ. Appendix 2B summarizes consolidation procedures using the cost method. Regardless of the method the parent uses to account for its subsidiary investment, however, the consolidated statements will be the same because the investment and related accounts are eliminated in the consolidation process.

The approach followed to prepare a complete set of consolidated financial statements subsequent to a business combination is quite similar to that used to prepare a consolidated balance sheet as of the date of combination. However, in addition to the assets and liabilities, the revenues and expenses of the consolidating companies must be combined. As the accounts are combined, eliminations must be made in the consolidation worksheet so that the consolidated financial statements appear as if they are the financial statements of a single company.

When a full set of consolidated financial statements is prepared subsequent to the date of combination, two of the important concepts affecting the statements are those of consolidated net income and consolidated retained earnings.

Consolidated Net Income

All revenues and expenses of the individual consolidating companies arising from transactions with unaffiliated companies are included in the consolidated financial statements. The consolidated income statement includes 100 percent of the revenues and expenses regardless of the parent's percentage ownership. Similar to single-company financial statements, where the difference between revenues and expenses equals net income, revenues minus expenses in the consolidated financial statements equals consolidated net income. *Consolidated net income* is equal to the parent's income from its own operations, excluding any investment income from consolidated subsidiaries, plus the net income from each of the consolidated subsidiaries, adjusted for any differential write-off (which is zero in this chapter). Intercorporate investment income from consolidated subsidiaries included in the parent's net income under either the cost or equity method must be eliminated in computing consolidated net income to avoid double-counting.

If all subsidiaries are wholly owned, all of the consolidated net income accrues to the parent company, or the controlling interest. If one or more of the consolidated subsidiaries is less than wholly owned, a portion of the consolidated net income accrues to the non-controlling shareholders (as explained in Chapter 3). In that case, the income attributable to the noncontrolling interest is deducted from consolidated net income on the face of the income statement to arrive at consolidated net income attributable to the controlling interest.

Consolidated net income and consolidated net income attributable to the controlling interest are the same when all consolidated subsidiaries are wholly owned. For example, assume that Push Corporation purchases all of the stock of Shove Company at an amount equal to its book value. During 20X1, Shove reports net income of $25,000, while Push reports net income of $125,000, including equity-method income from Shove of $25,000. Consolidated net income for 20X1 is computed as follows:

Push's net income	$125,000
Less: Equity-method income from Shove	(25,000)
Shove's net income	25,000
Consolidated net income	$125,000

Note that when the parent company properly applies the equity method, consolidated net income is always equal to the parent's equity-method net income.

Consolidated Retained Earnings

The retained earnings figure reported in the consolidated balance sheet is the retained earnings attributable to the controlling interest. For subsidiaries that are not wholly owned, the noncontrolling stockholders' share of subsidiary retained earnings is included in the noncontrolling interest amount reported in the equity section of the consolidated balance sheet.

Consolidated retained earnings, as it appears in the consolidated balance sheet, is that portion of the consolidated enterprise's undistributed earnings accruing to the parent company shareholders. Consolidated retained earnings at the end of the period is equal to the beginning consolidated retained earnings balance plus consolidated net income attributable to the controlling interest, less dividends declared by the parent company.

Computing Consolidated Retained Earnings

Consolidated retained earnings is computed by adding together the parent's retained earnings from its own operations (excluding any income from consolidated subsidiaries recognized by the parent) and the parent's proportionate share of the net income of each subsidiary since the date of acquisition, adjusted for differential write-off and goodwill impairment. Consolidated retained earnings should be equal to the parent's equity-method retained earnings.

If the parent accounts for subsidiaries using the equity method on its books, the retained earnings of each subsidiary is completely eliminated when the subsidiary is consolidated. This is necessary because (1) retained earnings cannot be purchased, and so subsidiary retained earnings at the date of a business combination cannot be included in the combined company's retained earnings; (2) the parent's share of the subsidiary's income since acquisition is already included in the parent's equity-method retained earnings; and (3) the noncontrolling interest's share (if any) of the subsidiary's retained earnings is not included in consolidated retained earnings.

In the simple example given previously, assume that on the date of combination, January 1, 20X1, Push's retained earnings balance is $400,000 and Shove's is $250,000. During 20X1, Shove reports $25,000 of net income and declares $10,000 of dividends. Push reports $100,000 of separate operating earnings plus $25,000 of equity-method income from its 100 percent interest in Shove; Push declares dividends of $30,000. Based on this information, the retained earnings balances for Push and Shove on December 31, 20X1, are computed as follows:

	Push	Shove
Balance, January 1, 20X1	$400,000	$250,000
Net income, 20X1	125,000	25,000
Dividends declared in 20X1	(30,000)	(10,000)
Balance, December 31, 20X1	$495,000	$265,000

Consolidated retained earnings is computed by first determining the parent's retained earnings from its own operations. This computation involves removing from the parent's retained earnings the $25,000 of subsidiary income since acquisition recognized by the parent, leaving $470,000 ($495,000 − $25,000) of retained earnings resulting from the parent's own operations. The parent's 100 percent share of the subsidiary's net income since the date of acquisition is then added to this number, resulting in consolidated retained earnings of $495,000. We note that since this is the first year since the acquisition, the net income since the date of acquisition is just this year's income. Subsequent examples will illustrate how this calculation differs in later years. We also emphasize that since Push uses the fully adjusted equity method, this number is the same as the parent's equity-method retained earnings.

CONSOLIDATED FINANCIAL STATEMENTS—100 PERCENT OWNERSHIP, CREATED OR ACQUIRED AT BOOK VALUE

Each of the consolidated financial statements is prepared as if it is taken from a single set of books that is being used to account for the overall consolidated entity. There is, of course, no set of books for the consolidated entity, and as in the preparation of the consolidated balance sheet, the consolidation process starts with the data recorded on the books of the individual consolidating companies. The account balances from the books of the individual companies are placed in the three-part worksheet, and entries are made to eliminate the effects of intercorporate ownership and transactions. The consolidation approach and procedures are the same whether the subsidiary being consolidated was acquired or created.

To understand the process of consolidation subsequent to the start of a parent–subsidiary relationship, assume that on January 1, 20X1, Peerless Products Corporation acquires all of the common stock of Special Foods Inc. for $300,000, an amount equal to the book value of Special Foods on that date. At that time, Special Foods has $200,000 of common stock outstanding and retained earnings of $100,000, summarized as follows:

(P)	Fair value of consideration		$300,000
1/1/X1	Book value of shares acquired		
100%	Common stock—Special Foods	$200,000	
	Retained earnings—Special Foods	100,000	
(S)			300,000
	Difference between fair value and book value		$ 0

Peerless accounts for its investment in Special Foods stock using the equity method. Information about Peerless and Special Foods as of the date of combination and for the years 20X1 and 20X2 appears in Figure 2–8.

FIGURE 2–8
Selected Information about Peerless Products and Special Foods on January 1, 20X1, and for the Years 20X1 and 20X2

	Peerless Products	Special Foods
Common Stock, January 1, 20X1	$500,000	$200,000
Retained Earnings, January 1, 20X1	300,000	100,000
20X1:		
Separate Operating Income, Peerless	140,000	
Net Income, Special Foods		50,000
Dividends	60,000	30,000
20X2:		
Separate Operating Income, Peerless	160,000	
Net Income, Special Foods		75,000
Dividends	60,000	40,000

Initial Year of Ownership

On January 1, 20X1, Peerless records its purchase of Special Foods common stock with the following entry:

(12)	Investment in Special Foods	300,000	
	Cash		300,000

Record purchase of Special Foods stock.

During 20X1, Peerless records operating earnings of $140,000, excluding its income from investing in Special Foods, and declares dividends of $60,000. Special Foods reports 20X1 net income of $50,000 and declares dividends of $30,000.

Parent Company Entries

Peerless records its 20X1 income and dividends from Special Foods under the equity method as follows:

(13)	Investment in Special Foods	50,000	
	Income from Special Foods		50,000

Record Peerless' 100% share of Special Foods' 20X1 income.

(14)	Cash	30,000	
	Investment in Special Foods		30,000

Record Peerless' 100% share of Special Foods' 20X1 dividend.

Consolidation Worksheet—Initial Year of Ownership

After all appropriate entries, including year-end adjustments, have been made on the books of Peerless and Special Foods, a consolidation worksheet is prepared as in Figure 2–9. The adjusted account balances from the books of Peerless and Special Foods are placed in the first two columns of the worksheet. Then all amounts that reflect intercorporate transactions or ownership are eliminated in the consolidation process.

The distinction between journal entries recorded on the books of the individual companies and the eliminating entries recorded only on the consolidation worksheet is an important one. Book entries affect balances on the books and the amounts that are carried to the consolidation worksheet; worksheet eliminating entries affect only those balances carried to the consolidated financial statements in the period. As mentioned previously, the eliminating entries presented in this text are shaded both when presented in journal entry form in the text and in the worksheet.

In this example, the accounts that must be eliminated because of intercorporate ownership are the stockholders' equity accounts of Special Foods, including dividends declared, Peerless' investment in Special Foods stock, and Peerless' income from Special Foods. However, different from previous examples, the book value portion of Peerless'

Advanced StudyGuide.com

investment has changed because earnings and dividends have adjusted the investment account balance. The book value portion of the investment account can be summarized as follows:

Book Value Calculations:

	Total Investment	=	Common Stock	+	Retained Earnings
Original book value	300,000		200,000		100,000
+ Net income	50,000				50,000
− Dividends	(30,000)				(30,000)
Ending book value	320,000		200,000		120,000

The beginning and ending balances in the investment account can be illustrated as follows:

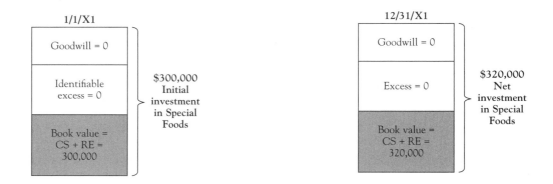

Under the equity method, Peerless recognizes its share (100 percent) of Special Foods' reported income. In the consolidated income statement, however, Special Foods' individual revenue and expense accounts are combined with Peerless' accounts. Peerless' equity method income from Special Foods, therefore, must be eliminated to avoid double-counting. Special Foods' dividends paid to the Peerless must be eliminated when consolidated statements are prepared so that only dividend declarations related to the parent's shareholders are treated as dividends of the consolidated entity. Thus, the basic eliminating entry removes both the equity method Income from Special Foods and Special Foods' dividends declared during the period:

Basic elimination entry:

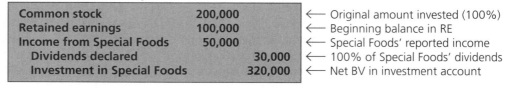

Common stock	200,000		← Original amount invested (100%)
Retained earnings	100,000		← Beginning balance in RE
Income from Special Foods	50,000		← Special Foods' reported income
Dividends declared		30,000	← 100% of Special Foods' dividends
Investment in Special Foods		320,000	← Net BV in investment account

The book value calculations in the chart above help to facilitate preparation of the basic elimination entry. Thus, the basic eliminating entry removes (1) Special Foods' equity accounts, (2) Special Foods' dividends declared, (3) Peerless' Income from Special Foods account, and (4) Peerless' Investment in Special Foods account. Note that we use blue shading in the numbers in the book value analysis that appear in the basic elimination entry. Since there is no differential in this example, the basic elimination entry completely eliminates the balance in Peerless' investment account on the balance sheet as well as the Income from Special Foods account on the income statement. Additional elimination entries will be necessary when there is a differential in Chapters 4 and 5.

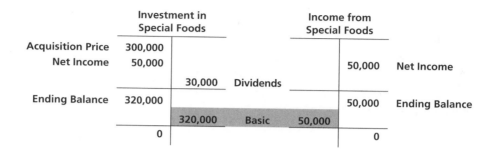

We now introduce one final elimination entry that is optional but that provides for a more "correct" consolidation. When the parent company acquires the subsidiary, the consolidated financial statements should appear as if all of the subsidiary's assets and liabilities were acquired at fair value as of the acquisition date. For example, if the acquisition were to be exercised as an acquisition of the assets instead of the stock of the company, each individual asset would be recorded by the acquiring company with a new basis equal to its fair value (and zero accumulated depreciation) on that date. Old book value and accumulated depreciation numbers from the seller would be disregarded. In the same way, when a company's stock is acquired in an acquisition, the consolidated financial statements should appear with all assets and liabilities recorded at their current fair market values. Thus, eliminating the old accumulated depreciation of the subsidiary as of the acquisition date and netting it out against the historical cost gives the appearance that the depreciable assets have been newly recorded at their fair value as of the acquisition date. In this example, the fair value of Special Foods' buildings and equipment is equal to their current book values. Special Foods' books indicate accumulated depreciation on the acquisition date of $300,000. Thus, the following elimination entry nets this accumulated depreciation out against the cost of the building and equipment.

Optional accumulated depreciation elimination entry:

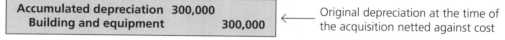

Original depreciation at the time of the acquisition netted against cost

Note that this worksheet elimination entry does not change the net buildings and equipment balance. Netting the pre-acquisition accumulated depreciation out against the cost basis of the corresponding assets merely causes the buildings and equipment to appear in the consolidated financial statements as if they had been revalued to their fair values on the acquisition date. This same entry would be included in each succeeding consolidation as long as the assets remain on Special Foods' books (always based on the acquisition date accumulated depreciation balance).

Worksheet Relationships

Both of the eliminating entries are entered in Figure 2–9 and the amounts totaled across each row and down each column to complete the worksheet. Some specific points to recognize with respect to the full worksheet are as follows:

FIGURE 2–9   December 31, 20X1, Equity-Method Worksheet for Consolidated Financial Statements, Initial Year of Ownership; 100 Percent Acquisition at Book Value

	Peerless Products	Special Foods	Elimination Entries DR	Elimination Entries CR	Consolidated
Income Statement					
Sales	$ 400,000	$200,000			$ 600,000
Less: COGS	(170,000)	(115,000)			(285,000)
Less: Depreciation Expense	(50,000)	(20,000)			(70,000)
Less: Other Expenses	(40,000)	(15,000)			(55,000)
Income from Special Foods	50,000		$ 50,000		0
Net Income	**$ 190,000**	**$ 50,000**	**$ 50,000**	**$ 0**	**$ 190,000**
Statement of Retained Earnings					
Beginning Balance	$ 300,000	$100,000	$100,000		$ 300,000
Net Income	190,000	50,000	50,000	$ 0	190,000
Less: Dividends Declared	(60,000)	(30,000)		30,000	(60,000)
Ending Balance	**$ 430,000**	**$120,000**	**$150,000**	**$ 30,000**	**$ 430,000**
Balance Sheet					
Cash	$ 210,000	$ 75,000			$ 285,000
Accounts Receivable	75,000	50,000			125,000
Inventory	100,000	75,000			175,000
Investment in Special Foods	320,000			$320,000	0
Land	175,000	40,000			215,000
Buildings & Equipment	800,000	600,000		300,000	1,100,000
Less: Accumulated Depreciation	(450,000)	(320,000)	$300,000		(470,000)
Total Assets	**$1,230,000**	**$520,000**	**$300,000**	**$620,000**	**$1,430,000**
Accounts Payable	$ 100,000	$100,000			$ 200,000
Bonds Payable	200,000	100,000			300,000
Common Stock	500,000	200,000	$200,000		500,000
Retained Earnings	430,000	120,000	150,000	$ 30,000	430,000
Total Liabilities & Equity	**$1,230,000**	**$520,000**	**$350,000**	**$ 30,000**	**$1,430,000**

1. Because of the normal articulation among the financial statements, the bottom-line number from each of the first two sections of the worksheet carries down to the next financial statement in a logical progression. As part of the normal accounting cycle, net income is closed to retained earnings, and retained earnings is reflected in the balance sheet. Therefore, in the consolidation worksheet, the net income is carried down to the retained earnings statement section of the worksheet, and the ending retained earnings line is carried down to the balance sheet section of the worksheet. Note that in both cases the entire line, including total eliminations, is carried forward.

2. Double-entry bookkeeping requires total debits to equal total credits for any single eliminating entry and for the worksheet as a whole. Because some eliminating entries extend to more than one section of the worksheet, however, the totals of the debit and credit eliminations are not likely to be equal in either of the first two sections of the worksheet. The totals of all debits and credits at the bottom of the balance sheet section are equal because the cumulative balances from the two upper sections are carried forward to the balance sheet section.

3. In the balance sheet portion of the worksheet, total debit balances must equal total credit balances for each company and the consolidated entity.

4. When the parent uses the full equity method of accounting for the investment, consolidated net income should equal the parent's net income and consolidated retained

earnings should equal the parent's retained earnings. This means the existing balance in subsidiary retained earnings must be eliminated to avoid double counting.

5. Certain other clerical safeguards are incorporated into the worksheet. The amounts reflected in the bottom line of the income statement section, when summed (algebraically) across, must equal the number reported as consolidated net income. Similarly, the amounts in the last line of the retained earnings statement section must equal consolidated retained earnings when summed across.

Second and Subsequent Years of Ownership

The consolidation procedures employed at the end of the second and subsequent years are basically the same as those used at the end of the first year. Adjusted trial balance data of the individual companies are used as the starting point each time consolidated statements are prepared because no separate books are kept for the consolidated entity. An additional check is needed in each period following acquisition to ensure that the beginning balance of consolidated retained earnings shown in the completed worksheet equals the balance reported at the end of the prior period. In all other respects, the eliminating entries and worksheet are comparable with those shown for the first year.

Parent Company Entries

We illustrate consolidation after two years of ownership by continuing the example of Peerless Products and Special Foods, based on the data in Figure 2–8. Peerless' separate income from its own operations for 20X2 is $160,000, and its dividends total $60,000. Special Foods reports net income of $75,000 in 20X2 and pays dividends of $40,000. Peerless records the following equity-method entries in 20X2:

(15)	Investment in Special Foods	75,000	
	Income from Special Foods		75,000
	Record Peerless' 100% share of Special Foods' 20X2 income.		

(16)	Cash	40,000	
	Investment in Special Foods		40,000
	Record Peerless' 100% share of Special Foods' 20X2 dividend.		

The balance in the investment account reported by Peerless increases from $320,000 on January 1, 20X2, to $355,000 on December 31, 20X2, and reported net income of Peerless totals $235,000 ($160,000 + $75,000).

Consolidation Worksheet—Second Year of Ownership

Figure 2–10 illustrates the worksheet to prepare consolidated statements for 20X2. The book value of Peerless' investment in Special Foods (which is equal to the book value of Special Foods' equity accounts) can be analyzed and summarized as follows:

Book Value Calculations:

	Total Investment	=	Common Stock	+	Retained Earnings
Original book value	320,000		200,000		120,000
+ Net income	75,000				75,000
− Dividends	(40,000)				(40,000)
Ending book value	355,000		200,000		155,000

The beginning and ending balances in the investment account can be illustrated as follows:

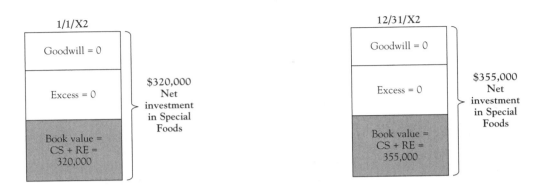

Again, the basic eliminating entry removes (1) Special Foods' equity accounts, (2) Special Foods' dividends declared, (3) Peerless' Income from Special Foods account, and (4) Peerless' Investment in Special Foods account:

Basic elimination entry:

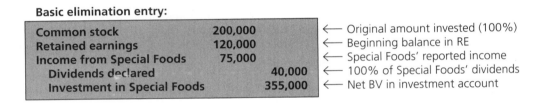

Common stock	200,000	← Original amount invested (100%)
Retained earnings	120,000	← Beginning balance in RE
Income from Special Foods	75,000	← Special Foods' reported income
Dividends declared	40,000	← 100% of Special Foods' dividends
Investment in Special Foods	355,000	← Net BV in investment account

As explained previously, since there is no differential in this example, the basic elimination entry completely eliminates the balance in Peerless' investment account on the balance sheet as well as the Income from Special Foods account on the income statement.

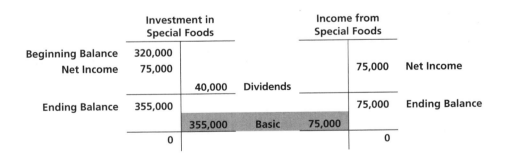

In this example, Special Foods had accumulated depreciation on the acquisition date of $300,000. Thus, we repeat the same accumulated depreciation elimination entry this year (and every year as long as Special Foods owns the assets) that we used in the initial year.

Optional accumulated depreciation elimination entry:

Accumulated depreciation	300,000	← Original depreciation at the time of
Building and equipment	300,000	the acquisition netted against cost

FIGURE 2–10 December 31, 20X2, Equity-Method Worksheet for Consolidated Financial Statements, Second Year of Ownership; 100 Percent Acquisition at Book Value

	Peerless Products	Special Foods	Eliminating Entries DR	Eliminating Entries CR	Consolidated
Income Statement					
Sales	$ 450,000	$300,000			$ 750,000
Less: COGS	(180,000)	(160,000)			(340,000)
Less: Depreciation Expense	(50,000)	(20,000)			(70,000)
Less: Other Expenses	(60,000)	(45,000)			(105,000)
Income from Special Foods	75,000		$ 75,000		0
Net Income	**$ 235,000**	**$ 75,000**	**$ 75,000**	**$ 0**	**$ 235,000**
Statement of Retained Earnings					
Beginning Balance	$ 430,000	$120,000	$120,000		$ 430,000
Net Income	235,000	75,000	75,000	$ 0	235,000
Less: Dividends Declared	(60,000)	(40,000)		40,000	(60,000)
Ending Balance	**$ 605,000**	**$155,000**	**$195,000**	**$ 40,000**	**$ 605,000**
Balance Sheet					
Cash	$ 245,000	$ 85,000			$ 330,000
Accounts Receivable	150,000	80,000			230,000
Inventory	180,000	90,000			270,000
Investment in Special Foods	355,000			$355,000	0
Land	175,000	40,000			215,000
Buildings & Equipment	800,000	600,000		300,000	1,100,000
Less: Accumulated Depreciation	(500,000)	(340,000)	$300,000		(540,000)
Total Assets	**$1,405,000**	**$555,000**	**$300,000**	**$655,000**	**$1,605,000**
Accounts Payable	$ 100,000	$100,000			$ 200,000
Bonds Payable	200,000	100,000			300,000
Common Stock	500,000	200,000	$200,000		500,000
Retained Earnings	605,000	155,000	195,000	$ 40,000	605,000
Total Liabilities & Equity	**$1,405,000**	**$555,000**	**$395,000**	**$ 40,000**	**$1,605,000**

After placing the two elimination entries in the consolidation worksheet, it is completed in the normal manner as illustrated in Figure 2–10. All worksheet relationships discussed in conjunction with Figure 2–9 continue in the second year as well. The beginning consolidated retained earnings balance for 20X2, as shown in Figure 2–10, should be compared with the ending consolidated retained earnings balance for 20X1, as shown in Figure 2–9, to ensure that they are the same.

Consolidated Net Income and Retained Earnings

In the consolidation worksheets illustrated in Figures 2–9 and 2–10, consolidated net income for 20X1 and 20X2 appears as the last number in the income statement section of the worksheets in the Consolidated column on the far right. The numbers can be computed as follows:

	20X1	20X2
Peerless' net income	$190,000	$235,000
Peerless' equity income from Special Foods	(50,000)	(75,000)
Special Foods' net income	50,000	75,000
Consolidated net income	$190,000	$235,000

In this simple illustration, consolidated net income is the same as Peerless' equity-method net income. Had Peerless used the cost method to account for its investment in Special Foods, the consolidated net income would not be the same as Peerless' net income.

In Figures 2–9 and 2–10, the ending consolidated retained earnings number is equal to the beginning balance of consolidated retained earnings plus consolidated net income, less dividends declared on the parent's common stock. It also can be computed as follows:

	20X1	20X2
Peerless' beginning retained earnings from its own operations	$300,000	$380,000
Peerless' income from its own operations	140,000	160,000
Peerless' income from Special Foods since acquisition (cumulative)	50,000	125,000
Peerless' dividends declared	(60,000)	(60,000)
Consolidated retained earnings	$430,000	$605,000

As with income, consolidated retained earnings is the same as the parent's equity-method retained earnings if the parent company uses the equity method. We note that the second year of this calculation illustrates how cumulative income from Special Foods (since the acquisition date) can be used to calculate ending retained earnings.

Summary of Key Concepts

Companies owning investments in the common stock of other companies generally report those investments by consolidating them or reporting them using the cost method (adjusted to market, if appropriate) or equity method, depending on the circumstances. Consolidation generally is appropriate if one entity controls the investee, usually through majority ownership of the investee's voting stock. The equity method is required when an investor has sufficient stock ownership in an investee to significantly influence the operating and financial policies of the investee but owns less than a majority of the investee's stock. In the absence of other evidence, ownership of 20 percent or more of an investee's voting stock is viewed as giving the investor the ability to exercise significant influence over the investee. The cost method is used when consolidation and the equity method are not appropriate, usually when the investor is unable to exercise significant influence over the investee. If the cost method is used in reporting an investment in common stock and the common stock is marketable, an adjustment to market is required for financial reporting purposes.

The cost method is similar to the approach used in accounting for other noncurrent assets. The investment is carried at its original cost to the investor. Consistent with the realization concept, income from the investment is recognized when distributed by the investee in the form of dividends.

The equity method is unique in that the carrying value of the investment is adjusted periodically to reflect the investor's changing equity in the underlying investee. Income from the investment is recognized by the investor under the equity method as the investee reports the income rather than when it is distributed.

Companies also have the choice of reporting nonconsolidated investments using the fair value option instead of the cost or equity method. Under the fair value option, the investment is remeasured to fair value at the end of each reporting period and the change in value recognized as an unrealized gain or loss in income.

Consolidated financial statements present the financial position and results of operations of two or more separate legal entities as if they were a single company. A consolidated balance sheet prepared on the date a parent acquires a subsidiary appears the same as if the acquired company had been merged into the parent.

A consolidation worksheet provides a means of efficiently developing the data needed to prepare consolidated financial statements. The worksheet includes a separate column for the trial balance data of each of the consolidating companies, a debit and a credit column for the elimination entries, and a column for the consolidated totals that appear in the consolidated financial statements. A three-part consolidation worksheet facilitates preparation of a consolidated income statement, retained earnings statement, and balance sheet, and it includes a section for each statement. Eliminating entries are needed in the worksheet to remove the effects of intercompany ownership and intercompany transactions so the consolidated financial statements appear as if the separate companies are actually one.

Key Terms

consolidated net income, *74*
consolidated retained
    earnings, *75*
consolidation, *55*
consolidation worksheet, *67*
corporate joint venture, *60*
cost method, *54*

eliminating entries, *69*
equity accrual, *61*
equity method, *55*
fully adjusted equity
    method, *86*
liquidating dividends, *57*
modified equity method, *85*

one-line consolidation, *65, 86*
parent, *55, 67*
significant influence, *55*
subsidiary, *55, 67*
unconsolidated subsidiary, *55*

Appendix 2A   Additional Considerations Relating to the Equity Method

Determination of Significant Influence

The general rule established in **APB 18 (ASC 323 and 325)** is that the equity method is appropriate when the investor, by virtue of its common stock interest in an investee, is able to exercise significant influence over the operating and financial policies of the investee. In the absence of other evidence, common stock ownership of 20 percent or more is viewed as indicating that the investor is able to exercise significant influence over the investee. However, the APB also stated a number of factors that could constitute other evidence of the ability to exercise significant influence:[11]

1. Representation on board of directors.

2. Participation in policy making.

3. Material intercompany transactions.

4. Interchange of managerial personnel.

5. Technological dependency.

6. Size of investment in relation to concentration of other shareholdings.

Conversely, the FASB provides in **FASB Interpretation No. 35 (ASC 323)** some examples of evidence that an investor is unable to exercise significant influence over an investee.[12] These situations include legal or regulatory challenges to the investor's influence by the investee, agreement by the investor to give up important shareholder rights, concentration of majority ownership among a small group of owners who disregard the views of the investor, and unsuccessful attempts by the investor to obtain information from the investee or representation on the investee's board of directors.

Alternative Versions of the Equity Method of Accounting for Investments in Subsidiaries

Companies are free to adopt whatever procedures they wish in accounting for investments in controlled subsidiaries on their books. Because investments in consolidated subsidiaries are eliminated when consolidated statements are prepared, the consolidated statements are not affected by the procedures used to account for the investments on the parent's books.

In practice, companies follow three different approaches in accounting for their consolidated subsidiaries:

1. Cost method.

2. Fully adjusted equity method.

3. Modified version of the equity method.

Several modified versions of the equity method are found in practice, and all usually are referred to as the *modified equity method.* Some companies apply the equity method without making adjustments for unrealized intercompany profits and the amortization of the differential.

---

[11] **APB 18,** para. 17. (ASC 323-10-15-6)

[12] *Financial Accounting Standards Board Interpretation No. 35,* "Criteria for Applying the Equity Method of Accounting for Investments in Common Stock," May 1981, para. 4. (ASC 323-10-15-10)

Others adjust for the amortization of the differential but omit the adjustments for unrealized intercompany profits. While modified versions of the equity method are not acceptable for financial reporting purposes, they may provide some clerical savings for the parent if used on the books when consolidation of the subsidiary is required.

Unrealized Intercompany Profits

The equity method as applied under **APB 18 (ASC 323 and 325)** often is referred to as a *one-line consolidation* because (*a*) the investor's income and stockholders' equity are the same as if the investee were consolidated and (*b*) all equity method adjustments are made through the investment and related income accounts, which are reported in only a single line in the balance sheet and a single line in the income statement.[13] The view currently taken in consolidation is that intercompany sales do not result in the realization of income until the intercompany profit is confirmed in some way, usually through a transaction with an unrelated third party. For example, if a parent company sells inventory to a subsidiary at a profit, that profit cannot be recognized in the consolidated financial statements until it is confirmed by resale of the inventory to an external party. Because profits from sales to related companies are viewed from a consolidated perspective as being unrealized until there is a resale to unrelated parties, such profits must be eliminated when preparing consolidated financial statements.

The consolidated financial statements are not the only ones affected, however, because **APB 18 (ASC 323 and 325)** requires that the income of an investor that reports an investment using the equity method must be the same as if the investee were consolidated. Therefore, the investor's equity-method income from the investee must be adjusted for unconfirmed profits on intercompany sales as well. The term for the application of the equity method that includes the adjustment for unrealized profit on sales to affiliates is *fully adjusted equity method.*

Adjusting for Unrealized Intercompany Profits

An intercompany sale normally is recorded on the books of the selling affiliate in the same manner as any other sale, including the recognition of profit. In applying the equity method, any intercompany profit remaining unrealized at the end of the period must be deducted from the amount of income that otherwise would be reported.

Under the one-line consolidation approach, the income recognized from the investment and the carrying amount of the investment are reduced to remove the effects of the unrealized intercompany profits. In future periods when the intercompany profit actually is realized, the entry is reversed.

Unrealized Profit Adjustments Illustrated

To illustrate the adjustment for unrealized intercompany profits under the equity method, assume that Palit Corporation owns 40 percent of the common stock of Label Manufacturing. During 20X1, Palit sells inventory to Label for $10,000; the inventory originally cost Palit $7,000. Label resells one-third of the inventory to outsiders during 20X1 and retains the other two-thirds in its ending inventory. The amount of unrealized profit is computed as follows:

Total intercompany profit	$10,000 − $7,000 = $3,000
Unrealized portion	$3,000 × 2/3 = $2,000

Assuming that Label reports net income of $60,000 for 20X1 and declares no dividends, the following entries are recorded on Palit's books at the end of 20X1:

(17)	Investment in Label Manufacturing	24,000	
	Income from Label Manufacturing		24,000
	Record equity-method income: $60,000 × 0.40		

(18)	Income from Label Manufacturing	2,000	
	Investment in Label Manufacturing		2,000
	Remove unrealized intercompany profit.		

[13] Although **APB 18 (ASC 323 and 325)** established the requirement for an equity-method investor's income and stockholders' equity to be the same as if the investee were consolidated, the FASB's recent decision to not permit the write-off of equity-method goodwill may lead to differences in situations in which such goodwill has been impaired.

If all the remaining inventory is sold in 20X2, the following entry is made on Palit's books at the end of 20X2 to record the realization of the previously unrealized intercompany profit:

(19)	Investment in Label Manufacturing Stock	2,000	
	Income from Label Manufacturing		2,000

Recognize realized intercompany profit.

Additional Requirements of APB 18 (ASC 323 and 325)

APB 18 (ASC 323 and 325), the main pronouncement on equity-method reporting, includes several additional requirements:

1. The investor's share of the investee's extraordinary items and prior-period adjustments should be reported as such by the investor, if material.

2. If an investor's share of investee losses exceeds the carrying amount of the investment, the equity method should be discontinued once the investment has been reduced to zero. No further losses are to be recognized by the investor unless the investor is committed to provide further financial support for the investee or unless the investee's imminent return to profitability appears assured. If, after the equity method has been suspended, the investee reports net income, the investor again should apply the equity method, but only after the investor's share of net income equals its share of losses not previously recognized.

3. Preferred dividends of the investee should be deducted from the investee's net income if declared or, whether declared or not, if the preferred stock is cumulative, before the investor computes its share of investee earnings.

APB 18 (ASC 323 and 325) also includes a number of required financial statement disclosures. When using the equity method, the investor must disclose[14]

1. The name and percentage ownership of each investee.

2. The investor's accounting policies with respect to its investments in common stock, including the reasons for any departures from the 20 percent criterion established by **APB 18 (ASC 323 and 325).**

3. The amount and accounting treatment of any differential.

4. The aggregate market value of each identified nonsubsidiary investment where a quoted market price is available.

5. Either separate statements for or summarized information as to assets, liabilities, and results of operations of corporate joint ventures of the investor, if material in the aggregate.

Investor's Share of Other Comprehensive Income

When an investor uses the equity method to account for its investment in another company, the investor's comprehensive income should include its proportionate share of each of the amounts reported as "Other Comprehensive Income" by the investee. For example, assume that Ajax Corporation purchases 40 percent of the common stock of Barclay Company on January 1, 20X1. For the year 20X1, Barclay reports net income of $80,000 and comprehensive income of $115,000, which includes other comprehensive income (in addition to net income) of $35,000. This other comprehensive income (OCI) reflects an unrealized $35,000 gain (net of tax) resulting from an increase in the fair value of an investment in stock classified as available-for-sale under the criteria established by **FASB 115.** In addition to recording the normal equity-method entries, Ajax recognizes its proportionate share of the unrealized gain on available-for-sale securities reported by Barclay during 20X1 with the following entry:

(20)	Investment in Barclay Stock	14,000	
	Unrealized Gain on Investee OCI Investments		14,000

Recognize share of investee's unrealized gain on available-for-sale securities.

---

[14] **FASB 159 (ASC 825)** requires most of the same disclosures for investments in common stock reported under the fair value option that otherwise would have been reported using the equity method.

Entry (20) has no effect on Ajax's net income for 20X1, but it does increase Ajax's other comprehensive income, and thus its total comprehensive income, by $14,000. Ajax will make a similar entry at the end of each period for its proportionate share of any increase or decrease in Barclay's accumulated unrealized holding gain.

Appendix 2B   Consolidation and the Cost Method

Advanced
StudyGuide
.com

Not all parent companies use the equity method to account for their subsidiary investments that are to be consolidated. The choice of the cost or equity method has no effect on the consolidated financial statements. This is true because the balance in the parent's investment account, the parent's income from the subsidiary, and related items are eliminated in preparing the consolidated statements. Thus, the parent is free to use either the cost method or some version of the equity method on its separate books in accounting for investments in subsidiaries that are to be consolidated.

Because the cost method uses different parent-company entries than the equity method, it also requires different eliminating entries in preparing the consolidation worksheet. Keep in mind that the consolidated financial statements appear the same regardless of whether the parent uses the cost or the equity method on its separate books.

CONSOLIDATION—YEAR OF COMBINATION

To illustrate the preparation of consolidated financial statements when the parent company carries its subsidiary investment using the cost method, refer again to the Peerless Products and Special Foods example. Assume that Peerless purchases 100 percent of the common stock of Special Foods on January 1, 20X1, for $300,000. At that date, the book value of Special Foods as a whole is $300,000. All other data are the same as presented in Figures 2–4 and 2–5.

Parent Company Cost-Method Entries

When the parent company uses the cost method, only two journal entries are recorded by Peerless during 20X1 related to its investment in Special Foods. Entry (21) records Peerless' purchase of Special Foods stock; entry (22) recognizes dividend income based on the $30,000 ($30,000 × 100%) of dividends received during the period:

(21)	Investment in Special Foods	300,000	
	Cash		300,000
	Record the initial investment in Special Foods.		

(22)	Cash	30,000	
	Dividend Income		30,000
	Record Peerless' 100% share of Special Foods' 20X1 dividend.		

No entries are made on the parent's books with respect to Special Foods income in 20X1, as would be done under the equity method.

Consolidation Worksheet—Year of Combination

Figure 2–11 illustrates the worksheet to prepare consolidated financial statements for December 31, 20X1, using the cost method. The trial balance data for Peerless and Special Foods included in the worksheet in Figure 2–11 differ from those presented in Figure 2–9 only by the effects of using the cost method rather than the equity method on Peerless' books. Note that all of the amounts in the Consolidated column are the same as in Figure 2–9 because the method used by the parent to account for its subsidiary investment on its books has no effect on the consolidated financial statements.

When a company uses the cost method, the basic elimination entry can be divided into two parts. The first eliminates the investment account. The investment elimination entry eliminates the balances in the stockholders' equity accounts of Special Foods and the balance in Peerless' investment account as of the date of combination. This elimination entry is the same each year (assuming there is no impairment of the investment account) since it relates to the original acquisition price and the original balances in Special Foods' equity accounts.

FIGURE 2–11   December 31, 20X1, Cost-Method Worksheet for Consolidated Financial Statements, Initial Year of Ownership; 100 Percent Acquisition at Book Value

	Peerless Products	Special Foods	Elimination Entries DR	CR	Consolidated
Income Statement					
Sales	$ 400,000	$200,000			$ 600,000
Less: COGS	(170,000)	(115,000)			(285,000)
Less: Depreciation Expense	(50,000)	(20,000)			(70,000)
Less: Other Expenses	(40,000)	(15,000)			(55,000)
Dividend Income	30,000		$ 30,000		0
Net Income	$ 170,000	$ 50,000	$ 30,000	$ 0	$ 190,000
Statement of Retained Earnings					
Beginning Balance	$ 300,000	$100,000	$100,000		$ 300,000
Net Income	170,000	50,000	30,000	$ 0	190,000
Less: Dividends Declared	(60,000)	(30,000)		30,000	(60,000)
Ending Balance	$ 410,000	$120,000	$130,000	$ 30,000	$ 430,000
Balance Sheet					
Cash	$ 210,000	$ 75,000			$ 285,000
Accounts Receivable	75,000	50,000			125,000
Inventory	100,000	75,000			175,000
Investment in Special Foods	300,000			$300,000	0
Land	175,000	40,000			215,000
Buildings & Equipment	800,000	600,000		300,000	1,100,000
Less: Accumulated Depreciation	(450,000)	(320,000)	$300,000		(470,000)
Total Assets	$1,210,000	$520,000	$300,000	$600,000	$1,430,000
Accounts Payable	$ 100,000	$100,000			$ 200,000
Bonds Payable	200,000	100,000			300,000
Common Stock	500,000	200,000	$200,000		500,000
Retained Earnings	410,000	120,000	130,000	$ 30,000	430,000
Total Liabilities & Equity	$1,210,000	$520,000	$330,000	$ 30,000	$1,430,000

Investment elimination entry:

Common stock	200,000	
Retained earnings	100,000	
Investment in Special Foods		300,000

The dividend elimination entry eliminates the dividend income recorded by Peerless during the period along with Special Foods' dividend declaration related to the stockholdings of Peerless.

Dividend elimination entry:

| Dividend income | 30,000 | |
| Dividends declared | | 30,000 |

Finally, the accumulated depreciation elimination entry is the same as under the equity method.

Optional accumulated depreciation elimination entry:

| Accumulated depreciation | 300,000 | |
| Building and equipment | | 300,000 |

As mentioned previously, the amounts in the Consolidated column of the worksheet in Figure 2–11 are the same as those in Figure 2–9 because the method used on the parent's books to account for the subsidiary investment does not affect the consolidated financial statements.

CONSOLIDATION—SECOND YEAR OF OWNERSHIP

Consolidation differences between cost-method accounting and equity-method accounting tend to be more evident in the second year of ownership simply because the equity method entries change every year while the cost method entries are generally the same (with the exception of recording the initial investment).

Parent Company Cost-Method Entry

Peerless only records a single entry on its books in 20X2 related to its investment in Special Foods:

| (23) | Cash | 40,000 | |
| | Dividend Income | | 40,000 |

Record Peerless' 100% share of Special Foods' 20X2 dividend.

Consolidation Worksheet—Second Year Following Combination

The worksheet elimination entries are identical to those used in the first year except that the amount of dividends declared by Special Foods in the second year is $40,000 instead of $30,000.

Investment elimination entry:

Common stock	200,000	
Retained earnings	100,000	
Investment in Special Foods		300,000

Dividend elimination entry:

| Dividend income | 40,000 | |
| Dividends declared | | 40,000 |

Optional accumulated depreciation elimination entry:

| Accumulated depreciation | 300,000 | |
| Building and equipment | | 300,000 |

Under the cost method, Peerless has not recognized any portion of the undistributed earnings of Special Foods on its parent company books. Therefore, Peerless' retained earnings at the beginning of the second year are less than consolidated retained earnings. Also, Peerless' Investment in Special Foods account balance is less than its 100% share of Special Foods' net assets at that date. The consolidation worksheet in Figure 2–12 demonstrates how the worksheet entries eliminate the balances reported by Peerless under the cost method.

Note that while the Consolidated column yields identical numbers to those found in Figure 2–10, the cost method does not maintain the favorable properties that exist when the equity method is employed. Specifically, the parent's net income no longer equals consolidated net income and the parent's retained earnings no longer equals consolidated retained earnings balance. Hence, while the procedures used under the cost method require less work, the parent company does not enjoy some of the favorable relationships among parent and consolidated numbers that exist under the equity method.

Questions

LO1 **Q2-1** What types of investments in common stock normally are accounted for using *(a)* the equity method and *(b)* the cost method?

LO1 **Q2-2** How is the ability to significantly influence the operating and financial policies of a company normally demonstrated?

FIGURE 2-12 **December 31, 20X1, Cost-Method Worksheet for Consolidated Financial Statements, Second Year of Ownership; 100 Percent Acquisition at Book Value**

	Peerless Products	Special Foods	Elimination Entries DR	Elimination Entries CR	Consolidated
Income Statement					
Sales	$ 450,000	$300,000			$ 750,000
Less: COGS	(180,000)	(160,000)			(340,000)
Less: Depreciation Expense	(50,000)	(20,000)			(70,000)
Less: Other Expenses	(60,000)	(45,000)			(105,000)
Income from Special Foods	40,000		$ 40,000		0
Net Income	**$ 200,000**	**$ 75,000**	**$ 40,000**	**$ 0**	**$ 235,000**
Statement of Retained Earnings					
Beginning Balance	$ 410,000	$120,000	$100,000		$ 430,000
Net Income	**200,000**	**75,000**	40,000	$ 0	235,000
Less: Dividends Declared	(60,000)	(40,000)		40,000	(60,000)
Ending Balance	**$ 550,000**	**$155,000**	**$140,000**	**$ 40,000**	**$ 605,000**
Balance Sheet					
Cash	$ 245,000	$ 85,000			$ 330,000
Accounts Receivable	150,000	80,000			230,000
Inventory	180,000	90,000			270,000
Investment in Special Foods	300,000			$300,000	0
Land	175,000	40,000			215,000
Buildings & Equipment	800,000	600,000		300,000	1,100,000
Less: Accumulated Depreciation	(500,000)	(340,000)	$300,000		(540,000)
Total Assets	**$1,350,000**	**$555,000**	**$300,000**	**$600,000**	**$1,605,000**
Accounts Payable	$ 100,000	$100,000			$ 200,000
Bonds Payable	200,000	100,000			300,000
Common Stock	500,000	200,000	$200,000		500,000
Retained Earnings	**550,000**	**155,000**	140,000	$ 40,000	605,000
Total Liabilities & Equity	**$1,350,000**	**$555,000**	**$340,000**	**$ 40,000**	**$1,605,000**

LO	Q	Question
LO3	Q2-3*	When is equity-method reporting considered inappropriate even though sufficient common shares are owned to allow the exercise of significant influence?
LO4	Q2-4	When will the balance in the intercorporate investment account be the same under the cost method and the equity method?
LO2, LO3	Q2-5	Describe an investor's treatment of an investee's prior-period dividends and earnings when the investor acquires significant influence through a purchase of additional stock.
LO2, LO3	Q2-6	From the point of view of an investor in common stock, what is a liquidating dividend? Is a liquidating dividend viewed in the same way by the investee?
LO2, LO3	Q2-7	What effect does a liquidating dividend have on the balance in the investment account under the cost method and the equity method?
LO2, LO3	Q2-8	How is the receipt of a dividend recorded under the equity method? Under the cost method?
LO5	Q2-9	How does the fair value method differ from the cost method and equity method in reporting income from nonsubsidiary investments?
LO3	Q2-10*	How does the fully adjusted equity method differ from the modified equity method?
LO4	Q2-11	Explain the concept of a one-line consolidation.
LO3	Q2-12*	What is the modified equity method? When might a company choose to use the modified equity method rather than the fully adjusted equity method?
LO3	Q2-13*	How are extraordinary items of the investee disclosed by the investor under equity-method reporting?

* Indicates that the item relates to material in the appendices.

LO6	**Q2-14**	How does an eliminating entry differ from an adjusting entry?
LO6, LO7	**Q2-15**	What portion of the balances of subsidiary stockholders' equity accounts is included in the consolidated balance sheet?
LO6	**Q2-16**	How does the elimination process change when consolidated statements are prepared after—rather than at—the date of acquisition?
LO7	**Q2-17**	What are the three parts of the consolidation worksheet, and what sequence is used in completing the worksheet parts?
LO6	**Q2-18**	How are a subsidiary's dividend declarations reported in the consolidated retained earnings statement?
LO7	**Q2-19**	How is consolidated net income computed in a consolidation worksheet?
LO6	**Q2-20**	Give a definition of *consolidated retained earnings*.
LO6, LO7	**Q2-21**	How is the amount reported as consolidated retained earnings determined?
LO7	**Q2-22**	Why is the beginning retained earnings balance for each company entered in the three-part consolidation worksheet rather than just the ending balance?

Cases

LO2, LO3   **C2-1**   **Choice of Accounting Method**

Understanding

Slanted Building Supplies purchased 32 percent of the voting shares of Flat Flooring Company in March 20X3. On December 31, 20X3, the officers of Slanted Building Supplies indicated they needed advice on whether to use the equity method or cost method in reporting their ownership in Flat Flooring.

Required

a. What factors should be considered in determining whether equity-method reporting is appropriate?

b. Which of the two methods is likely to show the larger reported contribution to Slanted's earnings in 20X4? Explain.

c. Why might the use of the equity method become more appropriate as the percentage of ownership increases?

LO2, LO3   **C2-2**   **Intercorporate Ownership**

Research

Most Company purchased 90 percent of the voting common stock of Port Company on January 1, 20X4, and 15 percent of the voting common stock of Adams Company on July 1, 20X4. In preparing the financial statements for Most Company at December 31, 20X4, you discover that Port Company purchased 10 percent of the common stock of Adams Company in 20X2 and continues to hold those shares. Adams Company reported net income of $200,000 for 20X4 and paid a dividend of $70,000 on December 20, 20X4.

Required

Most Company's chief accountant instructs you to review the current accounting literature, including pronouncements of the FASB and other appropriate bodies, and prepare a memo discussing whether the cost or equity method should be used in reporting the investment in Adams Company in Most's consolidated statements prepared at December 31, 20X4. Support your recommendations with citations and quotations from the authoritative financial reporting standards or other literature.

LO2   **C2-3**   **Application of the Equity Method**

Research

Forth Company owned 85,000 of Brown Company's 100,000 shares of common stock until January 1, 20X2, at which time it sold 70,000 of the shares to a group of seven investors, each of whom purchased 10,000 shares. On December 3, 20X2, Forth received a dividend of $9,000 from Brown. Forth continues to purchase a substantial portion of Brown's output under a contract that runs until the end of 20X9. Because of this arrangement, Forth is permitted to place two of its employees on the board of directors of Brown.

Required

Forth Company's controller is not sure whether the company should use the cost or equity method in accounting for its investment in Brown Company. The controller asked you to review the relevant accounting literature and prepare a memo containing your recommendations. Support your recommendations with citations and quotations from the appropriate authoritative financial reporting standards or other literature.

LO6

C2-4 Need for Consolidation Process

Communication

At a recent staff meeting, the vice president of marketing appeared confused. The controller had assured him that the parent company and each of the subsidiary companies had properly accounted for all transactions during the year. After several other questions, he finally asked, "If it has been done properly, then why must you spend so much time and make so many changes to the amounts reported by the individual companies when you prepare the consolidated financial statements each month? You should be able to just add the reported balances together."

Required

Prepare an appropriate response to help the controller answer the marketing vice president's question.

LO1

C2-5 Account Presentation

Research

Prime Company has been expanding rapidly and is now an extremely diversified company for its size. It currently owns three companies with manufacturing facilities, two companies primarily in retail sales, a consumer finance company, and two natural gas pipeline companies. This has led to some conflict between the company's chief accountant and its treasurer. The treasurer advocates presenting no more than five assets and three liabilities on its balance sheet. The chief accountant has resisted combining balances from substantially different subsidiaries and has asked for your assistance.

Required

Review the appropriate authoritative pronouncements or other relevant accounting literature to see what guidance is provided and prepare a memo to the chief accountant with your findings. Include citations to and quotations from the most relevant references. Include in your memo at least two examples of situations in which it may be inappropriate to combine similar-appearing accounts of two subsidiaries.

LO6

C2-6 Consolidating an Unprofitable Subsidiary

Research

Amazing Chemical Corporation's president had always wanted his own yacht and crew and concluded that Amazing Chemical should diversify its investments by purchasing an existing boatyard and repair facility on the lake-shore near his summer home. He could then purchase a yacht and have a convenient place to store it and have it repaired. Although the board of directors was never formally asked to approve this new venture, the president moved forward with optimism and a rather substantial amount of corporate money to purchase full ownership of the boatyard, which had lost rather significant amounts of money each of the five prior years and had never reported a profit for the original owners.

Not surprisingly, the boatyard continued to lose money after Amazing Chemical purchased it, and the losses grew larger each month. Amazing Chemical, a very profitable chemical company, reported net income of $780,000 in 20X2 and $850,000 in 20X3 even though the boatyard reported net losses of $160,000 in 20X2 and $210,000 in 20X3 and was fully consolidated.

Required

Amazing Chemical's chief accountant has become concerned that members of the board of directors or company shareholders will accuse him of improperly preparing the consolidated statements. The president does not plan to tell anyone about the losses, which do not show up in the consolidated income statement that the chief accountant prepared. You have been asked to prepare a memo to the chief accountant indicating the way to include subsidiaries in the consolidated income statement and to provide citations to or quotations from the authoritative accounting literature that would assist the chief accountant in dealing with this matter. You have also been asked to search the accounting literature to see whether any reporting requirements require disclosure of the boatyard in notes to the financial statements or in management's discussion and analysis.

Exercises

LO2, LO3

E2-1 Multiple-Choice Questions on Use of Cost and Equity Methods [AICPA Adapted]

Select the correct answer for each of the following questions.

1. Peel Company received a cash dividend from a common stock investment. Should Peel report an increase in the investment account if it uses the cost method or equity method of accounting?

	Cost	Equity
a.	No	No
b.	Yes	Yes
c.	Yes	No
d.	No	Yes

2. In 20X0, Neil Company held the following investments in common stock:

   - 25,000 shares of B&K Inc.'s 100,000 outstanding shares. Neil's level of ownership gives it the ability to exercise significant influence over the financial and operating policies of B&K.

   - 6,000 shares of Amal Corporation's 309,000 outstanding shares.

   During 20X0, Neil received the following distributions from its common stock investments:

November 6	$30,000 cash dividend from B&K
November 11	$1,500 cash dividend from Amal
December 26	3 percent common stock dividend from Amal
	The closing price of this stock was $115 per share.

   What amount of dividend revenue should Neil report for 20X0?

   a. $1,500.
   b. $4,200.
   c. $31,500.
   d. $34,200.

3. What is the most appropriate basis for recording the acquisition of 100 percent of the stock in another company if the acquisition was a noncash transaction?

   a. At the book value of the consideration given.
   b. At the par value of the stock acquired.
   c. At the book value of the stock acquired.
   d. At the fair value of the consideration given.

4. An investor uses the equity method to account for an investment in common stock. Assume that (1) the investor owns more than 50 percent of the outstanding common stock of the investee, (2) the investee company reports net income and declares dividends during the year, and (3) the investee's net income is greater than the dividends it declares. How would the investor's investment in the common stock of the investee company under the equity method differ at year end from what it would have been if the investor had accounted for the investment under the cost method?

   a. The balance under the equity method is higher than it would have been under the cost method.
   b. The balance under the equity method is lower than it would have been under the cost method.
   c. The balance under the equity method is higher than it would have been under the cost method, but only if the investee company actually paid the dividends before year end.
   d. The balance under the equity method is lower than it would have been under the cost method, but only if the investee company actually paid the dividends before year end.

5. A corporation exercises significant influence over an affiliate in which it holds a 40 percent common stock interest. If its affiliate completed a fiscal year profitably but paid no dividends, how would this affect the investor corporation?

   a. Result in an increased current ratio.
   b. Result in increased earnings per share.

c. Increase several turnover ratios.

d. Decrease book value per share.

6. An investor in common stock received dividends in excess of the investor's share of investee's earnings subsequent to the date of the investment. How will the investor's investment account be affected by those dividends under each of the following methods?

	Cost Method	Equity Method
a.	No effect	No effect
b.	Decrease	No effect
c.	No effect	Decrease
d.	Decrease	Decrease

7. An investor uses the cost method to account for an investment in common stock. A portion of the dividends received this year was in excess of the investor's share of investee's earnings subsequent to the date of investment. The amount of dividend revenue that should be reported in the investor's income statement for this year would be

a. Zero.

b. The total amount of dividends received this year.

c. The portion of the dividends received this year that was in excess of the investor's share of investee's earnings subsequent to the date of investment.

d. The portion of the dividends received this year that was not in excess of the investor's share of investee's earnings subsequent to the date of investment.

LO4

E2-2 Multiple-Choice Questions on Intercorporate Investments

Select the correct answer for each of the following questions.

1. Companies often acquire ownership in other companies using a variety of ownership arrangements. Equity-method reporting should be used by the investor whenever

a. The investor purchases voting common stock of the investee.

b. The investor has significant influence over the operating and financing decisions of the investee.

c. The investor purchases goods and services from the investee.

d. The carrying value of the investment is less than the market value of the investee's shares held by the investor.

2. The carrying amount of an investment in stock accounted for under the equity method is equal to

a. The original price paid to purchase the investment.

b. The original price paid to purchase the investment plus cumulative net income plus cumulative dividends declared by the investee since the date the investment was acquired.

c. The original price paid to purchase the investment plus cumulative net income minus cumulative dividends declared by the investee since the date the investment was acquired.

d. The original price paid to purchase the investment minus cumulative net income minus cumulative dividends declared by the investee since the date the investment was acquired.

LO3

E2-3 Multiple-Choice Questions on Applying Equity Method [AICPA Adapted]

Select the correct answer for each of the following questions.

1. Green Corporation owns 30 percent of the outstanding common stock and 100 percent of the outstanding noncumulative nonvoting preferred stock of Axel Corporation. In 20X1, Axel declared dividends of $100,000 on its common stock and $60,000 on its preferred stock. Green exercises significant influence over Axel's operations. What amount of dividend revenue should Green report in its income statement for the year ended December 31, 20X1?

a. $0.

b. $30,000.

c. $60,000.

d. $90,000.

2. On January 2, 20X3, Kean Company purchased a 30 percent interest in Pod Company for $250,000. Pod reported net income of $100,000 for 20X3 and paid a dividend of $10,000. Kean accounts for this investment using the equity method. In its December 31, 20X3, balance sheet, what amount should Kean report as its investment in Pod?

   a. $160,000.

   b. $223,000.

   c. $340,000.

   d. $277,000.

3. On January 1, 20X8, Mega Corporation acquired 10 percent of the outstanding voting stock of Penny Inc. On January 2, 20X9, Mega gained the ability to exercise significant influence over Penny's financial and operating decisions by acquiring an additional 20 percent of Penny's outstanding stock. The two purchases were made at prices proportionate to the value assigned to Penny's net assets, which equaled their carrying amounts. For the years ended December 31, 20X8 and 20X9, Penny reported the following:

	20X8	20X9
Dividends Paid	$200,000	$300,000
Net Income	600,000	650,000

   In 20X9, what amounts should Mega report as current year investment income and as an adjustment, before income taxes, to 20X8 investment income?

	20X9 Investment Income	Adjustment to 20X8 Investment Income
a.	$195,000	$160,000
b.	$195,000	$100,000
c.	$195,000	$ 40,000
d.	$105,000	$ 40,000

4. Investor Inc. owns 40 percent of Alimand Corporation. During the calendar year 20X5, Alimand had net earnings of $100,000 and paid dividends of $10,000. Investor mistakenly recorded these transactions using the cost method rather than the equity method of accounting. What effect would this have on the investment account, net earnings, and retained earnings, respectively?

   a. Understate, overstate, overstate.

   b. Overstate, understate, understate.

   c. Overstate, overstate, overstate.

   d. Understate, understate, understate.

5. A corporation using the equity method of accounting for its investment in a 40 percent–owned investee, which earned $20,000 and paid $5,000 in dividends, made the following entries:

Investment in Investee	8,000	
Equity in Earnings of Investee		8,000

Cash	2,000	
Dividend Revenue		2,000

   What effect will these entries have on the investor's statement of financial position?

   a. Financial position will be fairly stated.

   b. Investment in the investee will be overstated, retained earnings understated.

   c. Investment in the investee will be understated, retained earnings understated.

   d. Investment in the investee will be overstated, retained earnings overstated.

LO4

E2-4   Cost versus Equity Reporting

Winston Corporation purchased 40 percent of the stock of Fullbright Company on January 1, 20X2, at underlying book value. The companies reported the following operating results and dividend payments during the first three years of intercorporate ownership:

	Winston Corporation		Fullbright Company	
Year	Operating Income	Dividends	Net Income	Dividends
20X2	$100,000	$ 40,000	$70,000 ⟩ cost	⟮$30,000
20X3	60,000	80,000	40,000 ⟩	60,000
20X4	250,000	120,000	25,000	50,000

Required
Compute the net income reported by Winston for each of the three years, assuming it accounts for its investment in Fullbright using (*a*) the cost method and (*b*) the equity method.

LO2, LO3

E2-5   Acquisition Price

Phillips Company bought 40 percent ownership in Jones Bag Company on January 1, 20X1, at underlying book value. In 20X1, 20X2, and 20X3, Jones Bag reported net income of $8,000, $12,000, and $20,000, and dividends of $15,000, $10,000, and $10,000, respectively. The balance in Phillips Company's investment account on December 31, 20X3, was $54,000.

Required
In each of the following independent cases, determine the amount that Phillips paid for its investment in Jones Bag stock assuming that Phillips accounted for its investment using the (*a*) cost method and (*b*) equity method.

LO2, LO3

E2-6   Investment Income

Ravine Corporation purchased 30 percent ownership of Valley Industries for $90,000 on January 1, 20X6, when Valley had capital stock of $240,000 and retained earnings of $60,000. The following data were reported by the companies for the years 20X6 through 20X9:

Advanced
StudyGuide
.com

	Operating Income,	Net Income,	Dividends Declared	
Year	Ravine Corporation	Valley Industries	Ravine	Valley
20X6	$140,000	$30,000	$ 70,000	$20,000
20X7	80,000	50,000	70,000	40,000
20X8	220,000	10,000	90,000	40,000
20X9	160,000	40,000	100,000	20,000

Required
a. What net income would Ravine Corporation have reported for each of the years, assuming Ravine accounts for the intercorporate investment using (1) the cost method and (2) the equity method?

b. Give all appropriate journal entries for 20X8 that Ravine made under both the cost and the equity methods.

LO5

E2-7   Investment Value

Port Company purchased 30,000 of the 100,000 outstanding shares of Sund Company common stock on January 1, 20X2, for $180,000. The purchase price was equal to the book value of the shares purchased. Sund reported net income of $40,000, $30,000, and $5,000 for 20X2, 20X3, and 20X4, respectively. It paid a dividend of $25,000 in 20X2, but paid no dividends in 20X3 and 20X4.

Required

Compute the amounts Port Company should report as the carrying values of its investment in Sund Company at December 31, 20X2, 20X3, and 20X4.

LO2, LO3   **E2-8***   ## Income Reporting

Grandview Company purchased 40 percent of the stock of Spinet Corporation on January 1, 20X8, at underlying book value. Spinet recorded the following income for 20X9:

Income before Extraordinary Gain	$60,000
Extraordinary Gain	30,000
Net Income	$90,000

Required

Prepare all journal entries on Grandview's books for 20X9 to account for its investment in Spinet.

LO5   **E2-9**   ## Fair Value Method

Small Company reported 20X7 net income of $40,000 and paid dividends of $15,000 during the year. Mock Corporation acquired 20 percent of Small's shares on January 1, 20X7, for $105,000. At December 31, 20X7, Mock determined the fair value of the shares of Small to be $121,000. Mock reported operating income of $90,000 for 20X7.

Required

Compute Mock's net income for 20X7 assuming it uses

a. The cost method in accounting for its investment in Small.

b. The equity method in accounting for its investment in Small.

c. The fair value method in accounting for its investment in Small.

LO4, LO5   **E2-10**   ## Fair Value Recognition

Kent Company purchased 35 percent ownership of Lomm Company on January 1, 20X8, for $140,000. Lomm reported 20X8 net income of $80,000 and paid dividends of $20,000. At December 31, 20X8, Kent determined the fair value of its investment in Lomm to be $174,000.

Required

Give all journal entries recorded by Kent with respect to its investment in Lomm in 20X8 assuming it uses

a. The equity method.

b. The fair value method.

LO2, LO3   **E2-11***   ## Investee with Preferred Stock Outstanding

Reden Corporation purchased 45 percent of Montgomery Company's common stock on January 1, 20X9, at underlying book value of $288,000. Montgomery's balance sheet contained the following stockholders' equity balances:

Preferred Stock ($5 par value, 50,000 shares issued and outstanding)	$250,000
Common Stock ($1 par value, 150,000 shares issued and outstanding)	150,000
Additional Paid-In Capital	180,000
Retained Earnings	310,000
Total Stockholders' Equity	$890,000

Montgomery's preferred stock is cumulative and pays a 10 percent annual dividend. Montgomery reported net income of $95,000 for 20X9 and paid total dividends of $40,000.

Required

Give the journal entries recorded by Reden Corporation for 20X9 related to its investment in Montgomery Company common stock.

LO2, LO3 **E2-12*** ### Other Comprehensive Income Reported by Investee

Callas Corporation paid $380,000 to acquire 40 percent ownership of Thinbill Company on January 1, 20X9. The amount paid was equal to underlying book value. During 20X9, Thinbill reported operating income of $45,000, an increase of $10,000 in the market value of trading securities held for the year, and an increase of $20,000 in the market value of available-for-sale securities held for the year. Thinbill paid dividends of $9,000 on December 10, 20X9.

Required

Give all journal entries that Callas Corporation recorded in 20X9, including closing entries at December 31, 20X9, associated with its investment in Thinbill Company.

LO2, LO3 **E2-13*** ### Other Comprehensive Income Reported by Investee

Advanced
StudyGuide
.com

Baldwin Corporation purchased 25 percent of Gwin Company's common stock on January 1, 20X8, at underlying book value. In 20X8, Gwin reported a net loss of $20,000 and paid dividends of $10,000, and in 20X9 the company reported net income of $68,000 and paid dividends of $16,000. Gwin also purchased marketable securities classified as available-for-sale on February 8, 20X9, and reported an increase of $12,000 in their fair value at December 31, 20X9. Baldwin reported a balance of $67,000 in its investment in Gwin at December 31, 20X9.

Required

Compute the amount paid by Baldwin Corporation to purchase the shares of Gwin Company.

LO6 **E2-14** ### Basic Elimination Entry

On December 31, 20X3, Broadway Corporation reported common stock outstanding of $200,000, additional paid-in capital of $300,000, and retained earnings of $100,000. On January 1, 20X4, Johe Company acquired control of Broadway in a business combination.

Required

Give the eliminating entry that would be needed in preparing a consolidated balance sheet immediately following the combination if Johe acquired all of Broadway's outstanding common stock for $600,000.

LO6, LO7 **E2-15** ### Balance Sheet Worksheet

Blank Corporation acquired 100 percent of Faith Corporation's common stock on December 31, 20X2, for $150,000. Data from the balance sheets of the two companies included the following amounts as of the date of acquisition:

Item	Blank Corporation	Faith Corporation
Cash	$ 65,000	$ 18,000
Accounts Receivable	87,000	37,000
Inventory	110,000	60,000
Buildings and Equipment (net)	220,000	150,000
Investment in Faith Corporation Stock	150,000	
Total Assets	$632,000	$265,000
Accounts Payable	$ 92,000	$ 35,000
Notes Payable	150,000	80,000
Common Stock	100,000	60,000
Retained Earnings	290,000	90,000
Total Liabilities and Stockholders' Equity	$632,000	$265,000

At the date of the business combination, the book values of Faith's net assets and liabilities approximated fair value. Assume Faith Corporation's accumulated depreciation on buildings and equipment on the acquisition date was $30,000.

Required

a. Give the eliminating entry or entries needed to prepare a consolidated balance sheet immediately following the business combination.

b. Prepare a consolidated balance sheet worksheet.

LO3, LO6   E2-16   Consolidation Entries for Wholly Owned Subsidiary

Trim Corporation acquired 100 percent of Round Corporation's voting common stock on January 1, 20X2, for $400,000. At that date, the book values and fair values of Round's assets and liabilities were equal. Round reported the following summarized balance sheet data:

Assets	$700,000	Accounts Payable	$100,000
		Bonds Payable	200,000
		Common Stock	120,000
		Retained Earnings	280,000
Total	$700,000	Total	$700,000

Round reported net income of $80,000 for 20X2 and paid dividends of $25,000.

Required

a. Give the journal entries recorded by Trim Corporation during 20X2 on its books if Trim accounts for its investment in Round using the equity method.

b. Give the eliminating entries needed at December 31, 20X2, to prepare consolidated financial statements.

LO3, LO6   E2-17   Basic Consolidation Entries for Fully Owned Subsidiary

Amber Corporation reported the following summarized balance sheet data on December 31, 20X6:

Assets	$600,000	Liabilities	$100,000
		Common Stock	300,000
		Retained Earnings	200,000
Total	$600,000	Total	$600,000

On January 1, 20X7, Purple Company acquired 100 percent of Amber's stock for $500,000. At the acquisition date, the book values and fair values of Amber's assets and liabilities were equal. Amber reported net income of $50,000 for 20X7 and paid dividends of $20,000.

Required

a. Give the journal entries recorded by Purple on its books during 20X7 if it accounts for its investment in Amber using the equity method.

b. Give the eliminating entries needed on December 31, 20X7, to prepare consolidated financial statements.

Problems

LO2, LO3   P2-18   Retroactive Recognition

Idle Corporation has been acquiring shares of Fast Track Enterprises at book value for the last several years. Data provided by Fast Track included the following:

	20X2	20X3	20X4	20X5
Net Income	$40,000	$60,000	$40,000	$50,000
Dividends	20,000	20,000	10,000	20,000

Fast Track declares and pays its annual dividend on November 15 each year. Its net book value on January 1, 20X2, was $250,000. Idle purchased shares of Fast Track on three occasions:

Date	Percent of Ownership Purchased	Amount Paid
January 1, 20X2	10%	$25,000
July 1, 20X3	5	15,000
January 1, 20X5	10	34,000

Required

Give the journal entries to be recorded on Idle's books in 20X5 related to its investment in Fast Track.

LO5

P2-19   Fair Value Method

Gant Company purchased 20 percent of the outstanding shares of Temp Company for $70,000 on January 1, 20X6. The following results are reported for Temp Company:

	20X6	20X7	20X8
Net income	$40,000	$35,000	$60,000
Dividends paid	15,000	30,000	20,000
Fair value of shares held by Gant:			
January 1	70,000	89,000	86,000
December 31	89,000	86,000	97,000

Required

Determine the amounts reported by Gant as income from its investment in Temp for each year and the balance in Gant's investment in Temp at the end of each year assuming Gant uses the following methods in accounting for its investment in Temp:

a. Cost method.

b. Equity method.

c. Fair value method.

LO5

P2-20   Fair Value Journal Entries

Marlow Company acquired 40 percent of the voting shares of Brown Company on January 1, 20X8, for $85,000. The following results are reported for Brown Company:

	20X8	20X9
Net income	$20,000	$30,000
Dividends paid	10,000	15,000
Fair value of shares held by Marlow:		
January 1	85,000	97,000
December 31	97,000	92,000

Required

Give all journal entries recorded by Marlow for 20X8 and 20X9 assuming it uses the fair value method in accounting for its investment in Brown.

LO3

P2-21*   Other Comprehensive Income Reported by Investee

Dewey Corporation owns 30 percent of the common stock of Jimm Company, which it purchased at underlying book value on January 1, 20X5. Dewey reported a balance of $245,000 for its investment in Jimm Company on January 1, 20X5, and $276,800 at December 31, 20X5. During 20X5, Dewey and Jimm Company reported operating income of $340,000 and $70,000, respectively. Jimm received dividends from investments in marketable equity securities in the amount of $7,000 during 20X5. It also reported an increase of $18,000 in the market value of its portfolio of trading securities and an increase in the value of its portfolio of securities classified as available-for-sale. Jimm paid dividends of $20,000 in 20X5. Ignore income taxes in determining your solution.

Required

a. Assuming that Dewey uses the equity method in accounting for its investment in Jimm, compute the amount of income from Jimm recorded by Dewey in 20X5.

b. Compute the amount added to the investment account during 20X5.

c. Compute the amount reported by Jimm as other comprehensive income in 20X5.

d. If all of Jimm's other comprehensive income arose solely from its investment in available-for-sale securities purchased on March 10, 20X5, for $130,000, what was the market value of those securities at December 31, 20X5?

LO3, LO6 **P2-22*** ### Equity-Method Income Statement

Wealthy Manufacturing Company purchased 40 percent of the voting shares of Diversified Products Corporation on March 23, 20X4. On December 31, 20X8, Wealthy Manufacturing's controller attempted to prepare income statements and retained earnings statements for the two companies using the following summarized 20X8 data:

	Wealthy Manufacturing	Diversified Products
Net Sales	$850,000	$400,000
Cost of Goods Sold	670,000	320,000
Other Expenses	90,000	25,000
Dividends Paid	30,000	10,000
Retained Earnings, 1/1/X8	420,000	260,000

Wealthy Manufacturing uses the equity method in accounting for its investment in Diversified Products. The controller was also aware of the following specific transactions for Diversified Products in 20X8, which were not included in the preceding data:

1. On June 30, 20X8, Diversified incurred a $5,000 extraordinary loss from a volcanic eruption near its Greenland facility.

2. Diversified sold its entire Health Technologies division on September 30, 20X8, for $375,000. The book value of Health Technologies division's net assets on that date was $331,000. The division incurred an operating loss of $15,000 in the first nine months of 20X8.

3. On January 1, 20X8, Diversified switched from FIFO inventory costing to the weighted-average method. Had Diversified always used the weighted-average method, prior years' income would have been lower by $20,000.

4. During 20X8, Diversified sold one of its delivery trucks after it was involved in an accident and recorded a gain of $10,000.

Required

a. Prepare an income statement and retained earnings statement for Diversified Products for 20X8.

b. Prepare an income statement and retained earnings statement for Wealthy Manufacturing for 20X8.

LO3, LO6, LO7 **P2-23** ### Consolidated Worksheet at End of the First Year of Ownership (Equity Method)

Peanut Company acquired 100 percent of Snoopy Company's outstanding common stock for $300,000 on January 1, 20X8, when the book value of Snoopy's net assets was equal to $300,000. Peanut uses the equity method to account for investments. Trial balance data for Peanut and Snoopy as of December 31, 20X8, are as follows:

	Peanut Company		Snoopy Company	
	Debit	Credit	Debit	Credit
Cash	$ 130,000		$ 80,000	
Accounts Receivable	165,000		65,000	
Inventory	200,000		75,000	
Investment in Snoopy Stock	355,000		0	
Land	200,000		100,000	
Buildings and Equipment	700,000		200,000	
Cost of Goods Sold	200,000		125,000	
Depreciation Expense	50,000		10,000	
Selling & Administrative Expense	225,000		40,000	
Dividends Declared	100,000		20,000	
Accumulated Depreciation		$ 450,000		$ 20,000
Accounts Payable		75,000		60,000
Bonds Payable		200,000		85,000
Common Stock		500,000		200,000
Retained Earnings		225,000		100,000
Sales		800,000		250,000
Income from Snoopy		75,000		0
Total	$2,325,000	$2,325,000	$715,000	$715,000

Required

a. Prepare the journal entries on Peanut's books for the acquisition of Snoopy on January 1, 20X8, as well as any normal equity method entry(ies) related to the investment in Snoopy Company during 20X8.

b. Prepare a consolidation worksheet for 20X8 in good form.

LO3, LO6, LO7

P2-24

Consolidated Worksheet at End of the Second Year of Ownership (Equity Method)

Peanut Company acquired 100 percent of Snoopy Company's outstanding common stock for $300,000 on January 1, 20X8, when the book value of Snoopy's net assets was equal to $300,000. Problem 2-23 summarizes the first year of Peanut's ownership of Snoopy. Peanut uses the equity method to account for investments. The following trial balance summarizes the financial position and operations for Peanut and Snoopy as of December 31, 20X9:

	Peanut Company		Snoopy Company	
	Debit	Credit	Debit	Credit
Cash	$ 230,000		$ 75,000	
Accounts Receivable	190,000		80,000	
Inventory	180,000		100,000	
Investment in Snoopy Stock	405,000		0	
Land	200,000		100,000	
Buildings and Equipment	700,000		200,000	
Cost of Goods Sold	270,000		150,000	
Depreciation Expense	50,000		10,000	
Selling & Administrative Expense	230,000		60,000	
Dividends Declared	225,000		30,000	
Accumulated Depreciation		$ 500,000		$ 30,000
Accounts Payable		75,000		35,000
Bonds Payable		150,000		85,000
Common Stock		500,000		200,000
Retained Earnings		525,000		155,000
Sales		850,000		300,000
Income from Snoopy		80,000		0
Total	$2,680,000	$2,680,000	$805,000	$805,000

Required

a. Prepare any equity method journal entry(ies) related to the investment in Snoopy Company during 20X9.

b. Prepare a consolidation worksheet for 20X9 in good form.

LO3, LO6, LO7

P2-25 **Consolidated Worksheet at End of the First Year of Ownership (Equity Method)**

Paper Company acquired 100 percent of Scissor Company's outstanding common stock for $370,000 on January 1, 20X8, when the book value of Scissor's net assets was equal to $370,000. Paper uses the equity method to account for investments. Trial balance data for Paper and Scissor as of December 31, 20X8, are as follows:

	Paper Company		Scissor Company	
	Debit	**Credit**	**Debit**	**Credit**
Cash	$ 122,000		$ 46,000	
Accounts Receivable	140,000		60,000	
Inventory	190,000		120,000	
Investment in Scissor Stock	438,000		0	
Land	250,000		125,000	
Buildings and Equipment	875,000		250,000	
Cost of Goods Sold	250,000		155,000	
Depreciation Expense	65,000		12,000	
Selling & Administrative Expense	280,000		50,000	
Dividends Declared	80,000		25,000	
Accumulated Depreciation		$ 565,000		$ 36,000
Accounts Payable		77,000		27,000
Bonds Payable		250,000		100,000
Common Stock		625,000		250,000
Retained Earnings		280,000		120,000
Sales		800,000		310,000
Income from Scissor		93,000		0
Total	$2,690,000	$2,690,000	$843,000	$843,000

Required

a. Prepare the journal entries on Paper's books for the acquisition of Scissor on January 1, 20X8 as well as any normal equity method entry(ies) related to the investment in Scissor Company during 20X8.

b. Prepare a consolidation worksheet for 20X8 in good form.

LO3, LO6, LO7

P2-26 **Consolidated Worksheet at End of the Second Year of Ownership (Equity Method)**

Paper Company acquired 100 percent of Scissor Company's outstanding common stock for $370,000 on January 1, 20X8, when the book value of Scissor's net assets was equal to $370,000. Problem 2-25 summarizes the first year of Paper's ownership of Scissor. Paper uses the equity method to account for investments. The following trial balance summarizes the financial position and operations for Paper and Scissor as of December 31, 20X9:

	Paper Company		Scissor Company	
	Debit	**Credit**	**Debit**	**Credit**
Cash	$232,000		$116,000	
Accounts Receivable	165,000		97,000	
Inventory	193,000		115,000	
Investment in Scissor Stock	515,000		0	
Land	250,000		125,000	
Buildings and Equipment	875,000		250,000	

(continued)

	Debit	Credit	Debit	Credit
Cost of Goods Sold	$ 278,000		$178,000	
Depreciation Expense	65,000		12,000	
Selling & Administrative Expense	312,000		58,000	
Dividends Declared	90,000		30,000	
Accumulated Depreciation		$ 630,000		$ 48,000
Accounts Payable		85,000		40,000
Bonds Payable		150,000		100,000
Common Stock		625,000		250,000
Retained Earnings		498,000		188,000
Sales		880,000		355,000
Income from Scissor		107,000		0
Total	$2,975,000	$2,975,000	$981,000	$981,000

Required

a. Prepare any equity method journal entry(ies) related to the investment in Scissor Company during 20X9.

b. Prepare a consolidation worksheet for 20X9 in good form.

LO2, LO6, LO7   **P2-27***   **Consolidated Worksheet at End of the First Year of Ownership (Cost Method)**

Peanut Company acquired 100 percent of Snoopy Company's outstanding common stock for $300,000 on January 1, 20X8, when the book value of Snoopy's net assets was equal to $300,000. Peanut uses the cost method to account for investments. Trial balance data for Peanut and Snoopy as of December 31, 20X8, are as follows:

	Peanut Company		Snoopy Company	
	Debit	Credit	Debit	Credit
Cash	$ 130,000		$ 80,000	
Accounts Receivable	165,000		65,000	
Inventory	200,000		75,000	
Investment in Snoopy Stock	300,000		0	
Land	200,000		100,000	
Buildings and Equipment	700,000		200,000	
Cost of Goods Sold	200,000		125,000	
Depreciation Expense	50,000		10,000	
Selling & Administrative Expense	225,000		40,000	
Dividends Declared	100,000		20,000	
Accumulated Depreciation		$ 450,000		$ 20,000
Accounts Payable		75,000		60,000
Bonds Payable		200,000		85,000
Common Stock		500,000		200,000
Retained Earnings		225,000		100,000
Sales		800,000		250,000
Dividend Income		20,000		0
Total	$2,270,000	$2,270,000	$715,000	$715,000

Required

a. Prepare the journal entries on Peanut's books for the acquisition of Snoopy on January 1, 20X8 as well as any normal cost method entry(ies) related to the investment in Snoopy Company during 20X8.

b. Prepare a consolidation worksheet for 20X8 in good form.

LO2, LO6, LO7   **P2-28***   **Consolidated Worksheet at End of the Second Year of Ownership (Cost Method)**

Peanut Company acquired 100 percent of Snoopy Company's outstanding common stock for $300,000 on January 1, 20X8, when the book value of Snoopy's net assets was equal to $300,000.

Problem 2-25 summarizes the first year of Peanut's ownership of Snoopy. Peanut uses the cost method to account for investments. The following trial balance summarizes the financial position and operations for Peanut and Snoopy as of December 31, 20X9:

	Peanut Company		Snoopy Company	
	Debit	Credit	Debit	Credit
Cash	$ 230,000		$ 75,000	
Accounts Receivable	190,000		80,000	
Inventory	180,000		100,000	
Investment in Snoopy Stock	300,000		0	
Land	200,000		100,000	
Buildings and Equipment	700,000		200,000	
Cost of Goods Sold	270,000		150,000	
Depreciation Expense	50,000		10,000	
Selling & Administrative Expense	230,000		60,000	
Dividends Declared	225,000		30,000	
Accumulated Depreciation		$ 500,000		$ 30,000
Accounts Payable		75,000		35,000
Bonds Payable		150,000		85,000
Common Stock		500,000		200,000
Retained Earnings		470,000		155,000
Sales		850,000		300,000
Dividend Income		30,000		0
Total	$2,575,000	$2,575,000	$805,000	$805,000

Required

a. Prepare any cost method journal entry(ies) related to the investment in Snoopy Company during 20X9.
b. Prepare a consolidation worksheet for 20X9 in good form.

Chapter **Three**

The Reporting Entity and Consolidation of Less-than-Wholly-Owned Subsidiaries with No Differential

Endless possibilities.™

THE COLLAPSE OF ENRON AND THE BIRTH OF A NEW PARADIGM

In February 2001 *Fortune* magazine named Enron the most innovative company in America for the sixth year in a row. Ten months later on December 2, 2001, Enron filed for bankruptcy, making it, at that time, the largest bankruptcy in history. What was the cause of this drastic turnaround? Did Enron just throw in the towel after six years of "innovation" and decide to call it quits? Sadly, this was not the case; something much more serious caused Enron's historic fall.

Enron came into being in 1985 when InterNorth acquired Houston Natural Gas. Originally, the company was headquarted in Omaha, but shortly after Kenneth Lay took over as CEO of the company, he moved its headquarters to Houston. Enron was originally in the business of transmitting electricity and natural gas throughout the United States, which it accomplished through its extensive network of pipelines and power plants. These types of services made up the bulk of Enron's revenues until management decided to branch out. In 1990, Enron began to serve as an intermediary for gas contracts.

Energy and gas prices have traditionally been extremely volatile. Companies didn't want to sign long-term contracts because of the large fluctuations in these prices. Enron would buy 30-day gas contracts from a variety of suppliers and then bundle these contracts to offer long-term prices to local utility companies. Basically, Enron accepted the price risk in exchange for a fee. Over time, the wholesale trading of energy contracts became an increasingly important part of Enron's business, as illustrated in the figure on the next page. For the 2000 fiscal year, Enron reported revenues of $93 billion from these "wholesale" activities and only $2.7 billion from its traditional piping business.

Even with these extreme revenues, Enron was forced to file for bankruptcy at the end of 2001. How did this happen? Enron used two clever accounting tricks to inflate its performance. First, managers used Special Purpose Entities (SPEs) to hide losses and move liabilities and impaired assets off Enron's books. We discuss SPEs in detail in this chapter. Second, they "grossed" up their revenues to make their performance look better than it actually was. That is, Enron reported the total value of the trades it facilitated not just its fee for its wholesale services.

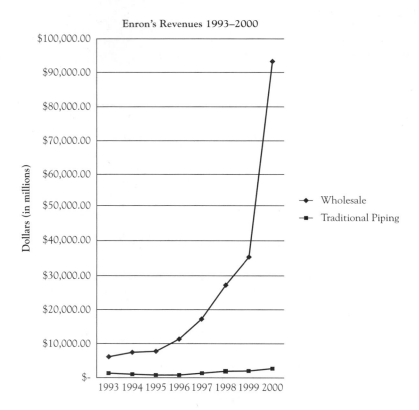

As a result of Enron's bankruptcy and the demise of its auditor, Arthur Andersen, over 100,000 jobs were lost (85,000 from Enron and 22,000 from Arthur Andersen), along with billions of dollars of investors' money. Accounting policies can have a significant influence on the economy. As Enron showed, careful manipulation of even a few simple rules can have catastrophic effects on individuals and the global economy. This chapter introduces new accounting rules for determining when a business entity must be consolidated that resulted from this and other accounting scandals. It also explores how the basic consolidation process differs when a subsidiary is only partially owned.

LEARNING OBJECTIVES

When you finish studying this chapter, you should be able to:

LO1 Understand and explain the usefulness and limitations of consolidated financial statements.

LO2 Understand and explain how direct and indirect control influence the consolidation of a subsidiary.

LO3 Understand and explain rules related to the consolidation of variable interest entities.

LO4 Understand and explain differences in consolidation rules under U.S. GAAP and IFRS.

LO5 Understand and explain differences in the consolidation process when the subsidiary is not wholly owned.

LO6 Understand and explain the differences in theories of consolidation.

LO7 Make calculations and prepare basic elimination entries for the consolidation of a less-than-wholly-owned subsidiary.

LO8 Prepare a consolidation worksheet for a less-than-wholly-owned consolidation.

THE USEFULNESS OF CONSOLIDATED FINANCIAL STATEMENTS

LO1

Understand and explain the usefulness and limitations of consolidated financial statements.

Chapter 2 introduced an example of a basic consolidation. We now provide more background. Consolidated financial statements are presented primarily for those parties having a long-run interest in the parent company, including the parent's shareholders, creditors, and other resource providers. Consolidated statements often provide the only means of obtaining a clear picture of the total resources of the combined entity that are under the parent's control and the results of employing those resources. Especially when the number of related companies is substantial, consolidated statements may provide the only means of conveniently summarizing the vast amount of information relating to the individual companies and how the positions and operations of the individual companies affect the overall consolidated entity.

Current and prospective stockholders of the parent company are usually more interested in the consolidated financial statements than those of the individual companies because the well-being of the parent company is affected by its subsidiaries' operations. When subsidiaries are profitable, profits accrue to the parent. However, the parent cannot escape the ill effects of unprofitable subsidiaries. By examining the consolidated statements, owners and potential owners are better able to assess how effectively management employs all the resources under its control.

The parent's long-term creditors also find the consolidated statements useful because the effects of subsidiary operations on the overall health and future of the parent are relevant to their decisions. In addition, although the parent and its subsidiaries are separate companies, the parent's creditors have an indirect claim on the subsidiaries' assets. The parent's short-term creditors, however, even though they also have an indirect claim on the subsidiaries' assets, are usually more interested in the parent's immediate solvency rather than its long-term profitability. Accordingly, they tend to rely more on the parent's separate financial statements, especially the balance sheet.

The parent company's management has a continuing need for current information both about the combined operations of the consolidated entity and about the individual companies forming the consolidated entity. For example, individual subsidiaries might have substantial volatility in their operations, and not until operating results and balance sheets are combined can the manager understand the overall impact of the activities for the period. On the other hand, information about individual companies within the consolidated entity also may be useful. For example, it may allow a manager to offset a cash shortfall in one subsidiary with excess cash from another without resorting to costly outside borrowing. The parent company's management may be particularly concerned with the consolidated financial statements because top management generally is evaluated, and sometimes compensated, based on the overall performance of the entity as reflected in the consolidated statements.

The creditors and any outside stockholders of subsidiaries generally are most interested in the separate financial statements of those subsidiaries. Subsidiary resource providers have no claim on the parent company unless the parent has provided guarantees or entered into other arrangements for the benefit of the subsidiaries.

LIMITATIONS OF CONSOLIDATED FINANCIAL STATEMENTS

While consolidated financial statements are useful, their limitations also must be kept in mind. Some information is lost any time data sets are aggregated; this is particularly true when the information involves an aggregation across companies that have substantially different operating characteristics. Some of the more important limitations of consolidated financial statements are as follows:

1. Because the operating results and financial position of individual companies included in the consolidation are not disclosed, the poor performance or position of one or more companies may be hidden by the good performance and position of others.

2. Not all the consolidated retained earnings balance is necessarily available for dividends of the parent because a portion may represent the parent's share of undistributed subsidiary earnings. Similarly, because the consolidated statements include the subsidiary's assets, not all assets shown are available for dividend distributions of the parent company.

3. Because financial ratios based on the consolidated statements are calculated on aggregated information, they are not necessarily representative of any single company in the consolidation, including the parent.

4. Similar accounts of different companies that are combined in the consolidation may not be entirely comparable. For example, the length of operating cycles of different companies may vary, causing receivables of similar length to be classified differently.

5. Additional information about individual companies or groups of companies included in the consolidation often is necessary for a fair presentation; such additional disclosures may require voluminous footnotes.

SUBSIDIARY FINANCIAL STATEMENTS

Some financial statement users may be interested in the separate financial statements of individual subsidiaries, either instead of or in addition to consolidated financial statements. While the parent company's management is concerned with the entire consolidated entity as well as individual subsidiaries, the creditors, preferred stockholders, and noncontrolling common stockholders of subsidiary companies are most interested in the separate financial statements of the subsidiaries in which they have an interest. Because subsidiaries are legally separate from their parents, a subsidiary's creditors and stockholders generally have no claim on the parent and the subsidiary's stockholders do not share in the parent's profits. Therefore, consolidated financial statements usually are of little use to those interested in obtaining information about the assets, capital, or income of individual subsidiaries.

CONSOLIDATED FINANCIAL STATEMENTS: CONCEPTS AND STANDARDS

LO2

Understand and explain how direct and indirect control influence the consolidation of a subsidiary.

Consolidated financial statements are intended to provide a meaningful representation of the overall position and activities of a single economic entity comprising a number of related companies. Current consolidation standards have been established by **Accounting Research Bulletin No. 51 (ASC 810)**, "Consolidated Financial Statements" (ARB 51),[1] issued in 1959; **FASB Statement No. 94 (ASC 840 and 810)**, "Consolidation of All Majority-Owned Subsidiaries" (FASB 94),[2] issued in 1987; and **FASB Statement No. 160 (ASC 810)**, "Noncontrolling Interests in Consolidated Financial Statements, an amendment of ARB No. 51 (ASC 810)" (FASB 160, ASC 810),[3] issued in 2007.[4] Under current standards, subsidiaries must be consolidated unless the parent is precluded from exercising control. When it is not appropriate to consolidate a subsidiary, it is reported as an intercorporate investment.

Traditional View of Control

Over the years, the single most important criterion for determining when an individual subsidiary should be consolidated has been that of control. **ARB 51 (ASC 810)** indicates

---

[1] *Accounting Research Bulletin No. 51(ASC 810)*, "Consolidated Financial Statements," Committee on Accounting Procedure, American Institute of Certified Public Accountants, August 1959.

[2] *Financial Accounting Standards Board Statement No. 94 (ASC 840 and 810)*, "Consolidation of All Majority-Owned Subsidiaries," October 1987.

[3] *Financial Accounting Standards Board Statement No. 160 (ASC 810)*, "Noncontrolling Interests in Consolidated Financial Statements, an amendment of ARB No. 51 (ASC 810)," December 2007.

[4] **FASB 141R (ASC 805)**, "Business Combinations," does not deal directly with consolidation standards, but many of its requirements have a significant impact on consolidated financial statements.

that consolidated financial statements normally are appropriate for a group of companies when one company "has a controlling financial interest in the other companies." It also states that "the usual condition for a controlling financial interest is ownership of a majority voting interest. . . ." In practice, control has been determined by the proportion of voting shares of a company's stock owned directly or indirectly by another company. This criterion was formalized by **FASB 94 (ASC 840 and 810),** which requires consolidation of all majority-owned subsidiaries unless the parent is unable to exercise control.

Although majority ownership is the most common means of acquiring control, a company may be able to direct the operating and financing policies of another with less than majority ownership, such as when the remainder of the stock is widely held. **FASB 94 (ASC 840 and 810)** does not preclude consolidation with less than majority ownership, but such consolidations have seldom been found in practice. More directly, **FASB 141R (ASC 805)** indicates that control can be obtained without majority ownership of a company's common stock.

Indirect Control[5]

The traditional view of control includes both direct and indirect control. **_Direct control_** typically occurs when one company owns a majority of another company's common stock. **_Indirect control_** or *pyramiding* occurs when a company's common stock is owned by one or more other companies that are all under common control. In each of the following examples, P Company controls Z Company. However, in each case, P Company does not own a direct interest in Z. Instead, P controls Z indirectly through ownership of other companies.

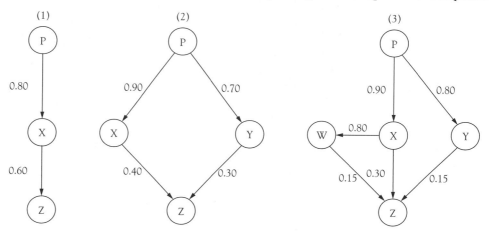

In (1), P owns 80 percent of X, which owns 60 percent of Z. Since P controls X and X controls Z, P indirectly controls Z. In (2), P owns 90 percent of X and 70 percent of Y; X owns 40 percent of Z; Y owns 30 percent of Z. Since P controls both X and Y and they, in turn, jointly control Z (with a combined ownership of 70 percent), P effectively controls Z through its two subsidiaries. In (3), P owns 90 percent of X and 80 percent of Y; X owns 80 percent of W and 30 percent of Z; Y owns 15 percent of Z; W owns 15 percent of Z. Since P controls both X and Y and they, in turn, jointly control Z (with a combined control of 60 percent—15 percent of which comes through X's subsidiary W), P effectively controls Z through its two subsidiaries. In each case, P controls Z either solely or in conjunction with other entities. As a result, P controls Z through its subsidiaries.

Ability to Exercise Control

Under certain circumstances, a subsidiary's majority stockholders may not be able to exercise control even though they hold more than 50 percent of its outstanding voting stock. This might occur, for instance, if the subsidiary was in legal reorganization or in bankruptcy; while the parent might hold majority ownership, control would rest with

---

[5] To view a video explanation of this topic, visit advancedstudyguide.com.

the courts or a court-appointed trustee. Similarly, if the subsidiary were located in a foreign country and that country had placed restrictions on the subsidiary that prevented the remittance of profits or assets back to the parent company, consolidation of that subsidiary would not be appropriate because of the parent's inability to control important aspects of the subsidiary's operations.

Differences in Fiscal Periods

A difference in the fiscal periods of a parent and subsidiary should not preclude consolidation of that subsidiary. Often the subsidiary's fiscal period, if different from the parent's, is changed to coincide with that of the parent. Another alternative is to adjust the financial statement data of the subsidiary each period to place the data on a basis consistent with the fiscal period of the parent. Both the Securities and Exchange Commission and current accounting standards permit the consolidation of a subsidiary's financial statements without adjusting the fiscal period of the subsidiary if that period does not differ from the parent's by more than three months and if recognition is given to intervening events that have a material effect on financial position or results of operations.

Changing Concept of the Reporting Entity

For nearly three decades, **ARB 51 (ASC 810)** served without significant revision as the primary source of consolidation policy. Over those years, many changes occurred in the business environment, including widespread diversification of companies and the increased emphasis on financial services by manufacturing and merchandising companies such as General Electric and Harley-Davidson.

In addition, the criteria used in determining whether to consolidate specific subsidiaries were subject to varying interpretations. Companies exercised great latitude in selecting which subsidiaries to consolidate and which to report as intercorporate investments. The lack of consistency in consolidation policy became of increasing concern as many manufacturing and merchandising companies engaged in "off-balance sheet financing" by borrowing heavily through finance subsidiaries and then excluding those subsidiaries from consolidation.

In 1982, the FASB began a project aimed at developing a comprehensive consolidation policy. In 1987, **FASB 94 (ASC 840 and 810),** requiring consolidation of all majority-owned subsidiaries, was issued to eliminate the inconsistencies found in practice until a more comprehensive standard could be issued. Unfortunately, the issues have been more difficult to resolve than anticipated. After grappling with these issues for more than two decades, the FASB has still been unable to provide a comprehensive consolidation policy.

Completion of the FASB's consolidation project has been hampered by, among other things, the inability to resolve issues related to two important concepts: (1) control and (2) the reporting entity. Regarding the first issue, the FASB has been attempting to move beyond the traditional notion of control based on majority ownership of common stock to requiring consolidation of entities under **effective control.** This idea reflects the ability to direct the policies of another entity even though majority ownership is lacking. Adopting the concept of effective control can lead to the consolidation of companies in which little, or even no, ownership is held and to the consolidation of entities other than corporations, such as partnerships and trusts. Although the FASB has indicated in its new standard on business combinations, **FASB 141R (ASC 805),** that control can be achieved without majority ownership, a comprehensive consolidation policy has yet to be achieved.

With respect to the second issue, defining the accounting entity would go a long way toward resolving the issue of when to prepare consolidated financial statements and what entities should be included. Unfortunately, the FASB has found both the entity and control issues so complex that they are not easily resolved and require further study. Accordingly, the FASB issued **FASB 160 (ASC 810),** which deals only with selected issues related to consolidated financial statements, leaving a comprehensive consolidation policy until a later time.

SPECIAL-PURPOSE AND VARIABLE INTEREST ENTITIES

While consolidation standards pertaining to related corporations have at times lacked clarity and needed updating, consolidation standards relating to partnerships or other types of entities such as trusts have been virtually nonexistent. Even corporate consolidation standards have not been adequate in situations in which other relationships such as guarantees and operating agreements overshadow the lack of a significant ownership element. As a result, companies such as Enron have taken advantage of the lack of standards to avoid reporting debt or losses by hiding them in special entities that were not consolidated. Although many companies have used special entities for legitimate purposes, financial reporting has not always captured the economic substance of the relationships. Only in the past few years have consolidation standards for these special entities started to provide some uniformity in the financial reporting for corporations having relationships with such entities.

ARB 51 (ASC 810) establishes consolidation standards in terms of one company controlling another and set majority voting interest as the usual condition leading to consolidation. Similarly, **FASB 94 (ASC 840 and 810)** requires consolidation for majority-owned subsidiaries. In recent years, however, new types of relationships have been established between corporations and other entities that often are difficult to characterize in terms of voting, controlling, or ownership interests. Such entities often are structured to provide financing and/or control through forms other than those used by traditional operating companies. Some entities have no governing boards, or they may have boards or managers with only a limited ability to direct the entity's activities. Such entities may be governed instead by their incorporation or partnership documents, or by other agreements or documents. Some entities may have little equity investment, and the equity investors may have little or no control over the entity. For these special types of entities, **ARB 51 (ASC 810)** does not provide a clear basis for consolidation.

These special types of entities have generally been referred to as *special-purpose entities (SPEs).* In general, SPEs are corporations, trusts, or partnerships created for a single specified purpose. They usually have no substantive operations and are used only for financing purposes. SPEs have been used for several decades for asset securitization, risk sharing, and taking advantage of tax statutes. Prior to 2003, no comprehensive reporting framework had been established for SPEs. Several different pronouncements from various bodies dealt with selected issues or types of SPEs, but the guidance provided by these issuances was incomplete, vague, and not always correctly interpreted in practice.

Off-Balance Sheet Financing

Imagine that Genergy, Inc., needs $1 billion to finance building a gas pipeline in central Asia. Potential investors may want their risk/reward exposure limited to the pipeline without other aspects of Genergy's business. They might also want the pipeline to be a self-supporting independent entity with cash flows that are separate from Genergy's other business activities, and they may want to eliminate the possibility that Genergy will sell the pipeline. These objectives might be achieved by forming an SPE or what the FASB refers to as a *variable interest entity (VIE),* with a charter that specifies these limited operating activities.

Once the VIE is established, the pipeline assets and the debt used to finance the pipeline may, under certain circumstances, be excluded from Genergy's balance sheet. In this manner, Genergy has achieved *off-balance sheet financing* of the pipeline. As long as the VIE is not consolidated, Genergy's financial statements will not reflect the assets, liabilities, cash flows, revenues, and expenses associated with owning and operating the pipeline. Further, any transactions between Genergy and the pipeline entity are not eliminated in preparing Genergy's financial statements.

Some estimates suggest that well over half of American companies use some type of off-balance sheet financing, involving perhaps trillions of dollars. These transactions are often facilitated by the use of some type of special entity, such as a VIE. There is concern that VIEs can be motivated either by a genuine business purpose, such as risk sharing among investors and isolation of project risk from company risk, or by a desire to meet specific financial reporting goals that may or may not be supported by the underlying economic substance of the transactions.

Companies might prefer to keep debt and the related assets financed by that debt off the balance sheet for a number of reasons, but the main one often has to do with making the company appear better to investors. One effect is to reduce the company's leverage and debt/equity ratios. Net income also may be increased as neither the interest on the debt nor the depreciation on the related assets is included in expenses. Further, the smaller asset base, because the assets are not shown on the balance sheet, combined with the higher net income produces a higher calculated return on assets.

Several means of keeping debt and related assets off a company's balance sheet have become common in practice. A company may lease assets from a third party such as a VIE, which borrows the money to buy the assets. Careful engineering of the lease terms so that it qualifies for treatment as an operating rather than a capital lease avoids recognition of the asset and lease obligation. Another possibility is for a company to sell assets such as accounts receivable outright rather than borrowing against them. A third option found with increasing frequency is for a company to create a new VIE and transfer both assets and liabilities to it. Not only does this allow the sponsoring corporation to remove the asset and related debt from its balance sheet, but the company also may be able to recognize a gain on the disposal of the asset.

Complex organizational structures increase the need for accounting standards aimed at ensuring that financial statements reflect the economic substance of those structures and the related transactions. However, the very complexity of these organizational structures makes the development of these standards a challenging endeavor.

Variable Interest Entities

In January 2003, the FASB issued **FASB Interpretation No. 46 (ASC 810),** "Consolidation of Variable Interest Entities, an interpretation of **ARB No. 51 (ASC 810),**" with a revised version issued in December 2003 **(FIN 46R, ASC 810).**[6] For clarification, the interpretation uses the term *variable interest entities* to encompass SPEs and any other entities falling within its conditions.

A *variable interest entity (VIE)* is a legal structure used for business purposes, usually a corporation, trust, or partnership, that either (1) does not have equity investors that have voting rights and share in all of the entity's profits and losses or (2) has equity investors that do not provide sufficient financial resources to support the entity's activities. In a variable interest entity, specific agreements may limit the extent to which the equity investors, if any, share in the entity's profits or losses, and the agreements may limit the control that equity investors have over the entity's activities. For the equity investment to be considered sufficient financial support for the entity's activities (condition 2), it must be able to absorb the entity's expected future losses. A total equity investment that is less than 10 percent of the entity's total assets is, in general, considered to be insufficient by itself to allow the entity to finance its activities, and an investment of more than 10 percent might be needed, depending on the circumstances.

A typical variable interest entity might be created (or sponsored) by a corporation for a particular purpose, such as purchasing the sponsoring company's receivables or leasing facilities to the sponsoring company. The sponsoring company may acquire little or no stock in the VIE. Instead, the sponsoring company may enlist another party to purchase most or all of the common stock. The majority of the VIE's capital, however, normally comes from borrowing. Because lenders may be reluctant to lend (at least at reasonable interest rates) to an entity with only a small amount of equity, the sponsoring

[6] *Financial Accounting Standards Board Interpretation No. 46 (ASC 810) (revised December 2003),* "Consolidation of Variable Interest Entities, an interpretation of **ARB No. 51 (ASC 810),**" December 2003.

company often guarantees the VIE's loans. Thus, the sponsoring company may have little or no equity investment in the VIE, but the loan guarantees represent a type of interest in the VIE.

A corporation having an interest in a VIE cannot simply rely on its percentage stock ownership, if any, to determine whether to consolidate the entity. Instead each party having a variable interest in the VIE must determine the extent to which it shares in the VIE's expected profits and losses. **FIN 46R (ASC 810, para. 2c)** defines a *variable interest* in a VIE as a contractual, ownership (with or without voting rights), or other money-related interest in an entity that changes with changes in the fair value of the entity's net assets exclusive of variable interests. In other words, variable interests increase with the VIE's profits and decrease with its losses. The VIE's variable interests will absorb portions of the losses, if they occur, or receive portions of the residual returns.

There are several different types of variable interests, some of which can be summarized as follows:

Type of Interest	Variable Interest?
Common stock, with no special features or provisions	Yes
Common stock, with loss protection or other provisions	Maybe
Senior debt	Usually not
Subordinated debt	Yes
Loan or asset guarantees	Yes

Common stock that places the owners' investment at risk is a variable interest. In some cases, certain common stock may have, by agreement, special provisions that protect the investor against losses or provide a fixed return. These special types of shares may not involve significant risk on the part of the investor and might, depending on the provisions, result in an interest that is not a variable interest. Senior debt usually carries a fixed return and is protected against loss by subordinated interests. Subordinated debt represents a variable interest because, if the entity's cash flows are insufficient to pay off the subordinated debt, the holders of that debt will sustain losses. They do not have the same protection against loss that holders of the senior debt have. Parties that guarantee the value of assets or liabilities can sustain losses if they are called on to make good on their guarantees, and, therefore, the guarantees represent variable interests.

The nature of each party's variable interest determines whether consolidation by that party is appropriate. An enterprise that will absorb a majority of the VIE's expected losses, receive a majority of the VIE's expected residual returns, or both, is called the ***primary beneficiary*** of the variable interest entity. The primary beneficiary must consolidate the VIE. If the entity's profits and losses are divided differently, the enterprise absorbing a majority of the losses will consolidate the VIE.

As an example of the financial reporting determinations of parties with an interest in a VIE, suppose that Young Company and Zebra Corporation, both financially stable companies, create YZ Corporation to lease equipment to Young and other companies. Zebra purchases all of YZ's common stock. Young guarantees Zebra a 7 percent dividend on its stock, agrees to absorb all of YZ's losses, and guarantees fixed-rate bank loans that are made to YZ. All profits in excess of the 7 percent payout to Zebra are split evenly between Young and Zebra.

In this case, the bank loans are not variable interests because they carry a fixed interest rate and are guaranteed by Young, a company capable of honoring the guarantee. Common stock of a VIE is a variable interest if the investment is at risk. In this case, Zebra's investment is not at risk, but it does share in the profits of YZ, and the amount of profits is not fixed. Therefore, the common stock is a variable interest. However, Zebra will not consolidate YZ because Zebra does not share in the losses, all of which Young will bear. Young would consolidate YZ because Young's guarantees represent a variable interest and it will absorb a majority (all) of the losses.

If consolidation of a VIE is appropriate, the amounts to be consolidated with those of the primary beneficiary are based on fair values at the date the enterprise first becomes the primary beneficiary. However, assets and liabilities transferred to a VIE by its primary beneficiary are valued at their book values, with no gain or loss recognized on the transfer. Subsequent to the initial determination of consolidation values, a VIE is accounted for in consolidated financial statements in accordance with **ARB 51 (ASC 810)** in the same manner as if it were consolidated based on voting interests. Intercompany balances and transactions are eliminated so the resulting consolidated financial statements appear as if there were just a single entity. These procedures are consistent with those used when consolidating parent and subsidiary corporations. Appendix 3A at the end of the chapter presents a simple illustration of the consolidation of a VIE.

IFRS Differences in Determining Control of VIEs and SPEs

LO4

Understand and explain differences in consolidation rules under U.S. GAAP and IFRS.

Although rules under international financial reporting standards (IFRS) for consolidation are generally very similar to those under U.S. GAAP, there are some important differences. The SEC's February 2010 working plan toward convergence in global accounting standards suggests that U.S. registrants could potentially be required to begin reporting under IFRS as early as 2015 or 2016. Therefore, understanding these differences is very important because students beginning their careers in the accounting profession will likely face this transition in the near future. In the meantime, the FASB and the IASB are working toward convergence of differences in existing rules within the consolidation area with an exposure draft on consolidation expected in the second quarter of 2010. While the proposed standard will remove many of these differences related to VIEs and SPEs, there are differences under the current standards. Figure 3–1 provides a summary of the main differences.

NONCONTROLLING INTEREST

LO5

Understand and explain differences in the consolidation process when the subsidiary is not wholly owned.

A parent company does not always own 100 percent of a subsidiary's outstanding common stock. The parent may have acquired less than 100 percent of a company's stock in a business combination, or it may originally have held 100 percent but sold or awarded some shares to others. For the parent to consolidate the subsidiary, only a controlling interest is needed. Those shareholders of the subsidiary other than the parent are referred to as "noncontrolling" or "minority" shareholders. The claim of these shareholders on the income and net assets of the subsidiary is referred to as the ***noncontrolling interest*** or the ***minority interest.*** Throughout this chapter and in subsequent chapters, whenever the acquired company is less-than-wholly-owned, we will frequently refer to the noncontrolling interest shareholders as the "NCI shareholders." The NCI shareholders clearly have a claim on the subsidiary's assets and earnings through their stock ownership. Because 100 percent of a subsidiary's assets, liabilities, and earnings is included in the consolidated financial statements, regardless of the parent's percentage ownership, the NCI shareholders' claim on these items must be reported.

Computation of Noncontrolling Interest

In uncomplicated situations, the noncontrolling interest's share of consolidated net income is a simple proportionate share of the subsidiary's net income. For example, if a subsidiary has net income of $150,000 and the NCI shareholders own 10 percent of the subsidiary's common stock, their share of income is $15,000 ($150,000 × 0.10).

The NCI shareholders' claim on the net assets of the subsidiary is based on the acquisition-date fair value of the noncontrolling interest, adjusted over time for a proportionate share of the subsidiary's income and dividends. The noncontrolling interest is discussed in more detail in Chapter 5.

Presentation of Noncontrolling Interest

Historically, the portion of the subsidiary's net income assigned to the noncontrolling interest normally has been deducted from the combined earnings of the entire entity

FIGURE 3–1 **Summary of Differences between IFRS and U.S. GAAP related to Control and VIEs**

Topic	U.S. GAAP	IFRS
Determination of Control	• Normally, control is determined by majority ownership of voting shares. • However, majority ownership may not indicate control of a VIE. • Thus, VIE rules must be evaluated first in all situations. • The primary beneficiary must consolidate a VIE. • The majority shareholder consolidates most non-VIEs. • Control is based on direct or indirect voting interests. • An entity with less than 50 percent ownership may have "effective control" through other contractual arrangements.	• Normally, control is determined by majority ownership of voting shares. • In addition to voting shares, convertible instruments and other contractual rights that could affect control are considered. • A parent with less than 50 percent of the voting shares could have control through contractual arrangements allowing control of votes or the board of directors. • Control over SPEs is determined based on judgment and relevant facts. • Substance over form considered in determining whether an SPE should be consolidated.
Related Parties	• Interests held by related parties and "de facto" agents may be considered in determining control of a VIE.	• There is no specific provision for related parties or de facto agents.
Definitions of VIEs versus SPEs	• SPEs can be VIEs. • Consolidation rules focus on whether an entity is a VIE (regardless of whether or not it is an SPE). • This guidance applies only to legal entities.	• Considers specific indicators of whether an entity has control of an SPE: (1) whether the SPE conducts activities for the entity, (2) whether the entity has decision-making power to obtain majority of benefits from the SPE, (3) whether the entity has the right to majority of benefits from the SPE, and (4) whether entity has majority of the SPE's residual or risks. • This guidance applies whether or not conducted by a legal entity.
Disclosure	• Disclosures required for determining control of a VIE. • Entities must disclose whether or not they are the primary beneficiary of related VIEs.	• No SPE-specific disclosure requirements. • There are specific disclosure requirements related to consolidation in general.
Accounting for Joint Ventures	• Owners typically share control (often with 50-50 ownership). • If the joint venture is a VIE, contracts must be considered to determine whether consolidation is required. • If the joint venture is not a VIE, venturers use the equity method. • Proportional consolidation generally not permitted.	• Joint ventures can be accounted for using either proportionate consolidation or the equity method. • Proportionate consolidation reports the venturer's share of the assets, liabilities, income, and expenses on a line-by-line basis based on the venturer's financial statement line items.

(including both the parent and subsidiary) to arrive at consolidated net income in the consolidated income statement. The label "consolidated net income" has sometimes been used in the past to refer to the parent's share of the consolidated entity's income. Even though income assigned to the noncontrolling interest does not meet the definition of an expense, it normally has been accorded this expense-type treatment. For example, Century Telephone generally has referred to the minority interest's share of income as an expense in the notes to its consolidated financial statements.

The FASB's new standard on reporting noncontrolling interests, **FASB 160 (ASC 810),** requires that the term "consolidated net income" be applied to the income available to all stockholders, with the allocation of that income between the controlling and noncontrolling stockholders shown. For example, assume that Parent Company owns

90 percent of Sub Company's stock, acquired without a differential, and that the two companies report revenues and expenses as follows:

	Parent	Sub
Revenues	$300,000	$100,000
Expenses	225,000	65,000

An abbreviated consolidated income statement for Parent and its subsidiary would appear as follows:

Revenues	$ 400,000
Expenses	(290,000)
Consolidated net income	$ 110,000
Less consolidated net income attributable to noncontrolling interest in subsidiary	(3,500)
Consolidated net income attributable to controlling interest	$ 106,500

The noncontrolling interest's claim on the net assets of the subsidiary was previously reported in the balance sheet most frequently in the "mezzanine" between liabilities and stockholders' equity. Some companies reported the minority interest as a liability, although it clearly did not meet the definition of a liability. **FASB 160 (ASC 810)** makes clear that the noncontrolling interest's claim on net assets is an element of equity, not a liability. It requires reporting the noncontrolling interest in equity, in the following manner:

Controlling interest:	
Common stock	$700,000
Additional paid-in capital	50,000
Retained earnings	80,000
Total controlling interest	$830,000
Noncontrolling interest in subsidiary	75,000
Total stockholders' equity	$905,000

Several different consolidation theories that affect the computation and treatment of the noncontrolling interest have been proposed. These theories are discussed briefly later in the chapter.

COMBINED FINANCIAL STATEMENTS

Financial statements are sometimes prepared for a group of companies when no one company in the group owns a majority of the common stock of any other company in the group. Financial statements that include a group of related companies without including the parent company or other owner are referred to as ***combined financial statements.***

Combined financial statements are commonly prepared when an individual, rather than a corporation, owns or controls a number of companies and wishes to include them all in a single set of financial statements. In some cases, a parent company may prepare financial statements that include only its subsidiaries, not the parent. In other cases, a parent may prepare financial statements for its subsidiaries by operating group, with all the subsidiaries engaged in a particular type of operation, or those located in a particular geographical region, reported together.

The procedures used to prepare combined financial statements are essentially the same as those used in preparing consolidated financial statements. All intercompany receivables and payables, intercompany transactions, and unrealized intercompany profits and losses must be eliminated in the same manner as in the preparation of consolidated statements. Although no parent company is included in the reporting entity, any intercompany ownership, and the associated portion of stockholders' equity, must be eliminated in the same way as the parent's investment in a subsidiary is eliminated in preparing consolidated financial statements. The remaining stockholders' equity of the companies in the reporting entity is divided into the portions accruing to the controlling and noncontrolling interests.

ADDITIONAL CONSIDERATIONS—DIFFERENT APPROACHES TO CONSOLIDATION

LO6

Understand and explain the differences in theories of consolidation.

Several different accounting theories have been suggested that might serve as a basis for preparing consolidated financial statements. The choice of theory can have a significant impact on the consolidated financial statements in cases when the parent company owns less than 100 percent of the subsidiary's common stock. This discussion focuses on three alternative theories of consolidation: (1) proprietary, (2) parent company, and (3) entity. The proprietary and entity theories may be viewed as falling near opposite ends of a spectrum, with the parent company theory falling somewhere in between. Until recently, the accounting profession had not adopted any of the three theories in its entirety, although practice was most closely aligned with the parent company approach. With the issuance of **FASB 141R (ASC 805)** in 2007, however, the FASB adopted the entity theory.

Theories of Consolidation

The ***proprietary theory*** of accounting views the firm as an extension of the owners. The firm's assets, liabilities, revenues, and expenses are viewed as those of the owners themselves. When applied to consolidated financial statements, the proprietary concept results in a ***pro rata consolidation*** in which the parent company consolidates only its proportionate share of a less-than-wholly-owned subsidiary's assets, liabilities, revenues, and expenses.

The ***parent company theory*** is perhaps better suited to the modern corporation and the preparation of consolidated financial statements than is the proprietary approach. The parent company theory recognizes that the parent has the ability to effectively control all of the assets and liabilities of a majority-owned subsidiary, not just a proportionate share, even though the parent does not actually own the subsidiary's assets or have any obligation for its liabilities. The consolidated financial statements include all of the subsidiary's assets, liabilities, revenues, and expenses. Separate recognition is given in the consolidated balance sheet to the noncontrolling interest's claim on the subsidiary's net assets and in the consolidated income statement to the earnings assigned to the NCI shareholders.

As a general ownership theory, the ***entity theory*** focuses on the firm as a separate economic entity rather than on the ownership rights of the shareholders. Emphasis under the entity approach is on the consolidated entity itself, with the controlling and NCI shareholders viewed as two separate groups, each having an equity interest in the consolidated entity. Neither of the two groups is emphasized over the other or over the consolidated entity. Accordingly, all of the assets, liabilities, revenues, and expenses of a less-than-wholly-owned subsidiary are included in the consolidated financial statements, with no special treatment accorded either the controlling or noncontrolling interest.

Comparison of Alternative Theories

Figure 3–2 provides a comparison of the amounts included in a consolidated balance sheet (lined areas) for a parent and less-than-wholly-owned subsidiary under the different approaches to consolidation. With the proprietary theory, only the parent's share of a subsidiary's assets and liabilities is included in the consolidated balance sheet, with

FIGURE 3–2
Recognition of Subsidiary Net Assets

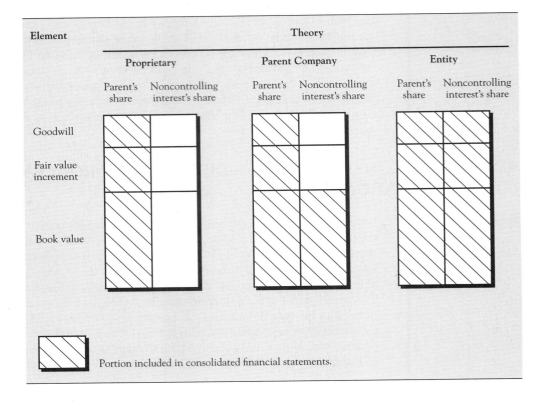

the amount based on the fair values of those assets and liabilities on the date majority ownership in the subsidiary is acquired. Goodwill is included for the excess of the purchase price over the fair value of the parent's share of the subsidiary's net identifiable assets. The portion of the subsidiary's identifiable assets and liabilities claimed by the noncontrolling interest is excluded from the consolidated balance sheet, as is any implied goodwill assignable to the noncontrolling interest.

The parent company approach includes all of the subsidiary's assets and liabilities in the consolidated balance sheet, as can be seen from the lined areas in Figure 3–2. However, only the parent's share of any fair value increment and goodwill is included. As a result, subsidiary assets are included at their full fair values only when the parent purchases full ownership of the subsidiary. The noncontrolling shareholders' claim is reported in the consolidated balance sheet based on a proportionate share of the book value of the subsidiary's net assets.

All subsidiary assets and liabilities are also included in the consolidated balance sheet under the entity approach. However, the amounts included are based on the full fair values at the date of combination, and the full amount of any goodwill is included regardless of the percentage ownership held by the parent. The amount of noncontrolling interest reported in the consolidated balance sheet is based on a proportionate share of the total amount of subsidiary net assets, including goodwill.

Figure 3–3 provides a comparison of amounts included in the consolidated income statement under the different approaches when a less-than-wholly-owned subsidiary is consolidated. In general, the income statement treatment is consistent with the balance sheet treatment shown in Figure 3–2 under each theory. As can be seen from the lined areas, the proprietary theory results in consolidation of just the parent's share of the revenues, expenses, and net income of the subsidiary. On the other hand, both the parent company and entity theories result in consolidation of all of the subsidiary's revenues and expenses, regardless of degree of majority ownership. Under the parent company theory, however, the noncontrolling interest's share of income is deducted to arrive at consolidated net income.

FIGURE 3–3
Recognition of
Subsidiary Income

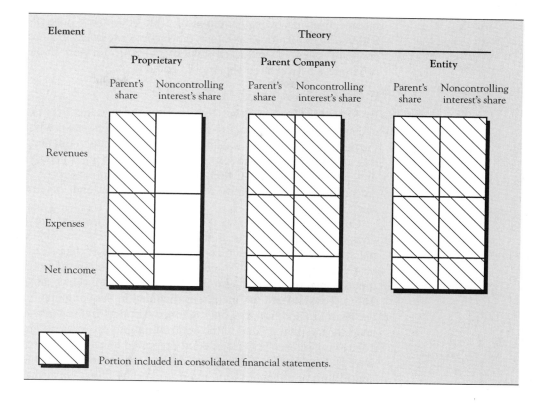

Figure 3–4 provides a numerical comparison of the different consolidation approaches. The example assumes that P Company acquires 80 percent of the stock of S Company on January 1, 20X1, for $96,000. On that date, S Company has a total fair value of $120,000 and the 20 percent noncontrolling interest has a fair value of $24,000. S Company holds assets with a book value of $100,000 and fair value of $120,000. The $20,000 fair value increment relates entirely to S Company's buildings and equipment, with a remaining life of 10 years. Straight-line depreciation is used. For the year 20X1, P Company reports

FIGURE 3–4
Illustration of the
Effects of Different
Approaches to the
Preparation of
Consolidated Financial
Statements

Item	Theory		
	Proprietary	Parent Company	Entity
Value of subsidiary net assets recognized at acquisition:			
Book value:			
$100,000 × 0.80	$ 80,000		
$100,000 × 1.00		$100,000	$100,000
Fair value increment:			
$20,000 × 0.80	16,000	16,000	
$20,000 × 1.00			20,000
Total net assets	$ 96,000	$116,000	$120,000
Amount of noncontrolling interest recognized at acquisition		$ 20,000	$ 24,000
Amount of fair value increment amortized*	$ 1,600	$ 1,600	$ 2,000
Consolidated net income	$222,400[a]	$222,400[a]	$228,000[b]
Income assigned to noncontrolling interest		$ 6,000[c]	$ 5,600[d]

[a]$222,400 = $200,000 + ($30,000 × 0.80) − $1,600*
[b]$228,000 = $200,000 + $30,000 − $2,000*
[c]$6,000 = $30,000 × 0.20
[d]$5,600 = ($30,000 − $2,000) × 0.20
*Amortization of fair value increment using straight-line basis over 10 years.

income from its own operations of $200,000, and S Company reports net income of $30,000. The example assumes the income includes no unrealized profits from intercompany sales. If unrealized intercompany profits were included in income, additional differences between the approaches could be seen.

Current Practice

FASB 141R (ASC 805) has significantly changed the preparation of consolidated financial statements subsequent to the acquisition of less-than-wholly-owned subsidiaries. In the past, only the parent's share of a subsidiary's fair value increment and goodwill at the date of combination was recognized, consistent with a parent company approach. Now, under **FASB 141R (ASC 805),** consolidation follows largely an entity-theory approach. Accordingly, the full entity fair value increment and the full amount of goodwill are recognized.

Current practice follows the entity approach in most important aspects, but it does deviate in certain respects. In the income statement, consolidated net income refers to the income of the consolidated entity as a whole, rather than just the parent's share as in the past. Still, more emphasis continues to be placed on the parent's share of consolidated net income than on the noncontrolling interest's share. For example, only the parent's portion of consolidated net income is included in the computation of consolidated earnings per share. In addition, the only retained earnings figure reported in the consolidated balance sheet is that related to the controlling interest, with all amounts relating to the noncontrolling interest's share of equity reported in a single figure. If a strict entity approach were followed, the emphasis would be on the entire entity without emphasizing either the controlling or noncontrolling interest over the other. Nevertheless, the current approach clearly follows the entity theory with minor modifications aimed at the practical reality that consolidated financial statements are used primarily by those having a long-run interest in the parent company.

THE EFFECT OF A NONCONTROLLING INTEREST

LO7

Make calculations and prepare basic elimination entries for the consolidation of a less-than-wholly-owned subsidiary.

When a subsidiary is less than wholly owned, the general approach to consolidation is the same as discussed in Chapter 2, but the consolidation procedures must be modified slightly to recognize the noncontrolling interest. Thus, the difference between the consolidation procedures illustrated in Chapter 2 and what we will demonstrate here is that we now have to account for the NCI shareholders' ownership in the income and net assets of the acquired company. Before examining the specific procedures used in consolidating a less-than-wholly-owned subsidiary, we discuss the computation of consolidated net income, consolidated retained earnings, and the noncontrolling interest's claim on income and net assets. We also discuss modifications to the consolidation worksheet.

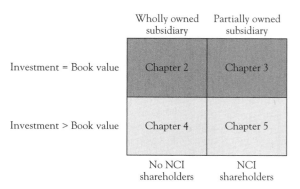

Consolidated Net Income

Consolidated net income, as it appears in the consolidated income statement, is the difference between consolidated revenues and expenses. In the absence of transactions between companies included in the consolidation, ***consolidated net income*** is equal to the parent's income from its own operations, excluding any investment income from consolidated subsidiaries, plus the net income from each of the consolidated subsidiaries.

When all subsidiaries are wholly owned, all of the consolidated net income accrues to the parent company, or the controlling interest. If one or more of the consolidated subsidiaries is less than wholly owned, a portion of the consolidated net income accrues to the NCI shareholders. In that case, the income attributable to the subsidiary noncontrolling interest is deducted from consolidated net income on the face of the income statement to arrive at consolidated net income attributable to the controlling interest.

Income attributable to a noncontrolling interest in a subsidiary is based on a proportionate share of that subsidiary's net income. The subsidiary's net income available to common shareholders is divided between the parent and noncontrolling stockholders based on their relative common stock ownership of the subsidiary. Note that the NCI shareholders in a particular subsidiary have a proportionate claim only on the income of that subsidiary and not on the income of the parent or any other subsidiary.

As an example of the computation and allocation of consolidated net income, assume that Push Corporation purchases 80 percent of the stock of Shove Company for an amount equal to 80 percent of Shove's total book value. During 20X1, Shove reports net income of $25,000, while Push reports net income of $120,000, including equity-method income from Shove of $20,000 ($25,000 × 0.80). Consolidated net income for 20X1 is computed and allocated as follows:

Push's net income	$120,000
Less: Equity-method income from Shove	(20,000)
Shove's net income	25,000
Consolidated net income	$125,000
Income attributable to noncontrolling interest	(5,000)
Income attributable to controlling interest	$120,000

Consolidated net income is equal to the separate income of Push from its own operations ($100,000) plus Shove's net income ($25,000). The $20,000 of equity-method income from Shove that had been recognized by Push must be excluded from the computation to avoid double-counting the same income. Consolidated net income is allocated to the noncontrolling stockholders based on their 20 percent share of Shove's net income. The amount of income allocated to the controlling interest is equal to the parent's income from its own operations ($100,000) and the parent's 80 percent share of Shove's income ($20,000).

Consolidated Retained Earnings

Advanced
StudyGuide
.com

The only retained earnings figure reported in the consolidated balance sheet is not entirely consistent with the computation of consolidated net income. Retained earnings in the consolidated balance sheet is that portion of the consolidated entity's undistributed earnings accruing to the parent's stockholders. It is calculated by adding the parent's share of subsidiary cumulative net income since acquisition to the parent's retained earnings from its own operations (excluding any income from the subsidiary included in the parent's retained earnings) and subtracting the parent's share of any differential write-off. Any retained earnings related to subsidiary NCI shareholders is included in the Noncontrolling Interest in Net Assets of Subsidiary amount reported in the equity section of the consolidated balance sheet. Thus, the consolidated retained earnings figure is more consistent with the parent company theory rather than the entity approach assumed in the computation of consolidated net income.

To illustrate the computation of consolidated retained earnings when a noncontrolling interest exists, assume that Push purchases 80 percent of Shove's stock on January 1,

20X1, and accounts for the investment using the equity method. Assume net income and dividends as follows during the two years following the acquisition:

	Push	Shove
Retained earnings, January 1, 20X1	$400,000	$250,000
Net income, 20X1	120,000	25,000
Dividends, 20X1	(30,000)	(10,000)
Retained earnings, December 31, 20X1	$490,000	$265,000
Net income, 20X2	148,000	35,000
Dividends, 20X2	(30,000)	(10,000)
Retained earnings, December 31, 20X2	$608,000	$290,000

Consolidated retained earnings at two years after the date of combination is computed as follows

Push's retained earnings, December 31, 20X2	$608,000
Equity accrual from Shove since acquisition ($25,000 + $35,000) × 0.80	(48,000)
Push's retained earnings from its own operations, December 31, 20X2	$560,000
Push's share of Shove's net income since acquisition ($60,000 × 0.80)	48,000
Consolidated retained earnings, December 31, 20X2	$608,000

We note several important points from the example. First, the subsidiary's retained earnings are not combined with the parent's retained earnings. Only the parent's share of the subsidiary's cumulative net income since the date of combination is included. Second, consolidated retained earnings are equal to the parent's retained earnings because the parent uses the equity method to account for its investment in the subsidiary. If the parent accounted for the investment using the cost method, the parent's retained earnings and consolidated retained earnings would differ. Finally, the cumulative income from the subsidiary recognized by the parent on its books must be removed from the parent's retained earnings to arrive at retained earnings from the parent's own operations so that all or part (depending on whether the equity or cost method is used) of the same income will not be included twice.

Worksheet Format

The same three-part worksheet described in Chapter 2 can be used when consolidating less-than-wholly-owned subsidiaries, with only minor modifications. The worksheet must allow for including the noncontrolling interest's claim on the income and net assets of the subsidiaries. The noncontrolling interest's claim on the income of a subsidiary is deducted from consolidated net income at the bottom of the worksheet's income statement section in the Consolidated column to arrive at consolidated net income attributable to the controlling interest. The noncontrolling interest's claim on the subsidiary's net assets is placed at the bottom of the worksheet's balance sheet section. The noncontrolling interest's claims on both income and net assets are entered in the worksheet through eliminating entries and then carried over to the Consolidated column. As discussed in Chapter 2, the amounts in the Consolidated column are used to prepare the consolidated financial statements.

CONSOLIDATED BALANCE SHEET WITH A LESS-THAN-WHOLLY-OWNED SUBSIDIARY

LO8

Prepare a consolidation worksheet for a less-than-wholly-owned consolidation.

In order to illustrate the consolidation process for a less-than-wholly-owned subsidiary, we use the Peerless-Special Foods example from Chapter 2. The only difference is that we assume that instead of acquiring all of the common stock of Special Foods, Peerless only buys 80 percent of the shares. Thus, we assume that the other 20 percent of the shares are widely held by other shareholders (the NCI shareholders).

80 Percent Ownership Acquired at Book Value

Peerless acquires 80 percent of Special Foods' outstanding common stock for $240,000, an amount equal to 80 percent of the fair value of Special Foods' net assets on January 1, 20X1. On this date, the fair values of Special Foods' individual assets and liabilities are equal to their book values. Because Peerless acquires only 80 percent of Special Foods' common stock, the Investment in Special Foods equals 80 percent of the total stockholders' equity of Special Foods ($200,000 + $100,000). We can summarize Special Foods' ownership as follows:

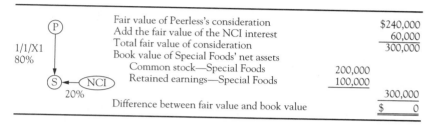

Fair value of Peerless's consideration		$240,000
Add the fair value of the NCI interest		60,000
Total fair value of consideration		300,000
Book value of Special Foods' net assets		
Common stock—Special Foods	200,000	
Retained earnings—Special Foods	100,000	
		300,000
Difference between fair value and book value		$ 0

Peerless records the 80 percent stock acquisition on its books with the following entry on January 1, 20X1:

(1)

Investment in Special Foods	240,000	
Cash		240,000

Record purchase of Special Foods stock.

The Basic Investment Elimination Entry

The basic elimination on the date of acquisition would be the same as the one illustrated in Chapter 2 except that the $300,000 book value of net assets is now jointly owned by Peerless (80 percent) and the NCI shareholders (20 percent). Thus, the original $300,000 credit to the Investment in Special Foods account from the wholly owned example in Chapter 2 is now "shared" with the NCI shareholders as shown in the breakdown of the book value of Special Foods:

Book Value Calculations:

	NCI 20% +	Peerless 80%	= Common Stock +	Retained Earnings
Original book value	60,000	240,000	200,000	100,000

Thus, the only eliminating entry in the worksheet removes the Investment in Special Foods Stock account and the subsidiary's stockholders' equity accounts and records the $60,000 NCI interest in the net assets of Special Foods.

Basic elimination entry:

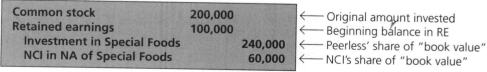

Common stock	200,000		← Original amount invested
Retained earnings	100,000		← Beginning balance in RE
Investment in Special Foods		240,000	← Peerless' share of "book value"
NCI in NA of Special Foods		60,000	← NCI's share of "book value"

In this example, Peerless' investment is exactly equal to its 80 percent share of the book value of net assets of Special Foods. Therefore, no goodwill is recorded and all assets and liabilities are simply combined from Special Foods' financial statements at their current book values. Again, in Chapters 4 and 5 we will explore situations where the acquiring company pays more than the book value of the acquired company's net assets. However, in Chapters 2 and 3, the excess value of identifiable net assets and goodwill will always be equal to zero. To maintain a consistent approach through all four chapters, we always illustrate the components of the acquiring company's investment, even though the acquiring company's investment will always be exactly equal to its share of the book value of net assets in Chapters 2 and 3. Therefore, the relationship between the fair value of the consideration given to acquire Special Foods, the fair value of Special Foods' net assets, and the book value of Special Foods' net assets can be illustrated as follows:

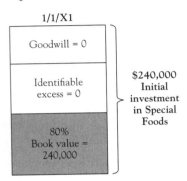

Therefore, the elimination entry simply credits the Investment in Special Foods Stock account (for the original acquisition price, $240,000), eliminating this account from Peerless' balance sheet.

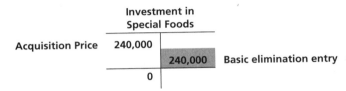

Remember that this entry is made in the consolidation worksheet, not on the books of either the parent or the subsidiary, and is presented here in T-account form for instructional purposes only. The investment account must be eliminated because, as explained in Chapter 2, from a single-entity viewpoint, a company cannot hold an investment in itself.

FIGURE 3–5   **Worksheet for Consolidated Balance Sheet, January 1, 20X1, Date of Combination; 80 Percent Acquisition at Book Value**

	Peerless Products	Special Foods	Elimination Entries		Consolidated
			DR	CR	
Balance Sheet					
Cash	110,000	50,000			160,000
Accounts Receivable	75,000	50,000			125,000
Inventory	100,000	60,000			160,000
Investment in Special Foods	240,000			240,000	0
Land	175,000	40,000			215,000
Buildings & Equipment	800,000	600,000			1,400,000
Less Accumulated Depreciation	(400,000)	(300,000)			(700,000)
Total Assets	**1,100,000**	**500,000**	**0**	**240,000**	**1,360,000**
Accounts Payable	100,000	100,000			200,000
Bonds Payable	200,000	100,000			300,000
Common Stock	500,000	200,000	200,000		500,000
Retained Earnings	300,000	100,000	100,000		300,000
NCI in NA of Special Foods				60,000	60,000
Total Liabilities & Equity	**1,100,000**	**500,000**	**300,000**	**60,000**	**1,360,000**

FIGURE 3–6
Consolidated Balance
Sheet, January 1, 20X1,
Date of Combination;
80 Percent Acquisition
at Book Value

PEERLESS PRODUCTS CORPORATION AND SUBSIDIARY				
Consolidated Balance Sheet				
January 1, 20X1				
Assets			Liabilities	
Cash		160,000	Accounts Payable	200,000
Accounts Receivable		125,000	Bonds Payable	300,000
Inventory		160,000	Stockholders' Equity	
Land		215,000	Common Stock	500,000
Buildings and Equipment	1,400,000		Retained Earnings	300,000
Accumulated Depreciation	(700,000)	700,000	NCI in NA of Special Foods	60,000
Total Assets		1,360,000	Total Liabilities and Equity	1,360,000

Consolidation Worksheet

Figure 3–5 presents the consolidation worksheet. As explained previously in Chapter 2, the investment account on the parent's books can be thought of as a single account representing the parent's investment in the net assets of the subsidiary, a *one-line consolidation.* In a full consolidation, the subsidiary's individual assets and liabilities are combined with those of the parent. Including both the net assets of the subsidiary, as represented by the balance in the investment account, and the subsidiary's individual assets and liabilities would double count the same set of assets. Therefore, the investment account is eliminated and not carried to the consolidated balance sheet.

The Consolidated Balance Sheet

Figure 3–6 presents the consolidated balance sheet as of the date of acquisition. Because no operations occurred between the date of combination and the preparation of the consolidated balance sheet, there is no income statement or statement of retained earnings.

CONSOLIDATION SUBSEQUENT TO ACQUISITION— 80 PERCENT OWNERSHIP ACQUIRED AT BOOK VALUE

Chapter 2 explains the procedures used to prepare a consolidated balance sheet as of the acquisition date. More than a consolidated balance sheet, however, is needed to provide a comprehensive picture of the consolidated entity's activities following acquisition. As with a single company, the set of basic financial statements for a consolidated entity consists of a balance sheet, an income statement, a statement of changes in retained earnings, and a statement of cash flows. Each of the consolidated financial statements is prepared as if it is taken from a single set of books that is being used to account for the overall consolidated entity. There is, of course, no set of books for the consolidated entity, and as in the preparation of the consolidated balance sheet, the consolidation process starts with the data recorded on the books of the individual consolidating companies. The account balances from the books of the individual companies are placed in the three-part worksheet, and entries are made to eliminate the effects of intercorporate ownership and transactions. The consolidation approach and procedures are the same whether the subsidiary being consolidated was acquired or created.

Initial Year of Ownership

Assume that Peerless has already recorded the acquisition on January 1, 20X1, and that during 20X1, Peerless records operating earnings of $140,000, excluding its income from investing in Special Foods, and declares dividends of $60,000. Special Foods reports 20X1 net income of $50,000 and declares dividends of $30,000.

Parent Company Entries

Peerless records its 20X1 income and dividends from Special Foods under the equity method as follows:

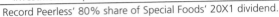

(2)	Investment in Special Foods	40,000	
	Income from Special Foods		40,000
	Record Peerless' 80% share of Special Foods' 20X1 income.		

(3)	Cash	24,000	
	Investment in Special Foods		24,000
	Record Peerless' 80% share of Special Foods' 20X1 dividend.		

Consolidation Worksheet—Initial Year of Ownership

After all appropriate equity method entries have been made on Peerless' books, the company can prepare a consolidation worksheet. Peerless begins the worksheet by placing the adjusted account balances from the books of Peerless and Special Foods in the first two columns of the worksheet. Then all amounts that reflect intercorporate transactions or ownership are eliminated in the consolidation process.

The distinction between journal entries recorded on the books of the individual companies and the eliminating entries recorded only on the consolidation worksheet is an important one. Book entries affect balances on the books and the amounts that are carried to the consolidation worksheet; worksheet eliminating entries affect only those balances carried to the consolidated financial statements in the period. As mentioned previously, the eliminating entries presented in this text are shaded when presented both in journal entry form in the text and in the worksheet.

In this example, the accounts that must be eliminated because of intercorporate ownership are the stockholders' equity accounts of Special Foods, including dividends declared, Peerless' investment in Special Foods stock, and Peerless' income from Special Foods. However, the book value portion of Peerless' investment has changed since the January 1 acquisition date because under the equity method, Peerless has adjusted the investment account balance for its share of earnings and dividends. The book value portion of the investment account can be summarized as follows:

Book Value Calculations:

	NCI 20%	+ Peerless 80%	= Common Stock	+ Retained Earnings
Original book value	60,000	240,000	200,000	100,000
+ Net income	10,000	40,000		50,000
− Dividends	(6,000)	(24,000)		(30,000)
Ending book value	64,000	256,000	200,000	120,000

Note that we shade the amounts in the book value analysis that appear in the basic elimination entry with a lighter font. The beginning and ending balances in the investment account can be illustrated as follows:

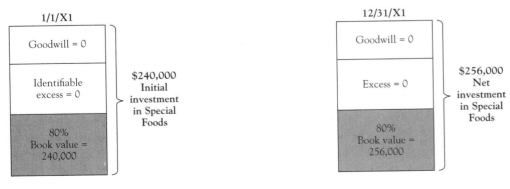

Under the equity method, the parent recognized on its separate books its share (80 percent) of the subsidiary's income. In the consolidated income statement, however, the individual revenue and expense accounts of the subsidiary are combined with those of the parent. Income recognized by the parent from all consolidated subsidiaries, therefore, must be eliminated to avoid double-counting. The subsidiary's dividends paid to the parent company must be eliminated when consolidated statements are prepared so that only dividend declarations related to the parent's shareholders are treated as dividends of the consolidated entity. Thus, the basic eliminating entry removes both the investment income reflected in the parent's income statement and any dividends declared by the subsidiary during the period:

Basic elimination entry:

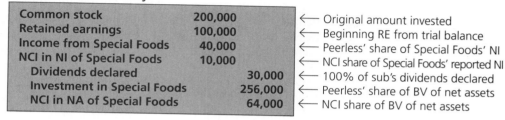

Common stock	200,000		← Original amount invested
Retained earnings	100,000		← Beginning RE from trial balance
Income from Special Foods	40,000		← Peerless' share of Special Foods' NI
NCI in NI of Special Foods	10,000		← NCI share of Special Foods' reported NI
Dividends declared		30,000	← 100% of sub's dividends declared
Investment in Special Foods		256,000	← Peerless' share of BV of net assets
NCI in NA of Special Foods		64,000	← NCI share of BV of net assets

Since there is no differential in this example, the basic elimination entry completely eliminates the balance in Peerless' investment account on the balance sheet as well as the Income from Special Foods account on the income statement. Note again that the parent's investment in the stock of a consolidated subsidiary never appears in the consolidated balance sheet and the income from subsidiary account never appears on the consolidated income statement.

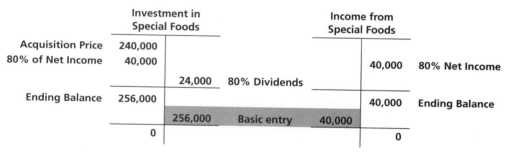

	Investment in Special Foods				Income from Special Foods	
Acquisition Price	240,000					
80% of Net Income	40,000				40,000	80% Net Income
		24,000	80% Dividends			
Ending Balance	256,000				40,000	Ending Balance
		256,000	Basic entry	40,000		
	0				0	

As explained in Chapter 2, when the parent company acquires the subsidiary, the consolidated financial statements should appear as if all of the subsidiary's assets and liabilities were acquired at fair value as of the acquisition date. If Peerless had purchased Special Foods' assets instead of its stock, the book value and accumulated depreciation amounts would have been ignored and the assets would have been recorded in Peerless' books at their current fair values as of the acquisition date. Following this logic, since Peerless did acquire Special Foods' stock, the consolidated financial statements should present all of Special Foods' assets and liabilities as if they had been recorded at their current fair market values on the acquisition date and then depreciated from that date forward. Thus, eliminating the old accumulated depreciation of the subsidiary as of the acquisition date and netting it out against the historical cost gives the appearance that the depreciable assets have been newly recorded at their fair value as of the acquisition date. In this example, Special Foods had accumulated depreciation on the acquisition date of $300,000. Thus, as explained in Chapter 2, the following elimination entry nets this accumulated depreciation out against the cost of the building and equipment.

Optional accumulated depreciation elimination entry:

Accumulated depreciation	300,000	
Building and equipment		300,000

← Original depreciation at the time of the acquisition netted against cost

Also as explained in Chapter 2, this worksheet elimination entry does not change the net buildings and equipment balance. Netting the pre-acquisition accumulated depreciation out against the cost basis of the corresponding assets merely causes the buildings and equipment to appear in the consolidated financial statements as if they had been revalued to their fair values on the acquisition date. This same entry would be included in each succeeding consolidation as long as the assets remain on Special Foods' books (always based on the accumulated depreciation balance as of the acquisition date).

We note that the only two changes on the worksheet when the subsidiary is only partially owned are that the income statement first calculates the consolidated net income ($190,000 in this example) and then deducts the portion attributable to the NCI shareholders to arrive at the portion attributable to the parent (controlling interest) as demonstrated in Figure 3–7. In this example, the final line of the income statement presents Peerless' share of the consolidated net income, $180,000. This amount should always equal the parent's net income in the first column of the worksheet

FIGURE 3–7   December 31, 20X1, Equity-Method Worksheet for Consolidated Financial Statements, Initial Year of Ownership; 80 percent Acquisition at Book Value

	Peerless Products	Special Foods	Elimination Entries DR	Elimination Entries CR	Consolidated
Income Statement					
Sales	400,000	200,000			600,000
Less COGS	(170,000)	(115,000)			(285,000)
Less Depreciation Expense	(50,000)	(20,000)			(70,000)
Less Other Expenses	(40,000)	(15,000)			(55,000)
Income from Special Foods	40,000		40,000		0
Consolidated Net Income	180,000	50,000	40,000	0	190,000
NCI in Net Income			10,000		(10,000)
Controlling Interest in Net Income	**180,000**	**50,000**	**50,000**	**0**	**180,000**
Statement of Retained Earnings					
Beginning Balance	300,000	100,000	100,000		300,000
Net Income	**180,000**	**50,000**	**50,000**	**0**	180,000
Less Dividends Declared	(60,000)	(30,000)		30,000	(60,000)
Ending Balance	**420,000**	**120,000**	**150,000**	**30,000**	**420,000**
Balance Sheet					
Cash	264,000	75,000			339,000
Accounts Receivable	75,000	50,000			125,000
Inventory	100,000	75,000			175,000
Investment in Special Foods	256,000			256,000	0
Land	175,000	40,000			215,000
Buildings & Equipment	800,000	600,000		300,000	1,100,000
Less Accumulated Depreciation	(450,000)	(320,000)	300,000		(470,000)
Total Assets	**1,220,000**	**520,000**	**300,000**	**556,000**	**1,484,000**
Accounts Payable	100,000	100,000			200,000
Bonds Payable	200,000	100,000			300,000
Common Stock	500,000	200,000	200,000		500,000
Retained Earnings	**420,000**	**120,000**	**150,000**	**30,000**	420,000
NCI in NA of Special Foods				64,000	64,000
Total Liabilities & Equity	**1,220,000**	**520,000**	**350,000**	**94,000**	**1,484,000**

(if the parent properly accounts for the investment in the subsidiary using the equity method on its own books).[7]

Second and Subsequent Years of Ownership

The consolidation procedures employed at the end of the second and subsequent years are basically the same as those used at the end of the first year. Adjusted trial balance data of the individual companies are used as the starting point each time consolidated statements are prepared because no separate books are kept for the consolidated entity. An additional check is needed in each period following acquisition to ensure that the beginning balance of consolidated retained earnings shown in the completed worksheet equals the balance reported at the end of the prior period. In all other respects the eliminating entries and worksheet are comparable with those shown for the first year.

Parent Company Entries

Consolidation after two years of ownership is illustrated by continuing the example of Peerless Products and Special Foods. Peerless' separate income from its own operations for 20X2 is $160,000, and its dividends total $60,000. Special Foods reports net income of $75,000 in 20X2 and pays dividends of $40,000. Equity-method entries recorded by Peerless in 20X2 are as follows:

| (4) | Investment in Special Foods | 60,000 | |
| | Income from Special Foods | | 60,000 |

Record Peerless' 80% share of Special Foods' 20X2 income.

| (5) | Cash | 32,000 | |
| | Investment in Special Foods | | 32,000 |

Record Peerless' 80% share of Special Foods' 20X2 dividend.

Peerless' reported net income totals $220,000 ($160,000 from separate operations + $60,000 from Special Foods).

Consolidation Worksheet—Second Year of Ownership

In order to complete the worksheet, Peerless must calculate the worksheet elimination entries using the following process. The book value of equity can be analyzed and summarized as follows:

Advanced
StudyGuide
.com

Book Value Calculations:

	NCI 20%	+ Peerless 80%	= Common Stock	+ Retained Earnings
Beginning book value	64,000	256,000	200,000	120,000
+ Net income	15,000	60,000		75,000
− Dividends	(8,000)	(32,000)		(40,000)
Ending book value	71,000	284,000	200,000	155,000

Thus, the balance in Peerless' Investment in Special Foods account increases from $256,000 to $284,000 in 20X2:

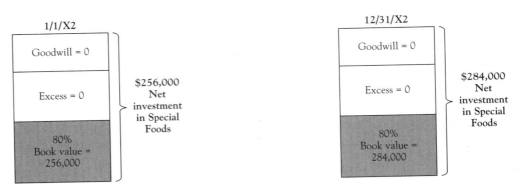

Thus, the basic eliminating entry removes both the investment income reflected in the parent's income statement and any dividends declared by the subsidiary during the period:

Basic elimination entry:

Common stock	200,000		← Original amount invested
Retained earnings	120,000		← RE from trial balance.
Income from Special Foods	60,000		← Peerless' share of Special Foods' NI
NCI in NI of Special Foods	15,000		← NCI share of Special Foods' reported NI
Dividends declared		40,000	← 100% of sub's dividends declared
Investment in Special Foods		284,000	← Peerless' share of BV of net assets
NCI in NA of Special Foods		71,000	← NCI share of BV of net assets

Since there is no differential in this example, the basic elimination entry completely eliminates the balance in Peerless' investment account on the balance sheet as well as the Income from Special Foods account on the income statement.

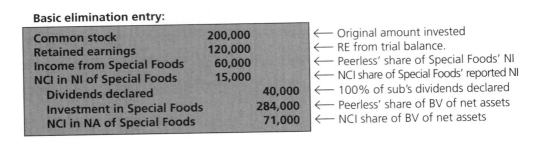

In this example, Special Foods had accumulated depreciation on the acquisition date of $300,000. Thus, we repeat the same accumulated depreciation elimination entry this year (and every year as long as Special Foods owns the assets) that we used in the initial year.

Optional accumulated depreciation elimination entry:

Accumulated depreciation	300,000		Original depreciation at the time of
Building and equipment		300,000	the acquisition netted against cost

After placement of the two elimination entries in the consolidation worksheet, the worksheet is completed in the normal manner as shown in Figure 3–8.

FIGURE 3–8   **December 31, 20X2, Equity-Method Worksheet for Consolidated Financial Statements, Second Year of Ownership; 80 percent Acquisition at Book Value**

	Peerless Products	Special Foods	Elimination Entries DR	Elimination Entries CR	Consolidated
Income Statement					
Sales	450,000	300,000			750,000
Less COGS	(180,000)	(160,000)			(340,000)
Less Depreciation Expense	(50,000)	(20,000)			(70,000)
Less Other Expenses	(60,000)	(45,000)			(105,000)
Income from Special Foods	60,000		60,000		0
Consolidated Net Income	220,000	75,000	60,000	0	235,000
NCI in Net Income			15,000		(15,000)
Controlling Interest Net Income	**220,000**	**75,000**	**75,000**	**0**	**220,000**
Statement of Retained Earnings					
Beginning Balance	420,000	120,000	120,000		420,000
Net Income	220,000	75,000	75,000	0	220,000
Less Dividends Declared	(60,000)	(40,000)		40,000	(60,000)
Ending Balance	**580,000**	**155,000**	**195,000**	**40,000**	**580,000**
Balance Sheet					
Cash	291,000	85,000			376,000
Accounts Receivable	150,000	80,000			230,000
Inventory	180,000	90,000			270,000
Investment in Special Foods	284,000			284,000	0
Land	175,000	40,000			215,000
Buildings & Equipment	800,000	600,000		300,000	1,100,000
Less Accumulated Depreciation	(500,000)	(340,000)	300,000		(540,000)
Total Assets	**1,380,000**	**555,000**	**300,000**	**584,000**	**1,651,000**
Accounts Payable	100,000	100,000			200,000
Bonds Payable	200,000	100,000			300,000
Common Stock	500,000	200,000	200,000		500,000
Retained Earnings	580,000	155,000	195,000	40,000	580,000
NCI in NA of Special Foods				71,000	71,000
Total Liabilities & Equity	**1,380,000**	**555,000**	**395,000**	**111,000**	**1,651,000**

Summary of Key Concepts

Consolidated financial statements present the financial position and results of operations of a parent and one or more subsidiaries as if they were actually a single company. As a result, a group of legally separate companies is portrayed as a single economic entity by the consolidated financial statements. All indications of intercorporate ownership and the effects of all intercompany transactions are excluded from the consolidated statements. The basic approach to the preparation of consolidated financial statements is to combine the separate financial statements of the individual consolidating companies and then to eliminate or adjust those items that would not appear, or that would appear differently, if the companies actually were one.

Current consolidation standards require that the consolidated financial statements include all companies under common control unless control is questionable. Consolidated financial statements are prepared primarily for those with a long-run interest in the parent company, especially the parent's stockholders and long-term creditors. While consolidated financial statements allow interested parties to view a group of related companies as a single economic entity, such statements have some limitations. In particular, information about the characteristics and operations of the individual companies within the consolidated entity is lost in the process of combining financial statements.

New types of business arrangements have proved troublesome for financial reporting. In particular, special types of entities, called *special-purpose entities* and *variable interest entities,* have been used to hide or transform various types of transactions, in addition to being used for many legitimate purposes such as risk sharing. Often these entities were disclosed only through vague notes to the financial statements. Reporting standards now require that the party that is the primary beneficiary of a variable interest entity consolidate that entity.

Several different theories or approaches underlie the preparation of consolidated financial statements, and the approach used can significantly affect the consolidated statements when the subsidiaries are not wholly owned. The proprietary and entity theories can be viewed as lying at opposite ends of a spectrum, with the parent company theory in the middle. Until recently, practice largely followed the parent company approach. Now, following issuance of **FASB 141R (ASC 805)** and **FASB 160 (ASC 810),** practice conforms most closely with the entity approach, but with a greater emphasis on the controlling interest than on the noncontrolling interest.

Key Terms

combined financial
  statements, *118*
consolidated net income, *123*
direct control, *111*
effective control, *112*
entity theory, *119*

indirect control, *111*
minority interest, *116*
noncontrolling interest, *116*
parent company theory, *119*
primary beneficiary, *115*
proprietary theory, *119*

pro rata consolidation, *119*
special-purpose entities
  (SPEs), *113*
variable interest entity
  (VIE), *114*

Appendix 3A Consolidation of Variable Interest Entities

The standards for determining whether a party with an interest in a variable interest entity (VIE) should consolidate the VIE were discussed earlier in the chapter. Once a party has determined that it must consolidate a VIE, the consolidation procedures are similar to those used when consolidating a subsidiary. As an illustration, assume that Ignition Petroleum Company joins with Mammoth Financial Corporation to create a special corporation, Exploration Equipment Company, that would lease equipment to Ignition and other companies. Ignition purchases 10 percent of Exploration's stock for $1,000,000, and Mammoth purchases the other 90 percent for $9,000,000. Profits are to be split equally between the two owners, but Ignition agrees to absorb the first $500,000 of annual losses. Immediately after incorporation, Exploration borrows $120,000,000 from a syndicate of banks, and Ignition guarantees the loan. Exploration then purchases plant, equipment, and supplies for its own use and equipment for lease to others. The balance sheets of Ignition and Exploration appear as follows just prior to the start of Exploration's operations:

Item	Ignition	Exploration
Cash and Receivables	$100,000,000	$ 23,500,000
Inventory and Supplies	50,000,000	200,000
Equipment Held for Lease		105,000,000
Investment in Exploration Equipment Co.	1,000,000	
Plant and Equipment (net)	180,000,000	1,350,000
Total Assets	$331,000,000	$130,050,000
Accounts Payable	$ 900,000	$ 50,000
Bank Loans Payable	30,000,000	120,000,000
Common Stock Issued and Outstanding	200,000,000	10,000,000
Retained Earnings	100,100,000	
Total Liabilities and Equity	$331,000,000	$130,050,000

Both Ignition and Mammoth hold variable interests in Exploration. Ignition's variable interests include both its common stock and its guarantees. Ignition is the primary beneficiary of Exploration because it shares equally in the profits with Mammoth but must absorb a larger share of the expected losses than Mammoth, through both its profit-and-loss-sharing agreement with Mammoth and its loan guarantee. Accordingly, Ignition must consolidate Exploration.

FIGURE 3–9
Balance Sheet
Consolidating a
Variable Interest
Entity

IGNITION PETROLEUM COMPANY
Consolidated Balance Sheet

Assets

Cash and Receivables	$123,500,000
Inventory and Supplies	50,200,000
Equipment Held for Lease	105,000,000
Plant and Equipment (net)	181,350,000
Total Assets	$460,050,000

Liabilities

Accounts Payable	$ 950,000	
Bank Loans Payable	150,000,000	
Total Liabilities		$150,950,000
Stockholders' Equity		
Common Stock	$200,000,000	
Retained Earnings	100,100,000	
Noncontrolling Interest	9,000,000	
Total Stockholders' Equity		309,100,000
Total Liabilities and Stockholders' Equity		$460,050,000

Ignition's consolidated balance sheet that includes Exploration appears as in Figure 3–9. The balances in Exploration's asset and liability accounts are added to the balances of Ignition's like accounts. Ignition's investment in Exploration is eliminated against the common stock of Exploration, and Exploration's remaining common stock is labeled as noncontrolling interest and reported within the equity section of the consolidated balance sheet.

Questions

LO1   **Q3-1**   What is the basic idea underlying the preparation of consolidated financial statements?

LO1   **Q3-2**   How might consolidated statements help an investor assess the desirability of purchasing shares of the parent company?

LO1   **Q3-3**   Are consolidated financial statements likely to be more useful to the owners of the parent company or to the noncontrolling owners of the subsidiaries? Why?

LO2   **Q3-4**   What is meant by "parent company"? When is a company considered to be a parent?

LO1   **Q3-5**   Are consolidated financial statements likely to be more useful to the creditors of the parent company or the creditors of the subsidiaries? Why?

LO2   **Q3-6**   Why is ownership of a majority of the common stock of another company considered important in consolidation?

LO2   **Q3-7**   What major criteria must be met before a company is consolidated?

LO3   **Q3-8**   When is consolidation considered inappropriate even though the parent holds a majority of the voting common shares of another company?

LO3   **Q3-9**   How has reliance on legal control as a consolidation criterion led to off-balance sheet financing?

LO3   **Q3-10**   What types of entities are referred to as *special-purpose entities*, and how have they generally been used?

LO3   **Q3-11**   How does a variable interest entity typically differ from a traditional corporate business entity?

LO3   **Q3-12**   What characteristics are normally examined in determining whether a company is a primary beneficiary of a variable interest entity?

LO2   **Q3-13**   What is meant by "indirect control"? Give an illustration.

LO4   **Q3-14**   What means other than majority ownership might be used to gain control over a company? Can consolidation occur if control is gained by other means?

LO5	**Q3-15**	Why must intercompany receivables and payables be eliminated when consolidated financial statements are prepared?
LO7	**Q3-16**	Why are subsidiary shares not reported as stock outstanding in the consolidated balance sheet?
LO8	**Q3-17**	What must be done if the fiscal periods of the parent and its subsidiary are not the same?
LO7	**Q3-18**	What is the noncontrolling interest in a subsidiary?
LO6	**Q3-19**	What is the difference between consolidated and combined financial statements?
LO6	**Q3-20**	How does the proprietary theory of consolidation differ from current accounting practice?
LO6	**Q3-21**	How does the entity theory of consolidation differ from current accounting practice?
LO6	**Q3-22**	Which theory of consolidation is closest to current accounting practice?

Cases

LO3, LO5   **C3-1**   **Computation of Total Asset Values**

Understanding

A reader of Gigantic Company's consolidated financial statements received from another source copies of the financial statements of the individual companies included in the consolidation. He is confused by the fact that the total assets in the consolidated balance sheet differ rather substantially from the sum of the asset totals reported by the individual companies.

Required

Will this relationship always be true? What factors may cause this difference to occur?

LO3   **C3-2**   **Accounting Entity [AICPA Adapted]**

Understanding

The concept of the accounting entity often is considered to be the most fundamental of accounting concepts, one that pervades all of accounting.

Required

a. (1) What is an accounting entity? Explain.
   (2) Explain why the accounting entity concept is so fundamental that it pervades all of accounting.
b. For each of the following, indicate whether the entity concept is applicable; discuss and give illustrations.
   (1) A unit created by or under law.
   (2) The product-line segment of an enterprise.
   (3) A combination of legal units.
   (4) All the activities of an owner or a group of owners.
   (5) The economy of the United States.

LO5   **C3-3**   **Recognition of Fair Value and Goodwill**

Research

March Corporation acquired 65 percent of Ember Corporation's ownership on January 2, 2008, for $708,500. At that time, Ember's net assets had a book value of $810,000 and a fair value of $960,000. The difference between the book value and fair value of Ember's net assets all related to depreciable assets. The total fair value of Ember's shares not acquired by March Corporation was $381,500.

    FASB Statement No. 141R (ASC 805), which was not in effect at the time of Ember's acquisition, requires recognition of 100 percent of the fair value of the assets and liabilities of an acquired company and 100 percent of the implied goodwill, even in less-than-100-percent acquisitions. Because March's top managers are considering additional acquisitions, they are concerned with how to account for those acquisitions under the FASB's current standards.

Required

Analyze how March's consolidated financial statements would have been different if March had acquired Ember after **FASB Statement No. 141R (ASC 805)** became effective. Prepare a memo to Mr. R. U. Cleer, CFO of March Corporation, explaining how the amounts appearing in the consolidated financial statements relating to Ember would differ between the prior reporting standards and those established by **FASB No. 141R (ASC 805).** Include in your memo citations to and quotations from the appropriate accounting literature.

LO5

Research

C3-4 Joint Venture Investment

Dell Computer Corp. and CIT Group, Inc., established Dell Financial Services L.P. (DFS) as a joint venture to provide financing services for Dell customers. Dell originally purchased 70 percent of the equity of DFS and CIT purchased 30 percent. In the initial agreement, losses were allocated entirely to CIT, although CIT would recoup any losses before any future income was allocated. At the time the joint venture was formed, both Dell and CIT indicated that they had no plans to consolidate DFS.

Required

a. How could both Dell and CIT avoid consolidating DFS?

b. Does Dell currently employ off-balance sheet financing? Explain.

LO5

Analysis

C3-5 Need for Consolidation [AICPA Adapted]

Sharp Company will acquire 90 percent of Moore Company in a business combination. The total consideration has been agreed on, but the nature of Sharp's payment has not. It is expected that on the date the business combination is to be consummated, the fair value will exceed the book value of Moore's assets minus liabilities. Sharp desires to prepare consolidated financial statements that will include Moore's financial statements.

Required

a. Explain how the amount of goodwill is determined.

b. From a theoretical standpoint, why should consolidated financial statements be prepared?

c. From a theoretical standpoint, what is usually the first necessary condition to be met before consolidated financial statements can be prepared?

LO1

Analysis

C3-6 What Company Is That?

Many well-known products and names come from companies that may be less well known or may be known for other reasons. In some cases, an obscure parent company may have well-known subsidiaries, and often familiar but diverse products may be produced under common ownership.

Required

a. Viacom is not necessarily a common name easily identified because it operates through numerous subsidiaries, but its brand names are seen every day. What are some of the well-known brand names from Viacom's subsidiaries? What changes occurred in its organizational structure in 2006? Who is Sumner Redstone?

b. ConAgra Foods, Inc., is one of the world's largest food processors and distributors. Although it produces many products with familiar names, the company's name generally is not well known. What are some of ConAgra's brand names?

c. What type of company is Yum! Brands, Inc.? What are some of its well-known brands? What is the origin of the company, and what was its previous name?

LO1

Analysis

C3-7 Subsidiaries and Core Businesses

During previous merger booms, a number of companies acquired many subsidiaries that often were in businesses unrelated to the acquiring company's central operations. In many cases, the acquiring company's management was unable to manage effectively the many diverse types of operations found in the numerous subsidiaries. More recently, many of these subsidiaries have been sold or, in a few cases, liquidated so the parent companies could concentrate on their core businesses.

Required

a. In 1986, General Electric acquired nearly all of the common stock of the large brokerage firm Kidder, Peabody Inc. Unfortunately, the newly acquired subsidiary's performance was very poor. What ultimately happened to this subsidiary of General Electric?

b. What major business has Sears, Roebuck been in for many decades? What other businesses was it in during the 1980s and early 1990s? What were some of its best-known subsidiaries during that time? Does Sears still own those subsidiaries? What additional acquisitions have occurred?

c. PepsiCo is best known as a soft-drink company. What well-known subsidiaries did PepsiCo own during the mid-1990s? Does PepsiCo still own them?

d. When a parent company and its subsidiaries are in businesses that are considerably different in nature, such as retailing and financial services, how meaningful are their consolidated financial statements in your opinion? Explain. How might financial reporting be improved in such situations?

LO4

C3-8 International Consolidation Issues

Research

The International Accounting Standards Board (IASB) is charged with developing a set of high-quality standards and encouraging their adoption globally. Standards promulgated by the IASB are called International Financial Reporting Standards (IFRS). The European Union (EU) requires statements prepared using IFRS for all companies that list on the EU stock exchanges. While the United States does not yet accept IFRS, the SEC has indicated that it is working toward allowing international companies that list on U.S. exchanges to use IFRS for financial reporting in the United States.

The differences between U.S. GAAP and IFRS are described in many different publications. For example, PricewaterhouseCoopers has a publication available for download on its Web site (http://www.pwc.com/us/en/issues/ifrs-reporting/publications/ifrs-and-us-gaap-similarities-and-differences-september-2009.jhtml) entitled "IFRS and U.S. GAAP: Similarities and Differences: September 2009" that provides a topic-based comparison. Based on the information in this publication or others, answer the following questions about the preparation of consolidated financial statements.

Required

a. Under U.S. GAAP, a two-tiered consolidation model is applied, one focused on voting rights and the second based on a party's exposure to risks and rewards associated with the entity's activities (the VIE model). Upon what is the IFRS framework based?

b. U.S. GAAP requires a two-step process to evaluate goodwill for potential impairment (as discussed in Chapter 1). What is required by IFRS with respect to goodwill impairment?

c. Under U.S. GAAP, noncontrolling interests are measured at fair value. What is required by IFRS?

LO3

C3-9 Off-Balance Sheet Financing and VIEs

Understanding

A variable interest entity (VIE) is a structure frequently used for off-balance sheet financing. VIEs have become quite numerous in recent years and have been the subject of some controversy.

Required

a. Briefly explain what is meant by off-balance sheet financing.

b. What are three techniques used to keep debt off the balance sheet?

c. What are some legitimate uses of VIEs?

d. How can VIEs be used to manage earnings to meet financial reporting goals? How does this relate to the importance of following the intent of the guidelines for consolidations?

LO6

C3-10 Alternative Accounting Methods

Analysis

The use of proportionate or pro rata consolidation generally has not been acceptable in the United States. Normally, a significant investment in the common stock of another company must be either fully consolidated or reported using the equity method.

Required

a. What method does Amerada Hess use to account for its investments in affiliates and joint ventures?

b. What method does EnCana Corporation use to account for its investments in jointly controlled ventures? In what country is EnCana based? Does this make a difference?

c. Should the method used to account for investments in affiliates be different depending on whether the affiliate is a corporation or an unincorporated partnership? Explain.

LO5

C3-11 Consolidation Differences among Major Companies

Research

A variety of organizational structures are used by major companies, and different approaches to consolidation are sometimes found. Two large and familiar U.S. corporations are Union Pacific and ExxonMobil.

Required

a. Many large companies have tens or even hundreds of subsidiaries. List the significant subsidiaries of Union Pacific Corporation.

b. Exxon Mobil Corporation is a major energy company. Does Exxon Mobil consolidate all of its majority-owned subsidiaries? Explain. Does Exxon Mobil consolidate any entities in which it does not hold majority ownership? Explain. What methods does Exxon Mobil use to account for investments in the common stock of companies in which it holds less than majority ownership?

Exercises

LO1

E3-1 Multiple-Choice Questions on Consolidation Overview [AICPA Adapted]

Select the correct answer for each of the following questions.

1. When a parent–subsidiary relationship exists, consolidated financial statements are prepared in recognition of the accounting concept of

   a. Reliability.
   b. Materiality.
   c. Legal entity.
   d. Economic entity.

2. Consolidated financial statements are typically prepared when one company has a controlling interest in another unless

   a. The subsidiary is a finance company.
   b. The fiscal year-ends of the two companies are more than three months apart.
   c. Circumstances prevent the exercise of control.
   d. The two companies are in unrelated industries, such as real estate and manufacturing.

3. Penn Inc., a manufacturing company, owns 75 percent of the common stock of Sell Inc., an investment company. Sell owns 60 percent of the common stock of Vane Inc., an insurance company. In Penn's consolidated statements, should consolidation accounting or equity-method accounting be used for Sell and Vane?

   a. Consolidation used for Sell and equity method used for Vane.
   b. Consolidation used for both Sell and Vane.
   c. Equity method used for Sell and consolidation used for Vane.
   d. Equity method used for both Sell and Vane.

4. Shep Company has a receivable from its parent, Pep Company. Should this receivable be separately reported on Shep's balance sheet and in Pep's consolidated balance sheet?

	Shep's Balance Sheet	Pep's Consolidated Balance Sheet
a.	Yes	No
b.	Yes	Yes
c.	No	No
d.	No	Yes

5. Which of the following is the best theoretical justification for consolidated financial statements?

   a. In form the companies are one entity; in substance they are separate.
   b. In form the companies are separate; in substance they are one entity.
   c. In form and substance the companies are one entity.
   d. In form and substance the companies are separate.

LO3

E3-2 Multiple-Choice Questions on Variable Interest Entities

Select the correct answer for each of the following questions.

1. Special-purpose entities generally

   a. Have a much larger portion of assets financed by equity shareholders than do companies such as General Motors.
   b. Have relatively large amounts of preferred stock and convertible securities outstanding.

  c. Have a much smaller portion of their assets financed by equity shareholders than do companies such as General Motors.

  d. Pay out a relatively high percentage of their earnings as dividends to facilitate the sale of additional shares.

2. Variable interest entities may be established as

  a. Corporations.

  b. Trusts.

  c. Partnerships.

  d. All of the above.

3. An enterprise that will absorb a majority of a variable interest entity's expected losses is called the

  a. Primary beneficiary.

  b. Qualified owner.

  c. Major facilitator.

  d. Critical management director.

4. In determining whether or not a variable interest entity is to be consolidated, the FASB focused on

  a. Legal control.

  b. Share of profits and obligation to absorb losses.

  c. Frequency of intercompany transfers.

  d. Proportionate size of the two entities.

LO5

E3-3 **Multiple-Choice Questions on Consolidated Balances [AICPA Adapted]**

Select the correct answer for each of the following questions.

1. Par Corporation owns 60 percent of Sub Corporation's outstanding capital stock. On May 1, 20X8, Par advanced Sub $70,000 in cash, which was still outstanding at December 31, 20X8. What portion of this advance should be eliminated in the preparation of the December 31, 20X8, consolidated balance sheet?

  a. $70,000.

  b. $42,000.

  c. $28,000.

  d. $0.

Items 2 and 3 are based on the following:

On January 2, 20X8, Pare Company acquired 75 percent of Kidd Company's outstanding common stock. Selected balance sheet data at December 31, 20X8, are as follows:

	Pare Company	Kidd Company
Total Assets	$420,000	$180,000
Liabilities	$120,000	$ 60,000
Common Stock	100,000	50,000
Retained Earnings	200,000	70,000
	$420,000	$180,000

2. In Pare's December 31, 20X8, consolidated balance sheet, what amount should be reported as minority interest in net assets?

  a. $0.

  b. $30,000.

  c. $45,000.

  d. $105,000.

3. In its consolidated balance sheet at December 31, 20X8, what amount should Pare report as common stock outstanding?

   a. $50,000.
   b. $100,000.
   c. $137,500.
   d. $150,000.

4. At the time Hyman Corporation became a subsidiary of Duane Corporation, Hyman switched depreciation of its plant assets from the straight-line method to the sum-of-the-years'-digits method used by Duane. As to Hyman, this change was a

   a. Change in an accounting estimate.
   b. Correction of an error.
   c. Change of accounting principle.
   d. Change in the reporting entity.

5. Consolidated statements are proper for Neely Inc., Randle Inc., and Walker Inc., if

   a. Neely owns 80 percent of the outstanding common stock of Randle and 40 percent of Walker; Randle owns 30 percent of Walker.
   b. Neely owns 100 percent of the outstanding common stock of Randle and 90 percent of Walker; Neely bought the Walker stock one month before the foreign country in which Walker is based imposed restrictions preventing Walker from remitting profits to Neely.
   c. Neely owns 100 percent of the outstanding common stock of Randle and Walker; Walker is in legal reorganization.
   d. Neely owns 80 percent of the outstanding common stock of Randle and 40 percent of Walker; Reeves Inc. owns 55 percent of Walker.

LO2, LO5 **E3-4** **Multiple-Choice Questions on Consolidation Overview [AICPA Adapted]**
Select the correct answer for each of the following questions.

1. Consolidated financial statements are typically prepared when one company has

   a. Accounted for its investment in another company by the equity method.
   b. Accounted for its investment in another company by the cost method.
   c. Significant influence over the operating and financial policies of another company.
   d. The controlling financial interest in another company.

2. Aaron Inc. owns 80 percent of the outstanding stock of Belle Inc. Compare the consolidated net earnings of Aaron and Belle (X) and Aaron's net earnings if it does not consolidate Belle (Y).

   a. X is greater than Y.
   b. X is equal to Y.
   c. X is less than Y.
   d. Cannot be determined.

3. On October 1, X Company acquired for cash all of Y Company's outstanding common stock. Both companies have a December 31 year-end and have been in business for many years. Consolidated net income for the year ended December 31 should include net income of

   a. X Company for three months and Y Company for three months.
   b. X Company for 12 months and Y Company for 3 months.
   c. X Company for 12 months and Y Company for 12 months.
   d. X Company for 12 months, but no income from Y Company until Y Company distributes a dividend.

4. Ownership of 51 percent of the outstanding voting stock of a company would usually result in

   a. The use of the cost method.

   b. The use of the lower-of-cost-or-market method.

   c. The use of the equity method.

   d. A consolidation.

LO7   **E3-5   Balance Sheet Consolidation**

On January 1, 20X3, Guild Corporation reported total assets of $470,000, liabilities of $270,000, and stockholders' equity of $200,000. At that date, Bristol Corporation reported total assets of $190,000, liabilities of $135,000, and stockholders' equity of $55,000. Following lengthy negotiations, Guild paid Bristol's existing shareholders $44,000 in cash for 80 percent of the voting common shares of Bristol.

Required

Immediately after Guild purchased the Bristol shares

a. What amount of total assets did Guild report in its balance sheet?

b. What amount of total assets was reported in the consolidated balance sheet?

c. What amount of total liabilities was reported in the consolidated balance sheet?

d. What amount of stockholders' equity was reported in the consolidated balance sheet?

LO7   **E3-6   Balance Sheet Consolidation with Intercompany Transfer**

Potter Company acquired 90 percent of the voting common shares of Stately Corporation by issuing bonds with a par value and fair value of $121,500 to Stately's existing shareholders. Immediately prior to the acquisition, Potter reported total assets of $510,000, liabilities of $320,000, and stockholders' equity of $190,000. At that date, Stately reported total assets of $350,000, liabilities of $215,000, and stockholders' equity of $135,000. Included in Stately's liabilities was an account payable to Potter in the amount of $15,000, which Potter included in its accounts receivable.

Required

Immediately after Potter acquired Stately's shares

a. What amount of total assets did Potter report in its balance sheet?

b. What amount of total assets was reported in the consolidated balance sheet?

c. What amount of total liabilities was reported in the consolidated balance sheet?

d. What amount of stockholders' equity was reported in the consolidated balance sheet?

LO7   **E3-7   Subsidiary Acquired for Cash**

Fineline Pencil Company acquired 80 percent of Smudge Eraser Corporation's stock on January 2, 20X3, for $72,000 cash. Summarized balance sheet data for the companies on December 31, 20X2, are as follows:

	Fineline Pencil Company		Smudge Eraser Corporation	
	Book Value	Fair Value	Book Value	Fair Value
Cash	$200,000	$200,000	$ 50,000	$ 50,000
Other Assets	400,000	400,000	120,000	120,000
Total Debits	$600,000		$170,000	
Current Liabilities	$100,000	100,000	$ 80,000	80,000
Common Stock	300,000		50,000	
Retained Earnings	200,000		40,000	
Total Credits	$600,000		$170,000	

Required

Prepare a consolidated balance sheet immediately following the acquisition.

LO7

E3-8 Subsidiary Acquired with Bonds

Byte Computer Corporation acquired 75 percent of Nofail Software Company's stock on January 2, 20X3, by issuing bonds with a par value of $50,000 and a fair value of $67,500 in exchange for the shares. Summarized balance sheet data presented for the companies just before the acquisition are as follows:

	Byte Computer Corporation		Nofail Software Company	
	Book Value	Fair Value	Book Value	Fair Value
Cash	$200,000	$200,000	$ 50,000	$ 50,000
Other Assets	400,000	400,000	120,000	120,000
Total Debits	$600,000		$170,000	
Current Liabilities	$100,000	100,000	$ 80,000	80,000
Common Stock	300,000		50,000	
Retained Earnings	200,000		40,000	
Total Credits	$600,000		$170,000	

Required

Prepare a consolidated balance sheet immediately following the acquisition.

LO7

E3-9 Subsidiary Acquired by Issuing Preferred Stock

Byte Computer Corporation acquired 90 percent of Nofail Software Company's common stock on January 2, 20X3, by issuing preferred stock with a par value of $6 per share and a market value of $8.10 per share. A total of 10,000 shares of preferred stock was issued. Balance sheet data for the two companies immediately before the business combination are presented in E3-8.

Required

Prepare a consolidated balance sheet for the companies immediately after Byte obtains ownership of Nofail by issuing the preferred stock.

LO3

E3-10 Reporting for a Variable Interest Entity

Gamble Company convinced Conservative Corporation that the two companies should establish Simpletown Corporation to build a new gambling casino in Simpletown Corner. Although chances for the casino's success were relatively low, a local bank loaned $140,000,000 to the new corporation, which built the casino at a cost of $130,000,000. Conservative purchased 100 percent of the initial capital stock offering for $5,600,000, and Gamble agreed to supply 100 percent of the management and guarantee the bank loan. Gamble also guaranteed a 20 percent return to Conservative on its investment for the first 10 years. Gamble will receive all profits in excess of the 20 percent return to Conservative. Immediately after the casino's construction, Gamble reported the following amounts:

Cash	$ 3,000,000
Buildings and Equipment	240,600,000
Accumulated Depreciation	10,100,000
Accounts Payable	5,000,000
Bonds Payable	20,300,000
Common Stock	103,000,000
Retained Earnings	105,200,000

The only disclosure that Gamble currently provides in its financial reports about its relationships to Conservative and Simpletown is a brief footnote indicating that a contingent liability exists on its guarantee of Simpletown Corporation's debt.

Required

Prepare a balance sheet in good form for Gamble immediately following the casino's construction.

LO7

E3-11 Consolidation of a Variable Interest Entity

Teal Corporation is the primary beneficiary of a variable interest entity with total assets of $500,000, liabilities of $470,000, and owners' equity of $30,000. Because Teal owns 25 percent of the VIE's voting stock, it reported a $7,500 investment in the VIE in its balance sheet. Teal reported total assets of $190,000 (including its investment in the VIE), liabilities of $80,000, common stock of $15,000, and retained earnings of $95,000 in its balance sheet.

Required

Prepare a condensed balance sheet in good form for Teal, taking into consideration that it is the primary beneficiary of the variable interest entity.

LO5, LO7

E3-12 Computation of Subsidiary Net Income

Frazer Corporation owns 70 percent of Messer Company's stock. In the 20X9 consolidated income statement, the noncontrolling interest was assigned $18,000 of income.

Required

What amount of net income did Messer Company report for 20X9?

LO5, LO7

E3-13 Incomplete Consolidation

Advanced
StudyGuide
.com

Belchfire Motors' accountant was called away after completing only half of the consolidated statements at the end of 20X4. The data left behind included the following:

Item	Belchfire Motors	Premium Body Shop	Consolidated
Cash	$ 40,000	$ 20,000	$ 60,000
Accounts Receivable	180,000	30,000	200,000
Inventory	220,000	50,000	270,000
Buildings and Equipment (net)	300,000	290,000	590,000
Investment in Premium Body Shop	150,000		
Total Debits	$890,000	$390,000	$1,120,000
Accounts Payable	$ 30,000	$ 40,000	
Bonds Payable	400,000	200,000	
Common Stock	200,000	100,000	
Retained Earnings	260,000	50,000	
Total Credits	$890,000	$390,000	

Required

a. Belchfire Motors acquired shares of Premium Body Shop at underlying book value on January 1, 20X1. What portion of the ownership of Premium Body Shop does Belchfire apparently hold?

b. Compute the consolidated totals for each of the remaining balance sheet items.

LO5, LO7

E3-14 Noncontrolling Interest

Sanderson Corporation acquired 70 percent of Kline Corporation's common stock on January 1, 20X7, for $294,000 in cash. At the acquisition date, the book values and fair values of Kline's assets and liabilities were equal, and the fair value of the noncontrolling interest was equal to 30 percent of the total book value of Kline. The stockholders' equity accounts of the two companies at the date of purchase are:

	Sanderson Corporation	Kline Corporation
Common Stock ($10 par value)	$400,000	$180,000
Additional Paid-In Capital	222,000	65,000
Retained Earnings	358,000	175,000
Total Stockholders' Equity	$980,000	$420,000

Required

a. What amount will be assigned to the noncontrolling interest on January 1, 20X7, in the consolidated balance sheet?

b. Prepare the stockholders' equity section of Sanderson and Kline's consolidated balance sheet as of January 1, 20X7.

c. Sanderson acquired ownership of Kline to ensure a constant supply of electronic switches, which it purchases regularly from Kline. Why might Sanderson not feel compelled to purchase all of Kline's shares?

LO7

E3-15   Computation of Consolidated Net Income

Ambrose Corporation owns 75 percent of Kroop Company's common stock, acquired at underlying book value on January 1, 20X4. At the acquisition date, the book values and fair values of Kroop's assets and liabilities were equal, and the fair value of the noncontrolling interest was equal to 25 percent of the total book value of Kroop. The income statements for Ambrose and Kroop for 20X4 include the following amounts:

	Ambrose Corporation	Kroop Company
Sales	$528,000	$150,000
Dividend Income	9,000	
Total Income	$537,000	$150,000
Less: Cost of Goods Sold	$380,000	$ 87,000
Depreciation Expense	32,000	20,000
Other Expenses	66,000	23,000
Total Expenses	$478,000	$130,000
Net Income	$ 59,000	$ 20,000

Ambrose uses the cost method in accounting for its ownership of Kroop. Kroop paid dividends of $12,000 in 20X4.

Required

a. What amount should Ambrose report in its income statement as income from its investment in Kroop using equity-method accounting?

b. What amount of income should be assigned to noncontrolling interest in the consolidated income statement for 20X4?

c. What amount should Ambrose report as consolidated net income for 20X4?

d. Why should Ambrose not report consolidated net income of $79,000 ($59,000 + $20,000) for 20X4?

LO7

Advanced
StudyGuide
.com

E3-16   Computation of Subsidiary Balances

Tall Corporation acquired 75 percent of Light Corporation's voting common stock on January 1, 20X2, at underlying book value. At the acquisition date, the book values and fair values of Light's assets and liabilities were equal, and the fair value of the noncontrolling interest was equal to 25 percent of the total book value of Light. Noncontrolling interest was assigned income of $8,000 in Tall's consolidated income statement for 20X2 and a balance of $65,500 in Tall's consolidated balance sheet at December 31, 20X2. Light reported retained earnings of $70,000 and additional paid-in capital of $40,000 on January 1, 20X2. Light did not pay dividends or issue stock in 20X2.

Required

a. Compute the amount of net income reported by Light for 20X2.

b. Prepare the stockholders' equity section of Light's balance sheet at December 31, 20X2.

LO7, LO8

E3-17   Subsidiary Acquired at Net Book Value

On December 31, 20X8, Banner Corporation acquired 80 percent of Dwyer Company's common stock for $136,000. At the acquisition date, the book values and fair values of all of Dwyer's assets and liabilities were equal. Banner uses the equity method in accounting for its investment. Balance sheet information provided by the companies at December 31, 20X8, is as follows:

	Banner Corporation	Dwyer Company
Cash	$ 74,000	$ 20,000
Accounts Receivable	120,000	70,000
Inventory	180,000	90,000
Fixed Assets (net)	350,000	240,000
Investment in Dwyer Company Stock	136,000	
Total Debits	$860,000	$420,000
Accounts Payable	$ 65,000	$ 30,000
Notes Payable	350,000	220,000
Common Stock	150,000	90,000
Retained Earnings	295,000	80,000
Total Credits	$860,000	$420,000

Required

Prepare a consolidated balance sheet for Banner at December 31, 20X8.

LO6

E3-18   Applying Alternative Accounting Theories

Noway Manufacturing owns 75 percent of Positive Piston Corporation's stock. During 20X9, Noway and Positive Piston reported sales of $400,000 and $200,000 and expenses of $280,000 and $160,000, respectively.

Required

Compute the amount of total revenue, total expenses, and net income to be reported in the 20X9 consolidated income statement under the following alternative approaches:

a. Proprietary theory.

b. Parent company theory.

c. Entity theory.

d. Current accounting practice.

LO6

E3-19   Measurement of Goodwill

Rank Corporation acquired 60 percent of Fresh Company's stock on December 31, 20X4. In preparing the consolidated financial statements at December 31, 20X4, goodwill of $240,000 was reported. The goodwill is attributable to Rank's purchase of Fresh shares, and the parent company approach was used in determining the amount of goodwill reported.

Required

Determine the amount of goodwill to be reported under each of the following consolidation alternatives:

a. Proprietary theory.

b. Entity theory.

c. Current accounting practice.

LO6

E3-20   Assets under Alternative Accounting Theories

Garwood Corporation acquired 75 percent of Zorn Company's voting common stock on January 1, 20X4. At the time of acquisition, Zorn reported buildings and equipment at book value of $240,000; however, an appraisal indicated a fair value of $290,000.

Required

If consolidated statements are prepared, determine the amount at which buildings and equipment will be reported using the following consolidation alternatives:

a. Entity theory.

b. Parent company theory.

c. Proprietary theory.

d. Current accounting practice.

LO6

E3-21 Reported Income under Alternative Accounting Theories

Placer Corporation acquired 80 percent of Billings Company's voting common stock on January 1, 20X4. Placer and Billings reported total revenue of $410,000 and $200,000 and total expenses of $320,000 and $150,000, respectively, for the year ended December 31, 20X4.

Required

Determine the amount of total revenue, total expense, and net income to be reported in the consolidated income statement for 20X4 under the following consolidation alternatives:

a. Entity theory.

b. Parent company theory.

c. Proprietary theory.

d. Current accounting practice.

LO7

E3-22 Acquisition of Majority Ownership

Lang Company reports net assets with a book value and fair value of $200,000 Pace Corporation acquires 75 percent ownership for $150,000. Pace reports net assets with a book value of $520,000 and a fair value of $640,000 at that time, excluding its investment in Lang.

Required

For each of the following, compute the amounts that would be reported immediately after the combination under current accounting practice:

a. Consolidated net identifiable assets.

b. Noncontrolling interest.

Problems

LO7

P3-23 Multiple-Choice Questions on Consolidated and Combined Financial Statements [AICPA Adapted]

Select the correct answer for each of the following questions.

1. What is the theoretically preferred method of presenting a noncontrolling interest in a consolidated balance sheet?

    a. As a separate item within the liability section.

    b. As a deduction from (contra to) goodwill from consolidation, if any.

    c. By means of notes or footnotes to the balance sheet.

    d. As a separate item within the stockholders' equity section.

2. Presenting consolidated financial statements this year when statements of individual companies were presented last year is

    a. The correction of an error.

    b. An accounting change that should be reported prospectively.

    c. An accounting change that should be reported by restating the financial statements of all prior periods presented.

    d. Not an accounting change.

3. A subsidiary, acquired for cash in a business combination, owned equipment with a market value in excess of book value as of the date of combination. A consolidated balance sheet prepared immediately after the acquisition would treat this excess as

    a. Goodwill.

    b. Plant and equipment.

    c. Retained earnings.

    d. Deferred credit.

4. Mr. Cord owns four corporations. Combined financial statements are being prepared for these corporations, which have intercompany loans of $200,000 and intercompany profits of $500,000. What amount of these intercompany loans and profits should be included in the combined financial statements?

	Intercompany	
	Loans	**Profits**
a.	$200,000	$ 0
b.	$200,000	$500,000
c.	$ 0	$ 0
d.	$ 0	$500,000

LO7

P3-24 Determining Net Income of Parent Company

Tally Corporation and its subsidiary reported consolidated net income of $164,300 for 20X2. Tally owns 60 percent of the common shares of its subsidiary, acquired at book value. Noncontrolling interest was assigned income of $15,200 in the consolidated income statement for 20X2.

Required

Determine the amount of separate operating income reported by Tally for 20X2.

LO7

P3-25 Reported Balances

Roof Corporation acquired 80 percent of the stock of Gable Company by issuing shares of its common stock with a fair value of $192,000. At that time, the fair value of the noncontrolling interest was estimated to be $48,000 and the fair values of Gable's identifiable assets and liabilities were $310,000 and $95,000, respectively. Gable's assets and liabilities had book values of $220,000 and $95,000, respectively.

Required

Compute the following amounts to be reported immediately after the combination

a. Investment in Gable reported by Roof.
b. Increase in identifiable assets of the combined entity.
c. Increase in total liabilities of the combined entity.
d. Goodwill for the combined entity.
e. Noncontrolling interest reported in the consolidated balance sheet.

LO7

P3-26 Acquisition Price

Darwin Company holds assets with a fair value of $120,000 and a book value of $90,000 and liabilities with a book value and fair value of $25,000.

Required

Compute the following amounts if Brad Corporation acquires 60 percent ownership of Darwin:

a. What amount did Brad pay for the shares if no goodwill and no gain on a bargain purchase are reported?
b. What amount did Brad pay for the shares if the fair value of the noncontrolling interest at acquisition is $54,000 and goodwill of $40,000 is reported?
c. What balance will be assigned to the noncontrolling interest in the consolidated balance sheet if Brad pays $73,200 to acquire its ownership and goodwill of $27,000 is reported?

LO3

P3-27 Consolidation of a Variable Interest Entity

On December 28, 20X3, Stern Corporation and Ram Company established S&R Partnership, with cash contributions of $10,000 and $40,000, respectively. The partnership's purpose is to purchase from Stern accounts receivable that have an average collection period of 80 days and hold them to collection. The partnership borrows cash from Midtown Bank and purchases the receivables without recourse but at an amount equal to the expected percent to be collected, less a financing fee of 3 percent of the gross receivables. Stern and Ram hold 20 percent and 80 percent of the ownership of the partnership, respectively, and Stern guarantees both the bank loan made to the partnership and a 15 percent annual return on the investment made by Ram. Stern receives any income in excess of the 15 percent return guaranteed to Ram. The partnership agreement provides

Stern total control over the partnership's activities. On December 31, 20X3, Stern sold $8,000,000 of accounts receivable to the partnership. The partnership immediately borrowed $7,500,000 from the bank and paid Stern $7,360,000. Prior to the sale, Stern had established a $400,000 allowance for uncollectibles on the receivables sold to the partnership. The balance sheets of Stern and S&R immediately after the sale of receivables to the partnership contained the following:

	Stern Corporation	S&R Partnership
Cash	$7,960,000	$ 190,000
Accounts Receivable	4,200,000	8,000,000
Allowance for Uncollectible Accounts	(210,000)	(400,000)
Other Assets	5,400,000	
Prepaid Finance Charges	240,000	
Investment in S&R Partnership	10,000	
Accounts Payable	950,000	
Deferred Revenue		240,000
Bank Notes Payable		7,500,000
Bonds Payable	9,800,000	
Common Stock	700,000	
Retained Earnings	6,150,000	
Capital, Stern Corporation		10,000
Capital, Ram Company		40,000

Required

Assuming that Stern is S&R's primary beneficiary, prepare a consolidated balance sheet in good form for Stern at January 1, 20X4.

LO3

P3-28 **Reporting for Variable Interest Entities**

Purified Oil Company and Midwest Pipeline Corporation established Venture Company to conduct oil exploration activities in North America to reduce their dependence on imported crude oil. Midwest Pipeline purchased all 20,000 shares of the newly created company for $10 each. Purified Oil agreed to purchase all of Venture's output at market price, guarantee up to $5,000,000 of debt for Venture, and absorb all losses if the company proved unsuccessful. Purified and Midwest agreed to share equally the profits up to $80,000 per year and to allocate 70 percent of those in excess of $80,000 to Purified and 30 percent to Midwest.

Venture immediately borrowed $3,000,000 from Second National Bank and purchased land, drilling equipment, and supplies to start its operations. Following these asset purchases, Venture and Purified Oil reported the following balances:

	Venture Company	Purified Oil Company
Cash	$ 230,000	$ 410,000
Drilling Supplies	420,000	
Accounts Receivable		640,000
Equipment (net)	1,800,000	6,700,000
Land	900,000	4,200,000
Accounts Payable	150,000	440,000
Bank Loans Payable	3,000,000	8,800,000
Common Stock	200,000	560,000
Retained Earnings		2,150,000

The only disclosure that Purified Oil currently provides in its financial statements with respect to its relationship with Midwest Pipeline and Venture is a brief note indicating that a contingent liability exists on the guarantee of Venture Company debt.

Required

Assuming that Venture is considered to be a variable interest entity and Purified Oil is the primary beneficiary, prepare a balance sheet in good form for Purified Oil.

LO7

P3-29 **Consolidated Income Statement Data**

Master Products acquired 80 percent ownership of LoCal Bakeries on January 1, 20X3, when the fair value of LoCal's depreciable assets was equal to book value.

	Master Products		LoCal Bakeries	
Sales		$ 300,000		$ 200,000
Cost of Goods Sold	$200,000		$130,000	
Depreciation Expense	40,000	(240,000)	30,000	(160,000)
Income before Income from Subsidiary		$ 60,000		
Net Income				$ 40,000

During 20X3, Master Products purchased a special imported yeast for $35,000 and resold it to LoCal for $50,000. LoCal did not resell any of the yeast before year-end.

Required

Determine the amounts to be reported for each of the following items in the consolidated income statement for 20X3:

a. Sales.

b. Investment income from LoCal Bakeries.

c. Cost of goods sold.

d. Depreciation expense.

LO7

P3-30 **Parent Company and Consolidated Amounts**

Quoton Corporation acquired 80 percent of Tempro Company's common stock on December 31, 20X5, at underlying book value. The book values and fair values of Tempro's assets and liabilities were equal, and the fair value of the noncontrolling interest was equal to 20 percent of the total book value of Tempro. Tempro provided the following trial balance data at December 31, 20X5:

	Debit	Credit
Cash	$ 28,000	
Accounts Receivable	65,000	
Inventory	90,000	
Buildings and Equipment (net)	210,000	
Cost of Goods Sold	105,000	
Depreciation Expense	24,000	
Other Operating Expenses	31,000	
Dividends Declared	15,000	
Accounts Payable		$ 33,000
Notes Payable		120,000
Common Stock		90,000
Retained Earnings		130,000
Sales		195,000
Total	$568,000	$568,000

Required

a. How much did Quoton pay to purchase its shares of Tempro?

b. If consolidated financial statements are prepared at December 31, 20X5, what amount will be assigned to the noncontrolling interest in the consolidated balance sheet?

c. If Quoton reported income of $143,000 from its separate operations for 20X5, what amount of consolidated net income will be reported for 20X5?

d. If Quoton had purchased its ownership of Tempro on January 1, 20X5, at underlying book value and Quoton reported income of $143,000 from its separate operations for 20X5, what amount of consolidated net income would be reported for 20X5?

LO7

P3-31 **Parent Company and Consolidated Balances**

Exacto Company reported the following net income and dividends for the years indicated:

Year	Net Income	Dividends
20X5	$35,000	$12,000
20X6	45,000	20,000
20X7	30,000	14,000

Advanced
StudyGuide
.com

True Corporation acquired 75 percent of Exacto's common stock on January 1, 20X5. On that date, the fair value of Exacto's net assets was equal to the book value. True uses the equity method in accounting for its ownership in Exacto and reported a balance of $259,800 in its investment account on December 31, 20X7.

Required

a. What amount did True pay when it purchased Exacto's shares?

b. What was the fair value of Exacto's net assets on January 1, 20X5?

c. What amount was assigned to the NCI shareholders on January 1, 20X5?

d. What amount will be assigned to the NCI shareholders in the consolidated balance sheet prepared at December 31, 20X7?

LO2, LO7 **P3-32** **Indirect Ownership**

Purple Corporation recently attempted to expand by acquiring ownership in Green Company. The following ownership structure was reported on December 31, 20X9:

Investor	Investee	Percentage of Ownership Held
Purple Corporation	Green Company	70
Green Company	Orange Corporation	10
Orange Corporation	Blue Company	60
Green Company	Yellow Company	40

The following income from operations (excluding investment income) and dividend payments were reported by the companies during 20X9:

Company	Operating Income	Dividends Paid
Purple Corporation	$ 90,000	$60,000
Green Company	20,000	10,000
Orange Corporation	40,000	30,000
Blue Company	100,000	80,000
Yellow Company	60,000	40,000

Required

Compute the amount reported as consolidated net income for 20X9.

LO6

P3-33 **Balance Sheet Amounts under Alternative Accounting Theories**

Parsons Corporation purchased 75 percent ownership of Tumble Company on December 31, 20X7, for $210,000. Summarized balance sheet amounts for the companies on December 31, 20X7, prior to the purchase, were as follows:

	Parsons Corporation	Tumble Company Book Value	Fair Value
Cash and Inventory	$300,000	$ 80,000	$ 80,000
Buildings and Equipment (net)	400,000	120,000	180,000
Total Assets	$700,000	$200,000	$260,000
Common Stock	$380,000	$ 90,000	
Retained Earnings	320,000	110,000	
Total Liabilities and Stockholders' Equity	$700,000	$200,000	

Required

If consolidated financial statements are prepared, determine the amounts that would be reported as cash and inventory, buildings and equipment (net), and goodwill using the following consolidation alternatives:

a. Proprietary theory.

b. Parent company theory.

c. Entity theory.

d. Current accounting practice.

LO7, LO8 **P3-34** **Consolidated Worksheet and Balance Sheet on the Acquisition Date (Equity Method)**

Advanced StudyGuide .com

Peanut Company acquired 90 percent of Snoopy Company's outstanding common stock for $270,000 on January 1, 20X8, when the book value of Snoopy's net assets was equal to $300,000. Peanut uses the equity method to account for investments. Trial balance data for Peanut and Snoopy as of January 1, 20X8, are as follows:

	Peanut Company	Snoopy Company
Assets		
Cash	55,000	20,000
Accounts Receivable	50,000	30,000
Inventory	100,000	60,000
Investment in Snoopy Stock	270,000	
Land	225,000	100,000
Buildings and Equipment	700,000	200,000
Accumulated Depreciation	(400,000)	(10,000)
Total Assets	1,000,000	400,000
Liabilities and Stockholders' Equity		
Accounts Payable	75,000	25,000
Bonds Payable	200,000	75,000
Common Stock	500,000	200,000
Retained Earnings	225,000	100,000
Total Liabilities and Equity	1,000,000	400,000

Required

a. Prepare the journal entry on Peanut's books for the acquisition of Snoopy on January 1, 20X8.

b. Prepare a consolidation worksheet on the acquisition date, January 1, 20X8, in good form.

c. Prepare a consolidated balance sheet on the acquisition date, January 1, 20X8, in good form.

LO7, LO8

Advanced
StudyGuide
.com

P3-35   Consolidated Worksheet at End of the First Year of Ownership (Equity Method)

Peanut Company acquired 90 percent of Snoopy Company's outstanding common stock for $270,000 on January 1, 20X8, when the book value of Snoopy's net assets was equal to $300,000. Peanut uses the equity method to account for investments. Trial balance data for Peanut and Snoopy as of December 31, 20X8, are as follows:

	Peanut Company		Snoopy Company	
	Debit	Credit	Debit	Credit
Cash	158,000		80,000	
Accounts Receivable	165,000		65,000	
Inventory	200,000		75,000	
Investment in Snoopy Stock	319,500		0	
Land	200,000		100,000	
Buildings and Equipment	700,000		200,000	
Cost of Goods Sold	200,000		125,000	
Depreciation Expense	50,000		10,000	
Selling & Administrative Expense	225,000		40,000	
Dividends Declared	100,000		20,000	
Accumulated Depreciation		450,000		20,000
Accounts Payable		75,000		60,000
Bonds Payable		200,000		85,000
Common Stock		500,000		200,000
Retained Earnings		225,000		100,000
Sales		800,000		250,000
Income from Snoopy		67,500		0
Total	2,317,500	2,317,500	715,000	715,000

Required

a. Prepare any equity method journal entry(ies) related to the investment in Snoopy Company for 20X8.

b. Prepare a consolidation worksheet for 20X8 in good form.

LO7, LO8

Advanced
StudyGuide
.com

P3-36   Consolidated Worksheet at End of the Second Year of Ownership (Equity Method)

Peanut Company acquired 90 percent of Snoopy Company's outstanding common stock for $270,000 on January 1, 20X8, when the book value of Snoopy's net assets was equal to $300,000. Problem 3-36 summarizes the first year of Peanut's ownership of Snoopy. Peanut uses the equity method to account for investments. The following trial balance summarizes the financial position and operations for Peanut and Snoopy as of December 31, 20X9:

	Peanut Company		Snoopy Company	
	Debit	Credit	Debit	Credit
Cash	255,000		75,000	
Accounts Receivable	190,000		80,000	
Inventory	180,000		100,000	
Investment in Snoopy Stock	364,500		0	
Land	200,000		100,000	
Buildings and Equipment	700,000		200,000	
Cost of Goods Sold	270,000		150,000	
Depreciation Expense	50,000		10,000	
Selling & Administrative Expense	230,000		60,000	

(continued)

	Peanut Company		Snoopy Company	
	Debit	Credit	Debit	Credit
Dividends Declared	225,000		30,000	
Accumulated Depreciation		500,000		30,000
Accounts Payable		75,000		35,000
Bonds Payable		150,000		85,000
Common Stock		500,000		200,000
Retained Earnings		517,500		155,000
Sales		850,000		300,000
Income from Snoopy		72,000		0
Total	2,664,500	2,664,500	805,000	805,000

Required

a. Prepare any equity method journal entry(ies) related to the investment in Snoopy Company during 20X9.

b. Prepare a consolidation worksheet for 20X9 in good form.

LO7, LO8   P3-37   Consolidated Worksheet and Balance Sheet on the Acquisition Date (Equity Method)

Paper Company acquired 80 percent of Scissor Company's outstanding common stock for $296,000 on January 1, 20X8, when the book value of Scissor's net assets was equal to $370,000. Paper uses the equity method to account for investments. Trial balance data for Paper and Scissor as of January 1, 20X8, are as follows:

	Paper Company	Scissor Company
Assets		
Cash	109,000	25,000
Accounts Receivable	65,000	37,000
Inventory	125,000	87,000
Investment in Scissor Stock	296,000	
Land	280,000	125,000
Buildings and Equipment	875,000	250,000
Accumulated Depreciation	(500,000)	(24,000)
Total Assets	1,250,000	500,000
Liabilities and Stockholders' Equity		
Accounts Payable	95,000	30,000
Bonds Payable	250,000	100,000
Common Stock	625,000	250,000
Retained Earnings	280,000	120,000
Total Liabilities and Equity	1,250,000	500,000

Required

a. Prepare the journal entry on Paper's books for the acquisition of Scissor Co. on January 1, 20X8.

b. Prepare a consolidation worksheet on the acquisition date, January 1, 20X8, in good form.

c. Prepare a consolidated balance sheet on the acquisition date, January 1, 20X8, in good form.

LO7, LO8   P3-38   Consolidated Worksheet at End of the First Year of Ownership (Equity Method)

Paper Company acquired 80 percent of Scissor Company's outstanding common stock for $296,000 on January 1, 20X8, when the book value of Scissor's net assets was equal to $370,000.

Paper uses the equity method to account for investments. Trial balance data for Paper and Scissor as of December 31, 20X8, are as follows:

	Paper Company		Scissor Company	
	Debit	Credit	Debit	Credit
Cash	191,000		46,000	
Accounts Receivable	140,000		60,000	
Inventory	190,000		120,000	
Investment in Scissor Stock	350,400		0	
Land	250,000		125,000	
Buildings and Equipment	875,000		250,000	
Cost of Goods Sold	250,000		155,000	
Depreciation Expense	65,000		12,000	
Selling & Administrative Expense	280,000		50,000	
Dividends Declared	80,000		25,000	
Accumulated Depreciation		565,000		36,000
Accounts Payable		77,000		27,000
Bonds Payable		250,000		100,000
Common Stock		625,000		250,000
Retained Earnings		280,000		120,000
Sales		800,000		310,000
Income from Scissor		74,400		0
Total	2,671,400	2,671,400	843,000	843,000

Required

a. Prepare any equity method journal entry(ies) related to the investment in Scissor Company for 20X8.

b. Prepare a consolidation worksheet for 20X8 in good form.

LO7, LO8   **P3-39**   **Consolidated Worksheet at End of the Second Year of Ownership (Equity Method)**

Paper Company acquired 80 percent of Scissor Company's outstanding common stock for $296,000 on January 1, 20X8, when the book value of Scissor's net assets was equal to $370,000. Problem 3-36 summarizes the first year of Paper's ownership of Scissor. Paper uses the equity method to account for investments. The following trial balance summarizes the financial position and operations for Paper and Scissor as of December 31, 20X9:

	Paper Company		Scissor Company	
	Debit	Credit	Debit	Credit
Cash	295,000		116,000	
Accounts Receivable	165,000		97,000	
Inventory	193,000		115,000	
Investment in Scissor Stock	412,000		0	
Land	250,000		125,000	
Buildings and Equipment	875,000		250,000	
Cost of Goods Sold	278,000		178,000	
Depreciation Expense	65,000		12,000	
Selling & Administrative Expense	312,000		58,000	
Dividends Declared	90,000		30,000	
Accumulated Depreciation		630,000		48,000
Accounts Payable		85,000		40,000

(continued)

	Paper Company		Scissor Company	
	Debit	Credit	Debit	Credit
Bonds Payable		150,000		100,000
Common Stock		625,000		250,000
Retained Earnings		479,400		188,000
Sales		880,000		355,000
Income from Scissor		85,600		0
Total	2,935,000	2,935,000	981,000	981,000

Required

a. Prepare any equity method journal entry(ies) related to the investment in Scissor Company during 20X9.

b. Prepare a consolidation worksheet for 20X9 in good form.

Chapter **Four**

Consolidation of Wholly Owned Subsidiaries Acquired at More than Book Value

HOW MUCH WORK DOES IT REALLY TAKE TO CONSOLIDATE? ASK THE PEOPLE WHO DO IT AT DISNEY

The Walt Disney Company, whose history goes back to 1923, is parent company to some of the most well-known businesses in the world. Best known for Walt Disney Studios, its world famous parks and resorts, its media operations, like the Disney Channel, and its consumer products, Disney is a widely diversified company. For example, did you know that Disney owns the ABC Television Network and is the majority owner of ESPN? While the consolidation examples you're working in class usually involve a parent company and a single subsidiary, Disney employs a dedicated staff at its Burbank, California headquarters each quarter to complete the consolidation of its five segments, each comprised of many subsidiaries, in preparation for its quarterly 10-Q and annual 10-K filings with the SEC. Preparation for the actual consolidation begins before the end of the fiscal period and soon after the end of the period each segment closes its books, including performing its own subsidiary-consolidations, works with the independent auditors, and prepares for the roll-up to the overall company consolidation. The work continues as the finance and accounting staff of approximately 100 men and women at the corporate offices review and analyze the results from the individual segments and work with segment financial staff to prepare what becomes the publicly disclosed set of consolidated financial statements.

However, the work doesn't all take place at the end of the fiscal period. The accounting system also tracks intercompany transactions throughout the period. The consolidation process requires the elimination of intercompany sales and asset transfers among others cost allocations (as discussed in Chapters 6 and 7). Tracking these transactions involves ongoing efforts throughout the period.

Finally, you may have read recently about Disney's acquisition of Marvel Entertainment in 2009 and its acquisition of Pixar Animation Studios in 2006. In these and other well-known acquisitions, Disney paid more than the book value of each acquired company's net assets to acquire them. Acquisition accounting rules require Disney to account for the full acquisition price—even though the acquired companies may continue to report their assets and liabilities on their separate books at their historical book

157

values. Thus, acquisition accounting requires Disney to essentially re-value the balance sheets of these companies to their amortized fair values in the consolidation process each period.

The bottom line is that preparation of Disney's publicly disclosed financial statements is the culmination of a lot of work by the segment and corporate accounting and finance staff. The issues mentioned here illustrate the complexity of a process that requires substantial team work and effort to produce audited financial statements that are valuable to an investor or interested accounting student. You'll learn in this chapter about the value-added activities during the consolidation process performed by the accounting staff at any well-known public company. This chapter also introduces differences in the consolidation process when there is a differential (i.e., the acquiring company pays more than the book value of the acquired company's net assets).

LEARNING OBJECTIVES

When you finish studying this chapter, you should be able to:

LO1   Understand and make equity-method journal entries related to the differential.

LO2   Understand and explain how consolidation procedures differ when there is a differential.

LO3   Make calculations and prepare elimination entries for the consolidation of a wholly owned subsidiary when there is a complex positive differential at the acquisition date.

LO4   Make calculations and prepare elimination entries for the consolidation of a wholly owned subsidiary when there is a complex bargain-purchase differential.

LO5   Prepare equity-method journal entries, elimination entries, and the consolidation worksheet for a wholly owned subsidiary when there is a complex positive differential.

LO6   Understand and explain the elimination of basic intercompany transactions.

LO7   Understand and explain the basics of push-down accounting.

DEALING WITH THE DIFFERENTIAL

This chapter continues to build upon the foundation established in Chapters 2 and 3 related to the consolidation of majority-owned subsidiaries. In Chapters 2 and 3, we focus on relatively simple situations where the acquisition price is exactly equal to the parent's share of the book value of the subsidiary's net assets. In Chapter 4, we relax this assumption and allow the acquisition price to differ from book value. As explained in Chapter 1, this allows for a "differential."

The Difference between Acquisition Price and Underlying Book Value

When an investor purchases the common stock of another company, the purchase price normally is based on the market value of the shares acquired rather than the book value of the investee's assets and liabilities. Not surprisingly, the acquisition price is usually different from the book value of the investor's proportionate share of the investee's net assets. This difference is referred to as a **differential.** The differential is frequently positive, meaning the acquiring company pays more than their share of the book value of the subsidiary's net assets. Note that in the case of an equity-method investment, the differential on the parent's books relates only to the parent's share of any difference between total investee's fair value and book value. The differential in the case of an equity-method investment is implicit in the investment account on the parent's books and is not recorded separately.

The cost of an investment might exceed the book value of the underlying net assets, giving rise to a positive differential, for any of several reasons. One reason is that the investee's assets may be worth more than their book values. Another reason could be the existence of unrecorded goodwill associated with the excess earning power of the investee. In either case, the portion of the differential pertaining to each asset of the investee, including goodwill, must be ascertained. When the parent company uses the equity-method, that portion of the differential pertaining to limited-life assets of the investee, including identifiable intangibles, must be amortized over the remaining economic lives of those assets. Any portion of the differential that represents goodwill (referred to as *equity-method goodwill*) is not amortized or written off because of impairment. However, an impairment loss on the investment itself should be recognized if it suffers a material decline in value that is other than temporary.

Amortization or Write-Off of the Differential[1]

When the equity-method is used, each portion of the differential must be treated in the same manner as the investee treats the assets or liabilities to which the differential relates. Thus, any portion of the differential related to depreciable or amortizable assets of the investee should be amortized over the remaining time that the cost of the asset is being allocated by the investee. Amortization of the differential associated with depreciable or amortizable assets of the investee is necessary on the investor's books to reflect the decline in the future benefits the investor expects from that portion of the investment cost associated with those assets. The investee recognizes the reduction in service potential of assets with limited lives as depreciation or amortization expense based on the amount it has invested in those assets. This reduction, in turn, is recognized by the investor through its share of the investee's net income. When the cost of the investor's interest in the investee's assets is greater than the investee's cost (as reflected in a positive differential), the additional cost must be amortized as well.

The approach to amortizing the differential that is most consistent with the idea of reflecting all aspects of the investment in just one line on the balance sheet and one line on the income statement is to reduce the income recognized by the investor from the investee and the balance of the investment account:

Income from Investee	XXXX	
Investment in Common Stock of Investee		XXX

The differential represents the amount paid by the investor in excess of the book value of the investment and is included in the investment amount. Hence, the amortization or reduction of the differential involves the reduction of the investment account. At the same time, the investor's net income must be reduced by an equal amount to recognize that a portion of the amount paid for the investment has expired.

[1] To view a video explanation of this topic, visit advancedstudyguide.com.

Treatment of the Differential Illustrated

To illustrate the equity-method when the cost of the investment exceeds the book value of the underlying net assets, assume that Ajax Corporation purchases 40 percent of the common stock of Barclay Company on January 1, 20X1, for $200,000. Barclay has net assets on that date with a book value of $400,000 and fair value of $465,000. Ajax's share of the book value of Barclay's net assets at acquisition is $160,000 ($400,000 × 0.40). A $40,000 differential is computed as follows:

Cost of investment to Ajax	$200,000
Book value of Ajax's share of Barclay's net assets	(160,000)
Differential	$ 40,000

The $65,000 excess of the fair value over the book value of Barclay's net assets consists of a $15,000 increase in the value of Barclay's land and a $50,000 increase in the value of Barclay's equipment. Ajax's 40 percent share of the increase in the value of Barclay's assets is as follows:

	Total Increase	Ajax's 40% Share
Land	$15,000	6,000
Equipment	50,000	20,000
	$65,000	$26,000

Thus, $26,000 of the differential is assigned to land and equipment, with the remaining $14,000 attributed to goodwill. The allocation of the differential can be illustrated as shown in the diagram.

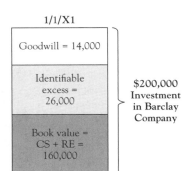

Although the differential relates to assets of Barclay, the additional cost incurred by Ajax to acquire a claim on the assets of Barclay is reflected in Ajax's investment in Barclay. No separate differential account is established, and no separate accounts are recorded on Ajax's books to reflect the apportionment of the differential to specific assets. Similarly, no separate expense account is established on Ajax's books. Amortization or write-off of the differential is accomplished by reducing Ajax's investment account and the income Ajax recognizes from its investment in Barclay.

Because land has an unlimited economic life, the portion of the differential related to land is not amortized. The $20,000 portion of the differential related to Barclay's equipment is amortized over the equipment's remaining life. If the equipment's remaining life is five years, Ajax's annual amortization of the differential is $4,000 ($20,000 ÷ 5).

Beginning in 1970, financial reporting standards required that goodwill be amortized over its useful life, not to exceed 40 years. In 2001, however, the FASB issued **Statement No. 142 (ASC 350),** "Goodwill and Other Intangible Assets," under which equity-method goodwill is neither amortized nor written off. That portion of the differential remains imbedded in the investment account. Thus, in this example, the only amortization of the differential is the $4,000 related to Barclay's equipment.

Barclay reports net income of $80,000 at year end and declares dividends of $20,000 during 20X1. Using the equity-method, Ajax records the following entries on its books during 20X1:

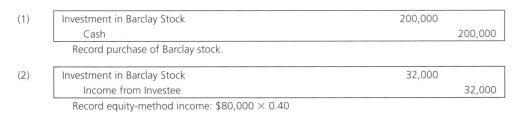

(1)	Investment in Barclay Stock	200,000	
	Cash		200,000
	Record purchase of Barclay stock.		

(2)	Investment in Barclay Stock	32,000	
	Income from Investee		32,000
	Record equity-method income: $80,000 × 0.40		

(3)

Cash	8,000	
Investment in Barclay Stock		8,000

Record dividend from Barclay: $20,000 × 0.40

(4)

Income from Investee	4,000	
Investment in Barclay Stock		4,000

Amortize differential related to equipment.

With these entries, Ajax recognizes $28,000 of income from Barclay and adjusts its investment in Barclay to an ending balance of $220,000.

The amortization on Ajax's books of the portion of the differential related to Barclay's equipment is the same ($4,000) for each of the first five years (20X1 through 20X5). This amortization stops after 20X5 because this portion of the differential is fully amortized after five years.

Notice that no special accounts are established on the books of the investor with regard to the differential or the amortization of the differential. The only two accounts involved are "Income from Investee" and "Investment in Barclay Stock." As the Investment in Barclay Stock account is amortized, the differential between the carrying amount of the investment and the book value of the underlying net assets decreases.

Disposal of Differential-Related Assets

Although the differential is included on the books of the investor as part of the investment account, it relates to specific assets of the investee. Thus, if the investee disposes of any asset to which the differential relates, that portion of the differential must be removed from the investment account on the investor's books. When this is done, the investor's share of the investee's gain or loss on disposal of the asset must be adjusted to reflect the fact that the investor paid more for its proportionate share of that asset than did the investee. For example, if in the previous illustration Barclay Company sells the land to which $6,000 of Ajax's differential relates, Ajax does not recognize a full 40 percent of the gain or loss on the sale. Assume that Barclay originally had purchased the land in 20X0 for $75,000 and sells the land in 20X2 for $125,000. Barclay recognizes a gain on the sale of $50,000, and Ajax's share of that gain is 40 percent, or $20,000. The portion of the gain actually recognized by Ajax, however, must be adjusted as follows because of the amount in excess of book value paid by Ajax for its investment in Barclay:

Ajax's share of Barclay's reported gain	$20,000
Portion of Ajax's differential related to the land	(6,000)
Gain to be recognized by Ajax	$14,000

Thus, if Barclay reports net income (including the gain on the sale of land) of $150,000 for 20X2, Ajax records the following entries (disregarding dividends and amortization of the differential relating to equipment):

(5)

Investment in Barclay Stock	60,000	
Income from Investee		60,000

Record equity-method income: $150,000 × 0.40

(6)

Income from Investee	6,000	
Investment in Barclay Stock		6,000

Remove differential related to Barclay's land that was sold.

The same approach applies when dealing with a limited-life asset. The unamortized portion of the original differential relating to the asset sold is removed from the investment account, and the investor's share of the investee's income is adjusted by that amount.

Note that the investor does not separately report its share of ordinary gains or losses included in the investee's net income, such as the gain on the sale of the fixed asset or the write-off of the unamortized differential. Consistent with the idea of using only a single line in the income statement to report the impact of the investee's activities on the investor, all such items are included in the Income from Investee account. Current standards do require the investor to report its share of an investee's extraordinary gains and losses, prior-period adjustments, and elements of other comprehensive income, if material to the investor, as separate items in the same manner as the investor reports its own.

Impairment of Investment Value

As with many assets, accounting standards require that equity-method investments be written down if their value is impaired. If the market value of the investment declines materially below its equity-method carrying amount, and the decline in value is considered other than temporary, the carrying amount of the investment should be written down to the market value and a loss recognized. The new lower value serves as a starting point for continued application of the equity-method. Subsequent recoveries in the value of the investment may not be recognized.

CONSOLIDATION PROCEDURES FOR WHOLLY OWNED SUBSIDIARIES ACQUIRED AT MORE THAN BOOK VALUE

LO2

Understand and explain how consolidation procedures differ when there is a differential.

Advanced StudyGuide .com

Many factors have an effect on the fair value of a company and its stock price, including its asset values, its earning power, and general market conditions. When one company acquires another, the acquiree's fair value usually differs from its book value, and so the consideration given by the acquirer does as well. As discussed in Chapter 1, this difference between the fair value of the consideration given and the book value of the acquiree's net identifiable assets is referred to as a *differential.*

The process of preparing a consolidated balance sheet immediately after a business combination is complicated only slightly when 100 percent of a company's stock is acquired at a price that differs from the acquiree's book value. To illustrate the acquisition of a subsidiary when the consideration given is greater than the book value of the acquiree, we use the Peerless-Special Foods example from Chapter 2. We assume that Peerless Products acquires all of Special Foods' outstanding stock on January 1, 20X1, by paying $340,000 cash, an amount equal to Special Foods' fair value as a whole. The consideration given by Peerless is $40,000 in excess of Special Foods' book value of $300,000. The resulting ownership situation can be viewed as follows:

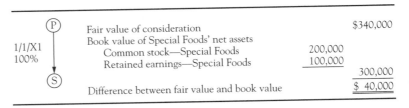

Peerless records the stock acquisition with the following entry:

In a business combination, and therefore in a consolidation following a business combination, the full amount of the consideration given by the acquirer must be assigned to the individual assets and liabilities acquired and to goodwill. In this example, the fair value of consideration given (the acquisition price) includes an extra $40,000 for appreciation in the value of the land since it was originally acquired by Special Foods. The relationship between the fair value of the consideration given for Special Foods, the fair value of Special Foods' net assets, and the book value of Special Foods' net assets can be illustrated as follows:

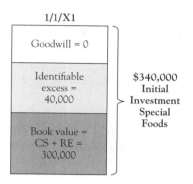

The consolidation worksheet procedures used in adjusting to the proper consolidated amounts follow a consistent pattern. The first worksheet entry (often referred to as the "basic" elimination entry) eliminates the book value portion of the parent's investment account and each of the subsidiary's stockholders' equity accounts. It is useful to analyze the investment account and the subsidiary's equity accounts as follows:

Book Value Calculations:

	Total Investment	=	Common Stock	+	Retained Earnings
Original book value	300,000		200,000		100,000

The worksheet entry to eliminate the book value portion of Peerless' investment account and the stockholders' equity accounts of Special Foods is as follows:

Basic elimination entry:

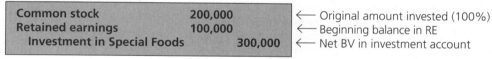

Common stock	200,000		← Original amount invested (100%)
Retained earnings	100,000		← Beginning balance in RE
Investment in Special Foods		300,000	← Net BV in investment account

When the acquisition-date fair value of the consideration is more than the acquiree's book value at that date, the second eliminating entry reclassifies the excess acquisition price to the specific accounts on the balance sheet for which the book values are not the same as their fair values on the acquisition date.[2] The differential represents (in simple situations involving a 100 percent acquisition) the total difference between the acquisition-date fair value of the consideration given by the acquirer and the acquiree's book value. In this example, the differential is the additional $40,000 paid by Peerless to acquire Special Foods because its land was worth $40,000 more than its book value as of the acquisition date. In preparing a consolidated balance sheet immediately after acquisition (on January 1, 20X1), the second elimination entry appearing

---

[2] Alternatively, a separate clearing account titled *Excess of Acquisition Consideration over Acquiree Book Value,* or just *Differential* can be debited for this excess amount. A subsequent entry can be used to reclassify the differential to the various accounts on the balance sheet that need to be re-valued to their acquisition date amounts. Note that the Differential account is simply a worksheet clearing account and is not found on the books of the parent or subsidiary and does not appear in the consolidated financial statements.

in the consolidation worksheet simply re-assigns this $40,000 from the investment account to the land account so that: (*a*) the Land account fully reflects the fair value of this asset as of the acquisition date and (*b*) the investment account is fully eliminated from Peerless' books:

Excess value reclassification entry:

Land	40,000	← Excess value assigned to land
Investment in Special Foods		40,000	← Reclassify excess acquisition price

Thus, these two elimination entries completely eliminate the balance in Peerless' investment account and the second entry assigns the differential to the land account.

Investment in Special Foods

Acquisition Price	340,000		
		300,000	Basic elimination entry
		40,000	Excess value reclassification entry
	0		

In more complicated examples where the fair values of various balance sheet accounts differ from book values, the excess value reclassification entry reassigns the differential to adjust various account balances to reflect the fair values of the subsidiary's assets and liabilities at the time the parent acquired the subsidiary and to establish goodwill, if appropriate.

Figure 4–1 illustrates the consolidation worksheet reflecting the allocation of the differential to the subsidiary's land.

The amounts reported in the consolidated balance sheet are those in the Consolidated column of the worksheet in Figure 4–1. Land would be included in the consolidated balance sheet at $255,000, the amount carried on Peerless' books ($175,000) plus the amount carried on Special Foods' books ($40,000) plus the differential reflecting the increased value of Special Foods' land ($40,000).

FIGURE 4–1 **Worksheet for Consolidated Balance Sheet, January 1, 20X1, Date of Combination; 100 Percent Acquisition at More than Book Value**

	Peerless Products	Special Foods	Elimination Entries DR	Elimination Entries CR	Consolidated
Balance Sheet					
Cash	10,000	50,000			60,000
Accounts Receivable	75,000	50,000			125,000
Inventory	100,000	60,000			160,000
Investment in Special Foods	340,000			300,000	0
				40,000	
Land	175,000	40,000	40,000		255,000
Buildings & Equipment	800,000	600,000			1,400,000
Less Accumulated Depreciation	(400,000)	(300,000)			(700,000)
Total Assets	**1,100,000**	**500,000**	**40,000**	**340,000**	**1,300,000**
Accounts Payable	100,000	100,000			200,000
Bonds Payable	300,000	100,000			300,000
Common Stock	500,000	200,000	200,000		500,000
Retained Earnings	300,000	100,000	100,000		300,000
Total Liabilities & Equity	**1,100,000**	**500,000**	**300,000**	**0**	**1,300,000**

This example is sufficiently simple that the assignment of the differential to land could be made directly in the basic eliminating entry rather than through the use of a separate entry. In practice, however, the differential often relates to more than a single asset, and the allocation of the differential may be considerably more complex than in this example. The possibilities for clerical errors are reduced in complex situations by making two separate entries rather than one complicated entry.

Treatment of a Positive Differential

The fair value, and hence acquisition price, of a subsidiary might exceed the book value for several reasons, such as the following:

1. Errors or omissions on the books of the subsidiary.
2. Excess of fair value over the book value of the subsidiary's net identifiable assets.
3. Existence of goodwill.

Errors or Omissions on the Books of the Subsidiary

An examination of an acquired company's books may reveal material errors. In some cases, the acquired company may have expensed rather than capitalized assets or, for other reasons, omitted them from the books. An acquired company that previously had been closely held may not have followed generally accepted accounting principles in maintaining its accounting records. In some cases, the recordkeeping may have simply been inadequate.

Where errors or omissions occur, corrections should be made directly on the subsidiary's books as of the date of acquisition. These corrections are treated as prior-period adjustments in accordance with **FASB Statement No. 16 (ASC 250),** "Prior Period Adjustments" (FASB 16, ASC 250). Once the subsidiary's books are stated in accordance with generally accepted accounting principles, that portion of the differential attributable to errors or omissions will no longer exist.

Excess of Fair Value over Book Value of Subsidiary's Net Identifiable Assets

The fair value of a company's assets is an important factor in the overall determination of the company's fair value. In many cases, the fair value of an acquired company's net assets exceeds the book value. Consequently, the consideration given by an acquirer may exceed the acquiree's book value. The procedures used in preparing the consolidated balance sheet should lead to reporting all of the acquired company's assets and liabilities based on their fair values on the date of combination. This valuation may be accomplished in one of two ways: (1) the assets and liabilities of the subsidiary may be revalued directly on the books of the subsidiary or (2) the accounting basis of the subsidiary may be maintained and the revaluations made each period in the consolidation worksheet.

Revaluing the assets and liabilities on the subsidiary's books generally is the simplest approach if all of the subsidiary's common stock is acquired. On the other hand, it generally is not appropriate to revalue the assets and liabilities on the subsidiary's books if there is a significant noncontrolling interest in that subsidiary. From a noncontrolling shareholder's point of view, the subsidiary is a continuing company, and the basis of accounting should not change. More difficult to resolve is the situation in which the parent acquires all of the subsidiary's common stock but continues to issue separate financial statements of the subsidiary to holders of the subsidiary's bonds or preferred stock. Revaluing the assets and liabilities of the subsidiary directly on the subsidiary's books is referred to as ***push-down accounting*** and is discussed later in this chapter.

When the assets and liabilities are revalued directly on the subsidiary's books, that portion of the differential then no longer exists. However, if the assets and liabilities are not revalued on the subsidiary's books, an entry to revalue those assets and allocate the differential is needed in the consolidation worksheet each time consolidated financial statements are prepared, for as long as the related assets are held.

Existence of Goodwill

If the acquisition-date fair value of the consideration exchanged for an acquired subsidiary is greater than the total fair value of the subsidiary's net identifiable assets, the difference is considered to be related to the future economic benefits associated with other assets of the subsidiary that are not separately identified and recognized and is referred to as *goodwill*. Thus, once a subsidiary's identifiable assets and liabilities are revalued to their fair values, any remaining debit differential is normally allocated to goodwill. For example, assuming that in the Peerless Products and Special Foods illustration the acquisition-date fair values of Special Foods' assets and liabilities are equal to their book values, then the $40,000 difference between the $340,000 consideration exchanged and the $300,000 fair value of the subsidiary's net identifiable assets should be attributed to goodwill. The following entry to assign the differential is needed in the consolidation worksheet prepared immediately after the combination:

Excess value reclassification entry:

Goodwill	40,000		← Excess value assigned to goodwill
Investment in Special Foods		40,000	← Reassign excess acquisition price

The consolidation worksheet is similar to Figure 4–1 except that the debit in the excess value reclassification worksheet entry would be to goodwill instead of land. Goodwill, which does not appear on the books of either Peerless or Special Foods, would appear at $40,000 in the consolidated balance sheet prepared immediately after acquisition.

In the past, some companies have included the fair-value increment related to certain identifiable assets of the subsidiary in goodwill rather than separately recognizing those assets. This treatment is not acceptable, and any fair-value increment related to an intangible asset that arises from a contractual or legal right or that is separable from the entity must be allocated to that asset.

Illustration of Treatment of a Complex Differential

LO3

Make calculations and prepare elimination entries for the consolidation of a wholly owned subsidiary when there is a complex positive differential at the acquisition date.

Advanced
StudyGuide
.com

In many situations, the differential relates to a number of different assets and liabilities. As a means of illustrating the allocation of the differential to various assets and liabilities, assume that the acquisition-date book values and fair values of Special Foods' assets and liabilities are as shown in Figure 4–2. The inventory and land have fair values in excess of their book values, while the buildings and equipment are worth less than their book values.

Bond prices fluctuate as interest rates change. In this example, the value of Special Foods' bonds payable is higher than the book value. This indicates that the nominal interest rate on the bonds is higher than the current market rate of interest, and, therefore, investors are willing to pay a price higher than par for the bonds. In determining the value of Special Foods, Peerless must recognize that it is assuming a liability that pays an interest rate higher than the current market rate. Accordingly, Special Foods' value will be less than if the liability carried a lower interest rate. The resulting consolidated financial statements must recognize the acquisition-date fair values of Special Foods' liabilities as well as its assets.

Assume that Peerless Products acquires all of Special Foods' capital stock for $400,000 on January 1, 20X1, by issuing $100,000 of 9 percent bonds, with a fair value of $100,000, and paying cash of $300,000. The resulting ownership situation can be pictured as follows with a $100,000 differential:

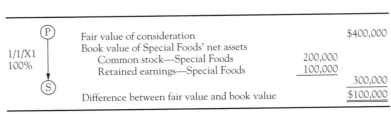

Fair value of consideration		$400,000
Book value of Special Foods' net assets		
Common stock—Special Foods	200,000	
Retained earnings—Special Foods	100,000	
		300,000
Difference between fair value and book value		$100,000

FIGURE 4–2
Differences between Book and Fair Values of Special Foods' Identifiable Assets and Liabilities as of January 1, 20X1, the Date of Combination

		Book Value	Fair Value	Difference between Fair Value and Book Value
Cash		$ 50,000	$ 50,000	
Accounts Receivable		50,000	50,000	
Inventory		60,000	75,000	$15,000
Land		40,000	100,000	60,000
Buildings and Equipment	600,000			
Accumulated Depreciation	(300,000)	300,000	290,000	(10,000)
		$500,000	$565,000	
Accounts Payable		$100,000	$100,000	
Bonds Payable		100,000	135,000	(35,000)
Common Stock		200,000		
Retained Earnings		100,000		
		$500,000	$235,000	$30,000

Peerless records the investment on its books with the following entry:

(8)	Investment in Special Foods	400,000	
	Bonds Payable		100,000
	Cash		300,000

Record purchase of Special Foods stock.

The fair value of the consideration that Peerless gave to acquire Special Foods' stock ($400,000) can be divided between the fair value of Special Foods' net assets ($330,000) and goodwill ($70,000), illustrated as follows:

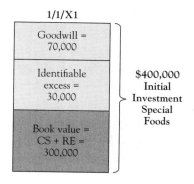

The total $400,000 consideration exceeds the book value of Special Foods' net assets by $100,000 (assets of $500,000 less liabilities of $200,000). Thus, the total differential is $100,000. The total fair value of the net identifiable assets acquired in the combination is $330,000 ($565,000 − $235,000), based on the data in Figure 4–2. The amount by which the total consideration of $400,000 exceeds the $330,000 fair value of the net identifiable assets is $70,000, and that amount is assigned to goodwill in the consolidated balance sheet. The book value portion of the acquisition price is $300,000:

Book Value Calculations:

	Total Investment	=	Common Stock	+	Retained Earnings
Original book value	300,000		200,000		100,000

Thus, the basic elimination entry is as follows:

Basic elimination entry:

Common stock	200,000	← Original amount invested (100%)
Retained earnings	100,000	← Beginning balance in RE
Investment in Special Foods		300,000 ← Net BV in investment account

The reclassification of the differential to the various accounts that are either over- or under-valued on Special Foods' balance sheet as of the acquisition date is more complicated than in the previous example. Thus, it is helpful to analyze the differential as follows:

Excess Value (Differential) Calculations:

Total Differential	=	Inventory	+	Land	+	Building	+	Goodwill	+	Bonds Payable
100,000		15,000		60,000		(10,000)		70,000		(35,000)

This analysis leads to the following reclassification entry to assign the $100,000 differential to the specific accounts that need to be "revalued" to reflect their fair values as of the acquisition date. Moreover, this entry completes the elimination of the investment account from Peerless' books.

Excess value (differential) reclassification entry:

Inventory	15,000		← Excess value assigned to inventory
Land	60,000		← Excess value assigned to land
Building		10,000	← Under-valuation assigned to building
Goodwill	70,000		← Excess value assigned to goodwill
Bonds Payable		35,000	← Excess liability associated with the bonds
Investment in Special Foods		100,000	← Re-assign excess acquisition price

In summary, these two elimination entries completely eliminate the balance in Peerless' investment account and the second entry assigns the differential to various balance sheet accounts. As in previous examples, it is helpful to visualize how the two elimination entries "zero out" the investment account:

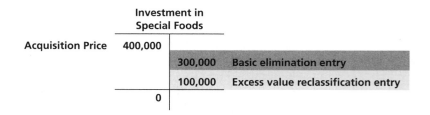

These entries are reflected in the worksheet in Figure 4–3. While the reclassification entry is somewhat more complex than in the previous example, the differential allocation is conceptually the same in both cases. In each case, the end result is a consolidated balance sheet with the subsidiary's assets and liabilities valued at their fair values at the date of combination.

FIGURE 4–3   Worksheet for Consolidated Balance Sheet, January 1, 20X1, Date of Combination; 100 Percent Acquisition at More than Book Value

	Peerless Products	Special Foods	Elimination Entries		Consolidated
			DR	CR	
Balance Sheet					
Cash	50,000	50,000			100,000
Accounts Receivable	75,000	50,000			125,000
Inventory	100,000	60,000	15,000		175,000
Investment in Special Foods	400,000			300,000	0
				100,000	
Land	175,000	40,000	60,000		275,000
Buildings & Equipment	800,000	600,000		10,000	1,390,000
Less Accumulated Depreciation	(400,000)	(300,000)			(700,000)
Goodwill			70,000		70,000
Total Assets	**1,200,000**	**500,000**	**145,000**	**410,000**	**1,435,000**
Accounts Payable	100,000	100,000			200,000
Bonds Payable	300,000	100,000			400,000
Premium on Bonds Payable				35,000	35,000
Common Stock	500,000	200,000	200,000		500,000
Retained Earnings	300,000	100,000	100,000		300,000
Total Liabilities & Equity	**1,200,000**	**500,000**	**300,000**	**35,000**	**1,435,000**

100 Percent Ownership Acquired at Less than Fair Value of Net Assets

It is not uncommon for companies' stock to trade at prices that are lower than the fair value of their net assets. These companies are often singled out as prime acquisition targets. The acquisition price of an acquired company may be less than the fair value of its net assets because some of the Acquiree's assets or liabilities may have been incorrectly specified or because the transaction reflects a forced sale where the seller was required to sell quickly and was unable to fully market the sale.

Obviously, if assets or liabilities acquired in a business combination have been incorrectly specified, the errors must be corrected and the assets and liabilities valued at their fair values. Once this is done, if the fair value of the consideration given is still less than the fair value of the net assets acquired, a gain attributable to the acquirer is recognized for the difference. In general, as discussed in Chapter 1, a business combination where (1) the sum of the acquisition-date fair values of the consideration given, any equity interest already held by the acquirer, and any noncontrolling interest is less than (2) the amounts at which the identifiable net assets must be valued at the acquisition date as specified by **FASB 141R (ASC 805)** (usually fair values) is considered a ***bargain purchase,*** and a gain attributable to the acquirer is recognized for the difference.

Illustration of Treatment of Bargain-Purchase Differential

Using the example of Peerless Products and Special Foods, assume that the acquisition-date book values and fair values of Special Foods' assets and liabilities are equal except that the fair value of Special Foods' land is $40,000 greater than its book value. On January 1, 20X1, Peerless acquires all of Special Foods' common stock for $310,000, resulting in a bargain purchase. The resulting ownership situation is as follows:

(P)	Fair value of consideration		$310,000
1/1/X1	Book value of Special Foods' net assets		
100%	Common stock—Special Foods	200,000	
	Retained earnings—Special Foods	100,000	
(S)			300,000
	Difference between fair value and book value		$ 10,000

Peerless records its investment in Special Foods with the following entry on its books:

(9)			
	Investment in Special Foods	310,000	
	Cash		310,000

Record purchase of Special Foods stock.

In this example, the acquisition-date fair value of Special Foods' net assets is greater than their book value by $40,000. However, the purchase price exceeds Special Foods' book value by only $10,000 and, thus, is less than the fair value of the net identifiable assets acquired. This business combination, therefore, represents a bargain purchase. All of the acquiree's assets and liabilities must be valued at fair value, which in this case requires only Special Foods' land to be revalued. Assuming push-down accounting is not employed, this revaluation is accomplished in the consolidation worksheet. The book value portion of the acquisition price is $300,000:

Book Value Calculations:

	Total Investment	=	Common Stock	+	Retained Earnings
Original book value	300,000		200,000		100,000

Thus, the basic elimination entry is the same as in previous examples:

Basic elimination entry:

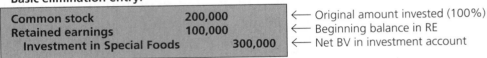

Common stock	200,000	← Original amount invested (100%)
Retained earnings	100,000	← Beginning balance in RE
Investment in Special Foods		300,000 ← Net BV in investment account

The reclassification of the net differential to the accounts that are either over- or under-valued on Special Foods' financial statements as of the acquisition date can be summarized as follows:

Excess Value (Differential) Calculations:

Net Differential	=	Land	−	Gain
10,000		40,000		(30,000)

In concept, this analysis leads to the following reclassification entry to assign the $10,000 net differential to the Land and Gain on Bargain Purchase accounts.

Excess value (differential) reclassification entry:

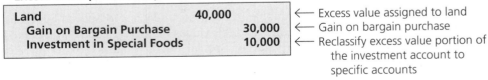

Land	40,000	← Excess value assigned to land
Gain on Bargain Purchase		30,000 ← Gain on bargain purchase
Investment in Special Foods		10,000 ← Reclassify excess value portion of the investment account to specific accounts

If the consolidation worksheet were prepared at the end of the year, the notion of recognizing a gain for the $30,000 excess of the $340,000 fair value of Special Foods' net assets over the $310,000 fair value of the consideration given by Peerless in the exchange would be correct. However, assuming the consolidation worksheet is prepared on the acquisition date (January 1, 20X1), the gain is carried directly to Retained Earnings because an income statement is not prepared on the acquisition date, only a balance sheet (since it is the first day of the year).[3]

In summary, these two elimination entries effectively eliminate the balance in Peerless' investment account and assign the net differential to the Land and Gain (or Retained Earnings) accounts. As in previous examples, it is helpful to visualize how the two elimination entries "zero out" the investment account:

Investment in Special Foods

Acquisition Price	310,000		
		300,000	Basic elimination entry
		10,000	Excess value reclassification
	0		

If the consideration given in the exchange had been less than the book value of Special Foods, the same procedures would be followed except the differential would have a credit balance.

CONSOLIDATED FINANCIAL STATEMENTS—100 PERCENT OWNERSHIP ACQUIRED AT MORE THAN BOOK VALUE

LO5

Prepare equity-method journal entries, elimination entries, and the consolidation worksheet for a wholly owned subsidiary when there is a complex positive differential.

Advanced
StudyGuide
.com

Most frequently, an investment in a subsidiary is acquired at a price that is in excess of the acquiree's book value. In consolidation, the excess or differential must be allocated to specific assets and liabilities, with the identifiable assets and liabilities revalued based on their acquisition-date fair values and any excess recognized as goodwill. If this revaluation is not accomplished on the separate books of the subsidiary through the use of push-down accounting, as illustrated in Appendix 4A, it must be made in the consolidation worksheet each time consolidated statements are prepared. In addition, if the revaluations relate to assets or liabilities that must be depreciated, amortized, or otherwise written off, appropriate entries must be made in the consolidation worksheet to reduce consolidated net income accordingly.

When an investor company accounts for an investment using the equity-method, as illustrated in Chapter 2, it records the amount of differential viewed as expiring during the period as a reduction of the income recognized from the investee. In consolidation, the differential is assigned to the appropriate asset and liability balances, and consolidated income is adjusted for the amounts expiring during the period by assigning them to the related expense items (e.g., depreciation expense).

Initial Year of Ownership

As an illustration of the acquisition of 100 percent ownership acquired at an amount greater than book value, assume that Peerless Products acquires all of Special Foods' common stock on January 1, 20X1, for $387,500, an amount $87,500 in excess of the book value. The acquisition price includes cash of $300,000 and a 60-day note for $87,500 (paid at maturity during 20X1). At the date of combination, Special Foods is holding the assets and liabilities shown in Figure 4–2. The resulting ownership situation is as follows:

Fair value of consideration			$387,500
Book value of Special Foods' net assets			
Common stock—Special Foods		200,000	
Retained earnings—Special Foods		100,000	
			300,000
Difference between fair value and book value			$ 87,500

1/1/X1 100%

[3] Note that if the acquisition were to take place at the end of the year, the gain would appear on the consolidated income statement in the acquisition year. In subsequent years, the credit for $30,000 would be assigned to retained earnings.

On the date of combination, all of Special Foods' assets and liabilities have fair values equal to their book values, except as follows:

	Book Value	Fair Value	Fair Value Increment
Inventory	$ 60,000	$ 65,000	$ 5,000
Land	40,000	50,000	10,000
Buildings and Equipment	300,000	360,000	60,000
	$400,000	$475,000	$75,000

Of the $87,500 total differential, $75,000 relates to identifiable assets of Special Foods. The remaining $12,500 is attributable to goodwill. The apportionment of the differential appears as follows: The entire amount of inventory to which the differential relates is sold during 20X1; none is left in ending inventory. The buildings and equipment have a remaining economic life of 10 years from the date of combination, and Special Foods uses straight-line depreciation. At the end of 20X1, Peerless' management determines that the goodwill acquired in the combination with Special Foods has been impaired. Management determines that a $3,000 goodwill impairment loss should be recognized in the consolidated income statement.

For the first year immediately after the date of combination, 20X1, Peerless Products earns income from its own separate operations of $140,000 and pays dividends of $60,000. Special Foods reports net income of $50,000 and pays dividends of $30,000.

Parent Company Entries

During 20X1, Peerless makes the normal equity-method entries on its books to record its purchase of Special Foods stock and its income and dividends from Special Foods:

(10)	Investment in Special Foods	387,500	
	Cash		300,000
	Notes Payable		87,500

Record the initial investment in Special Foods.

(11)	Investment in Special Foods	50,000	
	Income from Special Foods		50,000

Record Peerless' 100% share of Special Foods' 20X1 income.

(12)	Cash	30,000	
	Investment in Special Foods		30,000

Record Peerless' 100% share of Special Foods' 20X1 dividend.

In this case, Peerless paid an amount for its investment that was $87,500 in excess of the book value of the shares acquired. As discussed previously, this difference is a differential that is implicit in the amount recorded in the investment account on Peerless' books. Because Peerless acquired 100 percent of Special Foods' stock, Peerless' differential included in its investment account is equal to the total differential arising from the business combination. However, while the differential arising from the business combination must be allocated to specific assets and liabilities in consolidation, the differential on Peerless' books does not appear separate from the Investment in Special Foods account. A portion of the differential ($5,000) in the investment account on Peerless' books relates to a portion of Special Foods' inventory that is sold during 20X1. Because the asset to which that portion of the differential relates is no longer held by Special Foods at year-end, that portion of the differential is written off by reducing the investment account and Peerless' income from Special Foods. An additional $60,000 of the differential is attributable to the excess of the acquisition-date fair value over book value of Special Foods' buildings and equipment. As the service potential of the underlying assets expires, Peerless must amortize the additional cost it incurred because of the higher fair value of those assets. This is accomplished through annual amortization of \$6,000 (\$60,000 ÷ 10) over the remaining 10-year life beginning in 20X1. Finally, the goodwill is deemed to be impaired by \$3,000 and is also adjusted on Peerless' books.[4] Thus, the differential must be written off on Peerless' books to recognize the cost expiration related to the service expiration of Special Foods' assets to which it relates. Under the full equity-method, the differential is written off periodically from the investment account to Income from Special Foods to reflect these changes in the differential (\$5,000 inventory + \$6,000 depreciation + \$3,000 goodwill impairment = \$14,000):

(13)	Income from Special Foods	14,000	
	Investment in Special Foods		14,000

Record amortization of excess acquisition price.

Consolidation Worksheet—Year of Combination

The following diagrams illustrate the breakdown of the book value and excess value components of the investment account at the beginning and end of the year.

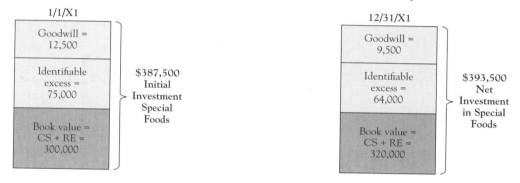

The book value component can be summarized as follows:

Book Value Calculations:

	Total Investment	=	Common Stock	+	Retained Earnings
Original book value	300,000		200,000		100,000
+ Net Income	50,000				50,000
– Dividends	(30,000)				(30,000)
Ending book value	320,000		200,000		120,000

This chart leads to the basic elimination entry. Note that we shade the numbers that appear in the elimination entry with a lighter font color to help the reader see how to construct the elimination entry.

Basic elimination entry:

Common stock	200,000		← Original amount invested (100%)
Retained earnings	100,000		← Beginning balance in RE
Income from Special Foods	50,000		← Special Foods' reported income
Dividends declared		30,000	← 100% of Special Foods' dividends
Investment in Special Foods		320,000	← Net BV in investment account

---

[4] Although the goodwill will be written down and a goodwill impairment loss recognized when preparing consolidated financial statements, the FASB has indicated that no equity-method adjustment should be made to reflect this impairment of goodwill. Some would argue that it would be inappropriate to treat the goodwill impairment in the same way as the other excess value components. However, for simplicity, since the investment account is eliminated in consolidation anyway, we choose to treat goodwill impairment like all other excess value components.

We then analyze the differential and its changes during the period:

Excess Value (Differential) Calculations:

	Total	= Inventory +	Land +	Building +	Acc. Depr. +	Goodwill
Beginning balance	87,500	5,000	10,000	60,000	0	12,500
− Changes	(14,000)	(5,000)			(6,000)	(3,000)
Ending balance	73,500	0	10,000	60,000	(6,000)	9,500

The entire differential amount assigned to the inventory already passed through cost of goods sold during the year. The only other amortization item—the excess value assigned to the building—is amortized over a 10-year period ($60,000 ÷ 10 = $6,000 per year). Finally, the goodwill is deemed to be impaired and worth only $9,500. Since the amortization of the differential was already written off from the investment account against the Income from Special Foods account, the changes are simply reclassified from the Income from Special Foods account to the various income statement accounts to which they apply during the consolidation process:

Amortized excess value reclassification entry:

Cost of goods sold	5,000	← Extra cost of goods sold
Depreciation expense	6,000	← Depreciation of excess building value
Goodwill impairment loss	3,000	← Goodwill impairment
Income from Special Foods	14,000	← See calculation above

Finally, the remaining unamortized differential is reclassified to the correct accounts based on the ending balances in the chart above:

Excess value (differential) reclassification entry:

Land	10,000	← Original calculated excess value.
Building	60,000	← Original calculated excess value.
Goodwill	9,500	← Calculated value from acquisition.
Accumulated depreciation	6,000	← = 60,000 ÷ 10 years
Investment in Special Foods	73,500	← Remaining balance in differential

In sum, these worksheet entries (1) eliminate the balances in the Investment in Special Foods and Income from Special Foods accounts, (2) reclassify the amortization of excess

	Inv. in Special Foods				Inc. from Special Foods	
Acquisition Price	387,500					
Net Income	50,000				50,000	80% Net Income
		30,000	Dividends			
		14,000	Excess Value	14,000		
			Amortization			
Ending Balance	393,500				36,000	Ending Balance
		320,000	Basic	50,000		
		73,500	Excess Reclass.		14,000	Excess Value
	0				0	

FIGURE 4–4 December 31, 20X1, Equity-Method Worksheet for Consolidated Financial Statements, Initial Year of Ownership; 100 Percent Acquisition at More than Book Value

	Peerless Products	Special Foods	Elimination Entries		Consolidated
			DR	CR	
Income Statement					
Sales	400,000	200,000			600,000
Less: COGS	(170,000)	(115,000)	5,000		(290,000)
Less: Depreciation Expense	(50,000)	(20,000)	6,000		(76,000)
Less: Other Expenses	(40,000)	(15,000)			(55,000)
Less: Impairment Loss			3,000		(3,000)
Income from Special Foods	36,000		50,000	14,000	0
Net Income	**176,000**	**50,000**	**64,000**	**14,000**	**176,000**
Statement of Retained Earnings					
Beginning Balance	300,000	100,000	100,000		300,000
Net Income	**176,000**	**50,000**	64,000	14,000	176,000
Less Dividends Declared	(60,000)	(30,000)		30,000	(60,000)
Ending Balance	**416,000**	**120,000**	**164,000**	**44,000**	**416,000**
Balance Sheet					
Cash	122,500	75,000			197,500
Accounts Receivable	75,000	50,000			125,000
Inventory	100,000	75,000			175,000
Investment in Special Foods	393,500			320,000	0
				73,500	
Land	175,000	40,000	10,000		225,000
Buildings & Equipment	800,000	600,000	60,000	300,000	1,160,000
Less Accumulated Depreciation	(450,000)	(320,000)	300,000	6,000	(476,000)
Goodwill			9,500		9,500
Total Assets	**1,216,000**	**520,000**	**379,500**	**699,500**	**1,416,000**
Accounts Payable	100,000	100,000			200,000
Bonds Payable	200,000	100,000			300,000
Common Stock	500,000	200,000	200,000		500,000
Retained Earnings	**416,000**	**120,000**	**164,000**	**44,000**	416,000
Total Liabilities & Equity	**1,216,000**	**520,000**	**364,000**	**44,000**	**1,416,000**

value to the proper income statement accounts, and (3) reclassify the remaining differential to the appropriate balance sheet accounts as of the end of the period.

As usual, we eliminate Special Foods' acquisition date accumulated depreciation against the Buildings and Equipment balance so that it will appear as if these fixed assets were recorded at their acquisition date fair values.

Optional accumulated depreciation elimination entry:

Accumulated depreciation	300,000	
Building and equipment		300,000

← Original depreciation at the time of the acquisition netted against cost

After the subsidiary income accruals are entered on Peerless' books, the adjusted trial balance data of the consolidating companies are entered in the three-part consolidation worksheet as shown in Figure 4–4. We note that because all inventory on hand on the date of combination has been sold during the year, the $5,000 of differential applicable to inventory is allocated directly to cost of goods sold. The cost of goods sold recorded on the books of Special Foods is correct for that company's separate financial statements. However, the cost of the inventory to the consolidated entity is viewed as being $5,000 higher, and this additional cost must be included in consolidated cost of goods sold. No worksheet entry is needed in future periods with respect to the inventory because the inventory has been expensed and no longer is on the subsidiary's books. The portion of the differential related to the inventory no longer exists on Peerless' books after 20X1 because it is removed from the investment account by the second elimination entry.

The differential assigned to depreciable assets must be charged to depreciation expense over the remaining lives of those assets. From a consolidated viewpoint, the acquisition-date fair value increment associated with the depreciable assets acquired becomes part of the assets' depreciation base. Depreciation already is recorded on the subsidiary's books based on the original cost of the assets to the subsidiary, and these amounts are carried to the consolidation worksheet as depreciation expense.

The difference between the $387,500 fair value of the consideration exchanged and the $375,000 fair value of Special Foods' net identifiable assets is assumed to be related to the excess earning power of Special Foods. This difference is entered in the worksheet in Figure 4–4. A distinction must be made between journal entries recorded on the parent's books under equity-method reporting and the eliminating entries needed in the worksheet to prepare the consolidated financial statements. Again, we distinguish between actual equity-method journal entries on the parent's books (not shaded) and worksheet elimination entries (shaded).

Consolidated Net Income and Retained Earnings

As can be seen from the worksheet in Figure 4–4, consolidated net income for 20X1 is $176,000 and consolidated retained earnings on December 31, 20X1, is $416,000. These amounts can be computed as shown in Figure 4–5.

Second Year of Ownership

The consolidation procedures employed at the end of the second year, and in periods thereafter, are basically the same as those used at the end of the first year. Consolidation two years after acquisition is illustrated by continuing the example used for 20X1. During 20X2, Peerless Products earns income from its own separate operations of $160,000 and pays dividends of $60,000; Special Foods reports net income of $75,000 and pays dividends of $40,000. No further impairment of the goodwill from the business combination occurs during 20X2.

FIGURE 4–5
Consolidated Net Income and Retained Earnings, 20X1; 100 Percent Acquisition at More than Book Value

Consolidated net income, 20X1:	
Peerless' separate operating income	$140,000
Special Foods' net income	50,000
Write-off of differential related to inventory sold during 20X1	(5,000)
Amortization of differential related to buildings and equipment in 20X1	(6,000)
Goodwill impairment loss	(3,000)
Consolidated net income, 20X1	$176,000
Consolidated retained earnings, December 31, 20X1:	
Peerless' retained earnings on date of combination, January 1, 20X1	$300,000
Peerless' separate operating income, 20X1	140,000
Special Foods' 20X1 net income	50,000
Write-off of differential related to inventory sold during 20X1	(5,000)
Amortization of differential related to buildings and equipment in 20X1	(6,000)
Goodwill impairment loss	(3,000)
Dividends declared by Peerless, 20X1	(60,000)
Consolidated retained earnings, December 31, 20X1	$416,000

Parent Company Entries

Peerless Products records the following entries on its separate books during 20X2:

(14)	Investment in Special Foods	75,000	
	Income from Special Foods		75,000
	Record Peerless' 100% share of Special Foods' 20X2 income.		

(15)	Cash	40,000	
	Investment in Special Foods		40,000
	Record Peerless' 100% share of Special Foods' 20X2 dividend.		

(16)	Income from Special Foods	6,000	
	Investment in Special Foods		6,000
	Record amortization of excess acquisition price.		

The changes in the parent's investment account during 20X2 can be summarized as follows:

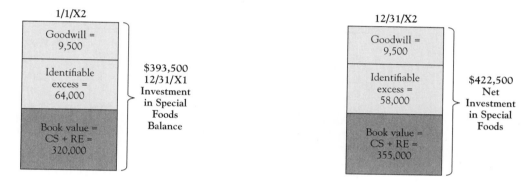

The book value component can be summarized as follows:

Book Value Calculations:

	Total Investment	=	Common Stock	+	Retained Earnings
Original book value	320,000		200,000		120,000
+ Net Income	75,000				75,000
− Dividends	(40,000)				(40,000)
Ending book value	355,000		200,000		155,000

The light-shaded numbers in this chart determine the basic elimination entry:

Basic elimination entry:

Common stock	200,000		← Original amount invested (100%)
Retained earnings	120,000		← Beginning balance in RE
Income from Special Foods	75,000		← Special Foods' reported income
Dividends declared		40,000	← 100% of Special Foods' dividends
Investment in Special Foods		355,000	← Net BV in investment account

The entire differential amount assigned to the inventory already passed through cost of goods sold during the prior year period. The only other amortization item is the excess value assigned to the building, which continues to be written off over a 10-year period ($60,000 \div 10 = \$6,000$) as illustrated in the following chart.

Excess Value (Differential) Calculations:

	Total	=	Land	+	Building	+	Acc. Depr.	+	Goodwill
Beginning balance	73,500		10,000		60,000		(6,000)		9,500
Changes	(6,000)						(6,000)		
Ending balance	67,500		10,000		60,000		(12,000)		9,500

Since the amortization of the differential was already written off from the investment account against the Income from Special Foods account, the change to the differential is simply reclassified from the Income from Special Foods account to the income statement account to which it applies during the consolidation process. Then, the remaining amount of the differential at year end is reclassified to the various balance sheet accounts to which they apply:

Amortized excess value reclassification entry:

Depreciation expense	6,000	← Extra depreciation expense
Income from Special Foods		6,000 ← See calculation above.

Excess value (differential) reclassification entry:

Land	10,000	← Original calculated excess value.
Building	60,000	← Original calculated excess value.
Goodwill	9,500	← Calculated value from acquisition.
Accumulated depreciation		12,000 ← = (60,000 ÷ 10 years) × 2 years
Investment in Special Foods		67,500 ← Remaining balance in differential

These elimination entries, (1) eliminate the balances in the Investment in Special Foods and Income from Special Foods accounts, (2) reclassify the amortization of excess value to the proper income statement accounts, and (3) reclassify the remaining differential to the appropriate balance sheet accounts as of the end of the accounting period. The following T-accounts illustrate how the three elimination entries "zero out" the equity-method investment and income accounts:

	Inv. in Special Foods				Inc. from Special Foods	
Acquisition Price	393,500					
Net Income	75,000				75,000	Net Income
		40,000	Dividends			
		6,000	Excess Price	6,000		
			Amortization			
Ending Balance	422,500				69,000	Ending Balance
		355,000	Basic	75,000		
		67,500	Excess Reclass.		6,000	Excess Value
	0				0	

Again, we repeat the same accumulated depreciation elimination entry this year (and every year as long as Special Foods owns the assets) that we used in the initial year.

Optional accumulated depreciation elimination entry:

Accumulated depreciation	300,000	← Original depreciation at the time of
Building and equipment		300,000 the acquisition netted against cost

FIGURE 4–6 December 31, 20X2, Equity-Method Worksheet for Consolidated Financial Statements, Second Year of Ownership; 100 Percent Acquisition at More than Book Value

	Peerless Products	Special Foods	Elimination Entries DR	Elimination Entries CR	Consolidated
Income Statement					
Sales	450,000	300,000			750,000
Less: COGS	(180,000)	(160,000)			(340,000)
Less: Depreciation Expense	(50,000)	(20,000)	6,000		(76,000)
Less: Other Expenses	(60,000)	(45,000)			(105,000)
Less: Impairment Loss					0
Income from Special Foods	69,000		75,000	6,000	0
Net Income	**229,000**	**75,000**	**81,000**	**6,000**	**229,000**
Statement of Retained Earnings					
Beginning Balance	416,000	120,000	120,000		416,000
Net Income	**229,000**	**75,000**	**81,000**	**6,000**	229,000
Less Dividends Declared	(60,000)	(40,000)		40,000	(60,000)
Ending Balance	**585,000**	**155,000**	**201,000**	**46,000**	**585,000**
Balance Sheet					
Cash	157,500	85,000			242,500
Accounts Receivable	150,000	80,000			230,000
Inventory	180,000	90,000			270,000
Investment in Special Foods	422,500			355,000	0
				67,500	
Land	175,000	40,000	10,000		225,000
Buildings & Equipment	800,000	600,000	60,000	300,000	1,160,000
Less Accumulated Depreciation	(500,000)	(340,000)	300,000	12,000	(552,000)
Goodwill			9,500		9,500
Total Assets	**1,385,000**	**555,000**	**379,500**	**734,500**	**1,585,000**
Accounts Payable	100,000	100,000			200,000
Bonds Payable	200,000	100,000			300,000
Common Stock	500,000	200,000	200,000		500,000
Retained Earnings	**585,000**	**155,000**	**201,000**	**46,000**	585,000
Total Liabilities & Equity	**1,385,000**	**555,000**	**401,000**	**46,000**	**1,585,000**

Consolidation Worksheet—Second Year Following Combination

The worksheet for the second year, 20X2, completes the two-year cycle as illustrated in Figure 4–6. Moreover, as can be seen from the worksheet, consolidated net income for 20X2 is $229,000 and consolidated retained earnings on December 31, 20X2, is $585,000 as illustrated in Figure 4–7.

FIGURE 4–7
Consolidated Net Income and Retained Earnings, 20X2; 100 Percent Acquisition at More than Book Value

Consolidated net income, 20X2:	
Peerless' separate operating income	$160,000
Special Foods' net income	75,000
Amortization of differential related to buildings and equipment in 20X2	(6,000)
Consolidated net income, 20X2	$229,000
Consolidated retained earnings, December 31, 20X2:	
Consolidated retained earnings, December 31, 20X1	$416,000
Peerless' separate operating income, 20X2	160,000
Special Foods' 20X2 net income	75,000
Amortization of differential related to buildings and equipment in 20X2	(6,000)
Dividends declared by Peerless, 20X2	(60,000)
Consolidated retained earnings, December 31, 20X2	$585,000

INTERCOMPANY RECEIVABLES AND PAYABLES

LO6

Understand and explain the elimination of basic intercompany transactions.

All forms of intercompany receivables and payables need to be eliminated when consolidated financial statements are prepared. From a single-company viewpoint, a company cannot owe itself money. If a company owes an affiliate $1,000 on account, one company carries a $1,000 receivable on its separate books and the other has a payable for the same amount. When consolidated financial statements are prepared, the following elimination entry is needed in the consolidation worksheet:

Accounts Payable	1,000	
Accounts Receivable		1,000

Eliminate intercompany receivable/payable.

If no eliminating entry is made, both the consolidated assets and liabilities are overstated by an equal amount.

If the intercompany receivable/payable bears interest, all accounts related to the intercompany claim must be eliminated in the preparation of consolidated statements, including the receivable/payable, interest income, interest expense, and any accrued interest on the intercompany claim. Other forms of intercorporate claims, such as bonds, are discussed in subsequent chapters. In all cases, failure to eliminate these claims can distort consolidated balances. As a result, the magnitude of debt of the combined entity may appear to be greater than it is, working capital ratios may be incorrect, and other types of comparisons may be distorted.

PUSH-DOWN ACCOUNTING

LO7

Understand and explain the basics of push-down accounting.

The term *push-down accounting* refers to the practice of revaluing an acquired subsidiary's assets and liabilities to their fair values directly on that subsidiary's books at the date of acquisition. If this practice is followed, the revaluations are recorded once on the subsidiary's books at the date of acquisition and, therefore, are not made in the consolidation worksheets each time consolidated statements are prepared.

Those who favor push-down accounting argue that the change in the subsidiary's ownership in an acquisition is reason for adopting a new basis of accounting for the subsidiary's assets and liabilities, and this new basis of accounting should be reflected directly on the subsidiary's books. This argument is most persuasive when the subsidiary is wholly owned, is consolidated, or has its separate financial statements included with the parent's statements.

On the other hand, when a subsidiary has a significant noncontrolling interest or the subsidiary has bonds or preferred stock held by the public, push-down accounting may be inappropriate. The use of push-down accounting in the financial statements issued to the noncontrolling shareholders or to those holding bonds or preferred stock results in a new basis of accounting even though, from the perspective of those statement users, the entity has not changed. From their viewpoint, push-down accounting results in the revaluation of the assets and liabilities of a continuing enterprise, a practice that normally is not acceptable.

SEC Staff Accounting Bulletin No. 54 requires push-down accounting whenever a business combination results in the acquired subsidiary becoming substantially wholly owned. The staff accounting bulletin encourages but does not require the use of push-down accounting in situations in which the subsidiary is less than wholly owned or the subsidiary has outstanding debt or preferred stock held by the public.

The revaluation of assets and liabilities on a subsidiary's books involves making an entry to debit or credit each asset and liability account to be revalued, with the balancing entry to a revaluation capital account. The revaluation capital account is part of the subsidiary's stockholders' equity. Once the revaluations are made on the books of the subsidiary, the new book values of the subsidiary's assets, including goodwill, are equal to the acquisition cost of the subsidiary. Thus, no differential arises in the consolidation process. The investment elimination entry in a consolidation worksheet prepared immediately after acquisition of a subsidiary and revaluation of its assets on its books might appear as follows:

Capital Stock—Subsidiary	XXX	
Retained Earnings	XXX	
Revaluation Capital	XXX	
Investment in Subsidiary Stock		XXX

Eliminate investment balance.

Note that the Revaluation Capital account, as part of the subsidiary's stockholders' equity, is eliminated in preparing consolidated statements. We provide a more detailed example of push-down accounting in Appendix 4A.

Summary of Key Concepts

Eliminating entries are needed in the worksheet to remove the effects of intercompany ownership and intercompany transactions so the consolidated financial statements appear as if the separate companies are actually one. Worksheet eliminating entries are needed to (1) eliminate the book value portion of the parent's subsidiary investment and the subsidiary's stockholders' equity accounts, (2) reclassify the amortization of excess value from the parent's income from subsidiary account to the correct income statement line items, (3) assign any remaining differential to specific assets and liabilities, and (4) net the original accumulated depreciation of the subsidiary as of the acquisition date against the historical cost of property, plant, and equipment.

Consolidated net income is computed in simple cases for a parent and a wholly owned subsidiary as the total of the parent's income from its own operations and the subsidiary's net income, adjusted for the write-off of differential, if appropriate. In this situation, consolidated retained earnings is computed as the total of the parent's retained earnings, excluding any income from the subsidiary, plus the subsidiary's cumulative net income since acquisition.

When a subsidiary is acquired for an amount greater than its book value, some parents may prefer to assign the differential to individual assets and liabilities directly on the books of the subsidiary at the time of acquisition, thereby eliminating the need for revaluation entries in the consolidation worksheet each period. This procedure is called push-down accounting.

Key Terms

bargain purchase, *169*
differential, *159*

goodwill, *166*

push-down accounting, *165*

Appendix 4A   Push-Down Accounting Illustrated

When a subsidiary is acquired in a business combination, its assets and liabilities must be revalued to their fair values as of the date of combination for consolidated reporting. If *push-down accounting* is employed, the revaluations are made as of the date of combination directly on the books of the subsidiary and no eliminating entries related to the differential are needed in the worksheets.

The following example illustrates the consolidation process when assets and liabilities are revalued directly on a subsidiary's books rather than using consolidation worksheet entries to accomplish the revaluation. Assume that Peerless Products purchases all of Special Foods' common stock on January 1, 20X1, for $370,000 cash. The purchase price is $70,000 in excess of Special Foods' book value. Of the $70,000 total differential, $10,000 is related to land held by Special Foods and $60,000 is related to buildings and equipment having a 10-year remaining life. Peerless accounts for its investment in Special Foods stock using the equity-method.

Peerless records the acquisition of stock on its books with the following entry:

(17)	Investment in Special Foods	370,000	
	Cash		370,000

Record the initial investment in Special Foods.

In contrast to a worksheet revaluation, the use of push-down accounting involves the revaluation of the assets on the separate books of Special Foods and alleviates the need for revaluation entries in the consolidation worksheet each period. If push-down accounting is used to revalue Special Foods' assets, the following entry is made directly on Special Foods' books:

(18)	Land	10,000	
	Buildings and Equipment	60,000	
	Revaluation Capital		70,000

Record the increase in fair value of land and buildings.

This entry increases the amount at which the land and the buildings and equipment are shown in Special Foods' separate financial statements and gives rise to a revaluation capital account that is shown in the stockholders' equity section of Special Foods' balance sheet. Special Foods records $6,000 additional depreciation on its books to reflect the amortization over 10 years of the $60,000 write-up of buildings and equipment. This additional depreciation decreases Special Foods' reported net income for 20X1 from $50,000 to $44,000.

Peerless records its income and dividends from Special Foods on its parent-company books:

(19)	Investment in Special Foods	44,000	
	Income from Special Foods		44,000

Record Peerless' 100% share of Special Foods' 20X1 income.

(20)	Cash	30,000	
	Investment in Special Foods		30,000

Record Peerless' 100% share of Special Foods' 20X1 dividend.

The equity-method income recorded by Peerless is less than had push-down accounting not been employed because Special Foods' income is reduced by the additional depreciation on the write-up of the buildings and equipment recorded on Special Foods' books. Because the revaluation is recorded on the subsidiary's books, Special Foods' book value is then equal to the fair value of the consideration given in the combination. Therefore, no differential exists, and Peerless need not record any amortization associated with the investment. The net amount of income from Special Foods recorded by Peerless is the same regardless of whether or not push-down accounting is employed. The book value portion of the investment account can be summarized as follows:

Book Value Calculations:

	Total Investment	=	Common Stock	+	Retained Earnings	+	Revaluation Capital
Original book value	370,000		200,000		100,000		70,000
+ Net Income	44,000				44,000		
− Dividends	(30,000)				(30,000)		
Ending book value	384,000		200,000		114,000		70,000

The basic elimination entry is very similar to the original example presented previously except that it must also eliminate Special Foods' revaluation capital account and the income from Special Foods is $6,000 lower due to the extra depreciation on the revalued building:

Basic elimination entry:

Common stock	200,000	
Retained earnings	100,000	
Revaluation Capital	70,000	
Income from Special Foods	44,000	
Dividends declared		30,000
Investment in Special Foods		384,000

Again, since there is no differential in this example, the basic elimination entry completely elimi-nates the balance in Peerless' investment account on the balance sheet as well as the Income from Special Foods account on the income statement.

	Investment in Special Foods			Income from Special Foods	
Acquisition Price	370,000				
Net Income	44,000			44,000	Net Income
		30,000	Dividends		
Ending Balance	384,000			44,000	Ending Balance
		384,000	Basic	44,000	
	0			0	

In addition, we include the normal accumulated depreciation elimination entry:

Optional accumulated depreciation elimination entry:

Accumulated depreciation	300,000	
Building and equipment		300,000

Figure 4–8 shows the consolidation worksheet prepared at the end of 20X1 and includes the effects of revaluing Special Foods' assets. Note that Special Foods' Land and Buildings and Equipment have been increased by $10,000 and $60,000, respectively. Also note the Revaluation

FIGURE 4–8 December 31, 20X1, Equity-Method Worksheet for Consolidated Financial Statements, Initial Year of Ownership; 100 Percent Acquisition at More than Book Value; Push-Down Accounting

	Peerless Products	Special Foods	Eliminating Entries		Consolidated
			DR	CR	
Income Statement					
Sales	400,000	200,000			600,000
Less: COGS	(170,000)	(115,000)			(285,000)
Less: Depreciation Expense	(50,000)	(26,000)			(76,000)
Less: Other Expenses	(40,000)	(15,000)			(55,000)
Income from Special Foods	44,000		44,000		0
Net Income	184,000	44,000	44,000	0	184,000
Statement of Retained Earnings					
Beginning Balance	300,000	100,000	100,000		300,000
Net Income	184,000	44,000	44,000	0	184,000
Less: Dividends Declared	(60,000)	(30,000)		30,000	(60,000)
Ending Balance	424,000	114,000	144,000	30,000	424,000
Balance Sheet					
Cash	140,000	75,000			215,000
Accounts Receivable	75,000	50,000			125,000
Inventory	100,000	75,000			175,000
Investment in Special Foods	384,000			384,000	0
Land	175,000	50,000			225,000
Buildings & Equipment	800,000	660,000		300,000	1,160,000
Less: Accumulated Depreciation	(450,000)	(326,000)	300,000		(476,000)
Total Assets	1,224,000	584,000	300,000	684,000	1,424,000
Accounts Payable	100,000	100,000			200,000
Bonds Payable	200,000	100,000			300,000
Common Stock	500,000	200,000	200,000		500,000
Retained Earnings	424,000	114,000	144,000	30,000	424,000
Revaluation Capital		70,000	70,000		0
Total Liabilities & Equity	1,224,000	584,000	414,000	30,000	1,424,000

Capital account in Special Foods' stockholders' equity. Because the revaluation was accomplished directly on the books of Special Foods, only the basic and the accumulated depreciation elimination entries are needed in the worksheet illustrated in Figure 4–8.

Questions

LO1   **Q4-1**   When is the carrying value of the investment account reduced under equity-method reporting?

LO1   **Q4-2**   What is a differential? How is a differential treated by an investor in computing income from an investee under (*a*) cost-method and (*b*) equity-method reporting?

LO1   **Q4-3**   Turner Manufacturing Corporation owns 100 percent of the common shares of Straight Lace Company. If Straight Lace reports net income of $100,000 for 20X5, what factors may cause Turner to report less than $100,000 of income from the investee?

LO1   **Q4-4**   What is the term *differential* used to indicate?

LO1   **Q4-5**   What conditions must exist for a negative differential to occur?

LO2   **Q4-6**   What portion of the book value of the net assets held by a subsidiary at acquisition is included in the consolidated balance sheet?

LO2   **Q4-7**   What portion of the fair value of a subsidiary's net assets normally is included in the consolidated balance sheet following a business combination?

LO3   **Q4-8**   What happens to the differential in the consolidation worksheet prepared as of the date of combination? How is it reestablished so that the proper balances can be reported the following year?

LO2   **Q4-9**   Explain why consolidated financial statements become increasingly important when the differential is very large.

LO3   **Q4-10**   Give a definition of *consolidated net income.*

LO5   **Q4-11**   When Ajax was preparing its consolidation worksheet, the differential was properly assigned to buildings and equipment. What additional entry generally must be made in the worksheet?

LO3, LO4   **Q4-12**   What determines whether the balance assigned to the differential remains constant or decreases each period?

LO7   **Q4-13**   What does the term *push-down accounting* mean?

LO7   **Q4-14**   Under what conditions is push-down accounting considered appropriate?

LO7   **Q4-15**   What happens to the differential when push-down accounting is used following a business combination?

Cases

LO1   **C4-1**   **Reporting Significant Investments in Common Stock**

Analysis   The reporting treatment for investments in common stock depends on the level of ownership and the ability to influence policies of the investee. The reporting treatment may even change over time as ownership levels or other factors change. When investees are not consolidated, the investments typically are reported in the Investments section of the investor's balance sheet. However, the investor's income from those investments is not always easy to find in the investor's income statement.

Required

a. Harley-Davidson, Inc., holds an investment in the common stock of Buell Motorcycle Company. How did Harley-Davidson report this investment before 1998? How does it report the investment now? Why did Harley change its method of reporting its investment in Buell?

b. How does Chevron Corporation account for its investments in affiliated companies? How does the company account for issuances of additional stock by affiliates that change the company's proportionate dollar share of the affiliates' equity? How does Chevron treat a differential associated with an equity-method investment? How does Chevron account for the impairment of an equity investment?

c. Prior to 1999, where did PepsiCo report its share of the net income or loss of its unconsolidated affiliates over which it exercised significant influence but not control? What rationale might be given for this treatment? How does PepsiCo now report this type of income?

d. Does Sears have any investments in companies that it accounts for using the equity-method? Where are these investments reported in the balance sheet, and where is the income from these investments reported in the income statement?

LO2

C4-2 Assigning an Acquisition Differential

Analysis

Ball Corporation's owners recently offered to sell 100 percent of their ownership to Timber Corporation for $450,000. Timber's business manager was told that Ball's book value was $300,000, and she estimates the fair value of its net assets at approximately $600,000. Ball has relatively old equipment and manufacturing facilities and uses a LIFO basis for inventory valuation of some items and a FIFO basis for others.

Required

If Timber accepts the offer and acquires a controlling interest in Ball, what difficulties are likely to be encountered in assigning the differential?

LO2

C4-3 Negative Retained Earnings

Understanding

Although Sloan Company had good earnings reports in 20X5 and 20X6, it had a negative retained earnings balance on December 31, 20X6. Jacobs Corporation purchased 100 percent of Sloan's common stock on January 1, 20X7.

Required

a. Explain how Sloan's negative retained earnings balance is reflected in the consolidated balance sheet immediately following the acquisition.

b. Explain how the existence of negative retained earnings changes the consolidation worksheet entries.

c. Can goodwill be recorded if Jacobs pays more than book value for Sloan's shares? Explain.

LO1

C4-4 Balance Sheet Reporting Issues

Judgment

Crumple Car Rentals is planning to expand into the western part of the United States and needs to acquire approximately 400 additional automobiles for rental purposes. Because Crumple's cash reserves were substantially depleted in replacing the bumpers on existing automobiles with new "fashion plate" bumpers, the expansion funds must be acquired through other means. Crumple's management has identified three options:

1. Issue additional debt.

2. Create a wholly owned leasing subsidiary that would borrow the money with a guarantee for payment from Crumple. The subsidiary would then lease the cars to the parent.

3. Create a trust that would borrow the money with a guarantee for repayment from Crumple and lease the cars to it. In the event of liquidation, the residual value of the trust would go to the Historical Preservation Society of Pleasantville.

The acquisition price of the cars is approximately the same under all three alternatives.

Required

a. You have been asked to compare and contrast the three alternatives from the perspective of

(1) The impact on Crumple's consolidated balance sheet.

(2) Their legal ramifications.

(3) The ability to control the maintenance, repair, and replacement of automobiles.

b. You are to consider any alternatives that might be used in acquiring the required automobiles.

c. You are to select the preferred alternative and show why it is the best choice.

LO1

C4-5 Subsidiary Ownership: AMR Corporation and International Lease

Research

Most subsidiaries are wholly owned, although only majority ownership is usually all that is required for consolidation. The parent's ownership may be direct or indirect. Frequently, a parent's direct subsidiaries have subsidiaries of their own, thus providing the parent with indirect ownership of the subsidiary's subsidiaries.

Required

a. AMR Corporation is one of the largest corporations in the United States, with significant visibility.

   (1) What is AMR Corporation's principal business?

   (2) What is the name of AMR's principal directly owned subsidiary?

   (3) In what city is AMR headquartered?

   (4) In what state is AMR incorporated?

   (5) Where are most of AMR's subsidiaries incorporated?

   (6) Where is AMR's common stock traded?

   (7) How many subsidiaries, if any, does AMR's principal subsidiary have?

   (8) Approximately what percentage of AMR's subsidiaries are wholly owned?

b. International Lease Finance Corporation is a very large leasing company. It leases equipment that everyone is familiar with and many have used.

   (1) Specifically, what is the principal business of International Lease Finance Corporation?

   (2) Who are the direct owners of International Lease?

   (3) In what city is International Lease headquartered?

   (4) In what state is International Lease incorporated?

   (5) Where is International Lease's common stock traded?

   (6) What company is the parent in the consolidated financial statements in which International Lease is included, and what is that company's principal business?

Exercises

LO1

E4-1 Cost versus Equity Reporting

Roller Corporation purchased 100 percent ownership of Steam Company on January 1, 20X5, for $270,000. On that date, the book value of Steam's reported net assets was $200,000. The excess over book value paid is attributable to depreciable assets with a remaining useful life of 10 years. Net income and dividend payments of Steam in the following periods were

Year	Net Income	Dividends
20X5	$20,000	$ 5,000
20X6	40,000	15,000
20X7	20,000	35,000

Required

Prepare journal entries on Roller Corporation's books relating to its investment in Steam Company for each of the three years, assuming it accounts for the investment using (a) the cost method and (b) the equity-method.

LO1

E4-2 Differential Assigned to Patents

Power Corporation purchased 100 percent of the common stock of Snow Corporation on January 1, 20X2, by issuing 45,000 shares of its $6 par value common stock. The market price of Power's shares at the date of issue was $24. Snow reported net assets with a book value of $980,000 on that date. The amount paid in excess of the book value of Snow's net assets was attributed to the increased value of patents held by Snow with a remaining useful life of eight years. Snow reported net income of $56,000 and paid dividends of $20,000 in 20X2 and reported a net loss of $44,000 and paid dividends of $10,000 in 20X3.

Required

Assuming that Power Corporation uses the equity-method in accounting for its investment in Snow Corporation, prepare all journal entries for Power for 20X2 and 20X3.

LO1

E4-3 Differential Assigned to Copyrights

Best Corporation acquired 100 percent of the voting common stock of Flair Company on January 1, 20X7, by issuing bonds with a par value and fair value of $670,000 and making a cash payment of $24,000. At the date of acquisition, Flair reported assets of $740,000 and liabilities of $140,000. The book values and fair values of Flair's net assets were equal except for land and copyrights. Flair's land had a fair value $16,000 greater than its book value. All of the remaining purchase price was attributable to the increased value of Flair's copyrights with a remaining useful life of eight years. Flair Company reported a loss of $88,000 in 20X7 and net income of $120,000 in 20X8. Flair paid dividends of $24,000 each year.

Required

Assuming that Best Corporation uses the equity-method in accounting for its investment in Flair Company, prepare all journal entries for Best for 20X7 and 20X8.

LO1

Advanced
StudyGuide
.com

E4-4 Differential Attributable to Depreciable Assets

Capital Corporation purchased 100 percent of Cook Company's stock on January 1, 20X4, for $340,000. On that date, Cook reported net assets of $300,000 valued at historical cost and $340,000 stated at fair value. The difference was due to the increased value of buildings with a remaining life of 10 years. During 20X4 and 20X5 Cook reported net income of $10,000 and $20,000 and paid dividends of $6,000 and $9,000, respectively.

Required

Assuming that Capital Corporation uses (*a*) the equity-method and (*b*) the cost method in accounting for its ownership of Cook Company, give the journal entries that Capital recorded in 20X4 and 20X5.

LO1

E4-5 Investment Income

Brindle Company purchased 100 percent of Monroe Company's voting common stock for $648,000 on January 1, 20X4. At that date, Monroe reported assets of $690,000 and liabilities of $230,000. The book values and fair values of Monroe's assets were equal except for land, which had a fair value $108,000 greater than book value, and equipment, which had a fair value $80,000 greater than book value. The remaining economic life of all depreciable assets at January 1, 20X4, was five years. The amount of the differential assigned to goodwill is not impaired. Monroe reported net income of $68,000 and paid dividends of $34,000 in 20X4.

Required

Compute the amount of investment income to be reported by Brindle for 20X4.

LO1

E4-6 Determination of Purchase Price

Branch Corporation purchased 100 percent of Hardy Company's common stock on January 1, 20X5, and paid $28,000 above book value. The full amount of the additional payment was attributed to amortizable assets with a life of eight years remaining at January 1, 20X5. During 20X5 and 20X6, Hardy reported net income of $33,000 and $6,000 and paid dividends of $15,000 and $12,000, respectively. Branch uses the equity-method in accounting for its investment in Hardy and reported a balance in its investment account of $161,000 on December 31, 20X6.

Required

Compute the amount paid by Branch to purchase Hardy shares.

LO1

E4-7 Correction of Error

During review of the adjusting entries to be recorded on December 31, 20X8, Grand Corporation discovered that it had inappropriately been using the cost method in accounting for its investment in Case Products Corporation. Grand purchased 100 percent ownership of Case Products on January 1, 20X6, for $56,000, at which time Case Products reported retained earnings of $10,000 and capital stock outstanding of $30,000. The differential was attributable to patents with a life of eight years. Income and dividends of Case Products were:

Year	Net Income	Dividends
20X6	$16,000	$6,000
20X7	24,000	8,000
20X8	32,000	8,000

Required

Give the correcting entry required on December 31, 20X8, to properly report the investment under the equity-method, assuming the books have not been closed. Case Products' dividends were declared in early November and paid in early December each year.

E4-8 Differential Assigned to Land and Equipment

Rod Corporation purchased 100 percent ownership of Stafford Corporation on January 1, 20X4, for $65,000, which was $10,000 above the underlying book value. Half the additional amount was attributable to an increase in the value of land held by Stafford, and half was due to an increase in the value of equipment. The equipment had a remaining economic life of five years on January 1, 20X4. During 20X4, Stafford reported net income of $12,000 and paid dividends of $4,500.

Required

Give the journal entries that Rod Corporation recorded during 20X4 related to its investment in Stafford Corporation, assuming Rod uses the equity-method in accounting for its investment.

E4-9 Equity Entries with Goodwill

Turner Corporation reported the following balances at January 1, 20X9:

Advanced
StudyGuide
.com

Item	Book Value	Fair Value
Cash	$ 45,000	$ 45,000
Accounts Receivable	60,000	60,000
Inventory	120,000	130,000
Buildings and Equipment	300,000	240,000
Less: Accumulated Depreciation	(150,000)	
Total Assets	$375,000	$475,000
Accounts Payable	$ 75,000	$ 75,000
Common Stock ($10 par value)	100,000	
Additional Paid-In Capital	30,000	
Retained Earnings	170,000	
Total Liabilities and Equities	$375,000	

On January 1, 20X9, Gross Corporation purchased 100 percent of Turner's stock. All tangible assets had a remaining economic life of 10 years at January 1, 20X9. Both companies use the FIFO inventory method. Turner reported net income of $16,000 in 20X9 and paid dividends of $3,200. Gross uses the equity-method in accounting for its investment in Turner.

Required

Give all journal entries that Gross recorded during 20X9 with respect to its investment assuming Gross paid $437,500 for the ownership of Turner on January 1, 20X9. The amount of the differential assigned to goodwill is not impaired.

E4-10 Multiple-Choice Questions on Consolidation Process

Select the most appropriate answer for each of the following questions.

1. Goodwill is

   a. Seldom reported because it is too difficult to measure.

   b. Reported when more than book value is paid in purchasing another company.

   c. Reported when the fair value of the acquiree is greater than the fair value of the net identifiable assets acquired.

   d. Generally smaller for small companies and increases in amount as the companies acquired increase in size.

2. [AICPA Adapted] Wright Corporation includes several subsidiaries in its consolidated financial statements. In its December 31, 20X2, trial balance, Wright had the following intercompany balances before eliminations:

	Debit	Credit
Current receivable due from Main Company	$ 32,000	
Noncurrent receivable from Main Company	114,000	
Cash advance to Corn Corporation	6,000	
Cash advance from King Company		$ 15,000
Intercompany payable to King Company		101,000

In its December 31, 20X2, consolidated balance sheet, what amount should Wright report as intercompany receivables?

a. $152,000.

b. $146,000.

c. $36,000.

d. $0.

3. Beni Corporation acquired 100 percent of Carr Corporation's outstanding capital stock for $430,000 cash. Immediately before the purchase, the balance sheets of both corporations reported the following:

	Beni	Carr
Assets	$2,000,000	$750,000
Liabilities	$ 750,000	$400,000
Common Stock	1,000,000	310,000
Retained Earnings	250,000	40,000
Liabilities and Stockholders' Equity	$2,000,000	$750,000

At the date of purchase, the fair value of Carr's assets was $50,000 more than the aggregate carrying amounts. In the consolidated balance sheet prepared immediately after the purchase, the consolidated stockholders' equity should amount to

a. $1,680,000.

b. $1,650,000.

c. $1,600,000.

d. $1,250,000.

Note: Questions 4 and 5 are based on the following information:
Nugget Company's balance sheet on December 31, 20X6, was as follows:

Assets		Liabilities and Stockholders' Equity	
Cash	$ 100,000	Current Liabilities	$ 300,000
Accounts Receivable	200,000	Long-Term Debt	500,000
Inventories	500,000	Common Stock (par $1 per share)	100,000
Property, Plant, and Equipment (net)	900,000	Additional Paid-In Capital	200,000
		Retained Earnings	600,000
Total Assets	$1,700,000	Total Liabilities and Stockholders' Equity	$1,700,000

On December 31, 20X6, Gold Company acquired all of Nugget's outstanding common stock for $1,500,000 cash. On that date, the fair (market) value of Nugget's inventories was $450,000, and the fair value of Nugget's property, plant, and equipment was $1,000,000. The fair values of all other assets and liabilities of Nugget were equal to their book values.

4. As a result of Gold's acquisition of Nugget, the consolidated balance sheet of Gold and Nugget should reflect goodwill in the amount of

a. $500,000.

b. $550,000.

c. $600,000.

d. $650,000.

5. Assuming that the balance sheet of Gold (unconsolidated) on December 31, 20X6, reflected retained earnings of $2,000,000, what amount of retained earnings should be shown in the December 31, 20X6, consolidated balance sheet of Gold and its new subsidiary, Nugget?

    a. $2,000,000.

    b. $2,600,000.

    c. $2,800,000.

    d. $3,150,000.

LO3, LO6   **E4-11**   **Multiple-Choice Questions on Consolidation [AICPA Adapted]**

Select the correct answer for each of the following questions.

1. On January 1, 20X1, Prim Inc. acquired all of Scrap Inc.'s outstanding common shares for cash equal to the stock's book value. The carrying amounts of Scrap's assets and liabilities approximated their fair values, except that the carrying amount of its building was more than fair value. In preparing Prim's 20X1 consolidated income statement, which of the following adjustments would be made?

    a. Decrease depreciation expense and recognize goodwill amortization.

    b. Increase depreciation expense and recognize goodwill amortization.

    c. Decrease depreciation expense and recognize no goodwill amortization.

    d. Increase depreciation expense and recognize no goodwill amortization.

2. The first examination of Rudd Corporation's financial statements was made for the year ended December 31, 20X8. The auditor found that Rudd had acquired another company on January 1, 20X8, and had recorded goodwill of $100,000 in connection with this acquisition. Although a friend of the auditor believes the goodwill will last no more than five years, Rudd's management has found no impairment of goodwill during 20X8. In its 20X8 financial statements, Rudd should report

	Amortization Expense	Goodwill
a.	$ 0	$100,000
b.	$100,000	$ 0
c.	$ 20,000	$ 80,000
d.	$ 0	$ 0

3. Consolidated financial statements are being prepared for a parent and its four subsidiaries that have intercompany loans of $100,000 and intercompany profits of $300,000. How much of these intercompany loans and profits should be eliminated?

	Intercompany Loans	Profits
a.	$ 0	$ 0
b.	$ 0	$300,000
c.	$100,000	$ 0
d.	$100,000	$300,000

4. On April 1, 20X8, Plum Inc. paid $1,700,000 for all of Long Corp.'s issued and outstanding common stock. On that date, the costs and fair values of Long's recorded assets and liabilities were as follows:

	Cost	Fair Value
Cash	$ 160,000	$ 160,000
Inventory	480,000	460,000
Property, plant and equipment (net)	980,000	1,040,000
Liabilities	(360,000)	(360,000)
Net assets	$1,260,000	$1,300,000

In Plum's March 31, 20X9, consolidated balance sheet, what amount of goodwill should be reported as a result of this business combination?

a. $360,000.

b. $396,000.

c. $400,000.

d. $440,000.

E4-12   **Eliminating Entries with Differential**

On June 10, 20X8, Tower Corporation acquired 100 percent of Brown Company's common stock. Summarized balance sheet data for the two companies immediately after the stock acquisition are as follows:

Item	Tower Corp.	Brown Company Book Value	Brown Company Fair Value
Cash	$ 15,000	$ 5,000	$ 5,000
Accounts Receivable	30,000	10,000	10,000
Inventory	80,000	20,000	25,000
Buildings and Equipment (net)	120,000	50,000	70,000
Investment in Brown Stock	100,000		
Total	$345,000	$85,000	$110,000
Accounts Payable	$ 25,000	$ 3,000	$ 3,000
Bonds Payable	150,000	25,000	25,000
Common Stock	55,000	20,000	
Retained Earnings	115,000	37,000	
Total	$345,000	$85,000	$ 28,000

Required

a. Give the eliminating entries required to prepare a consolidated balance sheet immediately after the acquisition of Brown Company shares.

b. Explain how eliminating entries differ from other types of journal entries recorded in the normal course of business.

E4-13   **Balance Sheet Consolidation**

Reed Corporation acquired 100 percent of Thorne Corporation's voting common stock on December 31, 20X4, for $395,000. At the date of combination, Thorne reported the following:

Cash	$120,000	Current Liabilities	$ 80,000
Inventory	100,000	Long-Term Liabilities	200,000
Buildings (net)	420,000	Common Stock	120,000
		Retained Earnings	240,000
Total	$640,000	Total	$640,000

At December 31, 20X4, the book values of Thorne's net assets and liabilities approximated their fair values, except for buildings, which had a fair value of $20,000 less than book value, and inventories, which had a fair value $36,000 more than book value.

Required

Reed Corporation wishes to prepare a consolidated balance sheet immediately following the business combination. Give the eliminating entry or entries needed to prepare a consolidated balance sheet at December 31, 20X4.

E4-14   **Acquisition with Differential**

Road Corporation acquired all of Conger Corporation's voting shares on January 1, 20X2, for $470,000. At that time Conger reported common stock outstanding of $80,000 and retained earnings of $130,000. The book values of Conger's assets and liabilities approximated fair values, except for land, which had a book value of $80,000 and a fair value of $100,000, and buildings, which had a book value of $220,000 and a fair value of $400,000. Land and buildings are the only noncurrent assets that Conger holds.

Required

a. Compute the amount of goodwill at the date of acquisition.
b. Give the eliminating entry or entries required immediately following the acquisition to prepare a consolidated balance sheet.

LO5

E4-15 Balance Sheet Worksheet with Differential

Blank Corporation acquired 100 percent of Faith Corporation's common stock on December 31, 20X2, for $189,000. Data from the balance sheets of the two companies included the following amounts as of the date of acquisition:

Item	Blank Corporation	Faith Corporation
Cash	$ 26,000	$ 18,000
Accounts Receivable	87,000	37,000
Inventory	110,000	60,000
Buildings and Equipment (net)	220,000	150,000
Investment in Faith Corporation Stock	189,000	
Total Assets	$632,000	$265,000
Accounts Payable	$ 92,000	$ 35,000
Notes Payable	150,000	80,000
Common Stock	100,000	60,000
Retained Earnings	290,000	90,000
Total Liabilities and Stockholders' Equity	$632,000	$265,000

At the date of the business combination, Faith's net assets and liabilities approximated fair value except for inventory, which had a fair value of $84,000, and buildings and equipment (net), which had a fair value of $165,000.

Required

a. Give the eliminating entry or entries needed to prepare a consolidated balance sheet immediately following the business combination.
b. Prepare a consolidation balance sheet worksheet.

LO3

E4-16 Worksheet for Wholly Owned Subsidiary

Gold Enterprises acquired 100 percent of Premium Builders' stock on December 31, 20X4. Balance sheet data for Gold and Premium on January 1, 20X5, are as follows:

	Gold Enterprises	Premium Builders
Cash and Receivables	$ 80,000	$ 30,000
Inventory	150,000	350,000
Buildings and Equipment (net)	430,000	80,000
Investment in Premium Stock	167,000	
Total Assets	$827,000	$460,000
Current Liabilities	$100,000	$110,000
Long-Term Debt	400,000	200,000
Common Stock	200,000	140,000
Retained Earnings	127,000	10,000
Total Liabilities and Stockholders' Equity	$827,000	$460,000

At the date of the business combination, Premium's cash and receivables had a fair value of $28,000, inventory had a fair value of $357,000, and buildings and equipment had a fair value of $92,000.

Required

a. Give all eliminating entries needed to prepare a consolidated balance sheet on January 1, 20X5.
b. Complete a consolidated balance sheet worksheet.
c. Prepare a consolidated balance sheet in good form.

LO3

E4-17 Computation of Consolidated Balances

Astor Corporation's balance sheet at January 1, 20X7, reflected the following balances:

Cash and Receivables	$ 80,000	Accounts Payable	$ 40,000
Inventory	120,000	Income Taxes Payable	60,000
Land	70,000	Bonds Payable	200,000
Buildings and Equipment (net)	480,000	Common Stock	250,000
		Retained Earnings	200,000
Total Assets	$750,000	Total Liabilities and Stockholders' Equity	$750,000

Phel Corporation, which had just entered into an active acquisition program, acquired 100 percent of Astor's common stock on January 2, 20X7, for $576,000. A careful review of the fair value of Astor's assets and liabilities indicated the following:

	Book Value	Fair Value
Inventory	$120,000	$140,000
Land	70,000	60,000
Buildings and Equipment (net)	480,000	550,000

Required

Compute the appropriate amount to be included in the consolidated balance sheet immediately following the acquisition for each of the following items:

a. Inventory.
b. Land.
c. Buildings and Equipment (net).
d. Goodwill.
e. Investment in Astor Corporation.

LO3, LO4

E4-18 Multiple-Choice Questions on Balance Sheet Consolidation

Top Corporation acquired 100 percent of Sun Corporation's common stock on December 31, 20X2. Balance sheet data for the two companies immediately following the acquisition follow:

Item	Top Corporation	Sun Corporation
Cash	$ 49,000	$ 30,000
Accounts Receivable	110,000	45,000
Inventory	130,000	70,000
Land	80,000	25,000
Buildings and Equipment	500,000	400,000
Less: Accumulated Depreciation	(223,000)	(165,000)
Investment in Sun Corporation Stock	198,000	
Total Assets	$844,000	$405,000
Accounts Payable	$ 61,500	$ 28,000
Taxes Payable	95,000	37,000
Bonds Payable	280,000	200,000
Common Stock	150,000	50,000
Retained Earnings	257,500	90,000
Total Liabilities and Stockholders' Equity	$844,000	$405,000

At the date of the business combination, the book values of Sun's net assets and liabilities approximated fair value except for inventory, which had a fair value of $85,000, and land, which had a fair value of $45,000.

Required

For each question, indicate the appropriate total that should appear in the consolidated balance sheet prepared immediately after the business combination.

1. What amount of inventory will be reported?

 a. $70,000.
 b. $130,000.
 c. $200,000.
 d. $215,000.

2. What amount of goodwill will be reported?

 a. $0.
 b. $23,000.
 c. $43,000.
 d. $58,000.

3. What amount of total assets will be reported?

 a. $84,400.
 b. $1,051,000.
 c. $1,109,000.
 d. $1,249,000.

4. What amount of total liabilities will be reported?

 a. $265,000.
 b. $436,500.
 c. $701,500.
 d. $1,249,000.

5. What amount of consolidated retained earnings will be reported?

 a. $547,500.
 b. $397,500.
 c. $347,500.
 d. $257,500.

6. What amount of total stockholders' equity will be reported?

 a. $407,500.
 b. $547,500.
 c. $844,000.
 d. $1,249,000.

LO3

E4-19 Wholly Owned Subsidiary with Differential

Canton Corporation is a wholly owned subsidiary of Winston Corporation. Winston acquired ownership of Canton on January 1, 20X3, for $28,000 above Canton's reported net assets. At that date, Canton reported common stock outstanding of $60,000 and retained earnings of $90,000. The differential is assigned to equipment with an economic life of seven years at the date of the business combination. Canton reported net income of $30,000 and paid dividends of $12,000 in 20X3.

Required

a. Give the journal entries recorded by Winston Corporation during 20X3 on its books if Winston accounts for its investment in Canton using the equity-method.

b. Give the eliminating entries needed at December 31, 20X3, to prepare consolidated financial statements.

LO5

E4-20 Basic Consolidation Worksheet

Blake Corporation acquired 100 percent of Shaw Corporation's voting shares on January 1, 20X3, at underlying book value. At that date, the book values and fair values of Shaw's assets and liabilities were equal. Blake uses the equity-method in accounting for its investment in Shaw. Adjusted trial balances for Blake and Shaw on December 31, 20X3, are as follows:

Item	Blake Corporation Debit	Blake Corporation Credit	Shaw Corporation Debit	Shaw Corporation Credit
Current Assets	$145,000		$105,000	
Depreciable Assets (net)	325,000		225,000	
Investment in Shaw Corporation Stock	170,000			
Depreciation Expense	25,000		15,000	
Other Expenses	105,000		75,000	
Dividends Declared	40,000		10,000	
Current Liabilities		$ 50,000		$ 40,000
Long-Term Debt		100,000		120,000
Common Stock		200,000		100,000
Retained Earnings		230,000		50,000
Sales		200,000		120,000
Income from Subsidiary		30,000		
	$810,000	$810,000	$430,000	$430,000

Required

a. Give all eliminating entries required on December 31, 20X3, to prepare consolidated financial statements.

b. Prepare a three-part consolidation worksheet as of December 31, 20X3.

LO5

E4-21 Basic Consolidation Worksheet for Second Year

Blake Corporation acquired 100 percent of Shaw Corporation's voting shares on January 1, 20X3, at underlying book value. At that date, the book values and fair values of Shaw's assets and liabilities were equal. Blake uses the equity-method in accounting for its investment in Shaw. Adjusted trial balances for Blake and Shaw on December 31, 20X4, are as follows:

Item	Blake Corporation Debit	Blake Corporation Credit	Shaw Corporation Debit	Shaw Corporation Credit
Current Assets	$210,000		$150,000	
Depreciable Assets (net)	300,000		210,000	
Investment in Shaw Corporation Stock	190,000			
Depreciation Expense	25,000		15,000	
Other Expenses	150,000		90,000	
Dividends Declared	50,000		15,000	
Current Liabilities		$ 70,000		$ 50,000
Long-Term Debt		100,000		120,000
Common Stock		200,000		100,000
Retained Earnings		290,000		70,000
Sales		230,000		140,000
Income from Subsidiary		35,000		
	$925,000	$925,000	$480,000	$480,000

Required

a. Give all eliminating entries required on December 31, 20X4, to prepare consolidated financial statements.

b. Prepare a three-part consolidation worksheet as of December 31, 20X4.

LO5

E4-22 Consolidation Worksheet with Differential

Kennelly Corporation acquired all of Short Company's common shares on January 1, 20X5, for $180,000. On that date, the book value of the net assets reported by Short was $150,000. The entire differential was assigned to depreciable assets with a six-year remaining economic life from January 1, 20X5.

The adjusted trial balances for the two companies on December 31, 20X5, are as follows:

Item	Kennelly Corporation Debit	Credit	Short Company Debit	Credit
Cash	$ 15,000		$ 5,000	
Accounts Receivable	30,000		40,000	
Inventory	70,000		60,000	
Depreciable Assets (net)	325,000		225,000	
Investment in Short Company Stock	195,000			
Depreciation Expense	25,000		15,000	
Other Expenses	105,000		75,000	
Dividends Declared	40,000		10,000	
Accounts Payable		$ 50,000		$ 40,000
Notes Payable		100,000		120,000
Common Stock		200,000		100,000
Retained Earnings		230,000		50,000
Sales		200,000		120,000
Income from Subsidiary		25,000		
	$805,000	$805,000	$430,000	$430,000

Kennelly uses the equity-method in accounting for its investment in Short. Short declared and paid dividends on December 31, 20X5.

Required

a. Prepare the eliminating entries needed as of December 31, 20X5, to complete a consolidation worksheet.

b. Prepare a three-part consolidation worksheet as of December 31, 20X5.

LO5

E4-23   Consolidation Worksheet for Subsidiary

Land Corporation acquired 100 percent of Growth Company's voting stock on January 1, 20X4, at underlying book value. Land uses the equity-method in accounting for its ownership of Growth. On December 31, 20X4, the trial balances of the two companies are as follows:

Item	Land Corporation Debit	Credit	Growth Company Debit	Credit
Current Assets	$ 238,000		$150,000	
Depreciable Assets	500,000		300,000	
Investment in Growth Company Stock	190,000			
Depreciation Expense	25,000		15,000	
Other Expenses	150,000		90,000	
Dividends Declared	50,000		15,000	
Accumulated Depreciation		$ 200,000		$ 90,000
Current Liabilities		70,000		50,000
Long-Term Debt		100,000		120,000
Common Stock		200,000		100,000
Retained Earnings		318,000		70,000
Sales		230,000		140,000
Income from Subsidiary		35,000		
	$1,153,000	$1,153,000	$570,000	$570,000

Required

a. Give all eliminating entries required on December 31, 20X4, to prepare consolidated financial statements.

b. Prepare a three-part consolidation worksheet as of December 31, 20X4.

LO7

E4-24 Push-Down Accounting

Jefferson Company acquired all of Louis Corporation's common shares on January 2, 20X3, for $789,000. At the date of combination, Louis's balance sheet appeared as follows:

Assets		Liabilities	
Cash and Receivables	$ 34,000	Current Payables	$ 25,000
Inventory	165,000	Notes Payable	100,000
Land	60,000	Stockholders' Equity	
Buildings (net)	250,000	Common Stock	200,000
Equipment (net)	320,000	Additional Capital	425,000
		Retained Earnings	79,000
Total	$829,000	Total	$829,000

The fair values of all of Louis's assets and liabilities were equal to their book values except for its fixed assets. Louis's land had a fair value of $75,000; the buildings, a fair value of $300,000; and the equipment, a fair value of $340,000.

Jefferson Company decided to employ push-down accounting for the acquisition of Louis Corporation. Subsequent to the combination, Louis continued to operate as a separate company.

Required

a. Record the acquisition of Louis's stock on Jefferson's books.

b. Present any entries that would be made on Louis's books related to the business combination, assuming push-down accounting is used.

c. Present, in general journal form, all elimination entries that would appear in a consolidation worksheet for Jefferson and its subsidiary prepared immediately following the combination.

Problems

LO5

P4-25 Assignment of Differential in Worksheet

Teresa Corporation acquired all the voting shares of Sally Enterprises on January 1, 20X4. Balance sheet amounts for the companies on the date of acquisition were as follows:

	Teresa Corporation	Sally Enterprises
Cash and Receivables	$ 40,000	$ 20,000
Inventory	95,000	40,000
Land	80,000	90,000
Buildings and Equipment	400,000	230,000
Investment in Sally Enterprises	290,000	
Total Debits	$905,000	$380,000
Accumulated Depreciation	$175,000	$ 65,000
Accounts Payable	60,000	15,000
Notes Payable	100,000	50,000
Common Stock	300,000	100,000
Retained Earnings	270,000	150,000
Total Credits	$905,000	$380,000

Sally Enterprises' buildings and equipment were estimated to have a market value of $175,000 on January 1, 20X4. All other items appeared to have market values approximating current book values.

Required

a. Complete a consolidated balance sheet worksheet for January 1, 20X4.

b. Prepare a consolidated balance sheet in good form.

LO3, LO4 **P4-26** ## Computation of Consolidated Balances

Retail Records Inc. acquired all of Decibel Studios' voting shares on January 1, 20X2, for $280,000. Retail's balance sheet immediately after the combination contained the following balances:

RETAIL RECORDS INC.
Balance Sheet
January 1, 20X2

Cash and Receivables	$120,000	Accounts Payable	$ 75,000
Inventory	110,000	Taxes Payable	50,000
Land	70,000	Notes Payable	300,000
Buildings and Equipment (net)	350,000	Common Stock	400,000
Investment in Decibel Stock	280,000	Retained Earnings	105,000
Total Assets	$930,000	Total Liabilities and Stockholders' Equity	$930,000

Decibel's balance sheet at acquisition contained the following balances:

DECIBEL STUDIOS
Balance Sheet
January 1, 20X2

Cash and Receivables	$ 40,000	Accounts Payable	$ 90,000
Inventory	180,000	Notes Payable	250,000
Buildings and Equipment (net)	350,000	Common Stock	100,000
Goodwill	30,000	Additional Paid-In Capital	200,000
		Retained Earnings	(40,000)
Total Assets	$600,000	Total Liabilities and Stockholders' Equity	$600,000

On the date of combination, the inventory held by Decibel had a fair value of $170,000, and its buildings and recording equipment had a value of $375,000. Goodwill reported by Decibel resulted from a purchase of Sound Stage Enterprises in 20X1. Sound Stage was liquidated and its assets and liabilities were brought onto Decibel's books.

Required

Compute the balances to be reported in the consolidated balance sheet immediately after the acquisition for:

a. Inventory.

b. Buildings and Equipment (net).

c. Investment in Decibel Stock.

d. Goodwill.

e. Common Stock.

f. Retained Earnings.

LO5 **P4-27** ## Balance Sheet Consolidation [AICPA Adapted]

Case Inc. acquired all Frey Inc.'s outstanding $25 par common stock on December 31, 20X3, in exchange for 40,000 shares of its $25 par common stock. Case's common stock closed at $56.50 per share on a national stock exchange on December 31, 20X3. Both corporations continued to operate as separate businesses maintaining separate accounting records with years ending December 31.

On December 31, 20X4, after year-end adjustments and the closing of nominal accounts, the companies had condensed balance sheet accounts (on the next page).

Additional Information

1. Case uses the equity-method of accounting for its investment in Frey.

2. On December 31, 20X3, Frey's assets and liabilities had fair values equal to the book balances with the exception of land, which had a fair value of $550,000. Frey had no land transactions in 20X4.

3. On June 15, 20X4, Frey paid a cash dividend of $4 per share on its common stock.

4. On December 10, 20X4, Case paid a cash dividend totaling $256,000 on its common stock.

	Case	Frey
Assets		
Cash	$ 825,000	$ 330,000
Accounts and Other Receivables	2,140,000	835,000
Inventories	2,310,000	1,045,000
Land	650,000	300,000
Depreciable Assets (net)	4,575,000	1,980,000
Investment in Frey Inc.	2,680,000	
Long-Term Investments and Other Assets	865,000	385,000
Total Assets	$14,045,000	$4,875,000
Liabilities and Stockholders' Equity		
Accounts Payable and Other Current Liabilities	$ 2,465,000	$1,145,000
Long-Term Debt	1,900,000	1,300,000
Common Stock, $25 Par Value	3,200,000	1,000,000
Additional Paid-In Capital	2,100,000	190,000
Retained Earnings	4,380,000	1,240,000
Total Liabilities and Stockholders' Equity	$14,045,000	$4,875,000

5. On December 31, 20X3, immediately before the combination, the stockholders' equity balance was:

	Case	Frey
Common Stock	$2,200,000	$1,000,000
Additional Paid-In Capital	1,660,000	190,000
Retained Earnings	3,166,000	820,000
	$7,026,000	$2,010,000

6. The 20X4 net income amounts according to the separate books of Case and Frey were $890,000 (exclusive of equity in Frey's earnings) and $580,000, respectively.

Required
Prepare a consolidated balance sheet worksheet for Case and its subsidiary, Frey, for December 31, 20X4. A formal consolidated balance sheet is not required.

LO5

P4-28 Consolidated Balance Sheet

Thompson Company spent $240,000 to acquire all of Lake Corporation's stock on January 1, 20X2. The balance sheets of the two companies on December 31, 20X3, showed the following amounts:

	Thompson Company	Lake Corporation
Cash	$ 30,000	$ 20,000
Accounts Receivable	100,000	40,000
Land	60,000	50,000
Buildings and Equipment	500,000	350,000
Less: Accumulated Depreciation	(230,000)	(75,000)
Investment in Lake Corporation	252,000	
	$712,000	$385,000
Accounts Payable	$ 80,000	$ 10,000
Taxes Payable	40,000	70,000
Notes Payable	100,000	85,000
Common Stock	200,000	100,000
Retained Earnings	292,000	120,000
	$712,000	$385,000

Lake reported retained earnings of $100,000 at the date of acquisition. The difference between the acquisition price and underlying book value is assigned to buildings and equipment with a remaining economic life of 10 years from the date of acquisition.

Required

a. Give the appropriate eliminating entry or entries needed to prepare a consolidated balance sheet as of December 31, 20X3.

b. Prepare a consolidated balance sheet worksheet as of December 31, 20X3.

LO5, LO6   P4-29   Comprehensive Problem: Consolidation in Subsequent Period

Thompson Company spent $240,000 to acquire all of Lake Corporation's stock on January 1, 20X2. On December 31, 20X4, the trial balances of the two companies were as follows:

Item	Thompson Company Debit	Thompson Company Credit	Lake Corporation Debit	Lake Corporation Credit
Cash	$ 74,000		$ 42,000	
Accounts Receivable	130,000		53,000	
Land	60,000		50,000	
Buildings and Equipment	500,000		350,000	
Investment in Lake Corporation Stock	268,000			
Cost of Services Provided	470,000		130,000	
Depreciation Expense	35,000		18,000	
Other Expenses	57,000		60,000	
Dividends Declared	30,000		12,000	
Accumulated Depreciation		$ 265,000		$ 93,000
Accounts Payable		71,000		17,000
Taxes Payable		58,000		60,000
Notes Payable		100,000		85,000
Common Stock		200,000		100,000
Retained Earnings		292,000		120,000
Service Revenue		610,000		240,000
Income from Subsidiary		28,000		
	$1,624,000	$1,624,000	$715,000	$715,000

Lake Corporation reported retained earnings of $100,000 at the date of acquisition. The difference between the acquisition price and underlying book value is assigned to buildings and equipment with a remaining economic life of 10 years from the date of acquisition. At December 31, 20X4, Lake owed Thompson $2,500 for services provided.

Required

a. Give all journal entries recorded by Thompson with regard to its investment in Lake during 20X4.

b. Give all eliminating entries required on December 31, 20X4, to prepare consolidated financial statements.

c. Prepare a three-part consolidation worksheet as of December 31, 20X4.

LO3, LO4   P4-30   Acquisition at Other than Fair Value of Net Assets

Mason Corporation acquired 100 percent ownership of Best Company on February 12, 20X9. At the date of acquisition, Best Company reported assets and liabilities with book values of $420,000 and $165,000, respectively, common stock outstanding of $80,000, and retained earnings of $175,000. The book values and fair values of Best's assets and liabilities were identical except for land which had increased in value by $20,000 and inventories which had decreased by $7,000. The estimated fair value of Best as a whole at the date of acquisition was $295,000.

Required

Give the eliminating entries required to prepare a consolidated balance sheet immediately after the business combination assuming Mason acquired its ownership of Best for:

a. $280,000.

b. $251,000.

LO6

P4-31 Intercorporate Receivables and Payables

Kim Corporation acquired 100 percent of Normal Company's outstanding shares on January 1, 20X7. Balance sheet data for the two companies immediately after the purchase follow:

	Kim Corporation	Normal Company
Cash	$ 70,000	$ 35,000
Accounts Receivable	90,000	65,000
Inventory	84,000	80,000
Buildings and Equipment	400,000	300,000
Less: Accumulated Depreciation	(160,000)	(75,000)
Investment in Normal Company Stock	305,000	
Investment in Normal Company Bonds	50,000	
Total Assets	$839,000	$405,000
Accounts Payable	$ 50,000	$ 20,000
Bonds Payable	200,000	100,000
Common Stock	300,000	150,000
Capital in Excess of Par		140,000
Retained Earnings	289,000	(5,000)
Total Liabilities and Equities	$839,000	$405,000

As indicated in the parent company balance sheet, Kim purchased $50,000 of Normal's bonds from the subsidiary immediately after it acquired the stock. An analysis of intercompany receivables and payables also indicates that the subsidiary owes the parent $10,000. On the date of combination, the book values and fair values of Normal's assets and liabilities were the same.

Required

a. Give all eliminating entries needed to prepare a consolidated balance sheet for January 1, 20X7.
b. Complete a consolidated balance sheet worksheet.
c. Prepare a consolidated balance sheet in good form.

LO5

P4-32 Balance Sheet Consolidation

On January 2, 20X8, Primary Corporation acquired 100 percent of Street Company's outstanding common stock. In exchange for Street's stock, Primary issued bonds payable with a par and fair value of $650,000 directly to the selling stockholders of Street. The two companies continued to operate as separate entities subsequent to combination.

Immediately prior to the combination, the book values and fair values of the companies' assets and liabilities were as follows:

	Primary Book Value	Primary Fair Value	Street Book Value	Street Fair Value
Cash	$ 12,000	$ 12,000	$ 9,000	$ 9,000
Receivables	41,000	39,000	31,000	30,000
Allowance for Bad Debts	(2,000)		(1,000)	
Inventory	86,000	89,000	68,000	72,000
Land	55,000	200,000	50,000	70,000
Buildings and Equipment	960,000	650,000	670,000	500,000
Accumulated Depreciation	(411,000)		(220,000)	
Patent				40,000
Total Assets	$741,000	$990,000	$607,000	$721,000
Current Payables	$ 38,000	$ 38,000	$ 29,000	$ 29,000
Bonds Payable	200,000	210,000	100,000	90,000
Common Stock	300,000		200,000	
Additional Paid-In Capital	100,000		130,000	
Retained Earnings	103,000		148,000	
Total Liabilities and Equity	$741,000		$607,000	

At the date of combination, Street owed Primary $6,000 plus accrued interest of $500 on a short-term note. Both companies have properly recorded these amounts.

Required

a. Record the business combination on the books of Primary Corporation.

b. Present in general journal form all elimination entries needed in a worksheet to prepare a consolidated balance sheet immediately following the business combination on January 2, 20X8.

c. Prepare and complete a consolidated balance sheet worksheet as of January 2, 20X8, immediately following the business combination.

d. Present a consolidated balance sheet for Primary and its subsidiary as of January 2, 20X8.

LO1

P4-33 **Consolidation Worksheet at End of First Year of Ownership**

Advanced
StudyGuide
.com

Mill Corporation acquired 100 percent ownership of Roller Company on January 1, 20X8, for $128,000. At that date, the fair value of Roller's buildings and equipment was $20,000 more than book value. Buildings and equipment are depreciated on a 10-year basis. Although goodwill is not amortized, the management of Mill concluded at December 31, 20X8, that goodwill involved in its acquisition of Roller shares had been impaired and the correct carrying value was $2,500.

Trial balance data for Mill and Roller on December 31, 20X8, are as follows:

Item	Mill Corporation		Roller Company	
	Debit	Credit	Debit	Credit
Cash	$ 19,500		$ 21,000	
Accounts Receivable	70,000		12,000	
Inventory	90,000		25,000	
Land	30,000		15,000	
Buildings and Equipment	350,000		150,000	
Investment in Roller Co. Stock	128,500			
Cost of Goods Sold	125,000		110,000	
Wage Expense	42,000		27,000	
Depreciation Expense	25,000		10,000	
Interest Expense	12,000		4,000	
Other Expenses	13,500		5,000	
Dividends Declared	30,000		16,000	
Accumulated Depreciation		$145,000		$ 40,000
Accounts Payable		45,000		16,000
Wages Payable		17,000		9,000
Notes Payable		150,000		50,000
Common Stock		200,000		60,000
Retained Earnings		102,000		40,000
Sales		260,000		180,000
Income from Subsidiary		16,500		
	$935,500	$935,500	$395,000	$395,000

Required

a. Give all eliminating entries needed to prepare a three-part consolidation worksheet as of December 31, 20X8.

b. Prepare a three-part consolidation worksheet for 20X8 in good form.

LO5

P4-34 **Consolidation Worksheet at End of Second Year of Ownership**

Mill Corporation acquired 100 percent ownership of Roller Company on January 1, 20X8, for $128,000. At that date, the fair value of Roller's buildings and equipment was $20,000 more than book value. Buildings and equipment are depreciated on a 10-year basis. Although goodwill is not amortized, the management of Mill concluded at December 31, 20X8, that goodwill involved in its acquisition of Roller shares had been impaired and the correct carrying value was $2,500. No additional impairment occurred in 20X9.

Trial balance data for Mill and Roller on December 31, 20X9, are as follows:

Item	Mill Corporation		Roller Company	
	Debit	Credit	Debit	Credit
Cash	$ 45,500		$ 32,000	
Accounts Receivable	85,000		14,000	
Inventory	97,000		24,000	
Land	50,000		25,000	
Buildings and Equipment	350,000		150,000	
Investment in Roller Co. Stock	142,500			
Cost of Goods Sold	145,000		114,000	
Wage Expense	35,000		20,000	
Depreciation Expense	25,000		10,000	
Interest Expense	12,000		4,000	
Other Expenses	23,000		16,000	
Dividends Declared	30,000		20,000	
Accumulated Depreciation		$ 170,000		$ 50,000
Accounts Payable		51,000		15,000
Wages Payable		14,000		6,000
Notes Payable		150,000		50,000
Common Stock		200,000		60,000
Retained Earnings		131,000		48,000
Sales		290,000		200,000
Income from Subsidiary		34,000		
	$1,040,000	$1,040,000	$429,000	$429,000

Required

a. Give all eliminating entries needed to prepare a three-part consolidation worksheet as of December 31, 20X9.

b. Prepare a three-part consolidation worksheet for 20X9 in good form.

c. Prepare a consolidated balance sheet, income statement, and retained earnings statement for 20X9.

LO5

P4-35 Comprehensive Problem: Wholly Owned Subsidiary

Power Corporation acquired 100 percent ownership of Upland Products Company on January 1, 20X1, for $200,000. On that date Upland reported retained earnings of $50,000 and had $100,000 of common stock outstanding. Power has used the equity-method in accounting for its investment in Upland.

Trial balance data for the two companies on December 31, 20X5 (on the next page).

Additional Information

1. On the date of combination, the fair value of Upland's depreciable assets was $50,000 more than book value. The differential assigned to depreciable assets should be written off over the following 10-year period.

2. There was $10,000 of intercorporate receivables and payables at the end of 20X5.

Required

a. Give all journal entries that Power recorded during 20X5 related to its investment in Upland.

b. Give all eliminating entries needed to prepare consolidated statements for 20X5.

c. Prepare a three-part worksheet as of December 31, 20X5.

Item	Power Corporation Debit	Power Corporation Credit	Upland Products Company Debit	Upland Products Company Credit
Cash and Receivables	$ 43,000		$ 65,000	
Inventory	260,000		90,000	
Land	80,000		80,000	
Buildings and Equipment	500,000		150,000	
Investment in Upland Products Stock	235,000			
Cost of Goods Sold	120,000		50,000	
Depreciation Expense	25,000		15,000	
Inventory Losses	15,000		5,000	
Dividends Declared	30,000		10,000	
Accumulated Depreciation		$ 205,000		$105,000
Accounts Payable		60,000		20,000
Notes Payable		200,000		50,000
Common Stock		300,000		100,000
Retained Earnings		318,000		90,000
Sales		200,000		100,000
Income from Subsidiary		25,000		
	$1,308,000	$1,308,000	$465,000	$465,000

LO5

P4-36 Comprehensive Problem: Differential Apportionment

Jersey Corporation acquired 100 percent of Lime Company on January 1, 20X7, for $203,000. The trial balances for the two companies on December 31, 20X7, included the following amounts:

Item	Jersey Corporation Debit	Jersey Corporation Credit	Lime Company Debit	Lime Company Credit
Cash	$ 82,000		$ 25,000	
Accounts Receivable	50,000		55,000	
Inventory	170,000		100,000	
Land	80,000		20,000	
Buildings and Equipment	500,000		150,000	
Investment in Lime Company Stock	240,000			
Cost of Goods Sold	500,000		250,000	
Depreciation Expense	25,000		15,000	
Other Expenses	75,000		75,000	
Dividends Declared	50,000		20,000	
Accumulated Depreciation		$ 155,000		$ 75,000
Accounts Payable		70,000		35,000
Mortgages Payable		200,000		50,000
Common Stock		300,000		50,000
Retained Earnings		290,000		100,000
Sales		700,000		400,000
Income from Subsidiary		57,000		
	$1,772,000	$1,772,000	$710,000	$710,000

Additional Information

1. On January 1, 20X7, Lime reported net assets with a book value of $150,000. A total of $20,000 of the acquisition price is applied to goodwill, which was not impaired in 20X7.

2. Lime's depreciable assets had an estimated economic life of 11 years on the date of combination. The difference between fair value and book value of tangible assets is related entirely to buildings and equipment.

3. Jersey used the equity-method in accounting for its investment in Lime.

4. Detailed analysis of receivables and payables showed that Lime owed Jersey $16,000 on December 31, 20X7.

Required

a. Give all journal entries recorded by Jersey with regard to its investment in Lime during 20X7.

b. Give all eliminating entries needed to prepare a full set of consolidated financial statements for 20X7.

c. Prepare a three-part consolidation worksheet as of December 31, 20X7.

LO7 **P4-37A** **Push-Down Accounting**

On December 31, 20X6, Greenly Corporation and Lindy Company entered into a business combination in which Greenly acquired all of Lindy's common stock for $935,000. At the date of combination, Lindy had common stock outstanding with a par value of $100,000, additional paid-in capital of $400,000, and retained earnings of $175,000. The fair values and book values of all Lindy's assets and liabilities were equal at the date of combination, except for the following:

	Book Value	Fair Value
Inventory	$ 50,000	$ 55,000
Land	75,000	160,000
Buildings	400,000	500,000
Equipment	500,000	570,000

The buildings had a remaining life of 20 years, and the equipment was expected to last another 10 years. In accounting for the business combination, Greenly decided to use push-down accounting on Lindy's books.

During 20X7, Lindy earned net income of $88,000 and paid a dividend of $50,000. All of the inventory on hand at the end of 20X6 was sold during 20X7. During 20X8, Lindy earned net income of $90,000 and paid a dividend of $50,000.

Required

a. Record the acquisition of Lindy's stock on Greenly's books on December 31, 20X6.

b. Record any entries that would be made on December 31, 20X6, on Lindy's books related to the business combination if push-down accounting is employed.

c. Present all eliminating entries that would appear in the worksheet to prepare a consolidated balance sheet immediately after the combination.

d. Present all entries that Greenly would record during 20X7 related to its investment in Lindy if Greenly uses the equity-method of accounting for its investment.

e. Present all eliminating entries that would appear in the worksheet to prepare a full set of consolidated financial statements for the year 20X7.

f. Present all eliminating entries that would appear in the worksheet to prepare a full set of consolidated financial statements for the year 20X8.

Kaplan CPA Review

SCHWESER

Kaplan CPA Review Simulation on Comprehensive Consolidation Procedures

Access to the online CPA Simulation can be attained by visiting the text's Web site: www.mhhe.com/baker1e

Situation

On January 1, Year One, Big Corporation acquires for $700,000 in cash all of the outstanding voting stock of Little Corporation. It was the first such acquisition for either company. On the day prior to the transaction, Big and Little reported assets of $2 million and $800,000, liabilities of $900,000 and $330,000, contributed capital of $300,000 and $100,000, and retained earnings of $800,000 and $370,000, respectively. Unless otherwise stated, assume Little Corporation holds a building with a book value of $200,000 but a fair value of $300,000. The building has a 10-year remaining life. All of Little's other assets and liabilities are fairly valued in its financial records.

Topics Covered in the Simulation

a. Computation of consolidated assets.

b. Goodwill measurement.

c. Computation of consolidated expenses.

d. Allocation of purchase differentials.

e. Equity-method reporting.

f. Valuation of other intangibles.

g. Determining when control exists.

h. Testing for goodwill impairment.

Chapter **Five**

Consolidation of Less-than-Wholly-Owned Subsidiaries Acquired at More than Book Value

CISCO ACQUIRES A CONTROLLING INTEREST IN NUOVA

In many of the examples of corporate acquisitions discussed so far, the acquiring company has purchased 100 percent of the outstanding stock of the acquired company. However, the buyer doesn't always acquire 100 percent ownership of the target company. For example, in 2006 Cisco Systems Inc. acquired 80 percent of Nuova Systems in order to take advantage of Nuova's innovative data center technology. The remaining 20 percent of the company was still held by individual investors. Cisco's initial investment in Nuova was $50 million. Accounting for this type of investment can be very complicated. First, Cisco's $50 million investment was not intended solely to purchase Nuova's tangible assets. Cisco also paid for Nuova's potential future earnings, for its innovation, and for the fair value of assets in excess of their book values as of the acquisition date. Because Cisco did not purchase 100 percent of Nuova, the Cisco consolidated financial statements in future years would have to account for the portion of the company owned by the non-controlling interest (NCI) shareholders. This chapter explores the consolidation of less-than-wholly-owned subsidiaries when there is a positive differential.

LEARNING OBJECTIVES

When you finish studying this chapter, you should be able to:

LO1 Understand and explain how the consolidation process differs when the subsidiary is less-than-wholly owned and there is a differential.

LO2 Make calculations and prepare elimination entries for the consolidation of a partially owned subsidiary when there is a complex positive differential.

LO3   Understand and explain what happens when a parent company ceases to consolidate a subsidiary.

LO4   Make calculations and prepare elimination entries for the consolidation of a partially owned subsidiary when there is a complex positive differential and other comprehensive income.

LO5   Understand and explain additional considerations associated with consolidation.

A NONCONTROLLING INTEREST IN CONJUNCTION WITH A DIFFERENTIAL

LO1

Understand and explain how the consolidation process differs when the subsidiary is less-than-wholly owned and there is a differential.

This chapter continues to build upon the foundation established in Chapters 2 through 4 related to the consolidation of majority-owned subsidiaries. In fact, Chapter 5 represents the culmination of our understanding of procedures associated with the consolidation process. Chapter 5 combines the complexities introduced in Chapters 3 and 4. Specifically, Chapter 5 examines situations where the acquiring company purchases less than 100 percent of the outstanding stock of the acquired company (similar to Chapter 3) and pays an amount greater than its proportionate share of the book value of net assets (resulting in a differential as introduced in Chapter 4). Once you master Chapter 5, you can handle virtually any consolidation problem!

	Wholly owned subsidiary	Partially owned subsidiary	
Investment = Book value	Chapter 2	Chapter 3	No differential
Investment > Book value	Chapter 4	Chapter 5	Differential
	No NCI shareholders	NCI shareholders	

CONSOLIDATED BALANCE SHEET WITH MAJORITY-OWNED SUBSIDIARY

The consolidation process for a less-than-wholly-owned subsidiary with a differential is the same as the process for a wholly owned subsidiary with a differential except that the claims of the noncontrolling interest must be included. The example of Peerless Products Corporation and Special Foods Inc. from Chapter 4 will serve as a basis for illustrating consolidation procedures when the parent has less than full ownership of a subsidiary. Assume that on January 1, 20X1, Peerless acquires 80 percent of the common stock of Special Foods for $310,000. At that date, the fair value of the noncontrolling interest is estimated to be $77,500. The ownership situation can be viewed as follows, where the total fair value indicated is equal to the sum of the fair value of the consideration given and the fair value of the noncontrolling interest:

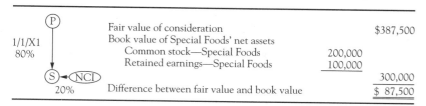

Fair value of consideration			$387,500
Book value of Special Foods' net assets			
Common stock—Special Foods		200,000	
Retained earnings—Special Foods		100,000	
			300,000
Difference between fair value and book value			$ 87,500

Peerless records the acquisition on its books with the following entry:

(1)			
	Investment in Special Foods	310,000	
	Cash		310,000
	Record purchase of Special Foods stock.		

FIGURE 5–1
Balance Sheets of Peerless Products and Special Foods, January 1, 20X1, Immediately after Combination

	Peerless Products	Special Foods
Assets		
Cash	$ 40,000	$ 50,000
Accounts Receivable	75,000	50,000
Inventory	100,000	60,000
Land	175,000	40,000
Buildings and Equipment	800,000	600,000
Accumulated Depreciation	(400,000)	(300,000)
Investment in Special Foods Stock	310,000	
Total Assets	$1,100,000	$500,000
Liabilities and Stockholders' Equity		
Accounts Payable	$ 100,000	$100,000
Bonds Payable	200,000	100,000
Common Stock	500,000	200,000
Retained Earnings	300,000	100,000
Total Liabilities and Equity	$1,100,000	$500,000

FIGURE 5–2
Values of Select Assets of Special Foods

	Book Value	Fair Value	Fair Value Increment
Inventory	$ 60,000	$ 65,000	$ 5,000
Land	40,000	50,000	10,000
Buildings and Equipment	300,000	360,000	60,000
	$400,000	$475,000	$75,000

The balance sheets of Peerless and Special Foods appear immediately after acquisition as in Figure 5–1. The fair values of all of Special Foods' assets and liabilities are equal to their book values except as shown in Figure 5–2.

The excess of the $387,500 total fair value of the consideration given and the non-controlling interest on the date of combination over the $300,000 book value of Special Foods is $87,500. Of this total $87,500 differential, $75,000 relates to the excess of the acquisition-date fair value over the book value of Special Foods' net identifiable assets, as can be seen from Figure 5–2. The remaining $12,500 of the differential, the excess of the consideration given and the noncontrolling interest over the fair value of Special Foods' net identifiable assets, is assigned to goodwill. Since Peerless only acquires 80 percent of Special Foods' outstanding common stock, Peerless' share of the total differential is $70,000 ($87,500 × 0.80). Specifically, Peerless' share of the excess fair value over book value of identifiable net assets is $60,000 ($75,000 × 0.80) and its share of the goodwill is $10,000 ($12,500 × 0.80). As a result, Peerless' acquisition price of $310,000 applies to the book value and differential components of Special Foods' fair value as follows:

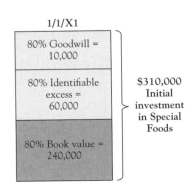

The book value component of the acquisition price is divided between Peerless and the noncontrolling interest as follows:

Book Value Calculations:

	NCI 20%	Peerless 80%	= Common Stock	+ Retained Earnings
Original book value	60,000	240,000	200,000	100,000

This analysis leads to the following basic elimination entry:

Advanced
StudyGuide
.com

Basic investment account elimination entry:[1]

Common stock	200,000		← Original amount invested (100%)
Retained earnings	100,000		← Beginning balance in RE
Investment in Special Foods		240,000	← Peerless' share of Special Foods' NA
NCI in NA of Special Foods		60,000	← NCI's share of BV

The differential can be allocated between Peerless and the noncontrolling interest as follows:

Excess Value (Differential) Calculations:

	NCI 20%	+ Peerless 80%	= Inventory	+ Land	+ Building	+ Acc. Depr.	+ Goodwill
Beginning balance	17,500	70,000	5,000	10,000	60,000	0	12,500

From this analysis, we can construct the excess value reclassification entry:

Excess value (differential) reclassification entry:

Inventory	5,000		← Original calculated excess value
Land	10,000		← Original calculated excess value
Building	60,000		← Original calculated excess value
Goodwill	12,500		← Calculated value from acquisition
Investment in Special Foods		70,000	← Peerless' share of differential
NCI in NA of Special Foods		17,500	← NCI's share of differential

As explained in Chapter 4, Special Foods had accumulated depreciation on the acquisition date of $300,000. The following elimination entry nets this accumulated depreciation out against the cost of the building and equipment.

Optional accumulated depreciation elimination entry:

Accumulated depreciation	300,000		← Original depreciation at the time of
Building and equipment		300,000	the acquisition netted against cost

Advanced
StudyGuide
.com

Figure 5–3 illustrates Peerless' consolidation worksheet on the date of acquisition at January 1, 20X1. Once the eliminating entries are placed in the worksheet, each row is summed across to get the consolidated totals. Note that the asset amounts included in the Consolidated column, and thus in the consolidated balance sheet, consist of book values for Peerless' assets and liabilities, plus acquisition-date fair values for Special Foods' assets and liabilities, plus goodwill.

---

[1] To view a video explanation of this topic, visit advancedstudyguide.com.

FIGURE 5–3 Worksheet for Consolidated Balance Sheet, January 1, 20X1, Date of Combination; 80 Percent Acquisition at More than Book Value

	Peerless Products	Special Foods	Elimination Entries		Consolidated
			DR	CR	
Balance Sheet					
Cash	40,000	50,000			90,000
Accounts Receivable	75,000	50,000			125,000
Inventory	100,000	60,000	5,000		165,000
Investment in Special Foods	310,000			240,000	0
				70,000	
Land	175,000	40,000	10,000		225,000
Buildings & Equipment	800,000	600,000	60,000	300,000	1,160,000
Less: Accumulated Depreciation	(400,000)	(300,000)	300,000		(400,000)
Goodwill			12,500		12,500
Total Assets	**1,100,000**	**500,000**	**387,500**	**610,000**	**1,377,500**
Accounts Payable	100,000	100,000			200,000
Bonds Payable	200,000	100,000			300,000
Common Stock	500,000	200,000	200,000		500,000
Retained Earnings	300,000	100,000	100,000		300,000
NCI in NA of Special Foods				60,000	77,500
				17,500	
Total Liabilities & Equity	**1,100,000**	**500,000**	**300,000**	**77,500**	**1,377,500**

CONSOLIDATED FINANCIAL STATEMENTS WITH A MAJORITY-OWNED SUBSIDIARY

LO2

Make calculations and prepare elimination entries for the consolidation of a partially owned subsidiary when there is a complex positive differential.

Consolidation subsequent to acquisition involves the preparation of a complete set of consolidated financial statements, as discussed in Chapter 4. To continue the illustration from the previous section beyond the date of acquisition, assume Peerless Products and Special Foods report the income and dividends during 20X1 and 20X2 shown in Figure 5–4. With respect to the assets to which the $87,500 differential relates, assume that the entire inventory is sold during 20X1, the buildings and equipment have a remaining economic life of 10 years from the date of combination, and straight-line depreciation is used. Further, assume that management determines at the end of 20X1 that the goodwill is impaired and should be written down by $3,125. Management has determined that the goodwill arising in the acquisition of Special Foods relates proportionately to the controlling and noncontrolling interests, as does the impairment. Finally, assume that Peerless accounts for its investment in Special Foods using the equity method.

Initial Year of Ownership

The business combination of Peerless Products and Special Foods occurs at the beginning of 20X1. Accordingly, Peerless records the acquisition on the acquisition date and recognizes income and dividends from Special Foods on its books for the entire year. Thus, the consolidated statements portray the two companies as if they were one entity for the entire year. The procedures are basically the same as those in Chapter 4 except the parent claims only its share of the subsidiary's income and dividends, and the consolidation procedures must allow for the claims of the noncontrolling shareholders as illustrated in Chapter 3.

Parent Company Entries

During 20X1, Peerless makes the usual equity-method entries to record income and dividends from its subsidiary, but, unlike in Chapter 4, Peerless must share Special Foods' income and dividends with the subsidiary's noncontrolling stockholders. Accordingly,

Advanced
StudyGuide
.com

FIGURE 5–4
Income and Dividend Information about Peerless Products and Special Foods for the Years 20X1 and 20X2

	Peerless Products	Special Foods
20X1:		
Separate operating income, Peerless	$140,000	
Net income, Special Foods		$50,000
Dividends	60,000	30,000
20X2:		
Separate operating income, Peerless	160,000	
Net income, Special Foods		75,000
Dividends	60,000	40,000

Peerless recognizes only its proportionate share of Special Foods' net income and dividends. Peerless records the following entries during 20X1:

(2)	Investment in Special Foods	40,000	
	Income from Special Foods		40,000
	Record Peerless' 80% share of Special Foods' 20X1 income.		

(3)	Cash	24,000	
	Investment in Special Foods		24,000
	Record Peerless' 80% share of Special Foods' 20X1 dividend.		

In addition, Peerless must write off a portion of the differential with the following entry:

(4)	Income from Special Foods	11,300	
	Investment in Special Foods		11,300
	Record amortization of excess acquisition price.		

Special Foods' undervalued inventory, comprising $5,000 of the total differential, was sold during the year. Therefore, Peerless' $4,000 portion ($5,000 × 80%) must be written off by taking it out of the investment account and reducing the parent's income from the subsidiary. Also, Peerless' $48,000 portion of the excess fair value of Special Foods' buildings and equipment must be amortized at $4,800 per year ($48,000 ÷ 10) over the remaining 10-year life. Finally, Peerless' portion of the goodwill impairment is included in this adjustment. The calculation of Peerless' share of the differential amortization is illustrated below in the "Excess Value (Differential) Calculations."

The following diagrams illustrate the breakdown of the book value and excess value components of the investment account at the beginning and end of the year.

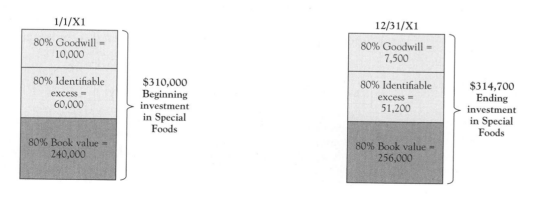

The book value component can be summarized as follows:

Book Value Calculations:

	NCI 20%	Peerless 80%	= Common Stock	+ Retained Earnings
Original book value	60,000	240,000	200,000	100,000
+ Net Income	10,000	40,000		50,000
− Dividends	(6,000)	(24,000)		(30,000)
Ending book value	64,000	256,000	200,000	120,000

The lighter shaded numbers in this chart comprise the basic elimination entry:

Basic investment account elimination entry:

Common stock	200,000		← Original amount invested (100%)
Retained earnings	100,000		← Beginning balance in RE
Income from Special Foods	40,000		← Peerless' share of Special Foods' NI
NCI in NI of Special Foods	10,000		← NCI's share of Special Foods' NI
Dividends declared		30,000	← 100% of Special Foods' dividends
Investment in Special Foods		256,000	← Peerless' share of Special Foods' NA
NCI in NA of Special Foods		64,000	← NCI's share of net amount of BV

We then analyze the differential and its changes during the period:

Excess Value (Differential) Calculations:

	NCI 20%	+ Peerless 80%	= Inventory	+ Land	+ Building	+ Acc. Depr.	+ Goodwill
Beginning Balance	17,500	70,000	5,000	10,000	60,000	0	12,500
Amortization	(2,825)	(11,300)	(5,000)			(6,000)	(3,125)
Ending Balance	14,675	58,700	0	10,000	60,000	(6,000)	9,375

The entire differential amount assigned to the inventory already passed through cost of goods sold during the year. The only other amortization item is the excess value assigned to the building, amortized over a 10-year period ($60,000 ÷ 10 = $6,000 per year). Finally, the goodwill is deemed to be impaired and worth only $9,375.

Since the amortization of the differential was already written off from the investment account against the Income from Special Foods account, the changes are simply reclassified from the Income from Special Foods account to the various income statement accounts to which they apply using the following worksheet entry:

Amortized excess value reclassification entry:

Cost of goods sold	5,000		← Extra cost of goods sold
Depreciation expense	6,000		← Depreciation of excess building value
Goodwill impairment loss	3,125		← Goodwill impairment
Income from Special Foods		11,300	← Peerless' share of amortization
NCI in NI of Special Foods		2,825	← NCI's share of amortization

Finally, the remaining unamortized differential is reclassified to the correct accounts based on the ending balances in the chart above:

Excess value (differential) reclassification entry:

Land	10,000		← Original calculated excess value
Buiding	60,000		← Original calculated excess value
Goodwill	9,375		← Calculated value from acquisition
Accumulated depreciation		6,000	← Excess building value ÷ 10 years
Investment in Special Foods		58,700	← Peerless' share of differential
NCI in NA of Special Foods		14,675	← NCI's share of differential

In sum, these worksheet entries (1) eliminate the balances in the Investment in Special Foods and Income from Special Foods accounts, (2) reclassify the amortization of excess value to the proper income statement accounts, and (3) reclassify the remaining differential to the appropriate balance sheet accounts as of the end of the accounting period. The following T-accounts illustrate how Peerless' equity method investment-related accounts are eliminated.

	Investment in Special Foods				Income from Special Foods	
Acquisition Price	310,000					
80% of NI	40,000				40,000	80% of NI
		24,000	80% of Div.			
		11,300	80% of Excess Amortization	11,300		
Ending Balance	314,700				28,700	Ending Balance
		256,000	Basic	40,000		
		58,700	Excess Value		11,300	"Amort. Excess Value"
	0		Reclassification		0	

Again, we repeat the same accumulated depreciation elimination entry this year (and every year as long as Special Foods owns the assets) that we used in the initial year.

Optional accumulated depreciation elimination entry:

Accumulated depreciation	300,000		← Original depreciation at the time of the acquisition netted against cost
Building and equipment		300,000	

Consolidation Worksheet—Initial Year of Ownership

After the subsidiary income accruals are entered on Peerless' books, the adjusted trial balance data of the consolidating companies are entered in the three-part consolidation worksheet as shown in Figure 5–5. The last column in the worksheet will serve as a basis for preparing consolidated financial statements at the end of 20X1.

Once the appropriate eliminating entries are placed in the consolidation worksheet in Figure 5–5, the worksheet is completed by summing each row across, taking into consideration the debit or credit effect of the eliminations.

Consolidated Net Income and Retained Earnings

As can be seen from the worksheet in Figure 5–5, consolidated net income for 20X1 is $175,875 and the amount of that income accruing to the controlling interest, shown as the last number in the income statement section of the worksheet in the Consolidated column, is $168,700. The amount of retained earnings reported in the consolidated balance sheet at December 31, 20X1, shown as the last number in the retained earnings section of the worksheet in the Consolidated column, is $408,700. Figure 5–6 illustrates the computation of these amounts.

Advanced
StudyGuide
.com

FIGURE 5–5   December 31, 20X1, Equity-Method Worksheet for Consolidated Financial Statements, Initial Year of Ownership; 80 Percent Acquisition at More than Book Value

	Peerless Products	Special Foods	Elimination Entries		Consolidated
			DR	CR	
Income Statement					
Sales	400,000	200,000			600,000
Less: COGS	(170,000)	(115,000)	5,000		(290,000)
Less: Depreciation Expense	(50,000)	(20,000)	6,000		(76,000)
Less: Other Expenses	(40,000)	(15,000)			(55,000)
Less: Impairment Loss			3,125		3,125
Income from Special Foods	28,700		40,000	11,300	0
Consolidated Net Income	168,700	50,000	54,125	11,300	175,875
NCI in Net Income			10,000	2,825	(7,175)
Controlling Interest in Net Income	**168,700**	**50,000**	**64,125**	**14,125**	**168,700**
Statement of Retained Earnings					
Beginning Balance	300,000	100,000	100,000		300,000
Net Income	**168,700**	**50,000**	64,125	14,125	168,700
Less: Dividends Declared	(60,000)	(30,000)		30,000	(60,000)
Ending Balance	**408,700**	**120,000**	**164,125**	**44,125**	**408,700**
Balance Sheet					
Cash	194,000	75,000			269,000
Accounts Receivable	75,000	50,000			125,000
Inventory	100,000	75,000			175,000
Investment in Special Foods	314,700			256,000	0
				58,700	
Land	175,000	40,000	10,000		225,000
Buildings & Equipment	800,000	600,000	60,000	300,000	1,160,000
Less: Accumulated Depreciation	(450,000)	(320,000)	300,000	6,000	(476,000)
Goodwill			9,375		9,375
Total Assets	**1,208,700**	**520,000**	**379,375**	**620,700**	**1,487,375**
Accounts Payable	100,000	100,000			200,000
Bonds Payable	200,000	100,000			300,000
Common Stock	500,000	200,000	200,000		500,000
Retained Earnings	**408,700**	120,000	164,125	44,125	408,700
NCI in NA of Special Foods				64,000	78,675
				14,675	
Total Liabilities & Equity	**1,208,700**	**520,000**	**364,125**	**122,800**	**1,487,375**

Second Year of Ownership

The equity-method and consolidation procedures employed during the second and subsequent years of ownership are the same as those used during the first year and are illustrated by continuing the Peerless Products and Special Foods example through 20X2. No further impairment of the goodwill arising from the business combination occurs in 20X2.

Parent Company Entries

Given the income and dividends as shown in Figure 5–4, Peerless Products records the following entries on its separate books during 20X2:

(5)	Investment in Special Foods	60,000	
	Income from Special Foods		60,000

Record Peerless' 80% share of Special Foods' 20X2 income.

FIGURE 5–6
Consolidated Net Income and Retained Earnings, 20X1; 80 Percent Acquisition at More than Book Value

Consolidated net income, 20X1:	
Peerless' separate operating income	$140,000
Special Foods' net income	50,000
Write-off of differential related to inventory sold in 20X1	(5,000)
Amortization of differential related to buildings and equipment in 20X1	(6,000)
Goodwill impairment loss	(3,125)
Consolidated net income	$175,875
Income to controlling interest, 20X1:	
Consolidated net income	$175,875
Income to noncontrolling interest	(7,175)
Income to controlling interest	$168,700
Consolidated retained earnings, December 31, 20X1:	
Peerless' retained earnings on date of combination, January 1, 20X1	$300,000
Income to controlling interest, 20X1	168,700
Dividends declared by Peerless, 20X1	(60,000)
Consolidated retained earnings	$408,700

(6)	Cash	32,000	
	Investment in Special Foods		32,000
	Record Peerless' 80% share of Special Foods' 20X2 dividend.		

(7)	Income from Special Foods	4,800	
	Investment in Special Foods		4,800
	Record amortization of excess acquisition price.		

Consolidation Worksheet—Second Year Following Combination

The consolidation procedures in the second year following the acquisition are very similar to those in the first year. Consistent with the process illustrated in 20X1, we follow the same process for 20X2. In order to determine the worksheet entries for 20X2, we first summarize the changes in the parent's investment account during 20X2 as follows:

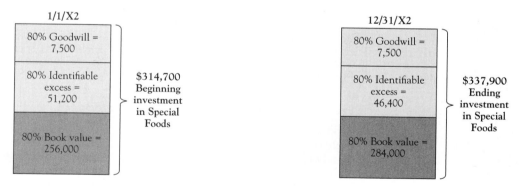

The book value component can be summarized as follows:

Book Value Calculations:

	NCI 20%	+ Peerless 80%	= Common Stock	+ Retained Earnings
Beginning book value	64,000	256,000	200,000	120,000
+ Net income	15,000	60,000		75,000
− Dividends	(8,000)	(32,000)		(40,000)
Ending book value	71,000	284,000	200,000	155,000

Advanced StudyGuide .com

The lighter shaded numbers in this chart comprise the basic elimination entry:

Basic elimination entry:

Common stock	200,000		← Original amount invested (100%)
Retained earnings	120,000		← Beginning RE from trial balance
Income from Special Foods	60,000		← Peerless' share of reported income
NCI in NI of Special Foods	15,000		← NCI's share of reported income
Dividends declared		40,000	← 100% of sub's dividends declared
Investment in Special Foods		284,000	← Peerless' share of Special Foods' NA
NCI in NA of Special Foods		71,000	← NCI's share of net amount of BV

The entire differential amount assigned to the inventory already passed through cost of goods sold during the prior year period. The only other amortization item is the excess value assigned to the building, which continues to be written off over a 10-year period ($60,000 ÷ 10 = $6,000).

Excess Value (Differential) Calculations:

	NCI 20%	+ Peerless 80%	= Land	+ Building	+ Acc. Depr.	+ Goodwill
Beginning Balances	14,675	58,700	10,000	60,000	(6,000)	9,375
Amortization	(1,200)	(4,800)			(6,000)	
Ending Balance	13,475	53,900	10,000	60,000	(12,000)	9,375

Since the amortization of the differential was already written off from the investment account against the Income from Special Foods account, the change to the differential is simply reclassified from the Income from Special Foods account to the income statement account to which it applies during the consolidation process. Then, the remaining amount of the differential is reclassified to the various balance accounts to which they apply:

Amortized excess value reclassification entry:

Depreciation expense	6,000		← Depreciation of excess building value
Income from Special Foods		4,800	← Peerless' share of amortization of diff.
NCI in NI of Special Foods		1,200	← NCI's share of amortization of differential

Excess value (differential) reclassification entry:

Land	10,000		← Original calculated excess value
Building	60,000		← Original calculated excess value
Goodwill	9,375		← Calculated value from acquisition
Accumulated depreciation		12,000	← = (Excess value ÷ 10 years) × 2 years
Investment in Special Foods		53,900	← Peerless' share of excess value
NCI in NA of Special Foods		13,475	← NCI's share of excess value

Again, these worksheet entries (1) eliminate the balances in the Investment in Special Foods and Income from Special Foods accounts, (2) reclassify the amortization of excess value to the proper income statement accounts, and (3) reclassify the remaining differential to the appropriate balance sheet accounts at the end of the accounting period. The following T-accounts illustrate how Peerless' Investment in Special Foods and Income from Special Foods accounts are eliminated.

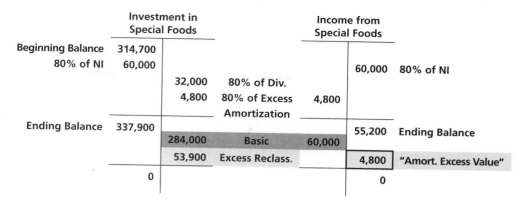

Again, we repeat the same accumulated depreciation elimination entry this year (and every year as long as Special Foods owns the assets) that we used in the initial year.

Optional accumulated depreciation elimination entry:

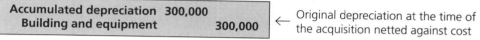

Accumulated depreciation	300,000	
Building and equipment		300,000

← Original depreciation at the time of the acquisition netted against cost

Figure 5–7 illustrates the worksheet to prepare a complete set of consolidated financial statements for the year 20X2.

Consolidated Net Income and Retained Earnings

Figure 5–8 shows the computation of 20X2 consolidated net income and consolidated retained earnings at the end of 20X2.

Consolidated Financial Statements

Figure 5–9 presents a consolidated income statement and retained earnings statement for the year 20X2 and a consolidated balance sheet as of December 31, 20X2.

DISCONTINUANCE OF CONSOLIDATION

LO3

Understand and explain what happens when a parent company ceases to consolidate a subsidiary.

A parent that has been including a subsidiary in its consolidated financial statements should exclude that company from future consolidation if the parent can no longer exercise control over it. Control might be lost for a number of reasons, such as the parent sells some or all of its interest in the subsidiary, the subsidiary issues additional common stock, the parent enters into an agreement to relinquish control, or the subsidiary comes under the control of the government or other regulator.

If a parent loses control of a subsidiary and no longer holds an equity interest in the former subsidiary, it recognizes a gain or loss for the difference between any proceeds received from the event leading to loss of control (e.g., sale of interest, expropriation of subsidiary) and the carrying amount of the parent's equity interest. If the parent loses control but maintains a noncontrolling equity interest in the former subsidiary, it must recognize a gain or loss for the difference, at the date control is lost, between (1) the sum of any proceeds received by the parent and the fair value of its remaining equity interest in the former subsidiary and (2) the carrying amount of the parent's total interest in the subsidiary.

FIGURE 5–7 December 31, 20X2, Equity-Method Worksheet for Consolidated Financial Statements, Second Year of Ownership; 80 Percent Acquisition at More than Book Value

	Peerless Products	Special Foods	Elimination Entries DR	Elimination Entries CR	Consolidated
Income Statement					
Sales	450,000	300,000			750,000
Less: COGS	(180,000)	(160,000)			(340,000)
Less: Depreciation Expense	(50,000)	(20,000)	6,000		(76,000)
Less: Other Expenses	(60,000)	(45,000)			(105,000)
Less: Impairment Loss					0
Income from Special Foods	55,200		60,000	4,800	0
Consolidated Net Income	215,200	75,000	66,000	4,800	229,000
NCI in Net Income			15,000	1,200	(13,800)
Controlling Interest Net Income	**215,200**	**75,000**	**81,000**	**6,000**	**215,200**
Statement of Retained Earnings					
Beginning Balance	408,700	120,000	120,000		408,700
Net Income	**215,200**	**75,000**	81,000	6,000	215,200
Less: Dividends Declared	(60,000)	(40,000)		40,000	(60,000)
Ending Balance	**563,900**	**155,000**	**201,000**	**46,000**	**563,900**
Balance Sheet					
Cash	221,000	85,000			306,000
Accounts Receivable	150,000	80,000			230,000
Inventory	180,000	90,000			270,000
Investment in Special Foods	337,900			284,000	0
				53,900	
Land	175,000	40,000	10,000		225,000
Buildings & Equipment	800,000	600,000	60,000	300,000	1,160,000
Less: Accumulated Depreciation	(500,000)	(340,000)	300,000	12,000	(552,000)
Goodwill			9,375		9,375
Total Assets	**1,363,900**	**555,000**	**379,375**	**649,900**	**1,648,375**
Accounts Payable	100,000	100,000			200,000
Bonds Payable	200,000	100,000			300,000
Common Stock	500,000	200,000	200,000		500,000
Retained Earnings	**563,900**	**155,000**	201,000	46,000	563,900
NCI in NA of Special Foods				71,000	84,475
				13,475	
Total Liabilities & Equity	**1,363,900**	**555,000**	**401,000**	**130,475**	**1,648,375**

FIGURE 5–8
Consolidated Net Income and Retained Earnings, 20X2; 80 Percent Acquisition at More than Book Value

Consolidated net income, 20X2:	
Peerless' separate operating income	$160,000
Special Foods' net income	75,000
Amortization of differential related to buildings and equipment in 20X2	(6,000)
Consolidated net income	$229,000
Income to controlling interest, 20X2:	
Consolidated net income	$229,000
Income to noncontrolling interest	(13,800)
Income to controlling interest	$215,200
Consolidated retained earnings, December 31, 20X2:	
Peerless' retained earnings on date of combination, January 1, 20X1	$300,000
Income to controlling interest, 20X1	168,700
Dividends declared by Peerless, 20X1	(60,000)
Consolidated retained earnings, December 31, 20X1	$408,700
Income to controlling interest, 20X2	215,200
Dividends declared by Peerless, 20X2	(60,000)
Consolidated retained earnings, December 31, 20X2	$563,900

FIGURE 5–9   **Consolidated Financial Statements for Peerless Products Corporation and Special Foods Inc., 20X2**

PEERLESS PRODUCTS CORPORATION AND SUBSIDIARY
Consolidated Income Statement
For the Year Ended December 31, 20X2

Sales		$750,000
Cost of Goods Sold		(340,000)
Gross Margin		$410,000
Expences:		
Depreciation and Amortization	$ 76,000	
Other Expenses	105,000	
Total Expenses		(181,000)
Consolidated Net Income		$229,000
Income to Noncontrolling Interest		(13,800)
Income to Controlling Interest		$215,200

PEERLESS PRODUCTS CORPORATION AND SUBSIDIARY
Consolidated Retained Earnings Statement
For the Year Ended December 31, 20X2

Retained Earnings, January 1, 20X2	$408,700
Income to Controlling Interest, 20X2	215,200
Dividends Declared, 20X2	(60,000)
Retained Earnings, December 31, 20X2	$563,900

PEERLESS PRODUCTS CORPORATION AND SUBSIDIARY
Consolidated Balance Sheet
December 31, 20X2

Assets			Liabilities		
Cash		$ 306,000	Accounts Payable	$200,000	
Accounts Receivable		230,000	Bonds Payable	300,000	
Inventory		270,000			$500,000
Land		225,000	Stockholders' Equity		
Buildings and Equipment	$1,160,000		Controling Interest		
Accumulated Depreciation	(552,000)		Common Stock	$500,000	
		608,000	Retained Earnings	563,900	
Goodwill		9,375	Total Controling Interest		1,063,900
			Noncontroling Interest		84,475
Total Assets		$1,648,375	Total Liabilities and Equity		$1,648,375

As an example, assume that Peerless Products sells three-quarters of its 80 percent interest in Special Foods on January 1, 20X2, for $246,000, leaving it holding 20 percent of Special Foods' outstanding stock. On that date, assume that the fair value of Special Foods as a whole is $410,000 and the carrying amount of Peerless' 80 percent share of Special Foods is $317,200 (as shown earlier in the chapter). Assume the fair value of Peerless' remaining 20 percent interest in Special Foods is $82,000. Peerless' gain on the sale of Special Foods stock is computed as follows:

Cash proceeds received	$246,000
Fair value of Peerless' remaining equity interest in Special Foods	82,000
	$328,000
Peerless' total interest in Special Foods at date of sale	314,700
Gain on sale of 60 percent interest in Special Foods	$ 13,300

Peerless reports the $13,300 gain in 20X2 income.

TREATMENT OF OTHER COMPREHENSIVE INCOME

LO4

Make calculations and prepare elimination entries for the consolidation of a partially owned subsidiary when there is a complex positive differential and other comprehensive income.

FASB Statement No. 130 (ASC 220), "Reporting Comprehensive Income", requires that companies separately report *other comprehensive income,* which includes all revenues, expenses, gains, and losses that under generally accepted accounting principles are excluded from net income.[2] Comprehensive income is the sum of net income and other comprehensive income. **FASB 130 (ASC 220)** permits several different options for reporting comprehensive income, but the consolidation process is the same regardless of the reporting format.

Other comprehensive income accounts are temporary accounts that are closed at the end of each period. Instead of being closed to Retained Earnings as revenue and expense accounts are, other comprehensive income accounts are closed to a special stockholders' equity account, Accumulated Other Comprehensive Income.

Modification of the Consolidation Worksheet

When a parent or subsidiary has recorded other comprehensive income, the consolidation worksheet normally includes an additional section for other comprehensive income. This section of the worksheet facilitates computation of the amount of other comprehensive income to be reported; the portion, if any, of other comprehensive income to be assigned to the noncontrolling interest; and the amount of accumulated other comprehensive income to be reported in the consolidated balance sheet. Although this extra section of the worksheet for comprehensive income could be placed after the income statement section of the standard worksheet, the format used here is to place it at the bottom of the worksheet. If neither the parent nor any subsidiary reports other comprehensive income, the section can be omitted from the worksheet. When other comprehensive income is reported, the worksheet is prepared in the normal manner, with the additional section added to the bottom. The only modification within the standard worksheet is an additional stockholders' equity account included in the balance sheet portion of the worksheet for the cumulative effects of the other comprehensive income.

To illustrate the consolidation process when a subsidiary reports other comprehensive income, assume that during 20X2 Special Foods purchases $20,000 of investments classified as available-for-sale. By December 31, 20X2, the fair value of the securities increases to $30,000. Other than the effects of accounting for Special Foods' investment in securities, the financial statement information reported by Peerless Products and Special Foods at December 31, 20X2, is identical to that presented in Figure 5–8.

Adjusting Entry Recorded by Subsidiary

At December 31, 20X2, Special Foods recognizes the increase in the fair value of its available-for-sale securities by recording the following adjusting entry:

(8)	Investment in Available-for-Sale Securities	10,000	
	Unrealized Gain on Investments (OCI)		10,000

Record the increase in fair value of available-for-sale securities.

The unrealized gain is not included in the subsidiary's net income but is reported by the subsidiary as an element of other comprehensive income (OCI).

Adjusting Entry Recorded by Parent Company

In 20X2, Peerless records all its normal entries relating to its investment in Special Foods as if the subsidiary had not reported other comprehensive income. In addition, at December 31, 20X2, Peerless Products separately recognizes its proportionate share of

---

[2] Other comprehensive income elements include foreign currency translation adjustments, unrealized gains and losses on certain derivatives and investments in certain types of securities, and certain minimum pension liability adjustments.

the subsidiary's unrealized gain from the increase in the value of the available-for-sale securities:

(9)	Investment in Special Foods	8,000	
	Other Comprehensive Income from Special Foods		8,000

Record share of the increase in value of available-for-sale-securities held by subsidiary.

Consolidation Worksheet—Second Year Following Combination

The worksheet to prepare a complete set of consolidated financial statements for the year 20X2 is illustrated in Figure 5–10. In the worksheet, Peerless' balance in the Investment in Special Foods Stock account is greater than the balance in Figure 5–8. Specifically, because of the adjusting entry just mentioned, Peerless' $8,000 proportionate share of Special Foods' unrealized gain is included in the separate section of the worksheet for comprehensive income (Other Comprehensive Income from Subsidiary—Unrealized Gain on Investments). Special Foods' trial balance has been changed to reflect (1) the reduction in the cash balance resulting from the investment acquisition, (2) the investment in available-for-sale securities, and (3) an unrealized gain of $10,000 on the investment.

Consolidation Procedures

The normal eliminating entries (the basic elimination entry, the amortized excess cost reclassification entry, the differential reclassification entry, and the accumulated depreciation elimination entry) were used in preparing the consolidation worksheet for 20X2 presented in Figure 5–7. Although these entries remain unchanged in this example, they would have included the elimination of the beginning balance of the subsidiary's accumulated Other Comprehensive Income, if the subsidiary had had a balance as of the beginning of the period because that account is properly included in the subsidiary's stockholders' equity; further, a portion of the balance of that account would have been allocated to the beginning noncontrolling interest, as with the other stockholders' equity accounts of the subsidiary.

One additional entry is needed for the treatment of the subsidiary's other comprehensive income. First, the proportionate share of the subsidiary's other comprehensive income recorded by the parent in the adjusting entry previously mentioned must be eliminated to avoid double-counting the subsidiary's other comprehensive income. Thus, the adjusting entry is reversed in the worksheet. Moreover, a proportionate share of the subsidiary's other comprehensive income must be allocated to the noncontrolling interest:

Other comprehensive income entry:

OCI from Special Foods	8,000	
OCI to the NCI	2,000	
Investment in Special Foods		8,000
NCI in NA of Subsidiary		2,000

The amount of consolidated other comprehensive income reported in the consolidated financial statements is equal to the subsidiary's $10,000 amount. The noncontrolling interest's $2,000 proportionate share of the subsidiary's other comprehensive income is deducted to arrive at the $8,000 other comprehensive income allocated to the controlling interest.

While consolidated net income is the same in Figure 5–10 as in Figure 5–7, the other comprehensive income section of the worksheet in Figure 5–10 gives explicit recognition to the unrealized gain on available-for-sale securities held by Special Foods. This permits recognition in the consolidated financial statements under any of the alternative formats permitted by the FASB.

FIGURE 5–10   December 31, 20X2, Comprehensive Income Illustration, Second Year of Ownership; 80 Percent Acquisition at More than Book Value

	Peerless Products	Special Foods	Elimination Entries DR	Elimination Entries CR	Consolidated
Income Statement					
Sales	450,000	300,000			750,000
Less: COGS	(180,000)	(160,000)			(340,000)
Less: Depreciation Expense	(50,000)	(20,000)	6,000		(76,000)
Less: Other Expenses	(60,000)	(45,000)			(105,000)
Less: Impairment Loss					0
Income from Special Foods	55,200		60,000	4,800	0
Consolidated Net Income	215,200	75,000	66,000	4,800	**229,000**
NCI in Net Income			15,000	1,200	**(13,800)**
Controlling Interest in Net Income	215,200	75,000	81,000	6,000	215,200
Statement of Retained Earnings					
Beginning Balance	408,700	120,000	120,000		408,700
Add Net Income	**215,200**	**75,000**	81,000	6,000	215,200
Less: Dividends Declared	(60,000)	(40,000)		40,000	(60,000)
Ending Balance	563,900	155,000	201,000	46,000	563,900
Balance Sheet					
Cash	221,000	65,000			286,000
Accounts Receivable	150,000	80,000			230,000
Inventory	180,000	90,000			270,000
Investment in Subsidiary	345,900			284,000	0
				53,900	
				8,000	
Investment in AFS Securities		30,000			30,000
Land	175,000	40,000	10,000		225,000
Buildings & Equipment	800,000	600,000	60,000	300,000	1,160,000
Less: Accumulated Depreciation	(500,000)	(340,000)	300,000	12,000	(552,000)
Goodwill			9,375		9,375
Total Assets	1,371,900	565,000	379,375	657,900	1,658,375
Accounts Payable	100,000	100,000			200,000
Bonds Payable	200,000	100,000			300,000
Common Stock	500,000	200,000	200,000		500,000
Retained Earnings	**563,900**	155,000	201,000	46,000	563,900
Accumulated Other Comprehensive Income, 12/31/X2	8,000	10,000	10,000	0	8,000
NCI in NA of Special Foods				71,000	86,475
				13,475	
				2,000	
Total Liabilities & Equity	1,371,900	565,000	411,000	130,475	1,658,375
Other Comprehensive Income					
Accumulated Other Comprehensive Income, 1/1/X2	0	0			0
Other Comprehensive Income from Special Foods	8,000		8,000		0
Unrealized Gain on Investments		10,000			10,000
Other Comprehensive Income to NCI			2,000		(2,000)
Accumulated Other Comprehensive Income, 12/31/X2	**8,000**	**10,000**	**10,000**	**0**	**8,000**

Consolidated financial statements for the other comprehensive income example are presented in Figure 5–11. Note that consolidated other comprehensive income includes the full $10,000 unrealized gain. The noncontrolling interest's share is then deducted,

FIGURE 5–11

Consolidated Financial Statements for Peerless Products Corporation and Special Foods Inc., 20X2, Including Other Comprehensive Income

PEERLESS PRODUCTS CORPORATION AND SUBSIDIARY
Consolidated Income Statement
For the Year Ended December 31, 20X2

Sales		$750,000
Cost of Goods Sold		(340,000)
Gross Margin		$410,000
Expences:		
Depreciation and Amortization	$ 76,000	
Other Expenses	105,000	
Total Expenses		(181,000)
Consolidated Net Income		$229,000
Income to Noncontrolling Interest		(13,800)
Income to Controlling Interest		$215,200

PEERLESS PRODUCTS CORPORATION AND SUBSIDIARY
Consolidated Statement of Comprehensive Income
For the Year Ended December 31, 20X2

Consolidated Net Income	$229,000
Other Comprehensive Income:	
Unrealized Gain on Investments	10,000
Total Consolidated Comprehensive Income	$239,000
Less: Comprehensive Income Attribute to Noncontrolling Interest	15,800
Comprehensive Income Attribute to Controlling Interest	$223,200

PEERLESS PRODUCTS CORPORATION AND SUBSIDIARY
Consolidated Statement of Financial Position
December 31, 20X2

Assets		
Cash		$ 286,000
Accounts Receivable		230,000
Inventory		270,000
Investment in Available-for-Sale Securities		30,000
Land		225,000
Buildings and Equipment	$1,160,000	
Accumulated Depreciation	(552,000)	608,000
Goodwill		9,375
Total Assets		$1,658,375
Liabilities		
Accounts Payable	$ 200,000	
Bonds Payable	300,000	
Total Liabilities		$ 500,000
Stockholders' Equity		
Controlling Interest:		
Common Stock	$ 500,000	
Retained Earnings	563,900	
Accumulated Other Comprehensive Income	8,000	
Total Controlling Interest	$1,071,900	
Noncontrolling Interest	86,475	
Total Stockholders' Equity		1,158,375
Total Liabilities and Stockholders' Equity		$1,658,375

along with its share of consolidated net income, to arrive at the consolidated comprehensive income allocated to the controlling interest. The amount of other comprehensive income allocated to the controlling interest is carried to the Accumulated Other Comprehensive Income that is reported in the consolidated balance sheet, while the noncontrolling interest's share is included in the Noncontrolling Interest amount in the consolidated balance sheet. The FASB requires that the amount of each other comprehensive income element allocated to the controlling and noncontrolling interests be disclosed in the consolidated statements or notes.

Consolidation Worksheet—Comprehensive Income in Subsequent Years

Each year following 20X2, Special Foods will adjust the unrealized gain on investments on its books for the change in fair value of the available-for-sale securities. For example, if Special Foods' investment increased in value by an additional $5,000 during 20X3, Special Foods would increase by $5,000 the carrying amount of its investment in securities and recognize as an element of 20X3's other comprehensive income an unrealized gain of $5,000. Under equity-method recording, Peerless would increase its Investment in Special Foods Stock account and record its $4,000 share of the subsidiary's other comprehensive income.

The eliminating entries required to prepare the consolidation worksheet at December 31, 20X3, would include the normal eliminating entries (the basic elimination entry, the amortized excess cost reclassification entry, the differential reclassification entry, and the accumulated depreciation elimination entry). In addition, the basic elimination entry would be expanded to eliminate the subsidiary's $10,000 beginning Accumulated Other Comprehensive Income balance and to increase the noncontrolling interest by its proportionate share of the subsidiary's beginning Accumulated Other Comprehensive Income amount ($10,000 × 0.20). The Other Comprehensive Income eliminating entry allocates the 20X3 other comprehensive income:

Other comprehensive income entry:

OCI from Special Foods	4,000	
OCI to the NCI	1,000	
Investment in Special Foods		4,000
NCI in NA of Subsidiary		1,000

ADDITIONAL CONSIDERATIONS

LO5

Understand and explain additional considerations associated with consolidation.

Chapters 3, 4, and 5 provide a conceptual foundation for preparing consolidated financial statements and a description of the basic procedures used in preparing consolidated statements. Before moving on to intercompany transactions in Chapters 6 and 7, several additional items should be considered to provide completeness and clarity.

Subsidiary Valuation Accounts at Acquisition

FASB 141R (ASC 805) indicates that all assets and liabilities acquired in a business combination should be valued at their acquisition-date fair values and no valuation accounts are to be carried over. While the application of this rule is clear-cut in merger-type business combinations, its application in consolidation following a stock acquisition is less clear. A subsidiary maintains an ongoing set of books and, unless push-down accounting is employed, it will carry forward its accounts. For some valuation accounts, such as accumulated depreciation, theory has dictated that the acquisition-date amount of the valuation account should be offset against the related asset account each time consolidated statements are prepared. Nevertheless, as an expediency, and because of a lack of materiality, companies generally have not made this offset, with no effect on the net amount of the asset. That is not expected to change under **FASB 141R (ASC 805).** For some other valuation accounts, depending on their nature and materiality, and how the amounts work out over time, they may have to be offset each time consolidated statements are prepared, at least for some number of periods. This is the reason for the optional accumulated depreciation elimination entry.

Negative Retained Earnings of Subsidiary at Acquisition

A parent company may acquire a subsidiary with a negative or debit balance in its retained earnings account. An accumulated deficit of a subsidiary at acquisition causes no special problems in the consolidation process. The basic investment account elimination entry is the same in the consolidation worksheet except that the debit balance in the subsidiary's Retained Earnings account is eliminated with a credit entry. Thus, the basic investment account elimination entry appears as follows:

Basic investment account elimination entry:

Common stock	XX	
Income from Special Foods	XX	
NCI in NI of Special Foods	XX	
Retained earnings		XX
Dividends declared		XX
Investment in Special Foods		XX
NCI in NA of Special Foods		XX

Other Stockholders' Equity Accounts

The discussion of consolidated statements up to this point has dealt with companies having stockholders' equity consisting only of retained earnings and a single class of capital stock issued at par. Typically, companies have more complex stockholders' equity structures, often including preferred stock and various types of additional contributed capital. In general, all stockholders' equity accounts accruing to the common shareholders receive the same treatment as common stock and are eliminated at the time common stock is eliminated.

Subsidiary's Disposal of Differential-Related Assets

The disposal of an asset usually has income statement implications. If the asset is held by a subsidiary and is one to which a differential is assigned in the consolidation worksheet, both the parent's equity-method income and consolidated net income are affected. On the parent's books, the portion of the differential included in the subsidiary investment account that relates to the asset sold must be written off by the parent under the equity method as a reduction in both the income from the subsidiary and the investment account. In consolidation, the portion of the differential related to the asset sold is treated as an adjustment to consolidated income.

Inventory

Any inventory-related differential is assigned to inventory for as long as the subsidiary holds the inventory units. In the period in which the inventory units are sold, the inventory-related differential is assigned to Cost of Goods Sold, as illustrated previously in Figure 5–5.

The inventory costing method used by the subsidiary determines the period in which the differential cost of goods sold is recognized. When the subsidiary uses FIFO inventory costing, the inventory units on hand on the date of combination are viewed as being the first units sold after the combination. Therefore, the differential normally is assigned to cost of goods sold in the period immediately after the combination. When the subsidiary uses LIFO inventory costing, the inventory units on the date of combination are viewed as remaining in the subsidiary's inventory. Thus, when the subsidiary uses LIFO inventory costing, the differential is not assigned to cost of goods sold unless the inventory level drops below its level at the date of combination.

Fixed Assets

A differential related to land held by a subsidiary is added to the Land balance in the consolidation worksheet each time a consolidated balance sheet is prepared. If the subsidiary sells the land to which the differential relates, the differential is treated in the consolidation worksheet as an adjustment to the gain or loss on the sale of the land in the period of the sale.

To illustrate, assume that on January 1, 20X1, Pluto purchases all the common stock of Star at $10,000 more than book value. All the differential relates to land that Star had purchased earlier for $25,000. So long as Star continues to hold the land, the $10,000 differential is assigned to Land in the consolidation worksheet. If Star sells the land to an unrelated company for $40,000, the following entry is recorded on Star's books:

(10)	Cash	40,000	
	Land		25,000
	Gain on Sale of Land		15,000
	Record sale of Land.		

While a gain of $15,000 is appropriate for Star to report, the accounting basis of the land to the consolidated entity is $35,000 ($25,000 + $10,000). Therefore, the consolidated enterprise must report a gain of only $5,000. To reduce the $15,000 gain reported by Star to the $5,000 gain that should be reported by the consolidated entity, the following elimination is included in the consolidation worksheet for the year of the sale:

Eliminate gain on sale of land:

| Gain on Sale of Land | 10,000 | |
| Income from Star | | 10,000 |

If, instead, Star sells the land for $32,000, the $7,000 ($32,000 − $25,000) gain recorded by Star is eliminated, and a loss of $3,000 ($32,000 − $35,000) is recognized in the consolidated income statement. The eliminating entry in this case is

Eliminate gain and record loss on sale of land:

Gain on Sale of Land	7,000	
Loss on Sale of Land	3,000	
Income from Star		10,000

When the equity method is used on the parent's books, the parent must adjust the carrying amount of the investment and its equity-method income in the period of the sale to write off the differential, as discussed in Chapter 2. Thereafter, the $10,000 differential no longer exists.

The sale of differential-related equipment is treated in the same manner as land except that the amortization for the current and previous periods must be considered.

Summary of Key Concepts

The procedures and worksheet for consolidating less-than-wholly-owned subsidiaries are the same as discussed in Chapter 4 for wholly owned subsidiaries, with several modifications. The worksheet elimination entries are modified to include the noncontrolling shareholders' claim on the income and assets of the subsidiary. The noncontrolling interest has a claim on subsidiary assets based on its acquisition-date fair value. If the acquisition-date fair value of the consideration given in a business combination, plus the fair value of any noncontrolling interest, exceeds the book value of the subsidiary, the difference is referred to as a differential and increases both the controlling and noncontrolling interests. The subsidiary's assets and liabilities are valued in consolidation based on their full acquisition-date fair values, with goodwill recognized at acquisition for the difference between (1) the sum of the fair value of the consideration given in the combination and the fair value of the noncontrolling interest and (2) the fair value of the subsidiary's net identifiable assets. Any subsequent write-off of the differential reduces both the controlling and noncontrolling interests.

Consolidated net income is equal to the parent's income from its own operations plus the subsidiary's net income adjusted for any amortization or write-off of the differential. The amount of consolidated net income attributable to the noncontrolling interest is equal to the noncontrolling interest's proportionate share of the subsidiary's net income less a proportionate share of any differential write-off. The income attributable to the controlling interest is equal to consolidated net income less the income attributable to the noncontrolling interest.

A subsidiary's other comprehensive income for the period must be recognized in consolidated other comprehensive income and allocated between the controlling and noncontrolling interests. The consolidation worksheet is modified to accommodate the other comprehensive income items by adding a special section at the bottom.

Key Term

other comprehensive income, *220*

Questions

LO1	**Q5-1**	Where is the balance assigned to the noncontrolling interest reported in the consolidated balance sheet?
LO1	**Q5-2**	Why must a noncontrolling interest be reported in the consolidated balance sheet?
LO1	**Q5-3**	How does the introduction of noncontrolling shareholders change the consolidation worksheet?
LO1	**Q5-4**	How is the amount assigned to the noncontrolling interest normally determined when a consolidated balance sheet is prepared immediately after a business combination?
LO2	**Q5-5**	What portion of consolidated retained earnings is assigned to the noncontrolling interest in the consolidated balance sheet?
LO2	**Q5-6**	When majority ownership is acquired, what portion of the fair value of assets held by the subsidiary at acquisition is reported in the consolidated balance sheet?
LO2	**Q5-7**	When majority ownership is acquired, what portion of the goodwill reported in the consolidated balance sheet is assigned to the noncontrolling interest?
LO2	**Q5-8**	How is the income assigned to the noncontrolling interest normally computed?
LO2	**Q5-9**	How is income assigned to the noncontrolling interest shown in the consolidation worksheet?
LO2	**Q5-10**	How are dividends paid by a subsidiary to noncontrolling shareholders treated in the consolidation worksheet?
LO5	**Q5-11**	Does a noncontrolling shareholder have access to any information other than the consolidated financial statements to determine how well the subsidiary is doing? Explain.
LO4	**Q5-12**	How do other comprehensive income elements reported by a subsidiary affect the consolidated financial statements?
LO4	**Q5-13**	What portion of other comprehensive income reported by a subsidiary is included in the consolidated statement of comprehensive income as accruing to parent company shareholders?

LO5 **Q5-14†** Prior to the adoption of **FASB 141R (ASC 805),** how was the amount of the differential determined?

LO5 **Q5-15†** Prior to the adoption of **FASB 141R (ASC 805),** how was the amount reported as goodwill determined when majority ownership was acquired at an amount greater than book value?

LO5 **Q5-16†** Prior to the adoption of **FASB 141R (ASC 805),** how was the amount of consolidated net income of a less-than-wholly-owned subsidiary determined?

LO5 **Q5-17*** What effect does a negative retained earnings balance on the subsidiary's books have on consolidation procedures?

LO5 **Q5-18*** What type of adjustment must be made in the consolidation worksheet if a differential is assigned to land and the subsidiary disposes of the land in the current period?

Cases

LO2 **C5-1 Consolidation Worksheet Preparation**

Analysis The newest clerk in the accounting office recently entered trial balance data for the parent company and its subsidiaries in the company's consolidation program. After a few minutes of additional work needed to eliminate the intercompany investment account balances, he expressed his satisfaction at having completed the consolidation worksheet for 20X5. In reviewing the printout of the consolidation worksheet, other employees raised several questions, and you are asked to respond.

Required

Indicate whether each of the following items can be answered by looking at the data in the consolidation worksheet (indicate why or why not):

a. Is it possible to tell if the parent is using the equity method in recording its ownership of each subsidiary?

b. Is it possible to tell if the correct amount of consolidated net income has been reported?

c. One of the employees thought the parent company had paid well above the fair value of net assets for a subsidiary purchased on January 1, 20X5. Is it possible to tell by reviewing the consolidation worksheet?

d. Is it possible to determine from the worksheet the percentage ownership of a subsidiary held by the parent?

LO2 **C5-2 Consolidated Income Presentation**

Research Standard Company has a relatively high profit margin on its sales, and Jewel Company has a substantially lower profit margin. Standard holds 55 percent of Jewel's common stock and includes Jewel in its consolidated statements. Standard and Jewel reported sales of $100,000 and $60,000, respectively, in 20X4. Sales increased to $120,000 and $280,000 for the two companies in 20X5. The average profit margins of the two companies remained constant over the two years at 60 percent and 10 percent, respectively.

Standard's treasurer was aware that the subsidiary was awarded a major new contract in 20X5 and anticipated a substantial increase in net income for the year. She was disappointed to learn that consolidated net income allocated to the controlling interest had increased by only 38 percent even though sales were 2.5 times higher than in 20X4. She is not trained in accounting and does not understand the fundamental processes used in preparing Standard's consolidated income statement. She does know, however, that the earnings per share figures reported in the consolidated income statement are based on income allocated to the controlling interest and she wonders why that number isn't higher.

Required

As a member of the accounting department, you have been asked to prepare a memo to the treasurer explaining how consolidated net income is computed and the procedures used to allocate income to the parent company and to the subsidiary's noncontrolling shareholders. Include in your memo citations to or quotations from the authoritative literature. To assist the treasurer in gaining a better understanding, prepare an analysis showing the income statement amounts actually reported for 20X4 and 20X5.

*Indicates that the item relates to "Additional Considerations."

†These questions may require Internet research.

LO1

Research

C5-3 Pro Rata Consolidation

Rose Corporation and Krome Company established a joint venture to manufacture components for both companies' use on January 1, 20X1, and have operated it quite successfully for the past four years. Rose and Krome both contributed 50 percent of the equity when the joint venture was created. Rose purchases roughly 70 percent of the output of the joint venture and Krome purchases 30 percent. Rose and Krome have equal numbers of representatives on the joint venture's board of directors and participate equally in its management. Joint venture profits are distributed at year-end on the basis of total purchases by each company.

Required

Rose has been using the equity method to report its investment in the joint venture; however, Rose's financial vice president believes that each company should use pro rata consolidation. As a senior accountant at Rose, you have been asked to prepare a memo discussing those situations in which pro rata consolidation may be appropriate and to offer your recommendation as to whether Rose should continue to use the equity method or switch to pro rata consolidation. Include in your memo citations of and quotations from the authoritative literature to support your arguments.

LO1

Communication

C5-4 Elimination Procedures

A new employee has been given responsibility for preparing the consolidated financial statements of Sample Company. After attempting to work alone for some time, the employee seeks assistance in gaining a better overall understanding of the way in which the consolidation process works.

Required

You have been asked to provide assistance in explaining the consolidation process.

a. Why must the eliminating entries be entered in the consolidation worksheet each time consolidated statements are prepared?

b. How is the beginning-of-period noncontrolling interest balance determined?

c. How is the end-of-period noncontrolling interest balance determined?

d. Which of the subsidiary's account balances must always be eliminated?

e. Which of the parent company's account balances must always be eliminated?

LO1

Research

C5-5 Changing Accounting Standards: Monsanto Company

Monsanto Company, a St. Louis–based company, is a leading provider of agricultural products for farmers. It sells seeds, biotechnology trait products, and herbicides worldwide.

Required

a. How did Monsanto Company report its income to noncontrolling (minority) shareholders of consolidated subsidiaries in its 2007 consolidated income statement?

b. How did Monsanto Company report its subsidiary noncontrolling (minority) interest in its 2007 consolidated balance sheet?

c. Comment on Monsanto's treatment of its subsidiary noncontrolling interest.

d. In 2007, Monsanto had several affiliates that were special purpose or variable interest entities. What level of ownership did Monsanto have in these entities? Were any of these consolidated? Why?

Exercises

LO1, LO2

E5-1 Multiple-Choice Questions on Consolidation Process

Select the most appropriate answer for each of the following questions.

1. If A Company acquires 80 percent of the stock of B Company on January 1, 20X2, immediately after the acquisition

   a. Consolidated retained earnings will be equal to the combined retained earnings of the two companies.

   b. Goodwill will always be reported in the consolidated balance sheet.

   c. A Company's additional paid-in capital may be reduced to permit the carryforward of B Company retained earnings.

   d. Consolidated retained earnings and A Company retained earnings will be the same.

2. Which of the following is correct?

   a. The noncontrolling shareholders' claim on the subsidiary's net assets is based on the book value of the subsidiary's net assets.

   b. Only the parent's portion of the difference between book value and fair value of the subsidiary's assets is assigned to those assets.

   c. Goodwill represents the difference between the book value of the subsidiary's net assets and the amount paid by the parent to buy ownership.

   d. Total assets reported by the parent generally will be less than total assets reported on the consolidated balance sheet.

3. Which of the following statements is correct?

   a. Foreign subsidiaries do not need to be consolidated if they are reported as a separate operating group under segment reporting.

   b. Consolidated retained earnings do not include the noncontrolling interest's claim on the subsidiary's retained earnings.

   c. The noncontrolling shareholders' claim should be adjusted for changes in the fair value of the subsidiary assets but should not include goodwill.

   d. Consolidation is expected any time the investor holds significant influence over the investee.

4. [AICPA Adapted] At December 31, 20X9, Grey Inc. owned 90 percent of Winn Corporation, a consolidated subsidiary, and 20 percent of Carr Corporation, an investee in which Grey cannot exercise significant influence. On the same date, Grey had receivables of $300,000 from Winn and $200,000 from Carr. In its December 31, 20X9, consolidated balance sheet, Grey should report accounts receivable from its affiliates of

   a. $500,000.

   b. $340,000.

   c. $230,000.

   d. $200,000.

LO1, LO2   **E5-2** **Multiple-Choice Questions on Consolidation [AICPA Adapted]**

Select the correct answer for each of the following questions.

1. A 70 percent owned subsidiary company declares and pays a cash dividend. What effect does the dividend have on the retained earnings and minority interest balances in the parent company's consolidated balance sheet?

   a. No effect on either retained earnings or minority interest.

   b. No effect on retained earnings and a decrease in minority interest.

   c. Decreases in both retained earnings and minority interest.

   d. A decrease in retained earnings and no effect on minority interest.

2. How is the portion of consolidated earnings to be assigned to the noncontrolling interest in consolidated financial statements determined?

   a. The parent's net income is subtracted from the subsidiary's net income to determine the noncontrolling interest.

   b. The subsidiary's net income is extended to the noncontrolling interest.

   c. The amount of the subsidiary's earnings recognized for consolidation purposes is multiplied by the noncontrolling interest's percentage of ownership.

   d. The amount of consolidated earnings on the consolidated worksheets is multiplied by the noncontrolling interest percentage on the balance sheet date.

3. On January 1, 20X5, Post Company acquired an 80 percent investment in Stake Company. The acquisition cost was equal to Post's equity in Stake's net assets at that date. On January 1, 20X5, Post and Stake had retained earnings of $500,000 and $100,000, respectively. During 20X5, Post had net income of $200,000, which included its equity in Stake's earnings, and declared dividends of $50,000; Stake had net income of $40,000 and declared dividends of $20,000. There were no other intercompany transactions between the parent and subsidiary. On December 31, 20X5, what should the consolidated retained earnings be?

a. $650,000.

b. $666,000.

c. $766,000.

d. $770,000.

Note: Items 4 and 5 are based on the following information:

On January 1, 20X8, Ritt Corporation acquired 80 percent of Shaw Corporation's $10 par common stock for $956,000. On this date, the fair value of the noncontrolling interest was $239,000, and the carrying amount of Shaw's net assets was $1,000,000. The fair values of Shaw's identifiable assets and liabilities were the same as their carrying amounts except for plant assets (net) with a remaining life of 20 years, which were $100,000 in excess of the carrying amount. For the year ended December 31, 20X8, Shaw had net income of $190,000 and paid cash dividends totaling $125,000.

4. In the January 1, 20X8, consolidated balance sheet, the amount of goodwill reported should be

a. $0.

b. $76,000.

c. $95,000.

d. $156,000.

5. In the December 31, 20X8, consolidated balance sheet, the amount of noncontrolling interest reported should be

a. $200,000.

b. $239,000.

c. $251,000.

d. $252,000.

LO2

Advanced
StudyGuide
.com

E5-3   Eliminating Entries with Differential

On June 10, 20X8, Game Corporation acquired 60 percent of Amber Company's common stock. The fair value of the noncontrolling interest was $32,800 on that date. Summarized balance sheet data for the two companies immediately after the stock purchase are as follows:

Item	Game Corp. Book Value	Amber Company Book Value	Amber Company Fair Value
Cash	$ 25,800	$ 5,000	$ 5,000
Accounts Receivable	30,000	10,000	10,000
Inventory	80,000	20,000	25,000
Buildings and Equipment (net)	120,000	50,000	70,000
Investment in Amber Stock	49,200		
Total	$305,000	$85,000	$110,000
Accounts Payable	$ 25,000	$ 3,000	$ 3,000
Bonds Payable	150,000	25,000	25,000
Common Stock	55,000	20,000	
Retained Earnings	75,000	37,000	
Total	$305,000	$85,000	$ 28,000

Required

a. Give the eliminating entries required to prepare a consolidated balance sheet immediately after the purchase of Amber Company shares.

b. Explain how eliminating entries differ from other types of journal entries recorded in the normal course of business.

LO2

E5-4   Computation of Consolidated Balances

Slim Corporation's balance sheet at January 1, 20X7, reflected the following balances:

Cash and Receivables	$ 80,000	Accounts Payable	$ 40,000
Inventory	120,000	Income Taxes Payable	60,000
Land	70,000	Bonds Payable	200,000
Buildings and Equipment (net)	480,000	Common Stock	250,000
		Retained Earnings	200,000
Total Assets	$750,000	Total Liabilities and Stockholders' Equity	$750,000

Ford Corporation entered into an active acquisition program and acquired 80 percent of Slim's common stock on January 2, 20X7, for $470,000. The fair value of the noncontrolling interest at that date was determined to be $117,500. A careful review of the fair value of Slim's assets and liabilities indicated the following:

	Book Value	Fair Value
Inventory	$120,000	$140,000
Land	70,000	60,000
Buildings and Equipment (net)	480,000	550,000

Goodwill is assigned proportionately to Ford and the noncontrolling shareholders.

Required

Compute the appropriate amount to be included in the consolidated balance sheet immediately following the acquisition for each of the following items:

a. Inventory.

b. Land.

c. Buildings and Equipment (net).

d. Goodwill.

e. Investment in Slim Corporation.

f. Noncontrolling Interest.

LO2

E5-5 Balance Sheet Worksheet

Power Company owns 90 percent of Pleasantdale Dairy's stock. The balance sheets of the two companies immediately after the Pleasantdale acquisition showed the following amounts:

	Power Company	Pleasantdale Dairy
Cash and Receivables	$ 130,000	$ 70,000
Inventory	210,000	90,000
Land	70,000	40,000
Buildings and Equipment (net)	390,000	220,000
Investment in Pleasantdale Stock	270,000	
Total Assets	$1,070,000	$420,000
Current Payables	$ 80,000	$ 40,000
Long-Term Liabilities	200,000	100,000
Common Stock	400,000	60,000
Retained Earnings	390,000	220,000
Total Liabilities and Stockholders' Equity	$1,070,000	$420,000

The fair value of the noncontrolling interest at the date of acquisition was determined to be $30,000. The full amount of the increase over book value is assigned to land held by Pleasantdale. At the date of acquisition, Pleasantdale owed Power $8,000 plus $900 accrued interest. Pleasantdale had recorded the accrued interest, but Power had not.

Required

Prepare and complete a consolidated balance sheet worksheet.

LO2

E5-6 Majority-Owned Subsidiary Acquired at Greater than Book Value

Zenith Corporation acquired 70 percent of Down Corporation's common stock on December 31, 20X4, for $102,200. The fair value of the noncontrolling interest at that date was determined to be $43,800. Data from the balance sheets of the two companies included the following amounts as of the date of acquisition:

Item	Zenith Corporation	Down Corporation
Cash	$ 50,300	$ 21,000
Accounts Receivable	90,000	44,000
Inventory	130,000	75,000
Land	60,000	30,000
Buildings and Equipment	410,000	250,000
Less: Accumulated Depreciation	(150,000)	(80,000)
Investment in Down Corporation Stock	102,200	
Total Assets	$692,500	$340,000
Accounts Payable	$152,500	$ 35,000
Mortgage Payable	250,000	180,000
Common Stock	80,000	40,000
Retained Earnings	210,000	85,000
Total Liabilities and Stockholders' Equity	$692,500	$340,000

At the date of the business combination, the book values of Down's assets and liabilities approximated fair value except for inventory, which had a fair value of $81,000, and buildings and equipment, which had a fair value of $185,000. At December 31, 20X4, Zenith reported accounts payable of $12,500 to Down, which reported an equal amount in its accounts receivable.

Required

a. Give the eliminating entry or entries needed to prepare a consolidated balance sheet immediately following the business combination.
b. Prepare a consolidated balance sheet worksheet.
c. Prepare a consolidated balance sheet in good form.

LO2

E5-7 Consolidation with Minority Interest

Temple Corporation acquired 75 percent of Dynamic Corporation's voting common stock on December 31, 20X4, for $390,000. At the date of combination, Dynamic reported the following:

Current Assets	$220,000	Current Liabilities	$ 80,000
Long-Term Assets (net)	420,000	Long-Term Liabilities	200,000
		Common Stock	120,000
		Retained Earnings	240,000
Total	$640,000	Total	$640,000

At December 31, 20X4, the book values of Dynamic's net assets and liabilities approximated their fair values, except for buildings, which had a fair value of $80,000 more than book value, and inventories, which had a fair value of $36,000 more than book value. The fair value of the noncontrolling interest was determined to be $130,000 at that date.

Required

Temple Corporation wishes to prepare a consolidated balance sheet immediately following the business combination. Give the eliminating entry or entries needed to prepare a consolidated balance sheet at December 31, 20X4.

LO2

E5-8 Worksheet for Majority-Owned Subsidiary

Glitter Enterprises acquired 60 percent of Lowtide Builders' stock on December 31, 20X4. Glitter acquired its shares for $90,000, the book value of the shares acquired. At that date, the fair value of the noncontrolling interest was equal to 40 percent of the book value of Lowtide. Balance sheet data for Glitter and Lowtide on January 1, 20X5, are as follows:

	Glitter Enterprises	Lowtide Builders
Cash and Receivables	$ 80,000	$ 30,000
Inventory	150,000	350,000
Buildings and Equipment (net)	430,000	80,000
Investment in Lowtide Stock	90,000	
Total Assets	$750,000	$460,000
Current Liabilities	$100,000	$110,000
Long-Term Debt	400,000	200,000
Common Stock	200,000	140,000
Retained Earnings	50,000	10,000
Total Liabilities and Stockholders' Equity	$750,000	$460,000

Required

a. Give all eliminating entries needed to prepare a consolidated balance sheet on January 1, 20X5.
b. Complete a consolidated balance sheet worksheet.
c. Prepare a consolidated balance sheet in good form.

LO2

E5-9 Multiple-Choice Questions on Balance Sheet Consolidation

Power Corporation acquired 70 percent of Silk Corporation's common stock on December 31, 20X2. Balance sheet data for the two companies immediately following the acquisition follow:

Item	Power Corporation	Silk Corporation
Cash	$ 44,000	$ 30,000
Accounts Receivable	110,000	45,000
Inventory	130,000	70,000
Land	80,000	25,000
Buildings and Equipment	500,000	400,000
Less: Accumulated Depreciation	(223,000)	(165,000)
Investment in Silk Corporation Stock	150,500	
Total Assets	$ 791,500	$405,000
Accounts Payable	$ 61,500	$ 28,000
Taxes Payable	95,000	37,000
Bonds Payable	280,000	200,000
Common Stock	150,000	50,000
Retained Earnings	205,000	90,000
Total Liabilities and Stockholders' Equity	$ 791,500	$405,000

At the date of the business combination, the book values of Silk's net assets and liabilities approximated fair value except for inventory, which had a fair value of $85,000, and land, which had a fair value of $45,000. The fair value of the noncontrolling interest was $64,500 on December 31, 20X2.

Required

For each question below, indicate the appropriate total that should appear in the consolidated balance sheet prepared immediately after the business combination.

1. What amount of inventory will be reported?
   a. $179,000.
   b. $200,000.
   c. $210,500.
   d. $215,000.

2. What amount of goodwill will be reported?
   a. $0.
   b. $28,000.
   c. $40,000.
   d. $52,000.

3. What amount of total assets will be reported?
   a. $1,081,000.
   b. $1,121,000.
   c. $1,196,500.
   d. $1,231,500.

4. What amount of total liabilities will be reported?
   a. $265,000.
   b. $436,500.
   c. $622,000.
   d. $701,500.

5. What amount will be reported as noncontrolling interest?
   a. $42,000.
   b. $52,500.
   c. $60,900.
   d. $64,500.

6. What amount of consolidated retained earnings will be reported?
   a. $295,000.
   b. $268,000.
   c. $232,000.
   d. $205,000.

7. What amount of total stockholders' equity will be reported?
   a. $355,000.
   b. $397,000.
   c. $419,500.
   d. $495,000.

LO2

E5-10   Basic Consolidation Entries for Majority-Owned Subsidiary

Farmstead Company reported the following summarized balance sheet data on December 31, 20X8:

Assets	$350,000	Account Payable	$ 50,000
		Common Stock	100,000
		Retained Earnings	200,000
Total	$350,000	Total	$350,000

On January 1, 20X9, Horrigan Corporation acquired 70 percent of Farmstead's stock for $210,000, the book value of the shares acquired. At that date the fair value of the noncontrolling interest was equal to 30 percent of the book value of Farmstead. Farmstead reported net income of $20,000 for 20X9 and paid dividends of $5,000.

Required

a. Give the equity-method journal entries recorded by Horrigan on its books during 20X9 related to its ownership of Farmstead.

b. Give the eliminating entries needed on December 31, 20X9, to prepare consolidated financial statements.

LO2 **E5-11** **Majority-Owned Subsidiary with Differential**

Canton Corporation is a majority-owned subsidiary of West Corporation. West acquired 75 percent ownership on January 1, 20X3, for $133,500. At that date, Canton reported common stock outstanding of $60,000 and retained earnings of $90,000, and the fair value of the noncontrolling interest was $44,500. The differential is assigned to equipment, which had a fair value $28,000 greater than book value and a remaining economic life of seven years at the date of the business combination. Canton reported net income of $30,000 and paid dividends of $12,000 in 20X3.

Required

a. Give the journal entries recorded by West during 20X3 on its books if it accounts for its investment in Canton using the equity method.

b. Give the eliminating entries needed at December 31, 20X3, to prepare consolidated financial statements.

LO2 **E5-12** **Differential Assigned to Amortizable Asset**

Major Corporation acquired 90 percent of Lancaster Company's voting common stock on January 1, 20X1, for $486,000. At the time of the combination, Lancaster reported common stock outstanding of $120,000 and retained earnings of $380,000, and the fair value of the noncontrolling interest was $54,000. The book value of Lancaster's net assets approximated market value except for patents that had a market value of $40,000 more than their book value. The patents had a remaining economic life of five years at the date of the business combination. Lancaster reported net income of $60,000 and paid dividends of $20,000 during 20X1.

Required

a. What balance did Major report as its investment in Lancaster at December 31, 20X1, assuming Major uses the equity method in accounting for its investment?

b. Give the eliminating entry or entries needed to prepare consolidated financial statements at December 31, 20X1.

LO2 **E5-13** **Consolidation after One Year of Ownership**

Pioneer Corporation purchased 80 percent of Lowe Corporation's stock on January 1, 20X2. At that date Lowe reported retained earnings of $80,000 and had $120,000 of stock outstanding. The fair value of its buildings was $32,000 more than the book value.

Pioneer paid $190,000 to acquire the Lowe shares. At that date, the noncontrolling interest had a fair value of $47,500. The remaining economic life for all Lowe's depreciable assets was eight years on the date of combination. The amount of the differential assigned to goodwill is not impaired. Lowe reported net income of $40,000 in 20X2 and declared no dividends.

Required

a. Give the eliminating entries needed to prepare a consolidated balance sheet immediately after Pioneer purchased Lowe stock.

b. Give all eliminating entries needed to prepare a full set of consolidated financial statements for 20X2.

LO2 **E5-14** **Consolidation Following Three Years of Ownership**

Knox Corporation purchased 60 percent of Conway Company ownership on January 1, 20X7, for $277,500. Conway reported the following net income and dividend payments:

Year	Net Income	Dividends Paid
20X7	$45,000	$25,000
20X8	55,000	35,000
20X9	30,000	10,000

On January 1, 20X7, Conway had $250,000 of $5 par value common stock outstanding and retained earnings of $150,000, and the fair value of the noncontrolling interest was $185,000. Conway held land with a book value of $22,500 and a market value of $30,000 and equipment with a book value of $320,000 and a market value of $360,000 at the date of combination. The remainder of the differential at acquisition was attributable to an increase in the value of patents, which had a remaining useful life of 10 years. All depreciable assets held by Conway at the date of acquisition had a remaining economic life of eight years.

Required

a. Compute the increase in the fair value of patents held by Conway.

b. Prepare the eliminating entries needed at January 1, 20X7, to prepare a consolidated balance sheet.

c. Compute the balance reported by Knox as its investment in Conway at January 1, 20X9.

d. Prepare the journal entries recorded by Knox with regard to its investment in Conway during 20X9.

e. Prepare the eliminating entries needed at December 31, 20X9, to prepare a three-part consolidation worksheet.

LO2

E5-15 Consolidation Worksheet for Majority-Owned Subsidiary

Proud Corporation acquired 80 percent of Stergis Company's voting stock on January 1, 20X3, at underlying book value. The fair value of the noncontrolling interest was equal to 20 percent of the book value of Stergis at that date. Proud uses the equity method in accounting for its ownership of Stergis during 20X3. On December 31, 20X3, the trial balances of the two companies are as follows:

Item	Proud Corporation		Stergis Company	
	Debit	Credit	Debit	Credit
Current Assets	$173,000		$105,000	
Depreciable Assets	500,000		300,000	
Investment in Stergis Company Stock	136,000			
Depreciation Expense	25,000		15,000	
Other Expenses	105,000		75,000	
Dividends Declared	40,000		10,000	
Accumulated Depreciation		$175,000		$ 75,000
Current Liabilities		50,000		40,000
Long-Term Debt		100,000		120,000
Common Stock		200,000		100,000
Retained Earnings		230,000		50,000
Sales		200,000		120,000
Income from Subsidiary		24,000		
	$979,000	$979,000	$505,000	$505,000

Required

a. Give all eliminating entries required as of December 31, 20X3, to prepare consolidated financial statements.

b. Prepare a three-part consolidation worksheet.

c. Prepare a consolidated balance sheet, income statement, and retained earnings statement for 20X3.

LO2

E5-16 Consolidation Worksheet for Majority-Owned Subsidiary for Second Year

Proud Corporation acquired 80 percent of Stergis Company's voting stock on January 1, 20X3, at underlying book value. The fair value of the noncontrolling interest was equal to 20 percent of the book value of Stergis at that date. Proud uses the equity method in accounting for its ownership of Stergis. On December 31, 20X4, the trial balances of the two companies are as follows:

Item	Proud Corporation		Stergis Company	
	Debit	Credit	Debit	Credit
Current Assets	$ 235,000		$150,000	
Depreciable Assets	500,000		300,000	
Investment in Stergis Company Stock	152,000			
Depreciation Expense	25,000		15,000	
Other Expenses	150,000		90,000	
Dividends Declared	50,000		15,000	
Accumulated Depreciation		$ 200,000		$ 90,000
Current Liabilities		70,000		50,000
Long-Term Debt		100,000		120,000
Common Stock		200,000		100,000
Retained Earnings		284,000		70,000
Sales		230,000		140,000
Income from Subsidiary		28,000		
	$1,112,000	$1,112,000	$570,000	$570,000

Required

a. Give all eliminating entries required on December 31, 20X4, to prepare consolidated financial statements.

b. Prepare a three-part consolidation worksheet as of December 31, 20X4.

Advanced
StudyGuide
.com

E5-17   Preparation of Stockholders' Equity Section with Other Comprehensive Income

Broadmore Corporation acquired 75 percent of Stem Corporation's common stock on January 1, 20X8, for $435,000. At that date, Stem reported common stock outstanding of $300,000 and retained earnings of $200,000, and the fair value of the noncontrolling interest was $145,000. The book values and fair values of Stem's assets and liabilities were equal, except for other intangible assets, which had a fair value $80,000 greater than book value and a 10-year remaining life. Broadmore and Stem reported the following data for 20X8 and 20X9:

	Stem Corporation			Broadmore Corporation	
Year	Net Income	Comprehensive Income	Dividends Paid	Operating Income	Dividends Paid
20X8	$40,000	$50,000	$15,000	$120,000	$70,000
20X9	60,000	65,000	30,000	140,000	70,000

Required

a. Compute consolidated comprehensive income for 20X8 and 20X9.

b. Compute comprehensive income attributable to the controlling interest for 20X8 and 20X9.

c. Assuming that Broadmore reported capital stock outstanding of $320,000 and retained earnings of $430,000 at January 1, 20X8, prepare the stockholders' equity section of the consolidated balance sheet at December 31, 20X8 and 20X9.

E5-18   Eliminating Entries for Subsidiary with Other Comprehensive Income

Palmer Corporation acquired 70 percent of Krown Corporation's ownership on January 1, 20X8, for $140,000. At that date, Krown reported capital stock outstanding of $120,000 and retained earnings of $80,000, and the fair value of the noncontrolling interest was equal to 30 percent of the book value of Krown. During 20X8, Krown reported net income of $30,000 and comprehensive income of $36,000 and paid dividends of $25,000.

Required

a. Present all equity-method entries that Palmer would have recorded in accounting for its investment in Krown during 20X8.

b. Present all eliminating entries needed at December 31, 20X8, to prepare a complete set of consolidated financial statements for Palmer Corporation and its subsidiary.

LO5

E5-19* Consolidation of Subsidiary with Negative Retained Earnings

General Corporation acquired 80 percent of Strap Company's voting common stock on January 1, 20X4, for $138,000. At that date, the fair value of the noncontrolling interest was $34,500. Strap's balance sheet at the date of acquisition contained the following balances:

STRAP COMPANY
Balance Sheet
January 1, 20X4

Cash	$ 20,000	Accounts Payable	$ 35,000
Accounts Receivable	35,000	Notes Payable	180,000
Land	90,000	Common Stock	100,000
Building and Equipment	300,000	Additional Paid-in Capital	75,000
Less: Accumulated Depreciation	(85,000)	Retained Earnings	(30,000)
Total Assets	$360,000	Total Liabilities and Stockholders' Equity	$360,000

At the date of acquisition, the reported book values of Strap's assets and liabilities approximated fair value.

Required
Give the eliminating entry or entries needed to prepare a consolidated balance sheet immediately following the business combination.

LO5

E5-20* Complex Assignment of Differential

On December 31, 20X4, Worth Corporation acquired 90 percent of Brinker Inc.'s common stock for $864,000. At that date, the fair value of the noncontrolling interest was $96,000. Of the $240,000 differential, $5,000 related to the increased value of Brinker's inventory, $75,000 related to the increased value of its land, $60,000 related to the increased value of its equipment, and $50,000 was associated with a change in the value of its notes payable due to increasing interest rates. Brinker's equipment had a remaining life of 15 years from the date of combination. Brinker sold all inventory it held at the end of 20X4 during 20X5; the land to which the differential related also was sold during the year for a large gain. The amortization of the differential relating to Brinker's notes payable was $7,500 for 20X5.

At the date of combination, Brinker reported retained earnings of $120,000, common stock outstanding of $500,000, and premium on common stock of $100,000. For the year 20X5, it reported net income of $150,000 but paid no dividends. Worth accounts for its investment in Brinker using the equity method.

Required
a. Present all entries that Worth would have recorded during 20X5 with respect to its investment in Brinker.
b. Present all elimination entries that would have been included in the worksheet to prepare a full set of consolidated financial statements for the year 20X5.

Problems

LO1

P5-21 Multiple-Choice Questions on Applying the Equity Method [AICPA Adapted]
Select the correct answer for each of the following questions.

1. On July 1, 20X3, Barker Company purchased 20 percent of Acme Company's outstanding common stock for $400,000 when the fair value of Acme's net assets was $2,000,000. Barker does not have the ability to exercise significant influence over Acme's operating and financial policies. The following data concerning Acme are available for 20X3:

	Twelve Months Ended December 31, 20X3	Six Months Ended December 31, 20X3
Net income	$300,000	$160,000
Dividends declared and paid	190,000	100,000

In its income statement for the year ended December 31, 20X3, how much income should Barker report from this investment?

a. $20,000.

b. $32,000.

c. $38,000.

d. $60,000.

2. On January 1, 20X3, Miller Company purchased 25 percent of Wall Corporation's common stock; no goodwill resulted from the purchase. Miller appropriately carries this investment at equity, and the balance in Miller's investment account was $190,000 on December 31, 20X3. Wall reported net income of $120,000 for the year ended December 31, 20X3, and paid dividends on its common stock totaling $48,000 during 20X3. How much did Miller pay for its 25 percent interest in Wall?

a. $172,000.

b. $202,000.

c. $208,000.

d. $232,000.

3. On January 1, 20X7, Robohn Company purchased for cash 40 percent of Lowell Company's 300,000 shares of voting common stock for $1,800,000 when 40 percent of the underlying equity in Lowell's net assets was $1,740,000. The payment in excess of underlying equity was assigned to amortizable assets with a remaining life of six years. The amortization is not deductible for income tax reporting. As a result of this transaction, Robohn has the ability to exercise significant influence over Lowell's operating and financial policies. Lowell's net income for the year ended December 31, 20X7, was $600,000. During 20X7, Lowell paid $325,000 in dividends to its shareholders. The income reported by Robohn for its investment in Lowell should be

a. $120,000.

b. $130,000.

c. $230,000.

d. $240,000.

4. In January 20X0, Farley Corporation acquired 20 percent of Davis Company's outstanding common stock for $800,000. This investment gave Farley the ability to exercise significant influence over Davis. The book value of the acquired shares was $600,000. The excess of cost over book value was attributed to an identifiable intangible asset, which was undervalued on Davis's balance sheet and had a remaining economic life of 10 years. For the year ended December 31, 20X0, Davis reported net income of $180,000 and paid cash dividends of $40,000 on its common stock. What is the proper carrying value of Farley's investment in Davis on December 31, 20X0?

a. $772,000.

b. $780,000.

c. $800,000.

d. $808,000.

LO1

P5-22 Amortization of Differential

Ball Corporation purchased 30 percent of Krown Company's common stock on January 1, 20X5, by issuing preferred stock with a par value of $50,000 and a market price of $120,000. The following amounts relate to Krown's balance sheet items at that date:

	Book Value	Fair Value
Cash and Receivables	$ 200,000	$200,000
Buildings and Equipment	400,000	360,000
Less: Accumulated Depreciation	(100,000)	
Total Assets	$ 500,000	
Accounts Payable	$ 50,000	50,000
Bonds Payable	200,000	200,000
Common Stock	100,000	
Retained Earnings	150,000	
Total Liabilities and Equities	$ 500,000	

Krown purchased buildings and equipment on January 1, 20X0, with an expected economic life of 20 years. No change in overall expected economic life occurred as a result of the acquisition of Ball's stock. The amount paid in excess of the fair value of Krown's reported net assets is attributed to unrecorded copyrights with a remaining useful life of eight years. During 20X5, Krown reported net income of $40,000 and paid dividends of $10,000.

Required

Give all journal entries to be recorded on Ball Corporation's books during 20X5, assuming it uses the equity method in accounting for its ownership of Krown Company.

LO1

P5-23   Computation of Account Balances

Easy Chair Company purchased 40 percent ownership of Stuffy Sofa Corporation on January 1, 20X1, for $150,000. Stuffy Sofa's balance sheet at the time of acquisition was as follows:

STUFFY SOFA CORPORATION
Balance Sheet
January 1, 20X1

Cash		$ 30,000	Current Liabilities	$ 40,000
Accounts Receivable		120,000	Bonds Payable	200,000
Inventory		80,000	Common Stock	200,000
Land		150,000	Additional Paid-In Capital	40,000
Buildings and Equipment	$ 300,000			
Less: Accumulated Depreciation	(120,000)	180,000	Retained Earnings	80,000
Total Assets		$560,000	Total Liabilities and Equities	$560,000

During 20X1 Stuffy Sofa Corporation reported net income of $30,000 and paid dividends of $9,000. The fair values of Stuffy Sofa's assets and liabilities were equal to their book values at the date of acquisition, with the exception of buildings and equipment, which had a fair value $35,000 above book value. All buildings and equipment had remaining lives of five years at the time of the business combination. The amount attributed to goodwill as a result of its purchase of Stuffy Sofa shares is not impaired.

Required

a. What amount of investment income will Easy Chair Company record during 20X1 under equity-method accounting?

b. What amount of income will be reported under the cost method?

c. What will be the balance in the investment account on December 31, 20X1, under (1) cost-method and (2) equity-method accounting?

LO1

P5-24   Multistep Acquisition

Jackson Corporation purchased shares of Phillips Corporation in the following sequence:

Date	Number of Shares Purchased	Amount Paid
January 1, 20X6	1,000 shares	$25,000
January 1, 20X8	500 shares	15,000
January 1, 20X9	2,000 shares	70,000

The book value of Phillips's net assets at January 1, 20X6, was $200,000. Each year since Jackson first purchased shares, Phillips has reported net income of $70,000 and paid dividends of $20,000. The amount paid in excess of the book value of Phillips's net assets was attributed to the increase in the value of identifiable intangible assets with a remaining life of five years at the date the shares of Phillips were purchased. Phillips has had 10,000 shares of voting common stock outstanding throughout the four-year period.

Required

Give the journal entries recorded on Jackson Corporation's books in 20X9 related to its investment in Phillips Corporation.

LO1

P5-25   Complex Differential

Essex Company issued common shares with a par value of $50,000 and a market value of $165,000 in exchange for 30 percent ownership of Tolliver Corporation on January 1, 20X2. Tolliver reported the following balances on that date:

TOLLIVER CORPORATION
Balance Sheet
January 1, 20X2

	Book Value	Fair Value
Assets		
Cash	$ 40,000	$ 40,000
Accounts Receivable	80,000	80,000
Inventory (FIFO basis)	120,000	150,000
Land	50,000	65,000
Buildings and Equipment	500,000	320,000
Less: Accumulated Depreciation	(240,000)	
Patent		25,000
Total Assets	$550,000	$680,000
Liabilities and Equities		
Accounts Payable	$ 30,000	$ 30,000
Bonds Payable	100,000	100,000
Common Stock	150,000	
Additional Paid-In Capital	20,000	
Retained Earnings	250,000	
Total Liabilities and Equities	$550,000	

The estimated economic life of the patents held by Tolliver is 10 years. The buildings and equipment are expected to last 12 more years on average. Tolliver paid dividends of $9,000 during 20X2 and reported net income of $80,000 for the year.

Required

Compute the amount of investment income (loss) reported by Essex from its investment in Tolliver for 20X2 and the balance in the investment account on December 31, 20X2, assuming the equity method is used in accounting for the investment.

LO1

P5-26   Equity Entries with Differential

On January 1, 20X0, Hunter Corporation issued 6,000 of its $10 par value shares to acquire 45 percent of the shares of Arrow Manufacturing. Arrow Manufacturing's balance sheet immediately before the acquisition contained the following items:

ARROW MANUFACTURING
Balance Sheet
January 1, 20X0

	Book Value	Fair Value
Assets		
Cash and Receivables	$ 30,000	$ 30,000
Land	70,000	80,000
Buildings and Equipment (net)	120,000	150,000
Patent	80,000	80,000
Total Assets	$300,000	
Liabilities and Equities		
Accounts Payable	$ 90,000	90,000
Common Stock	150,000	
Retained Earnings	60,000	
Total Liabilities and Equities	$300,000	

On the date of the stock acquisition, Hunter's shares were selling at $35, and Arrow Manufacturing's buildings and equipment had a remaining economic life of 10 years. The amount of the differential assigned to goodwill is not impaired.

In the two years following the stock acquisition, Arrow Manufacturing reported net income of $80,000 and $50,000 and paid dividends of $20,000 and $40,000, respectively. Hunter used the equity method in accounting for its ownership of Arrow Manufacturing.

Required

a. Give the entry recorded by Hunter Corporation at the time of acquisition.

b. Give the journal entries recorded by Hunter during 20X0 and 20X1 related to its investment in Arrow Manufacturing.

c. What balance will be reported in Hunter's investment account on December 31, 20X1?

P5-27 Equity Entries with Differential

Ennis Corporation acquired 35 percent of Jackson Corporation's stock on January 1, 20X8, by issuing 25,000 shares of its $2 par value common stock. Jackson Corporation's balance sheet immediately before the acquisition contained the following items:

JACKSON CORPORATION
Balance Sheet
January 1, 20X8

	Book Value	Fair Value
Assets		
Cash and Receivables	$ 40,000	$ 40,000
Inventory (FIFO basis)	80,000	100,000
Land	50,000	70,000
Buildings and Equipment (net)	240,000	320,000
Total Assets	$410,000	$530,000
Liabilities and Equities		
Accounts Payable	$ 70,000	$ 70,000
Common Stock	130,000	
Retained Earnings	210,000	
Total Liabilities and Equities	$410,000	

Shares of Ennis were selling at $8 at the time of the acquisition. On the date of acquisition, the remaining economic life of buildings and equipment held by Jackson was 20 years. The amount of the differential assigned to goodwill is not impaired. For the year 20X8, Jackson reported net income of $70,000 and paid dividends of $10,000.

Required

a. Give the journal entries recorded by Ennis Corporation during 20X8 related to its investment in Jackson Corporation.

b. What balance will Ennis report as its investment in Jackson at December 31, 20X8?

P5-28 Additional Ownership Level

Balance sheet and income and dividend data for Amber Corporation, Blair Corporation, and Carmen Corporation at January 1, 20X3, were as follows:

Account Balances	Amber Corporation	Blair Corporation	Carmen Corporation
Cash	$ 70,000	$ 60,000	$ 20,000
Accounts Receivable	120,000	80,000	40,000
Inventory	100,000	90,000	65,000
Fixed Assets (net)	450,000	350,000	240,000
Total Assets	$740,000	$580,000	$365,000
Accounts Payable	$105,000	$110,000	$ 45,000
Bonds Payable	300,000	200,000	120,000
Common Stock	150,000	75,000	90,000
Retained Earnings	185,000	195,000	110,000
Total Liabilities and Equity	$740,000	$580,000	$365,000
Income from Operations in 20X3	$220,000	$100,000	
Net Income for 20X3			$ 50,000
Dividends Declared and Paid	60,000	30,000	25,000

On January 1, 20X3, Amber Corporation purchased 40 percent of the voting common stock of Blair Corporation by issuing common stock with a par value of $40,000 and fair value of $130,000. Immediately after this transaction, Blair purchased 25 percent of the voting common stock of Carmen Corporation by issuing bonds payable with a par value and market value of $51,500.

On January 1, 20X3, the book values of Blair's net assets were equal to their fair values except for equipment that had a fair value $30,000 greater than book value and patents that had a fair value $25,000 greater than book value. At that date the equipment had a remaining economic life of eight years and the patents had a remaining economic life of five years. The book values of Carmen's assets were equal to their fair values except for inventory that had a fair value $6,000 in excess of book value and was accounted for on a FIFO basis.

Required

a. Compute the net income reported by Amber Corporation for 20X3, assuming the equity method is used by Amber and Blair in accounting for their intercorporate investments.

b. Give all journal entries recorded by Amber relating to its investment in Blair during 20X3.

LO1 **P5-29** **Correction of Error**

Hill Company paid $164,000 to acquire 40 percent ownership of Dale Company on January 1, 20X2. Net book value of Dale's assets on that date was $300,000. Book values and fair values of net assets held by Dale were the same except for equipment and patents. Equipment held by Dale had a book value of $70,000 and fair value of $120,000. All of the remaining purchase price was attributable to the increased value of patents with a remaining useful life of eight years. The remaining economic life of all depreciable assets held by Dale was five years.

Dale Company's net income and dividends for the three years immediately following the purchase of shares were

Year	Net Income	Dividends
20X2	$40,000	$15,000
20X3	60,000	20,000
20X4	70,000	25,000

The computation of Hill's investment income for 20X4 and entries in its investment account since the date of purchase were as follows:

		20X4 Investment Income
Pro rata income accrual ($70,000 × 0.40)		$28,000
Amortize patents ($44,000 ÷ 8 years)	$5,500	
Dividends received ($25,000 × 0.40)		10,000
20X4 investment income		$32,500

Investment in Dale Company

1/1/X2 purchase price	$164,000		
20X2 income accrual	16,000		
		Amortize patents	$5,500
20X3 income accrual	24,000		
		Amortize patents	5,500
20X4 income accrual	28,000		
		Amortize patents	5,500
12/31/X4 balance	$215,500		

Before making closing entries at the end of 20X4, Hill's new controller reviewed the reports and was convinced that both the balance in the investment account and the investment income that Hill reported for 20X4 were in error.

Required

Prepare a correcting entry, along with supporting computations, to properly state the balance in the investment account and all related account balances at the end of 20X4.

LO2

P5-30 Majority-Owned Subsidiary Acquired at Book Value

Cameron Corporation acquired 70 percent of Darla Corporation's common stock on December 31, 20X4, for $87,500. Data from the balance sheets of the two companies included the following amounts as of the date of acquisition:

Item	Cameron Corporation	Darla Corporation
Cash	$ 65,000	$ 21,000
Accounts Receivable	90,000	44,000
Inventory	130,000	75,000
Land	60,000	30,000
Buildings and Equipment	410,000	250,000
Less: Accumulated Depreciation	(150,000)	(80,000)
Investment in Darla Corporation Stock	87,500	
Total Assets	$692,500	$340,000
Accounts Payable	$152,500	$ 35,000
Mortgage Payable	250,000	180,000
Common Stock	80,000	40,000
Retained Earnings	210,000	85,000
Total Liabilities and Stockholders' Equity	$692,500	$340,000

At the date of the business combination, the book values of Darla Corporation's assets and liabilities approximated fair value, and the fair value of the noncontrolling interest was equal to 30 percent of the book value of Darla Corporation. At December 31, 20X4, Cameron reported accounts payable of $12,500 to Darla, which reported an equal amount in its accounts receivable.

Required

a. Give the eliminating entry or entries needed to prepare a consolidated balance sheet immediately following the business combination.

b. Prepare a consolidated balance sheet worksheet.

c. Prepare a consolidated balance sheet in good form.

LO2

P5-31 Majority-Owned Subsidiary Acquired at Greater Than Book Value

Porter corporation acquired 70 percent of Darla Corporation's common stock on December 31, 20X4, for $102,200. At that date, the fair value of the noncontrolling interest was $43,800. Data from the balance sheets of the two companies included the following amounts as of the date of acquisition:

Item	Porter Corporation	Darla Corporation
Cash	$ 50,300	$ 21,000
Accounts Receivable	90,000	44,000
Inventory	130,000	75,000
Land	60,000	30,000
Buildings and Equipment	410,000	250,000
Less: Accumulated Depreciation	(150,000)	(80,000)
Investment in Darla Corporation Stock	102,200	
Total Assets	$692,500	$340,000
Accounts Payable	$152,500	$ 35,000
Mortgage Payable	250,000	180,000
Common Stock	80,000	40,000
Retained Earnings	210,000	85,000
Total Liabilities and Stockholders' Equity	$692,500	$340,000

At the date of the business combination, the book values of Darla's assets and liabilities approximated fair value except for inventory, which had a fair value of $81,000, and buildings and equipment, which had a fair value of $185,000. At December 31, 20X4, Porter reported accounts payable of $12,500 to Darla, which reported an equal amount in its accounts receivable.

Required

a. Give the eliminating entry or entries needed to prepare a consolidated balance sheet immediately following the business combination.
b. Prepare a consolidated balance sheet worksheet.
c. Prepare a consolidated balance sheet in good form.

LO2

P5-32 Balance Sheet Consolidation of Majority-Owned Subsidiary

On January 2, 20X8, Total Corporation acquired 75 percent of Ticken Tie Company's outstanding common stock. In exchange for Ticken Tie's stock, Total issued bonds payable with a par value of $500,000 and fair value of $510,000 directly to the selling stockholders of Ticken Tie. At that date, the fair value of the noncontrolling interest was $170,000. The two companies continued to operate as separate entities subsequent to the combination.

Immediately prior to the combination, the book values and fair values of the companies' assets and liabilities were as follows:

	Total		Ticken Tie	
	Book Value	Fair Value	Book Value	Fair Value
Cash	$ 12,000	$ 12,000	$ 9,000	$ 9,000
Receivables	41,000	39,000	31,000	30,000
Allowance for Bad Debts	(2,000)		(1,000)	
Inventory	86,000	89,000	68,000	72,000
Land	55,000	200,000	50,000	70,000
Buildings and Equipment	960,000	650,000	670,000	500,000
Accumulated Depreciation	(411,000)		(220,000)	
Patent				40,000
Total Assets	$741,000	$990,000	$607,000	$721,000
Current Payables	$ 38,000	$ 38,000	$ 29,000	$ 29,000
Bonds Payable	200,000	210,000	100,000	100,000
Common Stock	300,000		200,000	
Additional Paid-in Capital	100,000		130,000	
Retained Earnings	103,000		148,000	
Total Liabilities and Equity	$741,000		$607,000	

At the date of combination, Ticken Tie owed Total $6,000 plus accrued interest of $500 on a short-term note. Both companies have properly recorded these amounts.

Required

a. Record the business combination on the books of Total Corporation.
b. Present in general journal form all elimination entries needed in a worksheet to prepare a consolidated balance sheet immediately following the business combination on January 2, 20X8.
c. Prepare and complete a consolidated balance sheet worksheet as of January 2, 20X8, immediately following the business combination.
d. Present a consolidated balance sheet for Total and its subsidiary as of January 2, 20X8.

LO2

P5-33 Incomplete Data

Blue Corporation acquired controlling ownership of Skyler Corporation on December 31, 20X3, and a consolidated balance sheet was prepared immediately. Partial balance sheet data for the two companies and the consolidated entity at that date follow:

BLUE CORPORATION AND SKYLER CORPORATION
Balance Sheet Data
December 31, 20X3

Item	Blue Corporation	Skyler Corporation	Consolidated Entity
Cash	$ 63,650	$ 35,000	$ 98,650
Accounts Receivable	98,000	?	148,000
Inventory	105,000	80,000	195,000
Buildings and Equipment	400,000	340,000	780,000
Less: Accumulated Depreciation	(215,000)	(140,000)	(355,000)
Investment in Skyler Corporation Stock	?		
Goodwill			9,000
Total Assets	$620,000	$380,000	$875,650
Accounts Payable	$115,000	$ 46,000	$146,000
Wages Payable	?	?	94,000
Notes Payable	200,000	110,000	310,000
Common Stock	120,000	75,000	?
Retained Earnings	115,000	125,000	?
Noncontrolling Interest			90,650
Total Liabilities and Equities	$?	$380,000	$875,650

During 20X3, Blue provided engineering services to Skyler and has not yet been paid for them. There were no other receivables or payables between Blue and Skyler at December 31, 20X3.

Required

a. What is the amount of unpaid engineering services at December 31, 20X3, on work done by Blue for Skyler?

b. What balance in accounts receivable did Skyler report at December 31, 20X3?

c. What amounts of wages payable did Blue and Skyler report at December 31, 20X3?

d. What was the fair value of Skyler as a whole at the date of acquisition?

e. What percentage of Skyler's shares were purchased by Blue?

f. What amounts of capital stock and retained earnings must be reported in the consolidated balance sheet?

LO2

P5-34 Income and Retained Earnings

Quill Corporation acquired 70 percent of North Company's stock on January 1, 20X9, for $105,000. At that date, the fair value of the noncontrolling interest was equal to 30 percent of the book value of North Company. The companies reported the following stockholders' equity balances immediately after the acquisition:

	Quill Corporation	North Company
Common Stock	$120,000	$ 30,000
Additional Paid-in Capital	230,000	80,000
Retained Earnings	290,000	40,000
Total	$640,000	$150,000

Quill and North reported 20X9 operating incomes of $90,000 and $35,000 and dividend payments of $30,000 and $10,000, respectively.

Required

a. Compute the amount reported as net income by each company for 20X9, assuming Quill uses equity-method accounting for its investment in North.

b. Compute consolidated net income for 20X9.

c. Compute the reported balance in retained earnings at December 31, 20X9, for both companies.

d. Compute consolidated retained earnings at December 31, 20X9.

e. How would the computation of consolidated retained earnings at December 31, 20X9, change if Quill uses the cost method in accounting for its investment in North?

LO2

Advanced StudyGuide .com

P5-35   Consolidation Worksheet at End of First Year of Ownership

Power Corporation acquired 75 percent of Best Company's ownership on January 1, 20X8, for $96,000. At that date, the fair value of the noncontrolling interest was $32,000. The book value of Best's net assets at acquisition was $100,000. The book values and fair values of Best's assets and liabilities were equal, except for Best's buildings and equipment, which were worth $20,000 more than book value. Buildings and equipment are depreciated on a 10-year basis.

Although goodwill is not amortized, the management of Power concluded at December 31, 20X8, that goodwill from its purchase of Best shares had been impaired and the correct carrying amount was $2,500. Goodwill and goodwill impairment were assigned proportionately to the controlling and noncontrolling shareholders.

Trial balance data for Power and Best on December 31, 20X8, are as follows:

Item	Power Corporation Debit	Power Corporation Credit	Best Company Debit	Best Company Credit
Cash	$ 47,500		$ 21,000	
Accounts Receivable	70,000		12,000	
Inventory	90,000		25,000	
Land	30,000		15,000	
Buildings and Equipment	350,000		150,000	
Investment in Best Co. Stock	96,375			
Cost of Goods Sold	125,000		110,000	
Wage Expense	42,000		27,000	
Depreciation Expense	25,000		10,000	
Interest Expense	12,000		4,000	
Other Expenses	13,500		5,000	
Dividends Declared	30,000		16,000	
Accumulated Depreciation		$145,000		$ 40,000
Accounts Payable		45,000		16,000
Wages Payable		17,000		9,000
Notes Payable		150,000		50,000
Common Stock		200,000		60,000
Retained Earnings		102,000		40,000
Sales		260,000		180,000
Income from Subsidiary		12,375		
	$931,375	$931,375	$395,000	$395,000

Required

a. Give all eliminating entries needed to prepare a three-part consolidation worksheet as of December 31, 20X8.

b. Prepare a three-part consolidation worksheet for 20X8 in good form.

LO2

Advanced
StudyGuide
.com

P5-36   Consolidation Worksheet at End of Second Year of Ownership

Power Corporation acquired 75 percent of Best Company's ownership on January 1, 20X8, for $96,000. At that date, the fair value of the noncontrolling interest was $32,000. The book value of Best's net assets at acquisition was $100,000. The book values and fair values of Best's assets and liabilities were equal, except for Best's buildings and equipment, which were worth $20,000 more than book value. Buildings and equipment are depreciated on a 10-year basis.

Although goodwill is not amortized, the management of Power concluded at December 31, 20X8, that goodwill from its purchase of Best shares had been impaired and the correct carrying amount was $2,500. Goodwill and goodwill impairment were assigned proportionately to the controlling and noncontrolling shareholders. No additional impairment occurred in 20X9.

Trial balance data for Power and Best on December 31, 20X9, are as follows:

Item	Power Corporation Debit	Power Corporation Credit	Best Company Debit	Best Company Credit
Cash	$ 68,500		$ 32,000	
Accounts Receivable	85,000		14,000	
Inventory	97,000		24,000	
Land	50,000		25,000	
Buildings and Equipment	350,000		150,000	
Investment in Best Co. Stock	106,875			
Cost of Goods Sold	145,000		114,000	
Wage Expense	35,000		20,000	
Depreciation Expense	25,000		10,000	
Interest Expense	12,000		4,000	
Other Expenses	23,000		16,000	
Dividends Declared	30,000		20,000	
Accumulated Depreciation		$ 170,000		$ 50,000
Accounts Payable		51,000		15,000
Wages Payable		14,000		6,000
Notes Payable		150,000		50,000
Common Stock		200,000		60,000
Retained Earnings		126,875		48,000
Sales		290,000		200,000
Income from Subsidiary		25,500		
	$1,027,375	$1,027,375	$429,000	$429,000

Required

a. Give all eliminating entries needed to prepare a three-part consolidation worksheet as of December 31, 20X9.

b. Prepare a three-part consolidation worksheet for 20X9 in good form.

c. Prepare a consolidated balance sheet, income statement, and retained earnings statement for 20X9.

LO2, LO5

P5-37   Comprehensive Problem: Majority-Owned Subsidiary

Master Corporation acquired 80 percent ownership of Stanley Wood Products Company on January 1, 20X1, for $160,000. On that date, the fair value of the noncontrolling interest was $40,000, and Stanley reported retained earnings of $50,000 and had $100,000 of common stock outstanding. Master has used the equity method in accounting for its investment in Stanley.

Trial balance data for the two companies on December 31, 20X5, are as follows:

Item	Master Corporation		Stanley Wood Products Company	
	Debit	Credit	Debit	Credit
Cash and Receivables	$ 81,000		$ 65,000	
Inventory	260,000		90,000	
Land	80,000		80,000	
Buildings and Equipment	500,000		150,000	
Investment in Stanley Wood Products Stock	188,000			
Cost of Goods Sold	120,000		50,000	
Depreciation Expense	25,000		15,000	
Inventory Losses	15,000		5,000	
Dividends Declared	30,000		10,000	
Accumulated Depreciation		$ 205,000		$105,000
Accounts Payable		60,000		20,000
Notes Payable		200,000		50,000
Common Stock		300,000		100,000
Retained Earnings		314,000		90,000
Sales		200,000		100,000
Income from Subsidiary		20,000		
	$1,299,000	$1,299,000	$465,000	$465,000

Additional Information

1. On the date of combination, the fair value of Stanley's depreciable assets was $50,000 more than book value. The differential assigned to depreciable assets should be written off over the following 10-year period.

2. There was $10,000 of intercorporate receivables and payables at the end of 20X5.

Required

a. Give all journal entries that Master recorded during 20X5 related to its investment in Stanley.
b. Give all eliminating entries needed to prepare consolidated statements for 20X5.
c. Prepare a three-part worksheet as of December 31, 20X5.

LO2

P5-38   Comprehensive Problem: Differential Apportionment

Mortar Corporation acquired 80 percent ownership of Granite Company on January 1, 20X7, for $173,000. At that date, the fair value of the noncontrolling interest was $43,250. The trial balances for the two companies on December 31, 20X7, included the following amounts:

Item	Mortar Corporation		Granite Company	
	Debit	Credit	Debit	Credit
Cash	$ 38,000		$ 25,000	
Accounts Receivable	50,000		55,000	
Inventory	240,000		100,000	
Land	80,000		20,000	
Buildings and Equipment	500,000		150,000	
Investment in Granite Company Stock	202,000			
Cost of Goods Sold	500,000		250,000	
Depreciation Expense	25,000		15,000	
Other Expenses	75,000		75,000	
Dividends Declared	50,000		20,000	
Accumulated Depreciation		$ 155,000		$ 75,000
Accounts Payable		70,000		35,000
Mortgages Payable		200,000		50,000
Common Stock		300,000		50,000
Retained Earnings		290,000		100,000
Sales		700,000		400,000
Income from Subsidiary		45,000		
	$1,760,000	$1,760,000	$710,000	$710,000

Additional Information

1. On January 1, 20X7, Granite reported net assets with a book value of $150,000 and a fair value of $191,250.

2. Granite's depreciable assets had an estimated economic life of 11 years on the date of combination. The difference between fair value and book value of Granite's net assets is related entirely to buildings and equipment.

3. Mortar used the equity method in accounting for its investment in Granite.

4. Detailed analysis of receivables and payables showed that Granite owed Mortar $16,000 on December 31, 20X7.

5. Assume that any goodwill impairment should be recorded as an adjustment in Mortar's equity method accounts along with the amortization of other differential components.

Required

a. Give all journal entries recorded by Mortar with regard to its investment in Granite during 20X7.

b. Give all eliminating entries needed to prepare a full set of consolidated financial statements for 20X7.

c. Prepare a three-part consolidation worksheet as of December 31, 20X7.

LO2

P5-39 Comprehensive Problem: Differential Apportionment in Subsequent Period

Mortar Corporation acquired 80 percent ownership of Granite Company on January 1, 20X7, for $173,000. At that date, the fair value of the noncontrolling interest was $43,250. The trial balances for the two companies on December 31, 20X8, included the following amounts:

Item	Mortar Corporation Debit	Credit	Granite Company Debit	Credit
Cash	$ 59,000		$ 31,000	
Accounts Receivable	83,000		71,000	
Inventory	275,000		118,000	
Land	80,000		30,000	
Buildings and Equipment	500,000		150,000	
Investment in Granite Company Stock	206,200			
Cost of Goods Sold	490,000		310,000	
Depreciation Expense	25,000		15,000	
Other Expenses	62,000		100,000	
Dividends Declared	45,000		25,000	
Accumulated Depreciation		$ 180,000		$ 90,000
Accounts Payable		86,000		30,000
Mortgages Payable		200,000		70,000
Common Stock		300,000		50,000
Retained Earnings		385,000		140,000
Sales		650,000		470,000
Income from Subsidiary		24,200		
	$1,825,200	$1,825,200	$850,000	$850,000

Additional Information

1. On January 1, 20X7, Granite reported net assets with a book value of $150,000 and a fair value of $191,250. The difference between fair value and book value of Granite's net assets is related entirely to Buildings and Equipment. Granite's depreciable assets had an estimated economic life of 11 years on the date of combination.

2. At December 31, 20X8, Mortar's management reviewed the amount attributed to goodwill and concluded goodwill was impaired and should be reduced to $14,000. Goodwill and goodwill impairment were assigned proportionately to the controlling and noncontrolling shareholders.

3. Mortar used the equity method in accounting for its investment in Granite.

4. Detailed analysis of receivables and payables showed that Mortar owed Granite $9,000 on December 31, 20X8.

5. Assume the goodwill impairment from the previous year was recorded as an adjustment in Mortar's equity method accounts along with the amortization of other differential components.

Required

a. Give all journal entries recorded by Mortar with regard to its investment in Granite during 20X8.

b. Give all eliminating entries needed to prepare a full set of consolidated financial statements for 20X8.

c. Prepare a three-part consolidation worksheet as of December 31, 20X8.

LO5

P5-40   **Subsidiary with Other Comprehensive Income in Year of Acquisition**

Amber Corporation acquired 60 percent ownership of Sparta Company on January 1, 20X8, at underlying book value. At that date, the fair value of the noncontrolling interest was equal to 40 percent of the book value of Sparta Company. Trial balance data at December 31, 20X8, for Amber and Sparta are as follows:

Item	Amber Corporation Debit	Amber Corporation Credit	Sparta Company Debit	Sparta Company Credit
Cash	$ 27,000		$ 8,000	
Accounts Receivable	65,000		22,000	
Inventory	40,000		30,000	
Buildings and Equipment	500,000		235,000	
Investment in Row Company Securities			40,000	
Investment in Sparta Company	108,000			
Cost of Goods Sold	150,000		110,000	
Depreciation Expense	30,000		10,000	
Interest Expense	8,000		3,000	
Dividends Declared	24,000		15,000	
Accumulated Depreciation		$140,000		$ 85,000
Accounts Payable		63,000		20,000
Bonds Payable		100,000		50,000
Common Stock		200,000		100,000
Retained Earnings		208,000		60,000
Other Comprehensive Income from Subsidiary (OCI)—Unrealized Gain on Investments		6,000		
Unrealized Gain on Investments (OCI)				10,000
Sales		220,000		148,000
Income from Subsidiary		15,000		
	$952,000	$952,000	$473,000	$473,000

Additional Information

Sparta purchased stock of Row Company on January 1, 20X8, for $30,000 and classified the investment as available-for-sale securities. The value of Row's securities increased to $40,000 at December 31, 20X8.

Required

a. Give all eliminating entries needed to prepare a three-part consolidation worksheet as of December 31, 20X8.

b. Prepare a three-part consolidation worksheet for 20X8 in good form.

c. Prepare a consolidated balance sheet, income statement, and statement of comprehensive income for 20X8.

LO5

P5-41

Subsidiary with Other Comprehensive Income in Year Following Acquisition

Amber Corporation acquired 60 percent ownership of Sparta Company on January 1, 20X8, at underlying book value. At that date, the fair value of the noncontrolling interest was equal to 40 percent of the book value of Sparta Company. Trial balance data at December 31, 20X9, for Amber and Sparta are as follows:

Item	Amber Corporation Debit	Amber Corporation Credit	Sparta Company Debit	Sparta Company Credit
Cash	$ 18,000		$ 11,000	
Accounts Receivable	45,000		21,000	
Inventory	40,000		30,000	
Buildings and Equipment	585,000		257,000	
Investment in Row Company Securities			44,000	
Investment in Sparta Company	116,400			
Cost of Goods Sold	170,000		97,000	
Depreciation Expense	30,000		10,000	
Interest Expense	8,000		3,000	
Dividends Declared	40,000		20,000	
Accumulated Depreciation		$ 170,000		$ 95,000
Accounts Payable		75,000		24,000
Bonds Payable		100,000		50,000
Common Stock		200,000		100,000
Retained Earnings		231,000		70,000
Accumulated Other Comprehensive Income		6,000		10,000
Other Comprehensive Income from Subsidiary (OCI)—Unrealized Gain on Investments		2,400		
Unrealized Gain on Investments (OCI)				4,000
Sales		250,000		140,000
Income from Subsidiary		18,000		
	$1,052,400	$1,052,400	$493,000	$493,000

Additional Information

Sparta purchased stock of Row Company on January 1, 20X8, for $30,000 and classified the investment as available-for-sale securities. The value of Row's securities increased to $40,000 and $44,000, respectively, at December 31, 20X8, and 20X9.

Required

a. Give all eliminating entries needed to prepare a three-part consolidation worksheet as of December 31, 20X9.

b. Prepare a three-part consolidation worksheet for 20X9 in good form.

Chapter Six

Intercompany Inventory Transactions

INVENTORY TRANSFERS AT TOYS Я US

Most people know the catchy jingle, "I don't want to grow up; I'm a Toys Я Us kid." Toys Я Us was originally a simple baby furniture warehouse started by Charles Lazarus in 1948. However, after a few years and numerous requests from customers, he expanded his business into toys. Quickly, toys became his staple product and he adopted the name "Toys Я Us," along with the supermarket model in 1957.

The business continued to expand and in 1978 Toys Я Us went public. During the 1980s, in an effort to further expand its business, Toys Я Us branched out into the clothing market with Kids Я Us stores (these stores were discontinued in 2003). It also opened two international stores in Singapore and Canada. The 1990s saw further expansion with the creation of the Babies Я Us brand which has since grown to more than 260 locations.

In its next effort to expand, Toys Я Us Inc. launched a subsidiary, Toysrus.com, in 1999 to capture a portion of the growing online toy retail market. As a subsidiary of Toys Я Us Inc., Toysrus.com acts independently of the parent company. However, the dotcom does not manufacture inventory or purchase it from outside sources; it receives its entire inventory from Toys Я Us Inc.

Because Toysrus.com is a wholly owned subsidiary of Toys Я Us Inc., transactions between the two companies are not considered "arm's length." They are related-party transactions and must be eliminated. Thus, the profit from intercompany inventory transfers is eliminated in preparing consolidated financial statements. This elimination is required because Toys Я Us Inc. and Toysrus.com, in essence, are the same company and a company cannot make a profit by selling inventory to itself. This elimination process becomes quite complicated and the procedures are slightly different for partially owned companies when the transactions are "upstream" (from subsidiary to parent). This chapter examines intercompany inventory transactions and the consolidation procedures associated with them.

LEARNING OBJECTIVES

When you finish studying this chapter, you should be able to:

LO1 Understand and explain intercompany transfers and why they must be eliminated.

LO2 Understand and explain concepts associated with inventory transfers and transfer pricing.

LO3 Prepare equity-method journal entries and elimination entries for the consolidation of a subsidiary following downstream inventory transfers.

LO4 Prepare equity-method journal entries and elimination entries for the consolidation of a subsidiary following upstream inventory transfers.

LO5 Understand and explain additional considerations associated with consolidation.

ToysRus

100%

ToysRus.com

OVERVIEW OF THE CONSOLIDATED ENTITY AND INTERCOMPANY TRANSACTIONS

LO1

Understand and explain intercompany transfers and why they must be eliminated.

The consolidated entity is an aggregation of a number of different companies. The financial statements prepared by the individual affiliates are consolidated into a single set of financial statements representing the financial position and operating results of the entire economic entity as if it were a single company.

A parent company and its subsidiaries often engage in a variety of transactions among themselves. For example, manufacturing companies often have subsidiaries that develop raw materials or produce components to be included in the products of affiliated companies. Some companies sell consulting or other services to affiliated companies. A number of major retailers, such as J. C. Penney Company, transfer receivables to their credit subsidiaries in return for operating cash. United States Steel Corporation and its subsidiaries engage in numerous transactions with one another, including sales of raw materials, fabricated products, and transportation services. Such transactions often are critical to the operations of the overall consolidated entity. These transactions between related companies are referred to as *intercompany* or *intercorporate transfers.*

Figure 6–1 illustrates a consolidated entity with each of the affiliated companies engaging in both intercompany transfers and transactions with external parties. From a consolidated viewpoint, only transactions with parties outside the economic entity are included in the income statement. Thus, the arrows crossing the perimeter of the consolidated entity in Figure 6–1 represent transactions that are included in the operating results of the consolidated entity for the period. Transfers between the affiliated companies, shown in Figure 6–1 as those arrows not crossing the boundary of the consolidated entity, are equivalent to transfers between operating divisions of a single company and are not reported in the consolidated statements.

FIGURE 6–1
Transactions of Affiliated Companies

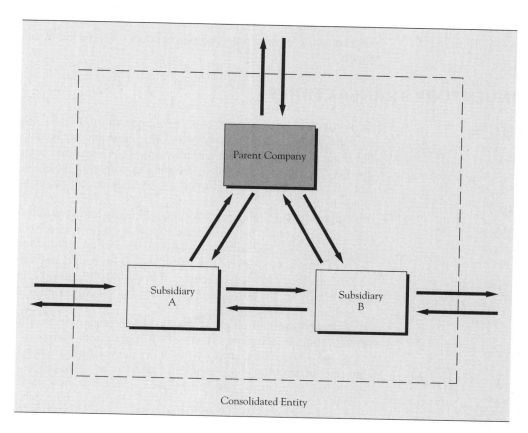

The central idea of consolidated financial statements is that they report on the activities of the consolidating affiliates as if the separate affiliates actually constitute a single company. Because single companies are not permitted to reflect internal transactions in their financial statements, consolidated entities also must exclude from their financial statements the effects of transactions that are totally within the consolidated entity. Building on the basic consolidation procedures presented in earlier chapters, this chapter and the next two deal with the effects of intercompany transfers. This chapter deals with intercompany inventory sales, and Chapter 7 discusses intercompany services and fixed asset sales.

Elimination of Intercompany Transfers

All aspects of intercompany transfers must be eliminated in preparing consolidated financial statements so that the statements appear as if they were those of a single company. **Accounting Research Bulletin No. 51,** "Consolidated Financial Statements" (ARB 51, ASC 810), mentions open account balances, security holdings, sales and purchases, and interest and dividends as examples of the intercompany balances and transactions that must be eliminated.[1]

No distinction is made between wholly owned and less-than-wholly-owned subsidiaries with regard to the elimination of intercompany transfers. The focus in consolidation is on the single-entity concept rather than on the percentage of ownership. Once the conditions for consolidation are met, a company becomes part of a single economic entity, and all transactions with related companies become internal transfers that must be eliminated fully, regardless of the level of ownership held.

Elimination of Unrealized Profits and Losses

Companies usually record transactions with affiliates on the same basis as transactions with nonaffiliates, including recognition of profits and losses. Profit or loss from selling an item to a related party normally is considered realized at the time of the sale from the selling company's perspective, but the profit is not considered realized for consolidation purposes until confirmed, usually through resale to an unrelated party. This unconfirmed profit from an intercompany transfer is referred to as ***unrealized intercompany profit.***

INVENTORY TRANSACTIONS

LO2

Understand and explain concepts associated with inventory transfers and transfer pricing.

Inventory transactions are the most common form of intercompany exchange. Conceptually, the elimination of inventory transfers between related companies is no different than for other types of intercompany transactions. All revenue and expense items recorded by the participants must be eliminated fully in preparing the consolidated income statement, and all profits and losses recorded on the transfers are deferred until the items are sold to a nonaffiliate.

The recordkeeping process for intercompany transfers of inventory may be more complex than for other forms of transfers. Companies often have many different types of inventory items, and some may be transferred from affiliate to affiliate. Also, the problems of keeping tabs on which items have been resold and which items are still on hand are greater in the case of inventory transactions because part of a shipment may be sold immediately by the purchasing company and other units may remain on hand for several accounting periods.

The worksheet eliminating entries used in preparing consolidated financial statements must eliminate fully the effects of all transactions between related companies. When there have been intercompany inventory transactions, eliminating entries are needed to remove the revenue and expenses related to the intercompany transfers recorded by the individual companies. The eliminations ensure that only the cost of the inventory to the

[1] *Accounting Research Bulletin No. 51,* "Consolidated Financial Statements," August 1959, para. 6. (ASC 810)

consolidated entity is included in the consolidated balance sheet when the inventory is still on hand and is charged to cost of goods sold in the period the inventory is resold to nonaffiliates.

Transfers at Cost

Merchandise sometimes is sold to related companies at the seller's cost or carrying value. When an intercorporate sale includes no profit or loss, the balance sheet inventory amounts at the end of the period require no adjustment for consolidation because the purchasing affiliate's inventory carrying amount is the same as the cost to the transferring affiliate and the consolidated entity. At the time the inventory is resold to a nonaffiliate, the amount recognized as cost of goods sold by the affiliate making the outside sale is the cost to the consolidated entity.

Even when the intercorporate sale includes no profit or loss, however, an eliminating entry is needed to remove both the revenue from the intercorporate sale and the related cost of goods sold recorded by the seller. This avoids overstating these two accounts. Consolidated net income is not affected by the eliminating entry when the transfer is made at cost because both revenue and cost of goods sold are reduced by the same amount.

Transfers at a Profit or Loss

Companies use many different approaches in setting intercorporate transfer prices. In some companies, the sale price to an affiliate is the same as the price to any other customer. Some companies routinely mark up inventory transferred to affiliates by a certain percentage of cost. Other companies have elaborate transfer pricing policies designed to encourage internal sales. Regardless of the method used in setting intercorporate transfer prices, the elimination process must remove the effects of such sales from the consolidated statements. Profit or loss from selling an item to a related party normally is considered realized at the time of the sale from the selling company's perspective, but the profit is not considered realized for consolidation purposes until confirmed, usually through resale to an unrelated party. This unconfirmed profit from an intercompany transfer is referred to as ***unrealized intercompany profit.***

When intercompany sales include unrealized profits or losses, the worksheet eliminations needed for consolidation in the period of transfer must adjust accounts in both the consolidated income statement and balance sheet:

Income statement: Sales and cost of goods sold. The sales revenue from the intercompany sale and the related cost of goods sold recorded by the transferring affiliate must be removed.

Balance sheet: Inventory. The profit or loss on the intercompany sale must be removed so the inventory is reported at the cost to the consolidated entity.

The resulting financial statements appear as if the intercompany transfer had not occurred.

Effect of Type of Inventory System

Most companies use either a perpetual or a periodic inventory control system to keep track of inventory and cost of goods sold. Under a perpetual inventory system, a purchase of merchandise is debited directly to the Inventory account; a sale requires a debit to Cost of Goods Sold and a credit to Inventory for the cost of the item. When a periodic system is used, a purchase of merchandise is debited to a Purchases account rather than to Inventory, and no entry is made to recognize cost of goods sold until the end of the accounting period.

The choice between periodic and perpetual inventory systems results in different entries on the books of the individual companies and, therefore, slightly different worksheet eliminating entries in preparing consolidated financial statements. Because most companies use perpetual inventory systems, the discussion in the chapter focuses on the consolidation procedures used in connection with perpetual inventories.

DOWNSTREAM SALE OF INVENTORY[2]

Advanced
StudyGuide
.com

For consolidation purposes, profits recorded on an intercorporate inventory sale are recognized in the period in which the inventory is resold to an unrelated party. Until the point of resale, all intercorporate profits must be deferred. When a sale is from a parent to a subsidiary, referred to as a *downstream sale,* any gain or loss on the transfer accrues to the parent company's stockholders. When the sale is from a subsidiary to its parent, an *upstream sale,* any gain or loss accrues to the subsidiary's stockholders. If the subsidiary is wholly owned, all gain or loss ultimately accrues to the parent company as the sole stockholder. If, however, the selling subsidiary is not wholly owned, the profit or loss on the upstream sale is apportioned between the parent company and the noncontrolling shareholders. Consolidated net income must be based on the realized income of the transferring affiliate. Because intercompany profits from downstream sales are on the parent's books, consolidated net income and the overall claim of parent company shareholders must be reduced by the full amount of the unrealized profits.

When a company sells an inventory item to an affiliate, one of three situations results: (1) the item is resold to a nonaffiliate during the same period, (2) the item is resold to a nonaffiliate during the next period, or (3) the item is held for two or more periods by the purchasing affiliate. We use the continuing example of Peerless Products Corporation and Special Foods Inc. to illustrate the consolidation process under each of the alternatives. Picking up with the example in Chapter 3, to illustrate more fully the treatment of unrealized intercompany profits, assume the following with respect to the Peerless and Special Foods example used previously:

1. Peerless Products Corporation purchases 80 percent of Special Foods Inc.'s stock on December 31, 20X0, at the stock's book value of $240,000. The fair value of Special Foods' noncontrolling interest on that date is $60,000, the book value of those shares.

2. During 20X1, Peerless reports separate income of $140,000 income from regular operations and declares dividends of $60,000. Special Foods reports net income of $50,000 and declares dividends of $30,000.

3. Peerless accounts for its investment in Special Foods using the equity method, under which it records its share of Special Foods' net income and dividends and also adjusts for unrealized intercompany profits using the fully adjusted equity method.

As an illustration of the effects of a downstream inventory sale, assume that on March 1, 20X1, Peerless buys inventory for $7,000 and resells it to Special Foods for $10,000 on April 1. Peerless records the following entries on its books:

	March 1, 20X1		
(1)	Inventory	7,000	
	Cash		7,000
	Record inventory purchase.		

	April 1, 20X1		
(2)	Cash	10,000	
	Sales		10,000
	Record sale of inventory to Special Foods.		

(3)	Cost of Goods Sold	7,000	
	Inventory		7,000
	Record cost of inventory sold to Special Foods.		

Special Foods records the purchase of the inventory from Peerless with the following entry:

	April 1, 20X1		
(4)	Inventory	10,000	
	Cash		10,000
	Record purchase of inventory from Peerless.		

[2] To view a video explanation of this topic, visit advancedstudyguide.com.

Resale in Period of Intercorporate Transfer

To illustrate consolidation when inventory is sold to an affiliate and then resold to a nonaffiliate during the same period, assume that on November 5, 20X1, Special Foods sells the inventory purchased from Peerless to Nonaffiliated Corporation for $15,000, as follows:

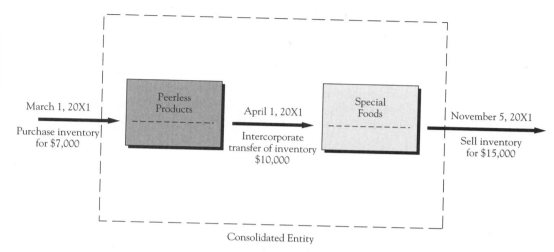

Consolidated Entity

Special Foods records the sale to Nonaffiliated with the following entries:

November 5, 20X1

(5)	Cash	15,000	
	Sales		15,000
	Record sale of inventory to Nonaffiliated.		

(6)	Cost of Goods Sold	10,000	
	Inventory		10,000
	Record cost of inventory sold to Nonaffiliated.		

A review of all entries recorded by the individual companies indicates that incorrect balances will be reported in the consolidated income statement if the effects of the intercorporate sale are not removed:

Item	Peerless Products	Special Foods	Unadjusted Totals	Consolidated Amounts
Sales	$10,000	$15,000	$25,000	$15,000
Cost of Goods Sold	(7,000)	(10,000)	(17,000)	(7,000)
Gross Profit	$ 3,000	$ 5,000	$ 8,000	$ 8,000

Although consolidated gross profit is correct even if no adjustments are made, the totals for sales and cost of goods sold derived by simply adding the amounts on the books of Peerless and Special Foods are overstated for the consolidated entity. The selling price of the inventory to Nonaffiliated Corporation is $15,000, and the original cost to Peerless Products is $7,000. Thus, gross profit of $8,000 is correct from a consolidated viewpoint, but consolidated sales and cost of goods sold should be $15,000 and $7,000, respectively, rather than $25,000 and $17,000. In the consolidation worksheet, the amount of the intercompany sale must be eliminated from both sales and cost of goods sold to correctly state the consolidated totals:

Sales	10,000	
Cost of Goods Sold		10,000

Note that this entry does not affect consolidated net income because sales and cost of goods sold both are reduced by the same amount. No elimination of intercompany profit is needed because all the intercompany profit has been realized through resale of the inventory to the external party during the current period.

Resale in Period following Intercorporate Transfer

When inventory is sold to an affiliate at a profit but is not resold during the same period, appropriate adjustments are needed to prepare consolidated financial statements in the period of the intercompany sale and in each subsequent period until the inventory is sold to a nonaffiliate. By way of illustration, assume that Peerless Products purchases inventory on March 1, 20X1 for $7,000 and sells the inventory during the year (on April 1) to Special Foods for $10,000. Special Foods sells the inventory to Nonaffiliated Corporation for $15,000 on January 2, 20X2, as follows:

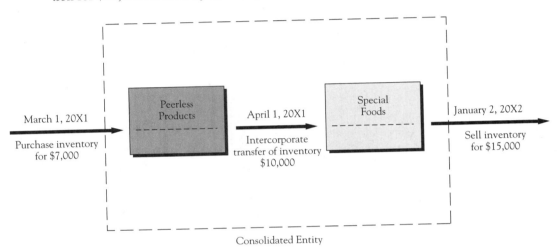

Consolidated Entity

During 20X1, Peerless records the purchase of the inventory and the sale to Special Foods with journal entries (1) through (3), given previously; Special Foods records the purchase of the inventory from Peerless with entry (4). In 20X2, Special Foods records the sale of the inventory to Nonaffiliated with entries (5) and (6), given earlier.

Equity-Method Entries—20X1

Using the equity method, Peerless records its share of Special Foods' income and dividends for 20X1:

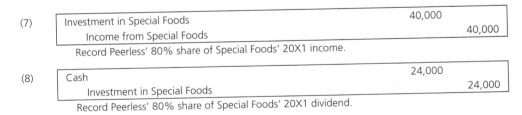

(7)	Investment in Special Foods	40,000	
	Income from Special Foods		40,000
	Record Peerless' 80% share of Special Foods' 20X1 income.		

(8)	Cash	24,000	
	Investment in Special Foods		24,000
	Record Peerless' 80% share of Special Foods' 20X1 dividend.		

As a result of these entries, the ending balance of the investment account is currently $256,000 ($240,000 + $40,000 − $24,000). However, since the downstream sale of inventory to Special Foods results in $3,000 of unrealized profits, Peerless makes an adjustment in the equity accounts to reduce the income from Special Foods on the income statement and Investment in Special Foods on the balance sheet by its share of the unrealized gross profit. Since this is a downstream transaction, the sale (and associated unrealized gross profit) resides on Peerless' income statement. Since we assume the NCI shareholders do not own Peerless stock, they do not share in the deferral of the unrealized profit. Under the fully adjusted equity method, Peerless defers the entire $3,000 using the following equity method entry:

(9)	Income from Special Foods	3,000	
	Investment in Special Foods		3,000

Defer unrealized gross profit on inventory sales to Special Foods not yet resold.

Note that this entry accomplishes two important objectives. First, since Peerless income is overstated by $3,000, the adjustment to Income from Special Foods offsets this overstatement so that Peerless bottom-line net income is now correct. Second, Special Foods' inventory is currently overstated by $3,000. Since the Investment in Special Foods account summarizes Peerless' investment in Special Foods' balance sheet, this reduction to the investment account offsets the fact that Special Foods' inventory (and thus entire balance sheet) is overstated by $3,000. Thus, after making this equity-method adjustment to defer the unrealized gross profit, Peerless' financial statements are now correctly stated. Therefore, Peerless' reported income will be exactly equal to the controlling interest in net income on the consolidated financial statements.

Consolidation Worksheet—20X1

We present the consolidation worksheet prepared at the end of 20X1 in Figure 6–2. The first two elimination entries are the same as we calculated in Chapter 3 with one minor exception. While the analysis of the "book value" portion of the investment account is the same, in preparing the basic elimination entry, we reduce the amounts in the Income from Special Foods and Investment in Special Foods by the $3,000 deferral.

Book Value Calculations:

	NCI 20% +	Peerless 80%	= Common Stock +	Retained Earnings
Original book value	60,000	240,000	200,000	100,000
+ Net income	10,000	40,000		50,000
− Dividends	(6,000)	(24,000)		(30,000)
Ending book value	64,000	256,000	200,000	120,000

Basic investment account elimination entry:

Common stock	200,000		← Original amount invested (100%)
Retained earnings	100,000		← Beginning balance in RE
Income from Special Foods	37,000		← Peerless' % of NI − Deferred GP
NCI in NI of Special Foods	10,000		← NCI share of Special Foods' NI
Dividends declared		30,000	← 100% of sub's dividends declared
Investment in Special Foods		253,000	← Net BV in investment − Deferred GP
NCI in NA of Special Foods		64,000	← NCI share of net amount of BV

FIGURE 6–2 December 31, 20X1, Consolidation Worksheet, Period of Intercompany Sale; Downstream Inventory Sale

	Peerless Products	Special Foods	Elimination Entries DR	Elimination Entries CR	Consolidated
Income Statement					
Sales	400,000	200,000	10,000		590,000
Less: COGS	(170,000)	(115,000)		7,000	(278,000)
Less: Depreciation Expense	(50,000)	(20,000)			(70,000)
Less: Other Expenses	(40,000)	(15,000)			(55,000)
Income from Special Foods	37,000		37,000		0
Consolidated Net Income	177,000	50,000	47,000	7,000	187,000
NCI in Net Income			10,000		(10,000)
Controlling Interest Net Income	**177,000**	**50,000**	**57,000**	**7,000**	**177,000**
Statement of Retained Earnings					
Beginning Balance	300,000	100,000	100,000		300,000
Net Income	**177,000**	**50,000**	57,000	7,000	177,000
Less: Dividends Declared	(60,000)	(30,000)		30,000	(60,000)
Ending Balance	**417,000**	**120,000**	**157,000**	**37,000**	**417,000**
Balance Sheet					
Cash	264,000	75,000			339,000
Accounts Receivable	75,000	50,000			125,000
Inventory	100,000	75,000		3,000	172,000
Investment in Special Foods	253,000			253,000	0
Land	175,000	40,000			215,000
Buildings & Equipment	800,000	600,000		300,000	1,100,000
Less: Accumulated Depreciation	(450,000)	(320,000)	300,000		(470,000)
Total Assets	**1,217,000**	**520,000**	**300,000**	**556,000**	**1,481,000**
Accounts Payable	100,000	100,000			200,000
Bonds Payable	200,000	100,000			300,000
Common Stock	500,000	200,000	200,000		500,000
Retained Earnings	**417,000**	**120,000**	157,000	37,000	417,000
NCI in NA of Special Foods				64,000	64,000
Total Liabilities & Equity	**1,217,000**	**520,000**	**357,000**	**101,000**	**1,481,000**

Advanced StudyGuide .com

Optional accumulated depreciation elimination entry:

Accumulated depreciation	300,000	
Building and equipment		300,000

← Original depreciation at the time of the acquisition netted against cost

Moreover, although Peerless recorded an equity-method entry to defer the unrealized gross profit, both the Income from Special Foods and Investment in Special Foods accounts are eliminated with the basic elimination entry. Peerless' Sales and Cost of Goods Sold amounts are still overstated (by $10,000 and $7,000, respectively). Moreover, Special Foods' ending inventory is still overstated by $3,000. Simply adding up the Peerless and Special Foods columns of the consolidation worksheet will result in overstated consolidated net income, total assets, and retained earnings. Therefore, we also record a new eliminating entry to correct the unadjusted totals to the appropriate consolidated amounts. In doing so, consolidated income is reduced by $3,000 ($10,000 − $7,000). In addition, ending inventory reported on Special Foods' books is stated at the intercompany exchange price rather than the historical cost to the consolidated entity. Until resold to an external party by Special Foods, the inventory must be reduced by the amount of unrealized intercompany profit each time consolidated statements are prepared.

Elimination of intercompany sales to Special Foods (still on hand in ending inventory):

Sales	10,000	
Cost of Goods Sold		7,000
Inventory		3,000

This elimination entry eliminates the effects of the intercompany inventory sale. The journal entries recorded by Peerless Products and Special Foods in 20X1 on their separate books will result in an overstatement of consolidated gross profit for 20X1 and the consolidated inventory balance at year-end unless the amounts are adjusted in the consolidation worksheet. The amounts resulting from the intercompany inventory transactions from the separate books of Peerless Products and Special Foods, and the appropriate consolidated amounts, are as follows:

Item	Peerless Products	Special Foods	Unadjusted Totals	Consolidated Amounts
Sales	$10,000	$ –0–	$10,000	$ –0–
Cost of Goods Sold	(7,000)		(7,000)	–0–
		–0–		
Gross Profit	$ 3,000	$ –0–	$ 3,000	$ –0–
Inventory	$ –0–	$10,000	$10,000	$7,000

The following T-accounts summarize the effects of all equity-method entries on Peerless' books as well as the basic elimination entry:

Consolidated Net Income—20X1

Consolidated net income for 20X1 is shown as $187,000 in the Figure 6–2 worksheet. This amount is computed and allocated as follows:

Peerless' separate income	$140,000
Less: Unrealized intercompany profit on downstream inventory sale	(3,000)
Peerless' separate realized income	$137,000
Special Foods' net income	50,000
Consolidated net income, 20X1	$187,000
Income to noncontrolling interest ($50,000 × 0.20)	(10,000)
Income to controlling interest	$177,000

Equity-Method Entries—20X2

During 20X2, Special Foods receives $15,000 when it sells to Nonaffiliated Corporation the inventory that it had purchased for $10,000 from Peerless in 20X1. Also, Peerless records its pro rata portion of Special Foods' net income ($75,000) and dividends ($40,000) for 20X2 with the normal equity-method entries:

(10)

Investment in Special Foods	60,000	
Income from Special Foods		60,000

Record Peerless' 80% share of Special Foods' 20X2 income.

(11)

Cash	32,000	
Investment in Special Foods		32,000

Record Peerless' 80% share of Special Foods' 20X2 dividend.

Under the fully adjusted equity method, once the inventory is sold to an unaffiliated party, the deferral in the equity method accounts is no longer necessary and is reversed out as follows:

(12)

Investment in Special Foods	3,000	
Income from Special Foods		3,000

Reverse the deferred gross profit from 20X1 on inventory sold to unaffiliated customers.

Consolidation Worksheet—20X2

Figure 6–3 illustrates the consolidation worksheet at the end of 20X2. The first two elimination entries are the same as those presented in Chapter 3 with one exception to the basic elimination entry. Whereas we subtracted the deferral of unrealized gross profit in 20X1, we now add back this deferral in the basic elimination entry for 20X2.

Book Value Calculations:

	NCI 20%	+ Peerless 80%	= Common Stock	+ Retained Earnings
Beginning book value	64,000	256,000	200,000	120,000
+ Net income	15,000	60,000		75,000
− Dividends	(8,000)	(32,000)		(40,000)
Ending book value	71,000	284,000	200,000	155,000

Basic elimination entry:

Common stock	200,000		← Original amount invested (100%)
Retained earnings	120,000		← Beginning balance in RE
Income from Special Foods	63,000		← Peerless' % of NI + 2001 reversal
NCI in NI of Special Foods	15,000		← NCI share of Special Foods' NI
Dividends declared		40,000	← 100% of sub's dividends declared
Investment in Special Foods		287,000	← Net investment + 2001 reversal
NCI in NA of Special Foods		71,000	← NCI share of ending book value

Optional accumulated depreciation elimination entry:

Accumulated depreciation	300,000	
Building and equipment		300,000

← Original depreciation at the time of the acquisition netted against cost

An additional elimination entry is needed to recognize the $3,000 of income that was deferred in 20X1. Whereas the inventory had not yet been sold to an unaffiliated customer in 20X1 and needed to be deferred, that inventory has now been sold in 20X2 and should be recognized in the consolidated financial statements.

FIGURE 6–3 December 31, 20X2, Consolidation Worksheet, Next Period Following Intercompany Sale; Downstream Inventory Sale

	Peerless Products	Special Foods	Elimination Entries DR	Elimination Entries CR	Consolidated
Income Statement					
Sales	450,000	300,000			750,000
Less: COGS	(180,000)	(160,000)		3,000	(337,000)
Less: Depreciation Expense	(50,000)	(20,000)			(70,000)
Less: Other Expenses	(60,000)	(45,000)			(105,000)
Income from Special Foods	63,000		63,000		0
Consolidated Net Income	223,000	75,000	63,000	3,000	238,000
NCI in Net Income			15,000		(15,000)
Controlling Interest Net Income	**223,000**	**75,000**	**78,000**	**3,000**	**223,000**
Statement of Retained Earnings					
Beginning Balance	417,000	120,000	120,000		417,000
Net Income	**223,000**	**75,000**	78,000	3,000	223,000
Less: Dividends Declared	(60,000)	(40,000)		40,000	(60,000)
Ending Balance	**580,000**	**155,000**	**198,000**	**43,000**	**580,000**
Balance Sheet					
Cash	291,000	85,000			376,000
Accounts Receivable	150,000	80,000			230,000
Inventory	180,000	90,000			270,000
Investment in Special Foods	284,000		3,000	287,000	0
Land	175,000	40,000			215,000
Buildings & Equipment	800,000	600,000		300,000	1,100,000
Less: Accumulated Depreciation	(500,000)	(340,000)	300,000		(540,000)
Total Assets	**1,380,000**	**555,000**	**303,000**	**587,000**	**1,651,000**
Accounts Payable	100,000	100,000			200,000
Bonds Payable	200,000	100,000			300,000
Common Stock	500,000	200,000	200,000		500,000
Retained Earnings	580,000	155,000	198,000	43,000	580,000
NCI in NA of Special Foods				71,000	71,000
Total Liabilities & Equity	**1,380,000**	**555,000**	**398,000**	**114,000**	**1,651,000**

Reversal of the 20X1 gross profit deferral:

Investment in Special Foods	3,000	
Cost of Goods Sold		3,000

Special Foods' unrealized intercompany profit included in beginning inventory was charged to Cost of Goods Sold when Special Foods sold the inventory during the period. Thus, consolidated cost of goods sold will be overstated for 20X2 if it is based on the unadjusted totals from the books of Peerless and Special Foods:

Item	Peerless Products	Special Foods	Unadjusted Totals	Consolidated Amounts
Sales	$ –0–	$ 15,000	$ 15,000	$ 15,000
Cost of Goods Sold	–0–	(10,000)	(10,000)	(7,000)
Gross Profit	$ –0–	$ 5,000	$ 5,000	$ 8,000

Unlike the period in which the intercompany transfer occurs, no adjustment to sales is required in a subsequent period when the inventory is sold to a nonaffiliate. The amount reported by Special Foods reflects the sale outside the economic entity and is the appropriate amount to be reported for consolidation. By removing the $3,000 of intercorporate profit from Cost of Goods Sold with this elimination entry, the original acquisition price paid by Peerless Products is reported, and $8,000 of gross profit is correctly reported in the consolidated income statement.

Once the sale is made to an external party, the transaction is complete and no adjustments or eliminations related to the intercompany transaction are needed in future periods. The following T-accounts illustrate the effects of all equity-method journal entries on Peerless' books as well as the elimination entries on the consolidation worksheet.

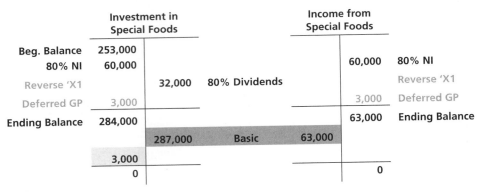

Consolidated Net Income—20X2

Consolidated net income for 20X2 is shown as $238,000 in the Figure 6–3 worksheet. This amount is verified and allocated as follows:

Peerless' separate income	$160,000
Realization of deferred intercompany profit on downstream inventory sale	3,000
Peerless' separate realized income	$163,000
Special Foods' net income	75,000
Consolidated net income, 20X2	$238,000
Income to noncontrolling interest ($75,000 × 0.20)	(15,000)
Income to controlling interest	$223,000

Inventory Held for Two or More Periods

Companies may carry the cost of inventory purchased from an affiliate for more than one accounting period. For example, the cost of an item may be in a LIFO inventory layer and would be included as part of the inventory balance until the layer is liquidated. Prior to liquidation, an eliminating entry is needed in the consolidation worksheet each time consolidated statements are prepared to restate the inventory to its cost to the consolidated entity. For example, if Special Foods continues to hold the inventory purchased from Peerless Products, the following eliminating entry is needed in the consolidation worksheet each time a consolidated balance sheet is prepared for years following the year of intercompany sale, for as long as the inventory is held:

Investment in Special Foods	3,000	
Inventory		3,000

This elimination entry simply corrects the balance in both the Inventory and Investment in Special Foods accounts. Whereas Peerless recorded an equity-method adjustment to defer the $3,000 of unrealized gross profit in the year of the intercompany inventory transfer by artificially decreasing the Investment in Special Foods to offset the overstated inventory balance on Special Foods' books, this entry simply corrects both accounts. No income statement adjustments are needed in the periods following the intercorporate sale until the inventory is resold to parties external to the consolidated entity.

UPSTREAM SALE OF INVENTORY

LO4

Prepare equity-method journal entries and elimination entries for the consolidation of a subsidiary following upstream inventory transfers.

Advanced
StudyGuide
.com

When an upstream sale of inventory occurs and the inventory is resold by the parent to a nonaffiliate during the same period, all the parent's equity-method entries and the eliminating entries in the consolidation worksheet are identical to those in the downstream case.

When the inventory is not resold to a nonaffiliate before the end of the period, worksheet eliminating entries are different from the downstream case only by the apportionment of the unrealized intercompany profit to both the controlling and noncontrolling interests. In this case, since the sale appears on Special Foods' income statement and since the NCI shareholders own 20 percent of Special Foods' outstanding shares, they are entitled to 20 percent of Special Foods' net income. Thus, the deferral of unrealized gross profits accrues to both Peerless and the NCI shareholders. In other words, the intercompany profit in an upstream sale is recognized by the subsidiary and shared between the controlling and noncontrolling stockholders of the subsidiary. Therefore, the elimination of the unrealized intercompany profit must reduce the interests of both ownership groups each period until the profit is confirmed by resale of the inventory to a nonaffiliated party.

We illustrate an upstream sale using the same example as used for the downstream sale except that the intercompany sale is made from Special Foods to Peerless. Assume Special Foods purchases the inventory on March 1, 20X1, for $7,000 and sells it to Peerless for $10,000 during the same year. Peerless holds the inventory until January 2 of the following year, at which time Peerless sells it to Nonaffiliated Corporation for $15,000.

Equity-Method Entries—20X1

Peerless Products records the following equity-method entries in 20X1:

(13)	Investment in Special Foods	40,000	
	Income from Special Foods		40,000
	Record Peerless' 80% share of Special Foods' 20X1 income.		

(14)	Cash	24,000	
	Investment in Special Foods		24,000
	Record Peerless' 80% share of Special Foods' 20X1 dividend.		

These entries are the same as in the illustration of the downstream sale. The only difference is that the fully adjusted equity method entry to defer the unrealized gross profit is only for Peerless' ownership percentage of Special Foods (80 percent). Thus, the deferral of Peerless relative share of the unrealized gross profit is $2,400 ($3,000 × 80%).

(15)	Income from Special Foods	2,400	
	Investment in Special Foods		2,400

Eliminate unrealized gross profit on inventory purchases from Special Foods.

Consolidation Worksheet—20X1

Advanced
StudyGuide
.com

We present the worksheet for the preparation of the 20X1 consolidated financial statements in Figure 6–4. The first two elimination entries are the same as we calculated in Chapter 3 with one minor exception. While the analysis of the "book value" portion of the investment account is the same, in preparing the basic elimination entry, we reduce the amounts in Peerless' Income from Special Foods and Investment in Special Foods accounts by Peerless' share of the deferral, $2,400 ($3,000 × 80%). We also reduce the NCI in Net Income of Special Foods and NCI in Net Assets of Special Foods by the NCI share of the deferral, $600 ($3,000 × 20%).

FIGURE 6–4 December 31, 20X1, Consolidation Worksheet, Period of Intercompany Sale; Upstream Inventory Sale

	Peerless Products	Special Foods	Elimination Entries		Consolidated
			DR	CR	
Income Statement					
Sales	400,000	200,000	10,000		590,000
Less: COGS	(170,000)	(115,000)		7,000	(278,000)
Less: Depreciation Expense	(50,000)	(20,000)			(70,000)
Less: Other Expenses	(40,000)	(15,000)			(55,000)
Income from Special Foods	37,600		37,600		0
Consolidated Net Income	177,600	50,000	47,600	7,000	187,000
NCI in Net Income			9,400		(9,400)
Controlling Interest Net Income	**177,600**	**50,000**	**57,000**	**7,000**	**177,600**
Statement of Retained Earnings					
Beginning Balance	300,000	100,000	100,000		300,000
Net Income	**177,600**	**50,000**	57,000	7,000	177,600
Less: Dividends Declared	(60,000)	(30,000)		30,000	(60,000)
Ending Balance	**417,600**	**120,000**	**157,000**	**37,000**	**417,600**
Balance Sheet					
Cash	264,000	75,000			339,000
Accounts Receivable	75,000	50,000			125,000
Inventory	100,000	75,000		3,000	172,000
Investment in Special Foods	253,600			253,600	0
Land	175,000	40,000			215,000
Buildings & Equipment	800,000	600,000		300,000	1,100,000
Less: Accumulated Depreciation	(450,000)	(320,000)	300,000		(470,000)
Total Assets	**1,217,600**	**520,000**	**300,000**	**556,600**	**1,481,000**
Accounts Payable	100,000	100,000			200,000
Bonds Payable	200,000	100,000			300,000
Common Stock	500,000	200,000	200,000		500,000
Retained Earnings	**417,600**	**120,000**	157,000	37,000	417,600
NCI in NA of Special Foods				63,400	63,400
Total Liabilities & Equity	**1,217,600**	**520,000**	**357,000**	**100,400**	**1,481,000**

Book Value Calculations:

	NCI 20% + Peerless 80%		= Common Stock + Retained Earnings	
Original book value	60,000	240,000	200,000	100,000
+ Net income	10,000	40,000		50,000
− Dividends	(6,000)	(24,000)		(30,000)
Ending book value	64,000	256,000	200,000	120,000

Basic investment account elimination entry:

Common stock	200,000		← Original amount invested (100%)
Retained earnings	100,000		← Beginning balance in RE
Income from Special Foods	37,600		← Peerless' % of NI − 80% Deferred GP
NCI in NI of Special Foods	9,400		← NCI share of NI − 20% Deferred GP
Dividends declared		30,000	← 100% of sub's dividends declared
Investment in Special Foods		253,600	← Net book value − 80% Deferred GP
NCI in NA of Special Foods		63,400	← NCI share of BV − 20% Deferred GP

Optional accumulated depreciation elimination entry:

Accumulated depreciation	300,000		← Original depreciation at the time of
Building and equipment		300,000	the acquisition netted against cost

The consolidation worksheet entry to correct for the intercompany sale is identical to the downstream case. The only difference is that the overstated Sales and Cost of Goods Sold numbers are now in the Special Foods' column of the consolidation worksheet and the overstated inventory is now in the Peerless column.

Eliminate inventory purchases from Special Foods (still on hand):

Sales	10,000	
Cost of Goods Sold		7,000
Inventory		3,000

Consolidated Net Income—20X1

We note that because the unrealized profit elimination is allocated proportionately between the controlling and noncontrolling interests in the upstream case, the income assigned to the noncontrolling shareholders is $600 ($3,000 × 0.20) less in Figure 6–4 for the upstream case than in Figure 6–2 for the downstream case. Accordingly, the amount of income assigned to the controlling interest is $600 higher. Note that consolidated net income and all other income statement amounts are the same whether the sale is upstream or downstream. Consolidated net income for 20X1 is shown in the worksheet as $187,000. Consolidated net income is computed and allocated to the controlling and noncontrolling stockholders as follows:

Peerless' separate income		$140,000
Special Foods' net income	$50,000	
Less: Unrealized intercompany profit on upstream inventory sale	(3,000)	
Special Foods' realized net income		47,000
Consolidated net income, 20X1		$187,000
Income to noncontrolling interest ($47,000 × 0.20)		(9,400)
Income to controlling interest		$177,600

Equity-Method Entries—20X2

Peerless recognizes its share of Special Foods' income ($75,000) and dividends ($40,000) for 20X2 with the normal equity-method entries:

(16)	Investment in Special Foods	60,000	
	Income from Special Foods		60,000
	Record Peerless' 80% share of Special Foods' 20X2 income.		

(17)	Cash	32,000	
	Investment in Special Foods		32,000
	Record Peerless' 80% share of Special Foods' 20X2 dividend.		

Under the fully adjusted equity method, Peerless reverses the deferred gross profit from 20X1 because this inventory has now been sold.

(18)	Investment in Special Foods	2,400	
	Income from Special Foods		2,400
	Reverse the deferred gross profit from 20X1 on inventory sold to unaffiliated customers.		

Consolidation Worksheet—20X2

Figure 6–5 illustrates the consolidation worksheet used to prepare consolidated financial statements at the end of 20X2. The first two elimination entries are the same as we prepared in Chapter 3 with the previously explained exception. While the analysis of the "book value" portion of the investment account is the same, in preparing the basic elimination entry, since the inventory sold to Peerless by Special Foods last year has now been sold to an unaffiliated party, we now increase the amounts in Peerless' Income from Special Foods and Investment in Special Foods accounts by Peerless' share of the deferral, $2,400 ($3,000 × 80%). We also increase the NCI in Net Income of Special Foods and NCI in Net Assets of Special Foods by the NCI share of the deferral, $600 ($3,000 × 20%).

Book Value Calculations:

	NCI 20%	+ Peerless 80%	= Common Stock	+ Retained Earnings
Beginning book value	64,000	256,000	200,000	120,000
+ Net income	15,000	60,000		75,000
− Dividends	(8,000)	(32,000)		(40,000)
Ending book value	71,000	284,000	200,000	155,000

FIGURE 6–5 December 31, 20X2, Consolidation Worksheet, Next Period following Intercompany Sale; Upstream Inventory Sale

	Peerless Products	Special Foods	Elimination Entries DR	Elimination Entries CR	Consolidated
Income Statement					
Sales	450,000	300,000			750,000
Less: COGS	(180,000)	(160,000)		3,000	(337,000)
Less: Depreciation Expense	(50,000)	(20,000)			(70,000)
Less: Other Expenses	(60,000)	(45,000)			(105,000)
Income from Special Foods	62,400		62,400		0
Consolidated Net Income	222,400	75,000	62,400	3,000	238,000
NCI in Net Income			15,600		(15,600)
Controlling Interest Net Income	222,400	75,000	78,000	3,000	222,400
Statement of Retained Earnings					
Beginning Balance	417,600	120,000	120,000		417,600
Net Income	222,400	75,000	78,000	3,000	222,400
Less: Dividends Declared	(60,000)	(40,000)		40,000	(60,000)
Ending Balance	580,000	155,000	198,000	43,000	580,000
Balance Sheet					
Cash	291,000	85,000			376,000
Accounts Receivable	150,000	80,000			230,000
Inventory	180,000	90,000			270,000
Investment in Special Foods	284,000		2,400	286,400	0
Land	175,000	40,000			215,000
Buildings & Equipment	800,000	600,000		300,000	1,100,000
Less: Accumulated Depreciation	(500,000)	(340,000)	300,000		(540,000)
Total Assets	1,380,000	555,000	302,400	586,400	1,651,000
Accounts Payable	100,000	100,000			200,000
Bonds Payable	200,000	100,000			300,000
Common Stock	500,000	200,000	200,000		500,000
Retained Earnings	580,000	155,000	198,000	43,000	580,000
NCI in NA of Special Foods			600	71,600	71,000
Total Liabilities & Equity	1,380,000	555,000	398,600	114,600	1,651,000

Advanced StudyGuide .com

Basic elimination entry:

Common stock	200,000	← Original amount invested (100%)
Retained earnings	120,000	← Beginning balance in RE
Income from Special Foods	62,400	← Peerless' % of NI + 80% 20X1 reversal
NCI in NI of Special Foods	15,600	← NCI % of NI + 20% 20X1 reversal
Dividends declared	40,000	← 100% of sub's dividends declared
Investment in Special Foods	286,400	← Net book value + 80% 20X1 reversal
NCI in NA of Special Foods	71,600	← NCI % of BV + 20% 20X1 reversal

Optional accumulated depreciation elimination entry:

Accumulated depreciation	300,000	← Original depreciation at the time of
Building and equipment	300,000	the acquisition netted against cost

Similar to the downstream example, the unrealized intercompany profit included in Peerless' beginning inventory was charged to Cost of Goods Sold when Peerless

sold the inventory during 20X2. Thus, consolidated cost of goods sold will be overstated for 20X2 if it is reported in the consolidated income statement at the unadjusted total from the books of Peerless and Special Foods. The following elimination
entry corrects Cost of Goods Sold and splits this adjustment proportionately between
Peerless' investment account and the NCI in Net Assets of Special Foods.

Reversal of 20X1 gross profit deferral:

Investment in Special Foods	2,400	
NCI in NA of Special Foods	600	
Cost of Goods Sold		3,000

The following t-accounts illustrate the effects of all equity method journal entries on
Peerless' books as well as the elimination entries on the consolidation worksheet.

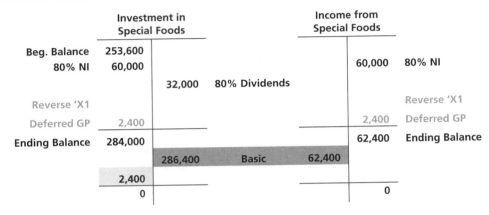

Consolidated Net Income—20X2

Consolidated net income for 20X2 is shown as $238,000 in the Figure 6–5 worksheet.
This amount is computed and allocated as follows:

Peerless' separate income		$160,000
Special Foods' net income	$75,000	
Realization of deferred intercompany profit on upstream inventory sale	3,000	
Special Foods' realized net income		78,000
Consolidated net income, 20X2		$238,000
Income to noncontrolling interest ($78,000 × 0.20)		(15,600)
Income to controlling interest		$222,400

ADDITIONAL CONSIDERATIONS

LO5

Understand and explain
additional consider-
ations associated with
consolidation.

The frequency of intercompany inventory transfers and the varied circumstances under
which they may occur raise a number of additional implementation issues. Several of
these are discussed briefly in this section.

Sale from One Subsidiary to Another

Transfers of inventory often occur between companies that are under common control
or ownership. When one subsidiary sells merchandise to another subsidiary, the eliminating entries are identical to those presented earlier for sales from a subsidiary to its
parent. The full amount of any unrealized intercompany profit is eliminated, with the
profit elimination allocated proportionately against the ownership interests of the selling
subsidiary.

As an illustration, assume that Peerless Products owns 90 percent of the outstanding stock of Super Industries in addition to its 80 percent interest in Special Foods. If Special Foods sells inventory at a $3,000 profit to Super Industries for $10,000 and Super Industries holds all of the inventory at the end of the period, the following elimination entry is among those needed in the consolidation worksheet prepared at the end of the period:

Eliminate intercompany inventory sales (still on hand):

Sales	10,000	
Cost of Goods Sold		7,000
Inventory		3,000

The $3,000 elimination of unrealized intercompany profit is allocated proportionately between the two shareholder groups of the selling affiliate. Consolidated net income is reduced by the full $3,000 unrealized intercompany profit. The income allocated to the controlling interest is reduced by Peerless' 80 percent share of the intercompany profit, or $2,400, and Special Foods' noncontrolling interest is reduced by its 20 percent share, or $600.

Costs Associated with Transfers

When one affiliate transfers inventory to another, some additional cost, such as freight, is often incurred in the transfer. This cost should be treated in the same way as if the affiliates were operating divisions of a single company. If the additional cost would be inventoried in transferring the units from one location to another within the same company, that treatment also would be appropriate for consolidation.

Lower of Cost or Market

A company might write down inventory purchased from an affiliate under the lower-of-cost-or-market rule if the market value at the end of the period is less than the intercompany transfer price. To illustrate this situation assume that a parent company purchases inventory for $20,000 and sells it to its subsidiary for $35,000. The subsidiary still holds the inventory at year-end and determines that its current market value (replacement cost) is $25,000.

The subsidiary writes the inventory down from $35,000 to its lower market value of $25,000 at the end of the year and records the following entry:

(19)	Loss on Decline in Inventory Value	10,000	
	Inventory		10,000
	Write down inventory to market value.		

While this entry revalues the inventory to $25,000 on the subsidiary's books, the appropriate valuation from a consolidated viewpoint is the $20,000 original cost of the inventory to the parent. Therefore, the following eliminating entry is needed in the consolidation worksheet:

Eliminate intercompany inventory sales (still on hand):

Sales	35,000	
Cost of Goods Sold		20,000
Inventory		5,000
Loss on Decline in Inventory Value		10,000

The inventory loss recorded by the subsidiary must be eliminated because the $20,000 inventory valuation for consolidation purposes is below the $25,000 market value of the inventory.

Sales and Purchases before Affiliation

Sometimes companies that have sold inventory to one another later join together in a business combination. The consolidation treatment of profits on inventory transfers that occurred before the business combination depends on whether the companies were at that time independent and the sale transaction was the result of arm's-length bargaining. As a general rule, the effects of transactions that are not the result of arm's-length bargaining must be eliminated. However, the combining of two companies does not necessarily mean that their prior transactions with one another were not conducted at arm's length. The circumstances surrounding the prior transactions, such as the price and quantity of units transferred, would have to be examined.

In the absence of evidence to the contrary, companies that have joined together in a business combination are viewed as having been separate and independent prior to the combination. Thus, if the prior sales were the result of arm's-length bargaining, they are viewed as transactions between unrelated parties. Accordingly, no elimination or adjustment is needed in preparing consolidated statements subsequent to the combination, even if an affiliate still holds the inventory.

Summary of Key Concepts	Consolidated financial statements are prepared for the consolidated entity as if it were a single company. Therefore, the effects of all transactions between companies within the entity must be eliminated in preparing consolidated financial statements. Each time consolidated statements are prepared, all effects of intercompany transactions occurring during that period, and the effects of unrealized profits from transactions in prior periods, must be eliminated. For intercompany inventory transactions, the intercompany sale and cost of goods sold must be eliminated. In addition, the intercompany profit may not be recognized in consolidation until it is confirmed by resale of the inventory to an external party. Unrealized intercompany profits must be eliminated fully and are allocated proportionately against the stockholder groups of the selling affiliate. If inventory containing unrealized intercompany profits is sold during the period, consolidated cost of goods sold must be adjusted to reflect the actual cost to the consolidated entity of the inventory sold; if the inventory is still held at the end of the period, it must be adjusted to its actual cost to the consolidated entity.

Key Terms	intercompany transfers, *255* intercorporate transfers, *255*	unrealized intercompany profit, *256*	downstream sale, *258* upstream sale, *258*

Appendix 6A Intercompany Inventory Transactions—Modified Equity Method and Cost Method

This appendix illustrates consolidation procedures under the modified (or sometimes called the basic) equity method and then the cost method. We use the upstream sale example presented earlier to illustrate these alternative methods. Assume that Special Foods purchases inventory for $7,000 in 20X1 and, in the same year, sells the inventory to Peerless Products for $10,000. Peerless Products sells the inventory to external parties in 20X2. Both companies use perpetual inventory control systems.

MODIFIED EQUITY METHOD

The journal entries on Peerless' books and the elimination entries in the consolidation worksheet are the same under the modified equity method as under the fully adjusted method except for differences related to unrealized intercompany profits. When using the fully adjusted equity method, the parent reduces its income and the balance of the investment account for its share of unrealized intercompany profits that arise during the period. Subsequently, the parent increases its income and the carrying amount of the investment account when the intercompany profits are realized through transactions with external parties. These adjustments related to unrealized gross profit on intercompany sales are omitted under the modified equity method. As a result, the worksheet entry in the second year to recognize the deferred gross profit from the first year is slightly different. Instead of recording a debit to the investment account, this debit goes to beginning retained earnings.

Modified Equity-method Entries—20X1

In 20X1, Peerless Products records the normal equity-method entries reflecting its share of Special Foods' income and dividends, but omits the additional entry to reduce income and the investment account by the parent's share of the unrealized intercompany profit arising during the year:

(19)	Investment in Special Foods	40,000	
	Income from Special Foods		40,000

Record Peerless' 80% share of Special Foods' 20X1 income.

(20)	Cash	24,000	
	Investment in Special Foods		24,000

Record Peerless' 80% share of Special Foods' 20X1 dividend.

Consolidation Elimination Entries—20X1

Figure 6–6 illustrates the consolidation worksheet for 20X1 under the modified equity method. The elimination entries are the same as we presented for the fully adjusted equity method with one minor exception. We do not reduce the amounts in Peerless' Income from Special Foods and Investment in Special Foods accounts by Peerless' share of the deferral, $2,400 ($3,000 × 80%),

FIGURE 6–6 December 31, 20X1, Modified Equity Method Consolidation Worksheet, Period of Intercompany Sale; Upstream Inventory Sale

	Peerless Products	Special Foods	Elimination Entries		Consolidated
			DR	CR	
Income Statement					
Sales	400,000	200,000	10,000		590,000
Less: COGS	(170,000)	(115,000)		7,000	(278,000)
Less: Depreciation Expense	(50,000)	(20,000)			(70,000)
Less: Other Expenses	(40,000)	(15,000)			(55,000)
Income from Special Foods	40,000		40,000		0
Consolidated Net Income	180,000	50,000	50,000	7,000	187,000
NCI in Net Income			9,400		(9,400)
Controlling Interest Net Income	180,000	50,000	59,400	7,000	177,600
Statement of Retained Earnings					
Beginning Balance	300,000	100,000	100,000		300,000
Net Income	180,000	50,000	59,400	7,000	177,600
Less: Dividends Declared	(60,000)	(30,000)		30,000	(60,000)
Ending Balance	420,000	120,000	159,400	37,000	417,600
Balance Sheet					
Cash	264,000	75,000			339,000
Accounts Receivable	75,000	50,000			125,000
Inventory	100,000	75,000		3,000	172,000
Investment in Special Foods	256,000			256,000	0
Land	175,000	40,000			215,000
Buildings & Equipment	800,000	600,000		300,000	1,100,000
Less: Accumulated Depreciation	(450,000)	(320,000)	300,000		(470,000)
Total Assets	1,220,000	520,000	300,000	559,000	1,481,000
Accounts Payable	100,000	100,000			200,000
Bonds Payable	200,000	100,000			300,000
Common Stock	500,000	200,000	200,000		500,000
Retained Earnings	420,000	120,000	159,400	37,000	417,600
NCI in NA of Special Foods				63,400	63,400
Total Liabilities & Equity	1,220,000	520,000	359,400	100,400	1,481,000

but we do reduce the NCI in Net Income of Special Foods and NCI in Net Assets of Special Foods by the NCI share of the deferral, $600 ($3,000 × 20%).

Book Value Calculations:

	NCI 20% + Peerless 80%	=	Common Stock + Retained Earnings	
Original book value	60,000	240,000	200,000	100,000
+ Net income	10,000	40,000		50,000
− Dividends	(6,000)	(24,000)		(30,000)
Ending book value	64,000	256,000	200,000	120,000

Basic investment account elimination entry:

Common stock	200,000		← Original amount invested (100%)
Retained earnings	100,000		← Beginning balance in RE
Income from Special Foods	40,000		← Peerless' % of NI
NCI in NI of Special Foods	9,400		← NCI share of NI − 20% Deferred GP
Dividends declared		30,000	← 100% of sub's dividends declared
Investment in Special Foods		256,000	← Net book value
NCI in NA of Special Foods		63,400	← NCI share BV − 20% Deferred GP

Optional accumulated depreciation elimination:

Accumulated depreciation	300,000	
Building and equipment		300,000

← Original depreciation at the time of the acquisition netted against cost

Eliminate inventory purchases from Special Foods (still on hand):

Sales	10,000	
Cost of Goods Sold		7,000
Inventory		3,000

Investment in Special Foods

Acquisition	240,000		
80% NI	40,000		
		24,000	80% Dividends
Ending Balance	256,000		
	256,000	Basic	
	0		

Income from Special Foods

	40,000	80% NI
	40,000	Ending Balance
40,000	Basic	
0		

Modified Equity-Method Entries—20X2

The equity method journal entries on Peerless' books are the same as illustrated previously, except that the adjustment for Peerless' share of the deferral is omitted:

(21)	Investment in Special Foods	60,000	
	Income from Special Foods		60,000

Record Peerless' 80% share of Special Foods' 20X2 income.

(21)	Cash	32,000	
	Investment in Special Foods		32,000

Record Peerless' 80% share of Special Foods' 20X2 dividend.

FIGURE 6–7 December 31, 20X2, Modified Equity-Method Consolidation Worksheet, Next Period following Intercompany Sale; Upstream Inventory Sale

	Peerless Products	Special Foods	Elimination Entries		Consolidated
			DR	CR	
Income Statement					
Sales	450,000	300,000			750,000
Less: COGS	(180,000)	(160,000)		3,000	(337,000)
Less: Depreciation Expense	(50,000)	(20,000)			(70,000)
Less: Other Expenses	(60,000)	(45,000)			(105,000)
Income from Special Foods	60,000		60,000		0
Consolidated Net Income	220,000	75,000	60,000	3,000	238,000
NCI in Net Income			15,600		(15,600)
Controlling Interest Net Income	**220,000**	**75,000**	**75,600**	**3,000**	**222,400**
Statement of Retained Earnings					
Beginning Balance	420,000	120,000	120,000		417,600
			2,400		
Net Income	**220,000**	**75,000**	**75,600**	**3,000**	222,400
Less: Dividends Declared	(60,000)	(40,000)		40,000	(60,000)
Ending Balance	**580,000**	**155,000**	**198,000**	**43,000**	**580,000**
Balance Sheet					
Cash	291,000	85,000			376,000
Accounts Receivable	150,000	80,000			230,000
Inventory	180,000	90,000			270,000
Investment in Special Foods	284,000			284,000	0
Land	175,000	40,000			215,000
Buildings & Equipment	800,000	600,000		300,000	1,100,000
Less: Accumulated Depreciation	(500,000)	(340,000)	300,000		(540,000)
Total Assets	**1,380,000**	**555,000**	**300,000**	**584,000**	**1,651,000**
Accounts Payable	100,000	100,000			200,000
Bonds Payable	200,000	100,000			300,000
Common Stock	500,000	200,000	200,000		500,000
Retained Earnings	**580,000**	**155,000**	**198,000**	**43,000**	580,000
NCI in NA of Special Foods			600	71,600	71,000
Total Liabilities & Equity	**1,380,000**	**555,000**	**398,600**	**114,600**	**1,651,000**

Consolidation Elimination Entries—20X2

Figure 6–7 illustrates the consolidation worksheet for 20X2 under the modified equity method. The first two elimination entries are the same with one exception. Since the inventory sold to Peerless by Special Foods last year has now been sold to an unaffiliated party, we now increase the NCI in Net Income of Special Foods and NCI in Net Assets of Special Foods by the NCI share of the deferral, $600 ($3,000 × 20%). However, we do not increase the amounts in Peerless' Income from Special Foods and Investment in Special Foods accounts by Peerless' share of the deferral, $2,400 ($3,000 × 80%).

Book Value Calculations:

	NCI 20% +	Peerless 80%	= Common Stock +	Retained Earnings
Beginning book value	64,000	256,000	200,000	120,000
+ Net income	15,000	60,000		75,000
− Dividends	(8,000)	(32,000)		(40,000)
Ending book value	71,000	284,000	200,000	155,000

Basic elimination entry:

Common stock	200,000		← Original amount invested (100%)
Retained earnings	120,000		← Beginning balance in RE
Income from Special Foods	60,000		← Peerless' % of NI
NCI in NI of Special Foods	15,600		← NCI % of NI + 20% 20X1 reversal
Dividends declared		40,000	← 100% of sub's dividends declared
Investment in Special Foods		284,000	← Net book value
NCI in NA of Special Foods		71,600	← NCI % of BV + 20% 20X1 reversal

Optional accumulated depreciation elimination entry:

Accumulated depreciation	300,000		← Original depreciation at the time of
Building and equipment		300,000	the acquisition netted against cost

Similar to 20X1, the unrealized intercompany profit included in Peerless' beginning inventory was charged to Cost of Goods Sold when Peerless sold the inventory during 20X2. Thus, consolidated cost of goods sold will be overstated for 20X2 if it is reported in the consolidated income statement at the unadjusted total from the books of Peerless and Special Foods. The following elimination entry corrects Cost of Goods Sold and splits this adjustment proportionately between beginning retained earnings and the NCI in Net Assets of Special Foods.

Reversal of 20X1 gross profit deferral:

Retained Earnings	2,400	
NCI in NA of Special Foods	600	
Cost of Goods Sold		3,000

COST METHOD

When using the cost method, the parent records dividends received from the subsidiary as income but makes no adjustments with respect to undistributed income of the subsidiary or unrealized intercompany profits. As an example of consolidation following an upstream intercompany sale of inventory when the parent accounts for its investment in the subsidiary using the cost method, assume the same facts as in previous illustrations dealing with an upstream sale.

Consolidation Elimination Entries—20X1

Figure 6–8 illustrates the consolidation worksheet for 20X1 under the cost method. The following eliminating entries are needed in the worksheet used to prepare consolidated financial statements for 20X1 using the cost method:

Investment elimination entry:

Common stock	200,000		← Original amount invested (100%)
Retained earnings	100,000		← RE on acquisition date.
Investment in Special Foods		240,000	← Original cost of investment
NCI in NA of Special Foods		60,000	← NCI share of acquisition date BV

Dividend elimination entry:

Dividend income	24,000		← Peerless' 80% share of dividends
NCI in NI of Special Foods	6,000		← NCI's 20% share of dividends declared
Dividends declared		30,000	← 100% of Special Foods' dividends

FIGURE 6–8 December 31, 20X1, Cost Method Consolidation Worksheet, Period of Intercompany Sale; Upstream Inventory Sale

	Peerless Products	Special Foods	Elimination Entries DR	Elimination Entries CR	Consolidated
Income Statement					
Sales	400,000	200,000	10,000		590,000
Less: COGS	(170,000)	(115,000)		7,000	(278,000)
Less: Depreciation Expense	(50,000)	(20,000)			(70,000)
Less: Other Expenses	(40,000)	(15,000)			(55,000)
Dividend Income	24,000		24,000		0
Consolidated Net Income	164,000	50,000	34,000	7,000	187,000
NCI in Net Income			6,000		(9,400)
			3,400		
Controlling Interest Net Income	**164,000**	**50,000**	**43,400**	**7,000**	**177,600**
Statement of Retained Earnings					
Beginning Balance	300,000	100,000	100,000		300,000
Net Income	**164,000**	**50,000**	43,400	7,000	177,600
Less: Dividends Declared	(60,000)	(30,000)		30,000	(60,000)
Ending Balance	**404,000**	**120,000**	**143,400**	**37,000**	**417,600**
Balance Sheet					
Cash	264,000	75,000			339,000
Accounts Receivable	75,000	50,000			125,000
Inventory	100,000	75,000		3,000	172,000
Investment in Special Foods	240,000			240,000	0
Land	175,000	40,000			215,000
Buildings & Equipment	800,000	600,000		300,000	1,100,000
Less: Accumulated Depreciation	(450,000)	(320,000)	300,000		(470,000)
Total Assets	**1,204,000**	**520,000**	**300,000**	**543,000**	**1,481,000**
Accounts Payable	100,000	100,000			200,000
Bonds Payable	200,000	100,000			300,000
Common Stock	500,000	200,000	200,000		500,000
Retained Earnings	**404,000**	**120,000**	143,400	37,000	417,600
NCI in NA of Special Foods				60,000	63,400
				3,400	
Total Liabilities & Equity	**1,204,000**	**520,000**	**343,400**	**97,000**	**1,481,000**

Assign Special Foods' undistributed income to NCI:

NCI in NI of Special Foods	3,400	
NCI in NA of Special Foods		3,400

← NCI's 20% share of undistributed NI − 20% 20X1 GP deferral
← NCI's 20% share of undistributed NI − 20% 20X1 GP deferral

Optional accumulated depreciation elimination entry:

Accumulated depreciation	300,000	
Building and equipment		300,000

← Original depreciation at the time of the acquisition netted against cost

Eliminate inventory purchases from Special Foods (still on hand):

Sales	10,000	
Cost of Goods Sold		7,000
Inventory		3,000

The investment elimination entry eliminates the original balances in Special Foods' equity section accounts as of the acquisition date. It simultaneously eliminates the Investment in Special Foods account and establishes the NCI in Net Assets account (for the NCI share of the Special Foods' net assets as of the acquisition date). The dividend elimination entry eliminates Special Foods' declared dividends and Peerless' dividend income and establishes the NCI in net income with the NCI share of dividends declared. While Peerless uses the cost method to account for its investment, the consolidated financial statements still must report the NCI shareholders' share of Special Foods' reported net income, while a portion of that income is allocated in the form of a dividend. Nevertheless, the NCI in Net income should report the NCI share of reported income (adjusted for the deferred gross profit on upstream intercompany sales). Thus, the third elimination entry assigns the NCI shareholders' 20 percent of the undistributed income (adjusted for 20 percent of the deferred gross profit) to both the NCI in Net Income of Special Foods and NCI in Net Assets of Special Foods. The optional accumulated depreciation and deferred gross profit elimination entries are the same as those explained for the fully adjusted equity method.

Consolidation Elimination Entries—20X2

Figure 6–9 illustrates the consolidation worksheet for 20X2 under the cost method. Elimination entries needed in the consolidation worksheet prepared at the end of 20X2 are as follows:

Investment elimination entry:

Common stock	200,000		← Original amount invested (100%)
Retained earnings	100,000		← RE on acquisition date
Investment in Special Foods		240,000	← Original cost of investment
NCI in NA of Special Foods		60,000	← NCI share of acquisition date BV

Dividend elimination entry:

Dividend income	32,000		← Peerless' 80% share of dividends
NCI in NI of Special Foods	8,000		← NCI's 20% share of dividends declared
Dividends declared		40,000	← 100% of Special Foods' dividends

Assign Special Foods' undistributed income to NCI:

NCI in NI of Special Foods	7,600		← NCI's 20% share of 20X2 undistributed NI + 20% Deferred GP reversal
Retained earnings	4,000		← NCI's 20% share of undistributed 20X1 income from Special Foods
NCI in NA of Special Foods		11,600	← NCI's 20% share of cumulative undistributed NI + 20% Deferred GP reversal

Optional accumulated depreciation elimination entry:

Accumulated depreciation	300,000		← Original depreciation at the time of the acquisition netted against cost
Building and equipment		300,000	

Reversal of 20X1 gross profit deferral:

Retained earnings	2,400	
NCI in NA of Special Foods	600	
Cost of Goods Sold		3,000

The investment and dividend elimination entries are the same as in 20X1. The third entry assigns cumulative undistributed net income from Special Foods. It assigns 20 percent of the 20X2 net income to the NCI shareholders and 20 percent of the 20X1 net income to retained earnings for the prior year. The accumulated depreciation elimination entry is the same as in 20X1. However, the last entry is identical to the entry under the modified equity method.

FIGURE 6–9   December 31, 20X2, Cost Method Consolidation Worksheet, Next Period Following Intercompany Sale; Upstream Inventory Sale

	Peerless Products	Special Foods	Elimination Entries DR	Elimination Entries CR	Consolidated
Income Statement					
Sales	450,000	300,000			750,000
Less: COGS	(180,000)	(160,000)		3,000	(337,000)
Less: Depreciation Expense	(50,000)	(20,000)			(70,000)
Less: Other Expenses	(60,000)	(45,000)			(105,000)
Dividend Income	32,000		32,000		0
Consolidated Net Income	192,000	75,000	32,000	3,000	238,000
			8,000		
NCI in Net Income			7,600		(15,600)
Controlling Interest Net Income	**192,000**	**75,000**	**47,600**	**3,000**	**222,400**
Statement of Retained Earnings					
Beginning Balance	404,000	120,000	100,000		417,600
			4,000		
			2,400		
Net Income	192,000	75,000	47,600	3,000	222,400
Less: Dividends Declared	(60,000)	(40,000)		40,000	(60,000)
Ending Balance	**536,000**	**155,000**	**154,000**	**43,000**	**580,000**
Balance Sheet					
Cash	291,000	85,000			376,000
Accounts Receivable	150,000	80,000			230,000
Inventory	180,000	90,000			270,000
Investment in Special Foods	240,000			240,000	0
Land	175,000	40,000			215,000
Buildings & Equipment	800,000	600,000		300,000	1,100,000
Less: Accumulated Depreciation	(500,000)	(340,000)	300,000		(540,000)
Total Assets	**1,336,000**	**555,000**	**300,000**	**540,000**	**1,651,000**
Accounts Payable	100,000	100,000			200,000
Bonds Payable	200,000	100,000			300,000
Common Stock	500,000	200,000	200,000		500,000
Retained Earnings	536,000	155,000	154,000	43,000	580,000
NCI in NA of Special Foods			600	60,000	71,000
				11,600	
Total Liabilities & Equity	**1,336,000**	**555,000**	**354,600**	**103,000**	**1,651,000**

Questions

Q6-1   Why must inventory transfers to related companies be eliminated in preparing consolidated financial statements?

LO2   **Q6-2**   Why is there a need for an eliminating entry when an intercompany inventory transfer is made at cost?

LO1   **Q6-3**   Distinguish between an upstream sale of inventory and a downstream sale. Why is it important to know whether a sale is upstream or downstream?

LO3   **Q6-4**   How do unrealized intercompany profits on a downstream sale of inventory made during the current period affect the computation of consolidated net income and income to the controlling interest?

LO4   **Q6-5**   How do unrealized intercompany profits on an upstream sale of inventory made during the current period affect the computation of consolidated net income and income to the controlling interest?

LO3, LO4   **Q6-6**   Will the elimination of unrealized intercompany profits on an upstream sale or on a downstream sale in the current period have a greater effect on income assigned to the noncontrolling interest? Why?

LO3   **Q6-7**   What eliminating entry is needed when inventory is sold to an affiliate at a profit and is resold to an unaffiliated party before the end of the period? (Assume both affiliates use perpetual inventory systems.)

LO3   **Q6-8**   What eliminating entry is needed when inventory is sold to an affiliate at a profit and is not resold before the end of the period? (Assume both affiliates use perpetual inventory systems.)

LO3, LO4   **Q6-9**   How is the amount to be reported as cost of goods sold by the consolidated entity determined when there have been intercorporate sales during the period?

LO3, LO4   **Q6-10**   How is the amount to be reported as consolidated retained earnings determined when there have been intercorporate sales during the period?

LO3, LO4   **Q6-11**   How is the amount of consolidated retained earnings assigned to the noncontrolling interest affected by unrealized inventory profits at the end of the year?

LO3, LO4   **Q6-12**   How do unrealized intercompany inventory profits from a prior period affect the computation of consolidated net income when the inventory is resold in the current period? Is it important to know if the sale was upstream or downstream? Why, or why not?

LO3, LO4   **Q6-13**   How will the elimination of unrealized intercompany inventory profits recorded on the parent's books affect consolidated retained earnings?

LO3, LO4   **Q6-14**   How will the elimination of unrealized intercompany inventory profits recorded on the subsidiary's books affect consolidated retained earnings?

LO5   **Q6-15***   Is an inventory sale from one subsidiary to another treated in the same manner as an upstream sale or a downstream sale? Why?

LO5   **Q6-16***   Par Company regularly purchases inventory from Eagle Company. Recently, Par Company purchased a majority of the voting shares of Eagle Company. How should it treat inventory profits recorded by Eagle Company before the day of acquisition? Following the day of acquisition?

Cases

LO2   **C6-1**   **Measuring Cost of Goods Sold**

Shortcut Charlie usually manages to develop some simple rule to handle even the most complex situations. In providing for the elimination of the effects of inventory transfers between the parent company and a subsidiary or between subsidiaries, Shortcut started with the following rules:

Judgment

1. When the buyer continues to hold the inventory at the end of the period, credit cost of goods sold for the amount recorded as cost of goods sold by the company that made the intercompany sale.
2. When the buyer resells the inventory before the end of the period, credit cost of goods sold for the amount recorded as cost of goods sold by the company that made the intercompany sale plus the profit recorded by that company.
3. Debit sales for the total amount credited in rule 1 or 2 above.

One of the new employees is seeking some assistance in understanding how the rules work and why.

Required

a. Explain why rule 1 is needed when consolidated statements are prepared.

b. Explain what is missing from rule 1, and prepare an alternative or additional statement for the elimination of unrealized profit when the purchasing affiliate does not resell to an unaffiliated company in the period in which it purchases inventory from an affiliate.

c. Does rule 2 lead to the correct result? Explain your answer.

d. The rules do not provide assistance in determining how much profit was recorded by either of the two companies. Where should the employee look to determine the amount of profit referred to in rule 2?

LO1   **C6-2**   **Inventory Values and Intercompany Transfers**

Research

Water Products Corporation has been supplying high-quality bathroom fixtures to its customers for several decades and uses a LIFO inventory system. Rapid increases in the cost of fixtures

*Indicates that the item relates to "Additional Considerations."

have resulted in inventory values substantially below current replacement cost. To bring its inventory carrying costs up to more reasonable levels, Water Products sold its entire inventory to Plumbers Products Corporation and purchased an entirely new supply of inventory items from Growinkle Manufacturing. Water Products owns common stock of both Growinkle and Plumbers Products.

Water Products' external auditor immediately pointed out that under some ownership levels of these two companies, Water Products could accomplish its goal and under other levels it could not.

Required

Prepare a memo to Water Products' president describing the effects of intercompany transfers on the valuation of inventories and discuss the effects that different ownership levels of Growinkle and Plumbers Products would have on the success of Water Products' plan. Include citations to or quotations from the authoritative accounting literature to support your position.

LO1

C6-3 **Intercompany Inventory Transfers**

Research

On December 20, 20X2, Evert Corporation paid Frankle Company $180,000 for inventory that Frankle had purchased for $240,000. Frankle had not previously recognized a loss and reduced the inventory's carrying value because the drop in prices was considered temporary. A resurgence in demand for the product occurred in early 20X3, and Evert sold the entire inventory for $310,000.

Evert owns 90 percent of Frankle's stock. Evert prepared consolidated financial statements at December 31, 20X2 and 20X3, but failed to make adjustments to the reported data provided by Evert and Frankle for the intercorporate sale.

Required

Prepare a memo to Evert's treasurer describing the required treatment of intercorporate sales of inventory. Include citations to or quotations from the authoritative accounting literature to support your position. You should include in your memo an analysis of the effects that eliminating the intercompany transfer would have had on Evert's reported revenues and expenses for 20X2 and 20X3 and on its balance sheet accounts at December 31, 20X2 and 20X3.

LO1

C6-4 **Unrealized Inventory Profits**

Understanding

Morrison Company owns 80 percent of Bloom Corporation's stock, acquired when Bloom's fair value as a whole was equal to its book value. The companies frequently engage in intercompany inventory transactions.

Required

Name the conditions that would make it possible for each of the following statements to be true. Treat each statement independently.

a. Income assigned to the noncontrolling interest in the consolidated income statement for 20X3 is greater than a pro rata share of the reported net income of Bloom.

b. Income assigned to the noncontrolling interest in the consolidated income statement for 20X3 is greater than a pro rata share of Bloom's reported net income, but consolidated net income is reduced as a result of the elimination of intercompany inventory transfers.

c. Cost of goods sold reported in the income statement of Morrison is greater than consolidated cost of goods sold for 20X3.

d. Consolidated inventory is greater than the amounts reported by the separate companies.

LO3, LO4

C6-5 **Eliminating Inventory Transfers**

Analysis

Ready Building Products has six subsidiaries that sell building materials and supplies to the public and to the parent and other subsidiaries. Because of the invoicing system Ready uses, it is not possible to keep track of which items have been purchased from related companies and which have been bought from outside sources. Due to the nature of the products purchased, there are substantially different profit margins on different product groupings.

Required

a. If no effort is made to eliminate intercompany sales for the period or unrealized profits at year-end, what elements of the financial statements are likely to be misstated?

b. What type of control system would you recommend to Ready's controller to provide the information needed to make the required eliminating entries?

c. Would it matter if the buyer and seller used different inventory costing methods (FIFO, LIFO, or weighted average)? Explain.

d. Assume you believe that the adjustments for unrealized profit would be material. How would you go about determining what amounts must be eliminated at the end of the current period?

LO1

C6-6

Analysis

Intercompany Profits and Transfers of Inventory

Many companies transfer inventories from one affiliate to another. Often the companies have integrated operations in which one affiliate provides the raw materials, another manufactures finished products, another distributes the products, and perhaps another sells the products at retail. In other cases, various affiliates may be established for selling the company's products in different geographic locations, especially in different countries. Often tax considerations also have an effect on intercompany transfers.

Required

a. Are Xerox Corporation's intercompany transfers significant? How does Xerox treat intercompany transfers for consolidation purposes?

b. How does ExxonMobil Corporation price its products for intercompany transfers? Are these transfers significant? How does ExxonMobil treat intercompany profits for consolidation purposes?

c. What types of intercompany and intersegment sales does Ford Motor Company have? Are they significant? How are they treated for consolidation?

Exercises

LO3, LO4

E6-1

Multiple-Choice Questions on Intercompany Inventory Transfers [AICPA Adapted]

Select the correct answer for each of the following questions.

1. Perez Inc. owns 80 percent of Senior Inc. During 20X2, Perez sold goods with a 40 percent gross profit to Senior. Senior sold all of these goods in 20X2. For 20X2 consolidated financial statements, how should the summation of Perez and Senior income statement items be adjusted?

   a. Sales and cost of goods sold should be reduced by the intercompany sales.

   b. Sales and cost of goods sold should be reduced by 80 percent of the intercompany sales.

   c. Net income should be reduced by 80 percent of the gross profit on intercompany sales.

   d. No adjustment is necessary.

2. Parker Corporation owns 80 percent of Smith Inc.'s common stock. During 20X1, Parker sold inventory to Smith for $250,000 on the same terms as sales made to third parties. Smith sold all of the inventory purchased from Parker in 20X1. The following information pertains to Smith's and Parker's sales for 20X1:

	Parker	Smith
Sales	$1,000,000	$700,000
Cost of Sales	(400,000)	(350,000)
Gross Profit	$ 600,000	$350,000

What amount should Parker report as cost of sales in its 20X1 consolidated income statement?

   a. $750,000.

   b. $680,000.

   c. $500,000.

   d. $430,000.

Note: Items 3 and 4 are based on the following information:
Nolan owns 100 percent of the capital stock of both Twill Corporation and Webb Corporation. Twill purchases merchandise inventory from Webb at 140 percent of Webb's cost.

During 20X0, Webb sold merchandise that had cost it $40,000 to Twill. Twill sold all of this merchandise to unrelated customers for $81,200 during 20X0. In preparing combined financial statements for 20X0, Nolan's bookkeeper disregarded the common ownership of Twill and Webb.

3. What amount should be eliminated from cost of goods sold in the combined income statement for 20X0?

   a. $56,000.
   b. $40,000.
   c. $24,000.
   d. $16,000.

4. By what amount was unadjusted revenue overstated in the combined income statement for 20X0?

   a. $16,000.
   b. $40,000.
   c. $56,000.
   d. $81,200.

5. Clark Company had the following transactions with affiliated parties during 20X2:

   - Sales of $60,000 to Dean Inc., with $20,000 gross profit. Dean had $15,000 of this inventory on hand at year-end. Clark owns a 15 percent interest in Dean and does not exert significant influence.

   - Purchases of raw materials totaling $240,000 from Kent Corporation, a wholly owned subsidiary. Kent's gross profit on the sales was $48,000. Clark had $60,000 of this inventory remaining on December 31, 20X2.

   Before eliminating entries, Clark had consolidated current assets of $320,000. What amount should Clark report in its December 31, 20X2, consolidated balance sheet for current assets?

   a. $320,000.
   b. $317,000.
   c. $308,000.
   d. $303,000.

6. Selected data for two subsidiaries of Dunn Corporation taken from the December 31, 20X8, preclosing trial balances are as follows:

	Banks Co. (Debits)	Lamm Co. (Credits)
Shipments to Banks	$ —	$150,000
Shipments from Lamm	200,000	—
Intercompany Inventory Profit on Total Shipments		50,000

Additional data relating to the December 31, 20X8, inventory are as follows:

Inventory acquired by Banks from outside parties	$175,000
Inventory acquired by Lamm from outside parties	250,000
Inventory acquired by Banks from Lamm	60,000

At December 31, 20X8, the inventory reported on the combined balance sheet of the two subsidiaries should be:

   a. $425,000.
   b. $435,000.
   c. $470,000.
   d. $485,000.

E6-2   Multiple-Choice Questions on the Effects of Inventory Transfers [AICPA Adapted]

Select the correct answer for each of the following questions.

1. During 20X3, Park Corporation recorded sales of inventory costing $500,000 to Small Company, its wholly owned subsidiary, on the same terms as sales made to third parties. At December 31, 20X3, Small held one-fifth of these goods in its inventory. The following information pertains to Park's and Small's sales for 20X3:

	Park	Small
Sales	$2,000,000	$1,400,000
Cost of Sales	(800,000)	(700,000)
Gross Profit	$1,200,000	$ 700,000

In its 20X3 consolidated income statement, what amount should Park report as cost of sales?

   a. $1,000,000.

   b. $1,060,000.

   c. $1,260,000.

   d. $1,500,000.

Note: Items 2 through 6 are based on the following information:

Selected information from the separate and consolidated balance sheets and income statements of Power Inc. and its subsidiary, Spin Company, as of December 31, 20X8, and for the year then ended is as follows:

	Power	Spin	Consolidated
Balance Sheet Accounts			
Accounts Receivable	$ 26,000	$ 19,000	$ 39,000
Inventory	30,000	25,000	52,000
Investment in Spin	53,000	—	—
Patents	—	—	20,000
NCI in NA of Spin	—	—	14,000
Stockholders' Equity	154,000	50,000	154,000
Income Statement Accounts			
Revenues	$200,000	$140,000	$308,000
Cost of Goods Sold	150,000	110,000	231,000
Gross Profit	$ 50,000	$ 30,000	$ 77,000
Income from Spin	7,400	—	—
Amortization of Patents	—	—	2,000
Net Income	33,000	15,000	40,000

Additional Information

During 20X8, Power sold goods to Spin at the same markup that Power uses for all sales. At December 31, 20X8, Spin had not paid for all of these goods and still held 37.5 percent of them in inventory.

Power acquired its interest in Spin on January 2, 20X5, when the book values and fair values of the assets and liabilities of Spin were equal, except for patents, which had a fair value of $28,000. The fair value of the noncontrolling interest was equal to a proportionate share of fair value of Spin's net assets.

2. What was the amount of intercompany sales from Power to Spin during 20X8?

   a. $3,000.

   b. $6,000.

   c. $29,000.

   d. $32,000.

3. At December 31, 20X8, what was the amount of Spin's payable to Power for intercompany sales?

   a. $3,000.

   b. $6,000.

    c. $29,000.

    d. $32,000.

4. In Power's consolidated balance sheet, what was the carrying amount of the inventory that Spin purchased from Power?

    a. $3,000.

    b. $6,000.

    c. $9,000.

    d. $12,000.

5. What is the percent of noncontrolling interest ownership of Spin?

    a. 10 percent.

    b. 20 percent.

    c. 25 percent.

    d. 45 percent.

6. Over how many years has Power chosen to amortize patents?

    a. 10 years.

    b. 14 years.

    c. 23 years.

    d. 40 years.

LO3

E6-3   Multiple-Choice Questions—Consolidated Income Statement

Select the correct answer for each of the following questions.

    Blue Company purchased 60 percent ownership of Kelly Corporation in 20X1. On May 10, 20X2, Kelly purchased inventory from Blue for $60,000. Kelly sold all of the inventory to an unaffiliated company for $86,000 on November 10, 20X2. Blue produced the inventory sold to Kelly for $47,000. The companies had no other transactions during 20X2.

1. What amount of sales will be reported in the 20X2 consolidated income statement?

    a. $51,600.

    b. $60,000.

    c. $86,000.

    d. $146,000.

2. What amount of cost of goods sold will be reported in the 20X2 consolidated income statement?

    a. $36,000.

    b. $47,000.

    c. $60,000.

    d. $107,000.

3. What amount of consolidated net income will be assigned to the controlling shareholders for 20X2?

    a. $13,000.

    b. $26,000.

    c. $28,600.

    d. $39,000.

LO4

E6-4   Multiple-Choice Questions—Consolidated Balances

Select the correct answer for each of the following questions.

    Lorn Corporation purchased inventory from Dresser Corporation for $120,000 on September 20, 20X1, and resold 80 percent of the inventory to unaffiliated companies prior to December 31, 20X1, for $140,000. Dresser produced the inventory sold to Lorn for $75,000. Lorn owns 70 percent of Dresser's voting common stock. The companies had no other transactions during 20X1.

1. What amount of sales will be reported in the 20X1 consolidated income statement?

    a. $98,000.

    b. $120,000.

    c. $140,000.

    d. $260,000.

2. What amount of cost of goods sold will be reported in the 20X1 consolidated income statement?

    a. $60,000.

    b. $75,000.

    c. $96,000.

    d. $120,000.

    e. $171,000.

3. What amount of consolidated net income will be assigned to the controlling interest for 20X1?

    a. $20,000.

    b. $30,800.

    c. $44,000.

    d. $45,000.

    e. $69,200.

    f. $80,000.

4. What inventory balance will be reported by the consolidated entity on December 31, 20X1?

    a. $15,000.

    b. $16,800.

    c. $24,000.

    d. $39,000.

LO4

E6-5   Multiple-Choice Questions—Consolidated Income Statement

Select the correct answer for each of the following questions.

    Amber Corporation holds 80 percent of the stock of Movie Productions Inc. During 20X4, Amber purchased an inventory of snack bar items for $40,000 and resold $30,000 to Movie Productions for $48,000. Movie Productions Inc. reported sales of $67,000 in 20X4 and had inventory of $16,000 on December 31, 20X4. The companies held no beginning inventory and had no other transactions in 20X4.

1. What amount of cost of goods sold will be reported in the 20X4 consolidated income statement?

    a. $20,000.

    b. $30,000.

    c. $32,000.

    d. $52,000.

    e. $62,000.

2. What amount of net income will be reported in the 20X4 consolidated income statement?

    a. $12,000.

    b. $18,000.

    c. $40,000.

    d. $47,000.

    e. $53,000.

3. What amount of income will be assigned to the noncontrolling interest in the 20X4 consolidated income statement?

    a. $7,000.

    b. $8,000.

    c. $9,400.

    d. $10,200.

    e. $13,400.

LO3

E6-6   Realized Profit on Intercompany Sale

Nordway Corporation acquired 90 percent of Olman Company's voting shares of stock in 20X1. During 20X4, Nordway purchased 40,000 Playday doghouses for $24 each and sold 25,000 of the doghouses to Olman for $30 each. Olman sold all of the doghouses to retail establishments prior to December 31, 20X4, for $45 each. Both companies use perpetual inventory systems.

Required

a. Give the journal entries Nordway recorded for the purchase of inventory and resale to Olman Company in 20X4.

b. Give the journal entries Olman recorded for the purchase of inventory and resale to retail establishments in 20X4.

c. Give the worksheet eliminating entry(ies) needed in preparing consolidated financial statements for 20X4 to remove all effects of the intercompany sale.

LO3

E6-7 Sale of Inventory to Subsidiary

Nordway Corporation acquired 90 percent of Olman Company's voting shares of stock in 20X1. During 20X4, Nordway purchased 40,000 Playday doghouses for $24 each and sold 25,000 of the doghouses to Olman for $30 each. Olman sold 18,000 of the doghouses to retail establishments prior to December 31, 20X4, for $45 each. Both companies use perpetual inventory systems.

Required

a. Give all journal entries Nordway recorded for the purchase of inventory and resale to Olman Company in 20X4.

b. Give the journal entries Olman recorded for the purchase of inventory and resale to retail establishments in 20X4.

c. Give the worksheet eliminating entry(ies) needed in preparing consolidated financial statements for 20X4 to remove the effects of the intercompany sale.

LO3

E6-8 Inventory Transfer between Parent and Subsidiary

Advanced
StudyGuide
.com

Karlow Corporation owns 60 percent of Draw Company's voting shares. During 20X3, Karlow produced 25,000 computer desks at a cost of $82 each and sold 10,000 desks to Draw for $94 each. Draw sold 7,000 of the desks to unaffiliated companies for $130 each prior to December 31, 20X3, and sold the remainder in early 20X4 for $140 each. Both companies use perpetual inventory systems.

Required

a. What amounts of cost of goods sold did Karlow and Draw record in 20X3?

b. What amount of cost of goods sold must be reported in the consolidated income statement for 20X3?

c. Give the worksheet eliminating entry or entries needed in preparing consolidated financial statements at December 31, 20X3, relating to the intercorporate sale of inventory.

d. Give the worksheet eliminating entry or entries needed in preparing consolidated financial statements at December 31, 20X4, relating to the intercorporate sale of inventory.

e. Give the worksheet eliminating entry or entries needed in preparing consolidated financial statements at December 31, 20X4, relating to the intercorporate sale of inventory if Draw had produced the computer desks at a cost of $82 each and sold 10,000 desks to Karlow for $94 each in 20X3, with Karlow selling 7,000 desks to unaffiliated companies in 20X3 and the remaining 3,000 in 20X4.

LO4

E6-9 Income Statement Effects of Unrealized Profit

Holiday Bakery owns 60 percent of Farmco Products Company's stock. During 20X8, Farmco produced 100,000 bags of flour, which it sold to Holiday Bakery for $900,000. On December 31, 20X8, Holiday had 20,000 bags of flour purchased from Farmco Products on hand. Farmco prices its sales at cost plus 50 percent of cost for profit. Holiday, which purchased all its flour from Farmco in 20X8, had no inventory on hand on January 1, 20X8.

Holiday Bakery reported income from its baking operations of $400,000, and Farmco Products reported net income of $150,000 for 20X8.

Required

a. Compute the amount reported as cost of goods sold in the 20X8 consolidated income statement.

b. Give the worksheet eliminating entry or entries required to remove the effects of the intercompany sale in preparing consolidated statements at the end of 20X8.

c. Compute the amounts reported as consolidated net income and income assigned to the controlling interest in the 20X8 consolidated income statement.

LO4

E6-10 Prior-Period Unrealized Inventory Profit

Holiday Bakery owns 60 percent of Farmco Products Company's stock. On January 1, 20X9, inventory reported by Holiday included 20,000 bags of flour purchased from Farmco at $9 per bag. By December 31, 20X9, all the beginning inventory purchased from Farmco Products had been baked into products and sold to customers by Holiday. There were no transactions between Holiday and Farmco during 20X9.

Both Holiday Bakery and Farmco Products price their sales at cost plus 50 percent markup for profit. Holiday reported income from its baking operations of $300,000, and Farmco reported net income of $250,000 for 20X9.

Required

a. Compute the amount reported as cost of goods sold in the 20X9 consolidated income statement for the flour purchased from Farmco in 20X8.

b. Give the eliminating entry or entries required to remove the effects of the unrealized profit in beginning inventory in preparing the consolidation worksheet as of December 31, 20X9.

c. Compute the amounts reported as consolidated net income and income assigned to the controlling interest in the 20X9 consolidated income statement.

LO3

Advanced
StudyGuide
.com

E6-11 Computation of Consolidated Income Statement Data

Prem Company acquired 60 percent ownership of Cooper Company's voting shares on January 1, 20X2. During 20X5, Prem purchased inventory for $20,000 and sold the full amount to Cooper Company for $30,000. On December 31, 20X5, Cooper's ending inventory included $6,000 of items purchased from Prem. Also in 20X5, Cooper purchased inventory for $50,000 and sold the units to Prem for $80,000. Prem included $20,000 of its purchase from Cooper in ending inventory on December 31, 20X5.

Summary income statement data for the two companies revealed the following:

	Prem Company	Cooper Company
Sales	$ 400,000	$ 200,000
Income from Cooper	20,500	
	$ 420,500	$ 200,000
Cost of Goods Sold	$ 250,000	$ 120,000
Other Expenses	70,000	35,000
Total Expenses	$(320,000)	$(155,000)
Net Income	$ 100,500	$ 45,000

Required

a. Compute the amount to be reported as sales in the 20X5 consolidated income statement.

b. Compute the amount to be reported as cost of goods sold in the 20X5 consolidated income statement.

c. What amount of income will be assigned to the noncontrolling shareholders in the 20X5 consolidated income statement?

d. What amount of income will be assigned to the controlling interest in the 20X5 consolidated income statement?

LO4

E6-12 Sale of Inventory at a Loss

The price of high-quality burnwhistles fluctuates substantially from month to month. As a result, it is not uncommon for a company that deals in burnwhistles to report a substantial gain in one period, followed by a substantial loss in the following period. The price of burnwhistles was relatively high during the first three months of 20X8, declined substantially for the next four months, and then recovered nicely by year-end. On February 6, 20X8, Trent Company purchased burnwhistles for $400,000 and sold them to Gord Corporation on July 10, 20X8, for $300,000. Gord held its purchase for several months before selling 60 percent to nonaffiliates for $360,000 in late November. The remaining units were held at year-end and are expected to be sold in early 20X9 for approximately $240,000. Gord owns 75 percent of the stock of Trent Company.

Required

a. Give the journal entries Trent and Gord recorded during 20X8 related to the initial purchase, intercorporate sale, and resale of inventory.

b. What amount should be reported as cost of goods sold in the 20X8 consolidated income statement?

c. If Gord reported operating income of $230,000 and Trent reported net income of $80,000, what amount of income should be assigned to the controlling interest in the 20X8 consolidated income statement?

d. Give the worksheet eliminating entry or entries needed in preparing consolidated financial statements for 20X8 to remove all effects of the intercompany transfer.

LO3, LO4   **E6-13   Intercompany Sales**

Hollow Corporation acquired 70 percent of Surg Corporation's voting stock on May 18, 20X1. The companies reported the following data with respect to intercompany sales in 20X4 and 20X5:

Year	Purchased by	Purchase Price	Sold to	Sale Price	Unsold at End of Year	Year Sold to Unaffiliated Co.
20X4	Surg Corp.	$120,000	Hollow Corp.	$180,000	$ 45,000	20X5
20X5	Surg Corp.	90,000	Hollow Corp.	135,000	30,000	20X6
20X5	Hollow Corp.	140,000	Surg Corp.	280,000	110,000	20X6

Hollow reported operating income (excluding income from its investment in Surg) of $160,000 and $220,000 in 20X4 and 20X5, respectively. Surg reported net income of $90,000 and $85,000 in 20X4 and 20X5, respectively.

Required

a. Compute consolidated net income for 20X4.

b. Compute the inventory balance reported in the consolidated balance sheet at December 31, 20X5, for the transactions shown.

c. Compute the amount included in consolidated cost of goods sold for 20X5 relating to the transactions shown.

d. Compute the amount of income assigned to the controlling interest in the 20X5 consolidated income statement.

LO4   **E6-14   Consolidated Balance Sheet Worksheet**

The December 31, 20X8, balance sheets for Doorst Corporation and its 70 percent owned subsidiary Hingle Company contained the following summarized amounts:

DOORST CORPORATION AND HINGLE COMPANY
Balance Sheets
December 31, 20X8

	Doorst Corporation	Hingle Company
Cash and Receivables	$ 98,000	$ 40,000
Inventory	150,000	100,000
Buildings and Equipment (net)	310,000	280,000
Investment in Hingle Company Stock	242,000	
Total Assets	$800,000	$420,000
Accounts Payable	$ 70,000	$ 20,000
Common Stock	200,000	150,000
Retained Earnings	530,000	250,000
Total Liabilities and Equity	$800,000	$420,000

Doorst acquired the shares of Hingle Company on January 1, 20X7. On December 31, 20X8, assume Doorst sold inventory to Hingle during 20X8 for $100,000 and Hingle sold inventory to Doorst for $300,000. Doorst's balance sheet contains inventory items purchased from Hingle for $95,000. The items cost Hingle $55,000 to produce. In addition, Hingle's inventory contains goods it purchased from Doorst for $25,000 that Doorst had produced for $15,000. Assume Hingle reported net income of $70,000 and dividends of $14,000.

Required

a. Prepare all eliminating entries needed to complete a consolidated balance sheet worksheet as of December 31, 20X8.

b. Prepare a consolidated balance sheet worksheet as of December 31, 20X8.

LO5

E6-15* Multiple Transfers between Affiliates

Klon Corporation owns 70 percent of Brant Company's stock and 60 percent of Torkel Company's stock. During 20X8, Klon sold inventory purchased in 20X7 for $100,000 to Brant for $150,000. Brant then sold the inventory at its cost of $150,000 to Torkel. Prior to December 31, 20X8, Torkel sold $90,000 of inventory to a nonaffiliate for $120,000 and held $60,000 in inventory at December 31, 20X8.

Required

a. Give the journal entries recorded by Klon, Brant, and Torkel during 20X8 relating to the intercorporate sale and resale of inventory.

b. What amount should be reported in the 20X8 consolidated income statement as cost of goods sold?

c. What amount should be reported in the December 31, 20X8, consolidated balance sheet as inventory?

d. Give the eliminating entry needed at December 31, 20X8, to remove the effects of the inventory transfers.

LO4

E6-16 Inventory Sales

Herb Corporation holds 60 percent ownership of Spice Company. Each year, Spice purchases large quantities of a gnarl root used in producing health drinks. Spice purchased $150,000 of roots in 20X7 and sold $40,000 of these purchases to Herb for $60,000. By the end of 20X7, Herb had resold all but $15,000 of its purchase from Spice. Herb generated $90,000 on the sale of roots to various health stores during the year.

Required

a. Give the journal entries recorded by Herb and Spice during 20X7 relating to the initial purchase, intercorporate sale, and resale of gnarl roots.

b. Give the worksheet eliminating entries needed as of December 31, 20X7, to remove all effects of the intercompany transfer in preparing the 20X7 consolidated financial statements.

LO4

E6-17 Prior-Period Inventory Profits

Home Products Corporation sells a broad line of home detergent products. Home Products owns 75 percent of the stock of Level Brothers Soap Company. During 20X8, Level Brothers sold soap products to Home Products for $180,000, which it had produced for $120,000. Home Products sold $150,000 of its purchase from Level Brothers in 20X8 and the remainder in 20X9. In addition, Home Products purchased $240,000 of inventory from Level Brothers in 20X9 and resold $90,000 of the items before year-end. Level Brothers' cost to produce the items sold to Home Products in 20X9 was $160,000.

Required

a. Give all worksheet eliminating entries needed for December 31, 20X9, to remove the effects of the intercompany inventory transfers in 20X8 and 20X9.

b. Compute the amount of income assigned to noncontrolling shareholders in the 20X8 and 20X9 consolidated income statements if Level Brothers reported net income of $350,000 for 20X8 and $420,000 for 20X9.

Problems

LO4

P6-18 Consolidated Income Statement Data

Sweeny Corporation owns 60 percent of Bitner Company's shares. Partial 20X2 financial data for the companies and consolidated entity were as follows:

	Sweeny Corporation	Bitner Company	Consolidated Totals
Sales	$550,000	$450,000	$820,000
Cost of Goods Sold	310,000	300,000	420,000
Inventory, Dec. 31	180,000	210,000	375,000

On January 1, 20X2, Sweeny's inventory contained items purchased from Bitner for $75,000. The cost of the units to Bitner was $50,000. All intercorporate sales during 20X2 were made by Bitner to Sweeny.

Required

a. What amount of intercorporate sales occurred in 20X2?

b. How much unrealized intercompany profit existed on January 1, 20X2? On December 31, 20X2?

c. Give the worksheet eliminating entries relating to inventory and cost of goods sold needed to prepare consolidated financial statements for 20X2.

d. If Bitner reports net income of $90,000 for 20X2, what amount of income is assigned to the noncontrolling interest in the 20X2 consolidated income statement?

LO4

P6-19 Unrealized Profit on Upstream Sales

Carroll Company sells all its output at 25 percent above cost. Pacific Corporation purchases all its inventory from Carroll. Selected information on the operations of the companies over the past three years is as follows:

Year	Carroll Company Sales to Pacific Corp.	Net Income	Pacific Corporation Inventory, Dec. 31	Operating Income
20X2	$200,000	$100,000	$ 70,000	$150,000
20X3	175,000	90,000	105,000	240,000
20X4	225,000	160,000	120,000	300,000

Pacific acquired 60 percent of the ownership of Carroll on January 1, 20X1, at underlying book value.

Required

Compute consolidated net income and income assigned to the controlling interest for 20X2, 20X3, and 20X4.

LO3, LO4

P6-20 Net Income of Consolidated Entity

Master Corporation acquired 70 percent of Crown Corporation's voting stock on January 1, 20X2, for $416,500. The fair value of the noncontrolling interest was $178,500 at the date of acquisition. Crown reported common stock outstanding of $200,000 and retained earnings of $350,000. The differential is assigned to buildings with an expected life of 15 years at the date of acquisition.

On December 31, 20X4, Master had $25,000 of unrealized profits on its books from inventory sales to Crown, and Crown had $40,000 of unrealized profit on its books from inventory sales to Master. All inventory held at December 31, 20X4, was sold during 20X5.

On December 31, 20X5, Master had $14,000 of unrealized profit on its books from inventory sales to Crown, and Crown had unrealized profit on its books of $55,000 from inventory sales to Master.

Master reported income from its separate operations (excluding income on its investment in Crown and amortization of purchase differential) of $118,000 in 20X5, and Crown reported net income of $65,000.

Required

Compute consolidated net income and income assigned to the controlling interest in the 20X5 consolidated income statement.

LO4

P6-21 Correction of Eliminating Entries

In preparing the consolidation worksheet for Bolger Corporation and its 60 percent owned subsidiary, Feldman Company, the following eliminating entries were proposed by Bolger's bookkeeper:

Cash	80,000	
Accounts Payable		80,000

To eliminate the unpaid balance for intercorporate inventory sales in 20X5.

Cost of Goods Sold	12,000	
Income from Subsidiary		12,000

To eliminate unrealized inventory profits at December 31, 20X5.

Income from Subsidiary	140,000	
Sales		140,000

To eliminate intercompany sales for 20X5.

Bolger's bookkeeper recently graduated from Oddball University, and while the dollar amounts recorded are correct, he had some confusion in determining which accounts needed adjustment. All intercorporate sales in 20X5 were from Feldman to Bolger, and Feldman sells inventory at cost plus 40 percent of cost. Bolger uses the fully adjusted equity method in accounting for its ownership in Feldman.

Required

a. What percentage of the intercompany inventory transfer was resold prior to the end of 20X5?

b. Give the appropriate eliminating entries needed at December 31, 20X5, to prepare consolidated financial statements.

LO3, LO4   **P6-22**   **Incomplete Data**

Lever Corporation acquired 75 percent of the ownership of Tropic Company on January 1, 20X1. The fair value of the noncontrolling interest at acquisition was equal to its proportionate share of the fair value of the net assets of Tropic. The full amount of the differential at acquisition was attributable to buildings and equipment, which had a remaining useful life of eight years. Financial statement data for the two companies and the consolidated entity at December 31, 20X6, are as follows:

LEVER CORPORATION AND TROPIC COMPANY
Balance Sheet Data
December 31, 20X6

Item	Lever Corporation	Tropic Company	Consolidated Entity
Cash	$ 67,000	$ 45,000	$112,000
Accounts Receivable	?	55,000	145,000
Inventory	125,000	90,000	211,000
Buildings and Equipment	400,000	240,000	680,000
Less: Accumulated Depreciation	(180,000)	(110,000)	(?)
Investment in Tropic Company	?		
Total Assets	$?	$320,000	$?
Accounts Payable	$ 86,000	$ 20,000	$ 89,000
Other Payables	?	8,000	?
Notes Payable	250,000	120,000	370,000
Common Stock	120,000	60,000	120,000
Retained Earnings	172,500	112,000	172,500
Noncontrolling Interest			44,500
Total Liabilities and Equity	$?	$320,000	$?

LEVER CORPORATION AND TROPIC COMPANY
Income Statement Data
For the Year Ended December 31, 20X6

Item	Lever Corporation	Tropic Company	Consolidated Entity
Sales	$420,000	$260,000	$650,000
Income from Subsidiary	32,250		
Total Income	$452,250	$260,000	$650,000
Cost of Goods Sold	$310,000	$170,000	$445,000
Depreciation Expense	20,000	25,000	50,000
Interest Expense	25,000	9,500	34,500
Other Expenses	22,000	15,500	37,500
Total Expenses	($377,000)	($220,000)	($567,000)
Consolidated Net Income			$ 83,000
Income to Noncontrolling Interest			(7,750)
Controlling Interest in Net Income	$ 75,250	$ 40,000	$ 75,250

All unrealized profit on intercompany inventory sales on January 1, 20X6, were eliminated on Lever's books. All unrealized inventory profits at December 31, 20X6, were eliminated on Tropic's books. Assume Lever uses the fully adjusted equity method and that Lever does not make the optional depreciation elimination worksheet entry.

Required

a. For the buildings and equipment held by Tropic when it was acquired by Lever and still on hand on December 31, 20X6, by what amount had they increased in value from their acquisition to the date of combination with Lever?

b. What amount should be reported as accumulated depreciation for the consolidated entity at December 31, 20X6 (assuming Lever does not make the optional accumulated depreciation elimination entry)?

c. If Tropic reported capital stock outstanding of $60,000 and retained earnings of $30,000 on January 1, 20X1, what amount did Lever pay to acquire its ownership of Tropic?

d. What balance does Lever report as its investment in Tropic at December 31, 20X6?

e. What amount of intercorporate sales of inventory occurred in 20X6?

f. What amount of unrealized inventory profit exists at December 31, 20X6?

g. Give the eliminating entry used in eliminating intercompany inventory sales during 20X6.

h. What was the amount of unrealized inventory profit at January 1, 20X6?

i. What balance in accounts receivable did Lever report at December 31, 20X6?

LO4

P6-23 **Eliminations for Upstream Sales**

Advanced StudyGuide .com

Clean Air Products owns 80 percent of the stock of Superior Filter Company, which it acquired at underlying book value on August 30, 20X6. At that date, the fair value of the noncontrolling interest was equal to 20 percent of the book value of Superior Filter. Summarized trial balance data for the two companies as of December 31, 20X8, are as follows:

	Clean Air Products		Superior Filter Company	
	Debit	Credit	Debit	Credit
Cash and Accounts Receivable	$ 145,000		$ 90,000	
Inventory	220,000		110,000	
Buildings and Equipment (net)	270,000		180,000	
Investment in Superior Filter Stock	268,000			
Cost of Goods Sold	175,000		140,000	
Depreciation Expense	30,000		20,000	
Current Liabilities		$ 150,000		$ 30,000
Common Stock		200,000		90,000
Retained Earnings		472,000		220,000
Sales		250,000		200,000
Income from Subsidiary		36,000		
Total	$1,108,000	$1,108,000	$540,000	$540,000

On January 1, 20X8, Clean Air's inventory contained filters purchased for $60,000 from Superior Filter, which had produced the filters for $40,000. In 20X8, Superior Filter spent $100,000 to produce additional filters, which it sold to Clean Air for $150,000. By December 31, 20X8, Clean Air had sold all filters that had been on hand January 1, 20X8, but continued to hold in inventory $45,000 of the 20X8 purchase from Superior Filter.

Required

a. Prepare all eliminating entries needed to complete a consolidation worksheet for 20X8.

b. Compute consolidated net income and income assigned to the controlling interest in the 20X8 consolidated income statement.

c. Compute the balance assigned to the noncontrolling interest in the consolidated balance sheet as of December 31, 20X8.

LO3, LO4   **P6-24   Multiple Inventory Transfers**

Ajax Corporation purchased at book value 70 percent of Beta Corporation's ownership and 90 percent of Cole Corporation's ownership in 20X5. At the dates the ownership was acquired, the fair value of the noncontrolling interest was equal to a proportionate share of book value. There are frequent intercompany transfers among the companies. Activity relevant to 20X8 follows:

Year	Producer	Production Cost	Buyer	Transfer Price	Unsold at End of Year	Year Sold
20X7	Beta Corporation	$24,000	Ajax Corporation	$30,000	$10,000	20X8
20X7	Cole Corporation	60,000	Beta Corporation	72,000	18,000	20X8
20X8	Ajax Corporation	15,000	Beta Corporation	35,000	7,000	20X9
20X8	Beta Corporation	63,000	Cole Corporation	72,000	12,000	20X9
20X8	Cole Corporation	27,000	Ajax Corporation	45,000	15,000	20X9

For the year ended December 31, 20X8, Ajax reported $80,000 of income from its separate operations (excluding income from intercorporate investments), Beta reported net income of $37,500, and Cole reported net income of $20,000.

Required

a. Compute the amount to be reported as consolidated net income for 20X8.

b. Compute the amount to be reported as inventory in the December 31, 20X8, consolidated balance sheet for the preceding items.

c. Compute the amount to be reported as income assigned to noncontrolling shareholders in the 20X8 consolidated income statement.

LO3, LO4   **P6-25   Consolidation with Inventory Transfers and Other Comprehensive Income**

On January 1, 20X1, Priority Corporation purchased 90 percent of Tall Corporation's common stock at underlying book value. At that date, the fair value of the noncontrolling interest was equal to 10 percent of the book value of Tall Corporation. Priority uses the equity method in accounting for its investment in Tall. The stockholders' equity section of Tall at January 1, 20X5, contained the following balances:

Common Stock ($5 par)	$ 400,000
Additional Paid-in Capital	200,000
Retained Earnings	790,000
Accumulated Other Comprehensive Income	10,000
Total	$1,400,000

During 20X4, Tall sold goods costing $30,000 to Priority for $45,000, and Priority resold 60 percent prior to year-end. It sold the remainder in 20X5. Also in 20X4, Priority sold inventory items costing $90,000 to Tall for $108,000. Tall resold $60,000 of its purchases in 20X4 and the remaining $48,000 in 20X5.

In 20X5, Priority sold additional inventory costing $30,000 to Tall for $36,000, and Tall resold $24,000 of it prior to year-end. Tall sold inventory costing $60,000 to Priority in 20X5 for $90,000, and Priority resold $48,000 of its purchase by December 31, 20X5.

Priority reported 20X5 income of $240,000 from its separate operations and paid dividends of $150,000. Tall reported 20X5 net income of $90,000 and comprehensive income of $110,000. Tall reported other comprehensive income of $10,000 in 20X4. In both years, other comprehensive income arose from an increase in the market value of securities classified as available-for-sale. Tall paid dividends of $60,000 in 20X5.

Required

a. Compute the balance in the investment account reported by Priority at December 31, 20X5.

b. Compute the amount of investment income reported by Priority on its investment in Tall for 20X5.

c. Compute the amount of income assigned to noncontrolling shareholders in the 20X5 consolidated income statement.

d. Compute the balance assigned to noncontrolling shareholders in the consolidated balance sheet prepared at December 31, 20X5.

e. Priority and Tall report inventory balances of $120,000 and $100,000, respectively, at December 31, 20X5. What amount should be reported as inventory in the consolidated balance sheet at December 31, 20X5?

f. Compute the amount reported as consolidated net income for 20X5.

g. Prepare the eliminating entries needed to complete a consolidation worksheet as of December 31, 20X5.

LO3, LO4   **P6-26**   **Multiple Inventory Transfers between Parent and Subsidiary**

Proud Company and Slinky Company both produce and purchase equipment for resale each period and frequently sell to each other. Since Proud Company holds 60 percent ownership of Slinky Company, Proud's controller compiled the following information with regard to intercompany transactions between the two companies in 20X5 and 20X6:

Year	Produced by	Sold to	Percent Resold to Nonaffiliate in 20X5	Percent Resold to Nonaffiliate in 20X6	Cost to Produce	Sale Price to Affiliate
20X5	Proud Company	Slinky Company	60%	40%	$100,000	$150,000
20X5	Slinky Company	Proud Company	30	50	70,000	100,000
20X6	Proud Company	Slinky Company		90	40,000	60,000
20X6	Slinky Company	Proud Company		25	200,000	240,000

Required

a. Give the eliminating entries required at December 31, 20X6, to eliminate the effects of the inventory transfers in preparing a full set of consolidated financial statements.

b. Compute the amount of cost of goods sold to be reported in the consolidated income statement for 20X6.

LO3, LO4   **P6-27**   **Consolidation Following Inventory Transactions**

Bell Company purchased 60 percent ownership of Troll Corporation on January 1, 20X1, for $82,800. On that date, the noncontrolling interest had a fair value of $55,200 and Troll reported common stock outstanding of $100,000 and retained earnings of $20,000. The full amount of the differential is assigned to land to be used as a future building site. Bell uses the fully adjusted equity method in accounting for its ownership of Troll. On December 31, 20X2, the trial balances of the two companies are as follows:

Item	Bell Company Debit	Bell Company Credit	Troll Corporation Debit	Troll Corporation Credit
Cash and Accounts Receivable	$ 69,400		$ 51,200	
Inventory	60,000		55,000	
Land	40,000		30,000	
Buildings and Equipment	520,000		350,000	
Investment in Troll Corporation Stock	103,780			
Cost of Goods Sold	99,800		61,000	
Depreciation Expense	25,000		15,000	
Interest Expense	6,000		14,000	
Dividends Declared	40,000		10,000	
Accumulated Depreciation		$175,000		$ 75,000
Accounts Payable		68,800		41,200
Bonds Payable		80,000		200,000
Bond Premium		1,200		
Common Stock		200,000		100,000
Retained Earnings		227,960		50,000
Sales		200,000		120,000
Income from Subsidiary		11,020		
	$963,980	$963,980	$586,200	$586,200

Troll sold inventory costing $25,500 to Bell for $42,500 in 20X1. Bell resold 80 percent of the purchase in 20X1 and the remainder in 20X2. Troll sold inventory costing $21,000 to Bell in 20X2 for $35,000, and Bell resold 70 percent prior to December 31, 20X2. In addition, Bell sold inventory costing $14,000 to Troll for $28,000 in 20X2, and Troll resold all but $13,000 of its purchase prior to December 31, 20X2.

Required

a. Record the journal entry or entries for 20X2 on Bell's books related to its investment in Troll Corporation, using the equity method.
b. Prepare the elimination entries needed to complete a consolidated worksheet for 20X2.
c. Prepare a three-part consolidation worksheet for 20X2.

LO3, LO4 **P6-28** **Consolidation Worksheet**

Crow Corporation purchased 70 percent of West Company's voting common stock on January 1, 20X5, for $291,200. On that date, the noncontrolling interest had a fair value of $124,800 and the book value of West's net assets was $380,000. The book values and fair values of West's assets and liabilities were equal, except for land that had a fair value $14,000 greater than book value. The amount attributed to goodwill as a result of the acquisition is not amortized and has not been impaired.

CROW CORPORATION AND WEST COMPANY
Trial Balance Data
December 31, 20X9

Item	Crow Corporation Debit	Crow Corporation Credit	West Company Debit	West Company Credit
Cash and Receivables	$ 81,300		$ 85,000	
Inventory	200,000		110,000	
Land, Buildings, and Equipment (net)	270,000		250,000	
Investment in West Company Stock	290,200			
Cost of Goods and Services	200,000		150,000	
Depreciation Expense	40,000		30,000	
Dividends Declared	35,000		5,000	
Sales and Service Revenue		$ 300,000		$200,000
Income from Subsidiary		24,500		
Accounts Payable		60,000		30,000
Common Stock		200,000		150,000
Retained Earnings		532,000		250,000
Total	1,116,500	1,116,500	$630,000	$630,000

On January 1, 20X9, Crow's inventory contained unrealized intercompany profits recorded by West in the amount of $30,000. West's inventory on that date contained $15,000 of unrealized intercompany profits recorded on Crow's books. Both companies sold their ending 20X8 inventories to unrelated companies in 20X9.

During 20X9, West sold inventory costing $37,000 to Crow for $62,000. Crow held all inventory purchased from West during 20X9 on December 31, 20X9. Also during 20X9, Crow sold goods costing $54,000 to West for $90,000. West continues to hold $20,000 of its purchase from Crow on December 31, 20X9. Assume Crow uses the fully adjusted equity method.

Required

a. Prepare all eliminating entries needed to complete a consolidation worksheet as of December 31, 20X9.
b. Prepare a consolidation worksheet as of December 31, 20X9.
c. Prepare a reconciliation between the balance in retained earnings reported by Crow on December 31, 20X9, and consolidated retained earnings.

LO3, LO4 **P6-29** **Computation of Consolidated Totals**

Bunker Corporation owns 80 percent of Harrison Company's stock. At the end of 20X8, Bunker and Harrison reported the following partial operating results and inventory balances:

	Bunker Corporation	Harrison Company
Total sales	$660,000	$510,000
Sales to Harrison Company	140,000	
Sales to Bunker Corporation		240,000
Net income		20,000
Operating income (excluding investment income from Harrison)	70,000	
Inventory on hand, December 31, 20X8, purchased from:		
Harrison Company	48,000	
Bunker Corporation		42,000

Bunker regularly prices its products at cost plus a 40 percent markup for profit. Harrison prices its sales at cost plus a 20 percent markup. The total sales reported by Bunker and Harrison include both intercompany sales and sales to nonaffiliates.

Required

a. What amount of sales will be reported in the consolidated income statement for 20X8?

b. What amount of cost of goods sold will be reported in the 20X8 consolidated income statement?

c. What amount of consolidated net income and income to controlling interest will be reported in the 20X8 consolidated income statement?

d. What balance will be reported for inventory in the consolidated balance sheet for December 31, 20X8?

LO3, LO4 **P6-30** ### Intercompany Transfer of Inventory

Pine Corporation acquired 70 percent of Bock Company's voting common shares on January 1, 20X2, for $108,500. At that date, the noncontrolling interest had a fair value of $46,500 and Bock reported $70,000 of common stock outstanding and retained earnings of $30,000. The differential is assigned to buildings and equipment, which had a fair value $20,000 greater than book value and a remaining 10-year life, and to patents, which had a fair value $35,000 greater than book value and a remaining life of five years at the date of the business combination. Trial balances for the companies as of December 31, 20X3, are as follows:

Item	Pine Corporation Debit	Pine Corporation Credit	Bock Company Debit	Bock Company Credit
Cash and Accounts Receivable	$ 15,400		$ 21,600	
Inventory	165,000		35,000	
Land	80,000		40,000	
Buildings and Equipment	340,000		260,000	
Investment in Bock Company Stock	109,600			
Cost of Goods Sold	186,000		79,800	
Depreciation Expense	20,000		15,000	
Interest Expense	16,000		5,200	
Dividends Declared	30,000		15,000	
Accumulated Depreciation		$140,000		$ 80,000
Accounts Payable		92,400		35,000
Bonds Payable		200,000		100,000
Bond Premium				1,600
Common Stock		120,000		70,000
Retained Earnings		127,900		60,000
Sales		260,000		125,000
Other Income		13,600		
Income from Subsidiary		8,100		
	$962,000	$962,000	$471,600	$471,600

On December 31, 20X2, Bock purchased inventory for $32,000 and sold it to Pine for $48,000. Pine resold $27,000 of the inventory during 20X3 and had the remaining balance in inventory at December 31, 20X3.

During 20X3, Bock sold inventory purchased for $60,000 to Pine for $90,000, and Pine resold all but $24,000 of its purchase. On March 10, 20X3, Pine sold inventory purchased for $15,000 to Bock for $30,000. Bock sold all but $7,600 of the inventory prior to December 31, 20X3. Assume Pine uses the fully adjusted equity method.

Required

a. Give all eliminating entries needed to prepare a full set of consolidated financial statements at December 31, 20X3, for Pine and Bock.

b. Prepare a three-part consolidation worksheet for 20X3.

LO3, LO4 **P6-31** ### Consolidation Using Financial Statement Data

Bower Corporation acquired 60 percent of Concerto Company's stock on January 1, 20X3, for $24,000 in excess of book value. On that date, the book values and fair values of Concerto's assets and liabilities were equal and the fair value of the noncontrolling interest was $16,000 in excess of book value. The full amount of the differential at acquisition was assigned to goodwill. At December 31, 20X6, the management of Bower reviewed the amount assigned to goodwill and concluded it had been impaired. They concluded the correct carrying value at that date should be $30,000 and the impairment loss should be assigned proportionately between the controlling and noncontrolling interests.

Balance sheet data for January 1, 20X6, and December 31, 20X6, and income statement data for 20X6 for the two companies are as follows:

BOWER CORPORATION AND CONCERTO COMPANY
Balance Sheet Data
January 1, 20X6

Item	Bower Corporation		Concerto Company	
Cash	$ 9,800		$ 10,000	
Accounts Receivable	60,000		50,000	
Inventory	100,000		80,000	
Total Current Assets		$169,800		$140,000
Land		70,000		20,000
Buildings and Equipment	$300,000		$200,000	
Less: Accumulated Depreciation	(140,000)	160,000	(70,000)	130,000
Investment in Concerto Company Stock		135,200		
Total Assets		$535,000		$290,000
Accounts Payable		$ 30,000		$ 20,000
Bonds Payable		120,000		70,000
Common Stock	$100,000		$ 50,000	
Retained Earnings	285,000	385,000	150,000	200,000
Total Liabilities and Stockholders' Equity		$535,000		$290,000

BOWER CORPORATION AND CONCERTO COMPANY
Balance Sheet Data
December 31, 20X6

Item	Bower Corporation		Concerto Company	
Cash	$ 26,800		$ 35,000	
Accounts Receivable	80,000		40,000	
Inventory	120,000		90,000	
Total Current Assets		$226,800		$165,000
Land		70,000		20,000
Buildings and Equipment	$340,000		$200,000	
Less: Accumulated Depreciation	(165,000)	175,000	(85,000)	115,000
Investment in Concerto Company Stock		139,600		
Total Assets		$611,400		$300,000
Accounts Payable		$ 80,000		$ 15,000
Bonds Payable		120,000		70,000
Common Stock	$100,000		$ 50,000	
Retained Earnings	311,400	411,000	165,000	215,000
Total Liabilities and Stockholders' Equity		$611,400		$300,000

BOWER CORPORATION AND CONCERTO COMPANY
Income Statement Data
Year Ended December 31, 20X6

Item	Bower Corporation		Concerto Company	
Sales		$400,000		$200,000
Income from Subsidiary		16,400		
		$416,400		$200,000
Cost of Goods Sold	$280,000		$120,000	
Depreciation and Amortization Expense	25,000		15,000	
Other Expenses	35,000	(340,000)	30,000	(165,000)
Net Income		76,400		$ 35,000

On January 1, 20X6, Bower held inventory purchased from Concerto for $48,000. During 20X6, Bower purchased an additional $90,000 of goods from Concerto and held $54,000 of its purchases on December 31, 20X6. Concerto sells inventory to the parent at 20 percent above cost.

Concerto also purchases inventory from Bower Corporation. On January 1, 20X6, Concerto held inventory purchased from Bower for $14,000, and on December 31, 20X6, it held inventory purchased from Bower for $7,000. Concerto's total purchases from Bower Corporation were $22,000 in 20X6. Bower Corporation sells items to Concerto Company at 40 percent above cost.

During 20X6, Bower paid dividends of $50,000, and Concerto paid dividends of $20,000. Assume Bower uses the fully adjusted equity method.

Required

a. Prepare all eliminating entries needed to complete a consolidation worksheet as of December 31, 20X6.

b. Prepare a three-part consolidation worksheet as of December 31, 20X6.

P6-32 **Intercorporate Transfer of Inventory**

Block Corporation was created on January 1, 20X0, to develop computer software. On January 1, 20X5, Foster Company purchased 90 percent of Block's common stock at underlying book value. At that date, the fair value of the noncontrolling interest was equal to 10 percent of the book value of Block Corporation. Trial balances for Foster and Block on December 31, 20X9, are as follows:

	20X9 Trial Balance Data			
	Foster Company		Block Corporation	
Item	Debit	Credit	Debit	Credit
Cash	$ 187,000		$ 57,400	
Accounts Receivable	80,000		90,000	
Other Receivables	40,000		10,000	
Inventory	137,000		130,000	
Land	80,000		60,000	
Buildings and Equipment	500,000		250,000	
Investment in Block Corporation Stock	234,900			
Cost of Goods Sold	593,000		270,000	
Depreciation Expense	45,000		15,000	
Other Expenses	95,000		75,000	
Dividends Declared	40,000		20,000	
Accumulated Depreciation		$ 155,000		$ 75,000
Accounts Payable		63,000		35,000
Other Payables		95,000		20,000
Bonds Payable		250,000		200,000
Bond Premium				2,400
Common Stock		210,000		50,000
Additional Paid-in Capital		110,000		
Retained Earnings		235,000		165,000
Sales		815,000		415,000
Other Income		26,000		15,000
Income from Subsidiary		72,900		
Total	2,031,900	2,031,900	$977,400	$977,400

During 20X9, Block produced inventory for $20,000 and sold it to Foster for $30,000. Foster resold 60 percent of the inventory in 20X9. Also in 20X9, Foster sold inventory purchased from Block in 20X8. It had cost Block $60,000 to produce the inventory, and Foster purchased it for $75,000. Assume Foster uses the fully adjusted equity method.

Required

a. What amount of cost of goods sold will be reported in the 20X9 consolidated income statement?

b. What inventory balance will be reported in the December 31, 20X9, consolidated balance sheet?

c. What amount of income will be assigned to noncontrolling shareholders in the 20X9 consolidated income statement?

d. What amount will be assigned to noncontrolling interest in the consolidated balance sheet prepared at December 31, 20X9?

e. What amount of retained earnings will be reported in the consolidated balance sheet at December 31, 20X9?

f. Give all eliminating entries required to prepare a three-part consolidation worksheet at December 31, 20X9.

g. Prepare a three-part consolidation worksheet at December 31, 20X9.

LO3

P6-33 **Consolidated Balance Sheet Worksheet [AICPA Adapted]**

The December 31, 20X6, condensed balance sheets of Pine Corporation and its 90 percent–owned subsidiary, Slim Corporation, are presented in the accompanying worksheet.

Additional Information

- Pine's investment in Slim was acquired for $1,170,000 cash on January 1, 20X6, and is accounted for by the equity method. The fair value of the noncontrolling interest at that date was $130,000.
- At January 1, 20X6, Slim's retained earnings amounted to $600,000, and its common stock amounted to $200,000.
- Slim declared a $1,000 cash dividend in December 20X6, payable in January 20X7.
- Slim borrowed $100,000 from Pine on June 30, 20X6, with the note maturing on June 30, 20X7, at 10 percent interest. Correct accruals have been recorded by both companies.
- During 20X6, Pine sold merchandise to Slim at an aggregate invoice price of $300,000, which included a profit of $60,000. At December 31, 20X6, Slim had not paid Pine for $90,000 of these purchases, and 5 percent of the total merchandise purchased from Pine still remained in Slim's inventory. Assume Pine uses the fully adjusted equity method.
- Pine's excess cost over book value of its investment in Slim has appropriately been identified as goodwill. At December 31, 20X6, Pine's management reviewed the amount attributed to goodwill and found no evidence of impairment.

Required

Complete the accompanying worksheet for Pine and its subsidiary, Slim, at December 31, 20X6.

PINE CORPORATION AND SUBSIDIARY
Consolidated Balance Sheet Worksheet
December 31, 20X6

	Pine Corporation	Slim Corporation	Adjustments and Eliminations Debit	Adjustments and Eliminations Credit	Consolidated
Assets					
Cash	105,000	15,000			
Accounts and Other Current Receivables	410,000	120,000			
Merchandise Inventory	920,000	670,000			
Plant and Equipment, Net	1,000,000	400,000			
Investment in Slim	1,257,000				
Totals	3,692,000	1,205,000			

(continued)

Liabilities and Stockholders' Equity:		
Accounts Payable and Other		
Current Liabilities	140,000	305,000
Common Stock ($10 par)	500,000	200,000
Retained Earnings	3,052,000	700,000
Totals	3,692,000	1,205,000

LO3, LO4 **P6-34**

Comprehensive Worksheet Problem

Randall Corporation acquired 80 percent of Sharp Company's voting shares on January 1, 20X4, for $280,000 in cash and marketable securities. At that date, the noncontrolling interest had a fair value of $70,000 and Sharp reported net assets of $300,000. Assume Randall uses the fully adjusted equity method. Trial balances for the two companies on December 31, 20X7, are as follows:

	Randall Corporation		Sharp Company	
Item	**Debit**	**Credit**	**Debit**	**Credit**
Cash	$ 130,300		$ 10,000	
Accounts Receivable	80,000		70,000	
Inventory	170,000		110,000	
Buildings and Equipment	600,000		400,000	
Investment in Sharp Company Stock	293,000			
Cost of Goods Sold	416,000		202,000	
Depreciation and Amortization	30,000		20,000	
Other Expenses	24,000		18,000	
Dividends Declared	50,000		25,000	
Accumulated Depreciation		$ 310,000		$120,000
Accounts Payable		100,000		15,200
Bonds Payable		300,000		100,000
Bond Premium				4,800
Common Stock		200,000		100,000
Additional Paid-in Capital				20,000
Retained Earnings		337,500		215,000
Sales		500,000		250,000
Other Income		20,400		30,000
Income from Sharp Company		25,400		
	1,793,300	1,793,300	$855,000	$855,000

Additional Information

1. The full amount of the differential at acquisition was assigned to buildings and equipment with a remaining 10-year economic life.

2. Randall and Sharp regularly purchase inventory from each other. During 20X6, Sharp sold inventory costing $40,000 to Randall Corporation for $60,000, and Randall resold 60 percent of the inventory in 20X6 and 40 percent in 20X7. Also in 20X6, Randall sold inventory costing $20,000 to Sharp for $26,000. Sharp resold two-thirds of the inventory in 20X6 and one-third in 20X7.

3. During 20X7, Sharp sold inventory costing $30,000 to Randall for $45,000, and Randall sold items purchased for $9,000 to Sharp for $12,000. Before the end of the year, Randall resold one-third of the inventory it purchased from Sharp in 20X7. Sharp continues to hold all the units purchased from Randall during 20X7.

4. Sharp owes Randall $10,000 on account on December 31, 20X7.

Required

a. Prepare the 20X7 journal entries recorded on Randall's books related to its investment in Sharp if Randall uses the equity method.

b. Prepare all eliminating entries needed to complete a consolidation worksheet as of December 31, 20X7.

c. Prepare a three-part consolidation worksheet as of December 31, 20X7.

d. Prepare, in good form, a consolidated income statement, balance sheet, and retained earnings statement for 20X7.

P6-35 ## Comprehensive Consolidation Worksheet; Equity Method [AICPA Adapted]

Fran Corporation acquired all outstanding $10 par value voting common stock of Brey Inc. on January 1, 20X9, in exchange for 25,000 shares of its $20 par value voting common stock. On December 31, 20X8, Fran's common stock had a closing market price of $30 per share on a national stock exchange. The acquisition was appropriately accounted for under the acquisition method. Both companies continued to operate as separate business entities maintaining separate accounting records with years ending December 31. Fran accounts for its investment in Brey stock using the equity method without adjusting for unrealized intercompany profits.

On December 31, 20X9, the companies had condensed financial statements as follows:

	Fran Corporation		Brey Inc.	
Income Statement	Dr	(Cr)	Dr	(Cr)
Net Sales		$(3,800,000)		$(1,500,000)
Income from Brey		(128,000)		
Gain on Sale of Warehouse		(30,000)		
Cost of Goods Sold	2,360,000		870,000	
Operating Expenses (including depreciation)	1,100,000		440,000	
Net Income		$ (498,000)		$ (190,000)
Retained Earnings Statement				
Balance, 1/1/X9		$ (440,000)		$ (156,000)
Net Income		(498,000)		(190,000)
Dividends Paid			40,000	
Balance, 12/31/X9		(938,000)		$ (306,000)
Balance Sheet				
Assets:				
Cash	$ 570,000		$ 150,000	
Accounts Receivable (net)	860,000		350,000	
Inventories	1,060,000		410,000	
Land, Plant, and Equipment	1,320,000		680,000	
Accumulated Depreciation	(370,000)		(210,000)	
Investment in Brey	838,000			
Total Assets	$ 4,278,000		$ 1,380,000	
Liabilities and Stockholders' Equity:				
Accounts Payable and Accrued Expenses		$(1,340,000)		$ (594,000)
Common Stock		(1,700,000)		(400,000)
Additional Paid-in Capital		(300,000)		(80,000)
Retained Earnings		(973,000)		(306,000)
Total Liabilities and Equity		$(4,278,000)		$(1,380,000)

Additional Information

There were no changes in the Common Stock and Additional Paid-in Capital accounts during 20X9 except the one necessitated by Fran's acquisition of Brey.

At the acquisition date, the fair value of Brey's machinery exceeded its book value by $54,000. The excess cost will be amortized over the estimated average remaining life of six years. The fair values of all of Brey's other assets and liabilities were equal to their book values. At December 31, 20X9, Fran's management reviewed the amount attributed to goodwill as a result of its purchase of Brey's common stock and concluded an impairment loss of $35,000 should be recognized in 20X9.

During 20X9, Fran purchased merchandise from Brey at an aggregate invoice price of $180,000, which included a 100 percent markup on Brey's cost. At December 31, 20X9, Fran owed Brey $86,000 on these purchases, and $36,000 of this merchandise remained in Fran's inventory. Assume Fran uses the fully adjusted equity method.

Required

Develop and complete a consolidation worksheet that would be used to prepare a consolidated income statement and a consolidated retained earnings statement for the year ended December 31, 20X9, and a consolidated balance sheet as of December 31, 20X9. List the accounts in the worksheet in the same order as they are listed in the financial statements provided. Formal consolidated statements are not required. Ignore income tax considerations. Supporting computations should be in good form.

LO5

P6-36A   Modified Equity Method

On December 31, 20X7, Randall Corporation recorded the following entry on its books to adjust from the fully adjusted equity method to the modified equity method for its investment in Sharp Company stock:

Investment in Sharp Company Stock	11,000	
Retained Earnings		8,400
Income from Sharp Company		2,600

Required

a. Adjust the data reported by Randall in the trial balance contained in Problem P6-34 for the effects of the preceding adjusting entry.

b. Prepare the journal entries that would have been recorded on Randall's books during 20X7 under the modified equity method.

c. Prepare all eliminating entries needed to complete a consolidation worksheet at December 31, 20X7, assuming Randall has used the modified equity method.

d. Complete a three-part consolidation worksheet as of December 31, 20X7.

LO5

P6-37A   Cost Method

The trial balance data presented in Problem P6-34 can be converted to reflect use of the cost method by inserting the following amounts in place of those presented for Randall Corporation:

Investment in Sharp Company Stock	$280,000
Retained Earnings	329,900
Income from Subsidiary	–0–
Dividend Income	20,000

Required

a. Prepare the journal entries that would have been recorded on Randall's books during 20X7 under the cost method.

b. Prepare all eliminating entries needed to complete a consolidation worksheet as of December 31, 20X7, assuming Randall uses the cost method.

c. Complete a three-part consolidation worksheet as of December 31, 20X7.

"A" indicates that the item relates to "Appendix A."

Chapter **Seven**

Intercompany Transfers of Services and Noncurrent Assets

MICRON'S INTERCOMPANY FIXED ASSET SALE

Micron Technology Inc., ranked number 423 in the 2009 Fortune 500 listing, was founded in Boise, Idaho, in 1978 and specializes in the fabrication of DRAM, SDRAM, flash memory, SSD, and CMOS semiconductor chips. Through a long series of acquisitions, Micron now owns many subsidiaries both in the United States and internationally. Micron also has several joint ventures with other companies. For example, in January 2006, Micron and Intel Corporation formed a new company called IM Flash Technologies, LLC, located in Lehi, Utah. A few years earlier in 2002, Micron acquired Toshiba's commodity DRAM operations located in Manassas, Virginia. This wholly owned subsidiary is now called Micron Technology Virginia.

In June 2009 IM Flash Technologies sold underutilized semiconductor manufacturing equipment to Micron Technology Virginia. The equipment originally cost $3,673,962 and had been assigned a five-year useful life. Since it had only been depreciated for approximately 25 months of its expected 60-month useful life, IM Flash Technologies determined that the equipment had a book value at the time of the transfer of $2,439,888. Given the agreed-upon fair market value and selling price of $1,500,000, IM Flash Technologies realized a loss of $939,888 on this intercompany asset sale. Since Micron Technology, Inc. owns more than 50 percent of IM Flash Technologies and 100 percent of Micron Technology Virginia, it consolidates both companies. Therefore, the loss on this sale between affiliated companies had to be eliminated in the consolidation process. This chapter explores the accounting for both depreciable and nondepreciable asset transfers among affiliated companies.

LEARNING OBJECTIVES

When you finish studying this chapter, you should be able to:

LO1 Understand and explain concepts associated with transfers of long-term assets and services.

LO2 Prepare equity-method journal entries and elimination entries for the consolidation of a subsidiary following an intercompany land transfer.

LO3 Prepare equity-method journal entries and elimination entries for the consolidation of a subsidiary following a downstream land transfer.

LO4 Prepare equity-method journal entries and elimination entries for the consolidation of a subsidiary following an upstream land transfer.

LO5 Prepare equity-method journal entries and elimination entries for the consolidation of a subsidiary following a downstream depreciable asset transfer.

LO6 Prepare equity-method journal entries and elimination entries for the consolidation of a subsidiary following an upstream depreciable asset transfer.

INTERCOMPANY LONG-TERM ASSET TRANSFERS

Understand and explain concepts associated with transfers of long-term assets and services.

The following illustrations provide an overview of the intercompany sale process using land as an example. Figure 7–1 shows a series of transactions involving a parent company and its subsidiary. Land first is purchased by Parent Company from an unrelated party, then sold to a subsidiary of Parent Company, and finally sold by the subsidiary to an unrelated party. The three transactions, and the amounts, are as follows:

T1—Purchase by Parent Company from outsider for $10,000.
T2—Sale from Parent Company to Subsidiary Corporation for $15,000.
T3—Sale from Subsidiary Corporation to outsider for $25,000.

FIGURE 7–1
Intercompany Sales

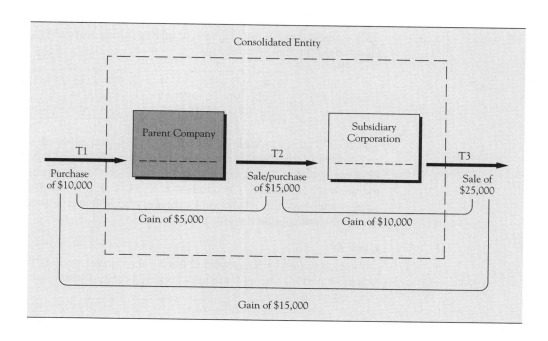

As shown in the following cases, the amount of gain reported by each of the individual companies and by the consolidated entity in a period depends on which of the transactions occur during that period.

Case A

All three transactions are completed in the same accounting period. The gain amounts reported on the transactions are:

Parent Company	$ 5,000 ($15,000 − $10,000)
Subsidiary Corporation	10,000 ($25,000 − $15,000)
Consolidated Entity	15,000 ($25,000 − $10,000)

The gain reported by each of the entities is considered to be realized because the land is resold to an unrelated party during the period. The total gain reported by the consolidated entity is the difference between the $10,000 price paid by the consolidated entity and the $25,000 price at which the consolidated entity sold the land to an outsider. This $15,000 gain is reported in the consolidated income statement. From a consolidated viewpoint, the sale from Parent Company to Subsidiary Corporation, transaction T2, is an internal transaction and is not reported in the consolidated financial statements.

Case B

Only transaction T1 is completed during the current period. The gain amounts reported on the transactions are:

Parent Company	$–0–
Subsidiary Corporation	–0–
Consolidated Entity	–0–

No sale has been made by either of the affiliated companies, and no gains are reported or realized. The land is reported both in Parent Company's balance sheet and in the consolidated balance sheet at its cost to Parent, which also is the cost to the consolidated entity.

Case C

Only transactions T1 and T2 are completed during the current period. The gain amounts reported on the transactions are:

Parent Company	$5,000 ($15,000 − $10,000)
Subsidiary Corporation	–0–
Consolidated Entity	–0–

The $5,000 gain reported by Parent Company is considered unrealized from a consolidated point of view and is not reported in the consolidated income statement because the land has not been resold to a party outside the consolidated entity. The land is carried on the books of Subsidiary Corporation at $15,000, the cost to Subsidiary. From a consolidated viewpoint, the land is overvalued by $5,000 and must be reported at its $10,000 cost to the consolidated entity.

Case D

Only transaction T3 is completed during the current period, T1 and T2 having occurred in a prior period. The gain amounts reported on the transactions in the current period are:

Parent Company	$ –0–
Subsidiary Corporation	10,000 ($25,000 − $15,000)
Consolidated Entity	15,000 ($25,000 − $10,000)

Subsidiary recognizes a gain equal to the difference between its selling price, $25,000, and cost, $15,000, while the consolidated entity reports a gain equal to the difference between its selling price of $25,000 and cost of $10,000.

From a consolidated viewpoint, the sale of an asset wholly within the consolidated entity involves only a change in the location of the asset and does not represent the culmination of the earning process. To culminate the earning process with respect to the consolidated entity, a sale must be made to a party external to the consolidated entity. The key to deciding when to report a transaction in the consolidated financial statements is to visualize the consolidated entity and determine whether a particular transaction occurs totally within the consolidated entity, in which case its effects must be excluded from the consolidated statements, or involves outsiders and thus constitutes a transaction of the consolidated entity.

INTERCOMPANY TRANSFERS OF SERVICES

Related companies frequently purchase services from one another. These services may be of many different types; intercompany purchases of consulting, engineering, marketing, and maintenance services are common.

When one company purchases services from a related company, the purchaser typically records an expense and the seller records revenue. When consolidated financial statements are prepared, both the expense and revenue must be eliminated. For example, if the parent sells consulting services to the subsidiary for $50,000, the parent would recognize $50,000 of consulting revenue on its books and the subsidiary would recognize $50,000 of consulting expense. In the consolidation worksheet, an eliminating entry would be needed to reduce both consulting revenue (debit) and consulting expense (credit) by $50,000. Because the revenue and expense are equal and both are eliminated, income is unaffected by the elimination. Even though income is not affected, the elimination is still important, however, because otherwise both revenues and expenses are overstated.

Generally, a simplistic approach is taken in eliminating intercompany transfers of services by assuming that the services benefit the current period and, therefore, any intercompany profit on the services becomes realized within the period of transfer. Accordingly, no eliminating entries relating to the current period's transfer of services are needed in future periods because the intercompany profit is considered realized in the transfer period.

Usually the assumption that the profit on intercompany sales of services is realized in the period of sale is a realistic assumption. In some cases, however, realization of intercompany profit on the services does not occur in the period the services are provided and the amounts are significant. For example, if the parent company charges a subsidiary for architectural services to design a new manufacturing facility for the subsidiary, the subsidiary would include that cost in the capitalized cost of the new facility. From a consolidated point of view, however, any profit the parent recognized on the intercompany sale of services (revenue over the cost of providing the service) would have to be eliminated from the reported cost of the new facility until the intercompany profit became realized. Realization would be viewed as occurring over the life of the facility. Thus, eliminating entries would be needed each year similar to those illustrated later in the chapter for intercompany transfers of fixed assets.

INTERCOMPANY LAND TRANSFERS[1]

LO2

Prepare equity-method journal entries and elimination entries for the consolidation of a subsidiary following an intercompany land transfer.

When intercorporate transfers of noncurrent assets occur, adjustments often are needed in the preparation of consolidated financial statements for as long as the assets are held by the acquiring company. The simplest example of an intercorporate asset transfer is the intercorporate sale of land.

Overview of the Profit Elimination Process

When land is transferred between related companies at book value, no special adjustments or eliminations are needed in preparing the consolidated statements. If, for

[1] To view a video explanation of this topic, visit advancedstudyguide.com.

Advanced
StudyGuide
.com

example, a company purchases land for $10,000 and sells it to its subsidiary for $10,000, the asset continues to be valued at the $10,000 original cost to the consolidated entity:

Parent		Subsidiary	
Cash 10,000		Land 10,000	
Land 10,000		Cash 10,000	

Because the seller records no gain or loss, both income and assets are stated correctly from a consolidated viewpoint.

Land transfers at more or less than book value do require special treatment in the consolidation process. The selling entity's gain or loss must be eliminated because the land is still held by the consolidated entity, and no gain or loss may be reported in the consolidated financial statements until the land is sold to a party outside the consolidated entity. Likewise, the land must be reported at its original cost in the consolidated financial statements as long as it is held within the consolidated entity, regardless of which affiliate holds the land.

As an illustration, assume that Peerless Products Corporation acquires land for $20,000 on January 1, 20X1, and sells the land to its subsidiary, Special Foods Incorporated, on July 1, 20X1, for $35,000, as follows:

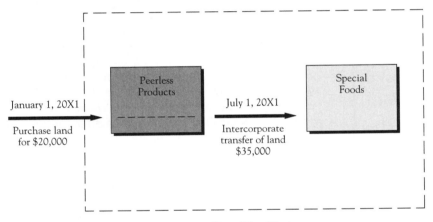

Consolidated Entity

Peerless records the purchase of the land and its sale to Special Foods with the following entries:

January 1, 20X1

(1)

Land	20,000	
Cash		20,000

Record land purchase.

July 1, 20X1

(2)

Cash	35,000	
Land		20,000
Gain on Sale of Land		15,000

Record sale of land to Special Foods.

Special Foods records the purchase of the land from Peerless as follows:

July1, 20X1

(3)

Land	35,000	
Cash		35,000

Record purchase of land from Peerless.

The intercorporate transfer leads to a $15,000 gain on Peerless' books and the carrying value of the land increases by the same amount on Special Foods' books. Neither of these amounts may be reported in the consolidated financial statements because the $15,000 intercompany gain is unrealized from a consolidated viewpoint. The land has not been sold to a party outside the consolidated entity but only transferred within; consequently, the land must still be reported in consolidated financial statements at its original cost to the consolidated entity. The gain should be eliminated in the preparation of consolidated statements and the land restated from the $35,000 recorded on Special Foods' books to its original cost of $20,000. This is accomplished with the following eliminating entry in the consolidation worksheet prepared at the end of 20X1:

Gain on Sale of Land	15,000	
Land		15,000

In addition, when intercompany gains or losses on asset transfers are incurred, the parent company can choose to use the fully adjusted equity method, which requires it to adjust its investment and income from subsidiary accounts to remove the unrealized gain.

July 1, 20X1

(4)	Income from Special Foods	15,000	
	Investment in Special Foods Stock		15,000

Defer gain on intercompany land sale to Special Foods.

This equity-method entry ensures that the parent company's income is exactly equal to the controlling interest in consolidated income on the consolidated financial statements.[2] Chapter 6 explains that the deferral of unrealized gross profit on intercompany inventory transfers is reversed in the subsequent accounting period if the inventory is sold to an outside party. Similarly, the deferral of gain on an intercompany asset transfer is reversed in the period in which the asset is sold to an outsider.

We use the fully adjusted equity method in all subsequent examples in the chapter. Another option is to ignore this unrealized gain on the parent company's books and only adjust for it in the consolidation worksheet under the modified equity method. We illustrate this approach in the appendix.

Assignment of Unrealized Profit Elimination

Unrealized intercompany gains and losses must be eliminated fully when preparing consolidated financial statements. Regardless of the parent's percentage ownership of a subsidiary, the full amount of any unrealized gains and losses must be eliminated and must be excluded from consolidated net income. Although the full amount of an unrealized gain or loss is excluded from consolidated net income, a question arises when the parent owns less than 100 percent of a subsidiary as to whether the unrealized profit elimination should reduce the controlling or noncontrolling interest, or both.

A gain or loss on an intercompany transfer is recognized by the selling affiliate and ultimately accrues to the stockholders of that affiliate. When a sale is from a parent to a subsidiary, referred to as a **downstream sale,** any gain or loss on the transfer accrues to the parent company's stockholders. When the sale is from a subsidiary to its parent, an **upstream sale,** any gain or loss accrues to the subsidiary's stockholders. If the subsidiary is wholly owned, all gain or loss ultimately accrues to the parent company as the sole stockholder. If,

[2] Students sometimes ask if this entry "double counts" the deferral of the gain since the gain is also eliminated in the consolidation worksheet. Note that this equity-method entry defers the gain on the parent's books to ensure that the parent's net income is accurate and equal to the parent's share of consolidated net income. Although the parent company records this deferral in its books, the investment in subsidiary and income from subsidiary accounts are eliminated in the consolidation process (i.e., they do not show up in the consolidated financial statements). Thus, the worksheet elimination entry is still necessary to ensure that the gain is removed from the consolidated financial statements. This explanation will be clearer in subsequent examples where we present the full consolidation worksheet.

however, the selling subsidiary is not wholly owned, the gain or loss on the upstream sale is apportioned between the parent company and the noncontrolling shareholders.

Generally, gains and losses are not considered realized by the consolidated entity until a sale is made to an external party. Unrealized gains and losses are eliminated in preparing consolidated financial statements against the interests of those shareholders who recognized the gains and losses in the first place: the shareholders of the selling affiliate. Therefore, the direction of the sale determines which shareholder group absorbs the elimination of unrealized intercompany gains and losses. Thus, unrealized intercompany gains and losses are eliminated in consolidation in the following ways:

Sale	Elimination
Downstream (parent to subsidiary)	Against controlling interest
Upstream (subsidiary to parent):	
Wholly owned subsidiary	Against controlling interest
Majority-owned subsidiary	Proportionately against controlling and noncontrolling interests

As an illustration, assume that Purity Company owns 75 percent of the common stock of Southern Corporation. Purity reports operating income from its own activities, excluding any investment income from Southern, of $100,000; Southern reports net income of $60,000. Included in the income of the selling affiliate is an unrealized gain of $10,000 on the intercompany transfer of an asset. If the sale is a downstream transfer, all unrealized profit is eliminated from the controlling interest's share of income when consolidated statements are prepared. Thus, consolidated net income is computed and allocated as follows:

Purity's separate income	$100,000
Less: Unrealized intercompany gain on downstream asset sale	(10,000)
Purity's separate realized income	$ 90,000
Southern's net income	60,000
Consolidated net income	$150,000
Income to noncontrolling interest ($60,000 × 0.25)	(15,000)
Income to controlling interest	$135,000

If, instead, the intercompany transfer is from subsidiary to parent, the unrealized profit on the upstream sale is eliminated proportionately from the interests of the controlling and noncontrolling shareholders. In this situation, consolidated net income is computed and allocated as follows:

Purity's separate income		$100,000
Southern's net income	$60,000	
Less: Unrealized intercompany gain on upstream asset sale	(10,000)	
Southern's realized net income		50,000
Consolidated net income		$150,000
Income to noncontrolling interest ($50,000 × 0.25)		(12,500)
Income to controlling interest		$137,500

Consolidated net income is the same whether the intercompany sale is upstream or downstream, but the allocation of the income reduction differs. Because Purity recognized all of the gain in the downstream case, the controlling interest's share of income is reduced by the full unrealized gain elimination. In the upstream case, the intercompany gain was recognized by Southern and shared proportionately by Southern's controlling and noncontrolling interests. Therefore, the elimination is made proportionately against the controlling and noncontrolling interests' share of income.

Note that unrealized intercompany gains and losses are always fully eliminated in preparing consolidated financial statements. The existence of a noncontrolling interest in a selling subsidiary affects only the allocation of the eliminated unrealized gain or loss and not the amount eliminated.

Income to the Noncontrolling Interest

The income assigned to the noncontrolling interest is the noncontrolling interest's proportionate share of the subsidiary's income realized in transactions with parties external to the consolidated entity. Income assigned to the noncontrolling interest in the downstream example is computed as follows:

Southern's net income	$60,000
Proportionate share to noncontrolling interest	× 0.25
Income assigned to noncontrolling interest	$15,000

Income assigned to the noncontrolling interest in the upstream example is computed as follows:

Southern's net income	$60,000
Less: Unrealized gain on upstream asset sale	(10,000)
Southern's realized net income	$50,000
Proportionate share to noncontrolling interest	× 0.25
Income assigned to noncontrolling interest	$12,500

In the downstream example, the $10,000 of unrealized intercompany profit is recognized on the parent company's books; therefore, the noncontrolling interest is not affected by the unrealized gain on the downstream intercompany transaction. The entire $60,000 of the subsidiary's income is realized in transactions with parties external to the consolidated entity. In the upstream example, the subsidiary's income includes $10,000 of unrealized intercompany profit. The amount of the subsidiary's income realized in transactions with external parties is only $50,000 ($60,000 less $10,000 of unrealized intercompany profit).

LO3

Prepare equity-method journal entries and elimination entries for the consolidation of a subsidiary following a upstream land transfer.

Advanced
StudyGuide
.com

Downstream Sale of Land

As in Chapter 6, assume that Peerless Products purchases 80 percent of the common stock of Special Foods on December 31, 20X0, for its book value of $240,000, and that the fair value of Special Foods' noncontrolling interest on that date is equal to its book value of $60,000. Assume that during 20X1, Peerless reports separate income of $140,000 income from regular operations and declares dividends of $60,000. Special Foods reports net income of $50,000 and declares dividends of $30,000. In addition, on July 1, 20X1, Peerless sells land to Special Foods for $35,000. Peerless had originally purchased the land on January 1, 20X1, for $20,000, resulting in an unrealized gain of $15,000.[3] Special Foods continues to hold the land through 20X1 and subsequent years.

Fully Adjusted Equity-Method Entries—20X1

During 20X1, Peerless records its share of Special Foods' income and dividends with the usual fully adjusted equity-method entries:

(5)	Investment in Special Foods	40,000	
	Income from Special Foods		40,000
	Record Peerless' 80% share of Special Foods' 20X1 income.		

[3] To avoid additional complexity, we assume the land's fair value is equal to its book value on the business combination date. As a result, there is no differential related to the land.

| (6) | Cash | 24,000 | |
| | Investment in Special Foods | | 24,000 |

Record Peerless' 80% share of Special Foods' 20X1 dividend.

Under the fully adjusted equity method, since the downstream sale of land to Special Foods results in a $15,000 unrealized gain, Peerless makes an adjustment in the equity accounts to reduce the income from Special Foods on the income statement and Investment in Special Foods on the balance sheet by its share of the unrealized gain. Since this is a downstream transaction, the sale (and associated unrealized gain) resides on Peerless' income statement. Since we assume the NCI shareholders do not own Peerless stock, they do not share in the deferral of the unrealized gain.

Under the fully adjusted equity method, Peerless Inc. defers the entire $15,000 using the following equity-method entry:

| (7) | Income from Special Foods | 15,000 | |
| | Investment in Special Foods | | 15,000 |

Defer gain on intercompany land sale to Special Foods.

Note that this entry accomplishes two important objectives. First, since Peerless' income is overstated by $15,000, the adjustment to Income from Special Foods offsets this overstatement so that Peerless' bottom-line net income is now correct. Second, Special Foods' land account is currently overstated by $15,000 (because the land was originally acquired by Peerless for $20,000, but it is now recorded at $35,000 on Special Foods' books). Since the Investment in Special Foods account summarizes Peerless' investment in Special Foods' balance sheet, this reduction to the investment account offsets the fact that Special Foods' land (and thus entire balance sheet) is overstated by $15,000. Thus, after making this equity-method adjustment to defer the unrealized gain on the sale of land, Peerless' financial statements are now correctly stated. Therefore, Peerless' reported income will be exactly equal to the controlling interest in net income on the consolidated financial statements.

On December 31, 20X1, the Peerless' equity-method accounts appear as follows:

	Investment in Special Foods				Income from Special Foods		
Acquisition	240,000						
80% NI	40,000					40,000	80% NI
		24,000	80% Dividends				
		15,000	Defer Gain	15,000			
Ending Balance	241,000					25,000	Ending Balance

Consolidation Worksheet—20X1

We present the consolidation worksheet prepared at the end of 20X1 in Figure 7–2. The first two elimination entries are the same as originally presented in Chapter 3 with one minor exception. While the analysis of the "book value" portion of the investment account is the same, in preparing the basic elimination entry, we reduce the amounts in the Income from Special Foods and Investment in Special Foods accounts by the $15,000 gain deferral.

Book Value Calculations:

	NCI 20%	+ Peerless 80%	= Common Stock	+ Retained Earnings
Original book value	60,000	240,000	200,000	100,000
+ Net income	10,000	40,000		50,000
− Dividends	(6,000)	(24,000)		(30,000)
Ending book value	64,000	256,000	200,000	120,000

Basic investment account elimination entry:

Common stock	200,000		← Original amount invested (100%)
Retained earnings	100,000		← Beginning RE from trial balance
Income from Special Foods	25,000		← Peerless' % of NI − Deferred Gain
NCI in NI of Special Foods	10,000		← NCI share of reported NI
Dividends declared		30,000	← 100% of sub's dividends declared
Investment in Special Foods		241,000	← Net BV − Deferred Gain
NCI in NA of Special Foods		64,000	← NCI share of net book value

Optional accumulated depreciation elimination entry:

Accumulated depreciation	300,000		← Original depreciation at the time of the acquisition netted against cost
Building and equipment		300,000	

Moreover, although Peerless recorded an equity-method entry to defer the unrealized gain on the sale of land, both the Income from Special Foods and Investment in Special Foods accounts are eliminated with the basic elimination entry. Therefore, based on the remaining numbers appearing in the trial balance, Peerless' income is overstated by the gain ($15,000). Moreover, Special Foods' land account is still overstated by $15,000. Simply adding up the Peerless and Special Foods columns of the consolidation worksheet will result in overstated consolidated net income, total assets, and retained earnings. Therefore, we also record an eliminating entry to correct the unadjusted totals to the appropriate consolidated amounts. In doing so, consolidated income is reduced by $15,000 when the gain is eliminated. In addition, land reported on Special Foods' books is stated at the intercompany sale price rather than the historical cost to the consolidated entity. Until resold to an external party by Special Foods, the carrying value of the land must be reduced by the amount of unrealized intercompany gain each time consolidated statements are prepared.

Eliminate gain on sale of land to Special Foods:

Gain on Sale of Land	15,000	
Land		15,000

In sum, because the land is still held within the consolidated entity, the $15,000 gain recognized on Peerless' books must be eliminated in the consolidation worksheet so that it does not appear in the consolidated income statement. Similarly, the land must appear in the consolidated balance sheet at its $20,000 original cost to the consolidated entity and, therefore, must be reduced from the $35,000 amount carried on Special Foods' books.

FIGURE 7–2 **December 31, 20X1, Consolidation Worksheet, Period of Intercompany Sale; Downstream Sale of Land**

	Peerless Products	Special Foods	Elimination Entries		Consolidated
			DR	CR	
Income Statement					
Sales	400,000	200,000			600,000
Less: COGS	(170,000)	(115,000)			(285,000)
Less: Depreciation Expense	(50,000)	(20,000)			(70,000)
Less: Other Expenses	(40,000)	(15,000)			(55,000)
Gain on Sale of Land	15,000		15,000		0
Income from Special Foods	25,000		25,000		0
Consolidated Net Income	180,000	50,000	40,000	0	190,000
NCI in Net Income			10,000		(10,000)
Controlling Interest Net Income	**180,000**	**50,000**	**50,000**	**0**	**180,000**
Statement of Retained Earnings					
Beginning Balance	300,000	100,000	100,000		300,000
Net Income	**180,000**	**50,000**	50,000	0	180,000
Less: Dividends Declared	(60,000)	(30,000)		30,000	(60,000)
Ending Balance	**420,000**	**120,000**	**150,000**	**30,000**	**420,000**
Balance Sheet					
Cash	299,000	40,000			339,000
Accounts Receivable	75,000	50,000			125,000
Inventory	100,000	75,000			175,000
Investment in Special Foods	241,000			241,000	0
Land	155,000	75,000		15,000	215,000
Buildings & Equipment	800,000	600,000		300,000	1,100,000
Less: Accumulated Depreciation	(450,000)	(320,000)	300,000		(470,000)
Total Assets	**1,220,000**	**520,000**	**300,000**	**556,000**	**1,484,000**
Accounts Payable	100,000	100,000			200,000
Bonds Payable	200,000	100,000			300,000
Common Stock	500,000	200,000	200,000		500,000
Retained Earnings	420,000	120,000	150,000	30,000	420,000
NCI in NA of Special Foods				64,000	64,000
Total Liabilities & Equity	**1,220,000**	**520,000**	**350,000**	**94,000**	**1,484,000**

Consolidated Net Income

The 20X1 consolidated net income is computed and allocated as follows:

Peerless' separate income	$155,000
Less: Unrealized intercompany gain on downstream land sale	(15,000)
Peerless' separate realized income	$140,000
Special Foods' net income	50,000
Consolidated net income, 20X1	$190,000
Income to noncontrolling interest ($50,000 × 0.20)	(10,000)
Income to controlling interest	$180,000

Noncontrolling Interest

The noncontrolling stockholders' share of consolidated net income is limited to their proportionate share of the subsidiary's income. Special Foods' net income for 20X1 is $50,000, and the noncontrolling stockholders' ownership interest is 20 percent. Therefore, income of $10,000 ($50,000 × 0.20) is allocated to the noncontrolling interest.

As shown in Figure 7–2, the total noncontrolling interest at the end of 20X1 is $64,000. Normally the noncontrolling interest's claim on the subsidiary's net assets at a particular date is equal to a proportionate share of the subsidiary's book value and remaining differential at that date. In this example, the subsidiary's acquisition-date fair value and book value are equal, and, thus, no differential is associated with the combination. Accordingly, the noncontrolling interest on December 31, 20X1, is equal to a proportionate share of Special Foods' book value:

Book value of Special Foods, December 31, 20X1:	
Common stock	$200,000
Retained earnings	120,000
Total book value	$320,000
Noncontrolling stockholders' proportionate share	× 0.20
Noncontrolling interest, December 31, 20X1	$ 64,000

The noncontrolling interest is unaffected by the unrealized gain on the downstream sale.

Upstream Sale of Land

An upstream sale of land results in the recording of an intercompany gain on the subsidiary's books. If the profits are unrealized from a consolidated viewpoint, they must not be included in the consolidated financial statements. Unrealized intercompany gains are eliminated from the consolidation worksheet in the same manner as in the downstream case. However, the gain elimination reduces both the controlling and the noncontrolling interests in proportion to their ownership.

When an upstream asset sale occurs and the asset is resold by the parent to a nonaffiliate during the same period, all the parent's equity-method entries and the eliminating entries in the consolidation worksheet are identical to those in the downstream case. When the asset is not resold to a nonaffiliate before the end of the period, worksheet eliminating entries are different from the downstream case only by the apportionment of the unrealized intercompany gain to both the controlling and noncontrolling interests. In this case, since the sale appears on Special Foods' income statement and since the NCI shareholders own 20 percent of Special Foods' outstanding shares, they are entitled to 20 percent of Special Foods' net income. Thus, the deferral of the unrealized gain accrues to both Peerless and the NCI shareholders. In other words, the intercompany gain on an upstream sale is recognized by the subsidiary and shared between the controlling and noncontrolling stockholders of the subsidiary. Therefore, the elimination of the unrealized intercompany profit must reduce the interests of both ownership groups each period until the profit is confirmed by resale of the asset to a nonaffiliated party.

The treatment of an upstream sale may be illustrated with the same example used to illustrate a downstream sale. In this case, Special Foods recognizes a $15,000 gain from selling the land to Peerless in addition to the $50,000 of income earned from its regular operations; thus, Special Foods' net income for 20X1 is $65,000. Peerless' separate income is $140,000 and comes entirely from its normal operations.

The upstream sale from Special Foods to Peerless is as follows:

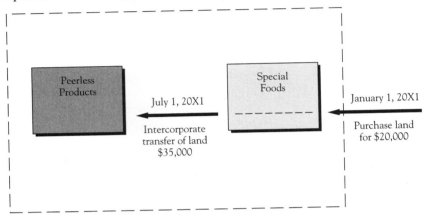

Consolidated Entity

Fully Adjusted Equity-Method Entries—20X1

During 20X1, Peerless records the normal entries under the fully adjusted equity method, reflecting its share of Special Foods' income and dividends:

(8)	Investment in Special Foods	52,000	
	Income from Special Foods		52,000
	Record Peerless' 80% share of Special Foods' 20X1 income.		

(9)	Cash	24,000	
	Investment in Special Foods		24,000
	Record Peerless' 80% share of Special Foods' 20X1 dividend.		

These entries are the same as in the illustration of the downstream sale. The only difference is in the fully adjusted equity-method entry to defer the unrealized gain. The difference is that deferral is only for Peerless' ownership percentage of Special Foods (80 percent). Thus, the deferral of Peerless' relative share of the unrealized gross profit is $12,000 ($15,000 × 0.80).

(10)	Income from Special Foods	12,000	
	Investment in Special Foods		12,000
	Eliminate unrealized gain on the sale of land to Special Foods.		

Peerless' equity-method accounts appear as follows at the end of 20X1:

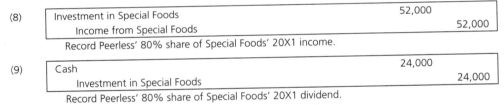

FIGURE 7–3   December 31, 20X1, Consolidation Worksheet, Period of Intercompany Sale; Upstream Sale of Land

	Peerless Products	Special Foods	Elimination Entries DR	Elimination Entries CR	Consolidated
Income Statement					
Sales	400,000	200,000			600,000
Less: COGS	(170,000)	(115,000)			(285,000)
Less: Depreciation Expense	(50,000)	(20,000)			(70,000)
Less: Other Expenses	(40,000)	(15,000)			(55,000)
Gain on Sale of Land		15,000	15,000		0
Income from Special Foods	40,000		40,000		0
Consolidated Net Income	180,000	65,000	55,000	0	190,000
NCI in Net Income			10,000		(10,000)
Controlling Interest Net Income	**180,000**	**65,000**	**65,000**	**0**	**180,000**
Statement of Retained Earnings					
Beginning Balance	300,000	100,000	100,000		300,000
Net Income	**180,000**	**65,000**	**65,000**	**0**	180,000
Less: Dividends Declared	(60,000)	(30,000)		30,000	(60,000)
Ending Balance	**420,000**	**135,000**	**165,000**	**30,000**	**420,000**
Balance Sheet					
Cash	299,000	110,000			339,000
Accounts Receivable	75,000	50,000			125,000
Inventory	100,000	75,000			175,000
Investment in Special Foods	256,000			256,000	0
Land	210,000	20,000		15,000	215,000
Buildings & Equipment	800,000	600,000		300,000	1,100,000
Less: Accumulated Depreciation	(450,000)	(320,000)	300,000		(470,000)
Total Assets	**1,220,000**	**535,000**	**300,000**	**571,000**	**1,484,000**
Accounts Payable	100,000	100,000			200,000
Bonds Payable	200,000	100,000			300,000
Common Stock	500,000	200,000	200,000		500,000
Retained Earnings	**420,000**	**135,000**	165,000	30,000	420,000
NCI in NA of Special Foods				64,000	64,000
Total Liabilities & Equity	**1,220,000**	**535,000**	**365,000**	**94,000**	**1,484,000**

Consolidation Worksheet—20X1

Figure 7–3 illustrates the consolidation worksheet prepared at the end of 20X1. The first two elimination entries are the same as we prepared in Chapter 3 with one minor exception. While the analysis of the "book value" portion of the investment account is the same, in preparing the basic elimination entry, we reduce the amounts in Peerless' Income from Special Foods and Investment in Special Foods accounts by Peerless' share of the deferral, $12,000 ($15,000 × 0.80). We also reduce the NCI in Net Income of Special Foods and NCI in Net Assets of Special Foods by the NCI's share of the deferral, $3,000 ($15,000 × 0.20).

Book Value Calculations:

	NCI 20%	+ Peerless 80%	= Common Stock	+ Retained Earnings
Original book value	60,000	240,000	200,000	100,000
+ Net income	13,000	52,000		65,000
− Dividends	(6,000)	(24,000)		(30,000)
Ending book value	67,000	268,000	200,000	135,000

Basic investment account elimination entry:

Common stock	200,000		← Original amount invested (100%)
Retained earnings	100,000		← Beginning RE from trial balance
Income from Special Foods	40,000		← Peerless' % of NI − 80% Def. Gain
NCI in NI of Special Foods	10,000		← NCI share of NI − 20% Def. Gain
Dividends declared		30,000	← 100% of sub's dividends declared
Investment in Special Foods		256,000	← Net BV − 80% Def. Gain
NCI in NA of Special Foods		64,000	← NCI share of BV − 20% Def. Gain

Optional accumulated depreciation elimination entry:

Accumulated depreciation	300,000		← Original depreciation at the time of
Building and equipment		300,000	the acquisition netted against cost

The consolidation worksheet entry to correct for the intercompany sale is identical to the downstream case. The only difference is that the unrealized gain (and overstated income) is now in Special Foods' column of the consolidation worksheet and the overstated land is now in Peerless' column.

Eliminate gain on purchase of land from Special Foods:

Gain on Sale of Land	15,000	
Land		15,000

Consolidated Net Income

When intercompany profits that are unrealized from a consolidated point of view are included in the income of a subsidiary, consolidated net income and the noncontrolling stockholders' share of income both must be adjusted for the unrealized profits. Consolidated net income for 20X1 is computed and allocated as follows:

Peerless' separate income		$140,000
Special Foods' net income	$65,000	
Less: Unrealized intercompany gain on upstream land sale	(15,000)	
Special Foods' realized net income		50,000
Consolidated net income, 20X1		$190,000
Income to noncontrolling interest ($50,000 × 0.20)		(10,000)
Income to controlling interest		$180,000

Consolidated net income in this year is the same whether or not there is an intercompany sale because the gain is unrealized. The unrealized gain must be eliminated fully, with consolidated net income based only on the realized income of the two affiliates.

Noncontrolling Interest

The income assigned to the noncontrolling shareholders is computed as their proportionate share of the realized income of Special Foods, as follows:

Special Foods' net income	$65,000
Less: Unrealized intercompany profit on upstream land sale	(15,000)
Special Foods' realized income	$50,000
Proportionate share to noncontrolling interest	× 0.20
Income to noncontrolling interest	$10,000

The total noncontrolling interest in the net assets of Special Foods is computed, in the absence of a differential, as the noncontrolling stockholders' proportionate share of the stockholders' equity of Special Foods, excluding unrealized gains and losses. On December 31, 20X1, the noncontrolling interest totals $64,000, computed as follows:

Book value of Special Foods, December 31, 20X1:	
Common stock	$200,000
Retained earnings	135,000
Total book value	$335,000
Unrealized intercompany gain on upstream land sale	(15,000)
Realized book value of Special Foods	$320,000
Noncontrolling stockholders' proportionate share	× 0.20
Noncontrolling interest, December 31, 20X1	$ 64,000

Eliminating the Unrealized Gain after the First Year

In the period in which unrealized profits arise from an intercorporate sale, worksheet eliminating entries are used in the consolidation process to remove the gain or loss recorded by the seller and to adjust the reported amount of the asset back to the price originally paid by the selling affiliate. Each period thereafter while the asset is held by the purchasing affiliate, the reported asset balance and the shareholder claims of the selling affiliate are adjusted to remove the effects of the unrealized gain or loss. Income in those subsequent periods is not affected. For example, if Special Foods continues to hold the land purchased from Peerless Products, the following eliminating entry is needed in the consolidation worksheet each time a consolidated balance sheet is prepared for years following the year of intercompany sale, for as long as the inventory is held:

Investment in Special Foods	15,000	
Land		15,000

This elimination entry simply corrects the balance in both the Land and Investment in Special Foods accounts. Whereas Peerless recorded an equity-method adjustment to defer the $15,000 of unrealized gain on the sale of land in the year of the intercompany land transfer by artificially decreasing the Investment in Special Foods to offset the overstated land balance on Special Foods' books, this entry simply corrects both accounts. No income statement adjustments are needed in the periods following the intercorporate sale until the inventory is resold to parties external to the consolidated entity.

In the upstream case, the subsidiary recognizes the intercompany gain. In the consolidation worksheet prepared in years subsequent to the intercompany transfer while the land is held by the parent, the unrealized intercompany gain is eliminated from the reported balance of the land and proportionately from the subsidiary ownership interests with the following entry:

Investment in Special Foods	12,000	
NCI in NA of Special Foods	3,000	
Land		15,000

All other elimination entries are made as if there is no unrealized intercompany gain.

Subsequent Disposition of the Asset

Unrealized profits on intercompany sales of assets are viewed as being realized at the time the assets are resold to external parties. When a transferred asset is subsequently sold to an external party, the gain or loss recognized by the affiliate selling to the external party must be adjusted for consolidated reporting by the amount of the previously unrealized (and deferred) intercompany gain or loss. While the seller's reported profit on the external sale is based on that affiliate's cost, the gain or loss reported by the consolidated entity is based on the cost of the asset to the consolidated entity, which is the cost incurred by the affiliate that purchased the asset originally from an outside party.

When previously unrealized intercompany profits are realized, the effects of the profit deferral must be reversed. At the time of realization, the full amount of the deferred intercompany profit is added back into the consolidated income computation and assigned to the shareholder interests from which it originally was eliminated.

To illustrate the treatment of unrealized intercompany profits once the transferred asset is resold, assume that Peerless purchases land from an outside party for $20,000 on January 1, 20X1, and sells the land to Special Foods on July 1, 20X1, for $35,000. Special Foods subsequently sells the land to an outside party on March 1, 20X5, for $45,000, as follows:

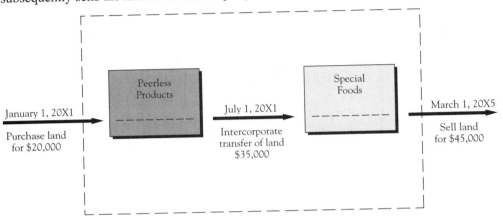

Consolidated Entity

Special Foods recognizes a gain on the sale to the outside party of $10,000 ($45,000 − $35,000). From a consolidated viewpoint, however, the gain is $25,000, the difference between the price at which the land left the consolidated entity ($45,000) and the price at which the land entered the consolidated entity ($20,000) when it was originally purchased by Peerless. Peerless would record an equity-method entry on its books to reverse the original deferral entry (7).

In the consolidation worksheet, the land no longer needs to be reduced by the unrealized intercompany gain because the gain now is realized and the consolidated entity no longer holds the land. Instead, the $10,000 gain recognized by Special Foods on the sale of the land to an outsider must be adjusted to reflect a total gain for the consolidated entity of $25,000. Thus, the following eliminating entry is made in the consolidation worksheet prepared at the end of 20X5:

Investment in Special Foods	15,000	
Gain on sale of land		15,000

All other elimination entries are the same as if there were no unrealized intercompany profits at the beginning of the period. No additional consideration need be given to the intercompany transfer in periods subsequent to the external sale. From a consolidated viewpoint, all aspects of the transaction are complete, and the profit is realized once the sale to an external party occurs.

In this example, if the sale to the external party had been made by Peerless following an upstream intercompany transfer from Special Foods, the worksheet treatment would be the same as in the case of the downstream transfer except that the debit would be prorated between Investment in Special Foods ($12,000) and NCI in Net Assets of Special Foods ($3,000) based on the relative ownership interests.

Investment in Special Foods	12,000	
NCI in NA of Special Foods	3,000	
Gain on sale of land		15,000

INTERCOMPANY TRANSFERS OF DEPRECIABLE ASSETS

Unrealized intercompany profits on a depreciable or amortizable asset are viewed as being realized gradually over the remaining economic life of the asset as it is used by the purchasing affiliate in generating revenue from unaffiliated parties. In effect, a portion of the unrealized gain or loss is realized each period as benefits are derived from the asset and its service potential expires.

The amount of depreciation recognized on a company's books each period on an asset purchased from an affiliate is based on the intercorporate transfer price. From a consolidated viewpoint, however, depreciation must be based on the cost of the asset to the consolidated entity, which is the asset's cost to the affiliate company that originally purchased it from an outsider. Eliminating entries are needed in the consolidation worksheet to restate the asset, associated accumulated depreciation, and depreciation expense to the amounts that would have appeared in the financial statements if there had been no intercompany transfer. Because the intercompany sale takes place totally within the consolidated entity, the consolidated financial statements must appear as if the intercompany transfer had never occurred.

Downstream Sale

LO5

Prepare equity-method journal entries and elimination entries for the consolidation of a subsidiary following a downstream depreciable asset transfer.

Advanced StudyGuide .com

We now modify the Peerless Products and Special Foods example to illustrate the downstream sale of a depreciable asset. Assume that Peerless sells equipment to Special Foods on December 31, 20X1, for $7,000, as follows:

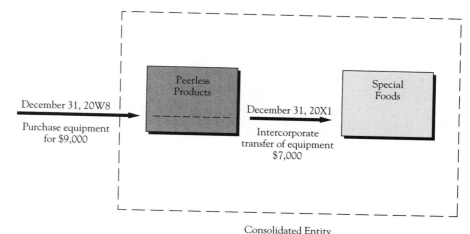

Consolidated Entity

The equipment originally cost Peerless $9,000 when purchased on December 31, 20W8, three years before the December 31, 20X1 sale to Special Foods. Assume that the equipment has been depreciated based on an estimated useful life of 10 years using the straight-line method with no residual value. The book value of the equipment immediately before the sale by Peerless is computed as follows:

Original cost to Peerless		$9,000
Accumulated depreciation on December 31, 20X1:		
Annual depreciation ($9,000 ÷ 10 years)	$900	
Number of years	× 3	
		(2,700)
Book value on December 31, 20X1		$6,300

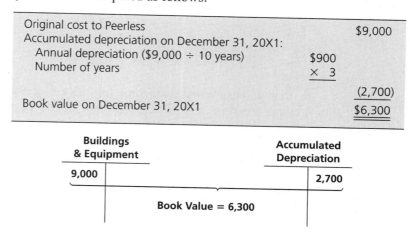

The gain recognized by Peerless on the intercompany sale of the equipment is

Sale price of the equipment	$7,000
Less: Book value of the equipment	(6,300)
Gain on sale of the equipment	$ 700

Separate-Company Entries—20X1

Special Foods records the purchase of the equipment at its cost:

December 31, 20X1

(11)	Equipment	7,000	
	Cash		7,000
	Record purchase of equipment.		

Special Foods does not depreciate the equipment during 20X1 because the equipment is purchased at the very end of 20X1. However, Peerless does record depreciation expense on the equipment for 20X1 because it holds the asset until the end of the year (and the 20X1 depreciation expense is recorded prior to calculating the gain on sale shown above):

December 31, 20X1

(12)	Depreciation Expense	900	
	Accumulated Depreciation		900
	Record 20X1 depreciation expense on equipment sold.		

Peerless also records the sale of the equipment at the end of 20X1 and recognizes the $700 ($7,000 − $6,300) gain on the sale:

December 31, 20X1

(13)	Cash	7,000	
	Accumulated Depreciation	2,700	
	Equipment		9,000
	Gain on Sale of Equipment		700
	Record sale of equipment.		

In addition, Peerless records the normal fully adjusted equity-method entries to recognize its share of Special Foods' income and dividends for 20X1:

(14)	Investment in Special Foods Stock	40,000	
	Income from Special Foods		40,000
	Record equity-method income: $50,000 × 0.80		

(15)	Cash	24,000	
	Investment in Special Foods Stock		24,000
	Record dividends from Special Foods: $30,000 × 0.80		

In order to ensure that its income for 20X1 is correct, under the fully adjusted equity method, Peerless also defers the gain on the intercompany sale of equipment as follows:

(16)	Income from Special Foods	700	
	Investment in Special Foods		700
	Defer unrealized gain on asset sale to Special Foods.		

Thus, Peerless' equity-method accounts appear as follows at the end of 20X1:

	Investment in Special Foods				Income from Special Foods	
Acquisition	240,000					
80% NI	40,000				40,000	80% NI
		24,000	80% Dividends			
		700	Defer Gain	700		
Ending Balance	255,300				39,300	Ending Balance

Consolidation Worksheet—20X1

Figure 7–4 illustrates the worksheet to prepare consolidated financial statements at the end of 20X1. In order to prepare the basic elimination entry, we first analyze the book value of Special Foods and allocate each component to Peerless and the NCI shareholders:

Book Value Calculations:

	NCI 20%	+ Peerless 80%	=	Common Stock	+ Retained Earnings
Original book value	60,000	240,000		200,000	100,000
+ Net income	10,000	40,000			50,000
− Dividends	(6,000)	(24,000)			(30,000)
Ending book value	64,000	256,000		200,000	120,000

The basic elimination entry is the same as illustrated in Chapter 3 except that we adjust the entries to the Investment in Special Foods and Income from Special Foods accounts for the gain that has been deferred on the intercompany asset sale:

Basic investment account elimination entry:

Common stock	200,000		← Original amount invested (100%)
Retained earnings	100,000		← Beginning RE from trial balance
Income from Special Foods	39,300		← Peerless' % of NI − Def. Gain
NCI in NI of Special Foods	10,000		← NCI share of reported NI
Dividends declared		30,000	← 100% of sub's dividends declared
Investment in Special Foods		255,300	← Net BV − Def. Gain
NCI in NA of Special Foods		64,000	← NCI share of net amount of BV

Optional accumulated depreciation elimination entry:

Accumulated depreciation	300,000		← Original depreciation at the time of
Building and equipment		300,000	the acquisition netted against cost

Although Peerless recorded an equity-method entry to defer the unrealized gain on the equipment sale, both the Income from Special Foods and Investment in Special Foods accounts are eliminated with the basic elimination entry. Peerless' income is overstated by the gain ($700). Moreover, Special Foods' Building and Equipment account is overstated by the same amount. Therefore we need an additional elimination entry to remove the gain that appears in Peerless' income statement and to correct the basis of the equipment on Special Foods' books to make it appear as if the asset had not been sold within the consolidated group. One way to calculate this elimination entry is to compare what actually happened (as recorded on the individual financial statements of the two companies) with how we want the transaction to appear in the consolidated financial statements. Whereas the equipment currently

FIGURE 7–4 December 31, 20X1, Consolidation Worksheet, Period of Intercompany Sale; Downstream

	Peerless Products	Special Foods	Elimination Entries DR	Elimination Entries CR	Consolidated
Income Statement					
Sales	400,000	200,000			600,000
Less: COGS	(170,000)	(115,000)			(285,000)
Less: Depreciation Expense	(50,000)	(20,000)			(70,000)
Less: Other Expenses	(40,000)	(15,000)			(55,000)
Gain on sale of fixed asset	700		700		0
Income from Special Foods	39,300		39,300		0
Consolidated Net Income	180,000	50,000	40,000	0	190,000
NCI in Net Income			10,000		(10,000)
Controlling Interest Net Income	**180,000**	**50,000**	**50,000**	**0**	**180,000**
Statement of Retained Earnings					
Beginning Balance	300,000	100,000	100,000		300,000
Net Income	180,000	50,000	50,000	0	180,000
Less: Dividends Declared	(60,000)	(30,000)		30,000	(60,000)
Ending Balance	**420,000**	**120,000**	**150,000**	**30,000**	**420,000**
Balance Sheet					
Cash	271,000	68,000			339,000
Accounts Receivable	75,000	50,000			125,000
Inventory	100,000	75,000			175,000
Investment in Special Foods	255,300			255,300	0
Land	175,000	40,000			215,000
Buildings & Equipment	791,000	607,000	2,000	300,000	1,100,000
Less: Accumulated Depreciation	(447,300)	(320,000)	300,000	2,700	(470,000)
Total Assets	**1,220,000**	**520,000**	**302,000**	**558,000**	**1,484,000**
Accounts Payable	100,000	100,000			200,000
Bonds Payable	200,000	100,000			300,000
Common Stock	500,000	200,000	200,000		500,000
Retained Earnings	420,000	120,000	150,000	30,000	420,000
NCI in NA of Special Foods				64,000	64,000
Total Liabilities & Equity	**1,220,000**	**520,000**	**350,000**	**94,000**	**1,484,000**

resides on Special Foods' books (valued at the acquisition price of $7,000 with no accumulated depreciation), we want it to appear in the consolidated financial statements as if it had not been transferred from Peerless to Special Foods (historical cost of $9,000 with accumulated depreciation of $2,700 as explained previously). The following T-accounts illustrate how to determine the correct elimination entry to defer the gain and correct the basis of the asset:

	Buildings & Equipment		Accumulated Depreciation	
Special Foods	7,000		Actual	0
	2,000			2,700
Peerless	9,000		"As if"	2,700

Eliminate gain on the equipment sold to Special Foods and correct the assets' basis:

Gain on Sale	700	
Buildings and Equipment	2,000	
Accumulated Depreciation		2,700

Separate-Company Entries—20X2

During 20X2, Special Foods begins depreciating the $7,000 cost of the equipment acquired from Peerless Products over its remaining life of seven years using straight-line depreciation. The resulting depreciation is $1,000 per year ($7,000 ÷ 7 years):

(17)	Depreciation Expense	1,000	
	Accumulated Depreciation		1,000
	Record depreciation expense for 20X2.		

Peerless records its normal equity-method entries for 20X2 to reflect its share of Special Foods' $74,000 income and dividends of $40,000. Note that Special Foods' net income is only $74,000 in 20X2 because it has been reduced by the $1,000 of depreciation on the transferred asset. Accordingly, Peerless' share of that income is $59,200 ($74,000 × 0.80).

(18)	Investment in Special Foods	59,200	
	Income from Subsidiary		59,200
	Record equity-method income: $74,000 × 0.80		

(19)	Cash	32,000	
	Investment in Special Foods		32,000
	Record dividends from Special Foods: $40,000 × 0.80		

Peerless must record one additional equity-method entry related to the transferred asset. Because the equipment was recorded at the time of the December 31, 20X1 sale on Special Foods' balance sheet at $7,000 (rather than the $6,300 book value at which it had been recorded on Peerless' books), Special Foods will record "extra" depreciation expense each year over the seven-year life of the asset. Special Foods' annual depreciation ($7,000 ÷ 7 years = $1,000 per year) is $100 per year higher than it would have been if Peerless had kept the equipment ($900 per year).

Gain =	÷ 7 =	**100**	**Extra depreciation**
700			
BV =	÷ 7 =	**900**	**Peerless' depreciation**
6,300			
		1,000	**Total depreciation**

Special Foods' extra depreciation essentially cancels out one-seventh of the unrealized gain. As a result, over the seven-year life of the asset, the unrealized gain is offset by the $700 of extra depreciation expense. Thus, in 20X2 (and each of the next six years) Peerless reverses out one-seventh of the gain deferral in it equity-method accounts as follows:

(20)	Investment in Special Foods	100	
	Income from Special Foods		100
	Reverse one-seventh of the deferred gain on fixed asset sold to Special Foods.		

Consolidation Worksheet—20X2

Figure 7–5 presents the consolidation worksheet for 20X2. The trial balance amounts from the Chapter 3 example have been adjusted to reflect the intercompany asset sale. In order to prepare the basic elimination entry, we again analyze the updated book value of Special Foods and examine the allocation of each component to Peerless and the NCI shareholders. Thus, in order to present the consolidated financial statements as if the equipment had not been transferred to Special Foods, we need to decrease depreciation expense to the amount Peerless would have recorded had the equipment stayed on its books.

Book Value Calculations:

	NCI 20%	+ Peerless 80%	= Common Stock	+ Retained Earnings
Beginning book value	64,000	256,000	200,000	120,000
+ Net income	14,800	59,200		74,000
− Dividends	(8,000)	(32,000)		(40,000)
Ending book value	70,800	283,200	200,000	154,000

The basic elimination entry is the same as illustrated in Chapter 3 except that we adjust the entries to the Investment in Special Foods and Income from Special Foods accounts for the extra $100 of depreciation for 20X2 associated with the asset transfer:

Basic investment account elimination entry:

Common stock	200,000		← Original amount invested (100%)
Retained earnings	120,000		← Beginning RE from trial balance
Income from Special Foods	59,300		← Peerless' % of NI + **extra depr.**
NCI in NI of Special Foods	14,800		← NCI share of reported NI
Dividends declared		40,000	← 100% of sub's dividends declared
Investment in Special Foods		283,300	← Net BV + **extra depr.**
NCI in NA of Special Foods		70,800	← NCI share of net amount of BV

Optional accumulated depreciation elimination entry:

Accumulated depreciation	300,000		← Original depreciation at the time of
Building and equipment		300,000	the acquisition netted against cost

In the 20X2 worksheet, two consolidation elimination entries are necessary. The first revalues the asset from its current book value on Special Foods' books to what its book value would have been if it had stayed on Peerless' books. The second corrects depreciation expense by adjusting it to what it would have been if the asset had stayed on Peerless' books. Again, T-accounts can be a helpful tool in figuring out the elimination entries:

	Buildings & Equipment			Accumulated Depreciation	
Special Foods	7,000		Actual		1,000
	2,000			100	2,700
Peerless	9,000		"As if"		3,600

Entries to adjust equipment and accumulated depreciation "as if" still on parent's books:

Investment in Special Foods	700	
Buildings and Equipment	2,000	
Accumulated Depreciation		2,700

Accumulated Depreciation	100	
Depreciation Expense		100

FIGURE 7–5 December 31, 20X2, Consolidation Worksheet, Next Period Following Intercompany Sale; Downstream Sale of Equipment

	Peerless Products	Special Foods	Elimination Entries DR	Elimination Entries CR	Consolidated
Income Statement					
Sales	450,000	300,000			750,000
Less: COGS	(180,000)	(160,000)			(340,000)
Less: Depreciation Expense	(49,100)	(21,000)		100	(70,000)
Less: Other Expenses	(60,000)	(45,000)			(105,000)
Income from Special Foods	59,300		59,300		0
Consolidated Net Income	220,200	74,000	59,300	100	235,000
NCI in Net Income			14,800		(14,800)
Controlling Interest Net Income	**220,200**	**74,000**	**74,100**	**100**	**220,200**
Statement of Retained Earnings					
Beginning Balance	420,000	120,000	120,000		420,000
Net Income	**220,200**	**74,000**	**74,100**	100	220,200
Less: Dividends Declared	(60,000)	(40,000)		40,000	(60,000)
Ending Balance	**580,200**	**154,000**	**194,100**	**40,100**	**580,200**
Balance Sheet					
Cash	298,000	78,000			376,000
Accounts Receivable	150,000	80,000			230,000
Inventory	180,000	90,000			270,000
Investment in Special Foods	282,600		700	283,300	0
Land	175,000	40,000			215,000
Buildings & Equipment	791,000	607,000	2,000	300,000	1,100,000
Less: Accumulated Depreciation	(496,400)	(341,000)	300,000	2,700	(540,000)
			100		
Total Assets	**1,380,200**	**554,000**	**302,700**	**586,000**	**1,651,000**
Accounts Payable	100,000	100,000			200,000
Bonds Payable	200,000	100,000			300,000
Common Stock	500,000	200,000	200,000		500,000
Retained Earnings	**580,200**	**154,000**	**194,100**	**40,100**	580,200
NCI in NA of Special Foods				70,800	70,800
Total Liabilities & Equity	**1,380,200**	**554,000**	**394,100**	**110,900**	**1,651,000**

Note that the debit to the investment account in the first elimination entry is equal to the amount of unrealized gain at the beginning of the year. Given the gain deferral entry in 20X1 under the fully adjusted equity method, the investment account is "artificially low" by $700. Thus, the basic elimination entry would "over-eliminate" this account. Therefore, the debit of $700 helps to eliminate the investment account. The debit to Buildings and Equipment in the first elimination entry is simply the difference between Special Foods' cost ($7,000) and peerless' historical cost ($9,000). The credit to accumulated depreciation in the first elimination entry represents the difference between what accumulated depreciation would have been if the asset had stayed on Peerless' books, $3,600 ($900 × 4 years) and the amount Special Foods actually recorded, $1,000, less the extra depreciation. Finally, the last elimination entry backs out the extra depreciation expense from Special Foods' income statement.

The following T-accounts illustrate how the worksheet entries eliminate the Investment in Special Foods and Income from Special Foods accounts:

Once all the eliminating entries have been made in the worksheet, the adjusted balances exclude the effects of the intercorporate transfer:

	Subsidiary Trial Balance	Elimination	Consolidated Amounts
Buildings and Equipment	$7,000	$2,000	$9,000
Accumulated Depreciation	(1,000)	(2,600)	(3,600)
Depreciation Expense	1,000	(100)	900

Consolidated Net Income and Retained Earnings

Computation of consolidated net income for 20X2 must include an adjustment for the realization of profit on the 20X1 sale of equipment to Special Foods:

Peerless' separate income	$160,900
Partial realization of intercompany gain on downstream sale of equipment	100
Peerless' separate realized income	$161,000
Special Foods' net income	74,000
Consolidated net income, 20X2	$235,000
Income to noncontrolling interest ($74,000 × 0.20)	(14,800)
Income to controlling interest	$220,200

Because Peerless adjusts its investment income from Special Foods for unrealized gains and losses under the fully adjusted equity method, Peerless' retained earnings account equals the amount that should be reported as consolidated retained earnings. This is one of the advantages of using the fully adjusted equity method. Appendix 7A illustrates procedures for the modified equity method.

Noncontrolling Interest

Income allocated to the noncontrolling stockholders in 20X2 is equal to their proportionate share of the subsidiary's realized and reported income. Special Foods' net income for 20X2 is $74,000, and the noncontrolling interest's 20 percent share is $14,800 ($74,000 × 0.20).

The total noncontrolling interest in the net assets of Special Foods at the end of 20X2 is $70,800, equal to the noncontrolling stockholders' proportionate share of the total book value of the subsidiary:

Book value of Special Foods, December 31, 20X2:	
Common stock	$200,000
Retained earnings	154,000
Total book value	$354,000
Noncontrolling stockholders' proportionate share	× 0.20
Noncontrolling interest, December 31, 20X2	$ 70,800

Normally the noncontrolling interest at a particular date is equal to a proportionate share of the subsidiary's book value plus the noncontrolling interest's share of the remaining differential at that date. In this example, however, no differential was recognized at the date of combination.

Consolidation in Subsequent Years

The consolidation procedures in subsequent years are quite similar to those in 20X2. As long as Special Foods continues to hold and depreciate the equipment (i.e., until the asset is fully depreciated), consolidation procedures include two objectives each year:

1. Restating the asset and accumulated depreciation balances.
2. Adjusting depreciation expense for the year.

Figure 7–6 summarizes the worksheet elimination entries at December 31st of each year from 20X1 to 20X8. Observation of the elimination entries from 20X2–20X8 illustrates a clear pattern. Since the extra depreciation recorded each year by Special Foods effectively cancels out one-seventh of the unrealized gain and since Peerless continues to record an equity method adjustment to recognize this "cancelling" of the unrealized gain (Entry #20), the debit to the Investment in Special Foods account and the credit to accumulated depreciation in the first elimination entry each decreases by $100 each year until the asset is fully depreciated and the intercompany gain is fully recognized. The second elimination entry to back out the extra depreciation is the same each year. After 20X8, no further equity-method entries are required on Peerless' books and no further elimination entries are required in consolidation related to this asset transfer.

Change in Estimated Life of Asset upon Transfer

When a depreciable asset is transferred between companies, a change in the remaining estimated economic life may be appropriate. For example, the acquiring company may use the asset in a different type of production process, or the frequency of use may change. When a change in the estimated life of a depreciable asset occurs at the time of an intercorporate transfer, the treatment is no different than if the change had occurred while the asset remained on the books of the transferring affiliate. The new remaining useful life is used as a basis for depreciation both by the purchasing affiliate and for purposes of preparing consolidated financial statements.

Upstream Sale

LO6

Prepare equity-method journal entries and elimination entries for the consolidation of a subsidiary following a downstream depreciable asset transfer.

The treatment of unrealized profits arising from upstream intercompany sales is identical to that of downstream sales except that the unrealized profit, and subsequent realization, must be allocated between the controlling and noncontrolling interests. We illustrate an upstream sale using the same example we demonstrated previously for the downstream sale. Assume that Special Foods sells equipment to Peerless Products for $7,000 on December 31, 20X1, and reports total income for 20X1 of $50,700 ($50,000 + $700),

FIGURE 7–6 Summary of Worksheet Elimination Entries over the Life of the Transferred Asset (Downstream Transfer)

20X1:

Gain on Sale	700	
Buildings and Equipment	2,000	
Accumulated Depreciation		2,700

Note: This is the acquisition date, so Special Foods has not recorded any depreciation.

	Build. & Equip.		Acc. Depr.	
Special Foods:	7,000	Actual		0
	2,000			2,700
Peerless:	9,000	"As if"		2,700

20X2:

Investment in Special Foods	700	
Buildings and Equipment	2,000	
Accumulated Depreciation		2,700

| Accumulated Depreciation | 100 | |
| Depreciation Expense | | 100 |

	Build. & Equip.		Acc. Depr.	
Special Foods:	7,000	Actual		1,000
	2,000		100	2,700
Peerless:	9,000	"As if"		3,600

20X3:

Investment in Special Foods	600	
Buildings and Equipment	2,000	
Accumulated Depreciation		2,600

| Accumulated Depreciation | 100 | |
| Depreciation Expense | | 100 |

	Build. & Equip.		Acc. Depr.	
Special Foods:	7,000	Actual		2,000
	2,000		100	2,600
Peerless:	9,000	"As if"		4,500

20X4:

Investment in Special Foods	500	
Buildings and Equipment	2,000	
Accumulated Depreciation		2,500

| Accumulated Depreciation | 100 | |
| Depreciation Expense | | 100 |

	Build. & Equip.		Acc. Depr.	
Special Foods:	7,000	Actual		3,000
	2,000		100	2,500
Peerless:	9,000	"As if"		5,400

20X5:

Investment in Special Foods	400	
Buildings and Equipment	2,000	
Accumulated Depreciation		2,400

| Accumulated Depreciation | 100 | |
| Depreciation Expense | | 100 |

	Build. & Equip.		Acc. Depr.	
Special Foods:	7,000	Actual		4,000
	2,000		100	2,400
Peerless:	9,000	"As if"		6,300

20X6:

Investment in Special Foods	300	
Buildings and Equipment	2,000	
Accumulated Depreciation		2,300

| Accumulated Depreciation | 100 | |
| Depreciation Expense | | 100 |

	Build. & Equip.		Acc. Depr.	
Special Foods:	7,000	Actual		5,000
	2,000		100	2,300
Peerless:	9,000	"As if"		7,200

20X7:

Investment in Special Foods	200	
Buildings and Equipment	2,000	
Accumulated Depreciation		2,200

| Accumulated Depreciation | 100 | |
| Depreciation Expense | | 100 |

	Build. & Equip.		Acc. Depr.	
Special Foods:	7,000	Actual		6,000
	2,000		100	2,200
Peerless:	9,000	"As if"		8,100

20X8:

Investment in Special Foods	100	
Buildings and Equipment	2,000	
Accumulated Depreciation		2,100

| Accumulated Depreciation | 100 | |
| Depreciation Expense | | 100 |

	Build. & Equip.		Acc. Depr.	
Special Foods:	7,000	Actual		7,000
	2,000		100	2,100
Peerless:	9,000	"As if"		9,000

including the $700 gain on the sale of the equipment. Special Foods originally purchased the equipment for $9,000 three years before the intercompany sale.[4] The book value of the equipment at the date of sale is as follows:

Original cost to Special Foods		$9,000
Accumulated depreciation on December 31, 20X1:		
Annual depreciation ($9,000 ÷ 10 years)	$900	
Number of years	× 3	
		(2,700)
Book value on December 31, 20X1		$6,300

Separate-Company Entries—20X1

Special Foods records depreciation on the equipment for the year and the sale of the equipment to Peerless on December 31, 20X1, with the following entries:

December 31, 20X1

(21)
Depreciation Expense	900	
Accumulated Depreciation		900

Record 20X1 depreciation expense on equipment sold.

December 31, 20X1

(22)
Cash	7,000	
Accumulated Depreciation	2,700	
Equipment		9,000
Gain on Sale of Equipment		700

Record sale of equipment.

Peerless records the purchase of the equipment from Special Foods with the following entry:

December 31, 20X1

(23)
Equipment	7,000	
Cash		7,000

Record purchase of equipment.

In addition, Peerless records the following fully adjusted equity-method entries on December 31, 20X1, to recognize its share of Special Foods' reported income and dividends:

(24)
Investment in Special Foods	40,560	
Income from Special Foods		40,560

Record Peerless' 80% share of Special Foods' 20X1 income: $50,700 × 0.80

(25)
Cash	24,000	
Investment in Special Foods		24,000

Record Peerless' 80% share of Special Foods' 20X1 dividend: $30,000 × 0.80

Finally, under the fully adjusted equity method Peerless records its share of the gain deferral from the purchase of the equipment from Special Foods.

(26)
Income from Special Foods	560	
Investment in Special Foods		560

Defer 80% of the unrealized gain on equipment purchase from Special Foods: $700 × 0.80

[4] To avoid additional complexity, we assume the equipment's fair value is equal to its book value on the business combination date. As a result, there is no differential related to the equipment.

These entries result in the following balances in the Investment in Special Foods and Income from Special Foods equity-method accounts:

	Investment in Special Foods				Income from Special Foods		
Acquisition	240,000						
80% NI	40,560					40,560	80% NI
		24,000	80% Dividends				
		560	Defer 80% Gain	560			
Ending Balance	256,000					40,000	Ending Balance

Consolidation Worksheet—20X1

Figure 7–7 illustrates the consolidation worksheet for 20X1. It is the same as the worksheet presented in Figure 7–5 except for minor modifications to reflect the upstream sale of the equipment. As usual, in order to prepare the basic elimination entry, we first analyze the book value of Special Foods and allocate each component to Peerless and the NCI shareholders:

Book Value Calculations:

	NCI 20%	+ Peerless 80%	= Common Stock	+ Retained Earnings
Original book value	60,000	240,000	200,000	100,000
+ Net income	10,140	40,560		50,700
− Dividends	(6,000)	(24,000)		(30,000)
Ending book value	64,140	256,560	200,000	120,700

The basic elimination entry is the same as illustrated in Chapter 3 except that we adjust both the controlling and noncontrolling interests in Special Foods' income and net assets by their respective shares of the gain that has been deferred on the intercompany asset sale:

Basic investment account elimination entry:

Common stock	200,000		← Original amount invested (100%)
Retained earnings	100,000		← Beginning RE from trial balance
Income from Special Foods	40,000		← Peerless' % of NI − 80% Def. Gain
NCI in NI of Special Foods	10,000		← NCI share of NI − 20% Def. Gain
Dividends declared		30,000	← 100% of sub's dividends declared
Investment in Special Foods		256,000	← Net BV − 80% Deferred Gain
NCI in NA of Special Foods		64,000	← NCI share of net BV − 20% Def. Gain

Optional accumulated depreciation elimination entry:

Accumulated depreciation	300,000		← Original depreciation at the time of
Building and equipment		300,000	the acquisition netted against cost

As illustrated previously, one way to calculate the gain elimination entry is to compare what actually happened (as recorded on the individual financial statements of the two companies) with how we want the transaction to appear in the consolidated financial statements. Whereas the equipment currently resides on Peerless' books (valued at the acquisition price of $7,000 with no accumulated depreciation), we want it to appear in the consolidated financial statements as if it had not been transferred from Special Foods to Peerless (historical cost of $9,000 with accumulated depreciation of $2,700, as explained previously). The following T-accounts

FIGURE 7–7   December 31, 20X1, Consolidation Worksheet, Period of Intercompany Sale; Upstream Sale of Equipment

	Peerless Products	Special Foods	Elimination Entries		Consolidated
			DR	CR	
Income Statement					
Sales	400,000	200,000			600,000
Less: COGS	(170,000)	(115,000)			(285,000)
Less: Depreciation Expense	(50,000)	(20,000)			(70,000)
Less: Other Expenses	(40,000)	(15,000)			(55,000)
Gain on sale of fixed asset		700	700		0
Income from Special Foods	40,000		40,000		0
Consolidated Net Income	180,000	50,700	40,700	0	190,000
NCI in Net Income			10,000		(10,000)
Controlling Interest Net Income	**180,000**	**50,700**	**50,700**	**0**	**180,000**
Statement of Retained Earnings					
Beginning Balance	300,000	100,000	100,000		300,000
Net Income	**180,000**	**50,700**	50,700	0	180,000
Less: Dividends Declared	(60,000)	(30,000)		30,000	(60,000)
Ending Balance	**420,000**	**120,700**	**150,700**	**30,000**	**420,000**
Balance Sheet					
Cash	257,000	82,000			339,000
Accounts Receivable	75,000	50,000			125,000
Inventory	100,000	75,000			175,000
Investment in Special Foods	256,000			256,000	0
Land	175,000	40,000			215,000
Buildings & Equipment	807,000	591,000	2,000	300,000	1,100,000
Less: Accumulated Depreciation	(450,000)	(317,300)	300,000	2,700	(470,000)
Total Assets	**1,220,000**	**520,700**	**302,000**	**558,700**	**1,484,000**
Accounts Payable	100,000	100,000			200,000
Bonds Payable	200,000	100,000			300,000
Common Stock	500,000	200,000	200,000		500,000
Retained Earnings	**420,000**	**120,700**	150,700	30,000	420,000
NCI in NA of Special Foods				64,000	64,000
Total Liabilities & Equity	**1,220,000**	**520,700**	**350,700**	**94,000**	**1,484,000**

illustrate how to determine the correct elimination entry to defer the gain and correct the basis of the asset:

	Buildings & Equipment			Accumulated Depreciation	
Peerless	7,000		Actual		0
	2,000				2,700
Special Foods	9,000		"As if"		2,700

Eliminate gain on the equipment sold to Special Foods and correct the assets' basis:

Gain on Sale	700	
Buildings and Equipment	2,000	
Accumulated Depreciation		2,700

As it turns out, the elimination entry for the upstream sale is exactly the same as the downstream example for 20X1.

As illustrated in Figure 7–7, the income assigned to the noncontrolling shareholders based on their share of Special Foods' realized income is computed as follows:

Net income of Special Foods for 20X1	$50,700
Unrealized gain on intercompany sale	(700)
Realized net income of Special Foods for 20X1	$50,000
Noncontrolling stockholders' proportionate share	× 0.20
Income to noncontrolling interest, 20X1	$10,000

In the upstream case, as in the downstream case, consolidated net income is reduced by the amount of the current period's unrealized gain on the intercompany transfer. However, in the upstream case the unrealized gain reduces both the controlling and noncontrolling interests proportionately because both are owners of Special Foods and shared in the gain. The allocation of Special Foods' income to the controlling and noncontrolling interests is based on Special Foods' realized net income after having deducted the unrealized gain. The computation and allocation of 20X1 consolidated net income is as follows:

Peerless' separate income		$140,000
Special Foods' net income	$50,700	
Less: Unrealized intercompany gain on upstream sale of equipment	(700)	
Special Foods' realized net income		50,000
Consolidated net income, 20X1		$190,000
Income to noncontrolling interest ($50,000 × 0.20)		(10,000)
Income to controlling interest		$180,000

Separate-Company Books—20X2

In the year following the intercorporate transfer, Special Foods reports net income of $75,900 (because the $900 of depreciation expense on the transferred asset is now on Peerless' income statement). In the upstream example, the extra $100 of depreciation expense now appears in Peerless' income statement:

Gain = 700	÷ 7 =	100	Extra depreciation
BV = 6,300	÷ 7 =	900	Special Foods' depreciation
		1,000	Total depreciation

Peerless records the normal fully adjusted equity-method entries on its books to recognize its share of Special Foods' 20X2 income and dividends. Moreover, it recognizes 80 percent of the deferred gain, $80 (($700 ÷ 7 years) × 0.80).

Peerless' extra depreciation essentially cancels out one-seventh of the unrealized gain. As a result, over the seven-year life of the asset, Peerless recognizes one-seventh of the gain deferral each year in its equity-method accounts:

(27)	Investment in Special Foods	80	
	Income from Special Foods		80
	Recognize 80% of 1/7 of the deferred gain on fixed asset purchased from Special Foods.		

At the end of 20X2, the Investment in Special Foods and Income from Special Foods accounts on Peerless' books appear as follows:

	Investment in Special Foods				Income from Special Foods	
Beg. Balance	256,000					
80% NI	60,720				60,720	80% NI
Realize		32,000	80% Dividends			Realize
80% of 1/7	80				80	80% of 1/7
Deferred Gain						Deferred Gain
Ending Balance	284,800				60,800	Ending Balance

Consolidation Elimination Entries—20X2

Figure 7–8 presents the consolidation worksheet for 20X2. We again analyze the updated book value of Special Foods and examine the allocation of each component to Peerless and the NCI shareholders. Also, in order to present the consolidated financial statements as if the equipment had not been transferred to Peerless, we need to decrease depreciation expense to the amount Special Foods would have recorded had the equipment stayed on its books.

Book Value Calculations:

	NCI 20%	+ Peerless 80%	= Common Stock	+ Retained Earnings
Beginning book value	64,140	256,560	200,000	120,700
+ Net income	15,180	60,720		75,900
− Dividends	(8,000)	(32,000)		(40,000)
Ending book value	71,320	285,280	200,000	156,600

The basic elimination entry is the same as illustrated in Chapter 3 except that we adjust the entries to the Investment in Special Foods and Income from Special Foods accounts for their 80 percent share of the extra $100 of depreciation for 20X2 associated with the asset transfer. Moreover, we add back 20 percent of the $100 of extra depreciation to the NCI in NI of Special Foods and NCI in NA of Special Foods:

Basic investment account elimination entry:

Common stock	200,000		← Original amount invested (100%)
Retained earnings	120,700		← Beginning RE from trial balance
Income from Special Foods	60,800		← Peerless' % of NI + 80% extra depr.
NCI in NI of Special Foods	15,200		← NCI share of NI + 20% extra depr.
Dividends declared		40,000	← 100% of sub's dividends declared
Investment in Special Foods		285,360	← Net BV + 80% extra depr.
NCI in NA of Special Foods		71,340	← NCI share of BV + 20% extra depr.

Optional accumulated depreciation elimination entry:

Accumulated depreciation	300,000		← Original depreciation at the time of
Building and equipment		300,000	the acquisition netted against cost

In the 20X2 worksheet, the same two consolidation elimination entries are necessary. The only difference from the downstream example is that the amount of deferred gain on Special Foods' equipment sale to Peerless at the beginning of the period ($700) is allocated between Peerless and the NCI shareholders based on their relative ownership

FIGURE 7–8 December 31, 20X2, Consolidation Worksheet, Next Period Following Intercompany Sale; Upstream Sale of Equipment

	Peerless Products	Special Foods	Elimination Entries DR	Elimination Entries CR	Consolidated
Income Statement					
Sales	450,000	300,000			750,000
Less: COGS	(180,000)	(160,000)		100	(340,000)
Less: Depreciation Expense	(51,000)	(19,100)			(70,000)
Less: Other Expenses	(60,000)	(45,000)			(105,000)
Income from Special Foods	60,800		60,800		0
Consolidated Net Income	219,800	75,900	60,800	100	235,000
NCI in Net Income			15,200		(15,200)
Controlling Interest Net Income	**219,800**	**75,900**	**76,000**	**100**	**219,800**
Statement of Retained Earnings					
Beginning Balance	420,000	120,700	120,700		420,000
Net Income	**219,800**	**75,900**	76,000	100	219,800
Less: Dividends Declared	(60,000)	(40,000)		40,000	(60,000)
Ending Balance	**579,800**	**156,600**	**196,700**	**40,100**	**579,800**
Balance Sheet					
Cash	284,000	92,000			376,000
Accounts Receivable	150,000	80,000			230,000
Inventory	180,000	90,000			270,000
Investment in Special Foods	284,800		560	285,360	0
Land	175,000	40,000			215,000
Buildings & Equipment	807,000	591,000	2,000	300,000	1,100,000
Less: Accumulated Depreciation	(501,000)	(336,400)	300,000	2,700	(540,000)
			100		
Total Assets	**1,379,800**	**556,600**	**302,560**	**588,060**	**1,651,000**
Accounts Payable	100,000	100,000			200,000
Bonds Payable	200,000	100,000			300,000
Common Stock	500,000	200,000	200,000		500,000
Retained Earnings	**579,800**	**156,600**	196,700	40,100	579,800
NCI in NA of Special Foods			140	71,340	71,200
Total Liabilities & Equity	**1,379,800**	**556,600**	**396,840**	**111,440**	**1,651,000**

percentages. Again, T-accounts can be a helpful tool in figuring out the elimination entries:

	Buildings & Equipment			Accumulated Depreciation	
Peerless	7,000		Actual		1,000
	2,000			100	2,700
Special Foods	9,000		"As if"		3,600

Entries to adjust equipment and accumulated depreciation "as if" still on parent's books:

Investment in Special Foods	560	
NCI in NA of Special Foods	140	
Buildings and Equipment	2,000	
Accumulated Depreciation		2,700

Accumulated Depreciation	**100**	
Depreciation Expense		**100**

As explained in the downstream example, the key to understanding these elimination entries is that the debit to the investment account in the first elimination entry is equal to Peerless' share of the unrealized gain at the beginning of the year. Given the gain deferral entry in 20X1 under the fully adjusted equity method, the investment account is "artificially low" by $560. Thus, the basic elimination entry would "overeliminate" this account. For this reason, the debit of $560 helps to eliminate the investment account.

Consolidated Net Income

Peerless Products' separate income for 20X2 is $159,000 after deducting an additional $1,000 for the depreciation on the transferred asset. Consolidated net income for 20X2 is computed and allocated as follows:

Peerless' separate income		$159,000
Special Foods' net income	$75,900	
Partial realization of intercompany gain on upstream sale of equipment	100	
Special Foods' realized net income		76,000
Consolidated net income, 20X2		$235,000
Income to noncontrolling interest ($76,000 × 0.20)		(15,200)
Income to controlling interest		$219,800

Noncontrolling Interest

The noncontrolling interest's share of income is $15,200 for 20X2, computed as the noncontrolling stockholders' proportionate share of the realized income of Special Foods ($76,000 × 0.20). Total noncontrolling interest in the absence of a differential is computed as the noncontrolling stockholders' proportionate share of the stockholders' equity of Special Foods, excluding unrealized gains and losses. On December 31, 20X2, the noncontrolling interest totals $71,200, computed as follows:

Book value of Special Foods, December 31, 20X2:	
Common Stock	$200,000
Retained earnings ($120,700 + $75,900 − $40,000)	156,600
Total book value	$356,600
Unrealized 20X1 intercompany gain on upstream sale	(700)
Intercompany gain realized in 20X2	100
Realized book value of Special Foods	$356,000
Noncontrolling stockholders' share	× 0.20
Noncontrolling interest, December 31, 20X2	$ 71,200

Consolidation in Subsequent Years

The consolidation procedures in subsequent years are quite similar to those in 20X2. Figure 7–9 summarizes the worksheet elimination entries at December 31st of each year from 20X2 to 20X8. We omit 20X1 because it is identical to the downstream entry reported in Figure 7–6. Observation of the elimination entries from 20X2–20X8 again illustrates a clear pattern. Since the extra depreciation recorded each year by Peerless effectively cancels out one-seventh of the unrealized gain and since Peerless continues to record an equity method adjustment to recognize this recognition of the unrealized gain (Entry #27), the sum of the debits to the Investment and NCI in NA of Special Foods accounts and the credit to accumulated depreciation in the first elimination entry each

FIGURE 7–9 Summary of Worksheet Elimination Entries over the Life of the Transferred Asset (Upstream Transfer)

20X2:

Investment in Special Foods	560	
NCI in NA of Special Foods	140	
Buildings and Equipment	2,000	
Accumulated Depreciation		2,700

Accumulated Depreciation	100	
Depreciation Expense		100

	Build. & Equip.			Acc. Depr.	
Peerless:	7,000		Actual		1,000
	2,000			100	2,700
Special Foods:	9,000		"As if"		3,600

20X3:

Investment in Special Foods	480	
NCI in NA of Special Foods	120	
Buildings and Equipment	2,000	
Accumulated Depreciation		2,600

Accumulated Depreciation	100	
Depreciation Expense		100

	Build. & Equip.			Acc. Depr.	
Peerless:	7,000		Actual		1,000
	2,000			100	2,600
Special Foods:	9,000		"As if"		4,500

20X4:

Investment in Special Foods	400	
NCI in NA of Special Foods	100	
Buildings and Equipment	2,000	
Accumulated Depreciation		2,500

Accumulated Depreciation	100	
Depreciation Expense		100

	Build. & Equip.			Acc. Depr.	
Peerless:	7,000		Actual		3,000
	2,000			100	2,500
Special Foods:	9,000		"As if"		5,400

20X5:

Investment in Special Foods	320	
NCI in NA of Special Foods	80	
Buildings and Equipment	2,000	
Accumulated Depreciation		2,400

Accumulated Depreciation	100	
Depreciation Expense		100

	Build. & Equip.			Acc. Depr.	
Peerless:	7,000		Actual		4,000
	2,000			100	2,400
Special Foods:	9,000		"As if"		6,300

20X6:

Investment in Special Foods	240	
NCI in NA of Special Foods	60	
Buildings and Equipment	2,000	
Accumulated Depreciation		2,300

Accumulated Depreciation	100	
Depreciation Expense		100

	Build. & Equip.			Acc. Depr.	
Peerless:	7,000		Actual		5,000
	2,000			100	2,300
Special Foods:	9,000		"As if"		7,200

20X7:

Investment in Special Foods	160	
NCI in NA of Special Foods	40	
Buildings and Equipment	2,000	
Accumulated Depreciation		2,200

Accumulated Depreciation	100	
Depreciation Expense		100

	Build. & Equip.			Acc. Depr.	
Peerless:	7,000		Actual		6,000
	2,000			100	2,200
Special Foods:	9,000		"As if"		8,100

20X8:

Investment in Special Foods	80	
NCI in NA of Special Foods	20	
Buildings and Equipment	2,000	
Accumulated Depr.		2,100

Accumulated Depreciation	100	
Depreciation Expense		100

	Build. & Equip.			Acc. Depr.	
Peerless:	7,000		Actual		7,000
	2,000			100	2,100
Special Foods:	9,000		"As if"		9,000

decreases by $100 each year until the asset is fully depreciated and the intercompany gain is fully recognized. The second elimination entry to back out the extra depreciation is the same each year. After 20X8, no further equity-method entries are required on Peerless' books and no further elimination entries are required in consolidation related to this asset transfer.

Asset Transfers before Year-End

In cases in which an intercorporate asset transfer occurs during a period rather than at the end, a portion of the intercompany gain or loss is considered realized in the period of the transfer. When this occurs, the worksheet eliminating entries at the end of the year must include an adjustment of depreciation expense and accumulated depreciation. The amount of this adjustment is equal to the difference between the depreciation recorded by the purchaser and that which would have been recorded by the seller during the portion of the year elapsing after the intercorporate sale.

For example, if the upstream equipment sale from Special Foods to Peerless had occurred on January 1, 20X1, rather than on December 31, 20X1, an additional eliminating entry (the second entry listed for every other year) would be needed in the consolidation worksheet on December 31, 20X1, to eliminate the "extra" depreciation.

INTERCOMPANY TRANSFERS OF AMORTIZABLE ASSETS

Production rights, patents, and other types of intangible assets may be sold to affiliated enterprises. Accounting for intangible assets usually differs from accounting for tangible assets in that amortizable intangibles normally are reported at the remaining unamortized balance without the use of a contra account. Other than netting the accumulated amortization on an intangible asset against the asset cost, the intercompany sale of intangibles is treated in the same way in consolidation as the intercompany sale of tangible assets.

Summary of Key Concepts

Transactions between affiliated companies within a consolidated entity must be viewed as if they occurred within a single company. Under generally accepted accounting principles, the effects of transactions that are internal to an enterprise may not be included in external accounting reports. Therefore, the effects of all transactions between companies within the consolidated entity must be eliminated in preparing consolidated financial statements.

The treatment of intercompany noncurrent asset transfers is similar to the treatment of intercompany inventory transfers discussed in Chapter 6. The elimination of intercompany transactions must include the removal of unrealized intercompany profits. When one company sells an asset to an affiliate within the consolidated entity, any intercompany profit is not considered realized until confirmed by subsequent events. If the asset has an unlimited life, as with land, the unrealized intercompany gain or loss is realized at the time the asset is resold to a party outside the consolidated entity. If the asset has a limited life, the unrealized intercompany gain or loss is considered to be realized over the remaining life of the asset as the asset is used and depreciated or amortized.

Consolidation procedures relating to unrealized gains and losses on intercompany transfers of assets involve worksheet adjustments to restate the assets and associated accounts, such as accumulated depreciation, to the balances that would be reported if there had been no intercompany transfer. In the period of transfer, the income assigned to the shareholders of the selling affiliate must be reduced by their share of the unrealized intercompany profit. If the sale is a downstream sale, the unrealized intercompany gain or loss is eliminated against the controlling interest. When an upstream sale occurs, the unrealized intercompany gain or loss is eliminated proportionately against the controlling and noncontrolling interests.

Key Terms

downstream sale, *311*   upstream sale, *311*

Appendix **7A** Intercompany Noncurrent Asset Transactions— Modified Equity Method and Cost Method

A parent company may account for a subsidiary using any of several methods. So long as the subsidiary is to be consolidated, the method of accounting for the subsidiary on the parent's books will have no impact on the consolidated financial statements. While the primary focus of this chapter is on consolidation using the fully adjusted equity method on the parent's books, two other methods are used in practice with some frequency as well. These methods are the modified equity method and the cost method.

MODIFIED EQUITY METHOD

A company that chooses to account for an investment using the modified equity method records its proportionate share of subsidiary income and dividends in the same manner as under the fully adjusted equity method. However, it does not record its share of any unrealized profits from intercompany transactions. Instead, these unrealized gains and losses are removed from the parent's retained earnings in the period after the intercompany sale. In the absence of these equity method adjustments, the parent's net income is usually not equal to the amount of consolidated net income allocated to the controlling interest.

As an illustration, assume the same facts as in the upstream sale of equipment discussed previously and reflected in the worksheets presented in Figures 7–7 and 7–8. Special Foods sells equipment to Peerless Products for $7,000 on December 31, 20X1, and reports total income for 20X1 of $50,700, including the $700 gain on the sale of the equipment. Special Foods originally purchased the equipment for $9,000 three years before the intercompany sale. Both companies use straight-line depreciation.

As illustrated previously, Special Foods records 20X1 depreciation on the equipment and the gain on the December 31, 20X1, sale of the equipment to Peerless with the following entries:

	December 31, 20X1		
(28)	Depreciation Expense	900	
	Accumulated Depreciation		900
	Record 20X1 depreciation expense on equipment sold.		

	December 31, 20X1		
(29)	Cash	7,000	
	Accumulated Depreciation	2,700	
	Equipment		9,000
	Gain on Sale of Equipment		700
	Record sale of equipment.		

Peerless records the purchase of the equipment from Special Foods with the following entry:

	December 31, 20X1		
(30)	Equipment	7,000	
	Cash		7,000
	Record purchase of equipment.		

Modified Equity-Method Entries—20X1

In addition, Peerless records the following modified equity-method entries on December 31, 20X1 to recognize its share of Special Foods' reported income and dividends:

(31)	Investment in Special Foods	40,560	
	Income from Special Foods		40,560
	Record Peerless' 80% share of Special Foods' 20X1 income: $50,700 × 0.80		

(32)	Cash	24,000	
	Investment in Special Foods		24,000
	Record Peerless' 80% share of Special Foods' 20X1 dividend: $30,000 × 0.80		

However, Peerless does not record an equity-method entry for its share of the gain deferral from the purchase of the asset from Special Foods.

Consolidation Elimination Entries—20X1

The consolidation worksheet elimination entries under the modified equity method are almost identical to those used under the fully adjusted equity method for 20X1 with one minor exception. We go through the exact same analysis of the book value of Special Foods and allocate each component to Peerless and the NCI shareholders:

Book Value Calculations:

	NCI 20%	+ Peerless 80%	= Common Stock	+ Retained Earnings
Original book value	60,000	240,000	200,000	100,000
+ Net income	10,140	40,560		50,700
− Dividends	(6,000)	(24,000)		(30,000)
Ending book value	64,140	256,560	200,000	120,700

The basic elimination entry under the modified equity method is identical to the basic elimination entry under the fully adjusted equity method with one minor exception. Since we don't make equity method adjustments for the unrealized gain in Peerless' books, we no longer adjust the entries to the Investment in Special Foods and Income from Special Foods accounts for the gain that has been deferred on the intercompany asset sale. Note that we continue to adjust the NCI shareholders' share of Special Foods' income and their share of Special Foods' book value of net assets:

Basic investment account elimination entry:

Common stock	200,000		← Original amount invested (100%)
Retained earnings	100,000		← Beginning RE from trial balance
Income from Special Foods	40,560		← Peerless' % of reported NI
NCI in NI of Special Foods	10,000		← NCI share of NI − 20% Def. Gain
Dividends declared		30,000	← 100% of sub's dividends declared
Investment in Special Foods		256,560	← Net BV left in the invest. acct.
NCI in NA of Special Foods		64,000	← NCI share of net BV − 20% Def. Gain

Optional accumulated depreciation elimination entry:

Accumulated depreciation	300,000		← Original depreciation at the time of the acquisition netted against cost
Building and equipment		300,000	

The following T-accounts illustrate that we arrive at the exact same answer in 20X1 for eliminating the intercompany gain on the sale of equipment from Special Foods to Peerless Products:

Eliminate gain on the equipment sold to Special Foods and correct the assets' basis:

Gain on Sale	700	
Buildings and Equipment	2,000	
Accumulated Depreciation		2,700

Figure 7–10 illustrates the consolidation worksheet for 20X1.

FIGURE 7–10   December 31, 20X1, Modified Equity Method Consolidation Worksheet, Period of Intercompany Sale; Upstream Sale of Equipment

	Peerless Products	Special Foods	Elimination Entries DR	Elimination Entries CR	Consolidated
Income Statement					
Sales	400,000	200,000			600,000
Less: COGS	(170,000)	(115,000)			(285,000)
Less: Depreciation Expense	(50,000)	(20,000)			(70,000)
Less: Other Expenses	(40,000)	(15,000)			(55,000)
Gain on Sale of Fixed Asset		700	700		0
Income from Special Foods	40,560		40,560		0
Consolidated Net Income	180,560	50,700	41,260	0	190,000
NCI in Net Income			10,000		(10,000)
Controlling Interest Net Income	**180,560**	**50,700**	**51,260**	**0**	**180,000**
Statement of Retained Earnings					
Beginning Balance	300,000	100,000	100,000		300,000
Net Income	**180,560**	**50,700**	**51,260**	**0**	180,000
Less: Dividends Declared	(60,000)	(30,000)		30,000	(60,000)
Ending Balance	**420,560**	**120,700**	**151,260**	**30,000**	**420,000**
Balance Sheet					
Cash	257,000	82,000			339,000
Accounts Receivable	75,000	50,000			125,000
Inventory	100,000	75,000			175,000
Investment in Special Foods	256,560			256,560	0
Land	175,000	40,000			215,000
Buildings & Equipment	807,000	591,000	2,000	300,000	1,100,000
Less: Accumulated Depreciation	(450,000)	(317,300)	300,000	2,700	(470,000)
Total Assets	**1,220,560**	**520,700**	**302,000**	**559,260**	**1,484,000**
Accounts Payable	100,000	100,000			200,000
Bonds Payable	200,000	100,000			300,000
Common Stock	500,000	200,000	200,000		500,000
Retained Earnings	**420,560**	**120,700**	**151,260**	**30,000**	420,000
NCI in NA of Special Foods				64,000	64,000
Total Liabilities & Equity	**1,220,560**	**520,700**	**351,260**	**94,000**	**1,484,000**

Modified Equity-Method Entries—20X2

In 20X2, Peerless records its share of Special Foods' $75,900 income and $40,000 of dividends as follows:

(33)	Investment in Special Foods	60,720	
	Income from Special Foods		60,720
	Record Peerless' 80% share of Special Foods' 20X2 income: $75,900 × 0.80		

(34)	Cash	32,000	
	Investment in Special Foods		32,000
	Record Peerless' 80% share of Special Foods' 20X2 dividend: $40,000 × 0.80		

Peerless does not make an entry under the modified equity method to increase income for the partial realization of the unrealized intercompany gain.

Consolidation Elimination Entries—20X2

In order to derive the elimination entries for the 20X2 worksheet, we again analyze the updated book value of Special Foods and examine the allocation of each component to Peerless and the NCI shareholders. Also, in order to present the consolidated financial statements as if the equipment had not been transferred to Peerless, we need to decrease depreciation expense to the amount Special Foods would have recorded had the equipment stayed on its books.

Book Value Calculations:

	NCI 20%	+ Peerless 80%	= Common Stock	+ Retained Earnings
Original book value	64,140	256,560	200,000	120,700
+ Net income	15,180	60,720		75,900
− Dividends	(8,000)	(32,000)		(40,000)
Ending book value	71,320	285,280	200,000	156,600

The basic elimination entry is the same as illustrated for the fully adjusted equity method except that we no longer adjust the entries to the Investment in Special Foods and Income from Special Foods accounts for their 80 percent share of the extra $100 of depreciation for 20X2 associated with the asset transfer. However, we continue to add back 20 percent of the $100 of extra depreciation to the NCI in NI of Special Foods and NCI in NA of Special Foods:

Basic investment account elimination entry:

Common stock	200,000		← Original amount invested (100%)
Retained earnings	120,700		← Beginning RE from trial balance
Income from Special Foods	60,800		← Peerless' share of reported NI
NCI in NI of Special Foods	15,200		← NCI share of NI + 20% extra depr.
Dividends declared		40,000	← 100% of sub's dividends declared
Investment in Special Foods		285,360	← Net BV left in the invest. acct.
NCI in NA of Special Foods		71,340	← NCI share of BV + 20% extra depr.

Optional accumulated depreciation elimination entry:

Accumulated depreciation	300,000		← Original depreciation at the time of
Building and equipment		300,000	the acquisition netted against cost

In the 20X2 worksheet, the only difference from the fully adjusted equity method example is that while the amount of deferred gain on Special Foods' equipment sale to Peerless at the beginning of the period ($700) is still allocated between Peerless and the NCI shareholders based on their relative ownership percentages, the amount accruing to Peerless is recorded as a decrease to beginning Retained Earnings rather than as a debit to the Investment in Special Foods account. Again, T-accounts can be a helpful tool in figuring out the elimination entries:

	Buildings & Equipment			Accumulated Depreciation	
Special Foods	7,000		Actual		1,000
	2,000			100	2,700
Peerless	9,000		"As if"		3,600

Entries to adjust equipment and accumulated depreciation "as if" still on parent's books:

Retained Earnings	560	
NCI in NA of Special Foods	140	
Buildings and Equipment	2,000	
Accumulated Depreciation		2,700

Accumulated Depreciation	100	
Depreciation Expense		100

Again, these elimination entries related to the intercompany asset sale are identical to those used under the fully adjusted equity method with the one exception that the debit for $560 in the first elimination entry goes to Retained Earnings rather than the Investment in Special Foods account.

Figure 7–11 illustrates the consolidation worksheet for 20X2.

COST METHOD

When using the cost method of accounting for an investment in a subsidiary, the parent records dividends received from the subsidiary during the period as income. No entries are made under the cost method to record the parent's share of undistributed subsidiary earnings, amortize differential, or remove unrealized intercompany profits.

To illustrate consolidation following an intercompany sale of equipment when the parent accounts for its subsidiary investment using the cost method, assume the same facts as in the previous illustrations of an upstream sale.

FIGURE 7–11 December 31, 20X2, Modified Equity Method Consolidation Worksheet, Next Period following Intercompany Sale; Upstream Sale of Equipment

	Peerless Products	Special Foods	Elimination Entries DR	CR	Consolidated
Income Statement					
Sales	450,000	300,000			750,000
Less: COGS	(180,000)	(160,000)			(340,000)
Less: Depreciation Expense	(51,000)	(19,100)		100	(70,000)
Less: Other Expenses	(60,000)	(45,000)			(105,000)
Income from Special Foods	60,720		60,720		0
Consolidated Net Income	219,720	75,900	60,720	100	235,000
NCI in Net Income			15,200		(15,200)
Controlling Interest Net Income	**219,720**	**75,900**	**75,920**	**100**	**219,800**
Statement of Retained Earnings					
Beginning Balance	420,560	120,700	120,700		420,000
			560		
Net Income	**219,720**	**75,900**	75,920	100	219,800
Less: Dividends Declared	(60,000)	(40,000)		40,000	(60,000)
Ending Balance	**580,280**	**156,600**	**197,180**	**40,100**	**579,800**
Balance Sheet					
Cash	284,000	92,000			376,000
Accounts Receivable	150,000	80,000			230,000
Inventory	180,000	90,000			270,000
Investment in Special Foods	285,280			285,280	0
Land	175,000	40,000			215,000
Buildings & Equipment	807,000	591,000	2,000	300,000	1,100,000
Less: Accumulated Depreciation	(501,000)	(336,400)	300,000	2,700	(540,000)
			100		
Total Assets	**1,380,280**	**556,600**	**302,000**	**587,980**	**1,651,000**
Accounts Payable	100,000	100,000			200,000
Bonds Payable	200,000	100,000			300,000
Common Stock	500,000	200,000	200,000		500,000
Retained Earnings	**580,280**	**156,600**	197,180	40,100	579,800
NCI in NA of Special Foods			140	71,340	71,200
Total Liabilities & Equity	**1,380,280**	**556,600**	**397,320**	**111,440**	**1,651,000**

Consolidation Elimination Entries—20X1

The following elimination entries would appear in the worksheet used to consolidate Peerless and Special Foods at the end of 20X1, assuming Peerless uses the cost method to account for its investment:

Investment elimination entry:

Common stock	200,000	
Retained earnings	100,000	
Investment in Special Foods		240,000
NCI in NA of Special Foods		60,000

Dividend elimination entry:

Dividend income	24,000	
NCI in NI of Special Foods	6,000	
Dividends declared		30,000

Assign undistributed income to NCI:

NCI in NI of Special Foods	4,000	
NCI in NA of Special Foods		4,000

Optional accumulated depreciation elimination entry:

Accumulated depreciation	300,000	
Building and equipment		300,000

Eliminate asset purchase from Special Foods:

Buildings and equipment	2,000	
Gain on Sale	700	
Accumulated Depreciation		2,700

The first four elimination entries are identical to those illustrated in Appendix 6A. They (1) eliminate the book value of Special Foods' equity accounts against the original investment account, (2) eliminate Special Foods' 20X1 dividends declared, (3) assign undistributed income to the NCI shareholders, and (4) eliminate accumulated depreciation recorded by Special Foods on fixed assets prior to Peerless' acquisition. Finally, the elimination entry related to the fixed asset transfer is identical to the one used under both the fully adjusted and modified equity methods.

Figure 7–12 illustrates the consolidation worksheet for 20X1.

Consolidation Elimination Entries—20X2

The following elimination entries would appear in the worksheet used to consolidate Peerless and Special Foods at the end of 20X2, assuming Peerless uses the cost method to account for its investment:

Basic elimination entry:

Common stock	200,000	
Retained earnings	100,000	
Investment in Special Foods		240,000
NCI in NA of Special Foods		60,000

Dividend elimination entry:

Dividend income	32,000	
NCI in NI of Special Foods	8,000	
Dividends declared		40,000

Assign prior undistributed income to NCI:

NCI in NI of Special Foods	7,200	
Retained earnings	4,140	
NCI in NA of Special Foods		11,340

FIGURE 7–12 December 31, 20X1, Cost Method Consolidation Worksheet, Period of Intercompany Sale; Upstream Sale of Equipment

	Peerless Products	Special Foods	Elimination Entries		Consolidated
			DR	CR	
Income Statement					
Sales	400,000	200,000			600,000
Less: COGS	(170,000)	(115,000)			(285,000)
Less: Depreciation Expense	(50,000)	(20,000)			(70,000)
Less: Other Expenses	(40,000)	(15,000)			(55,000)
Gain on sale of fixed asset		700	700		0
Dividend Income	24,000		24,000		0
Consolidated Net Income	164,000	50,700	24,700	0	190,000
NCI in Net Income			6,000		(10,000)
			4,000		
Controlling Interest Net Income	164,000	50,700	34,700	0	180,000
Statement of Retained Earnings					
Beginning Balance	300,000	100,000	100,000		300,000
Net Income	164,000	50,700	34,700	0	180,000
Less: Dividends Declared	(60,000)	(30,000)		30,000	(60,000)
Ending Balance	404,000	120,700	134,700	30,000	420,000
Balance Sheet					
Cash	257,000	82,000			339,000
Accounts Receivable	75,000	50,000			125,000
Inventory	100,000	75,000			175,000
Investment in Special Foods	240,000			240,000	0
Land	175,000	40,000			215,000
Buildings & Equipment	807,000	591,000	2,000	300,000	1,100,000
Less: Accumulated Depreciation	(450,000)	(317,300)	300,000	2,700	(470,000)
Total Assets	1,204,000	520,700	302,000	542,700	1,484,000
Accounts Payable	100,000	100,000			200,000
Bonds Payable	200,000	100,000			300,000
Common Stock	500,000	200,000	200,000		500,000
Retained Earnings	404,000	120,700	134,700	30,000	420,000
NCI in NA of Special Foods				60,000	64,000
				4,000	
Total Liabilities & Equity	1,204,000	520,700	334,700	90,000	1,484,000

Optional accumulated depreciation elimination entry:

Accumulated depreciation	300,000	
Building and equipment		300,000

Entries to adjust equipment and accumulated depreciation "as if" still on Peerless' books:

Retained Earnings	560	
NCI in NA of Special Foods	140	
Buildings and Equipment	2,000	
Accumulated Depreciation		2,700

Accumulated Depreciation	100	
Depreciation Expense		100

FIGURE 7–13   December 31, 20X2, Cost Method Consolidation Worksheet, Next Period following Intercompany Sale; Upstream Sale of Equipment

	Peerless Products	Special Foods	Elimination Entries		Consolidated
			DR	CR	
Income Statement					
Sales	450,000	300,000			750,000
Less: COGS	(180,000)	(160,000)			(340,000)
Less: Depreciation Expense	(51,000)	(19,100)		100	(70,000)
Less: Other Expenses	(60,000)	(45,000)			(105,000)
Dividend Income	32,000		32,000		0
Consolidated Net Income	191,000	75,900	32,000	100	235,000
NCI in Net Income			8,000		
			7,200		(15,200)
Controlling Interest Net Income	**191,000**	**75,900**	**47,200**	**100**	**219,800**
Statement of Retained Earnings					
Beginning Balance	404,000	120,700	100,000		420,000
			4,140		
			560		
Net Income	**191,000**	**75,900**	**47,200**	**100**	219,800
Less: Dividends Declared	(60,000)	(40,000)		40,000	(60,000)
Ending Balance	**535,000**	**156,600**	**151,900**	**40,100**	**579,800**
Balance Sheet					
Cash	284,000	92,000			376,000
Accounts Receivable	150,000	80,000			230,000
Inventory	180,000	90,000			270,000
Investment in Special Foods	240,000			240,000	0
Land	175,000	40,000			215,000
Buildings & Equipment	807,000	591,000	2,000	300,000	1,100,000
Less: Accumulated Depreciation	(501,000)	(336,400)	300,000	2,700	(540,000)
			100		
Total Assets	**1,335,000**	**556,600**	**302,000**	**542,700**	**1,651,000**
Accounts Payable	100,000	100,000			200,000
Bonds Payable	200,000	100,000			300,000
Common Stock	500,000	200,000	200,000		500,000
Retained Earnings	**535,000**	**156,600**	**151,900**	**40,100**	579,800
NCI in NA of Special Foods			140	60,000	71,200
				11,340	
Total Liabilities & Equity	**1,335,000**	**556,600**	**352,040**	**100,100**	**1,651,000**

Again, the first four elimination entries are identical to those illustrated in Appendix 6A. They (1) eliminate the book value of Special Foods' equity accounts against the original investment account, (2) eliminate Special Foods' 20X1 dividends declared, (3) assign undistributed income to the NCI shareholders, and (4) eliminate accumulated depreciation recorded by Special Foods on fixed assets prior to Peerless' acquisition. Finally, the elimination entries related to the fixed asset transfer is identical to the one used under the modified equity method.

Figure 7–13 illustrates the consolidation worksheet for 20X2.

Questions

LO1	Q7-1	When are profits on intercorporate sales considered to be realized? Explain.
LO2	Q7-2	What is an upstream sale? Which company may have unrealized profits on its books in an upstream sale?
LO1	Q7-3	What dollar amounts in the consolidated financial statements will be incorrect if intercompany services are not eliminated?

LO1 **Q7-4** How are unrealized profits on current-period intercorporate sales treated in preparing the income statement for (*a*) the selling company and (*b*) the consolidated entity?

LO1 **Q7-5** How are unrealized profits treated in the consolidated income statement if the intercorporate sale occurred in a prior period and the transferred item is sold to a nonaffiliate in the current period?

LO1 **Q7-6** How are unrealized intercorporate profits treated in the consolidated statements if the intercorporate sale occurred in a prior period and the profits have not been realized by the end of the current period?

LO2 **Q7-7** What is a downstream sale? Which company may have unrealized profits on its books in a downstream sale?

LO2, LO3 **Q7-8** What portion of the unrealized intercorporate profit is eliminated in a downstream sale? In an upstream sale?

LO2 **Q7-9** How is the effect of unrealized intercorporate profits on consolidated net income different between an upstream and a downstream sale?

LO4 **Q7-10** Unrealized profits from a prior-year upstream sale were realized in the current period. What effect will this event have on income assigned to the noncontrolling interest in the consolidated income statement for the current period?

LO6 **Q7-11** A subsidiary sold a depreciable asset to the parent company at a profit in the current period. Will the income assigned to the noncontrolling interest in the consolidated income statement for the current period be more than, less than, or equal to a proportionate share of the reported net income of the subsidiary? Why?

LO6 **Q7-12** A subsidiary sold a depreciable asset to the parent company at a profit of $1,000 in the current period. Will the income assigned to the noncontrolling interest in the consolidated income statement for the current period be more if the intercorporate sale occurs on January 1 or on December 31? Why?

LO5 **Q7-13** If a company sells a depreciable asset to its subsidiary at a profit on December 31, 20X3, what account balances must be eliminated or adjusted in preparing the consolidated income statement for 20X3?

LO5 **Q7-14** If the sale in the preceding question occurs on January 1, 20X3, what additional account will require adjustment in preparing the consolidated income statement?

LO5, LO6 **Q7-15** In the period in which an intercorporate sale occurs, how do the consolidation eliminating entries differ when unrealized profits pertain to an intangible asset rather than a tangible asset?

LO3, LO5 **Q7-16** When is unrealized profit on an intercompany sale of land considered realized? When is profit on an intercompany sale of equipment considered realized? Why do the treatments differ?

LO5, LO6 **Q7-17** In the elimination of a prior-period unrealized intercorporate gain on depreciable assets, why does the debit to the Investment account decrease over time?

LO6 **Q7-18A** A parent company may use on its books one of several different methods of accounting for its ownership of a subsidiary: (*a*) cost method, (*b*) modified equity method, or (*c*) fully adjusted equity method. How will the choice of method affect the reported balance in the investment account when there are unrealized intercorporate profits on the parent's books at the end of the period?

Cases

LO6 **C7-1** **Correction of Elimination Procedures**

Plug Corporation purchased 60 percent of Coy Company's common stock approximately 10 years ago. On January 1, 20X2, Coy sold equipment to Plug for $850,000 and recorded a $150,000 loss *Research* on the sale. Coy had purchased the equipment for $1,200,000 on January 1, 20X0, and was depreciating it on a straight-line basis over 12 years with no assumed residual value.

In preparing Plug's consolidated financial statements for 20X2, its chief accountant increased the reported amount of the equipment by $150,000 and eliminated the loss on the sale of equipment recorded by Coy. No other eliminations or adjustments related to the equipment were made.

Required

As a member of the audit firm Gotcha and Gotcha, you have been asked, after reviewing Plug's consolidated income statement, to prepare a memo to Plug's controller detailing the elimination

"A" indicates that the item relates to "Appendix A."

procedures that should be followed in transferring equipment between subsidiary and parent. Include citations to or quotations from the authoritative literature to support your recommendations. Your memo should include the correct eliminating entry and explain why each debit and credit is needed.

LO2

C7-2 Elimination of Intercorporate Services

Research

Dream Corporation owns 90 percent of Classic Company's common stock and 70 percent of Plain Company's stock. Dream provides legal services to each subsidiary and bills it for 150 percent of the cost of the services provided. During 20X3, Classic recorded legal expenses of $80,000 when it paid Dream for legal assistance in an unsuccessful patent infringement suit against another company, and Plain recorded legal expenses of $150,000 when it paid Dream for legal work associated with the purchase of additional property in Montana to expand an existing strip mine owned by Plain. In preparing the consolidated statements at December 31, 20X3, no eliminations were made for intercompany services. When asked why no entries had been made to eliminate the intercompany services, Dream's chief accountant replied that intercompany services are not mentioned in the company accounting manual and can be ignored.

Required

Prepare a memo detailing the appropriate treatment of legal services provided by Dream to Plain and Classic during 20X3. Include citations to or quotations from authoritative accounting standards to support your recommendations. In addition, provide the eliminating entries at December 31, 20X3, and 20X4, needed as a result of the services provided in 20X3, and explain why each debit or credit is necessary.

LO2

C7-3 Noncontrolling Interest

Understanding

Current reporting standards require the consolidated entity to include all the revenues, expenses, assets, and liabilities of the parent and its subsidiaries in the consolidated financial statements. When the parent does not own all of a subsidiary's shares, various rules and procedures exist with regard to the assignment of income and net assets to noncontrolling shareholders and the way in which the noncontrolling interest is to be reported.

Required

a. How is the amount of income assigned to noncontrolling shareholders in the consolidated income statement computed if there are no unrealized intercorporate profits on the subsidiary's books?

b. How is the amount reported for the noncontrolling interest in the consolidated balance sheet computed if there are no unrealized intercorporate profits on the subsidiary's books?

c. What effect do unrealized intercorporate profits have on the computation of income assigned to the noncontrolling interest if the profits arose from a transfer of (1) land or (2) equipment?

d. Are the noncontrolling shareholders of a subsidiary likely to find the amounts assigned to them in the consolidated financial statements useful? Explain.

LO4

C7-4 Intercompany Sale of Services

Analysis

Diamond Manufacturing Company regularly purchases janitorial and maintenance services from its wholly owned subsidiary, Schwartz Maintenance Services Inc. Schwartz bills Diamond monthly at its regular rates for the services provided, with the services consisting primarily of cleaning, grounds keeping, and small repairs. The cost of providing the services that Schwartz sells consists mostly of salaries and associated labor costs that total about 60 percent of the amount billed. Diamond issues consolidated financial statements annually.

Required

a. When Diamond prepares consolidated financial statements, what account balances of Diamond and Schwartz related to the intercompany sale of services must be adjusted or eliminated in the consolidation worksheet? What impact do these adjustments or eliminations have on consolidated net income?

b. In the case of intercompany sales of services at a profit, at what point in time are the intercompany profits considered to be realized? Explain.

LO2

C7-5 Intercompany Profits

Companies have many different practices for pricing transfers of goods and services from one affiliate to another. Regardless of the approaches used for internal decision making and performance evaluation or for tax purposes, all intercompany profits, unless immaterial, are supposed to be

Analysis   eliminated when preparing consolidated financial statements until confirmed through transactions with external parties.

Required

a. Verizon Communications is in the telephone business, although it is larger and more diversified than many smaller telecommunications companies. How does it treat intercompany profits for consolidation?

b. Harley-Davidson operates in two business areas: (1) motorcycles and related products and (2) financial services. Does Harley eliminate all effects of intercompany transactions when preparing consolidated financial statements? Explain. What effect does its treatment have on consolidated net income?

Exercises

LO5, LO6

E7-1   Multiple-Choice Questions on Intercompany Transfers [AICPA Adapted]
For each question, select the single best answer.

1. Water Company owns 80 percent of Fire Company's outstanding common stock. On December 31, 20X9, Fire sold equipment to Water at a price in excess of Fire's carrying amount, but less than its original cost. On a consolidated balance sheet at December 31, 20X9, the carrying amount of the equipment should be reported at

   a. Water's original cost.
   b. Fire's original cost.
   c. Water's original cost less Fire's recorded gain.
   d. Water's original cost less 80 percent of Fire's recorded gain.

2. Company J acquired all of Company K's outstanding common stock in exchange for cash. The acquisition price exceeds the fair value of net assets acquired. How should Company J determine the amounts to be reported for the plant and equipment and long-term debt acquired from Company K?

	Plant and Equipment	Long-Term Debt
a.	K's carrying amount	K's carrying amount
b.	K's carrying amount	Fair value
c.	Fair value	K's carrying amount
d.	Fair value	Fair value

3. Port Inc. owns 100 percent of Salem Inc. On January 1, 20X2, Port sold delivery equipment to Salem at a gain. Port had owned the equipment for two years and used a five-year straight-line depreciation rate with no residual value. Salem is using a three-year straight-line depreciation rate with no residual value for the equipment. In the consolidated income statement, Salem's recorded depreciation expense on the equipment for 20X2 will be decreased by

   a. 20 percent of the gain on the sale.
   b. $33^{1}/_{3}$ percent of the gain on the sale.
   c. 50 percent of the gain on the sale.
   d. 100 percent of the gain on the sale.

4. On January 1, 20X0, Poe Corporation sold a machine for $900,000 to Saxe Corporation, its wholly owned subsidiary. Poe paid $1,100,000 for this machine, which had accumulated depreciation of $250,000. Poe estimated a $100,000 salvage value and depreciated the machine using the straight-line method over 20 years, a policy that Saxe continued. In Poe's December 31, 20X0, consolidated balance sheet, this machine should be included in fixed-asset cost and accumulated depreciation as

	Cost	Accumulated Depreciation
a.	$1,100,000	$300,000
b.	$1,100,000	$290,000
c.	$ 900,000	$ 40,000
d.	$ 850,000	$ 42,500

5. Scroll Inc., a wholly owned subsidiary of Pirn Inc., began operations on January 1, 20X1. The following information is from the condensed 20X1 income statements of Pirn and Scroll:

	Pirn	Scroll
Sales	$500,000	$300,000
Cost of Goods Sold	(350,000)	(270,000)
Gross Profit	$150,000	$ 30,000
Depreciation	(40,000)	(10,000)
Other Expenses	(60,000)	(15,000)
Income from Operations	$ 50,000	$ 5,000
Gain on Sale of Equipment to Scroll	12,000	
Income before Taxes	$ 62,000	$ 5,000

Equipment purchased by Scroll from Pirn for $36,000 on January 1, 20X1, is depreciated using the straight-line method over four years. What amount should be reported as depreciation expense in Pirn's 20X1 consolidated income statement?

a. $50,000.

b. $47,000.

c. $44,000.

d. $41,000.

LO2, LO6

E7-2 Multiple-Choice Questions on Intercompany Transactions

Select the correct answer for each of the following questions.

1. Upper Company holds 60 percent of Lower Company's voting shares. During the preparation of consolidated financial statements for 20X5, the following eliminating entry was made:

Investment in Lower	10,000	
Land		10,000

Which of the following statements is correct?

a. Upper Company purchased land from Lower Company during 20X5.

b. Upper Company purchased land from Lower Company before January 1, 20X5.

c. Lower Company purchased land from Upper Company during 20X5.

d. Lower Company purchased land from Upper Company before January 1, 20X5.

2. Middle Company holds 60 percent of Bottom Corporation's voting shares. Bottom has developed a new type of production equipment that appears to be quite marketable. It spent $40,000 in developing the equipment; however, Middle agreed to purchase the production rights for the machine for $100,000. If the intercompany sale occurred on January 1, 20X2, and the production rights are expected to have value for five years, at what amount should the rights be reported in the consolidated balance sheet for December 31, 20X2?

a. $0.

b. $32,000.

c. $80,000.

d. $100,000.

Note: Questions 3 through 6 are based on the following information:
On January 1, 20X4, Gold Company purchased a computer with an expected economic life of five years. On January 1, 20X6, Gold sold the computer to TLK Corporation and recorded the following entry:

Cash	39,000	
Accumulated Depreciation	16,000	
Computer Equipment		40,000
Gain on Sale of Equipment		15,000

TLK Corporation holds 60 percent of Gold's voting shares. Gold reported net income of $45,000, and TLK reported income from its own operations of $85,000 for 20X6. There is no change in the estimated economic life of the equipment as a result of the intercorporate transfer.

3. In the preparation of the 20X6 consolidated income statement, depreciation expense will be

   a. Debited for $5,000 in the eliminating entries.

   b. Credited for $5,000 in the eliminating entries.

   c. Debited for $13,000 in the eliminating entries.

   d. Credited for $13,000 in the eliminating entries.

4. In the preparation of the 20X6 consolidated balance sheet, computer equipment will be

   a. Debited for $1,000.

   b. Debited for $15,000.

   c. Credited for $24,000.

   d. Debited for $40,000.

5. Income assigned to the noncontrolling interest in the 20X6 consolidated income statement will be

   a. $12,000.

   b. $14,000.

   c. $18,000.

   d. $52,000.

6. Consolidated net income for 20X6 will be

   a. $106,000.

   b. $112,000.

   c. $120,000.

   d. $130,000.

LO3

E7-3 Elimination Entries for Land Transfer

Huckster Corporation purchased land on January 1, 20X1, for $20,000. On June 10, 20X4, it sold the land to its subsidiary, Lowly Corporation, for $30,000. Huckster owns 60 percent of Lowly's voting shares.

Required

a. Give the worksheet eliminating entries needed to remove the effects of the intercompany sale of land in preparing the consolidated financial statements for 20X4 and 20X5.

b. Give the worksheet eliminating entries needed on December 31, 20X4 and 20X5, if Lowly had initially purchased the land for $20,000 and then sold it to Huckster on June 10, 20X4, for $30,000.

LO2

E7-4 Intercompany Services

Power Corporation owns 75 percent of Swift Company's stock. Swift provides health care services to its employees and those of Power. During 20X2, Power recorded $45,000 as health care expense for medical care given to its employees by Swift. Swift's costs incurred in providing the services to Power were $32,000.

Required

a. By what amount will consolidated net income change when the intercompany services are eliminated in preparing Power's consolidated statements for 20X2?

b. What would be the impact of eliminating the intercompany services on consolidated net income if Power owned 100 percent of Swift's stock rather than 75 percent? Explain.

c. If in its consolidated income statement for 20X2 Power had reported total health care costs of $70,000, what was the cost to Swift of providing health care services to its own employees?

LO2

E7-5 Elimination Entries for Intercompany Services

On January 1, 20X5, Block Corporation started using a wholly owned subsidiary to deliver all its sales overnight to its customers. During 20X5, Block recorded delivery service expense of $76,000 and made payments of $58,000 to the subsidiary.

Required

Give the worksheet eliminating entries related to the intercompany services needed on December 31, 20X5, to prepare consolidated financial statements.

LO5

E7-6 Elimination Entries for Depreciable Asset Transfer: Year-End Sale

Pam Corporation holds 70 percent ownership of Northern Enterprises. On December 31, 20X6, Northern paid Pam $40,000 for a truck that Pam had purchased for $45,000 on January 1, 20X2. The truck was considered to have a 15-year life from January 1, 20X2, and no residual value. Both companies depreciate equipment using the straight-line method.

Required

a. Give the worksheet eliminating entry or entries needed on December 31, 20X6, to remove the effects of the intercompany sale.

b. Give the worksheet eliminating entry or entries needed on December 31, 20X7, to remove the effects of the intercompany sale.

LO4

E7-7 Transfer of Land

Bowen Corporation owns 70 percent of Roan Corporation's voting common stock. On March 12, 20X2, Roan sold land it had purchased for $140,000 to Bowen for $185,000. Bowen plans to build a new warehouse on the property in 20X3.

Required

a. Give the worksheet eliminating entries to remove the effects of the intercompany sale of land in preparing the consolidated financial statements at December 31, 20X2 and 20X3.

b. Give the worksheet eliminating entries needed at December 31, 20X3 and 20X4, if Bowen had initially purchased the land for $150,000 and sold it to Roan on March 12, 20X2, for $180,000.

LO5

E7-8 Transfer of Depreciable Asset at Year-End

Frazer Corporation purchased 60 percent of Minnow Corporation's voting common stock on January 1, 20X1. On December 31, 20X5, Frazer received $210,000 from Minnow for a truck Frazer had purchased on January 1, 20X2, for $300,000. The truck is expected to have a 10-year useful life and no salvage value. Both companies depreciate trucks on a straight-line basis.

Required

a. Give the worksheet eliminating entry or entries needed at December 31, 20X5, to remove the effects of the intercompany sale.

b. Give the worksheet eliminating entry or entries needed at December 31, 20X6, to remove the effects of the intercompany sale.

LO5

E7-9 Transfer of Depreciable Asset at Beginning of Year

Frazer Corporation purchased 60 percent of Minnow Corporation's voting common stock on January 1, 20X1. On January 1, 20X5, Frazer received $245,000 from Minnow for a truck Frazer had purchased on January 1, 20X2, for $300,000. The truck is expected to have a 10-year useful life and no salvage value. Both companies depreciate trucks on a straight-line basis.

Required

a. Give the worksheet eliminating entry or entries needed at December 31, 20X5, to remove the effects of the intercompany sale.

b. Give the worksheet eliminating entry or entries needed at December 31, 20X6, to remove the effects of the intercompany sale.

LO5

E7-10 Sale of Equipment to Subsidiary in Current Period

On January 1, 20X7, Wainwrite Corporation sold to Lance Corporation equipment it had purchased for $150,000 and used for eight years. Wainwrite recorded a gain of $14,000 on the sale. The equipment has a total useful life of 15 years and is depreciated on a straight-line basis. Wainwrite holds 70 percent of Lance's voting common shares.

Required

a. Give the journal entry made by Wainwrite on January 1, 20X7, to record the sale of equipment.

b. Give the journal entries recorded by Lance during 20X7 to record the purchase of equipment and year-end depreciation expense.

 c. Give the eliminating entry or entries related to the intercompany sale of equipment needed at December 31, 20X7, to prepare a full set of consolidated financial statements.

 d. Give the eliminating entry or entries related to the equipment required at January 1, 20X8, to prepare a consolidated balance sheet only.

LO6

E7-11 Upstream Sale of Equipment in Prior Period

Baywatch Industries has owned 80 percent of Tubberware Corporation for many years. On January 1, 20X6, Baywatch paid Tubberware $270,000 to acquire equipment that Tubberware had purchased on January 1, 20X3, for $300,000. The equipment is expected to have no scrap value and is depreciated over a 15-year useful life.

 Baywatch reported operating earnings of $100,000 for 20X8 and paid dividends of $40,000. Tubberware reported net income of $40,000 and paid dividends of $20,000 in 20X8.

Required

 a. Compute the amount reported as consolidated net income for 20X8.

 b. By what amount would consolidated net income change if the equipment sale had been a downstream sale rather than an upstream sale?

 c. Give the eliminating entry or entries required to eliminate the effects of the intercompany sale of equipment in preparing a full set of consolidated financial statements at December 31, 20X8.

LO5

E7-12 Elimination Entries for Midyear Depreciable Asset Transfer

Kline Corporation holds 90 percent ownership of Andrews Company. On July 1, 20X3, Kline sold equipment that it had purchased for $30,000 on January 1, 20X1, to Andrews for $28,000. The equipment's original six-year estimated total economic life remains unchanged. Both companies use straight-line depreciation. The equipment's residual value is considered negligible.

Required

 a. Give the eliminating entry or entries in the consolidation worksheet prepared as of December 31, 20X3, to remove the effects of the intercompany sale.

 b. Give the eliminating entry or entries in the consolidation worksheet prepared as of December 31, 20X4, to remove the effects of the intercompany sale.

LO2

E7-13 Consolidated Net Income Computation

Verry Corporation owns 75 percent of Spawn Corporation's voting common stock. Verry reported income from its separate operations of $90,000 and $110,000 in 20X4 and 20X5, respectively. Spawn reported net income of $60,000 and $40,000 in 20X4 and 20X5, respectively.

Required

 a. Compute consolidated net income and the income assigned to the controlling interest for 20X4 and 20X5 if Verry sold land with a book value of $95,000 to Spawn for $120,000 on June 30, 20X4.

 b. Compute consolidated net income and the amount of income assigned to the controlling interest in the consolidated statements for 20X4 and 20X5 if Spawn sold land with a book value of $95,000 to Verry for $120,000 on June 30, 20X4.

LO2

Advanced
StudyGuide
.com

E7-14 Elimination Entries for Intercompany Transfers

Grand Delivery Service acquired at book value 80 percent of the voting shares of Acme Real Estate Company. On that date, the fair value of the noncontrolling interest was equal to 20 percent of Acme's book value. Acme Real Estate reported common stock of $300,000 and retained earnings of $100,000. During 20X3 Grand Delivery provided courier services for Acme Real Estate in the amount of $15,000. Also during 20X3, Acme Real Estate purchased land for $1,000. It sold the land to Grand Delivery Service for $26,000 so that Grand Delivery could build a new transportation center. Grand Delivery reported $65,000 of operating income from its delivery operations in 20X3. Acme Real Estate reported net income of $40,000 and paid dividends of $10,000 in 20X3.

Required

 a. Compute consolidated net income for 20X3.

 b. Give all journal entries recorded by Grand Delivery Service related to its investment in Acme Real Estate assuming Grand uses the fully adjusted equity method in accounting for the investment.

 c. Give all eliminating entries required in preparing a consolidation worksheet as of December 31, 20X3.

LO6

Advanced
StudyGuide
.com

E7-15 Sale of Building to Parent in Prior Period

Turner Company purchased 70 percent of Split Company's stock approximately 20 years ago. On December 31, 20X8, Turner purchased a building from Split for $300,000. Split had purchased the building on January 1, 20X1, at a cost of $400,000 and used straight-line depreciation on an expected life of 20 years. The asset's total estimated economic life is unchanged as a result of the intercompany sale.

Required

a. What amount of depreciation expense on the building will Turner report for 20X9?

b. What amount of depreciation expense would Split have reported for 20X9 if it had continued to own the building?

c. Give the eliminating entry or entries needed to eliminate the effects of the intercompany building transfer in preparing a full set of consolidated financial statements at December 31, 20X9.

d. What amount of income will be assigned to the noncontrolling interest in the consolidated income statement for 20X9 if Split reports net income of $40,000 for 20X9?

e. Split reports assets with a book value of $350,000 and liabilities of $150,000 at January 1, 20X9, and reports net income of $40,000 and dividends of $15,000 for 20X9. What amount will be assigned to the noncontrolling interest in the consolidated balance sheet at December 31, 20X9, assuming the fair value of the noncontrolling interest at the date of acquisition was equal to 30 percent of the book value of Split Company?

LO5

E7-16 Intercompany Sale at a Loss

Parent Company holds 90 percent of Sunway Company's voting common shares. On December 31, 20X8, Parent recorded a loss of $16,000 on the sale of equipment to Sunway. At the time of the sale, the equipment's estimated remaining economic life was eight years.

Required

a. Will consolidated net income be increased or decreased when eliminating entries associated with the sale of equipment are made at December 31, 20X8? By what amount?

b. Will consolidated net income be increased or decreased when eliminating entries associated with the sale of equipment are made at December 31, 20X9? By what amount?

LO6

E7-17 Eliminating Entries Following Intercompany Sale at a Loss

Brown Corporation holds 70 percent of Transom Company's voting common stock. On January 1, 20X2, Transom paid $300,000 to acquire a building with a 15-year expected economic life. Transom uses straight-line depreciation for all depreciable assets. On December 31, 20X7, Brown purchased the building from Transom for $144,000. Brown reported income, excluding investment income from Transom, of $125,000 and $150,000 for 20X7 and 20X8, respectively. Transom reported net income of $15,000 and $40,000 for 20X7 and 20X8, respectively.

Required

a. Give the appropriate eliminating entry or entries needed to eliminate the effects of the intercompany sale of the building in preparing consolidated financial statements for 20X7.

b. Compute the amount to be reported as consolidated net income for 20X7 and the income to be allocated to the controlling interest.

c. Give the appropriate eliminating entry or entries needed to eliminate the effects of the intercompany sale of the building in preparing consolidated financial statements for 20X8.

d. Compute consolidated net income and the amount of income assigned to the controlling shareholders in the consolidated income statement for 20X8.

LO4

E7-18 Multiple Transfers of Asset

Swanson Corporation purchased land from Clayton Corporation for $240,000 on December 20, 20X3. This purchase followed a series of transactions between Swanson-controlled subsidiaries. On February 7, 20X3, Sullivan Corporation purchased the land from a nonaffiliate for $145,000. It sold the land to Kolder Company for $130,000 on October 10, 20X3, and Kolder sold the land to Clayton for $180,000 on November 27, 20X3. Swanson has control of the following companies:

Subsidiary	Level of Ownership	20X3 Net Income
Sullivan Corporation	80 percent	$120,000
Kolder Company	70 percent	60,000
Clayton Corporation	90 percent	80,000

Swanson reported income from its separate operations of $150,000 for 20X3.

Required

a. At what amount should the land be reported in the consolidated balance sheet as of December 31, 20X3?

b. What amount of gain or loss on sale of land should be reported in the consolidated income statement for 20X3?

c. What amount of income should be assigned to the controlling shareholders in the consolidated income statement for 20X3?

d. Give any elimination entry related to the land that should appear in the worksheet used to prepare consolidated financial statements for 20X3.

LO6

E7-19 Elimination Entry in Period of Transfer

Blank Corporation owns 60 percent of Grand Corporation's voting common stock. On December 31, 20X4, Blank paid Grand $276,000 for dump trucks Grand had purchased on January 1, 20X2. Both companies use straight-line depreciation. The eliminating entry included in preparing consolidated financial statements at December 31, 20X4, was

Trucks	24,000	
Gain on Sale of Trucks	36,000	
Accumulated Depreciation		60,000

Required

a. What amount was paid by Grand to purchase the trucks on January 1, 20X2?

b. What was the economic life of the trucks on January 1, 20X2?

c. Give the worksheet eliminating entry needed in preparing the consolidated financial statements at December 31, 20X5.

LO6

E7-20 Elimination Entry Computation

Stern Manufacturing purchased an ultrasound drilling machine with a remaining 10-year economic life from a 70 percent owned subsidiary for $360,000 on January 1, 20X6. Both companies use straight-line depreciation. The subsidiary recorded the following entry when it sold the machine to Stern:

Cash	360,000	
Accumulated Depreciation	150,000	
Equipment		450,000
Gain on Sale of Equipment		60,000

Required

Give the worksheet elimination entry or entries needed to remove the effects of the intercorporate sale of equipment when consolidated financial statements are prepared as of (a) December 31, 20X6, and (b) December 31, 20X7.

LO5, LO6

E7-21 Using the Eliminating Entry to Determine Account Balances

Pastel Corporation acquired a controlling interest in Somber Corporation in 20X5 for an amount equal to its underlying book value. At the date of acquisition, the fair value of the noncontrolling interest was equal to its proportionate share of the book value of Somber Corporation. In preparing a consolidated balance sheet worksheet at January 1, 20X9, Pastel's controller included the following eliminating entry:

Equipment	53,500	
Investment in Somber Corp.	9,450	
Noncontrolling Interest	1,050	
Accumulated Depreciation		64,000

A note at the bottom of the consolidation worksheet at January 1, 20X9, indicates the equipment was purchased from a nonaffiliate on January 1, 20X1, for $120,000 and was sold to an affiliate on December 31, 20X8. The equipment is being depreciated on a 15-year straight-line basis. Somber reported stock outstanding of $300,000 and retained earnings of $200,000 at January 1, 20X9. Somber reported net income of $25,000 and paid dividends of $6,000 for 20X9.

Required

a. What percentage ownership of Somber Corporation does Pastel hold?

b. Was the parent or subsidiary the owner prior to the intercorporate sale of equipment? Explain.

c. What was the intercompany transfer price of the equipment on December 31, 20X8?

d. What amount of income will be assigned to the noncontrolling interest in the consolidated income statement for 20X9?

e. Assuming Pastel and Somber report depreciation expense of $15,000 and $9,000, respectively, for 20X9, what depreciation amount will be reported in the consolidated income statement for 20X9?

f. Give all eliminating entries needed at December 31, 20X9, to prepare a complete set of consolidated financial statements.

LO2

E7-22 Intercompany Sale of Services

Norgaard Corporation is provided management consulting services by its 75 percent owned subsidiary, Bline Inc. During 20X3, Norgaard paid Bline $123,200 for its services. For the year 20X4, Bline billed Norgaard $138,700 for such services and collected all but $6,600 by year-end. Bline's labor cost and other associated costs for the employees providing services to Norgaard totaled $91,000 in 20X3 and $112,000 in 20X4. Norgaard reported $2,342,000 of income from its own separate operations for 20X4, and Bline reported net income of $631,000.

Required

a. Present all elimination entries related to the intercompany sale of services that would be needed in the consolidation worksheet used to prepare a complete set of consolidated financial statements for 20X4.

b. Compute consolidated net income for 20X4 and the amount of income assigned to the controlling interest.

LO3, LO6

E7-23A Modified Equity Method and Cost Method

Newtime Products purchased 65 percent of TV Sales Company's stock at underlying book value on January 1, 20X3. At that date, the fair value of the noncontrolling interest was equal to 35 percent of the book value of TV Sales. TV Sales reported shares outstanding of $300,000 and retained earnings of $100,000. During 20X3, TV Sales reported net income of $50,000 and paid dividends of $5,000. In 20X4, TV Sales reported net income of $70,000 and paid dividends of $20,000.

The following transactions occurred between Newtime Products and TV Sales in 20X3 and 20X4:

1. TV Sales sold camera equipment to Newtime for a $40,000 profit on December 31, 20X3. The equipment had a five-year estimated economic life remaining at the time of intercompany transfer and is depreciated on a straight-line basis.

2. Newtime sold land costing $30,000 to TV Sales on June 30, 20X4, for $41,000.

Required

a. Assuming that Newtime uses the modified equity method to account for its investment in TV Sales:

(1) Give the journal entries recorded on Newtime's books in 20X4 related to its investment in TV Sales.

(2) Give all eliminating entries needed to prepare a consolidation worksheet for 20X4.

b. Assuming that Newtime uses the cost method to account for its investment in TV Sales:

   (1) Give the journal entries recorded on Newtime's books in 20X4 related to its investment in TV Sales.

   (2) Give all eliminating entries needed to prepare a consolidation worksheet for 20X4.

Problems

LO6

P7-24   Computation of Consolidated Net Income

Petime Corporation acquired 90 percent ownership of United Grain Company on January 1, 20X4, for $108,000 when the fair value of United's net assets was $10,000 greater than its $110,000 book value. The increase in value was attributed to amortizable assets with a remaining life of 10 years. At that date, the fair value of the noncontrolling interest was equal to $12,000.

During 20X4, United sold land to Petime at a $7,000 profit. United Grain reported net income of $19,000 and paid dividends of $4,000 in 20X4. Petime reported income, exclusive of its income from United Grain, of $34,000 and paid dividends of $15,000 in 20X4.

Advanced
StudyGuide
.com

Required

a. Compute the amount of income assigned to the controlling interest in the consolidated income statement for 20X4.

b. By what amount will the 20X4 income assigned to the controlling interest increase or decrease if the sale of land had been from Petime to United Grain and the gain on the sale of land had been included in Petime's $34,000 income?

LO5

P7-25   Subsidiary Net Income

Bold Corporation acquired 75 percent of Toll Corporation's voting common stock on January 1, 20X4, for $348,000, when the fair value of its net identifiable assets was $464,000 and the fair value of the noncontrolling interest was $116,000. Toll reported common stock outstanding of $150,000 and retained earnings of $270,000. The excess of fair value over book value of Toll's net assets was attributed to amortizable assets with a remaining life of 10 years. On December 31, 20X4, Toll sold a building to Bold and recorded a gain of $20,000. Income assigned to the noncontrolling shareholders in the 20X4 consolidated income statement was $17,500.

Required

a. Compute the amount of net income Toll reported for 20X4.

b. Compute the amount reported as consolidated net income if Bold reported operating income of $234,000 for 20X4.

c. Compute the amount of income assigned to the controlling interest in the 20X4 consolidated income statement.

LO6

P7-26   Transfer of Asset from One Subsidiary to Another

Pelts Company holds a total of 70 percent of Bugle Corporation and 80 percent of Cook Products Corporation stock. Bugle purchased a warehouse with an expected life of 20 years on January 1, 20X1, for $40,000. On January 1, 20X6, it sold the warehouse to Cook Products for $45,000.

Required

Complete the following table showing selected information that would appear in the separate 20X6 income statements and balance sheets of Bugle Corporation and Cook Products Corporation and in the 20X6 consolidated financial statements.

	Bugle Corporation	Cook Products Corporation	Consolidated Entity
Depreciation expense			
Fixed assets—warehouse			
Accumulated depreciation			
Gain on sale of warehouse			

LO6

P7-27   Consolidated Eliminating Entry

In preparing its consolidated financial statements at December 31, 20X7, the following eliminating entries were included in the consolidation worksheet of Master Corporation:

Buildings	140,000	
Gain on Sale of Building	28,000	
Accumulated Depreciation		168,000

| Accumulated Depreciation | 2,000 | |
| Depreciation Expense | | 2,000 |

Master owns 60 percent of Rakel Corporation's voting common stock. On January 1, 20X7, Rakel sold Master a building it had purchased for $600,000 on January 1, 20X1, and depreciated on a 20-year straight-line basis. Master recorded depreciation for 20X7 using straight-line depreciation and the same useful life and residual value as Rakel.

Required

a. What amount did Master pay Rakel for the building?

b. What amount of accumulated depreciation did Rakel report at January 1, 20X7, prior to the sale?

c. What annual depreciation expense did Rakel record prior to the sale?

d. What expected residual value did Rakel use in computing its annual depreciation expense?

e. What amount of depreciation expense did Master record in 20X7?

f. If Rakel reported net income of $80,000 for 20X7, what amount of income will be assigned to the noncontrolling interest in the consolidated income statement for 20X7?

g. If Rakel reported net income of $65,000 for 20X8, what amount of income will be assigned to the noncontrolling interest in the consolidated income statement for 20X8?

LO6

P7-28 **Multiple-Choice Questions**

Select the correct answer for each of the following questions.

1. In the preparation of a consolidated income statement:
   a. Income assigned to noncontrolling shareholders always is computed as a pro rata portion of the reported net income of the consolidated entity.
   b. Income assigned to noncontrolling shareholders always is computed as a pro rata portion of the reported net income of the subsidiary.
   c. Income assigned to noncontrolling shareholders in the current period is likely to be less than a pro rata portion of the reported net income of the subsidiary in the current period if the subsidiary had an unrealized gain on an intercorporate sale of depreciable assets in the preceding period.
   d. Income assigned to noncontrolling shareholders in the current period is likely to be more than a pro rata portion of the reported net income of the subsidiary in the current period if the subsidiary had an unrealized gain on an intercorporate sale of depreciable assets in the preceding period.

2. When a 90 percent owned subsidiary records a gain on the sale of land to an affiliate during the current period and the land is not resold before the end of the period:
   a. Ninety percent of the gain will be excluded from consolidated net income.
   b. Consolidated net income will be increased by the full amount of the gain.
   c. A proportionate share of the unrealized gain will be excluded from income assigned to noncontrolling interest.
   d. The full amount of the unrealized gain will be excluded from income assigned to noncontrolling interest.

3. During 20X5, Subsidiary Corporation sells land to Parent Corporation and records a gain of $15,000 on the sale. Subsidiary reports 20X5 net income of $55,000. Parent holds 60 percent of the voting shares of Subsidiary. Parent plans to build a new general headquarters on the land in 20X7. If no adjustment is made for unrealized profits in preparing the consolidated financial statements as of December 31, 20X5:
   a. Consolidated net income will be overstated by $15,000.
   b. Consolidated retained earnings will be overstated by $15,000.
   c. Income assigned to the noncontrolling interest in the consolidated income statement will be overstated by $9,000.
   d. Consolidated net income will be overstated by $9,000.
   e. Both answers *a* and *b* are correct.

4. Minor Company sold land to Major Company on November 15, 20X4, and recorded a gain of $30,000 on the sale. Major owns 80 percent of Minor's common shares. Which of the following statements is correct?

   a. A proportionate share of the $30,000 must be treated as a reduction of income assigned to the noncontrolling interest in the consolidated income statement unless the land is resold to a nonaffiliate in 20X4.

   b. The $30,000 will not be treated as an adjustment in computing income assigned to the non-controlling interest in the consolidated income statement in 20X4 unless the land is resold to a nonaffiliate in 20X4.

   c. In computing consolidated net income it does not matter whether the land is or is not resold to a nonaffiliate before the end of the period; the $30,000 will not affect the computation of consolidated net income in 20X4 because the profits are on the subsidiary's books.

   d. Minor's trial balance as of December 31, 20X4, should be adjusted to remove the $30,000 gain since the gain is not yet realized.

5. Lewis Company owns 80 percent of Tomassini Corporation's stock. You are told that Tomassini has sold equipment to Lewis and that the following eliminating entries are needed to prepare consolidated statements for 20X9:

Equipment	20,000	
Gain on Sale of Equipment	40,000	
Accumulated Depreciation		60,000

Accumulated Depreciation	5,000	
Depreciation Expense		5,000

Which of the following is incorrect?

   a. The parent paid $40,000 in excess of the subsidiary's carrying amount to acquire the asset.

   b. From a consolidated viewpoint, depreciation expense as Lewis recorded it is overstated.

   c. The asset transfer occurred in 20X9 before the end of the year.

   d. Consolidated net income will be reduced by $40,000 when this entry is used as an eliminating entry.

LO6

P7-29 **Intercompany Services Provided to Subsidiary**

During 20X4, Plate Company paid its employees $80,000 for work done in helping its wholly owned subsidiary build a new office building that was completed on December 31, 20X4. Plate recorded the $110,000 payment from the subsidiary for the work done as service revenue. The subsidiary included the payment in the cost of the building and is depreciating the building over 25 years with no assumed residual value.

Required

Present the eliminating entries needed at December 31, 20X4 and 20X5, to prepare Plate's consolidated financial statements.

LO4, LO5

Advanced
StudyGuide
.com

P7-30 **Consolidated Net Income with Intercorporate Transfers**

In its 20X7 consolidated income statement, Bower Development Company reported consolidated net income of $961,000 and $39,000 of income assigned to the 30 percent noncontrolling interest in its only subsidiary, Subsidence Mining, Inc. During the year, Subsidence had sold a previously mined parcel of land to Bower for a new housing development; the sales price to Bower was $500,000, and the land had a carrying amount at the time of sale of $560,000. At the beginning of the previous year, Bower had sold excavation and grading equipment to Subsidence for $240,000; the equipment had a remaining life of six years as of the date of sale and a book value of $210,000. The equipment originally had cost $350,000 when Bower purchased it on January 2, 20X2. The equipment never was expected to have any salvage value.

Bower had acquired 70 percent of the voting shares of Subsidence 12 years earlier when the fair value of its net assets was $200,000 greater than book value and the fair value of the noncontrolling interest was $60,000 more than a proportionate share of the book value of

Subsidence's net assets. All the excess over the book value was attributable to intangible assets with a remaining life of 10 years from the date of combination. Both parent and subsidiary use straight-line amortization and depreciation. Assume Bower uses the fully adjusted equity method.

Required

a. Present the journal entry made by Bower to record the sale of equipment in 20X6 to Subsidence.

b. Present all elimination entries related to the intercompany transfers of land and equipment that should appear in the consolidation worksheet used to prepare a complete set of consolidated financial statements for 20X7.

c. Compute Subsidence's 20X7 net income.

d. Compute Bower's 20X7 income from its own separate operations, excluding any investment income from its investment in Subsidence Mining.

LO4, LO5 | **P7-31** | **Preparation of Consolidated Balance Sheet**

Lofton Company owns 60 percent of Temple Corporation's voting shares, purchased on May 17, 20X1, at book value. At that date, the fair value of the noncontrolling interest was equal to 40 percent of the book value of Temple Corporation. The companies' permanent accounts on December 31, 20X6, contained the following balances:

	Lofton Company	Temple Corporation
Cash and Receivables	$101,000	$ 20,000
Inventory	80,000	40,000
Land	150,000	90,000
Buildings and Equipment	400,000	300,000
Investment in Temple Corporation Stock	141,000	
	872,000	$450,000
Accumulated Depreciation	$135,000	$ 85,000
Accounts Payable	90,000	25,000
Notes Payable	200,000	90,000
Common Stock	100,000	200,000
Retained Earnings	347,000	50,000
	$872,000	$450,000

On January 1, 20X2, Lofton paid $100,000 for equipment with a 10-year expected total economic life. The equipment was depreciated on a straight-line basis with no residual value. Temple purchased the equipment from Lofton on December 31, 20X4, for $91,000. Assume Lofton did not change the estimated useful life of the equipment.

Temple sold land it had purchased for $30,000 on February 23, 20X4, to Lofton for $20,000 on October 14, 20X5. Assume Lofton uses the fully adjusted equity method.

Required

a. Prepare a consolidated balance sheet worksheet in good form as of December 31, 20X6.

b. Prepare a consolidated balance sheet as of December 31, 20X6.

LO4, LO5 | **P7-32** | **Consolidation Worksheet in Year of Intercompany Transfer**

Prime Company holds 80 percent of Lane Company's stock, acquired on January 1, 20X2, for $160,000. On the acquisition date, the fair value of the noncontrolling interest was $40,000. Lane reported retained earnings of $50,000 and had $100,000 of common stock outstanding. Prime uses the fully adjusted equity method in accounting for its investment in Lane.

Trial balance data for the two companies on December 31, 20X6, are as follows:

	Prime Company		Lane Company	
Item	**Debit**	**Credit**	**Debit**	**Credit**
Cash and Accounts Receivable	$ 113,000		$ 35,000	
Inventory	260,000		90,000	
Land	80,000		80,000	
Buildings and Equipment	500,000		150,000	
Investment in Lane Company Stock	191,600			
Cost of Goods Sold	140,000		60,000	
Depreciation and Amortization	25,000		15,000	
Other Expenses	15,000		5,000	
Dividends Declared	30,000		5,000	
Accumulated Depreciation		$ 205,000		$ 45,000
Accounts Payable		60,000		20,000
Bonds Payable		200,000		50,000
Common Stock		300,000		100,000
Retained Earnings		322,000		95,000
Sales		240,000		130,000
Gain on Sale of Equipment		20,000		
Income from Subsidiary		7,600		
Total	$1,354,600	$1,354,600	$440,000	$440,000

Additional Information

1. At the date of combination, the book values and fair values of all separately iden-tifiable assets and liabilities of Lane were the same. At December 31, 20X6, the management of Prime reviewed the amount attributed to goodwill as a result of its purchase of Lane stock and concluded an impairment loss of $18,000 should be rec-ognized in 20X6 and shared proportionately between the controlling and noncontrol-ling shareholders.

2. On January 1, 20X5, Lane sold land that had cost $8,000 to Prime for $18,000.

3. On January 1, 20X6, Prime sold to Lane equipment that it had purchased for $75,000 on Janu-ary 1, 20X1. The equipment has a total economic life of 15 years and was sold to Lane for $70,000. Both companies use straight-line depreciation.

4. There was $7,000 of intercompany receivables and payables on December 31, 20X6.

Required

a. Give all eliminating entries needed to prepare a consolidation worksheet for 20X6.

b. Prepare a three-part worksheet for 20X6 in good form.

c. Prepare a consolidated balance sheet, income statement, and retained earnings statement for 20X6.

LO4, LO5   **P7-33**   **Consolidation Worksheet in Year Following Intercompany Transfer**

Prime Company holds 80 percent of Lane Company's stock, acquired on January 1, 20X2, for $160,000. On the date of acquisition, Lane reported retained earnings of $50,000 and $100,000 of common stock outstanding, and the fair value of the noncontrolling interest was $40,000. Prime uses the fully adjusted equity method in accounting for its invest-ment in Lane.

Trial balance data for the two companies on December 31, 20X7, are as follows:

	Prime Company		Lane Company	
Item	**Debit**	**Credit**	**Debit**	**Credit**
Cash and Accounts Receivable	$ 151,000		$ 55,000	
Inventory	240,000		100,000	
Land	100,000		80,000	
Buildings and Equipment	500,000		150,000	
Investment in Lane Company Stock	201,600			
Cost of Goods Sold	160,000		80,000	
Depreciation and Amortization	25,000		15,000	

(continued)

Other Expenses	20,000		10,000	
Dividends Declared	60,000		35,000	
Accumulated Depreciation		$ 230,000		$ 60,000
Accounts Payable		60,000		25,000
Bonds Payable		200,000		50,000
Common Stock		300,000		100,000
Retained Earnings		379,600		140,000
Sales		250,000		150,000
Income from Subsidiary		38,000		
Total	$1,457,600	$1,457,600	$525,000	$525,000

Additional Information

1. At the date of combination, the book values and fair values of Lane's separately identifiable assets and liabilities were equal. The full amount of the increased value of the entity was attributed to goodwill. At December 31, 20X6, the management of Prime reviewed the amount attributed to goodwill as a result of its purchase of Lane stock and recognized an impairment loss of $18,000. No further impairment occurred in 20X7.

2. On January 1, 20X5, Lane sold land that had cost $8,000 to Prime for $18,000.

3. On January 1, 20X6, Prime sold to Lane equipment that it had purchased for $75,000 on January 1, 20X1. The equipment has a total 15-year economic life and was sold to Lane for $70,000. Both companies use straight-line depreciation.

4. Intercorporate receivables and payables total $4,000 on December 31, 20X7.

Required

a. Prepare a reconciliation between the balance in Prime's Investment in Lane Company Stock account reported on December 31, 20X7, and the book value of Lane.

b. Prepare all worksheet eliminating entries needed as of December 31, 20X7, and complete a three-part consolidation worksheet for 20X7.

L03, LO4   **P7-34**   **Intercorporate Sales in Prior Years**

On January 1, 20X5, Pond Corporation acquired 80 percent of Skate Company's stock by issuing common stock with a fair value of $180,000. At that date, Skate reported net assets of $150,000. The fair value of the noncontrolling interest was $45,000. Assume Pond uses the fully adjusted equity method. The balance sheets for Pond and Skate at January 1, 20X8, and December 31, 20X8, and income statements for 20X8 were reported as follows:

20X8 Balance Sheet Data

	Pond Corporation		Skate Company	
	January 1	December 31	January 1	December 31
Cash	$ 40,400	$ 68,400	$ 10,000	$ 47,000
Accounts Receivable	120,000	130,000	60,000	65,000
Interest and Other Receivables	40,000	45,000	8,000	10,000
Inventory	100,000	140,000	50,000	50,000
Land	50,000	50,000	22,000	22,000
Buildings and Equipment	400,000	400,000	240,000	240,000
Accumulated Depreciation	(150,000)	(185,000)	(70,000)	(94,000)
Investment in Skate Company Stock	185,600	200,100		
Investment in Tin Co. Bonds	135,000	134,000		
Total Assets	921,000	982,500	$320,000	$340,000
Accounts Payable	$ 60,000	$ 65,000	$ 16,500	$ 11,000
Interest and Other Payables	40,000	45,000	7,000	12,000
Bonds Payable	300,000	300,000	100,000	100,000
Bond Discount			(3,500)	(3,000)
Common Stock	150,000	150,000	30,000	30,000
Additional Paid-in Capital	155,000	155,000	20,000	20,000
Retained Earnings	216,000	267,500	150,000	170,000
Total Liabilities and Equities	921,000	982,500	$320,000	$340,000

20X8 Income Statement Data				
	Pond Corporation		**Skate Company**	
Sales		$450,000		$250,000
Income from Subsidiary		22,500		
Interest Income		14,900		
Total Revenue		487,400		$250,000
Cost of Goods Sold	$285,000		$136,000	
Other Operating Expenses	50,000		40,000	
Depreciation Expense	35,000		24,000	
Interest Expense	24,000		10,500	
Miscellaneous Expenses	11,900	(405,900)	9,500	(220,000)
Net Income		$ 81,500		$ 30,000

Additional Information

1. In 20X2 Skate developed a patent for a high-speed drill bit that Pond planned to market more extensively. In accordance with generally accepted accounting standards, Skate charges all research and development costs to expense in the year the expenses are incurred. At January 1, 20X5, the market value of the patent rights was estimated to be $50,000. Pond believes the patent will be of value for the next 20 years. The remainder of the differential is assigned to buildings and equipment, which also had a 20-year estimated economic life at January 1, 20X5. All of Skate's other assets and liabilities identified by Pond at the date of acquisition had book values and fair values that were relatively equal.

2. On December 31, 20X7, Pond sold a building to Skate for $65,000 that it had purchased for $125,000 and depreciated on a straight-line basis over 25 years. At the time of sale, Pond reported accumulated depreciation of $75,000 and a remaining life of 10 years.

3. On July 1, 20X6, Skate sold land that it had purchased for $22,000 to Pond for $35,000. Pond is planning to build a new warehouse on the property prior to the end of 20X9.

4. Both Pond and Skate paid dividends in 20X8.

Required

a. Give all eliminating entries required to prepare a three-part consolidation working paper at December 31, 20X8.

b. Prepare a three-part worksheet for 20X8 in good form.

LO3, LO6

P7-35 **Intercorporate Sale of Land and Depreciable Asset**

Topp Corporation acquired 70 percent of Morris Company's voting common stock on January 31, 20X3, for $158,900. Morris reported common stock outstanding of $100,000 and retained earnings of $85,000. The fair value of the noncontrolling interest was $68,100 at the date of acquisition. Buildings and equipment held by Morris had a fair value $25,000 greater than book value. The remainder of the differential was assigned to a copyright held by Morris. Buildings and equipment had a 10-year remaining life and the copyright had a five-year life at the date of acquisition.

Trial balances for Topp and Morris on December 31, 20X5, are as follows:

	Topp Corporation		**Morris Company**	
	Debit	**Credit**	**Debit**	**Credit**
Cash	$ 15,850		$ 58,000	
Accounts Receivable	65,000		70,000	
Interest and Other Receivables	30,000		10,000	
Inventory	150,000		180,000	
Land	80,000		60,000	
Buildings and Equipment	315,000		240,000	
Bond Discount			15,000	
Investment in Morris Company Stock	157,630			
Cost of Goods Sold	375,000		110,000	
Depreciation Expense	25,000		10,000	

(continued)

Interest Expense	24,000		33,000	
Other Expense	28,000		17,000	
Dividends Declared	30,000		5,000	
Accumulated Depreciation—Buildings and Equipment		$ 120,000		$ 60,000
Accounts Payable		61,000		28,000
Other Payables		30,000		20,000
Bonds Payable		250,000		300,000
Common Stock		150,000		100,000
Additional Paid-in Capital		30,000		
Retained Earnings		165,240		100,000
Sales		450,000		190,400
Other Income		28,250		
Gain on Sale of Equipment				9,600
Income from Subsidiary		10,990		
Total	$1,295,480	$1,295,480	$808,000	$808,000

Topp sold land it had purchased for $21,000 to Morris on September 20, 20X4, for $32,000. Morris plans to use the land for future plant expansion. On January 1, 20X5, Morris sold equipment to Topp for $91,600. Morris purchased the equipment on January 1, 20X3, for $100,000 and depreciated it on a 10-year basis, including an estimated residual value of $10,000. The residual value and estimated economic life of the equipment remained unchanged as a result of the transfer and both companies use straight-line depreciation. Assume Topp uses the fully adjusted equity method.

Required

a. Compute the amount of income assigned to the nonconcontrolling interest in the consolidated income statement for 20X5.

b. Prepare a reconciliation between the balance in the Investment in Morris Company Stock account reported by Topp at December 31, 20X5, and the underlying book value of net assets reported by Morris at that date.

c. Give all eliminating entries needed to prepare a full set of consolidated financial statements at December 31, 20X5, for Topp and Morris.

d. Prepare a three-part worksheet for 20X5 in good form.

LO3, LO6

P7-36 Incomplete Data

Partial trial balance data for Mound Corporation, Shadow Company, and the consolidated entity at December 31, 20X7, are as follows:

Item	Mound Corporation	Shadow Company	Consolidated Entity
Cash	$ 65,300	$ 25,000	$ 90,300
Accounts Receivable	(d)	35,000	126,000
Inventory	160,000	75,000	235,000
Buildings and Equipment	345,000	150,000	(i)
Land	70,000	90,000	153,000
Investment in Shadow Company Stock	(f)		
Cost of Goods Sold	230,000	195,000	425,000
Depreciation Expense	45,000	10,000	52,000
Amortization Expense			(e)
Miscellaneous Expense	18,000	15,000	33,000
Dividends Declared	25,000	20,000	25,000
Income to Noncontrolling Interest			(l)
Copyrights			9,000
Total Debits	$1,180,900	$615,000	$1,674,200
Accumulated Depreciation	$ 180,000	$ 80,000	$ (j)
Accounts Payable	25,000	85,000	101,000
Common Stock	100,000	50,000	(a)

(continued)

Item	Mound Corporation	Shadow Company	Consolidated Entity
Additional Paid-in Capital	(b)	70,000	140,000
Retained Earnings	375,800	80,000	(k)
Income from Subsidiary	10,100		
Sales	343,000	(c)	593,000
Gain on Sale of Land	(g)		(h)
Noncontrolling Interest			86,400
Total Credits	$1,180,900	$615,000	$1,674,200

Additional Information

1. Mound Corporation acquired 60 percent ownership of Shadow Company on January 1, 20X4, for $106,200. Shadow reported net assets of $150,000 at that date, and the fair value of the noncontrolling interest was estimated to be $70,800. The full amount of the differential at acquisition is assigned to copyrights that are being amortized over a six-year life.

2. On August 13, 20X7, Mound sold land to Shadow for $28,000. Mound also has accounts receivable from Shadow on services performed prior to the end of 20X7.

3. Shadow sold equipment it had purchased for $60,000 on January 1, 20X4, to Mound on January 1, 20X6, for $45,000. The equipment is depreciated on a straight-line basis and had a total expected useful life of five years when Shadow purchased it. No change in life expectancy resulted from the intercompany transfer. Assume Mound uses the fully adjusted equity method.

4. Assume Mound Corp. does not use the optional accumulation depreciation elimination entry.

Required
Compute the dollar amount for each of the balances identified by a letter.

LO6

P7-37   Intercompany Sale of Equipment at a Loss in Prior Period
Block Corporation was created on January 1, 20X0, to develop computer software. On January 1, 20X5, Foster Company acquired 90 percent of Block's common stock at its underlying book value. At that date, the fair value of the noncontrolling interest was equal to 10 percent of the book value of Block Corporation. Trial balances for Foster and Block on December 31, 20X9, follow:

	Foster Company		Block Corporation	
	Debit	Credit	Debit	Credit
Cash	$ 82,000		$ 32,400	
Accounts Receivable	80,000		90,000	
Other Receivables	40,000		10,000	
Inventory	200,000		130,000	
Land	80,000		60,000	
Buildings and Equipment	500,000		250,000	
Investment in Block Corporation Stock	229,500			
Cost of Goods Sold	500,000		250,000	
Depreciation Expense	45,000		15,000	
Other Expense	95,000		75,000	
Dividends Declared	40,000		20,000	
Accumulated Depreciation		$ 155,000		$ 75,000
Accounts Payable		63,000		35,000
Other Payables		95,000		20,000
Bonds Payable		250,000		200,000
Bond Premium				2,400
Common Stock		210,000		50,000
Additional Paid-in Capital		110,000		
Retained Earnings		251,200		150,000
Sales		680,000		385,000
Other Income		26,000		15,000
Income from Subsidiary		51,300		
Total	$1,891,500	$1,891,500	$932,400	$932,400

On January 1, 20X7, Block sold equipment to Foster for $48,000. Block had purchased the equipment for $90,000 on January 1, 20X5, and was depreciating it on a straight-line basis with a 10-year expected life and no anticipated scrap value. The equipment's total expected life is unchanged as a result of the intercompany sale. Assume Foster uses the fully adjusted equity method.

Required

a. Give all eliminating entries required to prepare a three-part consolidated working paper at December 31, 20X9.

b. Prepare a three-part worksheet for 20X9 in good form.

LO2–LO6 **P7-38** **Comprehensive Problem: Intercorporate Transfers**

Rossman Corporation holds 75 percent of the common stock of Schmid Distributors Inc., purchased on December 31, 20X1, for $2,340,000. At the date of acquisition, Schmid reported common stock with a par value of $1,000,000, additional paid-in capital of $1,350,000, and retained earnings of $620,000. The fair value of the noncontrolling interest at acquisition was $780,000. The differential at acquisition was attributable to the following items:

Inventory (sold in 20X2)	$ 30,000
Land	56,000
Goodwill	64,000
Total Differential	$150,000

During 20X2, Rossman sold a plot of land to Schmid at a gain of $23,000 that it had purchased several years before; Schmid continues to hold the land. In 20X6, Rossman and Schmid entered into a five-year contract under which Rossman provides management consulting services to Schmid on a continuing basis; Schmid pays Rossman a fixed fee of $80,000 per year for these services. At December 31, 20X8, Schmid owed Rossman $20,000 as the final 20X8 quarterly payment under the contract.

On January 2, 20X8, Rossman paid $250,000 to Schmid to purchase equipment that Schmid was then carrying at $290,000. Schmid had purchased that equipment on December 27, 20X2, for $435,000. The equipment is expected to have a total 15-year life and no salvage value. The amount of the differential assigned to goodwill has not been impaired.

At December 31, 20X8, trial balances for Rossman and Schmid appeared as follows:

Item	Rossman Corporation Debit	Rossman Corporation Credit	Schmid Distributors Inc. Debit	Schmid Distributors Inc. Credit
Cash	$ 50,700		$ 38,000	
Current Receivables	101,800		89,400	
Inventory	286,000		218,900	
Investment in Schmid Stock	2,974,000			
Land	400,000		1,200,000	
Buildings and Equipment	2,400,000		2,990,000	
Cost of Goods Sold	2,193,000		525,000	
Depreciation and Amortization	202,000		88,000	
Other Expenses	1,381,000		227,000	
Dividends Declared	50,000		20,000	
Accumulated Depreciation		$ 1,105,000		$ 420,000
Current Payables		86,200		76,300
Bonds Payable		1,000,000		200,000
Common Stock		100,000		1,000,000
Additional Paid-in Capital		1,272,000		1,350,000
Retained Earnings, January 1		1,474,800		1,400,000
Sales		4,801,000		985,000
Other Income or Loss		90,000	35,000	
Income from Schmid		109,500		
Total	$10,038,500	$10,038,500	$5,431,300	$5,431,300

As of December 31, 20X8, Schmid had declared but not yet paid its fourth-quarter dividend of $5,000. Both companies use straight-line depreciation and amortization. Rossman uses the fully adjusted equity method to account for its investment in Schmid.

Required

a. Compute the amount of the differential as of January 1, 20X8.

b. Verify the balance in Rossman's Investment in Schmid Stock account as of December 31, 20X8.

c. Present all elimination entries that would appear in a three-part consolidation worksheet as of December 31, 20X8.

d. Prepare and complete a three-part worksheet for the preparation of consolidated financial statements for 20X8.

LO4, LO5 | **P7-39A** | **Modified Equity Method Computation of Retained Earnings following Multiple Transfers**

Great Company acquired 80 percent of Meager Corporation's common stock on January 1, 20X4, for $280,000. The fair value of the noncontrolling interest was $70,000 at the date of acquisition. Great's corporate controller has lost the consolidation files for the past three years and has asked you to compute the proper retained earnings balances for the consolidated entity at January 1, 20X8, and December 31, 20X8. The controller has been able to determine the following:

1. The book value of Meager's net assets at January 1, 20X4, was $290,000 and the fair value of its net assets was $325,000. This difference was due to an increase in the value of equipment. All depreciable assets had a remaining life of 10 years at the date of combination. At December 31, 20X8, Great's management reviewed the amount attributed to goodwill as a result of its purchase of Meager common stock and concluded an impairment loss of $17,500 should be recognized in 20X8 and shared proportionately between the controlling and noncontrolling shareholders.

2. Great uses the modified equity method in accounting for its investment in Meager.

3. Meager has reported net income of $30,000 and paid dividends of $20,000 each year since Great purchased its ownership.

4. Great reported retained earnings of $450,000 in its December 31, 20X7, balance sheet. For 20X8, Great reported operating income of $65,000 and paid dividends of $45,000.

5. Meager sold land costing $40,000 to Great for $56,000 on December 31, 20X7.

6. On January 1, 20X6, Great sold depreciable assets with a remaining useful life of 10 years to Meager and recorded a $22,000 gain on the sale.

Required

Compute the appropriate amounts to be reported as consolidated retained earnings at January 1, 20X8, and December 31, 20X8.

LO3, LO6 | **P7-40A** | **Consolidation Worksheet with Intercompany Transfers (Modified Equity Method)**

Mist Company acquired 65 percent of Blank Corporation's voting common stock on June 20, 20X2, at underlying book value. At that date, the fair value of the noncontrolling interest was equal to 35 percent of the book value of Blank Corporation. The balance sheets and income statements for the companies at December 31, 20X4, are as follows:

MIST COMPANY AND BLANK CORPORATION
Balance Sheets
December 31, 20X4

Item	Mist Company	Blank Corp.
Cash	$ 32,500	$ 22,000
Accounts Receivable	62,000	37,000
Inventory	95,000	71,000
Land	40,000	15,000
Buildings and Equipment (net)	200,000	125,000
Investment in Blank Corp. Stock	110,500	
Total Assets	$540,000	$270,000

(continued)

Accounts Payable	$ 35,000	$ 20,000
Bonds Payable	180,000	80,000
Common Stock, $5 par value	100,000	60,000
Retained Earnings	225,000	110,000
Total Liabilities and Stockholders' Equity	$540,000	$270,000

MIST COMPANY AND BLANK CORPORATION
Combined Income and Retained Earnings Statements
Year Ended December 31, 20X4

Item	Mist Company		Blank Corp.	
Sales and Service Revenue		$286,500		$128,500
Gain on Sale of Land		4,000		
Gain on Sale of Building				13,200
Income from Subsidiary		19,500		
		$310,000		$141,700
Cost of Goods and Services Sold	$160,000		$75,000	
Depreciation Expense	22,000		19,000	
Other Expenses	76,000	(258,000)	17,700	(111,700)
Net Income		$ 52,000		$ 30,000
Dividends Paid		(25,000)		(5,000)
Change in Retained Earnings		$ 27,000		$ 25,000

Additional Information

1. Mist uses the modified equity method in accounting for its investment in Blank.
2. During 20X4, Mist charged Blank $24,000 for consulting services to Blank during the year. The services cost Mist $17,000.
3. On January 1, 20X4, Blank sold Mist a building for $13,200 above its carrying value on Blank's books. The building had a 12-year remaining economic life at the time of transfer.
4. On June 14, 20X4, Mist sold land it had purchased for $3,000 to Blank for $7,000. Blank continued to hold the land at December 31, 20X4.

Required

a. Give all eliminating entries needed to prepare a full set of consolidated financial statements for 20X4.
b. Prepare a consolidation worksheet for 20X4.
c. Prepare the 20X4 consolidated balance sheet, income statement, and retained earnings statement.

LO6

P7-41A Modified Equity Method

On December 31, 20X7, Prime Company recorded the following entry on its books to adjust its investment in Lane Company from the fully adjusted equity method to the modified equity method:

Income from Lane Company	2,000	
Investment in Lane Company Stock	38,400	
Retained Earnings		40,400

Required

a. Adjust the data reported by Prime in the trial balance in Problem P7-33 for the effects of the adjusting entry presented above.
b. Prepare the journal entries that would have been recorded on Prime's books during 20X7 if it had always used the fully adjusted equity method.
c. Prepare all eliminating entries needed to complete a consolidation worksheet as of December 31, 20X7, assuming Prime has used the fully adjusted equity method.
d. Complete a three-part consolidation worksheet as of December 31, 20X7.

LO6 | **P7-42A** **Cost Method**

The trial balance data presented in Problem P7-33 can be converted to reflect use of the cost method by inserting the following amounts in place of those presented for Prime Company:

Investment in Lane Company Stock	$160,000
Retained Earnings	348,000
Income from Subsidiary	–0–
Dividend Income	28,000

Required

a. Prepare the journal entries that would have been recorded on Prime's books during 20X7 under the cost method.

b. Prepare all eliminating entries needed to complete a consolidation worksheet as of December 31, 20X7, assuming Prime has used the cost method.

c. Complete a three-part consolidation worksheet as of December 31, 20X7.

Chapter **Eight**

Multinational Accounting: Foreign Currency Transactions and Financial Instruments

Multi-Corporate
Entities

**Multinational
Entities**

**Foreign Currency
Transactions**

Translation of Foreign
Statements

Partnerships

Governmental
Entities

Microsoft®

MICROSOFT'S MULTINATIONAL BUSINESS

Microsoft was founded in 1975 by Bill Gates (a Harvard dropout) and Paul Allen (a Washington State dropout). In 1980 Microsoft teamed up with IBM and in 1981 the company released the first version of MS DOS for IBM PCs. The year 1983 was another big year for Microsoft with the release of Multi-Tool Word (later Microsoft Word). The first version of Microsoft Windows (Windows 1.0) was released two years later in 1985. When Microsoft went public in 1986, its shares began trading at $21.00 and closed that first day at $28.00. Interestingly, each of those original shares issued in 1986 would be worth approximately $9,000 today. At its peak, Microsoft was worth approximately $600 billion and Bill Gates was personally worth close to $90 billion.

Microsoft continued to update Windows and had a major breakthrough in 1995 with the release of Windows 95. Microsoft continued to improve the Windows operating system and Microsoft Office throughout the 1990s and into the first part of the 2000s. However, in 2001 Microsoft attempted to break into the gaming console market with the introduction of the Xbox. Finally, in 2006, the company introduced the Zune to compete with Apple's iPod. From its humble beginnings, Microsoft forged an empire that made its founder, Bill Gates, one of the most wealthy individuals in the world and made Microsoft Windows and Microsoft Office the standard operating system and day-to-day tools for most businesses as well as individuals around the world.

Right from the start, Microsoft saw the international market as an important part of its expansion. In fact, the company opened its first international office in Tokyo in 1978 and by 2009 over 40 percent of Microsoft's total revenues came from international sales and services. Because such a large proportion of Microsoft's revenues come from international transactions, foreign currency exchange rate fluctuations significantly affect reported income. The following graph illustrates the effect of foreign currency exchange rates on Microsoft's revenues from 2003 to 2009. For example, in 2008, exchange rates increased Microsoft's revenues by $1.6 billion. Multinational companies spend considerable time accurately accounting for foreign transactions and the effects that changes in exchange rates can have on their reported results.

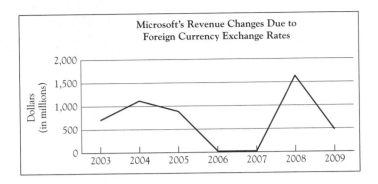

LEARNING OBJECTIVES

When you finish studying this chapter, you should be able to:

LO1   Understand how to make calculations using foreign currency exchange rates.

LO2   Understand the accounting implications of and be able to make calculations related to foreign currency transactions.

LO3   Understand how to hedge international currency risk using foreign currency forward exchange financial instruments.

LO4   Know how to measure hedge effectiveness, make interperiod tax allocations for foreign currency transactions, and hedge net investments in a foreign entity.

DOING BUSINESS IN A GLOBAL MARKET

LO1

Understand how to make calculations using foreign currency exchange rates.

Many companies, large and small, depend on international markets for acquiring goods and for selling their products and services. Every day the business press carries stories about the effects of export and import activity on the U.S. economy and the large flows of capital among the world's major countries. These reports often mention changes in the exchange rates of the major currencies of the world, such as, "The dollar weakened today against the yen." This chapter and Chapter 9 discuss the accounting issues affecting companies with international operations.

A company operating in international markets is subject to normal business risks such as lack of demand for its products in the foreign marketplace, labor strikes, and transportation delays in getting its products to the foreign customer. In addition, the U.S. entity may incur foreign currency risks whenever it conducts transactions in other currencies. For example, if a U.S. company acquires a machine on credit from an Italian manufacturer, the Italian company may require payment in euros. This means the U.S. company must eventually use a foreign currency broker or a bank to exchange U.S. dollars for euros to pay for the machine. In the process, the U.S. company may experience foreign currency gains or losses from fluctuations in the value of the U.S. dollar relative to the euro.

Foreign exchange markets are one of the most important and often misunderstood subjects in international business. Multinational enterprises (MNEs) entering into international transactions must agree with customers and suppliers on the currencies in which these transactions will be executed. Factors that affect this decision include familiarity with the foreign currency, the potential for gains and losses from changes in exchange rates, nationalistic pride, and practicality.

MNEs transact in a variety of currencies as a result of their export and import activities. There are approximately 150 different currencies around the world, but most international trade has been settled in six major currencies that have shown stability and general acceptance over time: the U.S. dollar, the British pound, the Canadian dollar, the Japanese yen, the Swiss franc, and the European euro.

The European euro (symbol €) is a relatively new currency introduced in 1999 to members of the European Union (EU) that wished to participate in a common currency. By 2002, euro notes and coins were introduced to be used in everyday trade. The EU is an organization of democratic member states from the European continent. The Union has grown over time and as of 2010 was composed of 27 member countries: Austria, Belgium, Bulgaria, Cyprus, Czech Republic, Denmark, Estonia, Finland, France, Germany, Greece, Hungary, Ireland, Italy, Latvia, Lithuania, Luxembourg, Malta, the Netherlands, Poland, Portugal, Romania, Slovakia, Slovenia, Spain, Sweden, and the United Kingdom. In addition, Croatia, Macedonia, and Turkey have applied for accession. The EU is a dominant economic force, rivaling the United States, and the euro is now as familiar to companies doing international business as the U.S. dollar. Currently, 16 of the 27 members of the EU use the Euro, and Estonia planned to adopt it in 2011.

The EU is one of several regional groupings, and these groupings are becoming increasingly important. The North American Free Trade Agreement (NAFTA) was approved by the U.S. Congress in 1993 and created a free-trade area of Canada, Mexico, and the United States, a market that exceeds 420 million people. Over time, the agreement will result in the elimination of tariffs (taxes) on goods shipped between these three countries. The Agreement on the South Asian Free Trade Area, or SAFTA, was created on January 1, 2006, and will be operational following ratification of the agreement by seven governments. SAFTA creates a framework for the creation of a free-trade zone covering 1.4 billion people in Bangladesh, Bhutan, India, the Maldives, Nepal, Pakistan, and Sri Lanka. The Association of Southeast Asian nations (ASEAN) created the ASEAN Free Trade Area (AFTA), which is a trade bloc agreement. The goal of AFTA is to increase ASEAN's competitive edge as a production base in the world market through the elimination, within ASEAN, of tariffs and nontariff barriers. AFTA currently is composed of Brunei, Cambodia, Indonesia, Laos, Malaysia, Myanmar, Philippines, Singapore, Thailand, and Vietnam. In January 2005, the Greater Arab Free Trade Area (also referred to as GAFTA) came into existence. GAFTA is a pact made by the Arab League to achieve a complete Arab economic bloc that can compete internationally. GAFTA is relatively similar to ASEAN.

Currency names and symbols often reflect a country's nationalistic pride and history. For example, the U.S. dollar receives its name from a variation of the German word *Taler,* the name of a silver piece that was first minted in 1518 and became the chief coin of Europe and the New World. Some historians suggest that the dollar symbol ($) is derived from a capital letter *U* superimposed over a capital letter *S.* The "greenback" as we know it today was first printed in 1862, in the midst of the Civil War, and now is issued by the 12 Federal Reserve banks scattered across the United States. The U.S. dollar can be identified in virtually every corner of the world because it has become one of the most widely traded currencies.

THE ACCOUNTING ISSUES

Accountants must be able to record and report transactions involving exchanges of U.S. dollars and foreign currencies. ***Foreign currency transactions*** of a U.S. company include sales, purchases, and other transactions giving rise to a transfer of foreign currency or the recording of receivables or payables that are *denominated*—that is, numerically specified to be settled—in a foreign currency. Because financial statements of virtually all U.S. companies are prepared using the U.S. dollar as the reporting currency, transactions denominated in other currencies must be restated to their U.S. dollar equivalents before they can be recorded in the U.S. company's books and included in its financial statements. This process of restating foreign currency transactions to their U.S. dollar–equivalent values is termed *translation.*

In addition, many large U.S. corporations have multinational operations such as foreign-based subsidiaries or branches. For example, a U.S. auto manufacturer may have manufacturing subsidiaries in Canada, Mexico, Spain, and Great Britain. The foreign subsidiaries prepare their financial statements in their home currencies. For example, the Mexican subsidiary reports its operations in pesos. The foreign currency amounts in the financial statements of these subsidiaries have to be translated, that is, restated, into their U.S. dollar equivalents before they can be consolidated with the financial statements of the U.S. parent company that uses the U.S. dollar as its reporting currency unit.

This chapter presents the accounting procedures for recording and reporting foreign transactions. Chapter 9 presents the procedures for combining or consolidating a foreign entity with a U.S. parent company. **FASB Statement No. 52 (ASC 830),** "Foreign Currency Translation" (FASB 52, ASC 830), issued in 1981, serves as the primary guide for accounting for accounts receivable and accounts payable foreign currency–denominated transactions that require payment or receipt of foreign currency. **FASB Statement No. 133 (ASC 815),** "Accounting for Derivative Instruments and Hedging Activities" (FASB 133, ASC 815), issued in 1998, guides the accounting for financial instruments specified as derivatives for the purpose of hedging certain items.

FOREIGN CURRENCY EXCHANGE RATES

Before 1972, most major currencies were valued on the basis of a gold standard whereby their international values were fixed per ounce of gold. However, in 1972, most countries signed an agreement to permit the values of their currencies to "float" based on the supply and demand for them. The resulting *foreign currency exchange rates* between currencies are established daily by foreign exchange brokers that serve as agents for individuals or countries wishing to deal in foreign currencies. Some countries, such as China, maintain an official fixed rate of currency exchange and have established fixed exchange rates for dividends remitted outside the country. These official rates may be changed at any time, and companies doing business abroad should contact the foreign country's government to ensure that the companies are in compliance with any currency exchange restrictions.

The Determination of Exchange Rates

A country's currency is much like any other commodity, and exchange rates change because of a number of economic factors affecting the supply of and demand for a nation's currency. For example, if a nation is experiencing high levels of inflation, the purchasing power of its currency decreases. This reduction in the value of a currency is reflected by a decrease in the positioning of that country's currency relative to other nations' currencies. Other factors causing exchange rate fluctuations are a nation's balance of payments, changes in a country's interest rate and investment levels, and the stability and process of governance. For example, if the United States had a higher average interest rate than that in Great Britain, the international investment community might seek to invest in the United States, thus increasing the demand for U.S. dollars relative to British pounds. The dollar would increase in value relative to the pound because of the increased demand. Exchange rates are determined daily and published in several sources, including *The Wall Street Journal.* Figure 8–1 presents an example of a typical daily business press report for selected foreign exchange rates. The rates illustrated in the table are current as of April 2010. Updated exchange rates may be obtained from most business publications, many metropolitan newspapers, and Web sites such as Yahoo! Finance.

Direct versus Indirect Exchange Rates

As indicated in Figure 8–1, the relative value of one currency to another may be expressed in two different ways: either *directly* or *indirectly.*

Direct Exchange Rate

The direct exchange rate (DER) is the number of *local currency units (LCUs)* needed to acquire one *foreign currency unit (FCU).* From the viewpoint of a U.S. entity, the

FIGURE 8–1 **Foreign Exchange Rates for Selected Major Currencies as of April 2010**

Country	Currency	Direct Exchange Rate (U.S. dollar equivalent)	Indirect Exchange Rate (currency per U.S. dollar)
Argentina	peso	0.2583	3.8713
Australia	dollar	0.9255	1.0805
Bahrain	dinar	2.6525	0.3770
Brazil	real	0.5672	1.7630
Canada	dollar	0.9999	1.0001
Chile	peso	0.0019	521
China	yuan renminbi	0.1465	6.8270
Colombia	peso	0.0005	1950.80
Czech Republic	koruna	0.0527	18.9670
Denmark	krone	0.1799	5.5595
Egypt	pound	0.1804	5.5442
Hong Kong	dollar	0.1288	7.7630
India	rupee	0.0226	44.2900
Indonesia	rupiah	0.0001	9009
Israel	new shekel	0.2688	3.7200
Japan	yen	0.0106	94.0300
1-month forward		0.009330	107.132
3-month forward		0.009350	106.935
6-month forward		0.00937	106.298
Malaysia	ringgit	0.3134	3.1910
Mexico	peso	0.0820	12.1886
Philippines	peso	0.0226	44.3100
Russia	ruble	0.0343	29.1213
South Korea	won	0.0009	1108.30
Sweden	krona	0.1396	7.1640
Switzerland	franc	0.9324	1.0725
Taiwan	dollar	0.0319	31.3350
Thailand	baht	0.0310	32.2200
United Kingdom	pound	1.5372	0.6505
1-month forward		1.94230	0.54485
3-month forward		1.93793	0.51602
6-month forward		1.93415	0.51702
Venezuela	bolivar	0.000466	2145.9230
Euro		1.3387	0.7470
1-month forward		1.4529	0.68875
3-month forward		1.454	0.68950
6-month forward		1.4559	0.69022
SDR		1.57435	0.635812

direct exchange rate can be viewed as the U.S. dollar cost of one foreign currency unit. The direct exchange rate ratio is expressed as follows, with the LCU, the U.S. dollar, in the numerator:

$$DER = \frac{\text{U.S. dollar−equivalent value}}{1\,\text{FCU}}$$

The direct exchange rate is used most often in accounting for foreign operations and transactions because the foreign currency–denominated accounts must be translated to their U.S. dollar–equivalent values. For example, if $1.20 can acquire €1 (1 European euro), the direct exchange rate of the dollar versus the European euro is $1.20, as follows:

$$\frac{\$1.20}{€1} = \$1.20$$

Indirect Exchange Rate

The indirect exchange rate (IER) is the reciprocal of the direct exchange rate. From the viewpoint of a U.S. entity, the indirect exchange rate is

$$IER = \frac{1\,FCU}{U.S.\,dollar - equivalent\,value}$$

For the European euro example, the indirect exchange rate is

$$\frac{€1}{\$1.20} = €0.8333$$

Another way to express this is

$$IER = \frac{Number\,of\,foreign\,currency\,units}{\$1}$$

$$= \frac{€0.8333}{\$1}$$

Thus, the indirect exchange rate of €0.8333 = $1 shows the number of foreign currency units that may be obtained for 1 U.S. dollar. People who travel outside the United States often use the indirect exchange rate.

Note that the direct and indirect rates are inversely related and that both state the same economic relationships between two currencies. For example, if the indirect exchange rate is given, the direct exchange rate may be computed by simply inverting the indirect exchange rate. If given the indirect exchange rate of €0.8333 (€0.8333/$1), the direct exchange rate can be computed as ($1/€0.8333) = $1.20. If given the direct exchange rate of $1.20, the indirect exchange rate can be computed as (€1/$1.20) = €0.8333. Again, the currency in the numerator identifies the direction of the exchange rate. In practice, a slight difference might exist in the inverse relationship because of brokers' commissions or small differences in demand for the two currencies.

Some persons identify the direct exchange rate as *American terms* to indicate that it is U.S. dollar–based and represents an exchange rate quote from the perspective of a person in the United States. The indirect exchange rate is sometimes identified as *European terms* to indicate the direct exchange rate from the perspective of a person in Europe, which means the exchange rate shows the number of units of the European's local currency units per one U.S. dollar. A guide to help remember the difference in exchange rates is to note that the U.S. dollar is the numerator for the direct rate or American terms (the foreign currency unit is in the denominator), and the foreign currency unit is in the numerator for the indirect rate or European terms (with the U.S. dollar in the denominator). The *terms currency* is the numerator and the *base currency* is the denominator in the exchange rate ratio. The numerator is the key to the identification of the rate.

Changes in Exchange Rates[1]

A change in an exchange rate is referred to as a *strengthening* or *weakening* of one currency against another. During the first decade of the new century, the relationship between the dollar and the euro was often volatile. For example, the exchange rate of the U.S. dollar versus the euro changed as follows during 2005 and 2006:

	January 2005	July 2005	January 2006	July 2006
Direct exchange rate (U.S. dollar equivalent of 1 euro)	$1.35	$1.20	$1.18	$1.28
Indirect exchange rate (euro per 1 U.S. dollar)	€0.74	€0.83	€0.85	€0.78

---

[1] To view a video explanation of this topic, visit advancedstudyguide.com.

Strengthening of the U.S. Dollar—Direct Exchange Rate Decreases

Between January 1, 2005, and July 1, 2005, the direct exchange rate decreased from $1.35 = €1 to $1.20 = €1, indicating that it took less U.S. currency ($) to acquire 1 European euro (€). In other words, the cost of 1 euro was $1.35 on January 1 but decreased to $1.20 on July 1. This means that the value of the U.S. currency rose relative to the euro. This is termed a *strengthening* of the dollar versus the euro. Alternatively, looking at the indirect exchange rate, 1 U.S. dollar could acquire 0.74 European euro on January 1, but it could acquire more euros, 0.83, on July 1. Thus, the relative value of the dollar versus the euro was greater on July 1 than on January 1.

Think of the strengthening of the U.S. dollar as

- Taking less U.S. currency to acquire one foreign currency unit.
- One U.S. dollar acquiring more foreign currency units.

Imports from Europe were less expensive for U.S. consumers on July 1 than on January 1 because of the strengthening of the dollar. For example, assume that a European manufacturer is selling a German-made automobile for €25,000. To determine the U.S. dollar–equivalent value of the €25,000 on January 1, the following equation is used:

$$\text{U.S. dollar– equivalent value} = \text{Foreign currency units} \times \text{Direct exchange rate}$$
$$\$33{,}750 = €25{,}000 \times \$1.35$$

Between January 1 and July 1, the direct exchange rate decreased as the dollar strengthened relative to the euro. On July 1, the U.S. dollar–equivalent value of the €25,000 is

$$\text{U.S. dollar– equivalent value} = \text{Foreign currency units} \times \text{Direct exchange rate}$$
$$\$30{,}000 = €25{,}000 \times \$1.20$$

Although a strengthening of the dollar is favorable for U.S. companies purchasing goods from another country, it adversely affects U.S. companies selling products in that country. Following a strengthening of the dollar, U.S. exports to Europe are more expensive for European customers. For example, assume a U.S. manufacturer is selling a U.S.-made machine for $10,000. To determine the foreign currency (euro) equivalent value of the $10,000 on January 1, the following equation is used:

$$\text{Foreign currency equivalent value} = \text{U.S. dollar units} \times \text{Indirect exchange rate}$$
$$€7{,}400 = \$10{,}000 \times €0.74$$

On July 1, after a strengthening of the dollar, the machine would cost the European customer €8,300, as follows:

$$\text{Foreign currency equivalent value} = \text{U.S. dollar units} \times \text{Indirect exchange rate}$$
$$€8{,}300 = \$10{,}000 \times €0.83$$

This substantial increase in cost could lead the European customer to decide not to acquire the machine from the U.S. company. Thus, a U.S. company's international sales can be seriously affected by changes in foreign currency exchange rates.

Weakening of the U.S. Dollar—Direct Exchange Rate Increases

Between July 1, 2005, and July 1, 2006, the direct exchange rate increased from $1.20 = €1 to $1.28 = €1, indicating that it took more U.S. currency to acquire 1 euro. On July 1, 2005, a euro cost $1.20, but on July 1, 2006, the relative cost for 1 euro increased to $1.28. This means that the value of the U.S. currency dropped relative to the

FIGURE 8–2
Relationships between Currencies and Exchange Rates

	January 2005	July 2005	July 2006
Direct exchange rate ($/€)	$1.35	$1.20	$1.28
Indirect exchange rate (€/$)	€0.74	€0.83	€0.78

Between January 1, 2005, and July 1, 2005—strengthening of the U.S. dollar:
  Direct rate decreases
    Dollar strengthens (takes less U.S. currency to acquire 1 euro)
  Indirect rate increases
    Euro weakens (takes more euros to acquire 1 U.S. dollar)
  Imports into United States normally increase in quantity
    Foreign goods imported into United States less expensive in dollars ($1 can acquire more)
  Exports from United States normally decrease in quantity
    U.S.-made exports more expensive (takes more euros to acquire goods)
Between July 1, 2005, and July 1, 2006—weakening of the U.S. dollar:
  Direct rate increases
    Dollar weakens (takes more U.S. currency to acquire 1 euro)
  Indirect rate decreases
    Euro strengthens (takes fewer euros to acquire 1 U.S. dollar)
  Imports into United States normally decrease in quantity
    Foreign goods imported into United States more expensive in dollars
  Exports from United States normally increase in quantity
    U.S.-made exports less expensive in euros

euro, termed a *weakening* of the dollar against the euro. Another way to view this change is to note that the indirect exchange rate decreased, indicating that on July 1, 2006, 1 dollar acquired fewer euros than it did on July 1, 2005. On July 1, 2005, 1 U.S. dollar could acquire 0.83 euro, but on July 1, 2006, 1 U.S. dollar could acquire fewer euros, 0.78, indicating that the relative value of the dollar dropped between July 1, 2005, and July 1, 2006.

Think of the weakening of the U.S. dollar as

- Taking more U.S. currency to acquire one foreign currency unit.
- One U.S. dollar acquiring fewer foreign currency units.

Figure 8–2 summarizes the relationships between currencies, imports, and exports.

During the latter part of the 1970s, the dollar consistently weakened against other major currencies because of several factors, including the high inflation the United States experienced. This weakening did help the U.S. balance of trade because it reduced the quantity of then more expensive imports, while making U.S.-made goods less expensive in other countries. In the first half of the 1980s, the dollar consistently strengthened relative to other currencies. Not only was the U.S. economy strong and producing goods more efficiently but also high interest rates attracted large foreign investment in the U.S. capital markets. A stronger dollar added to the foreign trade deficit by making imports less expensive and U.S.-made goods more expensive on the world market. Beginning in 1986 and continuing through the early 1990s, the dollar again weakened relative to the major international currencies. In the latter 1990s, the dollar generally strengthened because of the robustness of the U.S. economy, but in the early 2000s, the dollar again weakened because of the high trade deficit and the sluggish U.S. economy.

These changes in the international value of the dollar affect any consumer acquiring imported goods. A weakening dollar means that imports become more expensive while a strengthening dollar means that imports become less expensive. One reason the U.S. government may let the dollar weaken is to reduce the trade deficits. U.S. exporters can sell their goods more easily overseas, thus boosting their profitability. Imports should decrease because of the higher relative prices of the foreign-made goods, thus enhancing the demand for domestic-made goods within the United States. If the dollar weakens too far, overseas investors reduce their demand for dollar-dominated U.S. assets such as U.S.

stocks and bonds. The reduced investment demand may require an increase in bond interest rates to offset overseas investors' reduction in bond returns caused by the weakening dollar. An increase in interest rates may reduce economic investment within the United States. Finally a weakening dollar means that foreign travel becomes more expensive because of the reduction in the dollar's purchasing power. Thus, the U.S. government's management of the value of the dollar is a balancing act to achieve the needs of both U.S. businesses and U.S. consumers.

Spot Rates versus Current Rates

FASB 52 (ASC 830) refers to the use of both spot rates and current rates for measuring the currency used in international transactions. The *spot rate* is the exchange rate for immediate delivery of currencies. The *current rate* is defined simply as the spot rate on the entity's balance sheet date.

Forward Exchange Rates

A third exchange rate is the rate on future, or forward, exchanges of currencies. Figure 8–1 shows these exchange rates for the major international currencies for one month, three months, and six months forward. Active dealer markets in *forward exchange contracts* are maintained for companies wishing to either receive or deliver major international currencies. The forward rate on a given date is not the same as the spot rate on the same date. Expectations about the relative value of currencies are built into the forward rate. The difference between the forward rate and the spot rate on a given date is called the *spread.* The spread gives information about the perceived strengths or weaknesses of currencies. For instance, assume the spot rate for the Swiss franc is $1.1574 and the 30-day forward rate is $1.0576. The spread is the difference between these two numbers, or $0.0998. Because the forward rate is less than the spot rate, the expectation is that the dollar will strengthen against the franc in the next 30 days. The actual spot rate when the contract is due in 30 days may be higher or lower than the forward rate. By entering into the forward contract, the U.S. company gives up the chance of receiving a better exchange rate but also avoids the possibility of an exchange rate loss. This reduces the risk for the U.S. company.

For example, a U.S. company may have a liability in British pounds due in 30 days. Rather than wait 30 days to buy the pounds and risk having the dollar weaken in value relative to the pound, the company can go to a foreign exchange dealer and enter into a one-month forward exchange contract at the forward exchange rate in effect on the contract date. The United States has approximately 2,000 foreign exchange dealer institutions, of which about 200 are market-making, large banks such as Citibank, JP Morgan Chase, and Bank of America, which do the greatest volume of foreign exchange activity. The contract enables the buyer to receive British pounds from an exchange broker 30 days from the contract date at a price fixed now by the contract.

The next section of the chapter presents the accounting for import and export transactions and for forward exchange contracts.

FOREIGN CURRENCY TRANSACTIONS

LO2

Understand the accounting implications of and be able to make calculations related to foreign currency transactions.

As defined earlier, foreign currency transactions are economic activities denominated in a currency other than the entity's recording currency. These transactions include the following:

1. Purchases or sales of goods or services (imports or exports), the prices of which are stated in a foreign currency.
2. Loans payable or receivable in a foreign currency.
3. Purchase or sale of foreign currency forward exchange contracts.
4. Purchase or sale of foreign currency units.

One party in a foreign exchange transaction must exchange its own currency for another country's currency. Some persons use a shorthand to refer to foreign exchange transactions by using just the letters FX. This book uses the longer, more generally used description, which is *foreign exchange.*

For financial statement purposes, transactions denominated in a foreign currency must be translated into the currency the reporting company uses. Additionally, at each balance sheet date—interim as well as annual—account balances denominated in a currency other than the entity's reporting currency must be adjusted to reflect changes in exchange rates during the period since the last balance sheet date or since the foreign currency transaction date if it occurred during the period. This adjustment restates the foreign currency–denominated accounts to their U.S. dollar–equivalent values as of the balance sheet date. The adjustment in equivalent U.S. dollar values is a *foreign currency transaction gain or loss* for the entity when exchange rates have changed. For example, assume that a U.S. company acquires €5,000 from its bank on January 1, 20X1, for use in future purchases from German companies. The direct exchange rate is $1.20 = €1; thus the company pays the bank $6,000 for €5,000, as follows:

U.S. dollar – equivalent value = Foreign currency units × Direct exchange rate

$$\$6,000 \quad = \quad €5,000 \quad × \quad \$1.20$$

The following entry records this exchange of currencies:

	January 1, 20X1		
(1)	Foreign Currency Units (€)	6,000	
	Cash		6,000

The parenthetical notation (€) is used here after the debit account to indicate that the asset is European euros, but for accounting purposes it is recorded and reported at its U.S. dollar–equivalent value. This translation to the U.S. equivalent value is required in order to add the value of the foreign currency units to all of the company's other accounts that are reported in dollars.

On July 1, 20X1, the exchange rate is $1.100 = €1 as represented in the following time line:

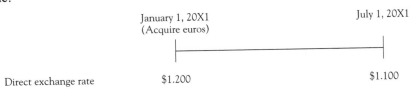

	January 1, 20X1 (Acquire euros)	July 1, 20X1
Direct exchange rate	$1.200	$1.100

The direct exchange rate has decreased, reflecting that the U.S. dollar has strengthened. On July 1, it takes less U.S. currency to acquire 1 euro than it did on January 1. If the dollar has strengthened, the euro has weakened. By holding the euros during a weakening of the euro relative to the dollar, the company experiences a foreign currency transaction loss, as follows:

Equivalent dollar value of € 5,000 on January 1:	
€ 5,000 × $1.200	$6,000
Equivalent dollar value of € 5,000 on July 1:	
€ 5,000 × $1.100	5,500
Foreign currency transaction loss	$ 500

If the U.S. company prepares financial statements on July 1, the following adjusting entry is required:

	July 1, 20X1		
(2)	Foreign Currency Transaction Loss	500	
	Foreign Currency Units (€)		500

The foreign currency transaction loss is the result of a foreign currency transaction and is included in this period's income statement, usually as a separate item under "Other Income or Loss." Some accountants use the account title Exchange Loss instead of the longer title Foreign Currency Transaction Loss. In this book, the longer, more descriptive account title is used to communicate fully the source of the loss. The Foreign Currency Units account is reported on the balance sheet at a value of $5,500, its equivalent U.S. dollar value on that date.

In the previous examples, the U.S. company used the U.S. dollar as its primary currency for performing its major financial and operating functions, that is, as its *functional currency.* Also, the U.S. company prepared its financial statements in U.S. dollars, its *reporting currency.* Any transactions denominated in currencies other than the U.S. dollar require translation to their equivalent U.S. dollar values. Generally, the majority of a business's cash transactions take place in the **local currency** of the country in which the entity operates. The U.S. dollar is the functional currency for virtually all companies based in the United States. A company operating in Germany would probably use the euro as its functional currency. *In this chapter, the local currency is assumed to be the entity's functional and reporting currency.* The few exceptions to this general case are discussed in Chapter 9.

Illustrations of various types of foreign currency transactions are given in the sections that follow. Note that different exchange rates are used to value selected foreign currency transactions, depending on a number of factors such as management's reason for entering the foreign currency transaction, the nature of the transaction, and the timing of the transaction.

Foreign Currency Import and Export Transactions

Advanced
StudyGuide
.com

Payables and receivables that arise from transactions with foreign-based entities and that are denominated in a foreign currency must be measured and recorded by the U.S. entity in the currency used for its accounting records—the U.S. dollar. The relevant exchange rate for settlement of a transaction denominated in a foreign currency is the spot exchange rate on the date of settlement. At the time the transaction is settled, payables or receivables denominated in foreign currency units must be adjusted to their current U.S. dollar–equivalent value. If financial statements are prepared before the foreign currency payables or receivables are settled, their account balances must be adjusted to their U.S. dollar–equivalent values as of the balance sheet date, using the current rate on the balance sheet date.

An overview of the required accounting for an import or export transaction denominated in a foreign currency, assuming the company does *not* use forward contracts, is as follows:

1. *Transaction date.* Record the purchase or sale transaction at the U.S. dollar–equivalent value using the spot direct exchange rate on this date.
2. *Balance sheet date.* Adjust the payable or receivable to its U.S. dollar–equivalent, end-of-period value using the current direct exchange rate. Recognize any exchange gain or loss for the change in rates between the transaction and balance sheet dates.
3. *Settlement date.* First adjust the foreign currency payable or receivable for any changes in the exchange rate between the balance sheet date (or transaction date if transaction occurs after the balance sheet date) and the settlement date, recording any exchange gain or loss as required. Then record the settlement of the foreign currency payable or receivable.

This adjustment process is required because the FASB adopted what is called the *two transaction approach,* which views the purchase or sale of an item as a separate transaction from the foreign currency commitment. By adopting the two-transaction approach to foreign currency transactions, the FASB established the general rule that foreign currency exchange gains or losses resulting from the revaluation of assets or liabilities denominated in a foreign currency must be recognized currently in the income statement of the period in which the exchange rate changes. A few exceptions to this general rule are allowed and are discussed later in this chapter.

FIGURE 8–3 Comparative U.S. Company Journal Entries for Foreign Purchase Transaction Denominated in Dollars versus Foreign Currency Units

If Denominated in U.S. Dollars	If Denominated in Japanese Yen

October 1, 20X1 (Date of Purchase)

Inventory 14,000
    Accounts Payable 14,000
	Inventory 14,000
	    Accounts Payable (¥) 14,000
	$14,000 = ¥2,000,000 × \$0.0070 spot rate

December 31, 20X1 (Balance Sheet Date)

No entry	Foreign Currency Transaction Loss .... 2,000 Accounts Payable (¥) .... 2,000 Adjust payable denominated in foreign currency to current U.S. dollar equivalent and recognize exchange loss: $ 16,000 = ¥2,000,000 × \$0.0080 Dec. 31 spot rate −14,000 = ¥2,000,000 × \$0.0070 Oct. 1 spot rate $ 2,000 = ¥2,000,000 × (\$0.0080 − \$0.0070)

April 1, 20X2 (Settlement Date)

	Accounts Payable (¥) .... 800 Foreign Currency Transaction Gain .... 800 Adjust payable denominated in foreign currency to current U.S. dollar equivalent and recognize exchange gain: $ 15,200 = ¥2,000,000 × \$0.0076 Apr. 1 spot rate −16,000 = ¥2,000,000 × \$0.0080 Dec. 31 spot rate $ 800 = ¥2,000,000 × (\$0.0076 − \$0.0080)
	Foreign Currency Units (¥) .... 15,200 Cash .... 15,200 Acquire FCU to settle debt: $15,200 = ¥2,000,000 × \$0.0076 April 1 spot rate

Accounts Payable 14,000
    Cash 14,000
	Accounts Payable (¥) 15,200
	    Foreign Currency Units (¥) 15,200

Illustration of Foreign Purchase Transaction

Figure 8–3 illustrates the journal entries used to measure and record a purchase of goods from a foreign supplier denominated either in the entity's local currency or in a foreign currency. On the left side of Figure 8–3, the transaction is denominated in U.S. dollars, the recording and reporting currency of the U.S. company; on the right side, the transaction is denominated in Japanese yen (¥). The U.S. company is subject to a foreign currency transaction gain or loss only if the transaction is denominated in the foreign currency. If the foreign transaction is denominated in U.S. dollars, no special accounting problems exist and no currency rate adjustments are necessary.

The following information describes the case:

1. On October 1, 20X1, Peerless Products, a U.S. company, acquired goods on account from Tokyo Industries, a Japanese company, for $14,000, or 2,000,000 yen.
2. Peerless Products prepared financial statements at its year-end of December 31, 20X1.
3. Settlement of the payable was made on April 1, 20X2.

The direct spot exchange rates of the U.S. dollar–equivalent value of 1 yen were as follows:

Date	Direct Exchange Rate
October 1, 20X1 (transaction date)	$0.0070
December 31, 20X1 (balance sheet date)	0.0080
April 1, 20X2 (settlement date)	0.0076

The following timeline may help to clarify the relationships between the dates and the economic events:

Accounts relating to transactions denominated in yen are noted by the parenthetical symbol for the yen (¥) after the account title. As you proceed through the example, you should especially note the assets and liabilities denominated in the foreign currency and the adjustment needed to reflect their current values by use of the U.S. dollar–equivalent rate of exchange.

Key Observations from Illustration

If the purchase contract is denominated in dollars, the foreign entity (Tokyo Industries) bears the foreign currency exchange risk. If the transaction is denominated in yen, the U.S. company (Peerless Products Corporation) is exposed to exchange rate gains and losses. The accounts relating to liabilities denominated in foreign currency units must be valued at the spot rate, with any foreign currency transaction gain or loss recognized in the period's income. The purchase contract includes specification of the denominated currency as the two parties agreed.

On October 1, 20X1, the purchase is recorded on the books of Peerless Products. The U.S. dollar–equivalent value of 2,000,000 yen on this date is $14,000 (¥2,000,000 × $0.0070).

On December 31, 20X1, the balance sheet date, the payable denominated in foreign currency units must be adjusted to its current U.S. dollar–equivalent value. The direct exchange rate has increased since the date of purchase, indicating that the U.S. dollar has weakened relative to the yen. Therefore, on December 31, 20X1, $16,000 is required to acquire 2,000,000 yen (¥2,000,000 × $0.0080), whereas, on October 1, 20X1, only $14,000 was required to obtain 2,000,000 yen (¥2,000,000 × $0.0070). This increase in the exchange rate requires the recognition of a $2,000 foreign currency transaction loss if the transaction is denominated in yen, the foreign currency unit. No entry is made if the transaction is denominated in U.S. dollars because Peerless has a liability for $14,000 regardless of the changes in exchange rates.

The payable is settled on April 1, 20X2. If the payable is denominated in U.S. dollars, no adjustment is necessary and the liability is extinguished by payment of $14,000. However, assets and liabilities denominated in foreign currency units must again be adjusted to their present U.S. dollar–equivalent values. The dollar has strengthened between December 31, 20X1, and April 1, 20X2, as shown by the decrease in the direct exchange rate. In other words, fewer dollars are needed to acquire 2,000,000 yen on April 1, 20X2, than on December 31, 20X1. Accounts Payable is adjusted to its current dollar value, and an $800 foreign currency transaction gain [¥2,000,000 × ($0.0076 − $0.0080)] is recognized for the change in rates since the balance sheet date. Peerless acquires 2,000,000 yen, paying an exchange broker the spot exchange rate of $15,200 (¥2,000,000 × $0.0076). Finally, Peerless extinguishes its liability denominated in yen by paying Tokyo Industries the 2,000,000 yen.

Understanding the revaluations may be easier by viewing the process within the perspective of a T-account. The following T-account posts the entries in Figure 8–3:

Accounts Payable (¥)			
		20X1	
		Oct. 1	14,000 (¥2,000,000 × $0.0070)
		Dec. 31	2,000 [¥2,000,000 × ($0.0080 − $0.0070)]
		Dec. 31	16,000 Balance (¥2,000,000 × $0.0080)
20X2			
Apr. 1			
[¥2,000,000 × ($0.0076 − $0.0080)]	800		
Apr. 1 settlement			
(¥2,000,000 × $0.0076)	15,200		
		Apr. 2	−0− Balance

Some accountants combine the revaluation and settlement entries into one entry. Under this alternative approach, the following entries would be made on April 1, 20X2, the settlement date, instead of the entries presented for that date in Figure 8–3:

(3)

April 1, 20X2		
Foreign Currency Units (¥)	15,200	
Cash		15,200

Acquire foreign currency.

(4)

Accounts Payable (¥)	16,000	
Foreign Currency Transaction Gain		800
Foreign Currency Units (¥)		15,200

Settle foreign currency payable and recognize gain from change in exchange rates since December 31, 20X1.

The final account balances resulting from the preceding one-entry approach and the two-entry approach used in Figure 8–3 are the same.

In summary, if the transaction is denominated in U.S. dollars, Peerless Products has no foreign currency exchange exposure; Tokyo Industries bears the risk of foreign currency exposure. If the transaction is denominated in yen, however, Peerless has a foreign currency exchange risk. The assets and liabilities denominated in foreign currency units must be valued at their U.S. dollar–equivalent values and a foreign currency transaction gain or loss must be recognized on that period's income statement.

MANAGING INTERNATIONAL CURRENCY RISK WITH FOREIGN CURRENCY FORWARD EXCHANGE FINANCIAL INSTRUMENTS

LO3

Understand how to hedge international currency risk using foreign currency forward exchange financial instruments.

Companies need to manage business risks. Derivative instruments are an important tool in managing risk. Companies operating internationally are subject not only to normal business risks but also to additional risks from changes in currency exchange rates. Therefore, multinational enterprises (MNEs) often use derivative instruments, including foreign currency–denominated forward exchange contracts, foreign currency options, and foreign currency futures, to manage risk associated with foreign currency transactions.

The accounting for derivatives and hedging activities is guided by three standards. **FASB Statement No. 133 (ASC 815),** "Accounting for Derivative Instruments and Hedging Activities" (FASB 133, ASC 815), defined derivatives and established the general rule of recognizing all derivatives as either assets or liabilities in the balance sheet and measuring those financial instruments at fair value. **FASB Statement No. 138**

(ASC 815), "Accounting for Certain Derivative Instruments and Certain Hedging Activities" (FASB 138, ASC 815), provided several amendments of importance to multinational entities. **FASB Statement No. 149 (ASC 815),** "Amendment of Statement 133 on Derivative Instruments and Hedging Activities" (FASB 149, ASC 815), considered a number of specific implementation issues.

A *financial instrument* is cash, evidence of ownership, or a contract that both (1) imposes on one entity a contractual obligation to deliver cash or another instrument and (2) conveys to the second entity that contractual right to receive cash or another financial instrument. Examples include cash, stock, notes payable and receivable, and many financial contracts.

A *derivative* is a financial instrument or other contract whose value is "derived from" some other item that has a variable value over time. An example of a derivative is a foreign currency forward exchange contract whose value is derived from changes in the foreign currency exchange rate over the contract's term. Note that not all financial instruments are derivatives.

The specific definition of a derivative is a financial instrument or contract possessing all of the following characteristics:

1. The financial instrument must contain one or more underlyings and one or more notional amounts, which specify the terms of the financial instrument.
   a. An *underlying* is any financial or physical variable that has observable or objectively verifiable changes. Currency exchange rates, commodity prices, index of prices or rates, days of winter warming, or other variables including the occurrence or nonoccurrence of a specified event such as the scheduled payment under a contract are examples of an underlying.
   b. A *notional amount* is the number of currency units, shares, bushels, pounds, or other units specified in the financial instrument.
2. The financial instrument or other contract requires no initial net investment or an initial net investment that is smaller than required for other types of contracts expected to have a similar response to changes in market factors. Many derivative instruments require no initial net investment or only a small investment for the time value of the contract (as discussed later in this chapter).
3. The contract terms: (*a*) require or permit net settlement, (*b*) provide for the delivery of an asset that puts the recipient in an economic position not substantially different from net settlement, or (*c*) allow for the contract to be readily settled net by a market or other mechanism outside the contract. For example, a forward contract requires the delivery of a specified number of shares of stock, but there is an option market mechanism that offers a ready opportunity to sell the contract or to enter into an offsetting contract.

Occasionally, a financial instrument may have an embedded derivative that must be separated, or bifurcated, from its host contract. An example of an embedded derivative is a company's issuing debt that includes regular interest as well as a potential premium payment based on the future price of a commodity such as crude oil. In this case, the contingent payment feature is a derivative. Another example is the debt agreement that specifies a principal, but whose interest rate is based on the U.S. LIBOR (London Interbank Offered Rate), which is a variable rate. In this case, the interest is the embedded derivative because its value, which is derived from the market, is variable.

Derivatives Designated as Hedges

Derivatives may be designated to hedge or reduce risks. Some companies obtain derivatives that are not designated as hedges but as speculative financial instruments. For example, a company may enter into a forward exchange contract that does not have any offsetting intent. In this case, the gain or loss on the derivative is recorded in periodic earnings.

Advanced
StudyGuide
.com

FASB 133 (ASC 815) provided specific requirements for classifying a derivative as a hedge. Hedge accounting offsets the gain (loss) on the hedged item with the loss (gain) on the hedging instrument. Hedges are applicable to (1) foreign currency exchange risk in which currency exchange rates change over time; (2) interest rate risks, particularly for companies owing variable-rate debt instruments; and (3) commodity risks whose future commodity prices may be quite different from spot prices.

For a derivative instrument to qualify as a hedging instrument, it must meet the following two criteria:

1. Sufficient documentation must be provided at the beginning of the hedge term to identify the objective and strategy of the hedge, the hedging instrument and the hedged item, and how the hedge's effectiveness will be assessed on an ongoing basis.

2. The hedge must be highly effective throughout its term. Effectiveness is measured by evaluating the hedging instrument's ability to generate changes in fair value that offset the changes in value of the hedged item. This effectiveness must be tested at the time the hedge is entered into, every three months thereafter, and each time financial statements are prepared. Effectiveness is viewed as the derivative instrument's ability to offset changes in the fair value or cash flows of the hedged item within the range between 80 and 125 percent of the change in value of the hedged item.

Derivatives that meet the requirements for a hedge and are designated as such by the company's management are accounted for in accordance with **FASB 133 (ASC 815)** and **FASB 138 (ASC 815),** as follows:

1. *Fair value hedges* are designated to hedge the exposure to potential changes in the fair value of (a) a recognized asset or liability such as available-for-sale investments or (b) an unrecognized firm commitment for which a binding agreement exists, such as to buy or sell inventory. The net gains and losses on the hedged asset or liability and the hedging instrument are recognized in current earnings on the statement of income. An example of a fair value hedge is presented in Appendix 8B using an option contract to hedge available-for-sale securities.

2. *Cash flow hedges* are designated to hedge the exposure to potential changes in the anticipated cash flows, either into or out of the company, for (a) a recognized asset or liability such as future interest payments on variable-interest debt or (b) a forecasted cash transaction such as a forecasted purchase or sale. A forecasted cash transaction is a transaction that is expected to occur but for which there is not yet a firm commitment. Thus, a forecasted transaction has no present rights to future benefits or a present liability for future obligations. **FASB 133 (ASC 815)** specifies that a derivative must be valued at its current fair market value. For cash flow hedges, changes in the fair market value of a derivative are separated into an effective portion and an ineffective portion. The net gain or loss on the effective portion of the hedging instrument should be reported in other comprehensive income. The gain or loss on the ineffective portion is reported in current earnings on the statement of income.

   The effective portion is defined as the part of the gain (or loss) on the hedging instrument that offsets a loss (or gain) on the hedged item. This portion of the change in the derivative's fair market value is related to the intrinsic value from changes in the underlying. Any remaining gain (or loss) on the hedging instrument is defined as the ineffective portion. This portion of the change in the derivative's fair market value is related to the time value of the derivative and reduces to zero at the derivative's expiration date. An example of determining the effective versus the ineffective portion of a change in value of a derivative is presented in Appendix 8B with regard to a cash flow hedge using an option to hedge an anticipated purchase of inventory.

3. *Foreign currency hedges* are hedges in which the hedged item is denominated in a foreign currency. Note that the incremental risk being hedged in a foreign currency hedge is the change in fair value or the change in cash flows attributable to the changes

in the foreign currency exchange rates. The following types of hedges of foreign currency risk may be designated by the entity:

a. A *fair value hedge* of a firm commitment to enter into a foreign currency transaction, such as a binding agreement to purchase equipment from a foreign manufacturer with the payable due in the foreign currency or a recognized foreign currency–denominated asset or liability (including an available-for-sale security). Just as with hedge accounting for firm commitments not involving foreign currency commitments in item (1) above, the gain or loss on the foreign currency hedging derivative and the offsetting loss or gain on the foreign currency–hedged item are recognized currently in earnings on the statement of income.

b. A *cash flow hedge* of a forecasted foreign currency transaction, such as a probable future foreign currency sale, the forecasted functional currency–equivalent cash flows associated with a recognized asset or liability, or a forecasted intercompany transaction. Just as with accounting for hedges of forecasted transactions not involving foreign currency commitments in item (2) above, the effective portion of the gain or loss on the foreign currency hedging derivative instrument is recognized as a component of other comprehensive income. The ineffective portion of the gain or loss is recognized currently in earnings.

   Cash flow hedges are used when all variability in the hedged item's functional currency–equivalent cash flows are eliminated by the effect of the hedge. Cash flow hedges with a derivative based only on changes in the exchange rates cannot be designated, for example, for a variable-rate foreign currency–denominated asset or liability because some of the cash flow variability is not covered with that specific hedge. However, foreign currency–denominated forward contracts can be used as cash flow hedges of foreign currency–denominated assets or liabilities that are fixed in terms of the number of foreign currency units.

c. A hedge of a net investment in a foreign operation. A derivative designated as hedging this type of foreign currency exposure has its gain or loss reported in other comprehensive income as part of the cumulative translation adjustment, as will be discussed in Chapter 9.

Forward Exchange Contracts

For the reporting year ended October 2009, the Foreign Exchange Committee of the New York Federal Reserve Board reported that the average daily volume in foreign exchange instruments totaled $675 billion, and the average daily volume in over-the-counter foreign exchange options totaled $25 billion.[2] The Chicago Mercantile Exchange (CME) is the world's largest and most diverse regulated foreign exchange trading market. The CME is an international marketplace that brings together buyers and sellers on its CME Globex electronic trading platform and on its trading floors. With $3.2 trillion traded daily, FX markets represent the largest class of assets in the world. In March 2010, CME foreign exchange products averaged a record 907,000 contracts per day, up 66 percent from the same period in 2009.[3]

Companies operating internationally often enter into forward exchange contracts with foreign currency brokers for the exchange of different currencies at specified future dates at specified rates. Forward exchange contracts are acquired from foreign currency brokers. Typically, these contracts are written for one of the major international currencies. They are available for virtually any time period up to 12 months forward, but most are for relatively shorter time periods, usually between 30 and 180 days. Forward exchange contracts can be entered into to receive foreign currency or to deliver foreign currency at a specified date in the future (the expiration date). The forward exchange rate differs

[2] Foreign Exchange Committee, FX Volume Survey, http://www.newyorkfed.org/FXC/volumesurvey/ (accessed May 17, 2010).

[3] CME Group, Quarterly FX Update, http://www.cmegroup.com/trading/fx/files/FX-260-Q4_FX_Quarterly_ Update.pdf (accessed May 17, 2010).

from the spot rate because of the different economic factors involved in determining a future versus spot rate of exchange. For hedging transactions, if the forward rate is more than the spot rate, the difference between the forward and spot rate is termed *premium on the forward exchange contract;* that is, the foreign currency is selling at a premium in the forward market. If the forward rate is less than the spot rate, the difference is a *discount on the forward exchange contract;* that is, the foreign currency is selling at a discount in the forward market.

FASB 133 (ASC 815) establishes a basic rule of fair value for accounting for forward exchange contracts. Changes in the fair value are recognized in the accounts, but the specific accounting for the change depends on the purpose of the hedge. For forward exchange contracts, the basic rule is to use the forward exchange rate to value the forward contract.

Multinational entities often use foreign currency forward contract derivatives. These contracts may be designated as hedging instruments or may not fulfill all the requirements for a hedge and would thus not be hedging instruments. The cases discussed in the next sections of this chapter illustrate the following:

Case 1: This case presents the most common use of foreign currency forward contracts, which is to manage a part of the foreign currency exposure from accounts payable or accounts receivable denominated in a foreign currency. Note that the company has entered into a foreign currency forward contract but that the contract does not qualify for or the company does not designate the forward contract as a hedging instrument. Thus, the forward contract is not a designated hedge but can offset most, if not all, foreign currency risks. The forward contract is valued using the forward rate, and changes in the market value of the forward contract are recognized currently in earnings on the statement of income. The foreign currency account payable or account receivable is revalued using the spot rate in accordance with **FASB 52 (ASC 830).**

Case 2: This case presents the accounting for an unrecognized firm commitment to enter into a foreign currency transaction, which is accounted for as a fair value hedge. A firm commitment exists because of a binding agreement for the future transaction that meets all requirements for a firm commitment. The hedge is against the possible changes in fair value of the firm commitment (e.g., the inventory to be purchased or the equipment to be acquired) from changes in the foreign currency exchange rates.

Case 3: This case presents the accounting for a forecasted foreign currency–denominated transaction, which is accounted for as a cash flow hedge of the possible changes in future cash flows. The forecasted transaction is *probable* but not a *firm* commitment. Thus, the transaction has not yet occurred nor is it assured; the company is *anticipating* a *possible* future foreign currency transaction. Because the foreign currency hedge is against the impact of changes in the foreign currency exchange rates used to predict the possible future foreign currency–denominated cash flows, it is accounted for as a cash flow hedge. **FASB 138 (ASC 815)** allows for the continuation of a cash flow hedge after the purchase or sale transaction occurs until settlement of the foreign currency–denominated account payable or receivable arising from the transaction. Alternatively, at the time the company enters into a binding agreement for the transaction that had been forecasted, the hedge can be changed to a fair value hedge, but any other comprehensive income recognized on the cash flow hedge to that date is not reclassified until the earnings process is completed.

Case 4: This case presents the accounting for foreign currency forward contracts used to speculate in foreign currency markets. These transactions are not hedging transactions. The foreign currency forward contract is revalued periodically to its fair value using the forward exchange rate for the remainder of the contract term. The gain or loss on the revaluation is recognized currently in earnings on the statement of income.

A time line of the possible points at which a company uses foreign currency contracts follows. Note that a company may use just one foreign currency forward contract during the time between each event and the final settlement of the foreign currency payable or receivable or may use more than one foreign currency forward contract during the time span presented. For example, a company could use one forward contract between the time of the forecast of the future transaction and the time it signs a binding agreement, or it could just continue with one forward contract the entire time between the date of the forecast and the final settlement.

Thus, the accounting for the hedge is based on the purpose for which the hedge, in this case a foreign currency forward contract, is entered into.

The following four cases illustrate the accounting for the major uses of forward exchange contracts.

Forecast expected future transaction. Enter into designated foreign currency forward contract.

Sign binding agreement for transaction. Enter into designated foreign currency forward contract.

Receive goods or services from transaction. Enter into undesignated foreign currency forward contract.

Settlement of foreign currency denominated payable or receivable.

Cash flow hedge of possible future foreign currency cash flow.

Fair value hedge of changes in value of goods or services due to possible changes in exchange rates.

Manage exposed position by entering into foreign currency forward contract.

Settle foreign currency payable or receivable.

(Case 3)

(Case 2)

(Case 1)

Case 1: Managing an Exposed Foreign Currency Net Asset or Liability Position: Not a Designated Hedging Instrument

A company that has more trade receivables or other assets denominated in a foreign currency than liabilities denominated in that currency incurs a foreign currency risk from its *exposed net asset position.* Alternatively, the company has an *exposed net liability position* if liabilities denominated in a foreign currency exceed receivables denominated in that currency.

The most common use of forward exchange contracts is for **managing an exposed foreign currency position, either a net asset or a net liability position.** Entering into a foreign currency forward contract balances a foreign exchange payable with a receivable in the same foreign currency, thus offsetting the risk of foreign exchange fluctuations. For example, a U.S. company acquiring goods from a Swiss company may be required to make payment in Swiss francs. If the transaction is denominated in Swiss francs, the U.S. company is exposed to the effects of changes in exchange rates between the dollar and the Swiss franc. To protect itself from fluctuations in the value of the Swiss franc, the U.S. company can enter into a forward exchange contract to receive francs at the future settlement date. The U.S. company then uses these francs to settle its foreign currency commitment arising from the foreign purchase transaction.

Alternatively, a U.S. company could have a receivable denominated in a foreign currency that it also could manage with a forward exchange contract. In this case, the U.S. company contracts to *deliver* foreign currency units to the forward exchange broker at a future date in exchange for U.S. dollars.

FASB 133 (ASC 815) specifies the general rule that the relevant exchange rate for measuring the fair value of a forward exchange contract is the *forward exchange rate* at each valuation date. Note that **FASB 52 (ASC 830)** specifies that the foreign currency–denominated account receivable or account payable from the exchange transaction is valued by using the *spot rate* at the valuation date. Forward contracts must be adjusted for changes in the fair value of the forward contract. Because of the two different currency exchange rates used—the spot and the forward—a difference normally exists between the amount of gain and loss. This difference should not be large but does create some volatility in the income stream.

Time Value of Future Cash Flows from Forward Contracts

One other item of note is that **FASB 133 (ASC 815)** requires the recognition of an interest factor if interest is significant. Thus, when interest is significant, companies should use the *present value* of the expected future net cash flows to value the forward contract. By using the present value, the company explicitly recognizes the time value of money. For the examples that follow and to focus on the main points of accounting for the hedges, interest was not considered to be significant. A comprehensive example using the time value of money to value a forward contract is presented in Appendix 8A.

Illustration of Managing an Exposed Net Liability Position

The following example shows the accounting for the management of an exposed foreign currency position with a forward exchange contract. For purposes of this example, assume the following:

1. On October 1, 20X1, Peerless Products purchases goods on account from Tokyo Industries in the amount of 2,000,000 yen.
2. This transaction is denominated in yen, and Peerless Products offsets its exposed foreign currency liability with a forward exchange contract for the receipt of 2,000,000 yen from a foreign exchange broker.
3. The term of the forward exchange contract equals the six-month credit period extended by Tokyo Industries.
4. December 31 is the year-end of Peerless Products, and the payable is settled on April 1, 20X2.

The relevant direct exchange rates are as follows:

	U.S. Dollar–Equivalent Value of 1 Yen	
Date	**Spot Rate**	**Forward Exchange Rate**
October 1, 20X1 (transaction date)	$0.0070	$0.0075 (180 days)
December 31, 20X1 (balance sheet date)	0.0080	0.0077 (90 days)
April 1, 20X2 (settlement date)	0.0076	

The following timeline summarizes these transactions:

10/1/X1 — Transaction date
- Incur liability denominated in yen.
- Sign 180-day forward exchange contract to receive yen.

12/31/X1 — Balance sheet date

4/1/X2 — Settlement date
- Obtain yen by settling forward exchange contract.
- Pay yen to settle account payable.

The following entries record the events for this illustration.

	October 1, 20X1		
(5)	Inventory	14,000	
	Accounts Payable (¥)		14,000
	Purchase inventory on account:		
	$14,000 = ¥2,000,000 × $0.0070 Oct. 1 spot rate		
(6)	Foreign Currency Receivable from Exchange Broker (¥)	15,000	
	Dollars Payable to Exchange Broker ($)		15,000
	Purchase forward contract to receive 2,000,000 yen:		
	$15,000 = ¥2,000,000 × $0.0075 forward rate		

FIGURE 8–4
T-Accounts for the
Illustration of the
Management of an
Exposed Net Liability

Foreign Currency Receivable from Broker (¥)				Accounts Payable (¥)			
(6)	15,000					(5)	14,000
(7)	400					(8)	2,000
Bal. 12/31	15,400					Bal. 12/31	16,000
		(9)	200	(10)	800		
		(12)	15,200	(13)	15,200		
Bal. 4/1	–0–					Bal. 4/1	–0–

Foreign Currency Units (¥)				Dollars Payable to Exchange Broker ($)			
						(6)	15,000
						Bal. 12/31	15,000
(12)	15,200	(13)	15,200	(11)	15,000		
Bal. 4/1	–0–					Bal 4/1	–0–

These entries record the purchase of inventory on credit, which is denominated in yen, and the signing of a six-month forward exchange contract to receive 2,000,000 yen in exchange for $15,000 (¥2,000,000 × $0.0075 forward rate). The amount payable to the exchange broker is denominated in U.S. dollars, whereas the receivable from the broker is denominated in yen. The entries for the transaction, the adjusting journal entries for the balance sheet date valuations, and the settlements of the forward contract and the accounts payable are posted to T-accounts in Figure 8–4.

The required adjusting entries on December 31, 20X1, Peerless' fiscal year-end, are

(7)
Foreign Currency Receivable from Exchange Broker (¥)	400	
Foreign Currency Transaction Gain		400

Adjust receivable denominated in yen to current U.S. dollar–
equivalent value using the forward rate, in accordance with
FASB 133:

$ 15,400 = ¥2,000,000 × $0.0077 Dec. 31 90-day forward rate

−15,000 = ¥2,000,000 × $0.0075 Oct. 1 180-day forward rate

$ 400 = ¥2,000,000 × ($0.0077 − $0.0075)

(8)
Foreign Currency Transaction Loss	2,000	
Accounts Payable (¥)		2,000

Adjust payable denominated in yen to current U.S. dollar–
equivalent value using the spot rate, in accordance with
FASB 52:

$ 16,000 = ¥2,000,000 × $0.0080 Dec. 31, spot rate

−14,000 = ¥2,000,000 × $0.0070 Oct. 1, spot rate

$ 2,000 = ¥2,000,000 × ($0.0080 − $0.0070)

Note that the foreign currency–denominated account payable is valued by using the spot rate. This is the valuation requirement specified in **FASB 52 (ASC 830).** The forward exchange contract is valued using the forward exchange rate for the remainder of the forward contract. This valuation basis is required by **FASB 133 (ASC 815).** The direct exchange spot rate has increased between October 1, 20X1, the date of the foreign currency transaction, and December 31, 20X1, the balance sheet date. As previously illustrated, this means that the U.S. dollar has weakened relative to the yen because it takes more U.S. currency to acquire 1 yen at year-end (¥1 = $0.0080) than at the initial date of the purchase transaction (¥1 = $0.0070), and a U.S. company with a liability in yen experiences an exchange loss. The U.S. dollar–equivalent values of the foreign currency–denominated accounts at October 1, 20X1, and December 31, 20X1, follow:

Accounts	U.S. Dollar–Equivalent Values of Foreign Currency–Denominated Accounts		Foreign Currency Transaction Gain (Loss)
	October 1, 20X1 (Transaction Date)	December 31, 20X1 (Balance Sheet Date)	
Foreign Currency Receivable from Exchange Broker (¥)	$15,000 (a)	$15,400 (b)	$ 400
Accounts Payable (¥)	14,000 (c)	16,000 (d)	(2,000)

(a) ¥2,000,000 × $0.0075 October 1, 180-day forward rate
(b) ¥2,000,000 × $0.0077 December 31, 90-day forward rate
(c) ¥2,000,000 × $0.0070 October 1, spot rate
(d) ¥2,000,000 × $0.0080 December 31, spot rate

On October 1, the U.S. dollar–equivalent value of the foreign currency receivable from the broker is $15,000. Because of the increase in the forward exchange rate of the yen relative to the dollar (i.e., the weakening of the dollar versus the yen), the U.S. dollar–equivalent value of the foreign currency receivable on December 31, 20X1, increases to $15,400, resulting in a foreign currency transaction gain of $400. For the U.S. company, the U.S. dollar–equivalent value of the liability has increased to $16,000, resulting in a $2,000 foreign currency transaction loss. Because of the differing valuation requirements of the forward contract and the exposed liability, the exchange gain of the accounts payable (¥) is not necessarily an exact offset of the exchange loss on the foreign currency receivable (¥).

The required entries on April 1, 20X2, the settlement date, are

(9)	Foreign Currency Transaction Loss	200	
	Foreign Currency Receivable from Exchange Broker (¥)		200

Adjust receivable to spot rate on settlement date:

$ 15,200 = ¥2,000,000 × $0.0076 Apr. 1, 20X2, spot rate
−15,400 = ¥2,000,000 × $0.0077 Dec. 31, 20X1, 90-day forward rate

$ 200 = ¥2,000,000 × ($0.0076 − $0.0077)

(10)	Accounts Payable (¥)	800	
	Foreign Currency Transaction Gain		800

Adjust payable denominated in yen to spot rate on settlement date:
¥2,000,000 × ($0.0076 − $0.0080)

(11)	Dollars Payable to Exchange Broker ($)	15,000	
	Cash		15,000

Deliver U.S. dollars to currency broker as specified in forward contract.

(12)	Foreign Currency Units (¥)	15,200	
	Foreign Currency Receivable from Exchange Broker (¥)		15,200

Receive ¥2,000,000 from exchange broker; valued at Apr. 1, 20X2, spot rate:
$15,200 = ¥2,000,000 × $0.0076

(13)	Accounts Payable (¥)	15,200	
	Foreign Currency Units (¥)		15,200

Pay 2,000,000 yen to Tokyo Industries, Inc., in settlement of liability denominated in yen.

The direct exchange spot rate has decreased from the $0.0080 rate on the balance sheet date to $0.0076 on April 1, 20X2, the settlement date, indicating that the U.S. dollar has strengthened relative to the yen. Fewer dollars are needed to acquire the same number of yen on the settlement date than were needed on the balance sheet date. The forward exchange contract becomes due on April 1, 20X2, and is now valued at the current spot rate. The difference between the 90-day forward rate on December 31, 20X1, and the spot rate at the date of the completion of the forward rate results in the loss of $200. The U.S. dollar–equivalent values of the foreign currency–denominated accounts on December 31, 20X1, and April 1, 20X2, follow:

	U.S. Dollar–Equivalent Values of Foreign Currency–Denominated Accounts		Foreign Currency Transaction Gain (Loss)
Accounts	**December 31, 20X1 (Balance Sheet Date)**	**April 1, 20X2 (Settlement Date)**	
Foreign Currency Receivable from Exchange Broker (¥)	$15,400 (a)	$15,200 (b)	$(200)
Accounts Payable (¥)	16,000 (c)	15,200 (d)	800

(a) ¥2,000,000 × $0.0077 December 31, 90-day forward rate
(b) ¥2,000,000 × $0.0076 April 1, 20X2, spot rate
(c) ¥2,000,000 × $0.0080 December 31, spot rate
(d) ¥2,000,000 × $0.0076 April 1, 20X2 spot rate

On December 31, 20X1, the U.S. dollar–equivalent value of the foreign currency receivable from the broker is $15,400. Because the yen weakened relative to the dollar, the foreign currency receivable on April 1, 20X2, is lower in U.S. dollar–equivalent value, and an exchange loss of $200 is recognized. The U.S. dollar–equivalent value of the foreign currency account payable is $16,000 on December 31, 20X1, but because the yen weakened (i.e., the dollar strengthened) during the period from December 31, 20X1, to April 1, 20X2, the U.S. dollar–equivalent value of the payable decreases to $15,200 on April 1, 20X2. This results in an $800 foreign currency transaction gain during this period.

Note that the total net foreign exchange transaction loss for the two years combined is $1,000 [20X1: $(2,000) plus $400; 20X2: $800 less $(200)]. This is the effect of the forward contract premium on October 1, 20X1, being taken into the earnings stream. Note the premium was for the difference between the forward rate ($0.0075) and the spot rate ($0.0070) at the date the forward contract was signed. At the April 1, 20X2, completion date, both of the foreign currency–denominated accounts are valued at the spot rate. Thus, the ¥2,000,000 × ($0.0070 − $0.0075) premium is the net effect on earnings over the term of the forward contract. The two accounts denominated in foreign currency start at different valuations but end using the same spot rate at the end of the term of the forward contract.

The forward exchange contract offsets the foreign currency liability position. On April 1, 20X2, Peerless pays the $15,000 forward contract price to the exchange broker and receives the 2,000,000 yen, which it then uses to extinguish its account payable to Tokyo Industries. Note that after settlement, all account balances in Figure 8–4 are reduced to zero.

If Peerless Products had a foreign currency receivable, it also could manage its exposed net asset position by acquiring a forward exchange contract to deliver foreign currency to the exchange broker. In this case, the forward currency payable to the exchange broker is denominated in the foreign currency. The forward exchange contract is settled when Peerless gives the broker the foreign currency units it has received from its customer. The foreign currency is then exchanged for U.S. dollars at the agreed-upon contractual rate from the forward exchange contract. The assets and liabilities denominated in foreign currency units must be revalued to their U.S. dollar–equivalent values in the same manner as for the import illustration. Recall that, for valuation purposes, **FASB 133 (ASC 815)** requires the use of the forward exchange rate for forward contracts and **FASB 52 (ASC 830)** requires the use of spot rates for exposed net asset or liability accounts arising from foreign currency transactions.

Formal Balance Sheets Reporting Net Amounts for Forward Exchange Contracts

FASB 133 (ASC 815) requires the recognition of all derivatives in the statement of financial position (the balance sheet) at net fair value. This means that the balance sheet presents the net of the forward contract receivable from the exchange broker against the dollars payable to the exchange broker. Some companies account for the forward exchange contract with only memorandum entries, using the philosophy that the contract is simply for the exchange of one currency for another. The underlying exposed accounts receivable or accounts payable denominated in foreign currency units are still presented. For example, a formal balance sheet prepared on October 1, 20X1, after the transactions recorded in entries (5) and (6) reports the following net amounts:

Assets		Liabilities	
Inventory	$14,000	Accounts Payable (¥)	$14,000

Under the net method of reporting the forward exchange contract, the gain or loss on the change in the value of the forward exchange contract must be recorded and reported in the balance sheet. The balance sheet prepared on December 31, 20X1, after posting entries (7) and (8) includes the following:

Assets		Liabilities and Equity	
Forward Exchange Contract (¥) (at net fair value)	$400	Accounts Payable (¥)	$16,000
		Retained Earnings (for net exchange loss)	(1,600)

Note that under the net approach to reporting, the forward exchange contract is valued at net fair value. The $2,000 foreign currency transaction loss on the account payable denominated in yen is partially offset with the $400 foreign currency transaction gain for the forward contract receivable in yen.

The net balance sheet presented on April 1, 20X2, immediately after entry (10) but before the settlement of the forward exchange contract and the accounts payable is

Assets		Liabilities and Equity	
Forward Exchange Contract (¥) (at net fair value)	$200	Accounts Payable (¥)	$15,200
		Retained Earnings (for amount of the premium)	(1,000)

The forward exchange contract is then settled by paying the exchange broker the $15,000 in U.S. dollars as initially contracted for in the forward exchange contract, receiving the 2,000,000 yen now valued at $15,200, and closing the net forward exchange contract for the difference of the $200.

The net approach is required for reporting derivative forward exchange contracts on the balance sheet. Nevertheless, we believe that recording both sides of the forward exchange contracts in the account maintains a full record of each side of the transaction.

Case 2: Hedging an Unrecognized Foreign Currency Firm Commitment: A Foreign Currency Fair Value Hedge

A company may expose itself to foreign currency risk *before* a purchase or sale transaction occurs. For example, a company may sign a noncancelable order to purchase goods from a foreign entity in the future to be paid for in the foreign currency. By agreeing to a purchase price in the present for a future purchase, the company has accepted an *identifiable foreign currency commitment* although the purchase has not yet occurred; that is, the purchase contract is still executory (unrecognized). The company will not have a liability obligation until after delivery of the goods, but it is exposed to changes in currency exchange rates before the transaction date (the date of delivery of the goods).

FASB 133 (ASC 815) specified the accounting requirements for the use of forward exchange contracts **hedging unrecognized foreign currency firm commitments.** The company can separate the commitment into its financial instrument (the obligation to pay yen) and nonfinancial asset (the right to receive inventory) aspects. The forward contract taken out is then a hedge of the changes in the fair value of the firm commitment for the foreign currency risk being hedged. A hedge of a firm commitment comes under the accounting for fair value hedges, and the forward contract is to be valued at its fair value.

It is interesting to note the different accounting treatment of a hedge of a forecasted transaction (cash flow hedge) versus that for a hedge of an unrecognized foreign currency firm commitment (fair value hedge). A *forecasted* transaction is *anticipated* but not *guaranteed.* The forecasted transaction may actually occur as anticipated, but a hedge of a forecasted transaction is accounted for as a cash flow hedge with the effective portion of the change in the hedge's fair value recognized in other comprehensive income. On the other hand, a firm commitment is an agreement with an unrelated party that is binding and usually legally enforceable. The agreement has the following characteristics:

1. The agreement specifies all significant terms such as the quantity, the fixed price, and the timing of the transaction. The price may be denominated in either the entity's functional currency or in a foreign currency.

2. The agreement must contain a penalty provision sufficiently large to make performance of the agreement probable.

A forecasted transaction may become a firm commitment if an agreement having these listed characteristics is made between the parties. Any cash flow hedge of the forecasted transaction may be changed to a fair value hedge when the firm commitment agreement is made. However, any amounts recorded in other comprehensive income under the cash flow hedge are not reclassified into earnings until the initially forecasted transaction impacts earnings.

FASB 131 (ASC 815) provides for management of an enterprise to select the basis by which the effectiveness of the hedge will be measured. Management may select the forward exchange rate, the spot rate, or the intrinsic value for measuring effectiveness. The examples used in this chapter use the forward rate, which is consistent with the general rule of valuing forward exchange contracts as specified in **FASB 133 (ASC 815).** The measure of the change in fair value of the forward contract uses the forward exchange rate for the remainder of the term and then, if interest is significant, the change in the forward rates is discounted to reflect the time value of money. The entries for a hedge of an identifiable foreign currency commitment are presented in the following illustration.

Illustration of Hedging an Unrecognized Foreign Currency Firm Commitment

For illustration purposes, the import transaction between Peerless Products and Tokyo Industries used throughout this chapter is extended with the following information:

1. On August 1, 20X1, Peerless contracts to purchase special-order goods from Tokyo Industries. Their manufacture and delivery will take place in 60 days (on October 1, 20X1). The contract price is 2,000,000 yen, to be paid by April 1, 20X2, which is 180 days after delivery.

2. On August 1, Peerless hedges its foreign currency payable commitment with a forward exchange contract to receive 2,000,000 yen in 240 days (the 60 days until delivery plus 180 days of credit period). The future rate for a 240-day forward contract is $0.0073 to 1 yen. The purpose of this 240-day forward exchange contract is twofold. First, for the

60 days from August 1, 20X1, until October 1, 20X1, the forward exchange contract is a hedge of an identifiable foreign currency commitment. For the 180-day period from October 1, 20X1, until April 1, 20X2, the forward exchange contract is a hedge of a foreign currency exposed net liability position.

The relevant exchange rates for this example are as follows:

Date	Spot Rate	U.S. Dollar–Equivalent Value of 1 Yen Forward Exchange Rate
August 1, 20X1	$0.0065	$0.0073 (240 days)
October 1, 20X1	0.0070	0.0075 (180 days)

A time line for the transactions follows:

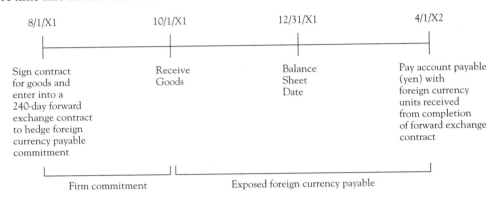

On August 1, 20X1, the company determines the value of its commitment to pay yen for the future accounts payable using the forward exchange rate. However, the payable is not recorded on August 1 because the exchange transaction has not yet occurred; the payable is maintained in memorandum form only. The forward exchange contract must be valued at its fair value. At the time the company enters into the forward exchange contract, the contract has no net fair value because the $14,600 foreign currency receivable equals the $14,600 dollars payable under the contract. The subsequent changes in the fair value of the forward contract are measured using the forward rate and then, if interest is significant, discounted to reflect the time value of money. For purposes of this illustration, we assume that interest is not significant and that hedge effectiveness is measured with reference to the change in the forward exchange rates.

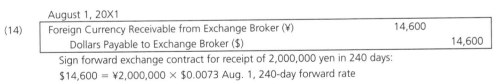

(14)

August 1, 20X1		
Foreign Currency Receivable from Exchange Broker (¥)	14,600	
Dollars Payable to Exchange Broker ($)		14,600

Sign forward exchange contract for receipt of 2,000,000 yen in 240 days:
$14,600 = ¥2,000,000 × $0.0073 Aug. 1, 240-day forward rate

On October 1, 20X1, the forward exchange contract is revalued to its fair value in accordance with **FASB 133**. The accounts payable in yen are recorded at the time the inventory is received.

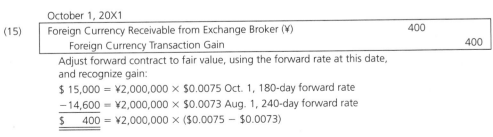

(15)

October 1, 20X1		
Foreign Currency Receivable from Exchange Broker (¥)	400	
Foreign Currency Transaction Gain		400

Adjust forward contract to fair value, using the forward rate at this date, and recognize gain:

$ 15,000 = ¥2,000,000 × $0.0075 Oct. 1, 180-day forward rate
−14,600 = ¥2,000,000 × $0.0073 Aug. 1, 240-day forward rate
$ 400 = ¥2,000,000 × ($0.0075 − $0.0073)

(16)

Foreign Currency Transaction Loss	400	
Firm Commitment		400

To record the loss on the financial instrument aspect of the firm commitment:

$15,000 = ¥2,000,000 × $0.0075 Oct. 1, 180-day forward rate

−14,600 = ¥2,000,000 × $0.0073 Aug. 1, 240-day forward rate

$ 400 = ¥2,000,000 × ($0.0075 − $0.0073)

The Firm Commitment account is a temporary account for the term of the unrecognized firm commitment. If it has a debit balance, it is shown in the assets section of the balance sheet; when it has a credit balance, as in this example, it is shown in the liability section of the balance sheet:

Assets		Liabilities and Equity	
Forward Exchange Contract (¥) (at net fair value)	$400	Firm Commitment	$400

Note that the $400 foreign currency transaction gain is offset against the $400 foreign currency transaction loss, resulting in no net effect on earnings.

The next entry records the receipt of the inventory and the recognition of the accounts payable in yen. Note that the temporary account, Firm Commitment, is closed against the purchase price of the inventory. The accounts payable are valued at the spot exchange rate in accordance with **FASB 52 (ASC 830).**

(17)

Inventory	13,600	
Firm Commitment	400	
Accounts Payable(¥)		14,000

Record accounts payable at spot rate and record inventory purchase:

$14,000 = ¥2,000,000 × $0.0070 Oct. 1, spot rate

Key Observations from Illustration

The August 1, 20X1, entry records the signing of the forward exchange contract that is used to hedge the identifiable foreign currency commitment arising from the noncancelable purchase agreement. In entries (15) and (16), the forward contract and the underlying hedged foreign currency payable commitment are both revalued to their current value, and the $400 gain on the forward contract offsets the $400 loss on the foreign currency payable commitment. Entry (17) records the accounts payable in yen at the current spot rate and records the $400 inventory net that resulted from the recognition of the $400 loss on the financial instrument aspect of the firm commitment in entry (16).

At this point, the company has an exposed net liability position, which is hedged with a forward exchange contract, and the subsequent accounting follows the accounting for an exposed foreign currency liability position as presented previously in Case 1. Figure 8–5 presents a side-by-side comparison of the journal entries for the forward contract and the unrecognized firm commitment, which are valued at the forward exchange rates. The exposed foreign currency–denominated account payable is recognized at the time the company receives the inventory and is valued using the spot exchange rate.

Case 3: Hedging a Forecasted Foreign Currency Transaction: A Foreign Currency Cash Flow Hedge

It is interesting to note the different accounting treatment of a hedge of a forecasted transaction as a cash flow hedge versus that of an identifiable foreign currency commitment as a fair value hedge. A forecasted transaction is anticipated but not guaranteed. The forecasted transaction may actually occur as anticipated, but a hedge of a forecasted transaction is accounted for as a cash flow hedge with the effective portion of the change in fair value of the hedging instrument recognized in other comprehensive income. This type of

FIGURE 8–5   Comparison of Journal Entries: Hedge of an Unrecognized Firm Commitment

Forward Exchange Contract (Use forward exchange rate)	Hedge of an Unrecognized Firm Commitment (Use forward exchange rate)

August 1, 20X1. Recognize forward exchange contract valued at forward rate.

(14)
Foreign Currency Receivable (¥)	14,600	
Dollars Payable to Exchange Broker		14,600

October 1, 20X1. Revalue foreign currency receivable and firm commitment hedge using forward rate.

(15)
Foreign Currency Receivable (¥)	400	
Foreign Currency Transaction Gain		400

(16)
Foreign Currency Transaction Loss	400	
Firm Commitment		400

Economic Management of an Exposed Foreign Currency Payable (Use spot exchange rate)

October 1, 20X1. Receive inventory, close firm commitment, and recognize foreign currency accounts payable.

(17)
Inventory	13,600	
Firm Commitment	400	
Accounts Payable (¥)		14,000

December 31, 20X1. Revalue forward contract using forward rate, and accounts payable in yen using spot rate.

(7)
Foreign Currency Receivable (¥)	400	
Foreign Currency Transaction Gain		400

(8)
Foreign Currency Transaction Loss	2,000	
Accounts Payable (¥)		2,000

April 1, 20X2. Revalue forward contract at its termination to spot rate, and accounts payable in yen to spot rate.

(9)
Foreign Currency Transaction Loss	200	
Foreign Currency Receivable (¥)		200

(10)
Accounts Payable (¥)	800	
Foreign Currency Transaction Gain		800

April 1, 20X2. Deliver $14,600 in U.S. dollars to exchange broker, receiving yen. Use yen to settle accounts payable.

(11)
Dollars Payable to Exchange Broker	14,600	
Cash		14,600

(12)
Foreign Currency Units (¥)	15,200	
Foreign Currency Receivable (¥)		15,200

(13)
Accounts Payable (¥)	15,200	
Foreign Currency Units (¥)		15,200

hedge is against the changes in possible future cash flow that may result from changes in the foreign currency exchange rate. A forecasted transaction may become a firm commitment if the parties make a binding agreement. Prior to **FASB 138 (ASC 815),** an entity could designate a forward foreign currency contract as a cash flow hedge if the purpose of the contract was offsetting forecasted cash flows, including transactions such as forecasted purchases or sales. Changes in the fair value of the cash flow hedge would be recognized as part of other comprehensive income. When the forecasted transaction became a firm commitment, the forward contract would be redesignated as a fair value hedge, and changes in the fair value of the contract would then be recognized in earnings. Any amount recorded in other comprehensive income under the cash flow hedge would not be reclassified into earnings until the initially forecasted transaction impacted earnings. If the forecasted foreign currency transaction did not occur and was not expected to occur in the future, the amount recorded in other comprehensive income would be reclassified into earnings. The forward rate was used to value the forward contract and the spot rate was used to value the account receivable or payable resulting from the transaction.

FASB 138 (ASC 815) allows management the additional option of designating the forward contract as a cash flow hedge from the time the contract is initially made until the final settlement of the payable or receivable, rather than requiring that the contract be redesignated as a fair value hedge when the forecasted transaction becomes a firm commitment. Changes in the value of the forward contract are measured using the forward exchange rate, while changes in the account payable or receivable are measured using the spot exchange rate. However, **FASB 138 (ASC 815)** requires that other comprehensive income from the forward contract revaluation be offset for any foreign exchange gain or loss on the account receivable or payable. Any remaining component of other comprehensive income is taken into the earnings stream only on final completion of the earnings process. Note that the forward contract must meet the requirements of a hedging instrument under the provisions of **FASB 133 (ASC 815),** including the designation and tests of effectiveness.

FASB 138 (ASC 815) allows management to (1) designate the forward contract as a cash flow hedge while it is a forecasted transaction and then redesignate it as a fair value hedge for the remainder of the contract or (2) designate the forward contract as a cash flow hedge for the entire period of time from the initial forecasting of the transaction through the eventual settlement of the receivable or payable. However, most companies regularly hedge their foreign currency receivables and payables and are likely to declare the forward contract as a continuing cash flow hedge in order to fully offset any gains or losses on changes in the fair value of the forward contract.

The following example is based on the data in Case 2 but adds the following assumption: the purchase of inventory is forecasted in August, but there is not a binding agreement for this purchase. Peerless Products Corporation enters into the 240-day forward exchange contract as a designated hedge against the future cash flows from the forecasted transaction, including the foreign currency–denominated accounts payable that would result from the purchase. Figure 8–6 presents the entries for this case, assuming that the hedge is designated as a cash flow hedge when the transaction is forecasted and then redesignated as a fair value hedge when the transaction occurs and the inventory is pur-

FIGURE 8–6 Journal Entries for Cash Flow Hedge Redesignated as Fair Value Hedge When a Forecasted Transaction Becomes a Transaction

FIGURE 8–7   Journal Entries for Cash Flow Hedge of a Forecasted Transaction

Entries for Forward Contract (Use forward exchange rate)	Entries for Foreign Currency Account Payable (Use spot rate)

August 1, 20X1. Acquire forward exchange contract valued at forward rate.

(14)
Foreign Currency Receivable (¥)	14,600	
Dollars Payable to Exchange Broker		14,600

October 1, 20X1. Receive inventory that was a forecasted transaction and recognize the foreign currency accounts payable at the spot rate.

(No revaluation of foreign currency receivable required at this date)

(17C)
Inventory	14,000	
Accounts Payable (¥)		14,000

December 31, 20X1. Revalue the forward contract to year-end fair value using the change in the forward rate since August 1 and recognize the effective portion of the change in value as other comprehensive income. Revalue accounts payable in yen using the spot rate. Then, in accordance with **FASB 133 (ASC 815),** reclassify a portion of the other comprehensive income to equally offset the foreign currency transaction loss recognized on the foreign currency payable that was remeasured using the spot exchange rate in accordance with **FASB 52 (ASC 830).**

(7C)
Foreign Currency Receivable (¥)	800	
Other Comprehensive Income		800

(¥2,000,000 × ($0.0077 − $0.0073))

(8)
Foreign Currency Transaction Loss	2,000	
Accounts Payable (¥)		2,000

(C)
Other Comprehensive Income	2,000	
Foreign Currency Transaction Gain		2,000

To offset loss on account payable.

April 1, 20X2. Revalue the forward contract at its termination using the spot rate and accounts payable in yen using the spot rate. Offset transaction gain on payable against other comprehensive income.

9(C)
Other Comprehensive Income	200	
Foreign Currency Receivable (¥)		200

(10)
Accounts Payable (¥)	800	
Foreign Currency Transaction Gain		800

(C)
Foreign Currency Transaction Loss	800	
Other Comprehensive Income		800

To offset gain on account payable.

April 1, 20X2. Deliver $14,600 in U.S. dollars to the exchange broker and receive yen. Use yen to settle accounts payable.

(11)
Dollars Payable to Exchange Broker	14,600	
Cash		14,600

(12)
Foreign Currency Units (¥)	15,200	
Foreign Currency Receivable (¥)		15,200

(13)
Accounts Payable (¥)	15,200	
Foreign Currency Units (¥)		15,200

Assumed sale of inventory and culmination of earnings process of other comprehensive income from forward contract.

Cost of Goods Sold	600	
Other Comprehensive Income		600

Cost of Goods Sold	14,000	
Inventory		14,000

chased. Figure 8–6 presents the entries for this case by bringing into the illustration Case 1 entries that would not change and noting the entries that would change with a *C* behind the entry number. Note that the entry on October 1 records the effect of the change in value of the forward contract as a component of Other Comprehensive Income.

Figure 8–7 presents the entries for this case assuming the hedge is designated as a cash flow hedge and remains as such between inception in August and final settlement in April. Figure 8–7 presents the entries for this case by bringing into the illustration Case 1 entries that would not change and noting the entries that would change with a letter *C* behind the entry number. Note the major differences in accounting for the forward contract as a cash flow hedge here versus as a fair value hedge in Case 2 are (1) the effective portion of the revaluation of the forward exchange contract is recorded in Other Comprehensive Income, (2) no firm commitment account exists under a forecasted transaction, (3) no revaluation of the forward contract receivable is required on October 1 and the inventory is recorded at its equivalent U.S. dollar cost determined at the spot rate, (4) there is an offset against Other Comprehensive Income to fully match the foreign currency transaction gain or loss recognized on the exposed foreign currency account payable, and (5) the $600 remaining balance in Other Comprehensive Income after the foreign currency payable is paid on April 1, 20X2, is finally reclassified into cost of goods sold at the time the inventory is sold, which is the culmination of the earnings process related to the cash flow hedge.

Case 4: Speculation in Foreign Currency Markets

An entity also may decide to speculate in foreign currency as with any other commodity. For example, a U.S. company expects that the dollar will strengthen against the Swiss franc, that is, that the direct exchange rate will decrease. In this case, the U.S. company might **speculate with a forward exchange contract** to sell francs for future delivery, expecting to be able to purchase them at a lower price at the time of delivery.

The economic substance of this foreign currency speculation is to expose the investor to foreign exchange risk for which the investor expects to earn a profit. The exchange rate for valuing accounts related to speculative foreign exchange contracts is the forward rate for the remaining term of the forward contract. The gain or loss on a speculative forward contract is computed by determining the difference between the forward exchange rate on the date of contract (or on the date of a previous valuation) and the forward exchange rate available for the remaining term of the contract. The forward exchange rate is used to value the forward contract.

Illustration of Speculation with Forward Contract

The following example illustrates the accounting for a U.S. company entering into a speculative forward exchange contract in Swiss francs (SFr), a currency in which the company has no receivables, payables, or commitments.

1. On October 1, 20X1, Peerless Products entered into a 180-day forward exchange contract to deliver SFr 4,000 at a forward rate of $0.74 = SFr 1, when the spot rate was $0.73 = SFr 1. Thus, the forward contract was to deliver SFr 4,000 and receive $2,960 (SFr 4,000 × $0.74).
2. On December 31, 20X1, the balance sheet date, the forward rate for a 90-day forward contract was $0.78 = SFr 1, and the spot rate for francs was $0.75 = SFr 1.
3. On April 1, 20X2, the company acquired SFr 4,000 in the open market and delivered the francs to the broker, receiving the agreed-upon forward contract price of $2,960. At this date, the spot rate was $0.77 = SFr 1.

A summary of the direct exchange rates for this illustration follows.

Date	U.S. Dollar–Equivalent of 1 Franc	
	Spot Rate	**Forward Rate**
October 1, 20X1	$0.73	$0.74 (180 days)
December 31, 20X1	0.75	0.78 (90 days)
April 1, 20X2	0.77	

A time line of the economic events is as follows:

The entries for these transactions are as follows:

October 1, 20X1

(18)

Dollars Receivable from Exchange Broker ($)	2,960	
Foreign Currency Payable to Exchange Broker (SFr)		2,960

Enter into speculative forward exchange contract:

$2,960 = SFr 4,000 × $0.74, the 180-day forward rate

December 31, 20X1

(19)

Foreign Currency Transaction Loss	160	
Foreign Currency Payable to Exchange Broker (SFr)		160

Recognize speculation loss on forward contract for difference
between initial 180-day forward rate and forward rate for
remaining term to maturity of contract of 90 days:

$160 = SFr 4,000 × ($0.78 − $0.74)

April 1, 20X2

(20)

Foreign Currency Payable to Exchange Broker (SFr)	40	
Foreign Currency Transaction Gain		40

Revalue foreign currency payable to spot rate at end of term of
forward contract:

$40 = SFr 4,000 × ($0.78 − $0.77)

(21)

Foreign Currency Units (SFr)	3,080	
Cash		3,080

Acquire foreign currency units (SFr) in open market when spot rate
is $0.77 = SFr1:

$3,080 = SFr 4,000 × $0.77 spot rate

(22)

Foreign Currency Payable to Exchange Broker (SFr)	3,080	
Foreign Currency Units (SFr)		3,080

Deliver foreign currency units to exchange broker in settlement of
forward contract:

$3,080 = SFr 4,000 × $0.77 spot rate

(23)

Cash	2,960	
Dollars Receivable from Exchange Broker ($)		2,960

Receive U.S. dollars from exchange broker as contracted.

Key Observations from Illustration

The October 1 entry records the forward contract payable of 4,000 Swiss francs to the exchange broker. The payables denominated in a foreign currency but must be translated into U.S. dollars used as the reporting currency of Peerless Products. For speculative contracts, the forward exchange contract accounts are valued to fair value by using the forward exchange rate for the remaining contract term.

The December 31 entry adjusts the payable denominated in foreign currency to its appropriate balance at the balance sheet date. The payable, Foreign Currency Payable to Exchange Broker, is adjusted for the increase in the forward exchange rate from October 1, 20X1. The foreign currency transaction loss is reported on the income statement, usually under "Other Income (Loss)."

Entry (20), the first April 1 entry, revalues the foreign currency payable to its current U.S. dollar–equivalent value using the spot rate of exchange and recognizes the speculation gain. Entry (21) shows the acquisition of the 4,000 francs in the open market at the spot rate of $0.77 = SFr 1. These francs will be used to settle the foreign currency payable to the exchange broker. The next two entries on this date, (22) and (23), recognize the settlement of the forward contract with the delivery of the 4,000 francs to the exchange broker and the receipt of the $2,960 agreed to when the contract was signed on October 1, 20X1. The $40 foreign currency transaction gain is the difference between

FIGURE 8–8 Foreign Exchange Matrix

Transactions or Accounts Denominated in Foreign Currency Units	Direct Exchange Rate Changes	
	Exchange Rate Increases (dollar has weakened)	Exchange Rate Decreases (dollar has strengthened)
Net monetary asset position, for example: (1) Foreign Currency Units (2) Accounts Receivable (3) Foreign Currency Receivable from Exchange Broker	EXCHANGE GAIN	EXCHANGE LOSS
Net monetary liability position, for example: (1) Accounts Payable (2) Bonds Payable (3) Foreign Currency Payable to Exchange Broker	EXCHANGE LOSS	EXCHANGE GAIN

the value of the foreign currency contract on December 31 using the forward rate and the value of the foreign currency units on April 1 using the spot rate.

Note that the company has speculated and lost because the dollar actually weakened against the Swiss franc. The net loss on the speculative forward contract was $120, which is the difference between the $160 loss recognized in 20X1 and the $40 gain recognized in 20X2.

Although this example shows a delivery of foreign currency units with a forward exchange contract, a company also may arrange a future contract for the receipt of foreign currency units. In this case, the October 1 entry is as follows:

	October 1, 20X1		
(24)	Foreign Currency Receivable from Exchange Broker (SFr)	2,960	
	Dollars Payable to Exchange Broker ($)		2,960

Sign forward exchange contract for future receipt of foreign currency units:
$2,960 = SFr 4,000 × $0.74

The remainder of the accounting is similar to that of a delivery contract except that the company records an exchange gain on December 31 because it has a receivable denominated in a foreign currency that has now strengthened relative to the dollar.

Foreign Exchange Matrix

The relationships between changes in exchange rates and the resulting exchange gains and losses are summarized in Figure 8–8. For example, if a company has an account receivable denominated in a foreign currency, the exposed net monetary asset position results in the recognition of an exchange gain if the direct exchange rate increases but an exchange loss if the exchange rate decreases. If a company offsets an asset denominated in a foreign currency with a liability also denominated in that currency, the company has protected itself from any changes in the exchange rate because any gain is offset by an equal exchange loss.

ADDITIONAL CONSIDERATIONS

LO4

Know how to measure hedge effectiveness, make interperiod tax allocations for foreign currency transactions, and hedge net investments in a foreign entity.

A Note on Measuring Hedge Effectiveness

FASB 133 (ASC 815) states that, at the beginning of each hedging transaction, a company must define the method it will use to measure the effectiveness of the hedge. *Effectiveness* means that there will be an approximate offset, within the range of 80 to 125 percent, of the changes in the fair value of the cash flows or changes in fair value to the risk being hedged. Effectiveness must be assessed at least every three months and when the company reports financial statements or earnings. A company may elect to choose from several different measures for assessing hedge effectiveness. The examples to this point in the chapter use the change in forward rates, but a company may use the change in spot prices or change in intrinsic value. The ***intrinsic value of a derivative*** is the value related to the changes in value of the underlying item. The ***time value of a derivative*** is related to the value assigned to the opportunity to hold the derivative open for a period of time. The time value expires over the term of the derivative and is zero at the derivative's maturity date. If the company uses spot prices for measuring hedge effectiveness, any difference between the spot price and the forward price is excluded from the assessment of hedge effectiveness and is included currently in earnings.

Interperiod Tax Allocation for Foreign Currency Gains (Losses)

Temporary differences in the recognition of foreign currency gains or losses between tax accounting and GAAP accounting require interperiod tax allocation. Generally, the accrual method of recognizing the effects of changes in exchange rates in the period of change differs from the general election for recognizing exchange gains for tax purposes in the period of actual conversion of the foreign currency–denominated item. The temporary difference is recognized in accordance with **FASB Statement No. 109 (ASC 740)**, "Accounting for Income Taxes" (FASB 109, ASC 740).

Hedges of a Net Investment in a Foreign Entity

In the earlier discussions of the use of forward exchange contracts as a hedging instrument, the exchange risks from transactions denominated in a foreign currency could be offset. This same concept is applied by U.S. companies that view a net investment in a foreign entity as a long-term commitment that exposes them to foreign currency risk. A number of balance sheet management tools are available for a U.S. company to hedge its net investment in a foreign affiliate. Management may use forward exchange contracts, other foreign currency commitments, or certain intercompany financing arrangements, including intercompany transactions. For example, a U.S. parent company could borrow 10,000 British pounds to hedge against an equivalent net asset position of its British subsidiary. Any effects of exchange rate fluctuations between the pound and the dollar would be offset by the investment in the British subsidiary and the loan payable.

    FASB 133 (ASC 815) specifies that for derivative financial instruments designated as a hedge of the foreign currency exposure of a net investment in a foreign operation, the portion of the change in fair value equivalent to a foreign currency transaction gain or loss should be reported in other comprehensive income. That part of other comprehensive income resulting from a hedge of a net investment in a foreign operation then becomes part of the cumulative translation adjustment in accumulated other comprehensive income. Chapter 9 presents both the translation adjustment portion of other comprehensive income and accumulated other comprehensive income.

Summary of Key Concepts	Virtually all companies have foreign transactions. The general rule is that accounts resulting from transactions denominated in foreign currency units must be valued and reported at their equivalent U.S. dollar values. Forward exchange contracts typically use the forward rate for determining current fair value. These accounts must be adjusted to recognize the effects of changes in the exchange rates. For fair value hedges, the gain or loss is taken into current earnings. For cash flow hedges, the gain or loss is taken into other comprehensive income for the period.

Key Terms	cash flow hedges, *388*
	current rate, *381*
	derivative, *387*
	fair value hedges, *388*
	financial instrument, *387*
		foreign currency exchange
		  rate, *376*
		foreign currency hedges, *388*
		foreign currency transaction
		  gain or loss, *382*
			foreign currency
			  transactions, *375*
			foreign currency unit
			  (FCU), *376*

Appendix **8A**   Illustration of Valuing Forward Exchange Contracts with Recognition for the Time Value of Money

This illustration uses the example of a hedge of an identifiable, unrecognized foreign currency commitment from the chapter to illustrate the present value of the forward exchange contract and hedge.

1. On August 1, 20X1, Peerless Products Corporation contracts to purchase special-order goods from Tokyo Industries. The manufacture and delivery of the goods will take place in 60 days (on October 1, 20X1). The contract price is 2,000,000 yen to be paid by April 1, 20X2, which is 180 days after delivery.

2. On August 1, 20X1, Peerless Products hedges its foreign currency payable commitment with a forward exchange contract to receive 2,000,000 yen in 240 days (the 60 days until delivery plus 180 days of credit period). The future rate for a 240-day forward contract is $0.0073 to 1 yen. The purpose of this 240-day forward exchange contract is twofold. First, for the 60 days from August 1, 20X1, until October 1, 20X1, the forward exchange contract is a hedge of an identifiable foreign currency commitment. For the 180-day period from October 1, 20X1, until April 1, 20X2, the forward exchange contract is a hedge of a foreign currency–exposed net liability position.

3. Peerless uses a discount interest rate of 10 percent to present value of the expected future cash flows from forward exchange contracts.

4. Peerless measures the effectiveness of hedges of identifiable, unrecognized firm commitments based on changes in the forward exchange rate.

The relevant exchange rates for this example are as follows:

U.S. Dollar–Equivalent Value of 1 Yen		
Date	**Spot Rate**	**Forward Exchange Rate**
August 1, 20X1	$0.0065	$0.0073 (240 days)
October 1, 20X1	0.0070	0.0075 (180 days)
December 31, 20X1 (balance sheet date)	0.0080	0.0077 (90 days)
April 1, 20X2 (settlement date)	0.0076	

The following timeline summarizes these transactions.

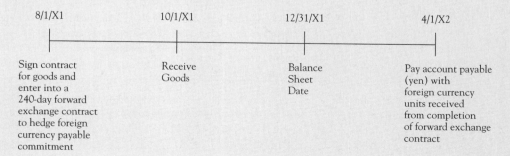

The computation of hedge effectiveness is performed using the changes in the forward exchange rate in accordance with the general requirements of **FASB 133 (ASC 815)** and the company's specific policies regarding measurement of effectiveness of the hedge by using the forward exchange rates.

	Change in the Fair Value of		
	Forward Contract Based on Changes in Forward Rate Gain (Loss)	**Firm Commitment Based on Changes in Forward Rate Gain (Loss)**	**Effectiveness Ratio for the Period**
October 1, 20X1	$380 (*a*)	$(380)	1.00
December 31, 20X1	400 (*b*)	No longer applicable because firm commitment was completed on October 1, 20X1.	
April 1, 20X2	(180) (*c*)		

(*a*) $380 = [($0.0075 − $0.0073) × ¥2,000,000] for the $400 cumulative, undiscounted gain from the change in the forward rates and then discounted at a 10 percent annual rate for the six-month period from October 1, 20X1, to April 1, 20X2, the completion date of the forward contract: NPV(0.05, 400) = $380.95, rounded.
(*b*) $400 = [($0.0077 − $0.0073) × ¥2,000,000] for the $800 cumulative, undiscounted gain from the change in the forward rates since entering the forward contract and then (1) discounted at a 10 percent annual rate for the three-month period from December 31, 20X1, to April 1, 20X2, NPV(0.025, 800) = $780.49, rounded; and then (2) subtract prior recognition of $380 reported for October 1, 20X1, in (a).
(*c*) $(180) = [($0.0076 − $0.0073) × ¥2,000,000] for the $600 cumulative gain from the change in the forward rate since entering the forward contract on August 1, 20X1, to the spot rate on April 1, 20X2, the completion of the forward contract; then subtract the prior recognition of $780 gain recognized previously in (a) and (b). This results in a loss of $(180) in the current period.

The amounts in the following entry on August 1, 20X1, are not present valued because the entry is a memorandum-type entry and because the interest factor will be taken into earnings through the changes in the fair value of the forward contract. Note that at the date of signing the forward contract, the net fair value of the forward contract is zero because the receivable and payable are equal to each other.

	August 1, 20X1		
(25)	Foreign Currency Receivable from Exchange Broker (¥)	14,600	
	Dollars Payable to Exchange Broker ($)		14,600

Sign forward exchange contract for receipt of 2,000,000 yen in 240 days:
$14,600 = ¥2,000,000 × $0.0073 Aug. 1, 240-day forward rate

On October 1, 20X1, the forward exchange contract will be revalued to its net fair value, recognizing the time value of money by using the present value of the expected future net cash flow from the forward contract. The temporary liability account, Firm Commitment, is also recorded at this time. Net present values can easily be computed using an electronic spreadsheet such as Excel and the Net Present Value (NPV) function.

	October 1, 20X1		
(26)	Foreign Currency Receivable from Exchange Broker (¥)	380	
	Foreign Currency Transaction Gain		380

Adjust forward contract to net fair value, using the present value of the change in the forward rates. [Item (*a*) in the hedge effectiveness illustration.]

(27)	Foreign Currency Transaction Loss	380	
	Firm Commitment		380

To record the loss on the financial instrument aspect of the firm commitment, using the present value of the change in the forward exchange rates. [Same amount as item (*a*) for this example because the effectiveness of the hedge on the firm commitment is assessed using the change in the forward exchange rates.]

On October 1, 20X1, the discounted net fair value of the forward contract is $380.

The next entry is to record the receipt of the inventory and the recognition of the accounts payable in yen. Note that the temporary account, Firm Commitment, is closed against the purchase price of the inventory.

(28)	Inventory	13,620	
	Firm Commitment	380	
	Accounts Payable (¥)		14,000

Record accounts payable at spot rate and the inventory purchase, closing the temporary liability account:
$14,000 = ¥2,000,000 × $0.0070 Oct. 1 spot rate

The required adjusting entries on December 31, 20X1, Peerless' fiscal year-end, are

(29)	Foreign Currency Receivable from Exchange Broker (¥)	400	
	Foreign Currency Transaction Gain		400

Adjust forward contract to net fair value, using the present value of the change in the forward rates. [Item (b) in the hedge effectiveness illustration.]

(30)	Foreign Currency Transaction Loss	2,000	
	Accounts Payable (¥)		2,000

Adjust payable denominated in yen to current U.S. dollar–equivalent value: $2,000 = ¥2,000,000 × ($0.0080 − $0.0070). No interest factor is used for this revaluation; thus, no present value computation is made.

On December 31, 20X1, the discounted net fair value of the forward contract is $780. The first required entry on April 1, 20X2, the settlement date, is

(31)	Foreign Currency Transaction Loss	180	
	Foreign Currency Receivable from Exchange Broker (¥)		180

Adjust forward contract for the change in the forward rate to the spot rate on settlement date: [Item (c) in the hedge effectiveness illustration.]

$0.0076 spot rate on 4/1/X2, the end of the forward contract
− 0.0073 forward rate on 8/1/X1, the beginning of the forward contract
$0.0003 × ¥2,000,000 = $ 600 cumulative change from 8/1/X1
−780 gains previously recognized
$(180) reduction (loss) this period

Note that at this point, the net foreign currency transaction gain on just the forward contract is $600. This is the difference between the time value of the forward contract (the $1,600 premium on the forward contract—$0.0073 forward rate less $0.0065 spot rate—when the forward contract was signed on August 1, 20X1, which is taken into earnings over the term of the forward contract) and the intrinsic value of the forward contract (the $2,200 difference between the spot rate of $0.0065 on August 1, 20X1, and the spot rate of $0.0076 on the forward contract completion date of April 1, 20X2). Another way to compute the net gain over the term of the forward contract is to compare the forward rate at the date the contract is signed ($0.0073) and the spot rate at the date the contract is completed ($0.0076). The net gain is $600 [¥2,000,000 × ($0.0073 − $0.0076)].

The following April 1, 20X2, entries complete the forward contract and the payment of the accounts payable that was denominated as ¥2,000,000.

(32)	Accounts Payable (¥)	800	
	Foreign Currency Transaction Gain		800

Adjust payable denominated in yen to spot rate on settlement date. No interest factor for this item.
$800 = ¥2,000,000 × ($0.0076 − $0.0080)

(33)	Dollars Payable to Exchange Broker ($)	14,600	
	Cash		14,600

Deliver U.S. dollars to currency broker as specified in forward contract.

(34)	Foreign Currency Units (¥)	15,200	
	Foreign Currency Receivable from Exchange Broker (¥)		15,200

Receive ¥2,000,000 from exchange broker; valued at Apr. 1, 20X2,
spot rate:
$15,200 = ¥2,000,000 × $0.0076

(35)	Accounts Payable (¥)	15,200	
	Foreign Currency Units (¥)		15,200

Pay 2,000,000 yen to Tokyo Industries, Inc., in settlement of liability
denominated in yen.

Appendix 8B Use of Other Financial Instruments by Multinational Companies

This chapter detailed the accounting for forward exchange contracts that were used to hedge exposed asset or liability positions or to hedge foreign currency commitments, or that were entered into for speculative purposes. Many multinational enterprises (MNEs) typically use financial instruments other than forward contracts to manage the risks associated with international transactions. A general definition of a financial instrument is that it is cash, stock, or a contract that imposes a contractual obligation to deliver or receive cash or another financial instrument to/from another entity. Examples of financial instruments are receivables/payables, bonds, shares of stock, foreign currency forward contracts, futures contracts, options, and financial swaps. A derivative financial instrument is when the value of a financial instrument is derived from some other item such as a contract valued on an index of stock values or futures contracts in which the value is determined by contemporary and predicted economic events. The other derivative financial instruments most often used by MNEs are futures, options, and swaps.

Accounting standard setters have had the daunting task of obtaining a consensus on the accounting, reporting, and disclosing of financial instruments. The FASB first placed the financial instrument project on its agenda in 1986 and has since continued to work on this project. Along the way, it issued **FASB Statement No. 105,** "Disclosure of Information about Financial Instruments with Off-Balance Sheet Risk" (FASB 105); **FASB Statement No. 107 (ASC 825),** "Disclosures about Fair Value of Financial Instruments" (FASB 107, ASC 825); and **FASB Statement No. 119,** "Disclosure about Derivative Financial Instruments and Fair Value of Financial Instruments" (FASB 119). In 1998, the FASB issued **FASB Statement No. 133 (ASC 815),** "Accounting for Derivative Instruments and Hedging Activities" (FASB 133, ASC 815). **FASB 133 (ASC 815)** supersedes **FASB Statement No. 80,** "Accounting for Future Contracts" (FASB 80); **FASB 105;** and **FASB 119.** In 1999, the FASB issued **FASB 137,** which delayed the implementation date of **FASB 133 (ASC 815)** for one year, until June 15, 2000, but **FASB 137** did not change any of **FASB 133**'s **(ASC 815)** requirements.

FASB 133 (ASC 815) specified four major decisions underlying the logic of the standard: (1) derivatives are assets or liabilities and should be reported in the financial statements; (2) fair value is the most relevant measure for financial instruments and the only relevant measure for derivatives, and adjustment to the carrying amount of hedged items should reflect offsetting changes in their fair value while the hedge is in effect; (3) only items that are assets or liabilities should be reported as such in the financial statements; and (4) special accounting for items designated as being hedged should be provided only for qualifying transactions, and an aspect of qualification should be an assessment of offsetting changes in fair values or cash flows. Thus, **FASB 133 (ASC 815)** has a general rule of fair value, requires the recognition of gains and losses for the changes in fair value, and limits the applications of hedge accounting. It defines *fair value* as the amount at which an asset (liability) could be bought (incurred) or sold (settled) in a current transaction between willing parties. Quoted market prices are typically the best evidence of fair value. In addition, **FASB 133 (ASC 815)** amended **FASB 107 (ASC 825)** to include specific disclosures about concentrations of credit risk of all financial instruments and encouraged disclosure about the market risk of all financial instruments. *Credit risk* is the loss that might occur if a party to the contract involving the entity fails to perform. *Market risk* is the loss that might occur from future changes in market prices that would impair the value of the financial instrument.

FASB Statement No. 138 (ASC 815), "Accounting for Certain Derivative Instruments and Certain Hedging Activities: An Amendment of FASB Statement No. 133" (FASB 138, ASC 815), issued in 2000, amended four smaller items in **FASB 133 (ASC 815)** in response to technical concerns raised by practitioners and preparers of the financial statements: (1) it broadened the application of the normal purchases and sales exception so that fewer of these contracts requiring delivery of non-financial assets would need to be accounted for as derivatives, (2) it redefined the interest rate risk to permit a benchmark risk-free interest rate to be the hedged risk, (3) it permitted hedging recognized foreign currency–denominated assets or liabilities with either cash flow or fair value hedges but still requires the foreign currency–denominated asset or liability to be valued according to the provisions of **FASB 52 (ASC 830),** and (4) it broadened the ability to hedge with intercompany derivatives.

FASB Statement No. 149 (ASC 815), "Amendment of Statement 133 on Derivative Instruments and Hedging Activities" (FASB 149, ASC 815), issued in 2003, presented a series of modifications resulting from implementation issues related to the definition of a derivative. **FASB 149 (ASC 815)** clarified several definitional issues but did not change the basic concepts presented in **FASB 133 (ASC 815).**

This appendix supplements the chapter by presenting a brief overview of futures, options, and swaps. It first gives brief definitions and descriptions. Next, it presents several examples of accounting for a hedge with a futures contract, a hedge with an option contract, and an interest-rate swap. Finally, it presents a description of the disclosure requirements that currently apply. A discussion of the detailed mechanics and risk ramifications of transactions that utilize these instruments is beyond the coverage of an advanced financial accounting textbook.

DEFINITIONS AND DESCRIPTIONS

A *derivative financial instrument* is an instrument whose value is based on or "derived from" the value of something else (an underlying). That underlying can be the value of another financial instrument, a commodity, an index, an asset, or a debt instrument. Because the derivative financial instrument has a value that is linked to the underlying, it makes the derivative a useful hedging instrument to offset the change in value of the hedged item. Examples of derivative financial instruments include futures, forward, swap, and option contracts; interest-rate caps; and fixed-rate loan commitments.

Forward and Futures Contracts

A forward contract is an agreement between a buyer and a seller that requires the delivery of some commodity at a specified future date at a price agreed to today (the exercise price). As presented in the chapter, foreign currency forward contracts are typically made with dealers of foreign exchange, and the contract is fulfilled at the end of the contract term by the exchanges of the currencies between the company and the dealer. Changes in the underlying market value of the foreign currency are recognized by the company holding the forward contract. The net fair value of a forward contract when it is written is zero because neither party pays anything and neither party receives anything. The contract is executory at this point. During the term of the forward contract, the net fair value changes based on the difference between a newly written forward contract for the remaining term and the original forward contract. At expiration, the forward contract's net fair value is the difference between the spot price and the original forward rate.

Futures are very similar to forward contracts except futures have standardized contract terms, they are traded on organized exchanges, and traders must realize any losses or gains on each and every trading day. Futures are contracts between two parties—a buyer and a seller—to buy or sell something at a specified future date, which is termed the *expiration date*. The contract trades on a futures exchange such as the Chicago Board of Trade (CBOT) or the Chicago Mercantile Exchange (CME). Futures contracts are actively traded in a number of commodities including grains and oilseeds, livestock and meat, food and fiber, and metals and energy. It is even possible to enter into futures contracts on foreign currencies. Companies trading in futures contracts are normally required to place cash in their margin accounts held by the brokerage exchange or a *clearing house,* and the gain (loss) on the futures contract is then added (subtracted) from the company's margin account. This margin account is settled daily for the changes in contract value. Margin accounts are maintained at some percentage (typically 2 to 5 percent) of the contract amount. Most investors do not expect to actually exchange the futures contract for the optioned item—the futures contract is simply an investment vehicle to ride the value curve of the optioned item—and they use a *closing transaction* to settle the futures contract. If a company is the purchaser of a futures contract, it is said to "go long" in a position. If a company contracts to sell with a futures contract, it is said to "go short." Futures contracts are sometimes referred to as *liquid forward contracts* because futures trade separately. The accounting for futures contracts is quite similar to accounting for foreign currency forward contracts.

Both futures and forward contracts are obligations to deliver a specified amount at a specified point in time. There is a potential for a gain under favorable circumstances and a potential for a loss under unfavorable circumstances. As presented in Chapter 8, not only the losses but also the gains are minimized by using foreign currency forward contracts. Forward contracts are commonly used for hedging foreign currency transactions because the forward contracts can be customized as to duration and amounts. Futures contracts are standardized as to duration and amount but are more readily accessible because of their wide acceptance in a futures exchange arena.

Option Contracts

An option contract between two parties—the buyer and the seller—gives the buyer (option holder) the right, but not the obligation, to purchase from or sell something to the option seller (option writer) at a date in the future at a price agreed to at the time the option contract is exchanged. Options can be written on a large variety of commodities such as grains, food and fibers, petroleum, livestock, metals, interest rates, and various foreign currencies. The option buyer pays the seller some amount of money, typically termed the "premium," for this right. An option to buy something is referred to as a "call"; an option to sell something is called a "put." Options trade on organized markets similar to the stock market. Exchanges on which options trade are the Chicago Board Options Exchange (CBOE), the Philadelphia Stock Exchange (PHLX), the American Stock Exchange (AMEX), and the Pacific Stock Exchange (PSE).

An option contract can give the buyer future control over a large number of shares or other items at the nominal cost of the option. This ability of the option for future control is the *time value* of the option. Over the option's term, the time value decreases to zero at the option's expiration date. Changes in the time value of the option are always taken to current earnings. The party selling the right is the writer; the party buying the right is the holder. The option holder has the right to exercise or not exercise the option. The holder of the option would not exercise the right embedded in the option if by doing so it would result in a loss. The option writer, however, is subject to risk because the option holder could exercise the option, forcing the writer to deliver under terms that are not favorable to the writer. An option's *intrinsic value* is directly related to the change in underlying value of the hedged item. The change in intrinsic value of a fair value hedge is taken to current earnings. The change in the effective portion of intrinsic value of a cash flow hedge is taken to other comprehensive income. An example of an option used as a hedge is presented later in this appendix.

The option is sold with a *strike price,* the price at which the holder has the option to buy or sell the item. If an investor holds a call option to purchase one share of Peerless Products stock for $5 a share from the writer, the holder may exercise that option when the market share price exceeds the strike price. If the market price is $6 a share, the holder will save $1 by exercising the option and purchasing the stock for $5. If the holder wishes to turn the savings into a cash profit, the investor would sell the share of stock, purchased for $5, on the market for $6. Alternatively, the holder of the option could directly sell the option for $1, its intrinsic value. When the market price is more than the strike price, the option to buy is "in the money." When the market price is less than the strike price, the option to buy is "out of the money."

If an investor is the holder of a put option to sell one share of Peerless Products for $5 a share to the writer, the holder will exercise that option when the share price is below the strike price. If the market price is $4 a share, the holder will make $1 by exercising the sell option at $5 per share rather than selling the share on the open market at $4 per share. When the market price is less than the option price, the option to sell is "in the money."

For the Peerless Products stock example, a summary of the relationship between the option type and the term used to describe the difference between the current market price of the underlying and the option's strike price is as follows:

Option	Current Market Price Equals the Option's Strike Price ($5 = $5)	Current Market Price Is More than the Option's Strike Price ($6 > $5)	Current Market Price Is Less than the Option's Strike Price ($4 < $5)
Call (buy)	At the money	In the money	Out of the money
Put (sell)	At the money	Out of the money	In the money

Options are typically purchased for a fee that is usually a small percentage of the optioned item's current value (e.g., 1 to 7 percent). The option's terms stipulate whether the option can

FIGURE 8–9
Features of Forwards, Futures, and Options

Type of Derivative	Features
Forwards	• Contracted through a dealer, usually a bank • Possibly customized to meet contracting company's terms and needs • Typically no margin deposit required • Must be completed either with the underlying's future delivery or net cash settlement
Futures	• Traded on an exchange and acquired through an exchange broker • Cannot be customized; for a specific amount at a specific date • Often company required to open a margin account with a small deposit so daily changes in futures value can be posted to the account • Usually settled with a net cash amount prior to maturity date; not expected to be completed by the underlying's future delivery
Options	• Traded on a variety of exchanges • Acquired on a large variety of commodities and major foreign currencies • Issued in two types: put (sell) and call (buy) • Option premium (fee) paid by the option holder to the writer (counterparty) for that right • Taker's or holder's loss limited to a maximum of the premium paid but virtually unlimited potential profit if underlying market moves in the option holder's desired direction • Grantor (counterparty or writer) offered potential to earn a maximum of the option premium and to lose a virtually unlimited amount if underlying market moves in the opposite direction than desired

be exercised at any time during the option period or only at the end of the exercise period. The minimum value of an option is zero because an option need not be exercised. Therefore, an option can never have a negative value, and the maximum loss of the holder of an option can incur is the premium initially paid for the option.

Figure 8–9 presents an overview of the major features of forwards, futures, and options.

Swaps

A *swap* is an arrangement by which two parties exchange cash flows over a period of time. Swaps can be designed to swap currencies, interest rates, or commodities. The two most common types of financial swaps used by companies are (1) currency swaps and (2) interest rate swaps. An example of a currency swap is Peerless Products Corporation's sale of products in Great Britain for which it receives pounds sterling. Another company located in London, England, sells products in the United States for which it receives U.S. dollars. A currency swap would occur, for example, if Peerless (a U.S. company) agrees that the periodic currency flows in pounds sterling from its Great Britain operations will be forwarded to its counterparty in Great Britain, and the dollar sales in the United States by the London company will be forwarded to Peerless, the U.S. company. At the end of each period, the two companies agree to settle up for any differences in the notional amount of the swap at the end of the period. Thus, both parties to this currency swap avoid dealing in other than their local currencies and avoid foreign currency exchange costs.

Another example of a swap is an interest-rate swap in which two parties agree to exchange the interest payments on a stated amount of principal (also called the "notional amount"). Typically, the swap is an exchange of a variable (floating) rate interest and a fixed-rate interest. For example, Peerless may issue variable-rate debt but wish to fix its interest rates because it believes the variable rate may increase. Peerless may enter into a contract with a counterparty that has a fixed-rate bond but is looking for a variable-rate interest because that company assumes the interest rates may decrease. Often the contract includes a financial intermediary to which net settlement payments are made and that charges a nominal fee for its services. Sometimes the counterparty is a dealer—a bank or an investment banking firm—that makes a market in swaps and other interest-rate derivatives. The notional amount (principal) is specified as the same for both parties, and Peerless fixes the interest rate on its notional amount while the counterparty obtains the variable rate it was seeking. Note that the debt is not being extinguished and

FIGURE 8–10   Overview of Three Types of Hedges

Type of Hedge	Basic Criteria	Recognition and Measurement
Fair value hedge	A hedge of the derivative instrument's exposure to changes in the fair value of an asset or liability, or of an unrecognized firm commitment.	Gain or loss on the hedging instrument, as well as the related loss or gain on the hedged item, should be recognized currently in earnings.
Cash flow hedge	Hedge the derivative instrument's exposure to variability in expected future cash flows of a recognized asset or liability, or of a forecasted transaction, that is attributable to a particular risk.	Gain or loss on the effective portion of hedge (e.g., the intrinsic value) is deferred and reported as a component of other comprehensive income. Any gain or loss on the derivative that is not offset by cash flow losses and gains on the hedged forecasted transaction (i.e., ineffective, including the time value of the option) is recognized currently in earnings.
Foreign currency hedge	A hedge of the foreign currency exposure of 1. An unrecognized firm commitment. 2. An available-for-sale security. 3. A forecasted transaction. 4. A net investment in a foreign operation.	The recognition and measurement differ by type of hedge: 1. This is a foreign currency fair value hedge. 2. This is a foreign currency cash flow hedge. 3. The gain or loss on the effective portion of the hedging derivative on a net investment in a foreign operative shall be reported as part of the translation adjustment component of other comprehensive income.

any fees paid to arrange the swap should be treated as debt issuance costs that are amortized over the term of the debt. Each company is still responsible for its actual interest payment to its creditor. The swap is merely an agreement for the net periodic settlement of the difference between the two interest rates and is done solely between the two companies that contracted for the interest swap. The simple swap of fixed- versus variable-interest rates is sometimes referred to as a *plain vanilla swap* or a *generic swap*. An interest rate swap is presented later in this appendix.

An overview of the accounting for the three major types of hedges is presented in Figure 8–10. Review this figure before proceeding to the examples.

EXAMPLE OF THE USE OF AN OPTION TO HEDGE AN ANTICIPATED PURCHASE OF INVENTORY: A CASH FLOW HEDGE

Assume that Peerless Products plans in 90 days to purchase 30,000 bushels of wheat that currently have a value of $75,000 (30,000 bushels × $2.50 spot price per bushel). Also assume that Peerless wants to lock in the value of the anticipated future purchase.

Peerless purchases a call option on wheat futures to hedge against a price change in the anticipated purchase of the inventory. If the price of wheat increases, the profit on the purchased call option will offset the higher price that Peerless would have to pay for the wheat. If the price of wheat decreases, Peerless loses the premium it paid for the call option but can then buy the wheat at a lower price.

On November 1, 20X1, Peerless purchases call options for a February 1, 20X2, call (90 days in the future) at a call price of $2.50. Peerless pays a premium of $0.05 per bushel, for a total cost of $1,500 (30,000 bushels × $0.05). The call options are for a notional amount of 30,000 bushels of wheat. Peerless specifies that the derivative qualifies for cash flow hedge accounting. It is a cash flow hedge because the option is hedging a forecasted, or planned, future transaction involving cash flows. Note that this example shows the entire $1,500 as the time value of the option; in other words, it sets a futures price equal to the current market price. This type of contract is sometimes termed "at the money," meaning it specifies the futures price of the underlying at the current market price. Thus, the value of the contract when it is signed is only with regard to the *time value* of the expectation that the actual future price of the commodity will differ from the current market price.

An overview of this hedge follows:

Hedging instrument	Call option on wheat futures
Hedged item	Forecasted purchase of wheat
Type of hedge	Cash flow hedge
Underlying	Price of a bushel of wheat
Notional amount	30,000 bushels of wheat
Time value at origin of hedge	$1,500, at the money
Valuation of call option	Fair value
If underlying increases in value	Call option increases in value
If underlying decreases in value	Call option decreases in value

Gain or loss on hedge:

Effective portion	To Other Comprehensive Income; related to change in intrinsic value of hedge
Ineffective portion	To current earnings; related to change in time value of hedge

The entry to record the purchase of the call options is as follows:

November 1, 20X1

(36)

Purchased Call Options	1,500	
Cash		1,500

To record the purchase of call options for 30,000 bushels of wheat at $2.50 per bushel in 90 days. The options are at the money; therefore, the $1,500 is all time value.

The fair market information for this example follows:

Fair Value Computations

	November 1, 20X1	December 31, 20X1	February 1, 20X2
Bushel of wheat Total: 30,000 bushels	$ 2.50	$ 2.60	$ 2.58
Call Option:			
Option market value (from market information)	$1,500	$3,700	$2,400
Less: Intrinsic value: [Number of bushels × (Market price − Strike price)]			
[30,000 bushels × ($2.50 − $2.50)]	–0–		
[30,000 bushels × ($2.60 − $2.50)]		(3,000)	
[30,000 bushels × ($2.58 − $2.50)]			(2,400)
Time value remaining	$1,500	$ 700	$ –0–

Note that for a cash flow hedge, the change in the intrinsic value (effective portion) is recognized in Other Comprehensive Income, and the change in the time value (ineffective portion) is recognized in current earnings.

At December 31, 20X1, the price of wheat increases to $2.60 per bushel. The *intrinsic value* is the change in value of the options due to the change in market value of the underlying. For cash flow hedges, the change in a derivative's intrinsic value is recorded in other comprehensive income. On December 31, the intrinsic value of the options is $3,000 (30,000 bushels × $0.10 increase).

FASB 133 (ASC 815) requires that hedging instruments be revalued to fair value at each balance sheet date. The change in value of the options is due to two factors: the change in the intrinsic value and the reduction of the time value. An option's time value decreases over its term and is zero when the options expire. At December 31, 20X1, the fair market value of the options is $3,700, meaning that the options' remaining time value is valued by the market at $700 ($3,700 fair value less $3,000 intrinsic value). **FASB 133 (ASC 815)** specifies that the $800 ($1,500 initial amount − $700 remaining) reduction in the time value portion of a derivative is recognized as part of current earnings. Entry (37) records the change in the value of the options to value them at their fair value at the balance sheet date.

	December 31, 20X1		
(37)	Purchased Call Options	2,200	
	Loss on Hedge Activity	800	
	Other Comprehensive Income		3,000

To revalue the options to their fair market value, recognizing the reduction
in time value and the increase in intrinsic value:
$2,200 = $3,700 current fair value of options less $1,500 balance on November 1
$800 = ($1,500 − $700 remaining) reduction in time value of options
$3,000 = 30,000 bushels × $0.10 increase in intrinsic value

Note that the increase in intrinsic value is recorded in Other Comprehensive Income pending the completion of the forecasted inventory transaction. The Other Comprehensive Income account is used to "store" the intrinsic value gains or losses on cash flow hedges until they are reclassified into earnings when the hedged transaction affects earnings.

At February 1, 20X2, the end of the 90 days, the price of wheat is $2.58 per bushel. The decrease in the intrinsic value of the call options is recorded as follows:

	February 1, 20X2		
(38)	Other Comprehensive Income	600	
	Purchased Call Options		600

To record the other comprehensive income, deferring the earning
recognition of the loss on the purchased call options:
$600 = 30,000 bushels × ($2.58 − $2.60)

The next entry (39) recognizes the expiration of the remaining amount ($700) of the time value of the purchased call option because the option has now expired. **FASB 133** specifies that the change in the time value portion of a derivative be recognized in current earnings.

	February 1, 20X2		
(39)	Loss on Hedge Activity	700	
	Purchased Call Options		700

To recognize the loss of the $700 remaining time value of the
purchased call options that have now expired.

Peerless now decides to sell the contracts for their intrinsic value of $2,400 [30,000 bushels × ($2.58 − $2.50 call price)]. In addition, Peerless acquires the 30,000 bushels of wheat at the current market price of $2.58 per bushel. The next entry records the sale of the purchased call options at their current market price.

	February 1, 20X2		
(40)	Cash	2,400	
	Purchased Call Options		2,400

To record the sale of the call options.

Peerless now purchases the 30,000 bushels of wheat at the current market price of $2.58 per bushel.

	February 1, 20X2		
(41)	Wheat Inventory	77,400	
	Cash		77,400

Finally, Peerless later sells the wheat at a price of $100,000 and records the sale as well as the reclassification of the other comprehensive income resulting from the purchased call options. Note that the other comprehensive income is taken into income only when the underlying item enters the income stream.

(42)	Cash	100,000	
	Sale		100,000

To record the sale of the 30,000 bushels of wheat.

(43)

Cost of Goods Sold	77,400	
Wheat Inventory		77,400

To recognize the cost of the wheat sold.

(44)

Other Comprehensive Income—Reclassification	2,400	
Cost of Goods Sold		2,400

To reclassify into earnings the other comprehensive income
from the cash flow hedge.

The reduction of the cost of goods sold increases net income for the period. The earning process for the other comprehensive income was the sale of the wheat. The hedge was successful. Peerless has a gain of $2,400 less the $1,500 it paid for the time value of the call options.

EXAMPLE OF AN OPTION CONTRACT TO HEDGE AVAILABLE-FOR-SALE SECURITIES: A FAIR VALUE HEDGE

Assume that on January 1, 20X1, Peerless purchases 100 shares of Special Foods stock at a cost of $25 per share. The company classifies these as available-for-sale securities because it does not intend to sell them in the near term. To protect itself from a decrease in the value of the investment, on December 31, 20X1, the company purchases, for a $300 premium, an at-the-money put option (i.e., option price is current market price), which gives it the right but not the obligation to sell 100 shares of Special Foods at $30 per share. The option expires on December 31, 20X3. The fair value of the investment and the option follow:

Fair Value Computations

	December 31		
	20X1	**20X2**	**20X3**
Special Foods shares:			
Per share	$ 30	$ 29	$ 26
Total (100 shares)	3,000	2,900	2,600
Put option:			
Market value (a)	$ 300	$ 340	$ 400
Less: Intrinsic value (b)	(–0–)	(100)	(400)
Time value (c)	$ 300	$ 240	$ –0–

(a) Market value is obtained from the current market price. There is a variety of option pricing models, such as the Black-Scholes model, to estimate the value of these options.
(b) Intrinsic value is the difference between the current market price and the option price times the number of shares. It is easy to compute at any point in the life of the option. For example, the intrinsic value on December 31, 20X2, is ($30 option price − $29 current market price) × 100 shares.
(c) The time value of the option reflects the effect of discounting the expected future cash flows and a portion for the expected volatility in the price of the underlying asset. A simple way to compute the value is that it is the difference between the option's market value and its intrinsic value.

Note that the time value at December 31, 20X1, is for the entire option price because the option was purchased for the current market price. The time value decreases to zero at the end of the option because no time element remains at that expiration point and the market value of the option is then based solely on its intrinsic value. Peerless exercises the option just before its expiration on December 31, 20X3, and delivers the Special Foods shares to the option writer.

Peerless determines the hedge effectiveness based on the changes in the option's intrinsic value. This is an acceptable method for determining effectiveness using options because of the ultimate value of the option being based on the price of the underlying asset in this example, the stock of Special Foods.

Hedge Effectiveness Analysis

Date	Change in Option's Intrinsic Value (Gain) Loss	Change in Value of Special Foods Shares (Gain) Loss	Effectiveness Ratio for Period
December 31, 20X2	$(100)	$100	1.00
December 31, 20X3	$(300)	$300	1.00

An overview of this hedge is

Hedging instrument	Put option on Special Foods stock
Hedged item	100 shares of Special Foods stock
Type of hedge	Fair value hedge
Underlying	Price of a share of Special Foods stock
Notional amount	100 shares of Special Foods stock
Time value at origin of hedge	$300, at the money
Valuation of put option	Fair value
If underlying increases in value	Put option decreases in value
If underlying decreases in value	Put option increases in value

Gain or loss on hedge:

Effective portion	To current earnings; related to change in intrinsic value of hedge
Ineffective portion	To current earnings; related to change in time value of hedge

The entries for this example follow:

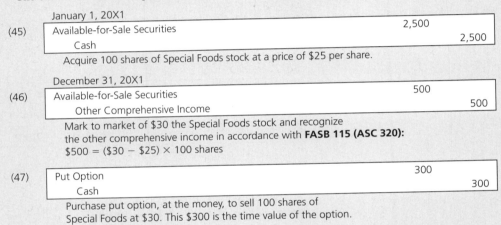

January 1, 20X1

(45)	Available-for-Sale Securities	2,500	
	Cash		2,500

Acquire 100 shares of Special Foods stock at a price of $25 per share.

December 31, 20X1

(46)	Available-for-Sale Securities	500	
	Other Comprehensive Income		500

Mark to market of $30 the Special Foods stock and recognize
the other comprehensive income in accordance with **FASB 115 (ASC 320):**
$500 = ($30 − $25) × 100 shares

(47)	Put Option	300	
	Cash		300

Purchase put option, at the money, to sell 100 shares of
Special Foods at $30. This $300 is the time value of the option.

Note that **FASB 133 (ASC 815)** amends **FASB 115 (ASC 320)** and requires the gain or loss on an available-for-sale security designated as a hedged item to be recognized in current earnings during the period. In entry (46), the marked-to-market value for the available-for-sale securities was recognized in other comprehensive income, in accordance with **FASB 115 (ASC 320).** As can be seen in entry (48), once available-for-sale securities are hedged in a fair value hedge, the gain or loss on marking to market must be taken to earnings for the period.

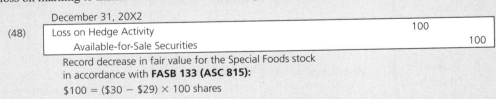

December 31, 20X2

(48)	Loss on Hedge Activity	100	
	Available-for-Sale Securities		100

Record decrease in fair value for the Special Foods stock
in accordance with **FASB 133 (ASC 815):**
$100 = ($30 − $29) × 100 shares

FASB 133 (ASC 815) specifies that the change in intrinsic value of fair value hedges be recognized currently in net earnings of the period. This is different from cash flow hedges in which the changes in intrinsic value were taken to other comprehensive income. Therefore, entry (49) recognizes the increase in the intrinsic value of this fair value hedge as a gain that will be closed to Retained Earnings.

December 31, 20X2

(49)	Put Option	100	
	Gain on Hedge Activity		100

Record increase in the intrinsic value of the put option.

(50)	Loss on Hedge Activity	60	
	Put Option		60

To record in earnings the ineffective portion of the change in
the fair value of the put options (i.e., the change in the time value).
$60 = $300 initial time value − $240 remaining time value

The entries for December 31, 20X3, continue the valuation process.

December 31, 20X3

(51)
Loss on Hedge Activity	300	
Available-for-Sale Securities		300

Mark to market of $26 the Special Foods stock and recognize the loss in earnings: $300 = ($26 − $29) × 100 shares

(52)
Put Option	300	
Gain on Hedge Activity		300

Record the increase in the intrinsic value of the put option.

(53)
Loss on Hedge Activity	240	
Put Option		240

Record in earnings the ineffective portion of the change in fair value of the put option (i.e., the change in the time value).

Entry (53) eliminates the remainder of the option's time value, which was initially $300. Entry (50) took $60 of the time value of the option against earnings of 20X2. Entry (53) takes the remainder into earnings of 20X3 because at the end of the option period, no time value remains. The only value of the put option at its term date is its intrinsic value.

(54)
Cash	3,000	
Put Option		400
Available-for-Sale Securities		2,600

Exercise the put option and delivery of the securities at a price of $30 per share.

(55)
Other Comprehensive Income	500	
Realized Gain on Sale of Securities		500

Reclassify the other comprehensive income on Special Foods' stock that was recorded on Dec. 31, 20X1, to earnings because the securities have now been sold.
$100 = ($30 − $29) × 100 shares

It is also important to note that **FASB 133 (ASC 815)** does not permit hedge accounting for hedges of trading securities. **FASB 115 (ASC 320)** requires that trading securities be marked to market with the gain or loss reported in net earnings for the period. Therefore, any gains or losses on financial instruments that are planned to hedge the risks of holding trading securities are always taken to net earnings for the period. Figure 8–11 presents an overview of the journal entries made for the hedged available-for-sale securities and for the hedging put option.

EXAMPLE OF AN INTEREST-RATE SWAP TO HEDGE VARIABLE-RATE DEBT: A CASH FLOW HEDGE

Advanced
StudyGuide
.com

Assume that on June 30, 20X1, Peerless borrows $5,000,000 of three-year, variable-rate debt with interest payments equal to the six-month U.S.$LIBOR (London Interbank Offered Rate) for the prior six months. The debt is not prepayable. The company then enters into a three-year interest-rate swap with First Bank to convert the debt's variable rate to a fixed rate. The swap agreement specifies that Peerless will pay interest at a fixed rate of 7.5 percent and receive interest at a variable rate equal to the six-month U.S.$LIBOR rate based on the notional amount of $5,000,000. Both the debt and the swap require interest to be paid semiannually on June 30 and December 31. Peerless specifies the swap as a cash flow hedge. A schematic of the swap relationships is presented in Figure 8–12.

The six-month U.S.$LIBOR rate and the market value of the swap agreement, as determined by a swap broker, follow for the first year of the swap agreement:

Date	Six-Month U.S. $LIBOR Rate	Swap Agreement Fair Value Asset (Liability)
June 30, 20X1	6.0%	$ –0–
December 31, 20X1	7.0	165,000
June 30, 20X2	5.5	(70,000)

FIGURE 8–11   Journal Entries for a Fair Value Hedge of Available-for-Sale Securities

Entries for Available-for-Sale Securities (hedged item)	Entries for Put Option Contract (hedging instrument)

January 1, 20X1. Acquire 100 shares of Special Foods stock as available-for-sale security.

(45)	Available-for-Sale Securities	2,500	
	Cash		2,500

December 31, 20X1. Revalue available-for-sale securities to market value in accordance with **FASB 115 (ASC 320)** and purchase put option for current market price of underlying.

(46)	Available-for-Sale Securities	500			(47)	Put Option	300	
	Other Comprehensive Income		500			Cash		300

December 31, 20X2. Revalue available-for-sale securities in accordance with **FASB 133 (ASC 815)** and adjust put option to current market value for increases in $100 intrinsic value and $60 reduction in time value of option.

(48)	Loss on Hedge Activity	100			(49)	Put Option	100	
	Available-for-Sale Securities		100			Gain on Hedge Activity		100
					(50)	Loss on Hedge Activity	60	
						Put Option		60

December 31, 20X3. Revalue available-for-sale securities and adjust put option to current market value for the $300 increase in intrinsic value and the $240 reduction in time value of the option.

(51)	Loss on Hedge Activity	300			(52)	Put Option	300	
	Available-for-Sale Securities		300			Gain on Hedge Activity		300
					(53)	Loss on Hedge Activity	240	
						Put Option		240

December 31, 20X3. Exercise put option and deliver 100 shares of stock at a $30 per share price. Reclassify other comprehensive income recognized in (46) on available-for-sale securities now sold.

(54)	Cash	3,000	
	Put Option		400
	Available-for-Sale Securities		2,600

(55)	Other Comprehensive Income	500	
	Realized Gain on Sale of Securities		500

**FIGURE 8–12
Fixed for Variable
Interest-Rate Swap on
$5,000,000 Notional
Amount**

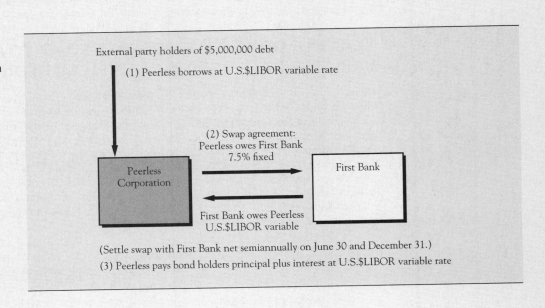

External party holders of $5,000,000 debt

(1) Peerless borrows at U.S.$LIBOR variable rate

(2) Swap agreement:
Peerless owes First Bank
7.5% fixed

Peerless Corporation

First Bank

First Bank owes Peerless
U.S.$LIBOR variable

(Settle swap with First Bank net semiannually on June 30 and December 31.)

(3) Peerless pays bond holders principal plus interest at U.S.$LIBOR variable rate

Note that Peerless must still pay the variable interest to the holders of the $5,000,000 debt. The interest-rate swap is just between Peerless and First Bank. The estimate of the fair value of the swap agreement was obtained from a broker-dealer of interest-rate swap agreements. Note that the value of the swap agreement to Peerless is positive if it believes that the variable rate will rise to higher than the fixed rate, but the swap agreement's value to Peerless is negative if it believes that the variable rate will remain lower than the fixed rate. Peerless' payments on the variable-rate debt and the net payments to First Bank on the interest-rate swap agreement are presented for the initial two semiannual periods:

	Interest Payments	
	December 31, 20X1	**June 30, 20X2**
Variable-rate interest payment	$150,000 (a)	$175,000 (b)
Interest-rate swap net payment	37,500 (c)	12,500
Total cash payment	$187,500 (d)	$187,500

(a) $150,000 = 5,000,000 × 0.06 × 6/12 months
(b) $175,000 = 5,000,000 × 0.07 × 6/12 months
(c) $37,500 = net payment required to First Bank for difference between variable and fixed interest rates
(d) $187,500 = 5,000,000 × 0.075 fixed rate × 6/12 months

Peerless recognizes interest expense based on the two factors of the variable rate plus the net payment or receipt from the swap agreement. In essence, Peerless has an interest expense equal to 7.5 percent of the notional amount of $5,000,000.

The entries to account for the first year of the interest-rate swap follow:

June 30, 20X1

(56)	Cash	5,000,000	
	Debt Payable		5,000,000
	Issue variable-rate debt.		

December 31, 20X1

(57)	Interest Expense	150,000	
	Cash		150,000
	Pay debt holders semiannual interest at a variable rate of 6.0 percent (from [a] in preceding table).		

(58)	Interest Expense	37,500	
	Cash		37,500
	Payment to First Bank for semiannual net settlement of swap agreement (from [c] in preceding table).		

(59)	Swap Agreement	165,000	
	Other Comprehensive Income		165,000
	Recognize change in fair value of swap agreement to other comprehensive income because the swap is a cash flow hedge.		

June 30, 20X2

(60)	Interest Expense	175,000	
	Cash		175,000
	Pay debt holders semiannual interest at a variable rate of 7.0 percent (from [b] in preceding table).		

(61)	Interest Expense	12,500	
	Cash		12,500
	Payment to First Bank for semiannual net settlement of swap agreement.		

(62)	Other Comprehensive Income	235,000	
	Swap Agreement		235,000
	Recognize decrease in fair value of swap agreement from $165,000 asset to $(70,000) liability to Other Comprehensive Income because the swap is a cash flow hedge.		

The swap agreement is reported on the balance sheet at its fair value. The amounts accumulated in Other Comprehensive Income are indirectly recognized in Peerless' earnings as periodic settlements of the payments required under the swap agreement are made, and the fair value of the swap agreement reaches zero at the end of the term of the agreement.

REPORTING AND DISCLOSURE REQUIREMENTS: DISCLOSURES ABOUT FAIR VALUE OF FINANCIAL INSTRUMENTS

FASB Statement No. 107 (ASC 825), "Disclosures about Fair Value of Financial Instruments," required disclosure of information pertaining to all financial instruments. This standard is the first to require information with respect to the current fair value of the financial instruments. Estimating fair value is of great practical difficulty because many financial instruments do not have a readily traded market from which to determine their value. Estimation methods are permitted, but if no estimation can be made, the reasons for the impracticality must be disclosed.

FASB 107 (ASC 825) does not permit the fair values of derivatives to be netted or aggregated with nonderivative financial instruments. The required disclosures are as follows:

1. The fair value based on quoted market prices. If fair value is not quoted, then a practical estimation is allowed.

2. Information relevant to the fair value such as carrying value, effective interest rate, maturity, and reasons why it is not practical to estimate, if such is the case.

3. Distinction between instruments held for trading or nontrading purposes.

FASB 133 (ASC 815) added a number of disclosures regarding derivatives and financial instruments. The company holding or issuing derivatives must disclose both its objectives for holding or issuing the instruments and the face or contract amount of the derivatives. The company also must distinguish between derivatives designated as fair value hedges, as cash flow hedges, as hedges of the foreign currency exposure of a net investment in a foreign operation, and all other derivatives. Specific disclosures are required for each type of hedge, but generally the company must disclose the purpose of the activity, the amount of any gains or losses recognized during the period (either in earnings or in other comprehensive income), and where those gains or losses and related assets and liabilities are reported in the statement of income and statement of financial position.

Companies operating internationally have increased risks when transacting in more than one currency. For that reason, a number of financial instruments are used in order to manage the increased risk. Chapter 8 presented the most commonly used financial instrument, the foreign currency forward exchange contract. This appendix briefly discussed several of the other major financial instruments used by multinational companies. It is certain that increased sophistication of the types of risk management tools will continue to occur in the business arena, and accountants must continue their efforts to understand and account for these instruments.

Questions

LO1 **Q8-1** Explain the difference between indirect and direct exchange rates.

LO2 **Q8-2** What is the direct exchange rate if a U.S. company receives $1.3623 in Canadian currency in exchange for $1.00 in U.S. currency?

LO1 **Q8-3** The U.S. dollar strengthened against the European euro. Will imports from Europe into the United States be more expensive or less expensive in U.S. dollars? Explain.

LO1 **Q8-4** Differentiate between a foreign transaction and a foreign currency transaction. Give an example of each.

LO1 **Q8-5** What types of economic factors affect currency exchange rates? Give an example of a change in an economic factor that results in a weakening of the local currency unit versus a foreign currency unit.

LO2 **Q8-6** How are assets and liabilities denominated in a foreign currency measured on the transaction date? On the balance sheet date?

LO2 **Q8-7** When are foreign currency transaction gains or losses recognized in the financial statements? Where are these gains or losses reported in the financial statements?

LO2 **Q8-8** Sun Company, a U.S. corporation, has an account payable of $200,000 denominated in Canadian dollars. If the direct exchange rate increases, will Sun experience a foreign currency transaction gain or loss on this payable?

LO3 **Q8-9** What are some ways a U.S. company can manage the risk of changes in the exchange rates for foreign currencies?

LO3 **Q8-10** Distinguish between an exposed net asset position and an exposed net liability position.

LO1 **Q8-11** Explain why a difference usually exists between a currency's spot rate and forward rate. Give two reasons this difference is usually positive when a company enters into a contract to receive foreign currency at a future date.

LO3 **Q8-12** A forward exchange contract may be used (*a*) to manage an exposed foreign currency position, (*b*) to hedge an identifiable foreign currency commitment, (*c*) to hedge a forecasted foreign currency transaction, or (*d*) to speculate in foreign currency markets. What are the main differences in accounting for these four uses?

LO2 **Q8-13** How—if at all—should the following items be reported on the financial statements?

a. Foreign Currency Receivable from Broker
b. Foreign Currency Transaction Loss
c. Foreign Currency Transaction Gain
d. Dollars Payable to Exchange Broker
e. Premium on Forward Contract
f. Foreign Currency Units
g. Accounts Payable (denominated in a foreign currency)

Cases

LO1 **C8-1** **Effects of Changing Exchange Rates**

Analysis Since the early 1970s, the U.S. dollar has both increased and decreased in value against other currencies such as the Japanese yen, the Swiss franc, and the British pound. The value of the U.S. dollar, as well as the value of currencies of other countries, is determined by the balance between the demand for and the supply of the currency on the foreign exchange markets. A drop in the value of the U.S. dollar has a widespread impact not only on consumers and businesses that deal with their counterparts overseas but also on consumers and businesses that operate solely within the United States.

Required

a. Identify the factors that influence the demand for and supply of the U.S. dollar on the foreign exchange markets.

b. Explain the effect a drop in value of the U.S. dollar in relation to other currencies on the foreign exchange markets has on

(1) The sales of a U.S. business firm that exports part of its output to foreign countries.

(2) The costs of a U.S. business firm that imports from foreign countries part of the inputs used in the manufacture of its products.

c. Explain why and how consumers and business firms that operate solely within the United States are affected by the drop in value of the U.S. dollar in relation to other currencies on the foreign exchange markets.

LO2 **C8-2** **Reporting a Foreign Currency Transaction on the Financial Statements [AICPA Adapted]**

Judgment On November 30, 20X5, Bow Company received goods with a cost denominated in pounds. During December 20X5, the dollar's value declined relative to the pound. Bow believes that the original exchange rate will be restored by the time payment is due in 20X6.

Required

a. State how Bow should report the impact, if any, of the changes in the exchange rate of the dollar and the pound on its 20X5 financial statements.

b. Explain why the reporting is appropriate.

LO1

C8-3   Changing Exchange Rates

Research

Search online to obtain and or prepare charts of the monthly average direct exchange rates for the past two years for the U.S. dollar versus (1) the Japanese yen, (2) the European euro, (3) the British pound, and (4) the Mexican peso. Your four charts should each have time on the horizontal axis and the direct exchange rate on the horizontal axis.

Questions for Discussion

a. Has the dollar strengthened or weakened during this time against each of the currencies?

b. What major economic or political factors could have caused the changes in the four foreign currencies' exchange rates versus the U.S. dollar?

c. Select one major factor from part (*b*) for each currency and present an argument showing how a change in that factor could cause the change in the exchange rate.

LO2

C8-4   Accounting for Foreign Currency–Denominated Accounts Payable

Research

Mardi Gras Corporation operates a group of specialty shops throughout the southeastern United States. The shops have traditionally stocked and sold kitchen and bath products manufactured in the United States. This year, Mardi Gras has established a business relationship with a manufacturing company in Lucerne, Switzerland, to purchase a line of luxury bath products to sell in its shops. As part of the business arrangement, payments by Mardi Gras are due 30 days after receipt of the merchandise, whose cost is quoted and payable in Swiss francs.

Mardi Gras records the purchases in inventory when it receives the merchandise and records a liability to the Swiss company, using the exchange rate for Swiss francs on the date the inventory purchase is recorded. When payment is made, Mardi Gras debits or credits to inventory any difference between the liability previously recorded and the dollar amount required to settle the liability in Swiss francs. Mardi Gras uses a perpetual inventory system and the FIFO method of inventory costing and can easily trace these adjustments to the specific inventory purchased.

Required

Obtain the most current accounting standards on accounting for foreign currency transactions. You can obtain access to accounting standards through the Financial Accounting Research System (FARS), from your library, or from some other source. As a staff accountant with the public accounting firm that audits Mardi Gras's annual financial statements, write a memo to Marie Lamont, the manager in charge of the audit, discussing the client's accounting for its transactions with the Swiss company. Support any recommendations with citations and quotations from the authoritative financial reporting standards.

LO3

C8-5   Accounting for Foreign Currency Forward Contracts

Research

Avanti Corporation is a small Midwestern company that manufactures wooden furniture. Tim Martin, Avanti's president, has decided to expand operations significantly and has entered into a contract with a German company to purchase specialty equipment for the expansion in manufacturing capacity. The contract fixes the price of the equipment at 4.5 million euros, and the equipment will be delivered in five months with payment due 30 days after delivery.

Tim is concerned that the value of the euro versus the U.S. dollar could increase during the six months between the date of the contract and the date of payment, thus increasing the effective price of the equipment to Avanti. Lindsay Williams, Avanti's treasurer, has suggested that the company enter into a forward contract to purchase 4.5 million euros in six months, thereby locking in an exchange rate for euros. Tim likes the idea of eliminating the uncertainty over the exchange rate for euros but is concerned about the effects of the forward contract on Avanti's financial statements. Because Avanti has not had previous experience with foreign currency transactions, Lindsay is unsure of what the financial statement effects are.

Required

Obtain the most current accounting standards on accounting for foreign currency forward contracts. You can obtain access to accounting standards through the FARS, from your library, or from some other source. Lindsay has asked you, as her assistant, to research the accounting for a foreign currency forward contract. Write a memo to her reporting on the results of your research. Support your recommendations with citations and quotations from the authoritative financial reporting standards.

LO3

C8-6   Accounting for Hedges of Available-for-Sale Securities

Research

Rainy Day Insurance Company maintains an extensive portfolio of bond investments classified as available-for-sale securities under **FASB 115 (ASC 320).** The bond investments have a variety of fixed interest rates and have maturity dates ranging from 1 to 15 years. Rainy Day acquired the bonds with the expectation that it could hold them until maturity or sell them any time that funds are required for unusually high insurance claims.

Because of the large dollar amount invested, Rainy Day is concerned about fluctuations in interest rates that affect the fair value of its bond portfolio. One of Rainy Day's investment professionals has proposed that the company invest in an interest rate futures contract to hedge its exposure to interest rate changes. Changes in the fair value of the futures contract would offset changes in the bond portfolio's fair value. If Rainy Day applies hedge accounting under **FASB 133 (ASC 815),** the income statement effect of changes in the fair value of the derivative would be offset by recording in earnings the changes in the fair value of the bond portfolio attributable to the hedged (interest rate) risk.

Required

Obtain the most current accounting standards on accounting for hedges of available-for-sale securities. You can obtain access to accounting standards through the FARS, from your library, or from some other source. Rainy Day's CFO, Mark Becker, has asked you, as an accountant in Rainy Day's investment division, to determine whether hedge accounting can be used in the scenario proposed. Write a memo to Mark, reporting on the results of your research. Support your recommendations with citations and quotations from the authoritative financial reporting standards.

Exercises

LO1

E8-1   Exchange Rates

Suppose the direct foreign exchange rates in U.S. dollars are

   1 British pound = $1.60
   1 Canadian dollar = $0.74

Required

a. What are the indirect exchange rates for the British pound and the Canadian dollar?

b. How many pounds must a British company pay to purchase goods costing $8,000 from a U.S. company?

c. How many U.S. dollars must be paid for a purchase costing 4,000 Canadian dollars?

LO1

E8-2   Changes in Exchange Rates

Upon arrival at the international airport in the country of Canteberry, Charles Alt exchanged $200 of U.S. currency into 1,000 florins, the local currency unit. Upon departure from Canteberry's international airport on completion of his business, he exchanged his remaining 100 florins into $15 of U.S. currency.

Required

a. Determine the currency exchange rates for each of the cells in the following matrix for Charles Alt's business trip to Canteberry.

b. Discuss and illustrate whether the U.S. dollar strengthened or weakened relative to the florin during Charles's stay in Canteberry.

c. Did Charles experience a foreign currency transaction gain or a loss on the 100 florins he held during his visit to Canteberry and converted to U.S. dollars at the departure date? Explain your answer.

	Arrival Date	Departure Date
Direct exchange rate		
Indirect exchange rate		

LO2

E8-3 Basic Understanding of Foreign Exposure

The Hi-Stakes Company has a number of importing and exporting transactions. Importing activities result in payables and exporting activities result in receivables. (LCU represents the local currency unit of the foreign entity.)

Required

a. If the direct exchange rate increases, does the dollar weaken or strengthen relative to the other currency? If the indirect exchange rate increases, does the dollar weaken or strengthen relative to the other currency?

b. Indicate in the following table whether Hi-Stakes will have a foreign currency transaction gain (G), loss (L), or not be affected (NA) by changes in the direct or indirect exchange rates for each of the four situations presented.

Transaction	Settlement Currency	Direct Exchange Rate		Indirect Exchange Rate	
		Increases	Decreases	Increases	Decreases
Importing	Dollar	_____	_____	_____	_____
Importing	LCU	_____	_____	_____	_____
Exporting	Dollar	_____	_____	_____	_____
Exporting	LCU	_____	_____	_____	_____

LO2

E8-4 Account Balances

Merchant Company had the following foreign currency transactions:

1. On November 1, 20X6, Merchant sold goods to a company located in Munich, Germany. The receivable was to be settled in European euros on February 1, 20X7, with the receipt of €250,000 by Merchant Company.

2. On November 1, 20X6, Merchant purchased machine parts from a company located in Berlin, Germany. Merchant is to pay €125,000 on February 1, 20X7.

The direct exchange rates are as follows:

November 1, 20X6	€1 = $0.60
December 31, 20X6	€1 = $0.62
February 1, 20X7	€1 = $0.58

Required

a. Prepare T-accounts for the following five accounts related to these transactions: Foreign Currency Units (€), Accounts Receivable (€), Accounts Payable (€), Foreign Currency Transaction Loss, and Foreign Currency Transaction Gain.

b. Within the T-accounts you have prepared, appropriately record the following items:

1. The November 1, 20X6, export transaction (sale).

2. The November 1, 20X6, import transaction (purchase).

3. The December 31, 20X6, year-end adjustment required of the foreign currency–denominated receivable of €250,000.

4. The December 31, 20X6, year-end adjustment required of the foreign currency–denominated payable of €125,000.

5. The February 1, 20X7, adjusting entry to determine the U.S. dollar–equivalent value of the foreign currency receivable on that date.

6. The February 1, 20X7, adjusting entry to determine the U.S. dollar–equivalent value of the foreign currency payable on that date.

7. The February 1, 20X7, settlement of the foreign currency receivable.

8. The February 1, 20X7, settlement of the foreign currency payable.

LO2

E8-5 Determining Year-End Account Balances for Import and Export Transactions

Delaney Inc. has several transactions with foreign entities. Each transaction is denominated in the local currency unit of the country in which the foreign entity is located. For each of the following independent cases, determine the December 31, 20X2, year-end balance in the appropriate accounts for the case. Write "NA" for "not applicable" in the space provided in the following chart if that account is not relevant to the specific case.

Case 1. On November 12, 20X2, Delaney purchased goods from a foreign company at a price of LCU 40,000 when the direct exchange rate was 1 LCU = $0.45. The account has not been settled as of December 31, 20X2, when the exchange rate has decreased to 1 LCU = $0.40.

Case 2. On November 28, 20X2, Delaney sold goods to a foreign entity at a price of LCU 20,000 when the direct exchange rate was 1 LCU = $1.80. The account has not been settled as of December 31, 20X2, when the exchange rate has increased to 1 LCU = $1.90.

Case 3. On December 2, 20X2, Delaney purchased goods from a foreign company at a price of LCU 30,000 when the direct exchange rate was 1 LCU = $0.80. The account has not been settled as of December 31, 20X2, when the exchange rate has increased to 1 LCU = $0.90.

Case 4. On December 12, 20X2, Delaney sold goods to a foreign entity at a price of LCU 2,500,000 when the direct exchange rate was 1 LCU = $0.003. The account has not been settled as of December 31, 20X2, when the exchange rate has decreased to 1 LCU = $0.0025.

Required

Provide the December 31, 20X2, year-end balances on Delaney's records for each of the following applicable items:

	Accounts Receivable	Accounts Payable	Foreign Currency Transaction Exchange Loss	Foreign Currency Transaction Exchange Gain
Case 1	_____	_____	_____	_____
Case 2	_____	_____	_____	_____
Case 3	_____	_____	_____	_____
Case 4	_____	_____	_____	_____

LO2

E8-6 Transactions with Foreign Companies

Harris Inc. had the following transactions:

1. On May 1, Harris purchased parts from a Japanese company for a U.S. dollar equivalent value of $8,400 to be paid on June 20. The exchange rates were

May 1	1 yen = $0.0070
June 20	1 yen = 0.0075

2. On July 1, Harris sold products to a Brazilian customer for a U.S. dollar equivalent of $10,000, to be received on August 10. Brazil's local currency unit is the real. The exchange rates were

July 1	1 real = $0.20
August 10	1 real = 0.22

Required

a. Assume that the two transactions are denominated in U.S. dollars. Prepare the entries required for the dates of the transactions and their settlement in U.S. dollars.

b. Assume that the two transactions are denominated in the applicable local currency units of the foreign entities. Prepare the entries required for the dates of the transactions and their settlement in the local currency units of the Japanese company (yen) and the Brazilian customer (real).

Advanced
StudyGuide
.com

LO2

E8-7 Foreign Purchase Transaction

On December 1, 20X1, Rone Imports, a U.S. company, purchased clocks from Switzerland for 15,000 francs (SFr), to be paid on January 15, 20X2. Rone's fiscal year ends on December 31, and its reporting currency is the U.S. dollar. The exchange rates are

December 1, 20X1	1 SFr = $0.70
December 31, 20X1	1 SFr = 0.66
January 15, 20X2	1 SFr = 0.68

Required

a. In which currency is the transaction denominated?

b. Prepare journal entries for Rone to record the purchase, the adjustment on December 31, and the settlement.

LO2

E8-8 Adjusting Entries for Foreign Currency Balances

Chocolate De-lites imports and exports chocolate delicacies. Some transactions are denominated in U.S. dollars and others in foreign currencies. A summary of accounts receivable and accounts payable on December 31, 20X6, before adjustments for the effects of changes in exchange rates during 20X6, follows:

Accounts receivable:	
In U.S. dollars	$164,000
In 475,000 Egyptian pounds (E£)	$ 73,600
Accounts payable:	
In U.S. dollars	$ 86,000
In 21,000,000 yen (¥)	$175,300

The spot rates on December 31, 20X6, were

E£1 = $0.176

¥1 = $0.0081

The average exchange rates during the collection and payment period in 20X7 are

E£1 = $0.18

¥1 = $0.0078

Required

a. Prepare the adjusting entries on December 31, 20X6.

b. Record the collection of the accounts receivable in 20X7.

c. Record the payment of the accounts payable in 20X7.

d. What was the foreign currency gain or loss on the accounts receivable transaction denominated in E£ for the year ended December 31, 20X6? For the year ended December 31, 20X7? Overall for this transaction?

e. What was the foreign currency gain or loss on the accounts receivable transaction denominated in ¥? For the year ended December 31, 20X6? For the year ended December 31, 20X7? Overall for this transaction?

f. What was the combined foreign currency gain or loss for both transactions? What could Chocolate De-lites have done to reduce the risk associated with the transactions denominated in foreign currencies?

LO3

E8-9 Purchase with Forward Exchange Contract

Merit & Family purchased engines from Canada for 30,000 Canadian dollars on March 10, with payment due on June 8. Also, on March 10, Merit acquired a 90-day forward contract to purchase 30,000 Canadian dollars at C$1 = $0.58. The forward contract was acquired to manage Merit & Family's exposed net liability position in Canadian dollars, but it was not designated as a hedge. The spot rates were

March 10	C$1 = $0.57
June 8	C$1 = $0.60

Required

Prepare journal entries for Merit & Family to record the purchase of the engines, entries associated with the forward contract, and entries for the payment of the foreign currency payable.

LO3

E8-10 Purchase with Forward Exchange Contract and Intervening Fiscal Year-End

Pumped Up Company purchased equipment from Switzerland for 140,000 francs on December 16, 20X7, with payment due on February 14, 20X8. On December 16, 20X7, Pumped Up also acquired a 60-day forward contract to purchase francs at a forward rate of SFr 1 = $0.67. On December 31, 20X7, the forward rate for an exchange on February 14, 20X8, is SFr 1 = $0.695. The spot rates were

December 16, 20X7	1 SFr = $0.68
December 31, 20X7	1 SFr = 0.70
February 14, 20X8	1 SFr = 0.69

Part I

Assume that the forward contract is not designated as a hedge but is entered into to manage the company's foreign currency–exposed accounts payable.

a. Prepare journal entries for Pumped Up to record the purchase of equipment; all entries associated with the forward contract; the adjusting entries on December 31, 20X7; and entries to record the revaluations and payment on February 14, 20X8.

b. What was the effect on the statement of income of the foreign currency transactions, including both the accounts payable and the forward contract, for the year ended December 31, 20X7?

c. What was the overall effect on the statement of income of these transactions from December 16, 20X7, to February 14, 20X8?

Part II

Now assume the forward contract is designated as a cash flow hedge of the variability of the future cash flows from the foreign currency account payable. The company uses the forward exchange rate to assess effectiveness.

Required

Prepare journal entries for Pumped Up to record the purchase of equipment; all entries associated with the forward contract; the adjusting and reclassification entries on December 31, 20X7; and entries to record the revaluations and payment on February 14, 20X8.

LO2

E8-11 Foreign Currency Transactions [AICPA Adapted]

Select the correct answer for each of the following questions.

1. Dale Inc., a U.S. company, bought machine parts from a German company on March 1, 20X1, for 30,000 euros, when the spot rate for euros was $0.4895. Dale's year-end was March 31, when the spot rate was $0.4845. On April 20, 20X1, Dale paid the liability with 30,000 euros acquired at a rate of $0.4945. Dale's income statements should report a foreign exchange gain or loss for the years ended March 31, 20X1 and 20X2 of

	20X1	20X2
a.	$0	$0
b.	$0	$150 loss
c.	$150 loss	$0
d.	$150 gain	$300 loss

2. Marvin Company's receivable from a foreign customer is denominated in the customer's local currency. This receivable of 900,000 local currency units (LCU) has been translated into $315,000 on Marvin's December 31, 20X5, balance sheet. On January 15, 20X6, the receivable was collected in full when the exchange rate was 3 LCU to $1. The journal entry Marvin should make to record the collection of this receivable is

		Debit	Credit
a.	Foreign Currency Units	300,000	
	Accounts Receivable		300,000
b.	Foreign Currency Units	300,000	
	Exchange Loss	15,000	
	Accounts Receivable		315,000
c.	Foreign Currency Units	300,000	
	Deferred Exchange Loss	15,000	
	Accounts Receivable		315,000
d.	Foreign Currency Units	315,000	
	Accounts Receivable		315,000

3. On July 1, 20X1, Black Company lent $120,000 to a foreign supplier, evidenced by an interest-bearing note due on July 1, 20X2. The note is denominated in the borrower's currency and was equivalent to 840,000 local currency units (LCU) on the loan date. The note principal was appropriately included at $140,000 in the receivables section of Black's December 31, 20X1, balance sheet. The note principal was repaid to Black on the July 1, 20X2, due date when the exchange rate was 8 LCU to $1. In its income statement for the year ended December 31, 20X2, what amount should Black include as a foreign currency transaction gain or loss on the note principal?

    a. $0.
    b. $15,000 loss.
    c. $15,000 gain.
    d. $35,000 loss.

4. If 1 Canadian dollar can be exchanged for 90 cents of U.S. currency, what fraction should be used to compute the indirect quotation of the exchange rate expressed in Canadian dollars?

    a. 1.10/1.
    b. 1/1.10.
    c. 1/.90.
    d. 0.90/1.

5. On July 1, 20X4, Bay Company borrowed 1,680,000 local currency units (LCU) from a foreign lender evidenced by an interest-bearing note due on July 1, 20X5, which is denominated in the currency of the lender. The U.S. dollar equivalent of the note principal was as follows:

Date	Amount
7/1/X4 (date borrowed)	$210,000
12/31/X4 (Bay's year-end)	240,000
7/1/X5 (date repaid)	280,000

In its income statement for 20X5, what amount should Bay include as a foreign exchange gain or loss on the note principal?

    a. $70,000 gain.
    b. $70,000 loss.
    c. $40,000 gain.
    d. $40,000 loss.

6. An entity denominated a sale of goods in a currency other than its functional currency. The sale resulted in a receivable fixed in terms of the amount of foreign currency to be received. The exchange rate between the functional currency and the currency in which the transaction was denominated changed. The effect of the change should be included as a

    a. Separate component of stockholders' equity whether the change results in a gain or a loss.
    b. Separate component of stockholders' equity if the change results in a gain, and as a component of income if the change results in a loss.

c. Component of income if the change results in a gain, and as a separate component of stockholders' equity if the change results in a loss.

d. Component of income whether the change results in a gain or a loss.

7. An entity denominated a December 15, 20X6, purchase of goods in a currency other than its functional currency. The transaction resulted in a payable fixed in terms of the amount of foreign currency, and was paid on the settlement date, January 20, 20X7. The exchange rates between the functional currency and the currency in which the transaction was denominated changed at December 31, 20X6, resulting in a loss that should

a. Not be reported until January 20, 20X7, the settlement date.

b. Be included as a separate component of stockholders' equity at December 31, 20X6.

c. Be included as a deferred charge at December 31, 20X6.

d. Be included as a component of income from continuing operations for 20X6.

LO2

E8-12   Sale in Foreign Currency

Marko Company sold spray paint equipment to Spain for 5,000,000 pesetas (P) on October 1, with payment due in six months. The exchange rates were

October 1, 20X6	1 peseta = $0.0068
December 31, 20X6	1 peseta = 0.0078
April 1, 20X7	1 peseta = 0.0076

Required

a. Did the dollar strengthen or weaken relative to the peseta during the period from October 1 to December 31? Did it strengthen or weaken between January 1 and April 1 of the next year?

b. Prepare all required journal entries for Marko as a result of the sale and settlement of the foreign transaction, assuming that its fiscal year ends on December 31.

c. Did Marko have an overall net gain or net loss from its foreign currency exposure?

LO2

Advanced
StudyGuide
.com

E8-13   Sale with Forward Exchange Contract

Alman Company sold pharmaceuticals to a Swedish company for 200,000 kronor (SKr) on April 20, with settlement to be in 60 days. On the same date, Alman entered into a 60-day forward contract to sell 200,000 SKr at a forward rate of 1 SKr = $0.167 in order to manage its exposed foreign currency receivable. The forward contract is not designated as a hedge. The spot rates were

| April 20 | SKr 1 = $0.170 |
| June 19 | SKr 1 = 0.165 |

Required

a. Record all necessary entries related to the foreign transaction and the forward contract.

b. Compare the effects on net income of Alman's use of the forward exchange contract versus the effects if Alman had not used a forward exchange contract.

LO2

E8-14   Foreign Currency Transactions [AICPA Adapted]

Choose the correct answer for each of the following questions.

1. On November 15, 20X3, Chow Inc., a U.S. company, ordered merchandise FOB shipping point from a German company for 200,000 euros. The merchandise was shipped and invoiced on December 10, 20X3. Chow paid the invoice on January 10, 20X4. The spot rates for euros on the respective dates were

November 15, 20X3	$0.4955
December 10, 20X3	0.4875
December 31, 20X3	0.4675
January 10, 20X4	0.4475

In Chow's December 31, 20X3, income statement, the foreign exchange gain is

   a. $9,600.

   b. $8,000.

   c. $4,000.

   d. $1,600.

2. Stees Corporation had the following foreign currency transactions during 20X2. First, it purchased merchandise from a foreign supplier on January 20, 20X2, for the U.S. dollar equivalent of $90,000. The invoice was paid on March 20, 20X2, at the U.S. dollar equivalent of $96,000. Second, on July 1, 20X2, Stees borrowed the U.S. dollar equivalent of $500,000 evidenced by a note that was payable in the lender's local currency on July 1, 20X4. On December 31, 20X2, the U.S. dollar equivalents of the principal amount and accrued interest were $520,000 and $26,000, respectively. Interest on the note is 10 percent per annum. In Stees's 20X2 income statement, what amount should be included as a foreign exchange loss?

   a. $0.

   b. $6,000.

   c. $21,000.

   d. $27,000.

3. On September 1, 20X1, Cott Corporation received an order for equipment from a foreign customer for 300,000 local currency units (LCU) when the U.S. dollar equivalent was $96,000. Cott shipped the equipment on October 15, 20X1, and billed the customer for 300,000 LCU when the U.S. dollar equivalent was $100,000. Cott received the customer's remittance in full on November 16, 20X1, and sold the 300,000 LCU for $105,000. In its income statement for the year ended December 31, 20X1, Cott should report a foreign exchange gain of

   a. $0.

   b. $4,000.

   c. $5,000.

   d. $9,000.

4. On April 8, 20X3, Trul Corporation purchased merchandise from an unaffiliated foreign company for 10,000 units of the foreign company's local currency. Trul paid the bill in full on March 1, 20X4, when the spot rate was $0.45. The spot rate was $0.60 on April 8, 20X3, and was $0.55 on December 31, 20X3. For the year ended December 31, 20X4, Trul should report a transaction gain of

   a. $1,500.

   b. $1,000.

   c. $500.

   d. $0.

5. On October 1, 20X5, Stevens Company, a U.S. company, contracted to purchase foreign goods requiring payment in pesos one month after their receipt in Stevens's factory. Title to the goods passed on December 15, 20X5. The goods were still in transit on December 31, 20X5. Exchange rates were 1 dollar to 22 pesos, 20 pesos, and 21 pesos on October 1, December 15, and December 31, 20X5, respectively. Stevens should account for the exchange rate fluctuations in 20X5 as

   a. A loss included in net income before extraordinary items.

   b. A gain included in net income before extraordinary items.

   c. An extraordinary gain.

   d. An extraordinary loss.

6. On October 2, 20X5, Louis Co., a U.S. company, purchased machinery from Stroup, a German company, with payment due on April 1, 20X6. If Louis's 20X5 operating income included no foreign exchange gain or loss, then the transaction could have

   a. Resulted in an extraordinary gain.

   b. Been denominated in U.S. dollars.

   c. Caused a foreign currency gain to be reported as a contra account against machinery.

   d. Caused a foreign currency translation gain to be reported as a separate component of stockholders' equity.

7. Cobb Co. purchased merchandise for 300,000 pounds from a vendor in London on November 30, 20X5. Payment in British pounds was due on January 30, 20X6. The exchange rates to purchase 1 pound were as follows:

	November 30, 20X5	December 31, 20X5
Spot rate	$1.65	$1.62
30-day rate	1.64	1.59
60-day rate	1.63	1.56

In its December 31, 20X5, income statement, what amount should Cobb report as a foreign exchange gain?

a. $12,000.
b. $9,000.
c. $6,000.
d. $0.

LO3

E8-15 Sale with Forward Contract and Fiscal Year-End

Jerber Electronics Inc. sold electrical equipment to a Dutch company for 50,000 guilders (G) on May 14, with collection due in 60 days. On the same day, Jerber entered into a 60-day forward contract to sell 50,000 guilders at a forward rate of G1 = $0.541. The forward contract is not designated as a hedge. Jerber's fiscal year ends on June 30. The forward rate on June 30 for an exchange on July 13 is G1 = $0.530. The spot rates follow:

May 14	G1 = $0.530
June 30	G1 = 0.534
July 13	G1 = 0.525

Required

a. Prepare journal entries for Jerber to record (1) the sale of equipment, (2) the forward contract, (3) the adjusting entries on June 30, (4) the July 13 collection of the receivable, and (5) the July settlement of the forward contract.
b. What was the effect on the income statement in the fiscal year ending June 30?
c. What was the overall effect on the income statement from this transaction?
d. What would have been the overall effect on income if the forward contract had not been acquired?

LO3

E8-16A Hedge of a Purchase (Commitment without and with Time Value of Money Considerations)

On November 1, 20X6, Smith Imports Inc. contracted to purchase teacups from England for 30,000 pounds (£). The teacups were to be delivered on January 30, 20X7, with payment due on March 1, 20X7. On November 1, 20X6, Smith entered into a 120-day forward contract to receive 30,000 pounds at a forward rate of £1 = $1.59. The forward contract was acquired to hedge the financial component of the foreign currency commitment.

Additional Information for the Exchange Rate

1. Assume the company uses the forward rate in measuring the forward exchange contract and for measuring hedge effectiveness.
2. Spot and exchange rates follow:

Date	Spot Rate	Forward Rate for March 1, 20X7
November 1, 20X6	£1 = $1.61	£1 = $1.59
December 31, 20X6	£1 = 1.65	£1 = 1.62
January 30, 20X7	£1 = 1.59	£1 = 1.60
March 1, 20X7	£1 = 1.585	

"A" indicates that the item relates to "Appendix A."

Required

a. What is Smith's net exposure to changes in the exchange rate of pounds for dollars between November 1, 20X6, and March 1, 20X7?

b. Prepare all journal entries from November 1, 20X6, through March 1, 20X7, for the purchase of the subassemblies, the forward exchange contract, and the foreign currency transaction. Assume Smith's fiscal year ends on December 31, 20X6.

Note: Requirement (c) requires information from Appendix 8A.

c. Assume that interest is significant and the time value of money is considered in valuing the forward contract and hedged commitment. Use a 12 percent annual interest rate. Prepare all journal entries from November 1, 20X6, through March 1, 20X7, for the purchase of the subassemblies, the forward exchange contract, and the foreign currency transaction. Assume Smith's fiscal year ends on December 31, 20X7.

LO3

E8-17 Gain or Loss on Speculative Forward Exchange Contract

On December 1, 20X1, Sycamore Company acquired a 90-day speculative forward contract to sell 120,000 European euros (€) at a forward rate of €1 = $0.58. The rates are as follows:

Date	SpotRate	Forward Rate for March 1
December 1, 20X1	€1 = $0.60	€1 = $0.58
December 31, 20X1	€1 = 0.59	€1 = 0.56
March 1, 20X2	€1 = 0.57	

Advanced
StudyGuide
.com

Required

a. Prepare a schedule showing the effects of this speculation on 20X1 income before income taxes.

b. Prepare a schedule showing the effects of this speculation on 20X2 income before income taxes.

LO3

E8-18 Speculation in a Foreign Currency

Nick Andros of Streamline Company suggested that the company speculate in foreign currency as a partial hedge against its operations in the cattle market, which fluctuates like a commodity market. On October 1, 20X1, Streamline bought a 180-day forward contract to purchase 50,000,000 yen (¥) at a forward rate of ¥1 = $0.0075 when the spot rate was $0.0070. Other exchange rates were as follows:

Date	Spot Rate	Forward Rate for March 31, 20X2
December 31, 20X1	$0.0073	$0.0076
March 31, 20X2	0.0072	

Required

a. Prepare all journal entries related to Streamline Company's foreign currency speculation from October 1, 20X1, through March 31, 20X2, assuming the fiscal year ends on December 31, 20X1.

b. Did Streamline Company gain or lose on its purchase of the forward contract? Explain.

LO3

E8-19 Forward Exchange Transactions [AICPA Adapted]

Select the correct answer for each of the following questions.

1. The following information applies to Denton Inc.'s sale of 10,000 foreign currency units under a forward contract dated November 1, 20X5, for delivery on January 31, 20X6:

	11/1/X5	12/31/X5
Spot rates	$0.80	$0.83
30-day forward rate	0.79	0.82
90-day forward rate	0.78	0.81

Denton entered into the forward contract to speculate in the foreign currency. In its income statement for the year ended December 31, 20X5, what amount of loss should Denton report from this forward contract?

a. $400.

b. $300.

c. $200.

d. $0.

2. On September 1, 20X5, Johnson Inc. entered into a foreign exchange contract for speculative purposes by purchasing 50,000 European euros for delivery in 60 days. The rates to exchange U.S. dollars for euros follow:

	9/1/X5	9/30/X5
Spot rate	$0.75	$0.70
30-day forward rate	0.73	0.72
90-day forward rate	0.74	0.73

In its September 30, 20X5, income statement, what amount should Johnson report as foreign exchange loss?

a. $2,500.

b. $1,500.

c. $1,000.

d. $500.

Note: Items 3 through 5 are based on the following:

On December 12, 20X5, Dahl Company entered into three forward exchange contracts, each to purchase 100,000 francs in 90 days. The relevant exchange rates are as follows:

	Spot Rate	Forward Rate for March 12, 20X6
December 12, 20X5	$0.88	$0.90
March 31, 20X2	0.98	0.93

3. Dahl entered into the first forward contract to manage the foreign currency risk from a purchase of inventory in November 20X5, payable in March 20X6. The forward contract is not designated as a hedge. At December 31, 20X5, what amount of foreign currency transaction gain should Dahl include in income from this forward contract?

a. $0.

b. $3,000.

c. $5,000.

d. $10,000.

4. Dahl entered into the second forward contract to hedge a commitment to purchase equipment being manufactured to Dahl's specifications. At December 31, 20X5, what amount of foreign currency transaction gain should Dahl include in income from this forward contract?

a. $0.

b. $3,000.

c. $5,000.

d. $10,000.

5. Dahl entered into the third forward contract for speculation. At December 31, 20X5, what amount of foreign currency transaction gain should Dahl include in income from this forward contract?

a. $0.

b. $3,000.

c. $5,000.

d. $10,000.

Problems

LO2

P8-20 Multiple-Choice Questions on Foreign Currency Transactions

Jon-Jan Restaurants purchased green rice, a special variety of rice, from China for 100,000 renminbi on November 1, 20X8. Payment is due on January 30, 20X9. On November 1, 20X8, the company also entered into a 90-day forward contract to purchase 100,000 renminbi. The forward contract is not designated as a hedge. The rates were as follows:

Date	Spot Rate	Forward Rate
November 1, 20X8	$0.120	$0.126 (90 days)
December 31, 20X8	0.124	0.129 (30 days)
January 30, 20X9	0.127	

Required
Select the correct answer for each of the following questions.

1. The entry on November 1, 20X8, to record the forward contract includes a
   a. Debit to Foreign Currency Receivable from Exchange Broker, 100,000 renminbi.
   b. Debit to Foreign Currency Receivable from Exchange Broker, $12,600.
   c. Credit to Premium on Forward Contract, $600.
   d. Credit to Dollars Payable to Exchange Broker, $12,600.

2. The entries on December 31, 20X8, include a
   a. Debit to Financial Expense, $300.
   b. Credit to Foreign Currency Payable to Exchange Broker, $300.
   c. Debit to Foreign Currency Receivable from Exchange Broker, $300.
   d. Debit to Foreign Currency Receivable from Exchange Broker, $12,600.

3. The entries on January 30, 20X9, include a
   a. Debit to Dollars Payable to Exchange Broker, $12,000.
   b. Credit to Cash, $12,600.
   c. Credit to Premium on Forward Contract, $600.
   d. Credit to Foreign Currency Receivable from Exchange Broker, $12,600.

4. The entries on January 30, 20X9, include a
   a. Debit to Financial Expense, $400.
   b. Debit to Dollars Payable to Exchange Broker, $12,600.
   c. Credit to Foreign Currency Units (renminbi), $12,600.
   d. Debit to Foreign Currency Payable to Exchange Broker, $12,700.

5. The entries on January 30, 20X9, include a
   a. Debit to Foreign Currency Units (renminbi), $12,700.
   b. Debit to Dollars Payable to Exchange Broker, $12,700.
   c. Credit to Foreign Currency Transaction Gain, $100.
   d. Credit to Foreign Currency Receivable from Exchange Broker, $12,600.

LO2

P8-21 Foreign Sales

Tex Hardware sells many of its products overseas. The following are some selected transactions.

1. Tex sold electronic subassemblies to a firm in Denmark for 120,000 Danish krones (Dkr) on June 6, when the exchange rate was Dkr 1 = $0.1750. Collection was made on July 3, when the rate was Dkr 1 = $0.1753.

2. On July 22, Tex sold copper fittings to a company in London for 30,000 pounds (£), with payment due on September 20. Also, on July 22, Tex entered into a 60-day forward contract to sell 30,000 pounds at a forward rate of £1 = $1.630. The spot rates follow:

July 10	£1 = $1.580
September 20	£1 = $1.612

3. Tex sold storage devices to a Canadian firm for C$70,000 (Canadian dollars) on October 11, with payment due on November 10. On October 11, Tex entered into a 30-day forward contract to sell Canadian dollars at a forward rate of C$1 = $0.730. The forward contract is not designated as a hedge. The spot rates were as follows:

October 11	C$1 = $0.7350
November 10	C$1 = $0.7320

Required

Prepare journal entries to record Tex's foreign sales of its products, use of forward contracts, and settlements of the receivables.

LO2

P8-22 **Foreign Currency Transactions**

Globe Shipping, a U.S. company, is an importer and exporter. The following are some transactions with foreign companies.

1. Globe sold blue jeans to a South Korean importer on January 15 for $7,400, when the exchange rate was KRW1 = $0.185. Collection, in dollars, was made on March 15, when the exchange rate was $0.180.

2. On March 8, Globe purchased woolen goods from Ireland for 7,000 euros. The exchange rate was €1 = $0.622 on March 8, but the rate was $0.610 when payment was made on May 1.

3. On May 12, Globe signed a contract to purchase toys made in Taiwan for 80,000 Taiwan dollars (NT$). The toys were to be delivered 80 days later on August 1, and payment was due on September 9, which was 40 days after delivery. On May 12, Globe also entered into a 120-day undesignated forward contract to buy 80,000 Taiwan dollars at a forward rate of NT$1 = $0.0376. On August 1, the forward rate for a September 9 exchange is NT$1 = $0.0378. The spot rates were as follows:

May 12	NT$1 = $0.0370
August 1	NT$1 = 0.0375
September 9	NT$1 = 0.0372

4. Globe sold microcomputers to a German enterprise on June 6 for 150,000 euros. Payment was due in 90 days, on September 4. On July 6, Globe entered into a 60-day undesignated forward contract to sell 150,000 euros at a forward rate of €1 = $0.580. The spot rates follow:

June 6	€1 = $0.600
July 6	€1 = 0.590
September 4	€1 = 0.585

Required

Prepare all necessary journal entries for Globe to account for the foreign transactions, including the sales and purchases of inventory, forward contracts, and settlements.

LO2

P8-23A **Comprehensive Problem: Four Uses of Forward Exchange Contracts without and with Time Value of Money Considerations**

On December 1, 20X1, Micro World, Inc., entered into a 120-day forward contract to purchase 100,000 Australian dollars (A$). Micro World's fiscal year ends on December 31. The direct exchange rates follow:

Date	Spot Rate	Forward Rate for March 31, 20X2
December 1, 20X1	$0.600	$0.609
December 31, 20X1	0.610	0.612
January 30, 20X2	0.608	0.605
March 31, 20X2	0.602	

Required

Prepare all journal entries for Micro World, Inc., for the following *independent* situations:

a. The forward contract was to manage the foreign currency risks from the purchase of furniture for 100,000 Australian dollars on December 1, 20X1, with payment due on March 31, 20X2. The forward contract is not designated as a hedge.

b. The forward contract was to hedge a firm commitment agreement made on December 1, 20X1, to purchase furniture on January 30, with payment due on March 31, 20X2. The derivative is designated as a fair value hedge.

c. The forward contract was to hedge an anticipated purchase of furniture on January 30. The purchase took place on January 30, with payment due on March 31, 20X2. The derivative is designated as a cash flow hedge. The company uses the forward exchange rate to measure hedge effectiveness.

d. The forward contract was for speculative purposes only.

Note: Requirement (e) uses the material in Appendix 8A.

e. Assume that interest is significant and the time value of money is considered in valuing the forward contract. Use a 12 percent annual interest rate. Prepare all journal entries required if, as in requirement (*a*), the forward contract was to manage the foreign currency–denominated payable from the purchase of furniture for 100,000 Australian dollars on December 1, 20X1, with payment due on March 31, 20X2.

LO2

P8-24 **Foreign Purchases and Sales Transactions and Hedging**

Advanced
StudyGuide
.com

Part I

Maple Company had the following export and import transactions during 20X5:

1. On March 1, Maple sold goods to a Canadian company for 30,000 Canadian dollars (C$), receivable on May 30. The spot rates for marks were C$1 = $0.65 on March 1 and C$1 = $0.68 on May 30.

2. On July 1, Maple signed a contract to purchase equipment from a Japanese company for 500,000 yen. The equipment was manufactured in Japan during August and was delivered to Maple on August 30, with payment due in 60 days on October 29. The spot rates for yen were ¥1 = $0.102 on July 1, ¥1 = $0.104 on August 30, and ¥1 = $0.106 on October 29. The 60-day forward exchange rate on August 30, 20X5, was ¥1 = $0.1055.

3. On November 16, Maple purchased inventory from a London company for 10,000 pounds, payable on January 15, 20X6. The spot rates for pounds were £1 = $1.65 on November 16, £1 = $1.63 on December 31, and £1 = $1.64 on January 15, 20X6. The forward rate on December 31, 20X5, for a January 15, 20X6, exchange was £1 = $1.645.

Required

a. Prepare journal entries to record Maple's import and export transactions during 20X5 and 20X6.

b. What amount of foreign currency transaction gain or loss would Maple report on its income statement for 20X5?

Part II

Assume that Maple used forward contracts to manage the foreign currency risks of all of its export and import transactions during 20X5.

1. On March 1, 20X5, Maple, anticipating a weaker Canadian dollar on the May 30, 20X5, settlement date, entered into a 90-day forward contract to sell 30,000 Canadian dollars at a forward exchange rate of C$1 = $0.64. The forward contract was not designated as a hedge.

2. On July 1, 20X5, Maple, anticipating a strengthening of the yen on the October 29, 20X5, settlement date, entered into a 120-day forward contract to purchase 500,000 yen at a forward exchange rate of ¥1 = $0.105. The forward contract was designated as a fair value hedge of a firm commitment.

3. On November 16, 20X5, Maple, anticipating a strengthening of the pound on the January 15, 20X6, settlement date, entered into a 60-day undesignated forward exchange contract to purchase 10,000 pounds at a forward exchange rate of £1 = $1.67.

Required

a. Prepare journal entries to record Maple's foreign currency activities during 20X5 and 20X6.

b. What amount of foreign currency transaction gain or loss would Maple report on its income statement for 20X5, if Parts I and II of this problem were combined?

c. What amount of foreign currency transaction gain or loss would Maple report on its statement of income for 20X6, if Parts I and II of this problem were combined?

LO2

P8-25 **Understanding Foreign Currency Transactions**

Dexter Inc. had the following items in its unadjusted and adjusted trial balances at December 31, 20X5:

	Trial Balances	
	Unadjusted	Adjusted
Accounts Receivable (denominated in Australian dollars)	$42,000	$41,700
Dollars Receivable from Exchange Broker	40,600	?
Foreign Currency Receivable from Exchange Broker	82,000	81,000
Accounts Payable (denominated in South Korean wons)	80,000	?
Dollars Payable to Exchange Broker	?	?
Foreign Currency Payable to Exchange Broker	40,600	?

Additional Information

1. On December 1, 20X5, Dexter sold goods to a company in Australia for 70,000 Australian dollars. Payment in Australian dollars is due on January 30, 20X6. On the transaction date, Dexter entered into a 60-day forward contract to sell 70,000 Australian dollars on January 30, 20X6. The 30-day forward rate on December 31, 20X5, was A$1 = $0.57.

2. On October 2, 20X5, Dexter purchased equipment from a South Korean company for 400,000 South Korean wons (KRW), payable on January 30, 20X6. On the transaction date, Dexter entered into a 120-day forward contract to purchase 400,000 South Korean wons on January 30, 20X6. On December 31, 20X5, the spot rate was KRW1 = $0.2020.

Required

Using the information contained in the trial balances, answer each of the following questions:

a. What was the indirect exchange rate for Australian dollars on December 1, 20X5? What was the indirect exchange rate on December 31, 20X5?

b. What is the balance in the account Foreign Currency Payable to Exchange Broker in the adjusted trial balance?

c. When Dexter entered into the 60-day forward contract to sell 70,000 Australian dollars, what was the direct exchange rate for the 60-day forward contract?

d. What is the amount of Dollars Receivable from Exchange Broker in the adjusted trial balance?

e. What was the indirect exchange rate for South Korean wons on October 2, 20X5? What was the indirect exchange rate on December 31, 20X5?

f. What is the balance in the account Dollars Payable to Exchange Broker in both the unadjusted and the adjusted trial balance columns?

g. When Dexter entered into the 120-day forward contract to purchase 400,000 South Korean wons, what was the direct exchange rate for the 120-day forward contract?

h. What was the Accounts Payable balance at December 31, 20X5?

LO1, LO2, LO3

P8-26 **Matching Key Terms**

Match the items in the left-hand column with the descriptions/explanations in the right-hand column.

Items	Descriptions/Explanations
1. Direct exchange rate	A. Exchange rate for immediate delivery of currencies.
2. Indirect exchange rate	B. Imports and exports whose prices are stated in a foreign currency.
3. Managing an exposed net asset position	C. The primary currency used by a company for performing its major financial and operating functions.
4. Spot rates	D. U.S. companies prepare their financial statements in U.S. dollars.
5. Current rates	E. 1 European euro equals $0.65.
6. Foreign currency transaction gain	F. A forward contract is entered into when receivables denominated in European euros exceed payables denominated in that currency.
7. Foreign currency transaction loss	
8. Foreign currency transactions	G. Accounts that are fixed in terms of foreign currency units.
9. Hedging a firm commitment	H. 1 U.S. dollar equals 99 Japanese yen.
10. Functional currency	I. Spot rate on the entity's balance sheet date.
11. Speculating in a foreign currency	J. In an export or import transaction, the date that foreign currency units are received or paid, respectively.
12. Managing an exposed net liability position	K. A forward contract is entered into when payables denominated in British pounds exceed receivables denominated in that currency.
13. Settlement date	
14. Denominated	L. Reported when receivables are denominated in European euros and the euro strengthens compared to the U.S. dollar.
15. Reporting currency	
	M. A forward contract is entered into on May 1 that hedges an import transaction to occur on July 1.
	N. Forward contract in which no hedging is intended.
	O. Reported when payables are denominated in Swiss francs and the franc strengthens compared to the U.S. dollar.

LO3

P8-27B **Multiple-Choice Questions on Derivatives and Hedging Activities**

Select the correct answer for each of the following questions.

1. According to **FASB 133 (ASC 815),** which of the following is *not* an underlying?

    a. A security price.

    b. A monthly average temperature.

    c. The price of a barrel of oil.

    d. The number of foreign currency units.

2. The intrinsic value of a cash flow hedge has increased since the last balance sheet date. Which of the following accounting treatments is appropriate for this increase in value?

    a. Do not record the increase in the value because it has not been realized in an exchange transaction.

    b. Record the increase in value to current earnings.

    c. Record the increase to Other Comprehensive Income.

    d. Record the increase in a deferred income account.

3. The requirements for a derivative instrument include all but which of the following?

    a. Has one or more underlyings.

    b. Has one or more notional amounts.

    c. Requires an initial net investment equal to that required for other types of contracts that would be expected to have a similar response to changes in market factors.

    d. Requires or permits net settlement.

"B" indicates that the item relates to "Appendix B."

4. A decrease in the intrinsic value of a fair value hedge is accounted for as

   a. A decrease of current earnings.

   b. Not recorded because the exchange transaction has not yet occurred.

   c. A decrease of other comprehensive income.

   d. A liability to be offset with subsequent increases in the fair value of the hedge.

5. Changes in the fair value of the effective portion of a hedging financial instrument are recognized as a part of current earnings of the period for which of the following:

	Cash Flow Hedge	Fair Value Hedge
a.	Yes	Yes
b.	No	Yes
c.	Yes	No
d.	No	No

6. According to **FASB 133 (ASC 815),** for which of the following is hedge accounting not allowed?

   a. A forecasted purchase or sale.

   b. Available-for-sale securities.

   c. Trading securities.

   d. An unrecognized firm commitment.

LO3

Advanced
StudyGuide
.com

P8-28B   **A Cash Flow Hedge: Use of an Option to Hedge an Anticipated Purchase**

Mega Company believes the price of oil will increase in the coming months. Therefore, it decides to purchase call options on oil as a price-risk-hedging device to hedge the expected increase in prices on an anticipated purchase of oil.

On November 30, 20X1, Mega purchases call options for 10,000 barrels of oil at $30 per barrel at a premium of $2 per barrel, with a March 1, 20X2, call date. The following is the pricing information for the term of the call:

Date	Spot Price	Futures Price (for March 1, 20X2, delivery)
November 30, 20X1	$30	$31
December 31, 20X1	31	32
March 1, 20X2	33	

The information for the change in the fair value of the options follows:

Date	Time Value	Intrinsic Value	Total Value
November 30, 20X1	$20,000	$ –0–	$20,000
December 31, 20X1	6,000	10,000	16,000
March 1, 20X2		30,000	30,000

On March 1, 20X2, Mega sells the options at their value on that date and acquires 10,000 barrels of oil at the spot price. On June 1, 20X2, Mega sells the oil for $34 per barrel.

Required

a. Prepare the journal entry required on November 30, 20X1, to record the purchase of the call options.

b. Prepare the adjusting journal entry required on December 31, 20X1, to record the change in time and intrinsic value of the options.

c. Prepare the entries required on March 1, 20X2, to record the expiration of the time value of the options, the sale of the options, and the purchase of the 10,000 barrels of oil.

d. Prepare the entries required on June 1, 20X2, to record the sale of the oil and any other entries required as a result of the option.

P8-29B **A Fair Value Hedge: Use of an Option to Hedge Available-for-Sale Securities**

On November 3, 20X2, PRD Corporation acquired 100 shares of JRS Company at a cost of $12 per share. PRD classifies them as available-for-sale securities. On this same date, PRD decides to hedge against a possible decline in the value of the securities by purchasing, at a cost of $100, an at-the-money put option to sell the 100 shares at $12 per share. The option expires on March 3, 20X3. The fair values of the investment and the options follow:

	November 3, 20X2	December 31, 20X2	March 3, 20X3
JRS Company shares			
Per share:	$ 12	$ 11	$ 10.50
Put Option (100 shares)			
Market value	$100	$140	$150
Intrinsic value	–0–	100	150
Time value	$100	$ 40	$–0–

Required

a. Prepare the entries required on November 3, 20X2, to record the purchase of the JRS stock and the put options.

b. Prepare the entries required on December 31, 20X2, to record the change in intrinsic value and time value of the options, as well as the revaluation of the available-for-sale securities.

c. Prepare the entries required on March 3, 20X3, to record the exercise of the put option and the sale of the securities at that date.

P8-30B **Matching Key Terms—Hedging and Derivatives**

Match the items in the left-hand column with the descriptions/explanations in the right-hand column.

Items	Descriptions/Explanations
1. Put option	A. Hedge of the exposure to changes in the fair value of a recognized asset or liability or an unrecognized firm commitment.
2. Notional amount	
3. Intrinsic value	B. Hedge of the exposure to variable cash flows of a forecasted transaction.
4. Underlying	
5. Gains or losses on cash flow hedges	C. Derivative instrument that is part of a host contract.
	D. Specified interest rate, security price, or other variable.
6. Foreign currency hedge	E. Number of currency units, shares, bushels, or other units specified in the contract.
7. Fair value hedge	F. Recognized in current earnings in the period of the change in value.
8. Call option	
9. Effectiveness	G. Recognized in Other Comprehensive Income in the period of the change in value.
10. Time value	
11. Gains or losses on fair value hedges	H. Measure of the extent to which the derivative offsets the changes in the fair values or cash flows of the hedged item.
12. Cash flow hedge	I. Hedge of the net investment in foreign operations.
13. Interest rate swap	J. Conversion of a company's fixed-rate debt to a variable-rate debt.
14. Bifurcation	K. Option that provides the right to acquire an underlying at an exercise or strike price.
15. Embedded derivative	L. Option that provides the right to sell an underlying at an exercise or strike price.
	M. Value of an option due to the spread between the current market price of the hedged item and the option's strike price.
	N. Value of an option due to the opportunity to exercise the option over the term of the option period.
	O. Process of separating the value of an embedded derivative from its host contract.

LO3

P8-31 **Determining Financial Statement Amounts**

Kiwi Painting Company engages in a number of foreign currency transactions in euros (€). For each of the following independent transactions, determine the dollar amount to be reported in the December 31, 2004, financial statements for the items presented in the following requirements. The relevant direct exchange rates for the euro follow:

	September 1, 2004	November 30, 2004	December 31, 2004
Spot rate	$0.95	$1.05	$0.98
Forward rate for exchange on February 1, 2005	0.97	1.03	1.01

These are the independent transactions:

1. Kiwi entered into a forward exchange contract on September 1, 2004, to be settled on February 1, 2005, to hedge a firm foreign currency commitment to purchase inventory on November 30, 2004, with payment due on February 1, 2005. The forward contract was for 20,000 euros, the agreed-upon cost of the inventory. The derivative is designated as a fair value hedge of the firm commitment.

2. Kiwi entered into a forward exchange contract on September 1, 2004, to be settled on February 1, 2005, to hedge a forecasted purchase of inventory on November 30, 2004. The inventory was purchased on November 30 with payment due on February 1, 2005. The forward contract was for 20,000 euros, the expected cost of the inventory. The derivative is designated as a cash flow hedge to be continued through to payment of the euro-denominated account payable.

3. Kiwi entered into a forward contract on November 30, 2004, to be settled on February 1, 2005, to manage the financial currency exposure of a euro-denominated accounts payable in the amount of 20,000 euros from the purchase of inventory on that date. The payable is due on February 1, 2005. The forward contract is not designated as a hedge.

4. Kiwi entered into a forward contract on September 1, 2004, to speculate on the possible changes in exchange rates between the euro and the U.S. dollar between September 1, 2004, and February 1, 2005. The forward contract is for speculation purposes and is not a hedge.

Required

Enter the dollar amount that would be shown for each of the following items as of December 31, 2004. Compute the statement amounts net. For example, if the transaction generated both a foreign currency exchange gain and a loss, specify just the net amount that would be reported in the financial statements. If no amount would be reported for an item, enter NA for Not Applicable in the space.

	Transaction			
	1	**2**	**3**	**4**
Forward contract receivable	___	___	___	___
Inventory	___	___	___	___
Accounts payable (€)	___	___	___	___
Foreign currency exchange gain (loss), net	___	___	___	___
Other comprehensive income gain (loss), net	___	___	___	___

Chapter Nine

Multinational Accounting: Issues in Financial Reporting and Translation of Foreign Entity Statements

MCDONALD'S—THE WORLD'S FAST FOOD FAVORITE

McDonald's was founded in 1940 by two brothers, Dick and Mac McDonald, in San Bernardino, California. The McDonalds brothers introduced the "Speedee Service System" in 1948, which laid the groundwork for modern fast-food restaurants.

In 1954, the brothers were using eight Multimixer milkshake machines in their San Bernardino location. This piqued the interest of Ray Kroc, one of Multimixer's salesmen, so he headed to San Bernardino to see "what the devil was going on." Kroc was so impressed with the McDonald brothers' operation that he convinced them to allow him to franchise their restaurants throughout the country. In 1955, Kroc opened the first McDonald's franchise in Des Plaines, Illinois.

The chain grew slowly at first, operating only 34 restaurants at the end of 1958. However, in 1959, Kroc expanded aggressively, opening 67 new restaurants. Two years later, he bought out the McDonald brothers' interest for $2.7 million. And just four years later he took the company public. The rest of the 1960s saw continued success for McDonald's. In 1966, the company sold its one billionth hamburger and, in 1968, it introduced the famous Big Mac and opened its 1,000th restaurant.

The 1970s were not much different. By 1971, McDonald's was operating restaurants in all 50 states. The company introduced the Egg McMuffin and the Happy Meal in 1972 and 1979, respectively. Three years after the Egg McMuffin, the McDonald's drive thru was introduced and in 1976 McDonald's sold its 20 billionth hamburger. The 1980s started out strong with the unveiling of the McChicken in 1980. In 1985, McDonald's became one of the 30 companies comprising the Dow Jones Industrial Average.

The 1990s was a time of international growth for McDonald's. In 1992, 66 percent of McDonald's revenue came from U.S. sales. That number dropped to about 43 percent in 1998 and then to about 35 percent in 2009. In 1991, only 3,600 international locations were in operation, but by 1998 that number had more than tripled to 11,000. Clearly, McDonald's has become a symbol of globalization. With locations in virtually every country in the world, McDonald's is the epitome of a multinational corporation. Managing such a widespread global empire requires a detailed understanding of accounting and the effects of currency changes on the company's financial statements.

Differences in accounting standards across countries and jurisdictions can cause significant difficulties for multinational firms like McDonald's. In fact, one of the significant challenges McDonald's faces is the preparation of financial statements according to the differing standards in countries where its subsidiaries are located and the subsequent consolidation of these foreign-based financial statements. These and other significant problems that result from differences in accounting standards have generated significant interest in the harmonization of accounting standards globally.

In addition, because of its global presence, McDonald's has to constantly monitor fluctuations in foreign currencies. The table below from McDonald's 2009 Form 10-K shows the effects of translating subsidiaries' financial statements from foreign currencies to U.S. dollars. For example, revenues in 2009 were adversely affected by $1.34 billion as a result foreign currency fluctuations.

In millions, except per share data	Reported Amount			Currency Translation Benefit/(Cost)		
	2009	2008	2007	2009	2008	2007
Revenues	$22,745	$23,522	$22,787	$(1,340)	$441	$988
Company-operated margins	2,807	2,908	2,869	(178)	63	129
Franchised margins	5,985	5,731	5,036	(176)	120	179
Selling, general, & administrative expenses	2,234	2,355	2,367	75	(21)	(73)
Operating income	6,841	6,443	3,879	(273)	163	230
Income from continuing operations	4,551	4,313	2,335	(164)	103	138
Net income	4,551	4,313	2,395	(164)	103	138
Income from continuing operations per common share—diluted	4.11	3.76	1.93	(0.15)	0.09	0.12
Net income per common share—diluted	4.11	3.76	1.98	(0.15)	0.09	0.12

Accountants preparing financial statements of global companies must consider (1) differences across national boundaries in accounting principles and (2) differences in currencies used to measure the operations of companies operating in different countries. Translation or restatement into U.S. dollars is necessary before the foreign subsidiary financial statements can be consolidated with the U.S. parent company's statements, which are already reported in dollars. This chapter summarizes current efforts to develop a global set of high-quality accounting standards and explores the translation of financial statements of a foreign business entity into U.S. dollars.

LEARNING OBJECTIVES

When you finish studying this chapter, you should be able to:

LO1   Understand and explain differences between U.S. GAAP and international financial reporting standards (IFRS) and the expected timeline to global convergence.

LO2   Determine the functional currency and understand the ramifications of different functional currency designations.

LO3   Understand and explain the differences between translation and remeasurment.

LO4   Make calculations and translate financial statements of a foreign subsidiary.

LO5   Prepare consolidated financial statements including a foreign subsidiary after translation.

LO6   Make calculations and remeasure financial statements of a foreign subsidiary.

LO7   Prepare consolidated financial statements including a foreign subsidiary after remeasurement.

LO8   Understand other issues related to foreign operations including the hedging of a net investment in a foreign subsidiary.

DIFFERENCES IN ACCOUNTING PRINCIPLES

LO1

Understand and explain differences between U.S. GAAP and international financial reporting standards (IFRS) and the expected timeline to global convergence.

Methods used to measure economic activity differ around the world. A country's economic, legal, educational, and political systems; stages of technological development or sophistication; culture and tradition; and various other socioeconomic factors all influence the development of accounting standards and the accounting profession in that nation. These differences have led to significant diversity in accounting standards from one nation to another. The lack of a uniform set of accounting standards creates problems for companies, preparers, and users. Some countries develop their accounting principles based on the information needs of the taxing authorities. Other countries have accounting principles designed to meet the needs of the central government economic planners. U.S. accounting standards focus on the information needs of the common stockholder or the creditors.

Arthur Levitt, former chairman of the Securities and Exchange Commission (SEC), noted in 1999 that the world economy was in a period of profound change as the notion of distance as a barrier was no longer a relevant impediment to business growth and development. Levitt noted that the flow of capital is a critical factor in global economic development, which had created a compelling need for a common business reporting language. Indeed, Levitt stated that "new business opportunities demand financial reporting standards that supersede national borders and cultural customs. These standards are not merely an ideal for a better global marketplace—they are fundamental to its very existence."[1]

During the decade following Levitt's statement, significant strides have been taken to move toward a single set of globally accepted reporting standards. Important benefits can be realized from the adoption of globally consistent accounting standards. Expected benefits include continued expansion of capital markets across national borders. Countries where accounting principles do not currently focus on the needs of investors could more quickly achieve stable, liquid capital markets, which in turn should drive economic growth. Use of a single set of accounting standards should help investors to better evaluate opportunities across national borders, which also should facilitate a more efficient use of global capital. A set of global standards also should reduce reporting costs that corporations currently incur if they attempt to access capital in markets outside their home country because corporations will no longer need to produce multiple sets of financial statements using different sets of accounting standards. Financial statement users are likely to have more confidence in financial reporting if it conforms to standards that have gained wide global acceptance.

The major financial reporting model that will very likely become globally accepted is being developed by the International Accounting Standards Board (IASB). The IASB is an independent, privately funded accounting standards-setting body based in London. The mission of the IASB is to develop a single set of high-quality, understandable, and enforceable global accounting standards. Standards published by the IASB are called ***International Financial Reporting Standards (IFRS).*** The IASB is composed of 14 members who each serves a five-year term subject to one reappointment. Members are required to sever all employment relationships that might compromise their independent judgment in setting accounting standards. The IASB solicits input from the public when evaluating potential standards and publishes a discussion paper and/or an exposure draft that are subject to comment before issuing a final standard. The IASB also has an advisory council, the Standards Advisory Council, that is composed of approximately 40 individuals from geographically diverse countries and draws members from both countries that have adopted IFRS and those that have not. The IASB has a mandate from the International Organization

---

[1] Arthur Levitt, "Remarks to the American Council on Germany: Corporate Governance in a Global Arena," Speech by SEC Chairman, October 7, 1999, http://www.sec.gov/news/speech/speecharchive/1999/spch302.htm.

of Securities Commissions (IOSCO) to develop a high-quality set of international financial reporting standards, and this effort has the support of the U.S. regulators and standard setters.

There is already widespread acceptance of IFRS around the world as these standards are mandated or permitted in over 100 countries around the world. Beginning in 2005, the European Union mandated the use of IFRS for companies listing on stock exchanges in the EU, although the EU continues to accept statements prepared according to U.S. GAAP. The increasing use of IFRS is already significant for U.S. stock exchanges. According to the SEC there has been a significant increase in the number of foreign private issuers who file within the United States from a relative few companies in 2005 to approximately 110 in 2006.[2] These companies prepare financial statements that comply with IFRS as published by the IASB. Further, the Commission expects to see this number continue to increase in the future, particularly as Canada will adopt IFRS beginning in 2011; there currently are approximately 500 foreign private issuers from Canada. This movement to IFRS also has begun to affect U.S. issuers, in particular those with a significant global footprint. For instance, certain U.S. issuers may compete for capital globally in industry sectors in which a critical mass of non-U.S. companies report under IFRS. Also, U.S. issuers with subsidiaries located in jurisdictions that have moved to IFRS may prepare those subsidiaries' financial statements according to IFRS for purposes of local regulatory or statutory filings.

The FASB is working with the IASB to improve the quality of reporting standards and to "converge" their two sets of standards. In September 2002, the FASB issued the "Norwalk Agreement" in which both the FASB and the IASB pledged to work together both to improve the quality of their financial reporting standards and to converge the standards by working to minimize the differences between them. The convergence effort focuses on both the evaluation of existing standards and guidance for implementing current standards and new standards as they are developed. PricewaterhouseCoopers offers a publication on its Web site entitled "IFRS and US GAAP: similarities and differences: September 2010" that provides a topic-based comparison. This publication can be accessed on the Internet at http://www.pwc.com/us/en/issues/ifrs-reporting/publications/ifrs-and-us-gaap-similarities-and-differences-september-2010.jhtml.

Until 2007, the SEC required foreign issuers that do use U.S. GAAP to reconcile their financial statements to U.S. GAAP and to file this reconciliation with the SEC on a Form 20-F. On January 4, 2008, the SEC issued new rules that allow foreign private issuers to file statements prepared in accordance with IFRS as issued by the IASB without reconciliation to U.S. GAAP.[3] Removing the Form 20-F requirement reduces costs to foreign private issuers and encourages their continued participation in the U.S. public capital market, which is a benefit to investors by increasing investment possibilities and furthering the efficient allocation of capital.

In December 2007, the SEC held roundtable discussions with representatives from public companies, audit firms, investor groups, academia, rating agencies, the legal community, and government agencies to obtain feedback on whether public companies in the United States should be permitted or required to file their consolidated financial statements using IFRS as published by the IASB instead of U.S. GAAP. Among this group, there was overwhelming support for the use of a single set of global standards, and the majority of the panelists agreed that IFRS ultimately will be the standard.

In general, panelists at the SEC roundtable felt that U.S. corporations could be more competitive globally if they were permitted to use IFRS for financial reporting. Benefits expected to accrue to U.S. firms include

[2] Securities and Exchange Commission, "Concept Release on Allowing U.S. Issuers to Prepare Financial Statements in Accordance with International Financial Reporting Standards," p. 6, www.sec.gov/rules/concept/2007/33-8831.pdf.

[3] Securities and Exchange Commission, "Acceptance from Foreign Private Issuers of Financial Statements Prepared in Accordance with International Financial Reporting Standards without Reconciliation to U.S. GAAP," *Federal Register* 73, no. 3 (January 4, 2008), pp. 986–1012, www.sec.gov/rules/final/2008/33-8879fr.pdf.

- Increased quality of information available to investors.
- Reduced costs of compliance for companies that are currently using multiple reporting frameworks.
- Enhanced global capital markets.
- Easier access to capital in the global markets.
- Enhanced comparability across companies for users. SEC Chairman Cox noted that two-thirds of U.S. investors own securities of foreign companies, a 30 percent increase in the last five years.

Moreover, because the SEC now permits foreign private issuers to file their financial reports using IFRS without reconciliation, not allowing U.S. companies to report under IFRS could result in U.S. companies bearing costs not incurred by foreign private issuers. Some observers fear that the United States could even become marginalized if more countries move to IFRS but the United States does not. Not only are U.S. investors divesting themselves of U.S. holdings and investing in non-U.S. holdings, but more companies are electing to raise capital on non-U.S. exchanges. As recently as 2000, nine out of every 10 dollars raised for foreign companies through new stock offerings were done in New York. However, by 2005, nine out of every 10 dollars were raised through new company listings in London or Luxembourg.[4]

There are still significant issues that must be addressed before a decision about adoption of IFRS by U.S. corporations can be made. Extensive training for professionals, users, and even regulators may be necessary. Still, many believe that convergence to a single set of international standards is key to economic development. Among 143 worldwide leaders of the accounting profession representing 91 countries who responded to a survey conducted by the International Federation of Accountants, 89 percent indicated that convergence to international financial reporting standards was either important or very important for economic growth in their countries, and only 1 percent said it was not important.

Nevertheless, on February 24, 2010, the SEC issued a formal statement supporting convergence to a single set of global accounting standards. The SEC has directed its staff to prepare a work plan to allow it to decide on a mandate for accepting IFRS for U.S. registrants. This work plan outlines the activities the SEC staff will undertake to provide the SEC with information for determining whether, when, and how to incorporate IFRS into the reporting system in the United States. This work plan addresses six concerns from comments received on the SEC's IFRS Roadmap:

1. Sufficient development and application of IFRS for the U.S. domestic reporting system.
2. The independence of standard setting for the benefit of investors.
3. Investor understanding and education regarding IFRS.
4. Examination of the U.S. regulatory environment that would be affected by a change in accounting standards.
5. The impact on users, both large and small, including changes to accounting systems, changes to contractual arrangements, corporate governance considerations, and litigation contingencies.
6. Human capital readiness.

Each of these issues is significant. Nevertheless, the SEC is determined to work through these concerns with the intent of allowing firms to begin filing in the United States based on IFRS during the next four to five years. A diagram published by Deloitte provides a potential timeline for the adoption of IFRS in the United States.[5]

---

[4] Craig Karmin and Aaron Lucchetti, "New York Loses Edge in Snagging Foreign Listings," *The Wall Street Journal* (Eastern Edition), January 26, 2006, p. C1.

[5] See Deloitte, *IFRS Insights: Achieving a Global Standard* 15 (March/April 2010).

The SEC anticipates providing four to five years for IFRS adoption.

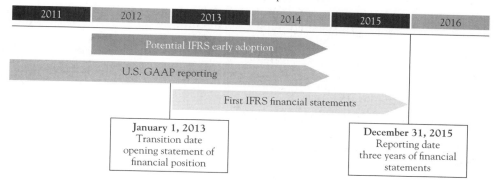

DETERMINING THE FUNCTIONAL CURRENCY

LO2

Determine the functional currency and understand the ramifications of different functional currency designations.

Imagine that you received 100 British pounds sterling in payment on an account in your London subsidiary on December 31, 20X1, and deposited it in a London bank. Assume that at the end of 20X1 the exchange rate is $1.80. To report the deposit on your 20X1 balance sheet stated in dollars, you would translate the deposit at the current rate and you would report an asset of $180. At the end of 20X2, assume you still have the 100 pounds sterling in the bank, but now the exchange rate is $1.70. To report the deposit on your 20X2 balance sheet, if you use the exchange rate at the end of 20X2, this amount would now translate into $170 and you would have an imbalance, also referred to as a *translation adjustment,* of $10 to deal with. If you translated at the historical rate, you would still translate into $180 and there would be no imbalance. Which is the correct exchange rate to use?

Date	Currency on Deposit	Current Exchange Rate	Dollar Equivalent
12/31/20X1	£100	$1.80	$180
12/31/20X2	100	1.70	170

Two major issues that must be addressed when financial statements are translated from a foreign currency into U.S. dollars are

1. Which exchange rate should be used to translate foreign currency balances to domestic currency?

2. How should translation gains and losses be accounted for? Should they be included in income?

There are three possible exchange rates that may be used in converting foreign currency values to the U.S. dollar. The *current rate* is the exchange rate at the end of the trading day on the balance sheet date. The *historical rate* is the exchange rate that existed when an initial transaction took place, such as the exchange rate on the date an asset was acquired or a liability was incurred. The *average rate* for the period is usually a simple average for a period of time and is usually the exchange rate used to measure revenues and expenses. Translation methods may employ a single rate or multiple rates. The translation adjustment created by the application of these exchange rates also must be reflected in the financial statements, as either a component of net income or a component of comprehensive income. The disposition of the translation adjustment will be discussed later in this chapter.

FASB Statement No. 52 (ASC 830), "Foreign Currency Translation" (FASB 52, ASC 830), provides specific guidelines for translating a foreign currency into U.S. dollars to allow preparation of consolidated financial statements measured, or denominated, in dollars. The purpose of **FASB 52 (ASC 830)** is to present results that are directionally

FIGURE 9–1 Functional Currency Indicators

Indicator	Factors Indicating Foreign Currency (Local Currency) Is the Functional Currency	Factors Indicating U.S. Dollar (Parent's Currency) Is the Functional Currency
Cash flows	Primarily in foreign currency and do not affect parent's cash flows	Directly impact the parent's current cash flows and are readily available to the parent company
Sales prices	Primarily determined by local competition or local government regulation; not generally responsive to changes in exchange rates	Responsive to short-term changes in exchange rates and worldwide competition
Sales markets	Active local sales markets for company's products; possibly, significant amounts of exports	Sales markets mostly in parent's country, or sales contracts are denominated in parent's currency
Expenses	Labor, materials, and other costs are primarily local costs	Production components generally obtained from the parent company's country
Financing	Primarily obtained from, and denominated in, local currency units; entity's operations generate funds sufficient to service financing needs	Primarily from the parent, or other dollar-denominated financing
Intercompany transactions and arrangements	Few intercompany transactions with parent	Frequent intercompany transactions with parent, or foreign entity is an investment or financing arm for the parent

sympathetic to the real economic effects of exchange rate movements. Additionally, **FASB 52 (ASC 830)** seeks to preserve financial results and relationships in the foreign financial statements through the translation process. For instance, if the gross margin on sales is positive when measured in the foreign currency, it should still be positive when sales and cost of goods sold are translated into dollars. The FASB adopted the concept of the *functional currency,* which is defined as "the currency of the primary economic environment in which the entity operates; normally that is the currency of the environment in which an entity primarily generates and receives cash."[6] The functional currency is used to differentiate between two types of foreign operations, those that are self-contained and integrated into a local environment and those that are an extension of the parent and integrated with the parent. A U.S. company may have foreign affiliates in many different countries. Each affiliate must be analyzed to determine its individual functional currency.

Figure 9–1 presents the six indicators that must be assessed to determine an entity's functional currency: cash flows, sales prices, sales markets, expenses, financing, and intercompany transactions. If a foreign affiliate uses the local currency for most of its transactions, and if the cash generated is not regularly physically returned to the parent in the United States, the local currency is usually the functional currency. Also, the foreign affiliate usually has active sales markets in its own country and obtains financing from local sources.

Some foreign-based entities, however, use a functional currency different from the local currency. For example, a U.S. company subsidiary in Venezuela may conduct virtually all of its business in Brazil, or a branch or a subsidiary of a U.S. company operating in Britain may well use the U.S. dollar as its major currency although it maintains its accounting records in British pounds sterling. The following factors indicate that the U.S. dollar is the functional currency for the British subsidiary: most of its cash transactions are in U.S. dollars; its major sales markets are in the United States; production components are generally obtained from the United States; and the U.S. parent is primarily responsible for financing the British subsidiary.

[6] *Financial Accounting Standards Board Statement No. 52,* "Foreign Currency Translation," 1981, para. 5.

The FASB adopted the functional currency approach after considering the following objectives of the translation process:

a. Provide information that is generally compatible with the expected economic effects of a rate change on an enterprise's cash flows and equity.

b. Reflect in consolidated statements the financial results and relationships of the individual consolidated entities as measured in their functional currencies in conformity with U.S. generally accepted accounting principles.[7]

The functional currency approach requires the foreign entity to translate all of its transactions into its functional currency. If an entity has transactions denominated in other than its functional currency, the foreign transactions must be adjusted to their equivalent functional currency value before the company may prepare financial statements.

Functional Currency Designation in Highly Inflationary Economies

An exception to the criteria for selecting a functional currency is specified when the foreign entity is located in countries such as Argentina and Peru, which have experienced severe inflation. Severe inflation is defined as inflation exceeding 100 percent over a three-year period.[8] The FASB concluded that the volatility of hyperinflationary currencies distorts the financial statements if the local currency is used as the foreign entity's functional currency. Therefore, in cases of operations located in highly inflationary economies, the reporting currency of the U.S. parent—the U.S. dollar—should be used as the foreign entity's functional currency. This exception prevents unrealistic asset values and income statement charges if the hyperinflation is ignored and normal translation procedures are used. For example, assume that a foreign subsidiary constructed a building that cost 1,000,000 pesos when the exchange rate was $0.05 = 1 peso. Further assume that because of hyperinflation in the foreign subsidiary's country, the exchange rate becomes $0.00005 = 1 peso. The translated values of the building at the time it was constructed and after the hyperinflation follow:

	Date of Construction		After Hyperinflation	
Amount (pesos)	Rate	Translated Amount	Rate	Translated Amount
1,000,000	$0.05	$50,000	$0.00005	$50

The translated values after the hyperinflation do not reflect the building's market value or historical cost. Thus, the FASB required the use of the U.S. dollar as the functional currency in cases of hyperinflation to give some stability to the financial statements.

Once a foreign affiliate's functional currency is chosen, it should be used consistently. However, if changes in economic circumstances necessitate a change in the designation of the foreign affiliate's functional currency, the accounting change should be treated as a change in estimate: current and prospective treatment only, no restatement of prior periods.

TRANSLATION VERSUS REMEASUREMENT OF FOREIGN FINANCIAL STATEMENTS[9]

LO3

Understand and explain the differences between translation and remeasurment.

Advanced
StudyGuide
.com

Two different methods are used to restate foreign entity statements to U.S. dollars: (1) the **translation** of the foreign entity's functional currency statements into U.S. dollars and (2) the **remeasurement** of the foreign entity's statements into the functional currency of the entity. After remeasurement, the statements must then be translated if the functional currency is *not* the U.S. dollar. No additional work is needed if the functional currency is the U.S. dollar.

Translation is the most common method used and is applied when the local currency is the foreign entity's functional currency. This is the normal case in which, for example, a

[7] *FASB 52*, para. 4.

[8] *FASB 52*, para. 11.

[9] To view a video explanation of this topic, visit advancedstudyguide.com.

U.S. company's French subsidiary uses the euro as its recording and functional currency. The subsidiary's statements must be translated from euros into U.S. dollars. To translate the financial statements, the company will use the current rate, which is the exchange rate on the balance sheet date, to convert the local currency balance sheet account balances into U.S. dollars. Any translation adjustment that occurs is a component of comprehensive income. Because revenues and expenses are assumed to occur uniformly over the period, revenues and expenses on the income statement are translated using the average rate for the reporting period. This translation method is called the ***current rate method.***

Remeasurement is the restatement of the foreign entity's financial statements from the local currency that the entity used into the foreign entity's functional currency. Remeasurement is required only when the functional currency is different from the currency used to maintain the books and records of the foreign entity. For example, a relatively self-contained Canadian sales branch of a U.S. company may use the U.S. dollar as its functional currency but may select the Canadian dollar as its recording and reporting currency. Of course, if the Canadian branch uses the U.S. dollar for both its functional and reporting currency, no translation or remeasurement is necessary: Its statements are already measured in U.S. dollars and are ready to be combined with the U.S. home office statements.

The method used to remeasure the financial statements from the local currency to the functional currency is called the ***temporal method.*** Monetary assets and liabilities are those that represent rights to receive or obligations to pay a fixed number of foreign currency units in the future. Under the temporal method, the current rate is usually used to translate these monetary amounts to the functional currency. Nonmonetary items include fixed assets, long-term investments, and inventories. These items are usually translated at the historical rate that existed when the assets originally were purchased or the liability originally was incurred. Revenues and expenses on the income statement are translated using the average rate for the reporting period. Any imbalance that occurs because of the application of the temporal method is included in the calculation of net income on the income statement.

The application of the temporal method converts a foreign currency to the functional currency. If the functional currency is the U.S. dollar, no additional adjustments are needed. If the functional currency is something other than the U.S. dollar, the current rate method must be applied to restate the financial information in U.S. dollars.

One application of remeasurement is for affiliates located in countries experiencing hyperinflation. For example, an Argentinian subsidiary of a U.S. parent records and reports its financial statements in the local currency, the Argentine peso. However, because the Argentine economy experiences inflation exceeding 100 percent over a three-year period, the U.S. dollar is specified as the functional currency for reporting purposes and the subsidiary's statements must then be remeasured from Argentine pesos into U.S. dollars.

The following table presents an overview of the methods a U.S. company would use to restate a foreign affiliate's financial statements in U.S. dollars.

Currency in Which the Foreign Affiliate's Books and Records Are Maintained	Functional Currency	Restatement Method
Local currency (i.e., currency of the country in which the foreign entity is located)	Local currency	Translate to U.S. dollars using current exchange rates
Local currency	U.S. dollar (such as required in hyperinflationary economies)	Remeasure from local currency to U.S. dollar
Local currency	Third country's currency (not LCU or U.S. dollar)	First, remeasure from the local currency into the functional currency, then translate from functional currency to U.S. dollars
U.S. dollar	U.S. dollar	No restatement is necessary; already in U.S. dollars

The conceptual reasons for the two different methods, translation and remeasurement, come from a consideration of the primary objective of the translation process: to provide information that shows the expected impact of exchange rate changes on the U.S. company's cash flows and equity. Foreign affiliates fall into two groups. Those in the first group are relatively self-contained entities that generate and spend local currency units. The local currency is the functional currency for this group of entities. These foreign affiliates may reinvest the currency they generate or may distribute funds to their home office or parent company in the form of dividends. Exchange rate changes do not directly affect the U.S. parent company's cash flows. Rather, the rate changes affect the foreign affiliate's net assets (assets minus liabilities) and, therefore, the U.S. parent company's net investment in the entity.

The second group of foreign affiliates is made up of entities that are an extension of the U.S. company. These affiliates operate in a foreign country but are directly affected by changes in exchange rates because they depend on the U.S. economy for sales markets, production components, or financing. For this group, the U.S. dollar is the functional currency. There is a presumption that the effect of exchange rate changes on the foreign affiliate's net assets will directly affect the U.S. parent company's cash flows, so the exchange rate adjustments are reported in the U.S. parent's income.

Translation and remeasurement include different adjustment procedures and may result in significantly different consolidated financial statements. Both methods are illustrated in this chapter.

TRANSLATION OF FUNCTIONAL CURRENCY STATEMENTS INTO THE REPORTING CURRENCY OF THE U.S. COMPANY

LO4

Make calculations and translate financial statements of a foreign subsidiary.

Most business entities transact and record business activities in the local currency. Therefore, the local currency of the foreign entity is its functional currency. The translation of the foreign entity's statement into U.S. dollars is a relatively straightforward process.

The FASB believes that the underlying economic relationships presented in the foreign entity's financial statements should not be distorted or changed during the translation process from the foreign entity's functional currency into the currency of the U.S. parent. For example, if the foreign entity's functional currency statements report a current ratio of 2:1 and a gross margin of 60 percent of sales, these relationships should pass through the translation process into the U.S. parent's reporting currency. It is important to be able to evaluate the performance of the foreign entity's management with the same economic measures used to operate the foreign entity. To maintain the economic relationships in the functional currency statements, the account balances must be translated by a comparable exchange rate.

The translation is made by using the current exchange rate for *all* assets and liabilities. This rate is the spot rate on the balance sheet date. The income statement items—revenue, expenses, gains, and losses—should be translated at the exchange rate on the dates on which the underlying transactions occurred, although for practical purposes an average exchange rate for the period may be used for these items with the assumption that revenues and expenses are recognized evenly over the period. However, if a material gain or loss results from a specific event, the exchange rate on the date of the event rather than the average exchange rate should be used to translate the transaction results.

The stockholders' equity accounts, other than retained earnings, are translated at historical exchange rates. The appropriate historical rate is the rate on the latter of the date the parent company acquired the investment in the foreign entity or the date the subsidiary had the stockholders' equity transaction. This is necessary to complete the elimination of the parent company's investment account against the foreign subsidiary's capital accounts in the consolidation process. The subsidiary's translated retained earnings are carried forward from the previous period with additions for this period's income and deductions for dividends declared during the period. Dividends are translated at the exchange rate on the date of declaration. It is interesting to observe that if the foreign entity has not paid its declared dividend by the end of its fiscal period, it has a dividends payable account that is translated at the current rate. Nevertheless, the dividend deduction from Retained Earnings is translated using the exchange rate on the date of dividend declaration.

In summary, the translation of the foreign entity's financial statements from its functional currency into the reporting currency of the U.S. company is made as follows:

Income statement accounts:	
Revenue and expenses	Generally, average exchange rate for period covered by statement
Balance sheet accounts:	
Assets and liabilities	Current exchange rate on balance sheet date
Stockholders' equity	Historical exchange rates

Because various rates are used to translate the foreign entity's individual accounts, the trial balance debits and credits after translation generally are not equal. The balancing item to make the translated trial balance debits equal the credits is called the ***translation adjustment.***

Financial Statement Presentation of Translation Adjustment

The translation adjustment resulting from the translation process is part of the entity's comprehensive income for the period. **FASB Statement No. 130 (ASC 220),** "Reporting Comprehensive Income" (FASB 130, ASC 220), issued in June 1997, defined comprehensive income to include all changes in equity during a period except those resulting from investments by owners and distributions to owners. ***Comprehensive income*** includes net income and ***"other comprehensive income"*** items that are part of the changes in the net assets of a business enterprise from nonowner sources (e.g., not additional capital investments and dividends) during a period. **FASB 130 (ASC 220)** requires the reporting of comprehensive income as part of the primary financial statements of the entity. The major items comprising the other comprehensive income items are the changes during the period in foreign currency translation adjustments, unrealized gains or losses on available-for-sale securities, revaluation of cash flow hedges, and adjustments in the minimum pension liability item.

FASB 130 (ASC 220) allows for several alternative presentation formats for comprehensive income. The single-statement, combined-income approach first presents the items composing net income and then has a section presenting the other comprehensive income items. An alternative, two-statement presentation first presents the computation of net income on one statement and then a related statement that begins with net income and reconciles to comprehensive income by reporting the other comprehensive income items separately. A third alternative, used by many companies, is just to present the items composing other comprehensive income in a schedule of accumulated other comprehensive income in the consolidated statement of shareholders' equity. An entity may present the components of other comprehensive income items net of tax or show the aggregate tax effects related to the total other comprehensive income items as one amount.

Each period's other comprehensive income (OCI) is closed to ***accumulated other comprehensive income*** (AOCI), which is displayed separately from other stockholders' equity items (e.g., capital stock, additional paid-in capital, and retained earnings). An appropriate title, such as "Accumulated Other Comprehensive Income," is used to describe this stockholders' equity item. The statement of changes in stockholders' equity opens with the accumulated balance of the other comprehensive income items at the beginning of the period, then includes the change in the translation adjustment and the additional other comprehensive income items during the period that were included in the period's comprehensive income, and ends with the accumulated other comprehensive income balance at the end of the period. The accumulated ending balance of the other

FIGURE 9–2
Balance Sheet Accounts for the Two Companies on January 1, 20X1 (Immediately before Acquisition of 100 percent of German Company's Stock by Peerless Products, a U.S. Company)

	Peerless Products	German Company
Cash	$ 350,000	€ 2,500
Receivables	75,000	10,000
Inventory	100,000	7,500
Land	175,000	–0–
Plant and Equipment	800,000	50,000
Total Debits	$1,500,000	€70,000
Accumulated Depreciation	$ 400,000	€ 5,000
Accounts Payable	100,000	2,500
Bonds Payable	200,000	12,500
Common Stock	500,000	40,000
Retained Earnings, 12/31/X0	300,000	10,000
Total Credits	$1,500,000	€70,000

comprehensive income items is then reported in the entity's balance sheet as part of the stockholders' equity section, usually after retained earnings. The discussion of the disclosure requirements presented later in this chapter demonstrates the financial statements for the Peerless Products Corporation example presented in the chapter.

LO5

Prepare consolidated financial statements including a foreign subsidiary after translation.

Illustration of Translation and Consolidation of a Foreign Subsidiary

In Chapter 8, the examples illustrated the effects of a dollar that was strengthening against the euro during 20X1. In the examples for the remainder of this chapter, the dollar weakens against the euro during 20X1. Thus, in Chapters 8 and 9, changes in exchange rates in both directions will have been illustrated.

To examine the consolidation of a foreign subsidiary, assume the following facts:

1. On January 1, 20X1, Peerless, a U.S. company, purchased 100 percent of the outstanding capital stock of German Company, a firm located in Berlin, Germany, for $63,000, which is $3,000 above book value. (The proof of the differential is shown at the end of the next section of the chapter.) The excess of cost over book value is attributable to a patent amortizable over 10 years. Balance sheet accounts in a trial balance format for both companies immediately *before* the acquisition are presented in Figure 9–2.

2. The local currency for German Company is the euro (€), which is also its functional currency.

3. On October 1, 20X1, the subsidiary declared and paid dividends of €6,250.

4. The subsidiary received $4,200 in a sales transaction with a U.S. company when the exchange rate was $1.20 = €1. The subsidiary still has this foreign currency on December 31, 20X1.

5. Relevant direct spot exchange rates ($/€1) are:

Date	Rate
January 1, 20X1	$1.20
October 1, 20X1	1.36
December 31, 20X1	1.40
20X1 average	1.30

Date-of-Acquisition Translation Worksheet

Figure 9–3 presents the translation of German Company's trial balance on January 1, 20X1. This illustration assumes that the subsidiary's books and records are maintained in European euros, the subsidiary's functional currency.

FIGURE 9–3
Worksheet to Translate Foreign Subsidiary on January 1, 20X1 (Date of Acquisition)
Functional Currency Is the European Euro

Item	Trial Balance, €	Exchange Rate, $/€	Trial Balance, $
Cash	2,500	1.20	3,000
Receivables	10,000	1.20	12,000
Inventory	7,500	1.20	9,000
Plant and Equipment	50,000	1.20	60,000
Total Debits	70,000		84,000
Accumulated Depreciation	5,000	1.20	6,000
Accounts Payable	2,500	1.20	3,000
Bonds Payable	12,500	1.20	15,000
Common Stock	40,000	1.20	48,000
Retained Earnings	10,000	1.20	12,000
Total Credits	70,000		84,000

Note: $1.20 is the direct exchange rate on January 1, 20X1.

The translation of the subsidiary's trial balance from the functional currency (€) into dollars, the U.S. parent's reporting currency, is made using the *current rate method*. Under acquisition accounting, the subsidiary's stockholders' equity accounts are translated using the current rate on the date of the parent company's purchase of the subsidiary's stock.

The entry made by Peerless Products to record the purchase of 100 percent of German Company's stock is

(1)
January 1, 20X1		
Investment in German Company Stock	63,000	
Cash		63,000

Purchase of German Company stock.

The differential on January 1, 20X1, the date of acquisition, is computed as follows:

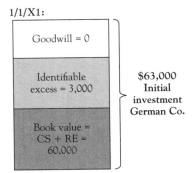

ⓟ	Fair value of consideration		$63,000
	Book value of shares acquired:		
1/1/X1	Common stock—German Co.	$48,000	
100%	Retained earnings—German Co.	12,000	
	Total	$60,000	
ⓢ	Percent of German Company's stock		
	acquired by Peerless Corporation	× 1.00	
	Book value acquired by Peerless Corporation		60,000
	Difference between fair value and book value		$ 3,000

A graphic representation of the acquisition is as follows:

1/1/X1:

Goodwill = 0

Identifiable excess = 3,000

Book value = CS + RE = 60,000

$63,000 Initial investment German Co.

Date-of-Acquisition Consolidated Balance Sheet

In order to prepare the elimination entries, we begin by analyzing the book value of the investment in German Company:

Book Value Calculations:

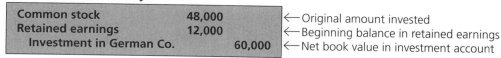

	Peerless 100%	=	Common Stock	+	Retained Earnings
Original book value	60,000		48,000		12,000

This leads to the basic elimination entry:

Basic elimination entry:

Common stock	48,000	← Original amount invested
Retained earnings	12,000	← Beginning balance in retained earnings
Investment in German Co.		60,000 ← Net book value in investment account

The differential is entirely attributable to the patent, $3,000, so the excess value reclassification entry is as follows:

Excess value reclassification entry:

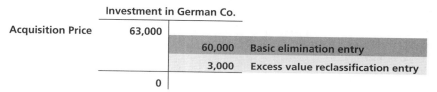

Patent	3,000	← Excess value assigned to patent
Investment in German Co.	3,000	← Reclassify excess acquisition price

These two worksheet entries eliminate the balance in Peerless' investment account and the second entry assigns the differential to the patent account.

Investment in German Co.			
Acquisition Price	63,000		
		60,000	Basic elimination entry
		3,000	Excess value reclassification entry
	0		

Finally, we include the optional accumulated depreciation elimination entry:

Optional accumulated depreciation elimination entry:

Accumulated depreciation	6,000	← Original depreciation at the time of the acquisition netted against cost
Building and equipment	6,000	

Figure 9–4 presents the consolidation worksheet on the acquisition date.

Subsequent to Date of Acquisition

The accounting subsequent to the date of acquisition is very similar to the accounting used for domestic subsidiaries. The major differences are due to the effects of changes in the exchange rates of the foreign currency.

Translation of Foreign Subsidiary's Postacquisition Trial Balance

Figure 9–5 illustrates the translation of German Company's December 31, 20X1, trial balance.

Note the account Foreign Currency Units in the trial balance of the German subsidiary. This account represents the $4,200 of U.S. dollars held by the subsidiary. Because this account is denominated in a currency other than the subsidiary's reporting currency, German Company made an adjusting journal entry to revalue the account from the amount originally recorded using the exchange rate on the date the company received the currency to that amount's equivalent exchange value at the end of the year.

The subsidiary made the following entry on its books when it received the U.S. dollars:

(2)	Foreign Currency Units ($)	3,500	
	Sales		3,500

Record sales and receipt of 4,200 U.S. dollars at spot exchange rate on the date of receipt: €3,500 = $4,200/$1.20 exchange rate.

FIGURE 9–4   January 1, 20X1, Worksheet for Consolidated Balance Sheet, Date of Acquisition
100 Percent Purchase at More Than Book Value

	Peerless Products	German Company	Elimination Entries DR	Elimination Entries CR	Consolidated
Balance Sheet					
Cash	287,000	3,000			290,000
Receivable	75,000	12,000			87,000
Inventory	100,000	9,000			109,000
Investment in German Co. Stock	63,000			60,000	0
				3,000	
Patent			3,000		3,000
Land	175,000				175,000
Plant & Equipment	800,000	60,000		6,000	854,000
Less: Accumulated Depreciation	(400,000)	(6,000)	6,000		(400,000)
Total Assets	**1,100,000**	**78,000**	**9,000**	**69,000**	**1,118,000**
Accounts Payable	100,000	3,000			103,000
Bonds Payable	200,000	15,000			215,000
Common Stock	500,000	48,000	48,000		500,000
Retained Earnings	300,000	12,000	12,000		300,000
Total Liabilities & Equity	**1,100,000**	**78,000**	**60,000**	**0**	**1,118,000**

FIGURE 9–5
December 31, 20X1, Translation of Foreign Subsidiary's Trial Balance
European Euro Is the Functional Currency

Advanced
StudyGuide
.com

Item	Balance, €	Exchange Rate	Balance, $
Cash	10,750	1.40	15,050
Foreign Currency Units	3,000	1.40	4,200
Receivables	10,500	1.40	14,700
Inventory	5,000	1.40	7,000
Plant and Equipment	50,000	1.40	70,000
Cost of Goods Sold	22,500	1.30	29,250
Operating Expenses	14,500	1.30	18,850
Foreign Currency Transaction Loss	500	1.30	650
Dividends Paid	6,250	1.36	8,500
Total Debits	123,000		168,200
Accumulated Depreciation	7,500	1.40	10,500
Accounts Payable	3,000	1.40	4,200
Bonds Payable	12,500	1.40	17,500
Common Stock	40,000	1.20	48,000
Retained Earnings (1/1)	10,000	(a)	12,000
Sales	50,000	1.30	65,000
Total	123,000		157,200
Accumulated Other Comprehensive Income—Translation Adjustment			11,000
Total Credits			168,200

(*a*) From the January 1, 20X1, translation worksheet.

At the end of the period, the subsidiary adjusted the foreign currency units (the U.S. dollars) to the current exchange rate ($1.40 = €1) by making the following entry:

(3)	Foreign Currency Transaction Loss	500	
	Foreign Currency Units ($)		500

Adjust account denominated in foreign currency units to current
exchange rate:

$4,200/$1.40	€3,000
Less: Preadjusted balance	(3,500)
Foreign currency transaction loss	€ (500)

The foreign currency transaction loss is a component of the subsidiary's net income, and the Foreign Currency Units account is classified as a current asset on the subsidiary's balance sheet. The subsidiary's net income consists of the following elements:

Sales	€50,000
Cost of Goods Sold	(22,500)
Operating Expenses	(14,500)
Foreign Currency Transaction Loss	(500)
Net Income	€12,500

Because the European euro is the foreign entity's functional currency, the subsidiary's statements must be translated into U.S. dollars using the current rate method. The assets and liabilities are translated using the current exchange rate at the balance sheet date ($1.40), the income statement accounts are translated using the average rate for the period ($1.30), and the stockholders' equity accounts are translated using the appropriate historical exchange rates ($1.20 and $1.36). The dividends are translated at the October 1 rate ($1.36), which was the exchange rate on the date the dividends were declared. The example assumes the dividends were paid on October 1, the same day they were declared. If the dividends had not been paid by the end of the year, the liability dividends payable would be translated at the current exchange rate of $1.40 = €1.

One of the analytical features provided by the current rate method is that many of the ratios management uses to manage the foreign subsidiary are the same in U.S. dollars as they are in the foreign currency unit. This relationship is true for the assets and liabilities of the balance sheet and the revenue and expenses of the income statement because the translation for these accounts uses the same exchange rate—the current rate for the assets and liabilities, and the average exchange rate for the income statement accounts. Thus, the *scale* of these accounts has changed but not their *relative amounts* within their respective statements. This relationship is not true when the ratio includes numbers from both the income statement and the balance sheet or when a stockholders' equity account is included with an asset or liability. The following table illustrates the relative relationships within the financial statements using the data in Figure 9–5:

	Measured in €	Measured in U.S. Dollars
Current ratio:		
Current assets	€29,250	$40,950
Current liabilities	€ 3,000	$ 4,200
Current ratio	9.75	9.75
Cost of goods sold as a percentage of sales:		
Cost of goods sold	€22,500	$29,250
Sales	€50,000	$65,000
Percent	45%	45%

The translation adjustment in Figure 9–5 arises because the investee's assets and liabilities are translated at the current rate, whereas other rates are used for the stockholders' equity and income statement account balances. Although the translation adjustment may be thought of as a balancing item to make the trial balance debits equal the credits, the effects of changes in the exchange rates during the period should be calculated to prove the accuracy of the translation process. This proof for 20X1, the acquisition year, is provided in Figure 9–6.

The proof begins with determination of the effect of changes in the exchange rate on the beginning investment and on the elements that alter the beginning investment. Note that only events affecting the stockholders' equity accounts will change the net assets investment. In this example, the changes to the investment account occurred from income of €12,500 and dividends of €6,250. No changes occurred in the stock outstanding during the year. The beginning net investment is translated using the exchange rate

FIGURE 9–6
**Proof of Translation
Adjustment as of
December 31, 20X1**
European Euro Is the
Functional Currency

PEERLESS PRODUCTS AND SUBSIDIARY
Proof of Translation Adjustment
Year Ended December 31, 20X1

	€	Translation Rate	$
Net assets at beginning of year	50,000	1.20	60,000
Adjustment for changes in net assets position during year:			
Net income for year	12,500	1.30	16,250
Dividends paid	(6,250)	1.36	(8,500)
Net assets translated at:			
Rates during year			67,750
Rates at end of year	56,250	1.40	78,750
Change in other comprehensive income— net translation adjustment during year			11,000
Accumulated other comprehensive income— translation adjustment, 1/1			–0–
Accumulated other comprehensive income— translation adjustment, 12/31 (credit)			11,000

at the beginning of the year. The income and dividends are translated using the exchange rate at the date the transactions occurred. The income was earned evenly over the year; thus the average exchange rate for the period is used to translate income. The ending net assets position is translated using the exchange rate at the end of the year. The cumulative translation adjustment at the beginning of the year is zero in this example because the subsidiary was acquired on January 1, 20X1.

The Accumulated Other Comprehensive Income—Translation Adjustment account has a credit balance because the spot exchange rate at the end of the first period of ownership is higher than the exchange rate at the beginning of the period or the average for the period. If the exchange rate had decreased during the period, the translation adjustment would have had a debit balance. Another way of determining whether the accumulated translation adjustment has a debit or credit balance is to use balance sheet logic. For example, the subsidiary's translated balance sheet at the beginning of the year would be

Translated Balance Sheet, 1/1/X1			
Net assets	$60,000	Common stock	$48,000
		Retained earnings	12,000
Total	$60,000	Total	$60,000

The translated balance sheet at the end of the year would be:

Translated Balance Sheet, 12/31/X1			
Net assets	$78,750	Common stock	$48,000
		Retained earnings	19,750
		Accumulated other comprehensive income— translation adjustment	11,000
Total	$78,750	Total	$78,750

Note that the $11,000 is a credit balance in order to make the balance sheet "balance."

Entries on Parent Company's Books

The parent company makes entries on its books to recognize the dollar equivalent values of its share of the subsidiary's income, amortization of the excess of cost over book value, a cumulative translation adjustment for the parent's differential, and the dividends received from the foreign subsidiary. In addition, the parent company must recognize its share of the translation adjustment arising from the translation of the subsidiary's financial statements. The periodic change in the parent company's translation adjustment from the foreign investment is reported as a component of the parent company's other comprehensive income.

The entries that Peerless Products makes to account for its investment in German Company follow. Peerless Products received the dividend on October 1, 20X1, and immediately converted it to U.S. dollars as follows:

	October 1, 20X1		
(4)	Cash	8,500	
	Investment in German Company Stock		8,500
	Dividend received from foreign subsidiary: €6,250 × $1.36 exchange rate		

	December 31, 20X1		
(5)	Investment in German Company Stock	16,250	
	Income from Subsidiary		16,250
	Equity in net income of German Co.: €12,500 × $1.30 average exchange rate		

(6)	Investment in German Company Stock	11,000	
	Other Comprehensive Income—Translation Adjustment		11,000
	Parent's share of change in translation adjustment from translation of subsidiary's accounts: $11,000 × 1.00		

If some time passed between the declaration and payment of dividends, the parent company would record dividends receivable from the foreign subsidiary on the declaration date. This account would be denominated in a foreign currency and would be adjusted to its current exchange rate on the balance sheet date and on the payment date, just like any other account denominated in a foreign currency. Any foreign transaction gain or loss resulting from the adjustment procedure would be included in the parent's income for the period.

The Differential

The allocation and amortization of the excess of cost over book value require special attention in the translation of a foreign entity's financial statements. The differential does not exist on the foreign subsidiary's books; it is part of the parent's investment account. However, the translated book value of the foreign subsidiary is a major component of the investment account on the parent's books and is directly related to a foreign-based asset. **FASB 52 (ASC 830)** requires that the allocation and amortization of the difference between the investment cost and its book value be made in terms of the functional currency of the foreign subsidiary and that these amounts then be translated at the appropriate exchange rates on the worksheet balance sheet date. The periodic amortization affects the income statement and is therefore measured at the average exchange rate used to translate other income statement accounts. On the other hand, the remaining unamortized balance of the differential is reported in the balance sheet and is translated at the current exchange rate used for balance sheet accounts. The effect of this difference in rates is shown in the parent company's translation adjustment as a revision of part of the parent's original investment in the subsidiary.

Peerless Products amortizes the patent over a five-year period. The patent amortization follows.

	European Euros	Translation Rate	U.S. Dollars
Income Statement			
Differential at beginning of year	€2,500	1.20	$3,000
Amortization this period (€5,000/5 years)	(500)	1.30	(650)
Remaining balances	€2,000		$2,350
Balance Sheet			
Remaining balance on 12/31/X1 translated at year-end exchange rates	€2,000	1.40	$2,800
Difference to other comprehensive income—translation adjustment (credit)			$ 450

Another way to view the differential adjustment of $450 is that it adjusts the parent company's differential, which is currently part of the investment account, to the amount necessary to prepare the consolidated balance sheet. In this example, if no differential adjustment is made, the patent on the consolidated balance sheet would be $2,350, which is incorrect. Because the balance sheet must report the patent translated at the end-of-period exchange rate of $2,800, the differential adjustment is made to properly report the amount in the consolidated balance sheet. Thus, the adjustment may be thought of as an adjustment necessary to obtain the correct amount of the differential to prepare the consolidated balance sheet. Depending on the direction of the changes in the exchange rate, the differential adjustment could be a debit or credit amount. In this case, the differential must be increased from $2,350 to $2,800, necessitating a debit of $450 to the investment account and a corresponding credit to the Other Comprehensive Income—Translation Adjustment account.

Entry (7) recognizes the amortization of the patent for the period. Entry (8) records the portion of the translation adjustment on the increase in the differential for the investment in the foreign subsidiary.

(7)
| Income from Subsidiary | 650 | |
| Investment in German Company Stock | | 650 |

Amortization of patent: $650 = €500 × $1.30 average exchange rate.

(8)
| Investment in German Company Stock | 450 | |
| Other Comprehensive Income—Translation Adjustment | | 450 |

Recognize translation adjustment on increase in differential.

It is important to note that the $450 translation adjustment from the differential is attributed solely to the parent company. Noncontrolling Interest is not assigned any portion of this translation adjustment. This $450 translation adjustment is attributable to the excess of cost paid over the book value of the assets and therefore is added to the differential, which is a component of the investment in the foreign subsidiary, thereby resulting in a debit to the investment account on the parent company's books.

The December 31, 20X1 balance in the Investment in German Company Stock account is $81,550 and the balance in Income from German Company is $15,600, as shown in the following T-accounts. A series of four worksheet entries (explained below) eliminates both accounts in the consolidation process.

	Investment in German Company				Income from German Company	
Acquisition 1/1/X1	63,000					
100% Net Income	16,250				16,250	**100% Net Income**
		8,500	**100% Dividends**			
German Co. Translation	11,000	650	**Excess Value**	650		
Differential Translation	450		**Amortization**			
Balance 12/31/X1	81,550				15,600	**Balance 12/31/X1**
		67,750	**Basic**	16,250		
		2,800	**Excess Reclass**		650	**"Amort. Excess Value"**
		11,000	**OCI**			
	0				0	

Note that the $11,450 Other Comprehensive Income—Translation Adjustment account balance in the parent company's books is composed of its share of the translation adjustment from translating the subsidiary's trial balance ($11,000) plus the parent company's adjustment ($450) due to the differential it paid for the investment.

During the parent company's closing entries process, the following two entries would be included to separately close net income from the subsidiary and the other comprehensive income arising from its investment in the subsidiary.

(9)

Income from Subsidiary	15,600	
Retained Earnings		15,600

To close net income from subsidiary:
$15,600 = $16,250 − $650

(10)

Other Comprehensive Income—Trans. Adjustment	11,450	
Accumulated OCI—Translation Adjustment		11,450

To close other comprehensive income resulting from the investment in the German subsidiary:
$11,450 = $11,000 + $450

Subsequent Consolidation Worksheet

The consolidation worksheet is prepared after the translation process is completed. The process of consolidation is the same as for a domestic subsidiary, except for two major differences: (1) The parent company will record its share of the translation adjustment arising from the translation of the foreign subsidiary's accounts. In this example, the parent owns 100 percent of the subsidiary, but, in cases of a less-than-wholly-owned subsidiary, the noncontrolling interest would be assigned its percentage share of the translation adjustment and (2) as shown previously, the patent amortization for the period is translated at the income statement rate (average for the period), whereas the ending patent balance is translated at the balance sheet rate (current exchange rate). Thus, a translation adjustment must be computed on the differential and assigned as part of the parent company's investment in the foreign subsidiary.

To prepare the elimination entries, we begin by analyzing the book value of the investment in German Company:

Book Value Calculations:

	Peerless 100%	=	Common Stock	+	Retained Earnings
Original book value	60,000		48,000		12,000
+ Net Income	16,250				16,250
− Dividends	(8,500)				(8,500)
Ending book value	67,750		48,000		19,750

This leads to the basic elimination entry:

Basic elimination entry:

Common stock	48,000		←Original amount invested
Retained earnings	12,000		←Beginning balance in retained earnings
Income from German Co.	16,250		←German Company's reported income
Dividends declared		8,500	←100% of German's dividends declared
Investment in German Co.		67,750	←Net book value in investment account

The differential of $3,000 is entirely attributable to the patent; nevertheless, since it arises from the acquisition of a foreign subsidiary, we provide calculations below that illustrate the translation adjustment for the differential:

Excess value (differential) calculation:

	Total Excess	=	Patent
Beginning excess value	3,000		3,000
− Amortization of differential	(650)		(650)
+ Differential translation adjustment	450		450
Ending excess value	2,800		2,800

Amortized excess value reclassification entry:

Operating expense	650		←Amortization of patent
Income from German Co.		650	←Elimination of patent amortization

Excess value (differential) reclassification entry:

Patent	2,800		←Excess value assigned to patent
Investment in German Co.		2,800	←Reclassify excess acquisition price

In addition, we record the other comprehensive income entry illustrated in Chapter 5:

Other Comprehensive Income Entry:

OCI from German Co.	11,000	
Investment in German Co.		11,000

Finally, we include the optional accumulated depreciation elimination entry:

Optional accumulated depreciation elimination entry:

Accumulated depreciation	6,000		← Original depreciation at the time of the acquisition netted against cost
Building and equipment		6,000	

The worksheet is presented in Figure 9–7. The trial balance for German Company is obtained from the translated amounts computed earlier in Figure 9–5. The worksheet entries follow in journal entry form. These entries are *not* made on either company's books; they are only in the worksheet elimination columns.

When the parent company uses the equity method and no intercompany revenue transactions occur, the parent's net income and retained earnings equal the consolidated net income and consolidated retained earnings. This makes it possible to verify the amounts reported on the consolidated financial statements.

Noncontrolling Interest of a Foreign Subsidiary

Most U.S. companies prefer to own 100 percent of their foreign subsidiaries. Doing so provides for more efficient management of the subsidiary and no requirement to prepare separate financial statements of the subsidiary for a noncontrolling interest. If a foreign

FIGURE 9–7 December 31, 20X1, Consolidation Worksheet, Prepared after Translation of Foreign Statements

	Peerless Products	German Company	Elimination Entries DR	Elimination Entries CR	Consolidated
Income Statement					
Sales	400,000	65,000			465,000
Less: COGS	(170,000)	(29,250)			(199,250)
Less: Operating Expenses	(90,000)	(18,850)	650		(109,500)
Less: Foreign Currency Transaction Loss		(650)			(650)
Income from German Co.	15,600		16,250	650	0
Net Income	**155,600**	**16,250**	**16,900**	**650**	**155,600**
Statement of Retained Earnings					
Beginning Balance	300,000	12,000	12,000		300,000
Net Income	**155,600**	**16,250**	16,900	650	155,600
Less: Dividends Declared	(60,000)	(8,500)		8,500	(60,000)
Ending Balance	**395,600**	**19,750**	**28,900**	**9,150**	**395,600**
Balance Sheet					
Cash	425,500	15,050			440,550
Dollars Held by German Company		4,200			4,200
Receivables	75,000	14,700			89,700
Inventory	100,000	7,000			107,000
Investment in German Company Stock	81,550			67,750	0
				2,800	
				11,000	
Land	175,000				175,000
Patent			2,800		2,800
Plant & Equipment	800,000	70,000		6,000	864,000
Less: Accumulated Depreciation	(450,000)	(10,500)	6,000		(454,500)
Total Assets	**1,207,050**	**100,450**	**8,800**	**87,550**	**1,228,750**
Accounts Payable	100,000	4,200			104,200
Bonds Payable	200,000	17,500			217,500
Common Stock	500,000	48,000	48,000		500,000
Retained Earnings	**395,600**	**19,750**	28,900	9,150	395,600
Accumulated Other Comprehensive Income	11,450	11,000	**11,000**	**0**	11,450
Total Liabilities & Equity	**1,207,050**	**100,450**	**87,900**	**9,150**	**1,228,750**
Other Comprehensive Income					
Accumulated Other Comprehensive Income, 1/1/X1	0	0			0
Other Comprehensive Income Translation Adjustment	11,450	11,000	11,000		11,450
Accumulated Other Comprehensive Income, 12/31/X1	**11,450**	**11,000**	**11,000**	**0**	**11,450**

subsidiary was less-than-wholly-owned, however, the noncontrolling interest would be computed and accounted for just as it was in Chapter 3 of this text. The only difference is the allocation of the translation adjustment that arises from the translation of the foreign subsidiary's trial balance accounts. Thus, for example, if Peerless had an 80 percent interest in German Company and another investor owned a 20 percent noncontrolling interest, the noncontrolling interest would be allocated its percentage share of the translation adjustment through the elimination entry process. The noncontrolling interest on the consolidated balance sheet at year-end would include its share of the accumulated other comprehensive income from the translation adjustment, as follows:

Common stock ($48,000 × 0.20)		$ 9,600
Retained earnings:		
Beginning retained earnings ($12,000 × 0.20)	$2,400	
Add: Net income ($16,250 × 0.20)	3,250	
Less: Dividends ($8,500 × 0.20)	(1,700)	
Total retained earnings		3,950
Accumulated other comprehensive income—		
translation adjustment ($11,000 × 0.20)		2,200
Total noncontrolling interest		$15,750

REMEASUREMENT OF THE BOOKS OF RECORD INTO THE FUNCTIONAL CURRENCY

LO6

Make calculations and remeasure financial statements of a foreign subsidiary.

A second method of restating foreign affiliates' financial statements in U.S. dollars is remeasurement. Although remeasurement is not as commonly used as translation, some situations in which the functional currency of the foreign affiliate is not its local currency exist. Remeasurement is similar to translation in that its goal is to obtain equivalent U.S. dollar values for the foreign affiliate's accounts so they may be combined or consolidated with the U.S. company's statements. The exchange rates used for remeasurement, however, are different from those used for translation, resulting in different dollar values for the foreign affiliate's accounts.

The FASB provided examples of several situations requiring remeasurement:[10]

1. A foreign sales branch or subsidiary of a U.S. manufacturer that primarily takes orders from foreign customers for U.S.-manufactured goods, that bills and collects from foreign customers, and that might have a warehouse to provide for timely delivery of the product to those foreign customers. In substance, this foreign operation may be the same as the export sales department of a U.S. manufacturer.

2. A foreign division, branch, or subsidiary that primarily manufactures a subassembly shipped to a U.S. plant for inclusion in a product that is sold to customers located in the United States or in different parts of the world.

3. A foreign shipping subsidiary that primarily transports ore from a U.S. company's foreign mines to the United States for processing in a U.S. company's smelting plants.

4. A foreign subsidiary that is primarily a conduit for euro borrowings to finance operations in the United States.

In most cases, the foreign affiliate may be thought of as a direct production or sales arm of the U.S. company, but it uses the local currency to record and report its operations. In addition, foreign entities located in highly inflationary economies, defined as economies having a cumulative three-year inflation rate exceeding 100 percent, must use the dollar as their functional currency, and their statements are remeasured into U.S. dollars. Many South American countries have experienced hyperinflation, with some countries having annual inflation rates in excess of 100 percent. If the foreign affiliate uses the U.S. dollar as both its functional and its reporting currency, no remeasurement is necessary because its operations are already reported in U.S. dollars.

The remeasurement process should produce the same end result as if the foreign entity's transactions had been initially recorded in dollars. For this reason, certain transactions

---

[10] These examples were provided in the exposure draft of **FASB 52 (ASC 830)** but were not included in its final draft. The FASB did not want the examples to limit remeasurement to those cases in which the U.S. dollar is the functional currency.

FIGURE 9–8
Accounts to Be
Remeasured Using
Historical Exchange
Rates
Source: *FASB 52,*
para. 48.

Examples of Balance Sheet Nonmonetary Items
Marketable securities:
  Equity securities
  Debt securities not intended to be held until maturity
Inventories
Prepaid expenses such as insurance, advertising, and rent
Property, plant, and equipment
Accumulated depreciation on property, plant, and equipment
Patents, trademarks, licenses, and formulas
Goodwill
Other intangible assets
Deferred charges and credits, except deferred income taxes and policy acquisition costs for
  life insurance companies
Deferred income
Common stock
Preferred stock carried at issuance price
Examples of Revenue and Expenses Related to Nonmonetary Items
  Cost of goods sold
  Depreciation of property, plant, and equipment
  Amortization of intangible items such as patents, licenses, etc.
  Amortization of deferred charges or credits, except deferred income taxes and policy
    acquisition costs for life insurance companies

and account balances are restated to their U.S. dollar equivalents using a historical exchange rate, the spot exchange rate at the time the transaction originally occurred. The remeasurement process divides the balance sheet into monetary and nonmonetary accounts. Monetary assets and liabilities such as cash, short-term or long-term receivables, and short-term or long-term payables have their amounts fixed in terms of the units of currency. These accounts are subject to gains or losses from changes in exchange rates. Nonmonetary assets are accounts such as inventories and plant and equipment, which are not fixed in relation to monetary units.

The monetary accounts are remeasured using the current exchange rate. The appropriate historical exchange rate is used to remeasure nonmonetary balance sheet account balances and related revenue, expense, gain, and loss account balances. A list of the accounts to be remeasured with the appropriate historical exchange rate is provided in Figure 9–8.[11]

Because of the variety of rates used to remeasure the foreign currency trial balance, the debits and credits of the U.S. dollar–equivalent trial balance will probably not be equal. In this case, the balancing item is a ***remeasurement gain or loss,*** which is included in the period's income statement.

Statement Presentation of Remeasurement Gain or Loss

Any exchange gain or loss arising from the remeasurement process is included in the current period income statement, usually under "Other Income." Various account titles are used, such as Foreign Exchange Gain (Loss), Currency Gain (Loss), Exchange Gain (Loss), or Remeasurement Gain (Loss). The title Remeasurement Gain (Loss) is used here because it is most descriptive of the source of the item. The remeasurement gain or loss is included in the period's income because if the transactions had originally been recorded in U.S. dollars, the exchange gains and losses would have been recognized this period as part of the adjustments required for valuation of foreign transactions denominated in a foreign currency. Upon completion of the remeasurement process, the foreign entity's financial statements are presented as they would have been had the U.S. dollar been used to record the transactions in the local currency as they occurred.

[11] *FASB 52,* para. 48 (ASC 830-10-45-18).

FIGURE 9–9
December 31, 20X1, Remeasurement of the Foreign Subsidiary's Trial Balance
U.S. Dollar Is the Functional Currency

Item	Balance, €	Exchange Rate	Balance, $
Cash	10,750	1.40	15,050
Foreign Currency Units	3,000	1.40	4,200
Receivables	10,500	1.40	14,700
Inventory	5,000	1.38	6,900
Plant and Equipment	50,000	1.20	60,000
Cost of Goods Sold	22,500	(a)	28,100
Operating Expenses	14,500	(b)	18,600
Foreign Currency Transaction Loss	500	1.30	650
Dividends Paid	6,250	1.36	8,500
Total Debits	123,000		156,700
Accumulated Depreciation	7,500	1.20	9,000
Accounts Payable	3,000	1.40	4,200
Bonds Payable	12,500	1.40	17,500
Common Stock	40,000	1.20	48,000
Retained Earnings	10,000	(c)	12,000
Sales	50,000	1.30	65,000
Total	123,000		155,700
Remeasurement Gain			1,000
Total Credits			156,700

	In Euros	Exchange Rate	In Dollars
(a) Cost of Goods Sold:			
Beginning Inventory	7,500	1.20	9,000
Purchases	20,000	1.30	26,000
Goods Available	27,500		35,000
Less: Ending Inventory	(5,000)	1.38	(6,900)
Cost of Goods Sold	22,500		28,100
(b) Operating Expenses:			
Cash Expenses	12,000	1.30	15,600
Depreciation Expense	2,500	1.20	3,000
	14,500		18,600

(c) Carry forward from January 1, 20X1, worksheet.

Illustration of Remeasurement of a Foreign Subsidiary

German Company again is used, this time to present remeasurement of financial statements. The only difference between the previous example of translation and the current example is that the foreign subsidiary's functional currency is now assumed to be the U.S. dollar rather than the European euro. German Company maintains its books and records in euros to provide required reports to the German government. Because the dollar is the functional currency, German Company's financial statements will be remeasured into dollars. Once the foreign affiliate's statements are remeasured, the consolidation process is the same as for a domestic subsidiary.

Remeasurement of Foreign Subsidiary's Postacquisition Trial Balance

The subsidiary's trial balance must be remeasured from the European euro into the U.S. dollar as shown in Figure 9–9. The current exchange rate is used to remeasure the monetary accounts, and the appropriate historical exchange rates are used for each of the nonmonetary accounts.

Three items need special attention. First, the plant and equipment are remeasured using the historical rate on the date the parent company acquired the foreign subsidiary. If the subsidiary purchases any additional plant or equipment after the parent has acquired the subsidiary's stock, the additional plant or equipment will be remeasured using the exchange rate on the date of the purchase of the additional plant. The same cautionary note is applicable for the other nonmonetary items. It is important to maintain a record of the subsidiary's acquisition or disposition of nonmonetary assets and equities after the foreign subsidiary's stock is acquired to ensure use of the proper exchange rates to remeasure these items. Recall that the business combination was accounted for as a purchase; therefore, the appropriate historical rate is the spot rate on the date the parent purchased the foreign subsidiary's stock. If the combination had been accounted for as a pooling, the appropriate historical spot rates would be the rates on the dates the subsidiary originally issued the stock and acquired the nonmonetary assets, not the later date on which the parent company acquired the subsidiary's stock.

Second, the cost of goods sold consists of transactions that occurred at various exchange rates. The beginning inventory was acquired when the rate was $1.20 = €1. Inventory purchases were made at different times during the year, so the average rate of $1.30 was used for the remeasurement exchange rate. For purposes of illustration, the example assumes that ending inventory was acquired when the direct exchange rate was $1.38 = €1 and the FIFO inventory method is used.

Third, the operating expenses are also incurred at different exchange rates. The depreciation expense is remeasured at $1.20 = €1 because it is associated with a nonmonetary account, Plant and Equipment, which is remeasured at the historical exchange rate of $1.20 = €1. The average exchange rate is used to remeasure the remaining operating expenses because they are assumed to be incurred evenly throughout the period.

The remeasurement gain is recognized in this period's income statement. The remeasurement exchange gain is a balancing item to make total debits and total credits equal, but it can be proved by analyzing changes in the monetary items during the period.

Proof of Remeasurement Exchange Gain

Figure 9–10 provides a proof of this balancing item. The analysis primarily involves the monetary items because they are remeasured from the exchange rate at the beginning of the period, or on the date of the generating transaction to the current exchange rate at the end of the period. The increase or decrease in net monetary assets resulting from remeasurement is recognized as an exchange gain or loss in the current period.

Schedule 1 presents the net monetary positions at the beginning and end of the year. The €11,250 change in the net monetary position is the change from a net liability opening balance of €2,500 to a net monetary asset position ending balance of €8,750. Schedule 2 presents the detailed effects of exchange rate changes on the foreign entity's net monetary position during this period. The beginning net monetary position is included using the exchange rate at the beginning of the year. Then all increases and decreases in the net monetary accounts are added or deducted using the exchange rates at the time the transactions occurred. Other sources of increases or decreases in the monetary accounts would include financing and investing transactions such as purchases of plant or equipment, issuance of long-term debt, or selling stock. The computed net monetary position at the end of the year using the transaction date exchange rates ($11,250) is then compared with the year-end net monetary position using the year-end exchange rate ($12,250). Because of the increasing exchange rate, the net asset position at the year-end was higher when remeasured using the December 31, 20X1, exchange rate of $1.40. This means that the U.S. dollar–equivalent value of the net monetary assets at the end of the year increased from $11,250 to $12,250 and that a remeasurement gain of $1,000 should be recognized. If the U.S. dollar–equivalent value of the December 31, 20X1, exposed net monetary assets position, as remeasured with the December 31 exchange rate, would have been lower than the computed value of $11,250, then a remeasurement loss would have been recognized for the reduction in the U.S. dollar–equivalent value of the net assets.

FIGURE 9–10
Proof of the Remeasurement Exchange Gain for the Year Ended December 31, 20X1
Functional Currency Is the U.S. Dollar

Schedule 1
Statement of Net Monetary Positions

	End of Year	Beginning of Year
Monetary assets:		
Cash	€10,750	€ 2,500
Foreign currency units	3,000	–0–
Receivables	10,500	10,000
Total	€24,250	€12,500
Less: Monetary equities:		
Accounts payable	€ 3,000	€ 2,500
Bonds payable	12,500	12,500
Total	€15,500	€15,000
Net monetary liabilities		€ (2,500)
Net monetary assets	€ 8,750	
Increase in net monetary assets during year	€11,250	

Schedule 2
Analysis of Changes in Monetary Accounts

	€	Exchange Rate	U.S. $
Exposed net monetary liability position, 1/1	(2,500)	1.20	(3,000)
Adjustments for changes in net monetary position during year:			
Increases:			
From operations:			
Sales	50,000	1.30	65,000
From other sources	–0–		–0–
Decreases:			
From operations:			
Purchases	(20,000)	1.30	(26,000)
Cash expenses	(12,000)	1.30	(15,600)
Foreign currency transaction loss	(500)	1.30	(650)
From dividends	(6,250)	1.36	(8,500)
From other uses	–0–		–0–
Net monetary position prior to remeasurement at year-end rates			11,250
Exposed net monetary asset position, 12/31	8,750	1.40	12,250
Remeasurement gain			1,000

Prepare consolidated financial statements including a foreign subsidiary after remeasurement.

Advanced
StudyGuide
.com

Remeasurement Case: Subsequent Consolidation Worksheet

Figure 9–11 presents the consolidation worksheet for the remeasurement case. The accounts used for German Company in the consolidation worksheet come from the remeasured accounts computed in Figure 9–9. The remeasurement gain is included in the German subsidiary's trial balance because the source of this account is the remeasurement of the subsidiary's accounts.

In the consolidated income statement, the Remeasurement Gain account is usually offset against the foreign currency transaction loss account, generating, in this example, a net gain of $350 ($1,000 − $650). This gain is reported in the other income section of the income statement. The remaining consolidation process is identical to the process for a domestic subsidiary. Note that the $2,400 patent shown on the consolidated balance sheet is the unamortized portion of the initial $3,000 amount ($2,400 = $3,000 − $600). No special adjustments are required for the patent when using the remeasurement process.

FIGURE 9–11   **December 31, 20X1, Consolidation Worksheet, Prepared after Remeasurement of Foreign Statements**

	Peerless Products	German Company	Elimination Entries DR	Elimination Entries CR	Consolidated
Income Statement					
Sales	400,000	65,000			465,000
Less: COGS	(170,000)	(28,100)			(198,100)
Less: Operating Expenses	(90,000)	(18,600)	600		(109,200)
Less: Foreign Currency Transaction Loss		(650)			(650)
Remeasurement Gain		1,000			1,000
Income from German Co.	18,050		18,650	600	0
Net Income	**158,050**	**18,650**	**19,250**	**600**	**158,050**
Statement of Retained Earnings					
Beginning Balance	300,000	12,000	12,000		300,000
Net Income	**158,050**	**18,650**	19,250	600	**158,050**
Less: Dividends Declared	(60,000)	(8,500)		8,500	(60,000)
Ending Balance	**398,050**	**22,150**	**31,250**	**9,100**	**398,050**
Balance Sheet					
Cash	425,500	15,050			440,550
Dollars Held by German Company		4,200			4,200
Receivables	75,000	14,700			89,700
Inventory	100,000	6,900			106,900
Investment in German Company Stock	72,550			70,150	0
				2,400	
Land	175,000				175,000
Patent			2,400		2,400
Plant & Equipment	800,000	60,000		6,000	854,000
Less: Accumulated Depreciation	(450,000)	(9,000)	6,000		(453,000)
Total Assets	**1,198,050**	**91,850**	**8,400**	**78,550**	**1,219,750**
Accounts Payable	100,000	4,200			104,200
Bonds Payable	200,000	17,500			217,500
Common Stock	500,000	48,000	48,000		500,000
Retained Earnings	**398,050**	**22,150**	31,250	9,100	**398,050**
Total Liabilities & Equity	**1,198,050**	**91,850**	**79,250**	**9,100**	**1,219,750**

To prepare the elimination entries, we begin by analyzing the book value of the investment in German Company:

Book Value Calculations:

	Peerless 100%	=	Common Stock	+	Retained Earnings
Original book value	**60,000**		**48,000**		12,000
+ Net Income	18,650				**18,650**
− Dividends	(8,500)				(8,500)
Ending book value	70,150		48,000		**22,150**

This leads to the basic elimination entry:

Basic elimination entry:

Common stock	48,000		←Original amount invested
Retained earnings	12,000		←Beginning balance in retained earnings
Income from German Co.	18,650		←German Company's reported income
Dividends declared		8,500	←100% of German's dividends declared
Investment in German Co.		70,150	←Net book value in investment account

The differential is entirely attributable to the patent, $3,000; nevertheless, since it arises from the acquisition of a foreign subsidiary, we provide calculations below that illustrate the translation adjustment for the differential (amortized over a five year period):

Excess value (differential) calculations:

	Total Excess	=	Patent
Beginning excess value	3,000		3,000
− Amortization of differential ($3,000/5 years)	600		600
Ending excess value	2,400		2,400

Amortized excess value reclassification entry:

Operating expense	600	←Amortization of patent
Income from German Co.	600	←Elimination of patent amortization

Excess value (differential) reclassification entry:

Patent	2,400	←Excess value assigned to patent
Investment in German Co.	2,400	←Reclassify excess acquisition price

Finally, we include the optional accumulated depreciation elimination entry:

Optional accumulated depreciation elimination entry:

Accumulated depreciation	6,000	← Original depreciation at the time of
Building and equipment	6,000	the acquisition netted against cost

A comparison of Figures 9–7 and 9–11 shows that the foreign subsidiary's reported income differs between translation and remeasurement. The primary reason that the subsidiary's reported income is approximately 15 percent higher when the dollar is the functional currency ($18,650 versus $16,250 under translation) is that the U.S. dollar weakened against the European euro during the year. This results in a remeasurement gain for the subsidiary because it was transacting in the stronger currency (the euro) during the period. Furthermore, the subsidiary's cost of goods sold and operating expenses also are remeasured at a lower exchange rate, resulting in a higher income.

The following T-accounts illustrate the calculation of the ending balances for Peerless' Investment in German Company and Income from German Company accounts and how the worksheet entries eliminate their balances:

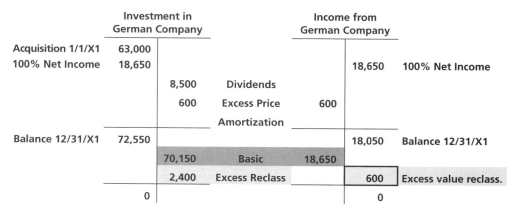

Figure 9–12's Consolidated Statement of Changes in Stockholder's Equity shows how the income statement and other comprehensive income accounts flow to the balance sheet equity ending balances.

FIGURE 9–12 **Consolidated Statement of Changes in Stockholders' Equity**

	Total	Comprehensive Income	Retained Earnings	Accumulated Other Comprehensive Income	Capital Stock
Beginning Balance	$800,000		$300,000	$ –0–	$500,000
Comprehensive Income:					
Net Income	155,600	$155,600	155,600		
Other Comprehensive Income:					
Foreign Currency Translation Adjustment	11,450	11,450		11,450	
Comprehensive Income		$167,050			
Dividends Declared on Common Stock	(60,000)		(60,000)		
Ending Balance	$907,050		$395,600	$11,450	$500,000

PEERLESS PRODUCTS AND SUBSIDIARY
Consolidated Statement of Changes in Equity
Year Ended December 31, 20X1

FIGURE 9–13 **Summary of the Translation and Remeasurement Processes**

Item	Translation Process	Remeasurement Process
Foreign entity's functional currency	Local currency unit	U.S. dollar
Method used	Current rate method	Monetary-nonmonetary method
Income statement accounts:		
Revenue	Weighted-average exchange rate	Weighted-average exchange rate, except revenue related to nonmonetary items (historical exchange rate)
Expenses	Weighted-average exchange rate	Weighted-average exchange rate, except costs related to nonmonetary items (historical exchange rate)
Balance sheet accounts:		
Monetary accounts	Current exchange rate	Current exchange rate
Nonmonetary accounts	Current exchange rate	Historical exchange rate
Stockholders' equity capital accounts	Historical exchange rate	Historical exchange rate
Retained earnings	Prior-period balance plus income less dividends	Prior-period balance plus income less dividends
Exchange rate adjustments arising in process	Translation adjustment accumulated in stockholders' equity	Remeasurement gain or loss included in period's income statement

Summary of Translation versus Remeasurement

When the functional currency is the dollar, the nonmonetary items on the balance sheet are remeasured using historical exchange rates. In this example, the direct exchange rate has increased during the period; therefore, the nonmonetary accounts are lower when remeasured than when translated. A summary of the differences between the translation and remeasurement methods is presented in Figure 9–13.

ADDITIONAL CONSIDERATIONS IN ACCOUNTING FOR FOREIGN OPERATIONS AND ENTITIES

LO8

Understand other issues related to foreign operations including hedging of a net investment in a foreign subsidiary.

This section covers special topics in accounting for multinational enterprises. Although many of these additional considerations are very technical, study of this section will complement your understanding of the many issues of accounting for foreign entities. For example, Figure 9–14 illustrates the two-statement approach to display comprehensive income.

FIGURE 9–14
Two-Statement
Approach to Display
Comprehensive Income

PEERLESS PRODUCTS AND SUBSIDIARY	
Consolidated Statement of Income	
Year Ended December 31, 20X1	
Sales	$465,000
Cost of Goods Sold	(199,250)
Gross Profit	265,750
Operating Expenses	(109,500)
Foreign Currency Transaction Loss	(650)
Consolidated Net Income to Controlling Interest	$155,600

PEERLESS PRODUCTS AND SUBSIDIARY	
Consolidated Statement of Comprehensive Income	
Year Ended December 31, 20X1	
Consolidated Net Income to Controlling Interest	$155,600
Other Comprehensive Income: Foreign Currency Translation Adjustment	$ 11,450
Comprehensive Income to Controlling Interest	$167,050

FOREIGN INVESTMENTS AND UNCONSOLIDATED SUBSIDIARIES

Most companies consolidate their foreign subsidiaries in conformity with **FASB Statement No. 94 (ASC 810 and 840),** "Consolidation of All Majority-Owned Subsidiaries" (FASB 94, ASC 810 and 840). In some cases these operations are not consolidated because of criteria that apply to foreign subsidiaries. Generally, a parent company consolidates a foreign subsidiary, except when one of the following conditions becomes so severe that the U.S. company owning a foreign company may not be able to exercise the necessary level of economic control over the foreign subsidiary's resources and financial operations to warrant consolidation:

1. Restrictions on foreign exchange in the foreign country.
2. Restrictions on transfers of property in the foreign country.
3. Other governmentally imposed uncertainties.

An unconsolidated foreign subsidiary is reported as an investment on the U.S. parent company's balance sheet. The U.S. investor company must use the equity method if it has the ability to exercise "significant influence" over the investee's financial and operating policies. If the equity method cannot be applied, the cost method is used to account for the foreign investment, recognizing income only as dividends are received.

When the equity method is used for an unconsolidated foreign subsidiary, the investee's financial statements are either remeasured or translated, depending on the determination of the functional currency. If remeasurement is used, the foreign entity's statements are remeasured in dollars and the investor records its percentage of the investee's income and makes necessary amortizations or impairments of any differential. A shortcut approach is available for translation: Multiply the foreign affiliate's net income measured in foreign currency units by the average exchange rate during the period and then recognize the parent company's percentage share of the translated net income. In addition, the investor must recognize its share of the translation adjustment arising from the translation of the foreign entity's financial statements. The investor's share of the translation adjustment from its foreign investees is reported on the investor's balance sheet as a separate component of stockholders' equity and as an adjustment of the carrying value of the investment account. The entries on the investor's books are the same under the equity method whether the subsidiary is consolidated or reported as an unconsolidated investment.

Liquidation of a Foreign Investment

The translation adjustment account is directly related to a company's investment in a foreign entity. If the investor sells a substantial portion of its stock investment,

FASB Interpretation No. 37 (ASC 830), "Accounting for Translation Adjustments upon Sale of Part of an Investment in a Foreign Entity" (FIN 37, ASC 830), requires that the pro rata portion of the accumulated translation adjustment account attributable to that investment be included in computing the gain or loss on the disposition of the investment. For example, if the parent company sold off 30 percent of its investment in a foreign subsidiary, 30 percent of the related cumulative translation adjustment would be removed from the translation adjustment account and included in determining the gain or loss on the disposition of the foreign investment.

HEDGE OF A NET INVESTMENT IN A FOREIGN SUBSIDIARY

FASB 133 (ASC 815) permits hedging of a net investment in foreign subsidiaries. For example, Peerless has a net investment of 50,000 in its German subsidiary for which it paid $66,000. Peerless could decide to hedge all, some, or none of this investment by accepting a liability in euros. Peerless could hedge its net asset investment by contracting for a forward exchange contract to sell euros, or the company could incur a euro-based liability. **FASB 133 (ASC 815)** states that the gain or loss on the effective portion of a hedge of a net investment is taken to other comprehensive income as part of the translation adjustment. However, the amount of offset to comprehensive income is limited to the translation adjustment for the net investment. For example, if the forward exchange rate is used to measure effectiveness, the amount of offset is limited to the change in spot rates during the period. Any excess on the ineffective portion of the hedge must be recognized currently in earnings.

For example, on January 1, 20X1, Peerless decides to hedge the portion of its investment that it just made in German Company that is related to the book value of German Company's net assets. Peerless is unsure whether the direct exchange rate for euros will increase or decrease for the year and wishes to hedge its net asset investment. On January 1, 20X1, Peerless' 100 percent ownership share of German Company's net assets is equal to €50,000 (€40,000 capital stock plus €10,000 retained earnings). Peerless borrows €50,000 at a 5 percent rate of interest to hedge its equity investment in German Company, and the principal and interest are due and payable on January 1, 20X2.

The entries on Peerless' books to account for this hedge of a net investment follow:

January 1, 20X1

(11)	Cash	60,000	
	Loan Payable (€)		60,000

  Borrow a euro-denominated loan to hedge net investment in German subsidiary:
  $60,000 = €50,000 × $1.20 spot rate

December 31, 20X1

(12)	Other Comprehensive Income	10,000	
	Loan Payable (€)		10,000

  Revalue foreign currency–denominated payable to end-of-period spot rate:
  $10,000 = €50,000 × ($1.40 − $1.20)

(13)	Interest Expense	3,250	
	Foreign Currency Transaction Loss	250	
	Interest Payable (€)		3,500

  Accrue interest expense and payable on euro loan:
  $3,250 = €50,000 × 0.05 interest × $1.30 average exchange rate
  $3,500 = €50,000 × 0.05 interest × $1.40 ending spot rate

(14)	Accumulated OCI—Translation Adjustment	10,000	
	Profit and Loss Summary (or Retained Earnings)	250	
	Foreign Currency Transaction Loss		250
	Other Comprehensive Income		10,000

  Close nominal accounts related to hedge of net investment in
  foreign subsidiary.

Then, when the principal and interest are paid on January 1, 20X2, Peerless makes the following entry:

	January 1, 20X2		
(15)	Interest Payable (€)	3,500	
	Loan Payable (€)	70,000	
	Cash		73,500

Pay principal and interest due on euro-denominated hedge:
$70,000 = $60,000 + $10,000

During 20X1, Peerless hedged a portion of its net asset investment in the foreign subsidiary. The dollar weakened against the euro (the direct exchange rate increased) and Peerless recognized a gain on a net asset investment in euros and a loss on a liability payable in euros. Without this hedge of the net investment, Peerless would have reported a $11,450 credit balance in the cumulative translation portion of accumulated other comprehensive income ($11,450 = $11,000 + $450 differential adjustment). With the hedge of its net investment, Peerless will report just $1,450 ($11,450 − $10,000 effect of hedge) as its change in the cumulative translation adjustment for 20X1. Thus, Peerless has balanced a portion of its net exposure on its January 1, 20X1, net asset investment in German Company.

Note also that the amount of the offset to other comprehensive income is limited to the effective portion of the hedge based on the revaluation of the net assets. Any excess, in this case the $250 loss on the revaluation of the interest payable in entry (14), is taken directly to current earnings on the income statement.

DISCLOSURE REQUIREMENTS

Peerless *Products*
Corporation

FASB 52 (ASC 830) requires the aggregate foreign transaction gain or loss included in income to be separately disclosed in the income statement or in an accompanying note. This includes gains or losses recognized from foreign currency transactions, forward exchange contracts, and any remeasurement gain or loss. If not disclosed as a one-line item on the income statement, this disclosure is usually a one-sentence footnote summarizing the company's foreign operations.

Under the translation method, the periodic change in the translation adjustment is reported as an element of other comprehensive income, as required by **FASB 130 (ASC 220).** Figure 9–14 presents the two-statement approach to displaying comprehensive income. The consolidated statement of comprehensive income presents the detail of the parent's other comprehensive income of $11,450. Figure 9–12 presents the statement of changes in equity that reconciles all of the elements of stockholders' equity. The balance sheet would then display the capital stock, retained earnings, and accumulated other comprehensive income in the stockholders' equity section. In addition, **FASB 52 (ASC 830)** requires footnote disclosure of exchange rate changes that occur after the balance sheet date and their effect on unsettled foreign currency transactions, if significant.

Statement of Cash Flows

The statement of cash flows is a link between two balance sheets. Individual companies have some latitude and flexibility in preparing the statement of cash flows. A general rule is that accounts reported in the statement of cash flows should be restated in U.S. dollars using the same rates as used for balance sheet and income statement purposes. Because the average exchange rate is used in the income statement and the ending spot exchange rate (current rate) is used in the balance sheet, a balancing item for the differences in exchange rates appears in the statement of cash flows. This balancing item can be analyzed and traced to the specific accounts that generate the difference, but it does not affect the net change in the cash flow for the period.

Lower-of-Cost-or-Market Inventory Valuation under Remeasurement

The application of the lower-of-cost-or-market rule to inventories requires special treatment when the recording currency is not the entity's functional currency and, therefore, the foreign entity's financial statements must be remeasured into the functional currency. The historical cost of inventories must first be remeasured using historical exchange rates to determine the functional currency historical cost value. Then these remeasured costs are compared with the market value of the inventories translated using the current rate. The final step is to compare the cost and market, now both in the functional currency, and to recognize any appropriate write-downs to market. The comparison is made in functional currency values, not local or recording currency values; therefore, it is possible to have a write-down appear in the functional currency statements but not on the subsidiary's books, or on the subsidiary's books but not in the consolidated statements.

To illustrate the application of the lower-of-cost-or-market method, assume that a German subsidiary acquired €5,000 of inventory when the direct exchange rate was $1.38 = €1. At the end of the year, the direct exchange rate had decreased to $1.20 = €1. The estimated net realizable value of the inventory (ceiling) is €5,500; its replacement cost is €5,000; and the net realizable value less a normal profit margin (floor) is €4,000. The valuation of the inventory is first specified in the local currency unit (euro), and then evaluated after remeasurement into its functional currency, the U.S. dollar, using the end-of-period exchange rate, as follows:

	€	Exchange	U.S. $
Historical cost	€5,000	$1.38	$6,900
Net realizable value (ceiling)	€5,500	$1.20	$6,600
Replacement cost	5,000	1.20	6,000
Net realizable value less normal profit (floor)	4,000	1.20	4,800

The market value of the inventory is €5,000, or $6,000 in U.S. dollars. Note that the subsidiary recorded no write-down because the historical cost of the inventory was the same as market. However, the comparison in functional currency (U.S. dollar) values shows that the U.S. parent requires a $900 write-down to write the inventory down from its functional currency historical cost of $6,900 to its functional currency market value of $6,000.

Intercompany Transactions

A U.S. parent or home office may have many intercompany sales or purchases transactions with its foreign affiliate that create intercompany receivables or payables. The process of translating receivables or payables denominated in a foreign currency was discussed in Chapter 8. For example, assume that a U.S. company has a foreign currency–denominated receivable from its foreign subsidiary. The U.S. company would first revalue the foreign currency–denominated receivable to its U.S. dollar equivalent value as of the date of the financial statements. After the foreign affiliate's statements have been translated or remeasured, depending on the foreign affiliate's functional currency, the intercompany payable and receivable should be at the same U.S. dollar value and can be eliminated.

FASB 52 (ASC 830) provides an exception when the intercompany foreign currency transactions will not be settled within the foreseeable future. These intercompany transactions may be considered part of the net investment in the foreign entity. The translation adjustments on these long-term receivables or payables are deferred and accumulated as part of the cumulative translation account. For example, a U.S. parent company may loan its German subsidiary $10,000 for which the parent does not expect repayment for the foreseeable future. Under the translation method, the dollar-denominated loan payable account of the subsidiary would first be adjusted for the effects of any changes in exchange rates during the period. Any exchange gain or loss adjustment relating to this intercompany note should be classified as part of the cumulative translation adjustment account in stockholders' equity, not in the subsidiary's net income for the period. The same result would occur whether the long-term intercompany financing was denominated in U.S. dollars or the local currency—in our example, the euro. Thus, where financing is regarded as part of the long-term investment in the foreign entity, any exchange gain or loss adjustments on that financing are accumulated in the cumulative translation adjustment account in stockholders' equity.

A particularly interesting problem arises when unrealized intercompany profits occur from transactions between the parent and foreign subsidiary. The problem is how to eliminate the profit across currencies that are changing in value relative to each other. For example, assume that the parent, Peerless Products Corporation, made a downstream sale of inventory to its German subsidiary. The goods cost the parent $10,000 but were sold to the subsidiary for €10,000 when the exchange rate was $1.30 = €1, resulting in an intercompany profit of $3,000 ($13,000 − $10,000). The goods are still in the subsidiary's inventory at the end of the year when the current exchange rate is $1.40 = €1. The relevant facts are summarized as follows:

	Measured in U.S. Dollars	Measured in European Euros
Initial inventory transfer date ($1.30 = €1):		
Selling price (€10,000 × $1.30)	$13,000	€10,000
Cost to parent	(10,000)	
Intercompany profit	$ 3,000	
Balance sheet date ($1.40 = €1):		
Inventory translation ($14,000 = €10,000 × $1.40)	$14,000	€10,000

There are two issues here:

1. At what amount should the ending inventory be shown on the consolidated balance sheet—the original intercompany transfer price of $13,000 (€10,000 × $1.30), the present equivalent exchange value of $14,000 (€10,000 × $1.40 current exchange rate), or some other amount?
2. What amount should be eliminated for the unrealized intercompany gain—the original intercompany profit of $3,000 or the balance sheet date exchange equivalent of the intercompany profit of $4,000 ($14,000 present exchange value less $10,000 original cost to parent)?

FASB 52 (ASC 830) provides the following guidance to answer these questions:[12]

> The elimination of intra-entity profits that are attributable to sales or other transfers between entities that are consolidated, combined, or accounted for by the equity method in the reporting entity's financial statements shall be based on the exchange rates at the dates of the sales or transfers. The use of reasonable approximations or averages is permitted.

Therefore, for the example, the eliminating entry for the intercompany profit is

Cost of Goods Sold	3,000	
Ending Inventory		3,000

The inventory is shown on the consolidated balance sheet at $11,000, which is a $1,000 increase over the initial cost to the parent company. This increase will result in a corresponding increase in a credit to the translation adjustment component of stockholders' equity. The FASB has stated that changes in exchange rates occurring *after* the date of the intercompany transaction are independent of the initial inventory transfer.

---

[12] *FASB 52,* para. 25 (ASC 830-30-45-10).

Income Taxes

Interperiod tax allocation is required whenever temporary differences exist in the recognition of revenue and expenses for income statement purposes and for tax purposes. Exchange gains and losses from foreign currency transactions require the recognition of a deferred tax if they are included in income but not recognized for tax purposes in the same period.

A deferral is required for the portion of the translation adjustment related to the subsidiary's undistributed earnings that are included in the parent's income. **APB Opinion No. 23 (ASC 740),** "Accounting for Income Taxes—Special Areas" (APB 23, ASC 740), presumes that a temporary difference exists for the undistributed earnings of a subsidiary unless the earnings are indefinitely reinvested in it. Deferred taxes need not be recognized if the undistributed earnings will be indefinitely reinvested in the subsidiary. However, if the parent expects eventually to receive the presently undistributed earnings of a foreign subsidiary, deferred tax recognition is required, and the tax entry recorded by the parent should include a debit to Other Comprehensive Income rather than to additional income tax, as follows:

(16)	Other Comprehensive Income—Translation Adjustment	X,XXX	
	Deferred Taxes Payable		X,XXX

Translation When a Third Currency Is the Functional Currency

There may be a few cases in which the foreign subsidiary maintains its books and records in the local currency unit but has a third currency as its functional currency. For example, assume that our subsidiary, German Company, maintains its records in its local currency, the euro. If the subsidiary conducts many of its business activities in the Swiss franc, management may conclude that the Swiss franc is the subsidiary's functional currency. If the entity's books and records are *not* expressed in its functional currency, the following two-step process must be used:

1. Remeasure the subsidiary's financial statements into the functional currency. In our example, the financial statements expressed in euros would be remeasured into Swiss francs. The remeasurement process would be the same as illustrated earlier in the chapter. The statements would now be expressed in the entity's functional currency, the Swiss franc.

2. The statements expressed in Swiss francs are then translated into U.S. dollars using the translation process illustrated in the chapter.

As indicated, this occurrence is not common in practice but is a consideration for foreign subsidiaries that have very significant business activities in a currency other than the currency of the country in which the subsidiary is physically located. This discussion indicates that it is important first to determine the foreign entity's functional currency before beginning the translation process.

Summary of Key Concepts

The restatement of a foreign affiliate's financial statements in U.S. dollars may be made using the translation or remeasurement method, depending on the foreign entity's functional currency. Most foreign affiliates' statements are translated using the current rate method because the local currency unit is typically the functional currency. If the U.S. dollar is the functional currency, remeasurement is used to convert the foreign entity's statements from the local currency into dollars. The choice of functional currency affects the valuations of the foreign entity's accounts reported on the consolidated financial statements.

Because translation or remeasurement is performed with different exchange rates applied to balance sheet and income statement accounts, a balancing item called a "translation adjustment" or "remeasurement gain or loss" is created in the process. The translation adjustment is proportionally divided between the parent company and the noncontrolling interest. The parent company's share, adjusted for the effects from the differential paid for the investment, is reported as a component of other comprehensive income and then accumulated in the stockholders' equity section of the consolidated balance sheet. The noncontrolling interest's share is a direct adjustment to noncontrolling interest reported in the consolidated balance sheet. The remeasurement gain or loss is reported in the consolidated statement of income.

Key Terms

accumulated other comprehensive income, *454*	functional currency, *450*	remeasurement, *451*
	historical rate, *449*	remeasurement gain or loss, *467*
average rate, *449*	International Financial Reporting Standards (IFRS), *446*	temporal method, *452*
comprehensive income, *454*		translation, *451*
current rate, *449*	other comprehensive income, *454*	translation adjustment, *449*
current rate method, *452*		

Questions

LO1   **Q9-1**   Why is there increasing interest in the adoption of a single set of high-quality accounting standards?

LO1   **Q9-2**   Briefly discuss the International Accounting Standards Board (IASB). What is its mission? What is the composition of the membership of the Board and how long do members serve? Where is the IASB located?

LO1   **Q9-3**   The IASB promulgates International Financial Reporting Standards (IFRS). Briefly describe the standard-setting process used by the IASB.

LO1   **Q9-4**   How widely used are IFRS? Can IFRS be used for listings on U.S. stock exchanges?

LO1   **Q9-5**   What is the attitude toward the possible use of IFRS in the United States?

LO1   **Q9-6**   What potential benefits might be achieved if U.S. firms are allowed to use IFRS?

LO2   **Q9-7**   Define the following terms: (*a*) local currency unit, (*b*) recording currency, and (*c*) reporting currency.

LO2   **Q9-8**   What factors are used to determine a reporting entity's functional currency? Provide at least one example for which a company's local currency may not be its functional currency.

LO3   **Q9-9**   Some accountants are seeking to harmonize international accounting standards. What is meant by the term *harmonize?* How might harmonization result in better financial reporting for a U.S. parent company with many foreign investments?

LO6   **Q9-10**   A Canadian-based subsidiary of a U.S. parent uses the Canadian dollar as its functional currency. Describe the methodology for translating the subsidiary's financial statements into the parent's reporting currency.

LO6   **Q9-11**   A U.S. company has a foreign sales branch located in Spain. The Spanish branch has selected the U.S. dollar for its functional currency. Describe the methodology for remeasuring the branch's financial statements into the U.S. company's reporting currency.

LO5   **Q9-12**   Discuss the accounting treatment and disclosure of translation adjustments. When does the translation adjustment account have a debit balance? When does it have a credit balance?

LO7   **Q9-13**   Where is the remeasurement gain or loss shown in the consolidated financial statements?

LO5   **Q9-14**   When the functional currency is the foreign affiliate's local currency, why are the stockholders' equity accounts translated at historical exchange rates? How is retained earnings computed?

LO5   **Q9-15**   Comment on the following statement: "The use of the current exchange rate method of translating a foreign affiliate's financial statements allows for an assessment of foreign management by the same ratio criteria used to manage the foreign affiliate."

LO5, LO7   **Q9-16**   A U.S. company paid more than book value in acquiring a foreign affiliate. How is this excess reported in the consolidated balance sheet and income statement in subsequent periods when the functional currency is the local currency unit of the foreign affiliate?

LO5

Q9-17 What is the logic behind the parent company's recognizing on its books its share of the translation adjustment arising from the translation of its foreign subsidiary?

LO8

Q9-18 Are all foreign subsidiaries consolidated? Why or why not?

LO8

Q9-19 Describe the accounting for a foreign investment that is not consolidated with the U.S. company.

LO8

Q9-20 Describe the basic problem of eliminating intercompany transactions with a foreign affiliate.

Cases

LO1

C9-1 **Comparison of U.S. GAAP and IFRS**

Research PricewaterhouseCoopers offers a publication on its Web site entitled "IFRS and US GAAP: similarities and differences: September 2010" that provides a topic-based comparison. Access this publication on the Web at http://www.pwc.com/us/en/issues/ifrs-reporting/publications/ifrs-and-us-gaap-similarities-and-differences-september-2010.jhtml. On pages 4–11 of this publication, there is a table of differences between U.S GAAP and IFRS by reporting issue. There is also a reference to the pages in the document where each of these items is explained in more detail. Select any three of the items and read about the nature of the differences. Prepare a short paper approximately 2–3 pages long that defines the nature of the differences and discusses what you have found.

LO1

C9-2 **Structure of the IASB**

Research The IASB Web site can be found at www.ifrs.org. At the top of the page, click on the link "About Us." Briefly describe the structure of the IASB.

LO1

C9-3 **IASB Deliberations**

Research The IASB Web site can be found at www.ifrs.org. Access the Web site and click on the link at the top of the page for Standards development/Work plan for IFRSs. You may also access this page by going directly to http://www.ifrs.org/Current+Projects/IASB+Projects/IASB+Work+Plan.htm. What are three projects currently on the active agenda that are being addressed by the IASB? What is the timetable identified for milestones on each of the projects? What is the status of the Conceptual Framework project?

LO2

C9-4 **Determining a Functional Currency**

Following are descriptions of several independent situations.

Judgment

1. Rockford Company has a subsidiary in Argentina. The subsidiary does not have much debt because of the high interest costs resulting from the average annual inflation rate exceeding 100 percent. Most of its sales and expense transactions are denominated in Argentinian pesos, and the subsidiary attempts to minimize its receivables and payables. Although the subsidiary owns a warehouse, the primary asset is inventory that it receives from Rockford. The Argentinian government requires all companies located in Argentina to provide the central government with a financial report using the Argentinian system of accounts and government-mandated forms for financial statements.

2. JRB International, located in Dallas, Texas, is the world's largest manufacturer of electronic stirrups. The company acquires the raw materials for its products from around the world and begins the assembly process in Dallas. It then sends the partially completed units to its subsidiary in Mexico for assembly completion. Mexico has been able to hold its inflation rate under 100 percent over the last three years. The subsidiary is required to pay its employees and local vendors in Mexican pesos. The parent company provides all financing for the Mexican subsidiary, and the subsidiary sends all of its production back to the warehouse in Dallas, from which it is shipped as orders are received. The subsidiary provides the Mexican government with financial statements.

3. Huskie Inc. maintains a branch office in Great Britain. The branch office is fairly autonomous because it must find its own financing, set its own local marketing policies, and control its own costs. The branch receives weekly shipments from Huskie Inc., which it then conveys to its customers. The pound sterling is used to pay the subsidiary's employees and to pay for the weekly shipments.

4. Hola Company has a foreign subsidiary located in a rural area of Switzerland, right next to the Swiss–French border. The subsidiary hires virtually all its employees from France and makes most of its sales to companies in France. The majority of its cash transactions are maintained in the European euro. However, it is required to pay local property taxes and sales taxes in Swiss francs and to provide annual financial statements to the Swiss government.

Required

For each of these independent cases, determine

a. The foreign entity's reporting currency in which its books and records are maintained.

b. The foreign entity's functional currency.

c. The process to be used to restate the foreign entity's financial statements into the reporting currency of the U.S.-based parent company.

LO4, LO5 **C9-5** **Principles of Consolidating and Translating Foreign Accounts [AICPA Adapted]**

Petie Products Company was incorporated in Wisconsin in 20X0 as a manufacturer of dairy supplies and equipment. Since incorporating, Petie has doubled in size about every three years and is

Understanding now considered one of the leading dairy supply companies in the country.

During January 20X4, Petie established a subsidiary, Cream Ltd., in the emerging nation of Kolay. Petie owns 90 percent of the outstanding capital stock of Cream; Kolay citizens hold the remaining 10 percent of Cream's outstanding capital stock, as Kolay law requires. The investment in Cream, accounted for by Petie using the equity method, represents about 18 percent of Petie's total assets at December 31, 20X7, the close of the accounting period for both companies.

Required

a. What criteria should Petie use in determining whether it would be appropriate to prepare consolidated financial statements with Cream Ltd. for the year ended December 31, 20X7? Explain.

b. Independent of your answer to part *a,* assume it has been appropriate for Petie and Cream to prepare consolidated financial statements for each year, 20X4 through 20X7. Before they can be prepared, the individual account balances in Cream's December 31, 20X7, adjusted trial balance must be translated into dollars. The kola (K) is the subsidiary's functional currency. For each of the following 10 accounts, taken from Cream's adjusted trial balance, specify what exchange rate (e.g., average exchange rate for 20X7, current exchange rate on December 31, 20X7) should be used to translate the account balance into dollars and explain why that rate is appropriate. Number your answers to correspond with these accounts.

(1) Cash in Kolay National Bank.

(2) Trade Accounts Receivable (all from 20X7 revenue).

(3) Supplies Inventory (all purchased during the last quarter of 20X7).

(4) Land purchased in 20X4.

(5) Short-Term Note Payable to Kolay National Bank.

(6) Capital Stock (no par or stated value and all issued in January 20X4).

(7) Retained Earnings, January 1, 20X7.

(8) Sales Revenue.

(9) Depreciation Expense (on buildings).

(10) Salaries Expense.

LO3 **C9-6** **Translating and Remeasuring Financial Statements of Foreign Subsidiaries [AICPA Adapted]**

Wahl Company's 20X5 consolidated financial statements include two wholly owned subsidiaries, Wahl Company of Australia (Wahl A) and Wahl Company of France (Wahl F). Functional curren-

Communication cies are the U.S. dollar for Wahl A and the European euro for Wahl F.

Required

a. What are the objectives of translating a foreign subsidiary's financial statements?

b. How are gains and losses arising from the translation or remeasurement of each subsidiary's financial statements measured and reported in Wahl's consolidated financial statements?

c. **FASB Statement No. 52 (ASC 830)** identifies several economic indicators to be considered both individually and collectively in determining the functional currency for a consolidated subsidiary. List three of these indicators.

d. What exchange rate is used to incorporate each subsidiary's equipment cost, accumulated depreciation, and depreciation expense in Wahl's consolidated financial statements?

LO5

C9-7 **Translation Adjustment and Comprehensive Income**

Analysis

Dundee Company owns 100 percent of a subsidiary located in Ireland. The parent company uses the Euro as the subsidiary's functional currency. At the beginning of the year, the debit balance in Accumulated Other Comprehensive Income—Translation Adjustment account, which was the only item in accumulated other comprehensive income, was $80,000. The subsidiary's translated trial balance at the end of the year is as follows:

	Debit	Credit
Cash	$ 50,000	
Receivables	24,700	
Inventories	60,300	
Property, Plant, and Equipment (net)	328,000	
Cost of Sales	285,000	
Operating Expenses (including depreciation)	140,000	
Dividends	12,000	
Current Payables		$ 16,000
Long-Term Payables		181,000
Capital Stock		100,000
Retained Earnings (1/1 balance)		135,000
Sales		560,000
Accumulated Other Comprehensive Income—Translation Adjustment	92,000	
	$992,000	$992,000

Required

a. Prepare the subsidiary's statement of income, ending in net income, for the year.

b. Prepare the subsidiary's statement of comprehensive income for the year.

c. Prepare a year-end balance sheet for the subsidiary.

d. **FASB 130 (ASC 220)** allows for alternative operating statement displays of the other comprehensive income items. Discuss the major differences between the one-statement format of the Statement of Income and Comprehensive Income versus the two-statement format of the Statement of Income with a separate Statement of Comprehensive Income.

LO5

C9-8 **Changes in the Cumulative Translation Adjustment Account**

The following footnote was abstracted from a recent annual report of Johnson & Johnson Company:

Understanding

Footnote 7: Foreign Currency Translation

For translation of its international currencies, the Company has determined that the local currencies of its international subsidiaries are the functional currencies except those in highly inflationary economies, which are defined as those which have had compound cumulative rates of inflation of 100% or more during the last three years.

In consolidating international subsidiaries, balance sheet currency effects are recorded as a separate component of stockholders' equity. This equity account includes the results of translating all balance sheet assets and liabilities at current exchange rates, except those located in highly inflationary economies, principally Brazil, which are reflected in operating results. These translation adjustments do not exist in terms of functional cash flows; such adjustments are not reported as part of operating results since realization is remote unless the international businesses were sold or liquidated.

An analysis of the changes during 20X3 and 20X2 in the separate component of stockholders' equity for foreign currency translation adjustments follows (with debit amounts in parentheses):

(Dollars in Millions)	20X3	20X2
Balance at beginning of year	$(146)	$ 134
Change in translation adjustments	(192)	(280)
Balance at end of year	$(338)	$(146)

Required

a. What is the main point of the footnote?

b. How is the footnote related to the concepts covered in the chapter?

c. List some possible reasons the company's translation adjustment decreased from a $134 million credit balance at the end of 20X1 to a $338 million debit balance at the end of 20X3.

d. Assume that the translated stockholders' equities of the foreign subsidiaries, other than the cumulative translation adjustment, remained constant from 20X1 through 20X3 at a balance of $500 million. What were the translated balances in the net assets (assets minus liabilities) of the foreign subsidiaries in each of the three years? What factors might cause the changes in the balances of the net assets over the three-year period?

e. How would changes in the local currency unit's exchange rate in the countries in which the company has subsidiaries affect the cumulative translation adjustment?

f. How could you verify the actual causal factors for the changes in the cumulative translation adjustment of Johnson & Johnson Company for the years presented? Be specific!

LO8

C9-9 Pros and Cons of Foreign Investment

Judgment

Many larger U.S. companies have significant investments in foreign operations. For example, McDonald's Corporation, the food service company, obtains 47 percent of its consolidated revenues and 44 percent of its operating income from, and has 45 percent of its invested assets in, non-U.S. locations. Unisys, the information systems company, obtains 51 percent of its consolidated revenues and 65 percent of its operating income from, and has 40 percent of its invested assets in, non-U.S. locations. Foreign operations impose additional types of operating risks to companies, including the risks from changes in the exchange rates for currencies, statutory acts by the foreign governments, and producing and marketing goods in an environment outside the United States.

With the passage of the North American Free Trade Agreement (NAFTA), more companies are confronted with the decision of whether or not to expand their production and marketing investments to Canada and Mexico.

Required

Using NAFTA as a discussion focus, address the following questions:

a. Explain why a U.S. company might find it advantageous to increase its production capacity of its subsidiaries in Mexico. Describe some circumstances under which it would be disadvantageous for a U.S. company to increase its investment in production subsidiaries located in Mexico.

b. In your opinion, would an increase in U.S. companies' investments in Mexico and Canada be good or bad for U.S. consumers?

c. What are some possible solutions to the possible problem of an increase in the U.S. unemployment rate if U.S. companies shift their production facilities to non-U.S. locations? Select one and discuss the pros and cons of that possible solution.

d. What conclusion can you draw from the attempts of the U.S. government to decrease barriers to international trade and investment? In your opinion, is this a good effort on the part of the government, or do you feel this effort should be changed?

LO2

C9-10 Determining an Entity's Functional Currency

Research

Maxima Corporation, a U.S. company, manufactures lighting fixtures and ceiling fans. Eight years ago, it set up a subsidiary in Mexico to manufacture three of its most popular ceiling fan models. When the subsidiary, Luz Maxima, was set up, it did business exclusively with Maxima, receiving shipments of materials from U.S. suppliers selected by Maxima and selling all of its production to Maxima. Maxima's management made a determination that its subsidiary's functional currency was the U.S. dollar.

During the past five years changes in Luz Maxima's operations have occurred. The subsidiary has developed relationships with suppliers within Mexico and is obtaining a significant percentage of its materials requirements from these suppliers. In addition, Luz Maxima has expanded its production by introducing a new product line marketed within Mexico and Central America. These products now make up a substantial percentage of the subsidiary's sales. Luz Maxima obtained long-term debt financing and a line of credit from several Mexican banks to expand its operations.

Prior to the preparation of Maxima's consolidated financial statements for the current year, Luz Maxima's financial statements, reported in Mexican pesos, must be converted into U.S. dollars. Maxima's CFO, Garry Parise, is concerned that Luz Maxima's functional currency may no longer be the U.S. dollar and that remeasurement of its financial statements may not be appropriate.

Required

Obtain the most current accounting standards on determining an entity's functional currency. You can obtain access to accounting standards through the Financial Accounting Research System (FARS), from your library, or from some other source. Garry has asked you, as an accountant in the controller's department, to research the functional currency issue. Write a memo to him, reporting on the results of your research. Support your recommendations with citations and quotations from the authoritative financial reporting standards.

LO5

C9-11 Accounting for the Translation Adjustment

Research

Sonoma Company has owned 100 percent of the outstanding common stock of Valencia Corporation, a Spanish subsidiary, for the past 15 years. The Spanish company's functional currency is the Euro, and its financial statements are translated into U.S. dollars prior to consolidation.

In the current year, Sonoma has sold 30 percent of Valencia's voting common stock to a nonaffiliated company. Sonoma's controller, Renee Voll, has calculated a gain on the sale of this portion of its investment in Valencia. The consolidated balance sheet at the end of last year contained a debit balance cumulative translation adjustment related to the Spanish subsidiary. Voll believes that the decrease in Sonoma's share of Valencia's translation adjustment will be automatically included in other comprehensive income as the year-end translation adjustment is calculated and that Sonoma's share is included in the consolidated financial statements. However, she has asked you, as an accountant in her department, to research the accounting for the translation adjustment as a result of the sale of a part of the investment in the Spanish subsidiary.

Required

Obtain the most current accounting standards on accounting for the translation adjustment resulting from translating the trial balance of a foreign affiliate. You can obtain access to accounting standards through the FARS, from your library, or from some other source. Write a memo to Renee reporting on the results of your research. Support your recommendations with citations and quotations from the authoritative financial reporting standards.

Exercises

LO4, LO6

E9-1 Multiple-Choice Questions on Translation and Remeasurement [AICPA Adapted]

For each of the seven cases presented below, work the case twice and select the best answer. First assume that the foreign currency is the functional currency; then assume that the U.S. dollar is the functional currency.

1. Certain balance sheet accounts in a foreign subsidiary of Shaw Company on December 31, 20X1, have been restated in U.S. dollars as follows:

	Restated at	
	Current Rates	**Historical Rates**
Accounts Receivable, Current	$100,000	$110,000
Accounts Receivable, Long-Term	50,000	55,000
Prepaid Insurance	25,000	30,000
Patents	40,000	45,000
Total	$215,000	$240,000

What total should be included in Shaw's balance sheet for December 31, 20X1, for the above items?

a. $215,000.
b. $225,000.
c. $230,000.
d. $240,000.

2. A wholly owned foreign subsidiary of Nick Inc. has certain expense accounts for the year ended December 31, 20X4, stated in local currency units (LCU) as follows:

	LCU
Depreciation of Equipment (related assets were purchased January 1, 20X2)	120,000
Provision for Uncollectible Accounts	80,000
Rent	200,000

The exchange rates at various dates were as follows:

	Dollar Equivalent of 1 LCU
January 1, 20X2	$0.50
December 31, 20X4	0.40
Average, 20X4	0.44

What total dollar amount should be included in Nick's statement of income to reflect the preceding expenses for the year ended December 31, 20X4?

a. $160,000.

b. $168,000.

c. $176,000.

d. $183,200.

3. Linser Corporation owns a foreign subsidiary with 2,600,000 local currency units (LCU) of property, plant, and equipment before accumulated depreciation on December 31, 20X4. Of this amount, 1,700,000 LCU were acquired in 20X2 when the rate of exchange was 1.5 LCU = $1, and 900,000 LCU were acquired in 20X3 when the rate of exchange was 1.6 LCU = $1. The rate of exchange in effect on December 31, 20X4, was 1.9 LCU = $1. The weighted average of exchange rates that were in effect during 20X4 was 1.8 LCU = $1. Assuming that the property, plant, and equipment are depreciated using the straight-line method over a 10-year period with no salvage value, how much depreciation expense relating to the foreign subsidiary's property, plant, and equipment should be charged in Linser's statement of income for 20X4?

a. $144,444.

b. $162,000.

c. $169,583.

d. $173,333.

4. On January 1, 20X1, Pat Company formed a foreign subsidiary. On February 15, 20X1, Pat's subsidiary purchased 100,000 local currency units (LCU) of inventory. Of the original inventory purchased on February 15, 20X1, 25,000 LCU made up the entire inventory on December 31, 20X1. The exchange rates were 2.2 LCU = $1 from January 1, 20X1, to June 30, 20X1, and 2 LCU = $1 from July 1, 20X1, to December 31, 20X1. The December 31, 20X1, inventory balance for Pat's foreign subsidiary should be restated in U.S. dollars in the amount of

a. $10,500.

b. $11,364.

c. $11,905.

d. $12,500.

5. At what rates should the following balance sheet accounts in the foreign currency financial statements be restated into U.S. dollars?

	Equipment	Accumulated Depreciation of Equipment
a.	Current	Current
b.	Current	Average for year
c.	Historical	Current
d.	Historical	Historical

6. A credit-balancing item resulting from the process of restating a foreign entity's financial statement from the local currency unit to U.S. dollars should be included as a (an)

   a. Separate component of stockholders' equity.

   b. Deferred credit.

   c. Component of income from continuing operations.

   d. Extraordinary item.

7. A foreign subsidiary of the Bart Corporation has certain balance sheet accounts on December 31, 20X2. Information relating to these accounts in U.S. dollars is as follows:

| | Restated at | |
	Current Rates	Historical Rates
Marketable Securities	$ 75,000	$ 85,000
Inventories, carried at average cost	600,000	700,000
Refundable Deposits	25,000	30,000
Goodwill	55,000	70,000
	$755,000	$885,000

What total should be included in Bart's balance sheet on December 31, 20X2, as a result of the preceding information?

   a. $755,000.

   b. $780,000.

   c. $870,000.

   d. $880,000.

LO4

E9-2 Multiple-Choice Questions on Translation and Foreign Currency Transactions [AICPA Adapted]

The following information should be used for questions 1, 2, and 3.

Select the best answers under each of two alternative assumptions: (*a*) the LCU is the functional currency and the translation method is appropriate or (*b*) the U.S. dollar is the functional currency and the remeasurement method is appropriate.

1. Refer to the preceding requirements. Gate Inc. had a credit adjustment of $30,000 for the year ended December 31, 20X2, from restating its foreign subsidiary's accounts from their local currency units into U.S. dollars. Additionally, Gate had a receivable from a foreign customer payable in the customer's local currency. On December 31, 20X1, this receivable for 200,000 local currency units (LCU) was correctly included in Gate's balance sheet at $110,000. When the receivable was collected on February 15, 20X2, the U.S. dollar–equivalent was $120,000. In Gate's 20X2 consolidated statement of income, how much should be reported as foreign exchange gain in computing net income?

   a. $0.

   b. $10,000.

   c. $30,000.

   d. $40,000.

2. Refer to the preceding requirements. Bar Corporation had a realized foreign exchange loss of $13,000 for the year ended December 31, 20X2, and must also determine whether the following items will require year-end adjustment:

   (1) Bar had a $7,000 credit resulting from the restatement in dollars of the accounts of its wholly owned foreign subsidiary for the year ended December 31, 20X2.

   (2) Bar had an account payable to an unrelated foreign supplier payable in the supplier's local currency. The U.S. dollar–equivalent of the payable was $60,000 on the October 31, 20X2, invoice date and $64,000 on December 31, 20X2. The invoice is payable on January 30, 20X3.

What amount of the net foreign exchange loss in computing net income should be reported in Bar's 20X2 consolidated statement of income?

a. $6,000.

b. $10,000.

c. $13,000.

d. $17,000.

3. Refer to the preceding requirements. The balance in Simpson Corp.'s foreign exchange loss account was $15,000 on December 31, 20X2, before any necessary year-end adjustment relating to the following:

(1) Simpson had a $20,000 debit resulting from the restatement in dollars of the accounts of its wholly owned foreign subsidiary for the year ended December 31, 20X2.

(2) Simpson had an account payable to an unrelated foreign supplier, payable in the supplier's local currency on January 27, 20X3. The U.S. dollar–equivalent of the payable was $100,000 on the November 28, 20X2, invoice date, and $106,000 on December 31, 20X2.

In Simpson's 20X2 consolidated income statement, what amount should be included as foreign exchange loss in computing net income?

a. $41,000.

b. $35,000.

c. $21,000.

d. $15,000.

4. When remeasuring foreign currency financial statements into the functional currency, which of the following items would be remeasured using a historical exchange rate?

a. Inventories carried at cost.

b. Trading securities carried at market values.

c. Bonds payable.

d. Accrued liabilities.

5. A foreign subsidiary's functional currency is its local currency, which has not experienced significant inflation. The weighted-average exchange rate for the current year would be the appropriate exchange rate for translating

	Sales to Customers	Wages Expense
a.	No	No
b.	Yes	Yes
c.	No	Yes
d.	Yes	No

6. The functional currency of Dahl Inc.'s subsidiary is the European euro. Dahl borrowed euros as a partial hedge of its investment in the subsidiary. In preparing consolidated financial statements, Dahl's debit balance of its translation adjustment exceeded its exchange gain on the borrowing. How should the translation adjustment and the exchange gain be reported in Dahl's consolidated financial statements?

a. The translation adjustment should be netted against the exchange gain, and the excess translation adjustment should be reported in the stockholders' equity section of the balance sheet.

b. The translation adjustment should be netted against the exchange gain, and the excess translation adjustment should be reported in the statement of income in computing net income.

c. The translation adjustment is reported as a component of other comprehensive income and then accumulated in the stockholders' equity section of the balance sheet, and the exchange gain should be reported in the statement of income in computing net income.

d. The translation adjustment should be reported in the statement of income, and the exchange gain should be reported separately in the stockholders' equity section of the balance sheet.

LO1–LO8

E9-3 **Matching Key Terms**

Match the descriptions of terms on the left with the terms on the right. Some terms may be used once, more than once, or not at all.

Descriptions of Terms	Terms
1. The group that has attempted to harmonize the world's many different accounting methods.	A. Financial Accounting Standards Board
2. The currency of the primary economic environment in which the entity operates.	B. Remeasurement gain or loss
3. The functional currency for a U.S. subsidiary located in a country with > 100 percent inflation over the last three years.	C. Translation adjustment
4. Translation of all assets and liabilities of a foreign subsidiary using the foreign exchange rate at the balance sheet date.	D. Current rate method
5. Restatement of the fixed assets and inventories of a foreign subsidiary into U.S. dollars using historical exchange rates.	E. Remeasurement method
6. Inclusion of this gain or loss on the U.S. company's statement of income as part of net income.	F. U.S. dollar
7. The item that balances the debits and credits of the foreign subsidiary's adjusted trial balance in U.S. dollars, assuming the functional currency is the currency of the foreign subsidiary's country.	G. Functional currency
8. The item that balances the debits and credits of the foreign subsidiary's adjusted trial balance in U.S. dollars, assuming the functional currency is the U.S. dollar.	H. International Accounting Standards Board
9. Translation of the statement of income accounts of a foreign subsidiary using the average exchange rate for the year.	I. International Managerial Accounting Society
10. Restatement of depreciation expense and cost of goods sold of a foreign subsidiary using historical exchange rates.	J. Functional currency indicators
11. An analysis of a foreign subsidiary's cash flows, sales prices, sales markets, expenses, and financing.	K. Historical rate method
12. The periodic change in this item reported as a component of other comprehensive income.	L. Cumulative transaction gain or loss

LO4, LO6

E9-4 **Multiple-Choice Questions on Translation and Remeasurement**

Use the following information for questions 1, 2, and 3.

Bartell Inc., a U.S. company, acquired 90 percent of the common stock of a Malaysian company on January 1, 20X5, for $160,000. The net assets of the Malaysian subsidiary amounted to 680,000 ringitts (RM) on the date of acquisition. On January 1, 20X5, the book values of the Malaysian subsidiary's identifiable assets and liabilities approximated their fair values. Exchange rates at various dates during 20X5 follow:

January 1	RM 1 = $0.21
December 31	RM 1 = $0.24
Average for 20X5	RM 1 = $0.22

1. Refer to the preceding information. On January 1, 20X5, how much goodwill was acquired by Bartell?

   a. $17,200.

   b. $31,480.

   c. $11,400.

   d. $25,360.

2. Refer to the preceding information. Assume that Bartell acquired $10,500 of goodwill on January 1, 20X5, and the goodwill suffered a 10 percent impairment loss in 20X5. If the functional currency is the Malaysian ringgit, how much goodwill impairment loss should be reported on Bartell's consolidated statement of income for 20X5?

    a. $1,050.

    b. $1,200.

    c. $1,100.

    d. $1,175.

3. Refer to the preceding information but now assume that the U.S. dollar is the functional currency. How much goodwill impairment loss should be reported on Bartell's consolidated statement of income in this situation?

    a. $1,050.

    b. $1,200.

    c. $1,100.

    d. $1,175.

Use the following information for questions 4, 5, 6, and 7.

    Mondell Inc., a U.S. company, acquired 100 percent of the common stock of a German company on January 1, 20X5, for $402,000. The German subsidiary's net assets amounted to 300,000 euros on the date of acquisition. On January 1, 20X5, the book values of its identifiable assets and liabilities approximated their fair values. As a result of an analysis of functional currency indicators, Mondell determined that the euro was the functional currency. On December 31, 20X5, the German subsidiary's adjusted trial balance, translated into U.S. dollars, contained $12,000 more debits than credits. The German subsidiary reported income of 25,000 euros for 20X5 and paid a cash dividend of 5,000 euros on November 30, 20X5. Included on the German subsidiary's income statement was depreciation expense of 2,500 euros. Mondell uses the fully adjusted equity method of accounting for its investment in the German subsidiary and determined that goodwill in the first year had an impairment loss of 10 percent of its initial amount. Exchange rates at various dates during 20X5 follow:

January 1	€1 = $1.20
November 30	€1 = 1.30
December 31	€1 = 1.32
Average for 20X5	€1 = 1.24

4. Refer to the preceding information. What amount should Mondell record as "income from subsidiary" based on the German subsidiary's reported net income?

    a. $31,000.

    b. $31,100.

    c. $33,000.

    d. $30,000.

5. Refer to the preceding information. The receipt of the dividend will result in

    a. A credit to the investment account for $6,200.

    b. A debit to the income from subsidiary account for $6,600.

    c. A credit to the investment account for $6,600.

    d. A credit to the investment account for $6,500.

6. Refer to the preceding information. On Mondell's consolidated balance sheet at December 31, 20X5, what amount should be reported for the goodwill acquired on January 1, 20X5?

    a. $37,660.

    b. $37,800.

    c. $41,580.

    d. $39,880.

7. Refer to the preceding information. In the stockholders' equity section of Mondell's consolidated balance sheet at December 31, 20X5, Mondell should report the translation adjustment as a component of other comprehensive income of

    a. $12,000.

    b. $15,920.

    c. $13,400.

    d. $8,080.

LO4, LO5

Advanced
StudyGuide
.com

E9-5   Translation

On January 1, 20X1, Popular Creek Corporation organized RoadTime Company as a subsidiary in Switzerland with an initial investment cost of Swiss francs (SFr) 60,000. RoadTime's December 31, 20X1, trial balance in SFr is as follows:

	Debit	Credit
Cash	SFr 7,000	
Accounts Receivable (net)	20,000	
Receivable from Popular Creek	5,000	
Inventory	25,000	
Plant and Equipment	100,000	
Accumulated Depreciation		SFr 10,000
Accounts Payable		12,000
Bonds Payable		50,000
Common Stock		60,000
Sales		150,000
Cost of Goods Sold	70,000	
Depreciation Expense	10,000	
Operating Expense	30,000	
Dividends Paid	15,000	
Total	SFr282,000	SFr282,000

Additional Information

1. The receivable from Popular Creek is denominated in Swiss francs. Popular Creek's books show a $4,000 payable to RoadTime.

2. Purchases of inventory goods are made evenly during the year. Items in the ending inventory were purchased November 1.

3. Equipment is depreciated by the straight-line method with a 10-year life and no residual value. A full year's depreciation is taken in the year of acquisition. The equipment was acquired on March 1.

4. The dividends were declared and paid on November 1.

5. Exchange rates were as follows:

January 1	SFr1 = $0.73
March 1	SFr1 = 0.74
November 1	SFr1 = 0.77
December 31	SFr1 = 0.80
20X1 average	SFr1 = 0.75

6. The Swiss franc is the functional currency.

Required

Prepare a schedule translating the December 31, 20X1, trial balance from Swiss francs to dollars.

LO4, LO5

E9-6   Proof of Translation Adjustment

Refer to the data in Exercise E9-5.

Required

a. Prepare a proof of the translation adjustment computed in Exercise E9-5.

b. Where is the translation adjustment reported on Popular Creek's consolidated financial statements and its foreign subsidiary?

LO6, LO7

E9-7   Remeasurement

Refer to the data in Exercise E9-5, but assume that the dollar is the functional currency for the foreign subsidiary.

Required

Prepare a schedule remeasuring the December 31, 20X1, trial balance from Swiss francs to dollars.

LO6, LO7   **E9-8**   **Proof of Remeasurement Gain (Loss)**

Refer to the data in Exercises E9-5 and E9-7.

Required

a. Prepare a proof of the remeasurement gain or loss computed in Exercise E9-7.

b. How should this remeasurement gain or loss be reported on Popular Creek's consolidated financial statements and the financial statements of its foreign subsidiary?

LO4, LO5   **E9-9**   **Translation with Strengthening U.S. Dollar**

Refer to the data in Exercise E9-5, but now assume that the exchange rates were as follows:

January 1	SFr1 = $0.80
March 1	SFr1 = 0.77
November 1	SFr1 = 0.74
December 31	SFr1 = 0.73
20X1 average	SFr1 = 0.75

The receivable from Popular Creek Corporation is denominated in Swiss francs. Popular Creek's books show a $3,650 payable to RoadTime.

Assume the Swiss franc is the functional currency.

Required

a. Prepare a schedule translating the December 31, 20X1, trial balance from Swiss francs to dollars.

b. Compare the results of Exercise E9-5, in which the dollar is weakening against the Swiss franc during 20X1, with the results in this exercise (E9-9), in which the dollar is strengthening against the Swiss franc during 20X1.

LO6, LO7   **E9-10**   **Remeasurement with Strengthening U.S. Dollar**

Refer to the data in Exercise E9-5, but now assume that the exchange rates were as follows:

January 1	SFr1 = $0.80
March 1	SFr1 = 0.77
November 1	SFr1 = 0.74
December 31	SFr1 = 0.73
20X1 average	SFr1 = 0.75

The receivable from Popular Creek is denominated in Swiss francs. Its books show a $3,650 payable to RoadTime.

Assume that the U.S. dollar is the functional currency.

Required

a. Prepare a schedule remeasuring the December 31, 20X1, trial balance from Swiss francs to dollars.

b. Compare the results of Exercise E9-7, in which the dollar weakens against the Swiss franc during 20X1, with the results in this exercise (E9-10), in which the dollar strengthened against the Swiss franc during 20X1.

LO5, LO7   **E9-11**   **Remeasurement and Translation of Cost of Goods Sold**

Duff Company is a subsidiary of Rand Corporation and is located in Madrid, Spain, where the currency is the Euro (€). Data on Duff's inventory and purchases are as follows:

Inventory, January 1, 20X7	€220,000
Purchases during 20X7	€846,000
Inventory, December 31, 20X7	€180,000

The beginning inventory was acquired during the fourth quarter of 20X6, and the ending inventory was acquired during the fourth quarter of 20X7. Purchases were made evenly over the year. Exchange rates were as follows:

Fourth quarter of 20X6	€1 = $1.29015
January 1, 20X7	€1 = $1.32030
Average during 20X7	€1 = $1.39655
Fourth quarter of 20X7	€1 = $1.45000
December 31, 20X7	€1 = $1.47280

Required

a. Show the remeasurement of cost of goods sold for 20X7, assuming that the U.S. dollar is the functional currency.

b. Show the translation of cost of goods sold for 20X7, assuming that the Spanish peseta is the functional currency.

LO4

E9-12 **Equity-Method Entries for a Foreign Subsidiary**

Thames Company is located in London, England. The local currency is the British pound (£). On January 1, 20X8, Dek Company purchased an 80 percent interest in Thames for $400,000, which resulted in an excess of cost-over-book value of $48,000 due solely to a trademark having a remaining life of 10 years. Dek uses the equity method to account for its investment.

Dek's December 31, 20X8, trial balance has been translated into U.S. dollars, requiring a translation adjustment debit of $6,400. Thames's net income translated into U.S. dollars is $60,000. It declared and paid a £15,000 dividend on May 1, 20X8.

Relevant exchange rates are as follows:

January 1, 20X8	£1 = $1.60
May 1, 20X8	£1 = $1.64
December 31, 20X8	£1 = $1.65
Average for 20X8	£1 = $1.63

Required

a. Record the dividend received by Dek from Thames.

b. Prepare the entries to record Dek's equity in the net income of Thames and the parent's share of the translation adjustment.

c. Show a calculation of the differential reported on the consolidated balance sheet of December 31, 20X8, and the translation adjustment from differential.

d. Record the amortization of the trademark on Dek's books.

e. Calculate the amount of the translation adjustment reported on the statement of comprehensive income as an element of other comprehensive income.

LO5

E9-13 **Effects of a Change in the Exchange Rate—Translation and Other Comprehensive Income**

Bentley Company owns a subsidiary in India whose balance sheets in rupees (R) for the last two years follow:

	December 31, 20X6	December 31, 20X7
Assets:		
Cash	R 100,000	R 80,000
Receivables	450,000	550,000
Inventory	680,000	720,000
Fixed Assets, net	1,000,000	900,000
Total Assets	R2,230,000	R2,250,000
Equities:		
Current Payables	R 260,000	R 340,000
Long-Term Debt	1,250,000	1,100,000
Common Stock	500,000	500,000
Retained Earnings	220,000	310,000
Total Equities	R2,230,000	R2,250,000

Bentley formed the subsidiary on January 1, 20X6, when the exchange rate was 30 rupees for 1 U.S. dollar. The exchange rate for 1 U.S. dollar on December 31, 20X6, and December 31, 2007, had increased to 35 rupees and 40 rupees, respectively. Income is earned evenly over the year, and the subsidiary declared no dividends during its first two years of existence.

Required

a. Present both the direct and the indirect exchange rate for the rupees for the three dates of (1) January 1, 20X6; (2) December 31, 20X6; and (3) December 31, 20X7. Did the dollar strengthen or weaken in 20X6 and in 20X7?

b. Prepare the subsidiary's translated balance sheet as of December 31, 20X6, assuming the rupee is the subsidiary's functional currency.

c. Prepare the subsidiary's translated balance sheet as of December 31, 20X7, assuming the rupee is the subsidiary's functional currency.

d. Compute the amount that 20X7's other comprehensive income would include as a result of the translation.

LO6

E9-14 Computation of Gain or Loss on Sale of Asset by Foreign Subsidiary

On December 31, 20X2, your company's Mexican subsidiary sold land at a selling price of 3,000,000 pesos. The land had been purchased for 2,000,000 pesos on January 1, 20X1, when the exchange rate was 10 pesos to 1 U.S. dollar. The exchange rate for 1 U.S. dollar was 11 pesos on December 31, 20X1, and 12 pesos on December 31, 20X2. Assume that the subsidiary had no other assets and no liabilities during the two years that it owned the land.

Required

a. Prepare all entries regarding the purchase and sale of the land that would be made on the books of the Mexican subsidiary whose reporting currency is the Mexican peso.

b. Determine the amount of the gain or loss on the transaction that would be reported on the subsidiary's remeasured statement of income in U.S. dollars, assuming the U.S. dollar is the functional currency. Determine the amount of the remeasurement gain or loss that would be reported on the remeasured statement of income in U.S. dollars.

c. Determine the amount of the gain or loss on the transaction that would be reported on the subsidiary's translated statement of income in U.S. dollars, assuming the Mexican peso is the functional currency. Determine the amount of the other comprehensive income that would be reported on the consolidated statement of other comprehensive income for 20X2.

LO8

E9-15* Intercompany Transactions

Hawk Company sold inventory to United Ltd., an English subsidiary. The goods cost Hawk $8,000 and were sold to United for $12,000 on November 27, payable in British pounds. The goods are still on hand at the end of the year on December 31. The British pound (£) is the functional currency of the English subsidiary. The exchange rates follow:

November 27	£1 = $1.60
December 31	£1 = 1.70

Required

a. At what dollar amount is the ending inventory shown in the trial balance of the consolidated worksheet?

b. What amount is eliminated for the unrealized intercompany gross profit, and at what amount is the inventory shown on the consolidated balance sheet?

Problems

LO4

P9-16 Parent Company Journal Entries and Translation

On January 1, 20X1, Par Company purchased all the outstanding stock of North Bay Company, located in Canada, for $120,000. On January 1, 20X1, the direct exchange rate for the Canadian dollar (C$) was C$1 = $0.80. North Bay's book value on January 1, 20X1, was C$90,000. The fair value of North Bay's plant and equipment was C$10,000 more than book value, and the plant

*Indicates that the item relates to "Additional Considerations."

and equipment are being depreciated over 10 years, with no salvage value. The remainder of the differential is attributable to a trademark, which will be amortized over 10 years.

During 20X1, North Bay earned C$20,000 in income and declared and paid C$8,000 in dividends. The dividends were declared and paid in Canadian dollars when the exchange rate was C$1 = $0.75. On December 31, 20X1, Par continues to hold the Canadian currency received from the dividend. On December 31, 20X1, the direct exchange rate is C$1 = $0.70. The average exchange rate during 20X1 was C$1 = $0.75. Management has determined that the Canadian dollar is the appropriate functional currency for North Bay Company.

Required

a. Prepare a schedule showing the differential allocation and amortization for 20X1. The schedule should present both Canadian dollars and U.S. dollars.

b. Par uses the fully adjusted equity method to account for its investment. Provide the entries that it would record in 20X1 for its investment in North Bay for the following items:

   (1) Purchase of investment in North Bay.
   (2) Equity accrual for Par's share of North Bay's income.
   (3) Recognition of dividend declared and paid by North Bay.
   (4) Amortization of differential.
   (5) Recognition of translation adjustment on differential.

c. Prepare a schedule showing the proof of the translation adjustment for North Bay as a result of the translation of the subsidiary's accounts from Canadian dollars to U.S. dollars. Then provide the entry that Par would record for its share of the translation adjustment resulting from the translation of the subsidiary's accounts.

d. Provide the entry required by Par to restate the C$8,000 in the Foreign Currency Units account into its year-end U.S. dollar–equivalent value.

LO4, LO5 **P9-17** **Translation, Journal Entries, Consolidated Comprehensive Income, and Stockholders' Equity**

On January 1, 20X5, Taft Company acquired all of the outstanding stock of Vikix, Inc., a Norwegian company, at a cost of $151,200. Vikix's net assets on the date of acquisition were 700,000 kroner (NKr). On January 1, 20X5, the book and fair values of the Norwegian subsidiary's identifiable assets and liabilities approximated their fair values except for property, plant, and equipment and patents acquired. The fair value of Vikix's property, plant, and equipment exceeded its book value by $18,000. The remaining useful life of Vikix's equipment at January 1, 20X5, was 10 years. The remainder of the differential was attributable to a patent having an estimated useful life of 5 years. Vikix's trial balance on December 31, 20X5, in kroner, follows:

	Debits	Credits
Cash	NKr 150,000	
Accounts Receivable (net)	200,000	
Inventory	270,000	
Property, Plant, and Equipment	600,000	
Accumulated Depreciation		NKr 150,000
Accounts Payable		90,000
Notes Payable		190,000
Common Stock		450,000
Retained Earnings		250,000
Sales		690,000
Cost of Goods Sold	410,000	
Operating Expenses	100,000	
Depreciation Expense	50,000	
Dividends Paid	40,000	
Total	NKr1,820,000	NKr1,820,000

Additional Information

1. Vikix uses the FIFO method for its inventory. The beginning inventory was acquired on December 31, 20X4, and ending inventory was acquired on December 15, 20X5. Purchases of NKr420,000 were made evenly throughout 20X5.

2. Vikix acquired all of its property, plant, and equipment on July 1, 20X3, and uses straight-line depreciation.

3. Vikix's sales were made evenly throughout 20X5, and its operating expenses were incurred evenly throughout 20X5.

4. The dividends were declared and paid on July 1, 20X5.

5. Taft's income from its own operations was $275,000 for 20X5, and its total stockholders' equity on January 1, 20X5, was $3,500,000. Taft declared $100,000 of dividends during 20X5.

6. Exchange rates were as follows:

July 1, 20X3	NKr1 = $0.15
December 30, 20X4	NKr1 = 0.18
January 1, 20X5	NKr1 = 0.18
July 1, 20X5	NKr1 = 0.19
December 15, 20X5	NKr1 = 0.205
December 31, 20X5	NKr1 = 0.21
Average for 20X5	NKr1 = 0.20

Required

a. Prepare a schedule translating the trial balance from Norwegian kroner into U.S. dollars. Assume the krone is the functional currency.

b. Assume that Taft uses the fully adjusted equity method. Record all journal entries that relate to its investment in the Norwegian subsidiary during 20X5. Provide the necessary documentation and support for the amounts in the journal entries, including a schedule of the translation adjustment related to the differential.

c. Prepare a schedule that determines Taft's consolidated comprehensive income for 20X5.

d. Compute Taft's total consolidated stockholders' equity at December 31, 20X5.

LO6, LO7   **P9-18**   ### Remeasurement, Journal Entries, Consolidated Net Income, and Stockholders' Equity

Refer to the information in Problem P9-17. Assume the U.S. dollar is the functional currency, not the krone.

Required

a. Prepare a schedule remeasuring the trial balance from Norwegian kroner into U.S. dollars.

b. Assume that Taft uses the fully adjusted equity method. Record all journal entries that relate to its investment in the Norwegian subsidiary during 20X5. Provide the necessary documentation and support for the amounts in the journal entries.

c. Prepare a schedule that determines Taft's consolidated net income for 20X5.

d. Compute Taft's total consolidated stockholders' equity at December 31, 20X5.

LO7   **P9-19**   ### Proof of Translation Adjustment

Refer to the information presented in Problem P9-17 and your answer to part *a* of Problem P9-17.

Required

Prepare a schedule providing a proof of the translation adjustment.

LO8   **P9-20**   ### Remeasurement Gain or Loss

Refer to the information given in Problem P9-17 and your answer to part *a* of Problem P9-18.

Required

Prepare a schedule providing a proof of the remeasurement gain or loss. For this part of the problem, assume that the Norwegian subsidiary had the following monetary assets and liabilities at January 1, 20X5:

Monetary Assets	
Cash	NKr 10,000
Accounts Receivable (net)	140,000

Monetary Liabilities	
Accounts Payable	NKr 70,000
Notes Payable	140,000

On January 1, 20X5, the Norwegian subsidiary has a net monetary liability position of NKr60,000.

LO4, LO5 **P9-21** **Translation and Calculation of Translation Adjustment**

On January 1, 20X4, Alum Corporation acquired DaSilva Company, a Brazilian subsidiary, by purchasing all the common stock at book value. DaSilva's trial balances on January 1, 20X4, and December 31, 20X4, expressed in Brazilian reals (BRL), follow:

	January 1, 20X4		December 31, 20X4	
	Debit	Credit	Debit	Credit
Cash	BRL 62,000		BRL 57,700	
Accounts Receivable (net)	83,900		82,000	
Inventories	95,000		95,000	
Prepaid Insurance	5,600		2,400	
Plant and Equipment	250,000		350,000	
Accumulated Depreciation		BRL 67,500		BRL 100,000
Intangible Assets	42,000		30,000	
Accounts Payable		20,000		24,000
Income Taxes Payable		30,000		27,000
Interest Payable		1,000		1,100
Notes Payable		20,000		20,000
Bonds Payable		120,000		120,000
Common Stock		80,000		80,000
Additional Paid-In Capital		150,000		150,000
Retained Earnings		50,000		50,000
Sales				500,000
Cost of Goods Sold			230,000	
Insurance Expense			3,200	
Depreciation Expense			32,500	
Amortization Expense			12,000	
Operating Expense			152,300	
Dividends Paid			25,000	
Total	BRL538,500	BRL538,500	BRL1,072,100	BRL1,072,100

Additional Information

1. DaSilva uses FIFO inventory valuation. Purchases were made uniformly during 20X4. Ending inventory for 20X4 is composed of units purchased when the exchange rate was $0.25.

2. The insurance premium for a two-year policy was paid on October 1, 20X3.

3. Plant and equipment were acquired as follows:

Date	Cost
January 1, 20X1	BRL200,000
July 10, 20X2	50,000
April 7, 20X4	100,000

4. Plant and equipment are depreciated using the straight-line method and a 10-year life, with no residual value. A full month's depreciation is taken in the month of acquisition.

5. The intangible assets are patents acquired on July 10, 20X2, at a cost of BRL60,000. The estimated life is five years.

6. The common stock was issued on January 1, 20X1.

7. Dividends of BRL10,000 were declared and paid on April 7. On October 9, BRL15,000 of dividends were declared and paid.

8. Exchange rates were as follows:

January 1, 20X1	BRL1 = $0.45
July 10, 20X2	BRL1 = 0.40
October 1, 20X3	BRL1 = 0.34
January 1, 20X4	BRL1 = 0.30
April 7, 20X4	BRL1 = 0.28
October 9, 20X4	BRL1 = 0.23
December 31, 20X4	BRL1 = 0.20
20X4 average	BRL1 = 0.25

Required

a. Prepare a schedule translating the December 31, 20X4, trial balance of DaSilva from reals to dollars.

b. Prepare a schedule calculating the translation adjustment as of the end of 20X4. The net assets on January 1, 20X4, were BRL280,000.

LO8 **P9-22** **Remeasurement and Proof of Remeasurement Gain or Loss**

Refer to the information in Problem P9-21. Assume that the dollar is the functional currency.

Required

a. Prepare a schedule remeasuring the December 31, 20X4, trial balance of DaSilva Company from reals to dollars.

b. Prepare a schedule providing a proof of the remeasurement gain or loss.

LO4, LO5 **P9-23** **Translation**

Alamo Inc. purchased 80 percent of the outstanding stock of Western Ranching Company, located in Australia, on January 1, 20X3. The purchase price in Australian dollars (A$) was A$200,000, and A$40,000 of the differential was allocated to plant and equipment, which is amortized over a 10-year period. The remainder of the differential was attributable to a patent. Alamo Inc. amortizes the patent over 10 years. Western Ranching's trial balance on December 31, 20X3, in Australian dollars is as follows:

	Debits	Credits
Cash	A$ 44,100	
Accounts Receivable (net)	72,000	
Inventory	86,000	
Plant and Equipment	240,000	
Accumulated Depreciation		A$ 60,000
Accounts Payable		53,800
Payable to Alamo Inc.		10,800
Interest Payable		3,000
12% Bonds Payable		100,000
Premium on Bonds		5,700
Common Stock		90,000
Retained Earnings		40,000
Sales		579,000
Cost of Goods Sold	330,000	
Depreciation Expense	24,000	
Operating Expenses	131,500	
Interest Expense	5,700	
Dividends Paid	9,000	
Total	A$942,300	A$942,300

Additional Information

1. Western Ranching uses average cost for cost of goods sold. Inventory increased by A$20,000 during the year. Purchases were made uniformly during 20X3. The ending inventory was acquired at the average exchange rate for the year.

2. Plant and equipment were acquired as follows:

Date	Cost
January 20X1	A$180,000
January 1, 20X3	60,000

3. Plant and equipment are depreciated using the straight-line method and a 10-year life, with no residual value.

4. The payable to Alamo is in Australian dollars. Alamo's books show a receivable from Western Ranching of $6,480.

5. The 10-year bonds were issued on July 1, 20X3, for A$106,000. The premium is amortized on a straight-line basis. The interest is paid on April 1 and October 1.

6. The dividends were declared and paid on April 1.

7. Exchange rates were as follows:

January 20X1	A$1 = $0.93
August 20X1	A$1 = 0.88
January 1, 20X3	A$1 = 0.70
April 1, 20X3	A$1 = 0.67
July 1, 20X3	A$1 = 0.64
December 31, 20X3	A$1 = 0.60
20X3 average	A$1 = 0.65

Required

a. Prepare a schedule translating the December 31, 20X3, trial balance of Western Ranching from Australian dollars to U.S. dollars.

b. Prepare a schedule providing a proof of the translation adjustment.

LO4

P9-24   Parent Company Journal Entries and Translation

Refer to the information given in Problem P9-23 for Alamo and its subsidiary, Western Ranching. Assume that the Australian dollar (A$) is the functional currency and that Alamo uses the fully adjusted equity method for accounting for its investment in Western Ranching.

Required

a. Prepare the entries that Alamo would record in 20X3 for its investment in Western Ranching. Your entries should include the following:

  (1) Record the initial investment on January 1, 20X3.
  (2) Record the dividend received by the parent company.
  (3) Recognize the parent company's share of the equity income of the subsidiary.
  (4) Record the amortizations of the differential.
  (5) Recognize the translation adjustment required by the parent from the adjustment of the differential.
  (6) Recognize the parent company's share of the translation adjustment resulting from the translation of the subsidiary's accounts.

b. Provide the necessary documentation and support for the amounts recorded in the journal entries, including a schedule of the translation adjustment related to the differential.

LO5

P9-25 **Consolidation Worksheet after Translation**

Refer to the information given in Problems P9-23 and P9-24 for Alamo and its subsidiary, Western Ranching. Assume that the Australian dollar (A$) is the functional currency and that Alamo uses the fully adjusted equity method for accounting for its investment in Western Ranching. A December 31, 20X3, trial balance for Alamo Inc. follows. Use this translated trial balance for completing this problem.

Item	Debit	Credit
Cash	$ 38,000	
Accounts Receivable (net)	140,000	
Receivable from Western Ranching	6,480	
Inventory	128,000	
Plant and Equipment	500,000	
Investment in Western Ranching	152,064	
Cost of Goods Sold	600,000	
Depreciation Expense	28,000	
Operating Expenses	204,000	
Interest Expense	2,000	
Dividends Declared	50,000	
Translation Adjustment	22,528	
Accumulated Depreciation		$ 90,000
Accounts Payable		60,000
Interest Payable		2,000
Common Stock		500,000
Retained Earnings, January 1, 20X3		179,656
Sales		1,000,000
Income from Subsidiary		39,416
Total	$1,871,072	$1,871,072

Required

a. Prepare a set of eliminating entries, in general journal form, for the entries required to prepare a comprehensive consolidation worksheet (including other comprehensive income) as of December 31, 20X3.

b. Prepare a comprehensive consolidation worksheet as of December 31, 20X3.

LO7

P9-26 **Remeasurement**

Refer to the information in Problem P9-23. Assume the U.S. dollar is the functional currency.

Required

a. Prepare a schedule remeasuring the December 31, 20X3, trial balance of Western Ranching from Australian dollars to U.S. dollars.

b. Prepare a schedule providing a proof of the remeasurement gain or loss. The subsidiary's net monetary liability position on January 1, 20X3, was A$80,000.

LO6

P9-27 **Parent Company Journal Entries and Remeasurement**

Refer to the information given in Problems P9-23 and P9-26 for Alamo and its subsidiary, Western Ranching. Assume that the U.S. dollar is the functional currency and that Alamo uses the fully adjusted equity method for accounting for its investment in Western Ranching.

Required

a. Prepare the entries that Alamo would record in 20X3 for its investment in Western Ranching. Your entries should do the following:

(1) Record the initial investment on January 1, 20X3.

(2) Record the dividend received by the parent company.

(3) Recognize the parent company's share of the equity income from the subsidiary.

(4) Record the amortizations of the differential.

b. Provide the necessary documentation and support for the amounts recorded in the journal entries.

Advanced
StudyGuide
.com

LO7

P9-28 **Consolidation Worksheet after Remeasurement**

Refer to the information given in Problems P9-23 and P9-27 for Alamo and its subsidiary, Western Ranching. Assume that the U.S. dollar is the functional currency and that Alamo uses the fully adjusted equity method for accounting for its investment in Western Ranching. A December 31, 20X3, trial balance for Alamo follows. Use this remeasured trial balance for completing this problem.

Item	Debit	Credit
Cash	$ 38,000	
Accounts Receivable (net)	140,000	
Receivable from Western Ranching	6,480	
Inventory	128,000	
Plant and Equipment	500,000	
Investment in Western Ranching	178,544	
Cost of Goods Sold	600,000	
Depreciation Expense	28,000	
Operating Expenses	204,000	
Interest Expense	2,000	
Dividends Declared	50,000	
Accumulated Depreciation		$ 90,000
Accounts Payable		60,000
Interest Payable		2,000
Common Stock		500,000
Retained Earnings, January 1, 20X3		179,656
Sales		1,000,000
Income from Subsidiary		43,368
Total	$1,875,024	$1,875,024

Required

a. Prepare a set of eliminating entries, in general journal form, for the entries required to prepare a three-part consolidation worksheet as of December 31, 20X3.

b. Prepare a three-part consolidation worksheet as of December 31, 20X3.

LO6, LO7

P9-29 **Foreign Currency Remeasurement [AICPA Adapted]**

On January 1, 20X1, Kiner Company formed a foreign subsidiary that issued all of its currently outstanding common stock on that date. Selected accounts from the balance sheets, all of which are shown in local currency units, are as follows:

	December 31	
	20X2	20X1
Accounts Receivable (net of allowance for uncollectible accounts of 2,200 LCU on December 31, 20X2, and 2,000 LCU on December 31, 20X1)	LCU 40,000	LCU 35,000
Inventories, at cost	80,000	75,000
Property, Plant, and Equipment (net of allowance for accumulated depreciation of 31,000 LCU on December 31, 20X2, and 14,000 LCU on December 31, 20X1)	163,000	150,000
Long-Term Debt	100,000	120,000
Common Stock, authorized 10,000 shares, par value 10 LCU per share; issued and outstanding, 5,000 shares on December 31, 20X2, and December 31, 20X1	50,000	50,000

Additional Information

1. Exchange rates are as follows:

January 1, 20X1–July 31, 20X1	2 LCU = $1
August 1, 20X1–October 31, 20X1	1.8 LCU = 1
November 1, 20X1–June 30, 20X2	1.7 LCU = 1
July 1, 20X2–December 31, 20X2	1.5 LCU = 1
Average monthly rate for 20X1	1.9 LCU = 1
Average monthly rate for 20X2	1.6 LCU = 1

2. An analysis of the accounts receivable balance is as follows:

	20X2	20X1
Accounts Receivable:		
Balance at beginning of year	LCU 37,000	
Sales (36,000 LCU per month in 20X2 and 31,000 LCU per month in 20X1)	432,000	LCU 372,000
Collections	(423,600)	(334,000)
Write-offs (May 20X2 and December 20X1)	(3,200)	(1,000)
Balance at end of year	LCU 42,200	LCU 37,000

	20X2	20X1
Allowance for Uncollectible Accounts:		
Balance at beginning of year	LCU 2,000	
Provision for uncollectible accounts	3,400	LCU 3,000
Write-offs (May 20X2 and December 20X1)	(3,200)	(1,000)
Balance at end of year	LCU 2,200	LCU 2,000

3. An analysis of inventories, for which the first-in, first-out inventory method is used, follows:

	20X2	20X1
Inventory at beginning of year	LCU 75,000	
Purchases (June 20X2 and June 20X1)	335,000	LCU375,000
Goods available for sale	LCU410,000	LCU375,000
Inventory at end of year	(80,000)	(75,000)
Cost of goods sold	LCU330,000	LCU300,000

4. On January 1, 20X1, Kiner's foreign subsidiary purchased land for 24,000 LCU and plant and equipment for 140,000 LCU. On July 4, 20X2, additional equipment was purchased for 30,000 LCU. Plant and equipment is being depreciated on a straight-line basis over a 10-year period, with no residual value. A full year's depreciation is taken in the year of purchase.

5. On January 15, 20X1, 7 percent bonds with a face value of 120,000 LCU were issued. These bonds mature on January 15, 20X7, and the interest is paid semiannually on July 15 and January 15. The first interest payment was made on July 15, 20X1.

Required

Prepare a schedule remeasuring the selected accounts into U.S. dollars for December 31, 20X1, and December 31, 20X2, respectively, assuming the U.S. dollar is the functional currency for the foreign subsidiary. The schedule should be prepared using the following form:

Item	Balance in LCU	Appropriate Exchange Rate	Remeasured into U.S. Dollars
December 31, 20X1:			
Accounts Receivable (net)			
Inventories			
Property, Plant, and Equipment (net)			
Long-Term Debt			
Common Stock			
December 31, 20X2:			
Accounts Receivable (net)			
Inventories			
Property, Plant, and Equipment (net)			
Long-Term Debt			
Common Stock			

LO4, LO5 **P9-30** ## Foreign Currency Translation

Refer to the information in Problem P9-29 for Kiner Company and its foreign subsidiary.

Required

Prepare a schedule translating the selected accounts into U.S. dollars as of December 31, 20X1, and December 31, 20X2, respectively, assuming that the local currency unit is the foreign subsidiary's functional currency.

LO1–LO8 **P9-31** ## Matching Key Terms

Match the items in the left-hand column with the descriptions/explanations in the right-hand column.

Items	Descriptions/Explanations
1. Current exchange rate	A. Method used to restate a foreign entity's financial statement when the local currency unit is the functional currency.
2. Foreign entity goodwill under translation	
3. Increase in the translation adjustment for the year	B. Method used to restate a foreign entity's financial statements when the U.S. dollar is the functional currency.
4. Other comprehensive income—translation adjustment	C. Currency of the environment in which an entity primarily generates and expends cash.
5. Translation	
6. Historical exchange rate	D. Is always the local currency unit of the foreign entity.
7. Foreign entity goodwill under remeasurement	E. Exchange rate at the end of the period.
8. Remeasurement	F. Exchange rate at the date of the asset acquisition or at the date of dividend declaration.
9. A decrease in the translation adjustment for the year	
10. Functional currency	G. Average exchange rate during the period.
	H. Periodic change in the cumulative translation adjustment.
	I. Method under which goodwill must be adjusted to the current exchange rate at the balance sheet date.
	J. Method under which goodwill is restated using the historical exchange rate.
	K. Increase of the exchange rate during the year.
	L. Decrease of the exchange rate during the year.

LO4

P9-32 **Translation Choices**

The U.S. parent company is preparing its consolidated financial statements for December 31, 20X4. The foreign company's local currency (LCU) is the functional currency. Information is presented in Data Set A and Data Set B.

Data Set A:

	Exchange Rate	Date
1.	LCU 0.74	June 16, 20X1: date foreign company purchased
2.	LCU 0.80	January 1, 20X4: beginning of current year
3.	LCU 0.87	March 31, 20X4
4.	LCU 0.86	June 12, 20X4
5.	LCU 0.85	Average for year 20X4
6.	LCU 0.84	November 1, 20X4
7.	LCU 0.83	December 31, 20X4: end of current year
8.	No translation rate is applied	

Data Set B:

a.	Accounts receivable outstanding from sales on March 31, 20X4.
b.	Sales revenue earned during year.
c.	Dividends declared on November 1, 20X4.
d.	Ending inventory balance from acquisitions through the year.
e.	Equipment purchased on March 31, 20X4.
f.	Depreciation expense on equipment.
g.	Common stock outstanding.
h.	Dividends payable from dividends declared on June 12, 20X4.
i.	Accumulated Other Comprehensive Income balance from prior fiscal year.
j.	Bond payable issued January 1, 20X4.
k.	Interest expense on the bond payable.

Required

a. Select the appropriate exchange rate from the amounts presented in Data Set A to prepare the translation worksheet for each of the accounts presented in Data Set B.

b. Determine the direct exchange rate for January 1, 20X4.

c. Determine whether the U.S. dollar strengthened or weakened during 20X4.

LO5

P9-33 **Proof of Translation Adjustment**

MaMi Co. Ltd. located in Mexico City is a wholly owned subsidiary of Special Foods, a U.S. company. At the beginning of the year, MaMi's condensed balance sheet was reported in Mexican pesos (MXP) as follows:

Assets	3,425,000	Liabilities	2,850,000
		Stockholders' Equity	575,000

During the year, the company earned income of MXP270,000 and on November 1 declared dividends of MXP150,000. The Mexican peso is the functional currency. Relevant exchange rates between the peso and the U.S. dollar follow:

January 1 (beginning of year)	$0.0870
Average for year	0.0900
November 1	0.0915
December 31 (end of year)	0.0930

Required

a. Prepare a proof of the translation adjustment, assuming that the beginning credit balance of the accumulated other comprehensive income—translation adjustment was $3,250.

b. Did the U.S. dollar strengthen or weaken against the Mexican peso during the year?

| Kaplan CPA Review | Please visit the text Web site for the online CPA Simulation: www.mhhe.com/baker1e. |

Kaplan CPA
Review

SCHWESER

Please visit the text Web site for the online CPA Simulation: www.mhhe.com/baker1e.

Situation

The Texas Corporation located in San Antonio has transactions both in the United States and in Mexico. The U.S. dollar is its functional currency. In addition, this company has a wholly owned subsidiary (Mexico, Inc.) located in Mexico. Consolidated financial statements are being prepared for year 1. The currency exchange rates are as follows for the current year (year 1M):

January 1, year 1	1 peso equals $0.088
Average for year 1	1 peso equals $0.090
November 1, year 1	1 peso equals $0.092
December 1, year 1	1 peso equals $0.094
December 31, year 1	1 peso equals $0.095
January 31, year 2	1 peso equals $0.098

Topics to be covered in simulation

- Sale to an unrelated company in Mexico.
- Purchase of equipment from an unrelated company in Mexico.
- Impact of the designation of the functional currency as the dollar or the peso.
- Translation of expenses from the peso to the dollar, assuming the peso is the functional currency.
- Translation of expenses from the peso to the dollar, assuming the dollar is the functional currency.
- Translation of fixed assets.
- Translation of liabilities.
- Translation adjustment.
- Functional currency.
- Forward exchange contracts.

Chapter Ten

Partnerships: Formation, Operation, and Changes in Membership

THE EVOLUTION OF PRICEWATERHOUSECOOPERS (PwC)

All of today's "Big 4" accounting firms are partnerships and all have evolved over time through continual mergers of existing accounting firms. PricewaterhouseCoopers (PwC) has a long history dating back to the mid-1800s. Samuel Price set up his own accounting practice in London in 1849. A few years later in 1854, William Cooper established his accounting practice in London as well. It would take nearly 150 years for these two firms to eventually come together. In fact, they competed with one another during most of this time.

Price, Holyland, and Waterhouse joined forces in 1865 to form what would eventually become Price, Waterhouse, & Company. It wasn't until 1957 that several large accounting firms would come together to form Coopers & Lybrand. These two firms became two of the "Big 8" and then the "Big 6" accounting firms. Throughout most of the 20th century, the profession was dominated by the "Big 8" accounting firms:

1. Arthur Andersen
2. Arthur Young & Co.
3. Coopers & Lybrand
4. Ernst & Whinney
5. Deloitte Haskins & Sells
6. Peat Marwick Mitchell
7. Price Waterhouse
8. Touche Ross

In 1989 due to intense competition, Ernst & Whinney merged with Arthur Young to form Ernst & Young. That same year, Deloitte, Haskins & Sells merged with Touche Ross to form Deloitte & Touche. These mergers narrowed the field to the "Big 6" and Price Waterhouse continued to compete with Coopers & Lybrand during the 1990s. Finally, in 1998, one of the largest mergers in the history of the public accounting profession occurred when Price Waterhouse merged with Coopers & Lybrand to form PricewaterhouseCoopers. This merger brought about the brief reign of the "Big 5" before the demise of Arthur Andersen in 2002 in the wake of the Enron scandal, which limited the playing field to the current "Big 4" accounting firms.

Most of the early mergers in the accounting profession were general partnerships. It wasn't until the 1990s that a new type of legal entity, the limited liability partnership (LLP), emerged, allowing some protection to partners for liabilities incurred by their partners. While only two states in the United States allowed LLPs in 1992, by the end of the decade, most had passed laws allowing LLPs. All of the Big 4 accounting firms are now LLPs.

The number of partnerships in the United States has been estimated to be between 1.5 and 2.0 million, second only to sole proprietorships, which number in excess of 15 million businesses. In contrast, there are about 1 million corporations in the United States. Accountants are often called on to aid in the formation and operation of partnerships to ensure proper measurement and valuation of the partnership's transactions. This chapter focuses on the formation and operation of partnerships, including accounting for the addition of new partners and the retirement of a present partner. Chapter 11 presents the accounting for the termination and liquidation of partnerships.

LEARNING OBJECTIVES

When you finish studying this chapter, you should be able to:

LO1 Understand and explain the nature and regulation of partnerships.

LO2 Understand and explain the differences among different types of partnerships.

LO3 Make calculations and journal entries for the formation of partnerships.

LO4 Make calculations and journal entries for the operation of partnerships.

LO5 Make calculations and journal entries for the allocation of partnership profit or loss.

LO6 Make calculations and journal entries to account for changes in partnership ownership.

THE NATURE OF THE PARTNERSHIP ENTITY

LO1

Understand and explain the nature and regulation of partnerships.

Partnerships are a popular form of business because they are easy to form and they allow several individuals to combine their talents and skills in a particular business venture. In addition, partnerships provide a means of obtaining more equity capital than a single individual can obtain and allow the sharing of risks for rapidly growing businesses.

Accounting for partnerships requires recognition of several important factors. First, from an accounting viewpoint, the partnership is a separate business entity. The Internal Revenue Code, however, views the partnership form as a conduit only, not separable from the business interests of the individual partners. Therefore, tax and financial accounting rules for specific events differ in several ways, such as the value assigned to assets contributed in the formation of the partnership. This chapter presents the generally accepted accounting principles of partnership accounting. We present a brief discussion of the tax aspects of a partnership in Appendix 10A.

Second, although many partnerships account for their operations using accrual accounting, some partnerships use the cash basis or modified cash basis of accounting. These alternatives are allowed because the partnership records are maintained for the partners and must reflect their information needs. The partnership's financial statements are usually prepared only for the partners but occasionally for the partnership's creditors. Unlike publicly traded corporations, most partnerships are not required to have annual audits of their financial statements. Although many partnerships adhere to generally accepted accounting principles (GAAP), deviations from GAAP are found in practice. The specific needs of the partners should be the primary criteria for determining the accounting policies to be used for a specific partnership.

The partnership form of business has several unique elements because of its legal and accounting status. The following section describes the major characteristics that distinguish the partnership form of organization.

Legal Regulation of Partnerships

Each state regulates the partnerships that are formed in it. Accountants advising partnerships must be familiar with partnership laws because these laws describe many of the rights of each partner and of creditors during the creation, operation, and liquidation of the partnership. Each state tends to begin with a uniform or model act and then modifies it to fit that state's business culture and history. The Uniform Partnership Act of 1914 served for many years as the model for defining the rights and responsibilities of the partners to each other and to the creditors of the partnership. In 1994 the National Conference of Commissioners on Uniform State Laws (NCCUSL) approved the first major revision of the model act to better reflect current business practices while also retaining many of the valuable provisions of the original act. This 1994 revision was titled the Revised Uniform Partnership Act (RUPA). During the next three years the NCCUSL continued to make small revisions of the model act and in 1997 it approved the final model as the ***Uniform Partnership Act of 1997 (UPA 1997).*** Most states have now adopted the UPA 1997 model partnership act because, although the UPA 1997 contains many of the features of the Uniform Partnership Act of 1914, the UPA 1997 reflects today's more complex partnership events and transactions, and stresses the fiduciary responsibilities of the partners to each other. The UPA 1997 will be used for discussion and illustration in this and the next chapter on partnerships.

Definition of a Partnership

Section 202 of the UPA 1997 states that ". . . the association of two or more persons to carry on as co-owners of a business for profit forms a partnership . . ." This definition encompasses three distinct factors:

1. *Association of two or more persons.* The "persons" are usually individuals; however, they also may be corporations or other partnerships.
2. *To carry on as co-owners.* This means that each partner has the apparent authority, unless restricted by the partnership agreement, to act as an agent of the partnership for transactions in the ordinary course of business of the kind carried on by the partnership. These transactions can legally bind the partnership to third parties.
3. *Business for profit.* A partnership may be formed to perform any legal business, trade, profession, or other service. However, the partnership must attempt to make a profit; therefore, not-for-profit entities such as fraternal groups may not be organized as partnerships.

Formation of a Partnership

A primary advantage of the partnership form of entity is ease of formation. The agreement to form a partnership may be as informal as a handshake or as formal as a many-paged partnership agreement. Each partner must agree to the formation agreement, and partners are strongly advised to have a formal written agreement to avoid potential problems that may arise during the operation of the business. It is usually true that if the potential partners cannot agree on the various operating aspects before a partnership is formed, many future disputes may arise that could cause severe management problems and that might seriously imperil the operations of the partnership.

The partnership agreement should include the following items:

1. The name of the partnership and the names of the partners.
2. The type of business to be conducted by the partnership and the duration of the partnership agreement.
3. The initial capital contribution of each partner and the method by which to account for future capital contributions.
4. A complete specification of the profit or loss distribution, including salaries, interest on capital balances, bonuses, limits on withdrawals in anticipation of profits, and the percentages used to distribute any residual profit or loss.
5. Procedures used for changes in the partnership, such as admission of new partners and the retirement of a partner.
6. Other aspects of operations the partners decide on, such as the management rights of each partner, election procedures, and accounting methods.

Each partner should sign the partnership agreement to indicate acceptance of the terms. A carefully prepared partnership agreement can eliminate many of the more common types of problems and disputes that may arise in the partnership's future operations.

Other Major Characteristics of Partnerships

After a state adopts the provisions of the UPA 1997, all partnerships formed in that state are regulated by the act. For partnerships that do not have a formal partnership agreement, the act provides the legal framework that governs the relationships among the partners and the rights of creditors of the partnership; in essence, the UPA 1997 becomes the partnership agreement for those partnerships that do not have one. The following presents the sections of the UPA 1997 applicable to the formation and operation of a partnership. Chapter 11 will present the sections of the UPA 1997 applicable to the dissolution and liquidation of a partnership.

1. *Partnership agreement.* The UPA 1997 governs in those partnership relations that are not specifically presented in the partnership agreement; thus, the UPA 1997 is used by the courts when there is no partnership agreement. There are several provisions of the UPA 1997 that are not waivable by partnership agreement. For example, a partnership may not restrict a partner's rights of access to the partnership's books and records, eliminate the obligations of partners for good faith and fair dealing with the other partners and the partnership, restrict any rights of third parties under the act, or reduce any legal rights of individual partners.

2. *Partnership as a separate entity.* A partnership is a separate business entity distinct from its partners. This **entity concept** means that a partnership can sue or be sued and that partnership property belongs to the partnership and not to any individual partner. Thus, there is no new partnership entity when there is a membership change in the partners (a new partner is admitted or a partner leaves the partnership).

3. *Partner is an agent of the partnership.* Each partner is an agent of the partnership for transactions of the kind carried on in the ordinary course of the partnership business, unless the partner did not have the authority to act for the partnership in that specific matter and the third party knew or had received a notification that the partner lacked authority. This agency relationship among the partners is very important. If the partnership determines that only specific partners shall have the authority for specific business transactions, then the partnership must make third parties aware of the limitations of authority of other partners. This notice should be in a public form either as a formal filing of a statement of partnership authority (discussed in the next point) or in direct communications with third parties. Otherwise, third parties may presume a partner has the authority to act as an agent for the partnership in those normal business transactions of the type engaged in for the business in which the partnership operates.

4. *Statement of partnership authority.* A **Statement of Partnership Authority** describes the partnership and identifies the specific authority of partners to transact specific types of business on behalf of the partnership. This voluntary statement is filed with the secretary of the state. The statement is a notice of any limitations on the rights of specific partners to enter into specific types of transactions. Partnerships should file these statements particularly for partnership transactions in real estate. The act states that a filed statement of partnership authority is sufficient constructive notice to third parties for partnership real estate transactions, but it is not necessarily sufficient notice for other types of partnership transactions.

5. *Partner's liability is joint and several.* All partners are liable jointly and severally for all obligations of the partnership unless otherwise provided by law. In the event a partnership fails and its assets are not sufficient to pay its obligations, partners are required to make contributions to the partnership in the proportion to which they share partnership losses. If a partner fails to make a contribution of the amount required, then all other partners must contribute in the proportion to which those partners share partnership losses. Partnership creditors must first be satisfied from partnership assets

and additional partner contributions are classified as partnership assets. However, a partner is liable for partnership liabilities incurred prior to that partner's admission into the partnership only to the extent of the partner's capital credit. A new partner is not personally liable for partnership debts incurred prior to that partner's admission into the partnership. If a partnership creditor takes legal action against an individual partner for a partnership obligation, the partnership creditor does not have any superior rights to the partner's individual assets. In this case, the partnership creditor joins with the other personal creditors.

6. *Partner's rights and duties.* Each partner is to have a capital account presenting the amount of that partner's contributions to the partnership, net of any liabilities, and the partner's share of the partnership profits or losses, less any distributions. The partner is entitled to an equal share of the profits or losses unless otherwise agreed to in the partnership agreement. New partners can be admitted only with the consent of all of the partners. Each partner has a right of access to the partnership's books and records, and each partner has a duty to act for the partnership in good faith and fair dealing.

7. *Partner's transferable interest in the partnership.* Under the entity approach to a partnership stated in the act, a partner is not a co-owner of any partnership property. This means that the only **transferable interest** of a partner is the partner's share of the profits and losses of the partnership and the right to receive distributions, including any liquidating distribution. A partner may not transfer any rights of management or authority to transact any of the partnership's business operations. Thus the partner's individual creditors may not attach any of the partnership's assets but a partner's personal creditor may obtain a legal judgment for attachment of the partner's transferable interest.

8. *Partner's dissociation.* A **partner's dissociation** means that the partner can no longer act on behalf of the partnership. A partner is dissociated from a partnership when any of the following events occurs: (*a*) the partner gives notice to the partnership of the partner's express will to withdraw as a partner; (*b*) the partner is expelled from the partnership in accordance with the partnership agreement, typically because the partner has violated some part of the partnership agreement or it becomes unlawful for the partnership to continue business with that partner; (*c*) one of several judicial determinations occurs (such as the partner committing a material breach of the partnership agreement or the partner engaging in serious conduct that materially and adversely affects the partnership); (*d*) the partner becomes a debtor in bankruptcy; or (*e*) the partner dies.

Types of Limited Partnerships

Many persons view the possibility of personal liability for a partnership's obligations as a major disadvantage of the general partnership form of business. For this reason, sometimes people become limited partners in one of the several limited partnership forms. A limited partnership (LP) is different from a limited liability partnership (LLP), or a limited liability limited partnership (LLLP). The variations are based on the degree of liability shield provided to the partners.

Limited Partnerships (LP)   In a limited partnership (LP), there is at least one general partner and one or more limited partners. The general partner is personally liable for the obligations of the partnership and has management responsibility. Limited partners are liable only to the extent of their capital contribution but do not have any management authority. The Uniform Limited Partnership Act of 2001 (ULPA 2001) is the model legal act used to regulate limited partnerships and has been adopted in many states. Accounting for the investment in a limited partnership is based on an evaluation of control. Typically, the general partner has the necessary elements of operational control of the limited partnership and will consolidate the investment on the general partner's books. The limited partners typically use the equity method to account for their investments.

However, in 2005, the Emerging Issues Task Force (EITF) reached consensus in **EITF Issue No. 04-05 (ASC 810)**, "Determining Whether a General Partner, or the General Partners as a Group, Controls a Limited Partnership or Similar Entity When the Limited Partners Have Certain Rights" (EITF 04-05, ASC 810). The EITF examined cases in which the limited partners have either (*a*) the ability to dissolve the limited partnership or to remove the general partners without cause (the so-called kick-out right) or (*b*) substantive participating rights to be actively engaged in the significant decisions of the limited partnership's business. In these two cases, the presumption of control by the general partners could be overcome and then each of the general partners would account for its investment in the limited partnership using the equity method of accounting. The identifier, LP or Limited Partnership, must be included in the name or identification of the limited partnership.

Limited Liability Partnerships (LLP) A limited liability partnership (LLP) is one in which each partner has some degree of liability shield. There are no general or limited partners in an LLP; thus each partner has the rights and duties of a general partner, but limited legal liability. A partner in a limited liability partnership is not personally liable for a partnership obligation. However, several states have defined that each partner in an LLP is fully liable for the obligations of the partnership, though not for acts of professional negligence or malpractice committed by other partners. Some legal support for the LLP came as a result of the fact that most professional service partnerships, such as accounting firms, have significant amounts of insurance to cover judgments in lawsuits and other losses from offering services. A limited liability partnership must identify itself as such by adding the LLP letters behind the name of the partnership in all correspondence or other means of identification of the firm. Virtually all large public accounting firms are LLPs. This designation has not changed the nature of accounting services provided to clients and has been generally accepted in the business market.

Limited Liability Limited Partnership (LLLP) In most states, a limited partnership may elect to become a limited liability limited partnership. In an LLLP, each partner is liable only for the business obligations of the partnership, and not for acts of malpractice or other wrongdealing by the other partners in the normal course of the partnership's business. The ULPA 2001 includes the regulatory guidance for LLLPs. The advantage of an LLLP is that general partners, even though responsible for management of the partnership, have no personal liability for partnership obligations, similar to the shield provided to limited partners. The identifier "LLLP" or the phrase "limited liability limited partnership" must be included in the name or identification of the entity.

Accounting and Financial Reporting Requirements for Partnerships

Most partnerships are small or medium-sized entities, although there are some large partnership entities. Partnerships do not issue stock and thus the information needs of a partnership are typically different from those of corporations that have stockholders. A partnership has much more flexibility to select specific accounting measurement and recognition methods and specific financial reporting formats.

If a partnership wishes to issue general-purpose financial statements for external users such as credit grantors, vendors, or others, then the partnership should use generally accepted accounting principles as promulgated by the FASB and other standard-setting bodies, and the independent auditor can issue an opinion that the statements are in accordance with generally accepted accounting principles. The FASB created the Private Company Financial Reporting Committee in June 2006 to provide input to the FASB on proposed and existing accounting standards as to their impact on nonpublic business entities. Thus, the FASB has a vehicle by which GAAP standards can be adapted to meet the cost/benefit perspective of nonpublic entities.

If a partnership has only internal reporting needs, then the accounting and financial reporting should meet those internal information needs of the partners. In this case, the partnership may use non-GAAP accounting methods and have financial reports in a format different from those required under GAAP. For example, some partnerships use the accounting methods prescribed by tax laws, thereby generating tax-based financial reports. Some partnerships use the cash-based accounting system, often with some adjustments, so the financial reports provide specific cash flow and cash positions. And other partnerships may use accounting methods that are proximate to GAAP, with some adjustments that fit the information needs of the partners, such as recognizing increases in the fair value of nonfinancial assets at the time of admission of a new partner. In these cases, if the financial statements are presented to users external to the partnership, such as banks, vendors, or regulatory bodies, it should be clearly identified on the statements what specific accounting methods were used by the entity so that the users are informed that the information presented in the financial statements does not conform to GAAP. An independent accountant's opinion on these financial statements also would have to disclose the specific accounting methods used or the deviations from GAAP that affected the amounts reported in the financial statements. It is up to the partners to determine their financial information needs and then the partnership accountant applies the necessary accounting measurement, recognition, and reporting methods that meet the partners' financial information needs.

International Financial Reporting Standards for Small and Medium-Sized Entities and Joint Ventures

In 2009, the International Accounting Standards Board issued "International Financial Reporting Standard for Small and Medium-sized Entities," more commonly known as **IFRS for SMEs.** SMEs are defined as those entities that (*a*) do not have public accountability (i.e., do not have stock or issue bonds in a public capital market) and (*b*) publish general-purpose financial statements for external users. This standard presents the definitions of items and accounting concepts that are quite similar to those already in the international financial accounting and reporting standards, except that less detail and fewer disclosures are mandated and more flexibility is provided for the formats of the financial statements. Moreover, **IAS 31** on the accounting for joint ventures, many of which are accounted as partnerships, also became effective in July 2009. Thus, the IASB is addressing the specific accounting and financial reporting requirements for SMEs and joint ventures that are required to provide general-purpose financial statements to external users. However, these standards do not apply to partnerships that do *not* have public accountability *and* do *not* issue general-purpose financial statements to external users.

ACCOUNTING FOR THE FORMATION OF A PARTNERSHIP[1]

LO3

Make calculations and journal entries for the formation of partnerships.

Advanced StudyGuide .com

At the formation of a partnership, it is necessary to assign a proper value to the noncash assets and liabilities contributed by the partners. Section 201 of the UPA 1997 specifies that a partnership is an entity distinct from its partners. Thus, an item contributed by a partner becomes partnership property. The partnership must clearly distinguish between capital contributions and loans made to the partnership by individual partners. Loan arrangements should be evidenced by promissory notes or other legal documents necessary to show that a loan arrangement exists between the partnership and an individual partner. Also, it is important to clearly distinguish between tangible assets that are owned by the partnership and those specific assets that are owned by individual partners but are used by the partnership. Accurate records of the partnership's tangible assets must be maintained.

FASB Statement No. 157 (ASC 820), "Fair Value Measurements" (FASB 157, ASC 820), continues the long-held accounting concept that the contributed assets should be valued at their fair values, which may require appraisals or other valuation techniques.

[1] To view a video explanation of this topic, visit advancedstudyguide.com.

Liabilities assumed by the partnership should be valued at the present value of the remaining cash flows.

The individual partners must agree to the percentage of equity that each will have in the net assets of the partnership. Generally, the capital balance is determined by the proportionate share of each partner's capital contribution. For example, if A contributes 70 percent of the net assets in a partnership with B, then A will have a 70 percent capital share and B will have a 30 percent capital share. In recognition of intangible factors, such as a partner's special expertise or necessary business connections, however, partners may agree to any proportional division of capital. Therefore, before recording the initial capital contribution, all partners must agree on the valuation of the net assets and on each partner's capital share.

Illustration of Accounting for Partnership Formation

The following illustration is used as the basis for the remaining discussion in this chapter. Alt, a sole proprietor, has been developing software for several types of computers. The business has the following account balances as of December 31, 20X0:

Cash	$ 3,000	Liabilities	$10,000
Inventory	7,000	Alt, Capital	15,000
Equipment	20,000		
Less: Accumulated Depreciation	(5,000)		
Total Assets	$25,000	Total Liabilities and Capital	$25,000

Alt needs additional technical assistance to meet the increasing sales and offers Blue an interest in the business. Alt and Blue agree to form a partnership. Alt's business is audited, and its net assets are appraised. The audit and appraisal disclose that $1,000 of liabilities have not been recorded, inventory has a market value of $9,000, and the equipment has a fair value of $19,000.

Alt and Blue prepare and sign a partnership agreement that includes all significant operating policies. Blue will contribute $10,000 cash for a one-third capital interest. The AB Partnership is to acquire all of Alt's business and assume its debts.

The entry to record the initial capital contribution on the partnership's books is

(1)
January 1, 20X1

Cash	13,000	
Inventory	9,000	
Equipment	19,000	
Liabilities		11,000
Alt, Capital		20,000
Blue, Capital		10,000

Record the formation of AB Partnership by capital contributions of Alt and Blue.

Key Observations from Illustration

Note that the partnership is an accounting entity separate from each of the partners and that the assets and liabilities are recorded at their market values at the time of contribution. No accumulated depreciation is carried forward from the sole proprietorship to the partnership. All liabilities are recognized and recorded.

The partnership's capital is $30,000. This is the sum of the individual partners' capital accounts and is the value of the partnership's assets less liabilities. The fundamental accounting equation—assets less liabilities equals capital—is used often in partnership accounting. Blue is to receive a one-third capital interest in the partnership with a contribution of $10,000. In this case, his capital interest equals his capital contribution.

Each partner's capital amount recorded does not necessarily have to equal his or her capital contribution. The partners could decide to divide the total capital equally regardless of the source of the contribution. For example, although Alt contributed $20,000 of the

$30,000 partnership capital, he could agree to $15,000 as his initial capital balance and permit Blue the remaining $15,000 as a capital credit. On the surface this may not seem to be a reasonable action by Alt, but it is possible that Blue has some particularly important business experience needed by the partnership and Alt agrees to the additional credit to Blue in recognition of his experience and skills. The key point is that the partners may allocate the capital contributions in any manner they desire. The accountant must be sure that all partners agree to the allocation and then record it accordingly.

ACCOUNTING FOR THE OPERATIONS OF A PARTNERSHIP

LO4

Make calculations and journal entries for the operation of partnerships.

A partnership provides services or sells products in pursuit of profit. These transactions are recorded in the appropriate journals and ledger accounts. Many partnerships use accrual accounting and generally accepted accounting principles to maintain their books because GAAP results in better measures of income over time. Some creditors, such as banks, and some vendors, such as large suppliers to the partnership, may periodically require audited financial statements, and if GAAP are used, the financial statements can then receive a "clean" or unqualified audit opinion. Furthermore, the partners can compare their business's GAAP-based financial statements against published financial profiles, such as Moody's or many published by the U.S. government, against other companies in the same line of business so that the partners can evaluate their respective financial performance and position.

But some partnerships use alternative non-GAAP methods such as the cash-basis method, or the modified cash-basis method. These two methods have simplified record-keeping requirements and can continuously provide the partners with the current cash position of their partnership. A small number of partnerships revalue all their assets at the end of each fiscal period in order to estimate the market value of their business as a whole at year-end. Some partnerships use federal income tax rules to account for transactions so the partners can determine the effects of transactions that will be reportable on their personal income tax returns. The accountant works with the partners to determine their specific information needs regarding the partnership and then applies the appropriate accounting and financial reporting methods to meet those needs.

Partners' Accounts

The partnership may maintain several accounts for each partner in its accounting records. These *partners' accounts* are capital, drawing, and loan accounts.

Capital Accounts

The initial investment of a partner, any subsequent capital contributions, profit or loss distributions, and any withdrawals of capital by the partner are ultimately recorded in the partner's capital account. Each partner has one capital account, which usually has a credit balance. On occasion, a partner's capital account may have a debit balance, called a *deficiency* or sometimes termed a *deficit,* which occurs because the partner's share of losses and withdrawals exceeds his or her capital contribution and share of profits. A deficiency is usually eliminated by additional capital contributions. The balance in the capital account represents the partner's share of the partnership's net assets.

Drawing Accounts

Partners generally make withdrawals of assets from the partnership during the year in anticipation of profits. A separate drawing account often is used to record the periodic withdrawals and is then closed to the partner's capital account at the end of the period. For example, the following entry is made in the AB Partnership's books for a $3,000 cash withdrawal by Blue on May 1, 20X1:

	May 1, 20X1		
(2)	Blue, Drawing	3,000	
	Cash		3,000
	Record Blue's withdrawal of $3,000.		

Noncash drawings should be valued at their market values at the date of the withdrawal. A few partnerships make an exception to the rule of market value for partners' withdrawals of inventory. They record withdrawals of inventory at cost, thereby not recording a gain or loss on these drawings.

Loan Accounts

The partnership may look to its present partners for additional financing. Any loans between a partner and the partnership should always be accompanied by proper loan documentation such as a promissory note. A loan from a partner is shown as a payable on the partnership's books, the same as any other loan. Unless all partners agree otherwise, the partnership is obligated to pay interest on the loan to the individual partner. Note that interest is *not* required to be paid on capital investments unless the partnership agreement states that capital interest is to be paid. The partnership records interest on loans as an operating expense. Alternatively, the partnership may lend money to a partner, in which case it records a loan receivable from the partner. Again, unless all partners agree otherwise, these loans should bear interest, and the interest income should be recognized on the partnership's income statement. The following entry is made to record a $4,000, 10 percent, one-year loan from Alt to the partnership on July 1, 20X1:

		July 1, 20X1		
(3)		Cash		4,000	
		Loan Payable to Alt			4,000
		Record loan agreement with partner Alt.		

The loan payable to Alt is reported in the partnership's balance sheet. A loan from a partner is a related-party transaction for which separate footnote disclosure is required, and it must be reported as a separate balance sheet item, not included with other liabilities.

ALLOCATING PROFIT OR LOSS TO PARTNERS

LO5

Make calculations and journal entries for the allocation of partnership profit or loss.

Advanced
StudyGuide
.com

Profit or loss is allocated to the partners at the end of each period in accordance with the partnership agreement. If the partnership does not have a formal partnership agreement, section 401 of the UPA 1997 indicates that all partners should share profits and losses equally. Virtually all partnerships have a profit or loss allocation agreement. The agreement must be followed precisely, and if it is unclear, the accountant should make sure that all partners agree to the profit or loss distribution. Many problems and later arguments can be avoided by carefully specifying the profit or loss distribution in the articles of copartnership.

A wide range of ***profit distribution plans*** is found in the business world. Some partnerships have straightforward distribution plans; others have extremely complex ones. It is the accountant's responsibility to distribute the profit or loss according to the partnership agreement regardless of how simple or complex that agreement is. Profit distributions are similar to dividends for a corporation: These distributions should not be included on the partnership's income statement regardless of how the profit is distributed. Profit distributions are recorded directly into the partner's capital accounts, not treated as expense items.

Most partnerships use one or more of the following distribution methods:

1. Preselected ratio.
2. Interest on capital balances.
3. Salaries to partners.
4. Bonuses to partners.

We note at the outset that the titles for these distribution methods can be deceiving. They simply describe different ways for allocating a fixed amount of partnership profit. For example, if a partnership earns $100,000 in profit for a given period, these methods are simply four different ways for dividing up the $100,000 among the partners.

Preselected ratios are usually the result of negotiations between the partners. Ratios for profit distributions may be based on the percentage of total partnership capital, time, and effort invested in the partnership, or a variety of other factors. Smaller partnerships often split profits evenly among the partners. In addition, some partnerships have different ratios if the firm suffers a loss rather than earns a profit. The partnership form of business allows a wide selection of profit distribution ratios to meet the partners' individual desires.

Distributing partnership income based on *interest on capital balances* simply means that the partners divide up some or all of the $100,000 among themselves based on the relative balances they have maintained in their capital accounts. This method recognizes the contribution of the partners' capital investments to the partnership's profit-generating capacity and requires the allocation of profits based on a fixed rate multiplied by the partner's capital account balance. This allocation of profits based on capital balances is generally not an expense of the partnership (like interest on a loan from a bank). It is simply a method for distributing profits.

If one or more of the partners' services are important to the partnership, the profit distribution agreement may provide for *salaries* or *bonuses.* Again, these represent fixed amounts allocated to partners from the $100,000 earned during the period. They are simply a form of profit distribution and not an expense of the partnership. Think of a salary as a fixed amount of company profits allocated to a given partner and a bonus as a portion of profits allocated to a partner based on a predetermined performance formula. Occasionally, the distribution process may depend on the size of the profit or may differ if the partnership has a loss for the period. For example, salaries to partners might be paid only if revenue exceeds expenses by a certain amount. The accountant must carefully read the partnership agreement to determine the precise profit distribution plan for the specific circumstances at the time.

The profit or loss distribution is recorded with a closing entry at the end of each period. The revenue and expenses are often closed into an income summary account that is then allocated to the partners' capital accounts based on the formula prescribed in the partnership agreement (which could include one or more of the four methods described above). If the partnership earns $100,000 for the period, the formula provided in the partnership agreement tells the accountant how to allocate this amount to the partners' capital accounts. Sometimes partnerships bypass the income summary account and close revenue and expense accounts directly to the partners' capital accounts. In the following examples, we use an income summary account. The balance in the income summary account (either net income or net loss) is closed and distributed to the partners' capital accounts.

Illustrations of Profit Allocation

During 20X1, the AB Partnership earns $45,000 of revenue and incurs $35,000 in expenses, leaving a profit of $10,000 for the year. Alt maintains a capital balance of $20,000 during the year, but Blue's capital investment varies during the year as follows:

Date	Debit	Credit	Balance
January 1			$10,000
May 1	$3,000		7,000
September 1		$500	7,500
November 1	1,000		6,500
December 31			6,500

The debits of $3,000 and $1,000 are recorded in Blue's drawing account; the additional investment is credited to his capital account.

Arbitrary Profit-Sharing Ratio

Alt and Blue could agree to share profits in a ratio unrelated to their capital balances or to any other operating feature of the partnership. For example, assume the partners agree to share profits or losses in the ratio of 60 percent to Alt and 40 percent to Blue. Some partnership agreements specify this ratio as 3:2. The following schedule illustrates how the net income is distributed using a 3:2 profit-sharing ratio:

	Alt	Blue	Total
Profit-sharing percentage	60%	40%	100%
Net income			$10,000
Allocate 60:40	$6,000	$4,000	(10,000)
Total	$6,000	$4,000	$ –0–

This schedule shows how net income is distributed to the partners' capital accounts. The actual distribution is accomplished by closing the Income Summary account. In addition, the drawing accounts are closed to the capital accounts at the end of the period.

December 31, 20X1

(4)	Blue, Capital	4,000	
	Blue, Drawing		4,000
	Close Blue's drawing account.		

(5)	Revenue	45,000	
	Expenses		35,000
	Income Summary		10,000
	Close revenue and expenses.		

(6)	Income Summary	10,000	
	Alt, Capital		6,000
	Blue, Capital		4,000
	Distribute profit in accordance with partnership agreement.		

Interest on Capital Balances

The partnership agreement may provide for interest to be credited on the partners' capital balances as part of the distribution of profits. The rate of interest is often a stated percentage, but some partnerships use a rate that is determined by reference to current U.S. Treasury rates or current money market rates.

As stated earlier, interest calculated on partners' capital is generally a form of profit distribution. The calculation is made after net income is determined in order to decide how to distribute the income.

Particular caution must be exercised whenever interest on capital balances is included in the profit distribution plan. For example, the amount of the distribution can be significantly different depending on whether the interest is computed on beginning capital balances, ending capital balances, or average capital balances for the period. Most provisions for interest on capital specify that a weighted-average capital should be used. This method explicitly recognizes the time span for which each capital level is maintained during the period. For example, Blue's weighted-average capital balance for 20X1 is computed as follows:

Date	Debit	Credit	Balance	Months Maintained	Months Times Dollar Balance
January 1			$10,000	4	$40,000
May 1	$3,000		7,000	4	28,000
September 1		$500	7,500	2	15,000
November 1	1,000		6,500	2	13,000
Total				12	$96,000
Average capital ($96,000 ÷ 12 months)					$ 8,000

Assume Alt and Blue agree to allocate profits first based on 15 percent on the weighted-average capital balances and then any remaining profit is to be distributed based on a 60:40 ratio; the distribution of the $10,000 profit would be calculated as follows:

	Alt	Blue	Total
Profit percentage	60%	40%	100%
Average capital	$20,000	$8,000	
Net income			$10,000
Interest on average capital (15%)	$ 3,000	$1,200	(4,200)
Residual income			$ 5,800
Allocate 60:40	3,480	2,320	(5,800)
Total	$ 6,480	$3,520	$ –0–

Salaries

Recall that salaries to partners are simply fixed amounts allocated to partners as part of the regular allocation of profits. They are generally included as part of the profit distribution plan to recognize and compensate partners for differing amounts of personal services provided to the business.

Section 401 of the UPA 1997 states that a partner is not entitled to compensation for services performed for the partnership except for reasonable compensation for services in winding up the business of the partnership. Some partnership agreements, however, do specify a management fee to be paid to a partner who provides very specific administration responsibilities.

As mentioned previously, a general precept of partnership accounting is that salaries to partners are not operating expenses but are part of the profit distribution plan. This precept is closely related to the proprietary concept of owner's equity. According to the proprietary theory, the proprietor invests capital and personal services in pursuit of income. The earnings are a result of those two investments. The same logic applies to the partnership form of organization. Some partners invest capital while others invest personal time. Those who invest capital are typically rewarded with interest on their capital balances; those who invest personal time are rewarded with salaries. However, both interest and salaries are a result of the respective investments and are used not in the determination of income but in the determination of the proportion of income to credit to each partner's capital account. An interesting question arises if the partnership experiences losses. Can salaries to the partners during the year be treated as a distribution of profits? Although any amounts actually paid to partners during the year are really drawings made in anticipation of profits, the agreed salary amounts usually are added to the loss and that total is then distributed to the partners' capital accounts. Caution should be exercised if the partnership experiences a loss during the year. Some partnership agreements specify different distributions for profit than for losses. The accountant must be especially careful to follow precisely the partnership agreement when distributing the period's profit or loss to the partners.

To illustrate the allocation of partnership profit based on salaries, assume that the partnership agreement provides for fixed allocations of $2,000 to Alt and $5,000 to Blue. Any remainder is to be distributed in the profit and loss–sharing ratio of 60:40 percent. The profit distribution is calculated as follows:

	Alt	Blue	Total
Profit percentage	60%	40%	100%
Net income			$10,000
Salary	$2,000	$5,000	(7,000)
Residual income			$ 3,000
Allocate 60:40	1,800	1,200	(3,000)
Total	$3,800	$6,200	$ –0–

Bonuses

Bonuses are sometimes used as a means of providing additional compensation to partners who have provided services to the partnership. Bonuses are typically stated as a percentage of income either before or after the bonus. Sometimes the partnership agreement requires a minimum income to be earned before a bonus is calculated. The bonus is easily calculated by deriving and solving an equation. To illustrate the difference between a bonus *before* and a bonus *after* subtracting the bonus, we provide the following example. Assume that a bonus of 10 percent of income in excess of $5,000 is to be credited to Blue's capital account before distributing the remaining profit. In Case 1, the bonus is computed as a percentage of income *before* subtracting the bonus. In Case 2, the bonus is computed as a percentage of income *after* subtracting the bonus.

Case 1.

$$\text{Bonus} = X\% \,(\text{NI} - \text{MIN})$$

where: X = The bonus percentage
   NI = Net income before bonus
   MIN = Minimum amount of income before bonus

$$\text{Bonus} = 0.10 \,(\$10,000 - \$5,000)$$
$$= \$500$$

Case 2.

$$\text{Bonus} = X\% \,(\text{NI} - \text{MIN} - \text{Bonus})$$
$$= 0.10 \,(\$10,000 - \$5,000 - \text{Bonus})$$
$$= 0.10 \,(\$5,000 - \text{Bonus})$$
$$= \$500 - 0.10 \,\text{Bonus}$$
$$1.10 \,\text{Bonus} = \$500$$
$$\text{Bonus} = \$454.55$$
$$\approx \$455$$

The distribution of net income based on Case 2 is calculated as follows:

	Alt	Blue	Total
Profit percentage	60%	40%	100%
Net income			$10,000
Bonus to partner		$ 455	(455)
Residual income			$ 9,545
Allocate 60:40	$5,727	$3,818	(9,545)
Total	$5,727	$4,273	$ –0–

Multiple Bases of Profit Allocation

Advanced
StudyGuide
.com

A partnership agreement may describe a formula describing several allocation procedures to be used to distribute profit. For example, assume the profit and loss agreement of the AB Partnership specifies the following allocation process:

1. Interest of 15 percent on weighted-average capital balances.
2. Salaries of $2,000 for Alt and $5,000 for Blue.
3. A bonus of 10 percent of profits to be paid to Blue on partnership income exceeding $5,000 before subtracting the bonus, partners' salaries, and interest on capital balances.
4. Any residual to be allocated in the ratio of 60 percent to Alt and 40 percent to Blue.

The partnership agreement also should contain a provision to specify the allocation process in the event that partnership income is not sufficient to satisfy all allocation procedures. Some partnerships specify a profit distribution to be followed but only to the extent possible (i.e., stop following the formula once profits are exhausted). Most agreements specify that the entire process is to be completed and any remainder at each step of the process (whether positive or negative) is to be allocated in the profit and loss ratio as illustrated in the following schedule:

	Alt	Blue	Total
Profit percentage	60%	40%	100%
Average capital	$20,000	$8,000	
Net income:			$10,000
Step 1:			
Interest on average capital (15 percent)	$ 3,000	$1,200	(4,200)
Remaining after step 1			$ 5,800
Step 2:			
Salary	2,000	5,000	(7,000)
Deficiency after step 2			$ (1,200)
Step 3:			
Bonus		500	(500)
Deficiency after step 3			$ (1,700)
Step 4:			
Allocate 60:40	(1,020)	(680)	1,700
Total	$ 3,980	$6,020	$ –0–

In this case, the first two distribution steps created a deficiency. The AB Partnership agreement provided that the entire profit distribution process must be completed and any deficiency distributed in the profit and loss ratio. A partnership agreement could specify that the profit distribution process should stop at any point in the event of an operating loss or the creation of a deficiency. Again, it is important for the accountant to have a thorough knowledge of the partnership agreement before beginning the profit distribution process.

Special Profit Allocation Methods

Some partnerships distribute net income on the basis of other criteria. For example, most public accounting partnerships distribute profit on the basis of partnership "units." A new partner acquires a certain number of units, and additional units are assigned by a firmwide compensation committee for obtaining new clients, for providing the firm with specific areas of industrial expertise, for serving as a local office's managing partner, or for accepting a variety of other responsibilities.

Other partnerships may devise profit distribution plans that reflect the earnings of the partnership. For example, some medical or dental partnerships allocate profit on the basis of billed services. Other criteria may be number or size of clients, years of service with the firm, or the partner's position within the firm. An obvious advantage of the partnership form of organization is the flexibility it allows partners for the distribution of profits.

PARTNERSHIP FINANCIAL STATEMENTS

A partnership is a separate reporting entity for accounting purposes, and the three financial statements—income statement, balance sheet, and statement of cash flows—typically are prepared for the partnership at the end of each reporting period. Interim statements also may be prepared to meet the partners' information needs. In addition to the three basic financial statements, a *statement of partners' capital* is usually prepared to present the changes in the partners' capital accounts for the period. The statement of partners' capital for the AB Partnership for 20X1 under the multiple-base profit distribution plan illustrated in the prior section follows:

AB PARTNERSHIP Statement of Partners' Capital For the Year Ended December 31, 20X1			
	Alt	Blue	Total
Balance, January 1, 20X1	$20,000	$10,000	$30,000
Add: Additional investment		500	500
Net income distribution	3,980	6,020	10,000
	$23,980	$16,520	$40,500
Less: Withdrawal		(4,000)	(4,000)
Balance, December 31, 20X1	$23,980	$12,520	$36,500

CHANGES IN MEMBERSHIP

LO6

Make calculations and journal entries to account for changes in partnership ownership.

Changes in the membership of a partnership occur with the addition of new partners or the dissociation of present partners. New partners are often a primary source of additional capital or needed business expertise. The legal structure of a partnership requires that the *admission of a new partner* be subject to the unanimous approval of the present partners. Furthermore, public announcements are typically made about new partner additions so that third parties transacting business with the partnership are aware of the partnership change. Section 306 of the Uniform Partnership Act of 1997 states that a person admitted as a new partner of an existing partnership is not personally liable for any partnership obligation incurred before the new partner was admitted. Thus, a new partner can be charged only up to the amount of his or her capital contribution at the time of admission for partnership liabilities existing prior to admission.

The retirement or withdrawal of a partner from a partnership is a dissociation of that partner. A partner's dissociation does not necessarily mean a dissolution and winding up of the partnership. Many partnerships continue in business and, under section 701 of the UPA 1997, the partnership may purchase the dissociated partner's interest at a *buyout price.* The buyout price is the estimated amount if (1) the assets were sold for a price equal to the greater of the liquidation value or the value based on a sale of the entire business as a going concern without the dissociated partner and (2) the partnership was wound up at that time, with payment of all the partnership's creditors and termination of the business. Partners who simply wish to leave a partnership may be liable to the partnership for damages to the partnership caused by a wrongful dissociation. A wrongful dissociation occurs when the dissociation is in breach of an express provision of the partnership agreement or, for partnerships formed for a definite term or specific undertaking, before the term or undertaking has been completed. There are also some events that require judicial dissolution and winding up of the partnership. These will be discussed in Chapter 11.

General Concepts to Account for a Change in Membership in the Partnership

The Partnership as an Entity Separate from the Individual Partners and the Use of GAAP

The Uniform Partnership Act of 1997 clearly defines a partnership as an entity separate from the individual partners. As such, the partnership entity does not change because of the addition or withdrawal of an individual partner. This is similar to the concept of the entity for the corporate form of business, in which the business is not necessarily revalued each time there is a change in stockholders.

Some partnerships choose to comply with generally accepted accounting principles (GAAP) in their accounting and financial reporting. These partnerships follow the same standards established by the FASB and other regulatory bodies as public companies. Often venture capital firms or other credit suppliers may require that the private partnership company comply with GAAP so that the partnership's financials can be compared with those of other public companies. Venture capital firms have a goal of eventually taking their investees public. Thus, if a partnership follows GAAP and is audited by external auditors, the partnership can receive an audit opinion stating that it is in conformity with generally accepted accounting principles.

A partnership following GAAP and defining its company as an entity separate from the individual partners would account for a change in membership in the same manner as a corporate entity would account for changes in its investors. Additional investments would be recognized at their fair values along with the related increase in the company's total capital.

Recognizing Decreases in Net Asset Revaluations There are a few situations under GAAP for recognizing decreases in the fair value of specific nonfinancial assets that may be triggered by a change in partnership membership. For example, **FASB Statement No. 142 (ASC 350),** "Goodwill and Other Intangible Assets" (FASB 142, ASC 350), presents procedures for recognizing impairments of currently held goodwill. **FASB Statement No. 144 (ASC 360),** "Accounting for the Impairment or Disposal of Long-Lived Assets" (FASB 144, ASC 360), presents the accounting standards for recognizing impairment losses on long-lived assets. Net asset revaluations performed using the appropriate accounting standards are in accordance with GAAP. However, there are no GAAP standards that provide for *increases* in the value of nonfinancial assets or recognition of new goodwill, solely due to a change in partnership membership.

Bonus Method The ***bonus method*** is sometimes agreed upon by the partners to record a change in the partnership membership. This method records an increase in the partnership's total capital only for the capital amount invested by the new partner, in accordance with GAAP. However, the bonus method assigns partners' capital account balances based on the partners' agreement, and it is often based on the value of the new partner's investment. In some cases, the current partners assign some of their capital to a new partner; in other cases, a new partner agrees to assign a portion of his or her capital interest to the prior partners. Thus, the bonus method does not violate GAAP because partners may legally assign any or all of their transferable partnership capital interest to other partners.

The Partnership as an Aggregate of Partners' Interests and the Use of Non-GAAP Accounting The partners in a private company may choose to follow non-GAAP accounting methods that meet their specific information needs. These partnerships may use the transactions surrounding the change of partnership members as an opportunity for recognizing increases in the fair value of the partnership's existing nonfinancial assets or for recording previously unrecognized goodwill.

Recognizing Increases in Net Asset Revaluations or Goodwill The practices of recognizing increases in a partnership's net assets using the ***net asset revaluation*** method, or recognizing previously unrecorded goodwill using the ***goodwill recognition*** method, are *not* in compliance with GAAP. Partnerships using these non-GAAP methods argue that revaluing all assets and liabilities at the time of the change in partnership membership states fully the true economic condition of the partnership at that point in time, and properly assigns the changes in asset and liability values and goodwill to the partners who have been managing the business during the time the changes in value occurred.

Partners in private companies have free choice as to how they may account for changes in partnership membership. As noted, a private partnership may use either GAAP or non-GAAP methods, based on the information needs of the partners. Because some partnerships do record increases in value by applying the net asset revaluation or goodwill recognition methods, the following sections of this chapter discuss these non-GAAP methods of accounting for the change in the partnership membership.

New Partner Purchases an Interest

An individual may acquire a partnership interest directly from one or more of the present partners. In this type of transaction, cash or other assets are exchanged outside the partnership, and the only entry necessary on the partnership's books is a reclassification of the total capital of the partnership. For example, a new partner, Cha, could purchase Blue's partnership interest directly from him (as depicted in the diagram). This simple example would result in an entry to remove Blue's capital account from the books with a debit and transfer the balance to Cha's new capital account with a credit.

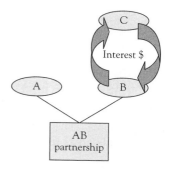

A concept used with some frequency is book value. The ***book value of a partnership*** is simply the total amount of the capital, which is also the amount of net assets (total assets minus total liabilities). Book value is important because it serves as a basis for asset and liability revaluations or goodwill recognition.

To provide a more complex example, assume that after operations and partners' withdrawals during 20X1 and 20X2, AB Partnership has a book value of $30,000 and profit percentages on January 1, 20X3, as follows:

	Capital Balance	Profit Percentage
Alt	$20,000	60
Blue	10,000	40
Total	$30,000	100

The following information describes the case:

1. On January 1, 20X3, Alt and Blue invite Cha to become a partner in their business. The resulting partnership will be called the ABC Partnership.

2. Cha purchases a one-fourth interest in the partnership capital directly from Alt and Blue for a total cost of $9,000, paying $5,900 to Alt and $3,100 to Blue. Cha will have a capital credit of $7,500 ($30,000 × 0.25) in a proportionate reclassification from Alt and Blue's capital accounts.

3. Cha will be entitled to a 25 percent interest in the profits or losses of the partnership. The remaining 75 percent interest will be divided between Alt and Blue in their old profit ratio of 60:40 percent. The resulting profit and loss percentages after the admission of Cha follow:

Partner	Profit Percentage
Alt	45 (75% of 0.60)
Blue	30 (75% of 0.40)
Cha	25
Total	100

In this example, Cha's 25 percent share of partnership profits or losses is the same as her one-fourth capital interest. These two percentage shares do not have to be the same. As described earlier in the chapter, a partner's capital interest may change over time because of profit distributions, withdrawals, or additional investments in capital. Furthermore, Cha could have acquired her entire capital interest directly from either partner. It is not necessary that a new partner directly purchasing an interest do so in a proportionate reclassification from each of the prior partners.

The transaction is between Cha and the individual partners and is not reflected on the partnership's books. The only entry in this case is to reclassify the partnership capital. Both Alt and Blue provide one-fourth of their capital to Cha, as follows:

	January 1, 20X3		
(7)	Alt, Capital	5,000	
	Blue, Capital	2,500	
	Cha, Capital		7,500

Reclassify capital to new partner:
From Alt: $5,000 = $20,000 \times 0.25$
From Blue: $2,500 = $10,000 \times 0.25$

In this case the capital credit to Cha is only $7,500, although $9,000 is paid for the one-fourth interest. The $9,000 payment implies that the fair value of the partnership is $36,000, calculated as follows:

$$\$9,000 = \text{Fair value} \times 0.25$$

$$\$36,000 = \text{Fair value}$$

The partnership's book value is $30,000 before Cha's investment. The payment of $9,000 is made directly to the individual partners, and it does not become part of the partnership's assets. The $6,000 difference between the partnership's fair value and its new book value could be due to understated assets or to unrecognized goodwill.

Recognizing Fair Value Increases in the Partnership's Net Assets (Non-GAAP)

Up to this point, the partnership is still following GAAP because the partners may legally assign any or all of their transferable partnership capital interest to other persons or among themselves as they agree. If the partners wish to be in accordance with GAAP, then they must follow the appropriate recognition and measurement methods for the net assets as prescribed in GAAP.

Assume that Alt and Blue decide to use the evidence from Cha's investment to recognize increases in fair values of the nonfinancial long-lived assets that have taken place before the admission of Cha. The partners have been informed by the partnership's accountant that this type of revaluation is not in accordance with GAAP. For example, if the partnership has land that is undervalued by $6,000 that it sells after Cha is admitted to the partnership, Cha will share in the gain on the sale according to the profit ratio. To avoid this possible problem, some partnerships revalue the assets at the time a new partner is admitted even if the new partner purchases the partnership interest directly from the present partners. In this case, Alt and Blue could recognize the increase in the value of the land immediately before the admission of Cha and allocate the increase to their capital accounts in their 60:40 profit ratio, as follows:

(8)	Land	6,000	
	Alt, Capital		3,600
	Blue, Capital		2,400

Revaluation of land before admission of new partner:
To Alt: $3,600 = $6,000 \times 0.60$
To Blue: $2,400 = $6,000 \times 0.40$

Note that the partnership's total resulting capital is $36,000 ($30,000 prior plus the $6,000 revaluation). The transfer of a one-fourth capital credit to Cha is recorded as follows:

(9)			
	Alt, Capital	5,900	
	Blue, Capital	3,100	
	Cha, Capital		9,000

Reclassify capital to new partner:
Cha = ($30,000 + $6,000) × 0.25 = $9,000
From Alt = ($20,000 + $3,600) × 0.25 = $5,900
From Blue = ($10,000 + $2,400) × 0.25 = $3,100

The partnership's accountant should ensure that sufficient evidence exists for any revaluation of assets and liabilities to prevent valuation abuses. Corroborating evidence such as appraisals or an extended period of excess earnings helps support asset valuations.

New Partner Invests in Partnership

A new partner may acquire a share of the partnership by investing in the business. In this case, the partnership receives the cash or other assets.

Advanced
StudyGuide
.com

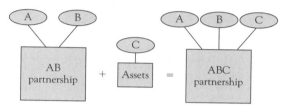

Three cases are possible when a new partner invests in a partnership:

Case 1. The new partner's investment equals the new partner's proportion of the partnership's book value.

Case 2. The investment is for *more* than the new partner's proportion of the partnership's book value. This indicates that the partnership's prior net assets are undervalued on the books or that unrecorded goodwill exists.

Case 3. The investment is for *less* than the new partner's proportion of the partnership's book value. This suggests that the partnership's prior net assets are overvalued on its books or that the new partner may be contributing goodwill in addition to other assets.

The first step in determining how to account for the admission of a new partner is to compute the ***new partner's proportion of the partnership's book value*** as follows:

$$\begin{array}{c}\text{New partner's} \\ \text{proportion of} \\ \text{the partnership's} \\ \text{book value}\end{array} = \left(\begin{array}{c}\text{Prior} \\ \text{capital of} \\ \text{present} \\ \text{partners}\end{array} + \begin{array}{c}\text{Investment} \\ \text{of new} \\ \text{partner}\end{array}\right) \times \begin{array}{c}\text{Percentage} \\ \text{of capital} \\ \text{to new} \\ \text{partner}\end{array}$$

The new partner's proportion of the partnership's book value is compared with the amount of the investment the new partner made to determine the procedures to be followed in accounting for his or her admission. Figure 10–1 presents an overview of the three cases presented above. Step 1 is to compare the new partner's investment with his or her proportion of the partnership's book value. Note that this is done before any revaluations or recognition of goodwill. Step 2 is to determine the specific admission method. Three different methods are available to the partnership to account for the admission of a new partner when a difference exists between the new partner's investment and his or her proportion of the partnership's book value. The three methods are (1) revalue net assets, (2) recognize goodwill, or (3) use the bonus method. Under the revaluation of net assets

FIGURE 10–1   Overview of Accounting for Admission of a New Partner

Step 1: Compare Proportionate Book Value and Investment of New Partner	Step 2: Alternative Methods to Account for Admission	Key Observations
Investment cost > Book value (Case 2)	1. Revalue net assets up to market value and allocate to prior partners. 2. Record unrecognized goodwill and allocate to prior partners. 3. Assign bonus to prior partners.	• Prior partners receive asset valuation increase, goodwill, or bonus indicated by the excess of new partner's investment over book value of the capital share initially assignable to new partner. • Recording asset valuation increase or prior partners' goodwill increases total resulting partnership capital.
Investment cost = Book value (Case 1)	1. No revaluations, bonus, or goodwill.	• No additional allocations necessary because new partner will receive a capital share equal to the amount invested. • Total resulting partnership capital equals prior partners' capital plus investment of new partner.
Investment cost < Book value (Case 3)	1. Revalue net assets down to market value and allocate to prior partners. 2. Recognize goodwill brought in by new partner. 3. Assign bonus to new partner.	• Prior partners are assigned the reduction of asset values occurring before admission of the new partner. Alternatively, new partner is assigned goodwill or bonus as part of admission incentive. • Recording asset valuation decrease reduces total resulting capital, while recording new partner's goodwill increases total resulting capital.

and goodwill recognition methods, the historical cost bases of the partnership's net assets are adjusted during the admission of the new partner. Some partners object to this departure from historical cost and prefer to use the bonus method, which uses capital interest transfers among the partners to align the total resulting capital of the partnership. Under the bonus method, net assets remain at their historical cost bases to the partnership. The choice of method of accounting for the admission of a new partner is up to the partners.

The accounting for the admission of a new partner parallels the accounting for an investment in the stock of another company. If a new partner pays more than book value, the excess of cost over book value, that is, the positive differential, may be due to unrecognized goodwill or to undervalued assets—the same cases as in accounting for the differential for stock investments. If book value equals the investment cost, then no differential exists, indicating that the book values of the net assets equal their fair values. If the new partner's investment is less than the proportionate book value, that is, an excess of book value over cost exists, the assets of the partnership may be overvalued. A concept unique to partnership accounting is the use of the bonus method. Figure 10–1 serves as a guide through the following discussion.

The AB Partnership example presented earlier is again used to illustrate the three cases. A review of the major facts for this example follows:

1. The January 1, 20X3, capital of the AB Partnership is $30,000. Alt's balance is $20,000, and Blue's balance is $10,000. Alt and Blue share profits in the ratio of 60:40.
2. Cha is invited into the partnership. Cha will have a one-fourth capital interest and a 25 percent share of profits. Alt and Blue will share the remaining 75 percent of profits in the ratio of 60:40, resulting in Alt having a 45 percent share of any profits and Blue having a 30 percent share.

Case 1. Investment Equals Proportion of the Partnership's Book Value

The total book value of the partnership before the admission of the new partner is $30,000, and the new partner, Cha, is buying a one-fourth capital interest for $10,000.

The amount of a new partner's investment is often the result of negotiations between the prior partners and the prospective partner. As with any acquisition or investment, the investor must determine its market value. In the case of a partnership, the prospective partner attempts to ascertain the market value and earning power of the partnership's net assets. The new partner's investment is then a function of the percentage of partnership capital being acquired. In this case, Cha must believe that the $10,000 investment required is a fair price for a one-fourth interest in the resulting partnership; otherwise, she would not make the investment.

After the amount of investment is agreed on, it is possible to calculate the new partner's proportionate book value. For a $10,000 investment, Cha will have a one-fourth interest in the partnership, as follows:

Investment in partnership	$10,000
New partner's proportionate book value: ($30,000 + $10,000) × 0.25	(10,000)
Difference (Investment = Book value)	$ –0–

Because the amount of the investment ($10,000) equals the new partner's 25 percent proportionate book value ($10,000 = $40,000 × 0.25), there is an implication that the net assets are fairly valued. Total resulting capital equals the prior partners' capital ($30,000) plus the new partner's tangible investment ($10,000). Note that the capital credit assigned to the new partner is her share of the total resulting capital of the partnership after her admission as partner. The entry on the partnership's books is

	January 1, 20X3		
(10)	Cash	10,000	
	Cha, Capital		10,000

Admission of Cha for one-fourth interest upon investment of $10,000.

The following schedule presents the key concepts in Case 1:

	Prior Capital	New Partner's Tangible Investment	New Partner's Proportion of Partnership's Book Value (25%)	Total Resulting Capital	New Partner's Share of Total Resulting Capital (25%)
Case 1 New partner's investment equals proportionate book value	$30,000	$10,000	$10,000		
No revaluations, bonus, or goodwill				$40,000	$10,000

Case 2. New Partner's Investment More than Proportion of the Partnership's Book Value

In some cases, a new partner may invest more in an existing partnership than his or her proportionate share of the partnership's book value. This means that the new partner perceives some value in the partnership that the books of account do not reflect.

For example, assume Cha invests $11,000 for a one-fourth capital interest in the ABC Partnership. The first step is to compare the new partner's investment with the new partner's proportionate book value, as follows:

Investment in partnership	$11,000
New partner's proportionate book value: ($30,000 + $11,000) × 0.25	(10,250)
Difference (Investment > Book value)	$ 750

Cha has invested $11,000 for an interest with a book value of $10,250, thus paying an excess of $750 over the present book value.

Generally, an excess of investment over the respective book value of the partnership interest indicates that the partnership's prior net assets are undervalued or that the partnership has some unrecorded goodwill. Three alternative accounting treatments exist in this case:

1. *Revalue net assets upward.* Under this alternative:
   a. Book values of net assets are increased to their market values.
   b. The prior partners' capital accounts are increased for their respective shares of the increase in the book values of the net assets.
   c. The partnership's total resulting capital reflects the prior capital balances plus the amount of asset revaluation plus the new partner's investment.

2. *Record unrecognized goodwill.* With this method:
   a. Unrecognized goodwill is recorded.
   b. The prior partners' capital accounts are increased for their respective shares of the goodwill.
   c. The partnership's total resulting capital reflects the prior capital balances plus the goodwill recognized plus the new partner's investment.

Under both of these methods, the partnership's assets (tangible and/or intangible) are revalued upward either to recognize unrecorded excess value or to record previously unrecorded goodwill. Thus, the size of the "pie" the partners are to divide among themselves becomes larger, so that their "slice" becomes proportionately larger.

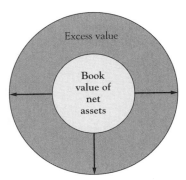

3. *Use bonus method.* Essentially, the bonus method is a transfer of capital balances among the partners. This method is used when the partners do not wish to record adjustments in asset and liability accounts or recognize goodwill. Thus, the size of the pie stays the same (the book value of existing equity plus the contribution of the new partner), but one or more partners will give some of his or her "slice" to the other partners.

Under this method:
   a. The prior partners' capital accounts are increased for their respective shares of the bonus paid by the new partner.
   b. The partnership's total resulting capital reflects the prior capital balances plus the new partner's investment.

The partnership may use any one of the three alternatives. The decision is usually a result of negotiations between the prior partners and the prospective partner. Some accountants criticize the revaluation of net assets or recognition of goodwill because it results in a marked departure from the historical cost principle and differs from the accepted accounting principles in **FASB Statement No. 142 (ASC 350)**, "Goodwill and Other Intangible Assets" (FASB 142, ASC 350), which prohibits corporations from recognizing goodwill that has not been acquired by purchase. Accountants who use the goodwill or asset revaluation methods argue that the goal of partnership accounting is to state fairly the relative capital equities of the partners, and this may require different accounting procedures from those used in corporate entities.

The accountant's function is to ensure that any estimates used in the valuation process are based on the best evidence available. Subjective valuations that could impair the fairness of the presentations made in the partnership's financial statements should be avoided or minimized.

Illustration of Revaluation of Net Assets Approach (Non-GAAP)

Assume that Cha paid a $750 *excess* ($11,000 − $10,250) over her proportionate book value because the partnership owns land on which are constructed warehouse buildings. The land has a book value of $4,000, but a recent appraisal indicates the land has a market value of $7,000. The partnership expects to continue using the land for warehouse space for as long as the business operates. The prior partners have been informed by their accountant that GAAP does not allow for *increasing* the value of nonfinancial, long-lived assets held and used in the operations of the business. But these prior partners decide to use the admission of the new partner to recognize the increase in the land's value and to assign this increase to the capital accounts of the prior partners. The increase in land value is allocated to the partners' capital accounts in the profit and loss ratio that existed during the time of the increase. Alt's capital is increased by $1,800 (60 percent of the $3,000 increase), and Blue's capital is increased by $1,200 (40 percent of the $3,000). The partnership makes the following entry for the revaluation of the land:

(11)	Land	3,000	
	Alt, Capital		1,800
	Blue, Capital		1,200

Revalue partnership land to market value.

Cha's $11,000 investment brings the partnership's total resulting capital to $44,000, as follows:

Prior capital of AB Partnership	$30,000
Revaluation of land to market value	3,000
Cha's investment	11,000
Total resulting capital of ABC Partnership	$44,000

Cha is acquiring a one-fourth interest in the total resulting capital of the ABC Partnership. Her capital credit, after revaluing the land, is calculated as follows:

$$\text{New partner's share of total resulting capital} = (\$30,000 + \$3,000 + \$11,000) \times 0.25 = \$11,000$$

The entry to record the admission of Cha into the partnership follows:

| (12) | Cash | 11,000 | |
| | Cha, Capital | | 11,000 |

Admission of Cha for one-fourth capital interest in ABC Partnership.

When the land is eventually sold, Cha will participate in the gain or loss calculated on the basis of the new $7,000 book value, which is the land's market value at the time of her admission into the partnership. The entire increase in the land value before Cha's admission belongs to the prior partners.

An important key to remember is that the new partner's capital account balance should be equal to his or her respective ownership percentage multiplied by either the book value of net assets (the small pie) under the bonus method or the revalued net assets (the large pie) under the revaluation or goodwill methods. In this case, the partners decided to revalue the balance sheet upward by recording the land's excess fair value at the time of Cha's admission. Thus, Cha's capital account balance upon admission is 25 percent of the newly expanded "pie" or $11,000.

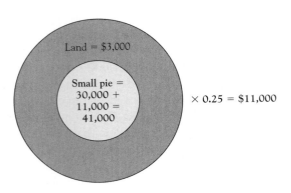

Illustration of Goodwill Recognition (Non-GAAP)   An entering partner may pay an extra amount to compensate the existing partners for unrecognized goodwill, indicated by the partnership's high profitability. Some partnerships use the change in membership as an opportunity to record unrecognized goodwill created by the prior partners. Recording unrecognized goodwill is used for partnership accounting to establish appropriate capital equity among the partners. As noted earlier, this is not in accordance with the rule established in **FASB 142 (ASC 350),** but the partners' information needs and the specific purposes of the partnership's financial statements could serve to support the use of this non-GAAP method.

Generally, the amount of goodwill is determined by negotiations between the prior and prospective partners and is based on estimates of future earnings. For example, the prior and new partners may agree that, due to the prior partners' efforts, the partnership has superior earnings potential and that $3,000 of goodwill should be recorded to recognize this fact. The new partner's negotiated investment cost will be based partly on the earnings potential of the partnership. Alternatively, goodwill may be estimated from the amount of the new partner's investment. For example, in this case, Cha is investing $11,000 for a one-fourth interest; therefore, she must believe the total resulting partnership capital is $44,000 ($11,000 ÷ 0.25). The estimated goodwill is $3,000:

Step 1	
25% of estimated total resulting capital	$ 11,000
Estimated total resulting capital ($11,000 ÷ 0.25)	$ 44,000
Step 2	
Estimated total resulting capital	$ 44,000
Total net assets not including goodwill ($30,000 prior plus $11,000 invested by Cha)	(41,000)
Estimated goodwill	$ 3,000

Another way to view the creation of goodwill at the time of a new partner's admission is to use a T-account form for the partnership's balance sheet. Any additional net assets, such as recognizing goodwill, must be balanced with additional capital, as follows:

		Balance Sheet			
Prior to admission of new partner Cha	Net assets	$30,000	Partners' capital	$30,000
New partner's cash investment	Cash	$11,000	New tangible capital	$11,000
Capital prior to recognizing goodwill		$41,000		$41,000
Estimated new goodwill	Goodwill	$ 3,000	Capital from goodwill	$ 3,000
Total resulting capital	Net assets	$44,000	Total resulting capital	$44,000

Once the new ABC Partnership's total resulting capital is estimated ($44,000), the new goodwill ($3,000) is the balance sheet balancing difference between the tangible capital ($41,000), which includes the new partner's cash investment and the estimated total resulting capital of ABC Partnership ($44,000).

The unrecorded goodwill is recorded, and the prior partners' capital accounts are credited for the increase in assets. The adjustments to the capital accounts are in the profit and loss ratio that existed during the periods the goodwill was developed. This increased Alt's capital by 60 percent of the goodwill and Blue's by 40 percent. The entries to record goodwill and the admission of Cha are as follows:

(13)	Goodwill	3,000	
	Alt, Capital		1,800
	Blue, Capital		1,200
	Recognize unrecorded goodwill.		

(14)	Cash	11,000	
	Cha, Capital		11,000
	Admission of Cha to partnership for a one-fourth capital interest: $44,000 × 0.25.		

Another reason for recording goodwill is that the new partner may want her capital balance to equal the amount of investment made. The investment is based on the market value of the partnership, and for this equality to occur, the partnership must restate its prior net assets to their fair values.

Again, it is important to note that the $11,000 credit to Cha's capital account is one-fourth of the total resulting capital of ABC Partnership of $44,000. Again, since the partners elected to revalue the balance sheet upward by recording goodwill, Cha's capital account balance is 25 percent of the larger pie (the newly expanded net assets).

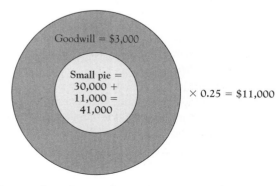

In future periods, any impairment loss of goodwill will be charged against partnership earnings before net income is distributed to the partners. Consequently, Cha's future profit distribution may be affected by the goodwill recognized at the time of her admission into the partnership.

Illustration of Bonus Method (GAAP)   Some partnerships are averse to recognizing asset revaluations or unrecorded goodwill when a new partner is admitted. Instead, they record a portion of the new partner's investment as a bonus to the existing partners to align the capital balances properly at the time of the new partner's admission. In this case, the $750 excess paid by Cha is a bonus allocated to the prior partners in their profit and loss ratio of 60 percent to Alt and 40 percent to Blue. ABC Partnership's total resulting capital consists of $30,000 prior capital of Alt and Blue plus the $11,000 investment of Cha. No additional capital is recognized by revaluing assets. Since the partners do not revalue the balance sheet, they will simply divide up the existing (small) pie based on their relative ownership percentages. Thus, Cha's capital account balance will be 25 percent of the small pie, $10,250.

$$\text{Small pie} = 30{,}000 + 11{,}000 = 41{,}000 \times 0.25 = \$10{,}250$$

The entry to record the admission of Cha under the bonus method is as follows:

(15)	Cash	11,000	
	Alt, Capital		450
	Blue, Capital		300
	Cha, Capital		10,250

Admission of Cha with bonus to Alt and Blue.

Cha may dislike the bonus method because her capital balance is $750 less than her investment in the partnership. This is a disadvantage of the bonus method.

The following schedule presents the key concepts for Case 2:

	Prior Capital	New Partner's Tangible Investment	New Partner's Proportion of Partnership's Book Value (25%)	Total Resulting Capital	New Partner's Share of Total Resulting Capital (25%)
Case 2					
New partner's investment greater than proportionate book value	$30,000	$11,000	$10,250		
1. Revalue assets by increasing land $3,000				$44,000	$11,000
2. Recognize $3,000 goodwill for prior partners				$44,000	$11,000
3. Bonus of $750 to prior partners				$41,000	$10,250

Case 3. New Partner's Investment Less than Proportion of the Partnership's Book Value

It is possible that a new partner may pay less than his or her proportionate share of the partnership's book value. For example, assume Cha invests $8,000 for a one-fourth capital interest in the ABC Partnership. The first step is to compare the new partner's investment with the new partner's proportionate book value, as follows:

Investment in partnership	$8,000
New partner's proportionate book value: ($30,000 + $8,000) × 0.25	(9,500)
Difference (Investment < Share of book value)	(1,500)

The fact that Cha's investment is less than the book value of a one-fourth interest in the partnership indicates that the partnership has overvalued net assets or the prior partners recognize that Cha is contributing additional value in the form of expertise or skills she possesses that are needed by the partnership. In this case, Cha is investing $8,000 in cash and an additional amount that may be viewed as goodwill.

As with Case 2, in which the investment is more than the book value acquired, there are three alternative approaches to account for the differential when the investment is less than the book value acquired. The three approaches are as follows:

1. *Revalue net assets downward.* Under this alternative:

    a. Book values of net assets are decreased to recognize the reduction in their values.

    b. The prior partners' capital accounts are decreased for their respective share of the decrease in the values of the net assets.

    c. The partnership's total resulting capital reflects the prior capital balances less the amount of the net asset valuation write-down plus the new partner's investment.

2. *Recognize goodwill brought in by the new partner.* In this approach:

    a. Goodwill or other intangible benefits brought in by the new partner are recorded and included in the new partner's capital account.

    b. The prior partners' capital accounts remain unchanged.

    c. The partnership's total resulting capital reflects the prior capital balances plus the new goodwill brought in plus the new partner's tangible investment.

3. *Use bonus method.* Under the bonus method:

    a. The new partner is assigned a bonus from the prior partners' capital accounts, which are decreased for their respective shares of the bonus paid to the new partner.

    b. The partnership's total resulting capital reflects the prior capital balances plus the new partner's investment.

Illustration of Revaluation of Net Assets Approach (GAAP)

Almost all of an entity's assets and liabilities have one or more generally accepted accounting principles for recognizing impairment losses or write-downs to fair value. Several examples of these GAAP are: recognizing a valuation loss on inventory valued using the lower-of-cost-or-market method, impairment losses on goodwill, impairment losses on long-lived assets used in the business, and losses on financial assets such as investments. Thus, recognizing decreases in the values of many assets is allowed by GAAP. The process of admitting a new partner is a common time for evaluating the fair values of the partnership's net assets and comparing those values with the book values.

Assume that the reason Cha paid only $8,000 for a one-fourth interest in the partnership is that equipment used in current production is recorded at a book value of $14,000 but has a fair value of only $8,000. The partners agree to recognize the impairment loss and write down the equipment to its fair value before the new partner's admission. The write-down is allocated to the prior partners in the profit and loss ratio that existed during the period of the decline in the fair value of the equipment: 60 percent to Alt and 40 percent to Blue. The write-down is recorded as follows:

(16)	Alt, Capital	3,600	
	Blue, Capital	2,400	
	Equipment		6,000

Recognize impairment loss on equipment.

Note that the partnership's total capital has now been reduced from $30,000 to $24,000 as a result of the $6,000 write-down. The value of Cha's share of total resulting capital of the ABC Partnership, *after the write-down,* is calculated as follows:

In this case the revaluation actually reduces the size of the pie. Cha's capital account is credited for 25 percent of $32,000 for $8,000.

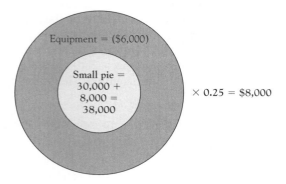

The entry to record the admission of Cha as a partner in the ABC Partnership is

(17)	Cash	8,000	
	Cha, Capital		8,000
	Admission of Cha to partnership.		

Cha's recorded capital credit is equal to her investment because the total partnership capital of $32,000 ($24,000 + $8,000) now represents the partnership's fair value.

Illustration of Recording Goodwill for New Partner (Non-GAAP)   The prior partners may offer Cha a one-fourth capital interest in the ABC Partnership for an $8,000 investment because Cha has essential business experience, skills, customer contacts, reputation, or other ingredients of goodwill that she will bring into the partnership. The amount of goodwill brought in by the new partner is usually determined through negotiations between the prior partners and the prospective partner. For example, Alt, Blue, and Cha may agree that Cha's abilities will generate excess earnings for the resulting ABC Partnership. They agree that Cha should be given $2,000 of goodwill recognition when she joins the partnership in recognition of her anticipated excess contribution to the partnership's future earnings. The negotiated goodwill is recognized and added to her tangible investment to determine the amount of capital credit.

Alternatively, the amount of goodwill brought in by the new partner may be estimated from the amount of the total capital being retained by the prior partners. In this case, the prior partners are retaining a 75 percent interest in the partnership and allowing the new partner a 25 percent capital interest. The dollar amount of the prior partners' 75 percent interest is $30,000. Cha's investment of $8,000 plus goodwill makes up the remaining 25 percent. The amount of goodwill that Cha brought into the partnership is determined as follows:

Step 1	
75% of estimated total resulting capital	$30,000
Estimated total resulting capital ($30,000 ÷ 0.75)	$40,000
Step 2	
Estimated total resulting capital	$40,000
Total net assets not including goodwill ($30,000 + $8,000)	(38,000)
Estimated goodwill	$ 2,000

Note that the goodwill estimate for the new partner is made using the information from the prior partners' interests. In Case 2, the estimate of goodwill to the prior partners was made using the information from the new partner's investment. The reason for this difference is that the best available information should be used for the goodwill estimates. If the new partner's goodwill is being estimated, it is not logical to use the new partner's tangible investment to estimate the total investment made by the new partner, including goodwill. That is circular reasoning that involves using a number to estimate itself. Furthermore, when goodwill is being assigned to the prior partners, it is not logical to use the existing capital of the prior partners to estimate their goodwill. A useful way to remember how to estimate goodwill is to use the opposite partner's information for the estimate. Use the new partner to estimate goodwill to prior partners; use prior partners to estimate goodwill to the new partner. Cha's capital account balance will be 25 percent of the newly revalued partnership balance sheet, $10,000.

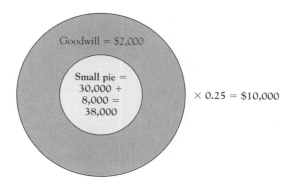

The entry to record the admission of Cha into the ABC Partnership is

(18)	Cash	8,000	
	Goodwill	2,000	
	Cha, Capital		10,000
	Admission of Cha to partnership.		

Note that the ABC Partnership's total resulting capital is now $40,000, with Alt and Blue together having a 75 percent interest and Cha having a 25 percent interest.

Illustration of Bonus Method (GAAP)   Cha's admission as a new partner with a one-fourth interest in the ABC Partnership for an investment of only $8,000 may be accounted for by recognizing a bonus given to Cha from the prior partners. The $1,500 bonus is the difference between the new partner's $9,500 book value and her $8,000 investment. The prior partners' capital accounts are reduced by $1,500 in their profit and loss ratio of 60 percent for Alt and 40 percent for Blue, and Cha's capital account is credited for $9,500, as follows:

(19)	Cash	8,000	
	Alt, Capital	900	
	Blue, Capital	600	
	Cha, Capital		9,500
	Admission of Cha to partnership.		

Note that the amount of the capital credit assigned to the new partner is her share of the total resulting capital (the small pie) since the partners did not elect to revalue the balance sheet other than to record Cha's capital contribution.

Small pie =
30,000 +
8,000 =
38,000   × 0.25 = $9,500

The following schedule presents the key concepts for Case 3:

	Prior Capital	New Partner's Tangible Investment	New Partner's Proportion of Partnership's Book Value (25%)	Total Resulting Capital	New Partner's Share of Total Resulting Capital (25%)
Case 3					
New partner's investment less than proportionate book value	$30,000	$8,000	$9,500		
1. Revalue assets by decreasing equipment by $6,000				$32,000	$ 8,000
2. Recognize goodwill of $2,000 for new partner				$40,000	$10,000
3. Bonus of $1,500 to new partner				$38,000	$ 9,500

Summary and Comparison of Accounting for Investment of New Partner

Figure 10–2 presents the entries made in each of the three cases discussed. In addition, the capital balance of each of the three partners immediately after the admission of Cha is presented to the right of the journal entries.

The following summarizes the alternative methods of accounting for the investment of a new partner:

Case 1. New partner's investment equals his or her proportion of the partnership's book value.

1. The new partner's capital credit equals his or her investment.
2. This case recognizes no goodwill or bonus.

Case 2. New partner's investment is more than his or her proportion of the partnership's book value.

1. The revaluation of an asset or recognition of goodwill increases the partnership's total resulting capital. The increase is allocated to the prior partners in their profit and loss ratio.
2. After recognition of the asset revaluation or unrecorded goodwill, the new partner's capital credit equals his or her investment and his or her percentage of the total resulting capital.
3. Under the bonus method, the partnership's total resulting capital is the sum of the prior partnership's capital plus the investment by the new partner. The capital credit recorded for the new partner is less than the investment but equals his or her percentage of the resulting partnership capital.

Case 3. New partner's investment is less than his or her proportion of the partnership's book value.

1. Under the revaluation of assets approach, the write-down of the assets reduces the prior partners' capital in their profit and loss ratio. The new partner's capital is then credited for the amount of the investment.
2. Under the goodwill method, goodwill is assigned to the new partner, and the total resulting capital of the partnership is increased. The new partner's capital is credited for his or her percentage interest in the total resulting capital of the partnership.
3. The bonus method results in a transfer of capital from the prior partners to the new partner. The new partnership's total resulting capital equals the prior capital plus the new partner's investment. The new partner's capital credit is more than the investment made but equals his or her percentage of the total resulting capital.

FIGURE 10–2
Summary of
Accounting for
Investment of New
Partner: Journal
Entries and Capital
Balances after
Admission of New
Partner

Case 1: New partner's investment equals proportionate book value. Cha invests $10,000 cash for one-fourth capital interest.

Cash	10,000		Alt	$20,000	
Cha, Capital		10,000	Blue	10,000	
			Cha	10,000	
			Total	$40,000	

Case 2: New partner's investment is greater than proportionate book value. Cha invests $11,000 cash for one-fourth capital interest.

(a)   Revalue net assets: (upward):

Land	3,000		Alt	$21,800	
Alt, Capital		1,800	Blue	11,200	
Blue, Capital		1,200	Cha	11,000	
Cash	11,000		Total	$44,000	
Cha, Capital		11,000			

(b)   Recognize goodwill for prior partners:

Goodwill	3,000		Alt	$21,800	
Alt, Capital		1,800	Blue	11,200	
Blue, Capital		1,200	Cha	11,000	
Cash	11,000		Total	$44,000	
Cha, Capital		11,000			

(c)   Bonus to prior partners:

Cash	11,000		Alt	$20,450	
Alt, Capital		450	Blue	10,300	
Blue, Capital		300	Cha	10,250	
Cha, Capital		10,250			
			Total	$41,000	

Case 3: New partner's investment is less than proportionate book value. Cha invests $8,000 cash for a one-fourth capital interest.

(a)   Revalue net assets: (downward)

Alt, Capital	3,600		Alt	$16,400	
Blue, Capital	2,400		Blue	7,600	
Equipment		6,000	Cha	8,000	
Cash	8,000		Total	$32,000	
Cha, Capital		8,000			

(b)   Recognize goodwill for new partner:

Cash	8,000		Alt	$20,000	
Goodwill	2,000		Blue	10,000	
Cha, Capital		10,000	Cha	10,000	
			Total	$40,000	

(c)   Bonus to new partner:

Cash	8,000		Alt	$19,100	
Alt, Capital	900		Blue	9,400	
Blue, Capital	600		Cha	9,500	
Cha, Capital		9,500	Total	$38,000	

Advanced
StudyGuide
.com

Determining a New Partner's Investment Cost

In the previous sections, the amount of the new partner's contribution has been provided. In some instances, accountants are asked to determine the amount of cash investment the new partner should be asked to contribute. The basic principles of partnership accounting provide the means to answer this question. For example, let's continue the basic example of partners Alt and Blue wishing to admit Cha as a new partner. The prior partnership capital was $30,000, and the partners wish to invite Cha into the partnership for a one-fourth interest.

Assume that the prior partners, Alt and Blue, agree that the partnership's assets should be revalued up by $3,000 to recognize the increase in value of the land held by the partnership. The question is how much Cha, the new partner, should be asked to invest for her one-fourth interest.

When determining the new partner's investment cost, it is important to note the total resulting capital of the partnership and the percentage of ownership interest retained by the prior partners. In this example, the prior partners retain a three-fourth interest in the resulting partnership, for which their 75 percent capital interest is $33,000, the $30,000 of prior capital plus the $3,000 from the revaluation of the land, as follows:

75% of total resulting capital	$33,000
	÷ 0.75
Total resulting capital (100%)	$44,000
Less prior partners' capital	(33,000)
Cash contribution required of new partner	$11,000

Note that this is simply another way to evaluate the admission process as discussed in the net asset revaluation illustration under Case 2.

In some cases, the bonus amount may be determined prior to the determination of the cash contribution required from the new partner. For example, assume that Alt and Blue agree to give Cha a bonus of $1,500 for joining the partnership. The following schedule determines the amount of cash investment required of Cha, the new partner:

Prior capital of Alt and Blue	$30,000
Less bonus given to Cha upon admission	(1,500)
Capital retained by Alt and Blue (75%)	$28,500
Total resulting capital ($28,500 ÷ 0.75)	$38,000
Less prior partners' capital	(28,500)
Capital credit required of new partner	$ 9,500
Less bonus to new partner from prior partners	(1,500)
Cash contribution required of new partner	$ 8,000

This second example is another way to view the bonus-to-new-partner method under Case 3 as presented. The key is to determine the amount of capital that the prior partners will retain for their percentage share in the partnership's total resulting capital after admitting the new partner. The new partner's cash contribution can be computed simply by determining the amount of the capital credit that will be assigned to him or her and then recognizing any bonuses that will be used to align the capital balances.

Dissociation of a Partner from the Partnership

When a partner retires or withdraws from a partnership, that partner is dissociated from the partnership. In most cases, the partnership purchases the dissociated partner's interest in the partnership for a buyout price. Section 701 of the UPA 1997 states that the buyout price is the estimated amount if (1) the assets of the partnership were sold at a price equal to the greater of the liquidation value or the value based on a sale of the entire business as a going concern without the dissociated partner and (2) the partnership was wound up at that time, with all partnership obligations settled. Note that goodwill may be included in the valuation. The partnership must pay interest to the dissociated partner from the date of dissociation to the date of payment. In cases of wrongful dissociation, the partnership may sue the partner for damages the wrongful dissociation causes the partnership.

In the case in which the partnership agrees to the dissociation and it is not wrongful, the accountant can aid in the computation of the buyout price. It is especially important to determine all existing liabilities on the dissociation date. The partnership agreement may include other procedures to use in the case of a partner dissociation, such as the specifics of valuation, the process of the acquisition of the dissociated partner's transferable value, and other aspects of the change in membership process.

Some partnerships have an audit performed when a change in partners is made. This audit establishes the existence of and the accuracy of the book values of the assets and liabilities. On occasion, accounting errors are found during an audit. Errors should be corrected and the partners' capital accounts adjusted based on the profit and loss ratio that existed in the period in which the errors were made. For example, if an audit disclosed that three years ago depreciation expense was charged for $4,000 less than it should have been, the error is corrected retroactively, and the partners' capital accounts are charged with their respective shares of the adjustment based on their profit and loss ratio of three years ago.

Generally, the continuing partners buy out the retiring partner either by making a direct acquisition or by having the partnership acquire the retiring partner's interest. If the continuing partners directly acquire the retiring partner's interest, the only entry on the partnership's books is to record the reclassification of capital among the partners. If the partnership acquires the retiring partner's interest, the partnership must record the reduction of total partnership capital and the corresponding reduction of assets paid to the retiring partner. Computation of the buyout price when a partner dissociates from the partnership can take the form of three possible scenarios. These are discussed next.

1. Buyout Price Equal to Partner's Capital Credit

Assume Alt retires from the ABC Partnership when his capital account has a balance of $55,000 after recording all increases in the partnership's net assets including income earned up to the date of the retirement. All partners agree to $55,000 as the buyout price of Alt's partnership interest. The entry made by the ABC Partnership is

(20)	Alt, Capital	55,000	
	Cash		55,000
	Retirement of Alt.		

If the partnership is unable to pay the total of $55,000 to Alt at the time of retirement, it must recognize a liability for the remaining portion.

2. Buyout Price Greater than Partner's Capital Credit

Assume Alt has a capital credit of $55,000 and all the partners agree to a buyout price of $65,000. Most partnerships would account for the $10,000 payment above Alt's capital credit ($65,000 paid − $55,000) as a capital adjustment bonus to Alt from the capital accounts of the remaining partners. In this case, the $10,000 would be allocated against the capital accounts of Blue and Cha in their profit ratio. Blue has a 30 percent interest, and Cha has a 25 percent interest in the net income of the ABC Partnership. The sum of their respective shares is 55 percent (30 percent + 25 percent), and their relative profit percentages, rounded to the nearest percentage, are 55 percent for Blue and 45 percent for Cha, computed as follows:

	Prior Profit Percentage	Remaining Profit Percentage
Alt	45	0
Blue	30	55 (30/55)
Cha	25	45 (25/55)
Total	100	100

The entry to record the retirement of Alt is

(21)	Alt, Capital	55,000	
	Blue, Capital	5,500	
	Cha, Capital	4,500	
	Cash		65,000

Retirement of Alt.

The $10,000 bonus paid to Alt is allocated to Blue and Cha in their respective profit ratios. Blue is charged for 55 percent, and Cha is charged for the remaining 45 percent.

Occasionally, a partnership uses the retirement of a partner to record unrecognized goodwill. In this case, the partnership may record the retiring partner's share only, or it may impute the entire amount of goodwill based on the retiring partner's profit percentage. If it imputes total goodwill, the remaining partners also receive their respective shares of the total goodwill recognized. Many accountants criticize recording goodwill on the retirement of a partner on the same theoretical grounds as they criticize recording unrecognized goodwill on the admission of a new partner. Nevertheless, partnership accounting sometimes uses all the recognition of goodwill at this event.

For example, if $65,000 is paid to Alt and only Alt's share of unrecognized goodwill is to be recorded, the partnership makes the following entries at the time of Alt's retirement:

(22)	Goodwill	10,000	
	Alt, Capital		10,000

Recognize Alt's share of goodwill.

(23)	Alt, Capital	65,000	
	Cash		65,000

Retirement of Alt.

3. Buyout Price Less than Partner's Capital Credit

Sometimes, the buyout price is less than a partner's capital credit. This could result if liquidation values of net assets are less than their book values or it may occur because the dissociating partner wishes to leave the partnership badly enough to accept less than his or her current capital balance. For example, Alt agrees to accept $50,000 as the buyout price for his partnership interest. The partnership should evaluate its net assets to determine if any impairments or write-downs should be recognized. If no revaluations of the net assets are necessary, then the $5,000 difference ($50,000 cash paid less $55,000 capital credit) is distributed as a capital adjustment to Blue and Cha in their respective profit and loss ratio.

Summary of Key Concepts

Accounting for partnerships recognizes the unique aspects of this form of business organization. Most states have enacted the major provisions of the Uniform Partnership Act of 1997 (UPA 1997). This act includes the rights and responsibilities of the partners, both with third parties and among the partners, and the rights of third parties, such as creditors, against the partnership. A partnership agreement is very important because many of the sections of the UPA 1997 can be waived with a formal partnership agreement. The partnership also should file a Statement of Partnership Authority with the secretary of the state and the clerk of the county in which the partnership business takes place. The UPA 1997 includes sections stating that the partnership is an entity distinct from its partners, that partners are agents of the partnership, that partners are personally liable for the partnership obligations that exceed the partnership's assets, that partnership profits or losses are shared equally, and that a partner may dissociate, in which case that partner no longer may share in the management of the partnership.

Partnerships use a wide variety of profit or loss distribution methods and accountants must ensure that the partnership agreement is followed closely. Most partnerships continue on in business when a partner dissociates (leaves the partnership) by purchasing the dissociated partner's interest at a buyout price based on the value of the partnership were it to wind up its business. Several methods of accounting are used to account for changes in partnership membership. Some partnerships use a net asset revaluation approach, sometimes including recognizing goodwill. The other major accounting approach used to account for changes in membership is the bonus method, which uses a reclassification of partner capital. Partnerships provide four financial statements: the statement of income, the balance sheet, the statement of cash flows, and a statement of partners' capital that presents the changes in the partners' capital accounts during the period.

Key Terms

admission of a new partner, *521*
bonus, *516*
bonus method, *522*
book value of a partnership, *523*
buyout price, *521*
entity concept, *509*
goodwill recognition, *522*

interest on capital balances, *516*
net asset revaluation, *522*
new partner's proportion of the partnership's book value, *525*
partners' accounts, *514*
partner's dissociation, *510*
preselected ratio, *516*
profit distribution plans, *515*

salary, *516*
statement of partners' capital, *520*
Statement of Partnership Authority, *509*
transferable interest, *510*
Uniform Partnership Act of 1997 (UPA 1997), *508*

Appendix 10A Tax Aspects of a Partnership

The Internal Revenue Service views the partnership form of organization as a temporary aggregation of some of the individual partners' rights. The partnership is not a separate taxable entity. Therefore, the individual partners must report their share of the partnership income or loss on their personal tax returns, whether withdrawn or not. This sometimes creates cash flow problems for partners who leave their share of income in the partnership and permit the partnership to use the income for growth. In such cases, the partners must pay income tax on income that was not distributed to them. However, this tax conduit feature also offers special tax features to the individual partners. For example, charitable contributions made by the partnership are reported on the partners' individual tax returns. Also, any tax-exempt income earned by the partnership is passed through to the individual partners.

This pass-through benefits individual partners when the business has an operating loss. The individual partners can recognize their shares of the partnership loss on their own tax returns, thereby offsetting other taxable income. If the business is incorporated, the loss does not pass through to the stockholders.

TAX BASIS OF ASSET INVESTMENTS

For capital investments, the accounting basis and the tax basis are computed differently. For tax purposes, a partnership must value the assets invested in the partnership at the tax basis of the individual partner who invests the assets. For example, assume that partner A contributes a building to the AB Partnership. The building originally cost $6,000 and has been depreciated $2,000, leaving a book value of $4,000. The building has a market value of $10,000. For tax purposes, the partnership records the building at $4,000, the adjusted basis of partner A.

This tax valuation differs from the amount that is recognized under generally accepted accounting principles. A basic concept in GAAP is to value asset transfers between separate reporting entities at their respective fair market values. In this case, the partnership records the building at its $10,000 fair value for accounting purposes. Most partnerships maintain their accounting records and financial statements using GAAP, and they use a separate adjusting schedule at the end of each period to report the results for tax purposes on Form 1065, the partnership tax information form.

In addition to asset transfers, a partnership also may assume the liabilities associated with an asset. For example, if the building was subject to a $2,000 mortgage, which the AB Partnership assumed with the building, partner A benefits because the other partners have assumed a portion of the mortgage that A originally owed entirely.

A partner's tax basis in a partnership is the sum of the following:

The partner's tax basis of any assets contributed to the partnership.

Plus: The partner's share of other partners' liabilities assumed by the partnership.

Less: The amount of the partner's liabilities assumed by the other partners.

To illustrate, A contributes the building discussed, which has an adjusted tax basis of $4,000 ($6,000 cost less $2,000 depreciation) and is subject to a mortgage of $2,000. The building's market value is $10,000. B contributes machinery that has a book value of $15,000 and a market value of $20,000 and is subject to a note payable of $5,000. The partners agree to share equally in the liabilities assumed by the AB Partnership. The tax basis of each partner in the partnership is calculated as follows:

	Partner A	Partner B
Tax basis of assets contributed	$4,000	$15,000
Partner's share of other partner's liabilities assumed by partnership:		
Partner A: (1/2 of $5,000)	2,500	
Partner B: (1/2 of $2,000)		1,000
Partner's liabilities assumed by other partners:		
Partner A: (1/2 of $2,000)	(1,000)	
Partner B: (1/2 of $5,000)		(2,500)
Tax basis of partner's interest	$5,500	$13,500

The tax basis of each partner is used for tax recognition of gains or losses on subsequent disposals of the partner's investment in the partnership.

For GAAP purposes, each partner's investment is based on the fair value of the assets less liabilities assumed. Thus, in the preceding case, partner A's accounting basis is $8,000 ($10,000 market value of the building less $2,000 mortgage), and partner B's accounting basis is $15,000 ($20,000 market value of the equipment less $5,000 note payable). Any asset disposal gain or loss in the accounting financial statements is based on the valuations made using GAAP. A separate schedule of tax bases for each of the partners is typically maintained in case the information is required for a partner's individual tax return.

S CORPORATIONS AND LIMITED LIABILITY COMPANIES

An S corporation is a corporate entity that elects to be taxed in the same manner as a partnership, with the shareholders including their share of corporate income or loss in their personal returns, whether or not the income has been distributed as dividends. This eliminates the double taxation of corporate income: first, as taxable income to the corporation and, second, as taxable dividend income to the shareholder. The S corporation form provides the shareholders with the liability limitation of an investment in a corporation. The Internal Revenue Service has certain qualifying criteria for S corporation status: (1) a maximum of 75 shareholders, all of whom must be either U.S. citizens or permanent resident aliens, is permitted; (2) only one class of stock may be issued; and (3) no more than 25 percent of the corporation's gross income can be derived from passive investment activities.

A limited liability company (LLC) is a relatively new form of corporate entity governed by the laws of the state in which it is formed. The LLC provides liability protection to its investors as well as the pass-through taxation benefits of partnerships and S corporations. However, each state has its own distinct set of laws governing LLCs, while the IRS has just one set of definitions for an S corporation. Over time, the LLC form of entity may gain in use.

Appendix **10B** Joint Ventures

A joint venture usually is a business entity owned and operated by a small group of investors as a separate and specific business project organized for the mutual benefit of the ownership group. Many joint ventures are short-term associations of two or more parties to fulfill a specific project, such as the development of real estate, joint oil or gas drilling efforts, the financing of a joint production center, or the financing of a motion picture effort. Many international efforts to expand production or markets involve joint ventures either with foreign-based companies or with foreign governments. A recent phenomenon is the formation of research joint ventures in which two or more corporations agree to share the costs and eventual research accomplishments of a separate research laboratory. The venturers might not have equal ownership interests; a venturer's share could be as low as 5 or 10 percent or as high as 90 or 95 percent. Many joint ventures of only two venturers, called 50 percent–owned ventures, divide the ownership share equally.

A joint venture may be organized as a corporation, partnership, or undivided interest. A corporate joint venture is usually formed for long-term projects such as the development and sharing of technical knowledge among a small group of companies. The incorporation of the joint venture formalizes the legal relationships between the venturers and limits each investor's liability to the amount of the investment in the venture. The venture's stock is not traded publicly, and the venturers usually have other business transactions between them. Accounting for a corporate joint venture is guided by **APB Opinion No. 18 (ASC 323),** "The Equity Method of Accounting for Investments in Common Stock" (APB 18, ASC 323), which requires that investors use the equity method to account for their investments in the common stock of corporate joint ventures.

When one corporation has control over another, the controlled corporation is considered a subsidiary rather than a corporate joint venture, even if it has a small number of other owners. A subsidiary should be consolidated by the controlling owner, and a noncontrolling interest recognized for the interests of other owners.

A partnership joint venture is accounted for as any other partnership. All facets of partnership accounting presented in the chapter apply to these partnerships, each of which has its own accounting records. Some joint ventures are accounted for on the books of one of the venturers; however, this combined accounting does not fully reflect the fact that the joint venture is a separate reporting entity. Each partner, or venturer, maintains an investment account on its books for its share of the partnership venture capital. The investment in the partnership account is debited for the initial investment and for the investor's share of subsequent profits. Withdrawals and shares of losses are credited to the investment account. The balance in the investment account should correspond to the balance in the partner's capital account shown on the joint venture partnership's statements.

In 1971, the AICPA issued **Accounting Interpretation No. 2,** "Investments in Partnerships and Ventures" (AIN 2 of APB 18, ASC 323), which stated that many of the provisions of **APB 18 (ASC 323)** are appropriate for accounting for investments in partnerships and unincorporated joint ventures. In particular, intercompany profits should be eliminated and the investor-partners should record their shares of the venture's income or loss in the same manner as with the equity method. For financial reporting purposes, if one of the investor-venturers in fact controls the joint venture, that venturer should consolidate the joint venture into its financial statements. If all investor-venturers maintain joint control, then the one-line equity method should be used to report the investment in the joint venture.

Accounting for unincorporated joint ventures that are undivided interests usually follows the method of accounting used by partnerships. An *undivided interest* exists when each investor-venturer owns a proportionate share of each asset and is proportionately liable for its share of each liability. Some established industry practices, especially in oil and gas venture accounting, provide for a pro rata recognition of a venture's assets, liabilities, revenue, and expenses. For example, assume that both A Company and B Company are 50 percent investors in a joint venture, called JTV, for the purposes of oil exploration. The JTV venture has plant assets of $500,000 and long-term liabilities of $200,000.

Therefore, both A Company and B Company have an investment of $150,000 ($300,000 × 0.50). Under the equity method, the investment is reported in A and B companies' balance sheets as a $150,000 investment in joint venture.

International Accounting Standard No. 31, "Interests in Joint Ventures" (IAS 31), specified the reporting of joint ventures under international accounting financial reporting standards. **IAS 31** identified three types of joint ventures: (*a*) *jointly controlled operations,* for which each venturer recognizes the assets that it controls and the liabilities it incurs and the expenses it incurs and its share of the joint venture's income; (*b*) *jointly controlled assets,* for which each venturer recognizes its share of the jointly controlled assets, any liabilities it has incurred plus its share of any liabilities incurred by the joint venture, and its share of the income together with its share of the expenses incurred from the operations of the joint venture plus any expenses that the individual venturer has incurred from its interest in the joint venture; and (*c*) *jointly controlled entities,* for which each venturer recognizes its interest in the joint venture using proportionate consolidation or the equity method.

Under the proportionate consolidation method, each venturer recognizes a pro rata share of the assets, liabilities, income, and expenses of the jointly controlled entity. This approach is illustrated in the JTV example. In this case, assets of $250,000 ($500,000 × 0.50) and liabilities of $100,000 ($200,000 × 0.50) are added to the present assets and liabilities of each investor-venturer. The proportionate share of the assets and liabilities should be added to similar items in the investor's financial statements. The same pro rata method is also used for the joint venture's revenue and expenses. A comparison of the equity method and the proportionate consolidation for venturer A Company is presented in Figure 10–3.

Joint ventures provide flexibility to their investors as to management, operations, and the division of profits or losses. However, companies need to be aware of **FASB Interpretation No. 46 (ASC 810),** "Consolidation of Variable Interest Entities: An Interpretation of ARB No. 51" (FIN 46, ASC 810), which was issued in 2003. In situations in which an investor does not have a majority stock ownership, there may exist contractual or other agreements specifying allocation of the entity's profits or losses. **FIN 46 (ASC 810)** specifies that consolidation of a variable interest entity (VIE) is required if an investor will absorb a majority of the entity's expected losses or receive a majority of the entity's expected return. Therefore, an equity investor not having a controlling financial interest may be determined to be the primary beneficiary of the VIE and thus be required to fully consolidate that entity.

Real estate development is often carried out through joint ventures. Accounting for noncontrolling interests in real estate joint ventures is guided by the AICPA's **Statement of Position 78-9 (ASC 970),** "Accounting for Investments in Real Estate Ventures" (SOP 78-9, ASC 970). **SOP 78-9 (ASC 970)** recommends that the equity method be used to account for noncontrolling investments in corporate or noncorporate real estate ventures.

A joint venture also makes additional footnote disclosures to present additional details about the joint venture's formation and operation, the methods of accounting it uses, and a summary of its financial position and earnings.

Another form of business association is the syndicate. Syndicates are usually short term and have a defined single purpose, such as developing a financing proposal for a corporation. Syndicates are typically very informal; nevertheless, the legal relationships between the parties should be clearly specified before beginning the project.

FIGURE 10–3
Comparative Balance Sheets for Reporting a Joint Venture

	Balance Sheets of A Company		
	Before Joint Venture	Equity Method	Proportionate Consolidation
Current Assets	$250	$100	$100
Property, Plant, and Equipment	400	400	650
Investment in Joint Venture	–0–	150	–0–
Total	$650	$650	$750
Current Liabilities	$100	$100	$100
Long-Term Debt	300	300	400
Stockholders' Equity	250	250	250
Total	$650	$650	$750

Questions

LO1	Q10-1	Why is the partnership form of business organization sometimes preferred over the corporate or sole proprietorship forms?
LO1	Q10-2	What is the Uniform Partnership Act of 1997 and what is its relevance to partnership accounting?
LO1	Q10-3	What types of items are typically included in the partnership agreement?
LO2	Q10-4	Define the following features of a partnership: (*a*) separate business entity, (*b*) agency relationship, and (*c*) partner's joint and several liability.
LO4	Q10-5	Under what circumstances would a partner's capital account have a debit, or deficiency, balance? How is the deficiency usually eliminated?
LO5	Q10-6	A partnership agreement specifies that profits will be shared in the ratio of 4:6:5. What percentage of profits will each partner receive? Allocate a profit of $60,000 to each of the three partners.
LO5	Q10-7	The Good-Nite partnership agreement includes a profit distribution provision for interest on capital balances. Unfortunately, the provision does not state the specific capital balance to be used in computing the profit share. What choices of capital balances are available to the partners? What is the preferred capital balance to be used in an interest allocation? Why?
LO4	Q10-8	Are salaries to partners a partnership expense? Why or why not?
LO6	Q10-9	Does a partner leaving the partnership require the partnership to dissolve and wind up its business? Explain how the partnership may purchase the dissociated partner's interest in the partnership.
LO4	Q10-10	What is the book value of a partnership? Does book value also represent the partnership's market value?
LO5	Q10-11	Present the arguments for and against the bonus method of recognizing the admission of a new partner.
LO6	Q10-12	In which cases of admission of a new partner does the new partner's capital credit equal the investment made? In which cases of admission of a new partner is the new partner's capital credit less than or more than the amount of the investment?
LO5	Q10-13	Aabel, a partner in the ABC Partnership, receives a bonus of 15 percent of income. If income for the period is $20,000, what is Aabel's bonus, assuming the bonus is computed as a percentage of income before the bonus? What is the bonus if it is computed as a percentage of income *after* deducting the bonus?
LO5	Q10-14	Caine, a new partner in the ABC Partnership, has invested $12,000 for a one-third interest in a partnership with a prior capital of $21,000. What is the ABC Partnership's implied fair value? If the partners agree to recognize goodwill for the difference between the book value and fair value, present the entries the ABC Partnership should make upon Caine's admission.
LO6	Q10-15A	S. Horton contributes assets with a book value of $5,000 to a partnership. The assets have a market value of $10,000 and a remaining liability of $2,000 that the partnership assumes. If the liability is shared equally with the other three partners, what is the basis of Horton's contribution for tax purposes? For GAAP purposes?
LO6	Q10-16B	What is a joint venture? How are corporate joint ventures accounted for on the books of the investor companies?

Cases

LO3	C10-1	**Partnership Agreement**

Judgment

J. Nitty and G. Gritty are considering the formation of a partnership to operate a crafts and hobbies store. They have come to you to obtain information about the basic elements of a partnership agreement. Partnership agreements usually specify an income and loss–sharing ratio. The agreements also may provide for such additional income and loss–sharing features as salaries, bonuses, and interest allowances on invested capital.

Required

a. Discuss why a partnership agreement may need features in addition to the income and loss–sharing ratio.

b. Discuss the arguments in favor of recording salary and bonus allowances to partners as expenses included in computing net income.

"A" indicates the material comes from Appendix 10A and "B" indicates the material comes from Appendix 10B.

c. What are the arguments against recording salary and bonus allowances to partners as partnership expenses?

d. Some partnership agreements contain a provision for interest on invested capital in distributing income to the individual partners. List the additional provisions that should be included in the partnership agreement so the interest amounts can be computed.

LO5

C10-2 **Comparisons of Bonus, Goodwill, and Asset Revaluation Methods**

Communication

Bill, George, and Anne are partners in the BGA Partnership. A difference of opinion exists among the partners as to how to account for the admission of Newt, a new partner. The three present partners have the following positions:

> Bill wants to use the bonus method.
> George believes the goodwill method is best.
> Anne wants to revalue the existing tangible assets.

You have been called in to advise the three partners.

Required

Prepare a memo discussing the three different methods of accounting for the admission of a new partner, including consideration of the effects on partnership capital in the year Newt is admitted, and the effects on the capital balances in future years.

LO1

C10-3 **Uniform Partnership Act Issues**

Research

(*Note:* Obtain a copy of the Uniform Partnership Act of 1997 [UPA 1997] for answering this case question. The UPA 1997 can be obtained from your university's general library, law library, or the Internet.)

You are in a group that is considering forming a partnership for the purpose of purchasing a coffee shop located near your campus. The coffee shop offers freshly brewed coffee and rolls in the morning and soup and sandwiches the remainder of the day. During your preliminary discussions, several issues have emerged for which your group needs additional information.

Required

Research and provide a written summary for the following:

a. Does, in fact, every partner have the right to serve as an agent of the partnership and bind the partnership by that individual partner's actions in carrying out the partnership business?

b. If a new partner is admitted after the partnership operates for a time, what is the new partner's liability for partnership obligations arising before his or her admission? What is the new partner's liability for obligations of the partnership incurred after his or her admission?

c. Should all partners be able to examine the accounting records (the partnership's books) at any time?

d. What happens if the term of the partnership is set at one year and the partners decide to continue doing business? Is a new partnership agreement necessary at that time?

e. What happens if an individual partner wishes to leave the partnership? Can that person just announce to the other partners that he or she no longer wishes to be in the partnership and will not be liable for any future partnership obligations? What are the rights of the other partners in this matter?

f. What items do you believe should be in the partnership agreement that would be prepared before actually agreeing to form the partnership?

LO5

C10-4 **Reviewing the Annual Report of a Limited Partnership**

Although few partnerships provide publicly available financial reports, some limited partnerships do provide their financial reports. These limited partnerships usually have a general partner or other major affiliate that has offered securities to the public, such as those offered by a real estate investment trust.

Using the SEC's EDGAR (www.sec.gov), obtain the annual report for Riverside Park Associates LP for the most recent year available. The form the entity filed is a 10-KSB, which is the small business annual filing.

Required

Answer each of the following questions from the information you obtain by analyzing the annual report of Riverside Park Associates LP.

a. Describe the business in which the limited partnership is engaged.

b. Identify the general partner of the limited partnership and describe the business relationships between the general partner and its major affiliates.

c. What percentage of the total number of outstanding units is owned by the general partner and its affiliates at the end of the year?

d. What amounts are presented for the net balances in the partners' capital accounts as presented on the year-end balance sheet? Discuss how a partnership can have deficit balances for its partnership capital.

e. Who provides management and administrative services for the limited partnership? What is the total amount of these charges for the year of your 10-KSB and the prior year? How much of these costs are charged in the determination of partnership income/loss? Where are the other costs charged to? Explain.

f. What is the profit allocation ratio between the general partner and the limited partners?

LO1

Understanding

C10-5 Defining Partners' Authority

Adam, Bob, and Cathy are planning to form a partnership to create a business that will retail cell phones in a new shopping center just completed in their city. They have been able to reach agreement on many issues, but Cathy is still concerned that Adam might become a little irresponsible and use his position as a partner, and the partnership's name, in business transactions that Cathy would not approve of for the partnership. Cathy feels that Adam has superb marketing skills that will benefit the business, but she wonders what Adam may do in regard to transactions with third parties on behalf of the partnership.

Required

Prepare a memo to Cathy discussing the rights of each partner to engage in transactions on behalf of the partnership and how a partnership can restrict a partner's authority to engage in specific types of transactions.

LO1

Understanding

C10-6 Preferences for Using GAAP for Partnership Accounting

You are providing accounting services for the JR Company partnership. The two partners, Jason and Richard, are thinking of adding a third partner to their business, and they have several questions regarding the use of generally accepted accounting principles (GAAP) for their partnership.

Required

Prepare a memo for the partners addressing each of the following questions from the partners.

a. Why are salaries to partners not shown on the partnership's Statement of Income prepared using GAAP?

b. Why should the partnership use GAAP to account for the admission of a new partner? Why is it not preferable for the partnership to recognize holding gains on its long-lived assets at the time of admitting the third partner? (The two partners argue that recognizing these gains now would allocate them to the partners who were growing the business prior to the admission of a new partner.)

c. Why should the partners and the partnership go through all the work of fully analyzing all the partnership's liabilities to ensure that there are no unrecognized liabilities at the time the new partner is admitted? (The two partners feel this is an unnecessary cost because if a supplier is not paid, then the supplier will simply send another bill in the future.)

LO1

Understanding

C10-7 Comparison of UPA 1997 with UPA 1914

One of the partners of the partnership for which you are the accountant asks you to compare the major features of the Revised Uniform Partnership Act of 1997 with those of the original Uniform Partnership Act of 1914.

Required

Using an Internet search engine or other database, do some research and provide a two- to three-page report comparing UPA 1997 and UPA 1914. Consider the following:

a. Determine whether the state in which your college or university is located has adopted the UPA 1997. (*Hint:* The National Conference of Commissioners on Uniform State Laws maintains a Web site with a few facts about the UPA 1997.)

b. Locate two articles that compare or contrast the UPA 1997 with the UPA 1914 and summarize the major differences in the two acts as discussed in the articles.

Exercises

LO3   **E10-1   Multiple-Choice on Initial Investment [AICPA Adapted]**

Select the correct answer for each of the following questions.

1. On May 1, 20X1, Cathy and Mort formed a partnership and agreed to share profits and losses in the ratio of 3:7, respectively. Cathy contributed a parcel of land that cost her $10,000. Mort contributed $40,000 cash. The land was sold for $18,000 immediately after formation of the partnership. What amount should be recorded in Cathy's capital account on formation of the partnership?

   a. $18,000.

   b. $17,400.

   c. $15,000.

   d. $10,000.

2. On July 1, 20X1, James and Short formed a partnership. James contributed cash. Short, previously a sole proprietor, contributed property other than cash, including realty subject to a mortgage, which the partnership assumed. Short's capital account at July 1, 20X1, should be recorded at

   a. Short's book value of the property at July 1, 20X1.

   b. Short's book value of the property less the mortgage payable at July 1, 20X1.

   c. The fair value of the property less the mortgage payable at July 1, 20X1.

   d. The fair value of the property at July 1, 20X1.

3. A partnership is formed by two individuals who were previously sole proprietors. Property other than cash that is part of the initial investment in the partnership is recorded for financial accounting purposes at the

   a. Proprietors' book values or the fair value of the property at the date of the investment, whichever is higher.

   b. Proprietors' book values or the fair value of the property at the date of the investment, whichever is lower.

   c. Proprietors' book values of the property at the date of the investment.

   d. Fair value of the property at the date of the investment.

4. Mutt and Jeff formed a partnership on April 1 and contributed the following assets:

	Mutt	**Jeff**
Cash	$150,000	$ 50,000
Land		310,000

   The land was subject to a $30,000 mortgage, which the partnership assumed. Under the partnership agreement, Mutt and Jeff will share profit and loss in the ratio of one-third and two-thirds, respectively. Jeff's capital account at April 1 should be

   a. $300,000.

   b. $330,000.

   c. $340,000.

   d. $360,000.

5. On July 1, Mabel and Pierre formed a partnership, agreeing to share profits and losses in the ratio of 4:6, respectively. Mabel contributed a parcel of land that cost her $25,000. Pierre contributed $50,000 cash. The land was sold for $50,000 on July 1, four hours after formation of the partnership. How much should be recorded in Mabel's capital account on the partnership formation?

   a. $10,000.

   b. $20,000.

   c. $25,000.

   d. $50,000.

E10-2 Division of Income—Multiple Bases

The partnership agreement of Angela and Dawn has the following provisions:

1. The partners are to earn 10 percent on the average capital.

2. Angela and Dawn are to earn salaries of $25,000 and $15,000, respectively.

3. Any remaining income or loss is to be divided between Angela and Dawn using a 70:30 ratio.

Angela's average capital is $50,000 and Dawn's is $30,000.

Required

Prepare an income distribution schedule assuming the income of the partnership is (*a*) $80,000 and (*b*) $20,000. If no partnership agreement exists, what does the UPA 1997 prescribe as the profit or loss distribution percentages?

E10-3 Division of Income—Interest on Capital Balances

Left and Right are partners. Their capital accounts during 20X1 were as follows:

Right, Capital					Left, Capital			
3/5	9,000	1/1	50,000		8/23	6,000	1/1	30,000
		7/6	7,000				4/3	8,000
		10/7	5,000				10/31	6,000

Partnership net income is $50,000 for the year. The partnership agreement provides for the division of income as follows:

1. Each partner is to be credited 8 percent interest on his or her average capital.

2. Any remaining income or loss is to be divided equally.

Required

Prepare an income distribution schedule.

E10-4 Distribution of Partnership Income and Preparation of a Statement of Partners' Capital

The income statement for the Apple-Jack Partnership for the year ended December 31, 20X5, follows:

APPLE-JACK PARTNERSHIP Income Statement For the Year Ended December 31, 20X5	
Net Sales	$300,000
Cost of Goods Sold	(190,000)
Gross Margin	$110,000
Operating Expenses	(30,000)
Net Income	$ 80,000

Additional Information for 20X5

1. Apple began the year with a capital balance of $40,800.

2. Jack began the year with a capital balance of $112,000.

3. On April 1, Apple invested an additional $15,000 into the partnership.

4. On August 1, Jack invested an additional $20,000 into the partnership.

5. Throughout 20X5, each partner withdrew $400 per week in anticipation of partnership net income. The partners agreed that these withdrawals are not to be included in the computation of average capital balances for purposes of income distributions.

Apple and Jack have agreed to distribute partnership net income according to the following plan:

	Apple	Jack
1. Interest on average capital balances	6%	6%
2. Bonus on net income before the bonus but after interest on average capital balances	10%	
3. Salaries	$25,000	$30,000
4. Residual (if positive)	70%	30%
Residual (if negative)	50%	50%

Required

a. Prepare a schedule that discloses the distribution of partnership net income for 20X5. Show supporting computations in good form. Round to the nearest dollar.

b. Prepare the statement of partners' capital at December 31, 20X5.

c. How would your answer to part *a* change if all of the provisions of the income distribution plan were the same except that the salaries were $30,000 to Apple and $35,000 to Jack?

LO1–LO5   **E10-5**   **Matching Partnership Terms with Their Descriptions**

Required

Match the descriptions of terms on the left with the terms on the right. A term may be used once, more than once, or not at all.

Descriptions of Terms	Terms
1. Item that occurs when the new partner's investment exceeds the new partner's capital credit.	A. General partner
2. Partner who cannot actively participate in the management of the partnership.	B. Note payable to a partner
3. The allocation of partnership profits and losses when nothing is stated in the partnership agreement.	C. Recognition of neither bonus nor goodwill
4. Item that occurs when the new partner's investment equals the new partner's capital credit and no change occurs in the old partners' capital balances.	D. Drawing account
5. Cost not deducted to determine the partnership's net income for the period.	E. Limited partner
6. Partner who actively participates in the partnership management and who is personally liable for the partnership's debts.	F. Bonus to old partners
7. Item that occurs when the new partner's capital credit exceeds the new partner's investment and no change occurs in the old partners' capital balances.	G. Interest on capital accounts
8. Account that increases when a partner takes assets out of the partnership in anticipation of partnership net income.	H. Partnership income or loss shared equally
9. Account that increases for the fair value of noncash assets invested by a partner.	I. New partner's goodwill recognized
10. Related-party transaction that must be disclosed in the notes to the financial statements.	J. Old partners' goodwill recognized
11. Item that occurs when the new partner's investment equals the new partner's capital credit and an increase occurs in the old partners' capital balances.	K. Partnership agreement
12. Item that occurs when the new partner's capital credit exceeds the new partner's investment and a decrease occurs in the old partners' capital balances.	L. Bonus to new partner
13. Recognition of an intangible asset upon a new partner's admission to the partnership that results in increases in the old partners' capital balances.	M. Capital account
14. Account closed to the capital account at year-end.	
15. Deduction of interest expense on this payable to determine the partnership's net income.	

LO6

E10-6 Admission of a Partner

In the GMP partnership (to which Elan seeks admittance), the capital balances of Mary, Gene, and Pat, who share income in the ratio of 6:3:1, are

Mary	$240,000
Gene	120,000
Pat	40,000

Required

a. If no goodwill or bonus is recorded, how much must Elan invest for a one-third interest?

b. Prepare journal entries for the admission of Elan if she invests $80,000 for a one-fifth interest and goodwill is recorded.

c. Prepare journal entries for the admission of Elan if she invests $200,000 for a 20 percent interest. Total capital will be $600,000.

d. Elan is concerned that she may be held liable for the partnership liabilities existing on the day she is admitted to the GMP partnership. She found nothing in the partnership agreement on this item. What does the UPA 1997 state with regard to the liability of a new partner for partnership obligations incurred prior to admission?

LO6

E10-7 Admission of a Partner

Pam and John are partners in the PJ's partnership, having capital balances of $120,000 and $40,000, respectively, and share income in a ratio of 3:1. Gerry is to be admitted into the partnership with a 20 percent interest in the business.

Required

For each of the following independent situations, first, record Gerry's admission into the partnership and, second, specify and briefly explain why the accounting method used in that situation is GAAP or non-GAAP.

a. Gerry invests $50,000, and goodwill is to be recorded.

b. Gerry invests $50,000. Total capital is to be $210,000.

c. Gerry purchases the 20 percent interest by directly paying Pam $50,000. Gerry is assigned 20 percent interest in the partnership solely from Pam's capital account.

d. Gerry invests $35,000. Total capital is to be $195,000.

e. Gerry invests $35,000, and goodwill is to be recorded.

f. Gerry invests $35,000. During the valuation process made as part of admitting the new partner, it is determined that the partnership's inventory is overvalued by $20,000 because of obsolescence. PJ's partnership uses the lower-of-cost-or-market value method for inventories.

LO6

E10-8 Multiple-Choice Questions on the Admission of a Partner

Select the correct answer for each of the following questions.

Note: The following balance sheet is for the partnership of Alex, Betty, and Claire in questions 1 and 2:

Cash	$ 20,000
Other Assets	180,000
	$200,000
Liabilities	$ 50,000
Alex, Capital (40%)	37,000
Betty, Capital (40%)	65,000
Claire, Capital (20%)	48,000
Total Liabilities and Capital	$200,000

(*Note:* Figures shown parenthetically reflect agreed profit and loss–sharing percentages.)

1. If the assets are fairly valued on this balance sheet and the partnership wishes to admit Denise as a new one-sixth-interest partner without recording goodwill or bonus, Denise should contribute cash or other assets of

   a. $40,000.

   b. $36,000.

   c. $33,333.

   d. $30,000.

2. If assets on the initial balance sheet are fairly valued, Alex and Betty give their consent, and Denise pays Claire $51,000 for her interest, the revised capital balances of the partners would be

   a. Alex, $38,000; Betty, $66,500; Denise, $51,000.

   b. Alex, $38,500; Betty, $66,500; Denise, $48,000.

   c. Alex, $37,000; Betty, $65,000; Denise, $51,000.

   d. Alex, $37,000; Betty, $65,000; Denise, $48,000.

3. On December 31, 20X4, Alan and Dave are partners with capital balances of $80,000 and $40,000, and they share profit and losses in the ratio of 2:1, respectively. On this date Scott invests $36,000 cash for a one-fifth interest in the capital and profit of the new partnership. The partners agree that the implied partnership goodwill is to be recorded simultaneously with the admission of Scott. The total implied goodwill of the firm is

   a. $4,800.

   b. $6,000.

   c. $24,000.

   d. $30,000.

4. Boris and Richard are partners who share profits and losses in the ratio of 6:4. On May 1, 20X9, their respective capital accounts were as follows:

Boris	$60,000
Richard	50,000

   On that date, Lisa was admitted as a partner with a one-third interest in capital and profits for an investment of $40,000. The new partnership began with a total capital of $150,000. Immediately after Lisa's admission, Boris's capital should be

   a. $50,000.

   b. $54,000.

   c. $56,667.

   d. $60,000.

5. At December 31, Rod and Sheri are partners with capital balances of $40,000 and $20,000, and they share profits and losses in the ratio of 2:1, respectively. On this date, Pete invests $17,000 in cash for a one-fifth interest in the capital and profit of the new partnership. Assuming that the bonus method is used, how much should be credited to Pete's capital account on December 31?

   a. $12,000.

   b. $15,000.

   c. $15,400.

   d. $17,000.

6. The capital accounts of the partnership of Ella, Nick, and Brandon follow with their respective profit and loss ratios:

Ella	$139,000	(.500)
Nick	209,000	(.333)
Brandon	96,000	(.167)

Tony was admitted to the partnership when he purchased directly, for $132,000, a proportionate interest from Ella and Nick in the net assets and profits of the partnership. As a result, Tony acquired a one-fifth interest in the net assets and profits of the firm. Assuming that implied goodwill is not to be recorded, what is the combined gain realized by Ella and Nick upon the sale of a portion of their interests in the partnership to Tony?

a. $0.

b. $43,200.

c. $62,400.

d. $82,000.

7. Fred and Ralph are partners who share profits and losses in the ratio of 7:3, respectively. Their respective capital accounts are as follows:

Fred	$35,000
Ralph	30,000

They agreed to admit Lute as a partner with a one-third interest in the capital and profits and losses, upon an investment of $25,000. The new partnership will begin with total capital of $90,000. Immediately after Lute's admission, what are the capital balances of Fred, Ralph, and Lute, respectively?

a. $30,000, $30,000, $30,000.

b. $31,500, $28,500, $30,000.

c. $31,667, $28,333, $30,000.

d. $35,000, $30,000, $25,000.

8. If A is the total capital of a partnership before the admission of a new partner, B is the total capital of the partnership after the investment of a new partner, C is the amount of the new partner's investment, and D is the amount of capital credit to the new partner, then there is

a. A bonus to the new partner if $B = A + C$ and $D < C$.

b. Goodwill to the old partners if $B > (A + C)$ and $D = C$.

c. Neither bonus nor goodwill if $B = A - C$ and $D > C$.

d. Goodwill to the new partner if $B > (A + C)$ and $D < C$.

LO6

E10-9   Withdrawal of a Partner

In the LMK partnership, Luis's capital is $40,000, Marty's is $50,000, and Karl's is $30,000. They share income in a 4:1:1 ratio, respectively. Karl is retiring from the partnership.

Advanced
StudyGuide
.com

Required

Prepare journal entries to record Karl's withdrawal according to each of the following independent assumptions:

a. Karl is paid $38,000, and no goodwill is recorded.

b. Karl is paid $42,000, and only his share of the goodwill is recorded.

c. Karl is paid $35,000, and all implied goodwill is recorded.

d. Prepare a one-paragraph note summarizing the guidance the UPA 1997 offers on computing the buyout price for a partner who is retiring from the partnership.

LO6

E10-10   Retirement of a Partner

On January 1, 20X1, Eddy decides to retire from the partnership of Cobb, Davis, and Eddy. The partners share profits and losses in the ratio of 3:2:1, respectively. The following condensed balance sheets present the account balances immediately before and, for six independent cases, after Eddy's retirement.

Accounts	Balances prior to Eddy's Retirement	Balances after Eddy's Retirement					
		Case 1	Case 2	Case 3	Case 4	Case 5	Case 6
Assets:							
Cash	$ 90,000	$ 10,000	$ 16,000	$ 25,000	$ 16,000	$ 50,000	$ 90,000
Other Assets	200,000	200,000	200,000	200,000	200,000	220,000	200,000
Goodwill	10,000	10,000	14,000	10,000	34,000	10,000	10,000
Total Assets	$300,000	$220,000	$230,000	$235,000	$250,000	$280,000	$300,000
Liabilities and Capital:							
Liabilities	$ 60,000	$ 60,000	$ 60,000	$ 60,000	$ 60,000	$ 60,000	$ 60,000
Cobb, Capital	80,000	74,000	80,000	83,000	92,000	110,000	80,000
Davis, Capital	90,000	86,000	90,000	92,000	98,000	110,000	160,000
Eddy, Capital	70,000	–0–	–0–	–0–	–0–	–0–	–0–
Total Liabilities and Capital	$300,000	$220,000	$230,000	$235,000	$250,000	$280,000	$300,000

Required

Prepare the necessary journal entries to record Eddy's retirement from the partnership for each of the six independent cases.

Problems

LO6

P10-11 Admission of a Partner

Debra and Merina sell electronic equipment and supplies through their partnership. They wish to expand their computer lines and decide to admit Wayne to the partnership. Debra's capital is $200,000, Merina's capital is $160,000, and they share income in a ratio of 3:2, respectively.

Required

Record Wayne's admission for each of the following independent situations:

a. Wayne directly purchases half of Merina's investment in the partnership for $90,000.

b. Wayne invests the amount needed to give him a one-third interest in the capital of the partnership if no goodwill or bonus is recorded.

c. Wayne invests $110,000 for a one-fourth interest. Goodwill is to be recorded.

d. Debra and Merina agree that some of the inventory is obsolete. The inventory account is decreased before Wayne is admitted. Wayne invests $100,000 for a one-fourth interest.

e. Wayne directly purchases a one-fourth interest by paying Debra $80,000 and Merina $60,000. The land account is increased before Wayne is admitted.

f. Wayne invests $80,000 for a one-fifth interest in the total capital of $440,000.

g. Wayne invests $100,000 for a one-fifth interest. Goodwill is to be recorded.

LO5

P10-12 Division of Income

C. Eastwood, A. North, and M. West are manufacturers' representatives in the architecture business. Their capital accounts in the ENW partnership for 20X1 were as follows:

C. Eastwood, Capital				A. North, Capital				M. West, Capital			
9/1	8,000	1/1	30,000	3/1	9,000	1/1	40,000	8/1	12,000	1/1	50,000
		5/1	6,000			7/1	5,000			4/1	7,000
						9/1	4,000			6/1	3,000

Required

For each of the following independent income-sharing agreements, prepare an income distribution schedule.

a. Salaries are $15,000 to Eastwood, $20,000 to North, and $18,000 to West. Eastwood receives a bonus of 5 percent of net income after deducting his bonus. Interest is 10 percent of ending capital balances. Eastwood, North, and West divide any remainder in a 3:3:4 ratio, respectively. Net income was $78,960.

b. Interest is 10 percent of weighted-average capital balances. Salaries are $24,000 to Eastwood, $21,000 to North, and $25,000 to West. North receives a bonus of 10 percent of net income after deducting the bonus and her salary. Any remainder is divided equally. Net income was $68,080.

c. West receives a bonus of 20 percent of net income after deducting the bonus and the salaries. Salaries are $21,000 to Eastwood, $18,000 to North, and $15,000 to West. Interest is 10 percent of beginning capital balances. Eastwood, North, and West divide any remainder in an 8:7:5 ratio, respectively. Net income was $92,940.

LO6

Advanced StudyGuide .com

P10-13   Determining a New Partner's Investment Cost

The following condensed balance sheet is presented for the partnership of Der, Egan, and Oprins, who share profits and losses in the ratio of 4:3:3, respectively.

Cash	$ 40,000	Accounts Payable	$150,000
Other Assets	710,000	Der, Capital	260,000
		Egan, Capital	180,000
		Oprins, Capital	160,000
Total Assets	$750,000	Total Liabilities and Capital	$750,000

Assume that the partnership decides to admit Snider as a new partner with a one-fourth interest.

Required

For each of the following independent cases, determine the amount that Snider must contribute in cash or other assets.

a. No goodwill or bonus is to be recorded.

b. Goodwill of $30,000 is to be recorded and allocated to the prior partners.

c. A bonus of $24,000 is to be paid by Snider and allocated to the prior partners.

d. The prior partners, Der, Egan, and Oprins, agree to give Snider $10,000 of goodwill upon admission to the partnership.

e. Other assets are revalued for an increase of $20,000, and goodwill of $40,000 is recognized and allocated to the prior partners at the time of the admission of Snider.

f. The partners agree that total resulting capital should be $820,000 and no goodwill should be recognized.

g. Other assets are revalued down by $20,000 and a bonus of $40,000 is paid to Snider at the time of admission.

LO5

Advanced StudyGuide .com

P10-14   Division of Income

Champion Play Company is a partnership that sells sporting goods. The partnership agreement provides for 10 percent interest on invested capital, salaries of $24,000 to Luc and $28,000 to Dennis, and a bonus for Luc. The 20X3 capital accounts were as follows:

Luc, Capital				Dennis, Capital			
8/1	15,000	1/1	50,000	7/1	10,000	1/1	70,000
		4/1	5,000			9/1	22,500

Required

For each of the following independent situations, prepare an income distribution schedule.

a. Interest is based on weighted-average capital balances. The bonus is 5 percent and is calculated on net income after deducting the bonus. In 20X3, net income was $64,260. Any remainder is divided between Luc and Dennis in a 3:2 ratio, respectively.

b. Interest is based on ending capital balances after deducting salaries, which the partners normally withdraw during the year. The bonus is 8 percent and is calculated on net income after deducting the bonus and salaries. Net income was $108,700. Any remainder is divided equally.

c. Interest is based on beginning capital balances. The bonus is 12.5 percent and is calculated on net income after deducting the bonus. Net income was $76,950. Any remainder is divided between Luc and Dennis in a 4:2 ratio, respectively.

LO6   **P10-15   Withdrawal of a Partner under Various Alternatives**

The partnership of Ace, Jack, and Spade has been in business for 25 years. On December 31, 20X5, Spade decided to retire from the partnership. The partnership balance sheet reported the following capital balances for each partner at December 31, 20X5:

Ace, Capital	$150,000
Jack, Capital	200,000
Spade, Capital	120,000

The partners allocate partnership income and loss in the ratio 20:30:50.

Required

Record Spade's withdrawal under each of the following independent situations.

a. Jack acquired Spade's capital interest for $150,000 in a personal transaction. Partnership assets were not revalued, and partnership goodwill was not recognized.

b. Assume the same facts as in part *a* except that partnership goodwill applicable to the entire business was recognized by the partnership.

c. Spade received $180,000 of partnership cash upon retirement. Capital of the partnership after Spade's retirement was $290,000.

d. Spade received $60,000 of cash and partnership land with a fair value of $120,000. The carrying amount of the land on the partnership books was $100,000. Capital of the partnership after Spade's retirement was $310,000.

e. Spade received $150,000 of partnership cash upon retirement. The partnership recorded the portion of goodwill attributable to Spade.

f. Assume the same facts as in part *e* except that partnership goodwill attributable to all the partners was recorded.

g. Because of limited cash in the partnership, Spade received land with a fair value of $100,000 and a note payable for $50,000. The carrying amount of the land on the partnership books was $60,000. Capital of the partnership after Spade's retirement was $360,000.

LO3–LO6   **P10-16   Multiple-Choice Questions—Initial Investments, Division of Income, Admission and Retirement of a Partner [AICPA Adapted]**

Select the correct answer for each of the following questions.

1. When property other than cash is invested in a partnership, at what amount should the noncash property be credited to the contributing partner's capital account?
    a. Contributing partner's tax basis.
    b. Contributing partner's original cost.
    c. Assessed valuation for property tax purposes.
    d. Fair value at the date of contribution.

2. William and Martha drafted a partnership agreement that lists the following assets contributed at the partnership's formation:

	Contributed by	
	William	**Martha**
Cash	$20,000	$30,000
Inventory		15,000
Building		40,000
Furniture and Equipment	15,000	

The building is subject to a $10,000 mortgage, which the partnership has assumed. The partnership agreement also specifies that profits and losses are to be distributed evenly. What amounts should be recorded as capital for William and Martha at the formation of the partnership?

	William	Martha
a.	$35,000	$85,000
b.	$35,000	$75,000
c.	$55,000	$55,000
d.	$60,000	$60,000

3. Smith and Duncan are partners with capital balances of $60,000 and $20,000, respectively. Profits and losses are divided in the ratio of 60:40. Smith and Duncan decided to form a new partnership with Johnson, who invested land valued at $15,000 for a 20 percent capital interest in the new partnership. Johnson's cost of the land was $12,000. The partnership elected to use the bonus method to record the admission of Johnson into the partnership. Johnson's capital account should be credited for

   a. $12,000.
   b. $15,000.
   c. $16,000.
   d. $19,000.

4. On April 30, 20X5, Apple, Blue, and Crown formed a partnership by combining their separate business proprietorships. Apple contributed $50,000 cash. Blue contributed property with a $36,000 carrying amount, a $40,000 original cost, and $80,000 fair value. The partnership accepted responsibility for the $35,000 mortgage attached to the property. Crown contributed equipment with a $30,000 carrying amount, a $75,000 original cost, and $55,000 fair value. The partnership agreement specifies that profits and losses are to be shared equally but is silent regarding capital contributions. Which partner has the largest April 30, 20X5, capital account balance?

   a. Apple.
   b. Blue.
   c. Crown.
   d. All capital account balances are equal.

Note: The following information is for questions 5 and 6:

The Moon-Norbert Partnership was formed on January 2, 20X5. Under the partnership agreement, each partner has an equal initial capital balance accounted for under the goodwill method. Partnership net income or loss is allocated 60 percent to Moon and 40 percent to Norbert. To form the partnership, Moon originally contributed assets costing $30,000 with a fair value of $60,000 on January 2, 20X5, and Norbert contributed $20,000 in cash. Partners' drawings during 20X5 totaled $3,000 by Moon and $9,000 by Norbert. Moon-Norbert's net income for 20X5 was $25,000.

5. Norbert's initial capital balance in Moon-Norbert is

   a. $20,000.
   b. $25,000.
   c. $40,000.
   d. $60,000.

6. Moon's share of Moon-Norbert's net income is

   a. $15,000.
   b. $12,500.
   c. $12,000.
   d. $7,800.

7. In the Crowe-Dagwood partnership, Crowe and Dagwood had a capital ratio of 3:1 and a profit and loss ratio of 2:1. They used the bonus method to record Elman's admittance as a new

partner. What ratio should be used to allocate, to Crowe and Dagwood, the excess of Elman's contribution over the amount credited to Elman's capital account?

a. Crowe and Dagwood's new relative capital ratio.

b. Crowe and Dagwood's new relative profit and loss ratio.

c. Crowe and Dagwood's old capital ratio.

d. Crowe and Dagwood's old profit and loss ratio.

8. Blue and Green formed a partnership in 20X4. The partnership agreement provides for annual salary allowances of $55,000 for Blue and $45,000 for Green. The partners share profits equally and losses in a 60:40 ratio. The partnership had earnings of $80,000 for 20X5 before any allowance to partners. What amount of these earnings should be credited to each partner's capital account?

	Blue	Green
a.	$40,000	$40,000
b.	$43,000	$37,000
c.	$44,000	$36,000
d.	$45,000	$35,000

9. When Jill retired from the partnership of Jill, Bill, and Hill, the final settlement of her interest exceeded her capital balance. Under the bonus method, the excess

a. Was recorded as goodwill.

b. Was recorded as an expense.

c. Reduced the capital balances of Bill and Hill.

d. Had no effect on the capital balances of Bill and Hill.

LO3–LO6 **P10-17** **Partnership Formation, Operation, and Changes in Ownership**

The partnership of Jordan and O'Neal began business on January 1, 20X7. Each partner contributed the following assets (the noncash assets are stated at their fair values on January 1, 20X7):

	Jordan	O'Neal
Cash	$ 60,000	$ 50,000
Inventories	80,000	–0–
Land	–0–	130,000
Equipment	100,000	–0–

The land was subject to a $50,000 mortgage, which the partnership assumed on January 1, 20X7. The equipment was subject to an installment note payable that had an unpaid principal amount of $20,000 on January 1, 20X7. The partnership also assumed this note payable. Jordan and O'Neal agreed to share partnership income and losses in the following manner:

	Jordan	O'Neal
Interest on beginning capital balances	3%	3%
Salaries	$12,000	$12,000
Remainder	60%	40%

During 20X7, the following events occurred:

1. Inventory was acquired at a cost of $30,000. At December 31, 20X7, the partnership owed $6,000 to its suppliers.

2. Principal of $5,000 was paid on the mortgage. Interest expense incurred on the mortgage was $2,000, all of which was paid by December 31, 20X7.

---

3. Principal of $3,500 was paid on the installment note. Interest expense incurred on the installment note was $2,000, all of which was paid by December 31, 20X7.

4. Sales on account amounted to $155,000. At December 31, 20X7, customers owed the partnership $21,000.

5. Selling and general expenses, excluding depreciation, amounted to $34,000. At December 31, 20X7, the partnership owed $6,200 of accrued expenses. Depreciation expense was $6,000.

6. Each partner withdrew $200 each week in anticipation of partnership profits.

7. The partnership's inventory at December 31, 20X7, was $20,000.

8. The partners allocated the net income for 20X7 and closed the accounts.

Additional Information

On January 1, 20X8, the partnership decided to admit Hill to the partnership. On that date, Hill invested $99,800 of cash into the partnership for a 20 percent capital interest. Total partnership capital after Hill was admitted totaled $450,000.

Required

a. Prepare journal entries to record the formation of the partnership on January 1, 20X7, and to record the events that occurred during 20X7.

b. Prepare the income statement for the Jordan-O'Neal Partnership for the year ended December 31, 20X7.

c. Prepare a balance sheet for the Jordon-O'Neal Partnership at December 31, 20X7.

d. Prepare the journal entry for the admission of Hill on January 1, 20X8.

P10-18A **Initial Investments and Tax Bases [AICPA Adapted]**

The DELS partnership was formed by combining individual accounting practices on May 10, 20X1. The initial investments were as follows:

	Current Value	Tax Basis
Delaney:		
Cash	$ 8,000	$ 8,000
Building	60,000	32,000
Mortgage payable, assumed by DELS	36,000	36,000
Engstrom:		
Cash	9,000	9,000
Office furniture	23,000	17,000
Note payable, assumed by DELS	10,000	10,000
Lahey:		
Cash	12,000	12,000
Computers and printers	18,000	21,000
Note payable, assumed by DELS	15,000	15,000
Simon:		
Cash	21,000	21,000
Library (books and periodicals)	7,000	5,000

Required

a. Prepare the journal entry to record the initial investments, using GAAP accounting.

b. Calculate the tax basis of each partner's capital if Delaney, Engstrom, Lahey, and Simon agree to assume equal amounts for the payables.

LO3–LO6 **P10-19** **Formation of a Partnership and Allocation of Profit and Loss**

Haskins and Sells formed a partnership on January 2, 20X3. Each had been a sole proprietor before forming their partnership.

Part I

Each partner's contributions follow. The amounts under the cost column represent the amounts reported on the books of each sole proprietorship immediately before the formation of the partnership.

	Cost	Fair Value
Haskins:		
Cash	$ 45,000	$ 45,000
Inventories (FIFO)	48,000	49,000
Trade accounts receivable	40,000	40,000
Allowance for uncollectible accounts	(1,500)	(2,000)
Building	550,000	370,000
Accumulated depreciation	(200,000)	
Mortgage on building assumed by partnership	(175,000)	(175,000)
Sells:		
Cash	$ 10,000	$ 10,000
Trade accounts receivable	30,000	30,000
Allowance for uncollectible accounts	(2,000)	(2,500)
Inventories (FIFO)	15,000	13,500
Note receivable due in 6 months	50,000	50,000
Temporary investments	100,000	81,500
Customer lists	–0–	60,000

Required

Using the preceding information, prepare a classified balance sheet as of January 2, 20X3, for the Haskins and Sells Partnership. Assume that $25,000 of the mortgage is due in 20X3 and that the customer lists are accounted for as an intangible asset to be amortized over a five-year period.

Part II

During 20X3, the Haskins and Sells Partnership reported the following information:

Revenues	$650,000
Cost of goods sold	320,000
Selling, general, and administrative expenses	70,000
Salaries paid to each partner (not included in selling, general, and administrative expenses):	
Haskins	90,000
Sells	70,000
Bonus paid to Haskins (not included in selling, general, and administrative expenses)	10% of net income
Withdrawals made during the year in addition to salaries:	
Haskins	10,000
Sells	5,000
Residual profit and loss–sharing ratio:	
Haskins	20%
Sells	80%

Required

a. Prepare an income statement for the Haskins and Sells Partnership for the year ended December 31, 20X3.

b. Prepare a schedule that shows how to allocate the partnership net income for 20X3.

c. What are the partners' capital balances that will appear on the December 31, 20X3, balance sheet?

d. Assume that the distribution of partnership net income remains the same (i.e., Haskins will continue to receive a 10 percent bonus and salaries will continue to be $90,000 and $70,000 to Haskins and Sells, respectively) and that the residual profit and loss–sharing ratio will continue to be 20:80. What would partnership net income have to be for each partner to receive the same amount of income?

Supplemental Problems for this chapter are available as part of the *Online Learning Center* on the textbook's Web site (URL: www.mhhe.com/baker1e).

Chapter Eleven

Partnerships: Liquidation

THE DEMISE OF LAVENTHOL & HORWATH

In 1990, when the "Big Six" accounting firms dominated the profession, Laventhol & Horwath was the seventh largest accounting firm with over 3,400 employees and a firm record $345.2 million in revenue. The Philadelphia-based accounting partnership had been in operation since 1915 and their prospects could not have been brighter. Serious problems began in October of 1989 when Laventhol was forced to pay over $30 million to nine banks that had relied on Laventhol's audit of a real estate corporation. Five months later the firmed negotiated a $13 million settlement with another group of plaintiffs. As the lawsuits continued to pile up, the strain on Laventhol increased.

In an effort to stay afloat following these large settlements, Laventhol announced a 10 percent across-the-board salary cut in October 1990. In fact, in a press release accompanying the cut, the firm was said it was "optimistic" about the future. Sadly, "the future" only lasted about a month. In November 1990 the firm fired the majority of its employees and filed for Chapter 11 bankruptcy protection in New York. At the time of the filing, Laventhol had 110 pending lawsuits and $75 million in debt.

LAVENTHOL & HORWATH

Because of the normal risks of doing business, the majority of partnerships begun in any year fail within three years and require dissolution and liquidation. The ending of a partnership's business is often an emotional event for the partners. The partners may have had high expectations and invested a large amount of personal resources and time in the business. The end of the partnership often is the end of those business dreams. Accountants usually assist in the winding down and liquidation process and must recognize the legitimate rights of and any amounts due to the many parties involved in the partnership: individual partners, creditors of the partnership, customers, and others doing business with the partnership.

The Uniform Partnership Act of 1997 has 71 sections, seven of which deal specifically with the dissolution and winding up of a partnership. Several sections discuss the specific rights of creditors of the partnership. Creditors have first claim to the partnership's assets. After the creditors are fully satisfied, any remaining assets are distributed to the partners based on the balances in their capital accounts. This chapter presents the concepts that accountants must know if they offer professional services to partnerships undergoing winding down and liquidation.

LEARNING OBJECTIVES

When you finish studying this chapter, you should be able to:

LO1 Understand and explain terms associated with partnership liquidations.

LO2 Make calculations related to lump-sum partnership liquidations.

LO3 Make calculations related to installment partnership liquidations.

OVERVIEW OF PARTNERSHIP LIQUIDATIONS

LO1

Understand and explain
terms associated with partnership liquidations.

The major provisions of the Uniform Partnership Act of 1997 (UPA 1997) have been adopted by most states and that act is used for the illustrations in this chapter. The chapter first presents the UPA 1997's major provisions regarding events and processes associated with partnership liquidations. After this overview, the chapter illustrates the winding-up process in both a lump-sum liquidation and an installment liquidation.

Dissociation, Dissolution, Winding Up, and Liquidation of a Partnership

Dissociation is the legal description of the withdrawal of a partner, including the following:

1. A partner's death.
2. A partner's voluntary withdrawal (i.e., a retirement).
3. A judicial determination, including (*a*) the partner engaged in wrongful conduct that materially and negatively affected the partnership, (*b*) the partner willfully committed a material breach of the partnership agreement, (*c*) the partner became a debtor in bankruptcy, or (*d*) an individual partner has become incapable of performing his or her duties under the partnership agreement.

Not all dissociations result in a partnership liquidation. Many partner dissociations involve only a buyout of the withdrawing partner's interest rather than a winding up and liquidation of the partnership's business.

Dissolution is the dissolving of a partnership. Events that cause dissolution and winding up of the partnership business are presented in section 801 of the UPA 1997, as follows:

1. In a partnership at will, a partner's express notice to leave the partnership. An at-will partnership is one in which there is, at most, only an oral understanding among the partners, and there is no definite term or specific task undertaking. A partnership agreement can eliminate this event as a cause for partnership dissolution by including, for example, a provision for a buyout of that partner's interest in the partnership.
2. In a partnership for a definite term or specific undertaking, dissolution takes place when (*a*) after a partner's death or wrongful dissociation, at least half of the remaining partners decide to wind up the partnership business, (*b*) all of the partners agree to wind up the partnership business, or (*c*) the term or specific undertaking has expired or been completed.
3. An event that makes it unlawful to carry on a substantial part of the partnership business.
4. A judicial determination that (*a*) the economic purpose of the partnership is unlikely to be achieved, (*b*) a partner has engaged in conduct relating to the partnership business that makes it impracticable to carry on the partnership business, or (*c*) it is not reasonably practicable to carry on the partnership business in conformity with the partnership agreement.

On dissolution, the partnership begins the winding up of the partnership's business.

Winding Up and Liquidation
Winding up and liquidation of the partnership begins after the dissolution of the partnership. The partnership continues for the limited purpose of winding up the business and completing work in process. The winding-up process includes the transactions necessary to liquidate the partnership such as the collection of receivables, including any receivables from partners; conversion of the noncash assets to cash; payment of the partnership's obligations; and the distribution of any remaining net balance to the partners, in cash, according to their capital interests. If the partnership agreement does not provide

for a special liquidation ratio, then profits or losses during the liquidation process are distributed in the normal profit and loss ratio that was used during the operation of the partnership.

Some terminating partnerships change to the liquidation basis of accounting once they no longer consider the business to be a going concern. At the point at which the liquidation basis of accounting is adopted, the partnership's assets are valued at their estimated net realizable liquidation values and liabilities at their estimated settlement amounts. Because of the apparent uncertainties in practice of specifically defining the point at which an entity is no longer a going concern, the FASB, decided (in March 2010) not to specifically define a going concern. Instead, the Board decided to require detailed disclosures when management, applying commercially reasonable business judgment, is aware of conditions and events that indicate, based on current facts and circumstances, that it is reasonably foreseeable that an entity may not be able to meet its obligations as they become due.

Loans to or from Partners   Under the UPA 1997, liabilities to partners for loans the partners have made to the partnership ("inside debt") have the same status as liabilities to the partnerships' third-party creditors ("outside debt"). In effect, UPA 1997 removes old rules formally subordinating inside debt to outside debt. However, a partner ultimately is personally liable for any outside debt that is still unsatisfied if the partnership has insufficient funds to satisfy all claims of outside creditors. The result is that the obligation to satisfy partnership debts effectively results in the equitable subordination of inside debt to outside debt when the partnership assets are insufficient to satisfy all obligations to non-partners. Even though the UPA 1997 indicates that partnership obligations to the individual partners must normally be paid during the winding up of the partnership on the same proportional basis as the other liabilities of the partnership, outside creditors frequently require partners to subordinate their receivables from the partnership. Thus, in all examples, we assume partners have agreed to subordinate their receivables from the partnership to outside debt. Therefore, we typically illustrate examples in which liquidation payments are made in the following order: (1) outside debt, (2) inside debt, and (3) partner's capital.

Deficits in Partners' Capital Accounts   As part of the liquidation process, each partner with a deficit in his or her capital account must make a contribution to the partnership to remedy that capital deficit. The partnership makes a liquidating distribution, in cash, to each partner with a capital credit balance. The UPA 1997 specifies cash for these liquidating distributions. If a partner fails to make a required contribution to remedy his or her capital deficit, all other partners must contribute, in the proportion to which those partners share partnership losses, the additional amount necessary to pay the partnership's obligations.

While the UPA 1997 does not provide for a formal offset of a loan payable to an individual partner with a deficit in his or her capital account, a failure to do so can result in inequalities. For example, assume a partnership owes a partner $10,000. If the partnership pays the partner the $10,000, it is possible that the partner could spend the money and subsequently become personally insolvent. Then, if the allocation of losses incurred on the sale of assets later results in a deficit balance in that partner's capital account, the other partners would have to absorb the deficit. Therefore, the legal doctrine of setoff effectively treats loans from partners to the partnership as additional capital investments that can be offset against a deficit capital account balance in order to avoid inequalities in the liquidation process.

Statement of Partnership Realization and Liquidation

To guide and summarize the partnership liquidation process, a ***statement of partnership realization and liquidation*** may be prepared. The statement, often called a "statement of liquidation," is the basis of the journal entries made to record the liquidation. It presents, in worksheet form, the effects of the liquidation on the balance sheet accounts of the partnership. The statement shows the conversion of assets into cash, the allocation of any gains or losses to the partners, and the distribution of cash to creditors and partners. This statement is a basic feature of accounting for a partnership liquidation and is presented and illustrated in the remainder of the chapter.

LUMP-SUM LIQUIDATIONS

LO2

Make calculations related to lump-sum partnership liquidations.

Advanced
StudyGuide
.com

A *lump-sum liquidation* of a partnership is one in which all assets are converted into cash within a very short time, creditors are paid, and a single, lump-sum payment is made to the partners for their capital interests. Although most partnership liquidations take place over an extended period, as illustrated later, the lump-sum liquidation is an excellent focal point for presenting the major concepts of partnership liquidation.

Realization of Assets[1]

Typically, a partnership experiences losses on the disposal of its assets. A partnership may have a "Going out of Business" sale in which its inventory is marked down well below normal selling price to encourage immediate sale. Often, the remaining inventory may be sold to companies that specialize in acquiring assets of liquidating businesses. The partnership's furniture, fixtures, and equipment also may be offered at a reduced price or sold to liquidators. Any goodwill on the partnership's books is generally written off at the time the partnership begins a liquidation because the entity is no longer a going concern.

The partnership attempts to collect its accounts receivable. Sometimes the partnership offers a large cash discount for the prompt payment of any remaining receivables whose collection may otherwise delay terminating the partnership. Alternatively, the receivables may be sold to a *factor*, a business that specializes in acquiring accounts receivable and immediately paying cash to the seller of the receivables. The partnership records the sale of the receivables as it would any other asset. Typically, the factor acquires only the best of a business's receivables at a price below face value, but some factors are willing to buy all receivables and pay a significantly lower price than face value.

The assets of the partnership, including any receivables from the partners and any contributions required of partners to remedy their capital deficits, are applied to pay the partnership's creditors. Loans to or from partners must be settled during the winding up process. Any remaining amount is then paid, in cash, to the partners in accordance with their rights to liquidating distributions. Section 807 of the UPA 1997 states that the liquidating distributions to the partners are to be made in cash.

Expenses of Liquidation

The liquidation process usually begins with scheduling the partnership's known assets and liabilities. The names and addresses of creditors and the amounts owed to each are specified. As diligent as the effort usually is, additional, unscheduled creditors may become known during the liquidation process. The liquidation process also involves some expenses, such as additional legal and accounting costs. The partnership also may incur costs of disposing of the business, such as special advertising and costs of locating specialized equipment dealers. These expenses are allocated to partners' capital accounts in the profit and loss distribution ratio.

Illustration of Lump-Sum Liquidation

The following illustration presents the liquidation of the ABC Partnership, whose partners, Alt, Blue, and Cha, decide to terminate the business on May 1, 20X5. The AB Partnership was formed on January 1, 20X1. Cha was admitted into the partnership on January 1, 20X3, and the name of the business was changed to the ABC Partnership. For purposes of this illustration, assume that Alt remained in the partnership and, in 20X4, the partners agreed to a realignment of their profit and loss–sharing percentages to more closely conform with each partner's efforts. The profit and loss–sharing percentages

---

[1] To view a video explanation of this topic, visit advancedstudyguide.com.

after realignment in 20X4 were as follows: Alt, 40 percent; Blue, 40 percent; and Cha, 20 percent. A condensed trial balance of the company on May 1, 20X5, the day the partners decide to liquidate the business, follows:

ABC PARTNERSHIP Trial Balance May 1, 20X5		
Cash	$ 10,000	
Noncash Assets	90,000	
Liabilities		$ 42,000
Alt, Capital (40%)		34,000
Blue, Capital (40%)		10,000
Cha, Capital (20%)		14,000
Total	$100,000	$100,000

The basic accounting equation, Assets − Liabilities = Owners' equity, applies to partnership accounting. In this case, owners' equity is the sum of the partners' capital accounts, as follows:

$$Assets - Liabilities = Owners'\ equity$$
$$\$100,000 - \$42,000 = \$58,000$$

The following three cases illustrate the partnership liquidation concepts used most commonly. Each case begins with the May 1, 20X5, trial balance of the ABC Partnership. The amount of cash realized from the disposal of the noncash assets is different for each of the three cases, and the effects of the different realizations are shown in the statement of partnership realization and liquidation presented for each case.

Case 1. Partnership Solvent and No Deficits in Partners' Capital Accounts

The noncash assets are sold for $80,000 on May 15, 20X5, at a $10,000 loss. The partnership's creditors are paid their $42,000 on May 20, and the remaining $48,000 cash is distributed to the partners on May 30, 20X5.

The statement of realization and liquidation for Case 1 is presented in Figure 11–1. Note that parentheses are used to indicate credit amounts in the worksheets used throughout this chapter. The statement includes only balance sheet accounts across the columns, with all noncash assets presented together as a single total. Once a business has entered liquidation, the balance sheet accounts are the only relevant ones; the income statement is for a going concern. The liquidation process is presented in the order of occurrence in the rows of the worksheet. Thus, the worksheet includes the entire realization and liquidation process and is the basis for the journal entries to record the liquidation.

Other important observations are as follows:

1. The preliquidation balances are obtained from the May 1, 20X5, trial balance.
2. When the partnership's noncash assets are sold, the $10,000 loss is allocated to the partners' capital accounts.
3. Creditors, including individual partners who have made any loans to the partnership, are paid before any cash is distributed to partners.
4. Payments to partners are made for their capital credit balances.
5. The postliquidation balances are all zero, indicating the accounts are all closed and the partnership is fully liquidated and terminated.

FIGURE 11–1 **Case 1. Partnership Solvent; No Deficits in Partners' Capital Accounts**

ABC PARTNERSHIP
Statement of Partnership Realization and Liquidation
Lump-Sum Liquidation

	Cash	Noncash Assets	Liabilities	Capital Balance		
				Alt, 40%	Blue, 40%	Cha, 20%
Preliquidation balances, May 1	10,000	90,000	(42,000)	(34,000)	(10,000)	(14,000)
Sales of assets and distribution of $10,000 loss	80,000	(90,000)		4,000	4,000	2,000
	90,000	–0–	(42,000)	(30,000)	(6,000)	(12,000)
Payment to creditors	(42,000)		42,000			
	48,000	–0–	–0–	(30,000)	(6,000)	(12,000)
Lump-sum payment to partners	(48,000)			30,000	6,000	12,000
Postliquidation balances	–0–	–0–	–0–	–0–	–0–	–0–

Note: Parentheses indicate credit amount.

The statement of partnership realization and liquidation is the basis for the following journal entries to record the liquidation process:

May 15, 20X5

(1)
Cash	80,000	
Alt, Capital	4,000	
Blue, Capital	4,000	
Cha, Capital	2,000	
Noncash Assets		90,000

Realization of all noncash assets of the ABC Partnership and distribution of $10,000 loss using profit and loss ratio.

May 20, 20X5

(2)
Liabilities	42,000	
Cash		42,000

Pay creditors.

May 30, 20X5

(3)
Alt, Capital	30,000	
Blue, Capital	6,000	
Cha, Capital	12,000	
Cash		48,000

Lump-sum payments to partners

Advanced
StudyGuide
.com

Case 2. Partnership Solvent and Deficit Created in Partner's Capital Account

A deficit in a partner's capital account can occur if the credit balance of that capital account is too low to absorb his or her share of losses. A capital deficit may be created at any time in the liquidation process. Such deficits may be remedied by either of the following two means:

1. The partner invests cash or other assets to eliminate the capital deficit.
2. The partner's capital deficit is distributed to the other partners in their resulting loss-sharing ratio.

The approach used depends on the solvency of the partner with the capital deficit. A partner who is personally solvent and has sufficient net worth to eliminate the capital deficit must make an additional investment in the partnership to cover the deficit. On the other hand, if the partner is personally insolvent—that is, personal liabilities exceed personal assets—section 807 of the UPA 1997 requires the remaining partners to absorb the insolvent partner's deficit by allocating it to their capital accounts in their resulting loss-sharing ratio.

The following lump-sum distribution illustrates these points:

1. The three partners' personal financial statements are as follows:

	Alt	Blue	Cha
Personal assets	$150,000	$ 12,000	$ 42,000
Personal liabilities	(86,000)	(16,000)	(14,000)
Net worth (deficit)	$ 64,000	$ (4,000)	$ 28,000

Blue is personally insolvent; Alt and Cha are personally solvent.

2. The partnership's noncash assets are sold for $35,000 on May 15, 20X5, and the $55,000 loss is allocated to the partners' capital accounts.
3. The partnership's creditors are paid $42,000 on May 20, 20X5.
4. Because Blue is personally insolvent, Blue's capital deficit of $12,000 is allocated to the other partners.
5. The remaining $4,000 cash is distributed as a lump-sum payment on May 30, 20X5.

The statement of partnership realization and liquidation for Case 2 is presented in Figure 11–2.

FIGURE 11–2   **Case 2. Partnership Solvent; Deficit Created in Personally Insolvent Partner's Capital Account**

ABC PARTNERSHIP
Statement of Partnership Realization and Liquidation
Lump-Sum Liquidation

	Cash	Noncash Assets	Liabilities	Capital Balance Alt, 40%	Blue, 40%	Cha, 20%
Preliquidation balances, May 1	10,000	90,000	(42,000)	(34,000)	(10,000)	(14,000)
Sales of assets and distribution of $55,000 loss	35,000	(90,000)		22,000	22,000	11,000
	45,000	–0–	(42,000)	(12,000)	12,000	(3,000)
Payment to creditors	(42,000)		42,000			
	3,000	–0–	–0–	(12,000)	12,000	(3,000)
Distribution of deficit of insolvent partner:					(12,000)	
40/60 × $12,000				8,000		
20/60 × $12,000						4,000
	3,000	–0–	–0–	(4,000)	–0–	1,000
Contribution by Cha to remedy capital deficit	1,000					(1,000)
	4,000	–0–	–0–	(4,000)	–0–	–0–
Lump-sum payment to partners	(4,000)			4,000		
Postliquidation balances	–0–	–0–	–0–	–0–	–0–	–0–

Note: Parentheses indicate credit amount.

The following observations emerge from this illustration:

1. The $55,000 loss on the realization of noncash assets is allocated in the partners' loss-sharing ratio of 40 percent for Alt, 40 percent for Blue, and 20 percent for Cha. Blue's $22,000 share of the loss on disposal creates a $12,000 deficit in his capital account. Blue is personally insolvent and is unable to make an additional investment to remove the capital deficit.

2. The partnership's creditors are paid before any distributions are made to the partners.

3. Blue's $12,000 deficit is distributed to Alt and Cha in their resulting loss-sharing ratio. Note that the UPA 1977 specifies the loss-sharing ratio be used for this allocation. Alt absorbs two-thirds (40/60) of Blue's deficit, and Cha absorbs one-third (20/60).

4. The distribution of Blue's deficit creates a deficit in Cha's capital account. Cha must contribute $1,000 to remedy her capital deficit.

5. A lump-sum payment is made to Alt for his $4,000 capital credit.

6. All postliquidation balances are zero, indicating the completion of the liquidation process.

Case 3. Partnership Is Insolvent and Deficit Created in Partner's Capital Account

Advanced StudyGuide .com

A partnership is insolvent when existing cash and cash generated by the sale of the assets are not sufficient to pay the partnership's liabilities. In this case, the individual partners are liable for the remaining unpaid partnership liabilities. The following illustration presents an insolvent partnership and a deficit in one of the partner's capital accounts.

1. Alt and Cha are personally solvent, and Blue is personally insolvent as in Case 2.
2. The noncash assets are sold for $20,000 on May 15, 20X5.
3. The partnership's creditors are paid $42,000 on May 20, 20X5.

The statement of partnership realization and liquidation for Case 3 is presented in Figure 11–3.

FIGURE 11–3   **Case 3. Partnership Insolvent; Deficit Created in Personally Insolvent Partner's Capital Account**

ABC PARTNERSHIP
Statement of Partnership Realization and Liquidation
Lump-Sum Liquidation

	Cash	Noncash Assets	Liabilities	Alt, 40%	Blue, 40%	Cha, 20%
Preliquidation balances, May 1	10,000	90,000	(42,000)	(34,000)	(10,000)	(14,000)
Sales of assets and distribution of $70,000 loss	20,000	(90,000)		28,000	28,000	14,000
	30,000	–0–	(42,000)	(6,000)	18,000	–0–
Distribution of deficit of insolvent partner:					(18,000)	
40/60 × $18,000				12,000		
20/60 × $18,000						6,000
	30,000	–0–	(42,000)	6,000	–0–	6,000
Contribution by Alt and Cha to remedy capital deficit	12,000			(6,000)		(6,000)
	42,000	–0–	(42,000)	–0–	–0–	–0–
Payment to creditors	(42,000)		42,000			
Postliquidation balances	–0–	–0–	–0–	–0–	–0–	–0–

Note: Parentheses indicate credit amount.

The following observations are made from this illustration:

1. The $70,000 loss is allocated to the partners in their loss-sharing ratio. This allocation creates a deficit of $18,000 in Blue's capital account.
2. Because Blue is personally insolvent, his $18,000 deficit is distributed to Alt and Cha in their loss-sharing ratio of 40:60 for Alt and 20:60 for Cha. The distribution of Blue's deficit results in a $6,000 deficit for Alt and a $6,000 deficit for Cha.
3. Alt and Cha make additional capital contributions to remedy their respective capital deficits of $6,000 and $6,000.
4. The $42,000 partnership cash now available is used to pay the partnership's creditors.
5. The postliquidation balances are zero, indicating completion of the partnership liquidation.

In Case 3, Alt and Cha each made additional capital contributions to eliminate their capital deficits. Whenever a partner must remedy another partner's capital deficit, the partner making the remedy has cause to bring suit against the failing partner. Blue's failure in the amount of $12,000 in Case 2, and $18,000 in Case 3, required Alt and Cha to remedy Blue's deficit. Alt and Cha can sue Blue and be included in the list of Blue's personal liabilities. Although Blue is personally insolvent, Alt and Cha may obtain a partial recovery of their amounts.

INSTALLMENT LIQUIDATIONS

LO3

Make calculations related to installment partnership liquidations.

An *installment liquidation* typically requires several months to complete and includes periodic, or installment, payments to the partners during the liquidation period. Most partnership liquidations take place over an extended period in order to obtain the largest possible amount from the realization of the assets. The partners typically receive periodic payments during the liquidation because they require funds for personal purposes.

Some partnerships using installment liquidations prepare a Plan of Liquidation and Dissolution prior to the beginning of the liquidation. This plan sets out the intended liquidation of its assets and the winding up of its affairs. The partners discuss and perhaps modify the plan, but an agreement of the partners is expected for the plan. And some partnerships, upon obtaining the consent of the partners to proceed with the installment liquidation, adopt the liquidation basis of accounting under which assets are stated at their estimated net realizable value and liabilities, including projected costs of liquidation, are stated at their estimated settlement amounts. These partnerships may prepare a Statement of Net Assets in Liquidation and a Statement of Changes in Net Assets in Liquidation. However, those partnerships using GAAP apply **FASB 144 (ASC 360),** "Accounting for the Impairment or Disposal of Long-Lived Assets" (FASB 144, ASC 360), to value their long-lived assets to be disposed of by sale. **FASB 144 (ASC 360)** states that these assets are to be classified separately and valued at the lower of carrying amount or fair value less costs to sell. And **FASB 146 (ASC 420),** "Accounting for Costs Associated with Exit or Disposal Activities" (FASB 146, ASC 420), requires that costs associated with an exit activity be recognized and measured at fair value in the period in which the liability is incurred, not in earlier periods when, for example, a restructuring plan is adopted. Most partnerships use the Statement of Partnership Realization and Liquidation during the installment liquidation process and recognize gains or losses from the liquidation events.

Installment liquidations involve the distribution of cash to partners before complete liquidation of the assets occurs. The accountant must be especially cautious when distributing available cash because future events may change the amounts to be paid to each partner. For this reason, the following practical guides are used to assist the accountant in determining safe installment payments to the partners:

1. Distribute no cash to the partners until all liabilities and actual plus potential liquidation expenses have been paid or provided for by reserving the necessary cash.
2. Anticipate the worst, or most restrictive, possible case before determining the amount of cash installment each partner receives:
   a. Assume that all remaining noncash assets will be written off as a loss; that is, assume that nothing will be realized on asset disposals.
   b. Assume that deficits created in the partners' capital accounts will be distributed to the remaining partners; that is, assume that deficits will not be eliminated by additional partner capital contributions.
3. After the accountant has assumed the worst possible cases, the remaining credit balances in capital accounts represent safe distributions of cash that may be distributed to partners in those amounts.

Advanced
StudyGuide
.com

Illustration of Installment Liquidation

The same illustration used in the lump-sum liquidation of the ABC Partnership is now used to illustrate liquidation in installments. Alt, Blue, and Cha decide to liquidate their business over a period of time and to receive installment distributions of available cash during the liquidation process.

ABC Partnership's condensed trial balance on May 1, 20X5, the day the partners decide to liquidate the business, follows. Each partner's profit and loss–sharing percentage is also shown.

ABC PARTNERSHIP Trial Balance May 1, 20X5		
Cash	$ 10,000	
Noncash Assets	90,000	
Liabilities		$ 42,000
Alt, Capital (40%)		34,000
Blue, Capital (40%)		10,000
Cha, Capital (20%)		14,000
Total	$100,000	$100,000

The following describes this case.

1. The partners' net worth statements on May 1, 20X5, are as follows:

	Alt	Blue	Cha
Personal assets	$150,000	$12,000	$42,000
Personal liabilities	(86,000)	(16,000)	(14,000)
Net worth (deficit)	$ 64,000	$ (4,000)	$28,000

Blue is personally insolvent; Alt and Cha are personally solvent.

2. The noncash assets are sold as follows:

Date	Book Value	Proceeds	Loss
5/15/X5	$55,000	$45,000	$10,000
6/15/X5	30,000	15,000	15,000
7/15/X5	5,000	5,000	

3. The creditors are paid $42,000 on May 20.
4. The partners agree to maintain a $10,000 cash reserve during the liquidation process to pay for any liquidation expenses.

FIGURE 11–4 | **Installment Liquidation Worksheet**

ABC PARTNERSHIP
Statement of Partnership Realization and Liquidation
Installment Liquidation

	Cash	Noncash Assets	Liabilities	Capital Balance Alt, 40%	Blue, 40%	Cha, 20%
Preliquidation balances, May 1	10,000	90,000	(42,000)	(34,000)	(10,000)	(14,000)
May 20X5:						
Sale of assets and distribution of						
$10,000 loss	45,000	(55,000)		4,000	4,000	2,000
	55,000	35,000	(42,000)	(30,000)	(6,000)	(12,000)
Payment to creditors	(42,000)		42,000			
	13,000	35,000	–0–	(30,000)	(6,000)	(12,000)
Payment to partners (Schedule 1,						
Figure 11–5)	(3,000)			3,000		
	10,000	35,000	–0–	(27,000)	(6,000)	(12,000)
June 20X5:						
Sale of assets and distribution of						
$15,000 loss	15,000	(30,000)		6,000	6,000	3,000
	25,000	5,000	–0–	(21,000)	–0–	(9,000)
Payment to partners (Schedule 2,						
Figure 11–5)	(15,000)			11,000		4,000
	10,000	5,000	–0–	(10,000)	–0–	(5,000)
July 20X5:						
Sale of assets at book value	5,000	(5,000)				
	15,000	–0–	–0–	(10,000)	–0–	(5,000)
Payment of $7,500 in liquidation						
costs	(7,500)			3,000	3,000	1,500
	7,500	–0–	–0–	(7,000)	3,000	(3,500)
Distribution of deficit of insolvent						
partner:					(3,000)	
40/60 × $3,000				2,000		
20/60 × $3,000						1,000
	7,500	–0–	–0–	(5,000)	–0–	(2,500)
Payment to partners	(7,500)			5,000		2,500
Postliquidation balances, July 31	–0–	–0–	–0–	–0–	–0–	–0–

Note: Parentheses indicate credit amount.

5. The partners agree to distribute the available cash at the end of each month; that is, installment liquidations will be made on May 31 and June 30. The final cash distributions to partners will be made on July 31, 20X5, the end of the liquidation process.

Figure 11–4 presents the statement of partnership realization and liquidation for the installment liquidation of the ABC Partnership.

Transactions during May 20X5

The events during May 20X5 result in a distribution of $3,000 to the partners. The procedure to arrive at this amount is as follows:

1. The sale of $55,000 of assets results in a loss of $10,000, which is distributed to the three partners in their loss-sharing ratio.
2. Payments of $42,000 are made to the partnership's creditors for the known liabilities.
3. Available cash is distributed to the partners on May 31, 20X5.

FIGURE 11–5 **Schedule of Safe Payment to Partners for an Installment Liquidation**

| | Partner | | |
	Alt 40%	Blue 40%	Cha 20%
ABC PARTNERSHIP			
Schedule of Safe Payment to Partners			
Schedule 1, May 31, 20X5			
Computation of distribution of cash available on May 31, 20X5:			
Capital balances, May 31, before cash distribution	(30,000)	(6,000)	(12,000)
Assume full loss of $35,000 on remaining noncash assets and $10,000			
in possible future liquidation expenses	18,000	18,000	9,000
	(12,000)	12,000	(3,000)
Assume Blue's potential deficit must be absorbed by Alt and Cha:		(12,000)	
40/60 × $12,000	8,000		
20/60 × $12,000			4,000
	(4,000)	–0–	1,000
Assume Cha's potential deficit must be absorbed by Alt	1,000		(1,000)
Safe payment to partners, May 31	(3,000)	–0–	–0–
Schedule 2, June 30, 20X5			
Computation of distribution of cash available on June 30, 20X5:			
Capital balances, June 30, before cash distribution	(21,000)	–0–	(9,000)
Assume full loss of $5,000 on remaining noncash assets and $10,000			
in possible future liquidation expenses	6,000	6,000	3,000
	(15,000)	6,000	(6,000)
Assume Blue's potential deficit must be absorbed by Alt and Cha:		(6,000)	
40/60 × $6,000	4,000		
20/60 × $6,000			2,000
Safe payment to partners, June 30	(11,000)	–0–	(4,000)

Note: Parentheses indicate credit amount.

Advanced
StudyGuide
.com

To determine the safe payment of cash to be distributed to partners, the accountant must make some assumptions about the future liquidation of the remaining assets. Under the assumption of the worst possible situation, the remaining $35,000 of assets will result in a total loss. Before making a cash distribution to the partners, the accountant prepares a *schedule of safe payments to partners* using the worst-case assumptions. Figure 11–5 presents the schedule of safe payments to partners as of May 31, 20X5.

The schedule of safe payments begins with the partners' capital balances as of May 31. The logic of using just the capital accounts comes from the accounting equation: Assets − Liabilities = Partners' capital balances. Thus, for example, if there was an increase in a liability that reduced the net assets, the equality of the accounting equation would also result in a decrease in the total of partners' capital balances. Because the partners' capital accounts are the focus of the payments to partners, it is unnecessary to include the assets and liabilities in the schedule of safe payments to partners. The schedule includes all the information necessary for partners to know how much cash they will receive at each cash distribution date.

Alt, Blue, and Cha agree to withhold $10,000 for possible liquidation expenses. In addition, the noncash assets have a remaining balance of $35,000 on May 31. A worst-case assumption is a complete loss on the noncash assets and $10,000 of liquidation expenses, totaling $45,000 of charges to be distributed to the partners' capital accounts. The capital accounts of Alt, Blue, and Cha would be charged for $18,000, $18,000, and $9,000, respectively, for their shares of the $45,000 assumed loss. These assumptions result in a pro forma deficit in Blue's capital account. This is not an actual deficit that must be remedied! It is merely the result of applying the worst-case assumptions.

Continuing such worst-case planning, the accountant assumes that Blue is insolvent (which happens to be true in this example) and distributes the pro forma deficit in Blue's capital account to Alt and Cha in their *loss-sharing ratio* of 40:60 to Alt and 20:60 to Cha. The resulting credit balances indicate the amount of cash that may be safely distributed to the partners. The May 31 cash distribution is shown in Figure 11–4. The available cash of $3,000 is distributed to Alt. The ending balances should satisfy the equality of assets and equities of the accounting equation. If the equality has been destroyed, an error has occurred that must be corrected before proceeding further. As of May 31, after the installment distribution, the accounting equation is

$$\text{Assets} - \text{Liabilities} = \text{Owners' equity}$$
$$\$45,000 - \$0 = \$45,000$$

Transactions during June 20X5

Figure 11–4 continues with transactions for June 20X5, as follows:

1. Noncash assets of $30,000 are sold on June 15 for a $15,000 loss, which is distributed to the partners in their loss-sharing ratio, resulting in a zero capital balance for Blue.
2. On June 30, 20X5, available cash is distributed as an installment payment to the partners.

The schedule of safe payments to partners as of June 30, 20X5, in Figure 11–5 shows how the amounts of distribution are calculated. A worst-case plan assumes that the remaining noncash assets of $5,000 must be written off as a loss and that the $10,000 cash in reserve will be completely used for liquidation expenses. This $15,000 pro forma loss is allocated to the partners in their loss-sharing ratio, which creates a $6,000 deficit in Blue's capital account. Continuing the worst-case scenario, it is assumed Blue will not eliminate this debit balance. Therefore, the $6,000 potential deficit is allocated to Alt and Cha in their resulting loss-sharing ratio of 40/60 to Alt and 20/60 to Cha. The resulting credit balances in the partners' capital accounts show the amount of cash that can be distributed safely. Only $15,000 of the available cash is distributed to Alt and Cha on June 30, as shown in Figure 11–4.

Transactions during July 20X5

The last part of Figure 11–4 shows the completion of the liquidation transactions during July 20X5:

1. The remaining assets are sold at their book value of $5,000.
2. Actual liquidation costs of $7,500 are paid and allocated to the partners in their loss-sharing ratio, creating a deficit of $3,000 in Blue's capital account. The remaining $2,500 of the $10,000 reserved for the expenses is released for distribution to the partners.
3. Because Blue is personally insolvent and cannot contribute to the partnership, the $3,000 deficit is distributed to Alt and Cha in their loss-sharing ratio. Note that this is an actual deficit, not a pro forma deficit.
4. The $7,500 of remaining cash is paid to Alt and Cha to the extent of their capital balances. After this last distribution, all account balances are zero, indicating the completion of the liquidation process.

Cash Distribution Plan

At the beginning of the liquidation process, accountants commonly prepare a ***cash distribution plan,*** which gives the partners an idea of the installment cash payments each will receive as cash becomes available to the partnership. The actual installment distributions are determined using the statement of realization and liquidation, supplemented with the schedule of safe payments to partners as presented in the preceding section of the chapter. The cash distribution plan is a pro forma projection of the application of cash as it becomes available.

Loss Absorption Power

A basic concept of the cash distribution plan at the beginning of the liquidation process is *loss absorption power (LAP).* An individual partner's LAP is defined as the maximum loss that the partnership can realize before that partner's capital account balance is extinguished. The LAP is a function of two elements, as follows:

$$LAP = \frac{\text{Partner's capital account balance}}{\text{Partner's loss share}}$$

For example, on May 1, 2005, Alt has a capital account credit balance of $34,000 and a 40 percent share in the losses of ABC Partnership. Alt's LAP is

$$LAP = \frac{\$34,000}{0.40} = \$85,000$$

This means that $85,000 in losses on disposing of noncash assets or from additional liquidation expenses would eliminate the credit balance in Alt's capital account, as follows:

$$\$85,000 \times 0.40 = \$34,000$$

Illustration of Cash Distribution Plan

The following illustration is based on the ABC Partnership example. A trial balance of its balance sheet accounts on May 1, 20X5, the day the partners decide to liquidate the business, is prepared.

ABC PARTNERSHIP Trial Balance May 1, 20X5		
Cash	$ 10,000	
Noncash Assets	90,000	
Liabilities		$ 42,000
Alt, Capital (40%)		34,000
Blue, Capital (40%)		10,000
Cha, Capital (20%)		14,000
Total	$100,000	$100,000

The partners ask for a cash distribution plan as of May 1, 20X5, to determine the distributions of cash as it becomes available during the liquidation process. Such a plan always provides for payment to the partnership's creditors before any distributions may be made to the partners. Figure 11–6 presents the cash distribution plan as of May 1, the beginning date of the liquidation process.

The important observations from this illustration are as follows:

1. Each partner's loss absorption power is computed as the partner's capital balance divided by that partner's *loss-sharing percentage.* Alt has the highest LAP ($85,000), Cha has the next highest ($70,000), and Blue has the lowest ($25,000). Each partner's LAP is the amount of loss that would completely eliminate his or her net capital credit balance. Alt is the least vulnerable to a loss, and Blue is the most vulnerable.

2. The least vulnerable partner is the first to receive any cash distributions after providing for creditors. Alt is the only partner to receive cash until his LAP is decreased to the level of the next highest partner, Cha. To decrease Alt's LAP by $15,000 requires

FIGURE 11–6 Cash Distribution Plan for Liquidating Partnership

ABC PARTNERSHIP
Cash Distribution Plan
May 1, 20X5

	Loss Absorption Power			Capital Balance		
	Alt	Blue	Cha	Alt	Blue	Cha
Loss-sharing percentages				40%	40%	20%
Preliquidation capital balances, May 1, 20X5				(34,000)	(10,000)	(14,000)
Loss absorption power (LAP)						
(Capital balance/Loss ratio)	(85,000)	(25,000)	(70,000)			
Decrease highest LAP to next-highest LAP:						
Decrease Alt by $15,000						
(cash distribution: $15,000 × 0.40 = $6,000)	15,000			6,000		
	(70,000)	(25,000)	(70,000)	(28,000)	(10,000)	(14,000)
Decrease LAPs to next-highest level:						
Decrease Alt by $45,000						
(cash distribution: $45,000 × 0.40 = $18,000)	45,000			18,000		
Decrease Cha by $45,000						
(cash distribution: $45,000 × 0.20 = $9,000)			45,000			9,000
	(25,000)	(25,000)	(25,000)	(10,000)	(10,000)	(5,000)
Decrease LAPs by distributing cash in the loss-sharing						
percentages	40%	40%	20%			

Summary of Cash Distribution Plan

Step 1: First $42,000 to creditors			
Step 2: Next $10,000 to liquidation expenses			
Step 3: Next $6,000 to Alt	6,000		
Step 4: Next $45,000 to Alt and Cha in their respective			
loss ratios ($27,000 now available)	18,000		9,000
Step 5: Any additional distributions in the partners'			
loss-sharing ratios	40%	40%	20%

Note: Parentheses indicate credit amount.

the payment of $6,000 ($15,000 × 0.40) to Alt. After payment of $6,000 to Alt, his new loss absorption power will be the same as Cha's, calculated as Alt's remaining capital balance of $28,000 divided by his loss-sharing percentage of 40 percent ($28,000/0.40 = $70,000).

3. Alt's and Cha's LAPs are now equal, and they will receive cash distributions until the LAP of each decreases to the next highest level, the $25,000 of Blue. Multiplying the loss absorption power of $45,000 ($70,000 − $25,000) by the two partners' loss-sharing ratios shows how much of the next available cash can be safely paid to each partner. Alt and Cha will receive cash distributions according to their loss-sharing ratios. As the next $27,000 of cash becomes available, it will be distributed to Alt and Cha in the ratio of 40:60 to Alt and 20:60 to Cha.

4. Finally, when all three partners have the same LAPs, any remaining cash is distributed according to their loss-sharing ratios.

The summary of the cash distribution plan on the bottom of Figure 11–6 is provided to the partners. From this summary, partners are able to determine the relative amounts each will receive as cash becomes available to the partnership.

Figure 11–7 presents the capital balances for each of the partners in the ABC Partnership during the installment liquidation period from May 1, 20X5, through July 31, 20X5. The installment payments to partners are computed on the statement of partnership realization and liquidation (Figure 11–4) using a schedule of safe distributions to partners

FIGURE 11–7 **Confirmation of Cash Distribution Plan**

ABC PARTNERSHIP
Capital Account Balances
May 1, 20X5, through July 31, 20X5

	Partner		
	Alt 40%	**Blue 40%**	**Cha 20%**
Preliquidation balances, May 1	(34,000)	(10,000)	(14,000)
May loss of $10,000 on disposal of assets	4,000	4,000	2,000
	(30,000)	(6,000)	(12,000)
May 31 distribution of $3,000 available cash to partners:			
First $3,000 (of $6,000 priority to Alt)	3,000		
	(27,000)	(6,000)	(12,000)
June loss of $15,000 on disposal of assets	6,000	6,000	3,000
	(21,000)	–0–	(9,000)
June 30 distribution of $15,000 available cash to partners:			
Next $3,000 (to complete Alt's $6,000 priority)	3,000		
Remaining $12,000:			
40/60 to Alt	8,000		
20/60 to Cha			4,000
	(10,000)	–0–	(5,000)
Liquidation cost of $7,500	3,000	3,000	1,500
	(7,000)	3,000	(3,500)
Distribution of Blue's actual deficit	2,000	(3,000)	1,000
	(5,000)	–0–	(2,500)
Final payment of $7,500 to partners on July 31, 20X5:			
40/60 to Alt	5,000		
20/60 to Cha			2,500
Postliquidation balances, July 31	–0–	–0–	–0–

Note: Parentheses indicate credit amount.

(Figure 11–5). Figure 11–7 shows that the actual distributions of available cash conform to the cash distribution plan prepared at the beginning of the liquidation process, with adjustment because of the actual deficit of Blue absorbed by Alt and Cha.

ADDITIONAL CONSIDERATIONS

Incorporation of a Partnership

As a partnership continues to grow, the partners may decide to incorporate the business to have access to additional equity financing, to limit their personal liability, to obtain selected tax advantages, or to achieve other sound business purposes. At the incorporation, the partnership is terminated, and the assets and liabilities are revalued to their fair values. The gain or loss on revaluation is allocated to the partners' capital accounts in the profit and loss–sharing ratio.

Capital stock in the new corporation is then distributed in proportion to the partners' capital accounts. The separate business entity of the partnership should now close its accounting records and the corporation, as a new business entity, should open its own new accounting records to record the issuance of its capital stock to the prior partners of the partnership.

The ABC Partnership's trial balance on May 1, 20X5, as shown previously, is used to illustrate incorporation of a partnership. Instead of liquidating the partnership as shown throughout the chapter, assume the partners agree to incorporate it.

The new corporation is to be called the Peerless Products Corporation. At the time of conversion from a partnership to a corporation, all assets and liabilities should be appraised and valued at their fair values. Any gain or loss must be distributed to the partners in their profit and loss–sharing ratios. Assume that the noncash assets have an $80,000 fair value. The $10,000 loss to fair value is allocated to the partners' capital accounts before the incorporation, as follows:

(4)			
	Alt, Capital	4,000	
	Blue, Capital	4,000	
	Cha, Capital	2,000	
	Noncash Assets		10,000

Recognize loss on reduction of assets to fair values

Of course, in practice, specific asset accounts are used instead of the general classification of noncash assets. Gains on asset revaluations also may occur when a successful partnership elects to incorporate.

The partnership's net assets have a fair value of $48,000 ($90,000 of assets less $42,000 of liabilities). The corporation issues 4,600 shares of $1 par common stock in exchange for the assets and liabilities of the ABC Partnership. The entry made by the Peerless Products Corporation to acquire the partnership's assets and liabilities in exchange for the issuance of the 4,600 shares of stock is

(5)			
	Cash	10,000	
	Noncash Assets	80,000	
	Liabilities		42,000
	Common Stock		4,600
	Paid-in Capital in Excess of Par		43,400

Issuance of stock for partnership's assets and liabilities.

The partners make the following entry on the partnership's books:

(6)			
	Investment in Peerless Products	48,000	
	Liabilities	42,000	
	Cash		10,000
	Noncash Assets		80,000

Receipt of stock in Peerless Products in exchange for partnership's net assets.

Recall that the noncash assets were reduced to their fair values in entry (4). To distribute the stock to the partners and close the partnership's books, the final entry is as follows:

(7)			
	Alt, Capital	30,000	
	Blue, Capital	6,000	
	Cha, Capital	12,000	
	Investment in Peerless		48,000

Distribution of Peerless Products stock to partners.

Summary of Key Concepts

The process of terminating and liquidating a partnership is often a traumatic time for partners. The Uniform Partnership Act of 1997 provides guidance for the liquidation process and specifies the legal rights of the partners and of partnership creditors.

Dissociation of a partner is his or her withdrawal, either voluntarily or involuntarily, from the partnership. Dissolution is the dissolving of a partnership. Not all dissociations and dissolutions require termination, which is the cessation of normal business functions, or liquidation, with the disposal of assets, payment of liabilities, and distribution of remaining cash to the partners. UPA 1997 defines a partnership as a legal entity apart from the individual partners. Therefore, unless required by judicial determination, termination and liquidation often can be avoided by carefully preparing the partnership agreement to allow continuation of the business when a partner retires or leaves the partnership. The most common reasons for involuntary liquidation are court decrees or the bankruptcy of the partnership.

Liquidation can involve a single lump-sum payment to partners. Most liquidations, however, take several months and involve installment payments to partners during the liquidation process.

Liquidations are facilitated by the preparation of the statement of partnership realization and liquidation, a worksheet summarizing the liquidation process and serving as a basis for the journal entries to record the events. Installment payments to partners are determined on a worst-case basis using a schedule of safe payments to partners, which assumes that all noncash assets will be written off and that partners with debit balances in their capital accounts will not be able to remedy the deficiencies.

A cash distribution plan provides information to partners about the installment payments they will receive as cash becomes available to the partnership. The plan is prepared at the beginning of the liquidation process. Actual cash distributions during the liquidation process are determined with the statement of partnership realization and liquidation. The concept of loss absorption power (LAP) is central to the development of the cash distribution plan. LAP is the amount of partnership loss required to eliminate a given partner's capital credit balance. The LAP is determined by dividing a partner's net capital credit balance by his or her loss-sharing percentage.

Key Terms	cash distribution plan, *573* dissociation (of a partner), *562* dissolution (of a partnership), *562* installment liquidation, *569*	loss absorption power (LAP), *574* lump-sum liquidation, *564* schedule of safe payments to partners, *572*	statement of partnership realization and liquidation, *563*

Appendix 11A   Partners' Personal Financial Statements

At the beginning of the liquidation process, partners are usually asked for personal financial statements to determine each partner's personal solvency. Guidelines for preparing personal financial statements are found in **Statement of Position 82-1 (ASC 274),** "Personal Financial Statements" (SOP 82-1, ASC 274).[2]

Personal financial statements consist of the following:

1. Statement of financial condition, or personal balance sheet, which presents the person's assets and liabilities at a point in time.
2. Statement of changes in net worth, or personal income statement, which presents the primary sources of changes in the person's net worth.

In addition to presenting a person's assets and liabilities, the statement of financial condition should include an estimate of the income taxes incurred as if all the assets were converted and the liabilities extinguished. The person's net worth would then be computed as assets less liabilities less estimated taxes (see Figure 11–8). In general, the accrual basis of accounting should be used to determine the person's assets and liabilities, and comparative statements are usually provided. However, unlike a balance sheet of a business that is based on historical cost, the assets in the personal statement of financial condition are stated at their estimated current values. The liabilities are stated at the lower of the discounted value of future cash payments or the current cash settlement amount. Included immediately below the liabilities are the estimated taxes that would be paid if all the assets were converted to cash and all the liabilities were paid.

Assets and liabilities are presented in their order of liquidity and maturity, not as current and noncurrent. **SOP 82-1 (ASC 274)** provides guidelines for determining the current value of a person's assets and liabilities. The primary valuation methods are discounted value of future cash flows, current market prices of marketable securities or other investments, and appraisals of properties. An investment in a separate business entity (e.g., a partnership) should be reported as a one-line, combined amount valued at the net investment's market value. The liabilities are stated at their discounted cash flow value or current liquidation value. The accountant uses applicable tax laws, carryover provisions, and other regulations to compute the estimated tax liability from the assumed conversion of assets and the assumed extinguishment of liabilities.

The statement of changes in net worth presents the major sources of income. It recognizes both realized and unrealized income. A commercial business's income statement may not recognize holding gains on some marketable securities, but such gains are recognized on an individual's statement of changes in net worth.

[2] *Accounting Standards Division of AICPA (Statement of Position 82-1),* "Accounting and Financial Reporting for Personal Financial Statements" (New York: AICPA, 1982).

FIGURE 11–8
Personal Statement of
Financial Condition

C. ALT
Statement of Financial Condition
May 1, 20X5 and 20X4

	Year	
	20X5	**20X4**
Assets		
Cash	$ 4,000	$ 2,500
Receivables	3,500	4,000
Investments:		
Marketable securities	5,000	4,000
ABC Partnership	34,000	26,000
Cash surrender value of life insurance	3,100	3,000
Residence	84,000	76,000
Personal effects	16,400	12,500
Total assets	$150,000	$128,000
Liabilities and Net Worth		
Charge accounts	$ 2,000	$ 3,000
Income taxes—current-year balance	1,200	800
10 percent note payable	6,000	10,000
Mortgage payable	60,000	62,000
Estimated income taxes on the difference between the estimated current values of assets and liabilities and their tax bases	16,800	12,200
Net worth	64,000	40,000
Total liabilities and net worth	$150,000	$128,000

ILLUSTRATION OF PERSONAL FINANCIAL STATEMENTS

The following illustration presents Alt's personal financial condition as of May 1, 20X5, the day the partners decide to liquidate the ABC Partnership. Alt's net worth on this date is as follows:

Personal assets	$150,000
Personal liabilities	(86,000)
Net worth	$ 64,000

Statement of Financial Condition

Alt's statement of financial condition on May 1, 20X5, is presented in Figure 11–8 along with the prior year's statement. The 20X5 statement illustrates the following:

1. Receivables due to Alt from other people have a present value of $3,500.

2. Alt has two investments, one of which is his interest in the ABC Partnership, valued at estimated current market value, which in this case also equals its book value of $34,000. The marketable security investments are shown at market value.

3. The cash surrender value of life insurance is presented net of any loans payable on the policies.

4. Alt's residence and personal effects are presented at their appraised values.

5. Liabilities are presented at their estimated current liquidation value or the discounted value of the future cash flows.

6. The estimated income taxes on the difference between the estimated current values of assets and liabilities and their tax bases represent the amount of income tax Alt would be liable for if all assets were converted to cash and all liabilities were paid.

7. Net worth is the difference between the estimated current value of Alt's assets and liabilities, including estimated tax.

FIGURE 11–9
Personal Statement of
Changes in Net Worth

C. ALT
Statement of Changes in Net Worth
For the Years Ended May 1, 20X5 and 20X4

	Year Ended May 1	
	20X5	20X4
Realized increases in net worth:		
Salary	$ 36,900	$ 34,900
Dividends and interest income	800	400
Distribution from ABC Partnership	3,000	1,000
Cash surrender value of life insurance	100	100
Gains on sales of marketable securities	1,400	1,200
	$ 42,200	$ 37,600
Realized decreases in net worth:		
Income taxes	$ 8,200	$ 7,800
Interest expense	1,400	700
Real estate taxes	2,400	2,200
Insurance payments (including $100 for increase in cash surrender value of life insurance)	400	300
Personal expenditures	18,800	18,600
	$(31,200)	$(29,600)
Net realized increase in net worth	$ 11,000	$ 8,000
Unrealized increases in net worth:		
Marketable securities	$ 1,600	$ 400
ABC Partnership	8,000	5,000
Residence	8,000	4,000
	$ 17,600	$ 9,400
Unrealized decreases in net worth:		
Increase in estimated income taxes on the difference between the estimated current values of assets and liabilities and their tax bases	(4,600)	(4,400)
Net unrealized increase in net worth	$ 13,000	$ 5,000
Net increase in net worth:		
Realized and unrealized	$ 24,000	$ 13,000
Net worth at beginning of period	40,000	27,000
Net worth at end of period	$ 64,000	$ 40,000

Statement of Changes in Net Worth

Alt's statement of changes in net worth, shown in Figure 11–9, illustrates the following:

1. The statement separates the realized and unrealized changes in net worth. Realized changes are cash flows to or from Alt that have already taken place. Unrealized changes are equivalent to holding gains or losses. They have not yet been converted to cash. For example, Alt received $3,000 from the ABC Partnership during the year ended May 1, 20X5. In addition, Alt's partnership interest increased by $8,000 during the year.

2. Alt had $42,200 of realized increases in net worth during the year ended May 1, 20X5. The primary source was a salary of $36,900 from full-time employment outside the ABC Partnership.

3. The major realized decrease in net worth during the year ended May 1, 20X5, was for personal expenditures of $18,800.

4. Unrealized increases of $17,600 during the year were primarily from an increase in the value of Alt's personal residence ($8,000) and an increase in the investment value of his partnership interest in the ABC Partnership ($8,000). Unrealized holding gains of $1,600 are available in Alt's investments in marketable securities.

5. The change in the estimated tax liability is an unrealized decrease because this amount is due only if Alt converts these assets to cash.

6. The net unrealized changes in net worth are added to the net realized changes in net worth to obtain the total change in Alt's net worth for each year. Alt's net worth increased by $13,000 during the year ended May 1, 20X4, and by $24,000 during the year ended May 1, 20X5.

Footnote Disclosures

Sufficient footnote disclosures should accompany the two personal financial statements. The footnotes should describe the following:

1. The methods used to value the major assets.

2. The names and the nature of businesses in which the person has major investments.

3. The methods and assumptions used to compute the estimated tax bases and a statement that the tax provision in an actual liquidation will probably differ from the estimate because the actual tax burden will then be based on actual realizations determined by market values at the point of liquidation.

4. Maturities, interest rates, and other details of any receivables and debt.

5. Any other information needed to present fully the person's net worth.

Questions

LO1	Q11-1	What are the major causes of a dissolution? What are the accounting implications of a dissolution?
LO1	Q11-2	During a partnership liquidation, do a partnership's liabilities to individual partners have a lower priority than the partnership's obligations to other, third-party creditors? Explain.
LO1	Q11-3	X, Y, and Z are partners. The partnership is liquidating, and Partner Z is personally insolvent. What implications may this have for Partners X and Y?
LO1	Q11-4	May an individual partner simply decide to leave a partnership? Does the partnership have any legal recourse against that partner? Explain.
LO1	Q11-5	Contrast a lump-sum liquidation with an installment liquidation.
LO1	Q11-6	How is a deficit in a partner's capital account eliminated if he or she is personally insolvent?
LO2–LO3	Q11-7	The DEF Partnership has total assets of $55,000. Partner D has a capital credit of $6,000, Partner E has a capital deficit of $20,000, and Partner F has a capital credit of $8,000. Is the DEF Partnership solvent or insolvent?
LO1	Q11-8	Assume that, because of a new law recently passed, the types of significant transactions in which a partnership engages are no longer lawful. Two of the five partners wish to have a winding up and termination of the partnership. Can these two partners require the partnership to terminate? Explain.
LO3	Q11-9	How are a partner's personal payments to partnership creditors accounted for on the partnership's books?
LO3	Q11-10	What is the purpose of the schedule of safe payments to partners?
LO2	Q11-11	In what ratio are losses during liquidation assigned to the partners' capital accounts? Is this ratio used in all instances?
LO3	Q11-12	The installment liquidation process uses a worst-case assumption in computing the payments to partners. What does this *worst-case assumption* mean?
LO3	Q11-13	Define *loss absorption power* and explain its importance in the determination of cash distributions to partners.
LO3	Q11-14	Partner A has a capital credit of $25,000. Partner B's capital credit is also $25,000. Partners A and B share profits and losses in a 60:40 ratio. Which partner will receive the first payment of cash in an installment liquidation?
LO3	Q11-15*	Explain the process of incorporating a partnership.

*Indicates that the item relates to "Additional Considerations."

Cases

LO1 **C11-1** **Cash Distributions to Partners**

The partnership of A. Bull and T. Bear is in the process of termination. The partners have disagreed on virtually every decision and have decided to liquidate the present business, with each partner taking his own clients from the partnership. Bull wants cash distributed as it becomes available; Bear wants no cash distributed until all assets are sold and all liabilities are settled. You are called in to aid in the termination and liquidation process.

Analysis

Required

How would you respond to each of the partners' requests?

LO2 **C11-2** **Cash Distributions to Partners**

Adam and Bard agreed to liquidate their partnership. You have been asked to assist them in this process, and you prepare the following balance sheet for the date of the beginning of the liquidation. The loss-sharing percentages are in parentheses next to the capital account balances.

Analysis

Cash	$ 40,000
Loan Receivable from Adam	10,000
Other Assets	200,000
Total	$250,000
Accounts Payable	$ 30,000
Loan Payable to Bard	100,000
Adam, Capital (50%)	80,000
Bard, Capital (50%)	40,000
Total	$250,000

Bard is demanding that the loan from him be paid before any cash is distributed to Adam. Adam believes the available cash should be paid to him until his capital account is reduced to $40,000, the same as Bard's. Adam will then pay the loan receivable to the partnership with the cash received. You have been asked to reconcile the argument.

Required

How would you advise in this case?

LO3 **C11-3*** **Incorporation of a Partnership**

After successfully operating a partnership for several years, the partners have proposed to incorporate the business and admit another investor. The original partners will purchase at par an amount of preferred stock equal to the book values of their capital interests in the partnership and common stock for the amount of the market value, including unrecognized goodwill, of the business that exceeds book value. The new investor will make an investment, at a 5 percent premium over par value, in both preferred and common stock equal to one-third of the total number of shares purchased by the original partners. The corporation will acquire all the partnership's assets, assume the liabilities, and employ the original partners and the new investor.

Required

a. Discuss the differences in accounts used and valuations expected in comparing the balance sheets of the proposed corporation and the partnership.

b. Discuss the differences that would be expected in a comparison of the income statements of the proposed corporation and the partnership.

LO2 **C11-4** **Sharing Losses during Liquidation**

Hiller, Luna, and Welsh are attempting to form a partnership to operate a travel agency. They have agreed to share profits in a ratio of 4:3:2 but cannot agree on the terms of the partnership agreement relating to possible liquidation. Hiller believes that it is best not to get into any arguments about potential liquidation at this time because the partnership will be a success and it is not necessary to think negatively at this point in time. Luna believes that in the event of liquidation, any losses should be shared equally because each partner would have worked equally for the partnership's success, or lack thereof. Welsh believes that any losses during liquidation should be distributed in the ratio of capital balances at the beginning of any liquidation because then the losses will be distributed based on a capital ability to bear the losses.

Research

You have been asked to help resolve the differences and to prepare a memo to the three individuals including the following items.

Required

a. Specify the procedures for allocating losses among partners stated in the Uniform Partnership Act of 1997 to be used if no partnership agreement terms are agreed upon regarding liquidation. (You may wish to access a copy of the Uniform Partnership Act of 1997 for this requirement.)

b. Critically assess each partner's viewpoint, discussing the pros and cons of each.

c. Specify another option for allocating potential liquidation losses not included in the positions currently taken by the three individuals. Critically assess the pros and cons of your alternative.

C11-5 **Analysis of a Court Decision on a Partnership Liquidation**

The *Mattfield v. Kramer Brothers* court case presents a number of the interesting legal issues that often arise from the dissolution of a partnership. The case was heard in the Supreme Court of the State of Montana in 2005 and decided on May 31, 2005, as Case 03-796. The decision of the court includes a summary of the disputes and lower court decisions.

The Montana State Supreme Court's decision is available at the FindLaw site. The easiest way to obtain the script of the decision is to search the Internet for the term "Mattfield v. Kramer Brothers" and then follow the link to the Court's 2005 decision. The legal briefs from each side that were presented to the Supreme Court may be obtained at the State Law Library of Montana site by searching the Internet for "State of Montana Law Library" or use the URL: http://courts.mt.gov/library, click on Cases, and then search using case number 03-796, or a text term such as Mattfield. The briefs will then be made available.

Required

Obtain a copy of the Montana Supreme Court decision in the *Mattfield v. Kramer Brothers* case. Then answer each of the following questions regarding the case.

a. Prepare a short summary of the history of the Kramer Brothers Co-Partnership from formation through the appeal to the Montana Supreme Court.

b. What type of partnership agreement existed? Recommend several provisions that you feel should have been included in a formal, written partnership agreement of the partnership.

c. At the time the case was appealed to the Supreme Court, did Bill Kramer still have an economic interest in the partnership? Explain.

d. What legal recourse did the other partners have at the time Don Kramer dissociated from the partnership in 1994?

e. In February 1997, why did Don Kramer's attorney, Floyd Brower, request copies of Ray Kramer's and Doug Kramer's personal tax returns?

f. Select and discuss two key points regarding partnership liquidations that are illustrated by this case and that you feel are important.

C11-6 **Reviewing the Liquidation Process of a Limited Partnership**

Some limited partnerships have SEC filing requirements because of selling partnership units or debt securities to the public. One such partnership was Fairfield Inn By Marriott Limited Partnership, which had a series of filings from January 1998 to May 2006. Using the SEC's EDGAR (www.sec.gov), obtain the annual report for this limited partnership for the year ended December 31, 2003, which was filed on May 14, 2004.

Required

Answer each of the following questions from the information you obtain by analyzing the 10-K of Fairfield Inn By Marriott Limited Partnership.

a. Describe the formation of the partnership, including the date of formation and the purpose for the limited partnership.

b. Who was the initial general partner? What was the general partner's initial percentage interest in the partnership? And who was general partner as of December 31, 2003?

c. What was the general partner's profit percentage? What economic reasons might the general partner have had for investing in this partnership?

   d. What were the major elements of the Restructuring Plan approved in 2001 by the limited partners?

   e. What were the major elements of the Plan of Liquidation that was initiated in 2003?

   f. The partnership adopted the liquidation basis of accounting beginning on September 30, 2003. Briefly describe the liquidation basis of accounting the partnership used.

   g. Compare the partnership's financial statements before and then after the September 30, 2003, adoption of the liquidation basis of accounting.

   h. The partnership filed a Form 15-12G on May 1, 2006. Obtain this filing. What is the purpose of this form that is required by the SEC?

Exercises

LO2

E11-1   Multiple-Choice Questions on Partnership Liquidations

Select the correct answer for each of the following questions.

Note: The following information is for questions 1, 2, and 3.

   The balance sheet for the partnership of Joan, Charles, and Thomas, whose shares of profits and losses are 40, 50, and 10 percent, is as follows:

Cash	$ 50,000	Accounts Payable	$150,000
Inventory	360,000	Joan, Capital	160,000
		Charles, Capital	45,000
		Thomas, Capital	55,000
Total Assets	$410,000	Total Liabilities and Equities	$410,000

Assume Charles is insolvent.

1. If the inventory is sold for $300,000, how much should Joan receive upon liquidation of the partnership?

   a. $48,000.

   b. $100,000.

   c. $136,000.

   d. $160,000.

2. If the inventory is sold for $180,000, how much should Thomas receive upon liquidation of the partnership?

   a. $28,000.

   b. $32,500.

   c. $37,000.

   d. $55,000.

3. The partnership will be liquidated in installments. As cash becomes available, it will be distributed to the partners. If inventory costing $200,000 is sold for $140,000, how much cash should be distributed to each partner at this time?

	Joan	Charles	Thomas
a.	$56,000	$70,000	$14,000
b.	$16,000	$20,000	$ 4,000
c.	$32,000	$ –0–	$ 8,000
d.	$20,000	$ –0–	$20,000

4. In accounting for partnership liquidation, cash payments to partners after all creditors' claims have been satisfied, but before the final cash distribution, should be according to

   a. The partners' relative profit and loss–sharing ratios.

   b. The final balances in partner capital accounts.

   c. The partners' relative share of the gain or loss on liquidations.

   d. Safe payments computations.

5. After all noncash assets have been converted into cash in the liquidation of the Adam and Kay Partnership, the ledger contains the following account balances:

	Debit	Credit
Cash	$47,000	
Accounts Payable		$32,000
Loan Payable to Adam		15,000
Adam, Capital	7,000	
Kay, Capital		7,000

Available cash should be distributed with $32,000 going to accounts payable and then

a. $15,000 to the loan payable to Adam.

b. $7,500 each to Adam and Kay.

c. $8,000 to Adam and $7,000 to Kay.

d. $7,000 to Adam and $8,000 to Kay.

Note: The following information is for questions 6 and 7.

F, A, S, and B are partners sharing profits and losses equally. The partnership is insolvent and is to be liquidated. The status of the partnership and each partner is as follows:

	Partnership Capital Balance	Personal Assets (exclusive of partnership interest)	Personal Liabilities (exclusive of partnership interest)
F	$(15,000)	$100,000	$40,000
A	(10,000)	30,000	60,000
S	20,000[a]	80,000	5,000
B	30,000[a]	1,000	28,000
Total	$ 25,000[a]		

[a] Deficit

6. The partnership creditors

a. Must first seek recovery against S because she is personally solvent and has a negative capital balance.

b. Will *not* be paid in full regardless of how they proceed legally because the partnership assets are less than the partnership liabilities.

c. Will have to share A's interest in the partnership on a pro rata basis with A's personal creditors.

d. Have first claim to the partnership assets before any partner's personal creditors have rights to the partnership assets.

7. The partnership creditors should seek recovery of their claims

a. From the partnership, including additional contributions from F and S.

b. From the personal assets of either F or A.

c. From the personal assets of either S or B.

d. From the personal assets of any of the partners for all or some of their claims.

LO3

E11-2 Multiple-Choice Questions on Partnership Liquidation [AICPA Adapted]

Select the correct answer for each of the following questions.

1. On January 1, 20X7, the partners of Casey, Dithers, and Edwards, who share profits and losses in the ratio of 5:3:2, decided to liquidate their partnership. On this date the partnership condensed balance sheet was as follows:

Assets		Liabilities and Capital	
Cash	$ 50,000	Liabilities	$ 60,000
Other Assets	250,000	Casey, Capital	80,000
		Dithers, Capital	90,000
		Edwards, Capital	70,000
Total	$300,000	Total	$300,000

On January 15, 20X7, the first cash sale of other assets with a carrying amount of $150,000 realized $120,000. Safe installment payments to the partners were made on the same date. How much cash should be distributed to each partner?

	Casey	Dithers	Edwards
a.	$15,000	$51,000	$44,000
b.	$40,000	$45,000	$35,000
c.	$55,000	$33,000	$22,000
d.	$60,000	$36,000	$24,000

2. In a partnership liquidation, the final cash distribution to the partners should be made in accordance with the

    a. Partners' profit and loss–sharing ratio.

    b. Balances of the partners' capital accounts.

    c. Ratio of the capital contributions by the partners.

    d. Ratio of capital contributions less withdrawals by the partners.

Note: The following information is for questions 3 through 5.

The balance sheet for the Art, Blythe, and Cooper Partnership is as follows. Figures shown parenthetically reflect agreed profit and loss–sharing percentages.

Assets		Liabilities and Capital	
Cash	$ 20,000	Liabilities	$ 50,000
Other Assets	180,000	Art, Capital (40%)	37,000
		Blythe, Capital (40%)	65,000
		Cooper, Capital (20%)	48,000
Total	$200,000	Total	$200,000

3. If the firm, as shown on the balance sheet, is dissolved and liquidated by selling assets in installments and if the first sale of noncash assets having a book value of $90,000 realizes $50,000 and all cash available after settlement with creditors is distributed, the respective partners would receive (to the nearest dollar)

	Art	Blythe	Cooper
a.	$8,000	$ 8,000	$ 4,000
b.	$6,667	$ 6,667	$ 6,666
c.	$ –0–	$13,333	$ 6,667
d.	$ –0–	$ 3,000	$17,000

4. If the facts are as in question 3 except that $3,000 cash is to be withheld, the respective partners would then receive (to the nearest dollar)

	Art	Blythe	Cooper
a.	$6,800	$ 6,800	$ 3,400
b.	$5,667	$ 5,667	$ 5,666
c.	$ –0–	$11,333	$ 5,667
d.	$ –0–	$ 1,000	$16,000

5. If each partner properly received some cash in the distribution after the second sale, if the cash to be distributed amounts to $12,000 from the third sale, and if unsold assets with an $8,000 book value remain, ignoring questions 3 and 4, the respective partners would receive

	Art	Blythe	Cooper
a.	$ 4,800	$ 4,800	$ 2,400
b.	$ 4,000	$ 4,000	$ 4,000
c.	37/150 of $12,000	65/150 of $12,000	48/150 of $12,000
d.	$ –0–	$ 8,000	$ 4,000

6. The following condensed balance sheet is presented for the partnership of Arnie, Bart, and Kurt, who share profits and losses in the ratio of 4:3:3, respectively:

Assets		Liabilities and Capital	
Cash	$100,000	Liabilities	$150,000
Other Assets	300,000	Arnie, Capital	40,000
		Bart, Capital	180,000
		Kurt, Capital	30,000
Total	$400,000	Total	$400,000

The partners agreed to dissolve the partnership after selling the other assets for $200,000. On dissolution of the partnership, Arnie should receive

a. $0.
b. $40,000.
c. $60,000.
d. $70,000.

LO2

E11-3 Computing Alternative Cash Distributions to Partners

Bracken, Louden, and Menser, who share profits and losses in a ratio of 4:3:3, are partners in a home decorating business that has not been able to generate the type of income hoped for by the partners. They have decided to liquidate the business and have sold all the assets except for their decorating equipment. All partnership liabilities have been settled and all the partners are personally insolvent. The decorating equipment has a book value of $40,000, and the partners have capital account balances as follows:

Bracken, capital	$25,000
Louden, capital	5,000
Menser, capital	10,000

Required

Determine the amount of cash each partner will receive as a liquidating distribution if the decorating equipment is sold for the amount stated in each of the following independent cases:

a. $30,000.
b. $21,000.
c. $7,000.

LO2

Advanced StudyGuide .com

E11-4 Lump-Sum Liquidation

Matthews, Mitchell, and Michaels are partners in the BG Land Development Company and share losses in a 5:3:2 ratio. The balance sheet on June 30, 20X1, when they decide to liquidate the business, is as follows:

Assets		Liabilities and Capital	
Cash	$ 20,000	Accounts Payable	$ 30,000
Noncash Assets	150,000	Mitchell, Loan	10,000
		Matthews, Capital	80,000
		Mitchell, Capital	36,000
		Michaels, Capital	14,000
Total Assets	$170,000	Total Liabilities and Equities	$170,000

The noncash assets are sold for $110,000.

Required

a. Prepare a statement of partnership realization and liquidation.
b. Prepare the required journal entries to account for the liquidation of the BG Land Development Company.

LO3

E11-5 **Schedule of Safe Payments**

After working for the In the Kitchen remodeling business for several years, Terry and Phyllis decided to go into business for themselves and formed the Kitchens Just for You partnership. Three years ago, they admitted Connie as a partner and recognized goodwill at that time because of her good client list for planned kitchen makeovers. However, they were not able to gain a sufficient market for new customers and on September 1, 20X9, they agreed to dissolve and liquidate the business. They decided on an installment liquidation in order to complete the projects already initiated. The balance sheet, with profit and loss–sharing percentages at the beginning of liquidation, is as follows:

KITCHENS JUST FOR YOU
Balance Sheet
September 1, 20X9

Assets		Liabilities and Equities	
Cash	$ 12,000	Accounts Payable	$ 43,000
Receivables	63,000	Connie, Loan	15,000
Terry, Loan	9,000	Terry, Capital (30%)	12,000
Inventory	48,000	Phyllis, Capital (50%)	36,000
Goodwill	28,000	Connie, Capital (20%)	54,000
Total Assets	$160,000	Total Liabilities and Equities	$160,000

Connie's loan was for working capital; the loan to Terry was for his unexpected personal medical bills.

During September 20X9, the first month of liquidation, the partnership collected $41,000 in receivables and decided to write off $12,000 of the remaining receivables. Sales of one-half of the book value of the inventory realized a loss of $4,000. The partners estimate that the costs of liquidating the business such as newspaper ads, signs, etc., are expected to be $6,000 for the remainder of the liquidation process.

Required
Prepare a schedule of safe payments to partners as of September 30, 20X9, to show how the available cash should be distributed to the partners.

LO3

E11-6 **Schedule of Safe Payments to Partners**

Partners Maness and Joiner have decided to liquidate their business. The ledger shows the following account balances:

Cash	$ 25,000	Accounts Payable	$15,000
Inventory	120,000	Maness, Capital	65,000
		Joiner, Capital	65,000

Advanced
StudyGuide
.com

Maness and Joiner share profits and losses in an 8:2 ratio. During the first month of liquidation, half the inventory is sold for $40,000, and $10,000 of the accounts payable is paid. During the second month, the rest of the inventory is sold for $30,000, and the remaining accounts payable are paid. Cash is distributed at the end of each month, and the liquidation is completed at the end of the second month.

Required
Prepare a statement of partnership realization and liquidation with a schedule of safe payments for the two-month liquidation period.

LO2

E11-7 **Alternative Profit and Loss–Sharing Ratios in a Partnership Liquidation**

Nelson, Osman, Peters, and Quincy have decided to terminate their partnership because of recurrent arguments among the partners. The partnership's balance sheet at the time they decide to wind up is as follows:

Cash	$ 17,000	Accounts Payable	$ 12,000
Noncash Assets	190,000	Nelson, Capital	15,000
		Osman, Capital	75,000
		Peters, Capital	75,000
		Quincy, Capital	30,000
Total Assets	$207,000	Total Liabilities and Equities	$207,000

During the winding up of the partnership, the other assets are sold for $100,000 and the accounts payable are paid. Osman and Peters are personally solvent, but Nelson and Quincy are personally insolvent.

Required

Determine the amount of cash each partner will receive from the final distributions of the partnership for each of the following independent cases of profit and loss ratios for Nelson, Osman, Peters, and Quincy.

a. The partners share profits and losses in the ratio of 3:3:2:2.

b. The partners share profits and losses in the ratio of 3:1:3:3.

c. The partners share profits and losses in the ratio of 3:1:2:4.

LO2

E11-8   Cash Distribution Plan

Adams, Peters, and Blake share profits and losses for their APB Partnership in a ratio of 2:3:5. When they decide to liquidate, the balance sheet is as follows:

Assets		Liabilities and Equities	
Cash	$ 40,000	Liabilities	$ 50,000
Adams, Loan	10,000	Adams, Capital	55,000
Other Assets	200,000	Peters, Capital	75,000
		Blake, Capital	70,000
Total Assets	$250,000	Total Liabilities and Equities	$250,000

Liquidation expenses are expected to be negligible. No interest accrues on loans with partners after termination of the business.

Required

Prepare a cash distribution plan for the APB Partnership.

LO3

E11-9   Confirmation of Cash Distribution Plan

Refer to the data in Exercise E11-8. During the liquidation process for the APB Partnership, the following events occurred:

1. During the first month of liquidation, noncash assets with a book value of $85,000 were sold for $65,000, and $21,000 of the liabilities were paid.

2. During the second month, the remaining noncash assets were sold for $79,000. The loan receivable from Adams was collected, and the rest of the creditors were paid.

3. Cash is distributed to partners at the end of each month.

Required

Prepare a statement of partnership realization and liquidation with a schedule of safe payments to partners for the liquidation period.

LO3

E11-10*   Incorporation of a Partnership

When Alice and Betty decided to incorporate their partnership, the trial balance was as follows:

	Debit	Credit
Cash	$ 8,000	
Accounts Receivable (net)	22,400	
Inventory	36,000	
Equipment (net)	47,200	
Accounts Payable		$ 17,200
Alice, Capital (60%)		62,400
Betty, Capital (40%)		34,000
Total	$113,600	$113,600

The partnership's books will be closed, and new books will be used for A & B Corporation. The following additional information is available:

1. The estimated fair values of the assets follow:

Accounts Receivable	$21,600
Inventory	32,800
Equipment	40,000

2. All assets and liabilities are transferred to the corporation.
3. The common stock is $10 par. Alice and Betty receive a total of 7,100 shares.
4. The partners' profit and loss–sharing ratio is shown in the trial balance.

Required

a. Prepare the entries on the partnership's books to record (1) the revaluation of assets, (2) the transfer of the assets to the A & B Corporation and the receipt of the common stock, and (3) the closing of the books.

b. Prepare the entries on A & B Corporation's books to record the assets and the issuance of the common stock.

LO3

E11-11A   Multiple-Choice on Personal Financial Statements [AICPA Adapted]
Select the correct answer for each of the following questions.

1. On December 31, 20X7, Judy is a fully vested participant in a company-sponsored pension plan. According to the plan's administrator, Judy has at that date the nonforfeitable right to receive a lump sum of $100,000 on December 28, 20X8. The discounted amount of $100,000 is $90,000 at December 31, 20X7. The right is not contingent on Judy's life expectancy and requires no future performance on Judy's part. In Judy's December 31, 20X7, personal statement of financial condition, the vested interest in the pension plan should be reported at

   a. $0.
   b. $90,000.
   c. $95,000.
   d. $100,000.

2. On December 31, 20X7, Mr. and Mrs. McManus owned a parcel of land held as an investment. The land was purchased for $95,000 in 20X0 and was encumbered by a mortgage with a principal balance of $60,000 at December 31, 20X7. On this date the fair value of the land was $150,000. In the McManuses' December 31, 20X7, personal statement of financial condition, at what amount should the land investment and mortgage payable be reported?

	Land Investment	Mortgage Payable
a.	$150,000	$60,000
b.	$ 95,000	$60,000
c.	$ 90,000	$ –0–
d.	$ 35,000	$ –0–

3. Rich Drennen's personal statement of financial condition at December 31, 20X6, shows net worth of $400,000 before consideration of employee stock options owned on that date. Information relating to the stock options is as follows:

   • Options are to purchase 10,000 shares of Oglesby Corporation stock.
   • Options' exercise price is $10 a share.
   • Options expire on June 30, 20X7.
   • Market price of the stock is $25 a share on December 31, 20X6.
   • Assume that exercise of the options in 20X7 would result in ordinary income taxable at 35 percent.

   After giving effect to the stock options, Drennen's net worth at December 31, 20X6, would be

   a. $497,500.
   b. $550,000.
   c. $562,500.
   d. $650,000.

"A" indicates that the item relates to "Appendix 11A."

4. Nancy Emerson owns 50 percent of the common stock of Marks Corporation. She paid $25,000 for this stock in 20X3. At December 31, 20X8, it was ascertained that her 50 percent stock ownership in Marks had a current value of $185,000. Marks's cumulative net income and cash dividends declared for the five years ended December 31, 20X8, were $300,000 and $30,000 respectively. In Nancy's personal statement of financial condition at December 31, 20X8, what amount should be reported as her net investment in Marks?

   a. $25,000.

   b. $160,000.

   c. $175,000.

   d. $185,000.

5. In a personal statement of financial condition, which of the following should be reported at estimated current values?

	Investments in Closely Held Business	Investments in Leaseholds
a.	Yes	Yes
b.	Yes	No
c.	No	No
d.	No	Yes

6. Personal financial statements should include which of the following statements?

	Financial Condition	Changes in Net Worth	Cash Flows
a.	No	Yes	Yes
b.	Yes	No	No
c.	Yes	Yes	No
d.	Yes	Yes	Yes

7. A business interest that constitutes a large part of an individual's total assets should be presented in a personal statement of financial condition as

   a. A single amount equal to the proprietorship equity.

   b. A single amount equal to the estimated current value of the business interest.

   c. A separate list of the individual assets and liabilities, at cost.

   d. Separate line items of both total assets and total liabilities, at cost.

8. Personal financial statements should report assets and liabilities at

   a. Historical cost.

   b. Historical cost and, as additional information, at estimated current values at the date of the financial statements.

   c. Estimated current values at the date of the financial statements.

   d. Estimated current values at the date of the financial statements and, as additional information, at historical cost.

9. The following information pertains to marketable equity securities owned by Kent:

	Fair Value at December 31		
Stock	20X3	20X2	Cost in 20X0
City Manufacturing Inc.	$95,500	$93,000	$89,900
Tri Corporation	3,400	5,600	3,600
Zee Inc.		10,300	15,000

The Zee stock was sold in January 20X3 for $10,200. In Kent's personal statement of financial condition at December 31, 20X3, what amount should be reported for marketable equity securities?

a. $93,300.

b. $93,500.

c. $94,100.

d. $98,900.

10. Personal financial statements should report an investment in life insurance at the

a. Face amount of the policy less the amount of premiums paid.

b. Cash value of the policy less the amount of any loans against it.

c. Cash value of the policy less the amount of premiums paid.

d. Face amount of the policy less the amount of any loans against it.

11. Mrs. Taft owns a $150,000 insurance policy on her husband's life. The cash value of the policy is $125,000, and there is a $50,000 loan against the policy. In the Tafts' personal statement of financial condition at December 31, 20X3, what amount should be shown as an investment in life insurance?

a. $150,000.

b. $125,000.

c. $100,000.

d. $75,000.

LO3 **E11-12A** **Personal Financial Statements**

Leonard and Michelle have asked you to prepare their statement of changes in net worth for the year ended August 31, 20X3. They have prepared the following comparative statement of financial condition based on estimated current values as required by **SOP 82-1 (ASC 274):**

LEONARD AND MICHELLE
Statement of Financial Condition
August 31, 20X3 and 20X2

		20X3		20X2
Assets				
Cash		$ 3,600		$ 6,700
Marketable securities		4,900		16,300
Residence		94,800		87,500
Personal effects		10,000		10,000
Cash surrender value of life insurance		3,200		5,600
Investment in farm business:				
Farmland	$42,000		$32,100	
Farm equipment	22,400		9,000	
Note payable on farm equipment	(10,000)		–0–	
Net investment in farm		54,400		41,100
Total assets		$170,900		$167,200
Liabilities and Net Worth				
Credit card		$ 2,400		$ 1,500
Income taxes payable		11,400		12,400
Mortgage payable on residence		71,000		76,000
Estimated income taxes on the difference between the estimated current values of assets and liabilities and their tax bases		19,700		16,500
Net worth		66,400		60,800
Total liabilities and net worth		$170,900		$167,200

Additional Information

1. Leonard and Michelle's total salaries during the fiscal year ended August 31, 20X3, were $44,300; farm income was $6,700; personal expenditures were $43,500; and interest and dividends received were $1,400.

2. Marketable securities purchased in 20X1 at a cost of $11,000 and with a current market value of $11,000 on August 31, 20X2, were sold on March 1, 20X3, for $10,700. No additional marketable securities were purchased or sold during the fiscal year.

3. The values of the residence and farmland are based on year-end appraisals.

4. On August 31, 20X3, Leonard purchased a used combine at a cost of $14,000. He made a $4,000 down payment and signed a five-year, 10 percent note payable for the $10,000 balance owed. No other farm equipment was purchased or sold during the fiscal year.

5. The cash surrender value of the life insurance policy increased during the fiscal year by $1,600. However, Leonard borrowed $4,000 against the policy on September 1, 20X2. Interest at 15 percent for the first year of this loan was paid when due on August 31, 20X3.

6. Federal income taxes of $12,400 were paid during the 20X3 fiscal year.

7. Mortgage payments made during the year totaled $9,000, which included payments of principal and interest.

Required

Using the comparative statement of financial condition and additional information provided, prepare the statement of changes in net worth for the year ended August 31, 20X3. (*Hint:* It will be helpful to use T-accounts to determine several realized and unrealized amounts. An analysis of the cash, personal effects, and credit card accounts should not be required to properly complete the statement.)

Problems

LO2

Advanced
StudyGuide
.com

P11-13 Lump-Sum Liquidation

The Carlos, Dan, and Gail (CDG) Partnership has decided to liquidate as of December 1, 20X6. A balance sheet as of December 1, 20X6, appears below:

CDG PARTNERSHIP Balance Sheet At December 1, 20X6		
Assets		
Cash		$ 25,000
Accounts Receivable (net)		75,000
Inventories		100,000
Property, Plant, and Equipment (net)		300,000
Total Assets		$500,000
Liabilities and Capital		
Liabilities:		
Accounts Payable		$270,000
Capital:		
Carlos, Capital	$120,000	
Dan, Capital	50,000	
Gail, Capital	60,000	
Total Capital		230,000
Total Liabilities and Capital		$500,000

Additional Information

1. The personal assets (excluding partnership capital interests) and personal liabilities of each partner as of December 1, 20X6, follow:

	Carlos	Dan	Gail
Personal assets	$250,000	$300,000	$350,000
Personal liabilities	(230,000)	(240,000)	(325,000)
Personal net worth	$ 20,000	$ 60,000	$ 25,000

2. Carlos, Dan, and Gail share profits and losses in the ratio 20:40:40.
3. All of the noncash assets were sold on December 10, 20X6, for $260,000.

Required

a. Prepare a statement of realization and liquidation for the CDG Partnership on December 10, 20X6.

b. Prepare a schedule of the net worth of each of the three partners as of December 10, 2006, after the liquidation of the partnership is completed.

Advanced
StudyGuide
.com

P11-14 Installment Liquidation [AICPA Adapted]

On January 1, 20X1, partners Art, Bru, and Chou, who share profits and losses in the ratio of 5:3:2, decide to liquidate their partnership. The partnership trial balance at this date is as follows:

	Debit	Credit
Cash	$ 18,000	
Accounts Receivable	66,000	
Inventory	52,000	
Machinery and Equipment (net)	189,000	
Accounts Payable		$ 53,000
Art, Capital		88,000
Bru, Capital		110,000
Chou, Capital		74,000
Total	$325,000	$325,000

The partners plan a program of piecemeal conversion of assets to minimize liquidation losses. All available cash, less an amount retained to provide for future expenses, is to be distributed to the partners at the end of each month. A summary of the liquidation transactions is as follows:

January 20X1

1. $51,000 was collected on accounts receivable; the balance is uncollectible.
2. $38,000 was received for the entire inventory.
3. $2,000 liquidation expenses were paid.
4. $50,000 was paid to creditors, after offset of a $3,000 credit memorandum received on January 11, 20X1.
5. $10,000 cash was retained in the business at the end of the month for potential unrecorded liabilities and anticipated expenses.

February 20X1

6. $4,000 liquidation expenses were paid.
7. $6,000 cash was retained in the business at the end of the month for potential unrecorded liabilities and anticipated expenses.

March 20X1

8. $146,000 was received on sale of all items of machinery and equipment.
9. $5,000 liquidation expenses were paid.
10. No cash was retained in the business.

Required

Prepare a statement of partnership liquidation for the partnership with schedules of safe payments to partners.

Advanced
StudyGuide
.com

LO3 **P11-15** **Cash Distribution Plan**

The partnership of Pen, Evan, and Torves has asked you to assist in winding up its business affairs. You compile the following information.

1. The trial balance of the partnership on June 30, 20X1, is

	Debit	Credit
Cash	$ 6,000	
Accounts Receivable (net)	22,000	
Inventory	14,000	
Plant and Equipment (net)	99,000	
Accounts Payable		$ 17,000
Pen, Capital		55,000
Evan, Capital		45,000
Torves, Capital		24,000
Total	$141,000	$141,000

2. The partners share profits and losses as follows: Pen, 50 percent; Evan, 30 percent; and Torves, 20 percent.

3. The partners are considering an offer of $100,000 for the accounts receivable, inventory, and plant and equipment as of June 30. The $100,000 will be paid to creditors and the partners in installments, the number and amounts of which are to be negotiated.

Required

Prepare a cash distribution plan as of June 30, 20X1, showing how much cash each partner will receive if the offer to sell the assets is accepted.

LO3 **P11-16** **Installment Liquidation**

Refer to the facts in Problem 11-15. The partners have decided to liquidate their partnership by installments instead of accepting the offer of $100,000. Cash is distributed to the partners at the end of each month. A summary of the liquidation transactions follows:

July

1. $16,500 collected on accounts receivable; balance is uncollectible.

2. $10,000 received for the entire inventory.

3. $1,000 liquidation expense paid.

4. $17,000 paid to creditors.

5. $8,000 cash retained in the business at the end of the month.

August

6. $1,500 in liquidation expenses paid.

7. As part payment of his capital, Torves accepted an item of special equipment that he developed, which had a book value of $4,000. The partners agreed that a value of $10,000 should be placed on this item for liquidation purposes.

8. $2,500 cash retained in the business at the end of the month.

September

9. $75,000 received on sale of remaining plant and equipment.

10. $1,000 liquidation expenses paid. No cash retained in the business.

Required

Prepare a statement of partnership realization and liquidation with supporting schedules of safe payments to partners.

LO3   **P11-17**   **Installment Liquidation**

The DSV Partnership decided to liquidate the partnership as of June 30, 20X5. The balance sheet of the partnership as of this date is presented as follows:

DSV PARTNERSHIP
Balance Sheet
At June 30, 20X5

Assets

Cash		$ 50,000
Accounts Receivable (net)		95,000
Inventories		75,000
Property, Plant, and Equipment (net)		500,000
Total Assets		$720,000

Liabilities and Partners' Capital

Liabilities:		
Accounts Payable		$405,000
Partners' Capital:		
D, Capital	$100,000	
S, Capital	140,000	
V, Capital	75,000	
Total Capital		315,000
Total Liabilities and Capital		$720,000

Additional Information

1. The personal assets (excluding partnership loan and capital interests) and personal liabilities of each partner as of June 30, 20X5, follow:

	D	S	V
Personal assets	$250,000	$450,000	$300,000
Personal liabilities	(270,000)	(420,000)	(240,000)
Personal net worth	$ (20,000)	$ 30,000	$ 60,000

2. The DSV Partnership was liquidated during the months of July, August, and September. The assets sold and the amounts realized follow:

Month	Assets Sold	Carrying Amount	Amount Realized
July	Inventories	$ 50,000	$ 45,000
	Accounts receivable (net)	60,000	40,000
	Property, plant, and equipment	400,000	305,000
August	Inventories	$ 25,000	$ 18,000
	Accounts receivable (net)	10,000	4,000
September	Accounts receivable (net)	$ 25,000	$ 10,000
	Property, plant, and equipment	100,000	45,000

Required

Prepare a statement of partnership realization and liquidation for the DSV Partnership for the three-month period ended September 30, 20X5. D, S, and V share profits and losses in the ratio 50:30:20. The partners wish to distribute available cash at the end of each month after reserving $10,000 of cash at the end of July and August to meet unexpected liquidation expenses. Actual liquidation expenses incurred and paid each month amounted to $2,500. Support each cash distribution to the partners with a schedule of safe installment payments.

LO3   **P11-18**   **Cash Distribution Plan**

Refer to the information contained in Problem 11-17. Assume the following amounts of cash were received during the months of July, August, and September from the sale of DSV Partnership's noncash assets:

July	$390,000
August	22,000
September	55,000

The partnership wishes to keep $10,000 of cash on hand at the end of July and August to pay for unexpected liquidation expenses.

It paid liquidation expenses of $2,500 at the end of each month, July, August, and September.

Required

a. Prepare a statement, as of June 30, 20X5, showing how cash will be distributed among partners as it becomes available.

b. Prepare schedules showing how cash is distributed at the end of July, August, and September 20X5.

LO1–LO3 **P11-19** **Matching**

Match the terms on the left with the descriptions on the right. Each description may be used only once (or not at all).

Terms	Descriptions of Terms
1. Dissolution	A. Sale of the partnership assets, payment of the partnership creditors, and the distribution of any remaining assets to partners.
2. Partner's loss absorption power	
3. Liquidation	B. Allocation to other partners in their profit and loss–sharing ratio if the partner is personally insolvent.
4. Statement of partnership realization and liquidation	C. Schedule that shows how cash is to be distributed as it becomes available during liquidation process.
5. Installment liquidation	D. Computed by dividing a partner's capital balance by that partner's loss-sharing ratio.
6. Cash distribution plan	E. Revaluation of a partnership's assets and liabilities to their market values.
7. Incorporation of a partnership	F. Change in the legal relationship between partners.
8. Partner's deficit in capital	G. End of the normal business function of the partnership.
9. Lump-sum liquidation	H. Liquidation in which all assets are converted into cash over a short time period, enabling all creditors to be paid, with any remaining cash being distributed according to the partner's capital balance.
10. Safe payments to partners	
	I. Cash payments to partners computed on the assumption that all noncash assets will be sold for nothing.
	J. Presents, in worksheet form, the effects of the liquidation process on the balance sheet accounts of the partnership.
	K. Liquidation in which cash is periodically distributed to partners during the liquidation process.

LO1 **P11-20** **Partnership Agreement Issues [AICPA Adapted]**

A partnership involves an association between two or more persons to carry on a business as co-owners for profit. Items 1 through 10 relate to partnership agreements.

The statement of facts for Parts A and B are followed by numbered sentences that state legal conclusions relating to those facts. Determine whether each legal conclusion is correct or not and mark it with the letter Y for yes, correct, or N for no, not correct.

Part A

Adams, Webster, and Coke were partners in the construction business. Coke decided to retire and found Black, who agreed to purchase his interest. Black was willing to pay Coke $20,000 and promised to assume Coke's share of all firm obligations.

Required (Use Y for yes and N for no)

1. Unless the partners agree to admit Black as a partner, she could not become a member of the firm.

2. The retirement of Coke would cause a dissolution of the firm.

3. The firm's creditors are third-party beneficiaries of Black's promise to Coke.

4. Coke would be released from all liability for the firm's debts if Black purchased his interest and promised to pay Coke's share of firm debts.

5. If the other partners refused to accept Black as a partner, Coke could retire, thereby causing a dissolution.

Part B

Carson, Crocket, and Kitt were partners in the importing business. They needed additional capital to expand and located an investor named White, who agreed to purchase a one-quarter interest in the partnership by contributing $50,000 in capital to the partnership. Before White became a partner, several large creditors had previously loaned money to the partnership. The partnership subsequently failed, and the creditors are now attempting to assert personal liability against White.

Required (Use Y for yes and N for no)

6. White is personally liable on all of the firm's debts contracted subsequent to his entry into the firm.

7. Creditors of the partnership prior to the admission of a new partner automatically continue to be creditors of the partnership after the admission of the new partner.

8. Creditors of the partnership that existed prior to White's entry can assert rights against his capital contribution.

9. White has personal liability for firm debts existing prior to his entry into the firm.

10. White must remain in the partnership for at least one year to be subject to personal liability.

Supplemental Problems for this chapter are available as part of the *Online Learning Center* on the textbook's Web site (URL: www.mhhe.com/baker1e).

Chapter **Twelve**

Governmental Entities: Introduction and General Fund Accounting

City of

San Diego

ACCOUNTING FOR THE BUSTLING CITY OF SAN DIEGO

The City of San Diego, California, is one of the most popular places to visit in the United States. The city has everything from beaches, lakes, and parks to a world-class zoo and pro sports teams. Because of its beauty and near perfect climate, San Diego is a popular location for visitors to hold meetings and conventions year round. It is also a very desirable place to live and work. With a population of 1.25 million, it is the seventh largest city in the United States and the second largest in California.

Have you ever considered what it takes to run a city of this size and diversity? In addition to maintaining the popular tourist attractions like beaches and parks, the city manages public pools, a cemetery, libraries, public transportation, youth recreation programs, law enforcement, emergency services, public utilities, airports, social services, schools, and countless other activities. In order to facilitate all of these programs, services, and activities, San Diego City has a long list of departments from Police to Lifeguard Services, and from Engineering to Environmental Services, to name a few. Naturally, the city has to report on its stewardship of these many activities, services, and programs to its citizens. Chapters 12 and 13 explore the financial reporting aspects of governmental units such as San Diego City, San Diego County, and the State of California.

Each of the 50 states follows relatively uniform accounting standards; however, some states have unique statutory provisions for selected items. Local governments are political subdivisions of state government. The 87,000-plus local governmental units in the United States are classified as (1) general-purpose local governments, such as counties, cities, towns, villages, and townships; (2) special-purpose local governments, such as soil conservation districts; and (3) authorities and agencies, such as the Port Authority of New York and New Jersey and local housing authorities. Authorities and agencies differ from other governmental units because they typically do not have taxing power and may sell only revenue bonds, not general obligation bonds.

The first part of this chapter introduces the accounting and reporting requirements for state and local governmental units. The major concepts of governmental accounting are discussed and illustrated first. The last part of this chapter presents a comprehensive illustration of accounting for the general fund of a city. The comprehensive illustration reviews and integrates the concepts presented in the first part of the chapter. Chapter 13 continues the comprehensive illustration to complete the discussion on state and local governmental accounting and reporting.

LEARNING OBJECTIVES

When you finish studying this chapter, you should be able to:

LO1   Understand and explain the basic differences between governmental and private sector accounting.

LO2   Understand and explain major concepts of governmental accounting.

LO3   Understand and explain the differences between the various governmental fund types.

LO4   Understand and explain basic concepts for financial reporting in governmental accounting.

LO5   Understand and explain the basic differences in the measurement focus and basis of accounting between governmental and private sector accounting.

LO6   Understand and explain basic budgeting concepts in governmental accounting.

LO7   Make calculations and record journal entries for the general fund.

LO8   Make calculations and record journal entries for basic interfund activities.

DIFFERENCES BETWEEN GOVERNMENTAL AND PRIVATE SECTOR ACCOUNTING

LO1

Understand and explain the basic differences between governmental and private sector accounting.

In the early 2000s, the combined annual spending of federal, state, and local governments exceeded $4.0 trillion. Governmental purchases of goods and services constitute approximately 20 percent of the total gross national product of the United States.[1]

Governmental entities have operating objectives different from those of commercial entities; therefore, governmental accounting is different from accounting for commercial enterprises. The major differences between governmental and for-profit entities are as follows:

1. Governmental accounting must recognize that governmental units collect resources and make expenditures to fulfill societal needs. Society expects governmental units to develop and maintain an infrastructure of highways, streets, and sewer and sanitation systems, as well as to provide public protection, recreation, and cultural services.

2. Except for some proprietary activities such as utilities, governmental entities do not have a general profit motive. Police and fire departments do not have a profit motive; instead these units must be evaluated on their abilities to provide for society's needs.

3. Governmental operations have legal authorization for their existence, conduct revenue-raising through the power of taxation, and have mandated expenditures they must make to provide their services. The governmental accounting system must make it possible to determine and demonstrate compliance with finance-related legal and contractual provisions. Governmental units are subject to extensive regulatory oversight through laws, grant restrictions, bond indentures, and a variety of other legal constraints.

4. Governmental entities use comprehensive budgetary accounting, which serves as a significant control mechanism and provides the basis for comparing actual operations against budgeted amounts. The budget is a legally established statutory control vehicle.

5. The primary emphasis in governmental fund accounting is to measure and report on management's stewardship of the financial resources committed to the objectives of the governmental unit. Accountability for the flow of financial resources is a chief objective of governmental accounting. The managers of the governmental unit must be able to show that they are in compliance with the many legal regulations governing its operations.

---

[1] Annual reports of the national income and product accounts, including aggregate revenues and expenditures of governmental entities, are presented in the *Survey of Current Business,* published periodically by the U.S. Department of Commerce.

6. Governmental entities typically are required to establish separate funds to carry out their various missions. Each fund is an independent accounting and fiscal entity and is responsible for using its own resources to accomplish its specific responsibilities.

7. Many fund entities do not record fixed assets or long-term debt in their funds. These fund entities record the purchase of assets such as equipment and buildings as expenditures of the period. A separate record of the fixed assets and long-term debt is maintained within the governmental unit.

8. An important objective of governmental financial reporting is accountability. Governments must be able to explain and justify to citizens and to other governments the raising and using of public resources. A key element of accountability is *interperiod equity* in which it is determined if current-year revenues are sufficient to pay for services provided during that year, or if future taxpayers will be required to assume burdens for services previously provided or deficits created in prior years.

HISTORY OF GOVERNMENTAL ACCOUNTING

Before 1984, the development of accounting principles for local governmental units was directed by the Municipal Finance Officers Association (MFOA). In 1934, the National Committee on Municipal Accounting, a committee of the MFOA, published the first statement on local governmental accounting. The report was entitled *A Tentative Outline— Principles of Municipal Accounting.* In 1968, the National Committee on Governmental Accounting, the successor committee, published *Governmental Accounting, Auditing, and Financial Reporting* (GAAFR). Some governmental accountants call it the "blue book" after the color of its cover. The GAAFR is periodically updated to include the most recent governmental financial reporting standards.

In 1974, the American Institute of Certified Public Accountants (AICPA) published an industry audit guide, *Audits of State and Local Governmental Units,* in which it stated that "except as modified in this guide, they (GAAFR) constitute generally accepted accounting principles."[2] In March 1979, the National Council on Governmental Accounting (NCGA) issued its **Statement No. 1,** "Governmental Accounting and Financial Reporting Principles" (NCGA 1), which established a set of accounting principles for governmental reporting.

In 1984, the Financial Accounting Foundation created a companion group to the Financial Accounting Standards Board. The Governmental Accounting Standards Board (GASB) is now responsible for maintaining and developing accounting and reporting standards for state and local governmental entities. In **GASB Statement No. 1,** "Authoritative Status of NCGA Pronouncements and AICPA Industry Audit Guide" (GASB 1), released in July 1984, the GASB stated that all NCGA statements and interpretations issued and in effect on that date were accepted as generally accepted accounting principles for governmental accounting. In 1985, the GASB published a codification of the existing GAAP for state and local governments entitled *Codification of Governmental Accounting and Financial Reporting Standards.* The first section of the codification is virtually identical to **NCGA 1** as amended by subsequent NCGA statements. Section 2 presents the financial reporting issues for governmental entities. Sections 3 and 4 present specific balance sheet and operating statement topics. The GASB continues to publish updated codifications periodically. The codification is an authoritative source for accounting and financial reporting principles for governmental units.

A very significant change in the governmental reporting model for governmental units was required by **GASB Statement 34,** "Basic Financial Statements—and Management's Discussion and Analysis—for State and Local Governments" (GASB 34), issued in 1999. **GASB 34** established government-wide financial statements to be prepared on the accrual basis of accounting and an array of fund-based financial statements. This standard also required several new footnote and schedule disclosures that increase the

[2] Committee on Governmental Accounting and Auditing, *Audits of State and Local Governmental Units* (New York: American Institute of Certified Public Accountants, 1974), pp. 8–9.

transparency of governmental reporting. The GASB continues to issue new standards to meet the information needs of citizens, creditors, and other users of the financial reports of governmental units.

Accounting for governmental entities is given the general name of *fund accounting* to distinguish it from accounting for commercial entities. This chapter first presents an overview of fund accounting, including accounting for typical transactions and providing required financial statements for a governmental entity. After introducing the major concepts of governmental accounting, a comprehensive illustration is presented of accounting and financial reporting for the general fund, typically the most important fund of most governmental entities. Chapter 13 presents the accounting for the remaining funds of a governmental entity and the required financial statements for a governmental entity. The comprehensive illustration provides integrated examples of the governmental accounting and financial reporting concepts that are discussed in the first part of this chapter. Some students may initially find governmental accounting to be quite different from the financial accounting learned in earlier accounting courses. However, after studying the concepts and working through the comprehensive illustration, the reasons and logic for fund accounting, and the content and form of the governmental financial statements, become more focused.

MAJOR CONCEPTS OF GOVERNMENTAL ACCOUNTING

LO2

Understand and explain major concepts of governmental accounting.

Governmental accounting is different from commercial accounting. Governmental entities use a fund-based accounting system in which some of the funds use a modified-accrual accounting method as opposed to the accrual method used by commercial entities. Also, the financial statements of governmental entities have a foundation in the individual funds but aggregate to a government-wide level. The following section discusses the major concepts for governmental accounting.

Elements of Financial Statements

In 2007, the GASB published **Concepts Statement No. 4,** "Elements of Financial Statements" (CON 4), that defined each of the seven elements of financial statements of state and local governments. Each definition uses the central focus of a *resource,* which is an item having a present capacity to provide, directly or indirectly, services for the governmental entity. This present service capacity may be in the form of direct provision of services as well as those items having the ability to affect cash flows in the future.

The *five elements of a statement of financial condition* are

1. *Assets* are resources with present service capacity that the entity presently controls.
2. *Liabilities* are present obligations to sacrifice resources that the entity has little or no discretion to avoid.
3. A *deferred outflow of resources* is a consumption of net assets that is applicable to a future reporting period.
4. A *deferred inflow of resources* is an acquisition of net assets that is applicable to a future reporting period.
5. *Net position* is the residual of all other elements presented in a statement of financial condition.

The *two elements of the resource flows statements* are

6. An *outflow of resources* is a consumption of net assets that is applicable to the current reporting period.
7. An *inflow of resources* is an acquisition of net assets that is applicable to the current reporting period.

The central focus of present service capacity for defining the elements of governmental financial statements is different from the focus used by the FASB in its **Statement of Financial Accounting Concepts No. 6,** "Elements of Financial Statements" (CON 6).

The FASB developed its definitions of the elements of financial statements based on the usefulness of financial reporting information to investors and creditors in making economic decisions for allocating scarce resources among alternative uses.

The GASB felt that its concepts statement provides a framework that will enhance consistency in setting future governmental accounting standards and serve as guidance for preparers and auditors when evaluating transactions that are not explicitly included in existing governmental accounting standards.

Expendability of Resources versus Capital Maintenance Objectives

The major differences between commercial and governmental accounting and reporting stem from the objectives of the entities. In commercial, profit-seeking enterprises, the measurement focus is on the flow of *all economic resources* of the firm. The accrual method of accounting is used to match the revenues and expenses during a period, with the purpose of measuring profitability. The company's balance sheet contains both current and noncurrent assets and liabilities, and the change in retained earnings reflects the company's ability to maintain its capital investment.

In contrast, the measurement focus for the governmental funds of a government entity is on changes in *current financial resources* available to provide services to the public in accordance with the government entity's legally adopted budget. The modified accrual method of accounting is used to measure the revenues that are available to finance current expenditures and the expenditures made during the period. The balance sheet reports only current assets, current liabilities, and a fund balance. Operating authorization for a fiscal period's transactions is initiated by the passage of a budget by the legislative governing body. Managers of governmental units must be fiscally accountable to show that resources are expended in compliance with the legal and financial restrictions placed on the governmental entity by its legislative body.

In 2006, the GASB published a White Paper that identified a number of key differences between financial reporting for governments and for-profit businesses.[3] The White Paper made the argument that users of governmental financial reports and users of business financial reports require substantially different financial and economic information in order to evaluate fiscal and operational performance. The White Paper expands on the differences stated in the list above and presents the GASB's perspective on the need for separate governmental accounting and financial reporting standards.

Definitions and Types of Funds

LO3

Understand and explain the differences between the various governmental fund types.

Fund accounting must recognize the unique aspects of governmental operations. Governmental units must provide a large range of services such as fire and police protection, water and sewerage, legal courts, and construction of public buildings and other facilities. In addition, governmental units receive their resources from many different sources and must make expenditures in accordance with legal restrictions.

The operations of a governmental unit also must be broken down into periodic reporting intervals of fiscal years because the management of these public operations may change as a result of elections or new appointments. Thus, governmental accounting must recognize the many different purposes, the different sources of revenue, the mandated expenditures, and the fiscal periodicity of the governmental unit. To accomplish the objectives of the governmental unit, the unit establishes a variety of *funds* as fiscal and accounting entities of the governmental unit. A fund is a separate accounting group with accounts to record the transactions and prepare the financial statements of a defined part of the governmental entity that is responsible for specific activities or objectives. Each fund records those transactions affecting its assets, related liabilities, and residual fund balance.

Different funds are established for the specific functions that a government must provide. Most funds obtain resources from taxes on property, income, or commercial sales; they also

[3] Governmental Accounting Standards Board, *Why Governmental Accounting and Financial Reporting Is—and Should Be—Different* (Norwalk, CT: GASB, 2006).

may obtain resources as grants from other governmental agencies, from fines or licenses, and from charges for services. Each fund must make its expenditures in accordance with its specified purposes. For example, a fund established for fire protection cannot be used to provide school buses for the local school. The fire department may make expenditures only as directly related to its function of providing fire protection.

Each governmental fund has its own asset and liability accounts and its own revenue and expenditures accounts. The term **expenditures** refers to decreases in net financial resources available under the current financial resources measurement focus. Expenditures are made in accordance with the budget established by the government unit's governing body, and the internal control structure of a vouchers payable system is generally used prior to payments to external vendors. Upon receipt and acceptance of the goods or services from the external vendor, the journal entry to recognize the approved expenditure is a debit to expenditures and a credit to vouchers payable. The increase in the payables decreases the net financial resources available. The payment of the vouchers payable must then be approved by the government's governing body.

Separate fund-based financial statements must be prepared for each fiscal period. In this manner, governing bodies or other interested parties may assess the fiscal and operating performance of each fund in fulfillment of the specific purposes for which each fund was established.

Governmental accounting systems are established on a fund basis in three major categories: governmental, proprietary, and fiduciary. Figure 12–1 presents an overview of each of the funds and provides a brief description of the types of activities accounted for in each fund.

Governmental Funds

Five types of **governmental funds** are used to provide basic governmental services to the public. These are (1) general fund, (2) special revenue funds, (3) capital projects funds, (4) debt service funds, and (5) permanent funds (see Figure 12–1). The number of governmental funds maintained by the governmental entity is based on its legal and operating requirements. Each governmental entity creates only one general fund, but it may create more than one of each of the other types of governmental funds based on the entity's specific needs. For example, some governmental entities establish a separate capital projects fund for each major capital project.

Proprietary Funds

Some activities of a governmental unit, such as the operation of a public swimming pool or a municipal water system, are similar to those of commercial enterprises. The objective of the governmental unit is to recover its costs in these operations through a system of user charges. The two types of **proprietary funds** typically used by governmental entities are enterprise funds and internal service funds (see Figure 12–1). Accounting and reporting for a proprietary fund are similar to accounting for a commercial operation. The balance sheet of each proprietary fund reports all assets, including long-term capital assets, and all liabilities, including long-term liabilities. Chapter 13 presents a complete discussion of proprietary funds.

Fiduciary Funds

Four types of **fiduciary funds** are provided for a governmental unit. Three are trust funds that account for financial resources maintained in trust by the government. These three are pension and other employee benefit trust funds, investment trust funds, and private-purpose trust funds. The fourth fiduciary fund, agency funds, is used to account for resources held by the government solely in a custodial capacity (see Figure 12–1). Note that the permanent fund, which is a governmental fund, includes resources that are legally restricted so that the governmental entity must maintain the principal and can use only the earnings from the fund's resources to benefit the government's programs for all of its citizens. The private-purpose trust funds include trusts under which the principal may or may not be expendable but for which the trust agreement specifies the principal, if expendable, and the earnings may be used only for the benefit of specific individuals, organizations, or other governments. Chapter 13 presents examples of fiduciary funds.

FIGURE 12–1   **Fund Structure**

Governmental Fund Types

1. General fund	Accounts for all financial resources except for those accounted for in another fund. Includes transactions for general governmental services provided by the executive, legislative, and judicial operations of the governmental entity.
2. Special revenue fund	Accounts for the proceeds of specific revenue sources that are restricted for specified purposes. Includes resources and expenditures for operations, such as public libraries, when a separate tax is levied for their support.
3. Capital projects fund	Accounts for financial resources for the acquisition or construction of major capital facilities that benefit many citizens, such as parks and municipal buildings. This fund is in existence only during the acquisition or construction of the facilities and is closed once the project is completed.
4. Debt service fund	Accounts for the accumulation of resources for, and the payment of, general long-term debt principal and interest. This fund is used for servicing the long-term debt of the government.
5. Permanent fund	Accounts for resources that are restricted such that only earnings, but not principal, may be used in support of governmental programs that benefit the government or its citizenry.

Proprietary Fund Types

6. Enterprise fund	Accounts for operations of governmental units that charge for services provided to the general public. Includes those activities financed in a manner similar to private business enterprises where the intent of the governing body is to recover the costs of providing goods or services to the general public on a continuing basis through user charges. Also includes those operations that the governing body intends to operate at a profit. Examples include sports arenas, municipal electric utilities, and municipal bus companies.
7. Internal service fund	Accounts for the financing of goods or services provided by one department or agency to other departments or agencies of the governmental unit. The services are usually provided on a cost-reimbursement basis and are offered only to other governmental agencies, not the general public. Examples are municipal motor vehicle pools, city print shops, and central purchasing operations.

Fiduciary Fund Types and Similar Component Units

8. Pension (and other employee benefit) trust fund	Accounts for resources required to be held in trust for the members and beneficiaries of pension plans, other post-employment benefit plans, or other employee benefit plans.
9. Investment trust fund	Accounts for the external portion of investment pools reported by the sponsoring government.
10. Private-purpose trust fund	Accounts for all other trust arrangements under which the fund's resources are to be used to benefit specific individuals, private organizations, or other governments, as specified in the trust agreement.
11. Agency fund	Accounts for assets held by a governmental unit in an agency capacity for employees or for other governmental units. An example is the city employees' payroll withholding for health insurance premiums.

FINANCIAL REPORTING OF GOVERNMENTAL ENTITIES[4]

LO4

Understand and explain basic concepts for financial reporting in governmental accounting.

Advanced
StudyGuide
.com

A governmental unit may have a variety of boards, commissions, authorities, or other component units under its control. The financial statements of a governmental entity are presented for the ***reporting entity,*** which consists of

1. The *primary government* such as a state government, a general-purpose local government, or a special-purpose local government that has a separately elected government body.

2. *Component units,* which are legally separate organizations for which the primary unit has financial accountability.

3. Other organizations that have a significant relationship with the primary government and need to be included in the primary government's financial statements to avoid misleading or incomplete financial representations. (More on these "other organizations" will be presented in Chapter 13.)

[4] To view a video explanation of this topic, visit advancedstudyguide.com.

GASB Statement No. 14, "The Financial Reporting Entity" (GASB 14), states that financial accountability exists for those component units if the primary government unit appoints a majority of an organization's governing body and

(*a*) is able to impose its will on the organization, or

(*b*) possesses a financial benefit or assumes a financial burden for the organization.

The *governmental financial reporting model* is specified in **GASB Statement No. 34,** "Basic Financial Statements—and Management's Discussion and Analysis—for State and Local Governments" (GASB 34). Figure 12–2 presents the names of the financial statements and the other major information specified by **GASB 34.** The reporting model has two integrated levels of financial statements.

1. The first level is the *fund-based financial statements* because governments continue to use fund-based accounting to record transactions in accordance with the legal or budgetary requirements established by their governing body. These fund-based financial statements demonstrate fiscal accountability of the management of each of the funds.

2. The second level is the *government-wide financial statements.* After preparing the fund-based financial statements, the government prepares reconciliation schedules to go from the governmental fund financial statements to the government-wide financial statements. In addition to the governmental funds, the reporting entity includes other funds in the government-wide financial statements. The government entity's capital assets, such as buildings and equipment, and long-term debt also are included in the government-wide financial statements. The government-wide financial statements demonstrate the operational accountability of the management of the governmental unit as a whole.

This chapter and the first part of Chapter 13 focus on the fund-based financial statements. After completing our discussion of each fund type in Chapter 13, the government-wide financial statements are presented.

Fund-Based Financial Statements: Governmental Funds

Two financial statements are required for the governmental funds: (1) balance sheet and (2) statement of revenues, expenditures, and changes in fund balance.

FIGURE 12–2
The Government
Reporting Model

1. Independent auditors' report
2. Management's Discussion and Analysis (required supplementary information)
3. Government-wide financial statements
   a. Statement of Net Assets
   b. Statement of Activities
4. Fund-based financial statements
   a. Governmental funds
      (1) Balance Sheet
      (2) Statement of Revenues, Expenditures, and Changes in Fund Balances
      (3) Reconciliation Schedules (of each of the two governmental fund-based statements to their related government-wide financial statements, either at the bottom of each of the two fund-based financial statements or in an accompanying schedule)
   b. Proprietary funds
      (1) Statement of Net Assets
      (2) Statement of Revenues, Expenses, and Changes in Fund Net Assets
      (3) Statement of Cash Flows
   c. Fiduciary funds
      (1) Statement of Fiduciary Net Assets
      (2) Statement of Changes in Fiduciary Net Assets
5. Notes to the financial statements
6. Required Supplementary Information (RSI) (in addition to the MD&A)
   a. Budgetary Comparison Schedules
   b. Information about Infrastructure Assets
   c. Information about Pensions

Balance Sheet for Governmental Funds

The format of the balance sheet, with added parenthetical guidance for learning assistance, for each of the governmental funds is

Balance Sheet for Governmental Funds		
Assets (financial resources available for current use; presented in order of liquidity)		$X,XXX
Total Assets		$X,XXX
Liabilities and Fund Balances		
Liabilities (due and expected to be paid from current financial resources; presented in order of due date)		$ XXX
Fund Balances		
Nonspendable	$XX	
Spendable:		
Restricted	XX	
Limited	XX	
Assigned	XX	
Unassigned	XX	XX
Total Liabilities and Fund Balances		$X,XXX

The five governmental funds use the ***current financial resources measurement focus.*** Under this method, the asset section of the balance sheet reports only financial assets such as cash or other assets that will convert into cash (e.g., receivables) in the normal course of operations over the near future. Some governments report inventories or other prepayments because these save the entity from the incurrence of future outflows of current financial resources. Long-term capital items such as equipment or buildings are not reported on the fund-based balance sheet because these amounts are no longer currently available for expenditure. However, the long-term capital assets of the governmental entity are scheduled and reported in the government-wide financial statements, as illustrated in Chapter 13.

The liability section of the balance sheet reports only those liabilities that have become due and that will require current financial resources to liquidate, such as vouchers payable or the current portion of long-term debt. A short-term debt often used in governmental funds is tax-anticipation notes. These notes represent loans obtained using future taxes as collateral for the notes. Most states restrict these borrowings to those taxes that have been levied but not yet collected. These notes payable are paid from the first tax collections of the tax levy to which the notes are related. The principal of long-term debt not due within the next year is not reported on the balance sheet because it will not be settled in the near term with current financial resources. However, the governmental unit's long-term debt is scheduled and is reported in the government-wide financial statements.

The third section of the balance sheet for the five governmental funds reports the net fund balance, which is the amount of the difference between reported assets and reported liabilities. **GASB 54** specifies that the fund balances for the governmental funds should be segregated into two categories:

1. *Nonspendable fund balances* represent amounts that are *(a)* not in spendable form, such as amounts related to inventories and prepaid items, or *(b)* required by legal or contractual provisions to be maintained intact, such as the principal of a permanent fund.

2. *Spendable fund balances* represent amounts that are available for spending. Amounts in this portion of the fund balance would be further classified as *(a)* restricted, *(b)* limited, *(c)* assigned, or *(d)* unassigned. The classification would

be based on an examination of requirements imposed by legal or contractual provisions and then of any constraints established by the governing body of the government entity.[5]

Statement of Revenues, Expenditures, and Changes in Fund Balance for Governmental Funds

This is often called the *operating statement* of the governmental funds, but the financial statements for the governmental funds use the full title. The statement of revenues, expenditures, and changes in fund balance has four major sections:

1. *Operating section.* The top section includes the revenues less expenditures for the period, with the difference shown as the excess (or deficiency) of revenues over expenditures.
2. *Other financing sources or uses.* This section includes nonrevenue items such as bond issue proceeds and interfund transfers. (Note that issuance of bonds and debt refundings of governmental long-term debt are shown in the other financing sources and uses section although the long-term debt is not shown on the fund's balance sheet.)
3. *Special and extraordinary items.* This section presents extraordinary items that are both unusual and infrequent, such as losses due to a hurricane. Special items are transactions or events within the control of management that are either unusual or infrequent in occurrence. An example of a special item would be the one-time sale of county park land.
4. *Fund balance.* The bottom portion presents both the beginning and the ending fund balance.

The format of the statement of revenues, expenditures, and changes in fund balance, with added parenthetical guidance, is

Statement of Revenues, Expenditures, and Changes in Fund Balance	
Revenues (recognized when both measurable and available; presented by source of revenue)	$XX,XXX
Expenditures (approved decreases in net financial resources; presented by function and character)	X,XXX
Excess of Revenues over Expenditures	$ XXX
Other Financing Sources or Uses (other increases or decreases in net financial resources available, such as bond issue proceeds and interfund transfers)	XX
Special Items and Extraordinary Items	(X)
Net Change in Fund Balance	$ XX
Fund Balance—Beginning	XXX
Fund Balance—Ending (reconciles to total fund balance on balance sheet)	$ XXX

Under the current financial resources measurement focus, revenues are recognized when they become both measurable and available to finance expenditures of the fiscal period. Profit-seeking businesses measure revenue by the accrual basis as it is earned, but the current financial resources measurement focus requires that the expected timing of the revenue-related inflow be evaluated. Availability means that the transaction will result in

---

[5] In March 2009, the GASB published a new standard, **GASB 54,** entitled "Fund Balance Reporting and Governmental Fund Type Definitions." This statement modifies the definitions of some of the governmental funds to make the definitions consistent across all government units. Furthermore, the standard establishes a fund balance classification system for the governmental fund types. Note that this statement applies only to the governmental fund types, not to proprietary or fiduciary fund types. The governmental fund balance classification system uses a hierarchy based on the extent to which a government is required to comply with constraints placed upon the use of resources reported in governmental funds. The hierarchy separates the fund balance between nonspendable and spendable resources. Note that the accounting is not changed by the proposed statement, only the presentation of the fund balances for the governmental funds.

financial resources collectible within the current period or soon thereafter in order to be used to pay liabilities of the current period.

The expenditure portion of the operating statement reports reductions in available current financial assets. Expenditures are recognized when approved services or goods are received by the governmental entity. Vouchers Payable or some other payable is credited when the expenditure is recognized. The increase in liabilities decreases the net financial resources still available for spending to meet the public purposes established by the governing body. Expenditures also include amounts to purchase capital assets such as trucks or buildings. These are expenditures because they result in a net outflow of current financial assets. Note that once the expenditure has been made for a capital asset, that amount is no longer currently available to spend. Thus, although an expenditure is recognized for the purchase of a capital asset, the capital asset (e.g., truck) is not reported on the governmental fund's balance sheet.

Other financing sources and uses, the second section of the operating statement under the current financial resources measurement focus, reports changes in current financial resources from nonrevenue items, such as sales of bonds or interfund transfers with other funds of the governmental entity. Note that under the current financial resources focus, the proceeds from a sale of bonds are reported in the operating statement, but the long-term bond payable is not reported in the liabilities on the governmental fund's balance sheet. Interfund transfers are discussed in depth later in this chapter.

The special items section presents unusual or infrequent items that affect the fund balance but are not revenue or expenditure items. Finally, the fund balance section presents the change in the fund balance to obtain the ending fund balance. The ending fund balance amount should reconcile to the total fund balance shown on the balance sheet.

After each governmental fund prepares its financial statements, it prepares a combined balance sheet and a combined operating statement. These combined statements include all the governmental funds. The format for the combined government funds statements is multicolumnar, with a separate column for each of the major governmental funds and a separate column for the aggregated nonmajor (small) governmental funds. The columns are then added together horizontally and a total column for each line item in the governmental funds is presented. We will illustrate combined governmental financial statements in Chapter 13.

MEASUREMENT FOCUS AND BASIS OF ACCOUNTING (MFBA)

LO5

Understand and explain the basic differences in the measurement focus and basis of accounting between governmental and private sector accounting.

Advanced
StudyGuide
.com

Because the concepts of *measurement focus* and *basis of accounting* are so important in understanding accounting for the various funds of state and local governments, a brief review of these two concepts is presented first. Then, coverage is provided of the accounting measurement and recognition requirements applicable to revenues and expenditures in the governmental funds.

The **basis of accounting** refers to the timing of recognizing a transaction for financial reporting purposes. For example, the cash basis recognizes revenue or expenditures when cash is received or paid. The accrual basis recognizes revenue or expenditures when the transaction or event takes place. The **modified accrual basis** is a hybrid system that includes some aspects of accrual accounting and some aspects of cash basis accounting. The modified accrual basis is used in funds that have a flow of *current financial resources measurement focus.* This measurement focus is on the flow of current financial resources and the proper expendability of the resources for designated purposes and determination of the available resources remaining to be expended. Expenditures recognized under the modified accrual basis are the amounts that would normally be liquidated with expendable available financial resources. The five governmental funds have this focus.

The accrual basis is used in funds that have a flow of **economic resources measurement focus.** This measurement focus is concerned with all economic resources available to a fund during a particular time period, thereby allowing for a comparison of revenues and expenses and a focus on maintenance of capital. The proprietary funds and fiduciary funds have this focus.

In addition, as is presented in Chapter 13, the government-wide financial statements are based on the accrual basis. This necessitates a reconciliation schedule for those items accounted for under the modified accrual basis for governmental fund accounting to obtain the accrual basis amount that is reported on the government-wide financials. The reconciliation schedule is discussed in more detail in Chapter 13.

Basis of Accounting—Governmental Funds

The current financial resources measurement focus and the modified accrual basis of accounting are used for the governmental funds financial statements. The modified accrual basis is applied as follows:

1. *Revenue* is recorded in the accounting period in which it is both measurable and available to finance expenditures made during the current fiscal period.

2. *Expenditures* are recognized in the period in which the liabilities are both measurable and incurred and are payable out of current financial resources.

Measurable means that the amount of the revenue or expenditure can be objectively determined. *Available* means due or past due and receivable within the current period and collected within the current period or expected to be collected soon enough thereafter to be used to pay current-period liabilities. The definition of "soon enough thereafter" has been stated for property taxes as a period of not more than 60 days after the end of the current fiscal period.

Recognition of Revenue

The accrual method of accounting recognizes revenues from exchange transactions (sales of goods or services) and from nonexchange transactions in which the government gives or receives value without directly receiving or giving equal value in exchange. In **GASB Statement 33,** "Accounting and Financial Reporting for Nonexchange Transactions" (GASB 33), issued in 1998, the GASB classified nonexchange transactions into four categories. **GASB 33** was written from the viewpoint of the accrual basis, and modifications are required to this statement when using the modified accrual basis of accounting. How revenues are recognized depends on the category. The four categories are discussed next.

1. *Derived tax revenues,* resulting from assessments on exchange transactions. Examples are income taxes and sales taxes.

    a. The *asset (cash or receivable) is recognized* when the underlying transaction occurs or resources are received, whichever comes first.

    b. *Revenue recognition* depends on the accounting basis used to measure the transaction. Under accrual accounting (proprietary and fiduciary funds), revenue is recognized when the underlying exchange transaction occurs. Under modified accrual accounting (governmental funds), revenue is recognized when the underlying exchange has occurred and the resources are available.

Resources received prior to the exchange transaction would be reported as deferred revenue (reported as a liability) until the revenue recognition requirement is met for the fund receiving the resources.

2. *Imposed nonexchange revenues,* resulting from assessments on nongovernmental entities, including individuals. Examples include property taxes and fines.

    a. The *asset (cash or receivable) is recognized* when the government has an enforceable legal claim to the resources or the resources are received, whichever comes first.

    b. *Revenue recognition* is made in the period when use of the resources for current expenditures is first permitted or required, or at the time the asset is recorded if no time restriction on the fund's use of the resources exists.

Resources received or recorded as receivables prior to the period in which they can be recognized as revenue should be reported as deferred revenues.

The next two categories have additional eligibility requirements that the providers of financial resources often impose. These eligibility requirements must be met before the transaction can be completed, that is, before the receiving governmental unit can recognize an asset and the associated revenue. The four types of eligibility requirements are typically (1) required characteristics of the recipient as specified by the provider of the financial resources (e.g., the receiving entity must be a school district), (2) time requirements for expending the resources (e.g., the resources must all be expended within a specific fiscal period), (3) reimbursements for only those costs determined to be allowable and incurred in conformity with a program's requirements, and (4) contingencies in which the recipient has met all actions required by the provider. If the recipient has met all of the eligibility requirements imposed by the provider, then the provider should recognize the liability (or decrease in assets) and expense, and the recipient should recognize the receivable (or increase in assets) and revenue at the time the eligibility requirements have been met. The two categories are as follows:

3. *Government-mandated nonexchange transactions,* resulting from one governmental unit's provision of resources to a governmental unit at another level and the requirement that the recipient use the resources for a specific purpose. An example of this type is federal programs that state or local governments are required to perform.

4. *Voluntary nonexchange transactions,* resulting from legislative or contractual agreements, other than exchanges. Examples include certain grants and private donations.

GASB Statement No. 36, "Recipient Reporting for Certain Shared Nonexchange Revenues" (GASB 36), issued in 2000, amended **GASB 33** for government-mandated and voluntary nonexchange situations in which a providing government provides part of its own derived tax units to recipients. Typically, the providing government provides the recipients with a periodic report of the amount of shared revenues the recipients should anticipate. **GASB 36** states that if the notification from the providing government is not available in a timely manner, the recipient governments should use a reasonable estimate of the amount to be accrued and not wait until the actual receipt of the cash resources.

The following examples present the accounting, under the modified accrual basis of accounting, as used in preparing the governmental funds financial statements.

1. *Property taxes.* Property taxes involve a series of steps that guide the recognition of the property tax asset and the property tax revenue. A typical process is as follows:

Year 1:

    Step 1: Levy filed for enforceable claims to property taxes for year 1.

    Step 2: Assessment notice presenting assessed value as of levy date is mailed to each property owner and any appeals are heard.

    Step 3: Property tax bills for year 1 mailed to each property owner. (Property tax on each property based on assessed value multiplied by the tax rate. The tax rate is determined based on the requirements specified in the levy request filed by each unit of government within the taxing district.)

Year 2:

    Step 4: First installment of property taxes for year 1 are due.

    Step 5: Second (and last) installment of property taxes for year 1 are due.

The levy creates an enforceable claim to the future collection of property taxes and a property tax receivable should be recorded at that date along with a deferred property tax revenue credit. As presented above, the property tax bill is mailed to each property owner in one fiscal period and the property taxes applicable to that fiscal period are then collected in the next fiscal period. There normally is a legally imposed time restriction on the use of the property tax resources until, in this example, year 2, at which time the resources become available for expenditure. In this example, property tax revenue would not be recognized until year 2 when the time restriction is extinguished. The year 2 entry would include a debit to deferred property tax revenue and a credit to property tax revenue. While this example presents the levy date in year 1 and the collection in year 2, some governmental entities do make the levy and the collection within the same fiscal period. The key to the timing of recognizing revenue from property taxes is to determine the fiscal period in which the use of the resources for current expenditures is permitted, not necessarily when the property taxes are levied or collected.

NCGA Interpretation No. 3, "Revenue Recognition—Property Taxes" (NCGA 3), specifies that property taxes must be collectible within a maximum of 60 days after the end of the current fiscal period in order to be recognized as revenue in the current period. Taxes collectible 60 days or more after the current period ends are recorded as deferred revenue for the current period and then accounted for as next period's revenue.

Revenue from another governmental unit or tax-exempt entity in lieu of taxes, such as a payment by a university to a city for police and fire protection, should be accrued and recorded as revenue when it becomes billable.

Revenue from property taxes should be recorded *net* of any uncollectibles or abatements. The Property Taxes Receivable account is debited for the full amount of the taxes levied, with estimated uncollectibles recorded separately in an allowance account reported as a contra account to the receivable.

2. *Interest on investments and delinquent taxes.* Interest on investments or delinquent property taxes is accrued in the period in which the interest is earned and available to finance expenditures in the period. The governmental funds may temporarily invest available cash in interest-generating financial instruments such as certificates of deposit and federal or state securities. Governmental entities should carefully determine the credit risks and market risks of possible investments to minimize their potential loss. Governmental funds report their own current and long-term financial investments and any accrued interest receivable as assets of the funds.

3. *Income taxes and sales taxes.* These derived tax revenues are recognized as assets under the modified accrual basis of accounting in the period in which the tax is imposed or when the resources are received, whichever comes first. These taxes must be available to finance expenditures made during the current fiscal period before recognition as revenue for the period. Income tax revenue should be reported net of any anticipated refunds to taxpayers. Sales taxes collected by another governmental unit (e.g., the state government) but not yet distributed should be accrued prior to receipt by the governmental unit to which they will be distributed (e.g., a city) if the taxes are both measurable and available for expenditure. Measurability in this case is based on an estimate of the sales taxes to be received, and availability is based on the ability of the governing entity (the city) to obtain current resources through credit by using future sales tax collections as collateral for the loan.

4. *Miscellaneous revenue.* Miscellaneous revenues such as license fees, fines, parking meter revenue, and charges for services are generally recorded when the cash is received because these cannot be predicted accurately. Often states take custody of private property when its legal owner cannot be found, as with unclaimed estates or abandoned bank accounts. The property is said to *escheat* (or revert) to the state government. The government should record the property as revenue at its fair market value less a liability for any anticipated claims from possible heirs or other claimants. States generally record the net revenue in the general fund, but some states prefer to account for these resources in a separate, private-purpose trust fund.

5. *Grants, entitlements, and shared revenue.* These are resources received from other governmental units. *Grants* are contributions from another governmental unit to be used for a specified purpose, activity, or facility. *Entitlements* are payments local governments are entitled to receive as determined by the federal government. *Shared revenue* is levied by one governmental unit but shared with others on some predetermined basis (e.g., revenue from taxes on the retail sale of gasoline collected by the state). Grants are recognized as

revenue in the period in which all eligibility requirements have been met. This may be at the point the grant is authorized, but, in practice, some governmental units wait until the cash is received because the grant may be withdrawn by the grantor. Some grants are made to reimburse a governmental unit for expenditures made in accordance with legal requirements. The revenue from such grants should be recognized only when the expenditure is made and all other eligibility requirements have been met. For example, a state government might agree to provide a grant for a local government's purchase of fire-fighting vehicles. Typically, the local government must meet all the requirements of the grant before it receives the monies from the state government. In these cases, the local government would record the grant revenue at the time it is received. In a few cases, such as a state grant of reimbursement for the purchase of the firefighting vehicles, the local government may receive grant monies before all the steps of the required expenditure are completed. In those few cases, the local government may be required to record the receipt of the grant monies as an unearned revenue (liability) until all the requirements have been met and the grant is expendable—at which time the unearned revenue is reclassified as earned revenue.

Proceeds from the sale of bonds are not revenue! These proceeds are reported as other financing sources on the statement of revenues, expenditures, and changes in fund balance. Although bond sales do increase the resources available for expenditure, bonds must be repaid, whereas revenue of the governmental unit does not need to be repaid.

Recognition of Expenditures

Under the modified accrual basis of accounting, expenditures are recorded in the period in which the related liability is both measurable and incurred. Specific examples are as follows:

1. Costs for personal services, such as wages and salaries, are generally recorded in the period paid because they are normal, recurring expenditures of a governmental unit.
2. Goods and services obtained from outside the governmental entity are recorded as expenditures in the period in which they are received.
3. Capital outlays for equipment, buildings, and other long-term facilities are recorded as expenditures in the period of acquisition.
4. Interest on long-term debt is recorded in the period in which it is legally payable.

Basis of Accounting—Proprietary Funds

The two major proprietary funds are the internal service fund and the enterprise fund. Proprietary funds are established for governmental operations that have a management focus of income determination and capital maintenance; therefore, the accrual method as used by profit–seeking corporate entities is used to account for these funds. Proprietary funds record their own long-term assets, and depreciation is recognized on these assets. Long-term debt is recorded and interest is accrued as it is for commercial operations.

Basis of Accounting—Fiduciary Funds

The accrual basis of accounting is used for all fiduciary funds. Agency funds are for those resources for which the governing unit is the temporary custodian. Agency funds have only assets and liabilities; no fund equity, revenue, or expenditures are used. An example of an agency fund is a county's billing and collecting taxes on behalf of other governmental entities, such as a city and a school district. After collection is completed on the "tax roll," the county properly distributes the taxes in accordance with each governmental entity's approved levy.

For fiduciary trust funds, the economic resources measurement focus and the accrual basis of accounting are used. Note that the fiduciary trust funds include those funds in which both the principal and income may be used for the benefit of specific individuals, organizations, or other governments, in accordance with the terms under which the trust fund was established. Agency and trust funds are discussed in depth in Chapter 13.

BUDGETARY ASPECTS OF GOVERNMENTAL OPERATIONS

LO6

Understand and explain
basic budgeting concepts in
governmental accounting.

Budgets are used in governmental accounting to assist in management control and to provide the legal authority to levy taxes, collect revenue, and make expenditures in accordance with the budget. Budgets establish the objectives and priorities of governing units.

For state governments, budgets are proposed by governors and debated by the legislative bodies. After passage, the budget usually becomes part of the fiscal period's state law. For local governments, the mayor or the major administrator may propose the budget. Public hearings and discussions of the budget are then held by governing boards such as the city council, county board, or township board prior to the adoption of the final budget.

A governmental unit may have several types of budgets, including the following:

1. *Operating budgets.* Operating budgets specify expected revenue from the various sources provided by law. The operating budget includes expected expenditures for various line items, such as payrolls of employees, supplies, and goods and services to be obtained from outside the governing unit. Operating budgets are used in the general fund, special revenue funds, and sometimes the debt service funds.

2. *Capital budgets.* A capital budget is prepared to provide information about proposed construction projects such as new buildings or street projects. Capital budgets are used in the capital projects funds.

Although budgets may be prepared for proprietary funds, these budgets do not serve as a primary control vehicle. Budgets in the proprietary funds are advisory in much the same way budgets are used in commercial entities.

Recording the Operating Budget

Budgets are such an important control vehicle that those governmental funds with legally adopted annual operating budgets should enter their budgets into the formal accounting records, although capital budgets are not normally entered. Recording the operating budgets permits better management control and facilitates a year-end comparison of budgeted and actual amounts. This comparison is part of the required supplementary information for the government reporting model for the funds that must have operating budgets. A budget-to-actual comparison provides an assessment of management's stewardship of the governmental entity and allows citizens and others to determine whether the governmental entity remained within its operating budgetary limits.

To help understand the process of accounting for operating budgets, this text uses the technique illustrated in *Governmental Accounting, Auditing, and Financial Reporting* (GAAFR),[6] in which the budgetary accounts are identified with all capital letters. Capitalization of the budgetary accounts clearly separates the budgetary nominal accounts from the operating accounts of the governmental unit. Although budgetary accounts are not capitalized in actual practice, this convention is helpful in learning the following material.

The recording of the operating budget for the general fund is shown with the following example. Assume that at January 1, 20X1, the first day of the new fiscal period, the city council of Barb City approves the operating budget for the general fund, providing for $900,000 in revenue and $850,000 in expenditures. Approval of the budget provides the legal authority to levy the local property taxes and to appropriate resources for the expenditures. The term *appropriation* is the legal description of the authority to expend resources. The entry made in the general fund's accounting records on this date is as follows:

	January 1, 20X1		
(1)	ESTIMATED REVENUES CONTROL	900,000	
	APPROPRIATIONS CONTROL		850,000
	BUDGETARY FUND BALANCE—UNASSIGNED		50,000
	Record general fund budget for year.		

[6] *Governmental Accounting, Auditing, and Financial Reporting* is updated periodically by the Government Finance Officers Association (Chicago).

Note the word CONTROL used as part of the account titles. In governmental accounting, control accounts often are used in the major journals, with subsidiary accounts recording the detail behind each control account. This method is similar to a commercial entity's using a control account for its accounts receivable and then using subsidiary ledgers for the specific customer transactions. Throughout this chapter, the control account level is illustrated to focus on the major issues. In practice, detailed accounting is maintained for each separate classification of revenue and appropriation, either in the major journal or in a subsidiary ledger. The AICPA uses both control-level accounts and budgetary accounts on the Uniform CPA Examination, although it does not capitalize the letters of the budgetary accounts used in the exam.

The ESTIMATED REVENUES CONTROL account is an *anticipatory asset;* that is, the governmental unit anticipates receiving resources from the revenue sources listed in the budget. The APPROPRIATIONS CONTROL account is an *anticipatory liability;* that is, the governmental unit anticipates incurring expenditures and liabilities for the budgeted amount. The excess of estimated revenues over anticipated expenditures is the budget surplus and is recorded to BUDGETARY FUND BALANCE—UNASSIGNED. Some approved budgets have budget deficits in which expected expenditures exceed anticipated revenue. These budgets are recorded with a debit to BUDGETARY FUND BALANCE—UNASSIGNED.

Recording the budget in the governmental entity's books makes the budget a formal accounting control mechanism for the fiscal period. In addition, having the budget in the accounting records provides the necessary information for the budgetary comparison schedules that are part of the required supplementary information (RSI) footnotes required by the government reporting model in **GASB 34.** At the end of the year, after the appropriate financial statements have been prepared, all the budgetary accounts are closed.

ACCOUNTING FOR EXPENDITURES

LO7

Make calculations and record journal entries for the general fund.

Advanced
StudyGuide
.com

The governmental funds use a variety of controls over expenditures to ensure that each expenditure is made in accordance with any legal restrictions on the fund.

The Expenditure Process

The expenditure process in governmental accounting comprises the following sequential steps: appropriation, encumbrance, expenditure, and disbursement.

Step 1. Appropriation

The budget provides the appropriating authority to make future expenditures. Operating budgets are prepared for the general, special revenue, and often the debt service funds. The capital projects fund prepares capital budgets.

The appropriation was recorded in the budget entry made previously in entry (1) for the general fund of Barb City. Recall that a total of $850,000 in anticipated expenditures was approved in the budget.

Step 2. Encumbrance

An **encumbrance** is a reservation of part of the budgetary appropriation and is recognized at the time an order is placed for goods or services. Encumbrances are a unique element of governmental accounting. Their purpose is to ensure that the expenditures within a period do not exceed the budgeted appropriations. The appropriation level was established by the approved budget and sets the legal maximum that may be expended for each budgeted item. The managers of the governmental unit must be sure that they do not exceed this budgetary authority. Thus, encumbrances provide a control system and safeguard for governmental unit administrators.

When an order is placed for goods or services to be received from outside the governmental unit, the budgeted appropriation is encumbered for the estimated cost of the order.

Encumbrances are of greatest use when an order is placed and a period of time expires before delivery. Payroll costs, immaterial costs, and costs for goods acquired from within the governmental entity typically are not encumbered because these are normal and recurring and the managers of the governmental unit are able to predict these costs based on past experiences and other administrative controls, such as employment agreements.

A sensible approach should be used with an encumbrance system. For example, it is not necessary to establish an individual encumbrance when an employee orders a pad of paper. Rather, a blanket purchase order with a maximum dollar amount, for example, a total of $500, should be prepared and encumbered, and then it can serve as the control for small, routine supply purchases. Encumbrances provide the unit administrators an important accounting control to fulfill their responsibilities to manage within an approved budget.

To illustrate encumbrance accounting, assume that on August 1, 20X1, Barb City completed a purchase order (PO) from an outside vendor for goods that are estimated to cost $15,000. The entry to record this application of part of the budgeted appropriation authority for the period is as follows:

	August 1, 20X1		
(2)	ENCUMBRANCES	15,000	
	BUDGETARY FUND BALANCE—ASSIGNED FOR ENCUMBRANCES		15,000

Record order for goods estimated to cost $15,000.

Note that the ENCUMBRANCES account is a budgetary account that is reserving part of the appropriation authority of the budget. For detailed accounting, governmental entities often maintain a subsidiary ledger including accounts for specific types of encumbrances to correspond to each specific type of appropriation. For purposes of this illustration, the single title ENCUMBRANCES is used to indicate a control-level account to focus attention on the major aspects of governmental accounting. In practice, very detailed account titles and classification numbers are used to fully account for each type of transaction. It is important to note that the BUDGETARY FUND BALANCE—ASSIGNED FOR ENCUMBRANCES is a *reservation (or restriction) of the budgetary fund balance,* not an actual liability.

Step 3. Expenditure

An expenditure and a corresponding liability are recorded when the governmental entity receives the goods or services ordered in step 2. When the goods are received, the encumbrance entry is reversed for the amount encumbered and the expenditure is recorded for the actual cost to the governmental entity. Although the actual cost is typically very close to the encumbered amount, some differences may exist because of partially completed orders, less expensive replacements, or unforeseen costs. Assume that the goods are received on September 20, 20X1, at an actual cost of $14,000. The entries to reverse the encumbrance for the goods and to record the actual expenditures are as follows:

	September 20, 20X1		
(3)	BUDGETARY FUND BALANCE—ASSIGNED FOR ENCUMBRANCES	15,000	
	ENCUMBRANCES		15,000

Reverse encumbrances for goods received.

(4)	Expenditures	14,000	
	Vouchers Payable		14,000

Receive goods at cost of $14,000.

At any time, the remaining appropriating authority available to the fund managers can be determined by the following equation:

$$\text{Appropriating authority remaining available} = \text{APPROPRIATIONS} - (\text{ENCUMBRANCES} + \text{Expenditures})$$

Step 4. Disbursement

A *disbursement* is the payment of cash for expenditures. Disbursements usually must be approved by the governing board or council as an additional level of control over expenditures.

Virtually all governmental entities use a comprehensive voucher system to control cash outflows. The governing board receives a schedule of vouchers to be approved for payment by vote of the board. This is usually one of the early agenda items in any board or council meeting as a vote is taken to "pay all bills." Checks are then written and delivered to the supplier of the goods. If the Barb City council approved the voucher at its October 8 meeting and a check was prepared in the amount of $14,000 and mailed on October 15, 20X1, the following entry records the disbursement:

	October 15, 20X1		
(5)	Vouchers Payable	14,000	
	Cash		14,000
	Payment of voucher for goods received.		

Classification of Expenditure Transactions and Accounts

Governmental accounting places many controls over expenditures, and much of the financial reporting focuses on the various aspects of an expenditure. Expenditures should be classified by fund, character, function (or program), organizational unit, activity, and principal classes of objects. Figure 12–3 describes the major expenditure classifications.

Many governmental units have a comprehensive chart of accounts with specific coding digits that provide the basis for classifying each expenditure. For example, an expenditure journal entry might specify the expenditure account to be charged as number 421.23-110. The chart of accounts shows that the 421.23 account is for public safety: police—crime control and investigation—patrol, as follows:

420. Public safety
    421. Police
        421.2 Crime control and investigation
        421.23 Patrol

The -110 suffix indicates that this expenditure is for personal services in the form of salaries and wages for regular employees. It is not unusual for some accounting systems to have 11- to 14-digit accounts classifying each individual transaction. The level of specificity in the chart of accounts depends on the particular governing entity's information needs. Classifying information with such specificity allows the governing entity to maintain complete database control over the expenditure information, which it can use at any time in aggregate or relational analysis. For the examples in this chapter, only the expenditure control level is presented; in practice, a complete specification of the expenditure is made.

Outstanding Encumbrances at the End of the Fiscal Period

In the previous Barb City example, the goods were received within the same fiscal period in which they were ordered. What happens if the goods are ordered in one fiscal year and received in the next year? In this case, the encumbrance is not reversed before the end of the fiscal period.

Accounting for these outstanding encumbrances depends on the governmental unit's policy. The government may allow outstanding encumbrances to lapse; that is, the governmental unit is not required to honor these encumbrances carried over to the new year, and the new year's budget must rebudget them. In virtually all cases, the encumbrances will be rebudgeted and honored; however, this policy specifically recognizes the legal authority of the new governing board to determine its own expenditures. A second method is to carry over the encumbrances as nonlapsing spending authority. This method

Advanced
StudyGuide
.com

FIGURE 12–3
Major Expenditure Classifications for Governmental Funds

Classification	Description
Fund	The fund is identified to show the specific source of the expenditure. For example, the general fund would be noted for expenditures from that fund.
Character	Character classifications are based primarily on the period the expenditures are anticipated to benefit. Four major character classifications are current, capital outlay, debt service, and intergovernmental.
Function (or program)	Functions are group-related activities directed at accomplishing a major service or regulatory responsibility. Standard classifications of function include general governmental; public safety; highway and streets; sanitation; health and welfare; culture and recreation; and education.
Organizational unit	Classifying by organizational unit maintains accountability by each unit director. The organizational unit is determined by the governmental unit's organization chart. For example, public safety could be broken down into police, fire, corrections, protective inspection (such as plumbing and electrical code inspections), and other protection (such as flood control, traffic engineering, and examination of licensed occupations).
Activity	Activities within a function are recorded to maintain a record of the efficiency of each activity. For example, the police function could be broken down into the following activities: police administration, crime control and investigation, traffic control, police training, support service (such as communication services and ambulance services), special detail services, and police station and building maintenance. Each of these activities could be broken down further, if desired.
Object class	Object class is a grouping of types of items purchased or services obtained. For example, operating expenditures include personal services, purchased and contractual services, and commodities. Each of these objects could be further broken down, depending on the information needs of the governing entity. For example, purchased services could include utility services, cleaning services (such as custodial, lawn care, and snow plowing), repair and maintenance services, rentals, construction services, and other purchased services, such as insurance or printing.

recognizes the practical aspects of encumbrances outstanding at the end of a fiscal period. Either method may be used in governmental accounting.

To illustrate the differences between the lapsing and nonlapsing methods of accounting for encumbrances, assume the following:

1. On August 1, 20X1, $15,000 of goods are ordered and an appropriate entry is made to record the encumbrance.
2. The goods have not been received on December 31, 20X1, the end of the fiscal period.
3. The goods are received on February 1, 20X2, at an actual cost of $14,000.

Figure 12–4 presents a comparison of the journal entries that would be required under each of the two methods of accounting for unfilled encumbrances at year-end.

Outstanding Encumbrances Lapse at Year-End

The closing entries on December 31, 20X1, close the remaining budgetary encumbrances and establish a reserve of the actual fund balance on the December 31, 20X1, balance sheet. Although the GAAFR recommends that a reserve for lapsing encumbrances be reported on the balance sheet, the GASB's codification allows the alternative of only footnote disclosure of lapsing orders at year-end that are expected to be honored in the next fiscal period. If only footnote disclosure is used, the governmental entity would have

FIGURE 12–4   **Comparison of Accounting for Lapsing and Nonlapsing Encumbrances at Year-End**

Item	Outstanding Encumbrances Lapse at Year-End	Outstanding Encumbrances Nonlapsing at Year-End
December 31, 20X1		

Close remaining budgetary encumbrances	BUDGETARY FUND BALANCE—
	ASSIGNED FOR
	  ENCUMBRANCES 15,000
	    ENCUMBRANCES 15,000
		BUDGETARY FUND BALANCE—
		ASSIGNED FOR
		  ENCUMBRANCES 15,000
		    ENCUMBRANCES 15,000

Reserve actual fund balance for outstanding encumbrances at end of 20X1 expected to be honored in 20X2	Fund Balance—Unassigned 15,000
	  Fund Balance—Assigned for
	    Encumbrances 15,000
		Fund Balance—Unassigned 15,000
		  Fund Balance—Assigned for
		    Encumbrances 15,000

January 1, 20X2		

Reverse prior year encumbrance reserve	Fund Balance—Assigned for
	  Encumbrances 15,000
	    Fund Balance—Unassigned 15,000	

Establish budgetary control over encumbrances renewed from prior period	ENCUMBRANCES 15,000
	  BUDGETARY FUND
	    BALANCE—ASSIGNED
	    FOR ENCUMBRANCES 15,000	

Reclassify reserve from prior year		Fund Balance—Assigned for
		  Encumbrances 15,000
		    Fund Balance—Assigned
		      for Encumbrances—20X1 15,000

February 1, 20X2		

Receive goods and remove budgetary reserve for encumbrances	BUDGETARY FUND BALANCE—
	ASSIGNED FOR
	  ENCUMBRANCES 15,000
	    ENCUMBRANCES 15,000	

Record actual expenditure for goods received	Expenditures 14,000
	  Vouchers Payable 14,000
		Expenditures—20X1 14,000
		  Vouchers Payable 14,000

December 31, 20X2		

Close expenditures account	Fund Balance—Unassigned 14,000
	  Expenditures 14,000
		Fund Balance—Assigned for
		  Encumbrances—20X1 15,000
		    Expenditures—20X1 14,000
		    Fund Balance—Unassigned 1,000

only the first closing entry on December 31, 20X1, to close out the budgetary accounts related to the encumbrance. No balance sheet reserve is established if the footnote disclosure alternative is used.

Normal procedure for many governmental entities is for the next year's governing board to meet after elections or appointments for the next year take place. This meeting is generally held shortly before the beginning of the next fiscal year so that the budget is effective beginning on January 1 of the next year. Thus, the incoming governing board will typically make a decision during the budget process as to whether or not year-end outstanding encumbrances will be honored in the next fiscal period. If the new governing board decides not to honor the 20X1 year-end outstanding encumbrances, then only the closing entry to close the remaining budgetary encumbrances would be made on December 31, 20X1. If the governmental entity uses the footnote disclosure alternative, no footnote disclosure in the 20X1 financial statements would be made for those outstanding encumbrances not expected to be renewed in the next fiscal year.

If the new governing board decides to honor the outstanding encumbrances from 20X1, then the outstanding encumbrances must be included in the 20X2 budgeted appropriations. An entry is made as of January 1, 20X2, to establish budgetary control over the expected expenditure. A "fresh start," new spending authority is established, and the sequence of entries continues as if this is a new purchase order effective for 20X2.

In the unusual case that the new governing board makes a decision as of January 1, 20X2, not to honor the outstanding encumbrances, and the December 31, 20X1, entry had already been recorded, then the following entry would be made as of January 1, 20X2, to record the cancellation of the outstanding encumbrance from 20X1:

		January 1, 20X2		
(6)		Fund Balance—Assigned for Encumbrances	15,000	
		Fund Balance—Unassigned		15,000

Eliminate reserve for outstanding encumbrances not being renewed.

If the January 1, 20X2, entries had already been made, and the governing board later decides not to honor the outstanding encumbrance from 20X1, reversing entries would be made to eliminate the actual fund balance reserve and the budgetary fund balance reserve that had been created on January 1, 20X2. If the governmental entity used only footnote disclosure in its 20X1 financial statements for the year-end outstanding encumbrances expected to be honored, then only a reversing entry would be required to reverse the January 1, 20X2, entry that had established the budgetary encumbrances and budgetary fund balance reserve. The governmental entity then simply cancels the order with the external vendor.

Outstanding Encumbrances Are Nonlapsing at Year-End

Some governing entities carry over the prior year appropriations authority as nonlapsing encumbrances. In this case, the budget for the second fiscal period does not show these carryovers because they arose from the appropriations authority of the prior year. The nonlapsing encumbrances are dated for the prior year to indicate they arose from that year's appropriating authority. Some governmental accountants believe this method is realistic for many situations in which orders placed with outside vendors cannot easily be canceled.

The 20X1 year-end closing entries presented in Figure 12–4 show the required reservation of the actual fund balance. Note that these are the same two entries made under the lapsing method with balance sheet recognition of the reserve of the fund balance. The differences between the two methods become apparent during the second fiscal period. Under the nonlapsing method, it is important to identify separately expenditures made from spending authority carried over from prior periods. Typically this is done in a reclassification entry on the first day of the second fiscal period, which dates the Fund Balance—Assigned for Encumbrances. No budgetary entry is made in the second year because the appropriation authority comes from the first year's budget. When the goods are received, the expenditures account is also dated to indicate that the expenditure authority emanated from 20X1.

At the end of 20X2, the Expenditures—20X1 account is closed directly to the Fund Balance—Assigned for Encumbrances—20X1. Note that the $1,000 difference between the actual $14,000 cost and the $15,000 assigned amount is closed to Fund Balance—Unassigned because the actual cost is less than the amount encumbered from the prior year's appropriation authority. If the actual cost is more than the reserve, the difference must be approved as part of the appropriation authority for 20X2.

Key Observations from the Illustrations

As a practical matter, almost all outstanding encumbrances at year-end are honored and completed in the next fiscal period. The method of accounting for open encumbrances at year-end is based on the governmental unit's budgetary policy, which may be affected by legal statutes controlling carryover of appropriating ability from one fiscal period to the next. Both methods are used in practice. It is important to note that, in this example, the 20X1 statement of revenues, expenditures, and changes in fund balance will report no expenditures relating to this item. In 20X2, $14,000 of expenditures will be recognized. Under the nonlapsing method, expenditures made in 20X2 but carried over from 20X1 encumbrances are dated to note they arose from 20X1's appropriations. The comprehensive illustration presented later in this chapter uses the lapsing method because of its widespread use.

Reporting of Encumbrances under the New Standard on Fund Balance Reporting

GASB 54 does not report any reserves of fund balance on the balance sheet. Rather, the amount of encumbrances is included as part of the spendable fund balance, usually in the assigned category. Only footnote disclosure is now used to report the aggregate amount of encumbrances, along with the required disclosures about other significant commitments. Since governments will continue to use encumbrance accounting because of the control and management information an encumbrance system provides, we continue to show encumbrance accounting even though encumbrances are no longer reported in the balance sheet. **GASB 54** does not restrict the accounting systems used by governments.

Expenditures for Inventory

Most governmental units maintain a small amount of inventory in office supplies. A first issue is to determine which of two methods should be followed to account for the expenditure of inventories. The first method recognizes the entire expenditure for inventory in the period the supplies are acquired. This is called the *purchase* method. The second method is the *consumption* method; it recognizes expenditures for only the amount of inventory used in the period. The specific method to follow depends on the governing unit's policy and how inventory expenditures are included in the budget.

A second issue is whether to show inventory as an asset on the balance sheet of the governmental funds. Inventory is not an expendable asset; that is, it may not be spent as the governing entity wishes. **NCGA 1** states that inventory should be shown on the balance sheets for governmental funds if the amount of inventory is material. Immaterial inventories need not be shown on the balance sheet. If the inventory is material, it is presented as an asset on the balance sheet; an amount equal to the inventory also should be shown as a reservation of the fund balance, indicating that that amount is no longer expendable.

Figure 12–5 presents the entries to account for inventories under both the purchase method and the consumption method. The illustration assumes that Barb City acquires $2,000 of inventory on November 1, 20X1, having held no inventory previously. On December 31, 20X1, the end of Barb City's fiscal year, a physical count shows $1,400 still in stock. During 20X2, $900 of this inventory is used, resulting in a $500 remaining balance of supplies on December 31, 20X2.

Purchase Method of Accounting for Inventories

Under the purchase method, the entire amount of inventory acquired is charged to Expenditures in the period acquired. On December 31, 20X1, the end of the fiscal year, an adjusting entry is made to recognize the $1,400 remaining inventory as an asset and to restrict the fund balance for the nonexpendable portion applicable to inventories.

The expenditure of $2,000 is closed into Fund Balance—Unassigned for 20X1 in a closing entry made at the end of the fiscal year. The December 31, 20X1, balance sheet includes the inventory of supplies as an asset in the amount of $1,400, and Fund Balance—Assigned for Inventories is shown as a fund balance reserve for $1,400. The 20X1 operating statement shows a $2,000 expenditure for supplies.

FIGURE 12–5 Comparison of Accounting for Inventories—Purchase versus Consumption Method

Item	Purchase Method of Accounting		Consumption Method of Accounting	
November 1, 20X1				
Record acquisition of $2,000 of inventory.	Expenditures Vouchers Payable	2,000 2,000	Expenditures Vouchers Payable	2,000 2,000
December 31, 20X1				
Recognize ending inventory of $1,400.	Inventory of Supplies Fund Balance— Nonspendable	1,400 1,400	Inventory of Supplies Expenditures	1,400 1,400
			Fund Balance—Unassigned Fund Balance—Nonspendable	1,400 1,400
December 31, 20X2				
Record remaining inventory of $500, with $900 of supplies having been consumed during 20X2.	Fund Balance—Nonspendable Inventory of Supplies	900 900	Expenditures Inventory of Supplies	900 900
			Fund Balance—Nonspendable Fund Balance—Unassigned	900 900

At the end of 20X2, an adjusting entry is made to recognize the use of the $900 of supplies of the $1,400 remaining from the 20X1 purchase. This entry reduces the reservation of the fund balance and decreases inventory. At the end of 20X2, Inventory of Supplies is $500, and Fund Balance—Assigned for Inventories is $500, for the remaining unused supplies.

In summary, the $2,000 expenditure is recognized in the period in which the supplies are purchased. No expenditures are recognized in subsequent periods although some of the supplies are used in those periods.

Consumption Method of Accounting for Inventories

Under the consumption method, expenditures for a period are reported only for the amount consumed. In this case, the budget for the period should be based on the expected amount of use so that the budgeted and actual amounts compared at the end of the year are on the same basis.

A net expenditure of $600 ($2,000 − $1,400) for supplies used is reported in 20X1, the year the supplies were acquired. With $500 of inventory remaining at the end of 20X2, an expenditure of $900 is reported in the 20X2 operating statement to show the amount of supplies consumed during 20X2. The consumption method relates the expenditures with the use of the inventory.

A comparison of selected account balances under the purchase method and consumption method shows the different amounts reported under these two methods:

	Purchase Method	Consumption Method
20X1:		
Expenditures	$2,000	$ 600
Inventory of Supplies	1,400	1,400
20X2:		
Expenditures	–0–	900
Inventory of Supplies	500	500

Note that the choice of methods has no effect on the balance sheet amounts; the only effect is on the period in which the expenditures for inventory are reported.

Both inventory methods are used in practice. The method used by a specific governmental unit depends on its budgeting policy. If the governmental unit includes all inventory acquisitions in its appropriations for the period, the purchase method should be used. If the governmental unit includes only the expected amount of inventory to be used during a period in that period's appropriations, the consumption method should be used.

Reporting of Inventory under the New Standard on Fund Balance Reporting

Inventories, if they are material in amount, are reported as an asset on the balance sheet. Under the proposed standard, reserves of fund balance are not reported on the face of the balance sheet. But the fund balance associated with inventories is reported in the non-spendable fund balance category.

Accounting for Fixed Assets

Governmental entities may acquire equipment that has an economic life of more than one year. Accounting for this acquisition depends on which fund expends the resources for the acquisition. The governmental funds are concerned with the expendability and control over available resources and account for the acquisitions of equipment as expenditures. In the governmental funds, the entire amount of the cost of the acquisition of equipment and other capital assets is recognized as an expenditure in the year the asset is acquired. No capital assets are recorded in the general fund; they are treated as expenditures of the period.

The proprietary funds are concerned with capital maintenance and account for acquisitions of capital assets in the same manner as commercial entities. Thus, the accounting for the purchase of a capital asset differs in the five governmental funds from the accounting used in the proprietary funds.

For example, assume that Barb City acquires a truck. The acquisition is made from the resources of, and is accounted for in, the general fund. The encumbrance is $12,000, but the actual cost is $12,500 because of minor modifications required by the city.

The general fund makes the following entries to account for the acquisition of the truck:

(7)	ENCUMBRANCES	12,000	
	BUDGETARY FUND BALANCE—ASSIGNED FOR ENCUMBRANCES		12,000

Order truck at estimated cost of $12,000.

(8)	BUDGETARY FUND BALANCE—ASSIGNED FOR ENCUMBRANCES	12,000	
	ENCUMBRANCES		12,000

Cancel reserve for truck received.

(9)	Expenditures	12,500	
	Vouchers Payable		12,500

Receive truck at actual cost of $12,500.

The truck is not recorded as an asset in the general fund; it is an expenditure in this fund. Sales of capital assets are recorded as a debit to Cash (or receivable) and a credit to Other Financing Sources—Sales of General Capital Assets for the amount received from the sale. If the amount from the sale is immaterial, the government entity may elect to record the credit to other revenues. A schedule of the acquisition or sale of capital assets by any governmental fund should be maintained, but that record is only for the government-wide financial statements, which do report the assets of a government unit.

Works of Art and Historical Treasures

For the purposes of government-wide financial statements, governments should capitalize works of art, historical treasures, and similar types of assets at their historical costs at acquisition or at their fair values at the date of the contribution. For example, if the general fund expended $10,000 for a work of art, it reports an expenditure for that amount. However, when preparing the government-wide financial statements, the cost of the work of art is reported as an asset of the government. If the assets are donated, contribution revenue is recognized in the government-wide financial statements.

The GASB provided practical guidance to the general rule of capitalizing works of art and historical treasures. For example, many collections have a very large number of items collected over long periods of time, and it is virtually impossible to determine the cost or fair value at the times of acquisition. A provision in **GASB 34** states that the government is not required but is still encouraged to capitalize a collection of art or historical treasures if the government meets all three of the following provisions: (1) holds the collection for public exhibition, education, or research; (2) protects and preserves the collection; and (3) has an organizational policy that requires the proceeds from sales of collection items to be used to acquire other items for collections. If contributed items are not capitalized, the government-wide financial statements report both a program expense and a contribution revenue for the fair market value of the item at the time of its donation.

Capitalized collections that are exhaustible, such as displays of works whose useful lives are reduced due to display, or used for education or research, should be depreciated over their estimated useful lives. Collections or individual items whose lives are inexhaustible are not depreciated.

Long-Term Debt and Capital Leases

Commercial, profit-seeking businesses recognize long-term debt and capital leases as noncurrent liabilities. The debt or capital lease is entered into to earn income, and the liability is recognized under the flow of economic resources measurement focus model. However, accounting for long-term liabilities in governmental funds is directly affected by the flow of current financial resources measurement focus model.

The governmental funds, which include the general fund, record the proceeds from a bond issue as a debit to Cash and a credit to Bond Issue Proceeds, an other-financing source. Bond issue proceeds are not revenue because the bonds must be repaid. Other financing sources are shown in the middle section of the statement of revenues, expenditures, and other changes in fund balances. Bonds are not reported on the governmental funds' balance sheets but only on the government-wide financial statements.

Capital leases are accounted for in a manner similar to long-term debt. If a proprietary fund (e.g., internal service or enterprise fund) enters into a capital lease, the lease is accounted for using methods similar to those used by commercial, profit-seeking entities, with the recording of an asset and a lease liability. However, if a governmental fund (e.g., general fund) enters into a capital lease, the capital lease is accounted for in a manner similar to a bond's accounting.

Investments

Some governmental entities maintain investments in stock or bond securities. The purpose of these investments typically is to obtain an investment return on available resources. **GASB Statement No. 31,** "Accounting and Financial Reporting for Certain Investments and for External Investment Pools" (GASB 31), established a general rule of fair market valuation for investments held by a government entity. The following investments are to be valued at fair value, if determinable, in the asset section of the balance sheet for the governmental entity: (1) investments in debt securities; (2) investments in equity securities (other than those accounted for under the equity method as provided for in **APB 18**),[7] including option contracts, stock warrants, and stock rights; (3) investments in open-end mutual funds; (4) investment pools in which a governmental entity combines with other investors; and (5) interest-earning investment contracts in which the value is affected by market (interest rate) changes. **GASB Statement No. 52,** "Land and Other Real Estate Held as Investments by Endowments" (GASB 52), extended the general rule of using fair value to real estate investments by endowments. The periodic changes in the fair value of all the types of investments included in **GASB 31** and **GASB 52** should be

---

[7] *APB Opinion No. 18* (ASC 325), "The Equity Method of Accounting for Investments in Common Stock," March 1971.

recognized as an element of investment income in the operating statement (or statement of activities) of each fund making the investment. In the case of an internal investment pool that combines the resources of several of the governmental entity's funds, for financial reporting purposes the pool's assets and its income are allocated to each individual fund based on its percentage of the total invested.

Many state and local governments have deposits and make investments that are open to a variety of risks. **GASB Statement No. 40,** "Deposit and Investment Risk Disclosures" (GASB 40), established detailed note disclosure requirements related to the following types of investment risks: credit risk (including concentrations of credit risk), interest rate risk, and foreign currency risk, as well as for deposit risks of custodial credit risk and foreign currency risk. The main objective of **GASB 40** is to require footnote disclosures of the policies and the profiles of the government's investment portfolios, such as the credit quality ratings debt securities and other fixed-income securities, and the terms of investments whose fair value is highly sensitive to changes in the interest rate.

INTERFUND ACTIVITIES

LO8

Make calculations and record journal entries for basic interfund activities.

Advanced
StudyGuide
.com

A basic concept in governmental accounting is that each fund is a separate entity and has separate sources of resources, sometimes including the power to levy and collect taxes. The revenues of each fund must then be expended in accordance with the budget and restrictions established by law. Because a single governmental entity has a number of separate funds, it sometimes becomes necessary to transfer resources from one fund to another. *Interfund activities* are resource flows between fund entities. In a consolidated financial statement for a commercial entity, intercompany transactions are eliminated to report only the effect of transactions with external entities. Governmental accounting, on the other hand, requires the separate maintenance and reporting of interfund items. The governing body must approve any interfund transfers and transactions to provide a public record and to prevent distortion of fund uses. Many governmental entities include interfund activities anticipated during a fiscal year in the operating budgets for the year. Budgetary entries for interfund activities are illustrated in the comprehensive example of Sol City presented later in this chapter. Interfund transfers must be accounted for carefully to ensure that the legal and budgetary restrictions are followed and that resources intended for one fund are not used in another.

GASB 34 establishes four types of interfund activities, as follows: (1) interfund loans, (2) interfund services provided and used, (3) interfund transfers, and (4) interfund reimbursements. A discussion of the four interfund items follows; they are illustrated in Figure 12–6.

(1) Interfund Loans

State law may allow lending or borrowing activities between funds. The loans must be repaid, usually within one year or before the end of the fiscal period. Loans and advances are not shown on a fund's statement of revenues, expenditures, and changes in fund balance; however, all outstanding loans or advances must be shown on the balance sheet as payables or receivables. Interest usually is not charged on interfund financing arrangements. If interest is charged, it is accounted for in the funds in the same manner as for other interest income or expense.

Some governmental entities distinguish between short-term and long-term financing arrangements by using the term "Advances to (or from)" to denote a long-term agreement and "Due to (or from)" for a short-term agreement.

The illustration of an interfund financing transaction in Figure 12–6 assumes that Barb City's general fund loans the internal service fund $4,000 for two months. The general fund reports a receivable for the amount of the loan until the loan is repaid.

FIGURE 12–6   Interfund Transactions and Transfers

Item	Entry in General Fund	Entry in Other Fund
		INTERNAL SERVICE FUND:

1. Interfund loan	Due from Internal Service Fund 4,000
	   Cash 4,000
		Cash 4,000
		   Due to General Fund 4,000

	Cash 4,000
	   Due from Internal Service
	   Fund 4,000
		Due to General Fund 4,000
		   Cash 4,000

		INTERNAL SERVICE FUND:

2. Interfund service provided and used	Expenditures 100
	   Due to Internal Service Fund 100
		Due from General Fund 100
		   Charge for Services 100

	Due to Internal Service Fund 100
	   Cash 100
		Cash 100
		   Due from General Fund 100

		CAPITAL PROJECTS FUND:

3. Interfund transfer	Other Financing Uses—Transfer
	  Out to Capital Projects Fund 10,000
	   Cash 10,000
		Cash 10,000
		   Other Financing Sources—
		   Transfer In from General
		   Fund 10,000

		CAPITAL PROJECTS FUND:

4. Interfund reimbursement	Cash 3,000
	   Expenditures 3,000
		Expenditures 3,000
		   Cash 3,000

(2) Interfund Services Provided and Used

These interfund activities are transactions that would be treated as revenue, expenditures, or expenses if they involved parties external to the governmental unit. These interfund activities are still reported as revenue, expenditures, or expenses but are different because they are entirely within the governmental unit. These interfund activities are often normal and recurring items, usually involving at least one proprietary fund. Three examples are as follows:

1. The general fund purchases goods or services from an internal service or enterprise fund.
2. Payments are made to the general fund from the enterprise fund for fire and police protection.
3. A transfer of resources from the general fund to the pension trust fund is made to pay for the city's cost of pension benefits for its employees. This is a cost associated with employee services provided to the city and is therefore an expenditure of the general fund.

Usually these transfers involve the recognition of a receivable or payable because of the time lag between the purchase of the services and the disbursement of funds. A "Due to (or from)" account is used for short-term interfund receivables and payables rather than a formal Vouchers Payable account.

The illustration of this type of interfund activity in Figure 12–6 assumes that Barb City's general fund uses an auto from the city motor pool. The motor pool operates as an internal service fund. The general fund is billed $100 based on mileage and pays the bill 30 days later.

(3) Interfund Transfers

The general fund often transfers resources into another fund to be used by the receiving fund for its own operations; occasionally, the general fund receives resources from other funds. These interfund transfers are not expected to be repaid. Such transfers are not fund revenues or expenditures but are instead called "interfund transfers." These transfers are classified under "Other Financing Sources or Uses" in the operating financial statements of the funds. The reason that the receiving fund does not recognize these transfers as revenue is that the issuing fund has already properly recognized these resources as revenue. Thus, the recording of these transfers as other financing sources eliminates the possibility of double counting the same resources as revenue in two different funds of the combined governmental entity. Examples include the following:

1. A transfer of resources, such as cash or other assets, is made from the general fund to an enterprise fund or internal service fund that has an operating deficit that must be eliminated.

2. A transfer of resources from the general fund to a capital projects fund is made to help finance new construction.

3. A transfer of resources from the general fund to the debt service fund is made to pay principal and interest.

The illustration of an interfund transfer in Figure 12–6 assumes that the general fund of Barb City agrees to provide $10,000 to the capital projects fund toward the construction of a new library. The Transfer Out account in the general fund is closed to its Unassigned Fund Balance at the end of the fiscal period. The capital projects fund also closes its Transfer In account at the end of the fiscal period to its Unassigned Fund Balance. These interfund transfers are not expected to be repaid.

(4) Interfund Reimbursements

A reimbursement transaction is for the reimbursement of a fund's expenditure or expense that was initially made from the fund but that is properly chargeable to another fund. These initial payments are sometimes made either because of improper classification to the wrong fund or for expediency within the governmental entity. The reimbursement from one fund to another is recorded as a reduction of the expenditure in the fund initially recording the expenditure and a recording of the expenditure in the proper fund for the appropriate amount. Two examples are as follows:

1. An expenditure properly chargeable to the special revenue fund is initially recorded and paid by the general fund, and the general fund subsequently is reimbursed by the special revenue fund.

2. The general fund records and pays for an expenditure to provide preliminary architectural work on the planning for a new sports arena. The sports arena enterprise fund later reimburses the general fund.

The illustration of an interfund reimbursement in Figure 12–6 assumes that the general fund of Barb City recorded a $3,000 expenditure for a bill from outside consultants that is later discovered to be properly chargeable to the capital projects fund. Upon notification, the capital projects fund reimbursed the general fund and properly recorded the expenditure in its fund.

OVERVIEW OF ACCOUNTING AND FINANCIAL REPORTING FOR THE GENERAL FUND

Figure 12–7 presents an overview of the accounting for the general fund, including accounting for the interfund activities on the general fund's operating statement, the statement of revenues, expenditures, and changes in fund balance. Note that the interfund loans are reported only on the fund's balance sheet.

The illustration uses the financial reporting requirements under **GASB 34.** The highlights of the proposed statement for fund balance reporting are covered in the additional

FIGURE 12–7
Overview of General Fund

Item	Description
Measurement focus	Flow of current financial resources—expendability.
Accounting basis	Modified accrual.
Budgetary basis	Operating budget.
Financial statements	1. Balance sheet.
	2. Statement of revenues, expenditures, and changes in fund balance.
Balance Sheet	
Current assets	Includes current financial resources such as cash, certificates of deposit, accrued property taxes receivable, and estimated allowance for uncollectible taxes. Interfund loans receivable are included as assets. Material inventories reported.
Long-term productive assets (buildings, etc.)	Fixed assets not reported in general fund.
Current liabilities	Vouchers payable is primary current liability. Interfund loans payable also included as liabilities.
Long-term debt	Governmental unit long-term debt not reported in general fund.
Fund balance	Unassigned fund balance and reservations of fund balance (e.g., encumbrances and inventories).
Statement of Revenues, Expenditures, and Changes in Fund Balance	
Revenue	Recorded when measurable and available under the modified accrual basis of accounting. Interfund services provided and used also included in revenues (or expenditures).
Expenditures	Recognized in period when measurable and fund liability arises.
Other financing sources and uses	Includes bond issue proceeds and interfund transfers.
Changes in fund balance	Reconciles changes in fund balance during period, including changes in reservations of fund balance.

considerations section of this chapter. Chapter 13 presents an example of the fund balance reporting for the governmental fund types under the proposed statement.

COMPREHENSIVE ILLUSTRATION OF ACCOUNTING FOR THE GENERAL FUND

The following example illustrates the accounting for the general fund of Sol City for the January 1, 20X2, to December 31, 20X2, fiscal year. The entries are presented by topic, not necessarily in chronological order. The balance sheet for the general fund as of December 31, 20X1, presented in Figure 12–8, represents the opening balances for fiscal 20X2.

Adoption of the Budget

The city council adopts the budget for fiscal 20X2 as presented in Figure 12–9. Charles Alt, an alderman of Sol City, voted in favor of adopting the budget. The budget summarizes the four major functions of the city: general government, streets and highways, public safety (fire and police), and sanitation. In the complete budget used by the city council, the expenditures in each of the four functions are broken down into the following categories: personal services, supplies, other services and charges, and capital outlay. The public safety budget includes a budgeted capital outlay of $50,000 for a new fire truck.

FIGURE 12–8
General Fund Balance Sheet at the Beginning of 20X2

SOL CITY General Fund Balance Sheet December 31, 20X1		
Assets:		
Cash		$ 50,000
Property Taxes Receivable—Delinquent	$100,000	
Less: Allowance for Uncollectibles—Delinquent	(5,000)	95,000
Inventory of Supplies		14,000
Total Assets		$159,000
Liabilities and Fund Balance:		
Vouchers Payable		$ 30,000
Fund Balance:		
Nonspendable:		
Supplies Inventory	$ 14,000	
Spendable:		
Assigned to:		
General Government Services	11,000	
Unassigned	104,000	129,000
Total Liabilities and Fund Balance		$159,000

FIGURE 12–9
General Fund Operating Budget for Fiscal 20X2

SOL CITY General Fund Operating Budget For Period of January 1, 20X2, to December 31, 20X2		
Estimated Revenue:		
Property Taxes	$775,000	
Grants	55,000	
Sales Taxes	25,000	
Miscellaneous	20,000	
Total Estimated Revenue		$875,000
Appropriations:		
General Government	$200,000	
Streets and Highways	75,000	
Public Safety	400,000	
Sanitation	150,000	
Total Appropriations		(825,000)
Excess of Estimated Revenue over Appropriations		$ 50,000
Other Financing Uses:		
Transfer out to Capital Projects Fund	$ (20,000)	
Transfer out to Initiate Internal Service Fund	(10,000)	
Total Other Financing Uses		(30,000)
Excess of Estimated Revenue and Interfund Transfers over Appropriations and Interfund Transfers		$ 20,000

Among the city's accounting policies, it elects to use the following:

1. *Consumption method for inventories.* The city budgets the supplies inventory on the consumption method, including only the costs of expected inventory use during the year.

2. *Lapsing method of accounting for encumbrances.* The city uses the lapsing method for accounting for any encumbrances outstanding at the end of fiscal periods. The APPROPRIATIONS CONTROL for fiscal 20X2 includes a reappropriation of the $11,000 of outstanding encumbrances as of December 31, 20X1.

3. *Use of control accounts.* The city uses a comprehensive system of control accounts for its major journals. The following accounts have extensive subsidiary ledgers that correspond to the entries made in the journal: ESTIMATED REVENUES CONTROL,

APPROPRIATIONS CONTROL, ENCUMBRANCES, and Expenditures. The specific details supporting each of these control accounts are maintained in the subsidiary records. For purposes of focusing on the major aspects of governmental accounting, the Sol City illustration includes the control-level entries only.

4. *Budgeted interfund activities.* The city includes in the budget all anticipated interfund activities during the fiscal year. The general fund is expected to have the following interfund transfers:

OTHER FINANCING USES:	
Transfer Out to Capital Projects Fund	$20,000
Transfer Out to Internal Service Fund	10,000

The interfund transfer out to the capital projects fund is to pay for the city's share of a municipal courthouse addition project, and the transfer out to the internal service fund is to initiate the internal service fund.

The following entries are made to record the budget and to renew the lapsing encumbrances from the prior period:

January 1, 20X2

(10)	ESTIMATED REVENUES CONTROL	875,000	
	APPROPRIATIONS CONTROL		825,000
	ESTIMATED OTHER FINANCING USES—TRANSFER OUT TO CAPITAL PROJECTS		20,000
	ESTIMATED OTHER FINANCING USES—TRANSFER OUT TO INTERNAL SERVICE		10,000
	BUDGETARY FUND BALANCE—UNASSIGNED		20,000

Record budget for fiscal 20X2.

(11)	Fund Balance—Assigned for Encumbrances	11,000	
	Fund Balance—Unassigned		11,000

Reverse prior-year encumbrances reserve.

(12)	ENCUMBRANCES	11,000	
	BUDGETARY FUND BALANCE—ASSIGNED FOR ENCUMBRANCES		11,000

Renew encumbrances from prior period as included in budgeted appropriations in 20X2.

(*Note:* The technique of capitalizing the account titles of all budgetary accounts continues through the comprehensive illustration. This technique is used in the text to assist differentiation of the budgetary from the operating accounts. In practice, the budgetary accounts are not capitalized.)

Property Tax Levy and Collection

Most municipalities obtain resources from property taxes, which are recorded as a receivable when an enforceable legal claim arises. Revenue is recorded if the property taxes are measurable and available for current expenditures. Recall that the 60-day rule for property taxes allows the recognition of revenue for the current fiscal period if the property taxes are expected to be collected within 60 days of the end of the current fiscal period. A deferred revenue account is credited if the property taxes are not available for current expenditures. For Sol City, the property taxes are due and available for use within the fiscal period and therefore are recorded as revenue as of the levy date. Note that a provision for uncollectibles must be recorded, and this provision is a reduction of property tax revenue, not a bad debts expense as in commercial accounting. Governmental funds have no such account as bad debts expense. The receivables are classified as current, collectible within this period, or delinquent, for past-due accounts.

The entries in Sol City's general fund for the transactions relating to property taxes are as follows:

(13)

Property Taxes Receivable—Current	785,000	
Allowance for Uncollectible Taxes—Current		10,000
Revenue—Property Tax		775,000

Property taxes levied for this fiscal year with a reduction from revenues for the estimated uncollectibles.

(14)

Cash	791,000	
Property Taxes Receivable—Current		695,000
Property Taxes Receivable—Delinquent		96,000

Collect portion of property taxes including $96,000 of past due accounts.

(15)

Allowance for Uncollectible Taxes—Delinquent	4,000	
Property Taxes Receivable—Delinquent		4,000

Write off remaining $4,000 of delinquent property taxes.

(16)

Allowance for Uncollectible Taxes—Delinquent	1,000	
Allowance for Uncollectible Taxes—Current	5,000	
Revenues—Property Tax		6,000

Revise estimate of uncollectibles from $10,000 to $5,000 and close remaining $1,000 balance of allowance account for delinquent accounts.

(17)

Property Taxes Receivable—Delinquent	90,000	
Allowance for Uncollectible Taxes—Current	5,000	
Property Taxes Receivable—Current		90,000
Allowance for Uncollectible Taxes—Delinquent		5,000

Reclassify remaining receivables and allowance account from current to delinquent.

Other Revenue

Other sources of income are grants from other governmental units, a portion of the sales tax collected on retail sales made within the city, and miscellaneous revenue from parking meters, fines, and licenses. Grants from other governmental units should be recognized as revenue when the grants become available and measurable. The city's policy is to recognize these grants as the monies are received because the grants may be withdrawn by the grantor at any time up to the actual transmittal of the monies. In our example, the city receives only 60 percent of the expected grant that had been budgeted at $55,000. Sales tax revenue may be accrued if the city can make a good estimate of the amount to be received and if the sales tax revenue is available for current expenditures. The city's policy is to recognize the sales taxes when received. Miscellaneous revenue is recognized as received.

The entries to record the other sources of income are as follows:

(18)

Cash	33,000	
Revenue—Grant		33,000

Receive only 60 percent of expected grant.

(19)

Cash	32,000	
Revenue—Sales Tax		32,000

Receive sales tax revenue from state.

(20)

Cash	18,000	
Revenue—Miscellaneous		18,000

Receive miscellaneous revenue from fines, license fees, minor disposals of equipment, and other sources.

Expenditures

The appropriations were recorded in the budget entry [entry (10)] with a renewal of the encumbrances carried over from the prior period under the lapsing method of accounting for encumbrances [entries (11) and (12)]. Orders for goods and services from outside vendors are encumbered, and a voucher system is used. Recall that a governmental entity typically does not encumber internal payroll.

Sol City makes the following entries for the encumbrances, expenditures, and disbursements made in the general fund during the year:

| (21) | ENCUMBRANCES | 210,000 | |
| | BUDGETARY FUND BALANCE—ASSIGNED FOR ENCUMBRANCES | | 210,000 |

Encumber for purchase orders for goods and services ordered from outside vendors.

| (22) | BUDGETARY FUND BALANCE—ASSIGNED FOR ENCUMBRANCES | 5,000 | |
| | ENCUMBRANCES | | 5,000 |

Reverse encumbrance for portion of order that is not deliverable because item has been discontinued.

| (23) | BUDGETARY FUND BALANCE—ASSIGNED FOR ENCUMBRANCES | 190,000 | |
| | ENCUMBRANCES | | 190,000 |

Reverse reserve for partial order of goods received.

| (24) | Expenditures | 196,000 | |
| | Vouchers Payable | | 196,000 |

Receive goods at actual cost of $196,000 that had been encumbered for $190,000. Difference due to increase in cost of items. Includes supplies for inventory.

| (25) | BUDGETARY FUND BALANCE—ASSIGNED FOR ENCUMBRANCES | 11,000 | |
| | ENCUMBRANCES | | 11,000 |

Reverse reserve for goods received that were ordered in prior year.

| (26) | Expenditures | 9,000 | |
| | Vouchers Payable | | 9,000 |

Receive goods ordered in prior year. Actual cost is $9,000 on encumbered amount of $11,000. Difference due to price reduction as part of special sale.

| (27) | Expenditures | 550,000 | |
| | Vouchers Payable | | 550,000 |

Payroll costs to employees for period.

| (28) | Vouchers Payable | 730,000 | |
| | Cash | | 730,000 |

Vouchers approved by city council and paid during period.

Acquisition of Capital Asset

The budget for the fire department includes $50,000 for a new fire truck. This capital outlay is accounted for as any other expenditure of available resources. The resources for the fire truck are encumbered when the order is placed with the truck manufacturer. The entries in the general fund for the fire truck acquisition are as follows:

| (29) | ENCUMBRANCES | 50,000 | |
| | BUDGETARY FUND BALANCE—ASSIGNED FOR ENCUMBRANCES | | 50,000 |

Order fire truck at estimated cost of $50,000

| (30) | BUDGETARY FUND BALANCE—ASSIGNED FOR ENCUMBRANCES | 50,000 | |
| | ENCUMBRANCES | | 50,000 |

Reverse reserve for fire truck received.

(31)	Expenditures	58,000	
	Vouchers Payable		58,000

Receive fire truck at actual cost of $58,000 due to approved
additional items required to meet new fire code.

(32)	Vouchers Payable	58,000	
	Cash		58,000

Voucher approved and disbursement made for fire truck.

Interfund Activities

The anticipated interfund items are included in the budget for the fiscal period. They include the estimated transfer out of $10,000 to initiate the internal service fund and the estimated transfer out of $20,000 for capital improvements to a capital projects fund. In addition to these transfers, the general fund also has an interfund transaction with the internal service fund for services received in the amount of $1,000, and it lends the enterprise fund $3,000.

The following entries in the general fund record the general fund's side of the interfund activities during the year. Chapter 13 continues the comprehensive example of Sol City and presents the entries for these interfund transactions and transfers in each of the related funds so that both sides of accounting for interfund items are illustrated for the Sol City example:

(33)	Other Financing Uses—Transfer Out to Internal Service Fund	10,000	
	Due to Internal Service Fund		10,000

Recognize the transfer out and associated liability to the internal
service fund as included in the budget.

(34)	Other Financing Uses—Transfer Out to Capital Projects Fund	20,000	
	Due to Capital Projects Fund		20,000

Recognize the transfer out and associated liability to the capital
projects fund as included in the budget.

(35)	Due to Internal Service Fund	10,000	
	Cash		10,000

Pay cash to internal service fund for payable from interfund transfer
out previously recognized.

(36)	Due to Capital Projects Fund	20,000	
	Cash		20,000

Pay cash to capital projects fund for payable from interfund transfer
out previously recognized.

(37)	Expenditures	1,000	
	Due to Internal Service Fund		1,000

Recognize payable for interfund supplies provided and used
(received from the internal service fund).

(38)	Due to Internal Service Fund	1,000	
	Cash		1,000

Pay cash to eliminate payable.

(39)	Due from Enterprise Fund	3,000	
	Cash		3,000

City Council approves loan to enterprise fund to be repaid in 90 days.

Adjusting Entries

Certain adjusting entries are required to state correctly the balance sheet items for the year. Assume that a physical count of the inventory shows an ending balance of $17,000 on December 31, 20X2. This is a net increase of $3,000 from the beginning balance of $14,000.

The policy of the general fund is to recognize inventory as an asset and to report a reserve against fund balance for the ending balance. Recall that the city is using the consumption method of accounting for inventories. The entries required to adjust the ending balance of the supplies inventory are as follows:

(40)	Inventory of Supplies	3,000	
	Expenditures		3,000

Adjust ending inventory to $17,000 and reduce expenditures to net amount consumed during the period.

(41)	Fund Balance—Unassigned	3,000	
	Fund Balance—Assigned for Inventories		3,000

Adjust the reserve for inventories from beginning balance of $14,000 to its ending balance of $17,000.

Closing Entries

The final set of entries closes the nominal accounts. The format presented first reverses the budget entry and then closes the operating revenues and expenditures. Some governmental entities close the accounts in a slightly different order by closing budgeted revenue against actual revenue and budgeted appropriations against actual expenditures. The specific order of closing the accounts has no impact on the final effect; all budgetary accounts and nominal operating accounts must be closed at year-end.

A preclosing trial balance is presented in Figure 12–10. Recall that the city is using the lapsing method of accounting for encumbrances open at the end of the fiscal year. The closing entries for the general fund of Sol City for fiscal 20X2 follow:

December 31, 20X2

(42)	APPROPRIATIONS CONTROL	825,000	
	ESTIMATED OTHER FINANCING USES—TRANSFER OUT TO CAPITAL PROJECTS	20,000	
	ESTIMATED OTHER FINANCING USES—TRANSFER OUT TO INTERNAL SERVICES	10,000	
	BUDGETARY FUND BALANCE—UNASSIGNED	20,000	
	ESTIMATED REVENUES CONTROL		875,000

Close budgetary accounts.

(43)	BUDGETARY FUND BALANCE—ASSIGNED FOR ENCUMBRANCES	15,000	
	ENCUMBRANCES		15,000

Close remaining encumbrances by reversing remaining budgetary balance.

(44)	Fund Balance—Unassigned	15,000	
	Fund Balance—Assigned for Encumbrances		15,000

Reservation of fund balance for encumbrances that lapse but are expected to be honored in 20X3.

(45)	Revenue—Property Tax	781,000	
	Revenue—Grant	33,000	
	Revenue—Sales Tax	32,000	
	Revenue—Miscellaneous	18,000	
	Expenditures		811,000
	Other Financing Uses—Transfer Out to Capital Projects Fund		20,000
	Other Financing Uses—Transfer Out to Internal Service Fund		10,000
	Fund Balance—Unassigned		23,000

Close operating statement accounts.

FIGURE 12–10
Preclosing Trial
Balance for General
Fund

SOL CITY
General Fund
Preclosing Trial Balance December 31, 20X2

	Debit	Credit
Cash	$ 102,000	
Property Taxes Receivable—Delinquent	90,000	
Allowance for Uncollectible Taxes—Delinquent		$ 5,000
Due from Enterprise Fund	3,000	
Inventory of Supplies	17,000	
Vouchers Payable		55,000
Fund Balance—Nonspendable		17,000
Fund Balance—Unassigned		112,000
Revenue—Property Tax		781,000
Revenue—Grant		33,000
Revenue—Sales Tax		32,000
Revenue—Miscellaneous		18,000
Expenditures	811,000	
Other Financing Uses—Transfer Out to Capital Projects Fund	20,000	
Other Financing Uses—Transfer Out to Internal Service Fund	10,000	
ESTIMATED REVENUES CONTROL	875,000	
APPROPRIATIONS CONTROL		825,000
ESTIMATED OTHER FINANCING USES—TRANSFER OUT TO CAPITAL PROJECTS		20,000
ESTIMATED OTHER FINANCING USES—TRANSFER OUT TO INTERNAL SERVICE		10,000
ENCUMBRANCES	15,000	
BUDGETARY FUND BALANCE—ASSIGNED FOR ENCUMBRANCES		15,000
BUDGETARY FUND BALANCE—UNASSIGNED		20,000
Total	$1,943,000	$1,943,000

The following reconciliation explains the calculation of the Fund Balance—Unassigned account balance:

Fund Balance—Unassigned

(41)	3,000	Bal. 1/1/X2	104,000
		(11)	11,000
(44)	15,000	Bal. Preclosing	112,000
		(45)	23,000
		Bal. 12/31/X2	120,000

General Fund Financial Statement Information

The general fund is always specified as a major governmental fund type. The two required statements for a major governmental fund are *(a)* the balance sheet and *(b)* the statement of revenues, expenditures, and changes in fund balance. For purposes of illustration, the two financial statements for the general fund are provided, applying the requirements of **GASB 34,** and then a presentation is made of the fund balance section of the balance sheet under the proposed governmental accounting statement on fund balance reporting and governmental fund type definitions.

The Balance Sheet

The balance sheet required under **GASB 34** is presented in Figure 12–11. This balance sheet includes the supplies inventory for $17,000 and the associated reservation of fund balance, reflecting that the portion of the fund balance already applied to inventory is not expendable. The $3,000 receivable from the interfund loan transaction with the enterprise fund is shown as a current asset. The outstanding encumbrances

FIGURE 12–11
General Fund Balance
Sheet Information at
the End of the Fiscal
Period

SOL CITY
General Fund
Balance Sheet Information December 31, 20X2

Assets:		
Cash		$102,000
Property Taxes Receivable—Delinquent	$ 90,000	
Less: Allowance for Uncollectibles—Delinquent	(5,000)	85,000
Due from Enterprise Fund		3,000
Inventory of Supplies		17,000
Total Assets		$207,000
Liabilities and Fund Balance:		
Vouchers Payable		$ 55,000
Fund Balance:		
Nonspendable:		
Supplies Inventory	$ 17,000	
Spendable:		
Assigned to:		
General Government Services	15,000	
Unassigned	120,000	152,000
Total Liabilities and Fund Balance		$207,000

of $15,000 are a reservation of fund balance indicating that a portion of the year's appropriation has been used but that the ordered goods or services have not yet been received.

The General Fund's Balance Sheet under GASB 54

The new statement on fund balance reporting and governmental fund type definitions does not change the reporting of assets or liabilities. It affects only the reporting of the fund balance for governmental fund types that includes the general fund. The fund balance section of the balance sheet could report only aggregate amounts for the nonspendable and spendable categories with detail presented in the footnotes. Alternatively, the balance sheet can report the detailed items within each category of the general fund balance. The nonspendable category includes the two classifications of amounts not in spendable form, such as inventories, or amounts that are legally or contractually required to be maintained. The spendable category includes resources that are in spendable form and are considered to be available for spending, such as fund balance related to cash, investments, and receivables. Amounts in the spendable fund balance category can then be classified as restricted, limited, assigned, or unassigned based on a hierarchy of the level of control over the spending of the resources.

Under the newly implemented **GASB 54,** reserves are not reported on the balance sheet; rather, the amount of encumbrances is reported in a footnote along with other commitments. The Sol City government has no restricted or limited spendable fund balances, but it does have an assigned amount for the amount of resources intended by the government to be used for the specific purpose of paying currently outstanding encumbrances from goods and services ordered to be used for general government functions.

The Statement of Revenues, Expenditures, and Changes in Fund Balance

This required statement is presented in Figure 12–12 and has the following sections:

1. *Operating section.* Revenues less expenditures, resulting in an excess of revenues over expenditures for the period. Expenditures include the interfund services provided and used, and separate reporting of outlays for capital assets.
2. *Other financing sources (uses).* This section includes interfund transfers and nonrevenue proceeds such as bond issues.

FIGURE 12–12
General Fund
Statement of Revenues,
Expenditures, and
Changes in Fund
Balance Information
for Fiscal 20X2

SOL CITY
Statement of Revenues, Expenditures, and Changes in Fund Balance Information
General Fund
For the Year Ended December 31, 20X2

Revenues:		
Property Taxes	$781,000	
Grants	33,000	
Sales Taxes	32,000	
Miscellaneous	18,000	
Total Revenues		$864,000
Expenditures:		
General Government	$206,000	
Streets and Highways	71,000	
Public Safety	335,000	
Sanitation	141,000	
Capital Outlay:		
Public Safety	58,000	
Total Expenditures		811,000
Excess of Revenues over Expenditures		$ 53,000
Other Financing Sources (Uses):		
Transfer Out to Capital Projects Fund	$ (20,000)	
Transfer Out to Internal Service Fund	(10,000)	
Total Other Financing Sources (Uses)		(30,000)
Net Change in Fund Balances		$ 23,000
Fund Balance, January 1		129,000
Fund Balance, December 31		$152,000

3. *Reconciliation of fund balance.* The ending balance in fund balances, including both assigned and unassigned, is reconciled for (a) the results of operations, (b) other financing sources or uses, and (c) special or extraordinary items in the period.

Revenues should be classified by major sources, and expenditures by character and major functions. Although the entries presented in the illustrations for Sol City did not break down the expenditures by function (general government, streets and highways, public safety, and sanitation), this breakdown is done in the actual governmental accounting process so each expenditure can be classified by both function and object (personal services, supplies, and other services and charges). The amounts presented in the expenditures section in Figure 12–12 are the assumed amounts from a comprehensive accounting system. Total expenditures do reconcile to the expenditures recorded in the Sol City illustration.

The statement of revenues, expenditures, and changes in fund balance presents the total fund balance, including both assigned and unassigned. Note that in this example, Sol City reported no extraordinary items or special items. Special items would include significant transactions or other events within the control of management that were either unusual in nature or infrequent in occurrence. An example of a special item could be a one-time sale of some city park land. If the city did have a special item or extraordinary item, it would be reported below the other financing sources (uses) section.

The General Fund's Statement of Revenues, Expenditures, and Changes in Fund Balance under the Proposed Statement

GASB 54 on governmental fund type balances does not require any changes in the statement of revenues, expenditures, and changes in fund balance. The reconciliation in this financial statement is to total fund balance, not to a specific classification of the fund balance. Therefore, this financial statement is the same under **GASB 54** as was previously required under **GASB 34**.

Summary of Key Concepts

Accounting for state and local governmental units requires the use of fund accounting to recognize properly the variety of services and objectives of the governmental unit. Funds are separate fiscal and accounting entities established to segregate, control, and account for resource flows. Three types of funds are used by governmental units: governmental funds, of which the general fund is usually the most important; proprietary funds; and fiduciary funds. The basis of accounting for each fund depends on the fund's objective. The current financial resources measurement focus and the modified accrual basis of accounting are used for the governmental fund financial statements. The economic resources measurement focus and accrual basis of accounting are used for the government-wide statements, the proprietary fund statements, and the fiduciary fund statements.

Under the modified accrual basis, revenue is recognized when it is both measurable and available for financing expenditures of the period. A major source of revenue is property tax levies, but other sources may include sales taxes; grants from other governmental units; and fines, licenses, or permits. Note that in the five governmental funds, the estimated uncollectible property taxes are a reduction of the property tax revenue, not an expense as in commercial accounting. Expenditures are recognized in the period in which the related liability is both measurable and incurred. The expenditure process usually begins with a budget, which establishes the spending authority for the fund. Encumbrances are used for purchases outside the governmental entity to recognize the use of a portion of the spending authority for the period and to avoid overspending the expenditure authority. Under current GAAFR, encumbrances outstanding at the end of a fiscal period are reported as a reserve of the fund balance and may be accounted for as lapsing or nonlapsing. Another type of fund balance reserve is a reserve for inventories, which is used if the amount of inventory is material.

The general fund is responsible for offering many of the usual services of governmental units. Fire and police protection, the local government's administrative and legislative functions, and many other basic governmental services are administered through the general fund. The general fund will provide balance sheet information and statement of revenues, expenditures, and changes in fund balances information to the governmental funds financial statements.

The government reporting model, as established by **GASB 34,** specifies that both fund-based financial statements and government-wide financial statements must be presented. The general fund uses the modified accrual basis of accounting to recognize revenue and expenditure transactions. Furthermore, no long-term capital assets or general long-term debt is recorded in the general fund. However, a reconciliation schedule will be required to go from the governmental fund types financial statements to the government-wide financial statements. The government-wide financial statements use the accrual basis of accounting and report all capital assets and all long-term debt. Government-wide financial statements are presented in Chapter 13 after the conclusion of that chapter's discussion of the remaining funds.

Interfund activities must be evaluated carefully to ensure that the legal and budgetary controls of the governmental unit are not violated. Four types of interfund activities exist: (1) interfund loans, (2) interfund services provided and used, (3) interfund transfers, and (4) interfund reimbursements. Outstanding interfund loans are presented as receivables or payables on the fund's balance sheet information. Interfund services provided and used are reported as part of the revenues and expenditures on the operating statements. Interfund transfers are reported separately in the other financing sources (uses) section of the operating statement. Interfund reimbursements are not reported separately on the fund's financial statements.

Key Terms

appropriation, *614*
basis of accounting, *609*
budgets, *614*
current financial resources measurement focus, *607*
disbursement, *617*
economic resources measurement focus, *609*
encumbrance, *615*

expenditure, *604*
fiduciary funds, *604*
fund-based financial statements, *606*
funds, *603*
governmental financial reporting model, *606*
governmental funds, *604*

government-wide financial statements, *606*
interfund activities, *625*
modified accrual basis, *609*
proprietary funds, *604*
reporting entity, *605*
reservation (or restriction) of the budgetary fund balance, *616*

Questions

| LO1 | **Q12-1** | What is a fund? How does a fund receive resources? |

LO1   **Q12-1**   What is a fund? How does a fund receive resources?

LO1   **Q12-2**   What are the 11 funds generally used by local and state governments? Briefly state the purpose of each fund.

LO1   **Q12-3**   Compare the modified accrual basis with the accrual accounting basis.

LO3   **Q12-4**   Which of the two, the modified accrual basis or the accrual basis, is used for funds for which expendability is the concern? Why?

LO5   **Q12-5**   When are property taxes recognized as revenue in the general fund?

LO4   **Q12-6**   How are taxpayer-assessed income and sales taxes recognized in the general fund? Why?

LO6   **Q12-7**   What is meant by "budgetary accounting"? Explain the accounting for expected revenue and anticipated expenditures.

LO6   **Q12-8**   Are all expenditures encumbered?

LO5   **Q12-9**   Why do some governmental units not report small amounts of supply inventories in their balance sheets?

LO6   **Q12-10**   What are the main differences between the lapsing and nonlapsing methods of accounting for encumbrances outstanding at the end of the fiscal year? What are the differences in accounting between the lapsing and nonlapsing methods when accounting for the actual expenditure in the subsequent year?

LO4   **Q12-11**   When is the expenditure for inventories recognized under the purchase method? Under the consumption method?

LO6   **Q12-12**   Explain the difference between an interfund services provided and used and an interfund transfer. Give examples of each.

LO4   **Q12-13**   Where is an interfund transfer reported on the general fund's financial statements?

LO4   **Q12-14**   The general fund agrees to lend the enterprise fund $2,000 for three months. How is this interfund loan reported on the financial statements of the general fund?

LO4   **Q12-15**   Explain how an expenditure may be classified by (1) function, (2) activity, and (3) object within the financial statements of a governmental unit.

Cases

LO6

C12-1 Budget Theory

Understanding

Governmental accounting gives substantial recognition to budgets, with budgets being recorded in the accounts of the governmental unit.

Required

a. What is the purpose of a governmental accounting system, and why is the budget recorded in the accounts of a governmental unit? Include in your discussion the purpose and significance of appropriations.

b. Describe when and how a governmental unit (1) records its budget and (2) closes out the budgetary accounts.

LO1

C12-2 Municipal versus Financial Accounting

Judgment

Wilma Bates is executive vice president of Mavis Industries Inc., a publicly held industrial corporation. She has just been elected to the city council of Gotham City. Before assuming office, she asks you to explain the major differences that exist in accounting and financial reporting for a large city when compared to accounting and reporting for a large industrial corporation.

Required

a. Describe the major differences that exist in the purpose of accounting and financial reporting and in the type of financial reports of a large city when compared to a large industrial corporation.

b. Why are inventories often ignored in accounting for local governmental units? Explain.

LO4

C12-3   Revenue Issues

Communication   The bookkeeper for the community of Spring Valley has asked for your assistance on the following items.

Required

Prepare a memo discussing the proper accounting and financial reporting in the general fund for each of the following items.

a. Property taxes receivable are recognized at the levy date. One percent of the levy is not expected to be collected.

b. Property taxes are collected in advance of the year in which they are expendable.

c. Sales tax revenues are received from the state, but the city is still owed another $15,000 by the state that will not be received until the next month.

d. An unexpected state grant is received to finance the purchase of fire prevention equipment. One-half of the grant is expended in this fiscal period, and the remainder is expected to be expended in the next fiscal period.

e. Interest is earned on short-term investments made from the general fund's resources.

f. A gift from a local citizen was given to be used for a new city park once the park has been completed. If the park is not constructed within two years, the gift must be returned to the grantor. It is expected that the park will be completed in the next fiscal period.

LO1

C12-4   Summarizing the Requirements of GASB 34

Research   You have a friend who was just elected to the County Board for your county. One of the first items of business for the County Board is to prepare a budget for the new fiscal period. Your friend does not understand the county governmental entity financial reporting requirements so you volunteer to assist by preparing a report on the financial statements and the management's discussion and analysis (MD&A) of the county government.

Required

Obtain the preface and summary of **GASB Statement 34,** "Basic Financial Statements—and Management's Discussion and Analysis—for State and Local Governments" (GASB 34). You may obtain these from the GASB's Web site (www.gasb.org), from your library, or from the GASB's Governmental Accounting Research System (GARS), a computer-based database sold by the GASB. Then answer the following questions.

a. GASB established the requirement for government annual reports to include a management's discussion and analysis (MD&A). Describe the purposes of the MD&A in a government's annual report.

b. GASB 34 discusses both fund financial statements and government-wide financial statements.

   (1) Discuss the major contents of the fund financial statements and why those statements are necessary in the government's annual report.

   (2) Discuss the major contents of the government-wide financial statements and why those statements are necessary in the government's annual report.

LO4

C12-5   Examining the General Fund Disclosures in a Comprehensive Annual Financial Report (CAFR)

Analysis   This case focuses on the general fund of a governmental unit.

Required

Using the Comprehensive Annual Financial Report (CAFR) for a governmental entity chosen by your instructor, answer the following questions that relate to the overall government and the governmental funds:

a. Find the budgetary comparison schedules for the general fund. Using these schedules, what were the estimated revenues and appropriations for the most recent fiscal year?

b. Using the same information as in question (*a*), list the amounts of any transfers in and transfers out that were budgeted for the most recent year.

c. Based on the notes following the financial statements, what is the policy of the general fund with respect to outstanding encumbrances at the end of the fiscal year?

d. On the balance sheet of the general fund at the end of the most recent fiscal year, what is the total amount reported for assets and for fund balance? Of the total amount reported for fund balance, how much is unassigned?

e. On the balance sheet of the general fund at the end of the most recent fiscal year, what is the amount reported for inventories? If inventories are reported, does the government use the purchase method or the consumption method?

f. Based on the notes following the financial statements, what is the government's revenue recognition policy with respect to property taxes in the general fund? What percentage of the property tax levy is estimated to be uncollectible?

g. Read the section of the CAFR that contains management's discussion and analysis. What reasons were given for the increase or decrease in general fund revenues for the most recent year?

h. Examine the statement of revenues, expenditures, and changes in fund balance for the most recent year. Compare the change in fund balance for the general fund with the amount of change in fund balance that was budgeted for the year. Were the government's general fund actual results better or worse than expected?

i. After revenue from taxes, what was the next most significant source of revenue for the general fund for the most recent year?

j. Has the general fund engaged in any interfund loans and advances? If yes, show the amounts that are owed to or by the general fund as of the end of the most recent year.

LO2 **C12-6** ## Examining Deposit and Investment Risk Disclosures of a Governmental Entity

Discovery

The financial reports of governmental entities must provide footnote disclosure of the deposit and investment risks faced by the entity. **GASB Statement No. 40,** "Deposit and Investment Risk Disclosures" (GASB 40), amended **GASB Statement No. 3,** "Deposits with Financial Institutions, Investments (including Repurchase Agreements) and Reverse Repurchase Agreements" (GASB 3).

The GASB requires disclosures of (*a*) the natures of the deposits and investment risks the governmental entity faces, (*b*) the policies of the governmental entity regarding each of those risks, and (*c*) specific disclosures such as credit ratings of investments in fixed income securities along with a schedule of maturity dates and fair values of these fixed income securities; the types of other investment securities held along with the amounts and fair values of those other investment securities; any concentrations of investments, other than those in U.S. government securities or in mutual or pooled investment funds, comprising 5 percent or more of total investments; and discussion of the risks from changing interest rates and changing foreign exchange rates.

Required

First, go to the GASB's Web site (www.gasb.org) and obtain the summaries of **GASB 40** and **GASB 3** (the GASB does not provide online access to their complete publications). Second, using an online search engine such as Google, locate the most recent annual report of a local government near your college or university. Then provide answers to the following questions.

a. List the types of deposit and investment risks addressed in **GASB 3** and **GASB 40.**

b. Explain why disclosures of information about these risks are important to the users of the government's financial statements.

The following questions should be answered using the footnote information for Deposits and Investments from your local government's most recent annual report.

c. Describe the types of deposit and investment risks of your local government.

d. Describe the policies your local government has for each type of risk identified.

e. Describe the types of specific disclosures of information for each type of risk identified.

Exercises

E12-1 Multiple-Choice Questions on the General Fund [AICPA Adapted]

Select the correct answer for each of the following questions.

1. One of the differences between accounting for a governmental (not-for-profit) unit and a commercial (for-profit) enterprise is that a governmental unit should

   a. *Not* record depreciation expense in any of its funds.
   b. Always establish and maintain complete self-balancing accounts for each fund.
   c. Use only the cash basis of accounting.
   d. Use only the modified accrual basis of accounting.

2. Belle Valley incurred $100,000 of salaries and wages for the month ended March 31, 20X2. How should this be recorded on that date?

	Debit	Credit
a. Expenditures—Salaries and Wages	100,000	
Vouchers Payable		100,000
b. Salaries and Wages Expense	100,000	
Vouchers Payable		100,000
c. Encumbrances—Salaries and Wages	100,000	
Vouchers Payable		100,000
d. Fund Balance	100,000	
Vouchers Payable		100,000

3. Which of the following expenditures is normally recorded on the accrual basis in the general fund?

   a. Interest.
   b. Personal services.
   c. Inventory items.
   d. Prepaid expenses.

4. Which of the following accounts of a governmental unit is credited when taxpayers are billed for property taxes?

   a. Estimated Revenue.
   b. Revenue.
   c. Appropriations.
   d. Fund Balance—Assigned for Encumbrances.

5. Fixed assets purchased from general fund revenue were received. What account, if any, should have been debited in the general fund?

   a. No journal entry should have been made in the general fund.
   b. Fixed Assets.
   c. Expenditures.
   d. Fund Balance—Unassigned.

6. The initial transfer of cash from the general fund in order to establish an internal service fund would require the general fund to credit Cash and debit

   a. Accounts Receivable—Internal Service Fund.
   b. Transfers Out.
   c. Budgetary Fund Balance—Assigned for Encumbrances.
   d. Expenditures.

E12-2 Matching for General Fund Transactions [AICPA Adapted]

For each general fund transaction listed in items 1 through 12, select the appropriate recording for the transaction listed next to letters A through O. A letter may be selected once, more than once, or not at all.

Transactions	Recording of Transactions
1. An interfund transfer out was made to the capital projects fund.	A. Credit Revenues
2. Approved purchase orders were issued for supplies.	B. Debit Expenditures
3. The above-mentioned supplies were received and the related invoices were approved.	C. Debit Encumbrances
4. Salaries and wages were incurred.	D. Debit Inventories
5. Cash was transferred to establish an internal service fund.	E. Debit Interfund Services Provided and Used
6. The property tax levy was passed by the city council and tax bills were sent to property owners.	F. Credit Budgetary Fund Balance—Unassigned
7. Property taxes for the current year were collected.	G. Debit Appropriations Control
8. Appropriations were recorded on adoption of the budget.	H. Credit Property Taxes Receivable—Current
9. Estimated revenues were recorded on adoption of the budget.	I. Credit Appropriations Control
10. There was an excess of estimated inflows over estimated outflows.	J. Credit Residual Equity Transfer Out
11. Invoices for computer equipment were received.	K. Debit Interfund Transfer Out
12. Received billing from water and sewer fund (enterprise fund) for using city water and sewer.	L. Credit Interfund Transfer Out
	M. Debit Estimated Revenues Control
	N. Debit Budgetary Fund Balance—Unassigned
	O. Debit Computer Equipment

LO6, LO7

E12-3 Multiple-Choice Questions on Budgets, Expenditures, and Revenue [AICPA Adapted]

Select the correct answer for each of the following questions.

1. Which of the following steps in the acquisition of goods and services occurs first?
   a. Appropriation.
   b. Encumbrance.
   c. Budget.
   d. Expenditure.

2. What account is used to earmark the fund balance to recognize the contingent obligations of goods ordered but not yet received?
   a. Appropriations.
   b. Encumbrances.
   c. Obligations.
   d. Fund Balance—Assigned for Encumbrances.

3. When the Estimated Revenues Control account of a governmental unit is closed out at the end of the fiscal year, the excess of estimated revenues over estimated appropriations is
   a. Debited to Fund Balance—Unassigned.
   b. Debited to Fund Balance—Assigned for Encumbrances.
   c. Debited to Budgetary Fund Balance—Unassigned.
   d. Credited to Fund Balance—Assigned for Encumbrances.

4. The Carson City general fund issued purchase orders of $630,000 to vendors for supplies. Which of the following entries should be made to record this transaction?

		Debit	Credit
a.	Encumbrances	630,000	
	Budgetary Fund Balance—Assigned for Encumbrances		630,000
b.	Expenditures	630,000	
	Vouchers Payable		630,000
c.	Expenses	630,000	
	Accounts Payable		630,000
d.	Budgetary Fund Balance—Assigned for Encumbrances	630,000	
	Encumbrances		630,000

5. The following balances are included in the subsidiary records of Dogwood's Parks and Recreation Department on March 31, 20X2:

Appropriations—Supplies	$7,500
Expenditures—Supplies	4,500
Encumbrances—Supply Orders	750

How much does the department have available for additional purchases of supplies?

   a. $0.

   b. $2,250.

   c. $3,000.

   d. $6,750.

6. The board of commissioners of the City of Elgin adopted its budget for the year ending July 31, 20X2, which indicated revenue of $1,000,000 and appropriations of $900,000. If the budget is formally integrated into the accounting records, what is the required journal entry?

   a. Memorandum entry only

b.	Appropriations Control	900,000	
	Budgetary Fund Balance—Unassigned	100,000	
	Estimated Revenues Control		1,000,000
c.	Estimated Revenues Control	1,000,000	
	Appropriations Control		900,000
	Budgetary Fund Balance—Unassigned		100,000
d.	Revenue Receivable	1,000,000	
	Expenditures Payable		900,000
	Budgetary Fund Balance—Unassigned		100,000

7. Which of the following accounts of a governmental unit is credited when the budget is recorded?

   a. Encumbrances.

   b. Budgetary Fund Balance—Assigned for Encumbrances.

   c. Estimated Revenue Control.

   d. Appropriations Control.

8. Which of the following accounts of a governmental unit is debited when supplies previously ordered are received?

   a. Encumbrances.

   b. Budgetary Fund Balance—Assigned for Encumbrances.

   c. Vouchers Payable.

   d. Appropriations Control.

9. Which of the following situations will increase the fund balance of a governmental unit at the end of the fiscal year?

   a. Appropriations are less than expenditures and budgetary fund balance is assigned for encumbrances.

b. Appropriations are less than expenditures and encumbrances.

c. Appropriations are more than expenditures and encumbrances.

d. Appropriations are more than estimated revenue.

10. Which of the following accounts of a governmental unit is credited to close it out at the end of the fiscal year?

a. Appropriations Control.

b. Revenue—Property Tax.

c. Budgetary Fund Balance—Assigned for Encumbrances.

d. Encumbrances.

LO2, LO7 **E12-4** **Multiple-Choice Questions on the General Fund**

Select the correct answer for each of the following questions.

1. The primary focus in accounting and reporting for governmental funds is on

a. Income determination.

b. Flow of financial resources.

c. Capital maintenance.

d. Transfers relating to proprietary activities.

2. The governmental fund measurement focus is on the determination of

	Income	Financial Position	Flow of Financial Resources
a.	Yes	Yes	No
b.	No	Yes	No
c.	No	No	Yes
d.	No	Yes	Yes

3. A Budgetary Fund Balance—Assigned for Encumbrances in excess of a balance of Encumbrances Control indicates

a. An excess of vouchers payable over encumbrances.

b. An excess of purchase orders over invoices received.

c. A recording error.

d. An excess of appropriations over encumbrances.

4. The Encumbrances Control account of a governmental unit is debited when

a. Goods are received.

b. A voucher payable is recorded.

c. A purchase order is approved.

d. The budget is recorded.

5. The following pertains to property taxes levied by Cedar City for the calendar year 20X6:

Expected collections during 20X6	$500,000
Expected collections during the first 60 days of 20X7	100,000
Expected collections during the remainder of 20X7	60,000
Expected collections during January 20X8	30,000
Estimated to be uncollectible (3/1/X7 through 1/1/X8)	10,000
Total levy	$700,000

What amount should Cedar report for 20X6 as revenues from property taxes?

a. $700,000.

b. $600,000.

c. $690,000.

d. $500,000.

6 Oak City issued a purchase order for supplies with an estimated cost of $5,000. When the supplies were received, the accompanying invoice indicated an actual price of $4,950. What amount should Oak debit (credit) to Budgetary Fund Balance—Assigned for Encumbrances after the supplies and invoice are received?

   a. $5,000.

   b. $(50).

   c. $4,950.

   d. $50.

7. For the budgetary year ending December 31, 20X6, Johnson City's general fund expects the following inflows of resources:

Property taxes, licenses, and fines	$9,000,000
Transfer in from internal service fund	500,000
Transfer in from debt service fund	1,000,000

   In the budgetary entry, what amount should Johnson record for estimated revenues?

   a. $9,000,000.

   b. $9,500,000.

   c. $10,500,000.

   d. $10,000,000.

8. Encumbrances outstanding at year-end in a state's general fund should be reported as a

   a. Liability in the general fund.

   b. Fund balance designation in the general fund.

   c. Fund balance reserve in the general fund.

   d. Liability in the general long-term debt account group.

9. Interperiod equity is an objective of financial reporting for governmental entities. According to the Governmental Accounting Standards Board, is interperiod equity fundamental to public administration? Is it a component of accountability?

	Fundamental to Public Administration	Component of Accountability
a.	Yes	Yes
b.	No	No
c.	Yes	No
d.	No	Yes

10. Which of the following statements is correct regarding comparability of governmental financial reports?

   a. Comparability is not relevant in governmental financial reporting.

   b. Differences between financial reports should be due to substantive differences in underlying transactions or the governmental structure.

   c. Selection of different alternatives in accounting procedures or practices account for the differences between financial reports.

   d. Similarly designated governments perform the same functions.

LO7

Advanced
StudyGuide
.com

E12-5   Encumbrances at Year-End

The City of Batavia ordered new computer equipment for $21,000 on November 3, 20X2. The equipment had not been received by December 31, 20X2, the end of Batavia's fiscal year.

Required

a. Assume that the city has a policy that outstanding encumbrances lapse at year-end.

   (1) Prepare the entry to record the encumbrance on November 3, 20X2.

   (2) Prepare the entries required on December 31, 20X2.

   (3) Assuming that the city council accepts outstanding encumbrances in its budget for the next fiscal period (20X3), prepare entries on January 1, 20X3.

(4) Prepare entries on January 18, 20X3, when the equipment was received with an invoice cost of $21,800 and accepted by the city.

(5) Prepare the closing entry on December 31, 20X3, to close the expenditures account.

b. Assume the city's policy is that outstanding encumbrances are nonlapsing.

(1) Prepare the entry to record the encumbrance on November 3, 20X2.

(2) Prepare the entries required on December 31, 20X2.

(3) Prepare the entry on January 1, 20X3, to classify the expenditure with 20X2, the year the encumbrance was initiated.

(4) Prepare the entry on January 18, 20X3, when the equipment was received for $21,800. The City Council approved the additional cost of $800 for the equipment as an addition to 20X3's expenditures.

(5) Prepare the closing entries on December 31, 20X3, to close the expenditures accounts.

c. Now assume the city has a policy that outstanding encumbrances are nonlapsing, but the 20X3 City Council decided, during its budget hearings for 20X3, not to accept the encumbrance for the computer equipment that had been ordered on November 3, 20X2.

(1) Prepare the entry required on January 1, 20X3, to cancel the encumbrance reserve for the equipment ordered on November 3, 20X2.

LO7

Advanced StudyGuide .com

E12-6 Accounting for Inventories of Office Supplies

Georgetown purchased supplies on August 8, 20X2, for $3,600. At the fiscal year-end on September 30, the inventory of supplies was $2,800.

Required

a. Assume that Georgetown uses the consumption method of accounting for inventories.

(1) Prepare the entry for the purchase on August 8, 20X2.

(2) Prepare the entries required on September 30, 20X2, including the closing of the Expenditures account.

(3) Assuming the supplies were used during 20X3, prepare the entries on September 30, 20X3.

b. Assume that Georgetown uses the purchase method of accounting for inventories.

(1) Prepare the entry for the purchase on August 8, 20X2.

(2) Prepare the entries required on September 30, 20X2, including the closing of the Expenditures account.

(3) Assuming the supplies were used during 20X3, prepare the entry on September 30, 20X3.

LO7

Advanced StudyGuide .com

E12-7 Accounting for Prepayments and Capital Assets

Required

Prepare journal entries for the Iron City general fund for the following, including any adjusting and closing entries on December 31, 20X1:

a. Acquired a three-year fire insurance policy for $5,400 on September 1, 20X1.

b. Ordered new furniture for the city council meeting room on September 17, 20X1, at an estimated cost of $15,600. The furniture was delivered on October 1, its actual cost was $15,200, its estimated life is 10 years, and it has no residual value.

c. Acquired supplies on November 4, 20X1, for $1,800. Iron City uses the consumption method of accounting. Supplies on hand on December 31, 20X1, were $1,120.

LO7

E12-8 Computation of Revenues Reported on the Statement of Revenues, Expenditures, and Changes in Fund Balance for the General Fund

Gilbert City had the following transactions involving resource inflows into its general fund for the year ended June 30, 20X8:

1. The general fund levied $2,000,000 of property taxes in July 20X7. The city estimated that 2 percent of the levy would be uncollectible and that $100,000 of the levy would not be collected until after August 31, 20X8.

2. On April 1, 20X8, the general fund received $50,000 repayment of an advance made to the internal service fund. Interest on the advance of $1,500 also was received.

3. During the year ended June 30, 20X8, the general fund received $1,800,000 of the property taxes levied in transaction (1).

4. The general fund received $250,000 in grant monies from the state to be used solely for the acquisition of computer equipment. During March 20X8, the general fund acquired computer equipment using $235,000 of the grant. The city has not yet determined the use of the remainder of the grant.

5. During the year ended June 30, 20X8, the general fund received $125,000 from the state as its portion of the sales tax. At June 30, 20X8, the state owed the general fund an additional $25,000 of sales taxes. The general fund does not expect to have the $25,000 available until early August 20X8.

6. In July 20X7, the general fund borrowed $800,000 from a local bank using the property tax levy as collateral. The loan was repaid in September 20X7, with the proceeds of property tax collections.

7. In February 20X8, a terminated debt service fund transferred $30,000 to the general fund. The $30,000 represented excess resources left in the debt service fund after a general long-term debt obligation had been paid in full.

8. On July 1, 20X7, the general fund estimated that it would receive $75,000 from the sale of liquor licenses during the fiscal year ended June 30, 20X8. For the year ended June 30, 20X8, $66,000 was received from liquor license sales.

9. The general fund received $15,000 in October 20X7, from one of the city's special revenue funds. The amount received represented a reimbursement for an expenditure of the special revenue fund that was paid by the city's general fund.

10. In July 20X7, the general fund collected $80,000 of delinquent property taxes. These property taxes were classified as delinquent on June 30, 20X7. In the entry to record the property tax levy in July 20X6, the general fund estimated that it would collect all property tax revenues by July 31, 20X7.

Required
Prepare a schedule showing the amount of revenue that should be reported by Gilbert's general fund on the statement of revenues, expenditures, and changes in fund balance for the year ended June 30, 20X8.

LO7

E12-9 **Computation of Expenditures Reported on the Statement of Revenues, Expenditures, and Changes in Fund Balance for the General Fund**

Advanced
StudyGuide
.com

Benson City had the following transactions involving resource outflows involving its general fund for the year ended June 30, 20X8:

1. During March 20X8, the general fund transferred $150,000 to a capital projects fund to help pay for the construction of a new police station.

2. During August 20X7, the general fund ordered computer equipment at an estimated cost of $200,000. The equipment was received in September 20X7, and an invoice for $202,000 was paid.

3. In November 20X7, the city authorized the establishment of an internal service fund for the maintenance of city-owned vehicles. The general fund was authorized to transfer $500,000 to the internal service fund in late November. Of this amount, $200,000 will be repaid by the internal service fund in two years with interest at 6 percent; the remaining $300,000 represents a permanent transfer to the internal service fund.

4. In May 20X8, the general fund made a $15,000 payment to one of the city's special revenue funds. The amount paid represented a reimbursement to the special revenue fund for expending $15,000 of its resources on behalf of the general fund.

5. During the year ended June 30, 20X8, the general fund received bills from the city's water department totaling $12,000. Of this amount, the general fund paid all but $500 by June 30, 20X8.

6. During the year ended June 30, 20X8, the general fund acquired supplies costing $35,000 and paid the salaries and wages of its employees totaling $900,000. The general fund uses the purchase method of accounting for its supplies. At June 30, 20X8, unused supplies in the general fund amounted to $5,000.

7. At June 30, 20X8, outstanding encumbrances for goods ordered in the general fund amounted to $25,000. Outstanding encumbrances do not lapse at the end of the fiscal year.

8. On March 15, 20X8, the general fund repaid a loan to a local bank. The amount paid was $265,000, of which $250,000 represented the principal borrowed. The general fund borrowed the money in July 20X7 and used collections of the property tax levy to repay the loan.

9. For the year ended June 30, 20X8, the general fund transferred $95,000 to the city's pension trust fund. The amount transferred represented the employer's contribution to the pension trust on behalf of the employees of the general fund.

10. During May 20X8, the general fund decided to lease several copying machines instead of purchasing them. The lease arrangement was properly accounted for as an operating lease. By June 30, 20X8, the general fund had made lease payments of $10,000 to the owner of the machines.

Required

Prepare a schedule showing the amount of expenditures that should be reported by Benson's general fund on the statement of revenues, expenditures, and changes in fund balance for the year ended June 30, 20X8.

LO7

E12-10   Closing Entries and Balance Sheet

The preclosing trial balance at December 31, 20X1, for Lone Wolf's general fund follows.

	Debit	Credit
Cash	$ 90,000	
Property Taxes Receivable—Delinquent	100,000	
Allowance for Uncollectibles—Delinquent		$ 7,200
Due from Other Funds	14,600	
Vouchers Payable		65,000
Due to Other Funds		8,400
Fund Balance—Unassigned		119,000
Property Tax Revenue		1,130,000
Miscellaneous Revenue		40,000
Expenditures	1,140,000	
Other Financing Uses—Transfer Out	25,000	
Estimated Revenues Control	1,200,000	
Appropriations Control		1,145,000
Estimated Other Financing Uses—Transfer Out		25,000
Encumbrances	32,000	
Budgetary Fund Balance—Assigned for Encumbrances		32,000
Budgetary Fund Balance—Unassigned		30,000
Total	$2,601,600	$2,601,600

Lone Wolf uses the purchase method of accounting for inventories and the lapsing method of accounting for encumbrances.

Required

a. Prepare the closing entries for the general fund.

b. Prepare a general fund–only balance sheet at December 31, 20X1.

LO7

E12-11   Statement of Revenues, Expenditures, and Changes in Fund Balance

Refer to the preclosing trial balance in Exercise 12-10. Assume that the balances on December 31, 20X0, were as follows:

Fund Balance—Assigned for Encumbrances	$28,000
Fund Balance—Unassigned	91,000

Required
Prepare a general fund–only statement of revenues, expenditures, and changes in fund balance for fiscal 20X1.

LO8

E12-12 **Matching Questions Involving Interfund Transactions and Transfers in the General Fund**

The general fund of Mattville had several interfund activities during the fiscal year ended June 30, 20X9. These interfund activities are presented in the left-hand column of the following table. A list of the types of interfund activities that occur in state and local governmental accounting is provided on the right. For each general fund transaction/transfer, select a letter from the list on the right that best describes the interfund activity.

General Fund Transactions and Transfers	Type of Interfund Transactions and Transfers
1. Received bills from an internal service fund for using city-owned vehicles.	A. Interfund loan
2. Transferred cash to start an enterprise fund. The enterprise fund does not have to return the cash to the general fund.	B. Interfund service provided and used
3. Received cash from a special revenue fund that was discontinued.	C. Interfund transfer
4. Transferred cash to a capital projects fund to help construct a building.	D. Interfund reimbursement
5. Transferred cash to a debt service fund to pay interest and principal of general long-term debt.	
6. Transferred cash to the pension trust fund representing the employer's contribution toward the pension of general fund employees.	
7. Transferred resources to an enterprise fund. It is expected that these resources will be repaid with interest.	
8. Transferred cash to a special revenue fund. The special revenue fund incurred and paid expenditures on behalf of the general fund.	
9. Received cash from an internal service fund. The cash received represented repayment of an advance made during the previous year.	
10. Received bills from an enterprise fund for using public parking facilities.	

Problems

LO7

Advanced StudyGuide .com

P12-13 **General Fund Entries [AICPA Adapted]**

The following information was abstracted from the accounts of the general fund of the City of Noble after the books had been closed for the fiscal year ended June 30, 20X2.

	Postclosing Trial Balance, June 30, 20X1	Transactions July 1, 20X1–June 30, 20X2		Postclosing Trial Balance, June 30, 20X2
		Debit	Credit	
Cash	$700,000	$1,820,000	$1,852,000	$668,000
Taxes Receivable	40,000	1,870,000	1,828,000	82,000
Total	$740,000			$750,000
Allowance for Uncollectible Taxes	$ 8,000	8,000	10,000	$ 10,000
Vouchers Payable	132,000	1,852,000	1,840,000	120,000
Fund Balance:				
Assigned for Encumbrances			70,000	70,000
Unassigned	600,000	70,000	20,000	550,000
Total	$740,000			$750,000

Additional Information

The budget for the fiscal year ended June 30, 20X2, provided for estimated revenue of $2,000,000 and appropriations of $1,940,000. Encumbrances of $1,070,000 were made during the year.

Required

Prepare proper journal entries to record the budgeted and actual transactions for the fiscal year ended June 30, 20X2. Include closing entries.

LO7

P12-14 **General Fund Entries [AICPA Adapted]**

The following trial balances were taken from the accounts of Omega City's general fund before the books had been closed for the fiscal year ended June 30, 20X2:

	Trial Balance July 1, 20X1	Trial Balance June 30, 20X2
Cash	$400,000	$ 700,000
Taxes Receivable	150,000	170,000
Allowance for Uncollectible Taxes	(40,000)	(70,000)
Estimated Revenues Control	—	3,000,000
Expenditures	—	2,900,000
Encumbrances	—	91,000
Total	$510,000	$6,791,000
Vouchers Payable	$ 80,000	$ 408,000
Due to Other Funds	210,000	142,000
Fund Balance—Assigned for Encumbrances	60,000	—
Fund Balance—Unassigned	160,000	220,000
Revenue from Taxes	—	2,800,000
Miscellaneous Revenues	—	130,000
Appropriations Control	—	2,980,000
Budgetary Fund Balance—Assigned for Encumbrances	—	91,000
Budgetary Fund Balance—Unassigned	—	20,000
Total	$510,000	$6,791,000

Additional Information

1. The estimated taxes receivable for the year ended June 30, 20X2, were $2,870,000, and the taxes collected during the year totaled $2,810,000. Miscellaneous revenue of $130,000 also was collected during the year.

2. Encumbrances in the amount of $2,700,000 were recorded. In addition, the $60,000 of lapsed encumbrances from the 20X1 fiscal year was renewed.

3. During the year, the general fund was billed $142,000 for services performed on its behalf by other city funds (debit Expenditures).

4. An analysis of the transactions in the Vouchers Payable account for the year ended June 30, 20X2, is as follows:

	Debit (Credit)
Current expenditures (liquidating all encumbrances to date except for renewed 20X1 commitment)	$(2,700,000)
Expenditures applicable to previous year	(58,000)
Vouchers for payments to other funds	(210,000)
Cash payments during year	2,640,000
Net change	$ (328,000)

5. On May 10, 20X2, encumbrances were recorded for the purchase of next year's supplies at an estimated cost of $91,000.

Required

On the basis of the data presented, reconstruct the original detailed journal entries that were required to record all transactions for the fiscal year ended June 30, 20X2, including the recording of the current year's budget. Do not prepare closing entries for June 30, 20X2.

LO7, LO8 **P12-15** **General Fund Entries and Statements**

The postclosing trial balance of the general fund of the town of Pine Ridge on December 31, 20X1, is as follows:

	Debit	Credit
Cash	$111,000	
Property Taxes Receivable—Delinquent	90,000	
Allowance for Uncollectibles—Delinquent		$ 9,000
Vouchers Payable		31,000
Fund Balance—Assigned for Encumbrances		21,000
Fund Balance—Unassigned		140,000
Total	$201,000	$201,000

Additional Information Related to 20X2

1. Estimated revenue: property taxes, $1,584,000 from a tax levy of $1,600,000 of which 1 percent was estimated uncollectible; sales taxes, $250,000; and miscellaneous, $43,000. Appropriations totaled $1,840,000; and estimated transfers out $37,000. Appropriations included outstanding purchase orders from 20X1 of $21,000. Pine Ridge uses the lapsing method for outstanding encumbrances.

2. Cash receipts: property taxes, $1,590,000, including $83,000 from 20X1; sales taxes, $284,000; licenses and fees, $39,000; and a loan from the motor pool, $10,000. The remaining property taxes from 20X1 were written off, and those remaining from 20X2 were reclassified.

3. Orders were issued for $1,800,000 in addition to the acceptance of the $21,000 outstanding purchase orders from 20X1. A total of $48,000 of purchase orders still was outstanding at the end of 20X2. Actual expenditures were $1,788,000, including $42,000 for office furniture. Vouchers paid totaled $1,793,000.

4. Other cash payments and transfers were as follows:

Loan to central stores	$13,000
Transfer out	37,000

Required

a. Prepare entries to summarize the general fund budget and transactions for 20X2.

b. Prepare a preclosing trial balance.

c. Prepare closing entries for the general fund.

d. Prepare a balance sheet for the general fund as of December 31, 20X2.

e. Prepare a statement of revenues, expenditures, and changes in fund balance for 20X2 for the general fund.

LO2–LO6 **P12-16** **Matching Governmental Terms with Descriptions**

Match the terms on the left with the descriptions on the right. A description may be used once or not at all.

Terms	Descriptions of Terms
1. Proprietary funds	A. Trust and agency funds.
2. Modified accrual method	B. Fiscal and accounting entities of a government.
3. Estimated revenues	C. Basis of accounting used by proprietary funds.
4. Appropriations	D. Example of this transaction when the general fund uses the services of an internal service fund.
5. Encumbrances	E. Expenditures for inventories representing the amount of inventories consumed during the period.
6. Expenditures	F. General, special revenue, debt service, capital projects funds, and permanent funds.
7. Budgetary fund balance—unassigned	G. Legal authority to make expenditures.
8. Consumption method for supplies inventories	H. Budgeted resource inflows.
	I. Revenues recognized when they are both measurable and available to finance expenditures made during the current period.
9. Nonlapsing encumbrances	J. Internal service and enterprise funds.
10. Interfund services provided or used	K. Expenditures for inventories representing the amount of inventories acquired during the current period.
11. Governmental funds	L. Reports government unit's infrastructure assets.
12. Interfund transfers	M. Recorded when the general fund orders goods and services.
13. Fiduciary funds	N. Appropriation authority that carries over to the next fiscal year for these orders.
14. Funds	O. Appropriation authority that does not carry over to the next fiscal year for these orders.
15. Government-wide financials	P. Type of transaction that occurs when the general fund makes a cash transfer to establish an internal service fund.
16. Accrual method	Q. Account debited in the general fund when an invoice is received for computer equipment.
	R. Account that would indicate a budget surplus or deficit in the general fund.

LO2–LO8   **P12-17**   **Identification of Governmental Accounting Terms**

For each of the following numbered statements, give the term(s) that is (are) described in the statement.

1. This is the set of financial statements that presents the governmental unit's infrastructure assets and long-term debt.

2. At the present time, this body has the authority to prescribe generally accepted accounting principles for state and local governmental entities.

3. This is a fiscal and an accounting entity with a self-balancing set of accounts recording cash and other financial resources with all related liabilities and residual equities or balances and changes therein that are segregated for the purpose of carrying on specific activities or attaining certain objectives in accordance with special regulations, restrictions, or limitations.

4. This type of interfund activity is accounted for as an expenditure or revenue.

5. These are the proprietary funds.

6. These are assets of the governmental unit and include roads, municipal buildings, sewer systems, sidewalks, and so forth.

7. These are the fiduciary funds.

8. This basis is used in funds that have a flow of financial resources measurement focus.

9. This is the measurement focus of government-wide financials.

10. This gives the governmental entity the legal right to collect property taxes.

11. These are the governmental funds.

12. This is subtracted from Property Taxes Receivable—Current to get the revenue from property taxes for the year.

13. This account is credited in the budget entry for the general fund if expected resource inflows exceed expected resource outflows.

14. This account is debited when the general fund records a purchase order for goods or services.

15. This method of accounting for supplies inventories in the general fund reports expenditures for supplies for only the amount used during the year.

16. This account is debited in the general fund when a transfer out is made to another fund.

17. This account is debited in the general fund when it records a billing from another fund for services that were provided to the general fund.

18. This is reported on the general fund balance sheet when assets exceed liabilities and assigned fund balance.

19. This account is debited in the general fund when fixed assets are acquired. Assume that a purchase order to acquire the fixed assets was not recorded.

20 This is the legal term that allows the general fund to make expenditures.

21. Under this method of accounting for encumbrances outstanding at year-end, expenditures are dated in the following year when the orders are received.

LO2–LO8   **P12-18**   **Questions on General Fund Entries [AICPA Adapted]**
The DeKalb City Council approved and adopted its budget for 20X2. The budget contained the following amounts:

Estimated revenues	$700,000
Appropriations	660,000
Authorized transfer out to the library debt service fund	30,000

During 20X2, various transactions and events occurred that affected the general fund.

Required
For items 1 through 39, indicate whether the item should be debited (D) or credited (C) or it is not affected (N).
Items 1 through 5 involve recording the adopted budget in the general fund.

1. Estimated Revenues.
2. Budgetary Fund Balance.
3. Appropriations.
4. Estimated Transfer Out.
5. Expenditures.

Items 6 through 10 involve recording the 20X2 property tax levy in the general fund. It was estimated that $5,000 would be uncollectible.

6. Property Tax Receivable.
7. Bad Debts Expense.
8. Allowance for Uncollectibles—Current.
9. Revenues.
10. Estimated Revenues.

Items 11 through 15 involve recording, in the general fund, encumbrances at the time purchase orders are issued.

11. Encumbrances.
12. Budgetary Fund Balance—Assigned for Encumbrances.
13. Expenditures.
14. Vouchers Payable.
15. Purchases.

Items 16 through 20 involve recording, in the general fund, expenditures that had been previously encumbered in the current year.

16. Encumbrances.
17. Budgetary Fund Balance—Assigned for Encumbrances.
18. Expenditures.
19. Vouchers Payable.
20. Purchases.

Items 21 through 25 involve recording, in the general fund, the transfer out of $30,000 made to the library debt service fund. (No previous entries were made regarding this transaction.)

21. Interfund Services Provided and Used.
22. Due from Library Debt Service Fund.
23. Cash.
24. Other Financing Uses—Transfer Out.
25. Encumbrances.

Items 26 through 35 involve recording, in the general fund, the closing entries (other than encumbrances) for 20X2.

26. Estimated Revenues.
27. Budgetary Fund Balance.
28. Appropriations.
29. Estimated Transfer Out.
30. Expenditures.
31. Revenues.
32. Other Financing Uses—Transfer Out.
33. Allowance for Uncollectibles—Current.
34. Bad Debt Expense.
35. Depreciation Expense.

Items 36 through 39 involve recording, in the general fund, the closing entry relating to the $12,000 of outstanding encumbrances at the end of 20X2 and an adjusting entry to reflect the intent to honor these commitments in 20X3.

36. Encumbrances.
37. Budgetary Fund Balance—Assigned for Encumbrances.
38. Fund Balance—Unassigned.
39. Fund Balance—Assigned for Encumbrances.

LO7–LO8   **P12-19**   ## Questions on Fund Items [AICPA Adapted]

The following information relates to actual results from Central Town's general fund for the year ended December 31, 20X1:

	Revenues	Expenditures and Transfers
Property tax collections:		
Current year taxes collected	$630,000	
Prior year taxes due 12/1/X0, collected 2/1/X1	50,000	
Current year taxes due 12/1/X1, collection expected by 2/15/X2	70,000	
Other cash receipts	190,000	
General government expenditures:		
Salaries and wages		$160,000
Other		100,000
Public safety and welfare expenditures:		
Salaries and wages		350,000
Other		150,000
Capital outlay		140,000
Transfer out to debt service fund		30,000

- Other cash receipts include a county grant of $100,000 for a specified purpose, of which $80,000 was expended; $50,000 in fines; and $40,000 in fees.

- General Government Expenditures—Other includes employer contributions to the pension plan and $20,000 in annual capital lease payments for computers over three years; the fair value and present value at lease inception is $50,000.

- Capital outlay is for police vehicles.

- Debt service represents annual interest payments due December 15 of each year on $500,000 face value, 6 percent, 20-year term bonds.

Capital Projects Fund

Central's council approved $750,000 for construction of a fire station to be financed by $600,000 in general obligation bonds and a $150,000 state grant. Construction began during 20X1, but the fire station was not completed until April 20X2. During 20X1, the following transactions were recorded:

State grant	$150,000
Bond proceeds	610,000
Expenditures	500,000
Unpaid invoices at year-end	30,000
Outstanding encumbrances at year-end, which do not lapse and are to be honored the following year	25,000

The unassigned fund balance in the capital projects fund at January 1, 20X1, was $110,000.

Required

For questions *a* through *i*, determine the December 31, 20X1, year-end amounts to be recognized in the particular fund. If the item is not reported in a particular fund but is reported on the government-wide financial statements, then specify the amount that would be reported on the government-wide financials. Select your answer from the list of amounts below the questions. An amount may be selected once, more than once, or not at all.

a. What amount was recorded for property tax revenues in the general fund?

b. What amount was recorded for other revenues in the general fund?

c. What amount was reported for capital leases of computers in the government-wide statement of net assets?

d. What amount was reported for the new police vehicles in the government-wide statement of net assets?

e. What amount was reported for the debt service interest payment in the debt service fund?

f. What was the total amount recorded for function expenditures in the general fund?

g. What amount was recorded for revenues in the capital projects fund?

h. What amount was reported for construction in progress in the government-wide statement of net assets?

i. What amount was reported as the Fund Balance—Unassigned at December 31, 20X1, in the capital projects fund?

Amounts
1. $0
2. $30,000
3. $50,000
4. $55,000
5. $60,000
6. $140,000
7. $150,000
8. $170,000
9. $190,000
10. $315,000
11. $345,000
12. $370,000
13. $500,000
14. $525,000
15. $630,000
16. $700,000
17. $710,000
18. $760,000

LO2–LO8   P12-20   **Identifying Types of Revenue Transactions**

Required

Using the requirements of **GASB Statement No. 33**, "Accounting and Financial Reporting for Nonexchange Transactions," classify each of the following independent transactions for the community of Fair Lake into the proper category of revenue as presented in the right-hand column.

Transactions	Types of Revenue
1. Property taxes were levied by the general fund.	A. Derived tax revenue
2. The electric utility (enterprise) fund billed the general fund for power usage.	B. Imposed nonexchange revenue
3. The city received a state grant for training its police force in additional security measures of public property.	C. Government-mandated nonexchange transaction
4. The city estimated its share of locally generated sales taxes that it expects to receive within the next month.	D. Voluntary nonexchange transaction
5. The city collected various fines it imposed during the period.	E. None of the above
6. The city sold excess office equipment from its municipal headquarters.	
7. The city received resources from the state that must be used to pay for local welfare costs.	
8. The city received a bequest from a local citizen to buy children's recreational items for the city park.	
9. The city collects its share of the local hotel taxes for which the proceeds are legislatively required to be used for a new community convention center.	
10. The state reimburses the city for specific costs related to extra security training of the city's fire department employees.	
11. The city receives its share of funds for environmental improvement resources under a state-required program.	
12. The city receives resources from the federal government to acquire new fire-prevention equipment. The equipment has not yet been acquired.	
13. The city receives grant monies under a state program encouraging cities to make their infrastructure assets wheelchair-accessible.	
14. A company that manufactures road-repaving materials gives the city a grant for the company to conduct a research project on the durability of various types of road repair materials.	

Supplemental Problems for this chapter are available as part of the *Online Learning Center* on the textbook's Web site (URL: www.mhhe.com/baker1e).

Chapter **Thirteen**

Governmental Entities: Special Funds and Government-wide Financial Statements

GOVERNMENTAL ACCOUNTING IN MARYLAND

In 1498, John Cabot was the first to explore the area that is now the state of Maryland. One of the original 13 colonies, Maryland began its provincial government after receiving its charter from King Charles I in 1632. The various governments of this geographical area have kept accounting records for nearly 400 years. The evolution from province to colony to state, along with a growing population, has led to increasingly more complex governmental functions and programs, which, in turn, have led to more complex accounting. However, it wasn't until the 20th century that standardized accounting standards for governmental entities became widely accepted.

While Chapter 12 discussed the various public services provided by the City of San Diego, the State of Maryland is even more complex and diverse. Consider the following representative sample of the varied activities administered by the State of Maryland:

- **Public Safety** (State Police, Prisons, Crime Prevention, Firearms Control)
- **Housing and Home Ownership** (Public Housing, Construction Regulation, Energy Programs)
- **Children and Parenting** (Adoption, Child Care Assistance, Foster Parenting)
- **Disabilities** (Special Olympics, Transportation for People with Disabilities, Disability Programs)
- **Assistance Programs** (Food Assistance, Energy Assistance, Homelessness Prevention)
- **Senior Citizens** (Assisted Living Programs, Home Nursing Programs, Senior Olympics)
- **Business** (Environmental Permits, Agriculture Licenses, Unemployment Programs)
- **Employment** (Employment of Minors, Equal Opportunity Programs, Injured Workers Programs)
- **Youth Education** (Pre-K through Grade 12, Public Schools)
- **Adult Learning** (Literacy Programs, Rehabilitation Services, English Language Schools)
- **Higher Education** (Colleges and Universities, Online Learning)
- **Financial Aid** (College Savings Programs, Grant and Loan Programs)

- **Travel and Tourism** (Maps and Travel Guides, Welcome Centers and Rest Areas, State Parks)
- **Recreation and Sports** (Camping Information, Fisheries Service, Golf Courses)
- **Arts and Culture** (Museums, Historical Locations, Maryland Science Center)

While this list is not exhaustive, it illustrates the diverse activities and programs overseen by the State. The disclosure of these many activities is a major part of the State's fiscal responsibility to its citizens. Maryland's 2009 Comprehensive Annual Financial Report (CAFR) is 172 pages long. It summarizes all of the activities of the different departments, programs, and entities affiliated with the state government. In addition to the general fund, discussed in Chapter 12, governments usually have a number of other funds. Maryland's 2009 CAFR contains government-wide financial statements, similar to consolidated financial statements in the private sector, as well as financial statements of these individual funds. This chapter presents the accounting and financial reporting requirements for (1) the four remaining governmental fund types, (2) the two proprietary fund types, and (3) the four fiduciary fund types.

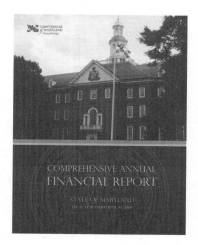

LEARNING OBJECTIVES

When you finish studying this chapter, you should be able to:

LO1   Understand and explain the differences in financial reporting requirements of the different fund types.

LO2   Make calculations and record journal entries for capital projects funds.

LO3   Make calculations and record journal entries for debt service funds.

LO4   Make calculations and record journal entries for permanent funds.

LO5   Understand and explain how governmental funds are reported and rules for separate reporting as major funds.

LO6   Make calculations and record journal entries for enterprise funds.

LO7   Understand and explain the financial reporting of proprietary funds.

LO8   Make calculations and record journal entries for internal service funds.

LO9   Make calculations and record journal entries for trust funds.

LO10 Make calculations and record journal entries for agency funds.

LO11 Understand and explain the preparation of government-wide financial statements.

LO12 Understand and explain the additional disclosures that accompany government-wide financial statements.

SUMMARY OF GOVERNMENTAL FUND TYPES

Figure 13–1 presents the typical fund organization for a local government.

In practice, the funds are often identified with the acronyms from the first letters of their titles, as follows:

Governmental Fund Types

GF   General fund
SRF   Special revenue funds
DSF   Debt service funds
CPF   Capital projects funds
PF   Permanent funds

Proprietary Fund Types

EF   Enterprise funds
ISF   Internal service funds

Fiduciary Fund Types

PTF   Pension trust funds
ITF   Investment trust funds
P-PTF Private-purpose trust funds
AF   Agency funds

A government should establish those funds required by law and the specific operating and management needs of the government entity. Unnecessary, additional funds add unneeded complexity and do not enhance the operational efficiency of the government. A general rule followed in many governmental entities is that all activities should be accounted for in the general fund unless specifically required by law or the different measurement focus used for proprietary and fiduciary funds. This rule does not prohibit the creation of additional funds but places a reasonable restraint on the proliferation of additional funds. The structure of funds discussed in this chapter is the typical one used in most state and local governmental systems.

One event may require entries in several funds. For example, the construction of a new municipal building through the issuance of general obligation bonds may require entries in both a capital project fund and a debt service fund. In addition, interfund activities require entries in two or more funds.

The governmental funds use the modified accrual basis of accounting, and the proprietary and fiduciary funds use the accrual basis of accounting. Governmental entities recognize estimated uncollectible amounts as a reduction of revenue, not as an expense. The five governmental funds do not report long-term assets or long-term

FIGURE 13–1
Funds for a
Governmental Entity

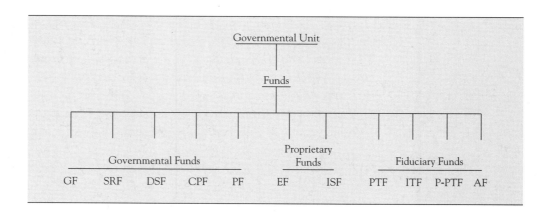

debt, but the government-wide statements do report them. Investments are reported in the appropriate funds and are valued at their fair market values at each balance sheet date. The government entity's financial report includes both fund-based and government-wide financial statements. The government-wide statements are prepared using the accrual basis of accounting. Reconciliation schedules are required to show the differences between the amounts reported in the governmental funds financial statements, presented using the modified accrual basis of accounting, and the amounts reported in the government-wide financial statements, presented using the accrual basis of accounting.

Some governmental units have pension trust funds for their employees. Accounting and reporting for pension trust funds is quite complex and beyond the scope of an advanced financial accounting course. Pension trust funds are covered briefly in the "Additional Considerations" section of this chapter.

This chapter continues the example of Sol City started in Chapter 12, where the entries and financial reports for the general fund were presented for 20X2. Sol City uses the lapsing method of accounting for encumbrances and the consumption method for inventories and records all expected budgetary accounts including anticipated interfund transactions. The techniques of capitalizing all budgetary accounts and recording journal entries at the control level are continued from Chapter 12. The financial statements for the illustration are prepared using the requirements of **GASB 34.** Many of the numbers for the Sol City example are assumed in order to focus on the main concepts of accounting and financial reporting for a governmental entity. Thus, some of the numbers cannot be computed from the data given. Instead, focus on the concepts being discussed. We present the fund balance reported for the governmental funds that is now required under the new **GASB 54.** The final section of this chapter presents the government-wide financial statements for Sol City.

Figure 13–2 presents an overview of the major accounting and financial standards for the individual funds. This figure can be used as a continual reference point during study of Chapter 13.

GOVERNMENTAL FUNDS WORKSHEETS

Each of the five governmental funds will report two *fund-based financial statements:* the balance sheet and the statement of revenues, expenditures, and changes in fund balance. Rather than presenting each of the separate governmental funds' financial statements in the chapter, we provide worksheets to summarize all governmental funds' financial statements. Specifically, Figure 13–3 presents the individual fund information that will be used to prepare the governmental funds' balance sheet. Figure 13–4 presents the individual governmental funds information that will be used to prepare the governmental funds' statement of revenues, expenditures, and changes in fund balance. The amounts for the general fund are taken from the information in Chapter 12. The amounts for the other funds will be developed throughout this chapter. We use these two worksheets throughout the chapter as the basis for preparing the governmental funds' financial statements that will be presented later in the chapter. The worksheets also include major funds tests that will be discussed later in the chapter. Thus, we develop the two worksheets through the discussions of each fund type in this chapter.

SPECIAL REVENUE FUNDS

Current governmental resources may be restricted to expenditure for specific purposes, such as development of the state highway system, maintenance of public parks, or operation of the public school system, city libraries, and museums. The necessary revenue often comes from special tax levies or federal or state governmental grants. Some minor revenue may be earned through user charges, but these charges are usually not sufficient to fully fund the service. *Special revenue funds* are used to account for such restricted

FIGURE 13–2 Overview of Accounting and Financial Reporting for Governments

	Governmental Funds					Proprietary Funds		Fiduciary Funds		Government-wide Financials
	General Fund	Special Revenue Funds	Capital Projects Funds	Debt Service Funds	Permanent Funds	Enterprise Funds	Internal Service Funds	Trust Funds	Agency Funds	
Basis of accounting	Modified accrual	Modified accrual	Modified accrual	Modified accrual	Modified accrual	Accrual	Accrual	Accrual	Accrual	Accrual
Budgetary basis recorded (budgetary accounts are typically used when a legally adopted annual operating budget is passed)	Operating budget often recorded	Operating budget often recorded	Capital budget usually not recorded	Not required	Not required	No	No	No	No	
Long-term productive assets (buildings, equipment, etc.) reported	No	No	No	No	No	Yes	Yes	Yes	No	Yes
Long-term debt reported	No	No	No	No	No	Yes	Yes	Yes	No	Yes
Encumbrances recorded	Yes	Yes	Possibly	Possibly	Possibly	No	No	No	No	
Financial Statements										
Balance sheet	X	X	X	X	X					
Statement of net assets						X	X			X
Statement of revenues, expenditures, and changes in fund balance	X	X	X	X	X					
Statement of revenues, expenses, and changes in fund net assets						X	X			
Statement of activities										X
Statement of cash flows						X	X			
Statement of fiduciary net assets								X	X	
Statement of changes in fiduciary net assets								X	X	

FIGURE 13–3 Worksheet for the Balance Sheet for the Governmental Funds

	Governmental Funds					Total Governmental Funds	Enterprise Fund	Total Governmental and Enterprise
	General	Special Revenue	Capital Projects	Debt Service	Permanent			
Assets								
Current								
Cash	102,000	15,000	16,000	2,000	13,000			
Property Taxes (net of allowances)	85,000	1,000		3,000				
Due from Enterprise Fund	3,000							
Inventory of Supplies	17,000							
Noncurrent								
Investment in Government Bonds					90,000			
Total Assets	207,000	16,000	16,000	5,000	103,000	347,000	140,000	487,000
Liabilities and Fund Balances								
Vouchers Payable	55,000	3,000						
Contract Payable—Retainage			10,000					
Total Liabilities	55,000	3,000	10,000	-0-	-0-	68,000	112,000	180,000
Fund Balances								
Nonspendable:								
Inventories	17,000							
Permanent Fund					103,000			
Spendable:								
Assigned to:								
General Government Services	15,000	6,000						
Debt Service				5,000				
Unassigned, reported in:								
General Fund	120,000							
Special Revenue Fund		7,000						
Capital Projects Fund			6,000					
Total Fund Balances	152,000	13,000	6,000	5,000	103,000	279,000		
Total Liabilities and Fund Balances	207,000	16,000	16,000	5,000	103,000	347,000		
Major Fund Tests on Total Assets:								
10% Test of Total Governmental or Enterprise	4.61%	4.61%	4.61%	1.44%	29.68%		100.00%	
5% Test of Governmental Plus Enterprise	3.29%	3.29%	3.29%	1.03%	21.15%		28.75%	
Major Fund Test (Yes or No)	Yes	No	No	No	Yes		Yes	
Major Fund Tests on Total Liabilities:								
10% Test of Total Governmental or Enterprise	4.41%	4.41%	14.71%	0.00%	0.00%		100.00%	
5% Test of Governmental Plus Enterprise	1.67%	1.67%	5.56%	0.00%	0.00%		62.22%	
Major Fund Test (Yes or No)	Yes	No	Yes	No	No		Yes	

FIGURE 13–4 Worksheet for the Statement of Revenues, Expenditures, and Changes in Fund Balances for the Governmental Funds

	Governmental Funds					Total Governmental Funds	Enterprise Fund	Total Governmental and Enterprise
	General	Special Revenue	Capital Projects	Debt Service	Permanent			
Revenues								
Property Taxes	781,000			33,000				
Sales Taxes	32,000	62,000						
Grants	33,000		10,000		8,000			
Miscellaneous	18,000							
Total Revenues	864,000	62,000	10,000	33,000	8,000	977,000	37,000	1,014,000
Expenditures								
Current								
General Government	206,000							
Streets and Highways	71,000							
Public Safety	335,000							
Sanitation	141,000							
Culture and Recreation		49,000			5,000			
Miscellaneous			124,000					
Debt Service								
Principal Retirement				20,000				
Interest Charges				10,000				
Capital Outlay	58,000							
Total Expenditures/Expenses	811,000	49,000	124,000	30,000	5,000	1,019,000	35,000	1,054,000
Excess (Deficiency) of Revenues over Expenditures	53,000	13,000	(114,000)	3,000	3,000	(42,000)		
Other Financing Sources (Uses)								
Proceeds of Bond Issue			102,000					
Transfers In			20,000	2,000				
Transfers Out	(30,000)		(2,000)					
Total Other Financing Sources and Uses	(30,000)	-0-	120,000	2,000	-0-	92,000		
Special Item								
Contribution					100,000	100,000		
Net Change in Fund Balances	23,000	13,000	6,000	5,000	103,000	150,000		
Fund Balances—Beginning	129,000	-0-	-0-	-0-	-0-	129,000		
Fund Balances—Ending	152,000	13,000	6,000	5,000	103,000	279,000		
Major Fund Tests on Total Revenues:								
10% Test of Total Governmental or Enterprise		6.35%	1.02%	3.38%	0.82%		100.00%	
5% Test of Governmental and Enterprise		6.11%	0.99%	3.25%	0.79%		3.65%	
Major Fund Test (Yes or No)	Yes	No	No	No	No		No	
Major Fund Tests on Total Expenditures/Expenses:								
10% Test of Total Governmental or Enterprise		4.81%	12.17%	2.94%	0.49%		100.00%	
5% Test of Governmental and Enterprise		4.65%	11.76%	2.85%	0.47%		3.32%	
Major Fund Test (Yes or No)	Yes	No	Yes	No	No		No	

resources. The governmental entity usually has a separate special revenue fund for each different activity of this type. Thus, a city may have several special revenue funds.

The accounting for special revenue funds is identical to the accounting for the general fund. The modified accrual basis of accounting is used, no fixed assets or depreciation are recorded, the operating budget is typically recorded in the accounts, and no long-term debt is recorded.

Special revenue fund accounting is not illustrated in the chapter because the principles for the special revenue fund are the same as those for the general fund as covered in Chapter 12. For purposes of the governmental funds statements, assume that $62,000 of property taxes were collected for the special revenue fund and that $49,000 was expended for the designated culture and recreation purposes for which the special revenue fund was established. The focus of this chapter is on the unique or interesting aspects of governmental accounting and financial reporting. Figure 13–3 presents the assumed numbers for the special revenue fund's balance sheet and Figure 13–4 presents the revenues ($62,000) and expenditures ($49,000) assumed for the special revenue fund.

CAPITAL PROJECTS FUNDS[1]

LO2

Make calculations and record journal entries for capital projects funds.

Advanced
StudyGuide
.com

Capital projects funds account for financial resources that are specified for the acquisition or construction of major capital facilities or improvements that benefit the public. Typical examples are the construction of libraries, civic centers, fire stations, courthouses, bridges, major streets, and city municipal buildings. A separate capital projects fund is created at the time the project is approved and ceases at its completion. Each project or group of related projects usually is accounted for in a separate capital projects fund.

Accounting for capital projects funds is similar to accounting for the general fund. The modified accrual basis of accounting is used, no fixed assets or depreciation are recorded in the capital projects funds, and no long-term debt is recorded in these funds. Capital projects funds, however, typically do not have annual operating budgets. Instead, a capital budget is prepared as a basis for selling bonds to finance a project, and the capital budget is the control mechanism for the length of the project. The capital budget for the project may, or may not, be formally recorded in the accounts. Theoretically, encumbrances are part of the budgetary system and should flow from the appropriating authority of the budget. However, encumbrances may be recorded even if the capital project budget is not recorded. Encumbrances maintain an ongoing accounting record of the expenditure commitments that have been made on a project and Sol City has a policy to use encumbrances in its capital projects funds. Sol City chose not to formally enter the project budget into the accounts.

The capital projects fund records capital outlays as expenditures. Thus, no fixed assets are recorded in this fund. A record of the construction in progress, however, may be maintained in memorandum format.

Illustration of Transactions

On January 1, 20X2, Sol City establishes a capital projects fund to account for a capital addition to the municipal courthouse. The expected cost of the addition is $120,000. A $100,000, 10 percent general obligation bond issue is sold at 102, for total proceeds of $102,000. The bond is a five-year serial bond with equal amounts of $20,000 to be paid each year, beginning on December 31, 20X2, until the debt is extinguished. The bond proceeds are not revenue to the capital projects fund; they are reported in the other financing sources section of the fund's statement of revenues, expenditures, and changes in fund balance. Any debt issue costs such as underwriting fees or attorney fees are recognized as expenditures when the liabilities are both measurable and incurred, and are payable out of current financial resources.

[1] To view a video explanation of this topic, visit advancedstudyguide.com.

The capital projects fund is not entitled to the $2,000 premium on the sale of bonds. This premium is transferred as a transfer out to the debt service fund immediately upon receipt. The debt service fund records the receipt of the transfer as a transfer in (see entry [15] later in this chapter). The premium is viewed as an adjustment of the interest rate, not as a part of the funds expendable by the capital projects fund. If bonds are sold at a discount, either the amount expended for the improvement must be decreased or the general fund must make up the difference to the face value of the bonds.

In addition, a federal grant for $10,000 is received as financial support for part of the capital addition, and the capital projects fund receives an interfund transfer in of $20,000 from the city's general fund. Recall that an interfund transfer is an interfund transaction in which resources are moved from one fund, usually from the general fund, to another fund to be used for the operations of the receiving fund. The general fund records this transfer of $20,000 as an interfund transfer out (see entry [34] in Chapter 12). The following entries are recorded for the 20X2 fiscal year.

Capital Projects Revenue and Bond Proceeds

The sale of the bonds and receipt of the federal grant and operating transfer in are recorded as follows:

(1)	Cash	102,000	
	Other Financing Sources—Bond Issue		100,000
	Other Financing Sources—Bond Premium		2,000
	Issue $100,000 of bonds at 102.		

(2)	Other Financing Uses—Transfer Out to Debt Service Fund	2,000	
	Cash		2,000
	Forward bond premium to debt service fund.		

(3)	Cash	10,000	
	Revenue—Federal Grant		10,000
	Receive federal grant to be applied to courthouse addition.		

(4)	Due from General Fund	20,000	
	Other Financing Sources—Transfer In from General Fund		20,000
	Establish receivable for interfund transfer in from general fund.		

(5)	Cash	20,000	
	Due from General Fund		20,000
	Receive transferred resources from general fund.		

Entry (3) recognizes the $10,000 grant from the federal government as revenue when the grant is received. Some grants from the federal government are termed "expenditure-driven" grants, for which revenue can be recognized only as expenditures are incurred in conformity with the grant agreement. For these expenditure-driven grants, the local governmental entity recognizes revenue only after the eligibility requirements for the government-mandated nonexchange transaction have been met: that is, the allowable expenditures have been made.

Capital Projects Fund Expenditures

The following encumbrances, expenditures, and disbursements are recorded in 20X2.

(6)	ENCUMBRANCES	110,000	
	BUDGETARY FUND BALANCE—ASSIGNED FOR ENCUMBRANCES		110,000
	Budgetary entry to record the issuance of a construction contract for $110,000.		

(7)	BUDGETARY FUND BALANCE—ASSIGNED FOR ENCUMBRANCES	110,000	
	ENCUMBRANCES		110,000
	Budgetary entry to record the completion of the construction project. Reverse reserve for encumbrances.		

(8)	Expenditures	118,000	
	Contract Payable		108,000
	Contract Payable—Retained Percentage		10,000

Actual construction cost of courthouse addition is $118,000.
Additional cost is approved. Contract terms include retained
percentage of $10,000 until full and final acceptance of project.

(9)	Expenditures	6,000	
	Vouchers Payable		6,000

Additional items for courthouse addition.

(10)	Vouchers Payable	6,000	
	Contract Payable	108,000	
	Cash		114,000

Pay current portion of construction contract and vouchers.

In entry (8), Contract Payable is credited for $108,000 for the current portion due, and Contract Payable—Retained Percentage is credited for $10,000. In entry (10), the $108,000 current portion of the contract liability is paid in full. A normal practice of governmental units is to have a retained percentage of the total amount due under a construction contract held back to ensure that the contractor fully completes the project to the satisfaction of the governmental unit. For example, a city may stipulate that 10 percent of the total contract price is retained until the project is fully completed and accepted. This retainage payable is released and paid upon final acceptance of the project by the governmental unit.

Closing Entries in the Capital Projects Fund

The nominal accounts are closed with the following entries:

(11)	Revenue—Federal Grant	10,000	
	Fund Balance—Unassigned	114,000	
	Expenditures		124,000

Close operating accounts of revenue and expenditures.

(12)	Other Financing Sources—Bond Issue	100,000	
	Other Financing Sources—Bond Premium	2,000	
	Fund Balance—Unassigned		102,000

Close other financing sources.

(13)	Other Financing Sources—Transfer In from General Fund	20,000	
	Other Financing Uses—Transfer Out to Debt Service Fund		2,000
	Fund Balance—Unassigned		18,000

Close interfund transfers.

No encumbrances are outstanding as of the end of the fiscal year. At this point, the Fund Balance—Unassigned account has a credit balance of $6,000. Upon completion and final approval of a capital project, the remaining fund balance is transferred either to the general fund or to the debt service fund, depending on the policy of the governmental unit. The transfer is a transfer out for the capital projects fund and a transfer in for the receiving fund because it involves the one-time transfer of the remaining resources in the capital projects fund. In the preceding example, Sol City decided that the fund should remain open through the first part of the next fiscal year in case any minor modifications of the new courthouse addition are required. If no further modifications are required, and the courthouse addition project is officially accepted, the $10,000 in the Contract Payable—Retained Percentage account is paid to the contractor. Any remaining resources in the capital projects fund are then transferred and the capital projects fund is closed.

Financial Statement Information for the Capital Projects Fund

The financial statement information for the capital projects funds is presented in Figure 13–3 for the balance sheet and in Figure 13–4 for the statement of revenues, expenditures, and changes in fund balances. The Sol City capital projects fund was created on January 1, 20X2, the date the capital addition was approved and the serial bonds were sold. Figure 13–3 shows that the only asset remaining in this fund on December 31, 20X2, is $16,000 of cash, which includes the $10,000 for the contract payable–retainage. Figure 13–4 for the capital projects fund column presents the $102,000 of proceeds from the bond issue, which is reported among other financing sources, with a reduction for the transfer out of the $2,000 premium to the debt service fund, and the transfer in of $20,000, netting against the large excess of expenditures over revenue in the amount of $114,000. The statement of revenues, expenditures, and changes in fund balance reconciles to the $6,000 fund balance at the end of the fiscal period.

DEBT SERVICE FUNDS

LO3

Make calculations and record journal entries for debt service funds.

Advanced
StudyGuide
.com

Debt service funds account for the accumulation and use of resources for the payment of general long-term debt principal and interest. A government may have several types of general long-term debt obligations, as follows:

1. *Serial bonds.* The most common form of debt issued by governments is in the form of serial bonds. The bonds are repaid in installments over the life of the debt. A serial bond is called "regular" if the installments are equal and "irregular" if they are not equal.
2. *Term bonds.* This form of debt is less frequent now than in the past. The entire principal of the debt is due at the maturity date.
3. *Special assessment bonds.* Special assessment bonds are secured by tax liens on the property located within the special assessment tax district. The governmental unit also may become obligated in some manner to assume the payment of the debt in the event of default by the property owners. Special assessment bonds may be used to finance capital projects or to acquire other assets such as ambulances or fire engines necessary to operate the governmental unit. Special assessment bonds sold to acquire enterprise fund assets, however, should be accounted for within the enterprise fund. The special assessment feature simply states the source of financing and means of repayment.
4. *Notes and warrants.* These consist of debt typically issued for one or two years. These debts are usually secured by specific tax revenue, which must first be used to repay the debt. Property tax anticipation warrants are an example.
5. *Capital leases.* Governmental entities must record capital leases in accordance with generally accepted accounting principles. These leases then become long-term liabilities of the governmental unit.

Some governmental entities service long-term debt directly from the general fund, thereby eliminating the need for a debt service fund as a separate fiscal, accounting, and reporting entity. However, if a governmental entity has several long-term general obligations outstanding, it may be required by bond indentures or other regulations to establish a separate debt service fund for each obligation to account for the proper servicing of each debt obligation.

The accounting and financial reporting for debt service funds are the same as for the general fund. The modified accrual basis of accounting is used, and only that portion of the long-term debt that has matured and is currently payable is recorded in the debt service funds.

Interest payable on long-term debt is not accrued; interest is recognized as a liability only when it comes due and payable. The "when due" recognition of interest matches the debt service expenditures with the resources accumulated to repay the debt. This approach prevents an understatement of the debt service fund balance. For example, if interest is accrued before it is actually due, the fund balance may show a deficit because of the excess of liabilities over assets. The function of the debt service fund is to accumulate resources to pay debt principal and interest as they become due. Thus, the when-due recognition of interest is consistent with the fund's objectives.

Illustration of Transactions

Sol City establishes a debt service fund to service the $100,000, five-year, 10 percent serial bond issued on January 1, 20X2, to finance the capital project courthouse addition. The bond initially sold at a premium of $2,000. The resources to pay the bond principal and interest as they become due will be obtained from a property tax levy specifically for debt service.

Adoption of Debt Service Fund Budget

Debt service funds are not required to adopt annual operating budgets because the fund's expenditures are generally mandated by bond agreements and an operating budget may be viewed as unnecessarily redundant. Nevertheless, there is no restriction against having an operating budget for the debt service fund as part of a comprehensive budgeting system for a governmental entity, as illustrated here.

The annual operating budget for the debt service fund is adopted at the time the fund is created to service the serial bonds sold for the courthouse addition. Appropriations of $30,000 are budgeted to pay $20,000 of maturing principal and $10,000 of interest for the year. Sol City budgets all expected interfund transactions, and the anticipated interfund transfer in of the $2,000 premium on the serial bonds sold is recorded with the budget:

(14)	ESTIMATED REVENUES CONTROL	30,000	
	ESTIMATED OTHER FINANCING SOURCES—TRANSFER IN	2,000	
	APPROPRIATIONS CONTROL		30,000
	BUDGETARY FUND BALANCE		2,000
	Adopt budget for 20X2.		

The budgetary accounts ESTIMATED REVENUES CONTROL and APPROPRIATIONS CONTROL are used to account for servicing serial bonds.

Debt Service Fund Revenue and Other Financing Sources

In this example, the debt service fund obtains revenue from a specified property tax levy. The bond premium received from the capital projects fund is recognized as a transfer in. Note that the capital projects fund records this transfer as an interfund transfer out (see entry [2] earlier in this chapter). The entries to record the receipt of the bond premium and the levy and collection of taxes are as follows:

(15)	Cash	2,000	
	Other Financing Sources—Transfer In from Capital Projects Fund		2,000
	Receive bond premium from capital projects fund.		

(16)	Property Taxes Receivable	35,000	
	Allowance for Uncollectible Taxes		5,000
	Revenue—Property Tax		30,000
	Levy property taxes and provide for allowance for uncollectible taxes. Estimated uncollectible property taxes reduce Revenue.		

(17)	Cash	30,000	
	Property Taxes Receivable		30,000
	Receive portion of property taxes.		

(18)	Property Taxes Receivable—Delinquent	5,000	
	Allowance for Uncollectible Taxes	5,000	
	Property Taxes Receivable		5,000
	Revenue—Property Tax		3,000
	Allowance for Uncollectible Taxes—Delinquent		2,000
	Reclassify remaining property taxes as delinquent and reduce allowance for uncollectible taxes from $5,000 to $2,000.		

Debt Service Fund Expenditures

The primary expenditures of the debt service fund are for the first annual payment of principal and for interest on the serial bonds payable. An encumbrance system is typically not used for matured principal and interest because the debt agreement serves as the expenditure control mechanism:

(19)	Expenditures—Principal	20,000	
	Matured Bonds Payable		20,000

Recognize matured portion of serial bond:
$100,000 ÷ 5 years

(20)	Expenditures—Interest	10,000	
	Matured Interest Payable		10,000

Recognize interest due this period:
$100,000 × 0.10 × 1 year

(21)	Matured Bonds Payable	20,000	
	Matured Interest Payable	10,000	
	Cash		30,000

Pay first year's installment plus interest on bond.

Closing Entries in the Debt Service Fund

The nominal accounts are closed as follows:

(22)	APPROPRIATIONS CONTROL	30,000	
	BUDGETARY FUND BALANCE	2,000	
	ESTIMATED REVENUES CONTROL		30,000
	ESTIMATED OTHER FINANCING SOURCES—TRANSFER IN		2,000

Close budgetary accounts.

(23)	Revenue—Property Tax	33,000	
	Expenditures—Principal		20,000
	Expenditures—Interest		10,000
	Fund Balance—Assigned for Debt Service		3,000

Close operating revenue and expenditures.

(24)	Other Financing Sources—Transfer In from Capital Projects Fund	2,000	
	Fund Balance—Assigned for Debt Service		2,000

Close interfund transfer.

If the debt service fund services term bonds, a different budgetary account system is used. The following budgetary entry would be made for term bonds for the periods prior to the maturity date:

REQUIRED CONTRIBUTIONS	XXX	
REQUIRED EARNINGS	XXX	
BUDGETARY FUND BALANCE		XXX

The budgetary amounts are determined based on a computation of the contributions needed each period to be invested, earning a given return to accumulate to the amount required for the payment of the bonds. The debt service fund may then receive resources from the general fund or from a tax levy, which it would invest until the term bonds became due. In the period the term bonds reach maturity, the debt service fund pays the matured principal and interest from its available resources. The debt service fund may make temporary investments of excess cash in order to maximize the return from its resources. These investments are reported as an asset of the debt service fund. Most temporary investments are made in low-risk U.S. Treasury securities or in certificates of deposit from larger banks. Interest income is accrued as earned. The investments are valued in accordance with **GASB Statement No. 31,** "Accounting for Financial Reporting for Certain Investments and for External Investment Pools" (GASB 31). The general valuation standard in **GASB 31** is fair value for most investments made by a governmental entity. However, an exception is allowed for governmental entities other than external investment pools, so that market investments may be reported at amortized cost, provided the investment has a remaining maturity of one year or less from the date of purchase. Unrealized gains or losses on investments are combined with realized gains or losses and are reported on the governmental entity's operating statements as net investment income or loss.

Financial Statement Information for the Debt Service Fund

The financial statement information for the debt service fund for the governmental funds is presented in Figure 13–3 for the balance sheet and in Figure 13–4 for the governmental funds statement of revenues, expenditures, and changes in fund balance.

PERMANENT FUNDS

LO4

Make calculations and record journal entries for permanent funds.

Advanced
StudyGuide
.com

Permanent funds are established in those cases in which there is a donor restriction that the fund principal must be preserved but the income from these permanent funds is required to be used to benefit the government's programs or its general citizenry. The donor-restricted donation may be from individuals, estates, and public or private organizations. Permanent funds are classified in the governmental funds category because the income resources in these funds are to be used toward the government's programs and services for its general citizenry. The modified accrual basis of accounting is used in this fund and the financial statements for the permanent funds are the same as for all other governmental funds.

Illustration of Transactions

On January 1, 20X2, Sol City receives a $100,000 bequest from a long-term city resident. The will stipulates that the $100,000 be invested and the income be used to provide for maintenance and improvement of the city park. Note that a private-purpose fund, which would be a fiduciary fund, is one in which the government is required to use the principal or earnings for the benefit of specific individuals, private organizations, or other designated governments, as stated in the trust agreement. This bequest is for the benefit of the general citizenry, however, and is established as a permanent fund that is a governmental fund type. The entries in this permanent fund during 20X2 are as follows:

(25)	Cash	100,000	
	Contributions		100,000
	Accept permanent fund resources.		

This contribution will be reported as a special item, after other financing sources and uses, toward the bottom of the statement of revenues, expenditures, and changes in fund balance.

Investment and Interest

The fund's resources are used to acquire $100,000 face value, high-grade, 8 percent governmental securities at 90 to yield an effective interest rate of 10 percent. Interest income is accrued under the modified accrual method, which means that the revenue recognition may be for only that amount of interest that is both measurable and available to finance expenditures made during the current fiscal period. Therefore, only the $8,000 of accrued interest receivable is available for expenditures this period, and the discount amortization would not be shown in the modified accrual basis financial statements.

| (26) | Investment in Bonds | 90,000 | |
| | Cash | | 90,000 |

Acquire $100,000 face value government securities at 90.

| (27) | Accrued Interest Receivable | 8,000 | |
| | Interest Revenue | | 8,000 |

Accrue interest:
$8,000 = $100,000 \times 0.08$, nominal (coupon) rate

| (28) | Cash | 8,000 | |
| | Accrued Interest Receivable | | 8,000 |

Collect accrued interest on securities.

Expenditures

The permanent trust fund expends $5,000 during the period for maintenance of the city park and recognizes the following entry:

| (29) | Expenditures | 5,000 | |
| | Cash | | 5,000 |

Expenditures made for maintenance of the city park.

The balance sheet information for the permanent fund as of December 31, 20X2, is presented in Figure 13–3. The entire amount of the fund balance for the permanent fund is classified as unspendable because the principal must be preserved and the income in this fund is required to be used for specified purposes. The information for the statement of revenues, expenditures, and changes in fund balance for the permanent fund is presented in Figure 13–4. Note that the $100,000 contribution is not part of operations but is reported at the bottom of the operating statement.

GOVERNMENTAL FUNDS FINANCIAL STATEMENTS

LO5

Understand and explain how governmental funds are reported and rules for separate reporting as major funds.

Advanced
StudyGuide
.com

GASB Statement No. 34, "Basic Financial Statements—and Management's Discussion and Analysis—for State and Local Governments" (GASB 34), requires two financial statements for the governmental funds. Figure 13–5 presents the first, the governmental funds balance sheet, and Figure 13–6 presents the second, the governmental statement of revenues, expenditures, and changes in fund balance. The worksheets in Figures 13–3 and 13–4 are the basis for preparing these two financial statements. In practice, the two financial statements will be prepared for each individual governmental fund and these individual fund statements are the foundation for the financial statements prepared for the governmental entity. But the fund-based financial statements for the governmental entity's annual report separately report only major governmental funds, not necessarily individually each of the five governmental funds. **GASB 34** specifies that the general fund is always a major fund. But some of the other governmental funds may not be determined to be major funds, and these nonmajor funds are aggregated and reported in a single column as other governmental funds. **GASB 34** establishes criteria that also encompass the enterprise funds. To determine which of the other governmental or specific enterprise funds are major, **GASB 34** specifies that *both* of the following criteria must be met:

1. *10 percent criterion:* Total assets, liabilities, revenues, or expenditures/expenses of that individual governmental or enterprise fund are at least 10 percent of the corresponding total (assets, liabilities, revenues, or expenditures/expenses) for all funds of that category or type (i.e., total governmental funds or total enterprise funds).
2. *5 percent criterion:* Total assets, liabilities, revenues, or expenditures/expenses of the individual governmental fund or enterprise fund are at least 5 percent of the corresponding total for all governmental *plus* enterprise funds combined.

FIGURE 13–5   **Governmental Funds Balance Sheet**

				Other Governmental Funds	Total Governmental Funds
	SOL CITY				
	Balance Sheet				
	Governmental Funds				
	December 31, 20X2				
	General	**Capital Projects**	**Permanent**	**Other Governmental Funds**	**Total Governmental Funds**
Assets					
Current					
Cash	$102,000	$16,000	$ 13,000	$17,000	$148,000
Property Taxes (net of allowances)	85,000			4,000	89,000
Due from Enterprise Fund	3,000				3,000
Inventory of Supplies	17,000				17,000
Noncurrent					
Investment in Government Bonds			90,000		90,000
Total Assets	$207,000	$16,000	$103,000	$21,000	$347,000
Liabilities and Fund Balances					
Vouchers Payable	55,000			3,000	$ 58,000
Contract Payable—Retainage		$10,000			10,000
Total Liabilities	$ 55,000	$10,000		$ 3,000	$ 68,000
Fund Balances:					
Nonspendable:					
Inventory	$ 17,000				$ 17,000
Permanent Fund Principal			$100,000		100,000
Spendable:					
Restricted for:					
Maintain City Park			3,000		3,000
Limited to:					
Culture & Recreation				$13,000	13,000
Assigned to:					
General Government	15,000				15,000
Courthouse Project		$ 6,000			6,000
Debt Service				5,000	5,000
Unassigned	120,000				120,000
Total Fund Balances	$152,000	$ 6,000	$103,000	$18,000	$279,000
Total Liabilities and Fund Balances	$207,000	$16,000	$103,000	$21,000	$347,000

Note that the major fund reporting requirements apply to a governmental or enterprise fund only if the same element (e.g., assets, liabilities, revenues, or expenditures/ expenses) exceeds both the 10 percent and the 5 percent criteria. These major funds tests are presented at the bottom of Figures 13–3 and 13–4. To prepare the tests, information is also required for the enterprise funds. The underlying transactions for Sol City's enterprise fund are presented in the next section of this chapter. The information for the total assets, liabilities, revenues, and expenses of Sol City's enterprise fund is taken from the enterprise fund's financial statement information. For right now, the information for the enterprise fund is presented solely to discuss the major funds tests. More detail on the enterprise fund will be presented immediately after the following discussion of the two major funds tests.

10 Percent Criterion Tests

To compute the 10 percent criterion tests for the five governmental funds, the denominators of the four tests (assets, liabilities, revenues, and expenditures) are the totals from the five governmental funds. For example, Figure 13–3 shows the total assets of the governmental funds as $347,000. Note again that the general fund is always a major fund, so no percentages need be computed for that fund. The 10 percent asset test shows that the permanent

FIGURE 13–6 Governmental Funds Statement of Revenues, Expenditures, and Changes in Fund Balance

<table>
<tr><td colspan="6" align="center">SOL CITY
Statement of Revenues, Expenditures, and Changes in Fund Balance
Governmental Funds
For the Year Ended December 31, 20X2</td></tr>
<tr><td></td><td align="center">General</td><td align="center">Capital
Projects</td><td align="center">Permanent</td><td align="center">Other
Governmental
Funds</td><td align="center">Total
Governmental
Funds</td></tr>
<tr><td>Revenues</td><td></td><td></td><td></td><td></td><td></td></tr>
<tr><td>Property Taxes</td><td>$781,000</td><td></td><td></td><td>$95,000</td><td>$ 876,000</td></tr>
<tr><td>Sales Taxes</td><td>32,000</td><td></td><td></td><td></td><td>32,000</td></tr>
<tr><td>Grants</td><td>33,000</td><td>$ 10,000</td><td></td><td></td><td>43,000</td></tr>
<tr><td>Miscellaneous</td><td>18,000</td><td></td><td>$ 8,000</td><td></td><td>26,000</td></tr>
<tr><td>Total Revenues</td><td>$864,000</td><td>$ 10,000</td><td>$ 8,000</td><td>$95,000</td><td>$ 977,000</td></tr>
<tr><td>Expenditures</td><td></td><td></td><td></td><td></td><td></td></tr>
<tr><td>Current</td><td></td><td></td><td></td><td></td><td></td></tr>
<tr><td>General Government</td><td>$206,000</td><td></td><td></td><td></td><td>$ 206,000</td></tr>
<tr><td>Streets and Highways</td><td>71,000</td><td></td><td></td><td></td><td>71,000</td></tr>
<tr><td>Public Safety</td><td>335,000</td><td></td><td></td><td></td><td>335,000</td></tr>
<tr><td>Sanitation</td><td>141,000</td><td></td><td></td><td></td><td>141,000</td></tr>
<tr><td>Culture and Recreation</td><td></td><td></td><td>$ 5,000</td><td>$49,000</td><td>54,000</td></tr>
<tr><td>Debt Service</td><td></td><td></td><td></td><td></td><td></td></tr>
<tr><td>Principal Retirement</td><td></td><td></td><td></td><td>20,000</td><td>20,000</td></tr>
<tr><td>Interest Charges</td><td></td><td></td><td></td><td>10,000</td><td>10,000</td></tr>
<tr><td>Capital Outlay</td><td>58,000</td><td>$ 124,000</td><td></td><td></td><td>182,000</td></tr>
<tr><td>Total Expenditures</td><td>$811,000</td><td>$ 124,000</td><td>$ 5,000</td><td>$79,000</td><td>$1,019,000</td></tr>
<tr><td>Excess (deficiency) of
Revenues over Expenditures</td><td>$ 53,000</td><td>$(114,000)</td><td>$ 3,000</td><td>$16,000</td><td>$ (42,000)</td></tr>
<tr><td>Other Financing Sources (Uses)</td><td></td><td></td><td></td><td></td><td></td></tr>
<tr><td>Proceeds of Bond Issue</td><td></td><td>$ 102,000</td><td></td><td></td><td>$ 102,000</td></tr>
<tr><td>Transfers In</td><td></td><td>20,000</td><td></td><td>$ 2,000</td><td>22,000</td></tr>
<tr><td>Transfers Out</td><td>$ (30,000)</td><td>(2,000)</td><td></td><td></td><td>(32,000)</td></tr>
<tr><td>Total Other Financing
Sources and Uses</td><td>$ (30,000)</td><td>$ 120,000</td><td>$ -0-</td><td>$ 2,000</td><td>$ 92,000</td></tr>
<tr><td>Contributions, Special Items
and Extraordinary Items:
Contribution</td><td></td><td></td><td>$100,000</td><td></td><td>$ 100,000</td></tr>
<tr><td>Net Change in Fund Balances</td><td>$ 23,000</td><td>$ 6,000</td><td>$103,000</td><td>$18,000</td><td>$ 150,000</td></tr>
<tr><td>Fund Balances—Beginning</td><td>129,000</td><td>-0-</td><td>-0-</td><td>-0-</td><td>129,000</td></tr>
<tr><td>Fund Balances—Ending</td><td>$152,000</td><td>$ 6,000</td><td>$103,000</td><td>$18,000</td><td>$ 279,000</td></tr>
</table>

fund meets the 10 percent criterion for total assets (29.68% = $103,000 ÷ $347,000). Continuing down to the liabilities, only the capital projects fund meets the 10 percent criterion for total liabilities (14.71% = $10,000 ÷ $68,000). Information in Figure 13–4 indicates that none of the nongeneral governmental funds meets the 10 percent criterion for revenues. For expenditures, the capital projects fund meets the 10 percent criterion for total expenditures (12.17% = $124,000 ÷ $1,019,000). Thus, the only two nongeneral governmental funds that meet the 10 percent criterion tests for a major fund are (1) the permanent fund (for total assets) and (2) the capital projects fund (for both total liabilities and for total expenditures).

5 Percent Criterion Tests

To compute the 5 percent criterion tests, the second group of major fund tests, the GASB specifies that the denominator of each of the four tests (assets, liabilities, revenues, and expenditures/expenses) is the combined total of each of these items for the five governmental funds *plus* the enterprise funds. For example, Figure 13–3 shows the combined total assets for the 5 percent asset test is $487,000 ($347,000 from the governmental funds plus $140,000 from the enterprise fund). For the nongeneral governmental funds, the permanent fund is the only one that meets the 5 percent criterion for total assets (21.15% = $103,000 ÷ $487,000). For total liabilities, the capital projects fund meets the 5 percent criterion (5.56% = $10,000 ÷ $180,000). Figure 13–4 shows that for revenues, the special revenue fund meets the 5 percent criterion (6.11% = $62,000 ÷ $1,014,000). For expenditures/expenses, only the capital projects fund meets the 5 percent criterion (11.76% = $124,000 ÷ $1,054,000).

Note that a governmental fund other than the general fund must meet *both* the 10 percent and the 5 percent criterion tests for at least one of the four financial statement items to be classified as a major fund. Thus, the following governmental funds are classified as major funds: (1) the general fund—always a major fund, (2) the capital projects fund (for liabilities and expenditures), and (3) the permanent fund (for assets). As shown in Figures 13–5 and 13–6, the governmental funds financial statements present details on these three funds. The two nonmajor funds, special revenue and debt service, are combined into a single Other Governmental Funds column. However, management of the governmental unit may elect to provide separate disclosure on any nonmajor fund that it believes is important for users of the financial statements to fully understand. **GASB 34** requires that a total for all governmental funds be provided. Note that enterprise funds are not governmental-type funds.

Governmental units are permitted to disclose, on the governmental funds' balance sheet, designations of unassigned funds. A designation is not a legal reservation or restriction but is similar to an appropriation of retained earnings for a commercial entity. The designation represents management's plans for the intended use of the resources and is a communication to users of the financial statements. However, designations are not permitted to be reported on the government-wide financial statements.

GASB 34 requires a reconciliation schedule to the government-wide financial statements to be presented either at the bottom of each of the two fund financial statements or in accompanying schedules. These two schedules reconcile the modified accrual basis of accounting used for the governmental funds to the accrual basis of accounting used for reporting in the two government-wide financial statements. The reconciliation schedules are presented later in this chapter within the discussion of presenting the government-wide financial statements.

ENTERPRISE FUNDS

LO6

Make calculations and record journal entries for enterprise funds.

Governments sometimes offer goods or services for sale to the public. The amounts charged to customers are intended to recover all or most of the cost of these goods or services. For example, a city may operate electric, gas, and water utilities; transportation systems such as buses, trains, and subways; airports; sports arenas; parking lots and garages; and public housing. Such operations are accounted for in *enterprise funds,* which differ from special revenue funds in that the costs of enterprise fund activities are recovered by user charges. Therefore, the primary difference between establishing a special revenue fund and an enterprise fund is the source of revenue.

Enterprise funds are one of the two proprietary fund types and have a measurement focus of all economic resources and use the accrual basis of accounting. Proprietary funds report fixed assets, which are depreciated, and long-term debt, if issued, and they focus on income determination and capital maintenance, the same as for commercial entities. The financial statements for proprietary funds are very similar to those for commercial entities: (1) the statement of net assets (balance sheet), (2) the statement of revenues, expenses, and changes in fund net assets (income statement), and (3) the statement of cash flows.

Budgeting in the proprietary funds also has the same role as in commercial entities. A budget may be prepared for management planning purposes; however, the budget is normally not entered into the accounts.

Illustration of Transactions

Sol City has a municipal water utility that it operates as an enterprise fund. The trial balance of the water utility as of January 1, 20X2, the first day of the 20X2 fiscal year, is presented here:

SOL CITY
Trial Balance for Water Utility Enterprise Fund
January 1, 20X2

Cash	$ 9,000	
Machinery and Equipment	94,000	
Buildings	40,000	
Accumulated Depreciation—Machinery and Equipment		$ 15,000
Accumulated Depreciation—Buildings		2,000
Bonds Payable, 5%		100,000
Net Assets:		
Invested in Capital Assets, Net of Related Debt		17,000
Unrestricted		9,000
Totals	$143,000	$143,000

One difference between balance sheet accounts for commercial entities and those for proprietary funds is the absence of a stockholders' equity section in governmental accounting. The general public is the theoretical owner of all governmental assets. Furthermore, no stock certificates are issued; therefore, a net assets section is used instead of common stock and additional paid-in capital. **GASB 34** requires the separate disclosure of the net assets invested in capital assets, net of related debt, which reports the book value (cost basis less accumulated depreciation) invested in capital assets such as land, buildings, machinery, equipment, and other tangible and intangible assets having expected useful lives exceeding one year. These resources are not readily available for other unrestricted uses as are the current assets. The related debt is that directly associated with the capital assets and is typically long-term in nature. For our example, assume the $100,000 of bonds payable is related to the $117,000 of net capital assets ($134,000 cost less $17,000 of accumulated depreciation). Other interesting differences are the large relative amounts of fixed assets and long-term debt because enterprise funds typically require large investments in productive assets in order to provide the necessary level of service to the public, and these investments are usually financed by long-term revenue bonds.

The water utility sells its product to the residents of Sol City based on a user charge. In addition to water revenue, the water utility receives a $3,000 short-term interfund loan from the general fund and obtains its office supplies from the city's centralized purchasing operation, which is accounted for as an internal service fund. During the year, the water utility acquires a new pump costing $6,000.

Enterprise Fund Revenues

The water utility provides service during the period and bills its customers for the amount of water used. The utility estimates that 7.5 percent of its billings will not be collected. Note that revenues are reported net of uncollectibles. These transactions are recorded as follows:

(30)	Accounts Receivable	40,000	
	Allowance for Uncollectibles		3,000
	Revenue—Water Sales		37,000

Bill customers for water used as indicated by meter readings.
Estimate $3,000 of billings will be uncollectible.

(31)	Cash	32,000	
	Accounts Receivable		32,000

Collect portion of accounts receivable.

Capital Asset Acquisition

The water utility acquires a new pump during the year.

(32)	Equipment	6,000	
	Vouchers Payable		6,000
	Receive new pump for well house.		

(33)	Vouchers Payable	6,000	
	Cash		6,000
	Pay voucher for new pump.		

Interfund Activities

Several interfund transactions occur during the year. First, in an interfund financing transaction, the water utility receives $3,000 from the general fund as a short-term loan to be repaid within 90 days. The general fund records this as a short-term receivable, Due from Enterprise Fund (see entry [39] in Chapter 12). Second, the utility acquires its office supplies from the internal service fund in an interfund services provided and used transaction. The internal service fund reports this as a revenue transaction (see entry [48] later in this chapter):

(34)	Cash	3,000	
	Due to General Fund		3,000
	Recognize payable for loan from general fund.		

(35)	Supplies Inventory	3,000	
	Due to Internal Service Fund		3,000
	Receive office supplies from centralized purchasing department at a cost of $3,000.		

(36)	Due to Internal Service Fund	2,000	
	Cash		2,000
	Approve payment of $2,000 to centralized purchasing department for supplies received.		

Enterprise Fund Expenses

The water utility fund incurs $9,000 of operating expenses during the period. In addition, several adjusting journal entries are required at the end of the fiscal year to recognize additional expenses. Note that these adjusting entries are similar to those of a commercial entity:

(37)	General Operating Expenses	9,000	
	Vouchers Payable		9,000
	Incur operating expenses during year.		

(38)	Vouchers Payable	6,000	
	Cash		6,000
	Pay approved vouchers for operating expenses.		

(39)	General Operating Expenses	3,000	
	Supplies Inventory		3,000
	Adjust for $3,000 of supplies consumed.		

(40)	Depreciation Expense	18,000	
	Accumulated Depreciation—Buildings		3,000
	Accumulated Depreciation—Machinery and Equipment		15,000
	Recognize depreciation expense for year.		

(41)	Interest Expense	5,000	
	Accrued Interest Payable		5,000
	Accrue interest on bond payable: $100,000 \times 0.05 \times 1$ year		

Closing and Reclassification Entries in the Enterprise Fund

The nominal accounts are closed, the period's profit or loss is determined, and, at the close of the fiscal year, the government reclassifies the various components of net assets based on the year-end amount of net assets invested in capital assets, net of related debt:

(42)	Revenue—Water Sales	37,000	
	General Operating Expenses		12,000
	Depreciation Expense		18,000
	Interest Expense		5,000
	Profit and Loss Summary		2,000

Close nominal accounts into profit and loss summary.

(43)	Profit and Loss Summary	2,000	
	Net Assets—Unrestricted		2,000

Close profit and loss summary into net assets.

(44)	Net Assets—Invested in Capital Assets, Net of Related Debt	12,000	
	Net Assets—Unrestricted		12,000

To reclassify net assets as of end of fiscal period:
12/31/X1 balance: $ 5,000 = $105,000 capital assets − $100,000 of related debt
1/1/X1 balance: 17,000 = $117,000 capital assets − $100,000 of related debt
                $12,000 = Decrease during period in net assets
                        invested in capital assets, net of related debt

Financial Statements for the Proprietary Funds

Three financial statements are required for the proprietary funds. If a governmental entity has more than one enterprise fund, each must be individually assessed by both the 10 percent criterion and the 5 percent criterion tests to determine whether it is a major fund. Sol City has only one enterprise fund. Figure 13–7 presents the statement of net assets for the enterprise proprietary fund and for the internal service proprietary fund that will be discussed in the next section of this chapter. Figure 13–8 presents the statement of revenues, expenses, and changes in fund net assets for Sol City's two proprietary funds. Figure 13–9 presents the statement of cash flows for these two proprietary funds.

The statement of net assets in Figure 13–7 is similar to that required for commercial entities. Proprietary funds report their own fixed assets, investments, and long-term liabilities. **GASB 34** specifies that the net assets section for the proprietary funds, which is presented below liabilities, be separated into three components: (1) invested in capital assets, net of related debt; (2) restricted because of restrictions beyond the government's control, such as externally imposed restrictions or legal requirements; and (3) unrestricted. **GASB Statement 46,** "Net Assets Restricted by Enabling Legislation" (GASB 46), issued in 2004, amended **GASB 34** with regard to net assets restricted by legally enforceable actions such as enabling legislation, which specifies that a government use resources only for the purposes as specified in the enabling legislation. **GASB 46** provides guidance for reporting the net assets so restricted and accounting for changes when new enabling legislation replaces the prior legislation. The key point is that **GASB 46** confirms the **GASB 34** requirement for separate disclosure of net assets restricted by legal requirements. For our example, there are no externally imposed or legal restrictions on net assets. The amount of the net assets invested in capital assets, net of related debt, is computed as capital assets less accumulated depreciation, less outstanding principal of related debt. For purposes of this example, assume that the information in Figure 13–7 shows that the enterprise fund has $5,000 of net assets invested in capital assets, net of related debt ($105,000 − $100,000), and the internal service fund has $2,000 invested in capital assets, net of related debt ($2,000 − $0).

FIGURE 13–7
Proprietary Funds Statement of Net Assets

SOL CITY
Statement of Net Assets
Proprietary Funds
December 31, 20X2

	Enterprise Fund	Internal Service Fund
Assets:		
Current Assets:		
Cash	$ 30,000	$ 4,000
Accounts Receivable (net)	5,000	
Due from Other Funds		1,000
Inventory of Supplies		6,000
Total Current Assets	$ 35,000	$11,000
Noncurrent Assets:		
Capital Assets:		
Machinery and Equipment	$100,000	$ 3,000
Less: Accumulated Depreciation	(30,000)	(1,000)
Buildings	40,000	
Less: Accumulated Depreciation	(5,000)	
Total Noncurrent Assets	$105,000	$ 2,000
Total Assets	$140,000	$13,000
Liabilities:		
Current Liabilities:		
Vouchers Payable	$ 3,000	$ 6,000
Accrued Interest Payable	5,000	
Due to Other Funds	4,000	
Total Current Liabilities	$ 12,000	$ 6,000
Noncurrent Liabilities:		
Bonds Payable, 5%	100,000	
Total Liabilities	$112,000	$ 6,000
Net Assets:		
Invested in Capital Assets, Net of Related Debt	$ 5,000	$ 2,000
Unrestricted	23,000	5,000
Total Net Assets	$ 28,000	$ 7,000

The statement of revenues, expenses, and changes in fund net assets is similar to the income statement for commercial entities. A separation of operating and nonoperating revenues and expenses is made to provide more information value regarding the operations of the proprietary funds. Contributions and transfers in or out are reported below the income (loss) line in the statement of revenues, expenses, and changes in fund net assets. Contributions would include any capital asset transfers from a governmental fund to a proprietary fund. For example, the general fund may transfer equipment to an enterprise fund. Note that the governmental funds describe the interfund transfers as other financing sources or uses, but the proprietary funds use only the terms *transfer in* or *transfer out* to describe these nonoperating interfund transactions. And both interest income and interest expense are reported as nonoperating items.

The statement of cash flows for enterprise funds is specified by **GASB Statement No. 9,** "Reporting Cash Flows of Proprietary and Nonexpendable Trust Funds and Governmental Entities That Use Proprietary Fund Accounting" (GASB 9). This standard provides a format that differs somewhat from the three-section format of the statement of cash flows for commercial entities. Because of the large number of capital asset acquisition and financing transactions in proprietary funds, the GASB specified four sections of the statement of cash flows, as follows:

FIGURE 13–8
**Proprietary Funds
Statement of
Revenues, Expenses,
and Changes in
Fund Net Assets**

	SOL CITY Statement of Revenues, Expenses, and Changes in Fund Net Assets Proprietary Funds For the Year Ended December 31, 20X2	
	Enterprise Fund	**Internal Service Fund**
Operating Revenues:		
Charges for Services	$37,000	$ 4,000
Total Operating Revenues	$37,000	$ 4,000
Operating Expenses:		
General Operating	$12,000	$ 4,000
Cost of Goods Sold		2,000
Depreciation	18,000	1,000
Total Operating Expenses	$30,000	$ 7,000
Nonoperating Revenue (Expenses):		
Interest Expense	$ (5,000)	
Total Nonoperating Expense	$ 5,000	
Income (Loss) before Contributions and Transfers	$ 2,000	$(3,000)
Transfer In		10,000
Change in Net Assets	$ 2,000	$ 7,000
Net Assets—Beginning	26,000	-0-
Net Assets—Ending	$28,000	$ 7,000

1. *Cash flows from operating activities.* This first section includes all transactions from providing services and delivering goods. **GASB 34** requires the use of the direct method of computing cash flows from operating activities. It includes cash flows from interfund operating transactions and reimbursements from other funds.

2. *Cash flows from noncapital financing activities.* This second section includes activities such as borrowing or repaying money for purposes other than to acquire, construct, or improve capital assets. It includes cash for financing activities received from, or paid to, other funds except that which is specified for capital asset use.

3. *Cash flows from capital and related financing activities.* This third section includes all activities clearly related to, or attributable to, the acquisition, disposition, construction, or improvement of capital assets. This section also includes the interest paid on borrowings for capital assets.

4. *Cash flows from investing activities.* This fourth section includes all investing activities, interest and dividend revenue, and acquisition and disposition of debt or equity instruments.

In addition to the statement of cash flows, proprietary funds also are required to provide a supplementary schedule that reconciles the cash flow from operating activities with the operating income or loss reported on the statement of revenues, expenses, and changes in fund net assets.

INTERNAL SERVICE FUNDS

LO8

Make calculations and record journal entries for internal service funds.

Internal service funds account for the financing of goods or services provided by one department or agency to other departments or agencies on a cost-reimbursement basis. These services are not available to the general public, making the internal service fund different from the enterprise fund. Examples are motor vehicle pools, central computer facilities, printing shops, and centralized purchasing and storage facilities. Separate internal service funds are established for each of these functions maintained by the local governmental unit.

FIGURE 13–9 **Proprietary Funds Statement of Cash Flows**

SOL CITY
Statement of Cash Flows
Proprietary Funds
For the Year Ended December 31, 20X2

	Enterprise Fund	Internal Service Fund
Cash Flows from Operating Activities:		
Receipts from Customers	$32,000	$ 3,000
Cash Payments for Goods and Services	(6,000)	(6,000)
Cash Paid to Internal Service Fund for Supplies	(2,000)	
Net Cash Provided (Used) by Operating Activities	$24,000	$(3,000)
Cash Flows from Noncapital Financing Activities:		
Cash Received from General Fund for Noncapital Loan	$ 3,000	$ 7,000
Net Cash Provided by Noncapital Financing Activities	$ 3,000	$ 7,000
Cash Flows from Capital and Related Financing Activities:		
Acquisition of Capital Asset	$ (6,000)	$(3,000)
Cash Received from General Fund for Capital Activity		3,000
Net Cash Provided (Used) for Capital Financing Activities	$ (6,000)	$ -0-
Cash Flows from Investing Activities	$ -0-	$ -0-
Net Increase in Cash	$21,000	$ 4,000
Balances—Beginning of Year	9,000	-0-
Balances—End of Year	$30,000	$ 4,000
Reconciliation of Operating Income to Net Cash Provided by Operating Activities:		
Operating Income	$ 7,000	$(3,000)
Adjustments to Reconcile Operating Income to Net Cash Provided (Used) by Operating Activities:		
Depreciation	18,000	1,000
Change in Assets and Liabilities:		
Increase in Net Accounts Receivable	(5,000)	
Increase in Due from Other Funds from Billings		(1,000)
Increase in Inventory of Supplies		(6,000)
Increase in Vouchers Payable	3,000	6,000
Increase in Due to Internal Service Fund	1,000	
Net Cash Provided (Used) by Operating Activities	$24,000	$(3,000)

Accounting and financial reporting for internal service funds are the same as for enterprise funds or for commercial entities. The accrual basis is used to measure revenue and expenses, and the balance sheet may include fixed assets, which are depreciated, and long-term debt, if issued. The statement of revenue, expenses, and changes in fund net assets reports the fund's income for the period. The statement of cash flows also is required.

Illustration of Transactions

Sol City decides to establish a centralized purchasing and storage function as an internal service fund. This centralized purchasing department provides office supplies to all other funds of the local government on a user-charge basis. After acquiring the necessary supplies, the centralized purchasing department makes the following sales:

Buying Fund	Selling Price	Cost to Internal Service Fund
General fund	$1,000	$ 500
Enterprise fund	3,000	1,500

The following entries are made during the year to record the activities of the centralized purchasing and storage department.

Establishment of Internal Service Fund and Acquisition of Inventories

The fund is started with a transfer in from the general fund in the amount of $10,000, which the internal service fund then uses to acquire inventory and equipment. The general fund records this interfund transfer as a transfer out (see entry [33] in Chapter 12):

(45)	Cash	10,000	
	Transfer In		10,000
	Receive interfund transfer in from general fund		
	to initiate centralized purchasing and storage function.		

(46)	Inventory	8,000	
	Vouchers Payable		8,000
	Acquire inventory of supplies.		

(47)	Machinery and Equipment	3,000	
	Vouchers Payable		3,000
	Acquire equipment.		

Internal Service Fund Revenue

The revenue of the internal service fund is earned by selling supplies to other funds and billing them for the value of the supplies. The billing rate is typically established at more than the operating costs of the internal service fund so that the fund may acquire replacement assets or new assets:

(48)	Due from General Fund	1,000	
	Due from Enterprise Fund	3,000	
	Charges for Services		4,000
	Recognize revenue from providing supplies		
	to general fund and enterprise fund.		

(49)	Cash	3,000	
	Due from General Fund		1,000
	Due from Enterprise Fund		2,000
	Collect portion of receivables.		

The general fund records the $1,000 for supplies as an interfund expenditures transaction (see entry [37] in Chapter 12). The enterprise fund records the $3,000 as an interfund inventory purchase transaction (see entry [35] earlier in this chapter).

Internal Service Fund Expenses

The internal service fund incurs $4,000 of operating expenses, including payroll, during the period. In addition, cost of goods sold of $2,000 and $1,000 of depreciation expense are recognized in adjusting entries. The $9,000 of vouchers paid include a voucher in the amount of $3,000 for the equipment acquired in entry (47) above:

(50)	General Operating Expenses	4,000	
	Vouchers Payable		4,000
	Incur operating expenses.		

(51)	Vouchers Payable	9,000	
	Cash		9,000
	Pay approved vouchers.		

(52)	Cost of Goods Sold	2,000	
	Inventory		2,000
	Recognize cost of supplies sold.		

(53)	Depreciation Expense	1,000	
	Accumulated Depreciation		1,000
	Depreciation of equipment.		

Closing Entries in the Internal Service Fund

The closing and reclassifying entries for the internal service fund follow. "Profit and Loss Summary" is used here in the closing process; however, some governmental units use the account called Excess of Net Revenues over Costs to perform the same function.

(54)	Charges for Services	4,000	
	Profit and Loss Summary	3,000	
	Cost of Goods Sold		2,000
	General Operating Expenses		4,000
	Depreciation Expense		1,000

Close revenue and expenses.

(55)	Transfer In	10,000	
	Profit and Loss Summary		3,000
	Net Assets—Unrestricted		7,000

Close profit and loss summary and transfer in to net assets.

(56)	Net Assets—Unrestricted	2,000	
	Net Assets—Invested in Capital Assets, Net of Related Debt		2,000

To reclassify net assets as of end of fiscal period:
$2,000 = $2,000 net capital assets − $0 related debt

Financial Statements for Internal Service Funds

The financial statements required for internal service funds are the same as those required for the enterprise fund. Figure 13–7 presents the statement of net assets, and Figure 13–8 presents the statement of revenues, expenses, and changes in fund net assets for the internal service fund. Figure 13–9 presents the statement of cash flows for the internal service fund.

TRUST FUNDS

LO9

Make calculations and record journal entries for trust funds.

Trust funds are a fiduciary fund type that accounts for resources held by a government unit in a trustee capacity. The governmental unit acts as a fiduciary for monies or properties held on behalf of individuals, employees, or other governmental agencies. The three main types of fiduciary trust funds are (1) pension and other employee benefit trust funds, (2) investment trust funds, and (3) private-purpose trust funds.

The accrual basis of accounting is used for the fiduciary funds, and the financial statements required for fiduciary funds are the statement of fiduciary net assets (Figure 13–10) and the statement of changes in fiduciary net assets (Figure 13–11). The statement of fiduciary

FIGURE 13–10
Fiduciary Funds
Statement of
Fiduciary Net Assets

SOL CITY Statement of Fiduciary Net Assets Fiduciary Funds December 31, 20X2		
	Private-Purpose Funds	**Agency Funds**
Assets:		
Cash	$ 1,600	$1,000
Investments, at Fair Value:		
Municipal Bonds	26,200	
Total Assets	$27,800	$1,000
Liabilities:		
Due to Insurance Company		$1,000
Total Liabilities	$ -0-	$1,000
Net Assets Held in Trust	$27,800	

FIGURE 13–11
**Fiduciary Funds
Statement of Changes
in Fiduciary Net Assets**

SOL CITY
Statement of Changes in Fiduciary Net Assets
Fiduciary Funds
For the Year Ended December 31, 20X2
Private-Purpose Fund

Additions:		
Contributions		$50,000
Investment Earnings:		
Increase in Fair Value of Investments	$1,200	
Interest	600	
Total Investment Earnings		1,800
Total Additions		$51,800
Deductions:		
Benefits		$23,000
Administrative Costs		1,000
Total Deductions		$24,000
Change in Net Assets		$27,800
Net Assets—Beginning of Year		-0-
Net Assets—End of Year		$27,800

net assets includes all trusts and agency funds. The statement of changes in fiduciary net assets includes only the trust funds because agency funds do not have a net asset balance; their assets must equal their liabilities. Agency funds are discussed after trust funds.

Private-purpose trust funds account for trust agreements for which the principal and/or income benefits specific individuals, private organizations, or other governments. Note that the benefit is limited to private, rather than general public, purposes. The trust agreement may require the principal to be preserved (i.e., nonexpendable principal), in which case an endowment is created. In other trust agreements, both the principal and income may be used for the specific purposes for which the trust was created. The governmental entity does not have to accept the donation if it is not consistent with the government's objectives. However, there are many cases in which a governmental entity accepts the donation and agrees to its provisions because of the benefits that can be achieved with the resources. For example, a citizen group may donate money to a city to be used for award recognition for businesses located in the downtown area that update and improve the appearances of their storefronts. The governmental entity is typically allowed to charge the private-purpose trust fund a fee for managing the trust's resources, which would include investing the resources and making the allowed expenditures from the resources.

An example of a private-purpose trust fund is illustrated in the next section of this chapter. Public employee pension funds are discussed in the "Additional Considerations" section later in the chapter.

Illustration of Private-Purpose Trust Fund

On January 1, 20X2, Sol City receives a $50,000 donation from Charles Alt, a citizen of Sol City. The terms of the trust agreement specify that the city is to use about $25,000 each year for the next two years to help alleviate the cost of transporting senior citizens to and from the senior citizens' center. The city accepts the donation and, as allowed by the trust agreement, invests $25,000 in highly rated bonds. The remaining $25,000 is deposited in a bank account that earns 4 percent interest. The terms of the trust agreement allow the city to deduct $1,000 per year for its administrative costs of managing the trust and the transportation services. During the first year, 20X2, $23,000 is paid out of the fund for transportation services. The fund pays out the remaining resources in 20X3.

(57)	Cash	50,000	
	Additions—Contributions		50,000

The city accepts a private-purpose trust fund of $50,000.

(58)

| Investment in Bonds | 25,000 | |
| Cash | | 25,000 |

The city invests half of the trust funds, as allowed
by the trust agreement.

(59)

| Cash | 600 | |
| Additions—Interest | | 600 |

Interest earned during the year on the monies deposited
in the bank is recognized from bank statements.

(60)

| Deductions—Transportation Benefits | 23,000 | |
| Cash | | 23,000 |

Transportation costs during the year are paid.

(61)

| Deductions—Administration Costs | 1,000 | |
| Cash | | 1,000 |

The $1,000 of administrative costs allowed to the
city are recognized and paid.

An adjusting journal entry is made on December 31, 20X2, to revalue the investment in
bonds to their fair values, as follows:

(62)

| Investment in Bonds | 1,200 | |
| Additions—Investment Revalued | | 1,200 |

The fair value of the investment in bonds increased by $1,200
by the end of the year.

Note that this private-purpose trust fund had an expendable principal as well as earnings. The requirement for a private-purpose trust fund is that its resources may be used only for specific individuals, organizations, or other governmental units as specified by the donor. Some private-purpose trust funds specify that the principal is nonexpendable and that only the earnings may be used for the private purpose. A private-purpose trust fund is differentiated from a permanent fund, which is part of the governmental funds, in the following manner. A permanent fund must maintain its principal, but the earnings are used to support the government's programs that benefit all citizens. A private-purpose trust fund must be used only for the specific purposes specified by the donor or grantor of the trust fund and is not available to support the government's general programs.

Figure 13–10 reports the statement of fiduciary net assets for the fiduciary funds for Sol City, including the private-purpose fund and agency fund. Figure 13–11 presents the statement of changes in fiduciary net assets for the private-purpose trust fund. Agency funds are presented in the next section of the chapter.

AGENCY FUNDS

LO10

Make calculations and record journal entries for agency funds.

Agency funds are a fiduciary fund type that accounts for resources held by a governmental unit as a custodial agent for individuals, private organizations, other funds, or other governmental units. Examples are tax collection funds that collect property taxes and then distribute them to local governmental units and employee benefit funds for such items as dental insurance or charitable contributions that employees authorize as withholdings from their paychecks.

The accrual basis of accounting is used to account for agency funds. Because agency funds are custodial in nature, assets always equal liabilities and there is no fund equity. The financial statement for agency funds is the statement of fiduciary net assets as presented in Figure 13–9. Note that there cannot be any net asset balance for agency funds; therefore, no statement of changes in fiduciary net assets is required for agency funds.

Illustration of Transactions in an Agency Fund

Sol City has established an agency fund to account for employees' share of health insurance, which is deducted from the employees' monthly paychecks and then forwarded to the insurance company on a quarterly basis. For this example, a total of $9,000 was deducted from the employees' paychecks, and $8,000 was paid to the insurance company in 20X2. The remaining $1,000 will be paid to the insurance company in the first quarter of 20X3.

Agency Fund Receipts and Disbursements

The receipts and disbursements in the agency fund during 20X2 are as follows:

(63)	Cash	9,000	
	Due to Insurance Company		9,000

Employees' contributory share of health
insurance deducted from payroll checks.

(64)	Due to Insurance Company	8,000	
	Cash		8,000

Pay liability to insurance company for
employees' share of insurance cost.

THE GOVERNMENT REPORTING MODEL

LO11

Understand and explain
the preparation of
government-wide
financial statements.

GASB 34 specifies the reporting model for governmental entities. All general-purpose units such as states, counties, and municipalities must provide all financial statements required in **GASB 34.** These statements are both the fund-based financial statements presented earlier in this chapter plus the government-wide financial statements that will be discussed in a following section of this chapter. Some special-purpose government units such as cemetery associations that are engaged in a single governmental activity are not required to provide the government-wide financial statements but still must provide fund-based financial statements. We now discuss four major issues arise in the government reporting model.

Four Major Issues

Issue 1: What Organizations Comprise the Reporting Entity?

The first issue to address is the determination of the *reporting entity* for which the statements will be provided. The primary government is part of the reporting entity, but this issue concerns what other boards, commissions, agencies, or authorities should be included with the reporting entity. **GASB 34** defines the reporting entity as (*a*) the primary government, such as a city, county, or state; (*b*) a component unit for which the primary government is financially accountable; and (*c*) any organization that has a significant relationship with the primary government and should be included to avoid misleading or incomplete financial statements.

Issue 2: What Constitutes Financial Accountability?

GASB Statement No. 14, "The Financial Reporting Entity" (GASB 14), states that financial accountability of the primary government for the component organization is evidenced by either *board appointment* or *fiscal dependence*. Financial accountability is evidenced when the primary government appoints a majority of the organization's governing board. Thus, the primary government has effective control over the organization, which in turn may provide specific benefits to, or may impose specific financial burdens on, the primary government. Financial accountability also may exist if the organization has a separately elected or appointed board but fiscally depends on the primary government for the financial resources required to operate.

The primary government's ability to impose its will on an organization is evidenced by such things as its ability to (1) remove appointed members of the organization's governing board, (2) approve or modify the organization's budget or approve rates or fee changes, (3) veto or overrule the decisions of the organization's governing body, or (4) appoint, hire, reassign, or dismiss those persons responsible for the organization's day-to-day operations. The potential for an organization to impose specific burdens on the primary government is evidenced by such things as the primary government's legal obligation or its assumption of the obligation to finance the deficits, or otherwise provide financial support to, the organization, or the primary government's obligation in some manner for the debt of the organization. These criteria indicate that when the primary governmental unit is financially accountable for legally separate organizations, those organizations should be included in the primary government's financial statements as ***component units.***

Issue 3: What Other Organizations Should Be Included in the Reporting Entity?

GASB 14 specifies a third category of organizations to be evaluated to determine if they are part of the reporting entity with the primary government. These are legally separate, tax-exempt entities for which the primary government is *not* financially accountable. **GASB Statement No. 39,** "Determining Whether Certain Organizations Are Component Units" (GASB 39), amended parts of **GASB 14** to more fully define what other organizations should be included in a government's reporting entity. In general, a legally separate, tax-exempt organization is reported as a component unit of the primary government if *all three* of the following characteristics are met:

1. The resources of the separate organization are held for the benefit of the primary government, its component units, or the persons served by the primary government or its component units.
2. The primary government, or its component units, is entitled to, or can use, a majority of the economic resources of the separate organization.
3. The economic resources of the separate organization that the primary government, or its component units, can use are significant to the primary government.

Examples of other organizations that should be included in the reporting entity include university foundations and university alumni associations.

Issue 4: How Should the Financial Results of the Component Units Be Reported?

The fourth issue is how to report the financial results of component units. A choice between two methods must be made: (1) ***discrete presentation*** in a separate column of the primary government's financial statements or (2) ***blended presentation*** by combining the organization's results into the primary government's financial results.

Most component units are discretely presented; however, the blending method should be used when the component unit is so intertwined with the primary government that, in essence, they are the same governmental unit. Blending should be used when either (1) the component unit's governing body is substantively the same as the primary government's governing body or (2) the component unit provides services entirely, or almost entirely, to the primary government or almost exclusively benefits the primary government. Some of these organizations are similar to the internal services fund. Component units may use governmental fund accounting or proprietary fund accounting, depending on their types of activities. Neither discretely presenting nor blending should change the measurement basis of the type of accounting used by the component unit; however, a general fund of a blended component unit should be reported as a special revenue fund for the primary government.

For purposes of the Sol City example, assume that the city has a separate library board responsible for managing the city library. The mayor appoints the library board, which must have its budget and tax levy approved by the mayor and council. In this case, the library is a component unit that will be discretely presented in a separate column of Sol City's two government-wide financial statements.

FIGURE 13–12 **The Comprehensive Annual Financial Report (CAFR)**

Section 1: Introductory Section This section contains organizational information and other preliminary items.

Section 2: Financial Section The financial section contains the following items:

1. Independent auditors report.
2. Management's discussion and analysis (required supplementary information) (**GASB 34**).
3. Government-wide financial statements.
   a. Statement of net assets (Figure 13–13).
   b. Statement of activities (Figure 13–14).
4. Fund-based financial statements.
   a. Governmental funds.
      (1) Balance sheet (Figure 13–5).
      (2) Statement of revenues, expenditures, and changes in fund balances (Figure 13–6).
      (3) Reconciliation schedules (Figures 13–15 and 13–16).
   b. Proprietary funds.
      (1) Statement of net assets (Figure 13–7).
      (2) Statement of revenues, expenses, and changes in fund net assets (Figure 13–8).
      (3) Statement of cash flows (Figure 13–9).
   c. Fiduciary funds.
      (1) Statement of fiduciary net assets (Figure 13–10).
      (2) Statement of changes in fiduciary net assets (Figure 13–11).
5. Notes to the financial statements (**GASB 34 and 38**).
6. Required supplementary information (RSI).
   a. Budgetary comparison schedules (Figure 13–17) (**GASB 41**).
   b. Information about infrastructure assets (**GASB 34** for modified approach).
   c. Information about pension funding progress and employer contributions to retirement and pension funds (**GASB 25, 27, 43, 45, and 50**).

Section 3: Combining and Individual Fund Financial Statements This section contains the financial statements of each individual fund as well as financial statements showing the combining of individual funds together as a fund type (e.g., combining all individual special projects fund into one fund).

Section 4: Statistical Section This section presents the economic condition reporting required by **GASB 44** to be presented in the statistical section of the annual report.

Government Financial Reports

The annual report of a governmental entity is termed the ***comprehensive annual financial report*** (CAFR). Figure 13–12 presents the components of the CAFR along with parenthetical information noting the figure number in the text, or the number of the GASB standard providing guidance on the information to be included in that item.

The GASB has continued to develop the reporting standards for the statistical section to make it more useful and comparative for users of the annual report. In 2004, the GASB issued **GASB Statement 44,** "Economic Condition Reporting: The Statistical Section—an Amendment of NCGA Statement 1" (GASB 44), which specifies the types of information that should be reported in each of the five sections of the statistical section: (1) financial trends information, (2) revenue capacity information, (3) debt capacity information, (4) demographic and economic information, and (5) operating information. The intent of this statement is to further improve the understandability and usefulness of this section by also requiring the governmental unit to add information about the sources of the data and the major assumptions used and expand explanations for any unusual information presented. Thus, the statistical section is an important part of the CAFR.

The fund-based financial statements were discussed previously in this chapter. The following discussion centers on the government-wide financials and the required supplementary information (RSI).

FIGURE 13–13 Government-wide Statement of Net Assets

		Primary Government		
SOL CITY **Statement of Net Assets** **December 20X2**	Governmental Activities	Business-type Activities	Total	Component Unit
Assets:				
Cash and Cash Equivalents	$ 152,000	$ 30,000	$ 182,000	$ 3,000
Receivables, Net	89,000	5,000	94,000	
Internal Balances	4,000	(4,000)	-0-	
Inventories	23,000		23,000	1,000
Investment in Government Bonds	91,000		91,000	
Capital Assets:				
Land and Infrastructure	3,000,000		3,000,000	
Depreciable Assets, Net	1,202,000	105,000	1,307,000	870,000
Total Assets	$4,561,000	$136,000	$4,697,000	$874,000
Liabilities:				
Vouchers Payable	$ 64,000	$ 3,000	$ 67,000	
Accrued Interest Payable		5,000	5,000	
Contract Payable—Retainage	10,000		10,000	
Noncurrent Liabilities:				
Due in More than 1 Year	80,000	100,000	180,000	$120,000
Total Liabilities	$ 154,000	$108,000	$ 262,000	$120,000
Net Assets:				
Invested in Capital Assets, Net of Related Debt	$4,122,000	$ 5,000	$4,127,000	$750,000
Restricted for:				
Debt Service	5,000		5,000	
Permanent Funds	103,000		103,000	
Unrestricted	177,000	23,000	200,000	4,000
Total Net Assets	$4,407,000	$ 28,000	$4,435,000	$754,000

Government-wide Financial Statements

The *government-wide financial statements* include (1) the statement of net assets and (2) the statement of activities. **GASB 34** requires that government-wide financial statements be prepared on the *economic resources measurement focus* with the accrual basis of accounting. *Note:* The fiduciary funds (e.g., private-purpose trust funds and agency funds) are *not* included in the two government-wide financial statements because fiduciary funds are not available to support government programs.

Statement of Net Assets

Figure 13–13 presents the statement of net assets for Sol City. Some important points regarding this statement of net assets follow:

1. *Format.* The format of the statement is Assets − Liabilities = Net assets. This focuses attention on the net assets of the government entity.
2. *Columnar presentation.* A columnar presentation is used because it emphasizes that the primary government has two different categories of activities, each needing a net asset base to support that category's activities, and the reporting entity's component units have their own net asset base.
   a. The primary government's activities are assigned to either governmental activities or business-type activities.
   b. The internal service funds are included as part of the governmental activities. This is because internal service funds provide service only to the governmental entity, not to external parties.

    c. The enterprise funds are presented as business-type activities of the primary government. This is because the enterprise funds offer services to the public, and thus they are more business oriented.

3. *Assets.* Reported assets include all types of assets of the governmental entity, including infrastructure such as roads, sewers, and so on. These capital assets are not reported in the governmental funds that, under the current financial resources measurement focus, record costs of capital assets as expenditures of the period. **GASB 34** requires that all capital and infrastructure assets be reported on the government-wide financial statements. Capital assets, such as buildings and equipment, will be depreciated and that depreciation will be presented as an expense on the government-wide statement of activities. Infrastructure assets are, by their definition, long-lived assets that can be maintained for a much longer time than capital assets. Roads can be paved over, bridges can be repaired, and water and sewer systems can be maintained.

Because of the difficulty in determining any reasonable estimated useful life for the infrastructure assets, **GASB 34** provides for two methods to account for the depreciating attribute of these infrastructure assets.

    a. Report estimated depreciation expense. The first method requires governments to estimate depreciation expense and report that estimated expense on the government-wide statement of activities.

    b. Modified approach. The second approach allows governments to avoid the requirement to estimate depreciation expense on infrastructure assets that are part of a network or subsystem of a network as long as the government manages those assets using an asset management system and the government can document that the assets are preserved approximately at, or above, a condition level established by the government. Under the modified approach, the government entity annually expenses actual repair and renewal costs associated with the infrastructure assets. Additions and improvements are added to the cost basis of the infrastructure asset. Required footnote disclosures include (1) an estimate of the amount required to maintain or preserve the infrastructure assets, along with the actual costs for each of the last five years, and (2) the presentation of condition assessments of the infrastructure assets for the last three years to show that these assets are indeed being maintained.

Many governments use the modified approach rather than the estimated depreciation expense method. Regardless of the method used for the depreciation element, the government must report the infrastructure assets in the asset section of the government-wide statement of net assets.

Note that Sol City distinguishes between its infrastructure assets and its buildings and equipment. Sol City has chosen to use the modified approach in recognizing the depreciating factors in its infrastructure assets. Thus, the depreciation expense reported on the statement of activities is only from the Depreciable Assets category, which includes items such as buildings and equipment. The asset, Internal Balances, represents interfund receivables/payables between the governmental activities and the business-type activities. In the Sol City example, the enterprise fund owes a total of $4,000 to other funds: $3,000 to the general fund for a loan and $1,000 to the internal fund for supplies purchases. Note again that the internal fund is considered a governmental activity because the internal fund provides services and supplies only to other entities within the government's reporting entity.

The asset Internal Balances represents interfund receivables/payables between the primary government's funds comprising the governmental activities (governmental funds plus internal service funds) and the funds comprising the business-type activities (the enterprise funds). These internal balances cancel out each other for the total column. **GASB Statement No. 37,** "Basic Financial Statements—and Management's Discussion and Analysis—for State and Local Governments: Omnibus" (GASB 37), issued in 2001, eliminated the requirement for capitalizing construction-period interest on capital assets used in governmental activities. Thus, on the government-wide financial statements, this interest is now shown as an indirect expense of the period in which it is incurred.

4. *Categories of net assets.* Net assets are separated into three categories, as follows:
   a. Invested in capital assets, net of related debt.
   b. Restricted (by external requirements of creditors, grantors, contributors, or other governmental entities).
   c. Unrestricted.

   Note that restricted and unrestricted do not mean the same things as assigned and unassigned as used for the fund-based statements.

Statement of Activities

The statement of activities for Sol City is presented in Figure 13–14. Important observations regarding this statement of activities follow:

1. *Accrual basis.* The full accrual basis of accounting is used to measure revenues and expenses for the government-wide statements. A reconciliation between the modified accrual basis of accounting for the governmental funds and the accrual basis of the government-wide statements is required.
2. *Format.* The format of the statement of activities is based on the functions or programs of the government entity.
   a. Program revenues are categorized by type, and the net expenses (revenues) are shown separately for each of the governmental and business-type activities.
   b. The internal service fund is blended into the Governmental Activities because this fund provides service solely within the governmental entity.
   c. The enterprise funds are presented in the Business-Type Activities column because this fund includes resources obtained by user charges to the public.
   d. Fiduciary funds are not reported on the statement of activities because these funds are not available to be used for providing governmental services.
   e. Note that the component unit, the city library, is discretely presented in its own column.
3. *Expenses.* The expenses include depreciation of the capital assets and expenses for any infrastructure assets. However, the expenses would not include any expenditures in the governmental funds that were made for long-term capital assets. For government-wide statements, these expenditures must be included as increases to long-term capital assets on the balance sheet.
4. *General revenues.* General revenues are reported separately on the bottom of the statement. These are revenues that are not directly tied to any specific program. **GASB 34** requires that contributions to permanent endowments, special items, and extraordinary items be reported in this section for the government-wide statements. Special items are events within the control of management that are either unusual in nature or infrequent in occurrence. Sol City has no special or extraordinary items, and the only contribution to a permanent endowment was the $100,000 contribution received by the permanent fund. Note that the amount of ending net assets reported in this statement articulates with the amount of ending net assets presented on the statement of net assets.

LO12

Understand and explain the additional disclosures that accompany government-wide financial statements.

Reconciliation Schedules

GASB 34 requires that two *reconciliation schedules* be presented to reconcile the net change in the total amounts reported on the governmental funds statements with the amounts reported on the government-wide statements. These reconciliation schedules may be presented as part of the governmental funds statements or in an accompanying schedule on the page immediately following the governmental fund financial statement it supports. The two required reconciliation schedules are as follows:

1. *Reconciliation schedule for Statement of Net Assets.* The first reconciliation schedule, the reconciliation between the fund balances reported for the governmental funds to the net assets for the government-wide financials, is presented in Figure 13–15. This schedule describes the adjustments necessary to move from the modified accrual

FIGURE 13–14 Government-wide Statement of Activities

Functions/Programs	Expenses	Program Revenues			Net (Expenses) Revenue and Changes in Net Assets			
		Charges for Services	Operating Grants and Contributions	Capital Grants and Contributions	Primary Government			Component Unit
					Governmental Activities	Business-Type Activities	Total	
Primary Government								
Governmental Activities:								
General Government	$212,000	$ 4,000	$23,000	$20,000	$(165,0000)		$ (165,000)	
Streets and Highways	71,000				(71,000)		(71,000)	
Public Safety	335,000				(335,000)		(335,000)	
Sanitation	141,000				(141,000)		(141,000)	
Culture and Recreation	54,000				(54,000)		(54,000)	
Depreciation of Capital Assets	120,000				(120,000)		(120,000)	
Interest on Long-Term Debt	10,000				(10,000)		(10,000)	
Total Government Activities	$943,000	$ 4,000	$23,000	$20,000	$ (896,000)		$ (896,000)	
Business-Type Activities:								
Water	$ 38,000	$40,000				$ 2,000	$ 2,000	
Total Business-Type Activities	$ 38,000	$40,000				$ 2,000	$ 2,000	
Total Primary Government	$981,000	$44,000	$23,000	$20,000	$ (896,000)	$ 2,000	$ (894,000)	
Component Unit:								
Library	$ 6,000	$ -0-						$ (6,000)
Total Component Unit	$ 6,000	$ -0-						$ (6,000)

General Revenues:		
Taxes:		
Property Taxes, Levied for General Purposes	$ 781,000	
Property Taxes, Levied for Special Purposes	62,000	
Property Taxes, Levied for Debt Service	33,000	
Sales Taxes	32,000	
Investment Earnings	9,000	
Miscellaneous Revenues	18,000	
Contribution	100,000	
Transfers between Governmental and Business-Type Funds	-0-	
Total General Revenues, Special Items, and Transfers	$1,035,000	
Change in Net Assets	$ 139,000	
Net Assets—Beginning	4,268,000	
Net Assets—Ending	$4,407,000	

(Business-Type Activities column: Total General Revenues $2,000; Change in Net Assets $2,000; Net Assets—Beginning 26,000; Net Assets—Ending $28,000)

(Total column: Total General Revenues $1,035,000; Change in Net Assets $ 141,000; Net Assets—Beginning 4,294,000; Net Assets—Ending $4,435,000)

(Component Unit column: Contribution $ 12,000; Change in Net Assets $ 6,000; Net Assets—Beginning 748,000; Net Assets—Ending $754,000)

FIGURE 13–15
Reconciliation
Schedule for the
Statement of
Net Assets

SOL CITY Reconciliation of the Balance Sheet of Governmental Funds to the Statement of Net Assets December 31, 20X2	
Fund balances reported in the governmental funds	$ 279,000
Amounts reported for the governmental activities in the statement of net assets are different because:	
Capital assets used in governmental activities are not financial resources and therefore are not reported in the governmental funds.	4,200,000
Internal service funds are used by management to charge the costs of certain activities, such as centralized purchasing and storage functions, to individual funds. The assets and liabilities of the internal service fund are included in governmental activities in the statement of net assets.	7,000
Long-term liabilities, including bonds payable, are not due and payable in the current period and therefore are not reported in the funds.	(80,000)
Interest on bonds in the permanent fund is recognized in that fund under the modified accrual basis but must be adjusted to the accrual basis for the government-wide financial statements.	1,000
Net assets of governmental activities	$4,407,000

basis used in the governmental funds to the accrual basis used for the government-wide statements. For example, the balance sheets of the government funds do not include infrastructure and capital assets. These costs are recognized as expenditures in the periods in which they are made. However, the government-wide statement of net assets must report the balance sheet date cost less depreciation of these infrastructure and capital assets. In addition, the government-wide statements must include the accounts of the internal service funds, which are separately reported from the governmental funds in the fund-based financial statements.

2. *Reconciliation schedule for Statement of Activities.* The second reconciliation schedule, the reconciliation between the net change in fund balances reported in the governmental funds' statement of revenues, expenditures, and changes in fund balance to the change in net assets reported in the government-wide financials, is presented in Figure 13–16. For example, interest revenue on the investment in bonds in the permanent fund was presented in that fund under the modified accrual basis for the amount of $8,000. However, under the accrual basis, the interest revenue would be computed based on the effective interest rate, with amortization of the discount, in the amount of $9,000 ($90,000 × 0.10). The difference of $1,000 is an adjustment both to the change in net assets and to the net assets.

Budgetary Comparison Schedule

GASB 34 requires that a *budgetary comparison schedule* be presented as required supplementary information for the general fund and for each special revenue fund that has a legally adopted annual budget. This schedule may be presented as a separate financial statement after the governmental funds financials or in the footnotes of the annual report. The budgetary comparison schedule for Sol City's general fund is presented in Figure 13–17.

Important observations regarding the budgetary comparison schedule follow:

1. **GASB 34** requires that both the original budget and the final budget be presented. The original budget is the first budget for the fiscal period adopted by the government entity. Through the year, many government entities will modify the original budget because of new events or changes in expectations. These changes must go through the legislative process of the government, such as the city council. For our example, no changes were made to the formal budget during the year.

2. The budgetary comparison schedule should be presented on the same format with the same terminology and classifications as the original budget.

FIGURE 13–16
Reconciliation
Schedule for the
Statement of
Revenues,
Expenditures,
and Changes in
Fund Balances

SOL CITY Reconciliation of the Statement of Revenues, Expenditures, and Changes in Fund Balances of Governmental Funds to the Statement of Activities For the Year Ended December 31, 20X2	
Net change in fund balances—governmental funds	$150,000
Governmental funds report capital outlays as expenditures. However, in the statement of activities, the costs of those assets are capitalized and depreciated over their estimated useful lives. This is the amount by which capital outlays in the governmental funds ($182,000) exceeded depreciation of the governmental assets ($119,000).	63,000
Bond proceeds provide current financial resources for the governmental funds. However, the issuance of debt increases long-term liabilities in the statement of net assets. Repayment of debt principal is an expenditure in the governmental funds, but the repayment reduces the long-term liabilities in the statement of net assets. This is the amount by which bond proceeds ($102,000) exceeded the net repayments of principal ($20,000).	(82,000)
Revenues in the statement of activities are recorded on the accrual basis. Interest revenue in the governmental funds is recorded on the modified accrual basis. This is the amount that accrual interest exceeded the interest recognized in the permanent funds.	1,000
Internal service funds are used by management to charge the costs of certain services, such as a centralized purchasing function, to individual funds. The net revenue (expense) of the internal service funds is reported with governmental activities.	7,000
Change in net assets of governmental activities	$139,000

3. A separate column for the variance between the final budget and the actual amounts is encouraged but not required. It is presented here to provide a complete presentation of the possible disclosures of a governmental entity.

FIGURE 13–17   **Budgetary Comparison Schedule**

	Budgeted Amount		Actual Amounts (Budgetary Basis)	Variance with Final Budget Positive (Negative)
SOL CITY Budgetary Comparison Schedule General Fund For the Year Ended December 31, 20X2				
	Original	Final		
Budgetary fund balance, January 1	$129,000	$129,000	$129,000	$ -0-
Resources (inflows):				
Property taxes	775,000	775,000	781,000	6,000
Grants	55,000	55,000	33,000	(22,000)
Sales taxes	25,000	25,000	32,000	7,000
Miscellaneous	20,000	20,000	18,000	(2,000)
Amounts available for appropriation	$875,000	$875,000	$864,000	$(11,000)
Charges to appropriations (outflows):				
General government	$200,000	$200,000	$206,000	$(6,000)
Streets and highways	75,000	75,000	71,000	4,000
Public safety	400,000	400,000	393,000	7,000
Sanitation	150,000	150,000	141,000	9,000
Nondepartmental:				
Transfers out to other funds	30,000	30,000	30,000	-0-
Total charges to appropriations	$855,000	$855,000	$841,000	$ 14,000
Budgetary fund balance, December 31	$149,000	$149,000	$152,000	$ 3,000

GASB Statement No. 41, "Budgetary Comparison Schedules—Perspective Differences" (GASB 41), amended **GASB 34** for state and local governments that have significantly different structures for budgetary purposes from the fund structures in **GASB 34.** These differences are termed perspective differences. A government with significant budgetary perspective differences such that the government cannot provide budgetary comparisons for the fund structure of the general fund and each special revenue fund is then required to present a budgetary comparison schedule in its required supplementary information based on the fund, program, or organizational structure that government uses for its legally adopted budget.

Management's Discussion and Analysis

GASB 34 specifies that the Management's Discussion and Analysis (MD&A) be included in the *required supplementary information (RSI)* of the government-wide financial statements. The MD&A is presented before the financial statements and provides an analytical overview of the government's financial and operating activities.

The MD&A discusses current-period operations and financial position and then compares those with the prior periods. The purpose of this RSI item is to provide users of the financial statements an objective discussion of whether the government's financial position has improved or deteriorated during the year. **GASB 37** states that the MD&A should be limited to the items specified in **GASB 34** rather than be used to present an abundance of other topics not specifically required. The GASB believes that additional discussions beyond those required might result in information that is not objective and cannot be directly analyzed. Governments that wish to provide additional information may do so in other supplementary information such as footnotes or transmittal letters.

Notes to the Government-wide Financial Statements

GASB Statement No. 34, "Basic Financial Statements—and Management's Discussion and Analysis—for State and Local Governments" (GASB 34), specified a number of required note disclosures in the government-wide financial statements that include the following:

1. Accounting and measurement policies used in the primary governmental entity.
2. Information about capital assets, including beginning and ending balances, along with capital acquisitions and sales during the year; and depreciation expense and accumulated depreciation.
3. For collections not capitalized, disclosures describing the collection, along with the reasons for not capitalizing these collections.
4. Note disclosures about long-term liabilities include a schedule of the beginning and ending balances along with increases or decreases during the year, for each long-term debt item; the current portion of each long-term item; and the amount of annual debt service required.
5. Disclosures about donor-restricted endowments should include net increases in investments for which the income is available for expenditure, and the policy for spending investment income.
6. Segment information is to be provided for the enterprise funds included in the government-wide financial statements.

GASB Statement No. 38, "Certain Financial Statement Note Disclosures" (GASB 38), was issued in June 2001 and stated that the required footnotes should be modified for the following:

1. In the summary of significant accounting policies, provide descriptions of the activities accounted for in the major funds, internal service fund type, and fiduciary fund types. This change is a result of **GASB 34**'s focus on major funds rather than all funds.
2. Delete the requirement to disclose the accounting policy for encumbrances in the summary of significant accounting policies (i.e., the lapsing or nonlapsing method).

3. Disclose the period of availability used for recording revenues in governmental funds.

4. Disclose debt service requirements to maturity, separately identifying principal and interest for each of the subsequent five years and in five-year increments thereafter and changes in variable-rate debt. In addition, governments should disclose the future minimum payments for each of the five succeeding years for capital and noncancelable operating leases.

5. Provide a schedule of changes in short-term debt during the year along with the purposes for which the debt was issued.

6. Add a disclosure of actions taken to address any significant violations of finance-related legal or contractual provisions to the footnote describing these significant violations.

7. Disclose details of the payable and receivable amounts for interfund balances and the purposes of the interfund transfers. In addition, disclosures should be made regarding the amounts of interfund transfers during the period along with a description and amount of significant transfers that are not expected to occur on a routine basis.

8. Provide details of the components of accounts payable so that the financial statement users can understand the timeliness and payment priorities of payables.

9. Provide details about significant individual accounts when their nature is obscured by aggregation. For example, more disclosure could be made for receivables that contain a myriad of different credit risks or liquidity attributes.

Other Financial Report Items

Governments may choose to provide additional information beyond that required as discussed previously. For example, some government entities present comprehensive annual financial reports (CAFRs), which include additional statistical information about the sources of revenues, property tax levies and property values, demographic statistics, and other miscellaneous statistics that management of the governmental entity believes will aid users of the financial report. Some governmental entities may additionally disclose financial statements for individual funds or combined by fund type. Some governments may go beyond the required footnote disclosures and provide additional schedules and information. As with commercial enterprises, it is up to the management of the governmental entity to determine how much additional disclosure it wishes to provide in its annual report.

Interim Reporting

Governmental entities generally are not required to publish interim reports, although many prepare monthly or quarterly reports to determine the current progress of compliance with legal and budgetary limitations and to plan for changes in events or developments that were not foreseen when the annual budget was prepared. Interim reports are a valuable internal management control instrument; they typically are not made available to the general public.

Auditing Governmental Entities

Most governmental entities are audited annually because of state or federal requirements or because long-term creditors demand audited statements as part of the debt agreements. The audit of a governmental entity is different from the audit of a commercial entity. The auditor not only must express an opinion on the fairness of the audited entity's financial statements in conformity with applicable accounting principles but also must assess the audited entity's compliance with legal or contractual provisions of state law, debt covenants, terms of grants from other governmental entities, and other restrictions on the governmental entity. The AICPA publishes the "State and Local Governments—Audit and Accounting Guide" that provides guidance relevant to audits of state and local governments. The guide includes planning the audit under the Risk Assessment Statements of Auditing Standards (SAS) in eight recent standards, number 104 through number 111. In addition, the guide defines internal control deficiencies for state and local governments.

The Single Audit Act of 1984 is a federal law specifying the audit requirements for all state and local governments receiving federal financial assistance. The audit act requires auditors to determine whether (1) the financial statements fairly present the government's financial condition, (2) the governmental entity has an internal control system to provide reasonable assurance that it is managing federal financial assistance programs in compliance with applicable laws and regulations, and (3) the governmental entity has complied with laws and regulations that may have a material effect on each federal program. The auditors issue not only the standard audit report but also special reports on items (2) and (3) above.

The Single Audit Act does not apply to all governmental entities receiving federal assistance. For fiscal years ending after December 31, 2003, governmental entities that expend $500,000 or more in federal awards in a year must have either a single or a program-specific audit for that year. A governmental entity is eligible for a program-specific audit only if the federal award is expended under a single federal program and that federal program's laws, regulations, or grant agreements do not require the governmental entity to have a financial statement audit. Otherwise a single audit is required. Governmental entities that expend less than $500,000 in federal awards in a year are exempt from the single audit requirement for that year. However, their records must be available for review or audit by officials from the federal agency, the pass-through entity providing the award, or the Government Accountability Office (GAO).

ADDITIONAL CONSIDERATIONS

Special-Purpose Governmental Entities

The accounting and financial reporting standards for general-purpose governments such as states, counties, and municipalities are discussed in this chapter and Chapter 12. However, a number of governments are ***special-purpose governments,*** which are legally separate entities. They may be component units of a general-purpose government or stand-alone governments apart from a general-purpose government. Special-purpose governments include governmental entities such as cemetery districts, levee districts, park districts, tollway authorities, and school districts. Some of these special-purpose government entities may be engaged in governmental activities that generally are financed through taxes, intergovernmental revenues, and other nonexchange revenues. These activities are usually reported in governmental or internal service funds. Some of these entities are engaged in business-type activities that are financed by fees charged for goods or services. These activities are usually reported in enterprise funds. **GASB 34** establishes specific reporting requirements for each of the following types of special-purpose governments:

1. Engaged in more than one governmental program or in both governmental and business-type activities: These governmental entities must provide both fund financial statements and government-wide financial statements as presented earlier in this chapter and in Chapter 12.

2. Engaged in a single governmental program (such as cemetery districts or drainage districts): These governmental entities may present a simplified set of government-wide and fund-based financial statements, often combining these two statements.

3. Engaged in only business-type activities: These governmental entities must present only the financial statements required for enterprise funds. Many public universities and public hospitals will be included in this category.

4. Engaged in only fiduciary-type activities: These governmental entities are not required to present the government-wide financials but must provide only the financial statements required for fiduciary funds. This category includes special-purpose governments responsible for managing pension funds.

Regardless of the category of special-purpose government entity, all governments must include in their financial reports the Management's Discussion and Analysis, the foot-notes, and any required supplementary information.

Financial Reporting for Pensions and OPEB Plans

Most states and many local governments provide a variety of pensions and other postem-ployment benefits (OPEB) to their employees. OPEBs include postemployment health care, life insurance, and other nonpension benefits for persons after retirement from the governmental unit. The GASB has a series of standards that prescribe the employer's accounting for these costs and the financial reporting by the entity that maintains the plans. In some cases, the governmental unit administers its own plans, such as a state-based pension plan covering all state employees in a specific employment category, while in other cases the governmental unit uses a multiemployer plan, such as a firefighter's retirement plan that includes firefighters from a number of cities.

Two GASB statements present the accounting and financial reporting requirements for the entity that administers the plan's assets and for the employer of the employees cov-ered by the plans. The first is **GASB Statement No. 25,** "Financial Reporting for Defined Benefit Pension Plans and Note Disclosures for Defined Contribution Plans" (GASB 25), which established the financial reporting requirements for pension plans. For defined benefit plans, the payout to the retirees is based on work-related factors such as number of years worked and is not related to the amount in the plan. For defined contribution plans, the payout is based on the amount accumulated for each employee. Some plans are contributory, in which the employees must make contributions, and some plans are noncontributory, in which the employer makes all the contributions. The second stan-dard is **GASB Statement No. 43,** "Financial Reporting for Postemployment Benefits Plans Other Than Pension Plans" (GASB 43), which provided financial reporting stan-dards for OPEB plans. The general principles in these two standards are similar. The entity that administers the plan must provide two categories of information in its financial reporting: *(a)* current financial information about plan assets and funding activities and *(b)* information about the funded position of the plan and the plan's progress in accumulat-ing sufficient financial resources to provide benefits when due. The two financial statements required for pension plans and other postemployment benefits plans are *(a)* a statement of plan net assets that provides information about the fair value and composition of the plan's assets and information about the plan's liabilities and *(b)* a statement of changes in plan net assets that provides information on the period's changes in the net assets of the plans. If a pension or OPEB plan is included within the reporting entity, that is, the governmental entity administers the plans, then the information for these two statements will be included with the other fiduciary funds in that fund's financial statements. The accrual method of accounting is required and informative footnotes must be provided.

Employer Accounting for Pensions and OPEB Plan Benefits

Two GASB statements present the standards for the employer's measurement and dis-play of accounting for the expenditures/expenses for the benefits and any related liabili-ties (or assets) for the difference between the expenditure/expenses recognition and the amount funded by the employer. The first is **GASB Statement No. 27,** "Accounting for Pensions by State and Local Governmental Employers" (GASB 27), which presents the standards for pensions. The second is **GASB Statement No. 45,** "Accounting and Financial Reporting by Employers for Postemployment Benefits Other Than Pensions" (GASB 45). The general principles for measurement, recognition, and display in these two standards are similar. The accrual method of accounting is typically used for the government-wide financial statements to measure the expenses of the employer for pen-sion costs for its employees and for the costs of other postemployment benefits for its employees. Actuarial assumptions are required under the accrual method. The state and local government employers must report the expense/expenditures and related liabilities (or assets) for both their pension benefits and their OPEBs.

Although **GASB 27** and **GASB 45** have many of the same measurement and display standards, there are some differences due to the differences in the nature of the specific benefits given by the employer. Accountants responsible for accounting for these two sets of postemployment benefits readily acknowledge that some plans and benefits can be quite complex and require detailed study of the specific requirements in the related GASB statements.

GASB Statement No. 50, "Pension Disclosures—an Amendment of GASB Statement No. 25 and No. 27" (GASB 50), requires additional disclosures for defined benefit plans and disclosures by the employers. The plans and the employers must present the following in their financial statements: *(a)* notes disclosing the funded status of the plan along with any actuarial methods and significant assumptions used to make the most recent actuarial valuation; *(b)* as RSI, a schedule of funding progress of defined benefit plans for which the annual required contribution of the employer is based on the aggregate actuarial cost method; *(c)* notes disclosing legal or contractual maximum contribution rates; and *(d)* notes disclosing changes in actuarial assumptions for successive years.

Accounting for Termination Benefits

Finally, termination benefits are sometimes offered by governmental entities when an employee is involuntarily terminated (i.e., fired or laid off) or voluntarily terminates in order to accept early-retirement benefits. These termination benefits may include health care–related programs, job transition costs, early retirement incentives, and other similar types of items. The accounting and reporting requirements for these benefits are presented in **GASB Statement No. 47,** "Accounting for Termination Benefits" (GASB 47). In the case of employees who voluntarily terminate, the employer recognizes a liability and expense when the employee accepts the offer and the amount can be estimated. The general measurement principle is that the dollar amount recognized should be the discounted present value of the estimated future payments.

Governmental entities may develop a plan for a reduction in their workforce that involves the involuntary termination of some employees. A liability and an expense should be recognized when the plan of termination is approved by the governing body, the plan has been communicated to the employees, and the amount can be estimated. For the government-wide financial statements, the accrual method is used to recognize the discounted present value of the estimated future payments.

Governmental entities have found that they must offer employees benefits similar to those offered in the private sector in order to attract and employ persons who would otherwise seek employment with business firms in the private sector. Thus, as the private sector changes what it offers employees, governmental entities will have to adjust what they offer to their employees.

Summary of Key Concepts	This chapter completes the discussion of accounting and financial reporting principles used by local and state governments. Governments may use five governmental fund types, two proprietary fund types, and four fiduciary fund types (including agency funds). The governmental funds use the modified accrual basis of accounting; the other funds use the accrual basis of accounting.

The government reporting model is currently specified in **GASB 34.** Both fund-based financial statements and government-wide financial statements are required. The government-wide statements are based on the accrual basis and present both long-term capital assets, including infrastructure assets, and long-term debt. Government entities must include required supplementary information (RSI) in their annual financial reports as specified by **GASB 34.** This RSI includes reconciliation schedules and a budgetary comparison schedule. A new GASB statement, GASB 54, specifies changes for fund balance reporting in the governmental fund types.

Key Terms	agency funds, *685*	discrete presentation, *687*	reporting entity, *686*
	blended presentation, *687*	enterprise funds, *675*	required supplementary
	budgetary comparison	fund-based financial	information (RSI), *695*
	schedule, *693*	statements, *661*	special-purpose
	capital projects funds, *665*	government-wide financial	governments, *697*
	component units, *687*	statements, *689*	special revenue funds, *661*
	comprehensive annual	internal service funds, *680*	trust funds, *683*
	financial report, *688*	permanent funds, *671*	
	debt service funds, *668*	reconciliation schedules, *691*	

Appendix 13A Other Governmental Entities—Public School Systems and the Federal Government

In addition to local and state governmental entities, two other governmental entities—public schools and the federal government—have pervasive influences on the lives of citizens. This appendix presents a brief overview of the basic accounting and financial reporting requirements for these two governmental entities.

PUBLIC SCHOOL SYSTEMS

In the United States today, more than 50 million students attend approximately 14,000 public elementary and secondary school systems employing about 2.5 million teachers and expending more than $100 billion annually. Many others attend one of the myriad of private schools formed by religious or other groups.

Accounting and Financial Reporting for Public School Systems

Accounting for public schools is similar to accounting for local or state governments. The modified accrual basis of accounting is used for most funds, and the financial statements for a school district are similar to those of a local government. More than half of school district revenue is obtained from local property taxes; the remaining sources are fees for services, state education aid, and federal grants to education. Most school districts have an elected school board that serves as a public policy-making body for the school system.

The fund structure for a school district is similar to the fund structure for a local or state government. School district funds include the general fund, special revenue funds, capital projects funds, debt service funds, enterprise funds, internal service funds, and trust and agency funds.

The school district's general fund resources are expended for costs directly associated with the education process: teachers' salaries, books and supplies, and other costs. Special revenue funds may include specific funds for operations, building, and maintenance (OBM) of the physical facilities of the school district, as well as the transportation special revenue fund, which is responsible for acquiring and maintaining the buses for transporting children to and from the schools.

Public school systems have a public hearing on the annual budget, which is then approved by the school board or other governing body. The budget specifies the revenue from the three basic sources: local property taxes and fees, state school aid, and federal sources. The expenditures are broken down into the following three dimensions: *program,* such as gifted, vocational, elementary, secondary, and adult/continuing education; *function,* such as guidance counselors, instructional staff, school administration, and student transportation; and *object,* such as salaries, employee benefits, purchased services, and supplies and materials.

The department of education of each state receives the annual reports from that state's school districts. Typically these financial statements must be audited by independent auditors. Many school districts are legally separate, fiscally independent, special-purpose government entities engaged in both governmental and business-type activities. These school districts have their own legally mandated budget process and tax levy authority, and they do not depend financially on another government entity. In these cases, school districts present their financial statements in accordance with **GASB 34,** which requires government-wide financial statements as well as fund financial statements. **GASB 34** also requires management's discussion and analysis, footnotes, and required supplementary information. School districts that are fiscally dependent and component units of a primary government entity, such as the city government in which the school is located, present their financial information within the primary government's financial statements, usually discretely presented in a column separate from the financial data of the primary government. Other statements required are the same as for other governmental units. In addition, the comprehensive annual financial report for a school district includes a variety of other disclosures relevant to the school district, such as the cost per student, the debt capacity of the district, and the assessed valuation of all property included in the school district.

Federal Government Accounting

An accounting structure for the federal government has been part of the U.S. statutes since 1789. The following individuals or entities have significant roles in the federal budgeting and expending process:

Executive Branch	Legislative Branch
President	Congress
Office of Management and Budget (OMB)	Government Accountability Office (GAO)
Secretary of the Treasury	Congressional Budget Office (CBO)
Federal agencies	

The fiscal period for the U.S. federal government is from October 1 to September 30 of the next calendar year. The president of the United States directs that the annual budget be prepared by the director of the Office of Management and Budget, who is a member of the president's staff. The director of the OMB then consults with the various federal agencies and the secretary of the treasury and prepares the budget that the president presents to Congress. The Congressional Budget Office then evaluates the executive budget and may propose that Congress present one of its own. After the legislative process runs its course and the budget is approved, Congress provides the authority for the executive branch to obtain revenue through taxation or other charges. The primary agency responsible for obtaining revenue is the Internal Revenue Service, which is an agency of the Department of the Treasury.

The appropriation-expenditure process is a little different for the federal government than for local government units. The federal budget provides the appropriation authority for the federal government. This appropriation authority is then allocated to the various agencies through a process of apportionments made by the Office of Management and Budget. The apportionment is then divided among the agency's programs and activities by a process of allotments. The agency then makes obligations by incurring costs for services provided. These obligations are then liquidated through the preparation of vouchers, which are submitted to the Department of the Treasury for payment.

The Federal Accounting Standards Advisory Board (FASAB) establishes the generally accepted accounting principles for federal financial reporting entities. In 1990, three federal government officials created the FASAB as a federal advisory committee. The three officials were the secretary of the treasury, the director of the Office of Management and Budget, and the comptroller general of the United States. The FASAB has issued over 30 statements and several technical releases establishing federal financial accounting standards. These standards are quite different from those for either profit-seeking entities (FASB) or state and local government entities (GASB) because of the many unique aspects of the federal government's operations.

The Department of Treasury annually issues the "Financial Report of the United States Government," which includes the auditor's report from the comptroller general of the United States. The financial report presents information on the federal government and its agencies, including a stewardship report and a statement of net cost by agency. The financial report is available on the Department of Treasury's Web site.

Audits of Federal Agencies

The comptroller general of the United States is the head of the Government Accountability Office (GAO). The GAO is an agency of the legislative branch of the federal government and works with the Department of the Treasury, an executive department, to develop and maintain the federal government's accounting system. The GAO reviews the accounting systems of each executive agency each year from both a financial and a compliance perspective. The compliance part of the audit ensures that the agency fulfilled all legal and budgetary restrictions. Exceptions are reported to Congress, which then communicates them to the executive branch, thus completing the cycle that began when the executive branch first proposed the annual budget to Congress.

Questions

LO1   **Q13-1**   In what circumstances would a governmental unit use a special revenue fund rather than a general fund?

LO1   **Q13-2**   Which governmental funds use operating budgets? Which use capital budgets?

LO3   **Q13-3**   How is interest on long-term debt accounted for in the debt service fund?

LO1   **Q13-4**   What are the major differences between a special revenue fund and an enterprise fund?

LO7   **Q13-5**   What is the basis of accounting in the proprietary funds? Why?

LO11   **Q13-6**   What financial statements must be prepared for the governmental funds? For the enterprise funds?

LO2   **Q13-7**   How are the proceeds from a bond issue accounted for in governmental funds? Where are these proceeds reported on the governmental funds' statement of revenues, expenditures, and changes in fund balance?

LO1   **Q13-8**   What are the primary differences between a permanent fund (governmental) and a private-purpose trust fund (fiduciary)?

LO11   **Q13-9**   Not all governmental funds need to be separately presented on the governmental funds financial statements. What are the two tests for determining major governmental funds for which separate disclosure is required?

LO11   **Q13-10**   How are contributions to governmental funds as well as special or extraordinary items reported on the governmental funds' statement of revenues, expenditures, and changes in fund balance?

LO10   **Q13-11**   Do agency funds have a net fund balance? Why or why not?

LO11   **Q13-12**   What are component units of a government, and how are these component units reported on the government-wide financial statements?

LO12   **Q13-13**   Reconciliation schedules are a required disclosure in the government-wide financial statements. What are the purpose and content of these reconciliation schedules?

LO12   **Q13-14**   **GASB 34** requires a budgetary comparison schedule for each governmental fund that has a legally adopted budget. Briefly describe this budgetary comparison schedule.

LO11   **Q13-15**   How are infrastructure and other long-term assets as well as general long-term debt reported on the government-wide financial statements?

Cases

LO1   **C13-1**   **Basis of Accounting and Reporting Issues**

Judgment   The accounting system of Barb City is organized and operated on a fund basis. Among the types of funds used are a general fund, a special revenue fund, and an enterprise fund.

Required

a. Explain the basic differences in revenue recognition between the accrual basis of accounting and the modified accrual basis of accounting in relation to governmental accounting.

b. What basis of accounting should be used for each of the following funds: (1) general fund, (2) special revenue fund, and (3) enterprise fund?

LO2, LO3, LO8   **C13-2**   **Capital Projects, Debt Service, and Internal Service Funds**

The funds of Lake City include a debt service fund, a capital projects fund, and an internal service fund.

Required

Understanding   a. Explain the use of capital projects funds. Include what they account for, the basis of accounting used, unusual entries and accounts, and their financial statements.

b. Explain the use of debt service funds. Include what they account for, the basis of accounting used, unusual entries and accounts, and their financial statements.

c. Explain the use of internal service funds. Include what they account for, the basis of accounting used, unusual entries and accounts, and their financial statements.

LO11

Research

C13-3 Discovery

This case provides learning opportunities using available databases and/or the Internet to obtain contemporary information about the topics in advanced financial accounting. Note that the Internet is dynamic and the specific Web site listed may change addresses. In that case, use a good search engine to locate the current address for the Web site.

Required

Access the Department of Treasury's Web site and scroll through until you locate the most recent "Financial Report of the United States Government" (http://fms.treas.gov/fr/index.html). Look over the report, especially the comptroller general's statement and the auditor's report, and then prepare a one- to two-page memo summarizing the major information items reported in the Financial Report of the United States Government.

LO11

Analysis

C13-4 Becoming Familiar with a Local Government's Comprehensive Annual Financial Report (CAFR)

Using the Internet, find the comprehensive annual financial report (CAFR) of a local government selected by your instructor. At a minimum, a CAFR will include (1) management's discussion and analysis (MD&A), (2) the basic financial statements—government-wide and fund-based financial statements, (3) notes to the basic financial statements, (4) other required supplementary information (RSI), and (5) the external auditor's opinion on the basic financial statements.

Required

Using the CAFR chosen by your instructor, answer the following questions that relate to the overall government and to the governmental funds:

a. Read the section of the report that contains management's discussion and analysis. Is your government a general purpose government? If yes, what types of services does your government provide?

b. What type of opinion was given by the external auditor on the basic financial statements? What responsibility did the auditor take with regard to MD&A and the other RSI?

c. Examine the financial statements for the funds. List the fund types used by your government.

d. From reading the notes that follow the government-wide and fund-based financial statements, what is the measurement focus and basis of accounting used by the governmental funds?

e. List the financial statements of the government that use the economic resources measurement focus and the accrual basis of accounting.

f. In addition to the general fund, list your government's other major governmental and proprietary funds.

g. Examine the government-wide financial statements. List any component units over which your government has fiscal accountability.

h. Examine the balance sheet of the governmental funds. What are the total assets and the total fund balance as of the most recent balance sheet date? How much of the total fund balance is assigned?

i. Examine the statement of revenues, expenditures, and changes in fund balance for the most recent year. How much of the total revenue came from taxes?

j. Examine the statement of revenues, expenditures, and changes in fund balance for the most recent year. How are expenditures classified?

k. Examine the statement of revenues, expenditures, and changes in fund balance for the most recent year. How much of the other financing sources resulted from transfers in?

l. Examine the statement of revenues, expenditures, and changes in fund balance for the most recent year. List any special items reported. What was the increase or decrease in fund balance for the year?

LO11

Discovery

C13-5 The GASB's Decision-Making Process

The Statements of Governmental Accounting Standards are the final step in the GASB's decision-making process. Standard setting has a number of specific steps, with open and thorough study of the issues, and with public participation and input encouraged throughout the process.

Required

Access the GASB's Web site at www.gasb.org; click on the "Education" tab and then on "How Standards are Set." Then read through the process described in the links on this page and prepare a one-page memorandum summarizing the steps the GASB takes before adopting a new governmental accounting standard.

LO11

C13-6 **Summarizing a Recent GASB Exposure Draft**

Discovery

The Governmental Accounting Standards Board places exposure drafts (EDs) of proposed future standards on its Web site. These exposure drafts provide an early view of the consensus viewpoints of the Board on a project. Accountants wishing to remain current in governmental accounting and auditing need to be aware of proposed governmental standards and their potential impacts on the accounting and reporting of the governmental entities with which the accountant is associated.

Required

Access the GASB's Web site at www.gasb.org; locate the most recent exposure draft of a proposed Statement. Read through the Summary presented at the front of the exposure draft and then prepare a one-page memorandum on what issues the proposed Statement is addressing; why the GASB feels the proposed Statement is needed; and the key provisions of the proposed Statement. Toward the bottom of your memorandum, place the expected effective date of the proposed Statement and, if included in the ED, the proposed transition implementation from current standards to the new standard.

Exercises

LO11

E13-1 **Multiple-Choice Questions on Government Financial Reporting**

Select the correct answer for each of the following questions.

1. The government-wide financial statements use the

   a. Economic resources measurement focus and the accrual basis of accounting.
   b. Current financial resources measurement focus and the accrual basis of accounting.
   c. Economic resources measurement focus and the modified accrual basis of accounting.
   d. Current financial resources measurement focus and the modified accrual basis of accounting.

2. The financial statements for the governmental funds use the

   a. Economic resources measurement focus and the accrual basis of accounting.
   b. Current financial resources measurement focus and the accrual basis of accounting.
   c. Economic resources measurement focus and the modified accrual basis of accounting.
   d. Current financial resources measurement focus and the modified accrual basis of accounting.

3. According to **GASB Statement No. 34,** infrastructure fixed assets

   a. Must be capitalized and depreciated.
   b. Must be capitalized, but governments do *not* have to depreciate them.
   c. May be capitalized and depreciated.
   d. Must be reported using the modified approach.

4. On which of the following government-wide financial statements would you find all liabilities of a state or local government?

   a. Statement of net assets.
   b. Statement of financial condition.
   c. Statement of activities.
   d. Statement of financial position.

5. On which of the following financial statements would you find all of the capital assets of a local government?

   a. Statement of net assets.
   b. Statement of financial condition.
   c. Statement of activities.
   d. Statement of financial position.

6. For which fund category is a statement of cash flows prepared?

   a. Governmental.
   b. Proprietary.
   c. Fiduciary.
   d. None of the above.

Note: Use the information below to answer questions 7 through 9.

The Village of Hampton reported the following data for its governmental activities for the year ended June 30, 20X5:

Item	Amount
Cash and cash equivalents	$ 1,880,000
Receivables	459,000
Capital assets	14,250,000
Accumulated depreciation	1,750,000
Accounts payable	650,000
Long-term liabilities	5,350,000

Additional data:
  All of the long-term debt was used to acquire capital assets.
  Cash of $654,000 is restricted for debt service.

7. On the statement of net assets prepared at June 30, 20X5, what amount should be reported for total net assets?

   a. $8,839,000.
   b. $7,804,000.
   c. $7,150,000.
   d. $8,189,000.

8. On the statement of net assets prepared at June 30, 20X5, what amount should be reported for net assets, invested in capital assets net of related debt?

   a. $8,839,000.
   b. $7,804,000.
   c. $7,150,000.
   d. $8,189,000.

9. On the statement of net assets prepared at June 30, 20X5, what amount should be reported for net assets, unrestricted?

   a. $1,685,000.
   b. $1,689,000.
   c. $1,035,000.
   d. $1,031,000.

10. Which of the following funds can be major funds assuming the appropriate tests are met?

    a. The parking meter special revenue fund and the water utility enterprise fund.
    b. The fire station capital projects fund and a property tax agency fund.
    c. The fire station bonds debt service fund and the city teachers pension trust fund.
    d. The local symphony permanent fund and the Edwina Williams private-purpose trust fund.

11. Where in the basic financial statements would you find a description of the measurement focus and the basis of accounting used in the government-wide financial statements?

    a. In the statement of net assets.
    b. In the statement of activities.
    c. In management's discussion and analysis.
    d. In the notes to the financial statements.

12. Where in the financial section of a CAFR would you find an analysis of the balances and transactions of individual funds?

    a. In the government-wide financial statements.
    b. In the fund financial statements.
    c. In management's discussion and analysis.
    d. In the notes to the financial statements.

LO1–LO3   **E13-2**   **Multiple-Choice Questions on Governmental Funds [AICPA Adapted]**

Select the correct answer for each of the following questions.

1. On December 31, 20X1, Tiffin Township paid a contractor $2,000,000 for the total cost of a new firehouse built in 20X1 on township-owned land. Financing was by means of a $1,500,000 general obligation bond issue sold at face amount on December 31, 20X1, with the remaining $500,000 transferred from the general fund. What should be reported on Tiffin's financial statements for the capital projects fund?

   a. Revenue, $1,500,000; Expenditures, $1,500,000.

   b. Revenue, $1,500,000; Other Financing Sources, $500,000; Expenditures, $2,000,000.

   c. Revenue, $2,000,000; Expenditures, $2,000,000.

   d. Other Financing Sources, $2,000,000; Expenditures, $2,000,000.

2. A debt service fund of a municipality is an example of which of the following types of funds?

   a. Fiduciary.

   b. Governmental.

   c. Proprietary.

   d. Internal service.

3. Revenue of a special revenue fund of a governmental unit should be recognized in the period in which the

   a. Revenue becomes available and measurable.

   b. Revenue becomes available for appropriation.

   c. Revenue is billable.

   d. Cash is received.

4. Taxes collected and held by a municipality for a school district would be accounted for in a(n)

   a. Enterprise fund.

   b. Intragovernmental (internal) service fund.

   c. Agency fund.

   d. Special revenue fund.

5. Interest expense on bonds payable should be recorded in a debt service fund

   a. At the end of the fiscal period if the interest due date does not coincide with the end of the fiscal period.

   b. When bonds are issued.

   c. When legally payable.

   d. When paid.

6. Which of the following funds does *not* have a fund balance?

   a. General fund.

   b. Agency fund.

   c. Special revenue fund.

   d. Capital projects fund.

LO6–LO8   **E13-3**   **Multiple-Choice Questions on Proprietary Funds [AICPA Adapted]**

Select the correct answer for each of the following questions.

1. Which of the following accounts could be included in the statement of net assets of an enterprise fund?

	Reserve for Encumbrances	Revenue Bonds Payable	Net Assets
a.	No	No	Yes
b.	No	Yes	Yes
c.	Yes	Yes	No
d.	No	No	No

2. Customers' meter deposits that cannot be spent for normal operating purposes would most likely be classified as restricted cash in the balance sheet of which fund?

   a. Internal service.

   b. Private-purpose trust.

   c. Agency.

   d. Enterprise.

3. Which fund is not an expendable fund?

   a. Capital projects.

   b. General.

   c. Special revenue.

   d. Internal service.

4. If a governmental unit established a data processing center to service all agencies within the unit, the data processing center should be accounted for as a(n)

   a. Capital projects fund.

   b. Internal service fund.

   c. Agency fund.

   d. Trust fund.

5. Recreational facilities run by a governmental unit and financed on a user-charge basis would be accounted for in which fund?

   a. General.

   b. Trust.

   c. Enterprise.

   d. Capital projects.

6. The Underwood Electric Utility Fund, which is an enterprise fund, had the following during its 20X1 fiscal year, ending at December 31, 20X1:

Prepaid insurance paid in December 20X1	$ 43,000
Depreciation for 20X1	129,000

   What amount should be reflected in the statement of revenues, expenses, and changes in fund net assets of the Underwood Electric Utility Fund for these items?

   a. $(43,000).

   b. $0.

   c. $129,000.

   d. $172,000.

7. Which of the following funds of a governmental unit uses the same basis of accounting as an enterprise fund?

   a. Special revenue.

   b. Internal service.

   c. Permanent trust.

   d. Capital projects.

8. Fixed assets utilized in a city-owned utility are accounted for in which of the following?

	Enterprise Fund	General Fund
a.	No	No
b.	No	Yes
c.	Yes	No
d.	Yes	Yes

9. Which of the following funds of a governmental unit would account for long-term debt in the accounts of the fund?

    a. Special revenue.

    b. Capital projects.

    c. Internal service.

    d. General.

LO8–LO10   **E13-4**   **Multiple-Choice Questions on Various Funds**

Use the information below to answer questions 1 and 2:

    On August 1, 20X6, the City of Rockhaven received $1,000,000 from a prominent citizen to establish a private-purpose trust fund. The donor stipulated that the cash be permanently invested and that the earnings from the investments be spent to support local artists. During the year ended June 30, 20X7, $50,000 of dividends were received from stock investments and $35,000 of interest was earned from bond investments. At June 30, $5,000 of the interest earned was not yet received. During the year ended June 30, 20X7, $75,000 was spent by the trust fund to support local artists.

1. For the year ended June 30, 20X7, the trust fund should report investment earnings of

    a. $80,000.

    b. $50,000.

    c. $85,000.

    d. $35,000.

2. For the year ended June 30, 20X7, the trust fund should report the $75,000 spent to support local artists as a

    a. Deduction.

    b. Contra contribution.

    c. Transfer out.

    d. Direct adjustment from fund balance.

3. Which of the following statements is (are) correct about agency funds?

    I. Agency funds should report investment earnings only when they are both measurable and available.

    II. Agency funds are reported on the proprietary funds' statement of cash flows.

    a. I only.

    b. II only.

    c. I and II.

    d. Neither I nor II.

Note: Use the following information to answer questions 4 through 8.

    On July 2, 20X6, the Village of Westbury established an internal service fund to service the data processing needs of the other village departments. The internal service fund received a transfer of $600,000 from the general fund and a $100,000 long-term advance from the water utility enterprise fund to acquire computer equipment. During July of 20X6, computer equipment costing $650,000 was acquired. The following events occurred during the year ended June 30, 20X7:

Charges for services to other departments for data processing services rendered	$100,000
Operating expenses (exclusive of depreciation expense)	45,000
Depreciation expense	40,000
Interest expense on the advance	5,000

At June 30, 20X7, all but $7,000 of the billings were collected, and all operating expenses and the interest expense were paid except for $3,000 of operating expenses.

4. For the year ended June 30, 20X7, what was the income of Westbury's internal service fund?

    a. $13,000.

    b. $6,000.

    c. $3,000.

    d. $10,000.

5. At June 30, 20X7, what total assets amount would appear on the internal service fund balance sheet?

    a. $700,000.

    b. $710,000.

    c. $713,000.

    d. $708,000.

6. Assume that the mayor's office and the police department were billed $55,000 for data processing work during the year ended June 30, 20X7. What account should be debited in the general fund to record these billings?

    a. Other Financing Use—Transfers Out.

    b. Expenditures.

    c. Due to Internal Service Fund.

    d. Operating Expenses.

7. Assume that the water utility, an enterprise fund, was billed $25,000 for data processing work during the year ended June 30, 20X7. What account should be debited in the enterprise fund to record these billings?

    a. Operating expenses.

    b. Other Financing Use—Transfers Out.

    c. Expenditures.

    d. Due to Internal Service Fund.

8. Assume that the income for Westbury's internal service fund was $10,000 for the year ended June 30, 20X7. What net assets should be reported on the internal service fund's statement of net assets at June 30, 20X7?

    a. $713,000.

    b. $610,000.

    c. $710,000.

    d. $613,000.

LO11

E13-5 **Multiple-Choice Questions on Financial Reporting Issues for Government-wide and Fund-Based Financial Statements**

Select the correct answer for each of the following questions.

1. Which of the following statements is correct?

    I. In the government-wide financial statements, internal service fund activities are reported in the governmental activities column.

    II. The total fund balance for the governmental funds that is reported on the governmental funds balance sheet will not equal the total net assets of governmental activities that is reported on the government-wide statement of net assets.

    a. I only.

    b. II only.

    c. I and II.

    d. Neither I nor II.

2. For the year ended June 30, 20X5, the internal service funds of Stanton Township reported an increase in net assets of $300,000 and ending net assets at June 30, 20X5, of $4,500,000. On the reconciliation of the balance sheet of the governmental funds to the statement of net assets as of June 30, 20X5, what amount should be added?

    a. $300,000.

    b. $4,200,000.

c. $4,500,000.

d. $4,800,000.

3. For the year ended June 30, 20X5, the enterprise funds of Stanton Township reported an increase in net assets of $300,000 and ending net assets at June 30, 20X5, of $4,500,000. The enterprise fund also reported net assets—unrestricted of $1,200,000 at June 30, 20X5, on its statement of net assets. On the reconciliation of the balance sheet of the governmental funds to the statement of net assets as of June 30, 20X5, what amount should be added?

a. $4,200,000.

b. $5,700,000.

c. $4,800,000.

d. $0.

4. Which of the following is true regarding permanent funds?

a. Permanent funds use modified accrual accounting.

b. The principal of permanent funds cannot be expended.

c. Dividend and interest income from permanent fund investments are used to benefit the government and its citizens.

d. All of the above.

Note: Use the information below to answer questions 5 through 7.

A water and sewer enterprise fund provided you with the following information for the year ended June 30, 20X5:

Customer receipts	$ 500,000
Dividends received from investments in common and preferred stock	25,000
Proceeds from issuance of revenue bonds (used for plant construction)	1,000,000
Proceeds of short-term notes (used to pay operating expenses)	30,000
Capital grant received from state (used for wastewater plant addition)	300,000
Paid interest on revenue bonds	40,000
Paid interest on short-term notes	1,000
Proceeds received from sale of Dell common stock	20,000
Acquired investments in corporate bonds	8,000
Made capital expenditures	600,000
Operating expenses paid	350,000
Depreciation expense for period	50,000

Answer the following questions about the amounts reported on the statement of cash flows for the water and sewer enterprise fund.

5. What amount should be reported for cash flows provided by operating activities?

a. $150,000.

b. $175,000.

c. $134,000.

d. $100,000.

6. What amount should be reported for cash flows provided by investing activities?

a. $12,000.

b. $45,000.

c. $17,000.

d. $37,000.

7. What amount should be reported for cash flows provided by capital and related financing activities?

a. $700,000.

b. $360,000.

c. $660,000.

d. $400,000.

8. Mary Smith donated cash of $1,000,000 to Elizabeth City with the stipulation that the contribution be invested and that earnings from the investment be spent for salaries for the City's symphony orchestra. The contribution was received on June 30, 20X4, and the cash received was invested in bonds on July 1, 20X4. The bonds were acquired at face value and pay interest at 6 percent on January 1 and July 1. At June 30, 20X5, the fair value of the bonds was $995,000. During the year ended June 30, 20X5, $20,000 was provided to the symphony orchestra to help pay salaries. On the statement of fiduciary net assets at June 30, 20X5, what would be the amount reported for net assets held in trust for the symphony orchestra?

   a. $1,060,000.

   b. $1,055,000.

   c. $1,025,000.

   d. $1,035,000.

LO2

Advanced
StudyGuide
.com

E13-6 Capital Projects Fund Entries and Statement

The City of Waterman established a capital projects fund for the construction of a ramp to be used for access by individuals with disabilities from the parking garage to the city's office building. The estimated cost of the ramp is $200,000. On January 1, 20X2, a 10 percent, $150,000 bond issue was sold at 104.0 with the premium transferred to the debt service fund. At that date, the county board provided a $50,000 grant. After a period of negotiation, the city council awarded a construction contract for $182,000 on April 5, 20X2. The ramp was completed on August 8, 20X2; its actual cost was $189,000. The city council approved payment of the total actual cost of $189,000. In addition to the $189,000, the ramp was carpeted with all-weather material at a cost of $5,500. On November 3, 20X2, the city council gave the final approval to pay for the ramp and the carpeting. After all bills were paid, the remaining fund balance was transferred to the debt service fund.

Required

a. Prepare entries for the capital projects fund for 20X2.

b. Prepare a statement of revenues, expenditures, and changes in fund balance for 20X2 for the capital projects fund.

LO3

Advanced
StudyGuide
.com

E13-7 Debt Service Fund Entries and Statement

The City of Waterman established a debt service fund to account for the financial resources used to service the bonds issued to finance the ramp (see Exercise 13-6). The 10 percent, $150,000 bond issue was sold at 104.0 on January 1, 20X2. It is a 10-year serial bond issue. The resources to pay the interest and annual principal will be from a property tax levy.

Additional Information

1. The operating budget for 20X2 included estimated revenue of $35,000. Budgeted appropriations included $15,000 for principal, $15,000 for interest, and $4,000 for other items. The budget also included an estimated transfer in of $5,000 from the capital projects fund.

2. The property tax levy was for $40,000 and an allowance for uncollectibles of $4,000 was established. Collections totaled $35,000. The remaining taxes were reclassified as delinquent and the allowance was reduced to $1,000. The bond premium was received from the capital projects fund.

3. The current portion of the serial bonds and the interest due this year were recorded and paid. Other expenses charged to the debt service fund totaled $1,700, of which $1,200 was paid.

4. The nominal accounts were closed.

Required

a. Prepare entries for the debt service fund for 20X2.

b. Prepare a balance sheet as of December 31, 20X2, for the debt service fund.

c. Prepare a statement of revenues, expenditures, and changes in fund balance for 20X2 for the debt service fund.

LO7

E13-8 Enterprise Fund Entries and Statements

Augusta has a municipal water and gas utility district (MUD). The trial balance on January 1, 20X1, was as follows:

	Debit	Credit
Cash	$ 92,000	
Accounts Receivable	25,000	
Inventory of Supplies	8,000	
Land	120,000	
Plant and Equipment	480,000	
Accumulated Depreciation		$ 80,000
Vouchers Payable		15,000
Bonds Payable, 6%		500,000
Net Assets:		
Invested in Capital Assets, Net of Related Debt		20,000
Unrestricted		110,000
Total	$725,000	$725,000

Advanced
StudyGuide
.com

Additional Information for 20X1

1. Charges to customers for water and gas were $420,000; collections were $432,000.

2. A loan of $30,000 for two years was received from the general fund.

3. The water and gas lines were extended to a new development at a cost of $75,000. The contractor was paid.

4. Supplies were acquired from central stores (internal service fund) for $12,400. Operating expenses were $328,000, and interest expense was $30,000. Payment was made for the interest and the payable to central stores, and $325,000 of the vouchers were paid.

5. Adjusting entries were as follows: for estimated uncollectible accounts receivable, $6,300; depreciation expense, $32,000; supplies expense, $15,200.

Required

a. Prepare entries for the MUD enterprise fund for 20X1, and prepare closing entries.

b. Prepare a statement of net assets for the fund for December 31, 20X1.

c. Prepare a statement of revenues, expenses, and changes in fund net assets for 20X1. Assume that the $500,000 of the 6 percent bonds is related to the net capital assets of land and of plant and equipment.

d. Prepare a statement of cash flows for 20X1.

LO2

E13-9   Interfund Transfers and Transactions

During 20X8, the following transfers and transactions between funds took place in the City of Matthew.

1. A $12,000 transfer was made on March 1 from the general fund to establish a building maintenance internal service fund. Matthew uses transfer accounts to account for this type of transfer.

2. On April 1, the general fund made an $8,000, six-month loan to the building maintenance service fund.

3. On April 15, $2,400 was transferred from the general fund to the debt service fund to pay interest.

4. On May 5, the Matthew transportation service fund billed the general fund $825 for April services.

Required

a. Prepare journal entries for the general fund and the other fund involved that should be recorded at the time of each transfer or transaction.

b. For each transfer or transaction, prepare the appropriate closing entries for the general fund and the other fund involved for the year ended June 30, 20X8.

LO8

E13-10   Internal Service Fund Entries and Statements

Bellevue City's printing shop had the following trial balance on January 1, 20X2:

	Debit	Credit
Cash	$ 24,600	
Due from Other Funds	15,600	
Inventory of Supplies	9,800	
Furniture and Equipment	260,000	
Accumulated Depreciation		$ 50,000
Vouchers Payable		12,000
Net Assets:		
Invested in Capital Assets (no related debt)		210,000
Unrestricted		38,000
Total	$310,000	$310,000

Advanced
StudyGuide
.com

Additional Information for 20X2

1. During 20X2, the printing shop acquired supplies for $96,000, furniture for $1,500, and a copier for $3,200.

2. Printing jobs billed to other funds amounted to $292,000; cash received from other funds, $287,300; costs of printing jobs, $204,000, including $84,000 of supplies; operating expenses, $38,000, including $8,400 of supplies; depreciation expense, $23,000; and vouchers paid, $243,000.

Required

a. Prepare entries for the printing shop for 20X2, including closing entries.

b. Prepare a statement of net assets for the fund on December 31, 20X2. No debt is related to the year-end amount of the fund's capital assets.

c. Prepare a statement of revenues, expenses, and changes in fund net assets for 20X2.

d. Prepare a statement of cash flows for 20X2.

LO11

E13-11 **Multiple-Choice Questions on Government-wide Financial Statements**
Note: Items 1 and 2 are based on the following:

Mountain View City is preparing its government-wide financial statements for the year. As of the year-end, the city has determined the following information for its capital assets, exclusive of its infrastructure assets:

Cost of capital assets acquired by governmental funds	$1,450,000
Accumulated depreciation on the capital assets	120,000
Outstanding debt related to the capital assets	780,000

1. On the government-wide statement of net assets for the year-end, what amount should be reported for capital assets in the Governmental Activities column?

   a. $550,000.

   b. $780,000.

   c. $1,330,000.

   d. $1,450,000.

2. On the government-wide statement of net assets for the year-end, what amount should be reported in the net assets section for the capital assets?

   a. $550,000.

   b. $780,000.

   c. $1,330,000.

   d. $1,450,000.

3. In accordance with **GASB 34,** "Basic Financial Statements—and Management's Discussion and Analysis—for State and Local Governments," which of the following statements is correct regarding the reporting of internal service funds?

I. The internal service fund should be discretely presented as part of the business-type activities of the government.

II. The internal service fund should be blended into the governmental activities.

a. I only.

b. II only.

c. I and II.

d. Neither I nor II.

Note: Items 4 and 5 are based on the following:

During the year, the City of Vero Beach sold bonds in its capital projects fund. The 6 percent, $500,000 par bonds were sold for 102. The effective interest rate was 5 percent.

4. How should the bonds be reported in the reconciliation schedule for the statement of revenues, expenditures, and changes in fund balance?

a. A decrease of $500,000 for the par value of the bonds.

b. A decrease of $30,000 for the interest paid on the bonds.

c. A decrease of $510,000 for the selling price of the bonds.

d. Not shown in this reconciliation schedule.

5. How should an interest adjustment be shown in the reconciliation of the balance sheet of governmental funds to the statement of net assets for the year?

a. A decrease of $30,000.

b. A decrease of $25,000.

c. A decrease of $5,000.

d. Not shown in this reconciliation schedule.

6. For which of the following should the accrual basis of accounting be used to measure financial performance?

	General Fund	Internal Service Fund	Government-wide Financial Statements
a.	Yes	Yes	Yes
b.	Yes	No	Yes
c.	No	No	No
d.	No	Yes	Yes

7. The City of Hastings has a separately elected school board that administers the city's schools. The city council must approve the school district's budget and tax levy. The school district's financial results should be reported in Hastings's financial statements in which way?

a. Included only as schedules in the footnotes of Hastings's financial reports.

b. Blended into Hastings's financial reports.

c. Discretely presented in Hastings's financial reports.

d. Not required to be presented in Hastings's financial reports.

8. Glen Valley City has properly adopted the modified approach to account for its infrastructure assets. Which of the following statements is correct about accounting for these infrastructure assets on the government-wide statement of activities?

I. Depreciation expense should be computed based on the assets' estimated useful lives and reported under the governmental activities column of the city's statement of activities.

II. The amount of the expenditures made for the infrastructure assets, except for additions and improvements, should be expensed in the period incurred.

a. I only.

b. II only.

c. I and II.

d. Neither I nor II.

9. A statement of cash flows is required for

	General Fund	Internal Service Fund	Government-wide Entity
a.	Yes	Yes	Yes
b.	No	Yes	Yes
c.	No	Yes	No
d.	Yes	No	No

10. Which of the following is reported as a restriction of net assets in the net assets section of the statement of net assets?

    a. A reservation of the fund balance in the general fund for $10,000 of encumbrances.

    b. A requirement in the permanent funds that the $100,000 principal of a bequest be maintained.

    c. A governing board decision that $15,000 of general fund resources should be assigned for planning for a city park.

    d. A governing board allocation of $4,000 to establish an internal services fund.

Problems

LO1

P13-12 **Adjusting Entries for General Fund [AICPA Adapted]**

On June 30, 20X2, the end of the fiscal year, the Wadsworth Park District prepared the following trial balance for the general fund:

	Debit	Credit
Cash	$ 47,250	
Taxes Receivable—Current	31,800	
Allowance for Uncollectibles—Current		$ 1,800
Temporary Investments	11,300	
Inventory of Supplies	11,450	
Buildings	1,300,000	
Estimated Revenues Control	1,007,000	
Appropriations Control		1,000,000
Revenue—State Grants		300,000
Bonds Payable		1,000,000
Vouchers Payable		10,200
Expenditures	848,200	
Debt Service from Current Funds	130,000	
Capital Outlays (Equipment)	22,000	
Revenue—Taxes		1,008,200
Fund Balance—Unassigned		81,800
Budgetary Fund Balance—Unassigned		7,000
Total	$3,409,000	$3,409,000

An examination of the records disclosed the following information:

1. The recorded estimate of losses for the current year taxes receivable was considered to be adequate.

2. The local governmental unit gave the park district 20 acres of land to be used for a new community park. The unrecorded estimated value of the land was $50,000. In addition, a state grant of $300,000 was received, and the full amount was used in payment of contracts pertaining to the construction of the park buildings. Purchases of playground equipment costing $22,000 were paid from general funds.

3. Five years ago, a 4 percent, 10-year sinking fund bond issue in the amount of $1,000,000 for constructing park buildings was sold; it is still outstanding. Interest on the issue is payable at maturity. Budgetary requirements of a contribution of $130,000 to the debt service

fund were met. Of this amount, $100,000 represents the fifth equal contribution for principal repayment.

4. Outstanding purchase orders not recorded in the accounts at year-end totaled $2,800.

5. A physical inventory of supplies at year-end revealed $6,500 of the supplies on hand.

6. Except where indicated to the contrary, all recordings were made in the general fund.

Required
Prepare the adjusting entries to correct the general fund records.

LO2–LO10   **P13-13**   **Entries for Funds [AICPA Adapted]**

Olivia Village was recently incorporated and began financial operations on July 1, 20X2, the beginning of its fiscal year. The following transactions occurred during this first fiscal year, July 1, 20X2, to June 30, 20X3:

1. The village council adopted a budget for general operations for the fiscal year ending June 30, 20X3. Revenue was estimated at $400,000. Legal authorizations for budgeted expenditures totaled $394,000.

2. Property taxes were levied in the amount of $390,000; 2 percent of this amount was estimated to prove uncollectible. These taxes are available as of the date of levy to finance current expenditures.

3. During the year, a village resident donated marketable securities valued at $50,000 to the village under the terms of a trust agreement. Those terms stipulated that the principal amount be kept intact. The use of revenue generated by the securities is restricted to financing college scholarships for needy students. Revenue earned and received on these marketable securities amounted to $5,500 through June 30, 20X3.

4. A general fund transfer of $5,000 was made to establish an internal service fund to provide for a permanent investment in inventory.

5. The village decided to install lighting in the village park through a special assessment project authorized to do so at a cost of $75,000. The city is obligated if the property owners default on their special assessments. Special assessment bonds were issued in the amount of $72,000, and the first year's special assessment of $24,000 was levied against the village's property owners. The remaining $3,000 for the project will be contributed from the village's general fund.

6. The special assessments for the lighting project are due over a three-year period, and the first year's assessments of $24,000 were collected. The $3,000 transfer from the village's general fund was received by the lighting capital projects fund.

7. A contract for $75,000 was let for the installation of the lighting. The capital projects fund was encumbered for the contract. On June 30, 20X3, the contract was completed and the contractor was paid.

8. During the year, the internal service fund purchased various supplies at a cost of $1,900.

9. Cash collections recorded by the general fund during the year were as follows:

Current property taxes	$386,000
Licenses and permit fees	7,000

The allowance for estimated uncollectible taxes is adjusted to $4,000.

10. The village council decided to build a village hall at an estimated cost of $500,000 to replace space occupied in rented facilities. The village does not record project authorizations. It was decided that general obligation bonds bearing interest at 6 percent would be issued. On June 30, 20X3, the bonds were issued at face value of $500,000, payable in 20 years. No contracts have been signed for this project, and no expenditures have been made, nor has an annual operating budget been prepared.

11. A fire truck was purchased for $15,000 and the voucher was approved and paid by the general fund. This expenditure was previously encumbered for $15,000.

Required

Prepare journal entries to record properly each of these transactions in the appropriate fund or funds of Olivia Village for the fiscal year ended June 30, 20X3.

Use the following funds: general fund, capital projects fund, internal service fund, and private-purpose trust fund. Each journal entry should be numbered to correspond to the transactions. Do not prepare closing entries for any fund. Your answer sheet should be organized using the following format:

Fund	Journal Entry

LO11

P13-14 **Entries to Adjust Account Balances [AICPA Adapted]**

You have been assigned by the town of Papillion to examine its June 30, 20X1, balance sheet. You are the first CPA to be engaged by the town, and you find that acceptable methods of municipal accounting have not been employed. The town clerk stated that the books had not been closed and presented the following preclosing trial balance of the general fund as of June 30, 20X1:

	Debit	Credit
Cash	$150,000	
Taxes Receivable—Current Year	59,200	
Allowance for Uncollectibles—Current		$ 18,000
Taxes Receivable—Delinquent	8,000	
Allowance for Uncollectibles—Delinquent		10,200
Estimated Revenues Control	310,000	
Appropriations Control		348,000
Donated Land	27,000	
Expenditures—Building Addition Constructed	50,000	
Expenditures—Serial Bonds Paid	16,000	
Other Expenditures	280,000	
Special Assessment Bonds Payable		100,000
Revenue		354,000
Accounts Payable		26,000
Fund Balance—Unassigned		82,000
Budgetary Fund Balance—Unassigned	38,000	
Total	$938,200	$938,200

Additional Information

1. The estimated losses of $18,000 for current-year taxes receivable were determined to be a reasonable estimate. The delinquent taxes allowance account should be adjusted to $8,000, the amount of the remaining delinquent taxes.

2. Included in the Revenue account is a credit of $27,000, representing the value of land donated by the state as a grant-in-aid for construction of a municipal park.

3. Operating supplies ordered in the prior fiscal year and chargeable to that year were received, recorded, and consumed in July 20X0. The outstanding purchase orders for these supplies, which were not recorded in the accounts on June 30, 20X0, amounted to $8,800. The vendors' invoices for these supplies totaled $9,400. Appropriations lapse one year after the end of the fiscal year for which they are made.

4. Outstanding purchase orders on June 30, 20X1, for operating supplies totaled $2,100. These purchase orders were not recorded on the books.

5. The special assessment bonds were sold in June 20X1 to finance a street-paving project. No contracts have been signed for this project, and no expenditures have been made from the capital projects fund. The city is obligated for the bonds if the property owners default.

6. The balance in the Revenue account includes credits for $20,000 for a note issued to a bank to obtain cash in anticipation of tax collections and for $1,000 for the sale of scrap iron from the town's water plant. The note was still outstanding on June 30, 20X1. The operations of the water plant are accounted for in the water fund.

7. The Expenditures—Building Addition Constructed account balance is the cost of an addition to the town hall building. This addition was constructed and completed in June 20X1. The general fund recorded the payment as authorized.

8. The Expenditures—Serial Bonds Paid account reflects the annual retirement of general obligation bonds issued to finance the construction of the town hall. Interest payments of $7,000 for the bond issue are included in other expenditures.

Required

a. Prepare the formal adjusting and closing journal entries for the general fund for the fiscal year ended June 30, 20X1.

b. The preceding information disclosed by your examination was recorded only in the general fund even though other funds were involved. Prepare the formal adjusting journal entries for any other funds involved.

LO2   **P13-15**   **Capital Projects Fund Entries and Statements**

During the fiscal year ended June 30, 20X3, West City Council authorizes construction of a new city hall building and the sale of serial bonds to finance the construction. The following transactions, related to financing and constructing the city hall, occur during fiscal 20X3:

1. On August 1, 20X2, West issues $5,000,000 of serial bonds for $5,080,000. Interest is payable annually, and the first retirement of $500,000 is due on July 31, 20X7. The premium is transferred to the debt service fund.

2. The old city hall, which had a recorded cost of $650,000, is torn down. The cost of razing the old building is $45,000, net of salvage value. This cost was included in the capital budget but was not encumbered. The cost is vouchered and paid.

3. West signs a contract with Roth Construction Company to build the city hall for $4,500,000. The contract cost is to be encumbered. Construction is to be completed during fiscal 20X4.

4. Roth Construction Company bills West $2,000,000 for construction completed during fiscal 20X3. Ten percent of the billings will be retained until final acceptance of the new city hall. The billing less the retainage was paid during the fiscal year.

Required

a. For each of these transactions, prepare the necessary journal entries for all the funds involved. Indicate the fund in which the entry is made by giving its initials in the left margin: CPF (capital projects fund) or DSF (debt service fund). Give the closing entries for the capital projects fund.

b. Prepare a balance sheet for the capital projects fund at June 30, 20X3.

c. Prepare a statement of revenues, expenditures, and changes in fund balance for the capital projects fund for the fiscal year ended June 30, 20X3.

 LO2–LO10   **P13-16**   **Recording Entries in Various Funds [AICPA Adapted]**

The following information relates to Vane City during the year ended December 31, 20X8:

Advanced
StudyGuide
.com

1. On October 31, 20X8, to finance the construction of a city hall annex, Vane issued 8 percent, 10-year general obligation bonds at their face value of $800,000. A contractor's bid of $750,000 was accepted for the construction of the annex. By year-end, one-third of the contract was completed at a cost of $246,000, all of which was paid on January 5, 20X9.

2. Vane collected $109,000 from hotel room taxes, restricted for tourist promotion, in a special revenue fund. The fund incurred and paid $81,000 for general promotions and $22,000 for a motor vehicle. Estimated revenues for 20X8 were $112,000, while appropriations were expected to be $108,000.

3. General fund revenues of $313,500 for 20X8 were transferred to a debt service fund and used to repay $300,000 of 9 percent, 15-year term bonds, which matured in 20X8, and to repay $13,500 of matured interest. The bond proceeds were used to construct a citizens' center.

4. At December 31, 20X8, Vane was responsible for $83,000 of outstanding encumbrances in its general fund. The city uses the nonlapsing method to account for its outstanding encumbrances.

5. Vane uses the purchases method to account for supplies in the general fund. At December 31, 20X8, an inventory indicated that the supplies inventory was $42,000. At December 31, 20X7, the supplies inventory was $45,000.

Required

For each numbered item above, make all the journal entries for the year ended December 31, 20X8, in all funds affected. Before each journal entry, identify the fund in which the journal entry is made. *Do not make any adjusting/closing entries for items (1), (2), and (3).*

LO2–LO10 | **P13-17** | **Matching Questions Involving Various Funds**

The numbered items listed on the left consist of a variety of transactions that occur in a municipality. The lettered items on the right consist of various ways to record the transactions. Select the appropriate method for recording each transaction. Some transactions have more than one correct answer. Some responses under Recording of Transactions may be used once, more than once, or not at all.

Transactions	Recording of Transactions
1. Term bond proceeds of $100,000 were received by the capital projects fund.	A. Debit expenditures in the general fund
2. Equipment costing $50,000 was acquired by the water utility, an enterprise fund.	B. Debit general operating expenses in the general fund
3. Land with a fair value of $500,000 was donated to the city to be used as a municipal park.	C. Debit equipment in the enterprise fund
4. Central stores, an internal service fund, received a transfer in of $750,000 from the general fund.	D. Debit equipment in the general fund
5. General obligation serial bonds of $250,000 matured and were paid by the debt service fund.	E. Debit building in the capital projects fund
6. Expenditures of $5,000,000 were incurred by the capital projects fund to construct a new city hall annex. The project was started and completed within the fiscal year.	F. Debit general operating expenses in the enterprise fund
7. The water utility, an enterprise fund, billed the mayor's office $200 for water usage.	G. Debit expenditures in the capital projects fund
8. The mayor's office received the billing in item 7.	H. Credit building in the capital projects fund
9. The tax agency fund received $250,000 of tax revenues that are to be distributed to the school districts within the municipality.	I. Debit expenditures in the debt service fund
10. Salaries and wages of $25,000 were incurred by the water utility enterprise fund.	J. Credit revenue in the private-purpose trust fund
	K. Credit revenue in the capital projects fund
	L. Credit other financing sources in the capital projects fund
	M. Credit transfers in in the internal services fund
	N. Debit revenue in the agency fund
	O. Credit due to other governmental units in the agency fund
	P. Credit revenue in the agency fund
	Q. Credit revenue in the enterprise fund
	R. Reported only on the government-wide financial statements

LO2–LO11 **P13-18** **Questions on Fund Transactions [AICPA Adapted]**

The following information relates to Dane City during its fiscal year ended December 31, 20X2:

1. On October 31, 20X2, to finance the construction of a city hall annex, Dane issued 8 percent, 10-year general obligation bonds at their face value of $600,000. Construction expenditures during the period equaled $364,000.

2. Dane reported $109,000 from hotel room taxes, restricted for tourist promotion, in a special revenue fund. The fund paid $81,000 for general promotions and $22,000 for a motor vehicle.

3. Dane transferred 20X2 general fund revenues of $104,500 to a debt service fund and used them to repay $100,000 of 9 percent, 15-year term bonds, and to pay $4,500 of interest. The bonds were used to acquire a citizens' center.

4. At December 31, 20X2, as a consequence of past services, city firefighters had accumulated entitlements for compensated absences of $86,000. General fund resources available at December 31, 20X2, are expected to be used to settle $17,000 of this amount, and $69,000 is expected to be paid out of future general fund resources.

5. At December 31, 20X2, Dane was responsible for $83,000 of outstanding general fund encumbrances, including the $8,000 for supplies that follow.

6. Dane uses the purchases method to account for supplies. The following information relates to supplies:

Inventory—1/1/X2	$ 39,000
—12/31/X2	42,000
Encumbrances outstanding—1/1/X2	6,000
—12/31/X2	8,000
Purchase orders during 20X2	190,000
Amount credited to vouchers payable during 20X2	181,000

Required

For items 1 through 10, determine the amounts based solely on the preceding information.

1. What is the amount of 20X2 general fund transfers out?

2. How much should be reported in 20X2 general fund liabilities from entitlements for compensated absences?

3. What is the 20X2 assigned amount of the general fund balance?

4. What is the 20X2 capital projects fund balance?

5. What is the 20X2 fund balance on the special revenue fund for tourist promotion?

6. What is the amount of 20X2 debt service fund expenditures?

7. What amount should be included in the government-wide financial statements for the cost of long-term assets acquired in 20X2?

8. What amount stemming from the 20X2 transactions and events decreased the long-term debt liabilities reported in the government-wide financial statements?

9. Using the purchases method, what is the amount of 20X2 supplies expenditures?

10. What was the total amount of 20X2 supplies encumbrances?

LO6–LO8 **P13-19** **Matching Questions Involving the Statement of Cash Flows for a Proprietary Fund**

The numbered items on the left consist of a variety of transactions that occurred in the water utility enterprise fund of Jeffersen City for the year ended June 30, 20X9. Items A, B, C, and D on the right represent the four categories of cash flows that are reported on the statement of cash flows for proprietary funds. Item E is for transactions that are not reported on the statement of cash flows. Assume that the direct method is used for disclosing cash flows from operating activities. For each transaction, select the appropriate letter to indicate where that transaction should be disclosed on the statement of cash flows or whether that item would not be reported on the statement of cash flows.

Transactions	Categories of Disclosure
1. Received $5,000,000 from revenue bonds to be used for construction of water treatment plant.	A. Operating activities
2. Paid $500,000 of salaries to employees of the water utility.	B. Noncapital financing activities
3. Received $1,000,000 state grant restricted for construction of water treatment plant.	C. Capital and related financing activities
4. Collected $2,500,000 of accounts receivable from households for use of city water.	D. Investing activities
5. Depreciation expense for the year amounted to $300,000.	E. Not reported on the statement of cash flows
6. Received $75,000 state grant restricted to the maintenance of fixed assets.	
7. Paid $250,000 of interest on the revenue bonds issued in item 1.	
8. Borrowed $125,000 from a local bank on revenue anticipation notes payable.	
9. Paid $5,000 of interest on the notes payable in item 8.	
10. Spent $1,200,000 of the revenue bonds for construction of the water treatment plant.	
11. Paid $5,000 fire insurance premium on June 30, 20X9, for next year's insurance coverage.	
12. Uncollected accounts receivable amounted to $135,000 on June 31, 20X9.	
13. Acquired $250,000 of state bonds as an investment of idle funds.	
14. Received $7,500 of interest on the state bonds in item 13.	
15. Received a $375,000 contribution from the city's general fund to be used for the construction of water treatment plant.	

LO2, LO3 **P13-20** **Matching Questions Involving the Statement of Revenues, Expenditures, and Changes in Fund Balance for a Capital Projects Fund and a Debt Service Fund**

The numbered items on the left consist of a variety of transactions and events that occurred in the capital projects and debt service funds of Walton City for the year ended June 30, 20X9. Items A, B, and C on the right represent three categories that are reported on the statement of revenues, expenditures, and changes in fund balance for capital projects and debt service funds. Item D is for transactions that are not reported on the statement of revenues, expenditures, and changes in fund balance for either debt service or capital projects funds. For each transaction, select the appropriate letter to indicate where that transaction should be reported on the statement of revenues, expenditures, and changes in fund balance or whether that item would not be reported on the statement.

Transactions/Events	Categories of Disclosure
1. The capital projects fund received the proceeds of general obligation bonds to be used for construction of a new courthouse.	A. Revenues
2. The capital projects fund accepted the lowest bid for the construction of the courthouse.	B. Expenditures
3. The capital projects fund received resources from the city's general fund to be used in the construction of the courthouse.	C. Other financing sources and uses
4. The bonds in item 1 were sold at a premium. The capital projects fund transferred the premium to the debt service	D. Not reported on the statement of revenues, expenditures, and changes in fund balance

(continued)

fund. Indicate how this transaction should be reported by the capital projects fund.

5. During the year ended June 30, 20X9, courthouse construction was completed.

6. In addition to the resources provided by the general obligation bonds and the general fund, the capital projects fund also received a state grant that it used to construct the courthouse.

7. The general fund of the city transferred a portion of the property tax collections to the debt service fund to be used to pay the principal and interest of the general obligation bonds issued in item 1.

8. The debt service fund acquired investments with part of the resources provided by the general fund.

9. Interest was earned on the investments acquired in item 8.

10. The debt service fund received the bond premium from the capital projects fund.

11. The debt service fund paid semiannual interest on the general obligation bonds on March 1, 20X9.

12. The debt service fund used a local bank to be its fiscal agent with regard to the recordkeeping activities related to the general obligation bonds issued in item 1. The bank charged a fee for this service.

13. As of June 30, 20X9, unmatured interest for four months was due on the general obligation bonds issued in item 1. Resources to pay this interest will be transferred to the debt service fund in the next fiscal year.

LO2–LO10 | **P13-21** | **Question on Fund Transactions [AICPA Adapted]**

Items 1 through 10 in the left-hand column represent various transactions pertaining to a municipality that uses encumbrance accounting. Items 11 through 20, also listed in the left-hand column, represent the funds and accounts used by the municipality. To the right of these items is a list of possible accounting and reporting methods.

Required

a. For each of the municipality's transactions (items 1 through 10), select the appropriate method for recording the transaction. A method of recording the transactions may be selected once, more than once, or not at all.

b. For each of the municipality's funds, accounts, and other items (items 11 to 20), select the appropriate method of accounting and reporting. An accounting and reporting method may be selected once, more than once, or not at all.

Transactions	Recording of Transactions
1. General obligation bonds were issued at par.	A. Credit Appropriations Control
2. Approved purchase orders were issued for supplies.	B. Credit Budgetary Fund Balance—Unassigned
3. Supplies in item 2 were received and the related invoices were approved.	C. Credit Expenditures Control
4. General fund salaries and wages were incurred.	D. Credit Deferred Revenues
5. The internal service fund had interfund billings.	E. Credit Interfund Revenues
6. Revenues were earned from a previously awarded grant.	F. Credit Tax Anticipation Notes Payable
7. Property taxes were collected in advance.	G. Credit Other Financing Sources
8. Appropriations were recorded on adoption of the budget.	H. Credit Other Financing Uses
9. Short-term financing was received from a bank, secured by the city's taxing power.	I. Debit Appropriations Control
10. There was an excess of estimated inflows over estimated outflows.	J. Debit Deferred Revenues
	K. Debit Encumbrances Control
	L. Debit Expenditures Control

Funds and Accounts	Accounting and Reporting
11. Enterprise fund fixed assets.	A. Accounted for in a fiduciary fund
12. Capital projects fund.	B. Accounted for in a proprietary fund
13. Permanent fund.	C. Accounts for permanent endowments that can be used for government programs
14. Infrastructure fixed assets.	
15. Enterprise fund cash.	D. Reported as an other financing use
16. General fund.	E. Accounted for in a special assessment fund
17. Agency fund cash.	F. Accounts for major construction activities
18. Transfer out from the general fund to the internal service fund.	G. Accounts for property tax revenues
	H. Accounts for payment of interest and principal on tax-supported debt
19. Special revenue fund (a major fund).	
20. Debt service fund (a major fund).	I. Accounts for revenues from earmarked sources to finance designated activities
	J. Reported in government-wide statements

LO5

P13-22 Major Fund Tests

The City of Somerset has the following fund information:

Fund	Assets	Liabilities	Revenues	Expenditures (Expenses)
General	$1,320,400	$ 878,300	$4,620,000	$4,550,000
Special revenue	27,000	19,000	327,000	328,000
Capital project—library	450,000	38,000	460,000	418,000
Capital project—arena	28,000	16,000	41,000	55,800
Debt service	41,000	-0-	331,000	290,000
Permanent	246,000	-0-	11,000	18,000
Enterprise—electric	2,640,000	1,800,700	289,000	245,000
Enterprise—water	1,356,000	1,100,000	329,000	298,000

Required

Apply the criteria specified in **GASB 34** to determine which of these funds meets the major fund reporting criteria.

LO12

P13-23 Reconciliation Schedules

The City of Sycamore is preparing its financial reports for the year and has requested that you prepare the reconciliation schedules to accompany its government-wide financial statements based on the following information:

1. The fund balances reported in the five governmental funds as of the end of the fiscal year total $888,400. The fund balances in governmental funds at the beginning of the year totaled $379,000.

2. The city has estimated its depreciation on capital assets to be $187,000 for the period. The city expended a total of $287,000 in capital outlays from the governmental funds. At year-end, the capital assets, net of depreciation, totaled $4,329,000. The internal service fund reported $18,000 of net capital assets. Total accumulated depreciation at year-end was $1,208,000.

3. The internal service fund reports $178,000 in total assets and $141,000 in total liabilities. The internal service fund reported $48,000 of revenues and $39,000 of expenses during the year.

4. The debt service fund paid $40,000 in interest during the year. Bonds with a face value of $500,000 and a coupon rate of 8 percent were sold at the beginning of the year at $460,000 for an effective interest rate of 10 percent. Interest is paid annually on the last day of the fiscal year. The bonds were sold to provide current financial resources for the governmental funds.

5. The permanent fund recorded interest received of $4,000 under the modified accrual basis of measurement. If the accrual basis of measurement had been used in the fund, an additional $1,000 of interest revenue would have been earned.

Required

a. Prepare a reconciliation schedule of the balance sheet of the governmental funds to the statement of net assets.

b. Prepare a reconciliation schedule of the statement of revenues, expenditures, and changes in fund balance of governmental funds to the statement of activities.

LO11, LO12   **P13-24**   **True/False Questions**

1. The budgetary comparison schedule in the government-wide financial statements requires only the final budget for the period and the actual amounts for the period.

2. The accrual basis of accounting is used in the government-wide financial statements.

3. A component unit of a primary government is a unit that is related to the primary government but is not financially accountable to the primary government.

4. The statement of net assets in the government-wide financial statements requires the net assets to be segregated as follows: assigned net assets (for items such as encumbrances and inventories) and unassigned net assets.

5. A major governmental fund that must be separately disclosed in the government-wide financial statements would be a fund that composed 5 percent of the total of the governmental funds.

6. Permanent governmental funds account for resources that have a principal that must be maintained and whose earnings are available for any government program that benefits all citizens.

7. The government unit's infrastructure and other fixed assets are reported on the government-wide statement of net assets.

8. The internal service fund is a proprietary fund and is not, therefore, shown in the Governmental Activities column of the government-wide statement of net assets.

9. In the reconciliation schedule for the statement of net assets, to reconcile from the net assets reported in the governmental funds to the net assets of governmental activities, capital assets used in governmental activities would be added.

10. In the reconciliation schedule for the statement of revenues, expenditures, and changes in fund balance, to reconcile from the net change in fund balances—governmental funds to the change in net assets of governmental activities, bond proceeds would be added back.

11. In the government-wide statement of activities, transfers between governmental and business-type funds must be reported as part of the change in net assets.

12. In the government-wide statement of activities, depreciation of fixed assets would equal the amount of the expenditures for assets made in the governmental funds.

13. The Management's Discussion and Analysis is a recommended but voluntary disclosure in the government-wide financial statements.

14. The government-wide statement of net assets includes the fiduciary funds of the government unit.

15. The format of the government-wide statement of activities is based on the programs of the government entity rather than the type of revenues of the government entity.

LO5   **P13-25**   **Determining Whether a Special Revenue Fund Is a Major Fund**

The City of Elmtree is preparing its financial statements for the year ended December 31, 20X2, and has asked for your assistance in determining whether its special revenue fund is a major or a nonmajor fund for the financial statements of its governmental funds. The city has provided the following information:

Items	Totals for Governmental Funds	Totals for Governmental and Enterprise Funds
Assets	$50,000,000	$80,000,000
Liabilities	22,000,000	37,000,000
Revenues	70,000,000	95,000,000
Expenditures/expenses	60,000,000	82,000,000

The special revenue fund reported the following amounts at December 31, 20X2 (assets and liabilities), and for the year ended December 31, 20X2 (revenues and expenditures):

Assets	$4,100,000
Liabilities	3,900,000
Revenues	6,700,000
Expenditures	6,500,000

Required
Determine whether the special revenue fund of Elmtree is a major fund for the 20X2 financial statements of the city's governmental funds.

LO11

P13-26 **Preparation of a Statement of Net Assets for a Governmental Entity**

Gibson City reported the following items at December 31, 20X2. It has no component units and does not depreciate its infrastructure fixed assets. All bonds—general obligation bonds and revenue—were issued to acquire capital assets. As of December 31, 20X2, net assets of $25,000 were restricted for road maintenance in special revenue funds, and net assets of $30,000 were restricted for debt service. Cash of $5,000 was restricted in business-type activities for plant maintenance.

	Governmental Activities	Business-Type Activities
Assets:		
Cash and cash equivalents	$ 68,000	$28,000
Taxes receivable (net)	52,000	
Accounts receivable (net)		12,000
Due from governmental activities		5,000
Inventories	10,000	7,000
Investments	25,000	15,000
Capital assets:		
Land	100,000	50,000
Infrastructure	60,000	
Other depreciable assets (net)	75,000	45,000
Liabilities:		
Vouchers payable	32,000	4,000
Accrued interest payable	1,500	2,000
Due to business-type activities	5,000	
Revenue bonds payable		80,000
General obligation bonds payable	60,000	

Required
Using the information provided, prepare in good form a statement of net assets for Gibson City at December 31, 20X2.

Kaplan CPA Review

Kaplan CPA Review Simulation on Governmental Accounting and Reporting

Access to the online CPA Simulation can be attained by visiting the text's Web site at www.mhhe.com/baker1e.

Situation
The City of Clarksville (Clarksville) is incorporated and has a December 31 year-end. The budget is approved by the City Council (Council) annually. For internal reporting purposes, Clarksville uses the modified accrual basis of accounting to record its general fund transactions. For external reporting purposes, Clarksville prepares a comprehensive annual financial report that includes both government-wide and fund-based financial statements.

The city has a policy that any amounts to be received within 60 days are viewed as currently being available.

At the beginning of Year One, the Council authorized the construction of a new recreation center. The estimated cost of the recreation center is $25 million. Clarksville plans to finance the construction by (1) combining bond proceeds with a state grant and (2) making a transfer from the general fund.

Topics Included in the Simulation

a. Assigning transactions in a proprietary fund to the appropriate classification on the statement of cash flows.

b. Evaluating the accuracy of recorded amounts in the governmental funds for recording budgets, the levy of taxes, and the collections of taxes.

c. Assigning nonexchange transactions to their correct categories of recognition.

d. Accounting for the construction of the new recreation center: issuance of the bonds, receipt of the state grant, accounting for the interfund transfer, and accounting for interest on the bonds.

e. Comparing fund-based reporting of the construction of the recreation center to that reportable on the government-wide financial statements.

f. Comparing the reporting of an acquisition of a capital asset on the fund-based financial statements with that on the government-wide financial statements.

g. Researching required disclosures in the comprehensive annual financial report for infrastructure assets under the modified approach.

Supplemental Problems for this chapter are available as part of the *Online Learning Center* on the textbook's Web site (URL: www.mhhe.com/baker1e).

Index

Page numbers followed by n indicate material in notes.